Encyclopedia of
New Religious Movements

New Religious Movements (NRMs) can involve vast numbers of followers and in many cases are radically changing the way people understand and practice religion and spirituality. Moreover, they are having a profound impact on the form and content of mainstream religion. The *Encyclopedia of New Religious Movements* provides uniquely global coverage of the phenomenon, with entries on over three-hundred movements from almost every country worldwide. Coverage includes movements that derive from the major religions of the world as well as neo-traditional movements, which are often overlooked in the study of NRMs.

In addition to the coverage of particular movements there are also entries on broad classifications and themes, and key topics, thinkers and ideas – the New Age Movement, Neo-Paganism, gender and NRMs, cyberspace religions, the Anti-Cult Movement, Swedenborg, Jung, de Chardin, Lovelock, Gurdjieff, al-Banna, Qutb.

The marked global approach and comprehensiveness of the encyclopedia enable an appreciation of the innovative energy of NRMs, of their extraordinary diversity, and the often surprising ways in which they can propagate geographically. A most ambitious publication of its sort, the *Encyclopedia of New Religious Movements* is a major addition to the reference literature for students and researchers in the field of religious studies and the social sciences.

Entries are cross-referenced, many with short bibliographies for further reading. There is a full index.

Peter B. Clarke is Professor Emeritus of the History and Sociology of Religion at King's College, University of London, UK and Professorial Member, Faculty of Theology, University of Oxford, UK. His latest book is *New Religious Movements in Global Perspective* (Routledge, 2006).

Encyclopedia of
New Religious Movements

Edited by
Peter B. Clarke

Routledge
Taylor & Francis Group

LONDON AND NEW YORK

First published 2006
by Routledge
2 Park Square, Milton Park, Abingdon, Oxon OX14 4RN

Simultaneously published in the USA and Canada
by Routledge
270 Madison Ave, New York, NY 10016

Routledge is an imprint of the Taylor and Francis Group

© 2006 Routledge

Typeset in Times New Roman and Optima by Taylor & Francis Books
Printed and bound in Great Britain by TJ International Ltd, Padstow, Cornwall

British Library Cataloguing in Publication Data
A catalogue record for this book is available from the British Library

Library of Congress Cataloging in Publication Data
A catalog record for this book has been requested

ISBN10: 0-415-26707-2
ISBN13: 9-78-0-415-26707-6

Taylor & Francis Group is the Academic Division of T&F Informa plc.

Contents

Introduction
New Religions as a global phenomenon

The apparent ease with which New Religious Movements (henceforth: NRMs) are 'invented' can be attributed in part to the increasingly global character of the contemporary world, which has witnessed the disembedding from their original cultural context and the wider circulation of religious beliefs and practices of every kind. This process of globalization has occasioned a shift in religions from geographically and culturally specific 'facts', that is from their being associated with one particular geographical and cultural zone such as the Middle East, Asia, the West, or Africa, to being a reality everywhere. Increasingly since the 1960s, Buddhism, Islam, and Hinduism have come to be seen less and less as exotic appendages to the religious culture of Western society, while the beliefs and practices associated with these religions, including the belief in reincarnation, the notion of God as impersonal, and the practices of yoga and vipassana or insight meditation are shared by a sizeable minority of the population of Western Europe, many of whom continue to identify themselves as Christians (Lambert 2004). Associated with this change, albeit less easily measured, are changes in spirituality, which include in the West a greater interest in an inner-directed kind of spirituality and in Asia in socially engaged spirituality.

Although the confluence, of historically unprecedented proportions, of religious systems and spiritualities has contributed, along with other processes that include modernization, urbanization, new developments in science and technology, economic migration, and legal changes such as the repeal of the Asian Exclusion Act in the United States in 1965, to make the phenomenon of NRMs a global one, there is, none the less, much variation in the structure, content, size, and in the goals of these religions and in their orientation towards the wider society.

Thus, while vast numbers of NRMs have either become or are in the process of becoming global religions, they manifest different characteristics in different parts of the world due to the process of domestication or to use Robertson's (1994) term 'glocalization'. This accounts for why Japanese NRMs develop a somewhat different reality in Brazil compared to Japan. In Brazil they display many more Catholic features, are more inclusive in terms of membership, and their ceremonies and rituals bear a close resemblance to those of Catholicism.

It is not possible even in an Encyclopedia to convey all the variation and variety of the NRMs that now exist. However, what can be done and has been attempted here, is to provide examples of the various kinds of NRMs that have arisen in different parts of the world in order to show how truly universal the phenomenon is, although the temptation to postulate a single general causal explanation for this widespread phenomenon, such as rapid social change is resisted. I will return briefly to this point later.

This Encyclopedia in addition to providing basic data on numerous NRMs from every continent also intends to offer the reader an idea of the direction taken by NRMs, which are often depicted as flowing directly from West to East, starting in the United States. In reality the flow resembles more a global labyrinth than a straight highway. Elsewhere (Clarke 2000) I wrote of reverse globalization in the case of Japanese NRMs to offset the widespread impression given at the time that everything had been moving from West to East. Even this was an oversimplification, movement is in all directions. For example, several Japanese NRMs including Sekai Kyûsei Kyô **(Church of World Messianity)** have arrived in parts of Africa including Angola, Mozambique, South Africa, the Democratic Republic of the Congo, and via the furthest point West of Japan, Brazil. By way of contrast the Brazilian NRM the **Santo Daime** movement has travelled with Brazilian-Japanese migrant workers to Japan.

The pathways taken by NRMs are endless, as are the interactions. These include the interactions of Korean spiritual beings and African spirits in the notorious **Lord's Resistance Army** in northern Uganda, the dynamic interaction of Rastafarian (see **Rastafarian movement**) and **Maori** religious worldviews, of African-Brazilian and Amerindian spiritual concepts and practices, and of the New Age Movement (NAM) with most forms of spirituality including various kinds of Islamic Sufism or mysticism and Native American religion. Through the NAM spiritualities of all

kinds have been carried from one part of the world to many others.

A feature of the contemporary religious environment is the ground being gained globally by what I have described above as inner-directed spirituality, much of which is based on the premise that the Self is the source of the supernatural. This kind of spirituality takes different forms and includes the use of various techniques such as the physical exercises of *t'ai chi* and *yoga*, which are designed to enable the practitioner to access and release the spiritual force that rests within the deepest layers of the self and apply it to the existential and emotional, and even material, areas of life. With this kind of spirituality comes a preference for a transpersonal understanding of transcendence over a theistic one, for experience over reason in spiritual matters and for knowing over believing, since logically experiencing the divine dispenses with the need for faith.

Although privatized and inner-directed, this form of spirituality, which is gaining ground in the West and contrasts with the previously mentioned socially engaged spirituality movements found in predominantly Buddhist countries, is not unconcerned with the condition of the world. Rather it holds to the view that self-transformation is the *sine qua non* of that social transformation which is anxiously awaited, an anxiety evident in the fundamental importance that countless NRMs give to the millenarian idea. Even those NRMs that derive from traditions where this belief is only adhered to in a weak sense, such as Buddhism, are, at least at the outset, passionately millenarian (see **Millenarianism**). While millenarianism is also a feature of almost all the NRMs that have been involved in violence, it must be stressed that it cannot be assumed that this belief predisposes a group to violent action. Many millenarian movements are pacific and among these are the Rastafarian movement, the **Mahdiyyat movement** and **Sekai Kyûsei Kyô**.

Being gripped by this belief in the imminent advent of the millennium as they are suggests that NRMs might best be understood if interpreted as ideologies of social transformation. This seems preferable to trying to understand them by classifying them according to their response to the world as 'world-denying', 'world-indifferent', and 'world-affirming' movements (Wallis 1984).

The previously mentioned option chosen by growing numbers for spirituality over religion and the stress on the need for a spirituality that is relevant and self-empowering clearly poses a threat to those long established religions whose doctrinal systems are tightly integrated and exclusive and whose identity depends not only on having a well defined, unambiguous set of teachings but also on clearly demarcated ritual boundaries. This is evident in the highly critical responses of some of the mainline Christian Churches, including the Catholic Church, to the previously mentioned **New Age Movement** (NAM). This notwithstanding, very few mainstream religions, and even the so called Traditional Religions, have remained uninfluenced by the NAM. Not only has the latter acted as a vehicle for the globalization of various forms of spirituality and religions, including Traditional Religions once closely associated with a specific ethnic group and territory such as Native American religion, but, at the same time, by a process of osmosis, it is fast becoming part of mainstream religion and culture.

Different interpretations of religious innovation and change

It is important to keep in mind when discussing what is meant by New Religion that religious innovation continues to be understood differently in different cultural and religious contexts and this despite the rapid pace of globalization. Newness or innovation in Oriental societies, and even to an extent in Islamic societies, often has more to do with orthopraxy than orthodoxy. **Engaged Buddhism**, for example, is not doctrinally speaking unorthodox but was perceived initially as a major religious innovation in Vietnam and Thailand, among other places, as was **Protestant Buddhism** in Sri Lanka and Raja **Yoga** in India.

Of course, a change in practice can also mean a change in understanding or belief. Theorists of 'Engaged Buddhism' insist, for example, that nirvana rather than constituting its goal should be seen as the means to the end of Buddhism which is social transformation.

There is much discussion concerning how the NRMs of today differ from those of the past. Wilson (1995) identified a number of characteristics that set contemporary NRMs in the West apart from past NRMs and existing mainstream religions. Often the differences are differences of emphasis, some of which characterize NRMs not only in the West but also across the world. One such difference is the stress placed by modern NRMs on the central role of lay people in their own spiritual advancement, accompanied by a de-emphasis on the significance of the role of the cleric. This is in line with the growing appeal of the previously mentioned inner-directed religion or religions of the True-Self. Although some NRMs may claim a unique legitimacy for their charismatic leader, who often seeks to strengthen their authority by asserting that access to secret but vital revelations or sources of wisdom that can only be had through the leader, most NRMs in theory stress that every individual is their own spiritual master.

Another general feature of contemporary NRMs that sets them apart from new movements of the past is their tendency to be more eclectic and more open to secular therapies, such as psychology, which they frequently fuse with their own spirituality. They often go beyond the purposes of psychology in making psychological techniques serve to uncover the 'god' within (Heelas 1997).

Different understandings of the principle of membership also distinguish most modern NRMs from traditional sects and cults in the Christian and other religious contexts. It is perfectly possible to be a member of several NRMs simultaneously, or even remain a member of the religion ascribed to one at birth and at the same time be a member of an NRM. This gives rise to a whole new understanding of the meaning of conversion and is of direct relevance to the **brainwashing** debate (Barker 1984). Modern NRMs are also organizationally different from those of the past, making greater use of more secular forms of management, administration, and assembly. Networking, rather than a focus on religion as community, also characterizes much modern religion. Indeed many NRMs, including Scientology, mirror in so much of their style, ethos, organization, orientation, and goals the wider society that Wilson (1990) describes them as modern 'secularized religions'.

Historically, moreover, NRMs, or as they were once called sects, strongly opposed either the Church or the society at large, or both, while contemporary ones are often more inclusive in every domain. Moreover although they profess to seek to transform the world many endorse the values of the existing order, catering to individualism and consumerism, the two dominant characteristics of contemporary society. Japan's NRMs, and they are not alone

in this regard, are frequently presented as offering benefits in keeping with the consumerist ethic of modern society and as providing religious legitimization for such benefits, and in this they bear a striking resemblance to the American Theology of Success or Glory movement, and according to Ezzy (2001) to several Wiccan groups in Australia.

Newness or innovation does not necessarily mean the introduction of new doctrines or ritual practices. As the entry on **New Religion** attempts to make clear, it can consist of innovative well established, time honoured beliefs and rituals, as in the case of the changes made to the traditional rite of possession (kamigakari) by Omoto's (Great Origin) founder Deguchi Nao (1837–1918) (Ooms 1993). While drawing on traditional Shinto beliefs of world transformation Deguchi Nao made a radical break with the traditional understanding of these beliefs and made the rituals associated with them serve different ends (Ooms 1993: 14–17).

This 'newness' in the Japanese context, as in others, cannot be understood without reference to past practice and belief. This notwithstanding, followers of Japanese NRMs are persuaded that the teachings to which they adhere are original in that they either contain newly discovered ancient and sacred foundational texts and/or provide for the first time the only complete and authentic interpretation of a particular ancient sacred text or tradition.

An example is Kofuku no Kogaku's (The Institute for Research in Human Happiness) claim to be presenting for the first time the true teachings of Buddha. Since they were not written down until one hundred years after his death, this movement believes these teachings were wrongly interpreted and a core element omitted – the teaching on love. The movement has now added this fundamentally important element for the first time to Buddhism's traditional three jewels and by so doing claims to have radically revised Buddhism.

Agonshu follows a similar line. Its founder Kiriyama Seiyu professed to have discovered new, hidden truths by reading early Buddhist texts known as the *Agama sutras*, texts which had been given little attention in Japan. Able to discern the hidden, inner meaning of these texts, Kiriyama claimed to have uncovered a direct and rapid road to Buddhahood for the living and just as importantly for the dead. This discovery has had consequences for Agonshu practice which places great stress on the pacification of the spirits of the dead and on the need to ensure that they attain Buddhahood (*jobutsu*), both of which are necessary if the living are to be at peace and secure well-being and prosperity (Reader 1991: 211).

NRMs, it has been emphasized, vary greatly from each other. However, religious innovation should not be seen on account of this as a disconnected series of ad hoc changes randomly introduced. Explicit mention has already been made of some of the innovations taking place globally including the growing emphasis on self-oriented spirituality and Engaged Buddhism. There is also a strong trend towards the greater democratization of religion found for example in Japanese Buddhism, evangelical Christianity in Latin America and in Muslim communities across the world.

The catalysts that have triggered this trend towards greater 'democratization' vary but almost everywhere they include increasing individualism and the declining importance of religion as the social cement of community due to ever-increasing institutional differentiation. Mainstream religion, associated in most people's minds with the old order to which it gave and continues to give

legitimacy, is increasingly regarded with indifference or seen as dysfunctional in terms of self-empowerment and progress. These processes have contributed to the decoupling of beliefs from those ecclesiastical institutions to which, for their validity and efficacy, they were once thought to be inextricably linked.

Out of all of this is emerging in the West a new cognitive style of being religious, which contrasts with that of theistic religions in particular. While the latter stress believing, NRMs are concerned with arriving at truth through experience. This holds for a disparate collection of NRMs including the Self-religions (see **Self-Religion, The Self, and self**); Neo-Hindu movements such as the **Bramakumaris** and **Hare Krishna** movements; Japanese NRMs including **Sekai Kyûsei Kyô** (Church of World Messianity), **Soka Gakkai** (Value Creation Society), and Perfect Liberty Kyodan; new Buddhist movements including the **Friends of the Western Buddhist Order**; metaphysical movements such as Transcendentalism and African-Caribbean derived movements including the **Rastafarian movement**; and psycho-therapeutic spiritual movements such as **Scientology** and Gurjieffian groups including The Work (see **Work, The**). Ouspensky (1987: 228) claimed that Gurdjieff was emphatic in his rejection of the traditional idea of faith and quotes him as saying:

> In properly organized groups no faith is required; what is required is simply a little trust and even that only for a little while, for the sooner a man begins to verify all he hears the better it is for him.

The cognitive style of many NRMs thus contrasts sharply with that of, for example, the traditional Christian understanding of the notion of faith in that it does not rest on recourse to divine revelation or on an external, divine source for what is believable or for a solution to the problem of meaning, most acute in the form of the problem of evil. Moral evil is widely understood to result from ignorance or lack of awareness of the true nature of the Self. This new cognitive style draws those who espouse it closer intellectually to Buddhism, and other religions of Oriental origin.

The dynamics of religious innovation, thus, are variable. They differ from one religious system to another and from one religious culture to another. The term 'new' also takes on different meanings depending on the movement and the context and is used not only to point to radical discontinuities or disconnections between the present and the past in terms of beliefs, rituals, and structures but also to the different use made in the present of the past and the 'new' meaning given to the practices and teachings derived therefrom.

Accounting for NRMs

The most common sociological explanation for the rise of NRMs interprets them as a response to the crises of identity, moral meaning and profound cultural upheaval brought about by *rapid* social change. While there is undoubtedly some merit in this kind of explanation it is, nevertheless, hardly sufficient as a general account of the phenomenon. Although it cannot be easily tested – not least because the subjective dimension of the impact of social change is not easily measured – there are instances where this kind of explanation does seem to elucidate what has happened, and these include the rise of Cargo cults in Melanesia (Worsley 1970) (see **Melanesia-millenarian ('Cargo') movements**) and of Independent Churches and Neo-Traditional movements in Africa (Turner 1991). But even in these cases the question arises as to whether it

was the *nature* of the change itself, its bearers and the methods used to implement it, rather than its rapidity that led to the outbreak of these movements. Moreover, there are also examples of religious change and innovation where rapid social change does not appear to have been the decisive factor, including in Medieval Europe (Cohn 1970) and in Japan in the late eighteenth century and first half of the nineteenth century (Inoue 1991).

Not only are there numerous cases for which the rapid social change explanation cannot account, but it also begs a number of fundamental questions of a historical and philosophical kind. It implicitly accepts the contrasts made between what is perceived on the one hand as dynamic modern society in a constant state of flux and upheaval, conditions which undermine identity and the moral and social structures that provide meaning and direction, against static so-called 'traditional' society in which everyone is sure not only of who they are, but also of their role and purpose. However, as Lewis (1971) points out, sects and cults in Traditional societies are often born of insufficient change. Furthermore, the rapid social change explanation tends to be reductionist in that it affords religion the status of an epiphenomenon by treating it as a kind of mechanism that is triggered by way of a response to bewilderment.

Although frequently seen as destructive of common values and aspirations NRMs, as we have seen, have also been accounted for, paradoxically, in terms of their mediating and integrative functions particularly during the late 1960s and 1970s in the West when, it is suggested, they socialized many counterculturalists in the values and work ethic of mainstream society and enabled them thereby to return to 'conventional' living (Robbins and Anthony 1978;

Tipton 1982). While some of the Self-religions, including *est* studied by Tipton (1982), fulfilled this function, this thesis is hardly supported by evidence from other movements irrespective of their religious and cultural origins.

Their diversity and the diverse contexts and cultures in which they arise rules out the possibility of finding a general explanation of the rise of NRMs as a whole. Like rapid social change theory, too much is claimed for globalization theory also (Robertson 1992), which provides little more than an explanation in particular contexts for the adaptation and application in a changed, modernized context of particular styles of religiosity. More attention to such apparently unrelated events as greater affluence, more opportunity for travel, changes in the immigration laws of a country, the effects of colonization and decolonization, and economic migration, may shed as much light on the rise of NRMs as the dislocating effects that follow from either globalization or rapid social change. But whatever lenses we use, we see the causes of what are truly complex phenomena only through a glass, darkly.

Size and impact

Some NRMs have attracted millions of adepts, others have remained numerically small, while others have become extinct. To explain this question of success and failure researchers have examined the various types of religious markets and the rational choices made by consumers of religion in those markets. A competitive religious market, it has been suggested (Stark and Finke 2000), makes for a buoyant religious economy and among the most successful religions competing in these markets, it has been argued (Iannacone 1995), are those with 'strict' teachings. Such religions are said to have greater appeal and attract more adherents than the more liberal types.

However, one needs to ask how this argument accounts for the relative success of much of Buddhism in the West, of movements such as **Seicho-no-Ie** (House of Growth) in Brazil, of Cao Daism in Vietnam, of hybrid Sufi movements in the United States and of the **New Age Movement** (NAM) everywhere. This would seem to contradict the strictness hypothesis. Moreover, as Wuthnow and Cadge (2004) point out, attention needs to be paid not only to strictness – a very difficult commodity to measure – but also to the efficiency with which religion is marketed. Also extremely relevant to understanding the reasons for the rise and decline of an NRM are the ways in which its teachings and practices are embedded in organizational structures, both those of its own making and those of the rest of society. Both Buddhism in the West and the NAM globally have been able to embed their teachings and practices comfortably in many of the organizational structures, including churches, of the wider society and this must in part explain their widespread appeal, as must the fact that they do not demand a radical break with the tradition to which practitioners belong and, therefore, avoid imposing a heavy burden on recruits in terms of their having to shed excessive amounts of cultural and spiritual capital (Stark 1996).

The question of the religious impact of NRMs has also been hotly debated. For some observers NRMs are explained as a sign of a revival of the sacred in the modern world that is pushing back the frontiers of secularization (Bell 1977; Stark and Bainbridge 1985). There is no clear consensus among scholars about the contribution of NRMs to this process of religious revival or whether such a process is under way. Research on contemporary religious practice and religious dispositions in Europe, the United States, and the West generally shows a decline in the public practice of Christianity and a move away from Christian orthodoxy and spirituality not, it is true, in the direction of no religion or spirituality, but towards more open-ended, synthetic forms of both (Lambert 2004). Only 10 per cent fewer Europeans believe in reincarnation – 22 per cent – than in the central Christian tenet of the resurrection of the body – 33 per cent, and while over 60 per cent believe in God, only 36 per cent believe in the traditional Christian idea of God as a personal God (Lambert 2004). Differing from Stark *et al.*, Wilson, among others, believes that NRMs have done little to reverse the process of secularization in Europe. On the contrary. If anything, they have, he argues (1991), advanced its course.

The numerical impact of NRMs is not widely understood. Often the membership figures given by observers are those of the movement's home base or country of origin and do not reflect its global membership. Several Japanese NRMs not only have several million members in Japan but a relatively large membership outside Japan for example in Brazil. The **Nation of Islam** (NOI), an African-American movement, also not only has some two million followers in the United States but also many followers in other parts of the world. A number of Chinese, Taiwanese, and African NRMs, likewise, have large home-based memberships of several million and many thousands of members mainly among ethnic Chinese and Africans abroad. The Brazilian Neo-Evangelical Church established in the 1970s, the **Universal Church of the Kingdom of God** (Igreja Universal do Reino de Deus, IURD), has millions of followers in Brazil and a large membership in several African countries, including the Ivory Coast.

When assessing the numerical impact of NRMs it is also important to keep in mind the extent to which they have indirectly influenced millions of people who do not formally belong. As was previously mentioned, through a process of osmosis many New Age ideas and practices have become part of mainstream society. Likewise Yoga and various other Oriental techniques, many of which, if not actually introduced to the West by NRMs, were made more widely available by them, are now accepted as part of mainstream culture. Gurdjieffian-derived techniques such as the Enneagram are also part of the spiritual direction offered by countless Catholic Orders, among other religious and secular bodies, worldwide.

Not only, then, are NRMs a global phenomenon in the sense that they have emerged in every continent, and within every continent in virtually every country, but also in terms of the influence they have had on the spiritual content and the spiritual practices of many beyond their home base. Sometimes this has been subtle and indirect, sometimes unmistakable and decisive, in shaping the content of modern religion and spirituality.

Peter B. Clarke
Oxford University

Bibliography and references

Barker, E. (1984) *The Making of a Moonie. Choice or Brainwashing?* Oxford: Blackwell.

Barker, E. (2002) 'Watching for Violence: A Comparative Analysis of the Roles of Five Types of Cult-Watching Groups' in D. G. Bromley and J. G. Melton (eds) *Cults, Religion and Violence*, Cambridge: Cambridge University Press, pp. 123–49.

Beckford, J. A. (2003) 'The Continuum Between Cults and Normal Religion' in L. L. Dawson (ed.) *Cults and New Religious Movements*, Oxford: Blackwell, pp. 26–33.

Beckford, J. A. (1985) *Cult Controversies. The Social Response to the New Religious Movements*, London: Tavistock Publications.

Bellah, R., Madsen, R., Sullivan, W., Swidler, A. and Tipton, S. (1985) *Habits of the Heart. Middle America Observed*, London: Hutchinson Education.

Bell, D. (1977) 'The Return of the Sacred?' *British Journal of Sociology* 28(4), 419–49.

Campbell, C. (1999) 'The Easternization of the West', in B. R. Wilson and J. Cresswell (eds), *New Religious Movements. Challenge and Response*, London: Routledge, pp. 35–49.

Clarke, P. B. and Somers, Jeffrey (eds) (1994) *Japanese New Religions in the West*, Eastbourne, Kent: Japan Library/Curzon Press.

Clarke, P. B. (1995) *Mahdism in West Africa. The Case of the Ijebu Prophet*, London: Luzac Oriental.

Clarke, P. B. (1997) (with E. Arweck) *New Religious Movements: An Annotated Bibliography*, Westport, CT: Greenwood Press.

Clarke, P. B. (1998) *New Trends and Developments: in the World of Islam*, London: Luzac Oriental.

Clarke, P. B. (1998) *New Trends and Developments in African Religions*, Westport, CT: Greenwood Press

Clarke, P. B. (1999) *An Annotated Bibliography of Japanese New Religions*, Eastbourne, Kent: Japan Library.

Clarke, P.B. (2000) (ed.) *Japanese New Religions. In Global Perspective*, Richmond: Curzon Press.

Cohn, N. (1970) *The Pursuit of the Millennium*, London: Paladin.

Durkheim, E. (1915) *The Elementary Forms of the Religious Life*, London: George Allen and Unwin

Ezzy, D. (2001) 'The Commodification of Witchcraft', *Australian Religion Studies Review*, 14(1) (Autumn), 31–45.

Groszos Ooms, E. (1993) *Women and Millenarian Protest in Meiji Japan*, Ithaca, NY: Cornell University, East Asia Program.

Hanegraaff, W. J. (1999) 'New Age Spiritualities as Secular Religion: A Historian's Perspective', *Social Compass*, 46(2), 145–60.

Heelas, P. (1991) 'Western Europe: Self-religions', in S. Sutherland and P. B. Clarke (eds) *The Study of Religion: Traditional and New Religion*, London: Routledge, pp. 167–73.

Heelas, P. (1997) *The New Age Movement*, Oxford: Blackwell.

Heelas, P. and Woodhead, L. (with Benjamin Steel *et al.*) (2005) *The Spiritual Revolution*, Oxford: Blackwell.

Iannacone, L. R. (1994) 'Why strict churches are strong', *American Journal of Sociology*, 99(5), 1180–211.

Inoue, N. (1991) (ed.) *New Religions: Contemporary Papers in Japanese Religions (2)*, Tokyo: Kokugakuin University, Institute for Japanese Culture and Classics.

Lambert, Y. (2004) 'A Turning Point in Religious Evolution in Europe', *Journal of Contemporary Religion*, 19(1), January, 29–47.

Martin, D. (1990) *Tongues of Fire*, Oxford: Basil Blackwell.

Maslow, A. (1970) *Motivation and Personality*, New York: Harper and Row.

Melton, J. Gordon (1990) *New Age Encyclopedia*, Detroit: Gale.

Ouspensky, P. D. (1987) *In Search of the Miraculous. Fragments of an Unknown Teaching*, London: Arkana Paperbacks.

Puttick, E. and Clarke, P. B. (eds) (1993) *Women as Teachers and Disciples in Traditional and New Religions*, Lewiston/Queenston/ Lampeter: Edwin Mellen Press.

Puttick, E. (1997) *Women in New Religions*, London: Macmillan.

Reader, I. (1991) *Religion in Contemporary Japan*, Basingstoke: Macmillan.

Richardson, J. (1996) 'Journalistic Bias Towards New Religious Movements in Australia', *Journal of Contemporary Religion*, 11(3), 209–303.

Richardson, J. (2004) *Regulating Religion: Case Studies from Around the Globe*, Amsterdam: Kluwer.

Robbins, T. and Dick, A. (1978) 'New Religious Movements and the Social System: Integration, Disintegration or Transformation', *Annual Review of the Social Sciences of Religion*, 21, 1–28.

Robbins, T. (1988) *Cults, Converts and Charisma*, London: Sage.

Robertson, R. (1992a) *Globalization: Social Theory and Global Culture*, London: Sage.

Robertson, R. (1992b) 'Globalization or glocalization', *Journal of International Communication*, 1, 33–52.

Sen, Amiya, P. (ed.) (2003) *Social and Religious Reform. The Hindus of British India*, Oxford: Oxford University Press.

Shimazono, S. (1999) '"New Age Movement" or New Spirituality Movements and Culture?' *Social Compass*, 46(2), 126–34.

Stark, R. and Bainbridge, W. S. (1985) *The Future of Religion*, Berkeley and Los Angeles: University of California Press.

Stark, R. and Bainbridge, W. S. (1987) *A Theory of Religion*, New York: Peter Lang.

Stark, R. and Finke, R. (2000) *Acts of Faith*, Berkeley and Los Angeles: University of California Press.

Tipton, S. M. (1982) *Getting Saved From the Sixties: Moral Meaning in Conversion and Cultural Change*, Berkeley: University of California Press.

Turner, H. W. (1967) *History of an Independent Church: The Church of the Lord Aladura*, Oxford: Clarendon Press.

Turner, H.W. (1991) 'Africa: New Religions', in S. R. Sutherland and P. B. Clarke (eds) *The Study of Religion: Traditional and New Religion*, London: Routledge, pp. 187–95.

Van Hove, H. (1996) 'Higher Realities and the Inner Self: One Quest? Transcendence and the Significance of the Body in the New Age Circuit', *Journal of Contemporary Religion*, 11(2), 185–95.

Wallis, R. (1976) *The Road to Total Freedom: A Sociological Analysis of Scientology*, London: Heinemann.

Wallis, R. (1984) *The Elementary Forms of the New Religious Life*, London: Routledge.

Werblowsky, R. J. Z. (1984) 'Religions New and Not so New: Fragments of an Agenda' in E. Barker (ed.) *New Religious Movements: A Perspective for Understanding Society*, New York, Toronto: Edwin Mellen, pp. 32–47.

Wilson B. R. (1970) *Religious Sects*, London: Weidenfeld & Nicolson.

Wilson, B. R. (1979) 'The Return of the Sacred?', *Journal for the Scientific Study of Religion* 18(3), 268–80.

Wilson, B. R. (1990) *The Social Dimensions of Sectarianism*, Oxford: Clarendon Press.

Wilson, B. R. (1991) 'Secularization: Religion in the Modern World', in S. R Sutherland and P. B Clarke (eds) *The Study of Religion: Traditional and New Religion*, London: Routledge, pp. 195–208

Wilson, B. R. (1992) 'The Changing Functions of Religion: Toleration and Cohesion in the Secularized Society', IOP. EC Lecture Series. The Wisdom of the East in Modern Society, Maidstone: Institute of Oriental Philosophy.

Wilson, B. R. (1993) 'Historical Lessons in the Study of Cults and Sects', in D. G Bromley and J. K. Hadden (eds) *Religion and Social Order*, 3, 53–85.

Wilson, B. R. and Dobbelaere, K. (1994) *A Time to Chant: The Soka Gakkai Buddhists in Britain*, Oxford: Oxford University Press.

Wilson, B. R. (1995) 'New Religions and the New Europe', in R. Towler (ed.) *New Religious Movements and the New Europe*, Aarhus: Aarhus University Press, pp. 11–31.

Worsley, P. (1970) *The Trumpet Shall Sound*, London: Paladin.

Wuthnow, R. (1978) *Experimentation in American Religion*, Berkeley: University of California Press.

Wuthnow, R. (1986) 'Religious Movements and counter-movements in America', in J. Beckford (ed.) *New Religious Movements and Rapid Social Change*, London: Sage, pp. 1–29.

Wuthnow, R. and Cadge, W. (2004) 'Buddhists and Buddhism in the United States: The Scope of Influence', *Journal for the Scientific Study of Religion*, 43(3) (Sept), 363–81.

How to Use this Encyclopedia

The encyclopedia is organized alphabetically to make for easy access to specific entries. The reader can search a specific entry by alphabetical order, or by using the index at the end of the volume. Cross-references are indicated in bold type in the body of each entry. References to further reading are also provided wherever these are available and considered relevant by the editor and contributors. Such further reading is supported by entries on literature on NRMs in French, German, Italian, Japanese, Portuguese and J. Gordon Melton's extensive and detailed resource guide to scholarly writings on NRMs. All entries are signed and the institutional affiliation of authors at the time of publication is provided on pp. xix–xxi. Entries range from short biographies to more detailed entries and overview essays for major subjects or themes. Biographical entries contain date and place of birth and death, wherever that information is available, the main profession of the individual and a concise description of their activities and works. Longer entries, indicated by italics in the list of entries, offer careful cross-referencing to enable the reader to pursue a topic in more detail across the volume.

This encyclopaedia takes a global perspective on the phenomenon of New Religious Movements (NRMs). It provides examples of NRMs that have become global cultures in their own right with millions, and even hundred of millions of followers. Not only are there over three hundred entries on various types of movement from almost every country in the world but there are also contributions on topics and themes directly associated with NRMs, such as spirituality, the New Age Movement (NAM), Neo-paganism, New Religion, New Religion as a global phenomenon, New Religion and gender, 'Protestant Buddhism', 'Engaged Buddhism', Modern Yoga, and Islamism. There are also entries on NRMs and cyberspace, NRMs and the law, NRMs and violence, the Anti-Cult Movement (ACM), and on the appropriateness or otherwise of terms used to describe NRMs such as sect and cult. There is also coverage of the key ideas of thinkers whose ideas have greatly influenced the development of NRMs including the Scientist and esotericist Emmanuel Swedenborg, the psychoanalyst Carl Gustav Jung, the Jesuit Pierre Teilhard de Chardin, the Scientist James Lovelock, author of one widely studied version of the Gaia hypothesis, George Ivanovitch Gurdjieff, founder of the Institute for the Harmonious Development of Man at Fontainebleau, and two of the most influential Islamist thinkers, the Egyptians Hassan al-Banna founder of the Muslim Brotherhood (Ikhwan) and Sayyid Qutb, an influential member of that same movement. Coverage is also given to movements that derive from all the major religions of the world and to Neo-Traditional movements. Movements often overlooked in the study of NRMs including Islamic derived NRMs such as the Nation of Islam, the Muslim Brotherhood, and Buddhist and Sikh derived NRMs are also included in the volume, as are movements from all the continents – from Caodaism in Asia (Vietnam) to the Santo Daime movement at the other side of the world in Brazil. This wide framework enables a better appreciation to be had of the innovative character of NRMs and of their diversity.

The global perspective taken in this volume sheds much light on aspects of NRMs that might otherwise remain obscure, including their significance and impact. They can be seen to be much more than small scale, marginal enterprises of little significance to all but a few. Instead they involve hundreds of millions of followers and in many cases are radically changing the way people understand and practise religion and spirituality. Moreover, many are having a profound impact on the form and content of much mainstream religion.

From a global vantage point one obtains a clearer picture of how vast and varied is the range of spiritual resources and technologies that are now being drawn upon in every part of the world. The global perspective also makes clear that there is no single source of NRMs or highway or route across the world that is favoured by them. They exist everywhere and move in all kinds of unexpected directions from Japan to Africa via Brazil for example and from Indonesia to Australia to Europe, others from Tibet to South Africa, from India to Mauritius and on to the West Indies.

Consultant Editors

Contributors

Afe Adogame
Bayreuth University, Germany

Akin Akinade
High Point University, North Carolina, USA

Allan Anderson
University of Birmingham, UK

Scott Appleby
University of Notre Dame, USA

Gideon Aran
The Hebrew University of Jerusalem, Israel

Elisabeth Arweck
University of Warwick, UK

Abamfo Atiemo
University of Ghana, Ghana

Kristin Aune
King's College, University of London, UK

Hans Baer
University of Arkansas, USA

Edward Bailey
Middlesex University, UK

Eileen Barker
London School of Economics, UK

David V. Barrett
London School of Economics, UK

Martin Baumann
University Bayreuth, Germany

Gwilym Beckerlegge
Open University, UK

Marion Bowman
Open University, UK

George Brandon
City University of New York, USA

David G. Bromley
Virginia Commonwealth University, USA

George Chryssides
University of Wolverhampton, UK

Peter Clarke
University of Oxford, UK

Dan Cohn-Sherbok
Lampeter University, UK

Simon Coleman
University of Sussex, UK

Catherine M. Cornille
Boston College, USA

Donald Cosentino
University of California Los Angeles, USA

Alberto Croisman
Universidade Federal de Santa Catarina, Brazil

Donal Cruise O'Brien
School of Oriental and African Studies, University of London, UK

Patricia Cunningham
London School of Economics, UK

Douglas J. Davies
Durham University, UK

Lorne Dawson
University of Waterloo, Canada

Elizabeth de Michelis
University of Cambridge, UK

CONTRIBUTORS

Elom Dovlo
University of Ghana, Ghana

Esther Foreman
London School of Economics, UK

Paul Freston
Federal University of Sao Carlos, Brazil

Masaki Fukui
King's College, University of London, UK

Catherine Garrett
University of Western Sydney, Australia

Paul Gifford
*School of Oriental and African Studies,
University of London, UK*

Emerson Giumbelli
Federal University of Rio de Janeiro, Brazil

Matthew Guest
University of Durham, UK

Malcolm Hamilton
University of Reading, UK

Helen Hardacre
Harvard University, USA

Graham Harvey
King Alfred's College, UK

Irving Hexham
University of Calgary, Canada

Richard Hoskins
King's College, University of London, UK

Julia Howell
Griffith University, Australia

Reinhart Hummel
*Evangelische Zentralstelle für
Weltanschauungsfragen, Germany*

Stephen Hunt
University of the West of England, UK

Keishin Inaba
Kobe University, Japan

Nabutaka Inoue
Kokugakin University, Japan

Massimo Introvigne
CESNUR, Turin, Italy

A. Hamish Ion
Royal Military College, Canada

Claude F. Jacobs
University of Michigan-Dearborn, USA

Christophe Jaffrelot
CNRS and FNSP/Sciences Po, Paris, France

Alan Johnson
The Oxford Centre for Mission Studies, UK

Daren Kemp
Researcher, London, UK

Alexandra Kent
Gothenburg University, Sweden

Ursula King
Universiy of Bristol, UK

Robert Kisala
Nanzan University, Japan

Ben Knighton
Oxford Centre for Mission Studies, UK

Kim Knott
University of Leeds, UK

Ioan M. Lewis
London School of Economics, UK

Rowland Littlewood
University College, London, UK

Phillip Lucas
Stetson University, USA

Roderick Main
University of Essex, UK

David Maxwell
Keele University, UK

Jean-François Mayer
University of Fribourg, Switzerland

J. Gordon Melton
*Institute of American Religion,
Santa Barbara, California, USA*

James Moore
Researcher, London, UK

R. David Muir
King's College, University of London, UK

Mark Mullins
Sophia University Tokyo, Japan

Matthews Ojo
Obafemi Awolowo University, Nigeria

Cephas Omenyo
University of Ghana, Ghana

Ari Pedro Oro
Federal University of Rio Grande do Sul at Porto Alegre, Brazil

Joanne Pearson
Cardiff University, UK

Karen Pechilis Prentiss
Drew University, New Jersey, USA

Jason Pelplinski
King's College, University of London, UK

Martyn Percy
University of Oxford, UK

Jennifer Porter
Memorial University of Newfoundland, Canada

Adam Possamai
University of Western Sydney, Australia

Elizabeth Puttick
Publisher, London, UK

Selva J. Raj
Albion College Michigan, USA

James T. Richardson
University of Nevada, USA

Donizete Rodrigues
University of Beira Interior, Portugal

Stuart Rose
Bath Spa University College, UK

Mikael Rothstein
University of Copenhagen, Denmark

Kathryn Rountree
Massey University at Albany, Auckland, New Zealand

Chris Rowland
University of Oxford, UK

Alexandra Ryan
Open University, UK

Maria Amelia Schmidt-Dickie
Universidade Federal de Santa Catarina, Brazil

Susumu Shimazono
University of Tokyo, Japan

Merril Singer
Hispanic Health Council Inc., New York, USA

Carlos Steil
Federal University of Rio Grande do Sul at Porto Alegre, Brazil

Steven Sutcliffe
University of Stirling, UK

Berend J. ter Haar
Leiden University, The Netherlands

Gerrie ter Haar
Institute of Social Studies, The Netherlands

Ronit Yoeli Tlalim
School of Oriental and African Studies, University of London, UK

Michael Walsh
Heythrop College, University of London, UK

Kathleen Walsh
Education Consultant, London, UK

Margit Warburg
University of Copenhagen, Denmark

Helen Waterhouse
Open University, UK

Rob Wheeler
Sea of Faith Movement

Paul Williams
University of Bristol, UK

Raymond Williams
Wabash College, USA

Ralph Woodhall
Selly Oak Colleges, University of Birmingham, UK

Peter Worsley
University of Manchester, UK

Yu-Shuang-Yao
Fo-Guang College, Ilan, Taiwan

Michael York
Bath Spa University, UK

PierLuigi Zoccatelli
CESNUR, Turin, Italy

List of Entries

Note: titles in italic indicate a major entry.

A COURSE IN MIRACLES
Daren Kemp

ADI DA
Stuart Rose

AETHERIUS SOCIETY
David V. Barrett

AFRICAN CHARISMATIC CHURCHES
Paul Gifford

AFRICAN INDEPENDENT CHURCHES
Cephas N. Omenyo

AFRICAN ORTHODOX CHURCH
Ben Knighton

AFRIKANIA MISSION
Elom Dovlo

AFTER-LIFE BELIEFS
Helen Waterhouse

AGE OF AQUARIUS
Michael York

AGONSHU
Peter B. Clarke

AHMADIYYA MOVEMENT
Peter B. Clarke

AKINSOWON, CHRISTIANA ABIODUN (MRS/CAPTAIN)
Matthews A. Ojo

AL-BANNA, HASSAN
Peter B. Clarke

AL-QAEDA (THE BASE)
Peter B. Clarke

ALPHA COURSE
Patricia Cunningham

THE AMA-NAZARETHA (THE NAZARETH BAPTIST CHURCH)
Irving Hexham

AMERICAN FAMILY FOUNDATION
David V. Barrett

AMORC
Massimo Introvigne

AMRITANANDAMAYI, MATA (AMMACHI)
Selva J. Raj

ANCIENT TEACHINGS OF THE MASTERS
PierLuigi Zoccatelli

ANTHROPOSOPHY
Alexandra E. Ryan

ANTI-CULT MOVEMENT
Elisabeth Arweck

APOSTLES' REVELATION SOCIETY
Elom Dovlo

APOSTOLIC CHURCH OF JOHANE MASOWE
Akintunde E. Akinade

ARCANUM NAMA SHIVAYA HINDU MISSION
Elom Dovlo

ARCHEOSOPHY
PierLuigi Zoccatelli

ARMSTRONG, HERBERT W.
David V. Barrett

ARYA SAMAJ
Kim Knott

ASAHARA SHOKO (MATSUMOTO, CHIZUO)
Susumu Shimazono

ASSAGIOLOI, ROBERTO
Peter B. Clarke

LIST OF ENTRIES

LIST OF ENTRIES

LIST OF ENTRIES

LIST OF ENTRIES

LIST OF ENTRIES

A COURSE IN MIRACLES

A Course in Miracles (the Course) is a lengthy channelled text, received by Dr Helen Schucman (1909–81) a psychologist at Columbia University in New York city between 1965 and 1972, which became especially popular in New Age circles (see **New Age Movement**). This entry briefly describes the nature of the Course, its history and leading interpreters in the broader movement it has inspired.

The Course is divided into three parts – the Text, the Workbook for Students and the Manual for Teachers – which were initially published separately but were subsequently collated in a single volume. The Course uses traditional Christian language and imagery, such as Father, Son, Holy Spirit, truth, grace, and forgiveness, but modifies traditional meanings to fit an idealist, neo-Gnostic worldview. Schucman is thought to have understood the entity which channelled the text to be Jesus, although she did

not publicize such an interpretation during her lifetime.

The Course describes its purpose as to train the mind to a different understanding of reality (Workbook: 1), and this formulation perhaps owes much to Schucman's profession as a research psychologist. The material world is said to be an illusory misunderstanding of the ego, both of which are in fact merely aspects of the one God. In the terminology of the Course, it is fear and guilt that creates the perception of a reality separate from God, and forgiveness that overcomes this delusion. Thinking in line with the thought of the Creator God can allow a miracle to happen – not a magical alteration of reality, but a real understanding of the illusory nature of the world.

The purpose of the Course is also described as salvation, and again this word should not be understood in its traditional Christian sense, but instead as attaining healing and wholeness through a correct perception of the world. In the psychological terminology also used in the Course, this is described as sanity, while false ideas or irrational delusions allow belief in the real existence of the material world.

Thus the Course shows some similarities to **Christian Science** and **New Thought**. It also owes philosophical debts to Plato, of whom Schucman was fond, René Descartes' method of doubt and analogy of the dream, and perhaps existentialism's concern for meaning in the world.

Bill Thetford (1922–88), Schucman's academic supervisor at the Department of Psychiatry at Columbia-Presbyterian Medical Center, New York, encouraged and assisted in the transcription of the Course. It was subsequently edited by Kenneth Wapnick (b. 1942), who like Schucman and Thetford came from a Jewish background. While Schucman and Thetford were then both agnostic (officially at least – Schucman continued Christian observances throughout her life), Wapnick had converted to Roman Catholicism and had seriously considered becoming a Trappist monk.

The Course was popularized by Judy Skutch Whitson (then Judy Skutch), and published in 1975. Skutch also had a Jewish background and an interest in parapsychology, having founded the Foundation for Parasensory Investigation in 1971, renaming it Foundation for Inner Peace (FIP) in 1975 on the advice of a communication received by Helen Schucman. The Foundation for *A Course in Miracles* (FACIM) was founded by Wapnick in 1983 as a sister, teaching arm of FIP. FACIM does not have members and should not be considered as a typical New Religious Movement in itself.

Wapnick is the foremost interpreter of the Course, and now vigorously defends the copyright interests in it, resulting in a number of lawsuits. Other well-known teachers inspired by the Course include Gerald Jampolsky, Marianne Williamson, and Chuck Spezzano.

There are many other institutions inspired by the Course, including the Miracle Distribution Center, Fullerton, California; The Foundation for Life Action, Los Angeles of Tara Singh; The Interfaith Fellowship, New York of Revd Jon Mundy and Revd Diane Berke; The Circle of Atonement, Sedona, Arizona of Robert Perry; The California Miracles Center, San Francisco, California of Revd Tony Ponticello; the controversial Endeavor Academy, Baraboo, Wisconsin of Chuck Anderson, known as 'Dear One'; and the Miracle Network, London, England.

The Course is also widely used by lone students, private study groups, many Christian churches – especially Unity churches – and twelve-step recovery programmes. Unlike Christian Science, which was inspired in a similar way by *Science and Health with Key to the Scriptures* (1875), it has not developed into a hierarchical church or even into a cohesive movement, and its long-term significance remains to be seen.

Further reading

Kemp, D. (2003) *New Age: A Guide – Alternative Spiritualities from Aquarian Conspiracy to Next Age*, Edinburgh: Edinburgh University Press.
Miller, D. P. (1997) *The Complete Story of The Course: The History, The People, and The Controversies behind A Course in Miracles*, Berkeley, CA: Fearless Books.

DAREN KEMP

ADI DA

The full self-given name of Adi Da is Ruchira Avatar Adi Da Samraj. The name means: Ruchira = shining or bright, avatar = a direct incarnation of God (see also **Mother Meera** and **Sai**

Baba, **Sathya**), Adi = first, Da = the Giver (God), and Samraj = divine ruler – hence, he claims to be the shining divine descent of the God-Man.

At birth in 1939 at Long Island, New York, he was given the name Franklin Albert Jones. As a baby, he says that he recollects being conscious of a divine state which he now calls the 'Bright'; at the age of two he decided to relinquish the bliss of this original state and enter the world. When 25 years old, Adi Da enrolled with his first spiritual teacher, Swami Rudrananda, which was followed four years later by entering a period of study with Swami Muktananda, and in 1970 he claims to have fully attained Self-realization. Two years later he started teaching and opened his first ashram in 1972. During this time he taught using the names Franklin Jones, Bubba Free John, Da Free John and Da Avabhasa.

In 1983, Adi Da moved to Fiji in the South Pacific, which has since become his primary residence – he became a Fijian citizen in 1993. Over the period of his life mostly in Fiji, Adi Da has written twenty-three 'source texts' – his writing is characterized by unorthodox word capitalization – five of which are described as the Heart of the Adidam Revelation. The titles of these works shed some light on his teachings: *Aham Da Asmi* (Beloved, I *Am* Da), *Ruchira Avatara Gita* (The Way Of The Divine Heart-Master), *Da Love-Ananda Gita* (The Free Gift Of The Divine Love-Bliss), *Hridaya Rosary* (Four Thorns Of Heart-Instruction) and *Eleutherios* (The *Only* Truth That Sets The Heart Free). All Adi Da's works are published by Adidam (the name given to the Adi Da community) through their Dawn Horse Press.

The community itself is spread world-wide, although mostly through the US. There are six main centres located in California, New Zealand, Australia, Holland, London, and Fiji, plus there are fourteen other centres, eight in the US (including Hawaii), two in Canada, two in Australia, and two in Continental Europe. In the UK, groups meet regularly in several towns and cities spread mostly in the south. The number of people involved in Adidam as a whole is not large because, as Georg Feuerstein points out in his chapter analysing Adi Da in *Holy Madness: The Shock Tactics and Radical Teachings of Crazy-wise Adepts, Holy Fools, and Rascal Gurus:* 'most people are in need of a prolonged period of intense preparation in which they must learn to discipline their attention and energy' (1992: 86).

To this end, Adi Da developed a structure to his teachings which he calls the Way of the Heart, the first step being a five-week introductory course, after which the aspirant can apply to become a pre-student, undertaking further courses, applying later again to become a student-novice. The highest level, or First Congregation, is comprised of those devotees who have fully dedicated their lives to Adi Da and are renunciants, although not necessarily celibate.

The levels of these teachings centre on the act and degree of surrender to Adi Da who demands a complete and uncompromising abandonment of the individual egoic self (see **Self-religion, The Self and self**) so, he claims, saving the person from all life's sorrow, despair, anger and lovelessness. In its place, the devotee is allowed to rest in Adi Da himself who, he says in *Da Love – Ananda Gita*, is the perfect one: 'I *Am* That Which Is Always Already The Case. I *Am* the Non-Separate and Only One, the "Bright" One, and Indivisible and Indestructible One, Who *Is* all and All. Therefore, surrender Only to *Me*, and accept all your experience *As* My own Play.'

Further reading

Feuerstein, G. (1992) *Holy Madness: The Shock Tactics and Radical Teachings of Crazy-wise Adepts, Holy Fools, and Rascal Gurus*, London: Arkana.
STUART ROSE

AETHERIUS SOCIETY

The Aetherius Society is one of the earliest and longest-lasting **UFO**-related religions. It is one of the few British NRMs (see **New Religious Movement**) to spread successfully to the USA and elsewhere in the world. It is also a rare example of a new religion making a smooth transition following the death of its founder.

In May 1954 George King (1919–97), who had practised yoga at a high level for ten years, heard a voice telling him 'Prepare yourself! You are to become the voice of Interplanetary Parliament!' A week later he was visited in his locked flat by 'an Indian Swami of world renown' who instructed him to form a group. Shortly after that he began receiving telepathic messages from Venus. King started holding public meetings in central London at which he gave messages from the Ascended Masters, and in 1955 he founded the Aetherius Society.

In its teachings the Aetherius Society is firmly in the tradition of those New Age groups (see **New Age Movement**) rooted in the **Theosophical** Society's reinterpretation of Eastern beliefs for the West. Our actions in this life determine our progression to the next; ideally through the lessons we learn in each successive life, we move up the scale until we eventually become Masters. The Ascended Masters (or Great White Brotherhood) are those who have reached the highest levels and now give guidance to those of us still working our way up. The Cosmic Hierarchy, or Interplanetary Parliament, is based on Saturn. Ascended Masters include Jesus and Buddha who came from Venus, Krishna from Saturn, and other great religious teachers of the past. The Aetherius Society sees each planet in our solar system as a different 'classroom'; when we have developed sufficiently through a succession of lives on Earth, we will move on to Venus or Mars to continue our development in a higher classroom.

Between 1958 and 1961, George King and other members of the Aetherius Society took part in Operation Starlight, in which they climbed eighteen mountains around the world and painted the Society's symbol, charging the mountains with spiritual power. Members still go on pilgrimages to these mountains.

The Aetherius Society helps the Ascended Masters in their constant battle against evil forces. In what is known as a Spiritual Push, through prayer and meditation members draw spiritual power (Prana) down to Earth from a huge (though invisible) spaceship, Satellite Three, which is in close orbit around our planet.

The most distinctive practice of the Aetherius Society is its use of Spiritual Energy Batteries. The prayers and chanting of members are focused through trained leaders, and poured into a battery where they can be stored indefinitely. In times of crisis, such as war, earthquake or famine, thousands of hours of stored prayer energy can be released in one moment.

Over the years George King accumulated a vast number of religious, chivalric and academic-sounding titles from a variety of unorthodox sources, such as Knight of the Grand Cross of Justice with Grand Collar in the Sovereign Military Orthodox Dynastic Imperial Constantinian Order of Saint Georges. The most significant of these was his consecration as a bishop from the Liberal Catholic Church; through this, the clergy of the Aetherius Society have legitimate Apostolic Succession. The Society today is run by three bishops, including the UK leader Richard Lawrence, and ten senior engineering officers, five in the UK and five in the USA, who have technical responsibility for the Society's missions, such as the prayer batteries. The board of directors is based in Los Angeles.

Since his death, George King has been recognized by the movement as an avatar of one of the Ascended Masters. He gave over 600 Cosmic Transmissions during his leadership, but these ceased with his death. The Aetherius Society treats King, and his messages, with great respect, and they still maintain all of his teachings, including the teaching that a Master will soon come to Earth openly, in a flying saucer. On a day-to-day basis, though, the emphasis has changed more to spiritual healing through the transfer of Prana, the universal life force; Richard Lawrence is a regular speaker and writer on healing in the wider New Age scene.

The worldwide membership of the Aetherius Society is 'in the thousands, but not tens of thousands', according to Lawrence. The USA, New Zealand and Africa have the largest concentration of members; in Britain there are 600–700 members, and around 8,000 on the mailing list.

Further reading

Barrett, D. V. (2001) *The New Believers*, London: Cassell.

King, G. and Lawrence, R. (1996) *Contacts With The Gods From Space*, Hollywood, CA: The Aetherius Society

DAVID V. BARRETT

AFRICAN CHARISMATIC CHURCHES

African charismatic churches is the label given to the wide variety of neo-pente-costal churches proliferating in Africa since about 1980. They vary in size from very small (the majority) to urban megachurches and even to what are effectively new denominations. There are variations across the continent (the phenomenon, for example, is more developed in Anglophone than Francophone countries), but all are distinguished for exuberant worship, media involvement, incessant evangelizing, particular theological ideas, and a general internationalizing ethos that differentiates them markedly from the **African Independent Churches** that have existed for over a century. African charismatic churches are dependent on gifted individuals, and almost a prototype is the Church of God Mission International founded by the late Benson Idahosa (1938–98) in Benin City in the 1960s; current paradigmatic examples are the **Living Faith World Outreach Centre (or Winners' Chapel)** founded in Lagos in 1983 by David Oyedepo (and which by 2000, only 16 years later, had spread to thirty-eight African countries); and the **Synagogue Church of All Nations** founded by the Prophet T. B. Joshua in 1994, also in Lagos.

The theology characteristic of these churches is, first, that of the **Health and Wealth gospel**, which teaches that a Christian has a right to success and plenty, which follow upon faith, or upon faith and on giving to God which through the inevitable functioning of the 'law of sowing and reaping' will bring wealth and victory. This 'law' has proved very effective in Africa, for all the concrete manifestations of this explosion – new churches, programmes, travel, music, vehicles, indeed an entire class of new religious professionals – have had to be paid for, and 'sowing' on the part of members has provided the means to pay for this explosion of Christianity at a time when investment in the continent has been pitifully small. If the form in which **prosperity theology** is expressed is often not very different from that articulated by its main US proponents Kenneth Hagin (1917–) or Kenneth Copeland (1937–), it must be said that its wide acceptance in Africa owes much to the underlying orientation of Africa's pre-Christian religion which was centred on this-worldly realities like fertility, abundance, long life.

The other prominent characteristic is **deliverance** theology. Since prosperity is considered the right of every believer, its absence requires explanation. Deliverance thinking explains that a Christian's rightful prosperity is often blocked by pervasive spiritual forces of which the believer may be unaware but which can be diagnosed and exorcised by an 'anointed man of God'. Evils may also arise from 'curses' incurred by the believer, again often unbeknown to her; these curses are often understood to arise from ancestors' involvement in 'witchcraft' or 'pagan practices'. This understanding fuels the particularly negative attitude of these churches to African traditions and culture (which gives rise to the paradox that the same churches which so denigrate African culture do much to perpetuate the traditional African religious world view). For most of these churches, all evils (physical sickness, of course, but now more commonly economic deprivation) are caused by such spiritual forces. The ubiquitous 'miracle crusades' associated with these churches consist mainly of casting out such demons.

Worship in these churches is participatory and exuberant (and sometimes though not invariably marked by the speaking in tongues characteristic of Pentecostal churches generally). The 'praise and worship' which constitutes at least a third of any service is backed not by drums, but by western instruments like electric guitars, and is characterised by modern hymns, often in English, which are repetitive and catchy. The music of these churches has frequently become a commercially significant element of a nation's recording industry. Nevertheless, the most important part of the service is unquestionably the sermon, usually delivered from at most a few notes, and ostensibly built on some biblical text or texts. (In keeping with the message of success, the biblical motifs stem largely from the Old Testament, and centre round OT examples like Abraham, Joseph, Joshua Moses, David, Solomon.) The music and the message constitute the greater part not only of the Sunday service but nearly all the many meetings throughout the week, even if labelled Bible Study or Women's Fellowship. Services may also be characterized by testimonies where believers speak of the marvels God has wrought for them; by an 'altar call' where those not yet 'born-again' can give their lives to Christ; by a warm welcome for all newcomers; and some services may include cures or deliverance.

In nearly all the established churches of this type, almost all such messages are taped if not videoed; these form the basis of the media involvement for which all these churches are known. In many African countries these church services constitute a good deal of the fare on radio and television, often supplemented with similar programmes from United States ministries. A comparison of these programmes reveals that the African media involvement is modelled on US paradigms. The same is true of the print media – in some countries, most Christian media is now of this charismatic type.

Institutionally, these churches were almost invariably founded by charismatic individuals (usually men, although occasionally women), in most cases with considerable leadership skills. Without such charisma and skills, given the competition, these churches quickly die. Because personalities are so crucial, co-operation between these churches is never easy, and in most cases goes no further than preaching at each other's conventions. For the same reason, Pentecostal or Evangelical or Charismatic Councils or other bodies established to represent these churches, rarely function with any force. Splits within these churches are frequent. With the increasing marginalization of Africa, it has become more desirable to form some links with similar US churches. Famous US preachers enhance African conventions, and some churches develop more lucrative links. The ethos of these groups has tended to become more authoritarian rather than more democratic, a tendency most marked since about 1995 with the increasing use of the term 'prophet' as a designation for these leaders.

Further reading

Gifford, P. (2003) *Ghana's New Christianity: Pentecostalism in a Globalising African Economy*, London: Hurst & Co.

PAUL GIFFORD

AFRICAN INDEPENDENT CHURCHES

The period from the late nineteenth century has witnessed the upsurge of a number of churches, which were indeed an African strand of a new development of Christianity. Mainly fabricated in Africa by Africans to suit the African context and described as 'a place to feel at home' these churches came to be referred to by various names such separatist, Ethiopian, Zionist, Spiritual, Prophetic Movements, Syncretistic Movement, Nativistic Churches, Messianic Movement, and Praying Churches. Others have classified the African Independent Churches (hereinafter referred to by the acronym AICs which in fact could stand for synonymous terms such as, African Instituted Churches; African Indigenous Churches; African Initiatives in Christianity) into two broad categories, namely, the Spirit-type (due to the centrality of the work and experience of the Holy Spirit among them) and Ethiopian type (because they were non-prophetic and often claimed ideological and religious links with Ethiopia Africa). The generally accepted term for these churches is African Initiated Churches.

The development of the AICs was essentially a paradigm shift and a challenge to the Eurocentric disposition of the mainline historic churches in Africa. A casual observer of the beliefs and practices of the AICs can be convinced about the resilience of the African indigenous worldview. Consequently, the AICs were perceived as authentic African expressions of Christianity. The effect of this new and contextual expression of Christianity on African Churches was the alarming rate of the exodus of members of the mainline historic churches to join some of the AICs.

Several factors accounted for the emergence of the AICs. The following are some of them.

In the first place, some of their leaders were nationalists who used religion as a protest against European colonial rule and as a means to pursue the policy of African self-expression and freedom from missionary control.

Second, the emergence of key charismatic leaders such as Garrick Braide (of Niger Delta in Nigeria) (see **Braide, Garrick Sokari**), William Wade Harris (a Kru from Liberia) (see **Harris, William Wadé**), and Simon Kimbangu (of Belgian Congo) (see **Kimbangu, Simon**) inspired some of their followers to start their own churches. Third, some African

Christians broke away from mainline historic churches in order to have the freedom to exercise their charismatic gifts, for the manifestation of which they felt the mainline churches did not create enough room within their framework. Fourth, some simply rebelled against the overtly Eurocentric brand of Christianity and sought to express Christianity in African terms. In the fifth place, the translation of the Bible into the mother tongues of various African ethnic groups enabled Africans to read the Bible in their own languages, thus they became more self-conscious as African and this provided them with a major impetus to form their own churches. Finally, crisis situations such as the deadly influenza epidemic that spread through West Africa in 1981 and to which orthodox medicine could not find a solution led people to seek healing through faith and other spiritual means. This development led to the emergence of prayer groups some of which later became independent churches.

Currently, there are a number of characteristics that make the AICs distinctive. Revelations through prophets and faith healing are two prominent features of the AICs. Indeed, the search for healing is the most common reason why people join the AICs. This led most of the AICs to establish healing centres or camps where patients could be kept for a period (sometimes for years), until they completely recovered. Healing is usually effected by praying and the laying on of hands. Most churches stress fasting in their healing process. They also practise anointing with oil, ritual bathing, and the drinking of blessed water. Most of the AICs also practise exorcism of evil spirits and cure confessed witches. Indeed exorcism is closely associated with healing since there is a strong belief among most Africans that mishap, evil, and ailment are caused by evil forces like witches and demons.

Spontaneity is the hallmark of the worship of the AICs. Their worship is vibrant and fascinating, full of lively African music, clapping and dancing which facilitates the active participation of members. Most of the songs used are traditional lyrics, which are usually spontaneous compositions that are accompanied by traditional musical instruments.

The AICs are noted for contextualizing Christianity 'from below'. Their sermons are deeply rooted in African primal culture and they are tailored to respond to the demands of their adherents. They are concerned to respond to the issues raised by the African worldview that contains a strong belief in malevolent spirits, witches and wizards. They attach great importance to the interpretation of dreams and visions.

Most AICs do not prohibit polygamy. Polygamists are admitted to all sacraments such as the Lord's Supper and they are allowed to take all offices including the office of a pastor/Prophet. AICs are also distinctive in African Christianity due to the prominent role that they give to women. Women are encouraged to participate in all activities and take up leadership roles in the churches. There are also numerous cases of women who were either founders or co-founders of AICs.

The AICs constitute a renewal movement that has sought to make Christianity more relevant to the African context. With the emergence of the AICs, the African worldview and African spirituality found fulfilment in a Christian way. The uniqueness of the AICs is found in the prominent use of traditional African beliefs, forms, symbols and practices, and the liberal interpretation of the Bible to respond to issues such as those posed by the spirit world in the African worldview. They are also noted for their emphasis on the Holy Spirit. This historical and spiritual significance, then, of the AICs is to be found in their having pioneered the movement to contextualize Christianity in Africa by offering an expression for the African spiritual quest for meaning in a Christian way.

Further reading

Baëta, C. G. (1962) *Prophetism in Ghana; A study of some Spiritual Churches*, London: SCM Press

Barret, D. B. (1968) *Schism and Renewal in Africa*, London: Oxford University Press

Turner, H. W. (1967) *African Independent Church*, 2 vols. London: Oxford University Press

CEPHAS N. OMENYO

AFRICAN ORTHODOX CHURCH

Founder: Alexander McGuire/
D. W. Alexander
Country: North America/Africa

The African Orthodox Church (AOC) represents a rarely successful move of African Independent Churches to join a mainstream denomination. It provided the best available legitimation for black Christian leaders to counter racial discrimination.

Origin: USA

In 1866 Alexander McGuire was born in Antigua, the eldest son of an Anglican plantation manager. He succeeded as a teacher, then as a minister in the Episcopalian Church of America. Seeking ecclesiastical freedom, he became Chaplain-General of Marcus Garvey's Universal Negro Improvement Association in New York. Neither it, nor the Roman, Orthodox, and Episcopal churches, would endorse his plans for a black church, so he convened a synod of all the Independent Episcopalian Churches. Over five days in September 1921 he underwent all the rites from baptism to enthronement as archbishop at the hands of Archbishop Metropolitan Joseph Vilatte of the American Catholic church, who enjoyed unbroken apostolic succession through the Syrian church of Antioch to St Peter. However only one bishop assisted in the consecration, leading later to criticisms that 'Patriarch' Alexander I's consecration was valid, but illegitimate. Clergy of the African Orthodox Church would emphasize the documentary evidence for its apostolic succession. It was not 'a little sect'. From the beginning it sought as a church, 'perpetually autonomous, autocephalous and controlled by negroes ... particularly to reach out and enfold the millions of African descent in both hemispheres'.

South Africa

The African Province only began with enquiries from well-educated men there, who learned of the AOC through reading Marcus Garvey's *The Negro World*. This contact with black theology made any African suspect with the colonial authorities. In South Africa Daniel Alexander was able to cross boundaries with his French passport and his coloured classification, being the son of a Roman Catholic of Martinique and a Cuban/Javan mother. He was ordained an Anglican priest in 1903, but left the church 11 years later to join the African Political Organization, soon ministering to a coloured church in Kimberley. He struggled for funds, members, and official recognition.

With the AOC Alexander believed that Africa belonged to the black races of the world; if the white colonial masters refused to leave the continent, they must be ousted. In 1924 McGuire appointed him Vicar Apostolic for South Africa, but Alexander had to take a £200 loan to go to New York for his consecration as Archbishop and Primate of the African Province in 1927. He received a rousing reception across southern Africa, being joined by Anglican priests and laymen. Yet buildings and funds eluded his authoritarian approach.

Uganda

Mukasa Spartas also became disenchanted with the Anglican church, seeking leadership in the redemption of Africa. He replied to McGuire that he wanted to be 'like that active son of South Africa', so Alexander made him a lay reader. On 6 January 29 Spartas formed the AOC in Uganda, and when he had paid his fare, impressed on Alexander to come to Uganda to ordain him in 1931. Spartas was made Archpriest and Vicar-General, but not the bishop that Alexander said that he desired. After a Greek told Spartas he was not using the Greek rite, he severed relations with Alexander in 1932 and sought recognition from the Orthodox Patriarch of Alexandria. By 1936 Spartas was claiming thirty centres, twenty-three church schools, and 5,000 members, spreading from Buganda to Busoga and Lango.

Kenya

In 1929 the female circumcision crisis provoked the exodus from the mission churches to the Agĩkũyũ **Karinga** movement. Though they started schools, they resolved that for seven years, they would do without church organization, as they had no well-educated men to take on the missionaries as equals.

However the Kikuyu Independent Schools Association (KISA) responded to the desire of its pupils like Kimani wa Kibero for baptism. They asked the Anglican Bishop of Mombasa to take two men for ordination training, but the mission churches did not want to foster an independent upstart. So they applied to Alexander for an apostolic church, as in the case of the AOC in Uganda, governed by Africans, of and for Africans. In November 1935 Spartas arrived bearing the hope that the 'Negro Race will set an example to the world, indicating what the race can do itself without any external assistance of another race' (Johnson 1999: 98).

Spartas survived the usual church disputes over money and translated McGuire's Divine Liturgy drawn from Roman, Anglican, and Orthodox sources. Meanwhile they used the *Gĩgĩkũyũ* Anglican prayer and hymn books. In nineteen months he baptized 8,000, including 646 on one Sunday, confirmed 300, married 150, and ordained five. Only two were well-educated, Philip Kiande, and Arthur Gatungu Gathuna. They accompanied him back to the coast and then set up the AOC of Kenya. The others resented Gathuna being ordained, when his Karinga people had refused to contribute to Alexander's fare, so formed their own church.

In 1938 the Syrian Patriarchate of Antioch excommunicated Vilatte and repudiated the AOC. Though Gathuna had already attracted a membership of 20,000, he soon joined with Spartas of Uganda to seek pure Greek Orthodox legitimation from the Patriarch of Alexandria. It took until 1946 to recognize their apostolic succession. Spartas became Bishop Christophoros of Niloupolis. By 1953 there were 30,000 members in Kenya, including 309 congregations and twenty-eight schools, but these were then banned for connections to Mau Mau oathing. Gathuna, to Spartas 'a pure Kikuyu', was arrested and detained until 1961. After post-independence growth to 250,000 members Gathuna was consecrated bishop in 1974, only to fall out with the Archbishop of East Africa on the issue of African accountability to 'foreign missionaries'. Gathuna was defrocked in 1987, while the leading clergy were reconciled to the Patriarch of Alexandria, who claimed authority over 300,000 Kenyans and 200,000 Ugandans in 2004.

In the USA the AOC has only 6,000 adherents, and perhaps 50,000 worldwide. Virtually all the AOC in Africa has been absorbed by the Greek Orthodox Church. Under a Cyprian Pope and Patriarch only Jonah of Uganda of the fifteen Metropolitans in Africa is black.

Further reading

Johnson, M. (1999) *Archbishop Daniel William Alexander and the African Orthodox Church*, London: International Scholars.

BEN KNIGHTON

AFRIKANIA MISSION

Afrikania Mission is a Neo-Traditional Movement established in Ghana in 1982 by a former Catholic Priest, Kwabena Damuah, who resigned from the church and assumed the traditional priesthood titles, *Osofo Okomfo*. The Mission aims to reform and update African traditional religion, and to promote nationalism and Pan-Africanism. Rather than being a single new religious movement, Afrikania also organizes various traditional shrines and traditional healers into associations bringing unity to a diffused system and thereby a greater voice in the public arena. Afrikania has instituted an annual convention for the traditional religion. It has become a mouthpiece of traditional religion in

Ghana through its publications, lectures, seminars, press conferences, and radio and television broadcast in which it advocates a return to traditional religion and culture as the spiritual basis for the development of Africa. The Mission is also known by other names such as AMEN RA (derived from Egyptian religion, and interpreted to mean 'God Centred'), Sankofa faith (implying a return to African roots for spiritual and moral values) and Godian Religion, which it adopted briefly during a period of association with **Godianism**, a Nigerian based neo-traditional Movement.

The previously mentioned Dr Kwabena Damuah (1930–92), a Roman Catholic Priest resigned from the Church and started the Mission in 1982. Damuah traces his religious evolution to the lingering influence of his father and grandfather who were herbalists and traditionalists and their simple yet effective ministration to people. Studying in America (1965–71) may also have made Damuah aware of his own identity as an African especially as this was during the time of Black power and the Civil Rights Movement. His doctoral thesis (Howard University 1971) on the Traditional Religion of the Wassa Amenfi of Western Ghana proposed that Africa's quest for identity and self-determination could best be achieved by a return to traditional spiritual roots. He attributed his immediate decision to form Afrikania Mission to attending a conference of religious leaders in Moscow (in 1981) where he noticed that almost everybody was Muslim, Hindu, Buddhist, or Christian but no one represented African Traditional Religion.

The teachings of the Movement can be found in the *Afrikania Handbook*, *Miracle at the Shrine* and the other pamphlets authored by Damuah and his successor Osofo Kofi Ameve. The Afrikania Handbook states, 'It is not a new

11

religion. It is traditional religion "come alive", reformed and updated. Afrikania is here not to destroy, but to fulfil the dream of a new Africa.'

The teachings, which are summarized into ten Articles of Faith, fourteen Pillars of life cover religious beliefs, socio-economic concerns and political activism though these often overlap. Recurrent in the pillars and articles are African values such as service to the community, respect for elders, etc. They also urge Africans to write wills to avoid litigation at death, to use time wisely and to engage in what is called agricultural evangelism, etc. They stress the efficacy and validity of African libation, prayer and sacrifices as well as other rituals. They recognize the mediation of the gods and ancestors. Among the latter, they list Pan-African figures such as Kwame Nkrumah, J. B. Danquah, K. A. Busia, Jomo Kenyatta, Malcolm X, etc. Afrikania Mission also promotes herbal medicine, which is closely associated with the traditional religion. Afrikania holds a Sunday forenoon worship service at various locations in big cities like Accra. In the Volta Region of Ghana the services are normally held on Sunday afternoon under the designation of Sankofa. The liturgy used during such services is similar to Christian services in structure, but is traditional in content.

Politically, Damuah initially saw the mission as a corollary to the ideals of the Jerry John Rawlings Revolution, which led to the formation of the Provisional National Defence Council (PNDC) government in Ghana. He joined the PNDC government in December 1981 and resigned in August 1982 before forming Afrikania Mission on 22 December 1982.

The movement is very nationalistic in its teaching promoting the tenets of Pan-Africanism and African emancipation. Its worship sites fly the Ghanaian national flag. The liturgical readings at worship are taken from the 'Egyptian book of the Dead', and a book of African Scriptures 'The Divine Acts' initiated by Damuah and developed by Kofi Ameve. They also use various pan-Africanist political literature.

In 1992 the founder Osofo Okomfo Damuah died. His succession led to a schism into two groups, the African Renaissance Mission led by Osofo Kofi Ameve and Afrikania Mission led by Osofo Dankama Quarm. The African Renaissance Mission, which has a larger following, reassumed the name Afrikania Mission in 2000. Under the leadership of His Holiness Osofo Kofi Ameve the Mission has gained a level of recognition as the mouthpiece of the traditional faith through its various activities. These include defending cultural practices especially against human rights activists, organizing training for prospective Afrikania priests, organizing the branches of the Mission in various areas of Ghana especially the Volta Region, and speaking on national issues such as religion in education, etc. They have also succeeded in organizing some traditional shrines and healers into associations and promote herbal healing as alternative medicine in Ghana. Afrikania also organizes an annual convention of traditional religions and are advocating for a traditional holiday in line with the national Christian and Muslim holidays. Afrikania also uses the media effectively and has a radio programme, the Afrikania Hour, through which it propagates its ideas. It has also acquired a site to build a University to study traditional culture and medicine in the Brong Ahafo Region of Ghana. Kofi Ameve died in 2003. In April 2004, the Mission elected a new leader, Osofo Komfo Atsu Kove. In his inaugural address, he noted the mainly adult membership of the Mission and promised to build schools that would nurture the youth and ensure the continuous growth of the Mission.

Afrikania Mission is significant for its intellectual support of traditional religion through literature, lectures, seminars, radio and television broadcast. Rather than being a single new religious movement, Afrikania also organizes various traditional shrines and traditional healers into associations in an attempt to bring unity to a diffused system and thereby give a greater voice to the traditional faith in the public arena. Though attempts to unite with Godianism of Nigeria have failed, the Mission still supports continental moves towards unity among the neo-traditional movements and is linked to groups and individuals in the African Diaspora some of whom/which support the movement financially.

Further reading

Bediako, K. (1995) *Christianity in Africa, The Renewal of a non-Western Religion*, Edinburgh: Orbis.

Gyanfosu, S. (2002) 'A Traditional Religion Reformed: Vicent Kwabena Damuah and the Afrikania Movement 1982–2000', in D. Maxwell with I. Lawrie (eds) *Christianity and the African Imagination*, Leiden: Brill.

ELOM DOVLO

AFTER-LIFE BELIEFS

The after-life beliefs of any NRM can be part of what makes it distinctive or, just as easily, can relate it to other movements or to a traditional religious worldview. Many NRMs follow a general trend within contemporary, Western religion which emphasizes the ways in which we experience this life, rather than anticipating and dwelling on destinations following death. With few exceptions, teachings about life after death receive less emphasis than learning and experience of this world and this life. After-life beliefs are, therefore, seldom prominent within the most accessible literature which such groups produce. However, most NRMs do hold beliefs about death and the after-life, which may be more or less central to their worldview and either vaguely held or worked out in detail. It sometimes happens that neophytes are attracted to a movement because of its after-life teachings. For example someone brought up within a Christian culture may be attracted by the idea of reincarnation as taught in NRMs which are influenced by Indian ideology.

After-life beliefs for all religions, both old and new, are based on just a few broad possibilities. These are: returning to earth as something or someone else; the passing of some element of a person – usually thought of as the soul – to somewhere else, including heavens and hells; integration or reintegration with the divine; and waiting in another place for future bodily or spiritual resurrection. In a very few movements, including some Pagan groups (see **Pagan Federation**), most of which teach a form of reincarnation, there are no teachings about an after-life since practitioners believe that this life is all there is and that death is the final end of individual existence.

NRMs which grow out of traditional religions usually take on the after-life beliefs which are taught in these traditions more generally. This means, for example, that the **Friends of the Western Buddhist Order**, the **New Kadampa Tradition** and other Buddhist derived NRMs teach rebirth in accordance with the teachings of the various schools of mainstream Buddhism from which they have developed. Within Hindu derived NRMs, for example, the **International Society for Krishna Consciousness** and the **Brahma Kumaris**, followers are taught well established Indian ideas about the nature of the continuity of life after death. The identities of these movements, as NRMs, do not depend upon their after-life teachings. Such teachings do not differentiate new movements from the mainstream.

In contrast, some NRMs teach distinctive ideas about what happens after death which do distinguish them from groups within the same broad religious family. An example of this is the **Church of Jesus Christ of Latter-Day Saints (Mormons)** who, based on an interpretation of the Christian Bible, teach that there are four possible final destinations for all people depending on their actions in this life: three realms of glory and outer darkness. It is essential for salvation that individuals are baptized and Mormons operate a system of proxy baptism in which living members of the church can be baptized on behalf of dead individuals thereby providing spirits awaiting final judgement with the opportunity to move into heaven. In this case, a Christian derived movement is clearly differentiated from more traditional Christian practice and doctrine by its distinctive after-life beliefs and the practices which relate to these.

Some NRMs show substantial influence from more than one of the major world-religions and their after-life beliefs reflect this. The Family Federation for World Peace and Unification (see **Unification Church/Moonies**) is influenced by Confucian ideas relating to ancestors as well as by a form of Christianity. In this NRM marriage is the focus for ritual activity on behalf of the dead. The movement teaches that it is not possible to enter the kingdom of heaven as an individual but only as part of a married couple. Living members may therefore be married to the dead in mass blessing ceremonies.

Movements which have no direct genealogy from broader religious traditions, including the, so called, self-religions (see **self-religion, the Self and self**), are not constrained by interpretations of traditional religious texts and ideas. Nonetheless, they do not necessarily move away from well established after-life beliefs. **Scientology**, for example, has a distinctive worldview and teaches distinctive practices aimed at individual development but it also teaches an unremarkable form of reincarnation in which past lives impact on experience in this life. NRMs vary considerably in their after-life beliefs but it is only where they have developed detailed teachings in this area that these beliefs form a distinctive part of their individual identities.

Further reading

Cohn-Sherbok, Dan and Lewis, Christopher (1995) *Beyond Death*, Basingstoke: Macmillan.

HELEN WATERHOUSE

AGE OF AQUARIUS

The Age of Aquarius is an astrological concept that relates to the myths concerning the 'ages of humanity'. Whether these various epochs represent historical periods or developmental stages (such as infancy, adolescence and adulthood), they manifest as recurring motifs that are found from Northern Borneo and the Hindu four *yugas* to the Aztec five eons and the five stages of the Mayan Great Cycle. In the West, the prevailing understanding of the 'ages of humanity' is taken from Hesiod (*Work and Days*) and depicts five historical epochs running successively from the Golden Age, Silver Age, Bronze Age, Heroic Age, and the Iron Age. This last is the dark times that humanity knows today – a time of work, loss, weariness, greed, crime, war, and death. It corresponds to the Hindu Kali Yuga, our own age of dissension, war, and immorality. But implicit in the 'ages of humanity' mythology is the cyclical notion and hope that a new 'golden age' will follow the war-torn and decadent times of the present era – an optimism that forms the **Theosophical** and **New Age** understandings of the coming Aquarian Age.

A further development to this scenario occurred through the thirteenth-century commentator on the Apocalypse, Joachim de Fiore (1145–1202). Instead of four ages of humanity, he described three and corresponded them to the Christian Trinity. Fiore's first age, that of God the Father, was the time of the ancient patriarchal ideal. It is followed by our present age, namely, that of God the Son – conforming to the birth of Jesus the Nazarene and the epoch in which the masses are to be freed from oppression. Fiore's third period is that of God the Holy Spirit. It is to be celebrated as the time of the Truth- or Mother-Principle. New Thought leader Emma Curtis Hopkins (1853–1925) maintained that the Age of the Spirit is the time for the rise of women. With New Thought constituting the mainstay of New Age affirmative spirituality, Fiore's third age has come frequently to be recognized as the New Age of Aquarius.

The notion of astrological ages develops from the astronomical feature known as the precession of the equinoxes, namely, the earlier occurrences of the equinoxes in each successive sidereal year. Since the earth functions as a tilting gyroscope, the direction in which the axis points changes along the ecliptic in a westerly direction, and the zodiacal constellations appear to rotate around the earth relative to any specific point (e.g., the spring equinoctial point). The timing of this zodiacal shift amounts to fifty seconds annually, approximately one degree every seventy-two years, one complete sign every 2,160 years, and a complete zodiacal revolution (one Platonic or great year) roughly every 26,000 years. Claudius Ptolemy defined the first thirty degrees of the sky as the sign Aries, and his tropical system of astronomy/astrology codified in the second century CE begins at the spring equinoctial point or zero degrees Aries. However, due to the retrograde motion caused by equinoctial precession, the sun is now in the sign of Pisces at the time of the vernal equinox around March 21. As long as it continues to be so, we are said to be in the Age of Pisces. However, when the zodiac precesses enough to cause the vernal equinoctial point to slip back into the sign that precedes Pisces, it is asserted by astrologers that we will then have entered into the Age of Aquarius which, in turn, is identified by many as the New Age.

In iconographic terms, the constellation of Aquarius is understood as Ganymede, the youth seized by Zeus/Jupiter to be cupbearer to the gods. In spiritual hermeneutics, this configuration has been reinterpreted to represent the servant of humanity pouring forth the water of knowledge to quench the world's thirst. The sign of Aquarius is ruled by the planet Uranus that, in the astrological register, signifies unexpected, dynamic and progressive change. Consequently, by aligning the New Age vision with the astrological Age of Aquarius, not only is the New Age grounded in a supposedly discernible astronomical event, but it is also linked to Uranian newness and transformation. However, the major difficulty involved is the location of the actual astronomical date for the equinoctial precession to the Aquarian constellation. British astrologer Nicholas Campion mentions at least seventy possibilities for the beginning of the Age of Aquarius covering a range of

1,500 years. One New Age interpretation holds that the entrance into the new age is an inner rather than outer conversion. As the New Age groups and/or movements constitute a diversified range of exegesis, there are those who expect the change to come through some kind of supernatural or millennial intervention (e.g., Ruth Montgomery (see **Montgomery, Ruth**), José Argüelles) – to a degree following Fiore. Others (such as Ram Dass) expect that the Aquarian entry is purely a spiritual event that depends on a sufficient number of individuals becoming aware of their 'higher selves' and undergoing the requisite personal transformation for a quantum shift in planetary consciousness. A third position is represented by Marilyn Ferguson (see **Ferguson, Marilyn**) who argues that a New Age will come about only through tough ecological reform and consciousness, social work, education, and the practical application of new ideas and innovations. From this last vantage point, the New Age of Aquarius is a social rather than supernatural or spiritual phenomenon.

Nevertheless, the fundamental understanding of the Age of Aquarius is astrological, and Campion suggests that the development of this constellational framing of time is a product of the theosophist and professional astrologer Alan Leo (William Frederick Allen, 1860–1917) who laid the foundations for the present-day understanding of 'astrological science'. In the course of the twentieth century, through its links with Theosophy, astrology became the *lingua franca* of the 1960s counterculture as well as the New Age movements that have descended from it. Its use of the astronomical phenomenon of the precession of the equinoxes has become the seminal framework within which the New Age of Aquarius has been heralded. However, one inconsistency in

identifying the Aquarian Age with the Golden Age is that the latter, traditionally presided over by Saturnus, ought properly to coincide with the Age of Capricorn – another 2,000 years or so after that of Aquarius.

Further reading

Bloom, W. (ed.) (1991) *The New Age: An Anthology of Essential Writings*, London: Rider.

Campion, N. (2000) 'The Beginning of the Age of Aquarius', *Correlation* 19(1), 7–16.

Ferguson, M. (1980) *The Aquarian Conspiracy: Personal and Social Transformation in Our Time*, Los Angeles: Tarcher.

York, M. (1995) *The Emerging Network: A Sociology of the New Age and Neo-pagan Movements*, Lanham, MD: Rowan and Littlefield.

MICHAEL YORK

AGONSHU

This Japanese new, new religion (shin shin shukyo) was established in its present form in 1978 by Kiriyama Seiyu (1921–), its founder and Kancho (leader). Kiriyama started an earlier movement in 1954 known as Kannon Jikeikai, Association for the Worship of Bodhisattva Kannon, who is regarded as the most potent symbol of compassion and mercy and a widely worshipped Buddhist figure not only in Japan but also among Japanese and their descendents abroad, including the United States and Brazil.

In the late 1970s Kiriyama claimed to have discovered the essentials of original, authentic Buddhism, by reading the Agama (Japanese Agon) sutras, early Buddhist texts which, he claimed, predate all previous Buddhist sutras, including the Lotus sutras which is much used in Japan. This discovery, Kiriyama claimed, provided him with an unrivalled understanding of the deeper meaning of Buddhism. In practice it meant the development of a system of beliefs and practices the principal aim of which is to ensure that the sufferings of the spirits of the dead are terminated and that they thereby attain jobutsu or Buddhahood.

In its teachings Agonshu stresses that all misfortunes and problems in life can be explained by reference to one's own or one's ancestors' karmic actions. Large scale goma rituals in which requests or petitions are inscribed on sticks or wood that are then burnt on a pyre while invocations are chanted, are performed every Friday in the Sohonzan Main Temple in Kyoto to eliminate negative ancestral karma and transform the sufferings of the spirits of the dead into *jobutsu* or buddhahood. The main annual festivals are the Star Festival (Hoshi Matsuri) on 11 February which consists of an outdoor goma ritual on a grand scale, the Flower Festival of 8 April to mark the Buddha's birthday, the Great Buddha Festival (Dai-Butsu Sai) of 5 May and the Tens of Thousands of Lanterns service held in Kyoto from 13–15 July and in Tokyo from 13–15 August, for the liberation and peace of ancestors' souls. Many of those who attend the Tens of Thousands of Lanterns festival at Kyoto also visit the Agon shu cemetery on the Kashihara hills northwest of the ancient capital city of Nara. The unique feature of this cemetery is that every tomb has what is called a '*Ho Kyo Into*' in which a small replica of the Busshari and its casket is placed.

Agonshu's principal object of veneration is the Shinsei-busshari (true Buddha relic), a casket said to contain an actual fragment of a bone of the Buddha, and hence his spirit. Three esoteric methods (shugyo) form the core of the training undertaken by recruits: jobutsu-ho which provides the necessary sensitivity and aptitude for spiritual enlightenment; *noyi hoju-ho*, a practice performed with the shinsei-busshari which enables one to achieve the happiness, good fortune and insight to cut loose from karma, an accomplishment rarely achieved, and *gumonji somei-ho*, a technique for developing profound wisdom and extraordinary mental awareness.

The estimated size of the membership of the movement in Japan is one million and Agonshu now has a modest following of between one hundred and one thousand members in several countries of the Far East, Asia, and Africa. It is also present in small numbers in Mongolia, Russia, the United States, Brazil, and several European countries. The movement is actively engaged in projects for the establishment of world peace and the reform of Buddhism through the teaching of the Agama sutras.

Agonshu is organized into main offices, branch offices, dojos or centres where teaching and training take place, and local offices. There are seven main offices in different regions of Japan, and its main religious centre is in Kyoto while its administrative headquarters are in both Tokyo and Kyoto.

Further reading

Reader, I. (1988) 'Agon Shu "The Rise of a Japanese 'New, New Religion'". Themes in the Development of Agon shu', *Japanese Journal of Religious Studies* 15(4), 231–61.

Reader, I. (1991) *Religion in Contemporary Japan*, Houndsmill, Basingstoke and London: Macmillan.

PETER B. CLARKE

AHMADIYYA MOVEMENT
Founder: Mirza Ghulam Ahmad
(c. 1839–1908)

The Ahmadiyya movement provided, from a Muslim theological point of view, one of the more unusual responses from among those that emerged in the

Asian subcontinent to modernization and westernization. The movement is regarded as unorthodox by Sunni Muslims principally on account of the claims made either by its founder Mirza Ghulam Ahmad (*c.* 1839–1908) from Qadian in Kashmir or on his behalf by his followers. Two of these claims in particular have given rise to strong opposition from Sunnis the first of which was a threefold claim to be at one and the same time the Promised Messiah of the Christians who looked forward to the Second Coming of Jesus, the Mahdi or God guided one of Islam, a reincarnation of Prophet Muhammad and an Avatar of the Hindu deity Krishna.

The second unorthodox claim that put Ghulam Ahmad outside the Muslim fold was his assertion that he was a prophet of God entrusted with mission to interpret Islam in accordance with the requirements of the new age. This second claim was in conflict with the Sunni position which holds that there can be no further prophets or no new revelation after the Prophet Muhammad, the last and final prophet. Ahmadis would see this as a misinterpretation of their position since for them their founder was an avatar or manifestation of the prophet and not a completely new prophet whose advent made the life and teachings of the Prophet Muhammad redundant. This understanding of his status, followers maintain, does not conflict with Muhammad being the seal of the prophets. Ghulam Ahmad's orthodoxy was also questioned over his claim that the era of jihad, in the sense of holy war, had come to an end.

In 1974 the Pakistani government declared the movement non-Muslim and forbade it to describe itself as a Muslim organization. Members are also officially prohibited from performing the hajj or pilgrimage to Mecca.

The Ahmadiyya began with a mission to halt the conversion of Muslims to Christianity using the strategy of modernizing Islam particularly in the field of education. In their schools they radically altered the Islamic curriculum by introducing Western subjects alongside the Islamic sciences. The movement was also concerned to stem the ever-growing number of young Muslims who, attracted by modernity, were abandoning Islam for Christianity which many of them regarded as more sophisticated and modern. The Ahmadiyya believed that by modernizing many of Islam's customs, practices, and ceremonies, and by adopting aspects of Western culture they could improve Islam's image and convince young Muslims that it was possible to be both Muslim and modern. Thus, the Ahmadiyya not only introduced a partly western curriculum into their schools but also encouraged western dress, and marriage and naming ceremonies modeled on those held in Christian churches.

The movement split in 1914 into Qadian and Lahore sections. The latter no longer accepting the claim to prophethood of the founder took the name of the Society for the Propagation of Islam. Following the partition of India in 1947 the Qadianis established their headquarters in Rabwah and the Lahoris in Lahore. Both sections are strongly missionary in orientation and heavily engaged in this work not only in South Asia but also in Africa, particularly West Africa, Europe, and the United States. One of the first Ahamadiyyah mosques to be built outside the subcontinent was erected in Woking, Surrey, England, in 1912. The movement claims to have at the time of writing more than 130 million members worldwide.

The leadership of the movement takes the form of a Caliphate which was instituted on the founder's death in 1908 and the current caliph is Mirza Tahir Ahmad (b. 1928).

Further reading

Mirza Bashir-Ud-Din, A. (1980) *Invitation to Ahmadiyya*, London and Boston: Routledge and Kegan Paul.

PETER B. CLARKE

AKINSOWON, CHRISTIANA ABIODUN (MRS/CAPTAIN)

Born: 25 December 1907; died 26 November 1994

Co-founder of the Cherubim and Seraphim churches, an African Independent Church

(see African Independent Churches)

Christiana Abiodun Emanuel (née Akinsowon), affectionately called by the title 'Captain', was the daughter of Yoruba Christian parents from Abeokuta. She was baptized into the Anglican Church in Lagos, spent her childhood in Porto-Novo, Ibadan and Lagos, and completed her elementary education in Lagos in 1920. Thereafter, she learnt sewing, but eventually took to trading while staying with her aunt in Lagos.

On 18 June 1925, after witnessing an annual religious procession of the Roman Catholics in Lagos, she claimed to have seen angels and then went into a prolonged trance. Unable to get help from the vicar of the Anglican Church, her guardians summoned Moses Orimolade (see **Orimolade, Moses**), an itinerant prophet. After Orimolade prayed, Abiodun regained consciousness, and then narrated, to the amazement of people, how she was taken to a 'celestial region' where angels ministered to her. Together with Orimolade, both continued to pray for people seeking various kinds of help.

An interdenominational group, Cherubim and Seraphim (C&S), was formed in September 1925 from among the enquirers. Abiodun played the role of a visionary, healer, and preacher within this group.

Young and energetic, Abiodun and her supporters undertook evangelistic tours into towns in the interior of Western Nigeria in early 1927. Through preaching and miraculous healing numerous C&S branches were established. Personality differences that were magnified by supporters of both leaders caused a split. After the parting of ways in early 1929, Abiodun led her own branch, Cherubim and Seraphim Society, until her death.

Married in January 1942 to George Orisanya Emanuel, a Lagos City Council civil servant, they had one daughter, Georgiana Yetunde.

As the first female to found a church in the country, Abiodun set the pace for the emergence of female religious leadership. By overriding cultural barriers against women in early twentieth-century Yoruba society, Abiodun became a change agent and a symbol of female empowerment, demonstrating the organizational abilities of women in social and religious matters.

Further reading

Omoyajowo, J. A. (1982) *Cherubim and Seraphim: The History of an African Independent Church*, New York: NOK Publishers International Ltd.

MATTHEWS A. OJO

AL-BANNA, HASSAN

(1906–49) Founder of the Muslim Brotherhood (Ikhwan al-Muslimin)

Hassan al-Banna whose writings and ideas have exercised a profound influence on radical Muslim thinking was born in 1906 in the small town of Damanhur about ninety miles from Cairo and received a traditional Islamic education. After training as a primary school teacher he later attended the prestigious Dar al-Ulum Teacher Training College in Cairo where he studied both western and Islamic subjects.

Al-Banna was himself greatly influenced by the strict, puritanical Islam taught by Hasanyn al-Hasafi (1848–1910) founder of the Hasafiyyah mystical brotherhood (*tariqa*) of which he himself was a member.

Al-Banna's period of study in Cairo in the 1920s and his experience of city life in Ismailia where he was appointed to teach at a secondary school in 1927 convinced him that Egyptian culture was in grave danger of being completely detached from its Islamic foundations. He believed that the country itself was in the grip of a profound moral crisis which he likened to an unstoppable storm, and pointed to false notions of individual and intellectual freedom, 'lewdness' imported by Europeans in the form of 'half naked women, liquor, theatres, dance halls, newspapers, novels and silly games' among other things, as the main reasons for this crisis.

Even more troubling and dangerous than these imports, Al-Banna was convinced, were the schools and scientific and cultural institutes which Europeans had established in the centre of the Islamic world. He believed these cultural, educational, and scientific institutions would prove to be far more detrimental to Islamic society in the longer term than any military or political power that the outsider might use to control it.

Thus, Hassan Al-Banna came to see his life's mission as the protection of Islamic society from the corrupting and corrosive influence of the non-Muslim and in particular western world, and as the transformation of Islamic society by a return to authentic Islam. For this purpose he set about establishing in 1928 the **Muslim Brotherhood** or (Ikhwan al-Muslimin). While over time this movement's activities would become more diverse and political it initially placed most stress on Islamic education which it believed would be its most effective weapon. What was provided was a complete and rounded education. Schools were opened for both sexes to train people to live according to Islamic faith and practice. The academic curriculum was supplemented with the teaching of practical or vocational courses in some colleges to enable Muslims to sever their dependence on western aid and products. In essence Al-Banna's message was that Islam was a comprehensive, a total way of life and had no need to rely on the support of the non-Muslim world.

The Brotherhood became increasingly involved in politics in the 1930s organizing mass demonstrations in against British influence and its policies in Palestine, and offering support both humanitarian and military to the Palestinians. For their part, those in power in Egypt were also aware of the growing number of militants in the Brotherhood some of whom supported the use of violence.

Al Banna was sent to jail for a short period in 1941 for organizing a demonstration against the British. This did little to restrain him and after his release he continued his campaign thereby contributing to the political turmoil that marked the 1940s. The political agitation intensified and turned violent in Egypt with the creation of the state of Israel in 1947. In 1948 the Egyptian Prime Minister was assassinated by a member of the Brotherhood and the movement was banned. A year later in 1949 Al-Banna who had campaigned fiercely against the creation of the state of Israel was shot dead, most likely in retaliation for the assassination just mentioned. The influence of Al-Banna's ideas has scarcely waned since his death and his message has continued to have a profound effect on the thinking of such militant Islamic reformers as Sayyid Qutb (see **Qutb, Sayyid**).

Further reading

Mitchell, R. P. (1969) *The Society of the Muslim Brothers*, London: Oxford University Press.

PETER B. CLARKE

AL-QAEDA (THE BASE)

Founder: Osama bin Laden (b. 1957)

Al-Qaeda is one of many of the so-called Islamist (see **Islamism**) groups – movements that are politically active in the cause of establishing an Islamic state – to have emerged in modern times. Others include the **Muslim Brotherhood** (Ikhwan al-Muslimin).

Not all Islamist groups have recourse to violent means to achieve their goal. In a departure from classical Islamic thought as expressed in the four Sunni schools of law (madhhabs) and a number of authentic traditions that convey the mind of the Prophet Muhammad on this subject, Al-Qaeda has legitimated the use of violence even against civilians as the suicide attacks on the twin towers in New York on 11 September 2001 so graphically illustrated.

Al-Qaeda originated in Afghanistan during the campaign to rid the country of the Russian army, which had invaded the territory in 1979. Freedom fighters composed of Afghani Muslims and Muslims from Arab countries and the rest of the world, collectively known as the *mujahideen* (those fighting jihad or holy war), backed with military hard-ware, logistical support and cash by the United States through the CIA, eventually forced the Russians to withdraw in 1989.

During the campaign against the 'secular' Soviets Osama bin Laden forged close links with a number of other jihadi groups including that led by the Egyptian medical doctor Ayman al-Zawahiri (b. 1951) founder of Egyptian Islamic Jihad and imprisoned in Egypt on suspicion of being involved in the assassination (1981) of President Anwar Sadat. Sayyid Qutb's writings (see **Qutb, Sayyid**) exercised a very strong influence on al-Zawahiri's thinking and in particular his observations on Islam and monotheism or belief in one God which he described as the core issue that separates Muslims from their enemies. Following Sayyid Qutb, al-Zawahiri insists that the true Muslim acknowledges that all power belongs to God and hence accepts the necessity of applying his law or *shari'a*, while others follow human, materialistic laws.

The relationship between bin Laden and al-Zawahiri matured in Afghanistan where they met in 1986 while the latter, a militant prior to his arrival, was rebuilding his Islamic Jihad movement which had been outlawed in Egypt. Like bin Laden, al-Zawahiri adopts a militant approach to the transformation of society along Islamic lines in that he is committed to the use of force against governments and political leaders, and even civilians.

Both men were greatly impressed by the philosophy and tactics of the conservative Taliban whose rise to power in Afghanistan had begun in the early 1990s and was completed by 1996. Al-Zawahiri's Islamic Jihad supported this new government's ban on women working and attending school or university and its laws enforcing their wearing of the veil. For its part the Taliban government facilitated the strengthening and training of his movement's members. Meanwhile, Osama bin Laden reached an agreement with Mullah Omar head of the Taliban which recognized him as the leader and protector of the Arab Afghans in the country. With its privileged position bin Laden's organization began to act as a state within a state.

The relationship between the two jihadi leaders, bin Laden and Al-Zawahiri, was formalized in 1998 with the signing of an agreement that united their movements which now formed the International Islamic Front for Jihad on Jews and Crusaders. The new movement issued a fatwa (a legal opinion on a point of law) that ordered Muslims to kill Americans whether soldiers or civilians and confiscate their wealth. America in the post-Cold War era is perceived as the leader of the West, of Christendom, of the Land of Unbelievers, the land of war (dar al harb). Innocent civilians are regarded as legitimate targets for attack for the reason that since they freely choose their rulers they must be held responsible for the deeds of the latter, a line of argument rejected by most Muslims including even many of those who would like to see the creation of an Islamic state in countries where the majority of the population is Muslim.

Al-Qaeda remains the name by which most observers refer to the movement started by bin Laden and he is seen as its all powerful and undisputed leader. This name has come to be used as an umbrella term for a vast array of radical Muslim groups worldwide, including the militant group led by Abu Musab al Zarqawi in Iraq which in 2004 assumed the name 'Al-Qaeda in Iraq' and its leader that of Emir or prince of Al-Qaeda in Iraq. This notwithstanding, it is not known how much control the Al-Qaeda leadership in Afghanistan has over the many activists who claim to carry out activities in its name. What is clear is that Osama bin Laden has become the most important and inspiring symbol for all those Muslims who espouse the use of warfare in pursuit of their goals.

Further reading

Al-Zayatt, M. (2004) *The Road to Al-Qaeda*, London: Pluto Press.
Lewis, B. (2004) *The Crisis of Islam*, London: Phoenix.

PETER B. CLARKE

ALPHA COURSE

The Alpha Course is a tool of evangelism first developed at an Anglican church, Holy Trinity, Brompton, in London, England in the late 1970s and later used by churches from every Christian denomination in 132 countries worldwide. It has been translated into fifty languages. Alpha is run largely by lay people meeting in churches, homes, on university campuses, in prisons and occasionally, even in workplaces. Each week for ten weeks, participants gather for an informal evening meal, listen to a talk and participate in a small group discussion. Newcomers are introduced to ideas central to conservative Protestant theology; namely, the authority of the Bible as the primary source of knowledge about God, the nature of Christ's mission as expiation for human sin, and the availability of salvation for those who repent and have faith. The fifteen talks on which the course is based are summarized in the book, *Questions of Life* (1993), written by curate Nicky Gumbel, who has led the course since the early 1990s. Christian doctrine which varies according to competing ecclesial traditions is not included. Most notably, there is no material on the sacraments, such as Baptism and the Eucharist, which figure prominently in Christian theology, but which are major points of disagreement amongst the denominations. Alpha for Catholics, meanwhile, is augmented with additions from the Roman Catholic catechism.

The Alpha Course was run for over a decade at Holy Trinity Church as a class for church members, before curate Nicky Gumbel decided the goal of the course should be religious conversion, rather than merely education. According to Alpha Course legend, this resulted from Gumbel's experience of the conversion *en masse*, of all the members of a small group he led in the early 1990s. The course was redesigned in content and format to make it more appealing to the un-churched. By 2002 it was estimated that 500,000 non-church members had taken the course. The number of converts is difficult to assess, in that no such records are kept. Meanwhile, as Alpha spread to more than 24,000 other registered locations throughout the world, Gumbel, the rector's assistant educated at Eton, Oxford and Cambridge, became somewhat of an international celebrity. A separate organization Alpha International, with its own director, was formed in 2002. However, the course continued to be substantially funded and led by Holy Trinity Church.

Practical Christianity

About two-thirds of those who take the course self-identify as Christians at the start, leading observers to conclude that Alpha is a revival movement, rather than a tool of conversion *per se*. Course organizers dispute this, asserting that newcomers are Christian in name only. This stems from a belief which prevails in the Evangelical wing of Protestantism, though not uniquely confined to it, that Christian identity is an existential decision, often expressed as a personal relationship with Jesus Christ. Being a Christian in more than a nominal way involves a significant level of commitment, expressed by regular engagement in practices of both corporate worship and personal piety. Consistent with this perspective, the main emphasis of Alpha is praxis rather than dogma. The focus of the course is to make Christian practices accessible to those who have had little religious experience, a status which increasingly typifies post-war Britons and most other western Europeans. Participants are given the opportunity to sing easily-mastered contemporary hymns, to read the bible, to formulate simple prayers and to discuss the deeper questions of life.

Furthermore, a significant amount of effort goes into demonstrating the social benefits of Christian membership, through fellowship and hospitality. Working to overcome negative stereotypes thought to be held by secular people about church-goers and their social functions, Alpha volunteers take care to prepare a comfortable, non-institutional social space and to present good quality meals. Small group leaders are trained to be supportive and non-confrontational. The goal is to create an atmosphere in which any objection or question about the Christian faith can be raised. Rather than theological argument, social inclusiveness and friendship are seen as the key to conversion.

In Gumbel's words, 'Alpha is friendship-based'. New recruits usually arrive by word of mouth, at the recommendation of a friend or relative who has taken the course. At Holy Trinity, where the average age on Alpha is about twenty-seven, many on the courses are recent arrivals in London and eager for new social ties. Participants form attachments both for the people they meet and for the course itself, commonly returning on subsequent courses as volunteers or to repeat the course. Meanwhile, entire small groups, or fragments thereof, may choose to stay together beyond Alpha, evolving into new cells of church congregations, becoming home groups and pastorates.

Charismatic element

In addition to the weekly evening meetings, Alpha offers a weekend retreat, which organizers believe has an important role in religious conversion. The early conversions witnessed on the course seem to have occurred during this event. As well as an opportunity for increased social bonding, the weekend provides training on empowerment by the Holy Spirit, a member of the Trinity, thought to be God active in the world. During a dramatic service, the physical presence of the Spirit, as experienced by the Apostles in the biblical book of Acts, is invoked and invited into the gathering. Manifestations such as speaking or singing in 'tongues', bodily swaying or becoming paralysed, crying and laughing, sensations of wind and heat, are all variously interpreted to be signs of direct religious experience. Newcomers are invited to share in these 'gifts' as well as those of prophecy and healing, which are also demonstrated during the course. The current of Pentecostalism running through the congregation of Holy Trinity and the Alpha Course reflects the influence of John Wimber, founder of the Vineyard Fellowship and also the **Toronto Blessing**, which has influenced other Anglican congregations. Meanwhile, those congregations which may be averse to charismatic displays, chose either to modify the content on the Holy Spirit, or to eliminate the retreat altogether.

Further reading

Gumbel, N. (1993) *Questions of Life*, Eastbourne: Kingsway Books.
Hunt, Stephen (2003) 'The Alpha Programme: Some Observations of State of the Art Evangelism in the UK', *Journal of Contemporary Religion* 18(1), 77–95.
Watling, Tony (2005) '"Experiencing" Alpha: Finding and Embodying the Spirit and Being Transformed – Empowerment and Control in a (Charismatic) Christian World view', *Journal of Contemporary Religion* 20(1), 91–109.

PATRICIA CUNNINGHAM

THE AMA-NAZARETHA (THE NAZARETH BAPTIST CHURCH)

Founder: Isaiah Mdliwamafa Shembe (1867–1935)

Country of origin: Zululand-Natal, South Africa

With over 1,000,000 followers The Ama-Nazaretha is the oldest continually existing African Independent Church and second largest, after the Zion Christian Church, in South Africa. It is known worldwide through the 1970s BBC film *Zulu Zion* and is unique among African New Religions because its sacred texts and oral histories were translated from original Zulu manuscripts into English by Dr Hans-Jürgen Becken and published at the request of Isaiah Shembe's successors.

Little is know about the founder's early life or religious background. He was born at Ntabamhlophe near Estcourt, Natal, of Zulu parents and died at Mikhaideni in Zululand. Shembe was involved with the Wesleyans and baptized by Baptists on 22 July 1906. Apparently he was an itinerant evangelist until he met a former Lutheran Rev. Nkabinde, whom he regarded as a 'Zulu prophet'. Through him Shembe developed a prophetic healing ministry around 1910. Sometime between then and early 1912, he founded The Ama-Nazaretha rooted in Zulu life and tradition. A few years later he bought a farm near Durban that became his holy city of Ekuphakameni. He also established an annual pilgrimage to the Holy Mountain of Nhlangakazi. Andreas Heuser in *Shembe, Gandhi und die Soldaten Gottes* (2003) shows that Gandhi and Shembe influenced each other.

Shembe was loved for his vivid parables, dramatic healings and uncanny insights. He composed, wrote, or dictated, many moving Zulu hymns, developed sacred dances and elaborate sacred costumes, based on Zulu traditions, to express the devotion of believers, insisted on health and dietary rules, including a prohibition on the eating of chicken, and created a liturgical calendar that omitted Christmas. These ideas came to him in vivid dreams. He argued with the Government over his refusal to allow his followers to be vaccinated in 1930 and won the dispute.

Shembe died from exhaustion on 2 May 1935 after spending weeks continually preaching and baptizing converts. A period of uncertainty gripped the church until his son Bishop Johannes Galilee Shembe (1904–76) assumed leadership. His death resulted in open warfare between the supporters of his son the Rt. Rev. Londaukosi Insikayakho (Londa) Shembe (1944–89), a lawyer, and J. G. Shembe's brother, Bishop Amos Khula Shembe (1907–96), a high school principal. Eventually the church properties were divided between the two rival groups. Around 75,000 members supported Londa; the majority joined Amos's church.

Londa Shembe was a charismatic leader who composed new hymns, invented dances and designed new church clothing. He said he was 'the Third Shembe' and that after his death the line of prophetic leadership would end and he speculated that the movement was an entirely new religion with either Jewish, or perhaps even Hindu, roots. He was assassinated on 7 April 1989.

Amos Shembe was more traditional preferring to move closer to historic Christianity. He placed greater emphasis on the Bible and Jesus. After his death in 1986 a fairly smooth transition occurred to the Rev. Vimbeni Mbusi Shembe (1945–) who now leads a thriving church.

G. C. Oosthuizen's *The Theology of a South African Messiah* (1967) argued that The Ama-Nazaretha were a new religion and not simply an African expression of Christianity. This led to a heated debate with Bishop Bengt Sundkler (d. 1995) who attacked Oosthuizen in his book *Zulu Zion and Some Swazi Zionists* (1976). The Zulu anthropologist, Absolom Vilakazi (d. 1993) continued the attack in *Shembe: The Revitalization of African Society* (1986, Braamfontein). Both claimed that Oosthuizen did not really understand Zulu idiom and implied he was an ethnocentric Afrikaner. Surprisingly, although they strongly disagreed with each other, both Amos and Londa Shembe agreed with Oosthuizen and said that Vilakazi's work was unacceptable. Amos argued that The Ama-Nazaretha were an entirely new form of African Christianity, and Londa believed his grandfather had founded a new religion. Carol Ann Muller has written about the role of women in the movement in her *Rituals of Fertility and the Sacrifice of Desire: Nazarite Women's Performance in South Africa* (1999). Other scholars have analysed different aspects of the movement which is probably the best known Indigenous/Independent Church in Africa.

Further reading

Heuser, A. (2003) *Shembe, Gandhi und die Soldaten Gottes*, Berlin: Waxmann.

Hexham, I. (ed.) (1994) *The Scriptures of the amaNazaretha of Ekuphakameni* (trans. L. Shembe and H-J. Becken), Calgary: Calgary University Press.

Hexham, I. *et al.* (eds.) (1996–2005) *Sacred History and Traditions of the AmaNazaretha*, Volumes 1–5 (trans. H-J. Becken), Lewiston: Edwin Mellen Press.

Muller, C. A. (1999) *Rituals of Fertility and the Sacrifice of Desire: Nazarite Women's Performance in South Africa,* Chicago: Chicago University Press.

Oosthuizen, G. C. (1967) *The Theology of a South African Messiah,* Leiden: E. J. Brill.

Sundkler, B. (1976) *Zulu Zion and Some Swazi Zionists,* London: Oxford University Press.

Vilakazi, A. (1986) *Shembe: The Revitalization of African Society,* Johannesberg: Skotaville.

IRVING HEXHAM

AMERICAN FAMILY FOUNDATION

The American Family Foundation (AFF) was founded in Massachusetts in 1979 by Kay Barney, the father of a young woman who had become involved with the Unification Church. For a time it was affiliated with the Citizens' Freedom Foundation (CFF) which later became the **Cult Awareness Network** (CAN). It also developed links with Evangelical Christian counter-cult movements such as the **Christian Research Institute**.

In 1980–1 Barney brought in psychology academics such as Dr John Clark and Dr Michael Langone, the current executive director. AFF's stated mission is 'to study psychological manipulation, especially as it manifests in cultic and related groups.' It also aims 'to help individuals and families adversely affected by psychologically manipulative groups and to protect society against the harmful implications of group-related manipulation and abuse'.

The AFF has a three-fold approach: 'research, education, and victim assistance'. As well as offering an information helpline, it organizes conferences and has published a number of books, including *Recovery From Cults* (1993), *Recovery From Abusive Groups* (1993), *Cults on Campus: Continuing Challenge* (1996), and *Cults and Psychological Abuse: A Resource Guide* (1999).

Unlike some other anti-cult organizations the AFF is conscious of the imprecision of meaning of the word 'cult' (see **Cult and New Religions**), and that different people use it in widely differing ways. Again unlike some other organizations, it makes good use of academics in the field, though at least some of these, such as sociology professor Benjamin Zablocki and psychology professor Margaret Singer, are supporters of the brainwashing or thought reform hypotheses, which most sociologists of religion believe to be discredited. Since the late 1990s, however, the AFF has also been in dialogue with academics from what it sees as the 'pro-cult' camp, and appears to be open to wider scholarly approaches than are usually found in anti-cult organizations.

The AFF's early magazine, *The Advisor*, was superseded by the *Cult Observer* in 1984, when it also began publishing the *Cultic Studies Journal*. In 2002 these were merged and replaced by the subscription online and print journal *Cultic Studies Review*. The AFF also provides a free emailed newsletter, *AFF Newsbriefs*. The AFF's website at *www.culticstudies.org* and *www.csj.org* contains several articles and offers AFF books and journals.

DAVID V. BARRETT

AMORC

Founder: Harvey Spencer Lewis
Country of origin: USA

AMORC, the Ancient and Mystical Order Rosae Crucis, is the largest among several organizations which claim a genealogy dating back to the Rosicrucian movement of the seventeenth century. It insists that it is not a religion, and that it comprises members ('students') from several different religious backgrounds. AMORC was founded in 1915 by Harvey Spencer Lewis (1883–1939), a New York advertising agent who had been a founding member of the New York Society of Psychical Research, after a visit to France, where he claimed to have been initiated into the Rosy Cross in an 'old tower' in Toulouse.

The Order later moved successively to San Francisco, Tampa (Florida), and (in 1927) to San Jose, California, where its world headquarters (including a temple, museum, library, and planetarium) have become one of the city's main tourist attractions. Following AMORC's success in the United States, several more or less independent AMORCs were established in Europe. Some of them later went their separate ways, but Lewis, working jointly with Jeanne Guesdon (1884–1955), was able to keep the large French-speaking branch within the main fold. He was succeeded as leader of AMORC ('Imperator') by his son, Ralph Maxwell Lewis (1904–1987).

When Ralph died, Gary L. Stewart, despite being only 34 years old, was elected Imperator with the support of Raymond Bernard, the powerful leader of the French-speaking branch. Stewart was soon in conflict with the Board of Directors, however, and in 1990 was ousted (going on to found a splinter group known as the Confraternity of the Rose Cross), and replaced by Raymond Bernard's son, Christian. The elder Bernard, in turn, distanced himself from AMORC and established a variety of separate organizations.

Most AMORC members enrol in correspondence courses and follow the instructions included in the Order's 'monographs'. For the first nine degrees, initiations may be self-conferred at home (although they may also be received in a temple). There are no initiations for the tenth, eleventh, and twelfth degrees because it is believed that the member, at this stage, is advanced enough to establish a direct contact with the occult hierarchy. AMORC teaches that, ideally, humans should reincarnate every 144 years. Each student's aim, rather than to escape from the cycle of reincarnations, is to be received into the Great White Brotherhood through a 'cosmic initiation'. AMORC insists that it is the heir to a tradition dating right back to ancient Egypt and the Pharaoh Tutmosis III (†1450 BC), and includes in its lineage of masters Jesus Christ himself. Astrology, occult anatomy, alchemy, and the study of the esoteric meaning of numbers, sounds, and geometrical shapes complete AMORC's teachings. Controversies notwithstanding, AMORC remains, by far, the largest Rosicrucian organization in the world, with hundreds of thousands of members (the figure of 'six million', often quoted, relates to the Order's mailing list), and maintains a very visible presence, thanks to its temples, publishing houses, and magazines, in several countries.

Further reading

Lewis, R. M. (1966) *Cosmic Mission Fulfilled*, San Jose, CA: Supreme Grand Lodge of AMORC.

MASSIMO INTROVIGNE

AMRITANANDAMAYI, MATA (AMMACHI)

Mata Amritanandamayi (Mother of Immortal Bliss) – affectionately called Amma or Ammachi (mother) – is a prominent contemporary religious leader, attracting devotees of all ages, races, religions, and walks of life. Known as the 'Hugging Saint' since she has literally embraced millions of devotees across the globe, Ammachi is regarded by her devotees as the embodiment of the Divine Mother. Born on 27 September 1953 into a poor, low caste family in rural Kerala, south India, Sudhamani – as she was known before her religious experience – rose from an impoverished childhood of abuse and rejection to great heights of spirituality. Her hagiographies stress that she was a spiritually gifted child who had an intense longing for union with the Divine. Following two watershed spiritual experiences in late 1975 in which she claimed to have experienced oneness initially with the Hindu god Krishna and later with the Divine Mother, Ammachi is said to reveal her true identity during a weekly ritual when she assumes the mood or form of the Divine Mother (Devi Bhava).

Ammachi's spiritual fame and mission spread, in India and abroad, as her devotees attributed miraculous powers that include clairvoyance, bilocation, levitation, dramatic healing of various physical and psychological disorders, and creating children for the childless. While the Amritpuri *ashram* (hermitage) instituted in 1981 in Kollam, Kerala serves as home for Ammachi and her growing global spiritual movement, numerous local and transnational congregations (*satsang*) – often under lay leadership – have emerged in India, Europe, Latin America, and North America. The movement also has a vast network of educational, social welfare, charitable, and medical institutions concentrated mainly in India. While religious power, authority, and leadership are consolidated in Ammachi, the temporal administration of her growing network of institutions is delegated to a band of trusted disciples.

Born and raised Hindu, Ammachi has introduced several creative innovations into the Hindu ritual tradition best exemplified in the Ammachi *darsan* or spiritual embrace that has become her spiritual trademark. Ammachi transmits her core spiritual message of unconditional love through the medium of the spiritual embrace. Involving intense physical contact in the form of hugging, kissing, and touching, *darsan* is also the most intimate and personal mode of interaction between Ammachi and her devotees. In redefining *darsan*, Ammachi – who is firmly grounded in the Hindu mystical, philosophical, and devotional traditions – defies and transcends orthodox Hindu norms concerning ritual purity, pollution, and bodily contact between the devotee and the embodied divine as well as Hindu social norms governing gender relations. Thus, Ammachi embodies, in her person, message, and rituals, the confluence of two distinct streams – of fidelity to tradition and defiance of tradition. Located at the juncture between tradition and change, Ammachi both supports and confounds the religious and social status quo through her simple message of unconditional love, embodied and transmitted through her innovative *darsan* ritual as well as through her ability to acculturate her message and medium to an ever widening global audience that extends beyond the Hindu and Indian frontiers. She is the recipient of several national and international awards, including the United Nation's Gandhi-King Award for Non-Violence in 2002.

Further reading

Amritaswarupananda, S. (1994) *Ammachi: A Biography of Mata Amritanandamayi*, San Ramon, California: Mata Amritananda-mayi Center.
http://www.ammachi.org/

SELVA J. RAJ

ANCIENT TEACHINGS OF THE MASTERS

The founder of ATOM (Ancient Teachings of the Masters) was Darwin Gross, who in 1971 received the 'Rod of Power' from Paul Twitchell (1908–71), the founder of **Eckankar**. Darwin Gross claims the title of 972nd Bourchakoum Master, the current heir to a line that includes a number of mysterious individuals. In 1983, after more than a decade as living as ECK Master and president of Eckankar, Gross was excluded from the group led by Harold Klemp (who in 1981 had been proclaimed ECK Master, although leaving Gross the role of president), but continues to this day to publish his writings and music through an organization called Sound Of Soul, with headquarters in Oak Grove (Oregon).

In 1989, Gross's 'path' was given its current name: ATOM (Ancient Teachings of the Masters). As a result of a lawsuit, Gross now calls himself the '972nd Living Master' but not 'ECK Master'. Today, ATOM has students in numerous countries/continents (United States, Australia, Africa, Europe) who make known the teachings of, and distribute the material written by, Darwin Gross, and organize international meetings and seminars.

ATOM's purpose is the realization of the Self, and the realization of God, in this life or the next (the movement believes in reincarnation of the soul). The individual recognizes that man's most important part is the soul, and learns the 'Soul movement'. The three pillars of the Teachings are Light, Sound and the Master. The student is given many spiritual exercises by means of which he/she can increase his/her level of understanding and knowledge. Daily meditation is the fundamental method for reinforcing the link with Light and Sound and with universal spiritual laws.

The essential aspects of ATOM's teachings are:

(a) the Sugmad, a name meaning God, the Divine Spirit that flows downward from the highest Source through to the worlds below;

(b) the Master, who is the manifestation of divinity on this Earth.

The master is guided spiritually by the 'Teachers' of the Ancient Teachings of the Masters, who – according to ATOM – are mentioned in the 'Nacaal Archives' hidden in Tibet, dating back about 35,000 years, and emanating from the planet Venus. The teachings are studied at home by means of monthly instalments, in 'discussion classes', or in Satsang classes. In the first six months of studying the instalments, the student receives his/her first initiation into the dream state. After two years of study, the student may receive the Light and Sound Initiation, through which he/she may become part of the cosmic Sound Current. After five years or more, he/she becomes eligible to receive the Soul Initiation.

The course of the initiation follows the 'God Worlds Chart', composed of thirteen levels, with a sound corresponding to each. For example, corresponding to the physical, astral, causal, mental, and ethereal levels are, respectively, thunder, the ocean's roar, the sound of bells, the flow of water, and the buzzing of bees, and the sound-words Alay, Kala, Aum, Mana, and Baju. When the individual has passed through the 'Tunnel of Yreka', and has entered the 'Soul Plane', he/she is free to move on his/her own. Beyond this world are invisible worlds, endless worlds, a God consciousness plane, the inaccessible, the nameless, the Sugmad Lok and lastly the world of Sugmad. At these levels, starting from that of the soul, correspond the sounds and melodies of a single note of the flute, a strong wind, a deep singing with closed mouth, thousands of violins, music for wind instruments, the sound of a vortex, music of the universe, and music of God. The corresponding sound-words are Sugma, Shanti, Hum, Aluk, Huk, Hu and, lastly, the Unspoken Word.

Further reading

Gross, D. (1997) *Principles Of The Ancient Teachings Of the Masters*, Oregon: Oak Grove.

PIERLUIGI ZOCCATELLI

ANTHROPOSOPHY

Anthroposophy is the name given to the 'spiritual science' developed by Austrian Rudolf Steiner (1861–1925). In Steiner's view, the natural world was guided by cosmic rhythms and he created anthroposophy with the aim of investigating the spiritual world without the partial and limited approaches of either science or mysticism alone. The basic tenets of anthroposophy were outlined in three of his key works: *Theosophy*, *Occult Science* and *Knowledge of the Higher Worlds*.

Steiner studied in Vienna, being particularly fascinated by the natural sciences and the German philosophical tradition. He worked on the team editing Goethe's complete works between 1890 and 1897 and his own work is considered to be an extension of Goethe, for example in his emphasis on understanding the experiential polarities of sensory information. Steiner was a moral individualist and believed in the necessity of awakening the spiritual faculties of human consciousness.

He had contact with **theosophy** and was asked to lead a new German Theosophical Society, which he developed with Marija von Sivers, whom he later married. Steiner differed from the theosophists, notably in their emphasis on Indian thought and on revelations (particularly those of Helena P. Blavatsky – see **Blavatsky, Helena**). Although Steiner was interested in Indian thought – one of his key projects was a remodelling of the concept of *karma* – he was more concerned with revitalizing the European Christian tradition.

Steiner's anthroposophical work centred around Dornach in Switzerland, where in 1913 construction began on his novel Goetheanum building and the Anthroposophical Society was founded. However, Steiner was never a member of the Society and remained independent, more concerned about social renewal and World War I than the Dornach community. After the first Goetheanum burned down in 1922, divisions within the Anthroposophical Society were apparent and in 1923 Steiner founded the General Anthroposophical Society to continue his ideals.

Steiner generated a number of artistic and social initiatives under the umbrella of anthroposophy, the most enduring of which is in the field of education. Steiner Schools focus on the creative, social and intellectual development of children, drawing on a wide curriculum. The first *Waldorfschule* was established in 1919 and over 880 Steiner schools exist worldwide, in countries as diverse as Brazil, Singapore, and Zimbabwe. The anthroposophical approach has also been successfully applied to special needs education and adult learning.

A second important initiative was the development of anthroposophical medicine with Dr Ita Wegman, a holistic system based on plants and minerals, most popular in Germany, Switzerland, and the Netherlands. Anthroposophical thought teaches that the human is composed of four bodies: the 'physical' or material body, the 'etheric' body of formative forces in living matter, the 'astral' body common to humans and animals and the 'ego', blending Jungian ideas of 'ego' and 'self'. Besides medicinal treatments the system advocates nutritional therapy, massage, counselling and artistic therapies, such as Steiner's movement therapy system 'Eurythmy'. The famous Weleda brand of medicines, founded in 1921 in Switzerland, is homoeopathically produced in line with the anthroposophical principles of biodynamic agriculture.

Further reading

McDermot, Robert (1992) 'Rudolf Steiner and Anthroposophy', in Antoine Faivre and Jacob Needleman (eds) *Modern Eastern Spirituality*, New York: Crossroads.

ALEXANDRA E. RYAN

ANTI-CULT MOVEMENT
FAIR
Cult Information Centre (CIC)

The 'anti-cult' movement (ACM) can be considered as the first social response to the phenomenon of New Religious Movements (NRMs) when they emerged in Western countries in the late 1960s and early 1970s. The term 'anti-cult movement' is generally used as a generic designation for any, usually secular, organized initiative opposed to at least some aspects of NRMs. This opposition combined with the conceptualization of NRMs as 'cults' gave rise to the notion of the ACM, a label to which some groups object, preferring descriptions such as 'cult concern', 'cult monitoring' or 'cult-watching' organization. However, the latter terms are generally understood to have a wider remit and to include organizations taking an academic approach to NRMs, such as INFORM (Information Network Focus on Religious Movements) and the (former) Centre for New Religious Movements at King's College, University of London.

Also, just as the study of NRMs requires careful differentiation between the various groups and movements subsumed under the heading 'NRMs', despite the 'generic' features they share, the study of the ACM requires equally careful distinctions between the various strands in the spectrum of organizations. Thus Introvigne's (1993, 1995a, 1995b) typology distinguishes between the secular anti-cult and the religious counter-cult, a distinction developed and refined further by Cowan (2002; 2003).

The first ACM groups were formed by concerned parents (and some sympathetic clergy) who were the first to experience the consequences of 'cult' membership in their families. These early self-help groups tended to be informal and to focus on adherence to a particular NRM, such as the Children of God (now The Family) – as in the case of FREECOG (Free Our Sons and Daughters from the Children of God) – or the Unification Church – as in the cases of CERF (Citizens Engaged in Reuniting Families) in the US and FAIR (Family Action Information & Resource) in the UK.

As the emergence of NRMs was first felt in the United States – a wave which slowly moved towards the United Kingdom and Continental Europe (see Arweck, 1999), it is here that the first groups formed in the 1970s (FREE-COG, CERF, American Family Foundation or AFF). Their aim was to support parents affected by 'cult' membership in their families, to gather and exchange information about the new religious groups (information which was not as readily available then as it is now), to find out about the whereabouts of their children, and to finds ways of getting them back. The groups became more established and expanded, both in terms of their structures and objectives, for example, FREECOG became Citizens' Freedom Foundation; they also developed connections with one another and formed networks and umbrella organizations, such as the Cult-Awareness Network (CAN), a process which was accompanied by a broadening of aims to include support and action from the wider society (the public and public authorities) which meant lobbying politicians, raising awareness locally, nationally, and internationally, campaigning for legal provisions, etc.

The ACM has sought to present a counterweight to NRMs, which they conceptualize as 'destructive cults' and thus see as harmful, if not dangerous. Generally speaking, the ACM's stance has been based on the idea that such groups actively recruit young people by applying a range of methods summarized under the heading 'brainwashing techniques' or 'thought reform' that keep members committed through 'mind control' or 'thought control' (see e.g. Conway and Siegelman, 1978; Hassan, 1988; Landau and Lalich, 1994; Singer and Lalich, 1995). Thus, it was argued, the only way to free someone from the 'clutches of a cult' was through 'deprogramming', a process designed to reverse 'brainwashing', which involved forcible physical and mental/emotional withdrawal through the agency of professional 'deprogrammers'. This model of (de)conversion is predicated on the notion of the individual as passive victim rather than active agent in the process of acquiring a religious affiliation – a model which has been at the centre of fiercely fought 'cult controversies' (Beckford, 1985) and one which has been at the centre of strong disagreement between the ACM and academic approaches to the study of NRMs. Although the ACM has not abandoned the 'brainwashing thesis', the practice of 'deprogramming' has given way – not least because of legal implications (a case of deprogramming led to the demise of CAN in 1996, although it was re-formed under new ownership and approach) – to **Exit Counseling**, an approach which is based on using information and communication to dissuade 'cult' members (see e.g. Giambalvo, 1992). However, it needs to be stressed that the practice of deprogramming was also controversial within the ACM and generally subscribed to by what might be described as the more radically inclined groups.

In Britain, the first 'anti-cult' group to form was FAIR (then Family, Action, Information & Rescue, changed to Family Action Information & Resource in 1994), founded in 1976 by Paul Rose, then a Member of Parliament who had unwittingly become the focus of 'cult concerns' after raising the issue in Parliament. At that time, FAIR constituted a coalition of concerned politicians, journalists, relatives of members, former members, some clergy, and parents, with the latter forming the main contingent and providing the funding. FAIR expanded by widening its remit to include all 'destructive cults', setting up a network of regional branches, and also working closely with evangelical groups. However, FAIR regards itself as non-religious in outlook, although its membership includes many committed Christians.

As it does not have charitable status, FAIR and its branches depend on voluntary donations from its *c.* 120 members, subscriptions to its quarterly newsletter, *FAIR News*, and the sale of occasional publications. FAIR's emphasis is on supporting families, while also providing information and counselling and educating the public about 'cults' and its own work. FAIR is embedded in a national and international network of similar organizations, maintaining links in the UK with 'cult concerned' organizations, such as Deo Gloria Outreach, Cultists Anonymous, Cult Information Centre (CIC), Reachout Trust, CONCERN, Housetop, the Dialogue Centre Dublin, and the Irish Family Foundation as well as ex-members' groups, such as EMERGE (Ex-Members of Extremist Religious Group), the Ex-Cult Members Support Group, TOLC (Triumph Over London Cults), and rehabilitation projects, such as Catalyst. Quite a number of the above organizations have either receded or folded, but CIC has remained one of the most active organizations. The creation of an umbrella group of 'Cult Concern Groups' in the UK was envisaged in the late 1980s, but did not progress beyond the preliminary stages.

On the European level, FAIR has co-operated with its counterparts, for example ADFI (Association pour la Défense de la Famille et de l'Individu) in France, *Elterninitiative* in Munich, Germany, the Panhellenic Parents Union (PPU) in Athens, and others. After the events of 1989 which opened the borders to the countries in Eastern Europe, links were expanded or formed with parents' groups there, a development which might be described as a process of exporting the 'anti-cult approach' to the East (see Shterin and Richardson, 2000).

FAIR is also a member of the European umbrella organization FECRIS (*Fédération Européenne des Centres de Recherche et d'Information*) which had its inaugural meeting in October 1994. Beyond the European level, FAIR has maintained connections with, for example, AFF in the US, Info-Culte in Canada, CCG (Concerned Christians Growth) Ministries in Australia, and the Free Mind Foundation in New Zealand.

The Cult Information Centre (CIC) was founded in 1987 by Ian Haworth, who has actively campaigned against 'cults' since 1978. CIC is a registered educational charity which is engaged in public education about the 'dangers of cults', dissemination through the media, consultancy work, family assistance, support for ex-cult members, and information (see Haworth, 2001). Unlike FAIR, CIC is not a parents' group, but acts as an agency for the provision of information and services.

Like other organizations (including NRMs), the ACM has made use of communications technology (electronic mail, internet facilities) to increase the dissemination of information and its ability to network, with most groups maintaining web sites (see, e.g., Cowan, 2001). Although the transformation of the organizations which have provoked their creation has been to some extent mirrored in the 'ant-cult groups' themselves, their *raison d'être* is ensured by the needs of those negatively affected by 'cult' membership – whether as parents or former members.

Further reading

Arweck, E. (1999) Responses to New Religious Movements in Britain and Germany, with special reference to the anti-cult movement and the churches, PhD thesis, University of London. To be published as *Researching NRMs: Responses and Redefinitions*, London: Routledge, 2005.

Beckford, J. A. (1985) *Cult Controversies: The Societal Response to the New Religious Movements*. London: Tavistock.

Conway, F. and Siegelman, J. (1978) *Snapping: America's Epidemic of Sudden Personality Change*, Philadelphia, PA: Lippincott.

Cowan, D. E. (2001) From Parchment to Pixels: The Christian Countercult on the Internet, paper presented to the International Conference of CESNUR, London; archived at http://www.cesnur.org/2001/london2001/cowan.htm

Cowan, D. E. (2002) 'Exits and Migrations: Foregrounding the Christian Counter-Cult', *Journal of Contemporary Religion* 17(3), 339–54.

Cowan, D. E. (2003) *Bearing False Witness? An Introduction to the Christian Countercult*, Westport, CT: Praeger.

Giambalvo, C. (1992) *Exit Counseling: A Family Intervention: How to Respond to Cult-Affected Loved Ones*, Bonita Springs, FL: American Family Foundation.

Hassan, S. (1988) *Combatting Cult Mind Control: Rescue and Recovery from Destructive Cults*, Rochester, VT: Park Street Press.

Haworth, I. (2001) *Cults: A Practical Guide*, London: Cult Information Centre.

Introvigne, M. (1993) 'Strange Bedfellows or Future Enemies?' *Update & Dialog on New Religious Movements* 3, 13–22.

Introvigne, M. (1995a) 'L'évolution du "mouvement contre les sectes" chrétien 1978–1993', *Social Compass* 42(2), 237–47.

Introvigne, M. (1995b) 'The Secular Anti-Cult and the Religious Counter-Cult Movement: Strange Bedfellows or Future Enemies?' in R. Towler (ed.) *New Religions and the New Europe*, Aarhus, Denmark: Aarhus University Press, 32–54.

Landau T., Janja, M. and Janja, L. (1994) *Captive Hearts, Captive Minds: Freedom and Recovery from Cults and Other Abuse Relationships*, Alameda, CA: Hunter House.

Shterin, M. S. and Richardson, J. T. (2000) 'Effects of the Western Anti-Cult Movement on Development of Laws Concerning Religion in Post-Communist Russia', *Journal of Church and State* 42(2), 247–71.

Singer, M. T. and Lalich, J. (1995) *Cults in Our Midst*, San Francisco: Jossey-Bass.

ELISABETH ARWECK

APOSTLES' REVELATION SOCIETY

The Apostles' Revelation Society (ARS) is an African Independent Church (AIC) founded in Ghana around 1945. Charles Kwabla Nutornti founded this church at Tadzewu in the Volta Region of Ghana where its Head office is located. Nutornti settled in Tadzevu in 1939 and founded a school and a prayer group. He initially voluntarily affiliated with the Ewe (now Evangelical) Presbyterian Church. In 1940 the prayer group received in a revelation the name Apostles' Revelation Society. In July 1943, Nutornti added the name Wovenu (meaning 'one who has received grace') to his names. In 1944 the movement came into conflict with the Ewe Presbyterian Church over Wovenu's spiritual practices, as well as the administration of a grant of money to the school he founded, from the colonial District Commissioner. Nutornutsi had a revelation at this time that transformed the group, the Apostles Revelation Society into a church. Wovenu died on 10 April 1999, and was succeeded by Apostle Amega. Seventeen principal officials bearing the title of Apostles run the Church. Below them are Regional Superintendents, Ministers, district and station pastors.

The church leaders, especially the founder, were renowned for their prophetic ability, healing and spiritual guidance to members. They also extended these spiritual resources to communities and groups that sought the guidance of the Church. In addition to the normal Christian sacraments, the ARS instituted additional ones, that sanctify traditional African practices. These include sacraments of insurance and protection for pregnancy, maidenhood, children, marriage and property. There are also foundation rites for putting up buildings, and acquiring the spirit of one's profession, etc. Many traditional rites of passage such as the outdooring of children, rites for twins, widowhood rites and the installation of traditional chiefs have been Christianized in the ARS.

The Church uses both Old and New Testament as the full basis of its faith and worship with the OT providing the basis of ARS culture. It also promotes traditional culture in a Christian way. For instance it has rules and codes of behaviour for its members as found in many AICs. Its code of conduct includes abstention from alcohol, worshipping barefoot, regular periods of fasting, and a dress code for the leadership. It also practises animal sacrifices. One of the purposes of a sacrificed sheep is to bring life and cleanliness to the individual and society. Also the sacrifice of coconuts, honey, and salt as burnt offering are meant to bring their sweet flavour into one's life.

ARS liturgy is rich in African imagery and symbolism. It incorporates forms of singing with drums and African musical instruments which are adapted to scriptural lyrics. The Lord's Prayer for instance is set to Anlo Ewe songs. The great Ewe poet Hesinor Vinorko Apaloo Akpa converted and joined the ARC in 1964 bringing into the Church his rich repertoire and gift in traditional composition. ARS has liturgy for many African events such as outdooring, and naming of children, the birth of twins, widowhood rites, elevation to traditional leadership, etc. Major celebrations of the Church include all Christian celebrations and a special end of year Anniversary Celebration, as well as a Founders' Day and Marriage Day. There are associations within the Church including a welfare group and an Associations of Traditional Chiefs, which is unique to the ARS.

The Church also encourages development in communities in which congregations are established. In addition to New Tadzewu, which serves as the Headquarters of the Church, the Church also developed four other new townships. It has established over fifty schools. The leader is also credited with the establishment of important markets in the Volta region thus boosting economic activity. It also promotes the provision of public conveniences and clean water for drinking. Members are themselves exhorted to hard work and to abjure laziness.

Though membership is drawn predominantly from the Ewe ethnic group, the Church has grown to embrace Akans and other Ethnic groups along the West Coast from the Ivory Coast to the Republic of Benin. ARS has around 638 branches in Ghana and several international branches in Canada, USA, England, Holland, Germany, France, and Belgium.

Further reading

Baëta, C. G. (1962) *Prophetism in Ghana*, London: SCM Press.
Fernandez, J. Y. (1970) 'Rededication and Prophetism in Ghana', in *Cahier d'Etudes Africaines*, X, 228–305.
Website: www.ars.

ELOM DOVLO

APOSTOLIC CHURCH OF JOHANE MASOWE

Founder: Johane Masowe
Country of origin: Zimbabwe

The Apostolic Church of Johane Masowe can be classified as one of the African Charismatic movements. It was through their Zion Churches that the Shona peoples produced their most powerful and creative independent movements. M. L. Daneel (1971, 1974, 1988) has comprehensively documented the legacy of these Pentecostal and

Charismatic Churches in his three-volume work, *Old and New in Southern Shona Independent Churches*. These Independent Churches have endeavored to incorporate African traditional worldviews into Christianity and have also provided Africans with a place to feel at home and exercise their spiritual creativity.

In the early 1930s, Shoniwa Moyo, a young Shona from Southern Zimbabwe claimed that he had died and had risen to life again. This resurrection experience occurred near Marimba Hill, where he had gone to pray and meditate. After this incredible religious experience, he was no longer Shoniwa, but Johane Masowe, the Messiah, Johane from the wilderness, or Johane the Baptist. He went around wearing a white robe and holding a Bible and a staff with a crucifix. Within a short time, he was able to attract many followers. Women followers wore white gowns and turbans, while the men went around with long beards and shaved heads.

The essence of his message revolved around the apocalyptic end of the wicked world. The day of judgment was near and people must repent. His most popular Bible verse was Revelation 4:5: 'And before the throne burn seven torches of fire, which are the seven spirits of God.' He was a spiritual maverick. He moved from one country to another creating an aura of mystery around himself. For much of his life, he could not be located. Even after his death, his radical ideas were still sustained by his followers. His popular appeal was rooted in the message of hope, deliverance, healing, and abundant life he offered his followers. He preached a message of a new age of freedom, justice, and self-sufficiency, which he described as the year of jubilee for African Christians. He rejected all Christian sacraments except Baptism. His followers believed in

Jehovah, observed Old Testament dietary laws, kept the Sabbath, and practiced polygamy. Johane was often described as the word, spirit, or star of God.

The poor and the oppressed were particularly attracted to his message of healing and holistic spirituality. The movement also included many celibate women, who were described as a 'collective ark'. Masowe's followers, known as the *vahosanna* (the hosannas) or as 'basketmakers' lived in their own separate communities and were self-reliant. They made baskets, furniture, and metalwares for sale. They were able to install their own electric generator. The industrial genius of the *vahosanna* was a remarkable phenomenon. They created independent financially viable communities.

Johane Masowe represents a bold affirmation of African agency in the transmission of Christianity. African prophets have been able to add unique perspectives to the shape and form of Christianity within the African continent.

Further reading

Daneel, M. L. (1971) *Old and New in Southern Shona Independent Churches. Vol. 1, Background and the Rise of the Major Movements,* The Hague: Mouton.

Daneel, M. L. (1974) *Old and New in Southern Shona Independent Churches. Vol. 2, Church Growth: Causative Factors and Recruitment Techniques,* The Hague: Mouton.

Daneel, M. L. (1988) *Old and New in Southern Shona Independent Churches. Vol. 3, Leadership and Fission Dynamics,* Gweru: Mambo Press.

Hastings, Adrian (1994) *The Church in Africa 1450–1950,* Oxford: Clarendon Press.

Isichei, Elizabeth (1995) *A History of Christianity in Africa,* Grand Rapids, MI: Wm. B. Eerdmans Publishing Co.

AKINTUNDE E. AKINADE

ARCANUM NAMA SHIVAYA HINDU MISSION

The Arcanum Nama Shivaya Hindu Mission (ANSHM) is a Saivite mission, founded by a Ghanaian in Ghana, West Africa with branches in the Ivory Coast and the Republic of Togo. The mission combines various features of Hinduism, Traditional Religion and Christianity. Its leader also practises esoteric and herbal healing.

Rev. Guru Janakananda Ramachandra Amankwa is the founder of ANSHM. He was born in 1948 and raised as a Presbyterian. He dates his Mission to a religious experience he had on the beach at Accra (capital of Ghana) in February 1963 in which a figure emerged from the sea, and instructed him in various spiritual matters. According to him, the figure later identified itself, as a deva, which made him link his new spiritual experiences to Hinduism. In subsequent visitations, he claims, the deva endowed him with knowledge of healing herbs and he began to pray for and heal people. In 1971 he began correspondence with a Swami, Jyotri Mayananda in India and received lessons on the Vedic path and healing. In 1978 he went to India to receive further tuition from the Swami. He returned to Ghana in 1979 and opened a temple in Accra in 1984.

ANSHM is a Saivite mission, recognizing Shiva as its object of worship and devotion. Members study the Vedas as sacred scriptures and a source of esoteric knowledge. They practise Yoga as a path that enhances human capacity and leads to enlightenment and freedom. They also adhere to other cardinal doctrines of Hinduism such as the doctrines of Samsara (rebirth) and Karma (law of cause and effect). Members are strict vegetarians.

The ANSHM is inclusivist in belief and practice. It holds a forenoon devotional worship on Sundays during which they use Hindu and Christian devotional choruses from a hymn book designed by the Guru. They also use modern musical instruments such as drums, keyboard, and guitar. Many of their choruses are popular Christian choruses with the name of Shiva substituted for that of Jesus. The intention is to make Christian converts feel no abrupt change from the contemporary Christian mode of worship in Ghana. The mission also frequently uses some Ghanaian traditional attributive appellations of God in its liturgical expressions.

Tuesdays and Thursdays are set apart for Healing. The psychical aspect of the healing takes place in the temple while herbal healing takes place in a small laboratory attached to the temple where the herbal drugs are made and administered to patients. Use of herbs adds African traditional elements to its healing procedures. Saturday is devoted to yoga classes for enrolled candidates.

The Mission is also called the 'Arcanum Church of All Religions Mission', indicating a general inclusive attitude to all religions. The African tenor of the movement is recognized on its letterhead, which describes it as 'A charitable reformed Hindu and African religious and philosophical organization incorporated in Ghana'. The Mission also has certain Christian features. The leader uses the title of 'Reverend' in addition to Guru and at times refers to the Mission as a Church. He also interprets the God Shiva as the Holy Spirit in Christianity. There is also a picture of St Anthony (recognized as an important mystic) on the altar of the temple.

Members of the Mission are recruited mostly from people who come for healing or seek the spiritual services of the leader. There are two types of membership, ordinary and life membership. Ordinary members are clients of the leader and occasional visitors, while life members are those who register to join the Mission. Life members undergo a spiritual formation programme beginning with the Mantra initiation, *diksa;* which introduces them to the use of the *mala* or rosary. Those who wish to pursue training in Yoga or priesthood are known as a *chela(s)* (learners) and are given two years' training as celibate religious students (*brahmacarin*) even if previously married. After the two years they are permitted to marry and/or go back to a normal householder's life (*grhasthya*). At 70 years, the person may take the vow of asceticism (*vanaprasthya*), and return to the celibate life (though may live at home) until death or he may choose to become a *sannyasin* (wandering ascetic) and live as a monk.

An Ivorian Guru, who was healed by the Ghanaian founder of the Mission, established and heads the branch in the Ivory Coast.

ELOM DOVLO

ARCHEOSOPHY

Following the esoteric revival promoted by the Theosophical sphere, a variety of Christian movements were created that expressed interest in esoteric subjects. These movements, critical of such a sphere, were nevertheless subjected to its influence. The Lotus + Cross Esoteric Order and the Archeosophic Association, both founded by Tommaso Palamidessi (1915–83) and each with original aspects, are part of this line.

Tommaso Palamidessi became interested in parapsychology and Eastern religions at an early age, and between 1945 and 1949 published a series of writings on yoga and tantrism. While in Turin, he often visited the Egyptian Museum and became fascinated first with Egyptology and then with alchemy. From the late 1950s on, he dedicated himself to the rediscovery of early Christian practices, and abandoned yoga. In 1968, he founded the Archeosophic Association in Rome. Thereafter, he studied iconographic art and music as a means to mystic and esoteric realization. After his death in 1983, his work was continued by his wife, Rosa Francesca Bordino (1916–99), his first disciple, whom he had married in 1947, and by Alessandro Benassai (1940–), his designated successor, who still guides the Archeosophic Association today. The Archeosophic Association currently has about 400 active members in Italy, in addition to groups in Germany, Portugal, and France.

Tommaso Palamidessi presented the archeosophic doctrine in pamphlets which he called *Notebooks* (about 40 in all, some of which were published in book form). Explicitly inspired by the early Church Fathers, and by a few aspects of ancient and modern Eastern orthodoxy, Palamidessi's works also include numerous theosophic and esoteric themes. God the Son, the eternal avatar, 'always the same', becomes incarnate 'when he wishes and when it is necessary to save mankind', in a historical personage: Rama, Krishna, Jesus, and perhaps tomorrow a 'future Messiah'. The avatars leave Churches ('Ekklesie') behind them, and have an external body and an esoteric internal body. This is particularly true of the Rosicrucians (see **AMORC**), an esoteric center that has withered over the years, thus necessitating a new epicenter.

The Lotus + Cross Esoteric Order was founded in 1948. By means of a particular discipline, the initiate readies her/himself for special experiences, such as the reading of the Akashic Archives – a concept previously proposed by Rudolf Steiner (1861–1925) (see **Anthroposophy**) –

the phenomena of doubling and out-of-body travel, the exact understanding of astrology, of theurgy, and of a 'higher spiritism', whereas common spiritual practices are discouraged. The lotus – which replaces the classic rose of the Rosicrucian tradition in its combination with the cross – is at times understood by Palamidessi as a symbol of reincarnation, of which traces are supposedly found in the Bible, and would therefore be compatible with Christianity. Archeosophy, in particular, teaches a technique for recovering the memory of one's past lives. Thanks to this technique, for example, Palamidessi supposedly discovered that he had been Origen (185–254), and the sixteenth century astrologer, doctor, and mathematician Girolamo Cardano (1501–76).

The initiate also studies the human body, alternative medicines, herbs, and nutrition. The archeosopher practises a series of daily spiritual exercises that includes a demanding regimen of prayer (inspired by the Eastern orthodox tradition and by Western monastic life), as well as a series of athletic and breathing exercises. Palamidessi's teachings also include a 'sexognosy' technique for building the 'body of light', similar to that of gnostic movements. The eschatology proposed by Palamidessi, is based on ideas of reincarnation and on the temporary nature of Hell. Souls that have restored their resemblance to God may also leave the reincarnation cycle, whereas a 'second death' at the end of time, at the Last Judgment, is not denied the blasphemous.

PIERLUIGI ZOCCATELLI

ARMSTRONG, HERBERT W.
(b. 1892; d. 1996)
Founder of the Worldwide Church of God

Born in Des Moines, Iowa of Quaker stock, Herbert W. Armstrong (the W

was an invented middle initial) became the founder and leader of a distinctively American heterodox Christian sect (see **Worldwide Church of God**) and its massive worldwide publishing and broadcasting effort. In his two-volume *Autobiography* he describes how in the early 1920s, after months of intensive study, he became convinced that the Bible was absolutely true, that God had ordained the Saturday Sabbath for all time, and that a true Christian must obey God's Law. He also decided that God's true Church must be called the Church of God, and in 1927 he joined a branch of the Church of God, Seventh Day, headquartered at Stanberry, Missouri, having fellowship with members between Salem and Eugene, Oregon. This was a Sabbatarian, millenarian Church which shared historical roots with the Seventh-day Adventist Church, though it had always been separate from it.

Armstrong began preaching in 1928, and was ordained a minister in the Church of God in 1931. In 1934 he began the two activities which were to characterize his own Church for the next half-century or more: the publication of the *Plain Truth* magazine (initially a mimeographed sheet with a print-run of 250) and *The World Tomorrow* radio programme on a small local radio station. Following disagreements with the Church of God, his ministerial credentials were revoked, and in 1937 Armstrong established his own Church, the Radio Church of God (renamed the Worldwide Church of God in 1968).

Armstrong was always a controversial figure. Although he claimed to have (re)discovered the true teachings of Christianity on his own, most of what became the core teachings of the Worldwide Church of God were taught by some of the leading ministers of the Church of God Seventh Day; he even reprinted one of their booklets under his own name. Similarly, he claimed to have worked out the distinctive British-Israelite ideas which underlay his Church's prophetic teachings through his own study, though they were taken almost directly from J. H. Allen's 1902 book *Judah's Sceptre and Joseph's Birthright*. Criticisms of Armstrong have included his authoritarian leadership and mercurial temperament, his love of expensive possessions, his hobnobbing with world leaders (described by his son as 'the world's most expensive autograph hunt'), and even accusations of incest with one of his daughters, which were never denied.

Further reading

Barrett, D. V. (2001) *The New Believers*, London: Cassell

DAVID V. BARRETT

ARYA SAMAJ

The Arya Samaj is a Hindu revivalist movement with its origins in north India in the nineteenth century, but with a global presence and purpose in the twenty-first. With its message of 'Back to the *Veda*', it has sought to purify Hindu practices, ideas, and institutions by rejecting what it sees as superstitious and superfluous and exhorting the nobility of early Indian, Vedic religion as articulated in its Ten Principles. With their focus on one God – whose qualities are being, intelligence, and bliss – on Vedic scripture, and an ethical lifestyle, these principles were the summation of *Satyarth Prakash* ('The Light of Truth'), the principal publication of the movement's founder, Swami Dayananda Saraswati (1824–83). Dayananda, after a period as an itinerant *sannyasi* (see **Sannyasin**), systematized his ideas on Vedic revival, and social and religious reform, and founded the Arya Samaj in Bombay

in 1875. It was in Punjab, however, where his forthright and uncompromising approach on the glory of the Vedic past and impoverishment of contemporary Hindu belief and practice, met with most success. He reviled Hindu idolatry and the caste system, and spoke out against missionary incursions on Hindus, whether Islamic or Christian. The popularity of his views allowed the Samaj to pursue a policy of *suddhi* or purification, which enabled those who had converted to return to the Hindu fold, and – in the case of those from low castes – to be invested with the sacred thread normally given only to higher castes. This battle for Indian souls led the Samaj to ally itself increasingly with the politics of Indian nationalism, particularly during the leadership of Lala Lajput Rai (1865–1928).

The Samaj has been successful in propagating neo-Vedic ritual and education in Hindu communities abroad as well as in India, and has active branches in the Caribbean, United States, Canada, United Kingdom, East Africa, South Africa, Hong Kong, and Australia. In its desire 'to promote, preserve, and realise the Vedic heritage', it works in sympathy with other *hindutva* or Hindu identity movements such as the **Vishva Hindu Parishad**.

Further reading

Jones, K. (1976) *Arya Dharm: Hindu Consciousness in Nineteenth Century Punjab*, Berkeley: University of California Press.

KIM KNOTT

ASAHARA SHOKO (NÉ MATSUMOTO, CHIZUO)

Asahara Shoku, founder of **Aum Shinrikyo** was born in 1955 in Kumamoto, Kyushu prefecture, to a poor family that made straw mats for a living. Poor sighted, he spent his primary and secondary school days in a boarding school for the blind. After finishing secondary education, he became a qualified masseur and went to Tokyo in 1977, where he married and took change of the running of a Chinese herbal medicine shop. Being interested in religion, he joined a Japanese new religion (shin shukyo) **Agonshu** around 1981 where he undertook with great eagerness and enthusiam training and practice. He was, however, dissatisfied with the poorly organized yoga training system and left the organization to form his own yoga training group in 1984. He soon claimed that he had attained *vimukti* (Buddhist emancipation) and began active propagation of his beliefs in 1986 and named his movement Aum Shinrikyo in 1987. Much of this movement's teaching was derived from Agon-shu.

Once optimistic about changing the world Asahara began to have serious doubts about the possibility of realizing a happy social life in this world and began to define *vimukti* as a process of both physical and mental transformation that lead to a dimension beyond this world, and urged the followers to devote themselves to training with a view to realizing this goal. He claimed to have attained *vimukti* and to be a guru after the manner of the Tibetan esoteric Buddhist tradition of gurus, and demanded absolute obedience of the followers.

Although Buddhism formed the core of his teachings these also included elements from other faiths including Hinduism and Christianity. Asahara even preached the accomplishment of the prophecy of the Revelation of St. John the Divine, and called himself the second advent of Jesus Christ.

Around 1989, he began reinterpreting traditional doctrines such as *poa* to justify violence and murder within the organization. He also emphasized the approaching final war that would destroy leaving behind to inherit the new world that would come into being only those disciples of his who were fully trained. Asahara was held responsible by the courts for, among other crimes, the massacre in Matsumoto, Nagano in 1994, and that in the subway station in central Tokyo in 1995, for which he is now incarcerated in prison.

Further reading

Reader, Ian (2000) *Religious Violence in Contemporary Japan. The Case of Aum-Shinrikyo*, Richmond: Curzon Press.
SUSUMU SHIMAZONO

ASSAGIOLI, ROBERTO
(1888–1976)

This Italian psychiatrist developed a system of psychotherapy known as **Psychosynthesis** which claims to be a more complete system than that developed by his teacher Freud, who failed to acknowledge the reality of the Higher Self (see **Self-Religion, The Self and self**) and focused almost exclusively on three dimensions of the human psyche, the id, super ego and the ego. In Freud's view religion and spirituality while they might on certain contexts and situations function positively, were far less significant to the integration and well being of the human being than a rational, mature consciousness under the control of a realistic ego. Carl Gustav **Jung**, also a former student of Freud who collaborated with him for some time before distancing himself from the master, developed his own theory of psychoanalysis which attached greater importance to religion and spirituality and was much more positive about the potential benefit they could have for the well being of the psyche. Jung became well known for his discovery of archetypes or symbols that lay deep down in the collective unconscious of human beings and that constituted images of certain psychological realities that were highly charged with psychodynamic energy. These included such images as Saviour, Guardian Angel, Son of God, and Mother.

Assagioli, who was born in Venice, was highly critical of Freud and sought to go beyond Jung claiming that the latter had failed to refine his theory of archetypes treating them as if they were undifferentiated. He located them all regardless of their spiritual nature or otherwise in one domain so to speak. He failed, **Wilber** claims, to differentiate archetypes of the higher spiritual realm – the supra conscious and transpersonal dimensions of the psyche – and those archetypes of the infra conscious and infra personal level, of the lower, mythological origin that may have existed from the beginning of human evolution.

Assagioli attempted to provide a much more refined, hierarchical map of the field of human consciousness in which the religious and spiritual were clearly located in their own particular realm. The map divided the psyche into six separate areas: the lower or infra consciousness where all instinctive and unconscious drives and repressed thoughts and feelings were stored; the middle unconscious or intermediate state between waking and sleeping to which individuals have access during their waking moments and where unconsciously they elaborate their thoughts and feelings about recent experiences; the higher unconsciousness, a mostly inaccessible place of highly developed spiritual forms, where lofty ideals and refined thoughts penetrate consciousness and from where thoughts, deeds and actions of a moral and spiritual worth and value derive, a place where the psychic ener-

gies both enhance and disrupt the functioning of the mind; the field of consciousness or part of the personality through which thoughts, images, feeling constantly ebb and flow and can be observed and analysed; the conscious self or ego or point from where we observe, regulate and make decisions about the content of our consciousness and from where we derive the feeling of 'I-ness'; the higher self or Self behind the 'I-ness' or self that keeps consciousness going when it is outside our control during for example sleep or hypnosis; and the collective unconscious which is the general or overall consciousness which relates an individual's consciousness to others and to the past, present and future.

Assagioli's principal objective was to turn psychology into a science that could integrate the human psyche's different fields of activity and functions and it was for this reason in particular that his introduction of the notion of the Higher Self was so central to his method of healing.

Further reading

Assagioli, Roberto (1971) *Psychosynthesis, A Manual of Principles and Techniques*, New York: Viking Press.

PETER B. CLARKE

ASSEMBLIES OF GOD
*Founders: E. N. Bell and
J. Roswell Flowers*

The Assemblies of God churches date their origins back to the Azusa Street, Los Angeles, Pentecostal awakening in 1906 (see **Azusa Street Revival**), although they did not formally come together to form an integrated movement until their first General Council in Hot Springs Arkansas in 1914. This

Council was assembled for the purpose of coordinating approaches to training, education, missionary strategy, and publishing. It was decided that the General Council would have control over these areas. The gathering adopted the periodical *The Word and Witness* edited by E. N. Bell as their official voice, a magazine that latter gave way to the *Pentecostal Evangel*.

The Assemblies adopted a congregational form of organization. An umbrella body in the form of a fifteen-member executive, which meets once a month, serves as the board of directors. The local churches are self-governing, retain considerable autonomy and are organized into districts covering every state in the United States. In 1998 the headquarters were moved to Springfield, Missouri.

The doctrinal and ritual foundations of the Assemblies were agreed in 1916 and include the belief that the Bible is the infallible word of God, that the Second Coming of Jesus is imminent, a belief in spiritual and the practices of baptism of the Holy Spirit by total immersion. Baptism in the Holy Spirit is accompanied by speaking in tongues known as glossolalia.

The missionary division of the movement was formally instituted in 1919 and today Assembly missionaries are working in virtually every country in the world. There is also a Division of Home missions that ministers to students, mixed cultural and ethnic groups and the military.

The estimated membership of the Assemblies of God in the United States is two and a half million and worldwide over 28 million.

Further reading

Hollenweger, W. (1988) *The Pentecostals*, Peabody, MA: Hendrickson Publishers.

PETER B. CLARKE

ATHLETES FOR CHRIST

In 1974, after having read Apostle Paul (the *Holy Bible*, the first letter of Paul to the Corinthians, 9:24), the former Brazilian F1 pilot, Alex Dias Ribeiro, member of the Baptist Church, started to spread the word of God in motor racing competitions. His personal logo was the inscription JESUS SAVES which he displayed on his car as well as on his competition clothing. He founded, together with the former football player, João Leite, in 1981. Alex Dias Ribeiro (now an F1 Pace Car pilot) has been the religious leader and pastor of the Athletes for Christ (AC) in different national and international events (Olympic Games, World Football Championships, Motoring championships).

Although it involves almost all sports (athletics, boxing, motoring, basketball, tennis), and well known sportsmen (Carl Lewis/Holyfield/Foreman, Ayrton Senna/Ary Vattanen, David Robinson, Michael Chang), the AC movement has always had a bigger impact in the football world than in any other branch of sport. Football has a common language which goes beyond racial, ethnic, social, and religious barriers. This NRM is now present in fifty countries, and is strongest in Portugal, Italy, Japan, and Spain. Considering all sports, there are at the moment 65,000 Athletes for Christ globally.

The strength of this religious movement became evident in the 1994 World Cup, in Los Angeles (USA), when a number of famous AC members (Muller, Taffarrel, Jorginho, Mazinho, Zinho, Paulo Sérgio, of the Brazilian team) took advantage of the most important world sports event (watched by over two billion people) to spread their evangelical message. At the end of the match they made a circle with the rest of the players for collective prayer to thank God for their fourth victory in a World Cup. In the 2002 World Cup, which took place in Japan and South Korea, the same ritual was once more accomplished.

The main objectives of this NRM are: to speak about Christ to sportsmen of all sports; to encourage and create conditions for the AC to evangelize their colleagues; to co-operate with Churches, Missions and Christian protestant organizations, to help in the creation and implementation of sports and leisure activities for the local communities; to encourage honesty and integrity in the practice of sports; to act as missionaries and make known across the world the message of salvation and to recruit other sportsmen and women to the AC as well as their supporters.

The Athletes for Christ is not strictly a religion nor a sect, nor is it a new Church. It is rather an evangelical movement which brings together supporters of the various protestant Churches, mainly of the Baptist Church. Nonetheless, integrated in the broad and diversified Neo-Evangelical movement, some Athletes for Christ have founded their own church, as in the case of Muller, a former Brazilian football national team player, who was a pastor of the 'Pentecostal Church Portas Abertas', and started his own 'Pentecostal Church of God' in Brazil.

According to the AC movement its mission is to take Christ's message to all those who practise sports, no matter what kind, professional or amateur.

Further reading

www.atletas.org.
www.netds.com.br/atletas

DONIZETE RODRIGUES

AUM SHINRIKYO (AUM OR ABSOLUTE OR SUPREME TRUTH MOVEMENT)

A new religion founded by **Asahara Shoko** (1955–) in the 1980s, this movement has become widely known for carrying out indiscriminate acts of violence using poisonous sarin gas and in particular for its attack on the Tokyo underground in March 1995. The leaders have since been arrested and many of them sentenced to death.

Asahara, the founder, who suffered from quasi blindness from birth, was born in Kumamoto in Kyushu prefecture and arrived in Tokyo in 1977 and opened a Chinese herbal medicine shop. He also had an ambition to enter Tokyo university which went unrealized and at the same time he was interested in religion. He joined **Agonshu**, a new religion around 1981. Dissatisfied with what he regarded as Agon-shu's poorly organized yoga training system he formed an independent yoga training group with the name of Aum Shinsen-no-kai (literally: Aum Mountain Hermits' Society). In 1986, Asahara claimed to have attained the state of *vimukti* (Buddhist emancipation) and began propagating his doctrines actively. He renamed his organization Aum Shinri-kyo in 1987.

During its early years, Aum Shinri-kyo's belief system differed little from that of Agon-shu and like the latter aimed at self-transformation by lessening or 'cutting one's bad karma'. Asahara, however, came in time to place a stronger emphasis on yoga training as the means to self-transformation. He also became more pessimistic about life in general and seems to have lost any hope he might once have had of the possibility of living a happy social life in this world.

Thus, the goal became life in another dimension and he defined *vimukti* as the process of physical and mental self transformation leading to a dimension beyond this world. Asahara was regarded as one who had attained *vimukti,* and in accordance with Tibetan esoteric Buddhism, he urged the followers to obey him as guru. Displaying a concern for the strict observance of the precepts of Buddhism, the organization claimed to be an authentic Buddhist organization despite its acceptance of Hindu beliefs including the belief in Shiva.

Asahara's pessimism became manifest in different ways including in his preaching about the imminent realization of the prophecy of the Revelation of St. John the Divine and his speaking of himself as the second advent of Jesus Christ.

How much these shifts in outlook contributed to the violence that the movement was to engage in is difficult to measure with any exactness. In 1988, when the movement's Mt. Fuji Headquarters and seminary were established, violence soon folowed and included the the death of a follower allegedly from harsh training practices. This death remained undisclosed and in February 1989, a follower who intended to report the case to authorities was reportedly lynched.

The meaning of doctrines was manipulated to justify such violence. *Poa*, for example, a ritual service for the recently dead to assist them in the passage to the world beyond, came to be interpreted as a salvific act and as meaning that in advanced Buddhist training a murder is permissible if it helps others to advance spiritually.

A further act of murder occurred in November 1989 when the movement's leadership ordered the death of the family of Tsutsumi Sakamoto, a lawyer who in response to an appeal from the families of followers who were concerned about their relatives and the movement's activities generally, had begun to examine and publicly criticize Aum. In addition to the movement's involvement in the murder of the Sakamotos, there was also growing public concern over its use of aggressive methods of propagation, its extraction by force of contributions from followers, and at the increase in the number of followers who had broken off all communication with their families.

In February 1990, Aum put forward many candidates for parliamentary elections and failed completely. This defeat clearly contributed to the movement becoming evermore introversionist and world-rejectionist. It was around this time that the organization purchased huge plots of land at several locations and built shelters to isolate its followers from society at large and began to equip itself with biological and chemical weapons and firearms. Around 1992, it began stressing that Armageddon was imminent. Soon it would turn its attention from murdering individuals and their families to murdering whole communities. In June 1994 a group of Aum devotees scattered sarin gas in Matsumoto city and this was followed in March 1995 with a sarin gas attack on the subway station of Kasumigaseki in the center of Tokyo. Asahara and the rest of the leadership were arrested and charged with the murders of several dozen people and other crimes, and found guilty. Other changes against Asahara remain to be brought.

At the end, thus, one of the main themes of Aum Shinrikyo came to be the spiritual emptiness of this world. It also came to emphasize the necessity of undergoing physically harsh training for spiritual advancement. At the height of its popularity it had a membership of about 10,000 in Japan and more –

around 40,000 – in Russia. The movement assumed the name Aleph in January 2000 and has now a much smaller membership.

Further reading

Reader, Ian (2000) *Religious Violence in Contemporary Japan. The Case of Aum-Shinrikyo*, Richmond: Curzon Press.

Shimazono, Susumu (1996) 'In the Wake of Aum: The Formation and Transformation of a Universe of Belief', in *Japanese Journal of Religious Studies*, Vol. 6, No. 3, pp. 389–412.

SUSUMU SHIMAZONO

AUROBINDO, SRI

Sri Aurobindo (1872–1950) was the co-founder of Auroville, which has become one of the most famous and highly regarded ashrams in India. He is also remembered for his teachings on **yoga** and a distinctive existential philosophy. Closely associated with him is Mira Richard (née Alfassa) (1878–1973), a Frenchwoman who became his disciple, co-founder and co-director of Auroville for many years.

Sri Aurobindo was born in Calcutta and educated in England (St Paul's school and Cambridge University), proving himself a precociously talented student. On his return to India in 1893 he became a radical Indian nationalist and journalist who campaigned for full independence. He was eventually arrested for sedition by the British authorities. During his imprisonment, he underwent a life-changing religious experience, and resolved to lead a life of spiritual teaching and leadership. To this end, on his release he moved to Pondicherry in what was then the French part of India. Here he attracted followers, but decided not to call them disciples for the time being.

Between 1914 and 1922 Sri Aurobindo wrote the bulk of his books, including *The Life Divine, The Synthesis of Yoga, Essays on the Gita, The Secret of the Veda, The Foundations of Indian Culture, The Future Poetry, The Human Cycle* and *The Ideal of Human Unity*. His writings are complex and high-level, open to different interpretations, but the main themes are clear. His philosophy is based on the principle of the evolution of consciousness, from pure matter, through animals, to humans. He believed that evolution would eventually culminate as the 'supermind', embodied in enlightened people in order to redeem all other forms of consciousness and matter. Such an outlook may well owe something to the philosophy of Nietzsche, whose 'superman' was destined to become 'the meaning of the earth'. Nietzsche's ideas were popular and influential at the time of Sri Aurobindo's writing phase.

The ordinary human mind was seen by Sri Aurobindo as being unstable, constantly changing its preferences, and displaying tendencies to make inappropriate choices regarding the future. The means of liberation from this chronic instability was to be yoga, the ancient Indian mind–body–spirit system, which he insisted should be carried out under the instruction, guidance and inspiration of a **guru**. Although India had produced sages and rishis (wise and holy men) for thousands of years, true widespread transformation for the majority was not considered possible until modern times. It is not clear why this is so, but Sri Aurobindo saw a conflict between the 'supranatural' force acting for change, and 'anti-divine' forces resisting change. This was his view of the Second World War when, in a reversal of his youthful attitudes, he strongly backed Britain against the Axis powers.

In 1914 Mira Richard arrived in Pondicherry from France. As a child she had had many psychic experiences, and later studied occultism in depth. Beginning as a disciple, she then became Sri Aurobindo's collaborator in the project to build an ashram, opened in 1926. Sri Aurobindo himself retired into seclusion soon after the ashram was set up, concentrating on his writing. Mira then became the ashram's main director and leading spokesperson, the formative influence who gave substance to Sri Aurobindo's teaching. Through her, the stated mission of the ashram was the goal of working towards a new world and a new humanity. She was referred to by all as 'The Mother', and claimed to have had visions of Sri Aurobindo before coming to India in which she realized that he was a present-day messiah or avatar (incarnation of God).

Since the death of its founders, Auroville has remained an active centre where about 1,200 people live, pursuing the life advocated by Sri Aurobindo of work, yoga and meditation. It now consists of several groups of buildings scattered around Pondicherry. There are many visitors from all around the world, who come and stay for varying periods of time. It is a registered charitable trust, and new members are appointed by the Government of India. The focal point of the ashram is the 'Samadhi' (tomb) of Sri Aurobindo and Mira Richard, where followers regularly gather for meditation.

The teachings of Sri Aurobindo as a new religious movement in the west were at their most influential in the 1960s and 1970s. Since then, other Indian spiritual teachers have had more impact, both within the discipline of yoga and generally. Nevertheless, he is seen by many students as having made one of the most important contributions to the philosophy of yoga since Patanjali, and his teachings remain part of the standard canon.

Further reading

Heehs, Peter (1989) *Sri Aurobindo: A Brief Biography*, Oxford and New York: Oxford University Press.

ELIZABETH PUTTICK

AZUSA STREET REVIVAL

The Azusa Street Revival in 1906–9, regarded by historians of religions as marking the beginning of twentieth-century Pentecostalism, has exercised a profound influence in the United States and beyond.

William Joseph Seymour (1870–1922), the central figure of the Revival was born to a family of emancipated slaves and grew up in the midst of violent racism. Seymour served as a pastor of a black Holiness Church in Jackson, Mississippi. He enrolled in a Bible College run by Charles Parham in Houston, Texas, around the time when glossolalia was being experienced as a sign of the power of the Holy Spirit at the College, which essentially became a major emphasis in Parham's teachings. In February 1906, Seymour became the pastor of the Church of Nazarene, which was a small black church in Los Angeles. He emphasized glossolalia as evidence of Spirit baptism during his Sunday sermons. Furthermore, conversion, sanctification, divine healing and the imminent return of Christ were themes that featured prominently during his evening teaching sessions. The emphases of Seymour's sermons incurred the displeasure of some which subsequently led to his being locked out of the mission. As a result he had to live with two black families while leading them in Bible study and prayer. Seymour is believed to have prayed for one Edward Lee who received healing and later was baptized in the Holy Spirit. This experience was later shared by others as well as Seymour himself. The next few days saw crowds of different races gathering to hear Seymour preach and to experience glossolalia, trances and healing.

The stupendous growth of adherents led them to arrange to have an abandoned Methodist Episcopal church at 312 Azusa Street leased to them for their meeting. They held three services each Sunday with attendances rising to over 800 with about 500 standing outside. The services of which Seymour was clearly in charge, were characterized by spontaneity. Sermons were generally not prepared in advance and extempore songs were mainly unaccompanied, there were testimonies, prayer, altar calls for salvation or sanctification or for baptism in the Holy Spirit. During prayer adherents claimed they fell under the power of the Holy Spirit.

The Azusa Street revival is significant for several reasons. First, it was at the heart of the emergence of the twentieth-century Pentecostal movement. Second, it was the first time that the press noticed the Pentecostal movement and thus gave it wide coverage thus attracting to it worldwide attention. The tremendous extent of its spread led to the emergence of several centers of Pentecostalism in cities throughout the United States. It also produced many Pentecostal denominations including white-oriented United Pentecostal Church and the Assemblies of God Church. Within five months of its birth, the revival had produced over thirty-eight missionaries who spread the Pentecostal message and experience in over fifty nations world-wide within two years.

Thirdly, the Azusa Street revival points to the black experiential origins of Pentecostalism thus, providing values and themes of the Pentecostal movement which distinctively belong to the black culture. Finally, the Azusa Street revival transcended geographical, racial and denominational barriers. There was a high sense of togetherness, irrespective of race and color and Christian profession. For instance, Germans and Jews, blacks and whites ate together in the little cottage at the rear of the church. The impact of the revival was thus felt initially among mainly Protestants. Roman Catholics were also to discover around the middle of the twentieth-century resources of renewal in Pentecostalism.

Further reading

Hollenweger, W. J. (1972) *The Pentecostals: The Charismatic Movement in the Churches*, Minneapolis, MN: Augsburg.

CEPHAS N. OMENYO

B

BABA RAM DAS
(a.k.a. Richard Alpert) (b. 1931)

Originally trained as a psychologist, Alpert was dismissed from his teaching position at Harvard University in 1963, as a consequence of experiments with LSD, together with his collaborator Timothy Leary. Alpert moved with Leary to the Ananda Ashram, in Millbrook, York, where he helped to found the League for Spiritual Discovery, which advocated the use of drugs for religious purposes. Alpert was one of the co-founders of the Original Neo-Kleptonian American Church, led by Art Kleps, and he co-authored *The Psychedelic Experience* (1964) with Leary and Ralph Metzner.

Leary and Alpert parted in 1967 when the latter embarked on a visit to India, where he met Neem Karoli Baba (1900?–73). Neem Karoli Baba caused Alpert to reject the use of hallucinogens, and Alpert became a disciple, assuming the name of Ram Das (meaning 'servant of God'). Ram Das studied various spiritual teachings, spanning Hinduism and Sufism, incorporating teachings of Jesus, as well as elements of Buddhism, particularly vipassana, and the Zen and Tibetan traditions.

Ram Das emphasized *karma yoga* (the spiritual path of deeds) and *sewa* (service to others). He established the Hanuman Foundation in 1973 (incorporated in 1974), which offered programmes principally for the dying and the bereaved. The foundation was so named after the Hindu deity Hanuman, who acted in service to the high god Ram. Ram Das also set up a Prison-Ashram Project, which sought to assist prisoners with their spiritual life. Ram Das made no claims to guruship or enlightenment, teaching that one's answers are to be found within oneself. Ram Das also lent his support to Larry Brilliant's Seva Foundation, set up to alleviate blindness.

Ram Das wrote several books, the best known of which is his partly-autobiographical *Be Here Now* (1971). *The*

Only Dance There Is (1976) and *Grist for the Mill* (1977) are both reconstructions of Neem Karoli Baba's talks, and *Miracle of Love* (1979) is a memoir of Neem Karoli Baba. In 1997 Ram Das suffered a stroke: his recovery was gradual and not wholly complete, but it caused him to author his most recent work *Still Here: Embracing Changing, Aging and Dying* (2000).

Further reading

Alpert, R. (Baba Ram Das) (1992) *Be Here Now*, Boulder, CO: Hanuman Foundation.

Alpert, R. (1976) *The Only Dance There Is*, New York: J. Aronson.

Alpert, R. (1977) *Grist for the Mill*, USA: Celestial Arts.

Alpert, R. (2000) *Still Here: Embracing, Chanhging, Aging and Dying*, New York: Riverhead Books.

Leary, T., Metzner, R. and Alpert, R. (1964) *The Psychedelic Experience: A Manual based on the Tibetan Book of the Dead*, Citadel Underground.

GEORGE CHRYSSIDES

BAHA'I

The Baha'i religion emerged from Shi'i Islam in the middle of the nineteenth century. It has developed into one of the more successful new religions, today claiming more than five million adherents. Its major goal is to create religious and political unity in the world and thereby promote a new and peaceful world civilization.

The Baha'i religion has its origins in nineteenth-century Iran in heterodox currents among the Shi'ites. In 1844 Ali Muhammad Shirazi (1819–50), called the Bab (the Arabic word *bab* means 'gate' and is a title indicating spiritual access to the Hidden Imam), declared himself to be a new source of divine revelations, and he soon attracted many followers. In a general climate of public unrest the millenarian Babi movement (see **millenarianism**) grew rapidly, and from 1848 the Babis were engaged in bloody fights with the Iranian government. After the execution of the Bab in 1850 the Babi movement was crushed, and the surviving Babi leaders were exiled to the neighbouring Ottoman Empire.

In exile an internal leadership conflict led to a schism around 1866 when Husayn-Ali Nuri (1817–92), called Baha'u'llah, declared that he was the new prophet whom the Bab had prophesied would appear. The great majority of Babis accepted Baha'u'llah as their new prophet and became known as Baha'is. Shortly after, the Ottoman authorities transferred Baha'u'llah to Akko north of Haifa in present-day Israel. Baha'u'llah remained there for the rest of his life, continuously working to change the Babi heritage into the new religion, Baha'i.

Through systematic mission initiated by Baha'u'llah's son and successor, Abdu'l-Baha (1844–1921), Baha'i gradually expanded outside its Middle Eastern environment. Baha'i missionaries came to the USA and Canada in the 1890s and to Western Europe around 1900. In 1910, Abdu'l-Baha moved the Baha'i administration to its present premises in Haifa on the slope of Mount Carmel. Abdu'l-Baha's grandson and successor, Shoghi Effendi (1897–1957), developed the Baha'i administration and mission further, and he translated many of the central Baha'i texts into English. In 1963, an interim leadership established the present collective leadership, the Universal House of Justice.

The Baha'i religion grew significantly from a few hundred thousand in the late 1950s to more than five million in the 1990s. Considerable growth has taken place in Africa, South Asia, and Latin America. In most countries, the majority of the Baha'is are native to the country, but there is usually also a significant contingent of foreign Baha'is, in particular expatriate Iranian Baha'is.

In Iran, the *c.* 300,000 Baha'is constitute the largest religious minority. They are considered heretics by the Muslim *ulama* (scholars), and they have been regularly persecuted. More than two hundred Baha'is have been killed since the Iranian revolution in 1979.

Contemporary Baha'i beliefs and religious practice

According to Baha'i doctrines the prophets of the major religions, such as Moses, Zoroaster, Buddha, Jesus, Muhammad, the Bab, and Baha'u'llah, are human manifestations of an invisible and indescribable deity called God. The belief in Baha'u'llah as a prophet coming after Muhammad is the reason why both Baha'is and Muslims agree that Baha'i is not an Islamic group.

According to Baha'i teachings every human being has a soul which comes into existence at conception and continues to exist after biological death. It is not reincarnated in another body but enters a new, non-material form of existence in the so-called Abha Kingdom. Here, it may progress until it attains God's presence.

Baha'i law regulates both community affairs and individual life among the Baha'is and resembles the Muslim *shari'a* in that respect. Central rituals, such as prayer, pilgrimage, and visits to holy places, also resemble Islamic practice. Baha'is are forbidden to drink alcohol, and the law prescribes a yearly fasting period, but otherwise the Baha'is have not retained the dietary prohibitions of Islam. In general, the Baha'is discourage the development of formalized collective rituals.

The basic social doctrines of Baha'i are often referred to as the 'twelve principles' (they are not fixed in word or order):

- Oneness of mankind;
- Independent investigation of truth;
- Common foundation of all religions;
- Oneness of religion;
- Essential harmony of science and religion;
- Equality of men and women;
- Elimination of the extremes of wealth and poverty;
- Elimination of prejudice of all kinds;
- Universal compulsory education;
- A spiritual solution of the economic problems;
- A universal auxiliary language;
- Universal peace upheld by a world government.

The Baha'i calendar was devised by the Bab. The Baha'i year has nineteen months, each consisting of nineteen days (the numbers nine and nineteen have a special significance for the Baha'is). At the first day of each month, local Baha'i communities celebrate the Nineteen Day Feast. In addition, the Baha'is commemorate the birth, death, and other major events associated with the Bab, Baha'u'llah, and Abdu'l-Baha.

Core activities in Baha'i religious life are the obligatory daily prayers and reading of the sacred texts, but it is also important to participate in the communal religious life, to contribute to the Baha'i funds, and to proselytize. The Baha'is largely recruit new members through their personal networks. They are also actively engaged in grass-root work at various international political events, such as the UN summits in the 1990s, and the Baha'i organization has official status as a nongovernmental organization in the UN system.

In their personal lives Baha'is are expected to work professionally and observe the general moral codes of the society they live in. They praise cultural pluralism, and pictures of people representing the most diverse ethnic groups are favourite Baha'i icons.

Organization

The Baha'i organization has doctrinal significance as a blueprint for the future politico-religious Baha'i world order. The lowest body is the local spiritual assembly whose nine elected members are responsible for all affairs of the local Baha'i community. There is no professionally educated clergy in Baha'i, and the members in turn lead the religious meetings. At the national level, the Baha'is elect a nine-member national spiritual assembly every year; this body has considerable authority. The world leadership is in the hands of the Universal House of Justice, a body of nine men (women are not eligible) elected for five-year periods by delegates. Thanks to its centralized organization the Universal House of Justice has been able to develop a high measure of doctrinal discipline and control among the Baha'is. This has caused some dissatisfaction, especially among Baha'i intellectuals with a liberal stance.

The Universal House of Justice is placed in the Baha'i World Centre in Haifa, a site with large monumental buildings, which also include the Shrine of the Bab. The Shrine of the Bab is considered the sacred centre of the world, and it is the architectural centrepiece of a remarkable complex of beautiful terraces and gardens stretching up the slope of Mount Carmel. The terraces were opened to the public in 2001.

The Baha'is have erected seven Baha'i temples around the world. They are unique pieces of architecture, with a regular nine-sided ground-plan and a central dome. They are open to the public, and several of them are tourist attractions.

Further reading

Cole, J. R. I. (1998) *Modernity and the Millennium. The Genesis of the Baha'i Faith in the Nineteenth-Century Middle East*, New York: Columbia University Press.

Smith, P. (1987) *The Babi and Baha'i Religions. From Messianic Shi'ism to a World Religion*, Cambridge: Cambridge University Press and George Ronald.

Walbridge, J. (1996) *Sacred Acts, Sacred Space, Sacred Time*, Oxford: George Ronald.

Warburg, M. (1995) 'Growth patterns of new religions: The case of Baha'i', in R. Towler (ed.) *New Religions and the New Europe*, Aarhus: Aarhus University Press.

MARGIT WARBURG

BAMBA MBACKÉ, AHMADU

Ahmadu Bamba Mbacké (1850/1–1927) a Muslim cleric of north-western Senegal, was the founder of the **Murid Movement**, a Sufi order but also a powerful political and economic organization. He built his following on the basis of his scholarship, also on the basis of miraculous feats in the face of the new French colonial authority in Senegal. He was twice exiled by the French (1895–1902, 1903–7) and spent the remainder of his life under a form of house arrest. He had been suspected by the colonial government of plotting armed resistance, but in fact was consistently the advocate of peaceful accommodation with French government. He opposed armed jihad as probably impious in practice, and saw no reason for Muslims to reject French government, as long as the French respected Muslim belief and practice. His appeal was above all to a Wolof following, and to the casualties of the defeated Wolof states, especially perhaps to the lower orders of Wolof society, to those of occupational caste or to (ex) slaves. Here was his charismatic clientele, but his appeal was to extend to all ranks of Wolof society, even beyond the boundaries of Wolof ethnicity (to the Serer in particular). He recommended hard work to his followers, agricultural labour in particular, to be combined with regular prayer: work was the way to survive, it was also the way to a life of dignity, the way away from vice. Murids were to become very effective economically as they followed his teaching, and the colonial government cautiously came to value Ahmadu Bamba as a Muslim leader with sound practical precepts. Since his death he is more respected than ever in Senegal, his image painted on buses and on houses. There are many Sufi heroes in Senegal, but he more than any has national status. **The Great Magal of Touba**, pilgrimage to his tomb, annually brings the country to a stop.

DONAL CRUISE O'BRIEN

BERG, DAVID BRANDT

David Brandt Berg (1919–94) was the founder and leader of The Children of God, later known as The Family (see **Family, The**). Raised in an Evangelical Christian environment (see **Evangelical Christianity**), Berg joined in missionary work from his early youth. After a brief period in the army, he served as a pastor in a mainstream church in Arizona, but influenced by socialist ideology he gradually developed a harsh opposition to the values of modern, Western society – 'The System' as he would later term it. From 1952–67 Berg worked as an assistant to tele-evangelist Fred Jordan (see **televangelism**). His career as a prophet and religious leader was inaugurated in the following years when he started evangelizing among the hippies of Southern California. He began receiving revelations and gradually developed a distinct theology based on his new insight. Initially he anticipated a major earthquake in California as the first apocalyptical sign, and later, as 'God's End Time Prophet', he would claim that the 'Battle of Armageddon' would be fought in 1993. Berg's eschatological emphasis was clearly nourished by his political identification of 'The System' and a general countercultural trend in his teachings is quite apparent.

However, it was Berg's strong interest in sex that came to identify his theology in the eyes of the public. He introduced sex as a missionary device, insisted that physical bonding was contained in the Christian concept of love, and he challenged the general sexual norms by favouring promiscuity. Rumours of paedophile relationships in his group flourished – sometimes with good reason. Berg's preoccupation with sex, however, has by and large been abandoned by his movement.

Berg's leadership was never direct or personal and most of his followers actually never saw him. His personal life was to a certain extend clouded in mystery, and when he died in 1994 and his photograph was circulated by his organization, inner-group followers said that he looked exactly as they had imagined. Berg was primarily accessible through his numerous writings, the so-called Mo-Letters, in which he would address all kinds of matters from a theological perspective in a rather crude and unsophisticated manner. According to The Family's home-page David Berg's 'lively, down-to-earth, and sometimes unconventional approach to heavenly matters makes his writings a unique contribution to Christian literature'.

MIKAEL ROTHSTEIN

BESANT, ANNIE

Annie Besant (1847–1933) is one of the most remarkable women in the history of religion: a political activist and social reformer who became a highly influential spiritual leader. During the course of her adventurous life, she moved from the Anglo-Catholicism of her girlhood, through marriage to and divorce from an Anglican clergyman, into radical atheism, followed by conversion to Theosophy which she ended up leading. All this at a time when the ideal female role was 'angel of the house'!

Besant's career began after her daughter's illness had led her into rejecting Christianity and ending her marriage. She moved to London, met Charles Bradlaugh (the leading Freethinker of the National Secular Society), and worked on his journal. In 1877 they were put on trial for publishing a book on birth control ('obscene libel'). Although they won the case, she was declared an unfit mother and lost custody of her daughter. Bitterly upset, she plunged into campaigning for a variety of social and feminist causes, including a famous victory for the London match girls in a strike against Bryant & May. She also became a member of the executive committee of the Fabian Society, a friend of G. B. Shaw, and founded a magazine to speak out for the poor and exploited.

In 1889, Annie Besant met Helena Blavatsky (see **Blavatsky, Helena**), and became converted to **Theosophy**. After Blavatsky's death the Society split into two branches, and Besant became the President of the main branch in Madras, India. Her main colleague was C. W. Leadbeater, a former Anglican minister who had been expelled from the Society for alleged paedophilia but was reinstated by Besant. Together they discovered and adopted Krishnamurti, whom they brought up to be the new World Teacher. Four years after Krishnamurti's rejection of this role, she died peacefully in Madras.

Besant's reputation has survived more widely in India than Britain. She played an active role in India's home rule movement, as well as campaigning for schools, women's rights, and other social reforms. Many Indian streets are named after her, and she also left an extensive written legacy, including an autobiography, translation of the Bhagavad Gita, and numerous books on esoteric spirituality.

ELIZABETH PUTTICK

BHAKTIVEDANTA, SWAMI

A. C. Bhaktivedanta Swami Prabhupada, as he is called on his many books, was the Bengali guru who travelled to the West and founded the Hare Krishna movement (see **International Society for Krishna Consciousness/ISKCON**). By the time of his death in 1977, he had established centres in America, Europe, Asia, Australasia, and Africa, and had returned to his native India with his young white disciples to revitalize the teachings of the sixteenth-century mystic, Chaitanya.

Born Abhay Charan De in Calcutta in 1896 Bhaktivedanta Swami worked as a chemist before coming across the Gaudiya Vaishnava Math, with its focus on Krishna worship, in the 1920s. He was initiated by Bhaktisiddhanta Saraswati in 1932, whilst still a family man. Following his guru's instructions, he began to write in English about *bhakti yoga*, devotion to Krishna, starting the magazine *Back to Godhead* in 1944. Several years later he decided to leave home and dedicate his life to Krishna, first by translating and publishing the *Bhagavata Purana*, and then by going to the West to preach. He became a *sannyasi* (see **Sannyasin**) in 1959, taking the name 'Bhaktivedanta Swami', and in 1965 made the long sea journey from India to the USA. (See **International Society for Krishna Consciousness, ISKCON** for his early American activities.) From 1966 to his death in 1977, as an elderly man, he preached, published (over 50 books), and initiated thousands of devotees worldwide into his new movement.

His achievements, in founding ISK-CON, making accessible some of the great works of devotional Hinduism to ordinary English speakers, and in effectively transmitting the teachings and practices of Krishna consciousness to the West and beyond, are described in his English biography, *Srila Prabhupada-lilamrta*, and discussed in the *Journal of Vaishnava Studies* (volume 6, number 2, 1998). Honoured by scholars as a sincere advocate of Gaudiya Vaishnavism, and loved and revered by his many devotees, Bhaktivedanta Swami saw himself first and foremost as his guru's disciple and Krishna's servant.

KIM KNOTT

BLACK HOLINESS– PENTECOSTAL MOVEMENT

The Holiness movement, which in large part emerged out of Methodism in the aftermath of the Civil War, was not specifically aimed at African Americans. Nevertheless, despite the close alliance between some of its adherents and the Ku Klux Klan, the Holiness movement did occasionally bring poor whites and blacks together in interracial revivals. Some blacks also established Holiness sects. Holiness sects elaborated upon John Wesley's emphasis on a 'second blessing', following conversion, and view 'sanctification' or 'holiness' as an inward experience produced by faith in the Holy Ghost. The United Holy church (established in 1886 in Method, North Carolina), was perhaps the earliest of the black Holiness sects.

While several black Holiness bodies arose out of the African Methodist Episcopal and African Methodist Episcopal Zion churches, most emerged as schisms from Baptist associations and conventions. For example, Charles H. Mason and Charles P. Jones started a black Holiness sect in the Mississippi Valley. Mason, who began his ministry in the Mt Gale Missionary Baptist Church in Preston, Arkansas, underwent sanctification in 1893. He joined Jones, J. A. Jeter, and W. S. Pleasant in conducting a Holiness-style revival in Jackson, Mississippi. After being expelled from the Baptist church, Mason and Jones established a congregation in Lexington, Mississippi, which they eventually named the Church of God but renamed it shortly thereafter the Church of God in Christ to distinquish it from the white-controlled Church of God.

Pentecostalism (see **Azusa Street Revival**) grew out of the Holiness movement and emphasizes the gifts of the Holy Spirit, particularly glossolalia or speaking-in-tongues, interpretation of tongues, prophecy, and divine healing, particularly in the form of laying-on-of-hands. Various scholars point to the establishment of Charles Fox Parham's Bible school in Topeka, Kansas, in 1901 as the beginning of modern Pentecostalism. While indeed Parham's teaching that glossolalia constitutes the only overt evidence of a convert's reception of the Holy Ghost played a significant role in the origin of Pentecostalism, the **Azusa Street Revival** of 1906–9 in Los Angeles under the leadership of William J. Seymour, a black Holiness preacher and former student at Parham's Houston Bible school, transformed it into a mass movement. The Revival attracted both poor blacks and whites from all over the United States and even other countries. Various Pentecostal sects owe their origins to the Revival. In 1907, Charles H. Mason, J. A. Jeter, and D. J. Young spoke in tongues during their five-week stay at the Azusa Street Mission. After he returned to his headquarters in Memphis, Mason asked an assembly of the Church of God in Christ (COGIC) that the sect become a Pentecostal group – a movement that forced his compatriot, C. P. Jones, to form the Church of Christ (Holiness) USA. Although specific black groups may refer to themselves as either Holiness or Pentecostal, many African Americans refer to them as Sanctified churches.

The initial interracial character of the Pentecostal movement began to break down in the year following the Revival. In 1914 COGIC-ordained white ministers formed the Assemblies of God in Hot Springs, Arkansas. The division along racial lines in 1924 of the Pentecostal Assemblies of the World formally ended the interracial period in American Pentecostalism. Although many black Holiness and Pentecostal churches emerged in the rural South, as a result of the Great Migration of African Americans to the cities of the North and the South in the early twentieth century, these churches were also established in urban areas across America. Sanctified churches have functioned for some time as a largely urban phenomenon. In addition to the Holiness and Pentecostal evangelists who followed the black migrants to the cities, countless numbers of new Sanctified sects appeared in the 'Promised Land' along with Father Divine, Daddy Grace, Prophet Jones, the Nation of Islam, and the Spiritual churches.

From its humble origins, COGIC has grown to the largest association within the black Holiness–Pentecostal movement. During the 1910s and 1920s, COGIC evangelists established congregations in New York, Chicago, Detroit, Dallas, Houston, Los Angeles, and many other US cities. In the 1920s, COGIC expanded its operations to the West Indies, Central America, and West Africa. COGIC claimed to have some 6,500,000 members in over 12,000 congregations in the mid-1990s and constitutes, along with the three National Baptist denominations and the three black Methodist denominations, one of the seven largest African American religious organizations in the United States. Despite the fact that most of its members are working-class blacks, it now also has a substantial number of professional and affluent members, including movie star Denzel Washington.

In contrast to COGIC, probably several hundred Sanctified sects exist in the United States, serving primarily working-class blacks.

Further reading

Paris, A. E. (1982) *Black Pentecostalism: Southern Religion in an Urban World*, Amherst: University of Massachusetts Press.

Sanders, C. J. (1996) *Saints in Exile: The Holiness-Pentecostal Experience in African American Religion and Culture*, New York: Oxford University Press.

HANS A. BAER

BLACK JEWISH MOVEMENTS

It is generally believed that the origins of Black Judaism lie in the identification of African slaves with the biblical Hebrews, including the period of Egyptian servitude and subsequent divine liberation. The imagery of African American Christianity, rooted in the experience of slavery and subsequent mistreatment, is filled with references to the suffering and great hopes of the Children of Israel. Folk preachers among the slaves are known to have been quite conversant with biblical stories and regularly incorporated them into their plantation sermons. Indeed, it is likely that the events and personalities of the Old Testament, including prophet figures like Moses, had a much more direct meaning for the slaves than for their white masters. While some researchers have suggested that the earliest Black Jewish groups might be traced either to the slaves of Jewish plantation owners or to individual African Americans who converted to Judaism, the earliest Black Jewish groups, in fact, were organized by working class men who only had limited contact with white Jewish congregations. Rather, their identification was with the Bible, usually both the Old and New Testaments.

The origin of Black Jewish groups in the United States can be traced as far back as the period just after the Civil War. By the turn of the twentieth century, there were several African American itinerant preachers traveling through the Carolinas claiming that Blacks were the lost sheep of the House of Israel. The oldest known Black Jewish sect, called the Church of the Living God, the Pillar Ground of Truth for All Nations, was started by an African American seaman and railroad worker named F. S. Cherry. His group was formed in Chattanooga, Tennessee in 1886. The second oldest Black Jewish group was probably the Church of God and Saints of Christ, founded by William S. Crowdy, a cook on the Santa Fe Railroad, in Lawrence, Kansas in 1896. Crowdy asserted that he was called by God to lead his people back to their historic religion and identity. Over the years, numerous other Black Jewish groups have emerged, many of them disappearing within a few years of their appearance. During the period from 1965–75, there was a notable jump in the number and size of Black Jewish groups, as African Americans searched for a new, more acceptable identity in the aftermath of the Civil Rights Movement. One of these, the Black Hebrew Israelites, migrated in the late 1960s to Liberia and then to Israel, where several thousand members of the group still live.

Throughout its history, Black Judaism has been a wellspring of new African American religious practice and ideology. Black Judaism has been characterized by a continual process of sectarian fragmentation and coalescence. Collectively, Black Jewish congregations exemplify a type of religious group that has been called *messianic nationalism* (see Baer and Singer 2002) because they unite a messianic faith with the goal of achieving cultural or even political independence. Generally, Black Jewish groups have at least some of the following characteristics:

1. belief in direct biological descent from the biblical Hebrews;
2. faith in the existence of a glorious African past and a subsequent 'fall' from divine grace;
3. rituals and symbols drawn from the Old Testament or contemporary Jewish practice;
4. millennial expectation of divine chastisement of external oppressors and a return to favor under the leadership of a divinely chosen leader;
5. assertion of Black sovereignty through the development of nationalist symbols, the launching of group owned businesses, and interest in territorial separation or even emigration; and

6. explicit rejection of certain social patterns (such as dietary practices) found in the wider African American community.

Despite these common features, Black Jewish groups differ in their beliefs, practices, objectives, and leadership, and intergroup conflict, including occasionally violent confrontations, is not unknown. Often, Black Jewish groups are highly syncretic, adopting their beliefs and practices from diverse sources, including non-Judaic sources such as Christianity and Islam. Consequently, in terms of their actual behavior, Black Jewish groups tend to fall somewhere along a continuum, with contemporary Jewish practice serving as one end, and ideas and rituals that have their source outside of Judaism as the far end of the continuum. As a result, practices at some Black Jewish synagogues appear much like ritual behavior at mainstream Jewish houses of worship, while other groups embrace numerous Christian rituals. Similarly, some groups identify with and seek approval from mainstream Judaism while others see white Jews as impostors.

Further reading

Baer, H. and Singer, M. (2002) *African American Religion: Varieties of Protest and Accommodation*, Second Edition. Knoxville, TN: University of Tennessee Press.
Freedberg, S. (1994) *Brother Love: Murder, Money and a Messiah*, New York: Pantheon Books.

MERRILL SINGER

BLACK MUSLIMS

The origins of the Black Muslim movement have been in dispute for many years. It is likely that some of the Africans brought as slaves to the New World were Muslims, however, it has never been established that they were the source of the black Islamic groups that began appearing in the US early in the twentieth century. At the same time, it is not unreasonable that some vestiges of Islamic belief did survive slavery and were passed down as cultural elements over the generations.

It is certain that one of the earliest organized black Islamic groups was founded by Timothy Drew. A black migrant from North Carolina, Drew, later known as Noble Drew Ali, launched the Caanite Temple in Newark in 1913. Drew taught his followers that they were not Negroes or Colored People, but were instead the noble descendants of ancient Moors from the shores of Africa. He stressed a number of symbols of nationhood, including a national flag (a star within a crescent on a field of red), a national dress (red fezzes and long beards), a holy book (a self-composed 'Koran'), and set of dietary practices (including abstinence from meat, eggs, alcohol, and tobacco). Elements of group belief and practice were drawn from Islam, Christianity, Freemasonry, Theosophy, and possibly Buddhism, suggesting the range of Drew's exposure. In 1916, Drew's group fragmented, with those loyal to him moving to Chicago and taking on the name Moorish Science Temple, a relatively successful organization that spread to and continues to function in a number of northern cities.

In size, scope, and worldwide publicity, Drew's group was soon surpassed by the Nation of Islam. The origin of the latter is cloudy, but appears to trace back to Wallace D. Fard, a Pakistani Muslim who entered the US in about 1913 and ultimately joined and became head of the Moorish Science Temple in Chicago. Unable to capture the national leadership of the group upon Drew's death, Fard moved to Detroit and established the Allah Temple of Islam and authored the volume *Secret Rituals of the Long-Found Nation of Islam*. In an effort to distance himself from one of his followers (who was arrested for performing a human sacrifice), Fard reconstituted his group as the Nation of Islam. Within four years, the group had 8,000 members.

When Fard disappeared in 1934, Elijah Poole, also a former member of the Moorish Science Temple, assumed leadership (after considerable conflict with several rivals and outsiders interested in controlling a burgeoning black movement). Poole taught that Fard was Allah and not a mere prophet of God, leading to a split in the group and a movement from Detroit to Chicago. From this new base, Poole, under the name of Elijah Muhammad and designated as a Messenger of Allah, spread the new gospel to a number of other cities.

Elijah Muhammad taught a non-orthodox, folk brand of Islam that explained that blacks were the original inhabitants of the earth, whites were the product of the experiments of a black scientist named Yakub 6,000 years ago, and that a coming millennium would return whites to dust and restore blacks to dominance. Like other messianic nationalist groups, the Nation of Islam under Elijah Muhammad stressed economic independence, a rigid moral code (which he nonetheless violated with regularity in his personal life), distinctive patterns of dress and behavior, and a rejection of slave names and attitudes. His movement proved to be quite appealing to a younger, more militant generation of African American youth during the 1960–70s, and the membership and holdings of the Nation of Islam swelled. Malcolm X emerged as a prominent and popular leader within the group while the conversion of Cassius Clay (Muhammad Ali), world heavyweight boxing champion, brought considerable attention to the Nation of Islam.

However, the disaffection of Malcolm X (in part because of Elijah Muhammad's shortcomings) and his subsequent assassination began a process of change. A number of groups splintered from the Nation of Islam, leading to the formation of a variety of black Islamic organizations. Upon Elijah Mohammad's death in 1975, his son, Wallace, took over, renamed the group the World Community of al-Islam in the West, and began to move the membership to a less militant, and more orthodox brand of Islam. While this transition was largely successful, and increased the appeal of the group to middle class African Americans, it led to the emergence of several confrontational splinter groups, like the one under Louis Farrakhan in 1978 (which took the old name of Nation of Islam).

Further reading

Evanzz, K. (1999) *The Messenger: Rise and Fall of Elijah Muhammad*, New York: Pantheon.

MERRILL SINGER

BLACK THEOLOGY

Modern Black Theology was born in the socio-political context of the Civil Rights Movement of the 1960s in America. During this period a number of Black theologians and religious protagonists became highly critical of racism in American society, Christianity and white theology. Some Black theologians were sympathetic to the 'Black Power' Movement for freedom and justice; others like James Cone (see **Cone, James**) and those on the National Committee of Negro Churchmen (later called National

Committee of Black Churchmen) went so far as to equate 'Black Power' with the Christian gospel. In doing so, they were breaking away from Dr Martin Luther King's opposition to the Black Power Movement's advocacy of reciprocal violence. After King's death (4 April 1968) a Black Theology movement developed and James Cone became its chief apostle with the publication of his *Black Theology and Black Power* in 1969 followed by *A Black Theology of Liberation* in 1970.

As a North American phenomenon Black Theology is a product of black Christian experience and reflection. Black Theology removed theological discourse from the abstract, 'objective' and the 'universal' and made the concrete, subjective particularity of black history, culture and experience part of the 'norms' and 'sources' of theology.

Black Theology is often called a 'theology of liberation'. In 1969 the National Committee of Black Churchmen defined Black Theology thus:

> Black Theology is a theology of black liberation. It seeks to plumb the black condition in the light of God's revelation in Jesus Christ, so that the black community can see that the gospel is commensurate with the achievement of black humanity. Black Theology is a theology of 'blackness'. It is the affirmation of black humanity that emancipates black people from white racism, thus providing authentic freedom for both white and black people.

Although the systematic development of what is termed 'Black Theology' is identified with the Civil Rights Movement, its critical content of freedom, justice and liberation in black social and religious thought predate this period. In Cornel West's widely acclaimed *Prophesy Deliverance: an Afro-American Revolutionary Christianity* (1982), he identifies four general stages in the development of the history, theology and politics of Black Theology.

In the first stage (1650–1863) the foundations of what can be called an embryonic Black theology of liberation were laid. As a critique of slavery in the New World, this early period saw a number of Black Christians using the Bible and its Old Testament narratives and gospel message of freedom as a weapon in their struggle against slavery and oppression. These included 'prophetic' Black Christians like Olaudah Equiano in Britain; Paul Bogle and Samuel Sharpe in the West Indies; and Sojourner Truth, Nat Turner and David Walker in America. In respect of liberation from white oppression Walker legitimized the use of force, arguing that the use of violence in pursuit of Black liberation from slavery and oppression were consistent with the Christian faith and black humanity. This current of black religious thought informed and divided the Civil Rights Movement in the 1960s. The question of violence and the meaning of reconciliation is also a critical issue for Black theologians like James Cone and J. Deotis Roberts

The second stage in the development of Black Theology (1864–1969) was very much concerned with critiquing institutional racism in America and the social and political structures which deprived the vast majority of black people of their political and economic rights. This post-Emancipation period of lynching, segregation, and the black struggle for equality witness the rise of a new and creative period in Black religious thought and political philosophy. Ethiopianism or the stress on African autonomy and independence (see **Ama-Nazaretha**) as a challenge to the racist theology of 'the curse of Ham', the 'Back to Africa Movement' of Marcus Garvey and the hegemony of Dr Martin Luther King's

non-violent philosophy are characteristic features of this stage in the development of Black theology.

Stages three (1969–77) and four (post-
1977) in the history of Black Theology is
characterized by a rich and varied theological and academic response to American theology and some of the traditional
topics of Christian theology such as
Christology, eschatology and theodicy in
light of black history and religious experience. Additionally, there were fecund
attempts to broaden the liberation ethic
of Black Theology beyond privileging
race and class in its critique of Western
capitalism and racism.

In the search for a balanced or holistic
Black Theology, 'Womanist' theologians like Delores Williams and Jacque-
lyn Grant argue the case for informing
black theological discourse with 'multi-
dialogical' perspectives which consider
the diversity of black social, political,
cultural, and sexual relations. The links
with 'Womanist Theology', 'Third World'
and other liberation theologies have provided a fuller matrix of consciousness in
black talk about God and liberation.

Christology and the thesis of the
'Black Messiah' occupy a controversial
place in Black Theology. Although there
are antecedents for this genre, its popularization and systematic exposition are
found in the writings of Revd Albert B.
Cleage and James Cone respectively. In
his controversial book *The Black Messiah* (1968) Cleage argued that Jesus was
a revolutionary Black leader and that he
wanted 'Black people to find their way
back to the historic Black Messiah'. In
essence, Cleage is arguing for a historical 'Black Messiah'. James Cone, on
the other hand, argues for a Messiah
who is symbolically and ontologically
'Black'. Theologically, says Cone, Jesus
is 'Black' because he *becomes one* with
the oppressed or with 'the least of these'
as stated in the parable of the Last

Judgment in Matthew 25:45. Herme-
neutically, Cone suggests that 'the least
in America' are literally and symbolically present in black people and Jesus
takes their suffering as his suffering.

For a theology that arose out of the
Black Church and the black religious
experience, the challenge facing 'Black
Theology' is how to make its insights
into some of the eternal truths of the
Gospel relevant to the Black Church
and the next generation of leaders as
well as a critical resource in the renewal
of the community.

Further reading

Cleage, A. B. (1968) *The Black Messiah*,
New Jersey: Africa World Press.
Cone, J. H (1969) *Black Theology and Black
Power*, New York: Harper & Row.
Cone, J. H. (1970) *A Black Theology of Lib-
eration*, Philadelphia: J. B. Lippincott.
Cone, J. H. (1975) *God of the Oppressed*,
Minneapolis: The Seabury Press.
Cone, J. H. and Wilmore, G. S. (eds) (1993)
*Black Theology: a Documentary History,
Volume 2:1980–1992*, Maryknoll: Orbis
Books.
Grant, J. (1989) *White Women's Christ and
Black Women's Jesus: Feminist Christol-
ogy and Womanist Response*, Atlanta:
Scholars Press.
Roberts, D. (1994) The *Prophethood of Black
Believers: An African American Political
Theology for Ministry*, Louisville: West-
minster/John Knox Press.
West, C. (1982) *Prophesy Deliverance: an
Afro-American Revolutionary Christianity*,
Phiiladelphia: Westminster.

R. DAVID MUIR

BLAVATSKY, HELENA

Helena Blavatsky (1831–91) was the
founder of **Theosophy**, a movement
which made the religions of Asia accessible to Western seekers for the first
time. She is a key figure in the history
of religion, and one of a minority of
women founders of new religions. She

was also a prolific writer of esoteric books, mostly still in print, of which the best known are her first, *Isis Unveiled* (1877), and *The Secret Doctrine* (1889).

Madame Blavatsky (as she is generally known) was born in the Ukraine. Her early life is mysterious, but seems to have been colourful and adventurous according to the many contradictory stories, which describe a chequered career as a novelist, circus performer, concert pianist and medium. In 1849 she married a state official whom she left after a year, and appears to have spent the next twenty-five years travelling throughout the world. She claimed that from childhood she had been endowed with remarkable psychic powers, and during her travels met various 'masters' (both living and discarnate) in London, Tibet, and India. In 1873 she arrived in New York where she met Henry Steel Olcott, with whom she founded the Theosophical Society in 1975. Three years later they left together for India, eventually settling in Madras, which is still the Society's world headquarters. They never married, and the relationship seems to have been spiritual and professional rather than sexual. Olcott was the first American to convert to Buddhism. Blavatsky continued to travel nonstop, writing and setting up new branches of Theosophy worldwide. Eventually she settled in London and established the European headquarters of the Theosophical Society, where she died in 1891.

Madame Blavatsky was a highly controversial figure, who has been regarded as a charlatan in her lifetime and later. In particular, her claimed psychic abilities have often been challenged and debunked, including a report by the Society for Psychical Research in London in 1885. The report caused substantial damage to her reputation, although the SPR published a rebuttal a hundred years later. Whatever the truth of her occult powers, Blavatsky's charisma and teachings had a tremendous impact on her followers and on later generations.

Further reading

Cranston, Sylvia (1995) *HPB: The Extraordinary Life and Influence of Helena Blavatsky*, New York: Tarcher

ELIZABETH PUTTICK

BLOOM, WILLIAM
(b. 1948)
New Age theorist and activist

William Bloom was born in London to a humanist family; his father was a psychiatrist and Bloom was educated at a private school. From the age of five he recalls profound spiritual experiences but later rejected these as a young man. He published fiction and was active in publishing and advice work in the counter-culture in the early 1970s before performing a six-month magical ritual in the western occult tradition in Morocco in 1973. This is described by Bloom in *The Sacred Magician: a ceremonial diary* (1992; first published in 1976 pseudonymously) which also recounts his enthusiastic discovery of Alice Bailey's writings and describes himself as a 'Gnostic or Rosicrucian' Christian.

Subsequently Bloom pursued community education and postgraduate study in London before co-founding the 'Alternatives' gathering in 1988 and leading it until 1994. 'Alternatives' became the most prominent New Age event in London (see **New Age Movement**) and consists in a weekly lecture evening held at St James's church, Piccadilly, regularly attended by two to three hundred people and featuring international speakers from New Age and Mind Body Spirit perspectives. 'Alternatives' has been broadly supported by the Anglican church leadership although there have been sporadic tensions with the mainstream Christian congregation.

Since the 1980s Bloom has been active at the **Findhorn community** and in Glastonbury, two major New Age sites in the UK, where he leads workshops and offers training in his own synthesis of New Age and esoteric Christian traditions. He has published a series of practical and theoretical books including *The Seeker's Guide: A New Age Resource Book* (co-edited, 1992), *First Steps: An Introduction to Spiritual Practice* (1993), *The Christ Sparks: The Inner Dynamics of Group Consciousness* (1995) and *The Endorphin Effect* (2001). He has also acted as a consultant for several UK television programmes and has been one of the most prominent popular theorists of New Age and holistic spirituality in the UK.

Further reading

Bloom, W. (1992) *The Sacred Magician: a ceremonial diary*, Glastonbury: Gothic Image.

Bloom, W. (1993) *First Steps: An Introduction to Spiritual Practice*, Findhorn Press.

Bloom, W. (1995) *The Christ Sparks: The Inner Dynamics of Group Consciousness*, Findhorn Press

Bloom, W. (2001) *The Endorphin Effect*, Llandeilo: Cygnus

Bloom, W. (ed.) (2001) *The Penguin Book of New Age and Holistic Writing*, Harmondsworth: Penguin

Bloom, W. and Button, J. (1992) *The Seeker's Guide: A New Age Resource Book*, London: HarperCollins.

STEVEN J. SUTCLIFFE

BRAHMA KUMARIS

(Daughters of Brahma)

Founder: Dada Lekhraj

Country of origin: India/Pakistan

The 'Brahma Kumaris' are a world-wide millenarian movement originating in the 1930s in Hyderabad (then north-west India, now Pakistan) in response to revelations of the Sindhi diamond merchant Dada Lekhraj (see **Lekhraj, Dada**). Drawing on the Hindu religious culture of its founder, the movement has nonetheless distinguished itself from Hinduism and projects itself as a vehicle for spiritual teaching rather than as a religion.

The Brahma Kumaris World Spiritual University, the movement's organizational basis, was founded in 1937 after a series of visions prompted Lekhraj to conclude his business career and devote himself wholly to spiritual life. Growing numbers of people began to share his devotions and the regular participants came to be known as the 'Om Mandali' ('Om Circle'). Lekhraj himself began to experience the regular in-dwelling of Shiva, whom he identified as 'The Supreme Soul' (more akin to the Christian One God than a deity in Hindu pantheism or henotheistic worship). As medium for the Divine, Lekhraj came to be known as 'Adi Dev' and 'Prajapita Brahma', or, affectionately, as 'Brahma Baba'.

By 1937 the circle had grown to such an extent that some formal administrative structure was required, and so Lekhraj founded the University. Lekhraj took the socially radical step of devolving its administration upon a 'Managing Committee' of nine women.

From the beginning, Lekhraj's gatherings had attracted disproportionate numbers of women. Remarkably in the predominantly patriarchial Indian subcontinent, Lekhraj not only welcomed their participation, but recognized women as spiritually superior to men. In women he saw a greater capacity for 'purity', especially through sexual renunciation, which he enjoined on all 'brahmins' (fully committed members).

The call for women brahmins (i.e., *kumari* or 'daughters') to remain celibate or chaste in marriage inverted prevailing social expectations that such renunciation was proper only for men and that the disposal of women's sexuality should remain with their fathers and husbands. The 'Anti-Om Mandali Committee' formed by outraged male family members violently persecuted Brahma Baba's group, prompting their flight to Karachi and withdrawal from society.

Intense world-rejection gradually eased after Partition in 1947, when the BKs moved from Pakistan to Mt Abu in India; there they gradually responded to calls to teach outsiders. Despite sporadic attempts to make their teachings known overseas, the movement was confined to India and Pakistan until 1971 when the first teachers were sent to the Indian migrant community in England and to Hong Kong. From England the movement spread around the world, initially by Western brahmins trained in London and a few Indian 'sisters.'

By 2003 the movement had branches in seventy countries across the world. The International Co-ordinating Office in London facilitates the activities of the 3,200 centres. The Management Office of the Administrative Head in Mt Abu has general oversight of the institution. Since the 1980s the BKs have undertaken major community service programmes that have eventuated in the University becoming recognized as an NGO in consultative status with United Nations bodies.

Local branches of the University focus on 'centres' where fully committed brahmins reside, run teaching programmes and facilitate group meditation. Newcomers have in the past been required to take the University's seven day course, where they are exposed to the BKs' beliefs and method of meditation or 'Raja Yoga.' ('Raja Yoga' is also another name for the movement.) (see **Yoga, Modern**)

The BK teachings revise Hindu beliefs in a Golden Age that deteriorates into successive ages in an endlessly recurring cycle of time; according to the movement, we are now in the worst age, on the eve of destruction, and only BKs, who have purified themselves through a vegetarian diet and chastity and cultivated 'soul consciousness', will be reborn in the Golden Age. Not enlightenment, but 'perfection' is the goal; from this will come life as a 'deity' in the heavenly world of the Golden Age.

Since the University spread to Western societies it has increasingly accommodated people with little interest in its theodicy but attracted to the practical applications of BK spiritual practices. The community service programmes of the 1980s and 1990s stimulated creative renderings of BK meditation as a tool for psychological health and eclectic spiritual exploration. The casual participants whom the BKs have attracted in this way probably made up the vast majority of the 450,000 people on the University's records at the turn of the century.

Further reading

Howell, J. and Nelson, P. (2000) The Brahma Kumaris in the Western World, Part II. *Research in the Social Scientific Study of Religion* 11, 225–39.

Walliss, J. (2002) *The Brahma Kumaris as a Reflexive Tradition*, Aldershot, Hampshire: Ashgate.

JULIA DAY HOWELL

BRAHMO SAMAJ

The first of the modern Hindu-related movements was inaugurated in 1828 in Bengal by a prominent reformer, Ram Mohan Roy (1772–1833). Taking his inspiration from the *Upanishads* and *vedanta* philosophy, but influenced by the English deist tradition of Unitarianism,

Roy favoured monotheism, the pursuit of reason, non-idolatrous worship, and social reform, particularly regarding the position of women. His openness to other religions and rejection of some Hindu teachings and practices – including karma, caste, and *sati* ('widow burning') – brought him into dispute with traditionalists, but his careful attention to scripture, in addition to reason, gave his movement appeal among those Bengalis eager to debate the future of Hinduism in the context of British rule and the challenges of modernism and Christianity. After Roy's death, the Samaj was led by Debendranath Tagore (1817–1905) and then by Keshab Chandra Sen (1838–84). Their differing views about whether members, most of whom were Brahmins, should relinquish their sacred threads typified their approaches to the purpose and direction of the Samaj, with Tagore favouring a more religiously conservative, and Sen a more socially radical approach. Following various disagreements within the Samaj, Sen formed a new branch, the Church of the New Dispensation, in 1878, in an attempt to synthesize aspects of Christianity, Islam, and Hinduism, and create a new universalism.

The Brahmo Samaj is of historical importance both as an indigenous modernist response to social and religious conditions in nineteenth-century India, and as a vehicle for innovation and debate among key intellectuals, spiritual seekers, and social reformers. Rabindranath Tagore, Dayananda Saraswati (**Arya Samaj**), Swami Vivekananda (see **Vivekananda, Swami**), and Gandhi were among those influenced by the movement which continued to grow slowly in and beyond India until the 1930s. As a small movement today, supported predominantly by Bengalis, it remains faithful to the principle of 'testing, questing, never resting, with open mind and open heart' (Sumit Chandra), and to the non-idolatrous worship of the one Brahman which meets its fullest expression in the *Upanishads*.

Further reading

Kopf, D. (1979) *The Brahmo Samaj and the Shaping of the Modern Indian Mind*, Princeton: Princeton University Press.

KIM KNOTT

BRAIDE, GARRICK SOKARI

Braide was born about 1882 of poor non-Christian parents. About 1890, he enrolled and later learnt to read and write at the Sunday school of St Andrews Anglican Church, Bakana, a Kalabari village in the riverine Niger Delta of Nigeria. He was baptized on 23 January 1910, had his confirmation in 1912, and thereafter became a lay preacher.

About 1912, claiming that God had commissioned him, he preached publicly at Bakana. He demanded confession of sins and the destruction of idols and charms as steps to becoming a Christian. Besides, he stipulated strict Sunday observances, encouraged regular prayers and fasting, and preached abstinence from alcoholic beverages, a rampant social evil.

Within a year, Braide had been accepted as a prophet, and his healing miracles confirmed this claim. From 1915, he visited other Kalabari towns conducting evangelistic campaigns and winning hundreds of converts into the Anglican churches. His call on the people to seek self-determination reawakened their hope of a truly indigenous church leadership. In 1915, he took the title Elijah II, and in the following year appointed evangelists, delegated healing power to them, and sent them out into other towns.

Braide's preaching stimulated a revival that peaked in February 1916, when James Johnson, the Diocesan Bishop took disciplinary actions against Braide and the clergy who supported him. Unable to contain the popular revolt that followed, Johnson appealed to the British colonial administration, and Braide was arrested in March 1916. Branded as a political agitator because his preaching against alcohol, an economic commodity, had reduced government revenues, he was tried and sentenced to six months' imprisonment. Further charges brought in November culminated in additional sentences.

Dissatisfied with the hypocrisy of the Anglican Church, Braide's followers about 1917 constituted themselves into the independent Christ Army Church. After his release from prison, Braide died of an illness on 15 November 1918.

Braide's revival was a challenge to a western Christianity that made church membership a long and tortuous journey of instructions in the catechisms and learning European manners. Conversely, Braide promoted a contextualized Christianity that was practical, while his healing and prophetic activities addressed some of the felt needs of the people, and partly stimulated Kalabari nationalism.

Further reading

Tasie, G. O. M. (1978) *Christian Missionary Enterprise in the Niger Delta 1864-1918*, Leiden: E. J. Brill.

MATTHEWS A. OJO

BRAINWASHING

Most people find certain actions, such as becoming a member of a fringe political or religious group, both shocking and unexplainable. The Romans believed that only witchcraft could explain why anybody would join such a bizarre cult as Christianity; later, when in power, Christians applied the same rationale to so-called heretics. In later centuries, the theory, which attributed conversion to 'strange' religions to witchcraft, became somehow secularized under the scientific name of mesmerism or hypnotism. Mormons, Seventh Day Adventists, and the more enthusiastic among the Protestant revival movements were among the religions accused of 'mesmerizing' converts. For Sigmund Freud (1856–1939), religion is the attempt to remain at a childish stage fixated on pleasure, rejecting pain and, with it, the real world. The religious illusion, however, does not arise spontaneously. On the contrary, Freud insisted that religion is instilled through manipulatory techniques that fix an individual in a permanent state of infantilism.

Around 1920, three members of the innermost circle of Freud's students, Paul Federn (1871–1950), Wilhelm Reich (1897–1957), and Erich Fromm (1900–1980), extended their teacher's critique of religious indoctrination methods to conservative politics and national-socialism. For these authors, belief in a totalitarian worldview is the product of a combination of three factors: authoritarian childhood education, the influence of popular culture and religion, and a cunning ideological indoctrination process that relies on this influence to manipulate followers for its own purposes. The debate on how the working classes could be indoctrinated into fascism was crucial for the formation of the Frankfurt School, a fusion of psychoanalysis and Marxism. The Nazi regime persecuted the leaders of the Frankfurt School both because they were political antagonists and because they were Jews; most of them migrated to the United States and continued their research there.

After the United States had replaced its anti-Nazi alliance with the Soviet Union with the Cold War, research on indoctrination focused on Communism. Frankfurt School theories on the authoritarian personality were further developed by Erik Homburger Erikson (1902–94), another Austrian-born psychoanalyst who coined the word 'totalismo' (totalism), in order to designate a black-and-white vision of the world divided between 'us' and 'them'. According to Erikson, the unresolved crises of childhood development, coupled to an authoritarian education and ideological manipulation, play a key role in the origin of totalism.

American psychiatrist Robert Jay Lifton (1926–) a friend and student of Erikson, published in 1961 *Thought Reform and the Psychology of Totalism. A Study of 'Brainwashing' in China,* the results of his study of twenty-five Westerners who had been detained in Chinese Communist jails, and of fifteen Chinese who had also undergone 'thought reform' processes, although outside of prison. Lifton did not present the Chinese Communist results as infallible, or even magical. Out of the forty subjects he studied, only two retained, after their release, a more favorable attitude toward Chinese Communism than they had before their indoctrination. Lifton also applied the result of his study of Chinese Communist indoctrination to religious 'cults', concluding that the roots of conversion to both these religions and Communism are to be found in the interaction of three elements: a 'philosophical motivation', a psychological predisposition, and totalitarian manipulation techniques.

In addition to Lifton, the work of Edgar H. Schein (1928–) was also influential. A US army psychologist, Schein was sent to Korea in 1953 to examine US prisoners of war who allegedly had been subjected to brainwashing (a word both he and Lifton eventually rejected). Schein concluded that most prisoners had only *stated* that they believed in Communism, simply in order to survive, without experiencing a 'genuine' conversion. Schein's main work on the topic was published in 1961 under the title *Coercive Persuasion*, and included Chinese thought reform processes together with Korean POW cases. The book discussed whether 'coercive persuasion' as practised in China or (North) Korea, differs from forms of indoctrination that are customarily accepted and practised in the West in schools, prisons, military academies, Catholic convents, the marketing of certain products, and corporate life. For Schein, in fact, the difference revolves around the *contents* of indoctrination much more than around the *method* of persuasion. 'Chinese Communist coercive persuasion' Schein concluded 'is not too different a process in its basic structure from coercive persuasion in institutions in our own society which are in the business of changing fundamental beliefs and values' (Schein *et al.* 1961: 282). Faced with Chinese practices, we claim to disapprove of a method of indoctrination, while in fact what we disapprove of is actually the doctrine inculcated through this method.

The word 'brainwashing' was coined during CIA efforts to use its own popular version of the totalitarian influence theory for Cold War propaganda, based on the reference to 'washing clean' the minds of the citizens in the well-known novel *1984* by George Orwell (the pen name of Eric Arthur Blair, 1903–50). Orwell's fictional account made a deep impression on Edward Hunter (1902–78), later a CIA agent whose cover job was that of reporter, first with English-language publications in China and later at the *Miami Daily News*. The expression *brainwashing* was first used by Hunter in the *Miami Daily News* on 24 September 1950, and later expanded on in many books. As Schein demonstrated in his 1961 book, 'brainwashing' does not translate from any Chinese expression related to thought reform, and Hunter coined it based on his reading of Orwell. For Hunter, there is no defense against brainwashing, and it can change anybody's ideology.

The CIA was aware that it needed scientific justification for theories originally put forth by a simple newspaper reporter. It researched the publications of European psychologists and psychoanalysts, such as Joost Abraham Maurits Meerloo (1903–76) from the Netherlands, and directly supported further research on the subject, *inter alia* by psychiatrist Louis Jolyon 'Jolly' West (1924–99,) who later served as a link with the anti-cult movement. Although researchers such as Meerloo tried to be careful, the CIA simply claimed that it had obtained 'scientific' confirmation of its propaganda. The CIA also commissioned expensive experiments in anticipation of a possible military and intelligence use of brainwashing, led by Donald Ewen Cameron (1901–67), a distinguished Montreal psychiatrist. In 1963, however, the CIA ended the controversial project, having concluded that by using the 'brainwashing' techniques, it was only possible to create individuals suffering from constant amnesia, who spent most of the day in a state of psycho-motor block, these 'vegetables' being thus totally useless for espionage or counter-espionage purposes. Indeed, it might be possible to 'wash' the brain until it loses its 'color' and becomes 'white', but it is not possible to 'recolor' it with new ideas contrary to the previous ones.

English psychiatrist William Walters Sargant (1907–88) first applied brainwashing models to religion in his 1957 book *The Battle for the Mind*. According to Sargant, the leading precursor of modern brainwashing techniques was John Wesley (1703–91), the founder of Methodism. Sargant also offered other examples from both Catholic and Protestant preachers. He was interested in religious conversion *in general*, rather than in differentiating between mainline religions and 'cults'. In the late 1960s, however, the **Anti-Cult Movement** quickly adopted brainwashing as a convenient explanation of why apparently normal young Americans were joining 'bizarre' cults. Prominent in this campaign was Margaret Thaler Singer, a clinical psychologist who had collaborated with Schein, and was adjunct professor at the University of California, Berkeley. She often appeared in court cases and, in a sense, invented a new profession as a psychologist in the service, for several years almost full-time, of anti-cult lawsuits and initiatives. Based on the brainwashing arguments, private vigilantes started kidnapping adult members of NRMs on behalf of their families, and subjected them to a sort of 'counter-brainwashing' technique which they called **Deprogramming**. The largest organization of the American anti-cult movement, the Cult Awareness Network, was often accused of referring families to deprogrammers, although courts were initially comparatively tolerant of the practice.

A frequent counter-expert (in the opposite camp of Singer's) in US court cases, forensic psychiatrist and NRM scholar Dick Anthony, persuasively demonstrated that while Singer claimed to apply to 'cults' the controversial but scholarly Lifton and Schein theories of totalitarian influence, she was in fact using the discredited CIA 'robot' model of brainwashing. Anthony was joined by the large majority of NRMs scholars, including Eileen Barker, who in 1984 offered an influential critique of brainwashing theories with respect to the Unification Church (see **Unification Church/Moonies**) in her book *The Making of a Moonie*. Criticism of the brainwashing model was also offered by the American Sociological Association and the American Psychological Association (APA). In 1983, APA accepted Singer's proposal of forming a task force, DIMPAC (Deceptive and Indirect Methods of Persuasion and Control) for the purpose of assessing the scientific status of these theories. On 11 May 1987 the BSERP (Board of Social and Ethical Responsibility for Psychology) of the APA, issued a Memorandum rejecting the DIMPAC report on the grounds that it 'lacks the scientific rigor and evenhanded critical approach necessary for APA imprimatur'. This rejection, and scholarly criticism in general, eventually reversed the trend in US courts. The decisive battle between the two camps took place in the US District Court for the Northern District of California in 1990, in the *Fishman* case, where a defendant in a fraud case offered as a defense that at the relevant time he had been subjected to Scientology 'brainwashing' (although Scientology had nothing whatsoever to do with Fishman's fraudulent activities). On 13 April 1990, Judge D. Lowell Jensen rejected the testimony of Singer and anti-cult sociologist Richard Ofshe from the case, quoting the APA position and Anthony's research. Jensen concluded that, while Margaret Singer claimed to derive her brainwashing theory from Lifton and Schein, in truth she was much closer to the non-scientific CIA and Hunter theories.

Although some later decisions deviated in varying degrees from it, so that the *Fishman* ruling did not spell out once and for all the death of the brainwashing theory, an important precedent (still relevant today) had been set in the United States that later triggered a chain of events which led to the end of deprogramming and even of the Cult Awareness Network (CAN). Caught red-handed in the act of referring a family to deprogrammers, CAN was sentenced to such a heavy fine that it was forced to file for bankruptcy. In 1996, the court-appointed trustee-in-bankruptcy sold by auction CAN's files, its name and its logo to a coalition of religious liberty activists led by Church of Scientology members.

Whilst in US courts the brainwashing theory lost its momentum in the 1990s, the suicides and homicides of the Solar Temple in 1994–5 gave it new impetus in Europe, where it influenced parliamentary reports (largely unaware of the complicated history of the US controversy) and even resulted in a controversial amendment to the French criminal code in 2001. In North America, a vocal minority of scholars who supported the anti-cult movement to varying degrees, including sociologists Stephen Kent and Benjamin Zablocki, tried to create a new respectability for the word 'brainwashing' by referring it not to conversion, but to difficulties created by NRMs for those wishing to leave them, by means of maximizing their exit costs. Although only a handful of academics accepted these theories, brainwashing explanations remain popular in some European political milieus and among the media, while acquiring a new currency to explain suicide terrorism in the wake of the events of 11 September 2001.

Further reading

Anthony, D. L. (1996) 'Brainwashing and Totalitarian Influence. An Exploration of Admissibility Criteria for Testimony in Brainwashing Trials', Ph.D. Diss., Berkeley: Graduate Theological Union.

Barker, E. (1984) *The Making of a Moonie. Choice or Brainwashing?*, Oxford: Basil Blackwell.

Lifton, R. J. (1961) *Thought Reform and the Psychology of Totalism. A Study of 'Brainwashing' in China*, New York: Norton.

Orwell, G. (1949) *Nineteen Eighty-Four*, London: Martin Secker & Warburg.

Sargant, W. (1997) *Battle for the Mind*, Cambridge, MA: Malor Books.

Schein, E. H., Schneier, I. and Barker, C. H. (1961) *Coercive Persuasion. A Socio-psychological Analysis of the 'Brainwashing' of American Civilian Prisoners by the Chinese Communists*, New York: Norton.

MASSIMO INTROVIGNE

BRANCH DAVIDIANS

The Branch Davidians and Waco will be synonymous for many years to come. Few people had heard of them before the armed siege which ended with a fireball and the deaths of around seventy-four people, including fifteen children, but millions saw this on television. In much the same way as the People's Temple and Jonestown fifteen years earlier, the Branch Davidians became a benchmark for 'killer cults', and for anti-cultists, and thereafter any heterodox movement became a potential Waco.

The Branch Davidians were an offshoot of an offshoot of the Seventh-day Adventist (SDA) movement. Victor Houteff (1886–1955), who felt that the SDA were compromising their beliefs and becoming too mainstream, was expelled from the SDA for his apocalyptic interpretations of Daniel and Revelation. With a dozen or so families he set up a movement called the Shepherd's Rod; in 1935 they moved from Los Angeles to set up a small community at Mount Carmel, near Waco, Texas, and in 1942 renamed themselves the Davidian Seventh-day Adventists, after the Kingdom of David.

After Houteff's death his widow Florence announced that the Second Coming would be in 1959. When this didn't occur, the movement fragmented; some members left, and several splinter groups were formed. One of these was led by Benjamin Roden, who told his followers to 'Get off the dead Rod and move on to a living Branch', and called his movement the Branch Davidians. After his death in 1978 he was succeeded by his widow Lois.

The man who was to become famous, or infamous, as David Koresh, was born Vernon Howell in 1959. He joined the Branch Davidians in 1983. Lois Roden had fallen out with her son George, who had announced he was the Messiah; Howell took Lois's side. After her death in 1986, George Roden forced Howell out of the community at gunpoint. The following year Roden tried to prove his power by raising a twenty-years-deceased member from the dead. Howell confronted Roden, and a gun battle ensued; Roden ended up in jail, and Howell was free to take over the movement at Mount Carmel.

In 1990 Howell changed his name to David Koresh. David was for King David, and Koresh after the Persian king Cyrus, who freed the Hebrews from their captivity in Babylon. He claimed that he understood the seven seals of Revelation chapters 5 and 6, and had the power to break the seventh seal (Revelation 8:1); he was the End-Time Messenger. He called himself the Lamb, but contrary to some reports, he never claimed to be God.

Koresh was a charismatic leader and an inspired speaker; he had an exhaustive knowledge of the Bible, and could preach for hours without notes. On recruitment trips, including Australia and the UK, he attracted more followers. (Around a third of those who died in the final conflagration were from Britain.)

Koresh had begun to establish his position in the movement back in 1984 when he had married the 14-year-old daughter of a senior elder in the Church; now he extended this dramatically. He announced he had the right to sleep with any woman in the movement in order to spread his holy seed. He is reported to have slept with at least fifteen, some the wives of members, and some very young, including the 12-year-old sister of his wife – thus giving legitimate ammunition to his critics.

The opposition to Koresh came initially from a former member who was offended by Koresh's sexual activity. He contacted other former members; completely unsubstantiated atrocity tales began to surface, of Koresh planning child sacrifices. In 1990 they hired a private investigator, who had meetings with various federal and state authorities, who decided there was no reason to take any action. They pursued two other avenues, an exposé TV documentary in Australia, and a custody case. A subsequent complaint in 1992 by the ex-husband of a member, of child abuse at Mount Carmel, was thoroughly investigated by the Texas Child Protective Services, who found no evidence to support the allegation. By this time Koresh's opponents were talking publicly in terms of 'mass suicide'. The FBI opened, then closed, an investigation.

In reaction to this continuing opposition, Koresh developed a siege mentality, and began to arm his members. Acting on a tip-off, the Bureau of Alcohol, Tobacco and Firearms (BATF) started an investigation in late 1992, but again found insufficient evidence for a search warrant. The BATF then turned to ex-members (one of whom had been deprogrammed (see **Deprogramming**)) and relatives of members – all opponents of Koresh – for further information.

On 28 February 1993 the BATF staged an armed raid on Mount Carmel, despite having lost the element of surprise essential to their operation. In the gunfight, four BATF agents were killed, and over a dozen injured; it is thought that six Branch Davidians were killed, and many injured, including Koresh, who was shot in the waist and the wrist. The FBI then put the compound under siege for fifty-one days. They cut off the water, and refused to allow baby food into the compound; other tactics included the playing of loud rock music and the amplified screams of dying rabbits. There were negotiations between the FBI and Koresh, but the FBI ignored representations by sociologists of religion and Sabbatarian academics with a specialist knowledge of Koresh's teachings.

Although injured, Koresh was working on 'the message of the seven seals' right up to the night before the FBI moved in on the morning of 19 April 1993. Tanks knocked down walls and fired CS gas into the compound. The stockpiled ammunition exploded, and the entire compound went up in a fireball. There are reports – denied by the FBI – that members trying to escape from the burning compound were shot. Although the official government report by former senator John C. Danforth concluded that 'the United States government is not responsible for the tragedy at Waco', he was highly critical of subsequent actions by the FBI, such as the loss of vital evidence. There is no doubt that, whoever started the fire that killed so many members, the entire situation was exacerbated by the clumsy and inappropriate behaviour of those in charge of the operation, based on unreliable evidence from opponents, and that the tragic outcome had been completely avoidable. Many questions still remain to be answered about the events at Waco. There have also been repercussions;

71

the Oklahoma bombing by Timothy McVeigh, which killed 168 people, was on the second anniversary of Waco.

There are several competing Branch Davidian groups still in existence, in the USA, the UK and Australia; the total number of members has been estimated as high as a thousand. There are also Davidian groups that are not Branch Davidian.

Further reading

Barrett, D. V. (2001) *The New Believers*, London: Cassell
Bromley, D. G. and Melton, J. G. (2002) *Cults, Religion & Violence*, Cambridge: Cambridge University Press.

DAVID V. BARRETT

BROTHERHOOD OF THE CROSS AND STAR

This movement of followers of Olumba Olumba Obu (b. 1918) began in Calabar, Nigeria in the late 1950s. It is also known as 'Christ Universal Spiritual School of Practical Christianity'. The leader and members insist that it should not be called a church but rather it aims to establish God's Reign throughout the world by uniting brothers and sisters in bonds of love. In this work, they believe their leader has a unique historic role to play.

There are many legends about Obu's childhood but reliable information is scanty. However, it is clear that, from the age of eighteen, he earned his living as a trader dealing in drapery. He was known for his conspicuous honesty and for his readiness to help anyone in need. He gradually gained popularity as an itinerant preacher. In the early 1940s he gave up his business and resolved to devote himself to teaching and praying, while visiting homes, and to a simple life style. Then, because many came to him to pray for healing and for deliverance from witchcraft, he gave up travelling and was able to set up a prayer house in Calabar which he called 'Bethel'. People from his home village of Biakpan who were living in the capital rallied to him and he thus became a leader in social development programmes. His movement was registered in 1956, under the name 'Brotherhood of the Cross and Star'; early publications explained the symbolism: 'Cross' as the sufferings of Jesus Christ on our behalf and also the hardships His followers suffer in His footsteps and 'Star' as the glory attained through these sufferings.

As followers became convinced that his was a divine brotherhood and that he personally shared in that divinity, the movement spread throughout Nigeria and to other countries and continents. Bethels were established and, although Obu no longer left Calabar, he was believed to visit them in the guise of a traveller or of one in need, so providing a motive for generous hospitality. The Brotherhood Printing Press in Calabar began to publish sermons of Obu and treatises by his followers. Here a distinctive pattern of thought appears, based on study of the Bible.

The most striking non-biblical component in this teaching is the importance assigned to re-incarnation. This may have been due to contact with Indian religious thought or with esoteric movements present in Nigeria but African scholar Mbon shows that elements of local tribal religion are a more likely influence. One publication from the Brotherhood Press, *The Gospel of 'Reincarnation'* (n.d.) by Ofem E Otu demonstrates an original development of this thinking which is no doubt due to the leader himself. The book presents Adam as a first 'divine incarnation' to be followed in series by Enoch, Noah, Melchisedech, Moses, Elijah, Christ

Jesus, and finally, Leader Obu. The eight are taken by this author to be 'God in mortalization', that is to say, God, who is otherwise omnipresent, on occasions enters particular mortal life. In the final entry, God has come to judge the living and the dead.

This particular teaching, naturally, met with disapproval by most churches in the country. There was a public confrontation in the streets of Calabar in 1977 with charges of blasphemy and some violence. But much of the other teaching in the literature from the Brotherhood Press must have been more acceptable.

The teaching has many elements derived from traditional culture, including belief in the presence of the 'living dead' at their meetings, in going barefoot as a sign of the holiness of the earth and in the prevalence of sorcery. But, like many African initiated churches (see **African Independent Churches** and **African Charismatic Churches**), it includes rejection of cultural fraternities and traditional divination. Unlike some, it is also against polygyny.

In moral teaching the movement lays great emphasis on the commandment to love unselfishly with generosity to the stranger and this seems to have borne fruit in practices of hospitality and care for those in distress. The frequent Brotherhood feasts constitute a ritual which Mbon compares to African symbolism used in oath taking, bonding the community: Obu says, 'They bring life and bind you together. There should be no divisions in the Bethel.'

Further reading

Mbon, F. M. (1992) *Brotherhood of the Cross and Star*, New York: P. Lang.
Otu, O. E. (n.d.) *The Gospel of 'Reincarnation'*, Brotherhood Press.

RALPH WOODHALL

BROTHERHOOD OF THE HOLY CROSS

Toward the end of 1971, the Upper Solimões Region of the Brazilian Amazon, located on the border between Peru and Colombia, underwent a period of religious effervescence that gave rise to a messianic movement known as the Brotherhood of the Holy Cross (BHC) which exists to this day.

The main protagonists of this movement were its founder, José Francisco da Cruz, the Tikuna Indians and a portion of the region's non-indigenous inhabitants.

Cruz was born in 1913 in Minas Gerais, the central region of Brazil. He received a religious education following the traditional Catholic model and in 1944 claimed to have visions in which Jesus ordered him to go out and preach the Gospel because the end of the world was near. In 1960, he began his life as a pilgrim traveling through South Central Brazil, Uruguay, Paraguay, and North Central Brazil. In 1969, he reached Peru where he lived until his expulsion at the end of 1971. Accompanied by dozens of his followers, he then descended the Solimões River, arriving at the Brazilian border where he was met by hundreds of people, among them, Tikuna Indians.

These Indians, the region's traditional inhabitants, today number around thirty thousand individuals. For many years, especially during the rubber boom at the beginning of the twentieth century, they lived under the white man's dominion. Their reaction to this situation took the form of messianic manifestations. Between the beginning of the twentieth century and 1960, there were seven of these manifestations. All of them failed but they kindled the group's messianic hopes so that when, in 1971, the Indians heard rumors that there was someone in Peru 'doing miracles' and that this person would 'soon reach them', they saw in that figure the culmination of their hopes not for liberation from the whites, but for the acquisition of civilization's goods and better conditions for their integration into regional society.

The region's non-indigenous social segments, heirs to a tradition of syncretic religiosity including various messianic and millenaristic elements, were also excited by the news that Cruz was arriving.

The arrival of the messianic caravan increased the mood of collective religious exaltation. There were dozens of boats in the fleet that accompanied the tall, thin, bearded prophet – a fifty-eight-year-old man, wearing a white tunic and bearing a Bible in his hands who, in an eloquent sermon, proceeded to deliver his doomsday message.

During all of 1972, Cruz preached in the region's towns and rural neighborhoods. In each of them he would solemnly raise a cross some fifteen feet in height. In 1973, Cruz settled on the Jui River, an affluent of the Içá River, which is, itself, a major affluent of the Solimões River. Here, he built a sacred city called the Vila União Paz e Amor – UPA – (Vila Union Peace and Love), residing there until his death on 23 June 1982. From there, he commanded his followers, organizing a general hierarchy of the BHC made up of patriarchs, delegates, novices, priests, and local directories.

From the Vila UPA, he would send messages through members of the hierarchy, claiming he had inaugurated the third and final reform of Christianity. The first came about with Jesus and the second with Luther. For him, the Cross and the Bible were the only true religious symbols. He announced for the year 2000 a 'flood of fire' which would destroy humanity and from which the Brotherhood's members would be the sole survivors. Today, the brothers assure us that the cataclysm was avoided thanks to their prayers. They preach puritanical conduct and the creation of a new religious, social, political, and economic order.

On the eve of his death, Cruz chose his successor – Valter Never, a Kambeva Indian, born in 1943, who at the time of writing is still the head of the Brotherhood. When it began, the BHC attracted most of the Tikuna as well as thousands of the region's other inhabitants, including members of the local elite. As time passed, the local elite as well as a number of Tikuna and lower income non-Indians abandoned the movement. Even so, the movement continues on, albeit divided into two major factions: the Peruvians and the Brazilians, each of which consider themselves the legitimate heirs to their founder's mission. The first group legitimates its claim by pointing out that Cruz spent three years in Peru; the second group underlines the fact that it was in Brazil that their founder was born, died and was buried. For this latter faction, the Vila UPA continues to be the sacred city. If, during the founder's lifetime, the town contained only a church and a few abodes today it is considerably bigger, with dozens of huts that house, people claim, a select group of the Brotherhood's adepts.

Further reading

Oro, A. P. (1989) *Na Amazonia um messias de índios e brancos. Traços para uma antropologia dos messianismos*, Publicado pela Editora Vozes, cidade de Petropolis (Rio de Janeiro), 207 pp.

ARI PEDRO ORO

BUDDHISM IN THE WEST

For the first time in its 2,500 years of history, Buddhism has become established on virtually every continent. During the twentieth century, Buddhists have set foot in Australia and New Zealand, in the Southern region of Africa, and in a multitude of European countries, as well as in South and North America. Just as Buddhism in no way forms a homogeneous religious tradition in Asia, the appearance of Buddhism outside of Asia is likewise marked by its heterogeneity and diversity. A plurality of Buddhist schools and traditions is observable in many 'Western' countries. The whole variety of Theravada, Mahayana, and Tibetan Buddhist traditions and schools can be found outside of Asia, often in one country and sometimes even in one major city such as London with some forty or fifty different Buddhist groups in a single place. Buddhists of the various traditions and schools have become neighbours and founded intra-Buddhist organizations – a rarity in Asia itself.

The history of knowledge about Buddhist concepts and practices in the West starts in classical times, though more information trickled into Europe with the reports by Jesuit missionaries working in Tibet, China, and Japan from the sixteenth century onwards. In the course of European colonial expansion, information was gathered about the customs and history of the peoples and regions that had been subjected to British, Portuguese, and Dutch domination. Around 1800, texts and descriptions about Indian religions had become known in literate and academic circles in Europe and an unquenchable enthusiasm for the East took hold. In the 1850s, Europe witnessed a boom of studies and translations, paving the way for an enhanced knowledge of and interest in the Buddhist teachings. 'Buddhism' – a concept coined by the French philologist Burnouf in 1844 – was essentially treated as a textual object, being located in books and Oriental libraries. On this basis, first translations reach the USA, praised by the transcendentalists (see **Transcendentalism**) Emerson (see **Emerson, Ralph Waldo**), Thoreau, and Whitman. Parallel and with no mutual contact, migrants from China and Japan arrived at the US-West coast, establishing their so-called 'joss-houses' where Buddhist, Taoist, and Chinese folk traditions mingled.

During the late nineteenth century, first Europeans and US-Americans, self-converted by reading Buddhist treatises, took up Buddhism as their guiding life-principle. Around the turn of the century, initial Buddhist institutions were founded, the first being the Society for the Buddhist Mission in Germany, established in 1903. During this time, a philosophical interest in Buddhist ideas and ethics dominated, based on the texts of the Pali canon. Starting in the 1950s, Buddhism in the West became plural and increasingly heterogeneous as Mahayana traditions from East Asia established centers and instituitions. In the US, lecture tours by the Japanese Zen teacher Daisetz Teitaro Suzuki (1870–1966) during the 1950s instigated an upsurge of interest in Zen concepts and meditation. At the same time, 'Beat Zen' and 'Square Zen' created by Allan Watts, Allen Ginsberg, and Jack Kerouac popularized Zen and attracted members of the emerging counter-culture. The boom of Zen Buddhism was followed by an upsurge of interest in Tibetan Buddhism starting in the mid-1970s. Within only two decades, converts to Tibetan Buddhism were able to found a multitude of centers and groups, at times outnumbering all other traditions in a given country, especially in Europe. This rapid increase led to a considerable rise in the number of Buddhist groups and centers, many of them composed of Buddhist converts. In Britain, for example, the number of organizations quintupled from seventy-four to 400 groups and centers (1979–2000). In Germany, interest in Buddhism resulted in an increase from some forty to more than 500 groups, meditation circles, centers, and societies (1975–2001). A similar explosive growth has been observed for the USA, and on a lesser scale for Australia also. In both South America and South Africa, interest in Buddhism has grown as well, beginning in the 1970s. Often neglected and hardly noticed, considerable numbers of Buddhists from Asian countries have come to Western Europe, North America, and Australia since the 1960s. In many nation states, immigrant or Asian Buddhists outnumber convert Buddhists by two or three times. Since the 1990s these Asian Buddhists started to strive for better public recognition and acknowledgment, building impressive temples and monasteries and engaging in debates about who represents Buddhism in the West.

In the early twenty-first century, a multitude of Buddhist schools and traditions have successfully settled in the West. The 'general traditions' of **Theravada**, **Mahayana** and Tibetan Buddhism (see **Vajrayana Buddhism**) are internally heavily subdivided according to country of origin (e.g. Laos, Burma, Sri Lanka, Thailand, etc.), lineage (e.g. Gelug, Karma Kagyu, Sakya, Nyingma; Rinzai, Soto, etc.), teacher (Asian and Western, manifold) and emphasis on specific Buddhist concepts and practices (e.g. Vipassana (see **Vipassana**); chanting; intellectualized reading). Flourishing in the West, these various Asian-derived schools and traditions to a large extent have not remained unchanged. Various sub-schools and sub-branches have evolved. In the course of time, a process of authentication of Western teachers by the Buddhist mother tradition in Asia has occurred. This has given birth to both traditionally oriented

centers and to independent centers, favoring innovative changes and the creation of a 'Western Buddhism'. With regard to the latter, mention could be made of the Insight Meditation Society in the USA or the **Friends of the Western Buddhist Order**, founded by the British Sangharakshita (b. 1925) in 1967 in London.

In the wake of public debates about new religious movements, some Buddhist schools and organizations have been faced with allegations of mind-control, sexual abuse and aggressive missionary methods. Soka Gakkai (Nichiren Buddhism), which has attracted considerable numbers of converts since the 1970s in Western countries, has been targeted by Christian 'sect experts', as have the Tibetan traditions of Karma Kagyu and its energetic Western spokesperson Ole Nydahl as well as the New Kadampa Tradition and its founder Geshe Kelsang Gyatso. Such criticism which most often has been based on testimonies by ex-members, can be taken as a further sign that since the late twentieth century Buddhism has succeeded in entering the religious mainstream in the West.

Further reading

Batchelor, S. (1994) *The Awakening of the West. The Encounter of Buddhism and Western Culture*, Berkeley, CA: Parallax Press.

Baumann, M. (2001) 'Global Buddhism. Developmental Periods, Regional Histories and a New Analytical Perspective', *Journal of Global Buddhism*, 2, 1–43.

Clasquin, M. and Krüger, K. (eds) (1999) *Buddhism and Africa*, Pretoria: University of South Africa.

Journal of Global Buddhism (since 2000), online www.globalbuddhism.org.

Prebish, C. S. (1999) *Luminous Passage. The Practice and Study of Buddhism in America*, Berkeley: University of California Press.

Prebish, C. S. and Tanaka, K. K. (eds) (1998) *The Faces of Buddhism in America*, Berkeley: University of California Press.

Prebish, C. S. and Baumann, M. (2002) *Westward Dharma. Buddhism Beyond Asia*, Berkeley: University of California Press.

Queen, C. S. (ed.) (2000) *Engaged Buddhism in the West*, Boston: Wisdom.

Spuler, M. (2003) *Developments in Australian Buddhism. Facets of the Diamond*, London: RoutledgeCurzon.

Rawlinson, A. (1997) *The Book of Enlightened Masters: Western Teachers in Eastern Traditions*, Chicago and La Salle, Ill.: Open Court.

Seager, R. H. (1999) *Buddhism in America*, New York: Columbia University Press.

MARTIN BAUMANN

BUILDERS OF THE ADYTUM

The Builders of the Adytum (BOTA), an American offshoot of the **Hermetic Order of the Golden Dawn**, was founded (originally as the School of Ageless Wisdom) in the early 1920s by Paul Foster Case (1884–1954). Case had been initiated into the Second Order of the Thoth-Hermes Temple of the Golden Dawn (Alpha et Omega) in New York in 1920. He was succeeded as leader of BOTA by Anne Davies, who extended his teachings until her own death in 1975.

According to the group's website at *www.BOTA.org*, the word 'Adytum' means 'the innermost part of the Temple, the Holy of Holies, that which is not made with hands'.

Through study, meditation, imagery and ritual, BOTA claims that its initiates expand their conscious awareness, with the effects of increasing their intelligence, improving their memory and aiding their ability to think more logically and clearly.

Much of the emphasis of BOTA is on the Kabbalah and Tarot. Among Case's books is *The Book of Tokens*, a collection of inspired meditations on the twenty-two Tarot cards of the Major Arcana.

As with many other **Esoteric movements**, membership initially is by correspondence course. Members first study and experiment in Hermetic psychology, which enables them to awaken 'the realization of what your inner powers are and always have been'. They then spend a year studying the Tarot, 'a complete record of the inner secrets of the Wise in picture form'. There is more advanced study in Tarot meditation, in healing through colour and sound, in the Tree of Life of the Kabbalah, and in Alchemy, 'the secrets of the process of spiritual unfoldment'. As the member progresses, there is the opportunity to join a study group. Initiates can also join a ritual group called a Pronaos.

The headquarters of Builders of the Adytum has been in Los Angeles since the 1930s. The largest centres of membership are New Zealand, the United States and Europe. The European headquarters is in France, with study groups and the higher-level Pronaos ritual groups throughout Europe, and teaching materials in French, German, Spanish, and Italian. The total membership worldwide is about 5,000.

DAVID V. BARRETT

BYAKKÔ SHINKÔ KAI

Founder: Goi Masahisa
Country of origin: Japan

One of Japan's new religions, Byakkô Shinkô Kai was founded in 1951 by Goi Masahisa (1916–80) who was born in Asakusa, a traditional shopping, entertainment, and residential district of Tokyo. Before he founded Byakkô Shinkô Kai, Goi Masahisa had been a member of several other of Japan's new religions.

Goi Masahisa came to know about the teachings concerning disease and recovery of Okada Mokichi, the founder of **Sekai Kyûsei Kyô** through one of his colleagues at the Hitachi company. In 1945, Goi Masahisa visited Okada Mokichi but was not impressed by him. At that time, he read the books written by Taniguchi Masaharu, the founder of **Seichô no Ie** and was impressed by his philosophy, and so became a member of Seichô no Ie. After devoting years of his life as a teacher of Seichô no Ie and to spiritual training, Goi Hasahisa gradually became skeptical about the teachings and developed his own way of contacting the spirits.

Eventually in 1949 Goi Masahisa received a divine revelation and attained enlightenment with emancipation from all karmic bonds. He received a special message from God: 'May Peace Prevail on Earth'. In 1951 the association, *Goi Sensei Sangô kai*, was established. The name of the association was later changed to Byakkô Shinkô Kai (White Light Association) and it became a religious juridical person in 1955. Since the passing of Goi Masahisa in 1980, Byakkô Shinkô Kai has been led by his adopted daughter, Saionji Masami. It is believed that Goi Masahisa sends spiritual messages to the Earth using Saionji as a medium. Saionji Masami conducts lectures throughout Japan and overseas, and the contents of the lectures as well as the teachings of Goi Masahisa are the guidelines for members.

Byakkô Shinkô Kai teaches that human beings derive from the universal *Kami* deity and that everybody has *Shugo-rei*, or guardian spirits, and *Shugo-shin*, or guardian deities, which always watch over and try to protect their charges. Therefore, Byakkô Shinkô Kai encourages members to pray to *Shugo-rei* and *Shugo-shin*. Directing one's thoughts towards *Shugo-rei* and *Shugo-shin* merits their help.

According to Byakkô Shinkô Kai, the world is divided into two realms: the physical realm and the Divine realm, and if light from the Divine realm is obscured and intercepted by negative karma, people become ill. Goi Masahisa believed that medical science must research into the impact of the physical realm on the mind. Byakkô Shinkô Kai also teaches that words and thoughts are waves vibrating at different frequencies and that prayer for world peace vibrating at the highest possible level has a purifying effect on people and the world.

Byakkô Shinkô Kai emphasizes world peace through the spiritual development of members, who are encouraged to develop and express their divinity, harmony, and true selves as a *Bun-rei*, a spirit derived from the universal Kami, or deity. It is believed that world peace can only be accomplished if the whirlpool of karmic waves circulating the earth are harmonized and purified through the peace prayer which is as follows: 'May peace prevail on earth. May peace be in our homes and countries. May our missions be accomplished. We thank thee, Guardian Deities and Guardian Spirits.' Byakkô Shinkô Kai distributes stickers and erects 'Peace Poles', on which the words '*Sekai Jinrui ga Heiwa de Arimasuyôni*, May Peace Prevail on Earth' are written, and has conducted world peace prayer ceremonies in such cities as Los Angeles, Assisi, and Paris.

The headquarters of Byakkô Shinnkô Kai is in Ichikawa-shi, Chiba prefecture, where there is a sacred training centre called *Hijirigaoka Dôjô*, or holy man hill training centre. There is also a training centre on the side of Mount Fuji. The movement's main activity is the peace prayer held weekly at *Hijirigaoka Dôjô* and a training centre on the side of Mount Fuji. Byakkô Shinnkô Kai claims to have some 500,000 members in Japan and around 1,000 members overseas particularly in the United States, South America, and Europe.

Further reading

Inaba, K. (2002) 'Byakkô Shinnkô Kai', in M. Baumann and G. Melton (eds) *Reli-* *gions of the World: A Comprehensive Encyclopedia of Beliefs and Practices,* Santa Barbara, CA: ABC-Clio.

Clarke, P. B. (1999) *An Annotated Bibliography of Japanese New Religions*, Eastbourne (Kent): Japan Library.

KEISHIN INABA

C

CADDY, EILEEN
(b. 1917)
New Age teacher and co-founder of the
Findhorn Community

Eileen Caddy (neé Combe) was born in 1917 in Alexandria, Egypt. She went to a private school in Ireland and attended church regularly with an aunt. In the 1930s her family moved to England to pursue Christian Science treatment for her brother's epilepsy. Caddy married an RAF officer involved in **Moral Re-armament** (MRA), known for its practice of 'quiet times' and 'guidance' sessions. On a tour of duty in Iraq she met Peter Caddy (see **Caddy, Peter**), also then in the RAF, who had additional interests in 'psychics, spiritualism and the occult' (Caddy 1988: 19). Through him she duly met Sheena Govan (1912–67), the daughter of an evangelical Scots family. In London in the late 1940s Govan taught Caddy a practical methodology of obtaining divine 'guidance' through discerning an inner, divine voice during periods of quiet sitting. Caddy made her first unambiguous contact with the 'god within' in 1953 in Glastonbury and subsequently perfected her technique as one of a small group of committed spiritual seekers attached to Govan in London and, later, the West Highlands of Scotland. This group became the nucleus of the **Findhorn Community** in 1962. A first book of spiritual messages obtained through Caddy's guidance, *God Spoke to Me*, was published in 1971. Apart from lecture tours with Peter Caddy, her second husband, Eileen Caddy has lived at Findhorn continuously where she has been a figure of stability in a fluid institution. She has published further collections of guidance including *Footprints on the Path* (1976) and *Opening Doors Within* (1987). Whilst immediately derived from Sheena Govan's teaching, her technique of 'guidance' is also influenced by the 'quiet times' of MRA and the curative mental power of Christian Science.

Further reading

Caddy, E. (1976) *Footprints on the Path,* Forres: Findhorn Press.

Caddy, E. (1987) *Opening Doors Within,* Forres: Findhorn Press.

Caddy, E. (1988) *Flight into Freedom,* Shaftesbury, Dorset: Element (reprinted in 2002 as *Flight into Freedom and Beyond,* Forres: Findhorn Press)

STEVEN J. SUTCLIFFE

CADDY, PETER

(b. 1917; d. 1994)

New Age activist and co-founder of the Findhorn Community

Peter Caddy was born in Ruislip, England, and grew up in a middle-class Methodist household. He attended public school, trained as a catering manager, and joined the RAF, with which he subsequently served in India and Iraq. He was exposed at an early age to alternative religion and healing through his father's use of homoeopathy, chiropractic and spiritual healing. Consequently Caddy recalled 'I began to question many of the things taught by conventional religions, and started my own search for the truth through many "ologies" and "isms"' (Caddy 1996: 25). Caddy's subsequent career in and on the fringes of new religions (see **New Religious Movement**) can be considered a prototype of the twentieth century 'spiritual seeker', spanning a spectrum of groups and practices in the UK from the **Rosicrucian Order, Crotona Fellowship** and **Moral Re-armament** in the 1930s and 1940s to **UFOs** and the **New Age Movement** in the 1950s and 1960s. In 1962 he co-founded the **Findhorn Community** in Scotland with his third wife Eileen Caddy (see **Caddy, Eileen**) and others. In 1979 he moved to the first of several American residences, first in Hawai'i, later at Mount Shasta in California – a popular site for alternative religions – where in 1982 he briefly established a community called 'Gathering of the Ways'. He continued to give talks and to 'network' in North America, Europe, Australasia, and after 1987, in India.

Caddy led a complex and variegated life; he was married five times, travelled internationally and was instrumental in publicizing the Findhorn community as a paradigmatic 'New Age' settlement in the 1960s. He was strongly influenced by a practical philosophy of positive thinking, intuitive guidance and strong leadership influenced by neo-Christian piety and New Age utopianism. In his normative biography as 'planetary citizen' (Caddy 1996: 427*ff*), he epitomizes the hybrid spirituality associated with 'New Age' and later popularized in 'mind body spirit' culture.

Further reading

Caddy, P. (1996) *In Perfect Timing: Memoirs of a Man for the New Millenium,* Forres (Moray): Findhorn Press

STEVEN J. SUTCLIFFE

CAMPUS CRUSADE FOR CHRIST

Campus Crusade for Christ (CCC), with headquarters in Orlando, Florida 'is an interdenominational ministry committed to helping take the gospel of Jesus Christ to all nations' (http://www.ccci.org/mission.html). As such, it is not a New Religion in terms of developing new doctrines or practices but is part of the post-World War II global missionary thrust of **Evangelical Christianity**. Founded in 1951 by Bill and Vonette Bright, CCC started as a ministry to college students at the University of California, Los Angeles and has grown to become one of the largest non-profit interdenominational organizations in the world with over 24,000 full-time staff, more than 500,000 trained volunteers, and a presence in 191 countries as of the year 2000 (http://home.cci.org/headquarters/).

In his 1970 book, *Come Help Change the World*, Bright relates that CCC was born out of a powerful spiritual experience in his final semester at seminary. While studying for an exam, at about midnight, without any warning he suddenly felt God's presence and 'had the overwhelming impression that the Lord had unfolded a scroll of instructions of what I was to do with my life' (Bright 1970: 26). He came away from this experience convinced that God was commanding him to help fulfil the Great Commission of Matthew 28:18–20 in this generation by winning and discipling the students of the world for Christ (1970: 26).

The name for this vision, Campus Crusade for Christ, was suggested to him by one of his professors from whom he had sought counsel concerning this experience (1970: 27). The initial campus ministry at UCLA in 1951 was very successful, and in keeping with the global vision given him, Bright made the decision to leave the fledgling work under the guidance of his wife Vonette while he went out and recruited their first group of staff. In 1952 five more campus ministries were opened and by 1960 they had a staff of 109, campus ministries in fifteen states on forty different campuses as well as Korea and Pakistan, and a weekly radio program (1970: 51).

Bright believes that one of the key elements to the success of CCC has been the commitment to comprehensive training. An important part of their training methodology has been the use of what Bright calls transferable concepts, by which he means 'a truth that

can be communicated to another, who in turn will communicate the same truth to another, generation after generation, without distorting or diluting the original truth' (1970: 77). The most well known and widely used of these transferable concepts has been a simple step-by-step presentation of the Gospel message that Bright wrote known as 'The Four Spiritual Laws'. This tract is the distilled essence of a presentation developed in 1957 called 'God's Plan for Your Life' that Bright developed as a result of reflecting on his own personal method for telling others about Christ. The four laws are: God loves you and has a wonderful plan for your life; humans are sinful and separated from God, thus we cannot know and experience God's love and plan for our lives; Jesus Christ is God's only provision for our sin, through him you can know and experience God's love and plan for your life; and finally we must individually receive Jesus Christ as Savior and Lord, then we can know and experience God's love and plan for us (1970: 46).

As a ministry with a world embracing vision CCC has featured strategic planning that is global in its scope and that is driven by an interpretation of the Great Commission that focuses on giving every person on earth a chance to hear the message of Jesus Christ. In the early 1970s a goal was set to train five million Christians by 1976 so that the task of world evangelization could be completed by 1980. A major part of the global strategy of CCC from the late 1970s to the present has been the development of the JESUS Project, dedicated to the translation, distribution and showing of the JESUS Film worldwide (http://www.jesusfilm.org/). As of October 2002 the film has been translated into 766 languages, with another 244 in progress, and a cumulative audience of five billion with 176 million decisions to follow

Christ recorded (http://www.jesusfilm.org/ progress/statistics.html). CCC's current goal is to 'help give every man, woman, and child in the entire world an opportunity to find new life in Jesus Christ' by the end of the first decade of the twenty-first century through their over fifty different ministries (http://www.ccci.org/ mission.html).

Further reading

Bright, B. (1970) *Come Help Change the World*, Old Tappan, NJ: Fleming H. Revell.

ALAN R. JOHNSON

CANDOMBLÉ

Candomblé, a term which initially referred to a dance and then a musical instrument, came to be applied to the ceremonies performed by Africans in Brazil. It is one of several varieties of African-Brazilian religion which were started in Brazil during the era of the trans-Atlantic slave trade (fifteenth to the nineteenth century). Historically, these religions are most widely practised in the northeast of Brazil, especially in the states of Bahia, Pernambuco, and Maranhao and differ in several respects from Umbanda (see **Umbanda**). Casas (houses), also known as *terreiros*, Candomblé communities and places of worship, have been in existence for some considerable time in São Paulo and as far south as Porto Alegre in the state of Rio Grande do Sul, and in other South American countries including Argentina and Uruguay, and in more recently the religion has spread to North America and Europe.

The most historic centre (terreiro) of African-Brazilian religion in existence today is probably the Casa das Minas in Sao Luiz de Maranhao, founded in the first half of the nineteenth century and identified by its use of rituals derived mainly from the Jeje culture of Dahomey (now the Republic of Benin) in West Africa. Later, around the middle of the nineteenth century, some of Brazil's foremost African-Brazilian religious centres including the Casa Branca (White House) and the Casa do Gantois, were founded in Salvador, capital of the state of Bahia, in northeast Brazil, which has come to be widely regarded as the spiritual home of the religion.

The practice of African-Brazilian religion predates these formal beginnings. African slaves from Central Africa (the Congo), from West Central Africa (mainly Angola), from a large area of West Africa, and from East Central Africa (mainly Mozambique), most of whom were baptized Catholics either before they were taken as slaves to Brazil or on arrival there, continued from the outset to perform their rituals while labouring on the sugar and tobacco plantations or working in the urban centres of the New World. From the second half of the nineteenth century the rituals and cosmology of the Yoruba people from the previously mentioned West African Republic of Benin (formerly Dahomey) and southwestern Nigeria were to have the greatest influence on the development of Candomblé in Bahia which, outside of Africa itself, has preserved in its most complete and authentic form the worship of Yoruba divinities or *orisha* (Portuguese: *orixas*).

Candomblé traditions are distinguished from each other not only according to the African tradition with which they are most closely associated historically, but also on the basis of the so-called 'nations' (Portuguese: *nacoẽs*) into which slaves were grouped and the practices they developed therein. In practice these nations were ethnically mixed. Other ways of distinguishing one tradition from another include the type of drums used in a terreiro and the way they are played, for example with or without drum sticks, and the language, dance, and music of the ceremonies. Thus, there is Candomble Nago or Yoruba Candomblé, Candomblé Jeje which, as we have seen, refers to a type of Dahomean (Republic of Benin) Candomblé, Angolan, and Congolese Candomblé and what is known as Candomblé-de-Caboclo, an essentially Amerindian based Candomblé in which the mediums are possessed by Amerindian spirits known popularly as *caboclos*. African-Brazilian practitioners of Candomblé, referred to as candomblistas, also reverence these Amerindian spirits or caboclos as the guardians of the original owners of the land to which their ancestors were sent as slaves.

A small number of casas or terreiros are dedicated exclusively to the veneration of ancestors (Yoruba: *egun*) as an independent cult and these are strongly opposed to any form of mixing of African and non-African traditions.

Candomblé has, however, close links with Catholicism and to a greater or lesser extent depending on the terreiro and its traditions with the Spiritist tradition of Allan Kardec (see **Kardec, Allan** and **Kardecism**), which is widespread throughout Brazil. Each Candomblé centre has a house of the ancestors usually situated away from the main place of worship. Candomblé centres have traditionally acknowledged correspondences between African gods and Catholic saints. There is much debate as to why this practice developed. Many suggest that it started a kind of smoke screen behind which slaves carried on the 'illegal' worship of their own gods. It is also possible that it served two very different but complementary ends by protecting both the African and the Brazilian Catholic identity of the slaves and their descendants.

The correspondences between African gods and Catholic saints often surprise and include the pairing of the violent and virile Yoruba god of thunder Shango (Portuguese: Xango) with the quiet, studious, pensive, balding, elderly St Jerome. The head of the Yoruba pantheon Oshala (Portuguese: Oxala) is paired with Christ and Yemanja, the mother of several orishas and goddess of the sea, corresponds with Our Lady of the Immaculate Conception.

Changed circumstances in the New World made for a change in emphasis regarding the functions of the orishas who came to be regarded much more as personal deities. Traditionally in Africa an orisha is associated either with a city or a 'nation' – Shango with Oyo and Yemanja with the Egba nation, and Oshala-Obatala with Ife. Orishas travelled with their followers and in this way devotion to them spread. Where, however, a person lived alone or with his immediate family the orisha would take on the characteristics of a personal divinity.

The result of the break up of the family unit through slavery was that each individual member of a terreiro known as a *filha* (daughter) or *filho* (son) *de santo* (saint) became personally responsible for fulfilling all the demands imposed by her/his orisha. A priestess or Mae de santo or the priest or Pae de santo, mother or father of the saint and/or divinity, and spiritual head of the terreiro respectively initiate into the cult those called to become a filha or filho de santo.

At the core of Candomblé religion is the mystical power (Yoruba: *ase*; Portuguese: *axe*) of the orishas or divinities transmitted to their descendants during possession. There are devotees who are not of African descent and for these possession cannot easily be explained by recourse to traditional theological ideas.

They can, however, claim to have certain personality traits and affinities of temperament in common with a particular orisha which would facilitate possession, the central rite and main purpose of Candomblé. In this case orishas come to be seen as archetypes of personality who manifest in their behaviour the fulfilment of latent tendencies that lie deep within their devotees and as providing a solution to unresolved personal conflicts that arise from the 'unnatural' rules which are designed to promote socially accepted behaviour. In this situation initiation and possession becomes a means of self-liberation enabling people to express their innermost tendencies, which are otherwise repressed.

The previously mentioned Yemanja, goddess of the sea, archetype, for example, is willful, rigorous, strong, protective, proud, and at times, impetuous and arrogant, and puts her friendships to the test. She bears grudges for a long time, and if she does forgive she never forgets. She is maternal and responsible, enjoys luxury, beautiful blue cloth and expensive jewels and tends to live beyond her means.

The gods can be understood from a number of perspectives. They can be seen, for example, as deified ancestors, and as natural entities and forces of nature. Certain trees such as the iroko are regarded as sacred, as is the wind.

Candomblé ceremonies are always preceded by a sacrifice which is followed by the rite known as the *pade* or dispatching of Eshu, the so called trickster god and messenger between the human and the divine whose demands need to be met if the proceedings are to go well and achieve the desired ends. The actual ceremony begins with the beating of the drums and the sounding of the *agogo*, a musical instrument made of metal and beaten with a metal stick. The drums which are 'baptized' possess ase (axe) or mystical power – the most important concept in Candomblé – which is maintained through sacrifices and offerings. The drums not only call upon the gods from Africa to possess their devotees, sounding the rhythm associated with each one of them, but also transmit their messages to them.

The purposes of Candomblé are many and in addition to that of preserving African identity, include culture and tradition, healing and the enabling of individuals to fulfil their identity. Without Candomblé, it is widely believed that African culture in the New World would have been extinguished, resulting in the loss of innumerable plants and herbs which are believed to have healing properties and which Ossaim, the god of vegetation, has the power release and apply. Today Candomblé priests and priestesses treat mainly psychological illnesses which it describes as 'illnesses of the gods', and the competence in this field of some of its healers is highly respected by modern medicine which makes use of its services.

Without Candomblé the discovery of a person's destiny through divination would also have become impossible leaving individuals without a sense of purpose and direction, and without explanations for their success and/or failure in relationships, careers, and indeed in all aspects of life. Further, often described as a 'beautiful religion' meaning rich in legend, dance, and music, Candomblé has greatly contributed to the survival of African mysticism, aesthetics, leisure activities, sculpture, art, and cuisine.

The relationship between religion and the economic life of a society has been the topic of much debate. Candomblé clearly has made and continues to make an indispensable contribution to the economic life of northeast Brazil, by among other things attracting, as it does, large numbers of tourists, many of whom are of African origin from the United States and in search of their roots.

Further reading

Bastide, R. (1971) *African Civilizations in the New World*, New York: Harper and Row.

Bastide, R. (1978) *The African Religions of Brazil*, Baltimore: Johns Hopkins University Press

Clarke. P. B. (1998) 'Accounting for Recent Anti-Syncretist Trends in Candomblé-Catholic Relations' in P. B. Clarke (ed.) *New Trends and Developments in African Religions*, Westport, CT: Greenwood Press, pp. 17–37.

Roberto, M. (1998) 'The Churchyfying of Candomblé: Priests, Anthropologists, and the Canonization of the African-Brazilian Memory in Brazil' in P. B. Clarke (ed.) *New Trends and Developments in African Religions*, Westport, CT: Greenwood Press, pp. 45–59.

PETER B. CLARKE

CAODAISM

Founder: Ngo Van Chieu

Country of origin: Vietnam

Caodaism – also known as Dao Cao Dai – first started in the French Colony of southern Vietnam in 1926 and is a new religion that has been revealed through séance, spiritism, and shamanic traditions. It gathered half a million members in the first four years of its existence. By the 1950s, it possessed its own army which had been trained by the Japanese during World War II.

Its founder, Ngo Van Chieu, was an official of the French colonial administration. He came into contact with a spirit called 'Cao Dai' – literally, 'high tower' – through séances. The spirit asked Chieu to adopt certain practices, including vegetarianism and ritual prayer four times a day. Caodists worship two spirit gods, Cao Dai and the Mother Goddess. They believe that by living a correct life they can escape the

cycle of reincarnation and become one with Cao Dai.

An eye surrounded by clouds was adopted as the symbol of this religion. It seeks the harmony of Buddhism, Confucianism, and Daoism while its doctrine is inclusive of Christianity in its French Catholic form and practice.

It first became a significant religion in Vietnam, and spread afterwards to Cambodia and Japan. After 1975, while the communists were attempting to dissolve the religion, it went global with the flood of refugees escaping Vietnam. For example, the first group of Caodaists in Australia met in Sydney in 1983 and founded the Australian Caodaist Association. One of their first activites was to sponsor the immigration of Vietnamese refugees and to establish contacts with Caodaists around the country. The Australian 2001 census puts the membership in the country at 819 – that is 145 less than from the 1996 census.

Its organizational structure is inspired by that of Roman Catholicism and the movement is led by a pope and cardinals. Its pantheon includes Buddha, Guan Di Gong – the warrior god, Lao-tzu, Confucius and Sun Yat Sen – the founder of the first Chinese republic, and Western figures such as Jesus, Joan of Arc, and Victor Hugo.

Firther reading

Fall, Bernard (1955) 'The Political Religious Sects of Vietnam', *Pacific Affairs*, XXVIII, pp. 235–43.

ADAM POSSAMAI

CATHOLIC APOSTOLIC CHURCH

Founders: Henry Drummond and others

Country of origin: England

The Catholic Apostolic Church is occasionally referred to as 'the Irvingite

Church', because of the influence, on its early beginnings, of the revival preached in London in 1832 by the Presbyterian Scottish revivalist Edward Irving (1792–1834). The Catholic Apostolic Church itself, however, does not accept the label 'Irvingite', and in fact Irving was not among its founders. A more crucial role was played by Henry Drummond (1786–1860), a rich lay prophecy buff, who organized a series of 'Prophetic Conferences' in his Albury Park mansion. In 1832, the enthusiasm generated by the Irving revival and by the report of several miraculous events around the UK, persuaded Drummond that the time was ripe for a new Christian dispensation. Based on prophetic words received by various participants in the Albury Park movement, a first new apostle was appointed in 1832, and an apostolic college of twelve (including Drummond, but not Irving) was established between 1832–5.

The twelve apostles set up what they called the Catholic Apostolic Church, and with it they achieved a particular success in Germany. Many were fascinated by the new church's liturgy, a carefully crafted worship system drawing its inspiration from Roman Catholic, Eastern Orthodox, and Anglican rituals. Although the calling of new apostles was controversial, the doctrines in fact remained very similar to those of the Church of England, with the obvious exceptions of the role of the apostles and of the urgent preaching of an imminent end of the world.

In fact, it is because the end of the world was near that Drummond and his friends taught that theirs was the last apostolic college, and that deceased apostles should not be replaced. Thus, when the last living Catholic Apostolic apostle, Francis Valentine Woodhouse (1805–1901) died, there were no apostles left to lead a declining church. This was a dramatic problem for the members, since only apostles could consecrate 'angels' (the equivalent of Roman Catholic or Anglican bishops), only 'angels' could ordain priests, and only priests could celebrate mass and administer the sacraments. The last 'angel' died in 1960, the last priest in 1971. This was the end of the magnificent Catholic Apostolic liturgy, although a small number of sub-deacons (the last deacon died in 1972) remained in Germany and led the community in singing hymns and reciting the litanies. Sermons preached before 1971, together with the Bible, continue to be read to a small number of loyal followers, who appreciate the High Church style of the Catholic Apostolic Church. Some of them would later join Anglican prophetic movements such as the Guild of Prayer for the Return of Our Lord, or an Eastern Orthodox Church, rather than the more populist **New Apostolic Church**, which between 1897–8 under the leadership of Fritz Krebs (1832–1905), solved the Catholic Apostolic dilemma by breaking with the London headquarters and calling new apostles.

Further reading

Flegg, C. G. (1992) *'Gathered Under Apostles'. A Study of The Catholic Apostolic Church*, Oxford: Clarendon Press.

MASSIMO INTROVIGNE

CATHOLIC CHARISMATIC RENEWAL

The Catholic Charismatic Renewal (CCR) began to take root on North American University campuses, among staff and students, in early 1967: in 1971 some 5,000 representatives from a dozen different countries attended the movement's annual conference at the University of Notre Dame in Indiana.

When, by 1976, the number attending had risen to 30,000 it was decided that annual gatherings should be held regionally around the world. By this time members of CCR could be found at the heart of RC academic, pastoral, and institutional life. Possibly for this reason, what some regarded as excesses of the movement were stemmed early on and CCR, while remaining broadly ecumenical, has continued to grow and flourish within the Catholic Church. CCR was able to develop as it did because of the reforms encouraged by the Second Vatican Council (1962–5).

Not only did Vatican II open up the possibility for Catholics to work ecumenically; it insisted that the laity are called to play a full part in building up the Church and endorsed the value of 'charismatic' gifts, enjoyed by clergy and laity alike, in this process. CCR has, from the beginning, run seminars, courses and retreats as well as prayer groups and more permanent residential communities. The boundaries of the movement have remained fairly fluid. 'Membership' figures are therefore difficult to calculate, but millions of Catholics worldwide have had some involvement.

While the charismatic movement as a whole has its roots in Pentecostalism, each of the denominational strands has distinctive features. CCR emphasizes the importance of the sacraments in mediating the grace of the Holy Spirit. It understands 'Baptism in the Spirit' as a particular release of the power of the Spirit received in sacramental baptism, an interpretation seen as totally in line with both Scripture and Catholic Tradition.

The Eucharist is central to the movement's life and worship and, for many groups, devotion the Virgin Mary is very important. Most of the groups and communities which make up CCR belong to one of several major coordinating bodies: *International Catholic Charismatic Renewal Services*, *International Catholic Programme of Evangelisation* and *Renouveau dans l'Esprit Sainte*. CCR, while remaining largely a lay movement, has enjoyed support and encouragement from clergy, bishops and the Pope: CCR leaders met regularly in Rome with Pope John Paul II.

The movement is seen as a major contributor to Church maintenance and renewal and, along with other new Catholic movements, a valuable source of vocations to the priesthood. Within CCR, The *Catholic Fraternity of Charismatic Covenant Communities and Fellowships* was the first organization to receive formal, canonical recognition. The *Fraternity* brings together Communities from Australia and New Zealand, Malaysia, North and South America, and Europe. The member Communities vary greatly among and within themselves in their structures, charisms and organization.

One of the largest is the *Emmanuel Community*, which itself has a multitude of communities in about forty countries involved in a wide range of evangelical activities. *Emmanuel*, which began in Paris in the 1970s runs the *International Summer Encounters* at Paray-le-Monial where from dioceses all over France and beyond more than 300,000 pilgrims gather each year. Its other ministries include the *Foundation of Love and Truth*, an organization of young people, engaged and married couples and families; *Presence and Witness*, which is concerned with the world of work; *Magnificat*, an association for artists and *Presence and Testimony*, which works to evangelize the media. *Emmanuel* also runs the new *School of Mission* at the St Laurence Centre in Rome. This was set up by the Pontifical Council for the Laity to 'give a Christian formation to young pilgrims for the Great Jubilee', and opened in October 1998 with twenty people nominated from dioceses, Roman Catholic Ecclesial Movements and New Communities around the world. Through a sub-group, *FIDESCO, Emmanuel* is also involved in evangelization and relief activities in many third world countries. It has over 200 priests and seminarians, almost that number of religious sisters and brothers, and about twenty permanent deacons among its 6,000 members and is charged with running some fifteen parishes.

Other Communities whose background is in CCR include the Community of the Beatitudes, formerly known as the Lion of Judah Community, the Christian Community of God's Delight, Word of Life, City of the Lord, Chemin Neuf, Pain de Vie, Community of Maria, and the Bethany Communities. Many of these have a presence around the world, and are involved in a range of ministries within the Church itself, in evangelization and in the social apostolate.

Further reading

Urquhart, Gordon (1995) *The Pope's Armada*, New York: Bantam Books.

KATHLEEN WALSH

CELESTIAL CHURCH OF CHRIST

(CCC)

Founder: Oschoffa, Samuel Bilewu Joseph (b. 1909; d. 1985)

Country of origin: Benin Republic

One of the most widespread indigenous prophetic-charismatic movements in West Africa is the CCC. It falls under the category of churches popularly known as *Aladura* (the prayer people) which emerged among the Yoruba in Western Nigeria. They are so called owing to their strong emphasis on prayer, healing, prophecy, visions, dreams. CCC was founded in 1947 through the charismatic initiative of a Yoruba 'carpenter-turned-prophet' Samuel Bilewu Oschoffa who claimed to have undergone his first visionary experience in a mangrove forest in Porto Novo (Dahomey) during his search for timber. Through this vision, he got a spiritual calling from God to embark on a 'special mission' and to found a church charged with 'cleansing the world'. Following this transformation, he received spiritual gifts of healing, prayer and prophecy and became famous for his healing miracles (i.e. raising the dead).

CCC started among the Egun and Yoruba peoples, and thus had its worldview largely shaped by these religiocultural backgrounds. Although the church had its origin in Porto Novo, it was its inception in Nigeria in 1950 that gained it popularity and fame. From its first base in Makoko-Lagos, it began to witness a phenomenal growth and spread first to virtually all Yoruba-speaking areas and later to other parts of Nigeria. As the church was spreading outside the Egun-Yoruba geo-ethnic context to other parts of Nigeria, parishes were being planted concurrently in the West African sub-region i.e. Togo, Côte d'Ivoire (Ivory Coast), Cameroon, Ghana, and Senegal. It also started to spread to the USA, Canada and to European countries (United Kingdom, Germany, Austria, Switzerland, and the Netherlands). Between 1976 and 1996, CCC parishes increased from 254 to 2,051. Of these, 1,744 are found in Nigeria alone while 307 parishes are scattered within the West Coast of Africa, Europe, America, Canada, and other parts of the world. Within five decades of its existence, the movement had transcended geo-ethnic boundaries with a membership running into several millions and over 4,000 parishes scattered worldwide.

CCC beliefs occupy an important place for its members as they lie behind the ritual practices, principle of membership, and decisions of the church. The Bible represent the basic source and foundation of their beliefs and modes of worship. The CCC Constitution (p. 29) explicitly states 'that the name and organisational structure of the church, its doctrines and rituals, are derived primarily from the inspiration of the Holy Spirit'. Apart from the centrality of God, Jesus Christ and the Holy Spirit, angelology occupies an important place in their belief system. CCC is structured around the centralized authority of the Pastor (Founder). As both the spiritual and administrative head of the church, the Pastor has the unchallengeable authority on all matters, and legitimates this authority through his personal charisma. The Pastor-in-Council under the ultimate authority of the Pastor represents the highest organ of government. The internal organization of the church provides a complex hierarchical structure that can be classified into the upper and lower cadres. CCC Worldwide is run through its international headquarters located at the Mission House in Ketu-Lagos. The Supreme headquarters is located in Porto-Novo by virtue of its birth there. Other sacred CCC places include the Celestial City (New Jerusalem) at Imeko, the International Camp Centre along the Lagos-Ibadan Expressway, and Mercy lands attached to each local parish of the church.

The demise of Pastor-Founder Oschoffa in 1985, marked a watershed in CCC's history as it struggled to deal with the problems of succession, continuity and the routinization of charisma. Abiodun Bada was enthroned as Oschoffa's successor in 1987, amidst leadership tussles and prolonged legal crisis, a position he held until his death in 2000. Bada's demise did not put an end to the legal crisis. The church hierarchy swung into action to fill the leadership vacuum created, and Philip Ajose who was until then the head of the CCC Overseas Diocesan headquarters in London, was enthroned in March 2001. Philip Ajose died on 2 March 2001, six days after he was officially installed Pastor of the CCC Worldwide. Following his death, a leadership vacuum was again created until January 2003 when Gilbert Jesse was appointed as the new spiritual head of the church.

Further reading

Adogame, A. U. (1999) *Celestial Church of Christ: The Politics of Cultural Identity in a West African Prophetic-Charismatic Movement*, Frankfurt a/M: Peter Lang.

Odeyemi, S. O. (1992) *The Coming of Oschoffa and the Birth of the Celestial Church of Christ*, Lagos.

AFE ADOGAME

CESNUR

Founder: Massimo Introvigne (b. 1955)
Country of origin: Italy

CESNUR, the Center for Studies on New Religions, is one of the largest international **information and research centres on NRMs**. It was established in 1988 through the efforts of Massimo Introvigne (b. 1955), an Italian NRMs scholar. CESNUR's original aim was to offer a professional association to scholars specialized in NRMs, contemporary esoteric, spiritual, and occult schools, and the new religious consciousness in general. It started as a small group of scholars predominantly active in Southern Europe. The first officers were, in addition to Introvigne himself, Swiss historian Jean-François Mayer, and Italian church historian and Catholic Bishop Giuseppe Casale, who later became Archbishop of Foggia. In 1988, Casale was appointed first president of CESNUR, with Introvigne serving as its managing director, a position he maintains to this day (in 1998, Casale became honorary president, and was replaced as president by Luigi Berzano, a professor of sociology at the University of Turin). Soon, however, the founders were joined by well-known scholars of new religious movements in the English-speaking world, including Eileen Barker and Gordon Melton.

CESNUR's first international conferences remained largely gatherings of scholars exchanging research news and information among themselves. In the 1990s, however, it became apparent that inaccurate information was being disseminated to the media and the public powers by activists associated with the international **Anti-Cult Movement**. Some NRMs were also disseminating unreliable or partisan information. CESNUR became more pro-active, and started supplying information beyond the boundaries of the academic world on a regular basis, opening an office in Turin in 1993 and organizing conferences and seminars for the general public in a variety of countries. In 1996, CESNUR gained official recognition as a public non-profit entity by the Italian authorities, which currently contribute to most of its projects. It is also financed by royalties from the sale of the books it publishes with different publishers, and by contributions from its members.

In 1996, CESNUR decided to publicly criticize the anti-cult approach to NRMs adopted by some European governments after the **Solar Temple** suicides and homicides in 1994, 1995 and 1997. In the wake of the controversies originating from the French parliamentary report on cults (1996), conferences were organized at the Sorbonne University on the anti-cult movement (1996), and in Paris

on the shortcomings of the brainwashing model (1997). Four well-attended press conferences were also organized in order to criticize the French report, two in Paris (one at the Senate), one in Brussels, and one in Geneva; a book in which leading international scholars criticized the French document was also published. These moves provoked a strong reaction from the international anti-cult movement and the French government itself, with several 'anti-CESNUR' Web sites and pages appearing on the Internet.

Today, CESNUR is a network of independent but related organizations in various countries (in addition to the international body headquartered in Italy, chapters have been legally incorporated in France and Latvia), dedicated to promoting NRMs research, to spreading information, and to exposing the very real problems associated with some movements, while at the same time defending everywhere the principles of religious liberty. Although established in 1988 by scholars who were mostly (but by no means all) Roman Catholic, CESNUR from its very beginning has had boards of directors which have included scholars representing a variety of religious persuasions. It is independent from any Church, denomination or religious movement, and its research is strictly secular although, of course, each director has his or her own opinions on religion, and remains free to express them anywhere he or she wishes.

Massimo Introvigne started collecting books on NRMs and esoteric movements in the 1970s. His collection now includes more than 20,000 volumes, plus complete, or semi-complete, series of more than 200 journals and magazines. While remaining his personal property, this collection is housed at the CESNUR library in Turin, Italy, which has officially been given public library status by the local authorities. Continuously updated and fully indexed on computer (the index is Web-accessible), it is regarded as the largest collection in Europe, and the second in the world, in its field. The library also includes a large collection of books and comics in the field of popular culture and supernatural fiction, a field which is also part of CESNUR's interests.

CESNUR's annual conference is the largest world gathering of those active in the field of studies on NRMs. Conferences have been held *inter alia* at the London School of Economics (1993 and 2001), the Federal University of Pernambuco in Recife, Brazil (1994), the State University of Rome (1995), the University of Montreal (1996), the Free University of Amsterdam (1997), the Industrial Union in Turin (1998), the Bryn Athyn College in Pennsylvania (1999), the University of Latvia in Riga (2000), the University of Utah and Brigham Young University (2002), and the University of Vilnius in Lithuania (2003). Special seminars are also organized periodically on single topics.

Finally, almost every week seminars or lectures are organized in Italy and elsewhere (including, increasingly, Eastern Europe), in order to introduce the basic concepts of a scholarly approach to NRMs to local scholars, students, government officers, professionals, priests, and pastors, as well as the general public. CESNUR co-operates regularly with law enforcement agencies (including the FBI's Critical Incident Analysis Group and Critical Incidents Response Group, for which CESNUR organized a seminar in 1999 in Virginia), supplying information and offering courses to agents.

CESNUR sponsors a wide range of publications, from the very scholarly to those intended for the general public. Its main project in Italian has been the monumental *Enciclopedia delle religioni in Italia* (2001), which was the Italian media's most reviewed non-fiction work in 2001. A collection of some forty monographs on single NRMs has also been published in Italian, with some of the titles also being translated into English, Spanish and French. The Web site *www.cesnur.org* welcomes yearly close to one million visitors, and has emerged as one of the main international Web references in its field.

Further reading

Introvigne, M., Zoccatelli, P.-L., Màcrina, N. M. and Roldán, V (2001) *Enciclopedia delle religioni in Italia*, Leumann (Torino): Elledici.

MASSIMO INTROVIGNE

CH'ONDOGYO
(Religion of the Heavenly Way.
Formerly Tonghak: Eastern Leaning)
Founder: Cho'oe Che-u (b. 1824; d. 1864)

Ch'ondogyo (Religion of the Heavenly Way) was founded in Korea as Tonghak (Eastern Learning) by Ch'oe Che-u (1824–64) in 1860, son of a well known Confucian scholar but regarded, none the less, as lower class on account of his mother's position as a concubine. Having despaired of finding an answer to society's ills in the traditional teachings of Buddhism, Confucianism, Taoism, Christianity, and Folk Religions, Ch'oe Che-u sought a remedy for society's ills in a new form of Eastern Learning.

The movement was particularly critical of the Christian concept of a transcendent God who stood apart from humanity and the natural world. God, Ch'oe Che-u believed, was the Great Totality innate in human beings, the 'Great I' to which everyone could aspire. And importantly, in terms of its millenarian belief, Tonghak taught that heaven and hell were not places that souls departed to after death but states that could be realized on earth, depending on behaviour. Chongdoryong (the one with God's truth) would, it was believed, proclaim from his position on Mount Kyerong, the *chongdo* or right way for the new heaven on earth in which all nations, laws, and teachings would be united. Unification was a constant theme in most nineteenth-century Korean new religion and is at the centre of **Unification Church (UC)** theology.

Tonghak's description of paradise on earth also displays a deep concern for the plight of the poorest, with the inconveniences and even intractable problems created by climate, and the forces of Nature generally, factors which fuel a desire to escape from disease and attain immortality. Also evident is a deep concern with the profound disruption to social and economic life and culture resulting from the introduction of a new form of exchange based on money, a new system of taxation and the threat to the Korean language posed by the opening up of the country to the West.

Though its teachings were contrasted with Western Learning/Christianity (*Sohak*) this new religion, like the Vietnamese movement **Caodaism**, contained ideas and practices derived from Catholicism, and from Confucianism, Buddhism, Taoism and Folk Religion. Claiming that he had been commissioned by the Lord of Heaven, the Great Totality, the ultimate energy (*chigi*) to save humanity from destruction Ch'oe Ch-eu devised the following mantra which encapsulated the movement's basic teachings:

> Infinite Energy being now within me, I yearn that it may pour into all living beings and all created things. Since this Energy abides in me, I am identified with God, and of one nature with all existence. Should I ever forget these things all existing things will know of it.

Tonghak was organized into branches or units (*jops*) of between thirty to fifty believers. The foundation date of the movement, 5 April, and the dates of the ordination of the leaders are kept as holy days. Services, as in Catholicism and other Christian denominations, were held on Sundays.

Amid strong opposition, at first from Confucian scholars and later from the government, the founder began spreading his message of the Eastern or Heavenly Way as opposed to the Western (Catholic Way), and predicting with the help of the Ch'amwisol – The Theory of Interpretation of Divinations – that the ruling Yi dynasty, after 500 years in power, would fall, and this happened to be in 1892. The government became increasingly hostile to what it considered to be 'subversive' teachings and in 1864 Ch'oe Che-u was executed and his followers either exiled or imprisoned.

Tonghak's core idea that all individuals possessed a God-like nature – or the doctrine that humans and God are one but different (*In Nae Chon*) – and were, therefore, equal in dignity and worth, had obvious revolutionary implications. It developed in followers the strong belief that injustice and inequality could and would be eradicated and that those responsible – in this case the ruling Yi dynasty – for the oppression that existed in Korea would be overthrown and punished. An invading force, it was predicted would destroy the oppressive old order and Tonghak members by the use of incantations and magical means would escape and as immortal beings would enjoy everlasting bliss in an earthly paradise (*Chisang Chonguk*).

A militant millenarian movement Tonghak, under the leadership of Chou Pong-jun, successor to Ch'oe Che-u, who enjoyed widespread support among the heavily taxed peasants, itself mounted a rebellion against the government to eradicate injustice and inequality. This was quashed but only with the assistance of Japanese and Chinese forces.

Though greatly reduced in numbers and forced to work underground Tonghak continued its campaigns against corruption and injustice and against foreign influence, and this resulted in further arrests, executions, and the exiling of leaders and members.

The outcome of such forceful repression was a change of name from Tonghak to Ch'ondogyo in 1904, principally for the purpose of convincing the government that it was now a nonpolitical, purely religious body. Its revised list of core beliefs, eight in all, included the belief that God and humanity were one, that mind and matter form a unity and the belief in the transmigration of the spirit. This new found religious orientation lasted for only a short time as political activities recommenced with the occupation of Korea by the Japanese in 1910. Tonghak/Ch'ondogyo became a resistance movement working for Korean independence underground against the Japanese occupation (1910–47). Though its headquarters are in Seoul, capital of South Korea, where it is estimated to have over one million members, Tonghak/Ch'ondogyo also has an estimated two million members in North Korea.

There are several interesting parallels between Tonghak/Ch'ondogyo beliefs and the **Unification Church**, and **Won Buddhism**.

Further reading

Grayson, J. H. (1989) *Korea: A Religious History*, Oxford: Oxford University Press.
Harvey, P. (1990) *An Introduction to Buddhism. Teachings, History and Practices*, Oxford: Oxford University Press.

PETER B. CLARKE

CHAOS MAGICK

Chaos Magick could be described as the union of traditional occult ideas (see **Esoteric Movements**) with applied postmodernism. Its most commonly quoted dictum is 'Nothing is True. Everything is Permitted.' As with Aleister Crowley's oft-quoted 'Do as thou wilt shall be the whole of the law' (borrowed from François Rabelais) this is easily misunderstood to be a recipe for hedonism and self-indulgence. With Crowley the caveat 'Love is the Law, Love under Will' clarifies the meaning. Wiccans and other Pagans usually preface Crowley's words with 'An [If] it hurt none …'. Chaos magicians make it clear that their own freedom of action must not be at the expense of anyone else's.

Chaos Magick is the creation of two magicians, Peter J. Carroll and Ray Sherwin, though Carroll is seen as its main theorist, with his books *Liber Null & Psychonaut*, *Liber Chaos*, and *Psybermagick*. Carroll and Sherwin were the founders in 1976 of the Illuminates of Thanateros (IOT), a magickal order for Chaos magicians, which has temples in the USA, UK, Australia, and several European countries.

Some Chaos magicians prefer the term Results Magic; they say that certain techniques produce magical results regardless of the belief system in which they are practised. They therefore encourage the use of anything and everything that is effective from all magical traditions. They are also happy to use popular culture, including science fiction and fantasy; some Chaos magicians, for example, work with the 'powers' in H. P. Lovecraft's fictional Cthulhu mythos. Their point is that all the great traditional magical systems were invented at some point; rather than slavishly following a ritual created by another magician little more than a century ago, as do many modern groups with a legacy in the **Hermetic Order of the Golden Dawn**, it makes more sense to create a ritual using symbolism that is relevant today, and which is personally significant to the magician. Carroll, who is a physicist, writes that 'It is techniques and intention that are important in successful magic.'

Chaos magicians say that extreme states of consciousness, which can be brought about by drumming, dancing, chanting, or other ritual activities, sometimes lead to para-psychological events. They make a conscious effort to harness these states to produce controlled results – hence the term Results Magic.

There is no creed in Chaos Magick, no set of beliefs which all must follow; such would be against the very ethos of Chaos Magick theory. It has been described as hands-on practical magic without religion. Many Chaos magicians have a grounding in Crowley; others come from a Wiccan background, or other areas of Paganism or the Occult. When practising Chaos Magick they will use those aspects of whatever system they have chosen to work in, that they have found to work, and discard those that don't.

One major influence on many Chaos magicians is the occult artist Austin Osman Spare (1886–1956), who did artwork for Crowley's magazine *The Equinox*, and who was also associated at various times with the occultist Kenneth Grant and the founder of modern Wicca, Gerald Gardner. Spare's philosophy and practices were a major influence on Carroll and Sherwin.

Further reading

Rabinovitch, Shelley and Lewis, James (2002) *The Encyclopedia of Modern Witchcraft and Neo-Paganism*, New York: Citadel Press.

DAVID V. BARRETT

CHARISMATIC MOVEMENTS

Movements that have emphasized the 'charismata' (the spiritual 'gifts' of healing, prophecy, glossolalia, interpretation of tongues, and words of wisdom) are to be found littered throughout the history of the Christian church and have frequently brought controversy regarding their authenticity and theological acceptability. More often than not, such movements are associated with renewal and sometimes sectarianism. Hence, the display of the charismata has been held by those involved (for example, in early Pentecostalism) as the true signs of the 'born again' believer and has separated the self-designated spiritual 'elite' from the worldliness of the established churches. Pre-dating Pentecostalism were Quakerism, Methodism, and the Holiness movements – all of which were identified with pietism, sectarianism, renewal, and evidence of the charismata.

The twentieth-century charismatic movement

The matter of the charismata has long been a major source of division between Christians who subscribe to the view that the charismata are 'for today', and those who hold the cessationist position – that the 'gifts' died out with the Apostolic age and were merely part of the 'signs and wonders' of the first-century church which legitimated and helped proselytize the gospel message. It was amidst such controversy that the so-called Charismatic Movement of the mid-twentieth century emerged.

The legendary beginnings of the Charismatic Movement (otherwise known as neo-Pentecostalism) are frequently traced to Episcopalian circles in the early 1960s with outbreaks of tongue-speaking in Van Nuys, California, and the Church of the Redeemer, Houston,

Texas. From these places of renewal, the identifiable features of the Charismatic Movement passed to Europe and elsewhere. However, a more reductionist account would identify the roots of the movement in the interaction between a number of major Pentecostal organizations and independent ministries on the one hand, and several leaders of the major mainline denominations on the other. Despite the diverse origins, what was designated 'charismatic renewal' was experienced in most strands of Christianity both sides of the Atlantic. The movement united the various Protestant denominations, and Roman Catholic and Orthodox Christians 'in the Spirit'. In addition, a parallel development occurred, perhaps even earlier, outside of the established denominations. This was the growth of the so-called **House Church Movement** which (in the case of Britain) had beginnings in Brethren circles and independent fellowships – attracting some Christians away from their denominational allegiances. Such a movement also had its counterparts elsewhere, most notably in the USA and South Africa.

Explaining the rise of the Charismatic Movement

There are various ways by which the broad Charismatic Movement can be accounted for. One is to interpret it as a periodic renewal movement within the Christian church. Hence, the emergence of such a movement in the 1960s was against a background of declining church attendance and membership. It essentially amounted to an attempt to break through tradition and ritualized and routinized procedures within the churches by rediscovering the spiritual experience of early Christianity in all its fullness. The denominational unity did not, however, extend to an agreement on moral and social issues and Biblical liberalism since charismatics have often proved ambivalent and inconsistent in these matters. For that reason, as well as an ecumenical stance and sometimes excessive emotionalism, it is difficult to regard the Charismatic Movement as fundamentalist (see **fundamentalism**) in the conventional meaning of the term.

An alternative way of viewing the Charismatic Movement is to designate it one of a number of **New Religious Movement**s arising in the 1960s, including those based on Eastern mysticism or more syncretic forms such as the Unification Church (see **Unification Church/ Moonies**). Like other NRMs, the Charismatic Movement arose to respond to unique spiritual needs; placing an emphasis on enthusiasm and emotionalism, collectivity, and an attempt to build its version of the Kingdom of God on earth. At the same time, such movements appealed to a largely middle-class clientele with an emphasis on healing and human potential albeit in a spiritual guise.

'Streams' within Charismatic renewal

Half a century of the Charismatic Movement has seen far-reaching transformations. While the movement in Western societies may have been in decline for some time, its international appeal continues unabated. There is good evidence that it peaked in the established churches in the mid-1970s, with the house churches reaching their apogee a decade latter. Since that time the movement has splintered and undergone a significant metamorphosis. In the mainline churches it has lost its exclusivism, while the insistence of speaking in tongues for all believers is no longer an imperative. However, the diluted teachings and culture are now discernible in many denominational churches through a joyous 'sing along' culture and theological emphasis on the Holy Spirit.

In the West, the movement has fragmented into discernible streams, largely outside of the denominations but sometimes influencing them. This includes the Vineyard Movement (see **vineyard ministries**) whose significance in the 1980s was a temporary preoccupation with 'signs and wonders' that enhanced the emphasis on healing and prophecy, all of which appeared to climax with the so-called 'Toronto Blessing' in the mid-1990s. Other important strands of the Charismatic Movement in the West that have come to have international repercussions are the Prosperity Gospel (see **prosperity theology**), Restorationism, the Prophetic Movement, the Third Wave Movement, a range of new black neo-Pentecostal churches (see **Black Holiness–Pentecostal Movement**), and the Alpha course programme.

The global significance of the Charismatic Movement

While the Charismatic Movement in the West has dampened down, its worldwide influence has continued unabated, with the total number of Charismatics and Pentecostals globally being in the region of three billion. Its emotional appeal, alongside a flexible theology, has ensured its formidable growth as the largest and fastest spreading expression of Christianity. Among those parts of the world where the Charismatic Movement has impacted are Latin America, Africa and the Pacific Rim. While recognizable in terms of core dogma, the expressions of the movement in very different social and cultural contexts in many ways marks a radical departure from that which began in the West. Thus, in Latin America an attractive articulation of the Charismatic Movement has spread rapidly at a time when traditional Catholicism and the more 'liberal' denominations have declined. In Africa, the movement has been extended by North American, European, and indigenous revivalists. On the Pacific Rim the movement has achieved growth through a mixture of the Prosperity Gospel and indigenous animism. The success of the broad Charismatic Movement in all these parts of the world, as in the West, has been its successful enculturation to diverse social environments, and its competitive edge in a 'free spiritual marketplace' in providing spiritual, material, and psychological benefits not just for the impoverished masses, but all sections of society.

Further reading

Cox, H. (1995) *Fire From Heaven*, Reading, MA: Addison-Wesley.
Martin, D. (1990) *Tongues of Fire*, Oxford: Blackwell.
Walker, A. (1985) *Restoring the Kingdom*, London: Hodder and Stoughton.

STEPHEN HUNT

CHERUBIM AND SERAPHIM CHURCHES

Beginning and growth

The Cherubim and Seraphim churches cover a variety of churches that traced their origin to the Aladura movement of the early twentieth century based in Lagos and led by Moses Orimolade (see **Orimolade, Moses**) and Christiana Abiodun Emanuel (nee Akinsowon) (see **Akinsowon, Christiana Abiodun (Mrs Captain)**). The churches' strong emphasis on prophetism, dreams, spirit possession, and healing were significant. Likewise, the experience of Abiodun and other women who functioned as founders, visionaries, and healers created a favourable situation for women's empowerment, and thus stimulated remarkable social and religious transformation in Nigeria.

The leader of the aladura or praying churches, Moses Orimolade was born about 1879 and baptized into the Anglican Church sometime in the 1890s. In 1919 he embarked on itinerant preaching in the interior of the country, and in July 1924 he arrived in the coastal city of Lagos. His activities centred on preaching against idolatry and praying for people with various needs.

In June 1925, a teenage girl, Abiodun Akinsowon went into a prolonged trance after witnessing an annual Roman Catholic carnival in Lagos. Confused about Abiodun's state and unable to get help from the vicar of the Anglican Church, her guardians summoned Orimolade for help. After Orimolade had prayed, Abiodun regained consciousness, and then narrated her strange experiences in the angelic heavens. Abiodun joined Orimolade and both continued to pray for enquirers and people with various needs. An interdenominational group formed from these enquirers was named *Egbe Serafu* (the Seraphim Society) on 9 September 1925. Another vision some months later modified the name to Cherubim and Seraphim (C&S). While Orimolade was the leader of the group conducting prayers and effecting healing, Christiana assisted as the visioner and preacher.

Early in 1926, Orimolade organized some active members into a Praying Band to assist him in praying for people, and to visit homes to pray for people without collecting or accepting any fees. Within two years, the group had achieved considerable popularity partly because of its colourful anniversary processions and the wearing of white robes, which ultimately became its uniform.

The commitment of members to prayers and chastity, and their denunciation of idolatry won the admiration of ministers from the mainline Protestant churches, where most of the early members had come from. However, opposition from the Anglican Church in particular later arose as a result of the veneration of angels and the devotion to Orimolade.

Early spread in Lagos was through personal contacts with Orimolade or Christiana. In early 1927, Christiana and her supporters embarked on evangelistic tours, which took them to various towns and cities in southwestern Nigeria including Abeokuta, Ibadan, Ile-Ife, Ilesa, Ijebu-Ode, and Ondo, where C&S branches were established. In subsequent years, other groups of evangelists were sent to the interior to strengthen existing branches and to establish new ones. As the membership increased, the group became formalized, and by 1928 the leaders had severed their Anglican connections.

Secessions and proliferation of C&S

Prophetism and charisma have largely determined the leadership. Without any formal training for the ministry, numerous prophets emerged claiming different kinds of spiritual authority. The first schism occurred when supporters of both Orimolade and Abiodun magnified the personality differences and suspicion existing between the old and illiterate Orimolade and the young, beautiful, educated Abiodun. In March 1929, the split was formalized when Orimolade wrote Abiodun asking her to go independent so that a peaceful atmosphere could prevail. Abiodun named her group Cherubim and Seraphim Society, while Orimolade's group was named the

Eternal Sacred Order of the Cherubim and Seraphim.

In 1930, Ezekiel Davies, the trusted leader of the Praying Band, broke away from Abiodun to establish the Praying Band of the Cherubim and Seraphim. In 1931, after C&S churches in seven important towns in the interior that were neutral to the crisis failed to bring about reconciliation in Lagos, they constituted themselves independently as the Western Conference of the Cherubim and Seraphim. Another secession occurred in 1932 when the Holy Flock of Christ seceded from the Praying Band, and shortly after Orimolade's death in October 1933, there was a further split over succession disputes among his followers. Splintering continued and by 1934 six independent groups had emerged; by 1968 these had increased to fourteen in Lagos alone. There also existed hundreds of prophets establishing C&S churches unaffiliated to any group.

Doctrinal emphases and practices

Among the core doctrinal emphases is the belief in the mediatory power of angels. This is evident from the outset in the choice of the name Cherubim and Seraphim, angels that surround the throne of God. The society also chose four angels – Michael, Gabriel, Uriel, and Raphael, rather than humans, as patrons. C&S further believes that individuals have guardian angels that provide them with spiritual assistance.

There is a strong belief in the existence of evil spiritual forces such as witches, wizards, and enemies who afflict people with illnesses and misfortunes. Hence, C&S's obsession with spiritual power and **healing** to counteract the activities of these satanic agents. Healing is largely carried out through prayers, fasting or the use of 'healing rituals' such as bathing in streams or the symbolic use of water, candles, and palm fronds. The church prohibits consultation with traditional diviner-healers, but allows the use of Western medicine.

Visions and dreams are important because most prophets centred their call and activities on these phenomena. Dreams reflect African traditional belief about communication with the supernatural realm. Members attach meaning to dreams and regularly consult prophets for the interpretation of these. Those possessed by the Holy Spirit can enter trance for several days during which they can have visionary experiences of past, present and future events.

Candles and incense feature in worship and they possess symbolic significance as representing divine power. The church premises are sacred places and shoes and menstruating women are excluded from such premises. Certain hilltops are also regarded as sacred, and it is common for prophets to hold special prayer sessions in these locations. Ecstatic spiritual experience, prolonged enthusiastic services full of singing and dancing, while reflecting the indigenous African pattern of worship, are also part of their Pentecostal features.

Conclusion

In an attempt at unifying all C&S factions in 1986 Captain Abiodun Emanuel, then the only living founder, was installed as the movement's supreme head worldwide. Though the membership was predominantly Yoruba in the early years of the movement, Cherubim and Seraphim is now an international movement.

Further reading

Omoyajowo, J. A. (1982) *Cherubim and Seraphim: The History of an African Independent Church*, New York: NOK Publishers International Ltd.

Peel, J. D. Y. (1968) *Aladura: A Religious Movement Among the Yoruba*, London: Oxford University Press.

MATTHEWS A. OJO

CH'I KUNG (QIGONG)

Ch'i kung (translated as 'energy work') is the name given to a number of meditative breathing and stretching exercises originating in China. Often categorized as a Chinese form of **Yoga**, *ch'i kung* systems share with martial arts such as *T'ai Chi Ch'uan* the aim of developing the fundamental energy (*ch'i*) of humans for physical and spiritual enhancement, or generating 'inner power' (*nei kung*). Exercises are based on the imitation of animal movements or natural processes and include simple standing postures and movement sequences, as well as particular breathing techniques.

The earliest archaeological evidence of *ch'i kung* practices dates to the fifth century BCE; a detailed manuscript from the second century BCE outlines various postures and designated therapeutic effects. *Ch'i kung* featured strongly in the theory and practice of Traditional Chinese Medicine, and was an integral element in the meditative rituals of religious Taoism. Five main schools of *ch'i kung* are recognized in China: Confucian, Taoist, Buddhist, medical, and martial.

Ch'i kung was driven underground during the Cultural Revolution (1966–69), but reappeared during the later twentieth century, for example as a meditative technique in the spiritual movement **Falun Gong**. However, it is chiefly influential as a health technique, and the late twentieth century saw the reintroduction of *ch'i kung* to many clinics and hospitals in China. In addition, the study of *ch'i kung* and the production of scientific evidence promoting its health effects became an ongoing project. A number of contested studies emerged during the 1990s, attesting to both the effects of personal *ch'i kung* practice, and instances of **Healing** produced by *ch'i* emitted from the hands of a master practitioner.

In the West, *ch'i kung* was little known until the 1980s, and experienced a surge of growth during the 1990s. A number of styles of *ch'i kung* are practised in Europe, with most practitioners adopting the art as a preventative holistic health tool (see **Holistic Health Movement**) and a remedy for a number of ailments. Its appeal is also as a meditative or spiritual technique, in line with the broader uptake of Asian meditative disciplines since the 1960s (see **Easternization**).

Further reading

Zixin, Lin (2000) *Ziqong: Chinese Medicine or Pseudoscience?* New York: Prometheus Books.

ALEXANDRA RYAN

CHINMOY, SRI

Chinmoy Kumar Ghose was born in East Bengal in 1931. At the age of twelve, his parents died, and he moved into the Sri Aurobindo (see **Aurobindo, Sri**) ashram in Pondicherry, where he lived for the next twenty years. Here he learned music, poetry, meditation and philosophy, and underwent various transformative experiences. In 1964 he moved to New York to 'share his inner wealth with sincere seekers' – one of the first Asian **Guru**s to move to the West in modern times.

Chinmoy sees 'aspiration of the heart towards higher realities and spirituality' as the primary driving force in religious, cultural, scientific, and even sporting fields. He teaches that people should 'live from the heart' in order to succeed in these fields and attain a balance between spiritual and daily life. World peace is an important aspiration. Chinmoy's philosophy is immanentist, a version of the 'god within', which has made it popular in New Age circles (see **New Age Movement**). However, it is less world-accepting than most Eastern-based movements popular in the West. Purity is paramount: the body and its instincts are considered impure, while the heart and soul are pure. Nevertheless, the body is essential to manifest the soul's divinity. This is similar to the Christian Manichean position (declared a heresy), and to another Westernized Hindu movement, the **Brahma Kumaris**. However, despite the emphasis on purity, there have been allegations of sexual abuse and other misconduct. However, he does not charge money for his lectures and concerts.

Chinmoy's headquarters are in New York, and there are centres in sixty countries. The movement has around 1,500 members and is actively proselytizing. For example, there used to be an advertising campaign on London buses and trains, and opportunities for putting up plaques in Chinmoy's name are actively pursued.

ELIZABETH PUTTICK

CHOPRA, DEEPAK

Deepak Chopra was born in India *c.* 1947. Although brought up as a Hindu at home, he was educated at a Catholic school run by Irish missionaries. His father was a prominent cardiologist in India, and the young Chopra went into medicine himself. He graduated from medical school in 1968, and travelled to the United States in 1970 where he specialized in endocrinology. He had a successful career, working very hard and acquiring many patients, but eventually becoming very stressed. This led to him consulting with a leading ayurvedic practitioner in 1981. Ayurveda is the ancient Indian holistic medical system, based on herbalism, astrology and diverse spiritual practices particularly yoga. Chopra had a strong experience with the treatment, which in the USA was largely promoted by the followers of **Transcendental Meditation** (TM).

Chopra was diagnosed as suffering from the stresses and strains of Western life, and was advised to take up meditation and change his diet, amongst other things, which he did. He met the guru Maharishi in 1984, and became a leading figure in the TM movement in the West until 1990, when he left. Chopra complained of 'being used' by some senior members of the movement as a figurehead, against his wishes. Nevertheless, he maintained his belief in the importance and effectiveness of ayurvedic medicine, despite scepticism from some of his medical colleagues, and he founded several institutes of ayurveda in the US, including one in San Francisco for the treatment of AIDS patients. He also retained a firm belief in the therapeutic value of meditation.

Chopra then became an outspoken critic of both Western medicine and the Western way of life. Like other practitioners in the **Holistic Health Movement**, he disapproved of the preoccupation of Western medicine with using powerful drugs to change the manifestations of an illness, without looking into root causes. He saw the problems of Western lifestyle as stemming from its high stress levels, the dominance of material goals over spiritual ones, and the abuse of the mind and body by poor diet and low-grade cultural input. Chopra's stated mission is 'bridging the technological miracles of the West with the wisdom of the East'. His approach is extremely successful, and he is widely regarded as a guru figure. Of his many books, the best known is 'The Seven Spiritual Laws of Success', which presents his ideas as a manual for self-development.

The 'brand name' for Chopra's work is Quantum Healing. He argues, for example, that spontaneous remissions of cancer in advanced sufferers can be explained best in quantum terms, using the power of the mind, and correcting wrong ideas. In his own words, taken from an interview:

> Quantum healing is healing the body-mind from a quantum level. That means from a level which is not manifest at a sensory level. Our bodies ultimately are fields of information, intelligence and energy. Quantum healing involves a shift in the fields of energy information, so as to bring about a correction in an idea that has gone wrong. So quantum healing involves healing one mode of consciousness, mind, to bring about changes in another mode of consciousness, body.

The creative power of consciousness in healing is seen as a non-dualistic approach, the 'bodymind' described above. Mind produces neuro-chemical brain events, which then transmit themselves to many other areas of the body, causing disease and discomfort. This in turns feeds back via the neuro-chemical system to the brain. Scientific support for this approach came from the work of Candace Pert, who demonstrated a link between brain and body through neuropeptides during the 1990s. This work was popularized by her in a best-selling book *The Molecules of Emotion* (1998), which was eagerly embraced by many prominent figures in the **New Age Movement**. Pert makes several (favourable) references to Chopra in her book. Of particular note is her account of the resistance and even hostility of many in the medical profession towards this new understanding, which Chopra himself must have encountered frequently.

Chopra runs the 'Center For Well-Being' in La Jolla, California, with its Director David Simon MD. Its stated aim is to integrate the best of Western medicine with natural healing traditions. He has written over twenty books, produced many audio and visual tapes, and gives talks to formal and informal events all over the world.

Further reading

Chopra, D., (1996) *The Seven Spiritual Laws of Success*, London: Bantam.
Pert, C. (Foreword by Deepak Chopra) (1998) *The Molecules of Emotion*, London: Simon & Schuster.

ELIZABETH PUTTICK

CHRIST APOSTOLIC CHURCH

Christ Apostolic Church which typically fused Pentecostal and African features in its doctrines and therapeutic practices was the largest African indigenous Church in Nigeria until the 1970s.

Essentially, the **Faith Tabernacle Church** (FTC) in Nigeria metamorphosed into the Christ Apostolic Church (CAC). The FTC affiliated with the British Apostolic Church (BAC) in 1931. As a result, seven Nigerian FTC pastors were made to undergo a second ordination as pastors and prophets during the visit of three British Apostolic leaders in 1931. Subsequently, the FTCs adopted the name Apostolic Church. Furthermore, George Perfect and Idris Vaughan arrived in Nigeria as resident missionary pastors of the BAC in July 1932. Their presence enhanced the relations between the British colonial authorities and the CAC and thereby increased the fortunes of the CAC. For instance pastor Babalola, who had been imprisoned by the British authorities, was released and was free to continue his evangelistic activities;

the church held vibrant evangelistic campaigns which enabled it to spread fast and establish several schools.

About six years after the affiliation, a number of crises which were mainly financial, administrative and doctrinal ensued which divided the local church leaders as well as the relations between the CAC and the BAC resident missionaries. The predominant factor was the accusation levelled against the BAC missionaries for taking drugs, particularly, quinine to prevent malaria fever. Since the CAC emphasized only divine healing, the action of the BAC missionaries was interpreted by some key leaders of the CAC, such as Babalola, as doctrinal infidelity. Consequently, such leaders and their followers (who formed the majority) broke away to form the Nigerian Apostolic Church (NAC) in 1939 while the others who sympathized with the missionaries remained with them under the name The Apostolic Church (TAC).

The evangelistic disposition of the NAC took it outside the bounds of Nigeria, particularly to Ghana. As a result, the nomenclature NAC which was seen as too nationalistic was changed, first to United Apostolic Church (UAC) in 1940 and later to Christ Apostolic Church (CAC) in 1941 when it was realized that the former initials were used by a major trading company.

As a typical African Pentecostal church, the bedrock of CAC is prayer, accompanied by fasting. The church believes all problems can be solved through prayer. It encourages the formation of 'Prayer Warrior' teams whose ministry is to pray fervently for the work of the church and for members of the church. The church encourages its members to withdraw to some designated hills and mountains (holy/sacred places) to pray and meditate. Such places sometimes have resident pastors or prophets/prophetesses who give pastoral assistance to those who patronize them. The CAC stresses the gifts of the Holy Spirit, particularly, the gifts of healing, and attaches great importance to dreams and visions. Resorting to divine healing without the use of medicine (traditional or Western orthodox) was strictly prescribed for members who were sick. However, since the 1970s this rule has been relaxed.

The CAC emphasizes a kind of holiness ethics which can be quite rigorous. It stresses monogamy and advocates that marriages should be blessed by the church. Divorce is not permitted except on the grounds of adultery and re-marriage of divorced members is disallowed. The church is strict on dress code for is female members and opposes the use of make-up and jewellery.

The CAC has lively evangelistic groups and activities. Such groups have contributed immensely to the numerical growth of the church and the establishment of branches of the church both in Nigeria and elsewhere including the Western world. A typical example of such groups is the World Soul Winning Evangelistic Ministry (WOSEM), which was established in 1974 and led by Timothy Obadare, a blind evangelist. The evangelistic associations are also often accompanied by Gospel music groups in their enterprises.

The CAC is administered by a leadership made up of the following in ascending order: Deacons, Elders, Teachers, Pastors, Evangelists, Prophets and Apostles. There is a central administration that posts pastors to the various assemblies. Individual assemblies of the church which enjoy a fair degree of autonomy send part of their tithes and offerings to the central administration.

The CAC is a typical African initiative in Christianity which provides a logical connection between traditional African and Christian spiritualities.

Further reading

Adegboyea, S. G. (1978) *Short History of the Apostolic Church of Nigeria*, Ibadan: Rosprint Industrial Press, Ltd.

Ayegboyin, D. and Ademola, I. (1997), *African Indigenous Churches*, Lagos: Greater Heights Publications.

Oshun, C. O. (1983) 'The Pentecostal Perspective of the Christ Apostolic Church', *Orita* 2(15), 105–14.

CEPHAS N. OMENYO

CHRISTAQUARIANS

Christaquarian is an alternative term for New Age Christian or Christian New Age and was first used in Kemp (2003). Although the term is therefore a neologism which is not used by practitioners themselves, the phenomenon to which it refers has been discernible at least since the 1960s and has earlier historical roots. This entry briefly summarizes typical Christaquarian beliefs, lists individuals, organizations and texts influential among them and considers some of the theoretical questions the term raises.

New Age (see **New Age Movement**), also known as the Age of Aquarius, is a New Socio-Religious Movement which emerged from the general cultic milieu as a distinct movement in its own right in the last three or four decades of the twentieth century. Typical examples of New Agers include Shirley MacLaine and David Spangler (see **Spangler, David**), and beliefs and practices include the healing power of crystals, reflexology, and meditation.

Mainstream Christianity has typically been hostile to the New Age, especially its evangelical or fundamentalist wings (see Saliba 1999). A number of Christian denominations have issued official reports on the New Age which generally rely on secondary sources and tend to warn Christians against it. The Christaquarian approach to the New Age is a minority approach but raises many interesting theological and sociological questions.

In the spirit of New Age anti-authoritarianism, Christaquarians are averse to hierarchical church structures and the imposition of creeds. It is therefore difficult to point to any representative leaders, organizations or definitive statements of belief.

Rev. Adrian B Smith (b. 1930) has discussed a New Age approach to Christianity in his many publications, including *A New Framework for Christian Belief* (Smith 2002), which has been used by a number of Christaquarian study groups. The themes covered include: a suggestion that the Universe is the primary source of revelation, which is limited by human experience and ongoing in nature; the idea that the Bible needs to be interpreted afresh by each age; that our perception of God is always evolving; that Jesus was limited by his humanity; and that other religions are paths to God. There is thus little in this exposition of Christaquarianism that cannot be found in earlier theological thought. What differs is that these beliefs are held together with an openness to other New Age ideas and practices.

Other Christians who take a New Age approach, and may therefore be considered Christaquarians even if they use neither of these terms themselves, include: **Matthew Fox** (b. 1940), who teaches an affirmative **Creation Spirituality**; Canon Peter Spink (b. *c.* 1930), of Winford Manor Retreat, formerly Omega Trust; Fr Diarmuid Ó'Murchú (b. 1952), influenced by Creation Spirituality and the Goddess movement; Paulo Coelho (b. 1947), the bestselling author; Dom Laurence Freeman (b. 1951), who teaches in the tradition of the Benedictine John Main's (1926–82) Christian Meditation; and William Johnston (b. 1925), who speaks about a 'new mysticism' or 'new religious consciousness'.

Institutions which have taken a New Age approach to Christianity include The Omega Order (now disbanded) of Canon Spink; the network Christians Awakening to a New Awareness (CANA), formerly known as Christians Awakening to a New Age (see Kemp 2003); the Quaker Universalist Group; the New Age Unitarian Network and the Unitarian Pagan Network, now known as the Unitarian Earth Spirit Network (UESN); and a number of Christian retreat centres. Again, not all these groups use the term 'New Age' to describe themselves.

Christaquarians typically lay claim to a historical tradition of esoteric and sometimes heretical Christianity, including the thought of: the Essenes, the Gnostics, Neoplatonists, Christian Qabbalah, the Rhineland Mystics, the Celtic tradition, Jacob Boehme, **Emanuel Swedenborg**, William Blake, **Theosophy**, **Anthroposophy**, the Arcane School, **Christian Science**, **New Thought**, **Carl Jung**, Edgar Cayce, **Dion Fortune** and **Pierre Teilhard de Chardin**. Obviously, such a diverse array of thinkers does not constitute a tangible historical succession except in terms of the history of ideas and similarities of thought.

Texts that are typically utilized by Christaquarians, although not necessarily in themselves explicitly either Christian or New Age, include: Helen Schucman's *A Course in Miracles* (1975); Neale Donald Walsch's *Conversations with God* series (1995, 1997, 1998); **David Spangler**'s *The Christ Experience and the New Age* (1967); and Levi Dowling's *The Aquarian Gospel of Jesus the Christ* (1907).

The notion of Christaquarians raises a number of theoretical considerations, both theological and sociological. Theologically, New Age beliefs tend to confront traditional Christian beliefs in a way that is difficult to reconcile. For example, New Age is often monist, while Christianity is almost exclusively dualist in its metaphysics. Similarly, it is often claimed that New Age is typically pantheist, while Christianity has almost without exception avoided such a view of God, even in its panentheist form exemplified by Matthew Fox. As a final example, the general New Age acceptance of reincarnation is difficult to reconcile with the central Christian beliefs in the resurrection of the body and life everlasting.

Sociologically, it is interesting to examine how such theological paradoxes are accommodated. Festinger's notion of 'cognitive dissonance', although his research methods have since been questioned, seems appropriate to explain how two (or more) apparently incompatible beliefs can be held by one individual at the same time. The question of imputing a label, such as Christaquarian, on to individuals who do not use that label themselves and may even be strongly against its application, is a problem that arises in studies of the New Age in general and in studies of other religious and social movements. As a third example of a sociological question raised by the term, we may consider its structural nature: is Christaquarianism a **New Religious Movement**, a sect, a denomination, a church, or can any other typology be applied, such as New Socio-Religious Movement? Further study of New Age Christianity is required before these and other questions can be answered.

Further reading

Dowling, L. (1972) *The Aquarian Gospel of Jesus the Christ* [1907], Camarillo, CA: DeVorss Publications.

Kemp, D. (2003) *The Christaquarians? A Sociology of Christians in the New Age*, London: Kempress (www.Christaquarian. net).

Kemp, D. (2004), *A New Age Christian Theology*, New Alresford: John Hunt Publishing.

Saliba, J. A. (1999) *Christian Responses to the New Age Movement: A Critical Assessment*, London: Geoffrey Chapman.

Smith, A. B (2002) *A New Framework for Christian Belief*, New Alresford: John Hunt Publishing.

Walsch, N. D. (1995, 1997, 1998) *Conversations with God* (series), Charlottesville, VA: Hampton Roads.

DAREN KEMP

CHRISTIAN CONGREGATION

The *Congregação Cristã* (henceforth Christian Congregation) is Brazil's oldest pentecostal church. The founder Luigi Francescon was an Italian emigrant to Chicago. He never lived in Brazil, but made eleven visits between 1910 and 1948. From a poor Catholic family in Údine, Francescon became a mosaicist in Chicago. He converted to Presbyterianism and later to a holiness church, before discovering pentecostalism (see **Azusa Street Revival**) in 1907. His missionary vocation came in a prophecy to evangelize the Italian world. After visiting Italian communities in the United States, he and a colleague went to Argentina and, in March 1910, to Brazil. Beginnings in São Paulo were not promising, and the first conversions were among Italians in the interior of Paraná state. Returning to São Paulo, Francescon preached in Italian at a Presbyterian Church in a heavily Italian working-class district, provoking a schism. The Christian Congregation (CC) was established with twenty members, of Presbyterian, Methodist, Baptist, and Catholic origin.

Francescon soon left Brazil, but through frequent visits he became the unifying point of the church. His brief history of the origins, written in 1942, is the only narrative text which the strongly oral culture of the CC has permitted. Francescon's survival for another 54 years were fundamental to the embedding of a church based on an oral and familial tradition.

The CC began totally Italian and spread into immigrant regions of São Paulo state. But it soon felt the need to guarantee survival by a transition to Portuguese, by means of a 'revelation' to the elders in 1935.

The 2000 census reported two-and-a-half million members of the CC in Brazil, making it the second largest non-Catholic church. It is still heavily concentrated in São Paulo and Paraná. It is overwhelmingly a rural and small town church, and whiter than most pentecostal groups. By 2000 it had spread to over thirty countries, being strong amongst the Brazilian diaspora (US, Paraguay, Japan) and in Latin America, Portugal, and Italy.

The CC rejects mass propaganda methods such as radio, television, open-air preaching or literature. Proselytism is exclusively inside the church or by personal contact. A strong belief in predestination undergirds this pattern. The conviction that God will bring in the people he desires to save has an effect on the CC's relationship to modernity, freeing from pressure to adapt methods constantly, in the name of evangelistic efficacy, to social change and technological advance. The price is that the CC grows more in small towns where family contacts still function well.

The CC gives a predominant role to direct inspiration. All church and many personal decisions must be confirmed by revelation. The preacher in a service is never chosen beforehand. All Christian literature is rejected, since culture is useless for faith. But 'prophecies unknown to the Word of God' are rejected, and inspirationism has managed to coexist with community.

Services follow a pietistic style, with emphasis on 'testimonies' and a rather solemn atmosphere. Much of the legalism of other pentecostals is rejected, including teetotalism and tithing. But men and women sit on separate sides in church, the women wearing veils. The CC does not cooperate with other churches. The emphasis on mutual assistance and the work ethic, although advantageous for social mobility, has not caused changes in worship style, behavioural norms or social appeal.

The organizational style of other pentecostal churches is considered human interference in the work of God. Bureaucracy is minimal and there are no pastors, only unpaid elders. Leadership is by seniority rather than by charisma or competence.

The familistic model limits growth in big cities by rejecting entrepreneurial techniques, but it also reduces schisms to a minimum. The absence of a paid pastorate minimizes power struggles by freeing them of careerist and economic elements.

Strong dualism in the form of the other or spiritual realm and the secular realm has protected the CC from the manipulation of religious status for personal and political ends. Extreme 'separation from the world' protects it from the desire for recognition and position.

Leaders of the CC are practically anonymous, but wealthy figures with time to dedicate to the church have been unofficial continuers of Francescon's role.

The CC affirms the duty to vote (compulsory in Brazil) but never indicates candidates. For many years it excommunicated members who stood for public office. An important factor in its apoliticism is rejection of the mass media, so readily associated with politics in Brazil. Its familial organization leaves no space for the political dreams of religious professionals. The operational cost of the church is low, diminishing the need for political contacts, and the dualistic ethos protects it from status anxiety.

Further reading

Martin, D. (1990) *Tongues of Fire*, Oxford: Blackwell.

Freston, Paul (2003) *Evangelicals and Politics in Asia, Africa and Latin America*, Cambridge: Cambridge University Press.

Rolim, Francisco Cartaxo (1990) 'Congregação Cristã no Brasil', in Lilah Ladin (ed.) *Sinais dos Tempos, Diversidade Religiosa no Brasil*, Rio de Janeiro: Instituto de Estudos da Religião, pp. 53–9.

PAUL FRESTON

CHRISTIAN GROWTH MINISTRIES

This Protestant evangelical Christian movement emerged out of the Pentecostalist and Charismatic Movements of the 1960s. The name was adopted in 1969 by four evangelical leaders: Charles Simpson, Bob Mumford, Derek Prince, and Don Basham; they were later joined by Ern Baxter, and collectively became known as the 'Fort Lauderdale Five' or the 'Shepherds of Fort Lauderdale'. These five leaders laid emphasis on Jesus Christ's 'Great Commission' to make disciples of all nations (Matthew 28: 19–20), and in 1970 made a 'covenant' with each other to offer mutual support in advancing Christ's kingdom. 'Covenant' was viewed as a key theme, together with submission, discipline and respect for authority. Spiritual discipline entailed 'discipling' and 'shepherding' – assigning each member to a spiritual supervisor ('shepherd'). The Five resisted setting up a new denomination with a shepherd–disciple structure, perceiving themselves as a trans-denominational, trans-local and trans-national movement. The magazine *New Wine* was the movement's principal vehicle of communication.

In 1973 Simpson and others formed the Gulf Coast Fellowship – a cluster of home churches. In 1976 Simpson moved to Mobile, Alabama, setting up the Covenant Church of Mobile in 1978. Basham, Mumford, and Baxter joined him, and their organization became known as Integrity Communications. Prince withdrew in 1984, and set up his own Derek Prince Ministries, with a particular concern to convert Jews. Mumford currently heads Life Changers, operating worldwide. His son Eric, who appears destined to take over the leadership, has focused particularly on the Ukraine. In 1999 Simpson resigned his duties at the Covenant Church of Mobile, to embark on international mission, and was succeeded by Oliver Heath.

The Christian Growth Movement has been described variously as a new Apostolic reformation, the New Paradigm Churches, and post-denominational Christianity. Whether the ideas are new is debatable; in particular, the CGM owes much to the Latter-Rain Movement, and Baxter previously worked with Latter-Rain leader William Branham. CGM's ideas on discipling have been influential, and were taken up by Promise Keepers and the International Churches of Christ.

Further reading

Prince, D. (1993). *The Spirit-filled Believer's Handbook,* Baldock, Herts: Derek Prince Publications.

GEORGE CHRYSSIDES

CHRISTIAN RESEARCH INSTITUTE

The Christian Research Institute (CRI), an American counter-cult organization, was founded in 1960 by Southern Baptist minister Walter Martin (1928–89), author of *The Kingdom of the Cults*. In some ways it is the most traditional of 'cult-watching' organizations in that its aim is to educate Christians about new religious movements by comparing their beliefs with those of Bible-based Evangelical Christianity, and showing where they have strayed from 'the truth'.

According to the CRI website, www.equip.org, Walter Martin was 'the first evangelical Christian clergy [*sic*] to recognize the threat and opportunity presented to the Christian church by cults and alternative religious systems'. Although his book, which has gone through numerous editions, was one of the most influential in its field, Martin was actually following in the well-trodden footsteps of other Christian writers such as William C. Irvine (*Heresies Exposed*, 1921, originally 1917 as *Timely Warnings*), J. K. van Baalen (*The Chaos of Cults*, 1938), J. Oswald Sanders (*Heresies and Cults*, 1948), and Horton Davies (*Christian Deviations: The Challenge of the Sects*, 1954), amongst others.

The stated mission of CRI today is 'To provide Christians worldwide with carefully researched information and well-reasoned answers that encourage them in their faith and equip them to intelligently represent it to people influenced by ideas and teachings that assault or undermine orthodox, biblical Christianity.'

CRI claims to be 'the largest, most effective apologetics ministry in the world'. Its current president, Hank Hanegraaff, runs a question-and-answer radio programme called *Bible Answer Man*. He has also written numerous books on aspects of Christian belief, against the Mormon Church, and against evolution. In his writings and broadcasts, as well as arguing against both 'pseudo-Christian cults' and non-Evangelical religious scholars, he has been heavily critical of some of the more controversial aspects of Evangelical Christianity, including the Toronto Blessing, faith healing, and deliverance, discipling, Word of Faith preachers such as Kenneth Hagin, Kenneth Copeland, and Oral Roberts, and the practice of setting the date of the End Times. Perhaps because of what some have called Hanegraaff's confrontational style, many CRI articles are responses to critics of CRI.

Further reading

Davies, H. (1954) *Christian Deviations: The Challenge of the Sects*, London: SCM.
Irvine, W. C. (1921) *Heresies Exposed*, New York: Loizeaux Brothers.
Martin, D. (1982) *Kingdom of the Cults*, Minneapolis: Bethany House.
Sanders, J. O. (1971) *Heresies and Cults* [1948], London: Lakeland
van Baalen, J. K. (1938) *The Chaos of Cults*, Grand Rapids, MI: Eerdmans.

DAVID V. BARRETT

CHRISTIAN SCIENCE

Christian Science is one of the half dozen nineteenth-century Christian sects which have survived in some strength into the twenty-first century, though membership appears to be declining.

Christian Science, or the Church of Christ, Scientist, was founded by Mary Baker Eddy (1821–1910) in 1879. (Eddy was her surname from her third marriage in 1877, and to avoid confusion she will be referred to as Eddy throughout.)

Eddy was born to Congregationalist parents in New Hampshire, USA. She was in ill health through the first few decades of her life. In 1862 she was healed of a crippling spinal disease by the mesmerist and faith healer Phineas P. Quimby, who taught that disease is caused by the faulty reasoning of the sufferer. Eddy spent two years lecturing on Quimby's work.

In February 1866, a month after Quimby's death, Eddy slipped on ice and fell badly. Reading her Bible a few days later she noticed the passage in Matthew 9:2–8 where Christ heals 'a man sick of the palsy'. 'The healing Truth dawned upon my sense,' she wrote, 'and the result was that I rose, dressed myself, and ever after was in better health than I had before enjoyed.' She began to formulate her teachings on 'the Christ Science, or divine laws of Life, Truth and Love', and in 1875 she published the first edition of *Science and Health with Key to the Scriptures*, the central text of Christian Science.

The main tenet of Christian Science is that God is Spirit and Truth and Love; anything that is not of spirit and truth and love is therefore not of God; therefore illness, not being of God, is illusory. If we recognize this, we will be healed.

Eddy set up the Christian Science Association in 1876, and founded the Church of Christ, Scientist, in 1879, moving it to Boston, Massachusetts in 1881. She set up the Massachusetts Metaphysical College, where she taught her beliefs and techniques to students from 1881 to 1889. She reorganized her Church in 1892, putting it under the direction of the *Church Manual* which is still in force today. Services today remain the same as a century ago, with set readings from the Bible and *Science and Health*, and no sermon.

From the start Eddy faced the criticism that she had appropriated the teachings of Phineas Quimby, though she denied this, stressing the differences rather than the similarities between

109

them. She also faced other problems. Some of her earliest students and closest colleagues left her organization to set up their own. The most significant of these was Emma Curtis Hopkins (1849–1925), formerly editor of the *Journal of Christian Science*; she left as early as 1885 to found the Emma Hopkins College of Metaphysical Science. Through Hopkins came the synthesis of the teachings of Eddy and Quimby, which became known as the **New Thought** movement; this spawned several Churches, including the Unity School of Christianity founded in 1903 by Charles and Myrtle Fillmore, and the Church of Religious Science, founded in 1948 by Ernest Holmes (1887–1960), author of the classic text in this field, *The Science of Mind* (1926).

The Church of Christ, Scientist, has a number of publications in addition to the well known daily newspaper *The Christian Science Monitor*; these include the weekly *Christian Science Sentinel*, the monthly *Christian Science Journal* and the *Christian Science Quarterly*. All members of the Church are required to buy these, unless this would cause them hardship.

The Church does not issue membership figures, but outside estimates appear to suggest that Church membership is declining quite rapidly, from 268,000 members in the 1930s to 150,000 members in 1992; some estimates in 1997 gave a worldwide membership as low as 100,000. Christian Science practitioners (trained healers) appear to have declined from *c.* 10,000 around 1950 to 2,600–3,000 in the early 1990s (source: http://www.adherents.com).

The declining membership is probably due to a number of factors. One is that spiritual healing, once almost the unique hallmark of Christian Science, is now widely available in many mainstream Christian Churches. Another is that the Church is still very rooted in its nineteenth-century origins, with services still following the exact format laid down by Mrs Eddy. A third is the perceived authoritarianism of the Church's Board, which caused a number of senior members to leave in the 1990s, in addition to a steady drift of ordinary members away from the Church, while still holding to its beliefs. Although numbers are difficult if not impossible to ascertain, one source has suggested that there may be more Christian Scientists outside the Church than within it.

Further reading

Barrett, David V. (2001) *The New Believers*, London: Cassell

DAVID V. BARRETT

CHURCH OF GOD MISSION INTERNATIONAL

The Independent Charismatic church in Nigeria is among the first and most influential new Pentecostal/Charismatic churches in Africa and provided a training base and model for hundreds of independent churches since (especially throughout West Africa). The Church of God Mission International was founded in Nigeria by Benson Idahosa (1938–98) in 1972. Idahosa, who became one of the best-known and first independent 'mega-church' preachers in Africa, attended the Christ for the Nations Institute in 1971, an independent Pentecostal college in Dallas, Texas founded by healing evangelist Gordon Lindsay (1906–73) and continued by his wife Freda (1916–). Idahosa's stay there was short-lived, however, and he returned to Nigeria after three months with an increased 'burden' for his people. He began the first of many mass evangelistic crusades for which he was so well known. He received considerable financial support from well-known independent Pentecostal preachers in the United States, including his mentors Gordon and Freda Lindsay, healing evangelist T. L. Osborne and televangelist Jim Bakker. By 1991 Idahosa had some 300,000 members and a headquarters in Benin City in southern Nigeria. There, a 'Miracle Center' was erected in 1975 with financial assistance from the USA, seating over 10,000. Thousands flocked there every week to receive their own personal miracles.

As part of the Miracle Centre, the church runs the All Nations for Christ Bible Institute, probably the most popular and influential Bible school in West Africa, from where hundreds of preachers fan out into different parts of the region, often to plant new independent Pentecostal churches. Idahosa became a Bishop in 1981 and later took the title Archbishop. He had both formal and unofficial links with other Charismatic churches throughout Africa. Idahosa's first 'crusade' in Accra in 1978 resulted in the subsequent formation of the first independent Charismatic churches there. Bishop Nicholas Duncan-Williams, formerly of the Church of Pentecost, is leader of one of the largest and earliest ones founded in 1980, Christian Action Faith Ministries, and he was trained at Idahosa's Bible Institute. Idahosa has traveled extensively in Africa and overseas, and has worked closely with Reinhard Bonnke, the German Pentecostal evangelist, whose controversial mass 'crusades' in Nigeria have provoked violent opposition from Nigerian Muslims. When Idahosa died suddenly in 1998, his wife, Margaret Idahosa, who had shared ministry and leadership with her husband since the church began, took his place as head and Bishop of the church. The church has declined to some extent since Benson Idahosa's

death in 1998 and has been divided by schisms.

Further reading

Anderson, A. (2001) *African Reformation: African Initiated Christianity in the 20th Century*, Trenton, NJ and Asmara, Eritrea: Africa World Press.

ALLAN ANDERSON

CHURCH OF JESUS CHRIST OF LATTER-DAY SAINTS (MORMONS)

The Church of Jesus Christ of Latter-day Saints (LDS) – the Mormons – was founded in North America in 1830 by six people; by the twenty-first century it numbered approximately eleven million worldwide. Its founder, Joseph Smith Jr (1805–44) received a series of visions. In the First Vision God the Father and his Son appeared in a pillar of light, gave Joseph a sense of the forgiveness of his sins and, in answer to his religious quest, announced that while all contemporary churches were misguided the truth would be revealed in due course. Later, the angel Moroni directed him to hidden records that became The Book of Mormon published in 1830. In two subsequent visions John the Baptist ordained Joseph and his friend Oliver Cowdery into the Aaronic Priesthood and the apostles Peter, James, and John ordained them into the Melchizedek Priesthood. Together these events restored true teachings and rituals that God had removed because of human disobedience.

Joseph called people to repent and gather in North America to await Christ's Second Coming. This Adventist and Millenarian (see **Millenarianism**) outlook reflected religion in Joseph's society. Many joined him: thousands of Europeans made the arduous journey by sea and by land. Joseph gave his closest followers additional distinctive rites including plural marriage or polygamy and rites called endowments that conferred a special status after death as the eternal couple advanced into a kind of god-like state along with their eternally expanding family. Importantly, baptism for the dead gave those who had died before hearing the Christian message the ability to accept it in the afterlife if their descendents performed the key rituals on their behalf in earthly temples. The growth in power of the early Mormons, as converts and migrants gathered in the Eastern States, along with their adoption of polygamy and secret rites caused opposition from other churches and, eventually, from the Federal Government. Joseph was killed while in prison in 1844 (and polygamy outlawed in the 1890s).

After a brief struggle Brigham Young (1801–77) led the majority of grief-stricken Saints west until they came to the Great Salt Lake Valley. There they established themselves, developing distinctive doctrines and practices associated with temples. Salt Lake City serves as the focus for the faith to this day. Some remained behind and formed other smaller groups, the best know coming to be The Reorganized Church of Jesus Christ of Latter Day Saints (RLDS, spelling its name differently from the Latter-day Saints) led by direct descendents of Joseph. At the turn of the twenty-first century the RLDS changed their name to The Community of Christ, reflecting their avoidance of the distinctive LDS doctrines and temple rites and their acceptance of all major points of doctrine concerning God, the Holy Trinity, and salvation, held by mainstream Christianity. This community, like the LDS, believes in continuous revelation through its prophet. One, in 1968, called members to build a new temple at the headquarters' town of Independence, Missouri – a temple that would be open to all and a place of learning and peace. More significant still was the decision to ordain women in 1985. Early in the twenty-first century the LDS emphasized the focus on Christ in its own name but maintained a strong commitment to male-focused priesthoods and to temples as places accessible only to members in good standing and as places existing to further the eternal destiny of families.

New revelations are rare amongst LDS, the most significant of the twentieth century came in 1978 when the ban on ordaining African males was lifted. New revelations appear in The Doctrine and Covenants. Along with The Pearl of Great Price and Book of Mormon these form the standard works of the church.

Organization

The Aaronic Priesthood – divided into deacon, teacher and priest – takes Mormon boys from the age of twelve to eighteen while the Melchizedek Priesthood covers all other worthy males. The Prophet and his Twelve Apostles along with what are called The Seventy are paid leaders of the church. All others are voluntary, unpaid 'laymen'. Geographically the church is divided into stakes and stakes into wards. The Stake President, supported by two counsellors, is responsible for the bishop (each with two counsellors) who runs each ward. Other organizations exist for adult women – The Relief Society – as well as for young men and young women. A unified programme of worship and instruction meets for a three-hour block on Sunday morning. This includes separate groups for men and women as well as a united Sacrament Meeting when bread and water are taken in remembrance of the atoning death of Christ and in the hope that his Spirit will be with members today. One night a week is without any church activity when the Family Home Evening takes place. Once a month a Fast and Testimony Meeting is held when members attest to their belief in God, Christ, the church and its leaders and what church life has done for them. After repentance and faith, initiation is by baptism by immersion and the laying on of hands for the giving of the Holy Ghost. Members follow the Word of Wisdom, a food code avoiding alcohol, tea and coffee, and tithe income to support the church financially. Many young adults serve a two-year period as full time missionaries, then return home, marry or continue their education. Education is encouraged as is marriage with another Mormon. Temple marriage seals people for time and eternity with the union as the basis for eternal progression of a united family group gaining a divine identity.

Further reading

Buerger, D. J. (1992) *The Mysteries of Godliness: A History of Mormon Temple Worship*, San Francisco: Smith Research Associates.

Bushman, R. L. (1984) *Joseph Smith and the Beginnings of Mormonism*, Urbana and Chicago: Chicago University Press.

Davies, D. J. (2000) *The Mormon Culture of Salvation*, Aldershot: Ashgate.

Shipps, J. (1985) *Mormonism,. The Story of a New Religious Tradition*, Urbana and Chicago: Chicago University Press.

DOUGLAS J. DAVIES

CHURCH OF PENTECOST

This church of Ghanaian origin was founded by James McKeown in 1953. The four main classical Pentecostal denominations in Ghana today are the Church of Pentecost, the Assemblies of God, the Apostolic Church of Ghana (see **Apostolic Church of Johane Masowe**), and the **Christ Apostolic Church**. Three of these are 'Apostolic' churches (so named because of their belief in the continued function of 'apostles' in the church) with origins in the work of a remarkable Ghanaian, Peter Anim (1890–1984) and his contemporary James McKeown (1900–89). Anim, regarded as the father of Pentecostalism in Ghana, came into contact with the publication of the **Faith Tabernacle Church** in Philadelphia, USA in about 1917. He received healing from stomach ailments in 1921 and resigned from the Presbyterian church to become an independent healing preacher who gathered a large following, adopting the name 'Faith Tabernacle' in 1922. Similar developments took place in Nigeria at the same time, when David Odubanjo became the leader of Faith Tabernacle there. Recognition was awarded these African leaders entirely through correspondence, as no personal visits were ever made from Philadelphia to West Africa.

In the meantime, Anim's evangelistic activities were creating churches throughout southern Ghana and as far as Togo in the east. When a report of the dismissal of the US leader of Faith Tabernacle for moral reasons reached Anim in 1930 he broke the connection and changed the name of his organization to Apostolic Faith, after the periodical *Apostolic Faith* from Portland, Oregon, to which he subscribed. In 1932 a Pentecostal revival broke out in Anim's church and many were baptized in the Spirit and spoke in tongues. Nigerian leader Odubanjo made contact with the Apostolic Church in the UK with a view to affiliation, and Anim and two leaders travelled to Lagos to meet their representatives in 1932. Anim affiliated with the Apostolic Church in 1935, and negotiated with the Bradford headquarters for missionaries to be sent to Ghana.

In 1937 James and Sophia McKeown arrived as these missionaries from Northern Ireland. When McKeown contracted malaria soon afterwards and was taken to hospital for treatment, Anim and his followers found this action as deviating from their under-standing of divine healing without the use of medicine. This led to the with-drawal of Anim and many of his mem-bers in 1939 to found the **Christ Apostolic Church**, some time before a different organization of the same name was founded in Nigeria for similar rea-sons. McKeown himself came into con-flict with the Apostolic Church over administrative protocol and seceded in 1953 to form the Gold Coast Apostolic Church (to be called after independence, the Ghana Apostolic Church). The church from which he seceded was known as the Apostolic Church of Ghana. In 1962 President Kwame Nkrumah intervened in a protracted legal battle over church properties between the two Apostolic churches and ordered McKeown to change the name to avoid confusion, when the name 'Church of Pentecost' (COP) was adop-ted. In 1971 the COP affiliated with the Elim Pentecostal Church in Britain, a cooperative arrangement that still exists. Elim have assisted in the areas of lea-dership training, radio ministry, and publishing, and there was, in 2003, one British Elim couple working in Pente-cost University College, the ministerial training college of the church.

From the beginning, although McKeown was Chairman of the church, he worked with an all-African executive council and Ghanaians took the initiatives for the expansion of the church. To all intents and purposes this was an autoch-thonous Ghanaian church. McKeown began to withdraw from his dominant

role in the church from the 1960s, when he would spend increasing amounts of time in Britain, eventually spending only half the year in Ghana. On his retire-ment and departure from Ghana in 1982, he was followed as Chairman by Apostle F. S. Safo (1982–7), Prophet M. K. Yeboah (1988–98), and Apostle Michael K. Ntumy, elected in 1998. Another important event occurred in 1969, when the three Anim-derived Apostolic churches and the **Assemblies of God** formed the Ghana Pentecostal Council. By 1998 150 denominations had joined this organization, a remark-able and unusual feat of Pentecostal and Charismatic ecumenism. The Church of Pentecost is today the second largest Christian denomination in Ghana, and will soon have more members than the Catholic Church. It is probably the most respected of the Pentecostal churches in Ghana.

Further reading

Anderson, A. (2001) *African Reformation: African Initiated Christianity in the 20th Century*, Trenton, NJ and Asmara, Eri-trea: Africa World Press.

Larbi, E. K. (2001) *Pentecostalism: The Eddies of Ghanaian Christianity*, Accra, Ghana: Centre for Pentecostal and Char-ismatic Studies.

ALLAN ANDERSON

CHURCH OF SATAN

The Church of Satan was founded by Anton LaVey in 1966 in California as the first organization that openly identi-fied itself with **Satanism**. Although it was structured as a series of local 'grot-tos' it was intended to foster individual-ism and self-achievement. LaVey disbanded the grotto system in 1975, after which the Church has existed only as an ever-changing network of indivi-duals who self-identify as members, perhaps read the works of Anton LaVey and/or magazines such as *The Black Flame*, and might communicate with each other by email. Such networks are less paradoxical in relation to individualism than the previous grotto system. In any form, the Church of Satan presents a 'sinister' image to the world, looking like Hollywood's archetypal or even clichéd Satanism. Inverted pentagrams, horned devils, nudity, blasphemy against Christian concepts of deity, and decency have been emblematic. In part, Anton LaVey's *The Satanic Bible* (1969) reads like an invocation and sermon inspired by reverence to a real Satan. A closer reading, however, reveals that belief in an actual devil, whether supernatural or otherwise, is unnecessary, and is increasingly explicitly rejected. Reference to Satan is a mask that needs to be seen through if people are to understand and achieve what LaVey intended. The Satanism of the Church of Satan can be summarized (with careful attention to context) in the first two of 'the Nine Satanic Statements' contained in *The Satanic Bible*:

1. Satan represents indulgence, instead of abstinence!
2. Satan represents vital existence, instead of spiritual pipe dreams! (LaVey 1969: 25).

This is carefully worded: Satan is a representation not a personal being. Thus Satanism in the Church of Satan neither encourages worship of the devil nor any attempt to emulate such a being.

The Church of Satan and all of LaVey's writings and organizing encourage individual self-exploration and self-expression. Excess and indulgence are modes of experimentation not metaphysical speculation or required modes of obedience. In this sense, the Church of Satan is comparable to self-religions (see **Self-Religion, The Self, and self**). Like

them, this kind of Satanism is primarily interested in the achievement of the full potential of each individual's inner or true 'self'. It offers a unique means of working towards that goal for those who are willing to transgress boundaries. LaVey wrote, 'One does not "find" oneself, One creates one's self' (1992: 44). In order to 'create one's self' people are encouraged to honestly indulge their desires. They are not offered a system of enlightenment or a technique for religious experience. The goal is the evolution of more individual selves. While this goal is like that of other self-religions, the method is radically different. This becomes most clear in contrast to the **New Age Movement** and New Age Movements in which the self is divinized and frequent reference to 'the light' encourage a rejection of carnality and 'lower' desires. The Church of Satan's Satanism is all about indulgence of precisely those attachments, activities and desires demonized by the wider society and mainstream religions. Nonetheless, LaVey and others in the Church of Satan encouraged a recognition that an experiment might lead to the realization that a particular desire was fruitless as a means of self-realization. One reason for the closure of the grotto system was that regular repetition of the same (perhaps transgressive) rituals proved counterproductive in the development of mature individuality. Furthermore, the Church's writings do suggest that individuals best achieve their greatest potential in chosen forms of sociality. Members are, therefore, encouraged to indulge in the context of a wider society that can be transgressed against *and* from an elective community or network of others whose wills and individualities are also to be respected.

Like other self-religions, the Church of Satan's Satanism inherits some of the interests and methods of earlier **esoteric** movements. The deliberate inversion of Christian religious acts (e.g. in the so-called 'Black Mass') may be little more than transgressive psychodrama, but there is an esoteric and magical undercurrent within the Church. This is demonstrated not primarily in the inclusion of alleged Satanic revelations in 'Enochian' or angelic language within LaVey's writings, but more in the use of ceremonial magic to effect changes according to the true will of the individual ritualist. However, the largest purpose of the Church of Satan is to provoke change in the name of the arch symbol of opposition to stasis: Satan.

Further reading

Harvey, G. (1995) 'Satanism in Britain Today', *Journal of Contemporary Religion* 10, 283–96.

LaVey, A. S. (1969) *The Satanic Bible,* New York: Avon Books.

LaVey, A. S. (1992) *The Devil's Notebook*, Portland, OR: Feral House.

GRAHAM HARVEY

CHURCH OF THE LIVING WORD

(a.k.a. The Living Word Fellowship, The Walk)

Founded by John Robert Stevens (1919–83), the Church of the Living Word, now known as the Living Word Fellowship, is an association of congregations in the Pentecostalist tradition (see **Azusa Street Revival** and **Charismatic Movements**), rather than a discrete denomination.

Born in Iowa, Stevens started his first church and wrote his first book, *To Be a Christian*, at the age of 14. He became an itinerant boy-evangelist, organizing tent meetings, and was ordained at age 18 by Dr. A. W. Courtcamp, Pastor of the Moline Gospel Temple in Moline, Illinois, a congregation whose roots lay in the Pentecostalist and Foursquare Gospel movements. At the age of 20, Stevens enrolled at the Life Bible College in Los Angeles, where he spent three semesters. In 1943 he helped to develop the Christian Tabernacle School in Daytona, Ohio, and became pastor at Oklahoma in a congregation that became affiliated to the International Foursquare Gospel Church.

He later became pastor of the Lynwood **Assemblies of God** in California, where he claimed to receive progressive revelations about entering a new age of the Spirit. This new age involved the purification of the churches, which would entail a return to first-century principles of Church government, in accordance with scripture. In particular, he became convinced that Churches were to be governed by elders, deacons, and other scriptural ministries, rather than congregational and denomination boards, and that they should celebrate the traditional Jewish festivals of Passover, Tabernacles, and the Day of Atonement. Such teachings brought him into conflict with the Assemblies of God, who revoked his pastorship in 1951. He then set about organizing his remaining supporters, establishing his own independent Grace Chapel of South Gate, California in the same year.

Stevens apparently received a vision in 1954, which provided an impetus for further growth. This vision resulted in a break with mainstream Christendom, which, he claimed had become apostate. He subsequently taught the need for a scriptural foundation to any work to be carried out by the Church. The Living Word Fellowship thoroughly deplores the 'fleshly emotions' that the churches encourage: secular entertainments such as bingo nights, barbecues, and church outings; the enormous variety of churches, which causes confusion, leading to apostasy; and especially the 'megachurches' and television churches, which promote cults of personalities rather than God.

The 1960s saw a further expansion of Stevens' work, with the influx of many young people. A vision of Jesus, which Stevens claimed in 1963, gave his work further impetus, and the 1970s saw a period of increased expansion, with a total of 100 associated congregations by 1977. The key doctrines of the Church of the Living Word are set out as a list of thirty-one principles in *To Every Man that Asketh* (1959). These are still used by the Living Word Fellowship as its statement of faith. The inerrancy of scripture forms the basis of its doctrines, together with belief in God as triune. The statement affirms the lostness of humanity, the substitutionary atonement by Jesus Christ, the need for conversion followed by water baptism, and life as 'a holy walk by the Holy Spirit for the believer'. Miracles and prophecy are affirmed, prophetic utterance being regarded as an important characteristic in worship. Particularly important is the statement's position on the Church: all members, without exception, are regarded as God's chosen priesthood (Exodus 19:6), and are 'anointed' for this role by laying on of hands. The Fellowship aims at world evangelism, in obedience to Christ's 'Great Commission' to preach the gospel to all nations (Matthew 28:19–20).

The organization is millennialist (see **Millenarianism**), teaching that humanity is living in the last days. It prefers the term 'first resurrection' to 'the rapture', since the latter expression is non-biblical. These end-times are characterized by a special visitation of Christ to the elect, in the same way as Stevens himself experienced him, and a gradual transition of believers' earthly bodies to 'spiritual bodies' (full resurrection bodies: 1 Corinthians 15: 42-44), making them

'manifest sons of God'. Such a transition entails the acquisition of special powers, such as controlling evil spirits and perceiving special vibrations around human bodies. In 1979 Stevens claimed to have broken through into the new kingdom, and become able to take members into it. Such claims caused Stevens to be criticized for occultism.

Following Stevens' death in 1983, the leadership passed to his wife Marilyn. The Fellowship currently claims some 5,000 members, and runs two schools, in San Diego and North Hills, California.

The name 'Church of the Living Word' also designates two other Christian fundamentalist organizations. The first originated as a house group in Euclid, New York in 1972, and with Robert J. Mazur as its first pastor, it gained early support from ex-hippies. It has now expanded to larger premises in Syracuse, New York. It is fundamentalist, with leanings towards Calvinism – affirming the 'universal depravity of man' and emphasizing hell – and the Holiness Movement, along with which it advocates the Spirit's sanctification and the acquisition of 'tongues of the Spirit'. The organization claims 'many hundreds of members' and owns its school for pupils of all ages.

The second was founded by L. T. and Weeda Moss in 1984. It is associated with the Word of Faith movement, and is affiliated to the International Convention of Faith Ministries (ICFM) and the Bethany Cell Church Network (BCCN). It is situated in Rio Grande Valley in Texas, and, in common with Stevens' organization, declares 'every believer a leader'.

Further reading

Hollenweger, Walter J. (1997) *Pentecostalism: Origins and Development Worldwide*, Peabody, MA: Hendrickson Publishers.

GEORGE CHRYSSIDES

CHURCH OF THE LORD (ALADURA)

A prophet-healing church, and a product of the Aladura (praying) movement in Western Nigeria in the early twentieth century, this church was founded by Josiah Olunlowo Ositelu (see **Ositelu, Josiah**). Born to Ijebu parents who were Ifa worshippers – Ifa is the diviner believed to have created the West African system of geomancy known as Ifa – on 15 May 1902, he was baptized in the Anglican Church in 1914. After completing his elementary education in 1919, he taught as a pupil teacher in several Anglican schools in Ijebuland.

Ositelu's visionary experiences that began in May 1925 led to his dismissal from teaching and exit from the Anglican Church. In June 1929, he began to preach publicly at Ogere, and in July 1930 the converts were constituted into a group named Church of the Lord (Aladura) in 1931. The church was rather peculiar because of its use of certain holy words, which Ositelu claimed to have received through vision. Among these were the unintelligible words such as *Arrabablalhhubab*, *gbanoyyamullah*, and *ahhojjammullah*, which were used in the Church's liturgy, thereby causing a parting of ways with the mainstream Aladura movement in 1931.

Its early spread was to Ibadan, Ijebu Ode and Abeokuta in southwestern Nigeria, and later to Lagos and other Yoruba towns in the 1940s. The early converts, most of whom had been members of the mainline Protestant churches, were attracted by Ositelu's prophecies, his demonstration of power through **healing** and the unmasking of witches. Ogere, the hometown of Ositelu, eventually became the headquarters of the church.

The expansion of the church to other West African countries began in 1947 when Adeleke Adejobi and S. O. Oduwole, two able Yoruba ministers arrived in Freetown, Sierra Leone in March 1947. They conducted prayer sessions for enquirers, and on 6 April, a church was established with forty members. S. O. Oduwole proceeded to Monrovia, Liberia, arriving on 3 April 1947. He centred his work on prayers and the healing of the sick, and despite great difficulties churches were ultimately established in Monrovia and in the interior of the country. From Freetown, Adejobi went to Ghana in March 1953 and established the church first in Takoradi, then Kumasi, where the church witnessed tremendous growth. Oduwole also extended the Liberian work to the coastal region of Ghana in June 1953 and this gave rise to disagreements with Adejobi's churches. Oduwole then extended the work to Lomé, Togo where a church was established in 1961, the first in any French-speaking country. Adejobi went to Glasgow, Scotland also in 1961 for theological training, and on 12 April 1964, he opened a branch in London, thus becoming the first African Independent Church in Europe (see **African Independent Churches**).

The church believes in dreams and visions as channels through which God makes himself known to humans. Most dreams and visions are facilitated by intense prayers, fasting, and the reading of psalms, and members are encouraged to record their dreams for later interpretation. The church is also Pentecostal (see **Azusa Street Revival**) because of the prolonged and enthusiastic services, the demonstration of the prophetic gifts, spirit possession and healing. Furthermore, the church prohibits membership in secret societies, any dealing with juju (magic), the wearing of shoes into the sanctuary, and the use of tobacco and cigarettes.

Healing constitutes a major pre-occupation in the church; hence thousands were drawn to the church through various experiences of healing. The belief in divine healing is strengthened with the complete rejection of all medicine whether Western or traditional African. Prayers lie at the root of all healing, and water, when blessed by the ministers, is frequently used sacramentally to convey healing.

The Mount Taborar festival, first celebrated in 1937 and held every August at Ogere, is the biggest event in the life of the church. The festival is devoted to the giving of special revelations, the fulfilment of vows, thanksgiving and celebration. This festival is preceded by a thirteen-day fast, which is celebrated at a special service in all branches of the church. The climax is the service held on the 22 August presided over by the Primate who would give special revelations received from God for the following year. In the 1990s, the Mount Taborar festival became a much-advertised event with the enlargement of the site, a piece of flat land and not a hill, which now lies close to a major motorway.

Ositelu and his church have made a significant contribution to the development of African Christianity both at home and abroad.

Further reading

Turner, H. W. (1967) *History of an African Independent Church: The Church of the Lord (Aladura)*, 2 vols, Oxford: Clarendon Press.

MATTHEWS A. OJO

CHURCH OF THE SACRED HEART

This church is also known as 'Children of the Sacred Heart' (*Bana Ba-Mutima*

in the language of the Bemba people in Zambia). The founder, Emilio Mulolani, born in 1923, came from a Catholic family and, as a child, he impressed his teachers in the junior seminary. But when he went to a senior seminary in Tanzania he was not accepted as suitable for ordination as a priest. However, he then served for years as a teacher and catechist. In 1954, after a vision, he founded a League of the Sacred Heart which aimed to combat alcoholism. He helped missionaries who lacked command of the local language. Many thought he was revealing parts of the Christian message deliberately hidden from them by the white priests. Among his followers, he had some who separated from their families and committed themselves to celibacy and the service of the poor.

There was growing tension with the bishops concerning the content of his preaching, although for some years he was using a language most missionaries did not know. He was anxious to remain a Catholic and actually set out on a pilgrimage on foot to Rome in order to appeal to the Pope; he returned after reaching Kenya. Finally, in 1958, he was excommunicated and sought government registration for his separate Catholic (not Roman) church. This was granted but in 1961 the church was struck off by the colonial government.

The points on which he took issue with church authority included the following: his 'enlargement' of the Trinity, exaggerations in devotion to Mary and, especially, neo-Gnostic dualism, suggesting that the Spirit is all that matters and bodily behaviour indifferent. Later, there were messianic hopes connected with his person. Because of Emilio's political stance as well as the disorderly behaviour of some followers, in 1974 the Zambian government made membership illegal. Underground activity continued and as late as 1984, the courts sanctioned secret assemblies with fines and imprisonment.

RALPH WOODHALL

CHURCH OF THE TWELVE APOSTLES

The Church of the Twelve Apostles also popularly referred to as 'Nackabah' is the first known African initiated church in Ghana. The Church exemplifies African initiative in Christianity by seeking to address the concerns and needs of African believers by making use of resources from the Bible and the African worldview. Although the African prophet William Wade Harris (see **Harris, William Wadé**) did not found a church but worked in close collaboration with Western missionaries, some of his followers started their own independent churches. Following on the visit of Harris to Axim and Apollonia districts, of Western Ghana in 1914, two of his earliest converts, Grace Tani and John Nackabar, started the church. The formal name of the church resulted from the practice of Harris appointing twelve apostles in each local congregation to cater for the pastoral needs of his converts.

Grace Tani was one of Harris's wives. A charismatic leader, she ministered to the needs of the members through divination and healing. Nackabar, after whom the church was nicknamed, assumed the administrative leadership of the church and was recognized as the main leader. Nackabar was succeeded by John Hackman, who in turn, appointed his nephew, Samuel Kofi Ansah as his successor before his death in June 1957. After the death of Ansah, the heads of the various districts started functioning independently of the headquarters of the church at Kadjabir in the Western Region of Ghana.

Essentially, for the Church, doctrine is secondary, and what is stressed is meeting the needs of their members such as healing the sick, casting out of evil spirits and the search for security and prosperity. The Church has two major sacred objects, namely, the Bible and the African dancing gourd-rattle (an African religious and secular musical instrument, made from a calabash with a 'neck', netted with strings of white beads which is rattled rhythmically to accompany singing and dancing). Every member is expected to possess these sacred objects. The Bible, for instance, is not primarily meant for reading, but is principally used as means of warding off evil from adherents; sick members are made to use it as pillow or put it under their pillow as part of the healing rituals. The noise of the rattle is believed to scare evil spirits and facilitate the healing process of believers. Interestingly most of the church's practices such as the use of the rattle are based not on African spirituality, but the Bible, as found in Exodus 15:20.

The Twelve Apostles Church enjoins adherents to observe certain food prohibitions such as abstinence from taking pork, stinking fish, shark's meat as well as snails, smoking, and the drinking of strong liquor. New dietary regulations are made as and when new revelations are received. The church attaches great importance to fasting. The leadership believes the 'Spirit' directs them as to what kind of fast (total abstinence or partial), the length of time that the fast should be embarked upon and the sort of people who should participate in the fast.

Neophytes are admitted without instructions, through special rituals, such as the marking of the sign of the cross on their foreheads in the name of the Trinity, a special ritual bath, and a special handshake by the leaders. Members observe a special code of ethics. Polygamous marriage and remarriage are not prohibited in the church.

The church has a sacred garden adjoining the regular place of worship where prayer meetings as well as healing services and other religious practices are held. A significant feature of this garden is a white wooden cross, located at the centre. Adherents lift basins of water towards it believing that the water will be consecrated and rendered efficacious for the purpose of healing. Furthermore, one striking feature of the church is the use of 'holy water', for protection against evil spirits as well as for divine healing. Adherents are made to carry 'holy water' on their heads, dance, and twist and swirl until they become ecstatic. At this point, their belief is that the Spirit falls on them. This event gives rise to violent outcries, shouts of joy, and convulsion in order for divine healing to be effected.

The emphasis on healing and warding off evil spirits by the Twelve Apostles Church is an attempt to address the concerns and needs of African believers in the context of the Church in Africa.

Further reading

Baëta, C. G. (1962) *Prophetism in Ghana*, London: SCM Press Ltd.
Debrunner, H. W. (1967) *A History of Christianity in Ghana*, Accra: Waterville.

CEPHAS N. OMENYO

CHURCH UNIVERSAL AND TRIUMPHANT

Founders: Mark and
Elizabeth Clare Prophet
Country of origin: United States

The Church Universal and Triumphant (CUT) is a unique New Age (see **New Age Movement**) religious organization that between 1990 and 2003 evolved into an entrepreneurial marketer of the teachings of its two founders, Mark L. Prophet (1918–73) and Elizabeth Clare Prophet (b. 1939). The group began its existence in 1958 as the Washington, DC-based Summit Lighthouse (SL). SL's teachings were rooted in such New Age forerunner traditions as **Theosophy**, **New Thought**, and the Saint Germain Foundation. Mark Prophet proclaimed the existence of a hierarchy of spiritual masters known as the Great White Brotherhood (see **Theosophy**). These 'ascended masters" avowed mission was to direct the spiritual evolution of humanity and to communicate their teachings through their selected messenger, Mark Prophet.

SL also taught the mystical power of the spoken word. Through verbal affirmations using the words 'I AM', the aspirant's intention could be connected to the Divine Self within, ensuring the ultimate material manifestation of this intention. Prophet called this practice 'positive decreeing' and offered it as a means for aspirants to change negative conditions in their lives and foster physical and spiritual healing. Decreeing remains the essential spiritual practice for CUT members. Prophet called the messages he received 'dictations' and sent them to disciples as small booklets entitled *Pearls of Wisdom*; *Pearls* is CUT's signature publication and is now available on CD ROM.

SL's mainly middle-aged, middle-class membership grew slowly from 1958 to 1966. During this time Prophet created an organization of students called the Keepers of the Flame Fraternity. Keepers gave a monthly tithe and received graded lessons on the path of ascension, decreeing, the ascended masters, and the spiritual mission of the United States in the emerging Golden Age. These lessons followed the well-established pattern of correspondence course esotericism pioneered by the Ancient and Mystical Order of Rosae Crucis (AMORC) (see **AMORC**). The fraternity in time would constitute the core group of Church Universal and Triumphant. Prophet met and married Elizabeth Wulf in 1963. Although he continued as the public messenger at SL's classes and services, he began privately to groom his wife as co-messenger.

A new wave of growth began in 1966 when SL moved to Colorado Springs. A coterie of counterculture youths moved into the Prophets' large mansion and became a committed core group around which the organization could expand its educational and initiatory outreach. During the late 1960s and early 1970s, the group hosted seasonal conclaves of students and inaugurated Montessori International to educate its children. Ascended Master University (later called Summit University) opened in 1972 and offered students intensive immersion in SL's teachings.

Mark Prophet's sudden death in 1973 brought Elizabeth Prophet into leadership of the movement. She changed the group's name to Church Universal and Triumphant, inaugurated Camelot, a New Age mystery school, in Malibu, California, and increased the group's publishing and missionary outreach. The signature books of this period, *Climb the Highest Mountain* and *The Great White Brotherhood in America*, proclaimed CUT as the true church of both Gautama Buddha and Jesus Christ in the dawning New Age. They also elaborated the ascended masters' teachings on spiritual initiation, the purpose of which was to reunite the human soul with its eternal I AM presence and foster ascension to higher realms of being. In the late 1970s Prophet encouraged her students to speak out against pornography, abortion, Communism, and terrorism. The church was unabashedly patriotic and affirmed America's special role in planetary spiritual evolution.

CUT received international notoriety in 1989 when Prophet predicted a possible global nuclear war and directed her followers to build fallout shelters in and around the church's international headquarters in southern Montana. By the time the 'shelter cycle' played itself out in the mid-1990s, CUT had lost a third of its membership, downsized its staff by 90 per cent, and had begun selling its Montana property to raise operating funds. A new phase of reorganization began in 1996 with the appointment of corporate executive Gilbert Cleirbault as president. Cleirbault turned CUT into an international distributor of the Prophets' teachings in audio, video, internet, and book formats. He also decentralized the organization with the intention of creating New Age spiritual communities around the globe. CUT's apocalyptic focus has softened, and its publications now promote a softer millennial (see **Millenarianism**) vision of global spiritual enlightenment. During 1998–9, Elizabeth Prophet relinquished both temporal and spiritual control of her church because of Alzheimer's disease. CUT has routinized her charisma with a revolving presidency, board of directors, and council of elders. Prophet currently resides in Bozeman, Montana, and remains a revered figure in the movement.

Further reading

Lewis, J. R. and Melton, J. G. (1994) *Church Universal and Triumphant in Scholarly Perspective*, Stanford, CA: Center for Academic Publication.

Prophet, E. C. (1976) *The Great White Brotherhood in the Culture, History and Religion of America*, Colorado Springs: The Summit Lighthouse.

PHILLIP CHARLES LUCAS

CIJI GONGDE HUI

Ciji Gongde Hui, The Buddhist
Compassionate Relief and Merit Society
Founder: Venerable Zhengyan
(or Cheng-Yen) (b. 1947)

Established in the eastern region of Taiwan, Ciji Gongde Hui (henceforth Ciji), The Buddhist Compassionate Relief and Merit Society (also known as the Buddhist Compassion Relief Tzu Chi Foundation) is the most successful of the Taiwanese Buddhist initiatives in **Engaged Buddhism**. A lay movement under the leadership of a Buddhist nun Dharma Master Zhengyan, Ciji has an estimated five million members world-wide and branches in thirty-four countries. One of its most important humanitarian activities is bone marrow donations. It has registered over 160,000 donors for this purpose. The scale of this movement's international humanitarian work is unprecedented in the history of Chinese Buddhism. Most of its members are ethnic Chinese.

A **Mahāyāna** Buddhist movement, Ciji was started in Hualien province, a deprived region in eastern Taiwan, in 1966 by the charismatic Taiwanese nun, the previously mentioned Dharma Master Zhengyan whose concern is more with the application than theory of Buddhist teachings. She engages rarely in theological discourse but stresses instead the fundamental importance of planting the seeds of good fortune, or *fu* meaning merit. Poor and the rich alike are reminded of the necessity to realize *fu* (*zhfu*), to appreciate *fu* (*xifu*) and to create *fu* (*zhaofu*) by cultivating self-awareness and by striving to improve their own and other people's material and spiritual condition, and that of society by, for example, creating harmony and helping others. The result has been the provision of free health care and vocational education for many of the poor of Taiwan and wherever the movement has established itself around the world.

The emphasis on Buddhism as a this-worldly, socially engaged religion is also a constant theme of Zhengyan's lectures and discussions. Asked by a medical student how he might be reborn as a human being her advice was that he should study hard now in order to be able to better care, when qualified, for his patients. The core Chinese virtue of filial piety and the importance of acquiring wisdom are also interpreted in such a way as to turn them into reasons for social action on behalf of others. Regarding the virtue of filial piety Zhengyan reminds her followers that their bodies are given them by their parents and the best way they can show gratitude to them is by helping others. Wisdom is to be acquired not only through study and meditation but also by performing good deeds and learning from one's interaction with others.

Master Zhengyan initiates only women, and having begun with just five disciples and thirty followers in 1966 there are now over 100 nuns as disciples and as was previously mentioned some five million followers. The preponderance of lay women in the administration under Zhengyan's leadership gives Ciji the appearance of a matriarchy. Most followers come to know this 'communitarian' organization through personal contact with existing members. Most of the membership in Taiwan are middle-aged, and are originally from rural areas and have been helped by the movement to establish contacts on arrival in the cities. Considerable numbers having come from poor backgrounds are now well to do, a majority earning above average incomes. For many who took on the challenge of being self-employed Ciji introduced them to helpful business contacts from among their new 'spiritual relatives' (*faqin*). Though not university graduates themselves a majority of Ciji families are committed to a university education for their children. Like Foguangshu, Ciji is not only one of the clearest examples of the objectives and strategies employed by Engaged Buddhism, but is also a classic illustration of the 'sect' as vehicle of upward social mobility, of the empowerment of women through a new religious movement (see **Gender and NRMs**), of the dynamics and impact of charismatic power, and of the increasingly global character of many Chinese New Religions. The movement is now established across Asia and in among other places North America and Europe.

Further reading

Clart, P. and Jones, C.B. (2003) *Religion in Modern Taiwan*, Honolulu: University of Hawai'i Press.
Huang, C. J. (2005). 'The Compassion Relief Diaspora' in L. Learman (ed.) *Buddhist Missionaries in the Era of Globalization*, Honolulu: University of Hawai'i Press, pp. 185–210.

PETER B. CLARKE AND
YU-SHUANG YAO

COHEN, ANDREW

Born in New York in 1955, Andrew Cohen is a western teacher with an Indian lineage, within the **guru**-disciple tradition but with a largely western following. He describes his enlightenment as coming shortly after meeting the guru H. W. L. Poonja in 1986, in India. Like many charismatic teachers, he claims revelations also came to him early in his life.

Poonjaji originally supported Cohen's vocation as a religious teacher, though there is disagreement as to whether he nominated Cohen as his successor.

However, they eventually parted acrimoniously. Cohen's account is that he was upset at what he saw as sexual misconduct by his teacher, combined with 'petty anger and jealousy'. However, he decided that such base attributes could co-exist with enlightenment in one person.

His philosophy is classical 'self-spirituality' (see **Self-Religion, The Self, and Self**) maintaining that 'only the self can know the self, and all else apart from the self is illusory, impermanent and therefore unreal'. He is one of a declining number of western teachers still advocating enlightenment as the primary goal of the spiritual life, easily attainable with the right approach. His main teaching method is lecturing to his followers, combined with meditation and other practices. He claims to be able to remove a person's karma accumulated over many lifetimes. Cohen's stated objective is to bring about a global spiritual revolution.

Andrew Cohen has a worldwide community of students formally called the International Fellowship for the Realization of Impersonal Enlightenment, also known as FACE (Friends of Andrew Cohen Everywhere). The headquarters is in Massachusetts, USA, offering a program of bi-annual retreats and public talks. His committed students live in communities managed by a leadership group, and Cohen himself is actively involved. The relationship is modeled on the devotional guru-disciple tradition found in Indian *Bhakti* yoga, although there is also an outer group of more loosely associated 'friends' including several celebrities. One of the movement's more successful ventures has been a magazine 'What is Enlightenment?', presenting articles on spirituality by a variety of writers and teachers, some very well known. However, Cohen says that few of these people are enlightened.

ELIZABETH PUTTICK

CONE, JAMES

James H. Cone is the founding figure of American 'Black Theology' of Liberation. Called the 'creator' of 'Black Theology' by the German theologian, Jurgen Moltmann, and 'the apostle to the Gentiles' by the African American theologian Albert Cleage, the theology of James Cone is one of the most challenging and significant contributions to modern theological discourse.

James Cone is Distinguished Professor of Systematic Theology at Union Theological Seminary in New York; he received his doctorate from Garrett-Northwestern in the USA with a thesis on the anthropology of Karl Barth. At the height of the Civil Rights Movement he published his *Black Theology and Black Power* (1969). This first book was unapologetically political; it radically identified the Black Power Movement with the Christian gospel. Indeed, Cone argued that the tenets of Black Power were not the antithesis of Christianity, rather it was 'Christ's central message to twentieth-century America'. Over the last three decades Cone has written a number of important books which systematically develop and widen this original perspective. These include *The Spirituals and the Blues: An Interpretation* (1972), *God of the Oppressed* (1975) and *For My People: Black Theology and the Black Church* (1984).

The message and methodology of Cone's first pioneering book and subsequent publications challenged traditional theology, and informed black religious thinking. Two principal themes are at the centre of Cone's theology. The first is the 'liberation' function of Christian theology; the second is God's relation to the oppressed in their pursuit of justice. Cone's central thesis is that God is 'the God of the oppressed' and the disinherited. The Exodus narratives in the Old Testament and the prophetic text quoted by Jesus in Luke 4:18 are critical in Cone's liberation hermeneutics. In the context of black people's struggle against slavery, racism, discrimination, and ontological negation Cone argues that the function of theology is to speak to these social realities in light of these two themes.

Cone defines 'Christian Theology' as 'a rational study of the being of God in the world in light of the existential situation of an oppressed community, relating the forces of liberation to the essence of the gospel, which is Jesus Christ'. The task of 'Black Theology' in this schema is twofold: it has to articulate the 'theological self-determination of black people'; it also has to provide ethical and religious categories for their liberation and search for 'black identity'.

Undoubtedly Cone's Black Liberation Theology was intended as an instrument in America's black revolution in the 1960s, as well as a theological paradigm for challenging racism and traditional white theology. Because Cone's theology is identified unreservedly with the goals of black and oppressed communities seeking liberation from injustice and oppression, it is open to the charge of being a theology of legitimation for radical black politics and ideology.

James Cone's Black Theology of liberation is 'a theology of and for the black community, seeking to interpret the religious dimensions of the forces of liberation in that community'. As such it is also a critique of 'white theology', especially in regard to the 'silence' of white theologians in the face of the historic oppression of Black people in America and the Diaspora. In classical Marxian terms Cone argues that there is a dialectical relationship between the socio-economic position of white theologians and the nature of their theologizing:

Because white theologians live in a society that is racist, the oppression of black people does not occupy an important item on their theological agenda… Because white theologians are well fed and speak for a people who control the means of production, the problem of hunger is not a theological issue for them.

(Cone 1975: 52)

In articulating new ways of talking about God and the black religious experience, Cone also enhanced black self-understanding, identity and spirituality. Ultimately, Cone saw his theology as a partial but critical answer to the black identity crisis in America. 'The search for black identity', says Cone, 'is the search for God, for God's identity is black identity.' By utilizing black history, 'the black experience' and culture as a 'source' for doing theology, in juxtaposition with Scripture, revelation and tradition, Cone opens new perspectives and methodological challenges to the discipline of systematic theology. The cadences of liberation informing Cone's theology are just as revolutionary and relevant today as they were when he published his first Black Theology books. This is because his central thesis is foundational to the Christian faith: God is a just God and in the struggle for justice God expects us to take sides.

Further reading

Cone, J. H. (1969) *Black Theology and Black Power*, Maryknoll: Orbis Books.
Cone, J. H. (1972) *The Spirituals and the Blues: An Interpretation*, Maryknoll: Orbis Books.
Cone, J. H. (1975) *God of the Oppressed*, Maryknoll: Orbis Books.
Cone, J. H. (1982) *My Soul Looks Back*, Nashville: Abingdon.
Cone, J. H. (1984) *For My People: Black Theology and the Black Church*, Maryknoll: Orbis Books.
Cone, J. H. (1986) *Speaking the Truth*, Grand Rapids: Eerdmans Publishing Co.

R. DAVID MUIR

CONFRATERNITY OF DEISTS

Founded in St Petersburg, Florida in 1967 by Paul Englert, a former Roman Catholic, the Confraternity draws on the deist tradition that emerged from the rationalism that prevailed in Britain and other parts of Europe – principally France and Germany – from the seventeenth century onwards. Influenced by the scientific advances of Bacon, Galileo, and Copernicus, Deists questioned the inerrancy of scripture and God's direct intervention in the world's affairs, for example by miracles. Reason rather than experiential revelation was the foundation of belief in a divine being. Lord Herbert of Cherbury (d. 1648), in his *De Veritate*, defined five principles of deism: belief in one supreme God; humankind's duty to revere him; practical morality as the principal effect of worship; forgiveness through repentance and abandonment of sins, rather than through an atoning sacrifice; and a just reward for good works, both in this life and life after death.

Other European deists included Anthony Collins (1676–1729) and Matthew Tindal (1657–1733) in England, and Jean-Jacques Rousseau (1712–78) and F. M. A. de Voltaire (1694–1778) in France. Deistic ideas gained momentum in the USA during the American Revolution and afterwards, and were influential on the notion of church–state separation, reflected in the US First Amendment of the American Constitution.

The Confraternity of Deists seeks to promote several of these principles of Deism. In common with the earlier deists it emphasizes the importance of the use of human reason, regarding intellectual achievements as the prime manifestation of God's glory. Being opposed to organized religion and believing in human progress, it regards free universities as its churches, and encourages the furtherance of knowledge and the arts. It holds that scriptures are literary works, written by human creators, rather than reliable guides to history, chronology, or religious truth. The Confraternity takes earlier deistic ideas further by denying the existence of sin as well as the need of a saviour, and rejecting the notion of any conscious state after death.

The organization has three centres – two on university campuses, and one at its headquarters, currently located at Homosassa Springs, Florida.

GEORGE CHRYSSIDES

CREATION SPIRITUALITY

Creation Spirituality, also known as Creation-Centred Spirituality, is a theological tradition 'rediscovered' by **Matthew Fox** (b. 1940), and not to be confused with the fundamentalist Christian theology of Creationism. This article gives a bare biography of Matthew Fox, briefly describes his theology and outlines the broader movement he has inspired.

Matthew Fox was born with the name Timothy and assumed the name Matthew on entry to the Dominican Order at the age of 19, being ordained in 1967. He completed his doctoral thesis in Paris in *Time Magazine* during 1958 on the subject of religion and spirituality, and self-published this as *Religion USA* in 1971 (Listening Press). His career has been as an educator and theologian, speaker and writer, and he is currently president of the University of Creation Spirituality in Oakland, California, and author of 25 books. A year of public silence was imposed on him by the Dominican Order in 1988–89, and he was eventually dismissed from the Order in 1993, becoming an Episcopal (Anglican) priest in 1994.

Creation Spirituality's central notion is that the Creation of the world was seen by God as good, an *Original Blessing* (Fox 1983), before it was condemned in Christian theology by Augustine and other Church fathers through the doctrine of Original Sin. All of Creation is therefore to be celebrated and enjoyed, whether through traditional Christian ceremonies re-presented through the use of multimedia techniques and equipment, or through the methods of other traditions such as Native American sweat lodges, dream quests and cosmic walks. Even sexuality (including homosexual sexuality), so long repressed by the Christian Churches and in orthodox theology the source of Original Sin, is celebrated as a blessing.

Fox's 1988 presentation of Creation Spirituality as *The Coming of the Cosmic Christ* (Harper & Row) is perhaps the most radical of his writings, re-interpreting traditional expositions of the ascended Christ as the foundation of panentheism – the belief that God is in all and all is in God – and distinguished from the heresy of pantheism (all is God). These notions are close to the thought of David Spangler (see **Spangler, David**) and other New Agers (see **New Age Movement**), although such links are not developed in this book.

Indeed, though early works were open to New Age, by the mid-1980s Matthew Fox was distancing himself from that movement at the same time as defending his association with **Starhawk**, a Wiccan (see **Wicca**). Instead, Matthew Fox suggests that Creation Spirituality is a central Christian tradition that has been suppressed by Church authorities throughout history. His role has been merely to 'rediscover' this tradition in

127

the works of earlier Christian theologians and in the Bible. Matthew Fox claims that what distinguishes a spirituality from a cult is precisely a tradition (Fox 1983: 21), and has published lengthy, original studies of Thomas Aquinas and Meister Eckhart.

In his autobiography (*Confessions*, 1996), Matthew Fox explains that his decision to move to the Anglican communion was confirmed by his plans to encourage the work of the Nine O'Clock Service in Sheffield, England, a community that was experimenting with rave worship and whose leader, Revd Chris Brain, was later accused of sexual impropriety.

Friends of Creation Spirituality, Inc. was founded by Matthew Fox in 1984 to educate the general public in Creation Spirituality through the presentation of multimedia resources including live performances, public forums and rituals. GreenSpirit was founded in 1987 as the Centre for Creation Spirituality at St James's Church, Piccadilly, London, England and became in 1994 a charitable membership organisation, The Association for Creation Spirituality, before changing to its present name. GreenSpirit welcomes followers of all traditions and none, and its members are particularly open to pagan traditions (see **Pagan Federation**), holding meetings linked to current ecological political issues and rituals which open awareness, often in lamentations, to injustices in the world.

Far from being simply followers of Matthew Fox, those inspired by Creation Spirituality now also value, for example, the theological approach to contemporary science – especially cosmology – represented by Thomas Berry and Brian Swimme, the writings of Deep Ecologists such as Joanna Macy, as well as campaigns for social justice championed by the Green movement and others. Creation Spirituality is confident of its importance for the future of Christian and non-Christian spiritualities, but its significance as a movement has been hampered to date by controversies surrounding Matthew Fox. Ironically, it may be these very controversies that have granted Creation Spirituality its wide popular audience.

Further reading

Blindell, G. (2000) *What is Creation Centred Spirituality?*, GreenSpirit Pamphlet No. 4, London: Association for Creation Spirituality (www.greenspirit.org.uk/books/).
Fox, M. (1983) *Original Blessing*, Santa Fe, NM: Bear and Co.
Fox, M. (1988) *The Coming of the Cosmic Christ*, New York: Harper & Row.
Fox, M. (1996) *Confessions*, San Francisco: Harper.

DAREN KEMP

CROWLEY, ALEISTER
(b. 1875; d. 1947)

Born Edward Alexander, the son of a brewer and Plymouth Brother, Aleister Crowley was a great influence on the development of magic (or 'magick') in the twentieth century. Crowley saw himself as the latest in a line of magicians that included John Dee, Cagliostro, and Eliphas Lévi, and he was the head of a number of magical orders.

In 1898, Crowley was initiated into the **Hermetic Order of the Golden Dawn**. His aptitude for magic paved his meteoric rise through the Order's grades of initiation, and after he was expelled from the Order (which he claimed had ceased to interest him), Crowley went on to found the Argenteum Astrum (Order of the Silver Star). Between 1909 and 1913, Crowley published many of the Golden Dawn's secret rituals in *The Equinox*, the journal of his Order. In 1912, Crowley joined the Ordo Templi

Orientis, a German system of occultism, becoming head of the Order in 1922. Considering himself to be the chosen prophet of a new aeon, the Age of Horus, Crowley founded the Abbey of Thelema at Cefalu in Sicily in 1920, influenced by François Rabelais' sixteenth-century novels, *Gargantua* and *Pantagruel*. He envisioned his Abbey as a magical colony from which to launch the new aeon, but was expelled by Mussolini in 1923.

A prolific writer, two of Crowley's most important works are *The Book of the Law*, which he claimed was dictated in 1904 by his Holy Guardian Angel, Aiwass, and *Magick in Theory and Practice*, self-published in 1929. The former contained his famous Law of Thelema: 'Do what thou wilt shall be the whole of the Law; Love is the Law, Love under Will'. Crowley also wrote a great deal of poetry, and was an accomplished mountaineer and practitioner of yoga, integrating Eastern philosophies and practices with the Western esoteric and magical theories which formed the foundation of his Thelema.

Further reading

Crowley, A. (1989) *The Confessions of Aleister Crowley: An Autohagiography* (eds) J. Symonds and K. Grant, with an Introduction by John Symonds, Harmondsworth: Arkana

Jo Pearson

CULT AND NEW RELIGIONS

The term 'cult' has become quite problematic in recent years, particularly within the United States (Richardson, 1993). It now is understood by most members of the general public, as well as policy makers and the media, as a term that refers to controversial groups that are odd and even dangerous to group members and others. Usually there is the assumption associated with the term that there is an all-powerful leader exercising inordinate influence over members of the group who were persuaded to join through the use of unethical processes referred to under the also negatively connoted rubric of '**brainwashing**' (Robbins and Anthony, 1982).

'Cult' has become a general term referring to a number of newer religious and quasi-religious groups that have attracted attention from the media and government officials in recent decades (Dillon and Richardson, 1994). Such groups as the **Unification Church** (known popularly as the 'Moonies'), **Scientology**, **Hare Krishna**, Divine Light Mission, The Way International, and International Community of Christ have been designated as cults by the media, often assisted by the efforts of the so-called **Anti-Cult Movement**. The negatively connoted term has become widely used for these and other newer, smaller, and more 'culturally oppositional' religious and quasi-religious groups (Campbell, 1972). The term has also been used to refer to the Manson group that murdered several Hollywood notables several decades ago, the **Branch Davidians** outside Waco, Texas, the Heavens Gate group that committed suicide in San Diego in the late 1990s, and the Solar Temple group that had several episodes of mass suicide and murders in the mid-1990s – all groups which were involved in very violent episodes. Thus the negative connotation of the term cult has been fostered by events involving some of the groups designated as cults by the media and policy makers.

The term cult has been used much less in some countries than in others, with the term sect being preferred as a somewhat negatively connoted term in Europe to refer to smaller controversial religious groups. The term in Europe includes both **New Religious Movements** (NRMs) and smaller non-traditional religious groups such as the Jehovah's Witnesses that have existed for some time in European countries. However, the term cult has become an important cultural export from the US in recent years. It appears that the designation given to the controversial groups within the American context has been transported around the world as part of the baggage associated with the information disseminated about these groups. Thus the cult term has become more diffused, leading to its more frequent use in other countries such as in Europe, Japan, and China, to refer to groups that are not positively sanctioned by the government and general society.

Most scholars prefer the term 'new religions' or 'New Religious Movements' (NRMs) to refer to the groups popularly known as cults. This term is somewhat imprecise, given that some of the 'new religions' claim heritages that are centuries old. However, the term does not have the negative connotation of the term cult.

Sociological history of the term cult

The term cult was first developed in the writings of Ernst Troeltsch (1931) and has been used since in other sociologically oriented writings since he wrote in the 1930s (i.e. Yinger, 1970; Wilson, 1970; Campbell, 1972). It has become something of a residual term in the traditional typology often referred to in the sociology of religion that includes such concepts as church, denomination, and sect (Niebuhr, 1929; Martin, 1962). As a technical term in sociology the characteristics of cult include: a small, transitory, amorphous group with porous or vague boundaries of belief and behavior. A few Scholars (Nelson, 1965) have taken issue with the transitory part

of this definition, however, noting that some cult-like groups last over time. Van Driel and Richardson (1988) offer a lengthy comparison of the characteristics of the terms sect and cult, highlighting major differences that include much more exclusiveness and firm boundaries in sect-like groups. It is worth noting that from a sociological point of view many of the NRM groups popularly referred to as cults are in fact sects according to the characteristics usually associated with that term.

Richardson (1978) adds another perspective as he states:

> The major criterion of the concept of cult is its oppositional nature: *A cult is a group that has beliefs and/or practices that are counter to those of the dominant culture. Beliefs and practices may also be in opposition to those of a subcultural group.* (emphasis in original)

This content oriented definitional approach, also used by other scholars such as Ellwood (1968), is useful in that it helps explain why otherwise small and relatively harmless groups may attract such attention and become the targets of normative efforts by media, government officials, and the general public. Such groups are viewed as threatening to dominant cultural values, and they have in recent decades attracted youth from dominant social classes in society.

The politics of the cult label

Groups successfully designated as cults are usually politically weak and cannot defend themselves well. They can become easy targets for politicians, traditional religious groups, the **Anti-Cult Movement**, or others seeking to use such controversial groups to further their own interests. This has been a common pattern in recent decades, especially in former Communist countries, as NRMs have become pawns in political battles for cultural dominance and hegemony in a number of societies (Dillon and Richardson, 1993; Shterin and Richardson, 2000; Richardson, 2004).

Controversial religious groups can be targeted by media calling attention to them, using labels that indicate their problematic nature. Politicians can decide to attack them, knowing that this can be done with impunity in most societies. The media usually follows the lead of opinion leaders and dominant groups in a society, thus contributing to the concern about such groups by labeling the targeted groups with terms such as cult. A 'moral panic' can ensue, which makes it very difficult for NRMs to receive fair treatment in legal actions that might be brought by the groups, or against them by others Richardson, 1991; Richardson, 2004).

Because of the problematic situation that exists with the use of the term cult, Richardson (1993) has recommended that scholars refrain from using the term when writing about NRMs. Or if scholars use the term, they should make clear that it is being used as a technical term, and not simply following – and promoting – the popular-negative usage of the term. Also, he makes another recommendation to disallow use of the label cult in legal actions involving minority religious groups, in order to avoid the baggage associated with that term becoming a factor in the legal action.

Further reading

Campbell, C. (1972) 'The Cult, the Cultic Milieu, and Secularization' in M. Hill (ed.), *A Sociological Yearbook of Religion in Britain*, London: SCM Press, pp. 119–136.

Dillon, J. and Richardson, J. T. (1994) 'The "Cult" Concept: A Politics of Representation Analysis', *SYZYGY: Journal of*

Alternative Religion and Culture 3, 185–198.

Ellwood, R. (1986) 'The Several Meanings of Cult', *Thought* LXI, 212–24.

Martin, D. (1962) 'The Denomination', *British Journal of Sociology* 13, 1–14.

Nelson, G. (1969) 'The Spiritualist Movement and the Need for a Redefinition of Cult', *Journal for the Scientific Study of Religion* 8, 152–60.

Niebuhr, H. R. (1929) *The Social Sources of Denominationalism*, New York: Holt, Rinehart & Winston.

Richardson, J. T. (2004) *Regulating Religion: Case Studies from Around the Globe*, Amsterdam: Kluwer.

Richardson, J. T. (1993) 'The Concept of Cult: From Socio-Technical to Popular-Negative', *Review of Religious Research* 34, 348–56.

Richardson, J. T. (1991) 'Cult/Brainwashing Cases and the Freedom of Religion', *Journal of Church and State* 33, 55–74.

Richardson, J. T. (1978) 'An Oppositional and General Conceptualization of Cult', *The Annual Review of the Social Sciences of Religion* 2, 29–52.

Robbins, T. and Anthony, D. (1982) 'Deprogramming, Brainwashing, and the Medicalization of Deviant Religion', *Social Problems* 29, 283–97.

Shterin, M. and Richardson, J. T. (2000) 'Effects of the Western Anti-Cult Movement on Development of Laws Concerning religion in Post-Communist Russia', *Journal of Church and State* 42, 247–72.

Van Driel, B. and Richardson, J. T. (1988) 'The Categorization of New Religious Movements in American Print Media', *Sociological Analysis* 49, 171–83.

Wilson, B. (1970) *Religious Sects*, New York: McGraw-Hill.

Yinger, M. (1970) *The Scientific Study of Religion*, London: Macmillan.

JAMES T. RICHARDSON

CULT AWARENESS NETWORK

The Cult Awareness Network (CAN) has been, in its various manifestations, one of the most controversial anti-cult organizations in America (see **Anti-Cult Movement**). Its present manifestation adds a bizarre twist to the story.

In 1972, a group of concerned parents of young people who had joined the (then) Children of God, formed an organization initially called Parents' Committee to Free Our Sons and Daughters from the Children of God – soon shortened to FREECOG. Parents of children who had joined other movements became involved, and in late 1973 FREECOG briefly became Volunteer Parents of America, before folding. Out of its ashes emerged a new organization, the Citizens Freedom Foundation (CFF). The CFF was initially based in California, and other similar organizations were formed by concerned parents elsewhere in the USA. During the mid-1970s several attempts were made to form umbrella groups, but none was successful.

During the 1970s some concerned parents of members of new religions (see **New Religious Movement**) engaged in two questionable practices. The first was to take their children (who were legal adults) to court to have them declared mentally unsound. The second was **Deprogramming**, a usually involuntary process of reverse indoctrination. Professional deprogrammers would sometimes forcibly kidnap young people and hold them against their will, haranguing them day and night to give up their beliefs.

The CFF was initially in favour of deprogramming, but when public opinion turned against it in the late 1970s, the CFF publicly dissociated itself from the practice, in favour of the more voluntary **exit counselling**. In 1984 the CFF renamed itself the Cult Awareness Network of the Citizens' Freedom Foundation, and then simply the Cult Awareness Network (CAN). Despite its public stance against deprogramming, there is evidence that CAN referred parents to deprogrammers.

In 1996 CAN was successfully sued, along with deprogrammer Rick Ross, over the attempted deprogramming of a member of an American Pentecostal Church. The million-dollar judgment bankrupted CAN. Its assets, including its name and helpline telephone number, were purchased at auction by a group which included members of the Church of **Scientology**, which had for some years been bitterly opposed to CAN. A new organization, the Religious Freedom Foundation was set up, using the operating name of the Cult Awareness Network. The new CAN, run by members of several religions, actively campaigns for tolerance for new religious movements, and against anti-cult individuals and organizations. It has been referred to as 'an anti-anti-cult group'.

Further reading

Melton, J. G. (1999) 'Anti-Cultists in the United States', in B. Wilson and J. Cresswell (eds) *New Religious Movements: Challenge and Response*, London: Routledge

DAVID V. BARRETT

CYBERSPACE RELIGIONS

The Internet has spread with an unprecedented rapidity, permanently altering the character of social life. Mass access to the Internet began in 1995 and by 2002 there were well over 500 million users. While active usage is dominated by Americans, Canadians, and Europeans, many other nations, like Brazil, Japan, and China, are fast becoming significant contributors to the development of cyberspace. At the beginning of the twenty-first century Internet usage is dominated by email and searches for information, but a growing number of users see the Internet as more than a tool. It is becoming an alternative living 'space' in which they can experience forms of social interaction that circumvent the physical, temporal, and social restrictions of their offline lives.

Religion is abundantly present on the World Wide Web, Internet chat and news groups. Religious and spiritual themes are one of the largest categories of classification on search engines and more people use the Internet for religious purposes than to do banking, trade stocks, or find dates (PEW, 2001). Every major world religion is represented, every major and minor Christian denomination, almost all new religious movements (see **New Religious Movement**), thousands of specific churches, and countless web pages operated by individual believers, self-declared gurus, prophets, shamans, apostates, and other moral entrepreneurs. In addition the net has spawned its own religious creations, from megasites of cyber-spirituality to virtual 'churches', and strictly online religions. To this mix we can add numerous commercial sites wishing to turn a profit by catering to our spiritual appetites, and sites launched to educate the public or to pursue a diverse array of religious causes (e.g., sites based on university courses or anti-cult crusades).

On the Internet people can:

- read about religion,
- talk with others about religion,
- download religious texts and documents,
- buy religious books and artifacts,
- see images of their religious leaders, watch video clips, and listen to religious music, sermons, prayers, testimonials, and discourses,
- take virtual tours of galleries of religious art or the interiors of religious buildings,
- search scriptures using electronic indexes,
- locate churches and religious centers,
- request intercessory prayers and rulings from religious authorities,
- participate in rituals, mediation sessions, and virtual pilgrimages.

In a mundane sense, it is clear people can practise their religion online. Individuals from widely disparate locations and backgrounds, for example, can meet online to interpret and debate the meaning of a staggering array of primary religious documents posted on the Internet. In fact never before have so many people had such easy and complete access to the religious literature of their own traditions and most others in the world. This new reality fundamentally changes the public context in which all religions will operate in the future.

Studies of virtual rituals, part of the more experiential elements of religious life, have come to more ambiguous conclusions. These cyber-rituals appear to be as efficacious as ones performed in real life. Observation and testimony suggest that they have the capacity to transform the mental and emotional state of participants in ways perceived to be authentic. Nonetheless, the reliance on computer-generated simulacra and exchanges of text messages to enact these rites appears rather contrived and limiting. Virtual rituals depend more on the imagination to work, but in continuity with the symbolic character of other forms of ritual. 'The medium is the message', as McLuhan (1965) declared, and the Internet induces an increased reflexivity in its users that may interfere with trust in authority and the release from inhibitions that fosters a sense of the sacred in offline contexts.

Consequently, cyberspace may be better suited to the needs and orientations of some religious traditions than others. Neo-pagan and Wiccan groups (see **Wicca**) are conspicuous online, while the Roman Catholic Church has officially proscribed the use of the Internet to hear confessions or perform the sacraments.

The Internet presents every religion, no matter how small, with a quick and economical means of establishing a global presence – by spreading their message and maintaining direct, interactive, and daily contact with officials and members. It allows groups to create and maintain a sense of community even though they are not physically co-present in any great numbers. It makes it easier to circumvent the control of broadcast media and information by traditional elites and commercial interests. By the same token, the breadth of information online and opportunities for 'boundary breaking' encounters with individuals from other cultures and religions can jeopardize the ability of religious authorities to shape the views of their members. The diffuse, largely unregulated, and easily accessed nature of computer-mediated communication poses new and serious challenges for the control of religious information and innovations, as well as the preservation of lines of authority within traditions. The Internet makes it easier for schisms to occur, for opponents and apostates to be heard, and information manipulated in defiance of the intentions of its creators. The sheer variety and cacophony of religious viewpoints expressed online can have a disillusioning effect.

As reliable empirical research displaces speculative discourses, efforts have begun to understand the Internet in the context of larger social-structural changes sweeping through late modern societies. There are positive feedback loops between the changes in society, technology, and religion that need to be delineated. Specialized, multiple, and partial social networks without clear geographical loci, for example, are increasingly displacing traditional communities in the social life of ordinary citizens. The Internet both fosters this change and buffers people from its consequences. The link to changes in religious sensibilities has yet to be adequately investigated.

Further reading

McLuhan, M. (1965) *Understanding Media*, New York: McGraw-Hill.

PEW Internet and American Life Project (2001) 'Cyberfaith: How Americans Pursue Religion Online', available online at www.pewinternet.org .

Dawson, L. L. and Cowan, D. E. (eds) (2004) *Religion Online*, New York: Routledge.

Hadden, J. K. and Cowan, D. E. (eds) (2000) *Religion on the Internet: Research Prospects and Promises*, New York: JAI Press.

Wellman, B. and Haythornthwaite, C. (eds) (2002) *The Internet in Everyday Life*, Oxford: Blackwell.

LORNE L. DAWSON

D

DAIMOKU (INVOCATION)

The Nichiren school of Buddhism developed and propagated by Nichiren Daishonin (1222–82) teaches that the Lotus Sutra contains the most important teachings of Buddha. This school further teaches that one can experience the deepest truth of Buddhism by chanting the name of the sutra while praying. The act of chanting *Nam Myoho Renge Kyo* is known as 'Daimoku'. This chanting is valued both by the traditional Nichiren schools and the new religions under the Nichiren umbrella such as **Soka Gakkai**, **Reiyû-kai**, **Rissho Kosei-kai**, and **Myochikai**.

While Daimoku (invocation) in the form of chanting the Mystic Law of *Nam-myoho Renge-Kyo* (meaning literally: Devotion to the Wonderful Law Lotus Sutra) was part of religious practices even before the thirteenth century, it was only after Nichiren that it assumed such importance and became such a frequent and widespread practice.

'Daimoku' resembles 'Nembutsu' which is practiced by the Jodo (Pure Land) and Jodo Shin Sects. 'Nembutsu' is the act of repeating the sacred name of Amitabha, the Buddha of salvation, with a view to being reborn in the Land of Happiness or Pure Land in the West. This practice and accompanying belief is based on the notion of that ordinary people living in the last days (*mappo*) of the Buddhist Law or *dharma*, since they are unable to afford the costs of full length training in Buddhism, can none the less achieve salvation simply through chanting 'Nembutsu'.

'Daimoku' means chanting the name of the Lotus Sutra, which describes the most important teachings of Sakyamuni Buddha, instead of a particular name of the Buddha. It is a practice, therefore, that is based on worship of the Lotus Sutra. Unlike 'Nembutsu' which expresses a desire for salvation in the other world, 'Daimoku' as a practice aims at salvation in this world in the form of obtaining divine favors such as curing illness and disease.

One of the reasons the Nichiren-inspired new religions (see **New Religion, Japan**) developed in modern Japan is that the practice of 'Daimoku' was familiar to modern Japanese. Moreover, many Nichiren-inspired new religions (see **New Religious Movement**) are lay Buddhist movements. The training and practices do not require advanced scholarly knowledge. They offer a type of Buddhism that ordinary people preoccupied with their families and occupations can practice without becoming priests and having to dedicate themselves exclusively to spiritual matters. For these and other reasons 'Daimoku' has spread remarkably in contemporary Japan thereby revitalizing a tradition that has existed since the thirteenth century.

SUSUMU SHIMAZONO

DALAI LAMA

For centuries the Buddhist monasteries in Tibet had been involved with political power. Faced with a military alliance aimed at destroying his Geluk school of Buddhism, the 'Great Fifth' Dalai Lama (1617–82) appealed for support from his Mongol devotees. These were led by the powerful Gushri Khan. He defeated the main rivals to Geluk hegemony and in 1642 gave control of Tibet over to the Dalai Lama. By most accounts the Dalai Lama was by the standards of his age a reasonably tolerant and benevolent ruler.

The Dalai Lamas are held by their followers to be advanced **Mahāyāna** *bodhisattvas* that is compassionate beings who so to speak have postponed their own entry into nirvana to help suffering humanity. Thus they are thought to be well on the way to Buddhahood, developing perfection in wisdom and compassion for the benefit of all sentient beings. It is this that justifies

doctrinally the socio-political involvement of the Dalai Lamas, as an expression of a bodhisattva's compassionate wish to help others.

A Dalai Lama is also held to be a *trulku*. In its Indian Buddhist origins this term refers to an emanation – or a 'transformation' body manifested by a Buddha in order to help ordinary sentient beings. In Tibetan Buddhism, however, the expression has come to be used to refer to a person who is considered to be a reincarnation of a previous teacher. The implication is that the previous teacher developed the ability through spiritual cultivation to control his or her rebirths in order to return to continue the bodhisattva path of helping others. Thus it happens that a child is identified as the reincarnation and trained to readopt his or her previous position and status. The trulkus form an important institution in the Tibetan Buddhist hierarchy, providing in particular a degree of 'hereditary' continuity within a political system that came to be dominated by celibate monks.

Finally, the Dalai Lama is thought to be a *trulba*. This is a much rarer phenomenon in Tibetan Buddhism. Tibetans normally speak of a *trulba* as an emanation of an important named 'transcendental' bodhisattva. It was the Fifth Dalai Lama who discovered through a revelation that the Dalai Lamas are *trulbas* of the Mahāyāna Bodhisattva Avalokiteśvara, the 'bodhisattva of compassion'. This status can entail seeing the Dalai Lama as literally Avalokiteśvara in person, in the form of a human monk. But there is also found a less exalted estimation of his status, as someone who has been blessed by Avalokiteśvara as the result of the Dalai Lama's strong vows of compassion in previous lives. A Dalai Lama is thereby enabled to act compassionately beyond his normal human capacity.

We should note here two things a Dalai Lama is *not*. First, he is not in any simple sense a 'god-king'. He may be a sort-of king, but he is not for Buddhism a god. Second, the Dalai Lama is not 'the Head of Tibetan Buddhism', let alone of Buddhism as a whole. There are many traditions of Buddhism. Some have nominated 'Heads'; some do not. Within Tibet too there are a number of traditions. The Head of the Geluk tradition is whoever is abbot of Ganden monastery, in succession to Tsong kha pa, the fourteenth/fifteenth century Geluk founder.

There have to date been fourteen Dalai Lamas, each one held to be his predecessor's reincarnation. The Third (1543–88) was the first actually to be called 'Dalai Lama'. *Dalai* means 'ocean', and is the Mongolian equivalent of the Tibetan *gyatso* that has normally been part of the names of the Dalai Lamas. When the Third Dalai Lama converted the Mongolian Altan Khan to his own brand of Buddhism the Mongolian-Tibetan hybrid title 'Dalai Lama' was bestowed by the latter upon the Third, who then in turn bestowed it retrospectively on his two previous recognized incarnations.

The Fifth Dalai Lama was the first to rule all Tibet. The Sixth Dalai Lama (1683–1706), like his predecessor, was intended to be Head of the Tibetan State, and a celibate Buddhist monk. However, he returned his monk's vows and preferred to drink alcohol and have fun. He also left behind him a racy reputation with the girls of Lhasa, the capital city of Tibet, and a small collection of unique love poetry. The Sixth disappeared in 1706 while under Mongol military escort, still in his early twenties. It was given out that he had died of illness. But the Dalai Lama was thought by some to have been murdered.

The other Dalai Lama who was particularly important was the Thirteenth (1876–1933). A strong ruler he tried, generally unsuccessfully, to modernize Tibet. The 'Great Thirteenth' also took advantage of weakening Chinese influence in the wake of the 1911 imperial collapse to reassert *de facto* what Tibetans have always considered to be truly the case, the complete independence of Tibet as a nation from China.

The current Fourteenth Dalai Lama (Tenzin Gyatso) was born in 1935. The Chinese invaded Tibet in the early 1950s and the Dalai Lama left Tibet in 1959. He now lives as a refugee in Dharamsala, North India, where he presides over the Tibetan Government in Exile. A learned and charismatic figure, he has been active in promoting the cause of his country's independence from China. He also promulgates Buddhism, world peace, and research into Buddhism and science, through his frequent travels, teaching, and books. Advocating 'universal responsibility and a good heart', he was awarded the Nobel Peace Prize in 1989.

Further reading

Dalai Lama (1990) *Dalai Lama, His Holiness the 14th Freedom in Exile: The Autobiography of the Dalai Lama of Tibet*, London, Sydney, Auckland, Toronto: Hodder and Stoughton

PAUL WILLIAMS

DAMANHUR

Damanhur, at first calling itself a 'city-state' or 'community of Aquarius', and now the Federation of Communities, was founded in 1976 in Valchiusella, 40 kilometers north of Turin, Italy, and can be considered to be a classic example of a post-**New Age Movement**. Its prefoundation roots lie in the studies and activities of Oberto Airaudi (1950–) and of the Horus Research and Information Service of Turin, devoted to parapsychology, esoteric studies and natural medicine.

At first, Damanhur (whose name – 'city of light' – derives from that of an ancient Egyptian city consecrated to the god Horus) had a very small population. Many communities and alternative movements were launched in the 1970s, but Damanhur remained true to itself, thanks to the central role that the spiritual and magical dimension of life and religious optimism has always played in its structure. Convinced that they were living at the dawn of the New Age (see **New Age Movement**), the Damanhurians created a self-sufficient microsociety in harmony with itself and with Nature. To immediately express their union with Nature and all forms of life, many Damanhurians gave themselves the names of animals, such as Raven, Nightingale, Ram, Gazelle, Phoenix, Unicorn and so on.

As Damanhur's population grew to more than a hundred, its first constitution was drawn up; ministers of agriculture, commerce, culture, foreign affairs, and finance were appointed, and an internal currency, the credit, was introduced. Damanhur began to consider itself to be a federation of communities with its own flag, and provided cultural, health, and educational facilities for its children. The citizens of Damanhur, who have amended their Constitution several times, now number more than 500; another 400 or so live in the vicinity. There are four types of citizenship: level A resident citizens, level B resident citizens, level C non-resident citizens, and level D non-resident citizens, depending on their degree of presence in Damanhur, their solidarity, and their respect for the principles and laws contained in its Constitution. As it grew, Damanhur became a reference community for thousands of visitors and supporters, who are received in several facilities/buildings with information services, exhibitions, and shops. Visitors can also enjoy a brief stay at Damanhur or attend some of the many courses and workshops given by Damanhur University throughout the year. The courses are organized according to subject matter: psychic sciences, paranormal studies, natural medicine, ecology, esoteric studies, and others. In recent years, the most popular courses have been art, esoteric and spiritual physics, and spiritual politics. Visitors to Damanhur have increased from about 7,000 in 1989 to 50,000 in 1997; this number was surpassed in 2000.

The core of Damanhurian thought is contained in the book entitled *The Horusian Way*, considered to be an initiatory path which, through the passing of tests and spiritual transformations, liberates individuals from their karmic cycle of reincarnations, allowing them, as their final goal, to become Consciousness, i.e., living participation in all forms. The Horusian Way contains eight fundamental questions: life as evolutive path, actions as continuous choices, the search for new logics for understanding reality, differences and complementarities between the feminine and masculine genders, creativity and continuous transformation, expansion of sensitivity, i.e. of the senses of man's multiple bodies, and uncertainty.

Every aspect of collective and individual life at Damanhur is accompanied by symbols and celebrations that also include a ritual moment: the most complex of these commemorate the two solstices and equinoxes, the commemoration of the deceased, and the founding of the community (coinciding with New Year's Day on 31 August). Alongside these major rituals, there is also a wide range of rituals linked to daily life, to the normal rhythms of time and work.

The place richest in symbols and rites is the Temple of Man: a large underground structure composed of rooms, laboratories and corridors. Begun in absolute secrecy in 1978, its construction was finally revealed by a former Damanhurian in 1992. A lawsuit based on accusations of presumed construction abuses has recently been settled, and building can now proceed much to the satisfaction of the community, divided into the Damjl, Etulte, Tentyris, Rama and Pan centers, in addition to a sixth community currently being formed in Berlin, Germany.

The imposing structure, which the media has at times called an 'underground city' illustrates Damanhur's attempt to physically represent its 'mystic pole'. Today, visitors to the Temple of Man are struck by the richness of its symbols and myths of various religions and traditions: signs of the 'sacred book' of Damanhur, salt of the earth, water, spheres, metals, mirrors. Following the revelation of the Temple's existence, Damanhur's forms of social participation and public identity have expanded, even to the extent of its forming its own political movement. The most politically and socially important event, was the election of a Damanhurian as mayor of Vidracco (the municipality in which the Temple of Man is located).

Further reading

Berzano, L. (1998) *Damanhur. Popolo e comunità*, Leumann (Torino): Elledici.

Merrifield, J. (1998) *Damanhur: The Real Dream*, London: Thorsons.

PIERLUIGI ZOCCATELLI

DEEPER LIFE BIBLE CHURCH

Deeper Life Bible Church, often abbreviated to 'Deeper Life', is one of the earliest independent Charismatic organizations in West Africa with vigorous evangelistic activities, a strong holiness ethos, and a sectarian orientation. Its growth is inextricably linked to the religious experience of the founder, William Folorunso Kumuyi.

W. F. Kumuyi

Born on 6 June 1941 of Ijesha parents then resident in Ijebuland, South-Western Nigeria, Kumuyi was brought up an Anglican, but claimed that he truly experienced conversion on 4 April 1964 after attending an Apostolic Faith Mission at Ikenne. After completing his secondary education at Mayflower School, Ikenne about 1963, the principal, Tai Solarin, a renowned atheist, sponsored his studies at the University of Ibadan, where he graduated with a first class degree in Mathematics in 1967. He taught for a few years at Mayflower School, then earned a postgraduate diploma in education in 1971, and thereafter was employed as a lecturer in the University of Lagos, Lagos.

Beginning and growth

From his involvement in the Charismatic Renewal, Kumuyi in early 1973 started a Bible study class that met on Monday evenings in his flat on the university campus. It witnessed tremendous growth within a year necessitating larger accommodation outside the campus. A widely-advertised camp meeting held in December 1975 and the adoption of a name, Deeper Christian Life Ministry, marked the beginning of an independent existence. Kumuyi left the Apostolic Faith Mission at this time when the church insisted that only ordained ministers could preach and evangelize. The group witnessed a steady growth as Bible study centres were established in other towns from mid-1976. Besides, the Easter retreat that began in 1976 and the December camp became regular annual events and created a bond that held the inter-denominational group together. The offer of free food, accommodation and transportation for those attending these meetings provided huge publicity. Never before had any Christian group offered such things to the public.

An effective literature ministry ensured the production and wide dissemination of many tracts and pamphlets written by Kumuyi. In addition, Kumuyi's sermons were produced on audiocassettes and distributed to distant places at cheap prices. Furthermore, a short-term ministerial training program offered in Lagos from the late 1970s attracted mostly college students, recent graduates, and other Africans.

Other African nationals resident in Nigeria also joined Deeper Life, and rapidly carried this religious innovation to their countries. For example, a Bible study group was established in Kumasi, Ghana in 1979, and a resident pastor was posted there in October 1980. There was rapid growth in Ghana from 5,704 members in seventy-two churches in 1988 to a membership of 20,832 in 270 churches in 1993.

In the early 1980s, missionaries were sent to some African countries to evangelize and establish more branches. By the mid-1980s Deeper Life groups had also been planted in the Philippines, England and the United States. These branches offered avenues for Africans in the Diaspora to express their religious experience within an indigenous setting.

The tremendous growth stimulated other developments, including the introduction of Sunday services on 7 November 1982. Again, early in 1983, Kumuyi created 5,000 Home Caring Fellowships throughout the country. These small groups meeting on Sunday evenings in homes afforded members the opportunity for close and personal relationships. New doctrinal emphases on **healing** and miracles strengthened internal cohesion and popularized Kumuyi's image. Other developments included the appointment of full time pastors to replace the non-salaried leaders, the acquisition of land, the erection of permanent buildings beginning first in Lagos, and a planned program of expansion.

Doctrinal emphases and practices

It was the doctrinal emphases of Deeper Life that actually gained it popularity from the mid-1970s. First, the emphasis on holiness, developed from Kumuyi's connection with the Apostolic Faith Mission, and its practical application that included a ban on the wearing of earrings for women, a ban on possessing and watching televisions, the prescription of a strict dress codes, the introduction of regulations regarding relations with non-Christians and the opposite sex, and the rejection of worldly values. Second, Kumuyi insisted on converts making amends for their past wrongs and mistakes, which he termed restitution. This emphasis challenged society's permissiveness and eventually created a new moral community among members. Cases of members who made restitution for such 'sins' as cheating in examinations, using forged certificates, and stealing from employers were widely reported as testimonies in the secular media. Third, Kumuyi placed great stress on self-discipline and on fidelity in marriage and piety in family life. Courtship was to be sanctioned by the church, preparation towards marriage should not involve going to marriage counselors or reading what Kumuyi called 'worldly' books, the wedding ceremony must be simple, full of godliness and not of festivities, and the use of wedding rings forbidden, as were polygamy and divorce. Kumuyi attempted to ensure adherence to this teaching with many booklets and regular seminars. Lastly, every member was encouraged to be an active evangelist on a daily basis regardless of the circumstances.

Conclusion

In October 1990, a decentralization program led to the establishment of additional branches in many towns, and subsequently an accelerated growth. The much-advertised International Church Growth Conference hosted by Deeper Life in Lagos in August 1992 further raised the public profile of the church. However, there were schisms in the 1990s led by some pastors in Nigeria and the United States. The proliferation of Charismatic organizations from the mid-1990s with more popular and contemporary emphases such as prosperity (see **prosperity theology**) and deliverance further retarded growth. Commencing in 2001, specialized programs were organized for youth and students to enlist more members.

Deeper Life doctrinal emphases and practices stimulated significant changes in Nigerian Christianity. While the stress on holiness sustained a personal morality and a pristine religious community, the evangelistic programs set the pace of growth strategy for other Charismatic organizations.

Further reading

Matthews, A. O. (1988) 'Deeper Christian Life Ministry: A Case Study of the Charismatic Movements in Western Nigeria', *Journal of Religion in Africa*, XVII(2), 141–62.

Matthews, A. O. (1992) 'Deeper Life Bible Church in Nigeria' in *New Dimensions in African Christianity*, P. Gifford (ed.) Nairobi: All African Conference of Churches, 135–56.

MATTHEWS A. OJO

DEGUCHI, NAO

Deguchi Nao (1836–1918) was the founder of Ōmoto (Great Origin) one of Japan's most significant new religions (see **New Religion, Japan**). Born into a poor rural family, Nao married a carpenter whose drinking and gambling left her the main breadwinner for a family of eight children at a time when Japanese society was undergoing massive transformation through industrialization. Unable to establish a foothold in the changing economy, the family's fortunes declined further. Nao was reduced to rag-picking; one son disappeared after an attempted suicide, another was killed in the Sino-Japanese War, and one daughter went mad.

At 53, Nao herself experienced numerous spirit possessions, and Ōmoto dates its founding from that time (1892). She identified the god of her revelations as Ushitora Konjin, also revered in Konkōkyō as a universal parent god mistakenly believed by many to be a mere directional deity guarding the northeast. Unlike any other popular understandings of this deity, Nao's Ushitora Konjin revealed that he intended to 'reform and renovate' (tatekae-tatenaoshi) the entire world in a millenarian (see **Millenarianism**) upheaval that would overthrow the current capitalist order and establish an agrarian utopia. In her writing *The Brush Tip* (*Ofudesaki*) Nao explained that a divine kingdom was to be established on earth and urged humanity to prepare themselves for its advent.

She proclaimed that Konjin was the ultimate deity, that Japan had become an evil society guided only by self interest, and she called for a 'renovation of the world', predicting an imminent apocalypse. She built a headquarters in the town of Ayabe, where followers formed a commune, and her revelations continued. The police saw a threat in her millenarian message and subjected Nao to repeated interrogation, also suppressing her following.

During her lifetime, Ōmoto remained a small rural group, but with the advent of Nao's co-founder and son-in-law Deguchi Onisaburô (see **Onisaburô**), it began to expand in urban society, and especially from around 1910 it grew dramatically into a highly influential movement. Many later leaders of new religious movements drew inspiration from Ōmoto.

Further reading

Ooms, E. G. (1993) *Women and Millenarian Protest in Meiji Japan: Deguchi Nao and Ōmotokyô*, Ithaca, NY: East Asia Program, Cornell University.

HELEN HARDACRE

DEIMA

This religion was founded by Bagué Honoyo (1892–1951) in the Ivory Coast. While she uses for official purposes the name Bagué Honoyo she is known among her followers by the more familiar name 'Marie Lalou'. Widowed by the mysterious disappearance of her husband and childless, she refused to marry which led to her being suspected of witchcraft and being treated as mad. She felt called to celibacy and a solitary life wandering in the forest. Marie Lalou had visions expressing the myths and symbolism of the forest dwellers and devoted herself to a struggle against sorcery and against buried fetishes that defile the earth. She was also looking for a basis on which whites and blacks could cooperate. Although often suffering rejection, she gathered small groups of disciples who valued her songs and her 'gospels', that is to say, the prophetic teaching which she revealed to them.

At a later stage, she was influenced by a passing missionary and absorbed some Christian teaching; she also gained a few literate followers.

In 1942, a congregation was formed around the founder and three male evangelists. Her teaching was preserved by oral tradition and a standard liturgy was developed for the movement; places of worship were built. After her death, the help of scholars towards putting their oral tradition in written form was welcomed by her congregation. In 1974 J. Girard published *Les Évangiles de la Prophétesse Bagué Honoyo* (The Gospels of the Prophetess Bagué), as a posthumous collection of her teachings approved by her congregation.

A central symbol used in the liturgy is the *Ku-Su* or 'Death Tree', a stripped palm tree stylized in the form of a cross. It has associations both with tradition and with Christian teaching. For the faithful it certainly recalls the death of Jesus but also crimes against nature including the burying of fetishes in the earth. Worshippers stand before *Ku-Su* to confess their sins, including the ecological ones, and to seek reconciliation. Friday worship is a special liturgy emphasizing sinfulness. Sunday is a more joyful day. For the everyday struggle against evil, fetishes and sorcery, there is sacramental use of symbols: ashes (*lalou*) are a cleansing agent. Water is prominent. The founder insisted that bottles of water ritually blessed (*deima*) were on sale (otherwise they would not be appreciated) but at a very small price. She also used cowry shells in divination.

Further reading

Girard, J. (ed.) (1974) *Les Évangiles de la Prophétesse Bagué Honoyo,* Grenoble: Presses Universitaires de Grenoble.

RALPH WOODHALL

DELIVERANCE (AND NEO-CHARISMATIC CHURCHES)

Deliverance is a popular practice in neo-charismatic churches in Africa and other places (see **African Charismatic Churches**). The practice thrives on the belief that malevolent supernatural forces can interfere in human affairs. Such interference may result in misfortunes such as persistent failures in a person's life, accidents, sicknesses, and premature deaths in families. In deliverance, the power of Jesus is invoked through prayer to liberate a person, situation or place disturbed as a result of such interference.

Deliverance is sometimes presented as a necessary rite for all new Christians. It is assumed that everybody, before conversion, has been involved in some of the things that make people vulnerable to demonic influences. Such things, designated 'demonic doorways', include cultural practices, traumatic experiences, immorality, and curses. The effects of such things are not automatically neutralized on one's conversion. It is therefore necessary to remove them through deliverance so that new believers may experience an uninterrupted flow of God's grace into their lives.

Believers seek deliverance from all kinds of evils including not only words and deeds considered 'sinful' by Christianity but also most of what modern psychology would diagnose as psychopathic behaviour or personality maladjustment. Also included are tragic events and conditions such as accidents, chronic illness and unstable marriages. Experiences such as spirit-possession, bad dreams, and haunted places are also handled through deliverance.

The actual act of deliverance often involves confession of sins, renunciation of occult involvement, prayer to 'break' covenants believed to have been made directly or indirectly with forces of darkness and laying-on of hands. People being delivered may cough out great quantities of phlegm, urinate, or perspire profusely and exhibit behaviour such as screaming, prolonged yawning, and weeping.

Deliverance may be seen as an alternative response to the same problems which psychology has tried to address. Morton Kelsey, in his work, *Discernment: A study in Ecstasy and Evil,* calls such problems, 'evils of the latter days'. He cites examples, 'floating anxiety and formless terror ... loss of meaning, futility and depression ... guilt and shame ... blind hate and hostility ... compulsion and neurosis...'.

For the African Charismatic Christian who lives with a keener awareness of the supernatural, deliverance is a relevant response to the problem of evil.

Further reading

Kelsey, M. T. (1978) *Discernment: A Study in Ecstasy and Evil,* New York: Paulist.

ABAMFO O. ATIEMO

DEPROGRAMMING

Deprogramming emerged in the early 1970s as a response to the rapid growth of **New Religious Movement**s (NRMs), popularly termed cults (see **cult and new religions**), through conversions of young adults in North America and Europe. Deprogramming involved the abduction and physical restraint of NRM members with the objective of inducing them to sever their membership ties. The practice was premised on the assumption that NRM affiliations were involuntary, the product of cultic programming (see **brainwashing**). Deprogrammers often were successful in achieving their objective of membership renunciation, and a major struggle over deprogramming continued through the 1970s and 1980s.

Proponents accused NRMs of kidnapping members through brainwashing, and opponents charged deprogrammers with kidnapping for faith breaking. When anti-cult activists were unable to secure legal protection for deprogramming, the practice gradually declined and was replaced by a non-coercive alternative termed exit counseling.

The anti-cult movement and deprogramming

The 1960s and 1970s were remarkable for their outpouring of religious innovation. The cohort of NRMs that appeared during this period drew upon the same wellspring of youthful discontent as had the 1960s countercultural movements. However, the counterculture did not offer long-term lifestyle solutions to participants and had begun to wane by the early 1970s. The appearance of a diverse array of NRMs at that time, many of which were of Asian origin, provided an alternative outlet through which to reject conventional lifestyles. The constituency for NRMs was predominantly well-educated, white, middle class, young adults. When these individuals appeared to be jettisoning carefully planned educational and occupational career plans for experimentation with NRMs, family members initially were mystified and disturbed by what they regarded as irrational and uncharacteristic behavior. Family members soon concluded that NRM affiliations were not voluntary at all but rather were the product of coercive mind control processes, which they termed brainwashing, employed by dangerous, predatory cults that were masquerading as authentic religions. Within a short time, family members had banded together into anticult associations dedicated to combating groups they designated as cults.

Over time grassroots anti-cult associations (see **Anti-Cult Movement**) coalesced into two primary organizations, the American Family Foundation (AFF) and the Cult Awareness Network (CAN), which had as their missions informing the public about the danger posed by cults and opposing the groups themselves. However, these organizations did not resolve the problem of families with relatives who already were cult members. Alongside the anti-cult associations, therefore, emerged a coterie of entrepreneurial intervention specialists who acted as agents of families that sought to extract individuals from NRMs. These deprogrammers, as they called themselves, had as their mission reversing cultic programming (brainwashing) and liberating individuals from cultic entrapment. As it developed, deprogramming involved gaining physical control over NRM members, often through physical abduction; taking them to a secluded, secure location; and then employing whatever forms of argumentation and influence would induce them to disaffiliate from the NRM. Deprogrammings were deemed 'successful' by proponents if they resulted in a renunciation of membership by the deprogrammee.

The advent of deprogramming

The invention of deprogramming is attributable to a single moral entrepreneur, Theodore Roosevelt 'Ted' Patrick, Jr. In 1971 Patrick was a community action worker in San Diego when members of his family were approached by recruiters from the Children of God (COG). He was disturbed by their reports of the encounter, and when by chance another parent appeared in his office to complain about a similar incident, he decided to personally investigate COG. Upon his return from a COG recruitment camp, he described

144

himself as having been a virtual prisoner and his exit as an 'escape'. He soon developed a crude theory of brainwashing that he initially thought described unique COG practices, but within a short time the theory was extended to a variety of groups that in his view employed similar tactics.

According to Patrick, brainwashing involved hypnosis through brain waves projected from a cult recruiter's eyes and fingertips. Once cults had individuals under their control, the groups programmed them through a combination of constant indoctrination, a totalistic environment and self-hypnosis that insured continued subservience. Based on this reasoning Patrick began developing a means of reversing cultic programming, which he termed deprogramming. According to Patrick the process involved opening up the individual's mind by providing alternative information. Once they were able to think and evaluate ideas again, he asserted, cult members would deprogram themselves and exit the cult. In reality, the process typically involved, as we have seen, abducting an individual, moving them to a remote location, and physically confining them for periods ranging from a few days to a few weeks until they agreed to renounce NRM membership. Patrick soon discovered, however, that many individuals needed further rehabilitation to insure that they were completely free of cultic influence. As a result, support facilities such as rehabilitation centers and halfway houses were created to monitor deprogrammees through the transition period.

Patrick claimed that he deprogrammed more than 1,600 NRM members personally, doubtless an exaggeration, and that his exploits earned him the moniker 'Black Lightning' from NRMs. Patrick's impact derived not only from his own deprogramming activity but also from training a coterie of others as deprogrammers. Ultimately Patrick was forced to give up his deprogramming activity as he was repeatedly arrested and prosecuted in civil and criminal cases, resulting in fines and prison sentences.

The organization and impact of deprogramming

In contrast to anti-cult associations, deprogrammers did not create formal organizations but rather operated independently as intervention agents for families. Typically a team of individuals was involved in a deprogramming. The team would include one or more people to provide security, assisting in the abduction and maintaining physical control during the deprogramming; one or more deprogrammers, who interacted directly with the deprogrammee; and one or more former members, who could be present at key moments to provide personal testimony to cultic brainwashing. Family members sometimes were involved at key points, particularly during the abduction in order to deflect legal prosecution and to reunite the family if the deprogramming was successful. Prior to the programming the security team had to discover a location from which the deprogrammee could be abducted, arrange for a secluded location where the deprogrammee could be held for whatever time was necessary; and prepare the family for the impending encounter.

Once the deprogramming sequence had commenced, the process sometimes extended over several days or occasionally even several weeks. During this period some combination of family members, deprogrammers, and former NRM members would use a combination of guilt, concern, argumentation, negative information about the group, testimonials from former members, and threats of continued confinement to convince the deprogrammee to disavow group membership. Given the size of the deprogramming team and the need for physical facilities, and the length of time potentially involved, deprogrammings often were relatively expensive. If rehabilitation facilities and staff were needed, the number of people and cost escalated even further.

Exactly how many deprogrammings have taken place is unknown, but they certainly number in the thousands. Deprogrammings were relatively more common in North America and Japan but quite rare in Europe. The number of incidents rose quickly in the early 1970s and then declined precipitously by the end of that decade. The increase in deprogrammings is attributable to the rapid flow of young adults into NRMs during the early 1970s, an expansion of the number of groups the anti-cult movement designated as cults, and a growth in the ranks of deprogrammers. Correspondingly, the subsequent decline was the result a decreasing flow of individuals into NRMs, increasing spontaneous defection rates, an inability of the anti-cult movement to gain legal sanction for deprogramming, increasing legal sanctions against deprogrammers, and the anti-cult movement's discovery that non-coercive tactics were about as successful in achieving member disaffiliation. Deprogramming was probably successful about two thirds of the time in inducing members to disavow membership in a NRM, although the process was much more successful with recent converts than established members.

Deprogramming had a variety of implications for both NRMs and the anti-cult movement. For larger NRMs the numerical impact of deprogramming was not significant since they were recruiting large numbers of converts and also experiencing a very high rate of spontaneous defection. Smaller groups that were targeted experienced a more substantial impact on membership size. In general deprogramming increased NRMs' seclusiveness, ironically exacerbating one of the characteristics that anti-cult activists decried. Deprogramming also intensified internal solidarity of targeted NRMs, adding to an already heightened sense of persecution in many cases. NRMs found deprogrammees who resisted the process and returned to their groups politically useful, treating them as returning heroes who would not capitulate to the tactics of deprogrammers. In some cases unsuccessful deprogrammings also yielded witnesses against deprogrammers in legal actions. Finally, coercive deprogrammings brought political support from civil libertarian groups that otherwise would not have allied themselves with NRMs.

For the anti-cult movement, deprogramming produced evidence that the battle against cults could be won, even if it was one person at a time. The deprogramming alternative gave the anti-cult associations a key resource to offer families who were prepared to take the accompanying risks. Successful deprogrammings also provided the anti-cult movement with a major source of confirmation for its brainwashing theory as well as evidence that the effects of brainwashing could be reversed. Former NRM members who politically allied themselves with the anti-cult movement became a primary source of atrocity stories that the ACM used to defend its ideology and practices. Apostate members were useful in generating solidarity within anti-cult ranks, sympathetic media coverage, and testimony at government hearings on the dangers of cults. Of course, successful deprogrammings were critical to the reputations of deprogrammers, who relied on past successes to convince families to undertake the risk and expense of a deprogramming to resolve their own family problems.

Deprogramming and the law

The legal struggle over deprogramming essentially rested on charges of kidnapping from both sides. From the point of view of anti-cult activists, brainwashing by cults essentially constituted psychological kidnapping. Brainwashed cult members lacked the capacity for independent, critical thought and were reduced to lives of dependence and servitude. Based on this assumption, extracting individuals, even if force was required was justified in order to restore their natural personalities and capacity for autonomy. From an NRM perspective, deprogrammers and their anti-cult allies were little more than religious faith breakers. For them, converts had the courage to fight off the brainwashing of a spiritually barren society in search of spiritually meaningful lives. Opposed to religious choices that they could not understand or accept, family members attempted to use force to compel conformity with lifestyles from which converts had sought to escape. Each side accused the other of using the color of law to protect its pernicious conduct, and the ensuing struggle was emotionally and morally charged.

Deprogramming obviously confronted the anti-cult movement with legal problems because it involved the physical abduction of legally adult individuals from groups that typically had been granted legal status as religious organizations. Abducting and challenging the faith of these individuals could clearly be interpreted as a challenge to the free exercise of religious belief. For a time deprogrammers operated with relative legal impunity as local law enforcement and judicial officials declined to become embroiled in what they regarded as family disputes. However, resistance to deprogramming gradually developed both in law enforcement agencies, which refused to extend private policing power to deprogrammers, and among the targeted groups.

A variety of legal strategies was tried, to permit deprogramming. Initially, family members requested writs of habeas corpus to compel NRMs to produce members in court, expecting that a direct, personal encounter would be sufficient to persuade NRM members to return home. This strategy soon failed as movements disavowed control over members or knowledge of their whereabouts. The next strategy was to seek judicial conservatorship or guardianship orders (originally created to give family members legal custody over senile elderly relatives) on grounds that NRM members were in fact mentally incapacitated by brainwashing. Conservatorship orders granted family members legal custody over an NRM member for a stipulated time period and thus avoided the necessity of coercion in order to conduct a deprogramming. For a time local courts did grant conservatorship orders, often in *ex parte* hearings, but gradually resistance to this use of these provisions mounted as NRMs provided members with legal counsel. A national campaign to include mind control as grounds for granting conservatorships in state law ultimately proved unsuccessful.

When the conservatorship strategy failed, the anti-cult movement turned to civil suits against NRMs. Taking advantage of a massive exodus from NRMs in the latter 1970s as well as successful deprogrammings, defecting members were encouraged to bring suits against their former groups. Generic charges, such as infliction of mental distress, were filed and anti-cult experts provided testimony on the psychological damage caused by brainwashing. There were some spectacular trial court victories, but verdicts were appealed, awards reduced, cases settled out of court. Gradually brainwashing testimony was excluded from trials on grounds that the theory was not scientifically recognized. As a result, the number of civil suits declined over time. In the absence of a statutory legal defense, individual deprogrammers tried a variety of strategies to avoid legal prosecution such as having family members present or involved in abductions and not initiating the deprogramming until the physical control had been established over the deprogrammee. When deprogrammers were arrested and prosecuted they were more likely to be charged with false imprisonment than kidnapping since they did not fit the standard profile of kidnapers or have obvious criminal motive. At trial deprogrammers often mounted a necessities defense, claiming that their actions, while technically violations, actually prevented the occurrence of a greater evil. This defense sometimes did convince sympathetic jurors to acquit but became increasingly problematic when brainwashing theory no longer received judicial recognition.

The demise of coercive deprogramming

Deprogrammings continued through the early 1990s despite their illegality and formal condemnation. In the absence of legal grounds for intervention and with therapists declining to be involved in non-consensual counseling, only deprogrammers were willing to act as agents for the family and intervene on its behalf. If families could not convince NRM members to agree to exit counseling, deprogramming and simply waiting for NRM experimentation to run its course were among the few alternatives. Anti-cult brainwashing ideology may well have contributed to the impetus for families to elect for deprogramming since they feared NRM members were in imminent danger, a fear to which deprogrammers could appeal. Some families therefore remained desperate enough to want to extract their kin from NRMs, taking the risks attending deprogramming. Another advantage to deprogramming was that there was less stigma attached to the deprogrammee and the family from an account of rescue from a predatory cult than to recovery from mental illness. Deprogrammers also counted on achieving successful deprogrammings, in which case there was no party interested in initiating prosecution. Ironically perhaps, deprogramming was brought to an end by a failed deprogramming. A civil suit was brought against CAN (Cult Awareness Network), through which a deprogramming referral had been arranged. The court judgment bankrupted CAN and eliminated the referral network through which deprogrammers had operated.

Further reading

Bromley, D. G. (ed.) (1998) *The Politics of Religious Apostasy*, Westport, CT: Praeger.

Bromley, D. G. (1988) 'Deprogramming as a Mode of Exit from New Religious Movements: The Case of the Unificationist Movement', in D. Bromley (ed.) *Falling From the Faith*, Newbury Park: Sage.

Patrick, T. with Dulack, T. (1976) *Let Our Children Go!*, New York: Ballantine Books.

Shupe, A. and Bromley, D. (1980) *The New Vigilantes*, Beverly Hills: Sage Publications.

DAVID G. BROMLEY

DINI YA MUSAMBWA

This religious movement which arose in western Kenya and Uganda, accused Christianity of being a 'white man's religion', and proposed a return to veneration of ancestors. It is a neo-primal movement (see **PRINERMs**). The founder was Elijah Masinde (1910–87) who was educated in a mission school and gained distinction playing for the national football team. He separated from the mission staff saying 'he believed in one God but not in one bible'.

Masinde embarked on a career both as independent preacher and as an agitator against colonialism. His position was that the white people had brought some good things but that it was time for them to go. He also criticized the authority given to chiefs. After independence, he was still an agitator against Kenyatta's policy of building a multi-racial society. Consequently, he spent many years in prison or detained in a mental institution. But by the end of his life he was revered by many as a prophet. There was a large attendance at his funeral.

The practice of this new religion centred on pilgrimages to Mount Elgon which was equated with Mount Zion ('Sayoni' in local speech). Here traditional sacrifices were offered. Masinde, however, was selective in his use of traditional religion. While rejecting Christianity (as the white man's religion) he maintained that the ancestral tradition in several respects resembled Christian practice and teaching. For instance, there was less emphasis on praying to ancestors and more to *Were* the High God. His close followers, in the early stages, saw his call as parallel to that of Moses, Jesus and Mohammed; for some of them, he was a messianic figure.

The movement continues to be active politically.

Further reading

Wipper, A. (1977) *Rural Rebels,* Oxford: Oxford University Press (ch. 11).

RALPH WOODHALL

DIVINE LIGHT MISSION

With a focus on self-awareness, Divine Light Mission – now known as Elan Vital – originated in north India and was brought to the West by the 13-year-old 'boy guru', Prem Pal Singh Rawat, and his followers in 1971. The mission was first established by Maharaji's father, Sri Hans ji Maharaj, to spread knowledge of a meditation technique, based on experience of the Divine Light, Music, Nectar, and the Holy Name, that he had learnt in the 1930s from a teacher in the Sant Mat, a Hindu-Sikh spiritual movement.

Under his mother's guidance, Prem Rawat, or 'Maharaji' as he became known, initially cultivated an Indian-oriented movement in the West, with *mahatmas* (teachers), *premis* (lovers of God), *satsang* (congregational religious discourse), and *ashrams* (spiritual communes). It grew quickly, with the influx of some 50,000 American followers within two years of its inception. Like other eastern spiritual imports, it was met with suspicion by some westerners because of its unfamiliar ideas and practices, and the ambiguity of its spiritual message and apparent materialism. In the 1980s Maharaji purged it of its Indian flavour. *Mahatmas* became 'instructors', *satsang* was replaced by the public forum, and *ashrams* were disbanded in favour of ordinary family life. Following his marriage to his key follower and secretary, Marolyn Johnson, Maharaji parted company with his mother, who returned to India, and the future of the mission in the West was in doubt.

However, renamed Elan Vital in the 1980s to reflect the shift from organized religion to the dissemination of a simple spiritual message, the movement continued to promote Maharaji's teachings through personal audiences and audio-visual media, with many thousands being introduced to the 'Knowledge' globally. For example, according to its publicity, in a two-month period in 2002 over 20,000 people were shown the technique, with many more attending his lectures.

Unlike many other leaders of NRMs, Maharaji has not published his teachings or systematized a body of ideas and practices. He is not associated with a community of believers or a formal religious institution. He remains a guru, one who guides others towards the inner light, with Elan Vital as an independent charitable organization that promotes his message.

KIM KNOTT

DRUIDRY

Very little is known about the original Celtic Druidry, which was an oral tradition celebrated mainly in nature. The Druids themselves seem to have combined the roles of priest, prophet, healer, philosopher, and lawgiver. Within the popular imagination, Druidry has positive associations of mistletoe, magic, forest groves, and stone circles; negative associations with human sacrifice and superstition; and jocular images of white robes and pointy hats. Most of these beliefs are mediated through Roman propaganda and the romantic reconstructions of the eighteenth-century revival. Contemporary Druidry looks back to its roots, but is pre-eminently a branch of neo-pagan nature spirituality (see **Neo-Paganism**).

Druidry is one of the two main movements under the neo-pagan umbrella, along with **Wicca** with which it has many similarities. Some pagans work within both traditions and create new syncretic groups drawing from both, sometimes including **Shamanism**. Despite its Celtic heritage, Druidry has become an international movement, particularly in English-speaking countries. There are around 300 Druid groups worldwide, about thirty-five based in Britain. Numbers are hard to estimate but may be around 10,000–15,000 in Britain. A few groups were founded in the eighteenth century (some even claim an unbroken Celtic lineage) but most are post-war creations. The largest is the Order of Bards, Ovates and Druids (OBOD), founded by Ross Nicholls in 1964 and now run by Philip Carr-Gomm, followed by the British Druid Order (BDO) founded by Philip Shallcrass in 1979. The most recent development in Britain is the Druid Network, set up in 2003 by Emma Restall Orr, former co-chief of the BDO, to provide a forum and represent Druidry as broadly as possible.

Druidry is a small, but by no means unified movement. There is a broad division between cultural, political, and spiritual groups. Cultural Druidry is represented by the Eisteddfod, whose main purpose is to promote Welsh culture and language. Their most high-profile recent member is Rowan Williams, Archbishop of Canterbury. Political orders are mainly focused on the battle to open Stonehenge for worship, but they also get involved in other social and environmental campaigns. Their most colourful activist is the self-styled King Arthur of Pendragon, who attracts wide media coverage. Religious views also vary enormously. Cultural groups tend to be secular, humanist, or Christian, while the political and spiritual groups are mainly pagan. Spiritual Druidry can be classified mainly under the neo-pagan and **New Age Movements**. However, even within pagan groups, some are animistic and shamanic while others are polytheistic, worshipping the ancient Celtic gods and goddesses and/or Gaia (as Earth Mother). Although the political and spiritual traditions have many common bonds, and united as a Council in the 1990s to campaign for Stonehenge, they have now split up again following disagreement regarding the balance of political and spiritual issues in Druidry. Structurally there are also many differences. Most groups have some form of initiation and priesthood, but the older orders tend to be more strictly organized and hierarchical, sometimes sexist, while the newer pagan orders are more open and fluid in structure, sometimes based on self-initiation.

Pagan Druidry has core beliefs and practices which most members would accept. Their common aim is the creation of a new indigenous spirituality based on the traditions, monuments, and landscapes of Britain. As exemplified by OBOD, there are three main types or style of Druid – Bards, Ovates, and Druids – all with different but interconnected roles. Although there are no formal sacred texts, all groups share a love of the Mabinogion, the collected Welsh myths. Like most pagans, their ritual comprises magic, divination (based on runes and the Celtic Ogham alphabet), and natural symbolism including the four elements. They celebrate the seasonal festivals of the 'wheel of the year', but their ceremony is always conducted outside within a circular sacred space ('nemeton'), mostly either in woodland groves (oak, ash, and yew being the favourite trees) or among one of Britain's many prehistoric stone monuments. Most important is Stonehenge, which some believe was erected by Druids (although the monument predates the Celts by a thousand years). As already mentioned, Stonehenge both unites and divides the Druid community, who hold divergent views regarding access and usage. Currently, controlled access is allowed for the summer solstice ceremony, which always attracts extensive media attention. Other important sites are Avebury, Glastonbury, and London's Primrose Hill – site of a Druidic ceremony since 1792.

Further reading

Hutton, Ronald (1991) *The Pagan Religions of the Ancient British Isles*, Oxford: Blackwell.

Harvey, Graham and Hardman, Charlotte (eds) (1995) *Pagan Pathways*, London: Thorsons.

ELIZABETH PUTTICK

E

EARTH PEOPLE OF TRINIDAD

It is often conjectured, by scholars and critics alike, that new religions can develop out of the delusions of mental illness. The classic suggestions however never give adequate descriptions of the psychopathology involved, either because of a historical lapse which means the study of the movement comes long after the initial inspiration (e.g. Sabbatai Svi), or the description of 'illness' is very loose, often no more than a lay assumption of 'abnormality' (the Vaihala Madness, the Doukhobors). An exception is the Trinidadian sect of the Earth People which was visited at its formation by an anthropologist and psychiatrist who provided a descriptive psychiatric diagnosis of the founder and all its members, using the World Health Organisation's international diagnostic instrument the Present State Examination (Littlewood, 1993). The founder had had an episode of thyrotoxicosis resulting in a clinical pattern of hypomania, whilst with one exception (a man with schizophrenia), both founder and members were subsequently shown to be psychologically normal.

The Earth People are an antinomian Africanist conununity settled on the north coast of Trinidad which originated in the visions of their leader Mother Earth (Jeanette MacDonald, 1934–84). From 1975 until 1976, she had experienced a series of revelations: she came to understand that the Christian teaching of God the Father as creator was false and that the world was the work of a primordial Mother, whom she identified with Nature and with the Earth. Nature gave birth to a race of Black people, but her rebellious Son (God) re-entered his Mother's womb to gain Her power of generation and succeeded by producing (or forcing Her to create) White people. The Whites, the Race of the Son, then enslaved the Blacks and have continued to exploit them. The Way of the Son is that of Science – of cities, clothes, schools, factories, and wage labour. The Way of The Mother is the Way of Nature – a return to the simplicity of the Beginning, a simplicity of nakedness, cultivation of the land by hand and with respect, and of gentle and non-exploiting human relationships.

The Son, in a continued quest for the power of generation, has recently entered into a new phase. He has now succeeded in establishing himself in Trinidad's Africans and Indians and is also on the point of replacing humankind altogether with computers and robots. Nature, who has borne all this out of love for the whole of Her creation, has finally lost patience. The current order of the Son will end in a catastrophic drought and famine, or a nuclear war, a destruction of the Son's work through his own agency, after which the original state of Nature will once again prevail.

Jeanette herself is a partial manifestation of The Mother who will fully enter into her only at the End. Her task at the time of ethnographic fieldwork (1980–2) was to facilitate the return to Nature by organizing the community known as Hell Valley, the Valley of Decision, to prepare for the return to the Beginning and to 'put out the life' to her people, the Black Nation, The Mother's Children.

She has to combat the false doctrines of existing religions which place the Son over the Mother and to correct the distorted teaching of the Bible where she is represented as the Devil (hence 'Hell Valley'). She stands for Life and Nature, in opposition to the Christian God who is really the Son, the principle of Science and Death. As the Devil she is opposed to churches and prisons, education and money, contemporary morals and fashionable opinions. Because God is 'right' Mother Earth teaches the Left, and the Earth People interchange various conventional oppositions: 'left' for 'right'; 'evil' or 'bad' for 'good'. Seeming obscen-

ities are only Natural words for She Herself is the Cunt, the origin of all life.

The exact timing of the End was uncertain but it was expected in Jeanette's physical lifetime. Then Time would end, Sickness would be healed and the Nation would speak one language. The Son will be exiled to his planet, the Sun, really the Planet of Ice which is currently hidden by Fire placed there by The Mother Fire – which will eventually return to where it belongs, back to the heart of the nurturant earth.

Mother Earth's revelations ceased in 1975–6 after an episode called The Miracle in which she brought the sun closer to the earth. At this time her family were still living with her in a deserted village some fifteen miles from the nearest settlement, and they were joined by an assortment of young men, mostly old friends and neighbours of hers from Port-of-Spain, together with **Rastafarians** attracted by a newspaper article written about this family going naked in the bush. Her ideas were now consolidated in reflection and debate. By 1978 her title of 'Mother Earth' was adopted, possibly after a recent Carnival masquerade which had portrayed a large fecund Earth Mother. Mother Earth continued to have visions in her dreams but these were similar to those of other members: premonitions and answers to the immediate organizational problems on which her attention was now focused. A confirmation of her status as divine Mother occurred with the Coming of the Makers (a group of visiting Rastas).

While around sixty people have been active Earth People at different times, in October 1981 twenty-two were resident in the Valley, with perhaps twenty sympathizers and occasional members in town.

There were annual naked marches into Port-of-Spain which sometimes ended in arrests with brief stays in the state psychiatric hospital for Mother Earth (with a variety of diagnoses), together with raids on the settlement by social workers which resulted in confinement of younger children to an orphanage: Mother Earth's youngest son escaped and trekked back to the community across the mountains. There were however supportive articles in two local periodicals, *Ras Tafari Speaks* and *The Bomb*. Trinidad's first prime minister had recently died and the government was preoccupied with an election: the Hell Valley group were left to themselves.

Only one other member of the group was female, with sixteen young male followers between 18 and 33, most previously associated with Rastafari or Spiritual Baptism, besides Mother Earth and her immediate family. The reason they gave for joining (to the visiting anthropologist in 1981) was the corruption and spiritual decay associated with the post-independence government, and a wish to return to a simpler *natural* lifestyle. In opposition to the *material* world, the group all went naked, sleeping out on the bare ground, and maintained themselves through fishing and cultivation of the land using only cutlasses.

The centre of the community was the old wooden house of the deserted village into which Mother Earth had moved in 1972, together with some added 'African' huts. For about half a mile in each direction, the secondary bush and scrub of the seasonal rain forest had been cleaned and a variety of trees and perennial cultigens were grown: medicine bushes; trees and plants for cordage and wrapping, and for basketry and calabashes; timber for building; plantain and banana; roots like cassava, sweet potatoes, dasheen, yam, tannia; aubergine, pineapple, tomato, pigeon peas, callaloo, okra; Indian corn, pumpkin,

ginger, sugar cane, christophene; trees bearing oranges, grapefruit, guava, nuts, mango, avocado, pawpaw, pomerac, tamarind and breadfruit; garlic and bushes with pepper, shadobenny and other herbs. Above the settlement, reaching into the lower reaches of the mountains of the northern range, were cocoa and coffee, cannabis and tobacco. In the nearby bush were cress and watermelon, mauby bark, mammy apple, passion fruit, star apple, nutmeg and soursap, whilst along the coast grew coconut and almond. The variety of crops, virtually every Trinidad food plant, perhaps justified the boast of the Earth People that they were living in the original Eden.

Although all members accepted Mother Earth's role as the Original Mother, the group were 'this worldly' in their emphasis on present cultivation of the land and on the preparation and consumption of food. Daily agricultural labour ended with a swim in the sea and Mother Earth ritually dealing out the cooked vegetable food to the group. The central 'rite of synthesis' (as anthropologists would put it) was this daily meal. The evening was passed with the smoking of cigars and ganja spliffs, and communal drumming and dancing with singing of their favourite anthems 'Beat them Drums of Africa', 'The Nation It Have No Food' and 'We Going Down Town to Free Up the Nation'. Each new member took a 'fruit name' – like Breadfruit, Coconut, Cassava, or Pumpkin. Relations between members were fairly egalitarian, and not especially 'religious', generally recalling those of the average Trinidad working-class family.

Supposedly the group were living in the Beginning of the End, a run-up to the eventual, very physical, end of the world, but little time was spent on millennial speculation. Painted words on the main house proclaimed 'Fock [*sic*]

God' – a sentiment in accord with the group's opposition to Christianity and Islam (although there was a more sympathetic attitude to Rastafari and Shango Baptism as being 'half-way there').

In 1982, with disputes in the group relating to differences in practical authority, and Mother Earth's continued illness, relations deteriorated, splits occurred and the settlement was burned. Mother Earth died of her illness in 1984, and by the late 1990s, the Earth People were split into four groups:

(i) Her biological sons and daughters living in the slum areas of town who visited the original site occasionally and went naked then;

(ii) A few members with some new recruits, going naked on the original site;

(iii) Rupert, her ex-partner, going naked with some new companions near his original village twenty miles away; and

(iv) A more 'Rasta-orientated' group in Port-of-Spain who were apparently clothed and who had repudiated Mother Earth's eschatological teaching.

For all four, what has remained central is less her personal messianic vision than some sense of a more 'natural' and 'African' style which her own life had embodied.

Beyond the particular doctrines of the group, they are of interest for suggesting that religions can occasionally originate in psychopathology when the illness is short-lived and the founder is already influential in a local milieu which is already open to unusual communications in a period of spiritual uncertainty, and the 'delusions' can to some extent be separated out from everyday life (Littlewood, 1993).

Further reading

Chevannes, B. (ed.) (1995) *Rastafari and Other African-Caribbean Worldviews*, London: Macmillan.

Littlewood, R. (1982) 'Minister Meets the Earth People', *Trinidad Guardian*, Port-of-Spain, 22 January.

Littlewood, R. (1982) 'Why We Don't Wear Clothes', *The Bomb*, Port-of-Spain, 22 January.

Littlewood, R. (1983) 'Earth People Split', *Trinidad Mirror*, Port-of-Spain, 4 February.

Littlewood, R. (1983) 'Paradise Lost', *Trinidad Express*, Port-of-Spain, 26 March.

Littlewood, R. (1985) 'Eddoes: Dasheen and Breadfruit in My Garden', *Trinidad Mirror*, Port-of-Spain, 6 August.

Littlewood, R. (1993) *The Work of Mother Earth in Trinidad: Pathology and Identity*, Cambridge: Cambridge University Press.

ROWLAND LITTLEWOOD

EASTERNIZATION

Easternization refers to the process by which religious and spiritual life in Western countries has been increasingly influenced by Eastern traditions even to the extent that it might be claimed that the traditional religious and spiritual ethos of Western civilization and culture are being supplanted by one which is essentially eastern in its fundamental characteristics. The Western transcendentalist, monistic, and personal conceptions of the divine is giving way to an immanentist, dualistic, and impersonal one.

History and background of the idea

From the latter half of the nineteenth century interest in and influences from Eastern religions and in particular Buddhism (see **Buddhism in the West**) have been steadily growing in the West. Movements such as **Theosophy** and **Transcendentalism** are notable examples. During the twentieth century some observers of this development saw in it signs of a transformation of Western thought along Eastern lines. The materialist West was thought to be spiritually bankrupt and undergoing a spiritual crisis which could be addressed by turning to Eastern traditions. Joseph Needham (1956), for example, expressed the view in *Science and Civilisation in China* (Volume 2) that the future belongs to Taoism. Geoffrey Parrinder has described the impact of Buddhism as a new Reformation (1964: 12 and 22). The rise of the New Religious Movements from the 1960s onwards, so many of which were influenced by Eastern religions led Jacob Needleman to speak of this period as witnessing a 'spiritual explosion' which recognized in Eastern religion the 'mystical core of all religion' (1977: xi).

Recent interpretations

A more radical variant of this thesis has recently been proposed by Colin Campbell. This alleges not only that the West has become subject to religious influences of Eastern provenance and inspiration but that the West is also undergoing a transformation of its religious life as a result of indigenous processes.

The traditional Western cultural paradigm no longer dominates in so-called 'Western' societies, but has been replaced by an 'Eastern' one. This fundamental change may have been assisted by the introduction of obviously Eastern ideas and influences into the West, but equally important have been internal indigenous developments within that system, developments that have precipitated this 'paradigm shift' (Campbell, 1999: 41).

> the dominant paradigm or 'theodicy' which has served the West effectively for 2,000 years has finally lost its grip over the majority of the population in Western Europe and North America. They no longer hold to a view of the world as divided into matter and spirit, and governed by an all powerful, personal, creator God; one who has set his creatures above the rest of creation. This vision has been cast aside and with it all justification for man's dominion over nature. In its place has been set the fundamentally Eastern vision of mankind as merely a part of the great interconnected web of sentient life.
>
> (Campbell, 1999: 47)

The contrast drawn between the Eastern and Western paradigm relies upon Max Weber's characterization of an Eastern ethos in which the divine is seen as impersonal and immanent in reality and a Western ethos in which it is seen as personal, transcendental, separate from and outside the world. The former is monistic and views the world as an interconnected, self-contained cosmos; the latter is dualistic viewing the world as governed, and even having been created, from somewhere else and by something beyond or above this world.

The process of Easternization in Campbell's sense is associated with a range of recent developments in Western thought; the rise of radical, holistic environmentalism or deep ecology (see **Gaia** and **Lovelock, James**); the emergence of the human potential and psychotherapy movements (see **Human Potential Movement**); declining belief in a personal God; and increasing belief in reincarnation.

Explanations of Easternization

A major cause of Easternization is said to be the fact that science has undermined traditional religion in the West while faith and trust in science has in turn weakened, leaving a gap to be filled. Eastern religion seems to offer a new paradigm which is not incompatible with science and, consequently, less vulnerable in the face of it. This has allowed Eastern religions to take advantage of the gaps in the scientific world view offering a more mystical orientation that Western religious traditions have lacked.

A second reason for the growing popularity of Eastern religious and spiritual ideas relates to the much vaunted process of globalization. The global extension of systems of communication leads to the global spread of ideas, practices, and cultural elements. For several hundred years the dominant flow has been perceived as being from West to East, producing a progressive Westernization of the planet but alongside this a reverse current flows exposing the West to Eastern influences including religious and spiritual ideas to which it has been increasingly receptive.

A third factor which may have increased this receptivity is the feminist movement and in particular eco-feminism. For those involved in such movements, the patriarchal attitudes of Western and Middle Eastern religious traditions – Judaism, Christianity, and Islam make them unattractive. Buddhism and Taoism, on the other hand strengthen anti-patriarchal sentiments; in the case of Buddhism, for example, its compassion and antipathy to violence and in the case of Taoism its emphasis upon feminine passivity and yielding above masculine strength and resistance.

A final factor which helps to account for Easternization is the emergence of the counter-culture of the 1960s and the fact that the traditions of the East offered this movement a spiritual alternative free of the negative associations of established Western religious traditions. The currents of thought that constitute Easternization often include an element of challenge to the mainstream, both religious and secular, in which much of their attraction lies.

The diversity of Eastern religion

There is, of course, no such thing as an Eastern religion or an Eastern tradition. Eastern religions are diverse. In so far as Eastern religions have influenced the West different traditions have done so to varying degrees at different times and in different ways.

The major contrast that can be drawn between Eastern religions is between those that developed in the Indian subcontinent and those of China. Certain ideas, particularly reincarnation and the self-orientation of human potential and psychotherapy, have been influenced by the Indian and Buddhist traditions, while others, particularly in the area of radical environmentalism, by the Chinese, and especially the Taoist, tradition.

What is imported from the East, also, is often a more refined, reformed and allegedly purified version which has been exported back to the East and then re-imported into the West as the 'authentic' tradition as opposed to folk or allegedly debased forms. This for example, it is claimed, is the case with 'Protestant Buddhism' as it has been called (see Gombrich and Obeyesekere, 1988; Southwold, 1983). In this case the 'authentic' tradition is very much more immanentist and monist than the indigenous tradition appears to have been.

Also, the appeal of Eastern religions in the West tends to be confined to limited sectors of the population rather than being in any sense a grass-roots movement (Bruce, 2000). Easternization is a process that affects, perhaps, only the Western spiritual intelligentsia rather than the society more generally.

Altered images

Some versions of the Easternization thesis, such as Campbell's, are quite radical in perceiving a fundamental and far reaching paradigm shift in spiritual ethos. At the other extreme are those who see it as rather superficial. What does seem quite clear, however, is that the process is not one of straightforward adoption of Eastern ideas in unmodified form and without a large degree of selectivity.

Eastern ideas are more often than not tailored to suit Western circumstances or interpreted in ways that fit the specific interests or prejudices of Western minds and thinkers. J. J. Clarke (1997: 186–90) discusses such processes in general terms while Bishop (1994) has done so quite systematically in the particular case of Tibetan Buddhism which becomes in Western consciousness a sort of museum of a fantasised past. Bryan Wilson (1990) has observed that Western versions of Buddhism lay little stress upon escape into nirvana or upon rebirth and more upon the achievement of a this-worldly enlightenment. Monastic Buddhism tends also, he notes, to attract less interest than the relevance of Buddhism for everyday life and he points out that the Friends of the Western Buddhist order have tended to play down the Buddhist tenet that life entails suffering because it is too depressing a sentiment for the Western mentality. Philip Mellor (1991) emphasizes the extent to which the members of this group interpret and practice Buddhism as a project for the development rather than transcendence of the self.

The teachings of Hinduism tend to be interpreted quite differently in the United States, as Lucy DuPertuis (1987) points out, to the way they are in India. Its devotees do not seek as their ultimate goal to transcend ordinary time, self and existence but have rather more this-worldly aims. Meditation, for example, becomes a panacea for the ills of modern urban civilization and a healthy alternative to tranquillizers offering relief from stresses without any fundamental change in lifestyle.

Western adoption of Eastern ideas, also, is highly selective. Belief in reincarnation, for example, seems to have few concrete implications for behaviour (see Walter, 2001; Walter and Waterhouse, 1999, 2001) and is not always accompanied by the idea of karma or of transmigration. When such ideas are associated with it they generally involve a one way process of mobility, namely upward. The idea of sinking to lower stations of human existence or to some non-human form of life is largely absent. Aspects of such beliefs, such as the idea that the disabled may well be suffering the effects of bad karma in previous lives and have, therefore, only themselves to blame are, in fact, deeply repugnant to Western values.

Another aspect of Eastern traditions that tends to be left aside when they are imported into the West is their renunciatory ideals. When and to the extent that these are sometimes extolled, for example fasting and dieting, it is for the most part very much an element in an eclectic mix, practised periodically and infrequently alongside relatively high levels of material consumption.

Related to this aversion to the ideals of renunciation is the West's equally strong reluctance to entertain the quietist ideals of Eastern traditions. While Taoist ideas may have been co-opted to some extent by the deep green movement it has shown relative indifference to Taoism's emphasis on passivity and non-activism. The West, as Campbell freely admits, remains firmly wedded to what he calls instrumental activism.

Further reading

Bruce, S. (2001) *God is Dead: Secularisation in the West*, Blackwell: Oxford: Blackwell. Chapter 5, 'The Easternization of the West'.

Campbell, C. (1999) 'The Easternization of the West', in B. Wilson and J. Cresswell (eds) *New Religious Movements: Challenge and Response*, London: Routledge.

Clarke, J. J. (1997) *Oriental Enlightenment: The Encounter Between Asian and Western Thought*, London: Routledge.

Hamilton, M. (1997) 'Easternization: critical reflections', *Religion*, 32/3 (July 2002), 243–58.

References

Bishop, P. (1994) *Dreams of Power: Tibetan Buddhism and the Western Imagination*, London: Athlone.

Bruce, S. (2000) 'The New Age and secularisation' in S. Sutcliffe and M. Bowman (eds) *Beyond New Age: Exploring Alternative Spirituality*, Edinburgh: Edinburgh University Press.

Campbell, C. (1999) 'The Easternization of the West' in B. Wilson and J. Cresswell (eds) *New Religious Movements: Challenge and Response*, London: Routledge.

Clarke, J. J. (1997) *Oriental Enlightenment: The Encounter Between Asian and Western Thought*, London: Routledge.

DuPertuis, L. G. (1987) 'American Adaptations of Hunduism', *Comparative Social Research* 10, 101–11.

Gombrich, R. F. and Obeyesekere, G. (1990) *Buddhism Transformed: Religious Change in Sri Lanka*, Princeton: Princeton University Press.

Mellor, P. A. (1991) 'Protestant Buddhism?: The Cultural Translation of Buddhism in England', *Religion* 21, 73–92.

Needham, J. (1956) *Science and Civilization in China*, vol. 2, *History of Scientific Thought*, London: Cambridge University Press.

Parrinder, E. G. (1964) *The Christian Debate: Light from the East*, London: Gollancz.

Southwold, M. (1983) *Buddhism in Life: The Anthropological Study of Religion and the Sinhalese Practice of Buddhism*, Manchester: Manchester University Press.

Walter, T. (2001) 'Reincarnation, modernity and identity', *Sociology* 35, 21–38.

Walter, T. and Waterhouse, H. (1999) 'A very private belief: reincarnation in contemporary England', *Sociology of Religion* 60, 187–97.

Walter, T. and Waterhouse, H. (2001) 'Lives-long learning: the effects of reincarnation belief on everyday life in England', *Religion*, 5, 85–101.

Wilson, B. (1990) 'The Western path of Buddhism', in *Buddhism Today: A Collection of Views from Contemporary Scholars*, Tokyo: The Institute of Oriental Philosophy.

MALCOLM HAMILTON

ECKANKAR

Eckankar was founded in the USA in 1965 by Paul Twitchell (see **Twitchell, Paul**), who pronounced himself the 971st Living Master in an unbroken line going back for millennia. It claims to be the root religion, 'the ancient teaching that is the source from which all religions and philosophies spring'. In fact its origins lie in the Sant Mat tradition, an esoteric movement with Hindu and Sikh roots, which dates back to the nineteenth century and has numerous variations. Before founding Eckankar Twitchell had belonged to the Self-Revelation Church of Absolute Monism, a Hindu movement led by Swami Premananda; to Ruhani Satsang, a Sant Mat movement founded by Kirpal Singh; and briefly to **Scientology**.

(Another modern organization with similar beliefs to Eckankar is MSIA (see, **Movement of Spiritual Inner Awareness (Insight)**), whose founder John-Roger was involved for a while with Eckankar. Elan Vital, formerly the **Divine Light Mission**, also teaches meditation techniques which are similar to those found in Sant Mat-derived movements.)

Eckankar teaches that through 'Soul Travel', the ability to be in two places at once, the inner self can travel independently of the body on the Astral and higher planes. This travel may occur during sleep; Eckankar teaches its members to recall and record their dreams. On these higher planes one may meet and learn from both the current Living Master and other Masters. These include such beings as Rebazar Tarzs, who is over 500 years old, Fubbi Quantz (over 1,000 years old) and Yaubl Sacabi (maybe 2,000 years old). These are among the Vairagi Masters, who are based in Tibet.

Through meditation and the chanting of the sound 'Hu', the sacred name of God, members can experience 'the Light and Sound of God'. These may be experienced through the physical senses, or internally, through visualization or guided meditation, or through lucid dreaming.

Twitchell wrote several books about the beliefs of Eckankar, including *The Spiritual Notebook* and *The Tiger's Fang*, and the first two volumes of the *Shariyat-Ki-Sugmad*, said to be the greatest of all sacred books, a distillation of all secret spiritual knowledge.

After Twitchell's death from a heart attack on 1971, the leadership passed to his appointed successor, Darwin Gross (Living Master No. 972), despite opposition from some senior members, some of whom left the movement. Gross was supported in his leadership bid by Twitchell's widow Gail, whom he married, though they were later divorced.

During Gross's time as leader there was a great deal of adverse publicity, mainly about the teachings of Eckankar having been borrowed from the Sant Mat movement Ruhani Satsang. Academic researcher David Lane wrote a book entitled *The Making of a Spiritual Movement: the Untold Story of Paul Twitchell and Eckankar* (1978) in which he demonstrated clearly not only that the main teachings of Eckankar were not newly-revealed after all, but could be found in other Sant Mat movements, but also that some of Twitchell's writings were direct plagiarizations of other people's works, including most of all the Sant Mat teacher Julian Johnson. For many years the movement ignored these criticisms, but later said that fragments

of the Truth can be found in all the world's religions, and that Twitchell had drawn these together. Moreover, the movements he had belonged to before founding Eckankar were part of his spiritual training,

Gross stepped down as leader in 1981, handing the rod of power of the Living Master to Harold Klemp; Gross continued as president until 1983, but in 1984 Klemp took full control, declared that Gross was no longer to be regarded as an Eck Master, and withdrew his books. Many members left at this time, confused at the 'deposing' of a Living Master. Gross set up a movement called Sounds of Soul, which later became Ancient Teachers of the Masters (ATOM); its teachings are broadly the same as those of Eckankar.

Klemp established himself firmly as the Living Master. He built the movement's Eck Temple at Chanhassen, MN, USA, he set up a system of Regional Eck Spiritual Aides (RESA) – representatives of the Living Master in different geographical areas – and he wrote a number of new books on Eckankar.

Although past Masters such as Twitchell (though not Gross) are regarded with respect, it is an important tenet of Eckankar that the teachings of the (current) Living Master supersede those of any of his predecessors. This allows the continued development of the teachings of the movement as well as, if necessary, the correction of past 'errors'.

Eckankar claims to have tens of thousands of members worldwide, many of whom also continue to be members of other religions.

Further reading

Barrett, D. V. (2001) *The New Believers*, London: Cassell
Lane, D. (1978) *The Making of a Spiritual Movement: the Untold Story of Paul*

Twitchell and Eckankar, Del Mar, CA: Del Mar Press.

Twitchell, P. (1979) *The Tiger's Fang*, Menlo Park: Illuminated Way Press.

Twitchell, P. (1988) *Shariyat-Ki-Sugmad*, Book Two. Minneapolis: Eckankar..

Twitchell, P. (1992) *The Spiritual Notebook*, Minneapolis: Eckankar.

DAVID V. BARRETT

ELEVENTH COMMANDMENT FELLOWSHIP

Founder: The Holy Order of MANS

Country of origin: United States

During its brief lifespan (1980–8), The Eleventh Commandment Fellowship (ECF) helped catalyze a concerted response to the ecological crisis from within the American Christian community. It was instrumental in forming an international coalition of religious and secular environmental groups, and in implementing an ethic of ecology that was rooted in the Jewish and Christian traditions.

The fellowship was an outgrowth of a prominent new religious movement of the 1960s, the Holy Order of MANS (HOOM). The order was founded in San Francisco in 1968 by Earl W. Blighton, and was organized as a non-denominational service and teaching community that resembled Catholic sub-orders such as the Jesuits and Franciscans. The group practiced a form of esoteric Christianity and celebrated seasonal festivals such as the solstices, equinoxes, and full moons with complex rites designed to expand the student's attunement to natural laws and processes. By the mid-1970s the order had established over sixty-four mission centers around the world and was best known for its service outreach, which included shelters for victims of domestic violence. Following Blighton's death in 1974, Vincent Rossi assumed control of

the movement and began to formulate a series of carefully articulated responses to pressing issues of the era. In 1979 he published 'The Eleventh Commandment: Toward an Ethic of Ecology', in the order's journal, *Epiphany*. The article communicated the group's vision of an authentic ecological lifestyle to both Christian and non-Christian thinkers and activists.

In the piece Rossi indicted American materialism and consumerism for crimes against the earth and its bio-systems. He called for a profound rethinking of Western culture's values and goals, and a global awakening to the divine presence in the natural world. In the spirit of the prophets of old, he proclaimed an eleventh commandment: 'The earth is the Lord's and the fullness thereof: Thou shall not despoil the earth, nor destroy the life thereon.' Through the efforts of a committed coterie of eco-monks and nuns, humankind could live in harmony with nature and create an economic system founded on sharing rather than competition.

The article also included an action plan that included educational workshops, a changeover to appropriate technologies, and efforts to organize spiritual communities of all stripes into an effective environmental action group. The ECF, founded in 1980, was the outgrowth of Rossi's call. During the first half of the 1980s, the fellowship spearheaded an ecumenical educational outreach to churches and parachurch agencies. The fellowship set up local chapters throughout the country, organized food cooperatives, helped plant community gardens in inner cities, and convened educational events to raise awareness concerning the environmental crisis. Its national office, under the leadership of Fred Kruger, published a newsletter, organized annual Earth Stewardship symposia in Northern California, and convened conferences throughout North America that brought together such luminaries of the ecological movement as Thomas Berry, Wendell Berry, Jeremy Rifkin, Calvin DeWitt of the Au Sable Institute, Joan Orgon, Sister Miriam MacGillis of Genesis Farm, Charlotte Black Elk, and Maria Artaza Paz of the National Council of Churches. Groups as diverse as the Gaia Institute, Native Americans for a Clean Environment, and the Mennonite Agricultural Concerns Committee co-sponsored these conferences with the ECF.

The high point of ECF's organizational efforts was the North American Conference on Christianity and Ecology (NACCE), which drew over five hundred people representing every major Christian denomination in North America to a retreat center in North Webster, Indiana, in August 1987. The working document produced by the conferees stated that God was calling humankind to:

1. preserve the earth's diverse life forms;
2. create an ecologically sustainable economy;
3. overcome the destruction of nature wherever it was occurring.

Because of a split between moderates and conservatives in the conference, a faction of NACCE members formed the North American Conference on Religion and Ecology (NACRE) to foster a more interfaith approach to eco-spirituality. When the HOOM transmogrified into an Eastern Orthodox Christian sect (Christ the Savior Brotherhood) in 1988, the ECF ultimately merged into the more Christian-centric NAACE.

The ECF's publications, workshops, and conferences helped spearhead a coordinated movement of regional and local religious/ecological groups in North America that continues to address the ecological crisis.

Further reading

Lucas, P. C. (1995) *The Odyssey of a New Religion: The Holy Order of MANS from New Age to Orthodoxy*, Bloomington: Indiana University Press.

Lucas, P. C. (1995) 'The Eleventh Commandment Fellowship: A New Religious Movement Confronts the Ecological Crisis', *Journal of Contemporary Religion*, 10(3), 229–41.

Rossi, V. (1981) 'The Eleventh Commandment: Toward an Ethic of Ecology', *Epiphany*, 1(4), 3–19.

PHILLIP CHARLES LUCAS

EMERSON, RALPH WALDO
(b. 1803; d. 1882)

Born in the vicarage of Boston's First Church, a Unitarian Church, in 1803. Ralph Waldo Emerson who was later to attend Harvard College was deeply influenced by the liberal theology of his father and the more conservative theological views of his Calvinist aunt, Mary Moody Emerson (1774–1863), who is described by her biographer, Cole (2002) as 'a founder of **Transcendentalism**'.

While struggling to resolve the intellectual problems that the conflict between the rational, liberal, Unitarian theology of his father and the conservative theology of his aunt posed for him Ralph Waldo Emerson toward the end of his time at Harvard in 1821 encountered the Swedenborgian Sampson Reed. Through Reed he came in contact with the writings of Emmanuel Swedenborg (1688–1771), and through reading these came close to having a conversion experience in that he began to adopt a spiritual outlook, and way of thinking and writing that were to set him apart from his New England theological heritage. He was opened up through his contact with Swedenborg's thinking to new modes of spiritual and religious expression, to new kinds of religious language and forms of symbolic expression, and philosophically, to what he considered to be a dynamic understanding of Platonism.

In 1836 Ralph Waldo Emerson set out in his book *Nature* the Swendenborgian doctrine of Correspondence – that Nature is a symbol of spirit – and at the same time challenged the authority of the Bible and the institutions which gave it legitimacy. Although he was later to reinterpret and refine Swedenborg's theory of Nature criticizing it for being too literal, Emerson's discovery of Swedenborg had clearly provided him with a compelling alternative understanding of reality derived from the Hermetic or Secret tradition to that of orthodox theology and philosophy. This intellectual shift was evident in his lecture series of 1845 on Representative Men in which he took Swedenborg as the representative mystic.

By the 1830s Ralph Waldo Emerson had come to see himself as both a poet and seer or prophet with a mission to warn society that it was in the danger of collapse. He defined Transcendentalism as a movement opposed to materialism and/or the getting and spending culture that he believed was destroying the cultural fabric of Western society and the prevailing views and values of the Enlightenment. More positively Transcendentalism was, he pointed out, concerned with the creation of a society founded on the principles of justice and morality and one free of all forms of spiritually inert ways of living and thinking.

Over time Emerson's thought became increasingly inclusive embracing as it did the classical and perennial views of mystics, neo-Platonist sages and philosophers from many different traditions and historical periods, among them Meister Eckhardt, John of the Cross, Theresa of Avila and Plotinus. He was also attracted by the Paganism of Egyptian, Greek and Roman antiquity, and by Roman Catholicism.

His wide range of theological and philosophical interests apart and his constant questioning of the nature of things, the one constant theme in Ralph Waldo Emerson's thought is monism, the idea that the world is the product of one mind and one will, active in all and everything from 'the ray of the star to each wavelet of the pool'.

Further reading

Albanese, C. (1977) *Corresponding Motion: Transcendental Religion in the New America*, Philadelphia: Temple University Press.
Alhstrom, S. E. (1985) 'Ralph Waldo Emerson and the American Transcendentalists', in *Nineteenth Century Religious Thought in the West*, Volume II (eds) N. Smart, J. Clayton, P. Sherry and S. T. Katz, Cambridge: Cambridge University Press, pp. 29–67.
Cole, P. (2002) *Mary Moody Emerson and the Origins of Transcendentalism: A Family History*, New York: Oxford University Press.

PETER B. CLARKE

ENGAGED BUDDHISM

The term Engaged Buddhism refers to the notion that Buddhist teachings and practices are not simply for the spiritual well being of the individual monk and the spiritual needs of those he serves but can also benefit the social, economic, and environmental aspects of life beyond the Sangha or monastic community. Some leading Buddhist theorists have gone so far as to question the pursuit of nirvana for its own sake maintaining that it is a means to an end and not the end being the establishment of a more just and equal society. Such thinking constitutes a powerful critique of those 'disengaged' Buddhist monks who have become totally preoccupied with their own spiritual advancement and neglect the needs and the suffering of others. Engaged Buddhism has taken root in many Asian countries and among Buddhists in the West. Here the coverage of this new emphasis on socially engaged Buddhism is confined to Vietnam.

The persecution and jailing of monks in 1963 in Vietnam by the Ngo Dinh Diem regime, and the self-immolation by fire in protest against this persecution and against the American War by several monks including Thich Quang Doc resulted not only in the full scale intervention of the United States in Vietnam but also in the establishment of the umbrella organization the Unified Buddhist Church of Vietnam (UBC) and/or the United or Unified Buddhist Congregation (UBC).

The original aims of this movement were threefold: to end the suppression of Buddhist activities by the Catholic authorities in South Vietnam, supported by the Americans, the creation from a disparate group of Buddhist and ethnic groups, of an integrated Buddhist response to the War and the promotion of Engaged Buddhism.

Despite internal differences over the role of Buddhism in politics the UBC became for a short time, under leaders that included Thich Tri Quang, Thich Tam Chau and Thich Nhat Hanh, the strongest voice in Vietnamese politics. In 1966 monks in their thousands were once again arrested and imprisoned and the UBC driven underground, from where it continued its engagement with society through relief work among those worst affected by the War.

After the fall of Saigon in 1975 the new, independent, socialist government was unprepared to tolerate such an effective and independent minded institution as the UBC and consequently

severely limited its activities. In 1981 the UBC was banned and replaced by a more manageable and compliant Buddhist Church of Vietnam which Buddhist groups were encouraged to join. The UBC continued on its struggle without official recognition for religious freedom and a more open society under the new socialist regime and this campaign reached the attention of many outside Vietnam as house arrests and imprisonment of monks became more frequent in the 1980s. These reached a turning point, in terms of international publicity, with the house arrest and imprisonment of the UBC leader, the Nobel Prize winner, Thich Quang Do, in 1992.

The global interest in Engaged Buddhism owes much to Thich Nhat Hanh's initiatives not only in Vietnam but also abroad, particularly in the United States and Europe. One of the founders in 1964 of the Van Hanh University in Saigon and the School for Social Service, which did much to promote Engaged Buddhism during the Vietnam War, Thich Nhat Hanh founded in 1965 a new branch of the Lam-Te movement, the Order of Interbeing (*Tiep Hien* Order) composed of monks and lay people, one of the principal aims of which was to further the cause of Engaged Buddhism. He has ordained over 100 monks into the Lam Te order since its foundation.

Prior to going into exile in 1966 Thich Nhat Hanh played a prominent role as a strategist and spokesperson for the Struggle Movement which sought to make known the Buddhist perspective on peace in Vietnam without supporting either North or South.

Elsewhere as in Thailand, Engaged Buddhism has taken the form of defending the forests from being cut down. In Sri Lanka, Buddhist initiative the Sarvodaya Shramadana Movement, under the leadership of Dr A. T. Ariyaratne, has linked together for almost half a century personal and social liberation. Many Buddhist associations including many Japanese lay Buddhist Movements are involved in peace work and in a worldwide campaign to abolish nuclear weapons.

Further reading

Queen, Christopher S. and King, Sallie B. (eds) (1996) *Engaged Buddhism: Buddhist Liberation Movements in Asia*, Albany: State University of New York Press.
Queen, Christopher S. (2000) *Engaged Buddhism in the West*, Boston, MA: Wisdom Publications.

PETER B. CLARKE

ENNEAGRAM

Like the **I-Ching** and the Kabbalist Tree of the *Sefirot*, G. I. Gurdjieff's (see **Gurdjieff, George Ivanovitch**) enneagram or nine-sided figure is a symbolic corollary to an inherently spiritual world view.

Presenting it to his private group of pupils in Moscow and Petrograd in 1916, Gurdjieff extolled it as a universal hieroglyph: an esoteric vehicle for transmitting objective knowledge to remote generations. His claim to be the first to advance the enneagram is persuasively supported by its perfect calibration with other uniquely Gurdjieffian models – those relating to cosmogony and cosmology; and to a human being's metabolic assimilation of food, air, and sensory impressions. Nor has success attended strenuous efforts to identify recognizable antecedents of the symbol in oriental mystical literature, neo-Platonism, Martinist, Rosicrucian, Theosophical, and Masonic sources.

Structure and application

However obscure its provenance and problematical its exegesis, the enneagram's geometrical and arithmetical basis are relatively straightforward. To construct it, describe a circle: divide its circumference into nine parts of equal length; successively number the dividing points clockwise from 1 to 9, so that 9 is uppermost; join points 9, 3 and 6 by straight lines to form an equilateral triangle with 9 at the apex; join the residual points by straight lines in the sequence 142857 to form an inverted hexagon (symmetrical about an imaginary diameter struck perpendicularly from 9). In relation to the digits 3 and 7 – which in Gurdjieff's model, as in metaphysical systems generally, are crucially important – this sequence 142857 has noteworthy properties (lost incidentally when transposed to notations other than denary). It deploys all digits except 3 and its positive multiples. In decimal terms, it results from dividing 1 (the Monad) by 7 (the octet). Cyclical progression yields every decimalized proper seventh (thus 2 sevenths = point 285714 recurring; 3 sevenths = point 428571 recurring and so on).

The particular enneagrammatic application which Gurdjieff emphasized was as a dynamic model for synthesizing, at macrocosmic and microcosmic level, his 'Law of Three' or Law of the Trinity and the 'Law of Seven' or Law of the Octave. The former is a ubiquitous sacred dialectic governing all transformations and built around his formulation: 'The higher blends with the lower in order to actualise the middle and thus becomes either higher for the preceding lower, or lower for the succeeding higher.' The Law of Seven, governing process, defies précis but stresses the ubiquitous discontinuity of vibrations; it has correlates with the Western musical scale (and with quantum theory and the periodic table of elements though Gurdjieff did not adduce these). It insists that no enterprise can be consummated merely on the strength of its

165

initial impetus but requires new shock or enthalpic input at pre-determined points.

Gurdjieff did not offer his enneagram only in dry schematic or arithosophical form. In 1919 in Tbilisi he had his pupil Alexandre de Salzmann make a drawing of the enneagram insetting a man 'consisting of' an eagle, lion, and bull – symbolizing respectively the intellectual, emotional, and motor functions (a design subsequently adopted as the programme cover of Gurdjieff's Institute). More significantly, he integrated the enneagram within his sacred dances or Movements. In 1922 at Fontainebleau-Avon, while planning his ballet *The Struggle of the Magicians*, he experimented with an evolution in which the dancers processed along the lines of the symbol marked on the Study House floor – a variation persuasively supporting the diagram's claim as a representation of perpetual motion. In 1924, Gurdjieff significantly climaxed his inaugural presentation of dances to a New York audience, with the enneagrammatic series called the 'Big Seven'.

Recourse to enneagrammatic 'multiplication' also characterizes the '39 Series', choreographed in Paris at the Salle Pleyel during the final decade of Gurdjieff's life (1939–49). A Gurdjieffian Movements' class (of however many horizontal rows) is characteristically deployed in six vertical files. In Movements entailing multiplication these six files are not successively designated 1, 2, 3, 4, 5, 6 but by the enneagram series 1, 4, 2, 8, 5, 7. During the dance, 'displacements' occur in which the files rapidly interchange position to reflect the ascending succession of sevenths. The resultant progressions make high demands on the dancers' attention; validate Gurdjieff's description of the enneagram as a *moving* symbol; and are deeply satisfying experientially and aesthetically.

The enneagram's authorized version

Gurdjieff died on 29 October 1949. For more than thirty-five years (a longish spell with new religions) expository material on the enneagram had remained hermetically sealed within its Work ambit (see **Work, The**). The ensuing three years initiated a measured dissemination of this hitherto recondite material to the public: in 1949 the original Petrograd exposition was published in *In Search of the Miraculous* which is P. D. Ouspensky's lucid and vibrant recapitulation of Gurdjieff's larger teaching (see **Ouspensky, Piotr Demianovich**); and 1952 saw the publication of fourteen solid enneagram dissertations by Ouspensky's pupil the distinguished psychotherapist Dr M. D. Nicoll (1884–1953). These two texts represent the Gurdjieffian hieroglyph's 'authorized version'; and, whatever one's view of symbolism generally or the enneagram specifically, it is hard to deny their intellectual coherence and essential dignity. On this sturdy and decent foundation, however, a whole cluster of baroque enneagram 'developments' would soon be reared by ideological entrepreneurs.

Heterodox Gurdjieffian extrapolation

The first innovators were (in a liberal sense) Gurdjieffians. Rodney Collin-Smith (1909–56), a precocious disciple of Ouspensky, emigrated to Mexico City and there in 1952 published *The Theory of Celestial Influence* (El Desarollo de la Luz). This astonishing but problematical work is essentially a Gurdjieffian *Systema Universi*, bearing comparison – both in its audacity and ultimate implausibility – with Bergson's 'Panpsychism', Comte's 'Panhylism', Fechner's 'Panentheism', and Hegel's 'Cosmosophy'. Significantly for later developments, it afforded the first account of the enneagram in Spanish. The Gurdjieffian spirit, although unaligned with any specific religion, is essentially Deistic and traditionalist; and in 1954 in Italy, Collin-Smith was received into the Roman Catholic Church. He now published his brief perfervid *Christian Mystery* which tendentiously gives an enneagrammatic form to the incarnation, passion, and resurrection of Christ. In 1957 the brilliant but eclectic Gurdjieffian John Godolphin Bennett (1897–1974) opened at his Institute for the Comparative Study of History, Philosophy and the Sciences, near London, his *Djamichunatra*, a lofty study hall constructed on enneagrammatic lines and oriented towards Gurdjieff's grave. This year found him well embarked on *The Dramatic Universe*, his own Brobdingnagian *Systema Universi* permeated with enneagrammatic speculation.

The enneagram and diversionary Neo-Sufism

All that was meretricious in the *nouvelle orientalisme* of the 1960s facilitated an orchestrated campaign by the ambitious half-Scottish half-Afghan 'Grand Sheikh' Idries Abutahir Shah (1924–96) to imply that he had somehow assumed Gurdjieff's mantle. Shah's self-advertisements and invertebrate 'Sufism' signified nothing in orthodox Islamic circles and were rejected wholesale by the British Gurdjieffian mainstream which he schemed to divert. The canard would never have taken hold had not Shah and his self-depiction first won flattering acceptance among a small but influential coterie of British intellectuals (including Doris Lessing), and second, chimed in with Bennett's extravagant millenarian and messianic fervour. Despite the lack of a credible proto-

enneagram within the treasure-house of traditional Muslim geometry (incidentally well reprised later during The World of Islam Festival of 1976), readers of Shah's literature met nudging allusion to 'the mystical *No-Koonja* the nine-fold *Naqsch* or Impress'. Shah's piracy had disproportionate consequences. Thanks arguably to a dereliction in intellectual and editorial vigilance there soon entered into even reputable reference books and encyclopaediae the tenacious misconception that Gurdjieff's teaching generally, and his enneagram specifically, are preponderantly Sufic in origin.

The new 'Enneagram of personality'

A drastic watershed in enneagram exegesis was imminent: the adoption of Gurdjieff's cherished talisman to support and market a nine-fold human typology. This innovation successively features Oscar Ichazo (b. 1931) a Bolivian esotericist; Claudio Naranjo a Chilean psychiatrist, Gestalt therapist and authority on psychotropic substances; and Helen Palmer a Berkeley 'intuitive' and former left-wing activist. The trio's inter-relationships – in descent from pupillage, through ideological appropriation and proprietorialism, to sharp dispute – seem neither historically transparent nor particularly edifying.

Independent biographical information concerning Ichazo is scant; and inconsistency characterizes his self-depiction. He variously claims to have been given Ouspensky's *In Search of the Miraculous* at the age of 19 – yet to have arrived independently at the 'enneagon' (his initial redesignation) 'before reading Gurdjieff'. Surreal assertions by his apologist John Lilly (d. 2001) – that he is instructed by Metraton the prince of archangels, guided by the Green *Qu'tub*, and has removed his karmic nodules by massaging his left foot with the handle of a mixing spoon – risk situating Oscar in the domain of 'crazy-wisdom', amply justifying his protest, years later, that he apprehends ultimate classification as a 'mystical fruitcake'.

Howsoever instructed or guided, Ichazo showed rare entrepreneurial resource (see **Hubbard, L. R.**) Still in his thirties, he elaborated a theory of personality types ostensibly related to the 'enneagon' and by 1968 was successfully propounding it to his *Instituto de Gnoseologica* in Arica, a Chilean fishing town. In expansionist mode he moved to New York City, reconstituted his enterprise as the Arica Institute Inc., and published *The Human Process for Enlightenment and Freedom* (1972).

An archetypical New Age spirit pervades this brochure-scale (120 pp.) production: it proposes seven 'enneagons' (domains, energies, divine principles, fixations, virtues, passions, and psycho-catalysers), each with nine points, altogether yielding sixty-three attributes or thematic foci. Mixed in are meditational *yantra* in psychedelic colours and photographs of Ichazo addressing rapt audiences while commending the mantra TOHAM KUM RAH. Yet, however dubious in presentation and specious in argumentation, this has proved a socially seminal work.

In Santiago in 1969 Naranjo heard Ichazo lecture on the 'enneagram of personality'. With his knowledge of clinical entities (schizoid, avoidant, compulsive, histrionic, etc.) he adroitly codified it and, with great success, began to proselytize in the Esalen Institute. He even gained a sympathetic hearing in important American Jesuit havens (e.g. theological centres at Berkeley, California, and Loyola University, Chicago) where the 'enneagon of the passions'

was deemed to reflect the scriptural seven deadly sins. Naranjo set up his own school called SAT (Seekers after Truth, cf. Gurdjieff's writings), with whom Palmer enjoyed a brief (10-day) contact.

From this juncture the neo-enneagram phenomenon burgeoned and it presently enjoys a vogue once accorded to **UFOs** and crop-circles. For its proponents it has proved gratifyingly marketable: books, tapes, videos, certification courses, study groups, workshops, seminars, retreats, magazines, conferences, Websites, and badges proliferate.

Notes towards an evaluation

As a geometric form expressing an arithmetical feature of denary notation the enneagram is unassailable: critique becomes admissible only when a particular symbolical significance is imputed and social consequences ensue.

In socio-analytical terms the Ichazo-Naranjo-Palmer neo-enneagram can be reasonably bracketed with the self-religions (see **Self-religion, The Self, and self**). Its typology is arguably closest to Sun-sign astrology in the tabloid press – tendentious because lacking an adequate substrate of scholarly or empiric validation. In 1991 the Second US Circuit Court ruled that 'Ichazo's attachment of labels to the enneagram figure contains the minimal degree of creativity necessary to make it copyrightable'. In 1996 Naranjo himself belatedly conceded 'the shallowness, bad taste, and general immaturity reflected in the current enneagram books and magazines'.

Predictably, Gurdjieffians deplore Ichazo's neo-enneagram: they perceive the original symbol's unacknowledged co-option as a usurpation; and its reduction to the commercial level as a prostitution. Ideologically they urge that the enneagram of personality overlooks the contrast between the hexagram's inner dynamic and the triangle's transcendence; and again, that personality was for Gurdjieff merely the mask (Latin *persona*) – his psychological address being to 'essence', the pupil's inexpungeable and fate-attracting particularity underlying the behavioural veneer. Indeed, given that the sixty-three attributes seem stuck around the symbol's circumference *au choix,* like bird-of-paradise feathers, Gurdjieffians hold that Ichazo's enneagram is to Gurdjieff's what New Guinea cargo-cults (see **cult and new religions**) are to aviation.

Gurdjieff's proto-ascription of meaning is opaque to comparable sociological scrutiny because the orthodox Work community is reclusive. As to the paradigm's philosophical or metaphysical weight, a provisional acknowledgement that all transformations entail dialectic and that all process has its cadences goes some distance towards habilitating Gurdjieff's Law of Three and the Law of Seven, so ingeniously reconciled in his enneagram. More work is needed.

Further reading

Blake, A. G. E. (1996) *The Intelligent Enneagram*, London and Boston: Shambhala.

Collin, R. (1954) *The Theory of Celestial Influence: Man, the Universe, and Cosmic Mystery*, London: Vincent Stuart.

Ichazo, O. (1972) *The Human Process for Enlightenment and Freedom*, New York: Arica Institute.

Nicoll, M. (1952), *Psychological Commentaries on the Teaching of Gurdjieff and Ouspensky* (Vol. Two), London: Vincent Stuart.

Ouspensky, P. D. (1949) *In Search of the Miraculous: Fragments of an Unknown Teaching*, London: Routledge & Kegan Paul.

Patterson, W. P. (1998) *Taking with the Left Hand: Enneagram Craze, People of the Bookmark, & The Mouravieff 'Phenomenon'*, Fairfax, California: Arete Communications.

JAMES MOORE

ESCRIVÁ DE BALAGUER, JOSEMARÍA

This saint and founder of Opus Dei was born in Barbastro, North-East Spain, on 9 January 1902 and died in Rome on 26 June 1975. In 1915 his family moved to Logroño, where three years later he entered the local seminary to study for the priesthood. He soon moved to the seminary at Zaragoza, and was ordained priest there in 1925. In addition to theology he studied law, and moved to Madrid to begin a doctorate which he finally completed in 1939. In the course of the Spanish Civil War he fled Madrid for France, though returned shortly afterwards to Burgos. There he completed his most important book, *Camino* ('The Way'), a collection of 999 maxims which became the main spiritual guide to members of Opus Dei. It is imbued with the mentality of militant Spanish Catholicism of the 1930s, and reflects Escrivá's theological conservatism. In the early 1940s he decided to add a society of priests to the membership of Opus because he felt he could not trust clergy other than those he had trained himself from the start to impart his spiritual doctrine. He was inspired to start Opus by a religious experience in Madrid on 2 October 1928. His first followers were young men who were living in the small university residence he had established, which was overseen by his mother and sister, though Opus itself did not fully take off until after the Civil War. From Burgos he moved back to Madrid, but established himself in Rome in 1947. From there he travelled widely encouraging the growth of his foundation. In 1968 he purchased the title of Marqués de Peralta. Escrivá enjoyed cult status among members of Opus Dei, and was revered as a saint by them soon after his death, if not before, though critics of his foundation pointed

169

to, among other aspects of his life, the purchase of the title of nobility as evidence that he was hardly endowed with the humility that Catholics expect from those presented to the Church for veneration. His beatification in 1992 was surrounded by controversy, not least by the almost unheard of speed with which Escrivá had reached the status of a 'Blessed'. His canonization – when he was declared a saint – in 2002 was rather less contentious.

MICHAEL WALSH

ESCUELA CIENTIFICA BASILIO

Founders: Eugenio Portal, Blanca Aubreton de Lambert

Country of origin: Argentina

The Escuela Cientifica Basilio is one of the largest Spiritualism organizations in the world (although it prefers to call its doctrine 'Higher Spiritualism'). Its origins can be traced back to a famous French spiritualist healer, Henry Jacob (1829–1913). One of Jacob's pupils, a medium called Blanche Aubreton de Lambert (1867–1920), migrated to Argentina during World War One, where she (using her Spanish name of Blanca) met Eugenio Portal (1867–1927), and started channelling the spirit of Eugenio's father, Pedro Basilio Portal (+ 1905). The spirit instructed Blanca and Eugenio on a new religion, or later, in the spirit's own words, on a resurgence of primitive Christianity which was said to have included doctrines later rejected by the Christian Church and typical of French Spiritism, such as reincarnation and contacts with the dead. The School, however, claims not to be 'Spiritist', but scientific and religious.

In 1917, Portal and Aubreton established their own organization in Buenos Aires under the name of Escuela Cientifica Basilio ('Basilio Scientific School').

It was not only Basilio who manifested himself through the mediumship of Aubreton and others: in fact, Jesus Christ, St Joseph, the Virgin Mary, and several characters from both sacred and secular history were regularly channelled. In 1925, the School was officially recognized as a spiritualist form of religion by the Argentinian government. A successful expansion followed, first to nearby Brazil, Paraguay, and Uruguay, and then to Europe and the US. Eugenio Portal died in 1927, and was succeeded by Italian-born Gerónimo Podestá (1890–1939) as the School's new Spiritual Director. The position was successively held by Hilario Fernández (1905–74), Mario Salvador Francisco Salierno (1925–87), and Ernesto Guido Boeri (b. 1935). Statistics are not released, but there are 343 local branches, and membership is estimated to be between 5,000 and 7,500. The school is not regarded as controversial in Argentina, although there are occasional attacks on it by Catholic critics. In 2002, however, the TV show *Punto DOC* on Argentine's Channel 2 included the School in a list of 'dangerous cults', thus causing a strong reaction among its members.

The doctrine of the School is derived from the French classical Spiritualism (known as 'Spiritism') of Allan Kardec (pseudonym of Hippolyte Denizard Léon Rivail, 1804–69) (see **Kardec, Allan**), which still inspires millions of followers of **Kardecism** throughout Latin America today. Like all Kardecist groups, the School is reincarnationist. A distinctive feature, however, is the School's claim to represent true Christianity, abandoned by the Christian Church in the fourth century. According to Portal and Aubreton, the first Christians did not at all regard Jesus Christ as God, this being a later deviation introduced by the post-Constantinian Church. The spirits, including that of the 'Venerable

Basilio' (i.e. Pedro Basilio Portal) manifested themselves in early twentieth century Argentina, in order to entrust the founders with the mission of restoring authentic primitive Christianity.

Further reading

Escuela Científica Basilio (1997) *Asociación Escuela Científica Basilio: Enseñanza Espiritual 'Hacia Dios por la Verdad y la Justicia', 80 años de Vida Institucional*, Buenos Aires: Asociación Escuela Científica Basilio.

MASSIMO INTROVIGNE

ESOTERIC MOVEMENTS

The word esoteric comes from the Greek for 'inner' or 'within', and refers to something taught to or understood by the inner circle or the initiated only, in contrast to exoteric (Greek: 'outside' or 'the outward form'), which is knowledge available to everyone. Many esoteric movements (and their detractors) also use the word 'occult', whose popular pejorative usage suggests association with the Devil or demons, but which actually simply means 'hidden' – i.e. secret knowledge.

Many esoteric movements today have their immediate roots in the late-nineteenth century organization, the **Hermetic Order of the Golden Dawn**; many claim spiritual roots over 2,000 years old; but the main historical background to most of today's movements lies in an extraordinary period from the late mediaeval, through the renaissance, to the hermetic philosophers of the seventeenth century.

The Gnostic beliefs of the first to third centuries, seen in such religions as the Manichaeans, resurfaced in the eleventh and twelfth centuries in the Bogomils of Bulgaria and Bosnia, and the better known Cathars of the Languedoc (now southern France). They believed they were the true Christians; the Roman Catholic Church disagreed, and in the only openly-declared Crusade of Christian against Christian (the Albigensian Crusade, beginning in 1209) the Cathars were brutally wiped out.

But the area of what is now southern France, northern Spain, and northern Italy was a melting pot of cultures and non-mainstream beliefs. As well as Gnostic Christians there were Moors and Jews, both of whom emphasized both scholarship and deep spirituality. The mysticism of Sufism and of the Kabbalah, which was developed in this same time and place, both stress a personal spiritual quest rather than conventional hierarchical organized religion. The heterodox fringes of the three Religions of the Book had a clear influence on each other.

From France also, in the late twelfth century, came the addition to the Arthurian mythos of the spiritual allegory of the Grail quest, and from northern Italy in the early fifteenth century came the Tarot, both of great importance in what was to become the Western Mystery Tradition.

In 1492 Spain and Portugal expelled their Jewish populations, who then travelled throughout Europe, settling in Germany, Poland, Italy, France, and to a lesser extent, England, taking their esoteric teachings with them; these also became of interest to heterodox Christian scholars.

During the fifteenth century many ancient teachings came to light, including neo-Platonic and neo-Pythagorian works; originally Greek and Egyptian, they had been preserved by Muslim scholars. In 1471 Marsilio Ficino translated the *Corpus Hermeticum* into Latin; thought at the time to have been written by (the mythical) Hermes Trismegistus at the time of Moses, this was actually a collection of Gnostic writings from the first four centuries of the Christian era, and was a distillation of Greek and Egyptian esoteric writing. It contains the teaching usually shortened to 'As above, so below', the linking of the divine macrocosm with the human microcosm, of the transcendent God with the immanence of God-within, the divine spark or Christ spark which esotericists, Gnostics and mystics of all religions identify within themselves.

Although their possession could lead to accusations of heresy, all of these teachings were available, to a greater or lesser extent, to the hermetic philosophers of the sixteenth and seventeenth centuries – scholars who blended a study of alchemy, astrology, heterodox spirituality, and the natural sciences. It was within this milieu that the Rosicrucian Manifestos (see **AMORC** and **Rosicrucian Order, Crotona Fellowship**) appeared in 1614, 1615, and 1616. It is highly improbable that Rosicrucians existed as such before the publication of these documents; but after their publication many of these scholars began to search for the non-existent secret brotherhood – and numerous new secret brotherhoods were formed. At the heart of Rosicrucian philosophy was the concept of scholars bringing good to the world by their study, their teachings and, through their own inner transformation, their subtle influence on others. These goals are much the same as those of Freemasonry which, almost certainly not coincidentally, began at roughly the same time. These precepts also found practical expression in the Royal Society, the first and still the most prestigious formal institution for the experimental study of science. Many of its early members also studied alchemy and heterodox religion – including Elias Ashmole, founder of the Ashmolean Museum in Oxford, and Isaac Newton. There were also close links between the Royal Society and Freemasonry; in the 1720s, around ninety of the first 250 fellows of the Royal Society were Freemasons.

Accompanying a fascination with Egyptology, the eighteenth and nineteenth centuries saw a resurgence of interest in esoteric study in France, both in the founding of organizations and in the interpretation of Tarot, which was connected with ancient Egyptian wisdom, specifically Hermes Trismegistus. One of the most significant figures, Éliphas Lévi, the author of the two-volume *Dogme et Ritual de la Haute Magie* (*Dogma and Ritual of High Magic*) (1855–6), made detailed connections between Tarot and the Kabbalah, and magical correspondences of astrology, colours, numbers and so on. From Lévi came the authority of esoteric lineage behind a number of organizations, including the *Fraternitas Rosae Crucis* in America. (Most Rosicrucian organizations claim a lineage – true or false – from older movements.)

The masonic connection continued in England with the founding in 1866 of *Societas Rosicruciana in Anglia*, an esoteric side degree of Freemasonry. Out of this was born, in 1888, the **Hermetic Order of the Golden Dawn**, which also drew heavily on the teachings of Éliphas Lévi. Although this only lasted, in its original incarnation, for about a decade, its influence has been enormous (see **Servants of the Light**, **Builders of the Adytum**, and **Chaos Magick** for just three of the many present-day movements which developed from the Golden Dawn). The influential twentieth century occultist Aleister Crowley (see **Crowley, Aleister**) was briefly a member of the Golden Dawn. He later headed the British branch of the *Ordo Templi Orientis*, which taught the theory and practice of sex magick.

In the past there was good reason for individuals and movements pursuing heterodox spiritual ideas to be careful about secrecy. From the mid-twentieth century onwards, societal changes including the reduction in power and influence of mainstream, orthodox religion, the increase in religious pluralism, and the belief that it is a good thing to challenge establishment ideas, have led to an increased openness about heterodox beliefs. The teachings of Éliphas Lévi, the Golden Dawn, Aleister Crowley and others are now readily available from bookshops. Although esoteric movements, sometimes called schools of occult science, still have an initiatory structure, with a progressive revelation of teachings to their members, this is more for the spiritual benefit of their students than to maintain secrecy. In reality, the words 'esoteric' and 'occult' no longer apply to the formerly hidden, heterodox spiritual teachings.

Further reading

Barrett, D. V. (1997) *Secret Societies*, London: Blandford/Cassell.

Matthews, C. and Matthews, J. (1986) *The Western Way: A Practical Guide to the Western Mystery Tradition, vol. 2 The Hermetic Tradition*, London: Arkana.

DAVID V. BARRETT

ESPIRITISMO

Espiritismo in Puerto Rico represents a dynamic, New World synthesis of indigenous spiritual beliefs dating to the period before the arrival of Columbus, African religious beliefs and rituals carried to the island by slaves, and eighteenth-century European ideas about communication with beings from the hidden spiritual realm. Although the wider spiritist movement found throughout the circum-Caribbean area, of which Puerto Rican Espiritismo is but one expression – including Black spiritual churches in the American South, Candomblé, Batuque, **Umbanda**, and Macumba in Brazil, Mexican Espiritualismo, **Vodun** in Haiti, Shango in Trinidad and Grenada, Kele in St. Lucia, and **Santería** in Cuba – is not a new religious movement, in that it is now several hundred years old, its various branches continue to change, spread, merge, and re-emerge in new guise, giving it the character of an emergent tradition.

The basic tenets of Espiritismo include the following:

1. each person is endowed with a spirit that continues to exist following the death of the corporal body;
2. spirits that do not complete their purpose while embodied as a particular human personality or because of some disruption (for example, because their body was subject to an untimely death or because of unresolved conflicts at the time of death) will cleave to the material realm rather than proceed on their enduring spiritual journey;
3. these spirits may disrupt the world of living people, causing sickness and misfortune;
4. additionally, these unhappy spirits may be ensnared by sorcerers to bring harm to their enemies;
5. also, people with developed spiritual ability, such as a medium or sorcerer, will have a relationship with a spirit familiar who may possess and use (e.g., to speak or carry out deeds) the body of their adherent, during which the style of speaking and acting will be expressed by their host's body; and
6. it is possible for a medium to communicate with the spirit realm to determine causes of sickness and misadventure, including sorcery,

as well appropriate ritual remedies to be used to reverse misfortune.

Spirits vary in their nature and origin; many are Nigerian Yoruban deities, called *orishas*, such as Obatala, Oduduwa, and Orunmila who are understood as having a parallel expression as a Catholic saint. Thus, the Yoruban god of thunder, Shango, is merged with Saint Barbara, despite the gender differences in these two figures. When mediums are possessed by St Barbara, they will exhibit the characteristic behaviors of Shango, including drinking rum, smoking cigars, and acting in a somewhat bellicose fashion, behaviors that may contrast sharply with the usual behavior of the person who is possessed. Whether of Catholic, Yoruban or other origin, spirits are venerated equally.

Worship in espiritismo is both home based and congregational. At home, adherents build altars, often in their bedroom on a bureau or even in a closet, to pay homage to guardian spirit familiars. Congregational worship is organized in *centros*. Observational studies have found that centros often are one-room storefront 'churches' led by a *patrino* (godfather) and/or a *madrina* (godmother). There may, in addition, be one or more additional mediums affiliated with the centro, including newer mediums who are in training. Centro adherents include both long-term and transitory individuals and family. Many people may visit a centro only for specific healings and only attend for a few days or weeks. Individuals who feel they have benefited from a healing may choose to begin training as a medium under the supervision of the patrino or madrina. Commonly centros are supported by the free-will donations of their members and contributions from successfully healed clients.

The focus of ritual within a centro is the *mesa blanca* (white table). On this table there may be a variety of objects, such as a large bowl of water (*fuente*) symbolizing the Espiritismo beliefs about clarity and purity. The water is used to diagnose and ritually cleanse clients of the negative vibrations given off by wayward spirits. When consulting with a client about the problems they are facing – such as bodily pains or depression, family or interpersonal conflicts, substance abuse problems, desire for love, or problems related to work – the lead medium is able to see the offending spirit in the bowl of water and to use this identification in initiating a set of spiritual efforts (such as baths, prayers, lighting of candles, sacrifices) to make the spirit leave. Also on the table, there commonly are statues of the centro's patron saint as well as of the guardian spirits of the lead medium(s), the madrina's primary spiritual guide.

Further reading

Koss-Chioino, J. (1992) *Women as Healers, Women as Patients: Mental Health Care and Traditional Healing in Puerto Rico*, Boulder: Westview Press.
Brandon, G. (1997) *Santeria from Africa to the New World*, Bloomington: Indiana University Press.

MERRILL SINGER

EVANGELICAL CHRISTIANITY

The word 'evangelical' derives from the Biblical Greek 'euangelion', meaning 'Gospel' or 'good news'. The term achieved prominence during the Reformation as a designation for those adhering to the teachings of the Reformers, i.e. a commitment to the authority of scripture, as the source of the Gospel, and to salvation by grace through faith, as the message of the Gospel. In this usage, 'evangelical' distinguished Protestants from both Catholic and Orthodox Christians, who emphasized the sacraments and adhered to a high ecclesiology. In modern times, the term has acquired a more specific meaning, referring to a conservative orientation to Christianity, centred on:

1. the authority of the Bible,
2. the need to be 'born again' and express a personal commitment to Christ, and
3. the need for a spiritually transformed life, incorporating both moral reform and an effort to bring others to the faith (evangelism).

The spread of such an evangelical style of Christian commitment among Roman Catholics – chiefly through the charismatic movement since the 1960s (see **Charismatic Movements**) – has challenged any rigidly Protestant understanding and reflects what has become a global movement across the denominations.

This movement emerged in the English-speaking world in the eighteenth century, shaped by seventeenth-century Puritanism and Calvinism, and by the religious revivals which occurred on both sides of the Atlantic from the seventeenth century onwards. In England, early evangelicalism was epitomized in John Wesley's Methodism, which stressed scriptural obedience, conversion as radical personal change, common fellowship and the importance of mission to the poor. A social agenda was further advanced through the established Church by prominent evangelical politicians such as William Wilberforce (1759–1833) and Lord Shaftesbury (1801–85), and through the inner-city work of the Church Pastoral Aid Society (founded 1836). In the USA, evangelical voluntary societies engaged in vigorous missionary efforts, both at home – through the distribution of tracts and the founding of Sunday schools – and abroad, through the preaching campaigns of figures such as Charles Finney (1759–1833). Moral reform was also a priority, not least through evangelical lobbying for legislation on issues such as temperance and Sabbath observance.

A change in direction occurred following the American revivalist movements and the Keswick Convention during the 1870s and 1880s. Both stressed the transforming experience of personal faith over social programmes, an agenda reflected in the preaching of the influential American Dwight L. Moody (1837–99). This was mirrored in a turn from post-millenialist teaching (see **Millenarianism**) – which affirmed social reform as a preparation for the second coming – to pre-millenialism, and the belief in Christ's return as the solution to society's moral and political evils. This strand of thought gained currency through the US-based fundamentalist movement (see **Fundamentalism**), which reacted against moral impurity in modern culture by affirming a return to Biblical teaching within a separatist model of Christian living.

While the fundamentalists gained more ground in the USA than in Britain, a parallel series of debates reflected a conservative/liberal divide on both sides of the Atlantic. In the UK, liberal evangelicals encouraged evangelical scholarship on a broad basis and accepted the findings of the Biblical critics. However, the post-war period saw the expansion of the conservative evangelical faction, gaining appeal through its response to the liberalism of the 1960s and headed by influential spokespersons such as John Stott (b. 1921). Moreover, the first National Evangelical Anglican Conference at Keele in 1967 consolidated the place of conservative evangelicals within the structures of the established Church of England. In the USA, fundamentalist separatism provoked a reactionary wing of 'neo-evangelicals' – including the evangelist Billy Graham – that was driven by a desire to evangelize in the wider culture. They found institutional voice in the National Association of Evangelicals (NAE), founded in 1942, and in the periodical *Christianity Today*. However, the movement in the USA has remained generally more conservative than its UK counterpart, so that Billy Graham's party is often associated with fundamentalism by less sympathetic British observers.

Anglo-American evangelicalism has given the movement its most focused identity, spreading its influence through global missionary endeavour. International conferences such as the 1974 International Congress on World Evangelization in Lausanne, which drew over 2,000 participants from 150 countries, have also affirmed a sense of unity and shared identity. This has emphasized Biblical authority and evangelism, but also social concern for the poor and oppressed.

However, it is a mistake to assume a unified global movement. For example, black evangelicals and much of the holiness/Pentecostal groups have developed apart from the organized evangelical/fundamentalist movement, although there are parallels in patterns of belief. Postwar diversification has also generated an increasing variety of evangelical strands, some of which mirror social class and regional differences. This is especially true of political orientations. In the USA, evangelicals encompass both the trenchant conservatives of the Moral Majority and the leftist radicals of Sojourners – a movement led by Jim Wallis (b. 1948), who attacks the **New Christian Right** for confusing consumerist values with the Gospel message. A renewed flexibility in

worship and mission, driven by the need for effective evangelism in increasingly secular cultures, has also encouraged a more positive engagement with movements outside the evangelical world.

Since the late twentieth century, the evangelical style of faith has become associated with some of the fastest growing Christian groups in the world. This is especially the case in the USA, in which some 35 per cent of the population are said to profess an evangelical commitment. South Africa, Brazil, the Philippines, and South Korea also have sizeable evangelical populations (Noll, 2001: 39–41). In the UK, figures are much lower – well under 10 per cent – although even here, evangelical churches demonstrate a greater resilience to forces of secularization than liberal and catholic parties.

Further reading

Bebbington, D. W. (1989) *Evangelicalism in Modern Britain – A History from the 1730s to the 1980s,* London: Unwin Hyman.

Noll, M. A., Bebbington, D. W. and Rawlyk, G. A. (eds) (1994) *Evangelicalism: Comparative Studies of Popular Protestantism in North America, The British Isles, and Beyond, 1700–1990,* Oxford and New York: Oxford University Press.

Noll, M. A. (2001) *American Evangelical Christianity: An Introduction,* Oxford, UK and Malden, MA: Blackwell.

MATHEW GUEST

EXIT COUNSELING

Exit counseling is a successor process to **Deprogramming** and is distinguished from it by the absence of the threat or exercise of coercive constraint. As described by its practitioners, exit counseling is premised on a voluntary relationship in which the NRM (see **New Religious Movement**) members consent to receive counseling concerning their

NRM affiliation and are provided with critical information and perspective concerning the groups in which they currently or formerly participated. Although non-coercive means are employed, the goal of exit counseling remains separation of individuals from NRMs.

Exit counseling was developed as an alternative to deprogramming for a variety of reasons. Despite a concerted effort, the **Anti-Cult Movement** was unable to develop legislative or judicial protection for deprogramming. As a result, deprogrammers confronted vigorous legal opposition from NRMs. Deprogramming presented anti-cult associations with public relations problems as well as a threat to their tax exempt status as educational organizations. Deprogrammers themselves also began to retreat from the rough and tumble tactics of the early 1970s as they sought to professionalize their practice as a means of gaining legitimacy. Finally, a recognition spread through anti-cult ranks that deprogramming might not be indispensable. As recruitment rates for NRMs began to wane, there were fewer converts to extract, and continuing high defection rates meant more spontaneous defections. Since deprogramming had always been most successful with novitiate members and less effective for longer term members, the compelling logic for deprogramming became questionable. When the Anti-Cult Movement discovered that non-coercive tactics produced comparable results and yielded a much lower risk of rupturing family relationships, the attractiveness of the exit counseling alternative increased.

Like deprogramming, exit counseling actually incorporates a relatively diverse set of perspectives and practices. The most organized network of exit counselors operates within the anti-cult movement from a mind control (**brainwashing**) perspective. As deprogramming gradually has given way to exit counseling, some exit counselors have exchanged the doctrinaire brainwashing approach for a more educational approach. Whichever framework is employed, individuals who are counseled are presumed to have lost their capacity for critical, independent thought. Exit counselors regard their objective as providing information critiquing the group on the assumption that members would not have access to such information. Another smaller and less well organized set of exit counselors operate from a religious perspective. For these counselors NRM (see **New Religious Movement**) members hold heretical religious beliefs, and the objective of counseling is to return NRM members to a conventional faith. Finally, there are some groups that offer transitional support to those exiting NRMs. Some formal organizations offer formal counseling as individuals seek to make the transition from NRM to conventional social lives. Other groups consist of networks of former members who share personal experiences of disillusionment, exploitation, and abuse. In some cases, groups consider both positive and negative aspects of members' experiences as they seek to assist individuals in assessing the meaning of their NRM careers. Most of these groups operate informally and have relatively short lifespans.

The process of exit counseling as practiced within the Anti-Cult Movement involved several stages. Although the extent of family preparation necessary for counseling is debated, many anti-cult affiliated exit counselors initially spend some time informing family members about what they regard as the manipulative practices and abuses of cults in general or the specific group involved. This initial family counseling is important since the family is the client and family support for the process is pivotal. The next step is to plan the means by which the voluntary involvement of the individual to be counseled can be elicited. This can be arranged in several ways. The family may approach the individual and negotiate an agreement to meet with the exit counselor. If that strategy does not appear promising, the family may arrange an occasion at which both exit counselor and family member are present and attempt to orchestrate an ostensibly serendipitous meeting. Alternatively, the family may invite the NRM member home and attempt to persuade them at that moment to accept exit counseling. Obviously the latter two strategies carry more risk of resistance and rejection.

Whichever approach is selected, at some point early in the process the NRM member must agree to continue the relationship, and the terms of the encounter must be specified. The NRM member may be confronted with a variety of moral, emotional, or intellectual appeals and pressures but not physical constraint. The third stage in the process involves a typically intense exchange between exit counselor and NRM member concerning the group and the individual's membership. Exit counselors assume that NRM members are unaware of negative aspects of the group, have been unable to discuss them with fellow members, or have become enmeshed in the movement to such an extent that they have lost the capacity for critical, independent reflection on their present course of action. The exit counselor therefore seeks to create 'balance' by providing information that challenges the individual's current perspective. Dialogue, discussion, and argumentation may continue as long as the NRM member consents. If at the end of the exit counseling the NRM member agrees to disaffiliate, additional counseling or time in a 'rehabilitation' facility may be negotiated.

Exit counseling is likely to remain controversial. For proponents it represents a legitimate remedy to manipulative and exploitive practices by cults; for opponents it is simply faith breaking concealing itself in a therapeutic guise. The practice is likely to continue, however, as it offers families a means of achieving their objective of separating members from NRMs without violating the law. The number of full-time exit counselors is relatively small as the demise of the **Cult Awareness Network** has eliminated a major source of network coordination. Hence the impact of exit counseling in the conflict between NRMs and their opponents is unlikely to be a decisive factor.

Further reading

Langone, M. (1994) *Recovery from Cults*, New York: W.W. Norton.
Rothbaum, S. (1988) 'Between Two Worlds: Issues of Separation and Identity after Leaving a Religious Community', in D. Bromley (ed.) *Falling from the Faith*, Newbury Park, CA: Sage Publications.

DAVID G. BROMLEY

EXTRATERRESTRIALS

Extraterrestrials are figures of religious significance in a number of new religious movements, including groups such as the **Raelian Church**, Unarius, the **Aetherius Society**, **Kofuku-no-Kagaku** (Institute for Research in Human Happiness) and **Heaven's Gate**. Although specific beliefs regarding extraterrestrials differ from group to group, there is also an underlying commonality to beliefs regarding extraterrestrials within these new religious movements.

Six factors drawn from the broader UFO movement (see **UFOs**) have influenced the perception of extraterrestrials among members of UFO groups and others. The first is the reported sighting of UFOs over Mt Rainer, Washington on 24 June 1947 that introduced the public to the term 'flying saucer', and the subsequent reported recovery of a crashed UFO on 3 July 1947 by the United States Military at Roswell, New Mexico. These events combined to produce the conviction among UFO believers that UFOs are the technologically sophisticated space craft of extraterrestrial visitors. The second is the emergence of the UFO contactee movement in the 1950s, characterized by claims to have met with and spoken to extraterrestrials. The contactees contributed an image of extraterrestrials as socially, morally and spiritually superior to human beings. The third factor is the emergence of the UFO abduction phenomenon in the 1960s, when stories of alien abduction and medical experimentation began to circulate. The UFO abduction phenomenon contributed two ideas: that extraterrestrials were interested in our genetic makeup; and that some extraterrestrials were not necessarily benevolent. The fourth factor is the widespread popularity of the ancient astronaut theory that emerged following the theatrical release of Erich von Däniken's *Chariots of the Gods? Unresolved Mysteries of the Past* (1969). This book popularized the thesis that religious texts and images record prehistoric contacts with extraterrestrials. The fifth factor is the return of the contactee phenomenon in the 1970s, with the added dimension of an ancient astronaut theme. Common to accounts of contactees in the 1970s are claims that extraterrestrials created human life from alien DNA. This conviction is prevalent in several organized UFO groups, including the Raelian Church. Finally, the sixth factor is the increased awareness in the 1980s of channeling as practiced within the **New Age Movement**. Channeling contributed the idea that

extraterrestrials need not be physically present on earth to communicate with human beings.

Based on these factors, the image of extraterrestrials that has emerged within new religious movements is of beings scientifically, technologically, morally, and spiritually superior to human beings. They are scientifically superior because their science has overcome the obstacle of intergalactic travel, circumventing the speed of light; and has overcome the mystery of interspecies reproduction, allowing the creation of human beings and genetic hybrids. Their technology is superior because it has created propulsion systems for UFOs which defy the laws of gravity and inertia, and other technological marvels such as robots, teleportation devices, and artificial gestation apparatus currently beyond human technological abilities. Extraterrestrials are understood within organized UFO religious groups to be concerned with human abuse of science and technology, particularly with threats of nuclear war and environmental catastrophe. Members of Unarius, the Aetherius Society, and the Raelian Church have all claimed to to have received scientific and technological guidance from extraterrestrials.

In addition to scientific and technological superiority, extraterrestrials are also considered to be morally and spiritually superior to human beings. They are morally superior to human beings because they have overcome poverty, prejudice, and war, and their societies are based on love for their fellow galactic beings. Moral guidance from extraterrestrials within organized UFO religious groups consists of urging us to love one another and end our warlike ways. Extraterrestrials are also spiritually superior to human beings, because they are understood to have reached a realization of their spiritual unity with one another and with the universe, and to act as guides so that humans might attain this awareness also. The moral and spiritual guidance received from extraterrestrials forms the basis of the religious dimensions of organized UFO groups.

Extraterrestrials are figures of reverence within organized UFO religious groups, but they are not objects of worship. Extraterrestrials are understood within an evolutionary framework suggesting they are simply farther along the scientific, biological and spiritual path of evolution than human beings. Consequently, they are conceptualized with organized UFO religious groups as guides, parents, teachers, brothers and sisters, but not as gods. Most organized UFO spiritual groups also believe in the existence of less evolved 'evil' alien entities who work to oppose our continued learning and spiritual evolution. The spiritual task of believers is often therefore to overcome evil alien influence under the guidance of benevolent alien teachings.

Further reading

Daniken, Erich von (1969) *Chariots of the Gods? Unresolved Mysteries of the Past* (trans. M. Heron), London: Souvenir Press.

Lewis, James (ed.) (1995) *The Gods have Landed: New Religions from Other Worlds*, Albany, NY: State University of New York Press.

JENNIFER E. PORTER

F

FAITH TABERNACLE CHURCH

Faith Tabernacle Church was a major indigenous African church that promised succour for adherents during the immediate post-World War One era which witnessed a major outbreak of the deadly influenza epidemic and its concomitant economic recession. Western medicine and mission founded churches proved quite incapable of handling the crisis. Most African Christians were convinced that the crisis had an important spiritual dimension. As a result, a number of prayer fellowships were formed in homes to pray for divine intervention. One Daddy Ali, who claimed to have had a religious experience during which God charged him to consecrate himself to be used as a vessel to heal the sick, organized one of such prayer fellowships at Ijebu-Ode (in the Southern part of Nigeria). Miss Sophia Odunlami, a member of the group, claimed she was directed to prescribe rain water and prayer for the purposes of faith healing. Testimonies of people who claimed that they received healing as a result of following her prescription drew large crowds to join the group. The group later assumed the name, *Egbe Okuta Iyebiye,* which is a Nigerian term, interpreted as the 'Precious Stone' or 'Diamond Society'.

The Diamond Society subscribed to *The Sword of the Spirit* magazine published by the Faith Tabernacle in Philadelphia, USA, because it realized that their beliefs resonated. Consequently, in 1921 the Diamond Society affiliated with the Faith Tabernacle, USA and changed its name to The Faith Tabernacle (FT) Nigeria. The FT Nigeria which initially operated as a renewal group within the Anglican Church clashed with the Church over the issue of infant baptism, having attributed the mysterious high mortality of children of the Anglican Church in that locality to infant baptism. The Anglican Bishop banned the group and the members of the group eventually became 'The Faith Tabernacle Church' (FTC), which held its first service as a church in 1922 at Ibadan. Subsequently, the FTC spread to many towns and cities in Nigeria.

The American FT adopted the Nigerian FTC and formally appointed some Nigerians as pastors to oversee all the FTCs in Nigeria. Relations between the Nigerian and the USA FT churches turned sour for three main reasons. First, after more than four years of fraternal relations, none of the American leaders had ever paid a pastoral visit to the young Nigerian church. Second, there were doctrinal differences. For instance, while the FTC stressed glossolalia, the American FT denounced it and taught that it was a Satanic delusion. Third, in 1925 there was a major leadership crisis in the FT headquarters, Philadelphia which further caused the American FT to lose control over the Nigerian FTC. A combination of the above factors led the Nigerian FTC to pull out of the relationship with the American FT around 1926.

The FTC witnessed a remarkable growth, with the emergence of the young Yoruba prophet Joseph Ayo Babalola, born in 1904, who appeared on the Nigerian religious scene in the late 1920s. Babalola claimed he experienced a spectacular divine call to the office of a prophet and evangelist. Consequent to that, he became an itinerant preacher, carrying a Bible and a bell. Initially, he operated in his local Anglican church by holding prayer and healing meetings. However, he was expelled by the Anglican Church due to his charismatic disposition, particularly, his healing practices which appeared strange to the Church.

In 1929, Babalola, joined the FTC in Ilesa, Nigeria. He played a leading role in a major revival that broke out in 1930 which brought the FTC into the limelight. It was alleged that Babalola raised to life a child who was being taken to the cemetery for burial. In his ministry, it is claimed that many were healed and he stressed the need for his hearers to renounce all evil practices and witchcraft.

The distinctive emphases of the FTC are: intense prayer and fasting as means of solving problems, 'believers' baptism' or baptism of adults who openly confess their faith in Jesus Christ and all the gifts of the Holy Spirit particularly divine (faith) healing and the outward manifestation of the baptism of the Holy Spirit. In their healing practices they resort to the use of aids such as water and oil and forbid adherents to use African traditional and Western orthodox medicine and healing practices. They insist on monogamous marriages which must be blessed by the church and disallow re-marriage of divorced people. The FTC demonstrated that African Christianity has the resources to deal with peculiar African problems and has the capacity to fulfil their aspirations.

Further reading

Ayegboyin, D. and Ishola, A. (1997) *African Indigenous Churches*, Lagos: Greater Heights Publications.

Clarke, P. B. (1986) *West Africa and Christianity*, London: Edward Arnold.

CEPHAS N. OMENYO

FALUN GONG

The Falun gong 法輪功 (The Practice of the Dharma Wheel) or Falun dafa 法輪大法 (The Great Teachings of the Dharma Wheel) was founded by **Li Hongzhi** 李洪志 in 1992 in the northeastern Chinese city of Changchun. It rapidly became a major popular movement, both in the People's Republic of China (PRC) itself and in overseas

Chinese communities all over the globe, reaching a total following of several millions. The movement has also been successful on a small scale among Westerners. It explicitly denies that it is religious in nature, because religion is associated by the educated urban population with superstition and backwardness. However, Li's teachings explain the cosmos and man's place and purpose in it in the same definitive way and with the same aim of giving meaning and direction that religious movements usually do. There is a foundation myth, cosmology, elaborate ethical thinking and ritual (its exercises and the public sit-ins that it already regularly held before persecution started in mid-1999 to defend its freedom of practice). The Falun Gong builds on traditional religious ideas in a number of ways, modifying them in the process, but does not advocate incense-burning.

In the movement's foundation myth the story is told of how Li Hongzhi acquired his knowledge and understanding of the teachings and the practices, leading up to his foundation of the movement and his career as a successful teacher until today. Because the movement sees its purpose as the transmission of objective truth, therefore the teacher occupies central stage as the only one who possesses this truth and can convey it to others. Much attention is paid to constructing the image of the teacher, through pictures, video- and audiotapes, books, the Internet and rare public appearances. This focus on the teacher fits both Buddhist and general Chinese educational practice, whether Confucian or Communist, in which the teacher is also always highly respected.

Central to the cosmology of the movement is the belief that everything and everybody in the universe is interconnected. We are the universe/cosmos (microcosm) and the universe/cosmos (macrocosm) is us. This cosmos can be called the Great Ultimate (*taiji* 太極, often written *Tai Chi*), which is represented as a circle containing both Yin and Yang (in contrasting colours or black and white, each with a dot of the other colour inside). The circular movements of the Falun Gong exercises enact the Great Ultimate, allowing the practitioner to draw in cosmic substance/ energy (*qi* 氣). All of this builds on common Chinese philosophical and religious ideas and is not at all unique to the Falun Gong.

More specific is Li Hongzhi's notion that the Great Ultimate is a manifestation of the Dharma Wheel (*falun* 法輪), which he represents symbolically with the *wan* (卍) character, as the Buddhist equivalent of the micro/macrocosm. He himself places this Dharma Wheel in the lower abdomen of new followers, if necessary from a great distance. The rotating movement is likened to the turning of the electrons in an atom, the planets around the sun, and the Milky Way as a whole. From this metaphor Li and his followers derive a sense of being scientific. Clockwise, the rotation takes in substance/energy (*qi*) from outside; counter clockwise, it emits energy. It is fed both by the influence of the teacher's own powerful Dharma Wheel and by the proper practice of the exercises, but only when and if accompanied by the cultivation of certain moral values.

The moral teachings build on the traditional Buddhist notion that our present life is determined by the effects of our actions in previous lives, which we carry with us through an endless chain of incarnations. These effects are called *karma* (*ye* 業) and as long as we produce *karma* we continue to be reborn. Li Hongzhi depicts this *karma* as something material (a black substance), which one can actually see. Getting rid of *karma* will increase one's *de* (德),

which is conventionally read as 'potency, potential', i.e. the ability to work good, but which Li explains as a kind of matter (a white substance). Although Li therefore gives the notions of *karma* and *de* or 'potency' a specific expression of his own, he certainly builds on existing ideas. His belief that *karma* is at the root of all our diseases is entirely consistent with Buddhist doctrine, as is his conclusion that therefore medical aid, though by no means prohibited, is rather pointless, since it cannot affect one's accumulated *karma*. When followers refuse medical aid they may seem to us to be eccentric, but actually are merely taking Buddhist notions to their logical conclusion.

Crucial to Li Hongzhi's teachings is his stress on moral attitude, which can be cultivated by attempting to bring to fruition in one's own life the three core values of 'truthfulness' (*zhen* 真), 'benevolence' (*shan* 善), and 'forbearance' (*ren* 忍). By practising 'forbearance' in stressful situations, in personal conflicts or by suffering persecution with equanimity it is possible to get rid of a great deal of *karma* and even absorb the *de* of one's persecutors. Clearly, this belief can be very inspirational in all kinds of stress situations that followers face in their workplaces and at home, including the terrible persecution that has been taking place from the late 1999 onwards.

At first sight the movement has little in the way of ritual, and it largely rejects the Chinese religious practice of burning incense, but its exercises to draw in cosmic substance (*qi*), its demonstrations already before persecution started, and its study groups carry a strong ritual dimension. The same could be said of its custom to compose and publicly announce (orally, in writing or on the web) lessons from their practice, a kind of confession ritual.

Nonetheless, we do well to keep in mind the movement's own rejection of the label 'religious' and its stress on being 'scientific' (*kexuede* 科學的), with its connotations of being objectively true and verifiable. It is the combination of providing answers to basic human emotional and intellectual needs with this claim of being true in a modern (or scientific) way that has formed much of the appeal of the Falun Gong movement.

Following a silent, 10,000 persons strong demonstration on 25 April 1999 outside the headquarters of the Chinese Communist Party (CCP) at Zhongnanhai in Beijing, the Falun Gong movement was prohibited. An intensive campaign of suppression followed, in the course of which many members were detained, placed in labour camps or locked up in psychiatric institutions, with hundreds of people dying in the process. Already some years previously, in 1996, Li Hongzhi had left the PRC for the United States. From there the movement has actively protested against the persecution. Inside the PRC itself, the movement carried out a series of hijackings of public television time in the midst of 2002, but otherwise those followers who have escaped persecution have gone underground or become inactive. It is believed that inside the PRC the movement has been more or less silenced, but outside it is still very much alive and continues to build a following. The US 'war on terrorism' since 11 September 2001 and the outbreak of SARS in early 2003 has meant that the international media have fallen silent regarding the suppression of Falun Gong, allowing China to deal with the movement in its own way.

The Falun Gong is sufficiently coherent in its teachings and its local networks of members cohesive enough, to allow it to be described as a movement. Although it lacks formalized institutions, the use of the Internet and other modern forms of communication have facilitated the creation of extensive networks of followers. The movement was not originally political in orientation, but clearly the ongoing persecution has forced it to resist and to take a stance on issues that are defined as political in the Chinese context. The way in which the Falun Gong has offered public resistance inside and outside China makes it a very special phenomenon, quite independent of the merits of its teachings and exercises.

Further reading

Penny, B. (2002) 'Falun Gong, prophecy and apocalypse', *East Asian History* 23.

Rahn, P. (2002) 'The Chemistry of a Conflict: The Chinese Government and the Falun Gong', *Terrorism and Political Violence*, 14(4), 41–65.

ter Haar, B. J. (n.d.) 'Falun Gong: Evaluation and Further References' at http://www. let.leidenuniv.nl/bth/falun.htm (including a bibliography and further WWW links).

Tong, J. (2002) 'An Organizational Analysis of the Falun Gong: Structure, Communications, Financing', *China Quarterly*, 171, 636–60.

BEREND J. TER HAAR

FAMILY, THE

The Family (officially The Fellowship of Independent Missionary Communities), formerly known as The Children of God and The Family of Love, came into being in California in the wake of the hippie movement of the late 1960s. Similar to other 'Jesus Freaks' the members practised communal living and incorporated principles of free sex and the use of drugs into a counter-cultural ideology based on the founding leader David Brandt Berg's (1919–94) (see **Berg, David Brandt**) understanding of Evangelical Christianity. Brandt – who was to become known to his followers as 'Dad', 'Moses David' or 'Father David' – was of a Christian Evangelical background himself, and was, prior to the foundation of his own movement, associated with several different Christian missionary organizations.

His teachings are in many ways anti-modern. Berg eschewed scholarly interpretations of the Bible, he counteracted evolutionary science, insisted that the Bible holds everything worth knowing and he identified the expansion of technology in society as a forerunner to the rise of Antichrist. On the other hand Berg, through his career, was able to relate his doctrines to the current societal situation, distributing his teachings in cartoon-like pamphlets and colourful posters. Modern myths such as tales of **UFOs** also became a part of the movement's ideological make-up.

After a few years among California's drop-outs, with whom Berg and his followers identified, the movement embarked on a journey around USA and ended up in Canada. Here Berg divorced his wife and married one of his followers, Karen Zerby. She became his partner, and since his death she has been the head of the organization. To her followers she is know as 'Maria'. Berg himself, though, is not entirely gone. Soon before he died he signed a charter containing all kinds of rules pertaining to the life of the movement, and inner-group members have declared that Berg's spiritual presence is felt through his legal advisers. While alive Berg was seen as a prophet with direct contact to God, and after his death he still represents the highest ideal to his followers.

From the early 1970s the globalization of Berg's movement developed rapidly and soon more than 200 communal 'homes' were established in almost fifty different countries around the world. This period in many ways was to determine the fate of the movement.

The theological emphasis on the world's imminent destruction, and the proclamation that Los Angeles would become completely destroyed in a major earthquake, caused The Children of God to become known as either crackpots or provocateurs. More important, however, was the strong emphasis on sexual liberality which dominated Berg's theological thinking. Inspired by Maria female members started proselytizing by offering 'physical love in the name of Jesus' – a practice that became known as 'flirty fishing' – to potential male converts, and in one of Berg's many written statements he proclaimed that sex was no sin at all. Soon the movement was accused of all kinds of deviant sexual practice and as the practice of 'flirty fishing' spread into all the countries where Berg's followers lived. The Children of God was soon to be almost universally described as a 'sex cult'. It is probably true that illegal sexual activities occurred. The majority of members, representing a sub-culture with close ties to the hippie generation, were in their mind simply applying another set of sexual values than those generally accepted. The emphasis on sex would greatly diminish during the mid-1980s (not least due to the spread of HIV/AIDS), but probably The Family will never be able to dissociate itself completely from this aspect of its past, even if 'flirty fishing' was totally abandoned in 1987.

During the 1990s the movement changed its image considerably. The theological emphasis turned away from the explicitly eschatological as the organization gradually became more institutionalized and mainstream. This is not to say that The Family has joined the ranks of more traditional Christian denominations, but since the millennium has failed to arrive members of the organization have come to realize that they have to live in an imperfect world, and so have adapted to the prevailing conditions. The practice of travelling

around the world was largely discontinued in the beginning of the 1990s. The Family was facing different kinds of campaigns launched by the **Anti-Cult Movement** in many places and, as one member said, 'there were no more places to flee to'. Consequently many of Berg's followers headed home to their native countries and settled. Some members however, have focused on the East European countries that had been out of reach until the ending of Soviet rule. As a consequence quite a number of members now live in the Ukraine, Russia, and other countries of the region where they do charity work.

Usually members of local congregations live together and their children typically receive home-based education highlighting the movement's continuing desire to disassociate itself from the surrounding society which has always been relevant to the movement's members. At the turn of the millennium, according to The Family, some 1,400 centres in almost ninety different countries were being run by 12,000 full-time members and associates. The real number is probably lower.

Further reading

Barrett, D. V. (2001) *The New Believers. Sects, 'Cults' and Alternative Religions*, London: Cassell.

Lewis, J. R. and Melton, J. G. (eds) (1994) *Sex, Slander and Salvation. Investigating The Family/The Children of God*, Stanford, California: Center for Academic Publication.

www.thefamily.org

MIKAEL ROTHSTEIN

FELLOWSHIP OF ISIS

Founded: 1976

Country of origin: Eire

The Fellowship of Isis was founded at the Spring Equinox of 1976 to promote closer communion between the Goddess and individuals. Its founders were the clergyman Lawrence Durdin-Robertson, along with his wife Pamela and his sister Olivia, cousins of the writer Robert Graves. Of Anglo-Irish aristocratic stock, the Robertsons claim a hereditary line to the priesthood of Ancient Egypt. The Fellowship was based at the family seat of Huntingdon Castle, Clonegal, Eire, which remains the Foundation Centre of the Fellowship and home of Olivia. Membership is free, and open to individuals of every religion, tradition and race; being inclusive, it counts Christians, Hindus, Witches, Pagans, and atheists among its members.

The Fellowship seeks to honour the good in all faiths, promote love, beauty, and truth, goodness, harmony, and wisdom, as well as to develop friendliness, psychic gifts, happiness, and compassion for all life. It contains within it the Order of Tara, devoted to the conservation of nature, and the Druid Clan of Dana which works to develop nature's psychic gifts.

By the year 2000 the Fellowship of Isis claimed over 17,000 members in ninety-three countries, making it the largest Goddess-centred organization in the world. Although Goddess-centred, the Fellowship concentrates on both female and male principles of divinity and is not exclusively orientated to the feminine. It is organized on a democratic basis, with both men and women initiated as priests and priestesses, and all members are considered equal. There are no vows required or commitments to secrecy.

From the Foundation Centre, the Fellowship has a network of affiliated Iseums, many of which are dedicated to a specific Goddess and/or God, and Lyceums of the College of Isis which carry out the liturgy and training of potential priests and priestesses. All are listed in the Fellowship's newsletter, *Isian News*. Correspondence courses are available, as well as a Lyceum Magi Degree system and an Iseum Initiate Level system, which contains thirty-three dramas of initiation.

Further reading

Robertson, O. ([1975], 1993), *The Call of Isis*, London: Neptune Press.

JO PEARSON

FERGUSON, MARILYN
(b. 1938)

Marilyn Ferguson was born in Grand Junction, Colorado and following her 1973 publication of *The Brain Revolution*, she became editor of the Los Angeles-based *Brain/Mind Bulletin* in 1975 and the *Leading Edge Bulletin* since 1980. She received her education from the University of Colorado and the University of California at Los Angeles. Ferguson is known principally for her understanding of the New Age (see **New Age Movement**) as the eventual product of a peaceful network of dissolving and re-coalescing holistic, spiritual and ecologically minded components. To this end, she published *The Aquarian Conspiracy: Personal and Social Transformation in the 1980s* in 1980 – the book for which she is chiefly known. In this work, Ferguson engineers and promotes the image of New Age 'global consciousness' as primarily a humanitarian and environmental movement. She calls for a new cultural paradigm that will emphasize a greater realization of the individual's physical, mental and spiritual potential. Her understanding of a 'spiritual conspiracy' is one that includes individuals, businesses and various organizations that have emerged to sponsor transformational and/or healing techniques. She acknowledges that this 'conspiracy' also comprises people who seek to market various New Age products ranging from crystals, incense and yoga to health foods and human potential therapy, but for Ferguson, New Age is less a spiritual movement as such than it is principally a social effort that seeks the conscious transformation of society itself. She has borrowed Thomas Kuhn's concept of the 'paradigm shift' as her central model in which sudden and innovative ways of thinking about old problems are given a rationalized basis and seen as the only viable means towards an improved future. Implicit in both Kuhn and Ferguson, though not explicitly presented as such in *The Aquarian Conspiracy*, is the theory of complexity as developed by the Santa Fe Institute in New Mexico. This deals with the kinds of spontaneous self-organization in which the whole becomes something more than simply the sum of its individual parts. For Ferguson, such automatic but natural and organic transformations are part of the dynamics of holism.

Translating the collective to the individualist level, Ferguson sees the deep inner change of personal consciousness as a form of shamanic transformation. She acknowledges that this shift is often deliberately sought through various 'psychotechnologies', and, as such, the New Age becomes for Ferguson a direct outgrowth of the counterculture of the 1960s with its drug culture and consciousness exploration. Through the incremental yet steady accumulation of new insights and ways of seeing, these shifts of perspective allow for the breaking of the kind of ingrained 'cultural trance' that allows parochial perceptions to become confused as universal truths (in complexity theory, the concept of 'lock-in'). In Ferguson's terminology, collective hypnotic stasis is potentially lethal to any society and any such sudden opening of group understanding can result in a 'collective paradigm shift' – a consensual transpersonal evolution that might occur 'when a critical number of thinkers has accepted [a] new idea'. Consequently, she welcomes conflict and struggle as themselves positive goads that can inspire and unfold social transformation. For Ferguson, the transcendent and holistic forms of consciousness and their non-linear dynamics are best apprehended through such phenomena as paradox, meditation and mystical experience, and in her understanding – a sort of pragmatic New Age outlook – the **Age of Aquarius** is a collective concern with both material well-being and psychological liberation. In this sense, and through her social activism, Ferguson's position escapes the essentially gnostic and **New Thought** underpinnings of much New Age thought and endeavour.

Ferguson's approach is essentially an activist one and stresses that we must become our own leaders. She supports non-violent resistance (Thoreau, Gandhi, and Martin Luther King) and a 'common sense science' as well as scientists who think like artists, musicians, and poets. She is a member of the Association of Humanistic Psychology as well as the Association of Transpersonal Psychology. She also serves on the board of directors for the Institute of Noetic Sciences. Her Aquarian perspective follows to a degree that of Ruth Montgomery (see **Montgomery, Ruth**) and argues that after the dark and violent age of Pisces, we are now on the brink of a new millennium of love and light. In 1990, she published her *Book of Pragmatics: Pragmatic Magic for Everyday Living*. Ferguson was designated in 1992 the 'Brain Trainer of the Year' by the American Society of Training and Development.

Further reading

Ferguson, M. (1973), *The Brain Revolution*, New York: Taplinger Publishing.

Ferguson, M. (1980, 1986), *Aquarian Conspiracy: Personal and Social Transformation in the 1980s*, Los Angeles: Tarcher.

Ferguson, M. (1990) *Book of Pragmatics: Pragmatic Magic for Everyday Living* New York: Pocket Books.

MICHAEL YORK

FINDHORN COMMUNITY

Founders: Peter Caddy, Eileen Caddy, Dorothy Maclean

Country of origin: Scotland/UK

The Findhorn Foundation Community (official title) is a colony of spiritual seekers in north-east Scotland that has been associated with New Age from the mid-1960s onwards (see **New Age Movement**): key activists with strong connections to Findhorn include George Trevelyan, David Spangler and William Bloom (see **Trevelyan, Sir George**; **Spangler, David**; **Bloom, William**). From basic beginnings in a solitary caravan Findhorn has grown into a substantial settlement inhabited by a steady turnover of participants exploring alternative spiritualities, holistic healing (see **Holistic Health Movement**), therapy, 'nature' and the arts. It is a major UK cross-roads for international networks of New Age practitioners whose beliefs and practices provide a cross-section of contemporary trends. Around two hundred people live in and around two compact sites. The majority is white, middle class, heterosexual and aged 30–45. Most come from the USA and north Europe (particularly England, Germany, and Scandinavia), although the demography is shifting as more Japanese, Brazilian, and East European nationals visit and settle. A countercultural orientation in the early 1970s is giving way to a more diverse economy of small businesses and private ownership. Findhorn now generally prefers to call itself a 'spiritual community', emphasizing interests in education, the environment, and various United Nations initiatives.

The settlement dates from November 1962 when Peter and Eileen Caddy (see **Caddy, Eileen**; **Caddy, Peter**) and their three children, and their Canadian colleague, Dorothy Maclean (b. 1920), occupied a caravan at Findhorn near Inverness. The group had recently managed a local hotel where they had for five years maintained telepathic contacts with internationally scattered mediums, occult 'masters' and UFO crew. This 'network of light' collectively anticipated an imminent planetary 'cleansing', to be followed by a 'New Age' for the surviving spiritual nucleus. Occult contact continued as Findhorn evolved into an organic garden and a venue for heterodox mediums, healers and thinkers. In the mid-1960s Findhorn made contact with other New Age groups and individuals in the UK and beyond, largely through the travels and correspondence of Peter Caddy. Spectacular growth occurred at the end of the decade when Findhorn was discovered by the hippie counterculture, who brought demographic stability (swelling colony numbers sixfold to around 120) and encouraged a hermeneutical shift in New Age (see **New Age Movement**) away from a post-apocalyptic utopia and towards this-worldly goals of healing, self-realization and egalitarian co-operation. Educational programmes were devised as a means to regulate visitor traffic and provide income. The Foundation was legally established in 1972; in 1975 it bought the hotel managed by the founders and in 1983 purchased the original caravan park. A variety of buildings have since been erected or bought and a total population of some two hundred has stabilized, although the original site continues to expand slowly as pockets of land become available.

The Findhorn Foundation organization revolves around a 'core' group of respected colony elders which functions as the custodian and guarantor of Findhorn's overall vision, and a management group which oversees practical decisions and Foundation infrastructure. Daily management of the latter is devolved to separate work departments in gardening, guest accommodation, housework and maintenance. Leadership is through 'focalizers', with decision-making based on consensus, derived from guidance obtained in meditation and from correct 'attunement' to 'spirit' or divine reality. Colony culture emphasizes the expression of emotion, bodily contact and self-reflexivity in speech and action: meditation, prayer, communing with nature, and studying various New Age texts are typical spiritual practices. Newcomers must attend an 'experience week' to learn loose behavioural codes and appropriate verbalization. The day-to-day running of Findhorn, communal meditation in the three dedicated 'sanctuaries', and the educational programme are regulated by routinized small group gatherings. This broadly oligarchic framework allows scope for institutional experiment whilst providing formal continuity. There are regular Foundation consultations on structure and goals and the dispersed local community of friends and affiliates has become a salient political force, both for internal Foundation policy and in the local Moray economy.

The original settlement, called 'The Park', contains caravans, chalets, and wooden houses, some Foundation-owned, others private. A Community Centre provides communal catering for Foundation employees and guests, the Universal Hall seats three hundred for conferences and meetings, and a sizeable organic foodstore and bookshop serves both residents and the local community. Communal meditation takes place in two sanctuaries. Turf-roofed and straw-bale buildings, an ecological sewage system and a wind-powered turbine attest to an expanding ecological agenda. The second site, known as 'Cluny', consists in the Victorian hotel building and garden grounds previously managed by the founders. The building itself contains several floors and around two hundred rooms; it accommodates the majority of Findhorn's visitors.

The Foundation depends financially upon turnover from its year-round programme of residential courses, conferences, and workshops. These are advertised in brochures distributed via an international mailing list of individuals, groups and organizations. The brochures also advertise Foundation training through a one year apprenticeship, after which one might become an employee of the Foundation, settle in the locality, or simply move on. An international directory of Foundation 'resource people' provides local contacts.

Despite popular perception of Findhorn as a 'community', the terms 'colony' or 'settlement' provide more precise descriptors since they better represent the population flux, the porous boundaries between colony and host culture, and the primary soteriological focus of Findhorn: the self-reflexive regeneration of individuals. Balancing the needs of colony and seekers through a period of considerable hermeneutical adjustment (from an 'other-worldly' to a 'this-worldly' interpretation of New Age) is a unique organizational achievement within New Age culture and justifies Findhorn's reputation as its most enduring and influential institutional expression.

Further reading

Findhorn Community (1988 [1976]) *The Findhorn Garden: Pioneering a New Vision of Humanity and Nature in Cooperation*, Forres (Moray): Findhorn Press.

Hawken, P. (1990 [1975]) *The Magic of Findhorn*, Glasgow: Fontana.

Sutcliffe, S. (2003) *Children of the New Age: A History of Spiritual Practices*, London: Routledge.

Walker, A. (ed.) (1994) *The Kingdom Within: A Guide to the Spiritual Work of the Findhorn Community*, Forres (Moray): Findhorn Press.

STEVEN J. SUTCLIFFE

FOCOLARE MOVEMENT

('focolare' = 'hearth' or 'home')

A movement in the Roman Catholic Church, formally known as The Work of Mary, Focolare was founded in Trent (Trento) in Northern Italy in 1943 by Chiara Lubich. In the midst of the bombed city she and a group of friends began working in the poorest areas of the city, trying to care for those hurt and to relieve their poverty, in response to Christ's command to love one another. In the evening they met together to read and reflect on the Bible. Their work began to attract other adherents and rapidly spread throughout Italy and, from 1952, throughout Europe.

The movement crossed the Atlantic in 1959, and has since reached over 180 countries. It claims some two million adherents or sympathizers. In 1948 in Rome Lubich met Igino Giordani, a Catholic activist, writer and member of the Italian parliament. He became the first married member of the organization which now embraces both married and celibate members, priests and members of religious orders, both male and female. The movement received formal approval from the Vatican in 1962. It now exists in eighteen separate divisions, among them The New Families Move-

ment launched in 1967 with, by now, some 300,000 members in most of the countries in which Focolare itself has been established.

It consists of family groups, with little overall structure, and organizes formation course for families and for engaged couples. It also encourages families to distribute surplus wealth to the poor, including in particular projects to aid children in countries in the process of development. The Parish Movement began in 1966, organizing families in parishes with the aim of renewing parish life. There are a thousand such parish groups in more than forty countries. The 'New Humanity Movement', inspired by the 1956 uprising in Hungary, engages focolarini (as the members are called) in social work, again with an emphasis on the developing world.

The organization has its own development agency, recognized as a formal Non-Governmental Organization (NGO) by the government of Italy and known from its Italian name as AMU ('Action for a United World'). A distinctive feature of Focolare is its 'small towns' known as 'Mariopolis' or 'city of Mary'. There are some twenty of these around the world, intended to be models of Christian communal living. The first, and best known, began at Loppiano near Florence in Italy in 1965. It now has around 800 inhabitants drawn from many nations. These are complete communities, with schools, small factories and so on: Loppiano even has its own radio station.

Focolare produces several magazines, its main one being *Città Nuova* ('New City'), which is also the title of its Italian publishing house. There is for the English-speaking world the New City Press in New York. Most full-time, unmarried members, those with the traditional vows of poverty, chastity, and obedience, live in groups in houses or apartments, though there is strict segregation of the sexes. Some continue to work in their chosen professions, but others are fully employed in running the various Focolare enterprises, such as the magazines, or in organizing the regular gatherings held for spiritual formation of members at the Mariopolis Centres.

There are frequent 'Genfests' for the 'New Generation' or youth movement of the Focolare, drawn very largely from children of members. In Europe Focolare enjoys considerable backing from Roman Catholic church leaders from the Pope down – Pope John Paul II was particularly supportive. Leaders of other Christian denominations have also endorsed Focolare, especially because it has, since the 1960s, extended its reach to non-Roman Catholics, and has engaged in ecumenical and inter-faith activity: the 'small town' of Mariopolis de Pace in the Philippines, for example, acts as a centre for dialogue with Eastern religions. In Latin America, on the other hand, it has been regarded by some as a conservative force, possibly because of the strict orthodoxy of its spirituality and possibly also because of its 'Economy of Communion' projects. These began in the early 1990s in the Brazilian city of São Paolo. They are an attempt to alleviate the poverty of those who dwell in the poorer districts of the city by harnessing the wealth and expertise of focolarini to establish small businesses, even in one instance a small business park, to provide employment. Critics, especially from the ranks of the Liberation Theologians, have seen these efforts as an attempt to improve conditions without challenging the political structures that underlie the poverty.

MICHAEL WALSH

FOREST MONKS

In Thailand, as in Sri Lanka, the long established view had been and continues to be that the Sangha or monastic community has special ritual and spiritual obligations to the laity. Historically and in modern times the most widely accepted view has been and is that monks should be *gramavasi* or reside in towns and villages for this purpose rather than *vanavasi* or residents of the forest where they meditate and are free of all responsibility to the laity. In practice they do serve the laity who seek them out for their prayers and spiritual blessings which are deemed to be more authentic than those of monks who dwell in urban temples.

The creation in the mid-nineteenth century of the Thammayuttika monastic *nikaya* or Order by the royal monk Mongkut, later King Rama IV (1851–68), restored the long established tradition, that of the forest monk or *thudong*, which had fallen into decline. This restoration resulted in among other developments countless itinerant monks practising *vipassana* or insight meditation as they wandered through the forests in robes made from rags following, they believed, the true path of the Buddha.

Forest monks who generally decry the institutionalized form of monasticism, particularly as lived by the urban monks, follow strictly the *vanavasi* ideal, the core of which is concentration on *vipasanna*, mendicancy, the use of rags for robes, and of urine for healing, and live a peripatetic existence in the forest. As in the Indian **Sanyassin** or renouncer tradition there is a turning away from society. Forest monks of Northeast Thailand can be highly critical of urban monastic life and dismissive of the monks who live that life describing them as 'useless' and only interested in money. The forest monks do not, however, disengage from society, and maintain that the monk should not only be preoccupied with his own spiritual progress but has a duty to engage with the spiritual and social concerns of the communities close to the forests that support them (see **Engaged Buddhism**).

Thus, forest monks serve their communities as teachers, healers, advisers, and counselors. They also either initiate or become involved in environmental projects and protest movements against, for example, deforestation, an activity that has led to confrontations with the Royal Forestry Department and even the military, as in the case of Phra Prachak Kutachitto. This monk who fought to save the Dong Yai Forest in the Northeast Province of Buri Ram, and who was later suspected of corruption, fought relentlessly under great pressure against the government's forced relocation programmes and eucalyptus schemes that he believed were detrimental to Dong Yai.

As was pointed out, the dilemma for monks who take to the forest is that they come to be regarded as especially pure in the sense of authentic, committed, and incorrupt, and consequently, tend to attract large numbers of people from the urban areas who believe that merit making, *tum bun,* performed with these monks as recipients of their gifts is highly efficacious. Several Thai forest monks have become well known and highly respected for their learning and piety both in Thailand and abroad, including Phra Ajaan Man Phuurithato (1870–1949), his disciple Ajaan Chan (1924–93) and Buddhadasa Bhikkhu. The latter's monastery at Wat Pah Nanachat attracts people from all over the world who are interested in being ordained as Buddhist monks. Ajaan Chan also founded the British Forest Sangha, branches of which have been established in California, Switzerland, Italy, New Zealand, and Australia.

Though close to people and often involved in their struggles forest monks can be extremely doctrinaire and critical of traditional rituals and beliefs, a well known example being Buddhadasa, founder of the Suan Mokkh temple in the south of Thailand. Buddhadasa's focus on the practical concerns of Buddhism such as economic and social inequalities, and corruption among the religious and civil leadership also constitute part of his appeal, although what has been construed as, if not approval of, then a failure to denounce political dictatorship, created serious problems for his more politically liberal supporters. Also much appreciated by his admirers was his belief in the possibility of enlightenment in this life, an insistence which, paradoxically, is believed to provide a more transcendental, spiritual version of Buddhism than that which focused mostly on meditation and the recitation of the suttas. For some (McCargo, 1999: 219), this understanding of enlightenment in the here and now forms part of an endeavour to create a more democratic foundation for the doctrine of karma.

Further reading

McCargo, D. (1999) 'The Politics of Buddhism in Southeast Asia' in J. Haynes (ed.) *Religion, Globalization and Political Culture in the Third World*, Houndsmill and London: Macmillan, pp. 213–39.

Swearer, D. (1991) 'Fundamentalistic Movements in Theravada Buddhism' in M. E. Marty and R. Scott Appleby (eds) *Fundamentalisms Observed*, Chicago: Chicago University Press, pp. 628–91.

Taylor, R. L. (1990) 'New Buddhist Movements in Thailand: an "individualistic revolution", reform and political dissonance', *Journal of Southeast Asian Studies*, 21(1), 140–43.

PETER B. CLARKE

FORTUNE, DION

(b. 1890; d. 1946)

Founder of the Fraternity of the Inner Light

Violet Mary Firth was born in Llandudno where her parents ran the Craigside

Hydrotherapeutic Establishment before moving to Bedford Park in London in 1906. The Firths were descended from a wealthy Sheffield steel-making family whose motto, 'Deo, non Fortuna' ('God, not Luck'), Violet took as her magical name on her initiation into the Alpha et Omega Temple of the Hermetic Order of the Golden Dawn in 1919. She adapted it slightly to Dion Fortune as a pen name for her occult writings, the name by which she is now commonly known. Her parents were Christian Scientists (see **Christian Science**), but Fortune never converted.

Fortune trained and practised as a psychoanalyst in London during the First World War, and later integrated her understanding of psychology with that of occultism. The latter interest stemmed from her own psychic experiences and reading in the library of the Theosophical Society (see **Theosophy**). After being a member of the Alpha et Omega until 1927, Fortune became president of the Christian Mystic Lodge of the Theosophical Society which within a year had become the independent Community of the Inner Light. It was later called the Guild of the Master Jesus and, after 1936, the Church of the Graal. Her own occult society, the **Fraternity of the Inner Light**, was ritually inaugurated in 1928.

Fortune's main teachings were that humanity was deity in the making and the universe an unfolding plan in the mind of God. This was framed within the Western Esoteric Tradition, which she saw as the whole spiritual experience of Western culture. She believed that the Hebrew **Kabbalah** was an authentic yoga of the West. Fortune expressed these ideas through her prolific writings, of which the best-known are her novels, particularly *The Sea Priestess* and *Moon Magic*, as well as *The Mystical Qabalah*. She identified herself as a priestess, and

is often considered to be a 'proto-Pagan' despite her blending of esoteric Christianity with occultism.

Further reading

Fortune, D. ([1935], 1987) *The Mystical Qabalah*, London: Aquarian
Fortune, D. (1978) *Sea Priestess*, York Beach, ME: Samuel Weiser.
Fortune, D. (2003) *Moon Magic*, York Beach, ME: Red Wheel/Weiser.
Knight, G. (2000) *Dion Fortune and the Inner Light*, Loughborough: Thoth Publications.

JO PEARSON

FOX, MATTHEW
(b. 1940)

Matthew Fox, born in Madison, Wisconsin, was ordained in 1967 as a Roman Catholic priest of the Dominican Order. He received his PhD from the Institute Catholique de Paris in 1970, studying with the great Dominican theologian M.-D. Chenu. He founded the Institute for Culture and **Creation Spirituality** in Chicago ten years after his ordination and through this became a self-appointed emissary to the New Age movement. Among the main influences on Fox are the ideas of Meister Johannes Eckhart, the thirteenth/ fourteenth century German Dominican mystic who, when accused of pantheism, successfully defended himself to the Vatican against charges of heresy. In 1983, Fox transferred his institute to the Holy Names College in Oakland, California. Because of his non-conformist teachings, however, the Vatican silenced Fox for a year from 15 December 1988. Subsequently, in 1994, after having left the Roman Catholic Church and Dominican Order, he was received as a priest of the Episcopal Church (US branch of the Anglican Communion) by the progressive Bishop William Swing of California. He currently serves as president of what has become the University of Creation Spirituality. He is also the co-chair of the Naropa University Oakland Campus – Naropa being the educational arm of the Vajradhatu Foundation that Tibetan Chögyam Trungpa Rinpoche founded in 1974 and now is headquartered in Boulder, Colorado. Fox has established Naropa's Master's Program.

The Friends of Creation Spirituality, Inc. was established in 1984 to educate the general public in creation-centred spirituality through the presentation of multimedia resources – including live performances, public forums and innovative liturgical rituals. In his 1983 *Original Blessing: A Primer in Creation Spirituality*, Fox shifted Christian emphasis from original sin to original blessing. He has sought to replace the Pauline and Augustine emphasis on the transmission of the error leading to Adam's fall and expulsion from paradise to one that celebrates God's manifold creativity and goodness. Fox's creation spirituality endeavours to blend Christian mysticism, feminism and environmentalism. In speaking of God, he prefers the pronoun 'she'. His message may be summed up as one of mystical, ecological and social justice. Creation Spirituality elucidates four spiritual pathways: the Via Positiva of awe, wonder, joy, and gratitude, the Via Negativa of darkness, silence, grief, pain, and release, the Via Creativa of creation, renewal, and rebirth, and the Via Transformativa of compassionate activity, manifestation of justice, and the celebratory act.

Fox has also engineered the 'reinvention of worship' through his Techno Cosmic Mass as a new liturgical form that employs the ritual circle and is intended to invoke the sacred into the total person (body, mind, heart, and soul). This mass blends Western liturgical forms with Eastern and indigenous spiritual constructs as well as multimedia technical imagery, dance and ecstatic music. Fox has described it as an 'interfaith, multi-cultural and intergenerational celebration', a democratic communal expression that is cosmologically oriented on the interconnection of all creation. In Fox's understanding, the mass as a drug-free, alcohol-free, and tobacco-fee event seeks to augment justice and compassion in the world by praising and thanking the Creator. It expresses the four spiritual journey pathways that Fox has articulated through his Creation Spirituality.

As a postmodern theologian, Fox is a prolific writer. Some of his nearly two dozen works include, beginning in 1972, *On Becoming a Musical, Mystical Bear: Spirituality American Style*; *A Spirituality Named Compassion*; *Passion for Creation: The Earth-Honoring Spirituality of Meister Eckhart*; *Meditations with Meister Eckhart*; his 1981 edited *Western Spirituality: Historical Roots, Ecumenical Routes*; *The Coming of the Cosmic Christ*; *Creation Spirituality: Liberating Gifts for the People of the Earth*; *Sheer Joy: Conversations with Thomas Aquinas on Creation Spirituality* – with an 'Afterword' by Bede Griffiths; *Wrestling with the Prophets*; *The Reinvention of Work*; *Natural Grace* – with Rupert Sheldrake; *The Physics of Angels: Exploring the Realm Where Science and Spirit Meet* – with Rupert Sheldrake; *Sins of the Spirit, Blessings of the Flesh* and, in 2000, *One River, Many Wells: Wisdom Springing from Global Faiths*. Through his books and worldwide talks, Fox has emerged as an articulate spokesperson for a grounded New Age perspective that combines the ecological and the mystical in a manner that bridges the traditional and innovative. His 1997 autobiography is titled *Confessions: The Making of a Post-Denominational Priest*.

Further reading

Fox, M. (1983) *Original Blessing: A Primer in Creation Spirituality Presented in Four Paths, Twenty-Six Themes, and Two Questions*, San Francisco: Bear & Co.; revised ed.: New York: Tarcher/Putnam, 2000.

Fox, M. (1997) *Confessions: The Making of a Post-Denominational Priest*, San Francisco: HarperCollins.

MICHAEL YORK

FRATERNITY OF THE INNER LIGHT

Founder: Dion Fortune

The Society and Fraternity of the Inner Light was founded by Dion Fortune (see **Fortune, Dion**) as a mystery school within the Western Esoteric Tradition in 1924. The Inner Light was based in Glastonbury and then London, and was intended to bridge the gap between Christian and Pagan doctrines, although it now has a Christian religious orientation. Prior to their publication by Israel Regardie in 1937–40, the Fraternity of the Inner Light used mainly Golden Dawn rituals (see **Hermetic Order of the Golden Dawn**); gradually, however, the Inner Light rituals altered until they bore no resemblance to those of the Golden Dawn.

The Society is the mundane vehicle for the Fraternity, running a supervised correspondence course which, if passed, leads to an interview by which successful students can become members of the Fraternity. Its principle aim is to expand psychic and spiritual consciousness, known as the 'inner planes', in order to aid the development of humanity. The application of spiritual principles to life on the physical level is thus emphasized. The Qabalistic Tree of Life is used as the chief training principle, expounded through Dion Fortune's textbook *The Mystical Qabalah*. Group meditation, symbolic visualization, and ritual are

key practices, based on the myths of ancient Greece and Egypt as the root of Western civilization, and the Arthurian legends and traditions associated with Glastonbury as the cultural heritage of the British Isles. Indeed, membership tends to be made up of people born and raised in Great Britain, as the Inner Light seeks to develop the consciousness of the Islands.

Service to the Great Work – dedicated service to God and the evolution of human consciousness – forms the basis of the Inner Light, which stresses that it is neither a social club nor a religious sect, self-help commune, psychical research organization, or alternative therapy centre. Rather, it aims to maintain and expand the bridge between outer physical life and spiritual forces through self-regeneration. This self-regeneration is based on Qabalistic principles, which teach that the human being consists of three basic elements. The first is the Incarnatory Personality, which is the normal human personality developed from birth and influenced by education, environment, and hereditary factors. The second is the Evolutionary Personality, Soul, Individuality, or Higher self. This is seen as encompassing in essence the experience of previous lives, demonstrating unique abilities which have been learned over successive reincarnations and learning the lessons of this and future incarnations. The third and final component is the Divine Spark or Spirit, to which the Incarnatory and Evolutionary Personalities should be in service. Its full expression is believed to produce genius and sanctity, but is thought to be rare in the world at this stage of human evolution.

Nevertheless, the development of this higher consciousness and its expression in the physical world is the main aim of the Inner Light. Beginning with the correspondence course on the Tree of Life, which takes a year to complete, members become disciplined in the practice of meditation and submit written reports at fortnightly intervals. Students should normally be at least 25 years of age, as a requirement of the Inner Light is the demonstration that a life has been established in the physical world prior to the development of the spiritual aspects of the personality. After successful completion of the study course, students can apply for and be interviewed for membership of the Fraternity. If admitted, training continues through the Three Degrees of the Lesser Mysteries, based loosely on Masonic symbolism, which are designed to develop and strengthen character, provide experience of ceremonial working, and develop visionary powers as a means to attaining higher consciousness. Each degree takes approximately one year, and includes meditation, practical group work once a month, and academic course work. After completion of the Lesser Mysteries, the Greater Mysteries can be embarked upon. In these Mysteries the Evolutionary Personality and the Spirit are worked on, and specialized work under the direction of the inner planes is conducted.

The Inner Light only charges fees for the supervised correspondence course, after which a voluntary donation can be made twice a year. Membership is open to both men and women on an equal standing, although preference is given to residents of the United Kingdom. An unsupervised correspondence course is available to anyone. The Society publishes a quarterly journal, available by subscription, and assists the continued publication of the works of its founder, Dion Fortune.

Further reading

Knight, G. (2000), *Dion Fortune and the Inner Light*, Loughborough: Thoth Publications.

Fortune, D. ([1935], 1987) *The Mystical Qabalah*, London: Aquarian
www.innerlight.org.uk

JO PEARSON

FRIENDS OF THE WESTERN BUDDHIST ORDER

The venerable Sangharakshita, born Dennis Lingwood in London in 1925 and having stayed for twenty years in India, founded the organization of the Friends of the Western Buddhist Order (FWBO) in London in 1967. The FWBO is not aligned to a specific Buddhist tradition in Asia, but rather strives to create a western form of Buddhist interpretation, practice, and organizational form.

The FWBO uses the texts of various Buddhist traditions. Basic to the FWBO is its reference to the spirit of the original teaching, as Sangharakshita calls it. This 'original teaching' and the 'spirit' are to be brought to light again, to be re-awakened. To this end, also western art and literature – among others, William Blake, Goethe, and Nietzsche – are introduced as so-called bridges to an understanding of the *dharma* (Buddhist teachings). This eclectic intra-Buddhist and inter-philosophical approach also applies to the practices favoured. Common are Buddhist meditation exercises from the Theravada tradition, especially those of the 'mindfulness of breathing' (Pali *anapna-sati*) and the 'cultivation of loving-kindness' (*metta bhavana*). Techniques from Zen and Tibetan traditions (e.g. visualization practices) are also used. Members regularly take part in *pujas* ('worship, devotional act'), which comprise chanting, bowing and prostration.

The Western Buddhist Order started in 1968 is the authoritative and organizational focal point of the movement. Order members are ordained, commit themselves to practice certain precepts and take the title *Dharmachari* and

197

Dharmacharini (male or female, '*Dharma-farer*') and a religious name in Sanskrit or Pali. Order members might be single or married, living in celibacy or being in full-time employment. Many, although not all, order members live together in residential communities. Such communities, most often single-sex, are usually found near a centre of the FWBO. The centres are visited by interested people and 'friends'. At the centres, order members offer regular programmes including meditation classes, public talks, study on Buddhist themes and texts and 'bodywork' such as Tai chi (see **Ch'i Kung**), **yoga**, and massage. In addition to the communities and the Buddhist centres, the FWBO has founded 'Right Livelihood' co-operatives, such as vegetarian restaurants, whole-food shops, or the successful wholesale and retail gift business Windhorse Trading in Cambridge (UK). The movement's three pillars of community, centre and co-operative aim to change the local environment as well as western society as a whole and to bring about a 'New Society'.

In the 1970s the FWBO started to establish communities in continental Europe and further afield. An especially strong branch exists in Western India, where Sangharakshita had supported Dr Ambedkar's conversion movement during the mid-1950s. Apart from Europe and India, institutions of the FWBO exist in Australia, New Zealand, Malaysia, Sri Lanka, Nepal, North and South America. In Britain, the movement has thirty-four centres and some twenty local groups (2000), and has become one of Britain's principal Buddhist organizations. Globally, there are about fifty-five city centres, fifteen retreat centres, numerous local groups and co-operatives. By late 2000, the order's size was approximately 900 members, and the number of supporters and Friends was estimated to be about 100,000, the vast majority of them being Buddhists in India. The FWBO has launched several journals, among them *Dharma Life*, and has a prolific book publication (Windhorse Publishing).

Since the 1990s, Sangharakshita started handing on responsibilities to senior order members whom he authorized to conduct ordinations and to take over the spiritual leadership of the movement. The selected members collectively comprise the Preceptors College Council (nineteen persons) based in Birmingham (UK). A core group of this Council, five men and three women, form the College of Public Preceptors. From this a chairperson is elected to take the headship of the order and thus of the entire movement. While in the future the chairperson will be elected by the whole college and council for a term of five years (re-electable), the first chairperson was chosen by Sangharakshita himself in 2000. This was Dharmachari Subhuti who is well known for his writings on contemporary Buddhism in the West.

Further reading

Sangharakshita (1990) *New Currents in Western Buddhism*, Glasgow: Windhorse.

Dharmachari, S. (1995) *Bringing Buddhism to the West. A Life of Sangharakshita*, Birmingham: Windhorse.

Batchelor, S. (1994) *The Awakening of the West. The Encounter of Buddhism and Western Culture*, Berkeley: Parallax, 323–40.

Baumann, M. (2000) 'Work as Dharma Practice: Right Livelihood Cooperatives of the FWBO', in C. S. Queen (ed.) *Engaged Buddhism in the West*, Boston: Wisdom Publishing, 372–93.

MARTIN BAUMANN

FUNDAMENTALISM

Fundamentalism describes a pattern or mode of religious faith and practice. As such, it does not technically indicate a 'new religious movement', nor is it simply a 'conservative', 'orthodox', or 'traditional' expression of religiosity. Rather, fundamentalism should be understood as a category by itself that originated in early twentieth-century American Protestantism, and which gained popular usage in the last quarter of the same century to demarcate a distinct brand of global religious resurgence. As of the beginning of the twenty-first century, groups that might properly be called fundamentalist were active in every major religious tradition in virtually every region of the world, ranking the rise of fundamentalism among the most significant developments in recent world history. Used properly, fundamentalism should be considered a fluid category of analysis rather than an absolute judgment, as individuals and groups may move in and out of fundamentalist-like beliefs and behaviors.

The term 'fundamentalism' was coined in 1920 by a group of Baptist evangelists and Bible teachers in the United States who battled against the encroachment of modernism into their denomination, particularly as it eroded the authority of scripture. This largely theological conflict was transformed into a clash between modern science and religion in the 1925 Scopes trial, which revolved around the teaching of Darwinian evolution in the public schools. After losing in the court of journalistic and public opinion, many fundamentalist groups retreated into quasi-seclusion, leaving the modernists to triumph in both the churches and in public life.

Because of the highly contextual origin of the term, many have wondered whether 'fundamentalism' can rightly describe any group outside the specific setting of North American Protestantism. Indeed, many Muslims, Jews, Hindus, and others to whom the term has been applied reject being classified by what is essentially an American-exported category. At the same time, some Protestant fundamentalists have grown uneasy with the designation, particularly since media depictions have imprecisely associated fundamentalism with radicalism and violence. However, given the lack of better terminology, fundamentalism has generally been retained in both scholarly and popular usage.

Several characteristics are common to fundamentalist movements across religious and geographical boundaries. Above all else, fundamentalists are concerned with the erosion of religion in society. In this sense fundamentalist movements are essentially defensive or reactive, as their very existence is based on fighting against the marginalization of their religious ideal, whether it be through the general processes of modernization and secularization, the secular state, or other religions and/or ethnic groups. This common concern about religion in the modern world should not, however, suggest that all fundamentalists are united by similar solutions to or even diagnoses of the problem; indeed, many of their specific goals are at cross-purposes with one another.

Fundamentalism is also characterized by selectivity, manifested in three different ways. First, fundamentalists should not be confused with restorationists or primitivists. Although they are defensive of their particular religious tradition and claim to be upholding both orthodoxy and orthopraxis, they are not primarily concerned with, nor committed to, a restoration of a golden era of pristine purity. Instead, they select and reshape particular aspects of the tradition that become their new standard. In so doing they will at times violate or significantly depart from other historic doctrines, practices, or behaviors of their tradition, and for this they are often criticized by their own co-religionists. In addition, while fundamentalists reject what they perceive to be the corrosive influences of modernity, they eagerly select and affirm certain aspects of the modern world that they use to further their own goals, whether it be technology, means of communication, or recruitment and organizational strategies. Finally, fundamentalists select certain processes or consequences of modernity as their specific target. In an attempt to describe their ambivalent relation with the modern world, it has been said that fundamentalists are 'anti-modern moderns'.

A fundamentalist's worldview is absolutist and dualistic. The world – along with its inhabitants – is uncompromisingly divided into light and darkness, good and evil. For fundamentalists the world outside their movement is polluted and sinful, although there may be gradations of contamination. They alternate between wanting to conquer, transform, or renounce this world, or simply create an entirely separate one of their own. Seeing themselves as an embattled minority, they often retreat into enclaves (that may or may not be territorial) in which they gain strength, nurture their followers, and develop strategies to interact with the outside world. These enclaves are distinguished by an elect, chosen membership, sharp boundaries, authoritarian organization, and strict behavior requirements. Not all fundamentalists are messianic, but they generally believe that history will have a dramatic culmination in which the good will triumph over evil, and eternal justice will vindicate them in the face of their enemies.

Although the rise of fundamentalism in the late twentieth century was often marked by the conflation of religion and politics, as in the **New Christian Right**, not all fundamentalist movements seek to gain political power, and some consider the modern state itself to be an abomination. Politics is seen as one among many tools available to further fundamentalists' goal of creating a society in which religion is the basis for a comprehensive system that includes law, polity, society, economy, and culture.

The mass media, particularly in the West, have often equated fundamentalism with violent fanaticism. Many fundamentalist groups have indeed used violence and terrorism to promote their end goals. However, it should be emphasized that fundamentalism as a designation does not in itself determine whether a group endorses violence, as many fundamentalists are primarily concerned with their members' spiritual welfare and promoting change through nonviolent means.

Further reading

Almond, G. A., Appleby, R. S. and Sivan, E. (2003) *Strong Religion: The Rise of Fundamentalisms around the World*, Chicago: University of Chicago Press.

Marty, M. E., and Appleby, R. S. (eds) (1991–1995) *The Fundamentalism Project*, 5 vols., Chicago: University of Chicago Press.

Marsden, G. M. (1980) *Fundamentalism and American Culture: The Shaping of Twentieth-Century Evangelicalism, 1870–1925*, Oxford: Oxford University Press.

R. SCOTT APPLEBY

G

GAIA

The Gaia hypothesis or theory that the earth along with its inhabitants is a single living organism is a combined development of environmental speculations contributed by James Lovelock (see **Lovelock, James**), Fritjof Capra, David Bohm and Rupert Sheldrake. Foremost is Lovelock who followed author William Golding's suggestion and selected the Greek earth-goddess designation, Gaia/Ge, for a planet-sized entity that could not be predicted from the sum of its parts. Lovelock promoted the idea that the entire range of living matter on the planet may be considered an organic entity in itself – one capable of manipulating the terrestrial atmosphere daily to fit and host earth's constituent parts. This manipulator Lovelock argued is life itself.

Related to the Gaia thesis are the ideas of Capra concerning matter and space as inseparable and independent parts of a single whole. Focusing on quantum field theory and its similarity to the unified ground concept of the Hindu *Brahman*, the Buddhist *Dharmakaya* and the Taoist *Tao*, Capra argues that particles are merely local condensations of the continuous fundamental medium present ubiquitously in space, the quantum field. Bohm likewise addresses the issue of undivided wholeness in his notion of the implicate order: the total order contained implicitly in each region of space and time. This order is not to be understood as simply the regular arrangement of objects or events but rather, in the sense of the hologram, as implicit/implicated multiple enfoldments. Bohm distinguishes between the explicate order of traditional physics and the implicate order of a super or holistic physics.

Sheldrake stresses a Platonic slant in considering morphogenetic fields as spatial structures (e.g., determinative plans or models) that are detectable only by their effects on material systems – analogous to gravitational and electromagnetic fields. Formulating a hypothesis of formative causation, Sheldrake suggests that morphogenetic fields operate causally in the development and maintenance of all systematic forms – from the most simple to the most complex. But rather than as pre-existing and changeless principles of order, he opens the possibility that previous similar forms may still operate causally across both space and time as a type of transphysical action.

The organic and innovative speculations of such modern-day thinkers have raised the consideration – both spiritual and ecological – of the earth as something more than simply its constituent parts: suggesting even the development of a super Gaian consciousness independent of humanity. To a degree, some of these thoughts have been prefigured in the evolutionary concepts of **Teilhard de Chardin** that trace a cosmic eventualizing process of matter (the geosphere) to the band of life that envelops the world (the biosphere) to an emerging mental envelope (the noosphere). While Teilhard's 'cosmogenesis' ultimately is superseded by a historical turning point toward greater unity and concentration, Gaian 'theogenesis' focuses instead on the build-up of matter, its vitalization and the ensuing hominization of life as a perpetually increasing complexity and development of consciousness.

In the broad range of the contemporary Alternative Spirituality network, Gaian exegesis varies greatly. For **Wicca** and broader-based Goddess Spirituality (see **Goddess Feminists** and **Goddess Movement**), Gaia as *terra mater* is either absorbed within or superseded by 'The Goddess' – an overarching construct comparable to Yahweh but now 'in a dress'. For traditional gnostics, Gaia is a phantom – the misreading of reality through our senses. For true lib-

eration, she/it is ultimately something from which to be emancipated. For the present-day, the more watered-down and less articulated form of Gnosticism, the **New Age Movement**, Gaia is the super-consciousness and balancing principle inherent in the earth and her eco-diversity as an interrelated and single system. Such Gaia spirituality manifests in concerns with geomancy or Chinese *feng-shui*, ley lines and vortexes, sacred centres and the attracting power of pilgrimage sites, earth-acupuncture to heal imbalances of the land using nodal points belonging to the planet's energy matrix, and the devic kingdom of nature spirits or elementals (e.g., fairies, angels, gnomes, etc.). Initially, the New Age orientation concentrated on the so-called 'higher realms' of etheric reality conforming to transcendental assumptions of religiosity and adopted a *soma sema* ('body is a tomb') attitude in which earth is understood as the 'lowest' and 'least advanced' frequency energy state. It contrasted with traditional, indigenous and geo-pagan forms of paganism that revere Gaia as earth-mother in which the tangible presence of deity is encountered in the theophany of nature. However, since especially the 1990s, **Neo-Paganism** has increasingly accepted a panentheistic combination of immanent and transcendent possibilities of deity, whilst New Age has steadily incorporated the notions of holistic science, complexity emergence and Gaia theory. In other words, as the two approaches grow more similar, New Age itself is becoming ever more comfortable with the concept of nature religion.

The worship of nature in today's world is as much political as spiritual (see **reclaiming**) – stressing environmental reformist and educational campaigns that range from simple recycling efforts and consumption reduction to such deep ecology activism as road protest movements, alternative and renewable energy lobbying and hands-on wilderness stewardship. Increasingly geo-centric Alternative Spirituality that engages with the sacred in daily life manifests notably in such centres as the Esalen, Naropa, and Whitney Institutes (USA), **Findhorn Foundation**, Schumacher College, and Sharpham (UK), Krishnamurti Centre and Bija Vidyapeeth (India), and Cortijo Romero (Spain) among others. The London-based Gaia Foundation is an international British charity serving as the European headquarters for a network of indigenous organizations, NGOs and policy-makers in Africa, Asia and Latin America who are dedicated to the protection of both democracy and cultural and biological diversity. Also in London, the Global Development Forum draws together various organizations, agencies and the general public to discuss ways of 'learning to manage a small planet'. Elsewhere, the Earth Council's International Secretariat (San José, Costa Rica) has issued the Earth Charter Document to form a global partnership to care for Earth. While not all these agencies consider an Earth Spirit as such, the Gaia concept of the interconnectedness of our living world remains the seminal inspiration.

Further reading

Bloom, W. (ed.) (1991) *The New Age: An Anthology of Essential Writings*, London: Rider.

Harvey, G. (1997) *Listening People, Speaking Earth: Contemporary Paganism*, London: Hurst.

Lovelock, J. (1982) *Gaia*, Oxford: Oxford University Press.

York, M. (2003) *Pagan Theology: Paganism as a World Religion*, New York: NYU Press.

MICHAEL YORK

GALLICAN CATHOLIC CHURCH
(*L'Église Catholique Gallicane*)

One of many churches that separated from the Catholic church in France in the nineteenth century the Gallican Catholic Church (GCC) established by the cleric Monseigneur François Chattel (1795–1857) traces the history of the principles on which it is founded to the late eighteenth century and even further back. It endorses for example the Four Gallican Articles drawn up by the renowned preacher and bishop, Jacques-Benize Bossuet (1627–1704) in 1682 and agreed upon by the French clergy of the day. These articles reject papal dominion over temporal affairs, insist that the decisions of a General Council of the Church are more authoritative than those of the Pope, that papal judgments are reversible and that the ancient liberties of the French Church are inviolable. Clearly, therefore, by accepting these articles of what is considered to be 'moderate' Gallicanism the GCC adopted a position that is incompatible with post Vatican Council I (1870) which proclaimed the dogma of papal infallibility.

This notwithstanding, the GCC which likens its stance towards Rome to that of the Anglican church in sixteenth century England claims never to have deviated from the authentic teachings of Jesus nor to have abandoned the long established liturgical traditions of the Catholic church. It sees itself as having followed a middle way between the popular piety of the middle ages and the more secular outlook of Modernism which sought to bring Catholic belief into line with contemporary thinking in philosophy, history and science. This movement which was condemned by Pope Pius X in 1907 endorsed biblical criticism common among Protestant theologians and was persuaded that the Gospel message rather than residing in its original core was continually unfolding under the guidance of the Holy Spirit.

The Gallican Catholic Church is presided over by a Primate and governed by bishops who have the authority to ordain priests. Its bishops, it claims, form part of the Apostolic succession and the validity of their ordination therefore cannot be denied. The GCC also insists that its teachings are also historically and doctrinally sound as they are based on all the dogmas of the Catholic church proclaimed since the Council of Nicaea (325) until Vatican Council 1 (1870).

Like other separatist Catholic movements in modern times including the **Lefebvre Movement** or order of St Pius X founded by the late Archbishop Marcel Lefebvre the GCC does not accept what it describes as the sacrilegious decisions of the Second Vatican Council (1962–5), particularly those relating to the celebration of the liturgy and the administration of the sacraments. On the contrary. It continues to administer the sacraments according to the sixteenth century rites laid down by the Council of Trent (1548 and 1568). Moreover, GCC refuses to accept any other interpretation of the Eucharist than that of its being a non-bloody sacrifice of Jesus' death on the Cross which he offered to God for the atonement of the sins of the world and also insists that its celebration must be carried in the traditional Tridentine way using what it defines as the sacred, universal language of Latin.

Its emphasis on tradition aside, certain of this Church's practices might appear to many mainstream Catholics to be liturgical novelties. It has introduced for example a ministry for animals, which it allows into the church on special days to receive sacramental blessings. This practice and that of healing have been greatly encouraged by the present Gallican Catholic archbishop of Paris, Mgr Dominique Philippe (b. 1951) who resides at and presides over the cathedral parish of Saint Rita, built in the neo-Gothic style of the late nineteenth century.

The Church's Gallicanism is expressed not only in its acceptance of the above mentioned Four Articles but also symbolically by the unfurling of the French national flag on the sanctuary of Saint Rita. The intention here, it is explained, is not to exclude anyone who is non-French from participation in its worship but to remind adepts that though open to all and ecumenical in spirit and outlook the GCC is French first. The Church though largely Caucasian (white) does have members from other racial background.

Further reading

MaCaffrey, James (1915) *History of the Catholic Church: From Renaissance to the French Revolution*, Dublin: Gill and Son, (2 vols), Vol. 1, chapter 7.

PETER B. CLARKE

GARDNER, GERALD BROSSEAU
(b. 1884; d. 1964)

Gerald Brosseau Gardner, publicist and perhaps founder of **Wicca**, was born in Great Crosby, Lancashire. He spent most of his asthmatic childhood in the care of his nursemaid, Josephine McCombie, going with her to Ceylon in 1900 when she married a tea planter. He taught himself to read and write, and remained in the Far East throughout his working life, moving from Ceylon to Borneo in 1908, and then on to Malaya in 1911. In 1927, on a visit to England, he married a nurse called Dorothea Frances Rosedale, usually called Donna, and when Gardner retired in 1936 she insisted that they return to England.

In retirement, Gardner lived in Highcliffe and London until moving to Castletown on the Isle of Man in 1954. He visited archaeological sites in the Near East, joined the Folklore Society (being elected to the council in 1946), the Co-Masons, the **Rosicrucian Fellowship of Crotona**, and the Druid Order. It was the Fellowship of Crotona which allegedly contained a hidden inner group of hereditary witches who initiated him in 1939, and whose rituals he wrote about in fictional form in the novel *High Magic's Aid* (1949) under the pseudonym Scire. The existence of this coven has neither been proved nor disproved.

Following the thesis of Egyptologist Margaret Murray, Gardner claimed that witchcraft had survived the Great Witch Hunt of early modern Europe and persisted in secret throughout history. However, it is largely undisputed that the development of **Wicca** was initiated by Gardner, influenced by Murray's 1921 publication *The Witch-cult in Western Europe*, and the work of Sir James Frazer, Charles Godfrey Leland, Jules Michelet, Robert Graves, and Aleister Crowley. He also drew heavily on images of witches and witchcraft throughout history.

However, Gardner was not able to publish more open accounts of witchcraft under his real name until the repeal of the 1736 Witchcraft Act in 1951 and its replacement with the Fraudulent Mediums Act, which gave freedom for individuals to practise witchcraft so long as no harm was done to person or property. No longer threatened by a law which enabled persecution of a person alleged to have magical powers, Gardner wrote *Witchcraft Today* which was published in 1954 and included an introduction by Murray, followed by *The Meaning of Witchcraft* in 1959.

Both books contained information on the Craft as it existed at that time. Gardner's books perpetuated the Murrayite theory and made use of Murray's scholastic weight to provide Wicca with a history and tradition which would defy accusations that Gardner had invented it. An apparent historical context for Gardner's Wicca had been found and given academic credibility, despite the fact that Murray's theory was never fully accepted in academic circles. Nevertheless, Murray's favourable reassessment of witchcraft provided the impetus for a surge of interest in this 'Dianic cult', just as Gardner had hoped.

Witchcraft Today vaulted Gardner into the public spotlight, and he made numerous media appearances. Believing witchcraft to be a dying religion, he propelled it into the public domain, initiated many new witches, and encouraged covens to spring up, operating according to the outlines provided in his books. By the mid-1950s, Gardner's love of publicity had drawn the religion to the attention of the public. In 1951, Gardner had become associated with the Museum of Witchcraft in Castletown and bought the premises when he moved there in 1954. Donna died in 1960, presumably having never been involved in her husband's interest in Wicca and subsequent revival of it. In the early 1960s Gardner's Wicca was exported to North America by one of his initiates, Raymond Buckland.

Gardner died in 1964, but his tradition of Gardnerian Wicca was firmly established, much to the annoyance of those who practised Traditional and Hereditary witchcraft, which was believed to be a witchcraft religion older than Gardner's Wicca. His belief in an underground Pagan nature/fertility cult which survived from pre-Christian times is a powerfully romanticized fiction, the aim of which was to make Wicca attractive to newcomers and thus prevent it from dying out. The growth of Wicca since the 1950s suggests that Gardner's activities in retirement were successful in terms of achieving this aim.

Further reading

Gardner, G. B. (1949) *High Magic's Aid*, London: Pentacle Enterprises.
Gardner, G. B. (1954) *Witchcraft Today*, London: Rider.
Gardner, G. B. (1957) *The Meaning of Witchcraft*, London: Aquarian

Jo Pearson

GEDATSUKAI

This Japanese new religion (see **New Religion (Japan)**) was founded by Okano Seiken (1881–1948). The term *gedatsu* is the Sino-Japanese translation of a Buddhist (Sanskrit) technical term meaning 'enlightenment'. While the group is often categorized as a new religion with origins in Esoteric Buddhism, its teachings and rituals are, in fact, composed of a mixture of Buddhism, Shinto and Confucianism. The group's headquarters is located at Kitamoto, Saitama Prefecture. Nominal membership numbered about 190,000 in 2002.

Okano was born in 1881 in what is present-day city of Kitamoto. Dropping out of elementary school before graduation, he left his family farm and moved to Tokyo, where he worked at a liquor store. In those early days of urban life, Okano attempted to start several new businesses, but failed. He finally succeeded in getting employment a shipping business, however, and established his own store in 1923.

Okano suffered from acute pneumonia in 1925 and was bedridden for three months, during which time his mother gave him *amacha* or hydrangea tea, resulting in a full recovery. Following the illness, Okano experienced a deepening interest in religious issues, visiting numerous Shinto shrines and Buddhist temples in the Kanto area of Japan, and associating with religious ascetics. He began religious austerities in the mountain area of Tanzawa in Kanagawa prefecture, and gradually gained a reputation for his ability to cure diseases. People with various ills heard the rumors and began visiting his residence in Setagaya Ward, Tokyo, seeking cures.

On a visit to a New Year's shrine in his homeland in 1929, Okano passed a small shrine where he experienced a heavenly revelation that a Great God would be revealed to the world through his work. In May in the same year, he also saw golden characters as he was writing. Okano gave his followers charms on which the characters were written, and discovered that they experienced a kind of mystical bodily vibration when handed the charms. This made him confident that the characters contained miraculous powers, and led him to establish the group Gedatsukai that year. Okano's wife, however, displayed strong antipathy to his deep religious concerns, leading to their divorce in 1931.

Okano started a unique form of religious austeries called 'Ongohou,' literally, the 'Precious Five Laws,' and instructed his followers in a specific ritual called '*Amacha kuyo*,' an offering of tea served to save spirits of the dead from suffering on account of the evil karma they have acquired while living. He also taught people to revere the native Japanese divinities or *kami*, and to respect ancestors and show gratitude and return thanks and gratitude for favors received. Okano also preached the importance of self-reflection, ridding the self of egoism and conforming to conventional ethics in human relations. After Okano's death in 1948, Okano Seiho (1939–) was appointed as organization president.

Gedatsukai is organized as a lay association, and maintains that life and religion exist on the same dimension. As a result, members are not rigidly bound to any particular Buddhist sect or other religion. They become members of Gedatsukai without changing any former religious affiliation, and while continuing to worship the traditional tutelary deity of their birthplace. They also pay worship to Japan's Imperial family, and thus regard the Grand Shrines of Ise, the Kashiwara shrine, and the temple Sennyuji as three sacred places for pilgrimage.

Major objects of worship in the group include Japan's 'heavenly deities and earthly deities' and the Five Buddhas (*Gochi-nyorai.*) as well as *Gedatsu Kongo,* the religious name given to Okano Seiken after his death. Most members live in Japan's Kanto area, with some others in the Tokai and Kansai areas, and other parts of Japan. The spiritual center (*dojo*) is located in the city of Kitamoto, and the group's most important religious services are held there. Other important facilities are located in the Shinjuku district of Tokyo, and function as centers of missionary activities and public relations. Four other *dojo* exist in Kyoto, Odawara, Nagoya, and Sapporo, and these are under the direct control of the group's headquarters. Together with these, nearly 400 branch churches have been established throughout Japan, as well as two churches overseas in California and Hawaii. Oversea Gedatsukai activities began during World War Two on the American west coast, primarily among Japanese-American residents.

Gedatsukai presently belongs to the Federation of New Religious Organizations of Japan (*Shin-shu-ren*). As one of the core member of the FNRS, the group carries out various social activities, including volunteer activities by young members, in association with the Federation.

Further reading

Earhart, H. Byron (1989) *Gedatsu Kai and Religion in Contemporary Japan*, Bloomington and Indianapolis: Indiana University Press.

NABUTAKE INOUE

GENDER AND NRMS

Like mainstream religious organizations in the West, the 'new religions' of the latter twentieth and early twenty-first century have displayed gender imbalances in leadership, lay participation and scope for authority afforded people in everyday life as women and men. Scholarly opinion has been divided, however, as to whether the new religions, competing with and sometimes explicitly challenging mainstream religions and secular society, have offered genuinely empowering alternatives to women or rather represent regressions into the patriarchy of the conservative mainstream.

Latter-day Western 'new religions', formed or imported into societies experiencing loosening family ties, rapidly changing sexual mores and greatly increased female participation in paid work outside the home, show great variety in gender norms and evaluations placed on women and men as spiritual beings. Indeed the new religious movements (NRMs) have provided some of the most notable sites for sexual and gender role experimentation in Western societies. However by no means all NRMs offer alternatives to conventional patriarchal institutions. Some offer, if anything, more highly structured and intensely patriarchal environments than most people experience in mainstream society.

This is particularly true of Asian-derived new religions launched since the mid-twentieth century when numerous Western countries lifted immigration restrictions on non-Europeans. Many Asian-derived NRMs imported in this era have introduced the conservative gender norms of their home countries. For example, the Indian-originated **International Society for Krishna Consciousness** (ISKCON) requires its Western converts to model their behaviour towards the opposite sex on traditional Vedic practice. Women are encouraged to achieve their limited spiritual potential through subservience to their husbands and ISKCON's male leadership. Celibacy, thought necessary for the rapid spiritual realization of Krishna consciousness and required for service as an initiating guru, is an ideal for men only. Buddhist orders imported into the West also carried requirements that women accede to male religious authority. The spiritual lineages that offered initiations were exclusively patrilineal and in their home countries treated nuns as inferior to monks.

Such Hindu- and Buddhist-derived movements, which in the West attached modern forms of formal organization to traditional personalistic master–disciple relationships, echoed the neo-conservative, patriarchal values evident in Pentecostal and evangelical Christianity and Jewish Orthodoxy that were also gaining in popularity in the latter twentieth century. In numerous cases, however, the exotic NRMs institutionalized those values in even more rigorous forms than the sectarian and neo-conservative Christian and Jewish movements. This prompted feminist scholars of the 1970s to see the popularity of new religious movements as a backlash against the renascent women's movement.

Nonetheless, subsequent scholarship, ranging more broadly across later twentieth century and contemporary NRMs, has called attention to striking exceptions to male monopoly of leadership in them, and in some has identified opportunities for at least partial female empowerment. Elizabeth Clare Prophet, for example, took over from her husband the leadership of their syncretistic **Church Universal and Triumphant** upon his death. Examples of female leadership can be found even in Hindu-derived movements, although these are not common. Thus Dada Lekhraj (see **Lekhraj, Dada**), spiritual leader of the **Brahma Kumaris**, gave the administration of the movement's formal organization over to a group of senior women adherents at its foundation in 1937, long before the movement came to the West in the 1970s. Similarly, the Bhagwan Shree Rajneesh (see **Rajneesh Movement**) from time to time placed his movement in the hands of female leaders. Moreover, Soto Zen and several other Buddhist movements in the West have responded to internal pressures from women converts for change, giving women unprecedented rights to confer initiations, lead lower level branches and devise new means of incorporating lay individuals and families into the religious community.

In some few cases, opportunities for women to act as leaders in the new religions have been underpinned by radical assertions of the spiritual superiority of women, as in the Brahma Kumari, Rajneesh and Mary Daly movements. Other NRMs like est, **Scientology**, and the **Raelian Church** promote belief in an essentially shared, gender-free spiritual nature. However, in the NRMs that first gained broad public notice in the 1970s and 1980s, beliefs in a special delegation of spiritual authority to men or the actual spiritual superiority of men have been more common, just as they have in the world religions from which many NRMs are descended.

The more loosely organized and substantially Western-sourced New Age (see **New Age Movement**) and neo-pagan movements (see **Neo-Paganism**) that gained increasing popularity in the final decades of the twentieth century have in contrast generally promoted redress of perceived male bias in other religions, thereby attracting sections of the secular women's movement as well as frustrated feminists from the mainstream religions. Neo-pagan groups in particular have mined Western and other peasant and tribal traditions for positive images of women's spirituality and promoted women as leaders in ritual and family life. Women's connection with material creation as birth givers is celebrated and often linked to the deep ecology movement's spiritualized embrace of nature. Perhaps alone amongst the NRMs, the neo-pagan groups cast their highest image of the divine as feminine, as the Goddess (see **Goddess Feminists** and **Goddess Movement**).

Clearly the variety in leadership patterns, family roles and constructions of men's and women's spiritual natures found in NRMs defies any categorical assessment of them as either havens for patriarchy or hothouses for women's empowerment. Even the internal complexity of individual movements (which, for example, may promote female leadership but focus on male images of divinity, or celebrate the sanctity of motherhood but regard sexuality as polluting) discredits such wholesale generalizations. Nonetheless, new religions, mobilizing as they often do high levels of motivation for personal change and commitment, have been attractive settings for reordering gender values, both in everyday life and in believers' relationships to the divine.

Further reading

Howell, J. (1998) 'Gender Role Experimentation in New Religious Movements: Clarification of the Brahma Kumari Case', *Journal for the Scientific Study of Religion*, 37(3), 453–61.

Palmer, S. (1994) *Moon Sisters, Krishna Mothers, Rajneesh Lovers. Women's Roles in New Religions*, Syracuse: Syracuse University Press.

Puttick, E. and Clarke, P. (eds) (1993) *Women as Teachers and Disciples in Traditional and New Religions*, Lampeter: Edwin Mellen Press.

JULIA DAY HOWELL

GLA SOGOHONBU

GLA was established in 1969, mainly by the original followers of Shinji Takahashi (1927–76), with the name *Daiuchû Shinko-kai*, meaning 'God Light Association of the Great Cosmos', and was later renamed in English as the God Light Association (GLA). GLA is a religious movement without any clear object of worship, which has instead an eclectic doctrine. Takahashi drew upon the ideas of various religious figures, such as the Buddha, Jesus and Moses, and included esoteric and quasi science fiction elements in his teachings, such as the idea of the immigration to earth of the first humans from another planet by UFO. The ultimate purpose of activities is the establishment of utopia on earth.

Takahashi was born as Haruo Takahashi into a farming family in Nagano Prefecture Japan in 1927. As a child, he underwent a number of religious experiences, including near death and out of the body experiences, after which he started visiting a nearby Shinto shrine to say prayers. He read electrical engineering at Nippon University and worked in several different lines of employment, later establishing his own electrical firm. He became aware of the 'Truth' and reached enlightenment in 1968, after which he started to teach a small number of enquirers. Sixty to seventy people started to gather to listen to Takahashi's sermons and the following year his believers volitionally formed a group, which became the GLA, and obtained official status as a religious organization in 1973.

Takahashi was believed by his followers to be the reincarnation of Gautama Buddha, and just before his death he claimed to be the incarnation of a great spiritual being, called El Ranty. His teaching is called *Shinri*, or God's Truth, which includes the important concept of the eternal lives of spirits that are reincarnated on earth as human beings. During his lecture meetings, Takahashi sometimes held spiritual dialogue sessions, called *reidô genshô*, in which he used a number of different 'foreign tongues'; allegedly talking with his believers in such languages as ancient Indian and Chinese. These sessions were performed as proof of the existence of the spirit world and the reincarnation of souls; the knowledge of foreign tongues was believed to come from their past lives.

Some observers point out that GLA's development coincided with a time when the occult was booming in Japan (Numata, 1987), and rather than his teachings it was probably Takahashi's psychic powers that attracted those who joined GLA.

He involved his daughter, Keiko (1956–), in GLA's activities, and she became known as Michael (after Archangel Michael). Takahashi died in 1969 at the age of forty-eight, as he had predicted, and Keiko, while still a university student, became her father's successor as leader of the GLA. A number of senior members, however, left GLA to establish their own movements. GLA's main office is in Tokyo and it has a membership of about 17,000 followers.

Further reading

Inoue, Nabutaka (2000) *Contemporary Japanese Religion*, Tokyo: Foreign Press Centre.

MASAKI FUKUI

GLASTONBURY

Glastonbury, a small town in the south west of England, has been dubbed the 'epicentre of the New Age in England' (see **New Age Movement**) and 'heart chakra of planet earth'. Such epithets are simply the latest claims made for a place which has been hailed over the centuries as the 'cradle of English Christianity'; the Isle of Avalon of Arthurian legend; and the New Jerusalem, where Christ will appear at his second coming.

Glastonbury's Christian credentials are based on the legend that merchant and provider of Christ's tomb, Joseph of Arimathea, came to Glastonbury after the crucifixion, building a simple church (on the site later occupied by Glastonbury Abbey) and bringing both the Grail (the chalice used at the Last Supper) and the Glastonbury Thorn, which flowers in spring and also around Christmastime. Some believe Joseph of Arimathea hid the Grail at Chalice Well, a chalybeate spring with red-staining waters. Further elaboration of this myth suggested that Jesus had accompanied Joseph to Glastonbury as a boy, inspiring William Blake (1757–1827) to write 'And did those feet in ancient time Walk upon England's mountains green?', and convincing some that Jesus will return there. Glastonbury also boasts connections with a number of Celtic saints, including St Bride. Glastonbury Abbey became a major medieval pilgrimage destination, but it was brutally suppressed in 1539 when Henry VIII 'dissolved' the Catholic monasteries and the Abbey fell into ruins.

In Arthurian legend, after his last battle, King Arthur was taken for healing to the Isle of Avalon, where some believe he remains, to return at some hour of great need. Rising out of the Somerset Levels, once a vast swamp with lagoons and waterways, Glastonbury was at one time an island or peninsula, leading some to identify Glastonbury with Avalon. The twelfth-century 'discovery' of the bodies of King Arthur and his queen in the grounds of Glastonbury Abbey seemed to confirm this.

From the late nineteenth/early twentieth centuries, a spate of esoteric religious activity commenced in Glastonbury, although it really flourished as a centre for a variety of spiritual seekers from the 1970s onwards. Glastonbury's credentials as an important site of New Age and alternative spirituality are myriad. Occultist Dion Fortune (see **Fortune, Dion**) lived in and was greatly influenced by Glastonbury; Eileen Caddy (see **Caddy, Eileen**) declared Glastonbury a 'Centre of Light', one point of a 'sacred triangle' involving the **Findhorn Community** and Iona. In the 1970s and 1980s the 'Ramala Teachers' were channelling messages to the Ramala Centre in Glastonbury. On 16 August 1987, hundreds gathered on Glastonbury Tor for the Harmonic Convergence as people attempted to 'activate' sacred sites around the world. Glastonbury is said to lie at the nodal point of significant leylines, which some claim gives it a particular 'energy' and healing powers, and there have been frequent rumours of UFO sightings (see **UFOs**).

Many now believe Glastonbury was a major pre-Christian site of Goddess worship (see **Goddess Movement**), and some maintain that Glastonbury was a huge centre of Druidic learning (see **Druidry**), attracting students from all over Europe and beyond. Contemporary Druids and Pagans of various types (see **Neo-Paganism**) converge on Glastonbury to celebrate the 'Celtic' or '8-fold calendar' of quarter days, equinoxes and solstices there, while what are perceived as pre-Christian customs and ritual are 'revived', 'reclaimed' or created. Various new religions (see **New Religious Move-**

ment) and assorted spiritual groups (ISKCON, **Baha'i**, **Sai Baba**, Sufi, Buddhist) have had a presence in Glastonbury over the years, and Christianity remains a vibrant force in the town, with a variety of denominations and Anglican and Roman Catholic Pilgrimages to the Abbey each summer.

Reflecting the 'topophilia' (love of place) of much contemporary spirituality, many feel that physically being in Glastonbury literally puts one in touch with the sacred. For some the most significant spot within Glastonbury is the Tor, a strangely contoured hill crowned by St Michael's Tower (all that remains of a medieval chapel). The Tor is variously regarded as a three-dimensional ceremonial maze, the entrance to the Other World, and a communication tower for alien contact. Others regard the Abbey ruins as its spiritual centre. The very landscape in and around Glastonbury is thought to reveal its sacred and special character through symbolic shapes and figures, either occurring naturally or meaningfully moulded in some previous era. What is seen and how it is interpreted depends on individual belief and perspective. At the start of the twentieth century, John Arthur Goodchild discerned the ancient 'Salmon of St Bride', a monument he considered equal in importance to Stonehenge. In the 1920s, artist Katherine Maltwood saw in Ordnance Survey maps of the Glastonbury area a variety of configurations in the landscape which she interpreted as a giant Zodiac, centred at nearby Butleigh, with a circumference of roughly 30 miles. Various versions of the Glastonbury Zodiac have developed subsequently, and many now believe that this Zodiac is the 'Round Table' of Arthurian myth. People discern at least two different Goddess (see **Goddess Movement**) figures in Glastonbury, one whose womb is covered by the Lady Chapel of the

Abbey, and another for whom Chalice Hill is her belly, with the red waters of Chalice Well as her menstrual flow.

A distinctive spiritual service industry has evolved in Glastonbury, including a huge range of healing, spiritual tour guides, specialist shops, and 'spiritual' Bed and Breakfast accommodation. The Isle of Avalon Foundation promotes spiritual education, with a diverse programme of lectures, workshops and training courses (e.g. Working with Angels and Nature Spirits, Tools for Remembering Past Lives, Firewalking, Tarot Counselling, Shamanic Practice).

Glastonbury in many ways epitomizes the 'mix and match' ethos of much contemporary spirituality, and 'spiritual tools' and services abound to assist individuals on their spiritual quest. Old myths are recycled and renewed – some say Jesus came to Glastonbury to attend the Druidic University, others believe that Arthur will return to Glastonbury to lead people into a New Age. For a great range of spiritual seekers, Glastonbury is a site of great national, indeed planetary, sacredness and significance.

Further reading

Benham, P. (1993) *The Avalonians*, Glastonbury: Gothic Image Publications.
Bowman, M. (2000) 'More of the same?: Christianity, Vernacular Religion and Alternative Spirituality in Glastonbury', in S. Sutcliffe and M. Bowman (eds) *Beyond New Age: Exploring Alternative Spirituality*, Edinburgh: Edinburgh University Press.
Bowman, M. (1993) 'Drawn to Glastonbury', in I. Reader and T. Walter (eds) *Pilgrimage in Popular Culture*, Basingstoke and London: Macmillan.

MARION BOWMAN

GNOSTIC MOVEMENT

This movement was founded by Víctor Manuel Gómez Rodríguez (1917–77) who was born in Santa Fé de Bogotà, in Colombia. As a youth, he was fascinated by spiritism and became a member of the Theosophical Society, which he left a few years later to join the Arnoldo Krumm-Heller (1876–1949) Fraternitas Rosicruciana Antiqua. In 1949, Gómez – having taken the esoteric name of Samael Aun Weor – founded the Universal Christian Gnostic Church in Mexico City, which over the years would assume other names following splintering within the 'Gnostic movement'.

With Samael Aun Weor's death, the movement underwent a ferocious battle of succession, and there are now scores of separate branches all over the world. Although these groups diverge – beyond questions of succession – on doctrinal matters as well, they share a veneration of Samael Aun Weor himself, and of his writings, which are worshipped as 'Kalki Avatar of the Age of Aquarius', 'Buddha Maitreya', and 'Logos of the planet Mars'. From the strictly phenomenological point of view, Samael Aun Weor's Gnostic thought combines elements deriving from the tradition of Gnostic Churches, from Arnoldo Krumm-Heller, from Tantrism, and from the Theosophical Society, without forgetting equally-important thelemitic influences (i.e., deriving from Aleister Crowley (1875–1947); (see **Ordo Templi Orientis**) as well as the teachings of George Ivanovitch Gurdjieff (1866?–1949) (see **Gurdjieff, George Ivanovitch**).

The synthesis of Samael Aun Weor's Gnostic teachings and of the schools based on them, is contained in the 'Three Factors for the Revolution of Consciousness', i.e.:

(a) the death of the individual's negative interior universe and the disintegration of all the psychological aggregates that prevent free circulation of energies and the reawakening of the 'objective consciousness';

(b) the birth of internal bodies or higher existential bodies of being, indispensable vehicles for dimensions higher than the physical dimension, thanks to the transmutation of creative energies by means of the practice of 'Arcane AZF', i.e., the practice of sexual excitation without orgasm, and elimination of psychological aggregates;

(c) sacrifice for the benefit of humanity in spreading eternal wisdom.

The path to Weor's Gnostic teachings is divided into three cycles, spread over a total of approximately fifty weekly sessions, similar in structure to a standard course of study: the 'first chamber' (exoteric circle) consists of three levels (A, B, and C) corresponding to three stages of learning of fundamental concepts. The 'second chamber' (mesoteric circle) is for those who, having understood the Gnostic teaching and put it into practice, and wish to experience the 'Three Factors for the Revolution of Consciousness'. Finally, the 'third chamber' (esoteric circle) is open to advanced students. The central practice is called Sahaja Maithuna, and consists of a complete sexual act between a man and a woman involving the sublimation of sexual energy without experiencing orgasm, thus realizing a 'transmutation' of sexual energy. As opposed to other esoteric spheres, Samael Aun Weor considered this path to sexual alchemy to be the only legitimate one: the others are rejected and even attacked as diabolic (presided over by a 'Black Lodge'). Drawing on a tantric tradition with a long history in oriental spirituality and in Western esotericism, Samael Aun Weor held that by avoiding emission of the sperm, sexual energy travels to the deepest fibers of the being and consciousness, rather than dispersing to the exterior, and is therefore reawa-

kened. A key element of Weor's Gnostic system is that it considers sexuality to be an eminent form of relationship with the transcendent ('sex is the creative function, by means of which the human being is a true God'), to the point that the dispersion of sexual energy outside these practices is considered to be the *causa causarum* of the loss of all internal powers, as well as of illnesses, old age, degeneration of vital functions, memory loss and, lastly, of death itself.

On the other hand, the practice of this alchemic method often provokes disagreement among the movement's various branches, which together could be seen as the world's largest 'Gnostic mass movement'. The international organization with the largest number of active members (approximately 18,000) is the Gnostic Institute of Anthropology, the legacy of Samael Aun Weor's wife, Arnolda Garro Gómez (1920–98), better known as Maestra Litelantes. Other important organizations include the AGEACAC (Asociación Gnóstica de Estudios Antropológicos y Culturales Asociación Civil), directed by Víctor Manuel Chavez, and the AGEAC (Asociación Gnóstica de Estudios Antropológicos, Científicos y Culturales), founded by Oscar Uzcátegui Quintero in Spain in 1992. Other branches of the Gnostic movement, although maintaining original aspects, are the CEG (Centro de Estudios Gnósticos), founded by Ernesto Barón, now present in over twenty countries around the world and growing rapidly, and the mosaic of realities traced to the teaching of the Colombian Joaquín Enrique Amortegui Valbuena (1926–2000), better known as V. M. Rabolú, who was one of Samael Aun Weor's main disciples, and whose branch is characterized by a particular apocalyptic and (see **Millenarianism**) millenarian trait.

Further reading

Zoccatelli, P.-L. (2000) 'Il paradigma esoterico e un modello di applicazione. Note sul movimento gnostico di Samael Aun Weor', *La Critica Sociologica*, 135, 33–49.

PierLuigi Zoccatelli

GOD IS LOVE

The *Igreja Pentecostal Deus é Amor* (Pentecostal Church God is Love) is a Brazilian pentecostal denomination founded in 1962 by David Miranda. Miranda, who still led the church in the early twenty-first century, was a southern Brazilian of rural extraction. In São Paulo, he converted from Catholicism to a small pentecostal church. In 1962, when 26 and unemployed, he used his severance pay to start a new church. This was a period when the first major pentecostal churches founded by Brazilians were springing up, especially in the industrial metropolis of São Paulo.

Miranda soon moved to a busy city-centre square; downtown passersby would be the church's base of expansion, and not a working-class suburb. The pentecostal message would be inserted into the gaps of the working world and the daily life of the street, and not only into the residential context. Extensive use was made of radio to divulge the church's activities. In 1979, the current 'World Headquarters' were acquired, an old warehouse that houses 10,000 people. Above the pulpit, there are numerous plaques with the names of radio stations which carry Miranda's programme, showing the centrality of this medium in the life of the church. In 1991, some fourteen of these radio stations belonged to the church. In the same year, God is Love claimed to have 5,000 churches in Brazil and to be present in seventeen foreign countries. By 2003, it claimed over 8,000 churches and a presence in 136 countries. These claims must

be treated with caution: the Brazilian census of 2000 showed it to have 800,000 members (only 4 per cent of Brazilian pentecostals), concentrated in the southeast of the country. It is undoubtedly strong in some neighbouring countries (especially Paraguay, Uruguay, and Peru) and has a presence in many African countries, including some predominantly Islamic areas of West Africa.

God is Love has a social arm known as Fundação Reviver, initiated in 1994 and presided over by the founder's wife. It also produces a news-sheet (*O Testemunho*) and a magazine (*Ide*). But its main investment has been in radio programmes and in the purchase of radio stations. Healing is adapted for the medium, but the link between radio and the church is maintained. Television, however, is not used at all, and members are forbidden to watch it. This is one manifestation of God is Love's strong *sectarianism*, also shown in relation to other churches (no collaboration, since they are all worldly) and to society (rigid formulas of 'separation from the world'). It offers an extremely legalistic recipe of sanctified life. Among the prohibitions: red clothes for men; games of any sort; contraceptives; heels of more than three centimetres when the heel is narrow, or four centimetres when broad. Female members aged 16 to 18 may marry a male member up to the age of 28, and so forth. For each rule, punishments are specified, generally suspension from membership.

Severity of rules grew from the 1980s and may be linked to attempts to increase resources. However, the stricter measures were not totally reducible to monetary calculations: one of the prohibitions is against carrying firearms, even at work. God is Love's attraction in a competitive religious market is mainly to the very poor and to those who feel they need a 'heavy doctrine' to keep them on the rails. The level of visible poverty is even greater in God is Love's services than in those of other major pentecostal churches in Brazil. Several elements are anticipations (but in a culturally outdated form) of the more successful **Universal Church of the Kingdom of God**: uniformed lay helpers, exorcisms at the front, interviews with the demons, the cry of 'burn' to make the demon leave its abode. It also anticipates the Universal Church in its frontal attack on Afro-Brazilian religions and in the recuperation of Catholic elements such as anointed objects and periods of special prayer analogous to the novenas.

For its methods, God is Love has paid the price of permanent isolation from the rest of the Brazilian Protestant world and from social respectability. Miranda himself has so far braked any *aggiornamento* of the church through his desire to maintain a strictly family business. Unlike some other pentecostal groups, it has not been able gradually to attract members of a slightly higher social level. Its organization is highly centralized on the person (or now, according to some, on the son-in-law) of the founder. Miranda has kept his distance from electoral politics, bucking the trend amongst most large pentecostal denominations since Brazil re-democratized in the 1980s.

Further reading

Rolim, Francisco Cartaxo (1990) 'Igreja Pentecostal Deus É Amor' in Lailah Landim (ed.) *Sinais Dos Tempos: Diversidade Religiosa no Brasil*, Rio de Janerio: Instituto de Estudos da Religião, pp. 59–65.

PAUL FRESTON

GODDESS FEMINISTS

Goddess feminists make up a substantial portion of the **Goddess Movement**; they are those within that movement whose feminist politics play a significant, integral role in their spirituality. They also form a sub-group within two much larger umbrella movements: **Neo-Paganism** and feminism. Goddess feminists, the great majority of whom are women, constitute the feminist wing of Neo-Paganism and, along with Christian and Jewish feminists, the spiritual wing of feminism. Goddess feminism has strong links with eco-feminism.

Many Goddess feminists regard Dianic **Wicca** or feminist witchcraft as synonyms for Goddess feminism. It should be noted, however, that there are Goddess feminists who are uncomfortable about or averse to adopting the label 'witch' because they consider its long-standing misogynous associations unhelpful to the feminist cause. Other Goddess feminists happily embrace the label 'witch' as a powerful symbol of independent female power and knowledge deemed illegitimate under patriarchy.

Goddess feminism arose in the United States in the late 1960s and drew on the countercultural ferment of the period. A number of women's liberation groups employed the acronym WITCH (Women's International Terrorist Conspiracy from Hell) for its dramatic symbolic value and the theatrical opportunities it leant to their protest activities. Later these political activists became interested in researching the atrocities of the European witch-hunts and in the possibility of pre-Christian matriarchal societies whose religions centred on a great Goddess. This appealed to women who were rejecting patriarchal religions along with patriarchal socio-political systems.

At Winter Solstice 1971, Zsuzsanna Budapest, a feminist and hereditary witch from Hungary, founded the Susan B. Anthony Coven (named after the American suffragist) and decided to make women's spiritual liberation her focus within the feminist movement. Another enormously influential figure within Goddess feminism has been **Starhawk** (Miriam Simos), a political activist and witch whose first book, *The Spiral Dance* (1989), set out the beliefs and ritual practices, based on those of Wicca, which are followed or adapted by many Goddess feminists. Goddess feminism differs significantly from Wicca, however, in that the Horned God has no role.

Goddess feminists are now found in all parts of the Western world and in parts of Asia. There is no over-arching organization and considerable variability in beliefs and practices exists. Many practise their spirituality independently, while others meet in autonomous groups, sometimes called feminist covens. Broadly, their beliefs are neo-pagan in that the earth and all of nature – indeed all matter and energy systems – are regarded as sacred and dynamically inter-connected. The worldview is holistic (transcending dualisms) and emphasizes the immanence of the sacred and cyclic (rather than linear) processes.

'The Goddess' is a multi-referential term. The earth is regarded as the sacred body of the Goddess possessing powers of fertility, generation and regeneration. As well as being Mother Earth, the Goddess is 'Mistress of Waters' and 'Queen of Heaven'. While incorporating both female and male (because the female gives birth to the male), the Goddess is also a metaphor for the strength, autonomy, beauty, and inherent divinity of women. She is regarded as a particularly empowering symbol for women raised in patriarchal religions where divinity is imaged as a singular, omnipotent male. The Goddess may also be conceived as one's Deep Self or True Self. While Goddess feminists frequently refer to 'the Goddess', they do not regard Her in monotheistic terms as a substitute for the Christian God, and are likely to regard themselves, like other neo-pagans, as pantheistic. Numerous goddesses from diverse ancient and contemporary religions are celebrated and invoked as expressions of the sacred feminine.

Politically, Goddess feminists are against all 'power-over' structures and forms of oppression. Rituals are preoccupied with healing women from the damaging effects of patriarchal oppression and enabling them to recognize themselves as 'Goddess' and discover their 'power within'. Equality and consensus decision-making are important ideals within groups; theoretically at least, groups are less hierarchical than Wiccan covens.

Goddess feminists have attracted criticism from other feminists, particularly Marxist feminists, who regard the embracing of any religion as counterproductive to feminist goals. They have also been criticized for holding utopian beliefs about ancient matriarchies, embracing essentialist ideas about women, and adopting a neo-colonialist position in relation to indigenous religions. They have vigorously refuted these criticisms.

Further reading

Budapest, Z. (1986) *The Holy Book of Women's Mysteries*, 2 vols. (2nd edn), Oakland, CA: Thesmophoria.

Eller, C. (1993) *Living in the Lap of the Goddess: The Feminist Spirituality Movement in America*, Boston: Beacon Press.

Spretnak, C. (ed.) (1982) *The Politics of Women's Spirituality: Essays on the Rise of Spiritual Power within the Feminist Movement*, New York: Doubleday.

Starhawk (1989) *The Spiral Dance: A Rebirth of the Ancient Religion of the Great Goddess* (2nd edn), San Francisco: Harper and Row.

KATHRYN ROUNTREE

GODDESS MOVEMENT

The spiritual beliefs and ritual practices of those who belong to the Goddess movement are essentially no different from those of **Goddess feminists**, and all Goddess feminists regard themselves as belonging to the Goddess movement. The difference between the two terms is one of emphasis: Goddess feminists explicitly stress their feminist politics whereas the term 'Goddess movement' draws attention to the spiritual or religious focus of the movement. It should be noted, however, that a feminist stance is fundamental to the Goddess movement and politics and religion are deeply integrated within it. The constituency of the Goddess movement includes more men than that of Goddess feminism, but women still far outnumber men within the Goddess movement.

The movement emerged in the United States in the late 1960s resulting from a confluence of neo-pagan ideas and practices with the spiritually-inclined portion of the women's liberation movement. Feminist authors like Mary Daly, Merlin Stone, Naomi Goldenberg, and Carol Christ were influential in the movement's early days, pointing out the damaging effects or irrelevance of male-identified religions, specifically Judeo-Christianity, for women, and championing an alternative woman-identified spirituality centred on the principle of the Sacred Feminine or 'the Goddess'. Neo-pagan authors – **Starhawk**, Z. Budapest and a raft of others on both sides of the Atlantic – introduced elements derived from **Wicca** into the movement.

The movement grew rapidly and is now represented in all Western societies and some Asian ones. The estimated population in the US is 500,000 and in the UK is 110–120,000 (Griffin 2000: 14). Along with most other branches of Neo-Paganism, the movement acknowledges 'the Goddess' as the pre-eminent symbol of divinity. It differs from **Wicca** and some other neo-pagan traditions in that the masculine principle or 'the God'

is given little or no recognition, gender bipolarity is not an important belief, rituals are less formally structured and more creative, there is no long process of education and initiation into a group, and there is not the array of lesser divinities, spirit beings, elementals, fairies and so on.

Participants in the Goddess movement say that Goddess religion is the oldest religion of all, with origins that extend back into the Paleolithic age and a worldview which resembles **shamanism**. Drawing on archaeological, ancient historical and classical research, they claim that for many thousands of years the religions of European societies centred on the worship of a great Goddess who was responsible for the generation, nurturance and re-generation of all life: wild plants, crops, animals and humans. In these societies the human feminine, as well as the divine feminine, was revered, women and men shared power equally, and community life was non-hierarchical and largely peaceful. The earth was considered sacred, Her seasons and cycles reverently acknowledged and celebrated.

This way of life is believed to have changed drastically in the Bronze Age when several waves of Indo-Europeans invaded southern Europe bringing with them warrior gods and patriarchal social systems and dealing a fatal blow to the older peaceful, matrifocal, Goddess-worshipping cultures. Archaeologist Marija Gimbutas has detailed this scenario extensively in a number of books, and her research is widely quoted and highly valued within the movement. Archaeologists outside the Goddess movement, however, including feminist archaeologists, have recently strongly criticized Gimbutas's methods and interpretations.

Nonetheless this history/mythology lends rhetorical power and inspiration to members of the contemporary Goddess movement, who claim that the time is now ripe for the Goddess's re-emergence. The demise of the Goddess is deemed to have been closely tied to the demise of women's position in society and the perspective which held the earth as sacred. Her return is seen as heralding a much needed re-valuing of women, a re-balancing of gender relations, a re-sacralization of nature and a re-conceptualization of human relations with the rest of the natural world.

The chief pre-occupation of the Goddess movement is to heal the damage caused by several thousand years of patriarchal religion and culture, especially its effects on women and the environment. Goddess rituals are created, often loosely based on a Wiccan structure (see **Wicca**), with the intent of empowering women to take control of their lives and to see themselves as divine.

The three core principles of Goddess religion, according to Starhawk (1989: 10), are immanence, interconnectedness and community. Immanence relates to the belief that 'the Goddess' is embodied in all of nature, including each person. Interconnection refers to the idea that all beings are linked and interdependent with all others in the cosmos to create one organic, living system (see **Gaia**). Community – which includes not only people but also animals, plants, soils and oceans – is a natural culmination of the other two principles, emphasizing the need to live with integrity, responsibility and an awareness that preserving the earth is essential to preserving human life.

The movement is highly eclectic in its employment of myths, goddesses and ritual practices from ancient and contemporary religions. Goddesses – whether ancient Greek, Celtic, Native American, Hindu, or Maori – may be invoked or prayed to as deities or regarded as archetypes of womanhood or tools for insight and inspiration. Because of this borrowing from numerous religious traditions, the Goddess movement has been accused of appropriating the cultural property of indigenous peoples and of appropriating and re-interpreting the past to serve contemporary social and spiritual agendas. Some within the movement are also concerned about these issues.

Further reading

Baring, A. and Cashford, J. (1991) *The Myth of the Goddess: Evolution of an Image*, London: Viking Arkana.

Christ, C. (1982) 'Why Women need the Goddess: Phenomenological, Psychological and Political Reflections', in C. Spretnak (ed.) *The Politics of Women's Spirituality: Essays on the Rise of Spiritual Power within the Feminist Movement*, New York: Anchor Books, Doubleday.

Griffin, W. (ed.) (2000) *Daughters of the Goddess: Studies of Healing, Identity and Empowerment*, Walnut Creek, CA: Altamira Press.

Raphael, M. (1999) *Introducing Thealogy: Discourse on the Goddess*, Sheffield: Sheffield Academic Press.

Starhawk (1989) *The Spiral Dance: A Rebirth of the Ancient Religion of the Great Goddess* (2nd edn), San Francisco: Harper & Row.

KATHRYN ROUNTREE

GODIANISM

Godianism is a neo-African traditional movement with its Head Office in Nigeria. It was originally known as the National Church, and later the National Church of Nigeria and Cameroons. Godianism propagates African Traditional Religion as a world religion and promotes an intellectual awakening of African cultural values. The movement is active in organizing a pan-African revival of traditional religion and culture and has formed a continental organization to unite all traditional religions in Africa called the Organization of Traditional Religions of Africa (OTRA). It is also known for its promotion of world peace. The leader of Godianism is Chief K. O. K. Onyioha (1923–2003).

Godianism traces its roots to the National Church, later known as the National Church of Nigeria and Cameroons. The church begun when mainline churches in Enugu and Yaba refused to hold a memorial service for twenty-two colliery miners who were shot by the colonial police in Enugu, Nigeria in 1949 while on strike as part of the nationalist struggle for independence. On 3 January 1950, the labour movement organized the service in an open field singing patriotic and traditional war songs and addressing their prayers to the God of Africa. They declared that the colonial church was not interested in the affairs of Africans and launched the National Church as the religious wing of the popular political party the National Council of Nigeria and Cameroons (NCNC), led by the veteran African politician, Dr Nnamdi Azikiwe. Initially, the church developed a liturgy that largely used traditional resources fused with the nationalist aspirations of the times. The African nationalist leaders were hailed as African Prophets and Messiahs in its liturgy.

In 1962 the Church changed its name to GODIANISM and appointed Chief K. O. K. Onyioha as its first high priest. The emphasis of the movement also shifted from political nationalism to the promotion of African traditional religion without losing sight of its goals of pan-Africanism and its advocacy for African culture.

Godianism propagates African Traditional Religion and also promotes an intellectual interpretation of African cultural values which includes the compilation of the oral scriptures of African peoples in a written form, and seeks to provide a harmonizing philosophy that would reform and perpetuate the liturgical variations in traditional religion. The movement in 1993 built a Godian Academy, which is situated at Ukwa Ukwu in Nkporo, Abia in Nigeria to facilitate learning and research and the showcasing of the spirituality of Africans. It thus promotes the publication of literary material such as the Godianism Series of Papers published after a conference in 1997. The movement has also developed its own Aquarian calendar using an African system of Igbo month names.

Godianism actively organizes a pan-African revival of traditional religion and culture through active participation in festivals such as Festac in Nigeria and Panafest in Ghana. It was instrumental in the formation of the Council of Religions in Nigeria and sponsored the building of shrines in that country. As we have seen, it also formed a continental organization to unite all traditional religions in Africa called the Organization of Traditional Religions of Africa (OTRA). In 1982 for instance, chief Anyioha negotiated with Osofo Okomfo Damuah of Ghana's **Afrikania Mission** and the latter agreed to join in the Godian mission. Godianism also links up through various projects with the African Diaspora.

The leader of the movement, Chief Onyioha travels widely in Africa, Europe, and North America promoting the ideals of the movement at educational institutions and international conferences. In the international arena Chief Onyioha works for world peace through the World Conference on Religion and Peace (WCRP). He addressed the special Session of the United Nations General Assembly on World Disarmament in 1978, and the World Conference of Leaders of World Major Religions in Tokyo,

Japan on the theme 'Principles of Peace and Disarmament' in 1981.

Though it begun as an African revivalist movement seeking to give identity, respectability and unity to the black race, Godianism has universalized its message by stressing love and harmony as the essence of true spirituality. It teaches that other religions such as Islam, Hinduism, and Christianity are liturgical variations and cultural expressions of the same spiritual truth. The movement sees itself in relation to other religions as a harmonizing power, which aims to bring about unity among all religions conceptual unity of all religions.

Further reading

Uka, E. M. (1998) 'Godianism and the Development of Modern African Studies', *Africania Marburgensia* 3, 1–2.
Online-Resource: http://www.godianism.org/
ELOM DOVLO

GRAIL MOVEMENT

Founder: Oskar Ernst Bernhardt
(b. 1875; d. 1941) (Alias Abd-ru-shin)

Oskar Ernst Bernhardt (1875–1941) was born in Bischofswerda, Germany, in 1875. Having travelled extensively, he published several novels and other works under the pen name of Abd-ru-shin ('Son of Light' in the Parsi language). In 1923, he circulated the first parts of *The Grail Message*, the publication of which continued through to 1937. A complicated esoteric work, which includes a history of the universe partially derived from the Theosophical Society (see **Theosophy**), and hinting at Berhnardt's own messianic role, it found interested readers within the esoteric milieu (see **Esoteric Movements**). Bernhardt decided to settle in Austria, at the Vomperberg (Tyrol), together with a handful of followers of what later became known as the Grail Movement. In 1938, Austria was occupied by Nazi Germany, the movement was banned, and Abd-ru-shin arrested. Released from jail in September 1938, he was banished firstly to Schlauroth, and then to Kipsdorf, where he died in 1941.

After World War Two, the Vomperberg centre was re-opened and the Movement re-established under the leadership of Maria Kauffer Freyer (née Taubert, and later adopted into the wealthy Kauffer family: 1887–1957), who had been Bernhardt's second wife. Maria's three children by her first marriage (Irmgard (1908–90), Alexander (1911–68) and Elizabeth (1912–2002) Freyer) also legally changed their surname from Freyer to Bernhardt. Maria died in 1957, and was succeeded first by Alexander and then by Irmgard (who signed herself as 'Irmingard'). The successions of Maria's children to her position were never recognized by a substantial part of the large Brazilian constituency of the movement which, under the leadership of Roselis von Sass (1906–97), created a splinter group under the name Ordem do Graal na Terra. Additional schisms also took place later in what is now the Czech Republic.

On her death in 1990, Irmingard left the Grail properties, including the Vomperberg, to Claudia-Maria (+ 1999), a natural child of Irmingard's adopted daughter Marga (both Claudia-Maria and her husband Siegfried (b. 1955) legally adopted the Bernhardt surname with Irmingard's blessing), while she bequeathed the copyrights on the Grail literature to an International Grail Foundation, led by Herbert Vollmann (1903–99, the husband of Irmingard's younger sister Elizabeth). Although Irmingard hoped that the Movement and the Foundation would peacefully cooperate, their co-existence was always uneasy and they finally split in 1999.

The Foundation remains the owner of the copyright on the founder's writings, and controls both the publishing house Stiftung Graalsbotschaf and the trademark 'International Grail Movement' in most English-speaking countries, where it operates under this name. This creates a certain amount of confusion with the rival International Grail Movement led by Siegfried Bernhardt from the Vomperberg, which legally controls the name outside of the English-speaking world. The total membership of the two main branches of the Grail Movement is currently 20,000. The international readership of *The Grail Message* is certainly much larger.

Further reading

Abd-ru-shin (1985) *In the Light of Truth. The Grail Message*. 3 vols. Vomperberg (Tyrol): Alexander Bernhardt.

MASSIMO INTROVIGNE

GREAT MAGAL OF TOUBA

The Great Magal of Touba is an annual pilgrimage to the tomb of **Ahmadu Bamba Mbacké** in that city's great mosque. It is the major annual event of the **Murid movement**, the affirmation of the movement's numbers and power, and it has become *the* Senegalese national event, three days when the country takes a breath. It is the commemoration of Ahmadu Bamba's return from exile under French colonial government (1902), and since Senegalese independence in 1960 it has increasingly been presented as a postcolonial assertion of Senegalese national dignity. Under the colonial government it was already the occasion for French authority to give the Murid movement the symbolic recognition of a strong official presence, and since national independence it has been the occasion for the government and for opposition parties to compete in their respect. It takes place over three days, the first two with more of a devotional character, religious singing, visits to the tomb and to individual living holy men; the third day given over to speakers, official presence, national radio and television. Murid power is the message to be conveyed here, the power of the number of people to be gathered together for this occasion, the power implicitly of their votes, of their economic production. The Great Magal is at its core a holy occasion, but it is also a political rally. The fact that it is located in Touba, not so long ago a village but now Senegal's second city in population size, supports the implicit affirmation of Murid power. Up to two million people have been in attendance at Great Magals of recent years, not all of them devout pilgrims it may safely be said. Pickpockets, street traders, magicians, as well as the politically ambitious, representatives of the caring professions, and the forces of order, most of human life is there.

DONAL CRUISE O'BRIEN

GURDJIEFF, GEORGE IVANOVITCH
(c. 1866–1949)

George Ivanovitch Gurdjieff was a teacher of temple dances, philosopher, composer, musicologist, therapist, and seminal twentieth century esotericist.

His oeuvre comprises one unperformed ballet, some 250 Sacred Dances, three posthumously published books, and 200 piano pieces. His fundamental challenge to humanity, posited within an awe-inspiring 'cosmology, is: awake from your unsuspected hypnotic sleep.

Gurdjieff was born to poor Greco-Armenian parents in Alexandropol on the Russo-Turkish border *c.* 1866 and died in Neuilly, Paris, on 29 October 1949. Our grasp of his Spartan childhood in Kars, his private education, and his *wanderjahre* relies on his a-historical, auto-mythopoeic *Meetings with Remarkable Men* (1963). Precociously seized by an 'irrepressible striving' to grasp the meaning of life, Gurdjieff became for twenty-five years (1885–1910) a fervent seeker after esoteric knowledge. He journeyed indefatigably throughout Asia, and in remote spiritual communities encountered profound traditional sources: 'In one place symbol, in another technique, and in another dance'. Three times he survived near-fatal bullet wounds. Though, soberingly, Gurdjieff's 'crucial decade' (1897–1907) in Central Asia lacks support in the journals of contemporary European explorers, his evocations ring true.

With Gurdjieff's arrival in Metropolitan Russia (*c.* New Year 1912) and his embarkation on the teaching of a hitherto unknown doctrine, biography slowly approaches objectivity. (Nevertheless doubt lingers over his marriage to Julia Osipovna Ostrowska.) In November 1914 Gurdjieff enticingly advertised his prospective ballet *The Struggle of the Magicians*. Consequently, in April 1915 Gurdjieff attracted the Russian author, journalist, and polymath Piotr Demianovich Ouspensky (1878–1947) (see **Ouspensky, Piotr Demianovich**); and in December 1916 the well-established Russian classical composer Thomas Alexandrovich de Hartmann (1885–1956) and his wife Olga Arkadievna (1885–1979). These war-time accessions bracket a concentrated teaching phase; never again will Gurdjieff so explicitly exhibit his teaching's arithosophical constituent and systemic integration, nor recruit pupils as contributive to its dissemination.

In 1917, uprooted by revolution and Civil War, Gurdjieff resourcefully extricated his nucleus of pupils via Georgia, Turkey, and Germany; and in 1922 settled permanently in France. Promptly he sited his Institute for the Harmonious Development of Man (founded Tbilisi, 1919) at the Prieure, Fontainebleau-Avon, where his reputation was first fanned then unjustly tarnished by the accession of the dying New Zealand writer Katherine Mansfield (1888–1923).

In 1924, shortly following the first of nine visits to New York, Gurdjieff survived a serious car accident; and – resolved to guarantee 'his teaching an enduring vehicle' – embarked on his vast trilogy *All and Everything*. His magnum opus *Beelzebub's Tales to His Grandson* (1950) employs 'celestial optics' to offer a radical critique of human life in which recognizable social values (pacifist, internationalist and so on) are spiritually posited.

Gurdjieff's followers deem his teaching to be implicated in the man himself as an actual incarnation of knowledge. He nevertheless bequeaths posterity a free-standing critique, nourishingly if contentiously explanatory on three levels: individual, social, and cosmic. This formal doctrine – enunciated most concentratedly in St Petersburg between February and June 1916, and reprised by Ouspensky in *In Search of the Miraculous* (1950) – integrates a semantic critique, a social critique, an epistemology, a mythopoeic cosmogony, a phenomenology of consciousness, and a practical *Existenzphilosophie*.

While knowledgeably saluting traditional spiritual Ways closely focused on the body, emotions, or intellect, Gurdjieff nevertheless propounds a 'Fourth Way' integrating all three; an evolutionary, dynamic, and redemptive psychology – not cultivated in religious seclusion (still less on the psychiatrist's couch) but in everyday life. The key concepts of Gurdjieffian psychology – self-observation, awakening, being, essence, presence, sensation, inner work, centres – contest ground already colonized by multiple preconceptions and misconceptions. It is hence vital to grasp that his seasoned pupils dedicated arduous years to arriving at empirically valid referents for these expressions.

The unique collaboration which produced the haunting 'Gurdjieff-de Hartmann music' ended in 1927. Nor did Gurdjieff write after 1935 when he completed *Life is Real Only Then, When 'I Am'* (1975). However his didactic recourse to sacred dance was life-long. These ensemble 'Movements' license no subjective expressionism; like Japanese *Kata* they are rigorously prescribed, some exemplifying the **Enneagram**, and demand mobilized attention. (Their character and quality appear in ten archival films made by Gurdjieff's senior pupil Jeanne de Salzmann (1889–1990)).

Although populist espousal of Gurdjieff's teaching is precluded by its undeniable elitism, in the laudatory sense, he stands at the root of a potent contemporary spiritual tradition whose vector resists scrutiny.

Further reading

Gurdjieff, G. I. (1981) *Life Is Real Only Then, When 'I Am'*, New York: E. P. Dutton.
Moore, J. (1991) *Gurdjieff: the Anatomy of a Myth*, Shaftesbury, Dorset, UK: Element Books.
Ouspensky, P. D. (1950) *In Search of the Miraculous: Fragments of an Unknown Teaching*, London: Routledge & Kegan Paul.

JAMES MOORE

GURU

Gurus originated during the Upanishadic era of Indian history, around the seventh century BCE. The term 'guru' is derived from the Sanskrit meaning weighty or substantial, and could therefore be translated as 'spiritual heavyweight'. Their original role was quite low-key, comparable to the spiritual directory of a Catholic monastery, but their status gradually evolved, peaking during the medieval period with the rise of *bhakti yoga* (the Hindu devotional traditional). Gurus were overshadowed by Islam and Christianity for the next few centuries, but revived with the growth of Hindu nationalism at the end of the nineteenth century.

The first Indian guru to arrive in the West was Vivekananda (see **Vivekananda Swami** and **Ramana Maharshi**) at the World Parliament of Religions in 1893, but the heyday was during the 1960s/70s counter-culture. These gurus were the pioneers and nucleus of the new religious movements (NRMs) of this era, which they founded. The first and most famous was the Maharishi Mahesh Yogi, guru to the Beatles and other celebrities. He was soon followed by Swami Prabhupada, founder of the **International Society for Krishna Conciousness** (ISKCON), again made famous by the Beatles; Guru Maharaji who founded the **Divine Light Mission** (later known as Elan Vital); Muktananda, and **Sathya Sai Baba**. By the late 1970s, the gurus and their NRMs were a well established force at the forefront of the alternative spirituality movement, and the most popular was **Osho**, founder of the **Rajneesh Movement**. Of all the gurus of this time, Osho best typified the characteristics of the guru as charismatic leader. Thousands of Westerners were attracted to these gurus, by their exoticism, differences from Christianity, the personal connection and teaching they offered, the emotional fulfillment of a devotional path, and the spiritual evolution obtainable from the range of techniques based on meditation.

The guru is a product of the Indian patriarchal social system, and has similar authority to a father in a family – closer to the Victorian paterfamilias than to a present-day 'new dad'. However, unlike the father or Brahmin priest, the basis of the guru's power was not law or tradition but charisma: belief in his self-declared enlightened status (sometimes endorsed by other gurus, especially within a lineage), also validated by demonstrations of psychic and spiritual power including 'miracles'. This is what the sociologist of religion Max Weber called 'charismatic authority'. Originally the role developed as a means of transmitting Hindu religion to boys and young men, who would live in the guru's *ashram,* or teaching centre, until they were ready to go out and teach in their own right. The task of the disciple (*chela*) was to be completely obedient to the guru, and to venerate him, normally recognizing him as a manifestation of a deity. Such devotion was considered essential to the proper transmission of the insights of the master to the student, a process known as *shaktipat* (from *shakti,* spiritual power). In India, *Bhakti yoga*, the medieval devotional tradition, originates from the guru–disciple relationship.

Gurus operate outside the traditional Brahmin hierarchy: not strictly as priests or spiritual teachers (*acharya*), but rather as masters of a particular path to enlightenment who have achieved a deep personal insight into the nature of being. Not all enlightened beings become gurus, but some have the skills and charisma to bring about a similar transformation in a student or disciple, by initiating them and guiding their personal development. They do not necessarily teach a fixed system of beliefs and practices, unlike for example a typical religious teacher within a monotheistic tradition. The guru may be a **yoga** teacher, or a tantric teacher, or follow another branch of Hinduism, or they might be an artist. It is not uncommon in India to go to a concert, and for the chief musician to announce the programme, introducing the other players as 'my disciples'.

Gurus typically offer at least two levels of commitment at initiation. The lower level is for lay followers who lead normal lives as associate disciples or friends (*mitra*). The second, more demanding level of discipleship calls for a new spiritual and personal identity, often including a new name and a break with one's past. What follows are years of arduous training and, as far as possible, the elimination of any trace of egotism. Such an approach is not readily accepted or understood in cultures based on the Western idea of enlightenment, scientific materialism and hedonism.

The concept of the guru has spread beyond Hinduism. Tibetan lamas, Japanese Zen roshis, Sufi and Taoist masters may be even more powerful and authoritarian figures than Indian gurus.

The word guru has been absorbed into colloquial English, and is now used to describe almost any charismatic leadership role, particularly 'business gurus' such as Tom Peters and Anthony Robbins. In the process the word has become secularized and trivialized, but retains its power within spiritual traditions.

ELIZABETH PUTTICK

GURUMAYI

Gurumayi is the current guru of the worldwide Siddha Yoga spiritual path and head of the multimillion dollar SYDA (Siddha Yoga Dham Associates) Foundation that supports the spiritual path. She is a young woman, a striking embodiment of beauty, humility, spiritual authority, and organizational leadership.

Her titles, the popular Gurumayi ('One Who is Immersed in the Guru') and the formal Swami Chidvilasananda ('The Bliss of the Play of Pure Consciousness'), capture the dynamic nature of the **guru**: the guru both experiences ultimate reality, and through the teacher–disciple relationship guides others to that transformative experience.

Gurumayi was born Malti Shetty to a Bombay restaurateur in 1955; her parents were devotees of Swami Muktananda, who was then the guru of Siddha Yoga, and brought her and three siblings to the ashram in nearby Ganeshpuri on weekends. After Swami Muktananda gave Malti formal initiation, through *shaktipat* (the bestowal of spiritual power), at the age of 14, she began to live at the ashram, where she performed intensive spiritual practices to purify her mind and body and to become attuned with her guru. She played a visible role in the Siddha Yoga program, as Swami Muktananda's translator (from 1975), as a lecturer on Sunday nights (from 1980), and as executive vice-president of SYDA Foundation (from 1981).

In May of 1982, Swami Chidvilasananda and her brother Swami Nityananda took their final monastic vows, and were consecrated as Swami Muktananda's designated successors. When the guru passed away on 2 October, the two were officially installed as the Siddha Yoga gurus. They worked together for three years, until, in disputed circumstances, Swami Nityananda resigned his position in October 1985. Since that time, Gurumayi has assumed sole leadership of Siddha Yoga and SYDA, aided by a corps of teaching swamis appointed by her guru, by volunteers who administer the programs and maintain the ashrams and centers throughout the world through *seva* (selfless service). Recently SYDA has appointed a CEO and CFO to assist Gurumayi.

Gurumayi continues her guru's format of transmitting *shaktipat* en masse to devotees in weekend intensive programs. The hallmarks of her leadership include her emphasis on *seva*, including programs such as the Prison Project and Prasad (assisting the poor); her numerous teaching and devotional publications, videos, and audiotapes; her Yearly Message, being a short phrase for the spiritual community's contemplation throughout the year; and her sophisticated use of communications technology, especially satellite technology, which transmits the guru's *shakti* during Intensive programs and public talks in real time.

KAREN PECHILIS PRENTISS

GUSH EMUNIM

Gush Emunim (the Bloc of the Faithful, henceforth GE), is a Jewish-Zionist messianic movement – also Fundamentalist (see **Fundamentalism**) – embracing a hawkish political program, effectively implemented in Israel since the 1970s, identified with the settlements in the 'Territories' (West Bank and Gaza) – the epicenter of the rage consuming the contemporary Middle East. Israel began its withdrawal from these settlements in August 2005.

GE acts out the frustrations of young Modern Orthodox Israelis who, prior to the 1970s, felt deprived of recognition and influence by the predominantly secular establishment and betrayed by their veteran leadership. It was also inspired by the patriotic exhilaration and a vague sense of religiosity which characterized Israel following the victory in the 1967 war and the consequent return to the Temple Mount and other sacred places of the Promised Land. Paradoxically, their diffuse structure became tightened only in the sobering aftermath of the 1973 war, the unprecedented territorial withdrawal and a profound

225

shock to the fundamental Zionist values and symbols. GE was one among several protest movements and organizers of grassroot non-violent uprisings calling for change of leadership, policies and of the political culture. In their heroic and charismatic formative years (1975–7), they expanded their popular base and formulated their methods and style, focusing on settlement and civil disobedience. Following the political upheaval of 1977, GE was partly coopted by the new establishment and underwent a spectacular expansion. The next one-and-a-half decades were marked by fluctuations in GE's popular support, political impact, institution building, and morale, with peaks, like during Sharon's incumbency as minister in charge of the settlements, when the GE and the official Israeli policies became almost indistinguishable in the 1980s, and ebbs, at the evacuation of Sinai in 1981, the Intifadah of 1987 and, of course, the Oslo Accords in 1993–5.

GE claims a morally superior stand not only in religious matters proper but in a variety of political and social issues which – they argue – are of profound religious significance. All things national have a Jewish, i.e. sacred, nature, currently hidden but soon to become obvious to all Jews and others, including local Arabs, who on reading this would cooperate in rebuilding the Temple. In the meantime, the avant-garde of the enlightened is called upon to promote the realization of this vision by ensuring Israeli strategic advantage and expanding its sovereignty over the 'Whole Land of Israel', including the 'Territories', seen as the biblical Judea and Samaria. From here, it's only one step to the vision of the ancient Hebrew Law as State Law. The GE motto is: 'the Torah (Jewish scripture of sacred law) of Israel to the People of Israel in the Land of Israel'. The latter component – the territorial sanctity – is highlighted as a pivotal religious tenet.

Aware of the pitfalls of antinomy, GE has become excessively orthodox, including intensive Torah study and rigorous halachic observance. It also cultivates selected messianic elements applying them to present-day reality. GE's enthno-national ultra-activism is messianic in its theology and its dynamics. Its outlook is founded on the teachings of R' A. Y. H. Kook (d. 1935), a Chief Rabbi, committed to nation-building in pre-state Palestine, a daring mystic and halachic innovator. His legacy, somewhat narrowly interpreted, was effectively preached by his son, R' Z. Y. H. Kook (d. 1982), and cultivated in Jerusalem's Merkaz Harav Yeshiva (Torah academy), from which it spread to revolutionary-type Zionist *yeshivas* (settlements) mushrooming all over the country, especially in the Territories since the 1970s.

The GE creed responds to the challenging religious paradox inherent in contemporary Israel as a Jewish – yet modern and secular – state, in which halachah is replaced by nationalism, citizenship, and democracy as criteria of collective identity. GE's creative solution to this dilemma combines traditional religiosity with sanctioning collaboration with the secular sector in exemplary devotion to the State, seeking to attract both the non-Zionist orthodox and the non-orthodox Zionists under their aegis. Contrary to its self-conception and public image, Israel is consecrated by GE's assuming secular Israelis to be 'saints despite themselves' through defining Zionism as an a priori millenarian (see **Millenarianism**) pursuit and the state organs as sublime media whose true mission is to bring redemption. The conquest and inhabitance of the mytho-historical Holy Land is seen as a critical precondition of the salvation of the people, then humanity, and finally the world. Territorial politics turn into an act of worship, a manifestation not only of old-time pioneer spirit, but also of rehabilitated 'authentic' Judaism. The endeavor of GE to reshape the regional map as well as the face of both Judaism and Zionism is nourished by security problems and a general sense of a social and moral crisis as well as cleavages within Israeli society.

The elementary cells of GE are a few dozen settlements and/or yeshivas. They are the hotbed of the movement's subculture, its reservoir of cadres, and the bridgehead for its operations. These are morally or politically supported by peripheries varying in size and commitment. In GE's rallies concerning urgent geo-political issues in the 1980s and 1990s participation exceeded 100,000. Single-issue parliamentary factions unofficially affiliated with the movement amounted to five to fifteen of the electorate. GE's disproportional impact is due to its skilful handling of public opinion and government officials, to an ingenious exploitation of political opportunities, and to quasi-military, often clandestine, sometimes illegal campaigns. Their *modus operandi* combines parliamentary and extra-parliamentary manipulation, ranging from international fundraisers to head-on collision with law and order agents or ideological opponents. Their most effective method has been the creation of a *fait accompli* reality in the territories.

Contrary to early expectations, very few secular Jews joined the movement. GE proper, numbering no more than several thousand, should be distinguished from Israel's National Camp (at times supported by half the country's population), from the Zionist Neo-Orthodox sector (roughly 10 per cent of Jewish Israelis, including segments which oppose GE), and from the 200,000 settlers in 120 or so settlements, mostly secular and not necessarily ideologically committed. Whereas GE consists of only a

portion of these three categories, its link with them is very significant.

In the last three decades of the twentieth century, GE was crucial in fashioning both religion and politics in Israel and it determined to a large degree the Middle Eastern geographic, demographic, strategic and moral reality. At present, GE is in crisis. It is challenged by political setbacks and ideological dilemmas that seem to produce demoralization, revisionism, possibly desperate actions. Decline has been mainly related on the one hand to the progress toward an Israeli–Palestinian peace agreement and to the intensification of the conflict, on the other. Both threaten the future of the settlements, thus jeopardizing the realization of redemption.

Further reading

Aran, G. (1991) 'Jewish–Zionist Fundamentalism' in M. Marty and S. Appleby (eds.) *Fundamentalisms Observed*, Chicago: University of Chicago Press.

GIDEON ARAN

GYPSIES AND PENTECOSTALISM

Originating from the United States, Pentecostalism (see **Azusa Street Revival**) has rapidly spread to other continents, giving birth to other churches, including the **Assemblies of God**. The great majority of those converted to Pentecostalism are (im)migrants, ethnic minorities, black people, Hispanic populations, and poor people in general. In this context, there is a close relation between Pentecostalism and the Gypsy people. Throughout its history, the Gypsies have always adapted themselves (without necessarily being converted) to the dominant religion of the country where they happen to settle. In Europe

227

they took to Catholicism, the major confession.

Nevertheless, in 1945, in the North of France, the presence of Gypsies in the services of the Assembly of God was registered, and their religious enthusiasm was said to be remarkable. In 1950, a gypsy mother took her dying son to the pastor Clément Le Cossec asking him to save the boy. The miraculous cure of the young boy (believed to be due to God's grace and the Holy Spirit) took place. The 'miracle' was widely publicized and led to a large number of gypsy conversions, thus giving birth to the Gypsy Evangelical Movement (GEM).

As a Pentecostal-protestant movement, the GEM depends in its ideological foundations on the authority of the Bible. It stresses the importance of the Holy Spirit; salvation as a gift of God; and the importance of evangelizing.

In 1968 Le Cossec founded the Gypsy Evangelical Mission as an independent body seperate from the Assemblies of God who refused to allow Gypsy pastors. The GEM started then forming its own gypsy pastors, who began to evangelize among their own community. Bible schools were started and his magazine *Vie et Lumière* was launched.

From 1959, the Gypsy Evangelical Movement started to spread to other countries, mainly to Spain, where a large gypsy community is settled. The evangelization process in Spain started in 1963, and was led by a group of gypsies who had been converted in France. The expansion of the GEM in Spain is remarkable: in less than one decade, the number of converts amounted to 5,000. In 1969 the movement was given official recognition and became the *Evangelical Church of Philadelphia*. According to more recent data, this Church now has 900 pastors, and 31,000 members in Spain.

Due to the strong historical, cultural and family links among the gypsy communities in the Iberian Peninsula, the Spanish Gypsy Evangelical movement began to enter Portugal towards the end of the 1960s. In 1974 the gypsy communities in Portugal formed an independent Church adopting then the name of *Gypsy Evangelical Church of Philadelphia of Portugal*. Today it has over fifty places of worship.

The reasons for this strong conversion process of the gypsies to Pentecostalism, not only in Europe but also in countries like Brazil or India, is very much linked to their situation of social, economic, and cultural deprivation. Pentecostal salvation also reinforces the social bounds and adapts itself to the ethnic and cultural specificities of minorities. Conversion to evangelical Christianity has minimized where the gypsies are concerned the most severe effects of marginalization.

Conversion to Pentecostalism has not, therfore, led to a loss of Gypsy identity. On the contrary, there seems to be a reinforcement of their ethnicity, a feeling of ethnic and cultural belonging in a group which wants to remain gypsy, while becoming evangelical.

Further reading

Rodrigues, D. and Santos, A. P. (2000) 'Being an Evangelical Gypsy: religiosity in a small gypsy community in Portugal', in D. Rodrigues and P. del Rio (eds) *The Religious Phenomenon: an interdisciplinary approach*, Madrid: Ed. Aprendizaje.
Williams, P. (ed.) (1989) *Tsiganes: Identité, Évolution*, Paris: Éditions Syros.

DONIZETE RODRIGUES

H

HARRIS, WILLIAM WADÉ
(b. c. 1860; d. 1929)

William Wadé Harris was a Liberian evangelist, from the Grebo (Kru) ethnic group. Harris claimed to have received his call to be an evangelist while serving a prison sentence for an alleged protest against the repressive policy of the Americo-Liberian authorities towards his Grebo ethnic group. Harris claimed that while in his prison cell the Angel Gabriel appeared to him in a trance and told him that God was coming to anoint him and he would be God's Prophet and baptize many. Harris is reported to have experienced the descent of the Holy Spirit upon him and to have spoken in tongues.

After his release from prison Harris commenced his preaching wearing a white robe and a turban and carrying a bamboo cross, a Bible and a calabash for baptism. He emphasized in his preaching belief in God and baptism, and the need to relinquish charms, amulets and fetishes. Harris had no intention of founding his own church and advised people to join existing churches, to keep Sunday holy and to respect the Bible. He exorcised, healed and performed miracles. He crossed to the Ivory Coast in 1913 and then to the Apolonia and Axim areas of Ghana in 1914 where he had a profound influence on the lives of people. In the Ivory Coast it is estimated that over 100,000 people were converted. It is reported that at Appolonia in the Western region of Ghana alone he baptized more than 36,000 adult-converts including chiefs.

Harris' ministry was perceived as offering responses to the deeply felt needs and aspirations of Africans and he made his preaching relate to the worldview of his converts. As a result an overwhelming number of converts flocked to him at a time when Western European missionaries were making little progress. Harris' significance is his understanding of the spiritual universe of Africans and the capacity he had to penetrate it. He exemplifies a new non-Western approach to evangelization of the Gospel in the African context.

Further reading

Shank, D. A. (1994) *Prophet Harris, the 'Black Elijah' of West Africa*, Leiden: Brill.

CEPHAS N. OMENYO

HEALING

The goal of many new religions is healing including medical healing but also more importantly psychotherapeutic healing and in particular healing the apparent split between the state in which we live, our temporal state, and an eternal state to which we seem to belong. In this sense, and in others, the goals of NRMs (New Religious Movements) are decidedly this-worldly.

This understanding of healing is attractive to those who are frustrated by the limits of biomedicine, and in particular its apparent inability to save the larger human being, and to the ever growing number of people in the West who believe in the divine nature of their true or real self, as opposed to the ego (see **Self-religion, The Self, and self** and **Self-Transformation**).

New religions are not all of one mind on the causes of sickness and misfortune and the means necessary for health and wholeness. Over time these views can change. Scholars have noted how movements that begin as 'secular' movements with this-worldly, non-spiritual ends turn to the pursuit of transcendental goals. Examples of this change in function and orientation include Synanon and **Scientology** (Wallis, 1977).

There are also examples of movements that started as thoroughgoing faith healing movements forbidding any use of modern medical cures but gradually came to adopt a more syncretistic outlook allowing adepts to have recourse in certain situations where certain types of illness were concerned to modern medicine. Examples of this shift include the **Worldwide Church of God** and/or Armstrongism and the Aladura (praying) churches. There are also many Japanese examples of this type of healing movement. Moreover, the power to heal has been an important means of legitimating the authority of founders of Japanese new religions, among others, and, it follows, an important motivation for joining a new religion (see **New Religion (Japan)**). It has been estimated that in the case of 52 per cent of the membership of Mahikari healing was the main motivation for joining (Davis, 1980: 103). In fact all of Japan's new religions have been established with a core of healing activity, an activity that is said to constitute one of the most effective means of maintaining the groups' membership.

There is considerable overlap on matters of healing between NRMs and both the Holistic Health Movement (HHM) and the **Human Potential Movement** (HPM). The HHM emerged in the 1960s in opposition to the free clinic movement, the former favouring a more client centred structure and approach than the largely physician oriented ethos and structure of the latter. The client was encouraged to take responsibility for her/his health.

As is the case of the **Self-Religions** and the **New Age Movement** (NAM), the HHM, which exists independently of both, is founded on the belief that the individual is responsible for her/his own actions, well being, quality of life and for discovering the path towards complete self realization (see **Self-Realization Fellowship**). From the outset there was a quasi-spiritual dimension to the HHM symbolized in the layout and design of its temples which were modelled on the

Greek healing temples of Aesculapius and in the healing practices which included meditation. The Meadowlark centre established in California in 1959 was designed in this way and emphasized meditation as an important element in physical and emotional healing. Important developments that influenced the growth of the HHM in Europe were the Westbank Healing and Teaching Centre in Fife, Scotland which started in 1959 and the Research Society for Natural Therapeutics (formerly the Naturopathic Research Group) also founded in 1959 in Bournemouth, England. The Esalen Institute established in Big Sur in California in 1962 by Michael Murphy and Richard Price is perhaps the best known HHM centre and many of the HHM's healers were taught and trained there.

The HHM has made considerable headway in creating nationwide networks across the United States and a large number of professional associations have been formed to bring therapists and practitioners together including the American Holistic Medical Association (AHMA) which was set up in 1978.

An essential element of the teaching of the HHM is that a person is a whole system composed of mental, physical, emotional and spiritual dimensions. Health itself is viewed not merely as an absence of disease but as a positive condition, which everyone should aim to achieve. Illness for its part is also to be seen in a positive light as an opportunity for learning.

In contrast with the idea of medicine as the means to cure specific diseases by the use of drugs and surgery or to maintain the status quo where an individual's health is 'good', the holistic movement seeks to advance beyond this static and passive view of health and healing to an approach that might be termed proactive and largely non-intrusive.

In recent times the established medical community has begun to accept holistic health concepts, methodologies, and techniques. Moreover, the keystone of holistic health, preventive medicine, has received greater emphasis in the wider society in educational, political and business circles, among others, during the past two decades. What has not been so widely accepted is the HHM's stress on the impact of the spiritual side of the individual on her/his physical and overall well-being. While there are exceptions, the approach of a majority of medical practitioners would appear to be largely mechanistic, in that it treats the individual as a composite of various interacting biochemical systems that can be patched up, adjusted, and readjusted or repaired by physical methods of intervention. As for spiritual ideas of human functioning these are dismissed as medieval superstition or passed over as interesting but marginal and 'deviant' forms of knowledge. This can have serious adverse consequences particularly for patients for whom the norm is to express their state of mind and physical and general well-being in spiritual or mythopoetical language.

There are signs of a change of attitude and outlook in this area also and especially in the field of psychoanalysis. Religious experience is no longer seen in Freudian terms as a one-way transference where the believer or devotee projects her/his instinctually based childhood fear and wishes on to a religious construct. Rather in the 'new' approach religious experience both reflects and is reflected in the self and, construed as a matrix of internalized relationships in which religious beliefs, practices, and experiences are seen to reflect the structure of this relational self. Even in the field of general medicine itself there is evidence of a change in understanding and outlook. One example is the American

231

Medical Association's adoption of the Alcoholics Anonymous definition of alcoholism as a threefold disease with physical, mental/emotional and spiritual aspects and its approach to arresting the disease. The latter involves not only the elimination of the physical part by eliminating the alcohol from the person's metabolism and the healing of the emotional problems that cause the person to want to anaesthetize her/his feelings by means of the 'group therapy' of the meetings but also by revitalizing the person's spiritual life by opening her or him up to some kind of conversion experience.

The recognition that the cause of an illness can be psychosomatic has long been accepted by psychotherapists, and the more medical practitioners turn to such explanations the more likely they are to see a role for the spiritual in the healing process.

The HHM sees most illnesses as resulting from a lack of equilibrium between the various elements that make up the individual. The lack of harmony between the individual and her/his environment, whether this be their social, cultural or natural environment, is also considered to be an important causal element.

This general understanding of sickness and health is found in 'traditional' societies and the HHM not only endorses the theory but also incorporates both the healers and the healing practices and techniques of these societies such as acupuncture into its programmes. Of course, the explanations for the efficacy of a particular practice such as acupuncture whose healing power is said to be derived from *chi* energy (see **Ch'i Kung** (Qigong)) are not always convincing and cannot always be verified or reconciled with western medical methods.

Holistic medicine, it should be noted, is not a catch all phrase for any and every alternative form of medicine or medical technique. The holistic approach is open ended in that it accepts the need to try various therapeutic techniques before settling on one specific set appropriate to the individual in question, and this it shares in common with many forms of traditional medicine.

There is no clear cut dividing line between the Holistic Health Movement and the Human Potential Movement (HPM) also known as the Growth Movement which became popular in the mid-1960s with the spread of Encounter Groups, Gestalt Therapy, Primal Therapy, Bioenergetics, and a myriad of other groups that sought to enable people to experience the deepest levels of their consciousness and being in a self-directed way. The HPM emerged in part because of a growing dissatisfaction with the narrow ends of psychoanalysis and behaviourism as practised at the time. These groups were motivated by the belief that human beings though born perfect became warped by their existence in society and particularly through its chief agent of socialization the nuclear family. While this idea dates back to Rousseau and beyond its more recent vehicles and the ones that were to have a profound influence on the development of the HPM were Reichian therapy, Gestalt psychology, Humanistic psychology, Existentialism, Gurdjieff's **The Work**, **Theosophy**, and various meditation and **yoga** groups of oriental origin.

Initially those who frequented HPM centres showed little concern for spiritual development in itself. But a change was to occur, the reasons for which is a subject of debate. Many of those who were to eventually join such new religions as the **Rajneesh Movement** were involved at first in the HPM which, as already pointed out, conceived of human health and wholeness in natural terms and pursued what were largely natural ends.

Many NRMs began as HPMs, among them The Process, Synanon, **Scientology** and Silva Mind Control (see **Silva Method**). Their goals were essentially naturalistic. While the ultimate objective was as previously noted the realization of the greatest possible amount of one's potential at every level, movements also claimed that their techniques would enable recruits to reap such this-worldly and natural rewards as greater success in examinations, in business, in personal relationships and other practical, 'materialistic' goals (Wallis, 1991).

While the extent of the shift varied from one group to another many essentially growth groups moved beyond the human potential stage into a more spiritual realm where a new understanding of the self and its development was cultivated. There are those who maintain that this change in orientation was a result in part of the frustration generated by the fact that the rewards movements claimed to be able to provide were very often not forthcoming (Stark and Bainbridge, 1985: 263–83). Moreover, their repeated failure to provide the benefits promised gave rise to a stock of disconfirming evidence that could be used against these movements and the only way to avoid this was to offer what are termed *compensators* of a less tangible, less verifiable kind, in other words supernatural or spiritual rewards (ibid.). This line of reasoning overlooks the great difficulties in disconfirming certain belief systems such as Scientology which postulate the existence of a previous life or previous lives that can always be invoked – in a way that is impossible to gainsay – to explain why a goal has not been achieved. People, moreover, cannot be so easily misled. If what they were seeking was a combination of purely materialistic, practical, instrumental rewards then surely they would not have remained part of a movement that abandoned this end in favour of expressive largely non-attainable goals.

HPM practitioners did not always make a clear-cut distinction between natural and supernatural goals. It would appear that it was not only the failure – and there was failure in the case of Synanon and other movements – of the HPM to supply the 'natural' rewards sought that motivated people to move into spiritual groups. The over-commercialization of the movement was also a factor in turning people away from the HPM to more identifiably spiritual movements, although the latter were in time to be charged with the same failing. While HPM goals were often perceived as worthwhile but it was a loose, diffuse movement that shunned any idea of limits on growth and encouraged continual experimentation. It was this outlook and spirit as much as anything else that created the demand for something more profound and deeper and facilitated the move by practitioners from an overriding concern with the natural to a deeper involvement in the spiritual.

The pursuit of more spiritual or supernatural goals did not, however, mean that the 'natural' HPM aim of realizing one's full potential was dismissed as worthless. It was a stage on the path that led beyond full self-development to radical self-transformation the realization of which required a change in perspectives and techniques. The spiritual techniques made available by the new religions of the psychological kind referred to variously as psycho-spiritual movements, psychological religions, self-religions or, as this writer would prefer to call them, religions of the True-Self, were often called upon to achieve this end. It is however true that in certain cases these religions were without anything resembling religious rituals in the traditional sense of the term and developed therapeutic techniques and practices that in themselves were devoid of any obvious religious features. This was largely the case with Scientology and similar movements. These movements did, none the less, develop a recognizably religious belief system drawing mainly on Eastern religious ideas.

Jung, Fromm, and Maslow among others had seen the possibility of a fruitful dialogue and exchange between Western psychology and Eastern spirituality before the new religions began to attempt to create a synthesis between the two. But in practice those interested in such a synthesis did little to develop one and tended to juxtapose the two approaches drawing on each independently of the other. As already noted, early HHM centres had sought to integrate the two but the real breakthrough came in the early 1970s when a number of religions of the radical self-transformative kind including the Rajneesh movement began to develop a psychospiritual therapeutic system founded on ideas of and the ways of realizing the Self derived from Eastern spirituality and on the 'new' and as yet fringe developments in psychotherapy in the West.

The Rajneesh Movement which attracted many of its adepts known at first as neo-sannyasins and later simply as **sannyasins** from the HPM movement became one of the foremost leaders of the movement for radical self-transformation through a combination of Eastern spiritual ideas and practices and psychotherapeutic theories and techniques. Wilhelm Reich exercised great influence on the founder of this movement, the Bhagwan Shree Rajneeh (see **Osho**) as he developed his Rajneesh therapeutic techniques, as did his disciple Alexander Lowen who developed the technique of bioenergetics. Gurdjieff's ideas, especially his view of the

individual as trapped by the mechanics of her/his socialized self, also had a strong impact.

The spiritual aspect of these therapies was not always very evident nor where it was in evidence was it always recognizably Eastern. This was the case with the highly energetic and controversial Rajneesh meditation technique of Dynamic meditation. Some of those who practised this technique found it disturbing and problematic while others who did not deny its potentially 'dangerous' and disturbing effects appear to have benefited from it. Dynamic meditation resembled closely the Reichian practice of using breathing to break down 'character armour' which inhibited the full development of the individual and of society. It was Reich's view that the inhibition of respiration was the principle mechanism of neurosis in society for it was in this way that the emotions, feelings, and sexuality were suppressed and repressed. In the Rajneesh understanding of spiritual development the technique enabled energy to be released which could then be directed to meditation, a view of meditation that clearly differs from traditional Hindu and Buddhist ideas of it.

The Rajneesh Movement also provided a vast array of psychotherapies which were also holistic in approach. Like the meditations these therapies were rooted in active, body based techniques such as bioenergetics and massage the aim of which was to awaken and release repressed energies and emotions.

There was also an important relational dimension to the therapies. This was developed particularly in the follow up groups in which the awakened and released energies and emotions were explored with a view to improving the quality of interpersonal relationships.

As in psychotherapy generally Rajneesh therapy was based on catharsis. However, catharsis was not seen as an end in itself but was placed in this instance within the much wider context of meditation. Rajneesh himself did not believe in catharsis for its own sake or that such cathartic programmes as those provided by Primal Therapy were in themselves actually effective or that they achieved what was ultimately desirable. This kind of cathartic endeavour was mechanical and on its own it simply dealt with the symptoms while his spiritual psychotherapies, he claimed, went to the very roots of the problem. The primary emphasis in the therapies was not so much on a quick but transient resolution of the problem as on finding deep down in the self the spiritual resources that could be drawn upon to construct a strong, deep, enduring psychological, and spiritual cathartic feeling.

There is no unanimity among psychologists as to whether catharsis is actually effective. As to Rajneeshian psychotherapy there are those who believe that it was not only ineffective but also caused harm and in essence was a form of violence used for purposes of control. It is worth noting that while some of those sannyasins who took part in the more adventurous therapy groups believed that they could be dangerous, in a physical sense, and even violent, almost all believed that the overall effect on them personally was positive. Moreover, in time a less frenetic, calmer, more controlled, more meditative approach became the norm. Other criticisms of the therapy were that far from opening up a real source of inner strength and power it functioned as a conversion technique inducing people who were not in a fit state to make a decision to take sannyas and become disciples of Rajneesh, and also as a means of inculcating submission and obedience to their master (see **brainwashing**). Clearly, healing and/or therapy can be and is used to legitimate or bolster power and authority and there are examples of this among new religions that are the creation of charismatic leaders.

Healing, thus, in the holistic sense of the term is a central part of the activity of many new movements.

Further reading

Davis, W. (1980) *Dojo: Magic and Exorcism in Modern Japan*, Stanford: Stanford University Press

Melton, J. G. (1990) *New Age Encyclopaedia*, Detroit: Gale Research Inc.

Puttick, E. (1994) 'Gender, Discipleship and Charismatic Authority in the Rajneesh Movement', PhD thesis, King's College, University of London.

Reader, I. (1991) *Religion in Contemporary Japan*, Basingstoke and London: Macmillan.

Robertson, R. (1994) 'Globalization or glocalization', *Journal of International Communication*, 1, 33–52.

Silva, J. and Miele, P. (1980) *The Silva Mind Control Method*, London: Granada.

Stark, R. and Bainbridge, W. S. (1985) *The Future of Religion*, Berkeley and Los Angeles: University of California Press.

Wallis, R. (1977) *The Road to Total Freedom: A Sociological Analysis of Scientology*, New York: Columbia University Press.

Wallis, R. (1991) 'New Religions in North America', in Stewart Sutherland and Peter Clarke (eds) *The Story of Religion, Traditional and New Religion*, London: Routledge.

PETER B. CLARKE

HEALTH AND WEALTH

The 'Health and Wealth' movement has gained a degree of prominence and can claim some limited influence within Christian fundamentalism (see **Fundamentalism**), Evangelicalism, Pentecostalism, and Charismatic Renewal (see **Catholic Charismatic Renewal**). Strictly speaking, there is no 'health and wealth' movement *per se*. It is, rather, an ideology that can be traced to several seminal preachers and teachers, who in turn advocate and emphasize slightly different doctrines and practices that are connected with the health and wealth concerns of Christians. The range and variants of belief and practice are considerable.

Some health and wealth exponents will argue that the Bible demands *tithing* (i.e., individuals giving 10 per cent of income). Correspondingly, those who fail to do this, it is argued, could not expect God to reward them with financial success, prosperity and good health. Put another way, 'godly giving' is the only real way of ensuring that God will bless the individual.

Other health and wealth exponents have more complex and novel ideologies. Some argue that God will not only match the gifts of believers with assurance and blessing, but will actually *multiply* those gifts, and return them to the individual. Exponents of this teaching – such as Morris Cerullo – have suggested that believers can expect a 'sevenfold' increase on their gift or investment. For every one dollar that believers donate, they could expect to receive the equivalent of seven back, either through promotion at work, good fortune, or other means. Ironically, Cerullo has appealed for such generous giving from supporters in order to help him evade the deepening debt that had threatened to curtail his ministry. A variant on this teaching would be the 'seed faith' practice of Oral Roberts. Believers are encouraged to make their offering, even if (or especially if) they are in financial difficulty. Only by giving will believers be able to receive – 'your return, poured into your lap, will be great, pressed down and running over' (Roberts, quoted in Hadden and Shupe, 1988: 31).

Others exponents have suggested that the gospel *guarantees* health and wealth to believers who have realized their sanctified and empowered status. Thus,

all the believer needs to do is have the necessary amount of faith to claim their God-given heritage – a mixture of heavenly and earthly rewards. Correspondingly, poverty is seen as the outcome of a lack of faith. The ultimate premise of the health and wealth ideology – sometimes called 'name it and claim it' – is that there is no blessing or gift that God would wish to deny [his] people, because God is a God of love, generosity, and abundance. 'God does not want you to be poor' is the frequently cited mantra of the movement. Again, examples of this in practice might include Oral Roberts' advocacy of a 'Blessing Pact'; in return for donations from believers, their financial, spiritual, relational and health concerns will be addressed.

The roots of the 'Health and Wealth' movement are complex. Culturally, they can be traced to the very origins of American entrepreneurial frontier religion – the independent preacher that went from town to town, 'selling' the gospel, and establishing networks of followers who supported the ministry by purchasing tracts and subscribing to newsletters that tended to develop distinctive and novel teachings that were not found within mainstream denominations. In a sense, the 'Health and Wealth' gospel can be said to be rooted in a distinctive 'American dream' (success, prosperity, etc.), though the movement is now encountered all over the world.

Besides a selective reading and interpretation of key biblical texts, other influences upon the movement have included Norman Vincent Peale ('the power of positive thinking'), whose legacy is most obviously manifest in Robert Schuller's ministry and the startling Crystal Cathedral in California. Another obvious influence upon the movement, sociologically, is a belief in an ever-growing economy. Although exponents of health and wealth would not explicitly articulate such a view, their actual assumption about investment and return assumes a pattern of economic growth. Correspondingly, a serious economic recession tends to lead to a downturn in the fortunes of health and wealth exponents, although we should note that some individuals will try and give more during times of hardship, as they believe that this will be their best means of returning to prosperity.

Health and wealth teaching has become an enduring feature of the Protestant Evangelical and Pentecostal landscape of North America. Pat Robertson, Kenneth Copeland, William Branham, and Oral Roberts are names that still command respect amongst some, while Jim Bakker, Morris Cerullo, and Jimmy Swaggart have suffered from financial and personal crises that have cast some doubt on the movement as a whole. Further afield, Paul Yonghi Cho, pastor of the world's largest church in Seoul, South Korea, continues to offer a distinctive brand of health and wealth teaching fused to Korean culture and its newly modernized economic expectations. In Brazil, Edir Macedo's Universal Church of the Kingdom of God claims more than six million followers spread over eighty-five countries. Macedo, a former sales assistant in a lottery shop, now heads a church that owns a bank, a soccer team and various media outlets (radio, TV, newspapers, etc.), with the organization having an estimated annual turnover of over US$1 billion. Bruce (1990) identifies three distinctive emphases that characterize the Health and Wealth movement. First, health and wealth teaching is linked to a revival of the Pentecostal emphasis on physical healing and well-being. Second, the teaching is linked to the 'discovery' that the Bible proclaims not only spiritual salvation for the believer, but also material and physical prosperity. Third, the teaching emphasizes 'positive confession' – a crude cocktail of confidence and assertion, under the guise of faith, that claims that in order to receive healing or wealth, the individual must *first* believe and act as though the miracle has already been effected, even if all the evidence still points to the contrary. The favoured biblical text that underpins this dogma is found in Mark 11: 24: '...whatever you desire, when you pray, believe that you shall receive them, and you shall have them...'. It is on the basis of this last point that the health and wealth movement is dubbed 'Name it and Claim it'.

Unsurprisingly, the health and wealth exponents have had many critics within Christianity. Liberation theologians (see **Liberation Theology**) have attacked the movement for its obsession with material prosperity, and its capacity to exploit the poor and vulnerable in developing nations and poor communities. Others have attacked the movement for its deficient hermeneutics, and for the psychological and pastoral damage that can be done to those who fail to receive either health or wealth, and are forced to conclude that this is their own fault, due to a lack of faith. Others regard the movement as a deviant form of Christian orthopraxy that is disreputable and highly manipulative.

In their defence, health and wealth exponents defend their stance as a 'daring' theology that testifies to the generosity and goodness of God. They speak of the 'universal law of divine reciprocity'. Or, as the old Pentecostal mantra puts it, 'as you sow, so shall you reap'.

These points aside, the teaching of the movement continues to have a beguiling and almost mesmerizing effect upon its followers. It offers a world-view – a kind of 'theological construction of reality' –

that is remarkably resistant to a reckoning with any antithesis, which is in turn centred upon a world that offers promises and guarantees about health and wealth, despite evidence to the contrary. To actualize their blessings, all the believer need do is 'plant the seed of faith', and give.

Thus, committed believers who follow the health and wealth teachings may find that they believe they will be cured of cancer, even though the disease is in their liver, and they have only days to live. Others will believe that by giving away their money, they will receive more. On a personal note, I can recall a conversation with a young man in 1987, who was a follower of the evangelist Reinhardt Bonnke. The follower explained to me that after the prayer rally at which Bonnke was speaking, he was going outside to collect his new car – a large Volvo estate – which God had promised him, to help him with his ministry. In prayer, God had apparently told him that all he needed to do was believe, and he would receive. As an act of faith, God had asked him to choose a colour scheme for the car, so he would recognize it as his. When he stepped out of the meeting, there was indeed a brand new Volvo parked outside the main exit. But as the follower explained to me afterwards, he knew it wasn't his – 'because it was the wrong colour'.

Further reading

Bruce, S. (1990) *Pray TV: Televangelism in America*, London: Routledge.

Hadden, J. and Shupe, A. (1988) *Tele-vangelism: Power and Politics on God's Frontier*, New York: Henry Holt.

McConnell, D. (1988) *A Different Gospel: A Historical and Biblical Analysis of the Modern Faith Movement*, Peabody, MA: Hendrickson.

MARTYN PERCY

HEATHENRY

Heathenry as a generic term includes the more specific Odinism and Asatru and other groups of movements from the same tradition. All such groups focus on Norse and Germanic mythology, and some prefer the generic term the Northern Tradition. They distinguish themselves from Paganism (see **Pagan Federation**) in that their religion is a recreated revival of genuine old beliefs from 2,000 years ago to 1,000 years ago, when they were supplanted by Christianity, rather than a modern new age creation; but they accept a comparison in that originally Paganism meant 'the religion of the people of the country', while Heathenry was 'the religion of the people of the heath'. Both, in that sense, could be called folk religions, and in practice the two appear to exist happily side by side. A closer comparison might be with modern North Americans who draw on Native American mythology (see **Peyote Cult**).

The gods and goddesses of Heathenry are the familiar figures found in the Norse poetic *Elder Edda* and prose *Younger Edda*, and the Germanic *Niebelungenlied*: Odin, Thor, Freya, Balder, etc. There tends to be a greater emphasis on those from the Aesir or Asa family of gods (hence Asatru), though some Heathens focus on the earlier family, the Vanir; their sister tradition is called Vanatru, and tends to have a greater emphasis on feminine mysteries and female ancestor work. But the different focus is on a continuum; although individual Heathens may have a preference for a particular god, they will work with other gods for different purposes.

As with Paganism, there is a strong emphasis on nature and on healing (see **healing**), and hence on magic. While Pagans and Occultists might use Tarot or the **Kabbalah** for magic, meditation and mysticism, Heathens use the Runes. Runes were the written language symbols – the letters – of the Norse people, but always had a strong magico-religious element; Odin, or Woden, the Allfather, hung upside down from the World Tree Yggdrasil for nine days and nights, impaled on his own spear, in order to gain wisdom, and was given (or was the creator of) the Runes. Rune magic is used for, amongst other things, healing and protection.

There is a large number of mainly small Heathen organizations; four of the most significant are the Odinic Rite, Odinshof, the Ring of Troth, and the Rune Gild. Numbers are difficult to estimate, but one leading British Heathen estimates that there are two or three thousand people in Britain with a serious interest in the Northern Tradition, and tens of thousands in northern Europe and the USA.

Partly because Heathenry is originally an ethnic tradition, and partly because the Nazis appropriated some of its symbolism and mythology (the SS symbol is a double Sigel rune – a perversion of its meaning not only of victory, but of vanquishing evil), there are some Heathen groups in Britain, Europe and the USA which are extreme right-wing – or perhaps extreme right-wing groups which make overt use of Heathen imagery. It is important to note that the majority of Heathen movements dissociate themselves completely from such groups.

DAVID V. BARRETT

HEAVEN'S GATE

Difficult to categorize in the swarm of new religious movements (see **New Religious Movement**), Heaven's Gate stands out as a unique – and sad – expression of modern, religious creativity. Although the group never managed to attract a larger membership (no more that sixty persons were members at one and the same time), it certainly captured the attention of the surrounding society on at least two different occasions.

The first was in September of 1975 when the group (at that time known as Human Individual Metamorphosis) caused alarm in the public because some thirty individuals had joined it after a public lecture in Walport, Oregon. According to a flow of newspaper articles, two strange persons, a man and a woman who called themselves Bo and Peep, had mesmerized people to the extent where they would abandon their ordinary lives and join the unknown religious movement. In reality, of course, the circumstances were far more complex, but it remains a fact that the two preachers called upon people to leave their homes and detach themselves from ordinary human emotions in order to reach an ultimate spiritual goal.

Bo and Peep – Marshal Herff Applewhite (1932–97) and Bonnie Lou Nettles (?–1985) – had met a few years earlier when the former, as a patient, attended a hospital where the latter was employed as a nurse. Together they came to understand that they were in fact the embodiment of 'the two witnesses' mentioned in Revelation 11, a pair who, according to Christian myths, would be martyred but subsequently resurrected, a process referred to as 'The Demonstration' by Appelwhite and Nettles. She had been active on the subcultural occult-metaphysical scene while his background was Presbyterian. His father had been a minister and, for at period of time, Applewhite was pursuing a ministerial career himself. Together, however, they formed a syncretistic belief system which ultimately focused on the elevation of the believers on to 'the next level'. It was believed that the faithful would be taken aboard a space craft where they would assume a cocoon-like state in order to transform their physical bodies in preparation for their rebirth. They believed heaven to be a physical location somewhere else in the universe, and prepared their followers to join them as crew members on a vessel heading for that place.

Soon, however, the group became silent and was more or less forgotten by the public. For a very brief period of time in 1980 members of the group suddenly visited their relatives after years of voluntary isolation. Then in 1993, the group resurfaced under the name Total Overcomers Anonymous and offered the world its last chance before 'The End' in a number of newspaper advertisements, and things became silent once again.

When the world heard of Applewhite and his followers again, they were all dead. On 26 March 1997 the bodies of thirty-nine men and women were found in a large house just outside San Diego. All were dressed in a kind of uniform with signs indicating that they were crew members of 'The Away Team'. Carefully produced videotapes and other readily available evidence explained what had happened. Applewhite, inspired by the intense interest about the passing Hale-Bopp comet, had come to the conclusion, that the long awaited space craft was approaching in the wake of the comet. He had therefore summoned his followers and told them that this was the time, and in full cooperation everyone had prepared his or her own death. They were 'stepping out of their physical containers' in order to reach the UFO (see **UFOs**) which was piloted by semi-divine creatures from TELAH; The Evolutionary Level Above Human.

Some of the males, Applewhite himself being one of them, were discovered to be eunuchs, and it is obvious that there was a general attempt to equalize the differences between the two sexes in the group. This led to the theory that Applewhite's extreme ideology had developed from sexual frustrations: His homosexuality was never accepted by his surroundings and on one occasion he had been expelled from the school where he was working because he was accused of illegitimate sexual contacts. A closer study of Heaven's Gate's belief system, however, makes it more likely that Applewhite and Nettles were counteracting sexuality in itself rather that certain aspects of it. The biological body was merely a container, an understanding apparently inspired by Romans 8:8 which states that those who 'are in the flesh' are on the wrong track.

Heaven's Gate's sad end is rather special but not entirely exceptional. The history of religions knows a number of theologically designed collective suicides, deaths by people's own hands based on hope, joy and the sense of religious fulfilment.

Further reading

Balch, Robert and Taylor, David (2002) 'Making Sense of Heaven's Gate Suicides', in David Bromley and Gordon J. Melton (eds) *Religion and Violence*, Cambridge: Cambridge University Press, pp. 209–28.

Lewis, J. R. (ed.) (2000) *UFOs and Popular Culture. An Encyclopedia of Contemporary Myth*, Santa Barbara: ABC-Clio.

Perkins, R. and Jackson, F. (1997) *Cosmic Suicide. The Tragedy and Transcendence of Heaven's Gate*, Dallas: The Pentaradial Press.

MIKAEL ROTHSTEIN

HERMETIC ORDER OF THE GOLDEN DAWN

The Hermetic Order of the Golden Dawn (HOGD) was founded in 1888 by three leaders of an esoteric side degree of Freemasonry, *Societas Rosicruciana in Anglia* (SRIA). Although in its original form it lasted barely a decade, its influence on current **esoteric movements** has been incalculable.

HOGD was founded on a deception. In 1887 one of its founders, Dr William Wynn Westcott, was supposedly given a 60-page enciphered manuscript containing fragments of 'Golden Dawn' rituals. He asked Samuel Liddell 'MacGregor' Mathers to flesh these out into full working rituals, and recruited the third founder, Dr William Robert Woodman, who was then Supreme Magus of SRIA. Rather like legitimizing a fake antique, between them they created a false provenance for HOGD in the form of 'Fräulein Sprengel', the non-existent head of a non-existent German occult order, the *Goldene Dämmerung*, who granted a charter to HOGD.

The main emphasis of the new society was the study of magical theory and ritual, including Tarot and the **Kabbalah**; its teachings drew on the writings of, amongst others, the French esotericist Éliphas Lévi. Unusually for such movements, especially considering its Masonic origins, its membership was open to women; significant members included the tea heiress Annie Horniman and the actress Florence Farr (mistress of George Bernard Shaw, amongst others).

In 1892 Woodman died. In 1896 Annie Horniman, who had been funding Mathers, fell out with him and left. In 1897 Westcott was told that his position in such a secret society was incompatible with his position as a senior London coroner; he too resigned. Mathers, who had become increasingly autocratic, was the sole remaining head, but he had moved to Paris. HOGD was already in a mess when, in 1898, a young poet, artist and mountaineer, Aleister Crowley (see **Crowley, Aleister**), joined. He rose through the five ranks of the outer order in six months, and demanded entrance to the inner order, the *Ordo Rosae, Rubae et Aureae Crucis* (RR et AC), which taught practical ritual magic, rather than just the theory of the outer circle. Crowley was turned down on the grounds of unsuitability. He went to Paris, where Mathers initiated him into the first grade of RR et AC; returning to London, he demanded the documentation relevant to the grade, and was again refused. His attempted physical takeover of the London temple led to ludicrous legal action. Things were made even worse by Mathers suddenly revealing the deception about Fräulein Sprengel. The remaining senior members expelled both Crowley and Mathers.

Annie Horniman returned and, with the poet W. B. Yeats, tried to sort out the mess.

Out of the ashes of HOGD came three organizations. The esoteric historian A. E. Waite took over the London temple and changed the emphasis from ritual magic to an esoteric Christian mystical path; from his renamed group later came the Fellowship of the Rosy Cross, whose members included the writers Charles Williams and Evelyn Underhill. Those who preferred the emphasis on magic formed Stella Matutina, the Order of the Morning Star; these included Yeats, and Israel Regardie, who was later to publish the entire HOGD teachings. Some loyal followers of Mathers formed a third group, the Alpha et Omega Temple, one of whose members, **Dion Fortune**, later founded what became the Society of the Inner Light (see **Servants of the Light**). Crowley, meanwhile, founded his own order, *Argenteum Astrum* (the Order of the Silver Star), and also became the British leader of the **Ordo Templi Orientis** (OTO).

241

Today, versions of the teachings of HOGD and its immediate successors can be found in a vast range of esoteric movements (e.g. see **Builders of the Adytum** and **Chaos Magick**), and also in some areas of Neo-Paganism, particularly Wicca; there are also several small groups calling themselves Golden Dawn.

Further reading

Barrett, D. V. (1997) *Secret Societies*, London: Blandford/Cassell.

Barrett, D. V. (2001) *The New Believers*, London: Cassell.

Gilbert, R. A. (1997) *Revelations of the Golden Dawn: The Rise and Fall of a Magical Order*, Slough: Quantum.

Regardie, Israel (1989, originally 1937–40) *The Golden Dawn* (6th edn), St Paul, MN: Llewellyn.

DAVID V. BARRETT

HINDU MONASTERY OF AFRICA

The Hindu Monastery of Africa (also known as the African Hindu Monastery) started as a small group of Ghanaians of mystical inclination in the late 1950s under the leadership of Kwesi Ninson. In 1975 Swami Krishnananda Saraswati, the leader of the **Divine Light Mission** initiated Ninson giving him the name of Swami Ghanananda Saraswati and also named the group the Hindu Monastery of Africa.

Swami Ghanananda Saraswati, the head of the Monastery was born in 1937. He traces a lineage of African Traditional Priests and herbalists. He developed interest and passion for mystical traditions and read widely about various forms of spirituality including oriental ones. He also corresponded with various Muslim and Hindu mystics seeking their guidance. In 1969 he went to study in the monasteries of Divine Life Society in Reshikas, India. When he returned to Ghana in 1971 the group he led which was originally Christian in inclination, was transformed into a Hindu group with a Monastery in Accra, the capital of Ghana.

In 1975 Swami Krishnananda Saraswati, the leader of the Divine Light Mission visited a group of orthodox Hindus (Indians) in Ghana and Ninson was introduced to him. He later initiated Ninson giving him the name of Swami Ghanananda Saraswati and also named the group the Hindu Monastery of Africa (HMA).

The HMA now has centres in five cities in Ghana and a branch in Lomé, capital of the Republic of Togo. The monastery claims a current membership of about 3,000.

The HMA follows the eternal law (*Sanatana Dharma*). Among the beliefs stressed are that every person is part of God and must strive to realize his God-nature and consciousness here on earth and that to arrive at God consciousness one has to transverse fourteen plains of consciousness and existence of which the 8th *Bhu* is the Earth. The Highest plane is *Satyam* where one has full consciousness of God. They subscribe to the doctrines of *Karma* and *Samsara* and teach various forms of **yoga** and stress the pursuance of right action *(Kama Yoga)*.

The group also observes various devotional practices. *Puja* which involves singing devotional songs and listening to a short lecture by a disciple takes place on Saturday afternoons. The devotional songs are a mixture of Hindu chants and popular Christian choruses whose lyrics have been altered with Hindu phrases. The *Howan* or divine service of five sacrifices is held on Sundays at 5.30 a.m. It is performed putting butter (*ghee*) into fire as a form of sacrifice to God. The Vedas and other devotional texts such as the Mahabharata are also read and discussed at this meeting. The group also practises meditation and concentration and uses the rosary (*mala*) as an aid. On initiation, devotees are normally given a name of God, which they repeat, meditatively with the aid of the rosary so as to be sanctified. A six-week course on *sanatana dharma* is part of the learning process for new devotees to ensure their knowledge of faith and religion. According to the HMA, their purpose is not to evangelize but to lead any interested person towards this goal whatever the faith to which they belong. The movement does not therefore actively engage in seeking converts though members may invite others to their meetings. The membership is predominantly literate. Among the members are bankers, accountants, government functionaries, market women, university professors, and business executives. The reputed spiritual potency of the leader draws many people to the monastery. The Swami is said to have great mystical powers and is reported to help people overcome misfortunes beyond their control, such as barrenness, witchcraft, evil spirits, and fatal diseases.

Swami Ghanananda Saraswati (also known as Guide Essel) as the spiritual head of the Group presides over all its divine services. There is an Executive Committee, which runs the day-to-day affairs of the Temples. Since the 1990s the President of the National Executive Committee is a professor of Physics at the University of Ghana. There is also a General Council, which meets twice a year to deliberate on the affairs of the monastery.

The group sees its main influence on society as coming from the ability to change the individual members' outlook on life and work through the teaching and practice of *Kama Yoga*, which eventually affects all their actions, and consequently the society in which they live. HMA also engages in charitable work through the distribution of food to the hungry and destitute, and through giving donations to various psychiatric hospitals, orphanages and leprosariums in Ghana.

ELOM DOVLO

HIZBOLLAH (PARTY OF GOD)

Founder: Shaykh Muhammad Husain Fadlallah (b. 1934)

The Hizbollah movement like AMAL (Groups for the Lebanese Resistance) which was established earlier in 1975, was initially centred on the Baalbek, a Shi'ite community in the Bezaa valley.

Although its roots go further back Shaykh Muhammad Husain Fadl Allah, known as al-Qaid, the wise jurist, formally established the movement in 1982. Fadl Allah was educated in Najaf the Iraqi city which houses one of Shi'ite Islam's holiest shrines. Fadl Allah who was persuaded that passivity ran counter to the true teachings of Shi'ite Islam in its pursuit of social justice which, he believed, clearly placed the responsibility for achieving this on Muslims themselves was to play a major role in the creation of Shi'ite activism in the Lebanon in modern times. He returned to live there permanently in the mid-1960s and began the task of activating and mobilizing Shi'ites and encouraging them to abandon their quietist passivity.

Hizbollah philosophy and strategy were greatly influenced by the Iranian revolution led by Ayatollah Khomeini, which began in 1979, and the Israeli invasion of southern Lebanon in 1982. These events turned Fadl Allah from a theoretician into an activist. By 1983 he had become the leading figure among Shi'ite militants and one of the three most important Shi'ite Muslim clerics in Lebanon. By 1985 he had acquired the title of Ayatollah, a title reserved for the highest ranking clerics in Shi'ite Islam. In 1992 the movement appointed Shaykh Hassan Nasrallah as its overall leader.

Hizbollah is organized into a consultative council of twelve members most of whom are clerics. Specialist committees deal with intelligence, military affairs, financial matters and social affairs. The movement takes the name Islamic jihad when engaged in military activities.

Hizbollah is best described as an Islamist movement (see **Islamism**) unlike the more secular AMAL movement which was taken over by the notorious militant Nabih Berri in 1980. The former seeks to establish a Muslim state and basing itself on various qura'nic injunctions including qu'ran 58: 19–20 sees itself as being engaged in a war against Satan. It is also persuaded that western powers are determined to destroy the teachings of Islam.

From the 1980s Hizbollah had become synonymous in the western media with terror. It was closely associated with the suicide bombing at the American base in Beirut in 1983 which resulted in the death of 241 American marines. It was also associated with the hijacking of airplanes and attacks on Jewish institutions in Argentina and played a lead role in the taking of western hostages. It has acquired a reputation as a committed, dedicated and effective force among militant Muslims largely for having forced the Israeli withdrawal from southern Lebanon.

Hizbollah has been one of the pioneers in modern times of the use of suicide bombers in its campaign against the Israeli occupation of the Lebanon and Palestine. The candidates chosen to be what are referred to as martyrs were almost always young males from relatively deprived backgrounds. This began to change when Kurdish rebels in Turkey introduced female suicide bombers in 1996, an innovation adopted by Palestinians for the first time in 2002. For their part pacifists argue that suicide in itself is contrary to Islamic teaching.

Although Hizbollah has links with Islamist and Jihadi movements that have used suicide bombing its justification of the use of this weapon did not extend to the Al-Qaeda alleged attack on the twin towers in New York on 11 September 2001. On the contrary. It condemned this attack as unlawful and un-Islamic.

Further reading

Sachedina, A. A. (1991) 'Activist Shi'ism in Iran, Iraq and Lebanon' in M. E. Marty and R. S. Appelby (eds) *Fundamentalisms Observed*, Chicago: University of Chicago Press, pp. 403–57.

PETER B. CLARKE

HOA HAO MOVEMENT
Founder: Huyen Phu So (b. 1919; d. 1947)

A twenty-year-old visionary, Huyen Phu So, founded the Hoa Hao Movement, in Hoa Hao village in 1939. A Buddhist reform movement, which developed a military wing, Hoa Hao believes itself to be a continuation of the Buu Son Ky Huong (Strange Fragrance of Precious Mountain) sect which was started in Vietnam in 1849. This continuity notwithstanding, Hoa Hao integrates its own interpretation of the Mahayana tradition with the traditional cult of the ancestors (see **Mahayana Buddhism**).

Hoa Hao refuses to accept the idea of an institutionalized order of monks separate from lay people. Thus, even the most dedicated of followers live in the world with their families and do not follow the monastic practice of shaving their heads. Like the **Santi Asoke** community of Thailand and the **Won Buddhist** movement in Korea there are no statues of the Buddha in Hoa Hao temples. Moreover, there are no symbols on the movement's rectagular, brown flag.

The message of Huyen Phu So which prophesied the coming of the Japanese and the defeat of the French appealed especially to sharecroppers and small farmers from the western Mekong Delta region. Growth at the beginning was rapid, the membership allegedly reaching 100,000 by 1940 and several hundred thousand by 1945. By the mid-1970s officials were claiming a membership of three million, no doubt an over-estimate of around two million. But a majority of the provinces of An Giang and Chau Doc were involved in the movement.

Like the Cao Dai Church (see **Caodaism**) the Hoa Hao movement, which eventually assumed the position of a state within a state, with its own bureaucracy, system of taxation and its own militia, frequently engaged in military action. It deployed its troops against the Communist Viet Minh who assassinated its prophet in 1947, and against all other comers including the French, the Vietnamese nationalist government and the Cao Dai.

During the American and/or Vietnam War this movement acted as a self-defense force protecting its territories from Viet Minh control. Meanwhile, it had changed, at least organizationally, from a religious sect to a church with a central administrative headquarters at Tay An Pagoda and with administrative committees in districts, villages and hamlets. Prayer towers were everywhere calling members to worship. Serious internal power struggles among parochial, conservative, aging leaders led to splintering and by the mid-1970s there were at least three sizeable factions. By this time the movement had virtually lost all of its political and military influence. More appealing, especially to students in the late 1970s were peace movements including that started by the 'coconut monk', Kien Hoa, who had a sanctuary dedicated to peace built on an island near Ben Tre.

The movement was only officially recognized by the Vietnamese government in 1999 after it had agreed to seek government approval for holding a congress in An Giang Province in that year. This led to criticism from a number of followers who rejected the decisions of the congress on the grounds that the movement was no longer independent and had succumbed to government pressure to accept its overall authority.

The Hoa Hao movement has many members overseas among diaspora Vietnamese and its international headquarters are in California in the United States. Statistics on membership vary with the official government figures claiming that there are 1.3 million members while the Hoa Hao authorities put the number at more than two million.

Further reading

Keyes, C. F. (1977) *The Golden Peninsula. Culture and Adaptation in Mainland Southeast Asia*, New York: Macmillan.

PETER B. CLARKE

HOLISTIC HEALTH MOVEMENT

The holistic health movement is perhaps the most successful development of the whole alternative spirituality movement. Like the **Human Potential Movement** and **New Age Movement** with which it is connected, it is less a coherent tradition than an umbrella term for an enormous range of schools, groups and practices, generally known simply as complementary health. As a movement it crosses boundaries between east and west, New Age and paganism, psychology and spirituality, body and soul, alternative and mainstream. Of all the movements of the last hundred years, holistic health is the most integrated and accepted in mainstream society.

The growth of complementary medicine can be attributed to several causes. First, the inability of allopathic medicine to treat many chronic, stress-related, mental and environmental illnesses has caused desperate patients to look elsewhere. Second, there is a rise in iatrogenic and hospital-acquired infections, combined with increasingly harmful side-effects from drugs and other mainstream treatments, particularly drugs. Perhaps most importantly, a personalized, attentive treatment regime appeals to many patients alienated by the dehumanizing routinization of standard healthcare. Complementary approaches are experienced as particularly beneficial when combined, as they often are, with an educational and spiritual dimension.

Holism derives from the etymologically related concepts of health, wholeness and holiness, integrated into a philosophy and praxis the 'whole person'. Its key doctrine is the validity and interconnection of all our faculties: physical, mental, emotional and spiritual. It is linked with the environmental movement through its belief in the intimate connection between personal and planetary healing, a belief shared with **shamanism** and **Neo-Paganism**. Holism also comprises an ongoing journey of self-development whose destination is the state Maslow called self-actualization (see **Maslow, Abraham**): functioning at the optimum level of health and happiness. The ideal is health defined as a positive state of wellbeing rather than a negative absence of symptoms. Holistic is also a synonym for alternative therapies, in which the healthcare professional or 'healer' and patient work as partners. Symptoms are not just eliminated or masked, but used as a guide to diagnose the root cause, and treatments are selected to support the body's natural healing system. Central precepts of the holistic health movement include:

- Health is a positive value, beyond the absence of disease or symptoms.
- Education and prevention are preferable to treatment.
- Health is only present to the degree that an individual's complete needs are met.
- Responsibility for health lies largely with the individual, determined by manageable lifestyle factors, particularly diet and nutrition. Many practitioners and patients eat organic food and may be vegetarian, vegan or macrobiotic.
- Illness and aging, like other major life events, offer opportunities for growth and self-discovery.
- Non-conventional health options and supportive therapies can work in conjunction with standard medical practices
- Mind and body directly affect each other as inseparable partners in producing health and/or illness.

The holistic health movement is rooted in ancient medical systems around the world. The Classical Greek physician Hippocrates defined a healthy life as in harmony with nature. Socrates warned against treating only one part of the body 'for the part can never be well unless the whole is well'. Traditional European medicine has been rediscovered, particularly the sixteenth century English herbalist from Culpeper, whose book is still taught on courses. Homeopathy was founded in the eighteenth century by Samuel Hahnemann (1745–1843), and is now one of the best established systems, used among others by the British royal family. Herbalism and homeopathy, along with osteopathy, chiropractic, therapeutic massage, shiatsu and acupuncture, are now recognized by the British Medical Association and available from the National Health Service. There are hundreds of other approaches of which some of the best known are: Alexander technique, aromatherapy, Feldenkrais method, naturopathy, radionics, reflexology, and **Reiki**. Fitness is an important element of the holistic lifestyle, and spiritually derived techniques such as **yoga** are particularly popular. Alongside the growth in healing services is a whole industry selling health products including chains of health stores. Aromatherapy in particular has made inroads into the beauty market, and multinational companies are manufacturing ranges available on the high street. However, many people prefer to obtain their products from organic and ethical sources.

Among the most fashionable current Asian therapies in holistic health circles are Chinese herbalism and Indian ayurvedic medicine, the latter popularized mainly by Deepak Chopra (see **Chopra, Deepak**). Although the holistic health movement is not an NRM, it does contain a number of highly charismatic practitioners who often become famous through their books and media appearances as well as their therapy, such as Chopra himself. Spiritual healing approaches, perhaps unsurprisingly, are particularly likely to produce 'gurus' such as Bernie Siegel, Caroline Myss, and Barbara Brennan – all bestselling authors. Conversely, there are attempts at regulation and institutionalization through bodies such as the British Complementary Medicine Association and the American Holistic Medicine Association.

The holistic health movement has been criticized because therapeutic outcomes are seldom subjected to rigorous statistical analysis, allowing practitioners to make unverifiable claims. Insofar as there have been proper evaluations, the results have been mixed. For example, one British study dismissed homeopathic remedies as no better than a placebo effect, although other research has yielded dramatic evidence of its curative potential. Holistic health practitioners claim that standard scientific methodologies are unsuitable for evaluating the multifaceted nature of their work. The movement has always defined itself to some extent in contrast to allopathic or scientific medicine. Although there has been tension and rivalry between the two systems, many allopathic family practices (up to 50 per cent in the UK) include the option of holistic treatments of many kinds. This is true not only in the western world, but also in Asia, especially China, where traditional acupuncture and herbal medicine may be on offer as well. There are also various attempts to synthesize the best aspects of each approach, such as Andrew Weil's Integrative Medicine. Holistic health has now grown to the point where around a fifth of British people have used complementary health products and services, and the numbers are comparable in other Western countries.

Further reading

Alster, Kristine Beyerman (1989) *The Holistic Health Movement*, Tuscaloosa: University of Alabama Press.

ELIZABETH PUTTICK

HOLY ORDER OF MANS
Founder: Earl W. Blighton (b. 1974)

One of the more influential new religions to emerge in the counterculture milieu of 1960s San Francisco, the Holy

Order of MANS (HOOM) (see also **Eleventh Commandment Fellowship**) transmogrified from a universalist initiatory order into an exclusivist Eastern Orthodox sect during its twenty-year life span (1968–88). The order's founder was Earl W. Blighton, a retired electrical engineer, social worker, and minister whose roots were in the Spiritualist, **Rosicrucian**, and **New Thought** movements. Blighton opened a small chapel near San Francisco's Tenderloin district at the height of the hippie explosion to minister to young runaways and street people. From these modest beginnings, Blighton formed a New Age monastic brotherhood in 1968 whose mission was to prepare the earth and its peoples for a coming Golden Age of spiritual enlightenment. This mission was to be accomplished through the transmission of ancient Christian 'mystery teachings' and initiations.

The movement's signature initiation, called 'illumination', was seen as an infusing of the initiate's physical and subtle bodies with the light of the Cosmic Christ. The order saw the widespread administration of this sacrament as necessary to prepare humanity for the radically changed vibratory level that would accompany the Golden Age.

The order spread quickly throughout the United States and Europe between 1969–74, establishing seminaries and mission stations in sixty major cities. A Discipleship and Christian Community movement that ministered to lay working families and single people expanded the order's outreach during the early 1970s.

Following Blighton's death in 1974 and the Jonestown mass suicides in 1978, the order sought a firmer footing in traditional Christian beliefs and practices. Blighton's successor, Vincent Rossi, experienced a personal conversion to Eastern Orthodoxy in the early

1980s, and gradually led the order into organizational unity with an independent Greek Orthodox jurisdiction headquartered in Queens, New York. The order changed its name to Christ the Savior Brotherhood in 1988 and proclaimed its new mission as a defender of traditional Christian Orthodoxy in an age of apostasy.

The order's development is an interesting case of the accommodation and identity distortion that new religions can experience during their founding generation in response to both internal and external pressures.

Further reading

Lucas, P. C. (1995) *The Odyssey of a New Religion: The Holy Order of MANS from New Age to Orthodoxy*, Bloomington: Indiana University Press.

PHILLIP CHARLES LUCAS

HONMICHI

A new religion established by Ohnishi Aijiro after separating from Tenrikyo. The Honmichi sect is the largest organization among those sects which have originated from within **Tenrikyo**. The group's headquarters are located in Takaishi, Osaka Prefecture, and it claims a nominal membership of about three hundred thousand as of 2002. The group is recognized as a religious juridical person by the Japanese Ministry of Education, Culture, Sports, Science and Technology.

The founder was born as Kataoka Aijiro in Nara prefecture in 1881 as the third son of the Kataoka family. On the occasion of an illness suffered by his mother, Kataoka sensed the hand of god and became a follower of Tenrikyo. Soon after the death of his mother, Kataoka decided to become a religious teacher for Tenrikyo, becoming engaged in activities called 'solitary missions' in

1900. He chose Gunma Prefecture for the purpose of his missionary efforts, returning to Nara in 1903 to marry Ohnishi Towo, adopting his wife's family name at that time. Soon after the marriage Ohnishi traveled to Yamaguchi Prefecture to assist a branch church of Tenrikyo. After learning the doctrines of Tenrikyo and the teachings of its founder Nakayama Miki, Ohnishi reached a new interpretation of the *Kanrodai*, a symbolic object constructed at Tenrikyo's organizational center and serving as its object of prayer. The *Kanrodai* had been constructed in 1914, one year after the date Miki had prophesied she would die at the age of 115 (she actually died in 1887 at the age of 90).

As a result of his study, Ohnishi came to conclusion that the *Kanrodai* indicated not only a special place, but also the special person who would act as mediator between god and human beings by transmitting the divine will. In 1914, Ohnishi came to hold the idea that he was the *kanrodai* in the latter sense, and thus the genuine successor of Nakayama Miki. Since Tenrikyo leaders could not accept his assertion and regarded his unique interpretation as heresy, they quickly divested him of his qualifications as a teacher.

Ohnishi returned to Nara prefecture, working as an elementary school teacher and at other jobs. He established a Study Group of Tenrikyo in 1925, with the aim of coming to a deeper understanding of Miki's teachings.

As part of his activities, Ohnishi related prophecies whose contents included claims that a war was coming and that the nation was destined to face a severe crisis. He also ordered his followers to deliver documents in which the divinity of the Emperor was denied. As a result, he and about 500 followers were arrested in 1928 on suspicion of lèse majesté. Although Ohnishi was found guilty in his first and second trials, he was acquitted by the prewar Supreme Court in 1930. Soon after his release, his movement resumed its activities, changing its name to Tenri Honmichi in 1936.

Ohnishi continued to order followers to distribute documents with contents almost identical to those before, however, and he and other group leaders were again arrested in a simultaneous nationwide crackdown, with charges again of lèse majesté and violation of the Peace Preservation Law. At the same time, the organization was ordered to disband. Following Japan's defeat in World War Two, all members of the group were released and subsequently acquitted. Reconstruction of the movement began in 1946, and the headquarters were established in Takaishi, Osaka Prefecture.

Ohnishi died in 1958 and was succeeded by his grandson Yasuhiko. Although the group had previously been rather closed and exclusive, it began to exhibit a higher degree of openness from the 1980s, making it possible for non-members to visit and observe group activities. The group's basic teachings are quite similar to those of Tenrikyo. Proselytizing activities are called *nihoigake* (literally 'spreading perfume'), and volunteer labor is called *hinokishin* (literally 'daily services') just as in Tenrikyo. The group's present vast shrine was constructed by the volunteer labor of group members. The group now possesses two branch churches and five branch offices, besides their headquarters in Japan and branches in foreign countries. Religious sessions are also held at some 230 places for the training and cultivation of believers. Members are distributed mainly in the Kansai region of Japan.

Based on Ohnishi's early predictions of events such as the coming of World War II, the group's religious thought includes a sort of eschatology that

249

continues to some degree even at present. Teachings include the prediction that the world will enter a culminating, final period, although the time frame is not specified; this will be followed by deluge and other natural disasters, a final war, the spread of epidemic diseases and the confusion of ideas among people. These eschatological ideas are understood as the terminal results of the *karma* which human beings will have accumulated until then.

The group Honbushin (originally known as Tenri Miroku Kai) separated from Honmichi in 1962 by claiming that Aijiro's second daughter, Ohnishi Tama, was Aijiro's genuine revealed successor. Claiming that Tama is a reincarnation of Nakayama Miki, this splinter group established headquarters in Okayama City.

Further reading

Shimazono, Susumu (2004) *From Salvation to Spirituality*, Melbourne: Trans Pacific Press.

NABUTAKE INOUE

HONOHANA SANPŌGYŌ

Honohana Sanpōgyō is a **New Religious Movement** established by Fukunaga Hogen in 1980. As a result of his arrest in 2001, the group was ordered to disband. Fukunaga was born in Yamaguchi prefecture in 1945 with the name Teruyoshi, but took. Hogen as a religious name meaning 'origin of dharma'. At the age of 19, Fukunaga went to Tokyo to work at the Toshiba company, and is said to have visited **Seicho-no-Ie** (Tokyo) and Shizen no Izumi (Yamaguchi) in his youth. Both groups are categorized as new religions (see **New Religion (Japan)**).

After leaving Toshiba in 1968, Fukunaga established a small company, but it failed and he went into bankruptcy in 1978. In deep despair over the business failure, Fukunaga is said to have attempted suicide, but then had a mystical experience. In this experience, he was visited in visions by high ranking Buddhist monks appearing one after another, culminating in the appearance of Jesus Christ. Jesus told Fukunaga to 'make the flower of dharma blossom among all human beings'. Fukunaga's followers interpret this message as the experience of a 'heavenly voice.'

A few months after the mystical visitation, Fukunaga began his new religious activities based on this 'revelation'. He explained that the voice was truly the voice of Heaven announced through the medium of his body. He also claimed that his movement was a 'supra-religion' because it transcended normal religions. Fukunaga published numerous books with the declared purpose of saving all human beings. Most of the books, authored at least nominally by Fukunaga, referred to methods of economic success or recovery from illness. Such titles as *How to Become a Millionaire* (1992) and *Heavenly Power Defeats Illness* (1992) are good examples of these tendencies.

In 1987, Fukunaga's group was registered as a religious juridical person recognized by the governor of Shizuoka Prefecture. The headquarters was located in Fuji City, and the grounds owned by the group were called the 'Village of the Heavenly Voice'.

In terms of doctrine and practice, Fukunaga's movement has little connection with traditional Japanese religions, Shrine Shinto or Buddhist denominations. Attracted by its unique teachings and methods of practice, the membership gradually grew, and is said to have reached some several thousands by the late 1990s. In 1986, the group began a new type of initiation which they called 'the five days' training' at the Village of the Heavenly Voice. The most important goal of the training was to modify the initiates' personalities by eradicating the former old-fashioned self and accepting a new way of thinking taught by Fukunaga.

At the same time, Fukunaga established a stock company called 'Earth Aid' in 1990, with the nominal aim of promoting environmental conservation. He has delivered lectures in many places and occasionally has appeared on television to publicize his message. He also divined fortunes under the pseudonym Kokushiin Josho, publishing such books as *Sole of the Foot Therapy for Cutting off Disease* in 1990 and *Mystery of Moon Power* in 1991.

Fukunaga taught his followers that all sufferings were the result of one's own behavior, and that Heaven imposed such sufferings as a means of informing humans of their imperfections. He also claimed that the heavenly voice teaches us the law of the macro-universe, warns us not to drift off course, and that it teaches us our faults without mercy. Moreover, he insisted that the heavenly voice was sometimes incompatible with social norms, since the heavenly law cannot be applied to morals and ethics invented by mere human beings. As a logical conclusion, he ordered members to follow his instructions regardless of whether or not they were compatible with conventional social norms.

In the latter half of the 1990s, however, criticism of the group increased rapidly as entry fees for the initiation seminars gradually inflated from one-million to over two-million yen. Fukunaga's 'sole of the foot therapy' became the focus of particular criticism because of the way he threatened clients, claiming that they might suffer cancer if they continued living as before, while they would be completely cured by experiencing his five days' seminar.

In 1996, former members who were of the Honohana group established an association together with other concerned individuals as a means of exchanging information about the its activities. The establishment of this association drew hundreds of inquiries from persons wanting to resolve various problems which they beleived resulted from their involvement with the group. Some ex-members filed legal actions at various local courts, claiming they had been deceived into donating millions of yen to the group.

Against the background of these charges, Fukunaga and leading members of Honohana were arrested for fraud in May, 2000. The religious corporation Honohana Sanpōgyō was disbanded in March, 2001 as the group itself and its corporation Earth Aids were recognized as carrying excessive debts.

Further reading

Inoue, Nabutake (2000) *Contemporary Japanese Religion*, Tokyo: Foreign Press Center.
                                    NABUTAKE INOUE

HOUSE CHURCH MOVEMENT

The British House Church Movement began in the late 1960s and 1970s, when, prompted by a spiritual experience they called 'baptism in the Holy Spirit', groups of adherents of **Evangelical Christianity** began to leave the established churches and congregate in houses; the term 'house church movement' comes from this practice.

Theologically, House Church Christians are Evangelicals whose focus on a fairly literal interpretation of the Bible is similar to that of **Fundamentalism**. More specifically, their beliefs share similarities with nineteenth-century Brethrenism and the Catholic Apostolic Church, as well as twentieth-century Classical Pentecostalism. Along with Classical Pentecostalists, House Church Christians believe that a conversion experience in which members forsake sin is necessary for entrance to the Christian community. They also perform believers' baptism in water and 'in the Holy Spirit' and practise the *charismata* or spiritual gifts such as speaking in tongues, prophecy and healing. These practices align them with the charismatic movement (see **Charismatic Movements**), with whom they are contemporaries. In common with Evangelical Christians, they actively engage in evangelism.

The House Church movement is distinguishable from other charismatic and Pentecostal forms of Christianity in three ways. First, they believe that denominations were not designed by God, and that denominational structures should be replaced simply by the 'kingdom of God' or Church. Second, they have a distinct theology of the church. Andrew Walker (1985) has called House Church members 'Restorationists' because of this. They aspire to 'restore the church' according to their understanding of the New Testament pattern of church life. In their leadership structure men referred to as apostles, around whom the small groups of Christians gathered, are responsible for overseeing networks of churches, which are led by men known as elders. The third – and sometimes controversial – distinctive feature is their exercise of **shepherding**, in which believers submit to the advice and guidance of those appointed as their leaders.

At its birth the House Church Movement was comprised mainly of young, predominantly middle class, people. Members have continued to adhere to a conservative sexual morality with an emphasis on marriage and family life.

They willingly commit substantial amounts of time and money to the local church, often giving a tithe of their income. For a minority, commitment extends to moving house to 'plant' congregations in new locations.

From the mid-1970s two main networks of House Churches emerged. In his pioneering work on the movement, *Restoring the Kingdom*, Walker (1985), influenced by Max Weber's concept of ideal types, terms the more conservative group 'R1'. Leaders of this group included Barney Coombs, Bryn Jones, Tony Morton, and Terry Virgo. 'R2', Walker's terminology for the more liberal group, included leaders Gerald Coates and John Noble.

They experienced rapid growth through the 1970s and early 1980s, attracting a combination of new converts and people who had left their previous churches. A dozen or so networks developed, notably New Frontiers International (formerly 'Coastlands', led by Terry Virgo), Pioneer (led by Gerald Coates), Salt and Light Ministries (led by Barney Coombs) c.net (formerly 'Cornerstone', led by Tony Morton) and Covenant Ministries (led by Bryn Jones). From the late 1980s growth slowed and fragmentation increased. 'R2' churches became more open and ecumenical, and less sectarian and paternalistic. Female leaders were admitted, and R2 churches showed increased interest in issues of social justice. They also adopted the title 'New Churches'. While 'R1' churches largely kept their original emphases, usage of the term 'New Church' expanded, and it quickly became an umbrella term used for what was previously the House Church Movement.

Today, a noticeable feature of these churches (particularly those of the 'R1' type) is their juxtaposition of a contemporary, experiential worship style with an emphasis on order, authority and a fundamentalist attitude to the Bible. Although their roots are different, they share a number of common features with churches from the Ichthus Christian Fellowship, **Vineyard Ministries** and the **Jesus Army**. While most congregations now worship in public buildings rather than houses, their emphasis on the local church as an extended family remains.

At the beginning of the new millennium, British 'new church' membership stands at 120–140,000; attendance is double this number. The largest network is Terry Virgo's New Frontiers International, with 300 congregations worldwide, the majority in Britain, and 25,000 British members.

Further reading

Walker, A. (1985) *Restoring the Kingdom: The Radical Christianity of the House Church Movement*, London: Hodder and Stoughton.

Walker, A. (2002) 'Crossing the Restorationist Rubicon: From House Church to New Church' in M. Percy and I. Jones (eds) *Fundamentalism, Church and Society*, London: SPCK.

KRISTIN J. AUNE

HOUSE OF THE GODDESS

The House of the Goddess (HOG) was, in its own words, 'a modern Pagan clan and temple' based in South London, England. Founded in 1985 by Shan Jayran, its Clan Mother or Priestess, to provide 'contact, support, learning and celebration to Pagans and the like-minded', HOG's emphasis was in teaching generic Paganism, particularly at an introductory level.

Although the temple was originally founded and built by women, when it opened as House of the Goddess it was for both women and men, emphasizing the importance of the masculine role within what many saw as a female-orientated religion – that they should be 'neither bully nor wimp, but powerful, wild, loving, sexual and supportive with room for doubt and uncertainty' – and experimenting with parallel women's and men's covens, masculine/God power chants, and men's workshops.

At the centre of HOG was Circlework, a practical workshop for newcomers to Paganism. The course introduced people to Paganism through small-group discussion and practical work, with the aim that they could then go on, if they chose, to pursue it in greater depth either within HOG itself or in any other tradition.

HOG also established a national contact network for Pagans, later to become Paganlink. It ran large seasonal festivals, both indoors and outdoors, across southern England and Wales, including an annual Pagan Halloween Festival, a national public weekend gathering of Pagan art, music, crafts, and community networking, culminating in a large public ritual.

HOG published several small books by Shan Jayran, including *Circlework*, *The Pagan Index*, a comprehensive listing of Pagan resources, groups and events in Britain, and *Which Craft?*, an introduction to the Craft, which included sections on the history of Paganism, and on its present-day beliefs.

Although House of the Goddess came to an end in 2000, it played a significant part in the wider development of Paganism in the 1980s and 1990s, in introducing Paganism to new followers, and in broadening public awareness of Paganism as a contemporary spiritual path, working, along with others, in national media representation of Pagans, especially addressing the moral panic over ritual child abuse. Its website is still available at www.hogonline.co.uk.

Further reading

Jayran, S. (1986) *Circlework: A DIY Hand-book of Ritual Psychology & Magic*, HOG/ Airlift 1986, 2nd ed. 1994.

DAVID V. BARRETT

HUBBARD, L. RON
(b. 1911; d. 1986)

Lafayette Ronald Hubbard, L. Ron Hubbard, founder of the Church of Scientology, was born 13 March 1911 in Tilden, Nebraska, USA, the son of Harry Ross Hubbard, a US naval officer, and his wife Ledora May Waterbury. Shortly after his birth, the family moved several times before finally establishing itself near Helena, the capital of Montana. Hubbard spent the next years in this rural setting, learning to ride and befriending the local Blackfoot Indians who – it is claimed – made him a blood brother. After about five years, further moves followed and in October 1923, Hubbard's father was ordered to Washington DC. During their journey east, the 12-year-old Hubbard met US navy commander Joseph 'Snake' Thompson, a friend of his father's, who is said to have studied with Freud in Vienna; he taught Hubbard everything he knew about psychoanalysis and Freudian psychology. This inspired Hubbard to engage in his own explorations of the human mind.

Hubbard's formal education seems to involve a number of schools: in 1925, he attended Queen Anne High school in Seattle, while in September 1927, he joined Helena High School (where he both contributed to and edited the school paper) and in 1929, he completed his high school education at Swaveley Prep School in Manassas, Virginia (February 1930) and Woodward School for Boys in Washington DC (June 1930). During that period, Hubbard undertook his first sea journeys abroad: in March 1927, he went to Guam to meet his father, with brief stops in Hawaii, Japan, China, Hong Kong, and the Philippines, and in 1928, he travelled in the Orient again for fourteen months. In the autumn of 1930, he enrolled at George Washington University (GWU), in the faculty for engineering, but left after two years, apparently without any qualification. However, while at university, he seems to have been quite involved in the social activities of university life, including writing, singing, and the presidency of the GWU Flying Club. His studies, such as a course in sub-atomic physics, provided technical language which became another cornerstone of his later thought and writings. In 1932, Hubbard's first non-fiction article appeared in the *Sportsman Pilot*, a couple of fictional stories followed in *The University Hatchet*, and he won the GWU Literary Award for a one-act play.

In 1933, Hubbard married his first wife (he was married three times) and, in order to earn a living, he began writing for popular pulp magazines. Using pen names, such as Winchester Remington Colt, Bernard Hubbel, René Lafayette, Scott Morgan, Kurt von Rachen, and John Seabrook, he produced stories which ranged from westerns to supernatural fantasies. In 1937, he published his first novel and his second novel was turned into a serial by Columbia Pictures; Hubbard moved to Hollywood for a brief spell to work on the screenplay for the serial and two further ones as well as an adventure film for Warner Brothers. Hubbard returned to film-making in the late 1970s.

After his return to New York, he began to contribute to *Astounding Science Fiction* (his first contribution appeared in July 1938) as well as to *Unknown*, a fantasy magazine (his first piece was published in June 1940). The editor of both publications, John W. Campbell, became a friend and later joined Hubbard's first Foundation, but their association did not last. Hubbard also became president of the New York chapter of the American Fiction Guild.

After he was he was elected as a member of the Explorers Club in 1940, Hubbard sailed under its banner as head of the Alaskan Radio Experimental Expedition. In June 1941, he was commissioned as a lieutenant (junior grade) in the US Naval Reserve and called to active duty after the attack on Pearl Harbour. After various postings, including command of a convoy escort, Hubbard spent the last months of the war at Oak Knoll Naval Hospital in Oakland, California, where – having time to reflect on the nature of the human mind – some of the ideas of Dianetics/**Scientology** began to form. Hubbard left the service in February 1946, with a small disability pension for a duodenal ulcer, and returned to his pre-war life of writing. His first marriage having ended, he married again.

In December 1945, just after having been discharged from Oak Knoll, Hubbard encountered the Agape Lodge in Pasadena, California, which had been set up by John W. (Jack) Parsons (1914–52). The Lodge was part of the **Ordo Templi Orientis** (OTO), a ritual magic group founded by **Aleister Crowley** (1875–1947), which practised 'real magick' (as opposed to stage magic). Although Hubbard apparently did not become a member, he assisted Parsons in several magical operations. However, in early 1946, Parsons and Hubbard parted company; their respective accounts differ as to the reasons for their discord. While some commentators see occult influences in Hubbard's teachings, others maintain that Scientology thought and practice are far removed from Crowley's teachings and show no direct connection with the OTO.

In 1948, Hubbard published a short book, *The Original Thesis*, which was circulated privately (now available as *The Dynamics of Life*). It presented early conclusions about the nature of 'human aberrations' and ideas about 'auditing' as a counselling technique. This led to the publication of *Dianetics: The Modern Science of Mental Health* in May 1950, which immediately became a bestseller, and to the creation of the Hubbard Dianetic Research Foundation in Elizabeth, New Jersey, where Hubbard trained 'auditors'. With Dianetics growing fast and a number of *Dianetics* inspired organizations forming, Hubbard launched a series of training lectures and published his 'Professional Course' in late 1950. In 1951, he continued with public lectures, published *Science of Survival* and *Self-Analysis*, and introduced the E-meter (electropsychometer), a device to measure emotional reactions – what the 'pre-Clear' mind does when that person is induced to think of something.

In 1951, the subject of reincarnation was intensely debated by the board of the Foundation, with some board members (among them John Campbell and Dr Joseph Winter, a physician who had written the preface to *Dianetics*) seeking to pass a resolution to ban the subject altogether. However, the idea of reincarnation became a basic element in Hubbard's framework of ideas. In 1952, Hubbard founded the Hubbard Association of Scientologists (to which 'international' was added later), launched the *Journal of Scientology*, and issued a series of technical publications for auditors. The term 'Scientology' indicated a new emphasis: while Dianetics concentrated on the mind as the mechanism which receives, records, and stores images of experiences ('engrams'), Scientology is concerned with the entity which observes the images which the mind stores (the 'thetan', a timeless being which needs to be liberated from traps into which man chooses to step), comparable to the notions of 'soul' or 'spirit'. Together with the idea of past lives, this concept introduced religious aspects so that in early 1954, the first local Church of Scientology was founded. However, there is a continuing debate over whether Scientology can indeed be considered a religion (and thus enjoy the status of a 'church').

In 1952, Hubbard travelled to England and opened a training centre in London and in 1955, Hubbard opened the Founding Church of Scientology in Washington DC with himself as its executive director. In the late 1950s, the international headquarters moved to Saint Hill Manor near East Grinstead, Sussex, England, where Hubbard lived for seven years.

Neither the American Psychiatric Association nor the American Medical Association were interested in Hubbard's Dianetics. Possibly as a result of the response from the established therapeutic professions, Hubbard showed a marked antagonism to medical practitioners and to psychiatrists in particular (see Wallis, 1976: 73–4), which is reflected in the campaigns of the Commission for Violations of Psychiatry against Human Rights (founded in 1972). In 1958, the Internal Revenue Service (IRS) withdrew the tax-exempt status of Scientology branches which set years of litigation in motion. Further, the Food and Drugs Administration (FDA) investigated the E-meter and claims about the beneficial effects of auditing. The seizure of E-meters and literature at the Washington branch in early 1963 by FDA agents led to protracted litigation. In the course of the 1960s, authorities in other countries launched investigations, for example, Australia, which prohibited the practice of Scientology (Anderson, 1965) for some time, New Zealand (Powles and Dumbleton, 1969),

and Britain where Scientology 'missionaries' from abroad were denied entry to the UK in 1968 (the recommendation of the Foster Report (Foster, 1971) to lift the ban did not come into effect until 1980). Given extensive newspaper coverage of the controversies surrounding Scientology and a set of books by highly critical authors (e.g. Malko, 1970; Cooper, 1971; Kaufmann, 1972), the Guardian Office was set in place in 1966. It launched an extensive programme of intelligence gathering, infiltration of government agencies, and alleged placing of disinformation. At the same time, Hubbard resigned all official administrative positions and withdrew to continue his development of advanced levels of training and to write. By that stage, he had produced books about the overall perspective and structure of the organization and published *The Bridge to Freedom* (1965), a chart which outlines the steps for personal progress (to reach the goal of 'Clear' and ultimately becoming an 'Operating Thetan') and training as an auditor (through a series of grades).

In 1967, Sea Org (Sea Organization) was set up, a kind of *élite* corps in uniform, drawn from the most dedicated and advanced members (they lived under para-military discipline and signed a contract for a million years), which was located on board three ships, the *Diana*, *Athena*, and *Apollo* (the latter as the flagship). Hubbard then announced the material of OT III (Operating Thetan III), a new level on the Bridge. After various sea voyages, life aboard the ships came to an end in 1975, when Hubbard suffered a stroke while on the *Apollo* near Curaçao and had to be taken ashore in Cabana, in the West Indies. Sea Org moved to the new Flag Land Base in Clearwater, Florida, where various properties, e.g. the Fort Harrison Hotel and the former Bank of Clearwater building, had been acquired through a third party, and Hubbard relinquished control of the organization.

In 1977, eleven Guardian Office officials were indicted in the US, including Hubbard's wife Mary Sue, and sentenced in late 1979 to 4–5 years in prison and fines. The disclosure of the illegal activities of the Guardian Office led to a major international reorganization, a series of civil lawsuits, and further negative publicity. Despite Hubbard's consent to the reforms, a substantial number of Scientologists left, some to set up their own groups or to turn critic (e.g. Atack, 1990). In the late 1960s and in the 1970s, Scientology had spread to Europe (by 1980, it was present in fifty-two countries) where the controversies became just as vehement as in the USA, revolving around issues, such as recruitment strategies, charitable status, excessively high course fees, etc.

Hubbard began life as a recluse. Officially the news was that he had gone away to write the sequel to *Battlefield Earth* (published in 1982), the ten-volume science-fiction novel, *Mission Earth*. He gave no press interviews and did not appear in public. Rumours abounded, first that he was drifting around the world aboard his boat, then that he was dead. His wife, released from prison after a year, had no idea where he was. In 1982, his eldest son, Ronald DeWolf (he was born in 1934 as L. Ron Hubbard Jr., had left the organization in 1960 and changed his name in 1972 to escape harassment from Scientology officials), filed a lawsuit claiming that his father was either dead or mentally incompetent, but the judge ruled that Hubbard was still alive. In 1983, he broke silence in an interview with the *Rocky Mountain News*, although the questions were submitted and answered in writing. During the last years of Hubbard's life, which he spent on a ranch in rural California outside San Luis Obispo (120 miles north of Los Angeles), only a small number of close associates had contact with him.

On 24 January 1986, Hubbard died at the age of 74. The official announcement on 27 January stated that 'L. Ron Hubbard discarded the body he had used in his lifetime for seventy four years ten months and eleven days. The body he had used to facilitate his existence in this universe had ceased to be useful and had, in fact, become an impediment to the work he must now do outside its confines. The being we knew as L. Ron Hubbard still exists' (Harrison, 1990: 69). His ashes were scattered at sea.

He left behind a wealthy organization which, despite being perceived as highly controversial and litigious, continued to expand: by 1992, it claimed to be represented in 74 countries (Church of Scientology International, 1992: 454–5), to have over 10,000 'contracted staff' (ibid.: 458), to attract thousands of people per year (see ibid.: 460), among them 'celebrity' members (e.g. John Travolta, Chick Chorea, Julia Migenes), and to distribute periodicals and Hubbard's books widely (see ibid.: 466–7), an organization which supports a number of projects which use Scientological principles (e.g. Narconon – a drug rehabilitation programme, ABLE – Association for Better Living and Education, Criminon for reform in prisons, etc.) and operates through a range of sub-organizations (e.g. Bridge Publications, NEW ERA Publications, Saint Hill Foundation, etc.). It is also an organization which has spawned a number of splinter and counter groups.

As a memorial to the founder, each branch maintains an office room, with a collection of Hubbard's books, a desk with writing utensils, and a picture of Hubbard, as if one day he might walk into the building to continue his work. Hubbard is said to have been awarded a number of prizes and honours beyond his lifetime. In 1993, the Moscow State University awarded Hubbard the first posthumous doctorate (for literature) in the history of the University and renamed its library for journalism 'L. Ron Hubbard Reading Room'. In 1997, a street in Hollywood, a cross-street to Sunset Boulevard, was renamed 'L. Ron Hubbard Way'.

Myths and legends which surround leaders of New Religious Movements (see **New Religious Movement**) play a significant role in shaping the perception of them, both in their lifetime and beyond their death. Hubbard is a good case in point, as his life story intertwines fact and fiction to such a degree that it needs painstaking research to separate the one from the other. He determined how his life and work should be remembered and this process is sustained by the continuous publication of biographical accounts by the organization he created.

Further reading

Anderson, K. V. (1965) *Report of the Board of Enquiry into Scientology*, Melbourne, Australia: Government Printer.

Atack, J. (1990) *A Piece of Blue Sky*, New York: Carol.

Bundesministerium für Familie, Senioren, Frauen und Jugend (1996) *Die Scientology-Organisation: Ziele, Praktiken und Gefahren* [The Scientology Organization: Aims, Practices, and Dangers], Cologne: Bundesverwaltungsamt.

Church of Scientology International (1992) *What is Scientology?* Los Angeles: Bridge Publications.

Cooper, P. (1971) *The Scandal of Scientology*, New York: Tower.

Foster, J. G. (1971) *Enquiry into the Practice and Effects of Scientology: Report by Sir John G. Foster, KBE, QC, MP*, London: HMSO.

Harrison, S. (1990) *'Cults': The Battle for God*. London: Christopher Helm.

Hubbard, L. R. (1950) *Dianetics: The Modern Science of Mental Health: A Hand-book of Dianetic Procedure*, Los Angeles: The American Saint Hill Organization.

Kaufmann, R. (1972) *Inside Scientology*, New York, London: Olympia.

Kent, S. (1996) 'Scientology's Relationship with Eastern Religious Traditions', *Journal of Contemporary Religion* 11(1), 21–36.

Littler, J. D. (1991) *The Church of Scientology: A Bibliography*, New York: Garland.

Malko, G. (1970) *Scientology: The Now Religion*, New York: Delacorte.

Melton, J. G. (2000) *The Church of Scientology*, Salt Lake City, UT: Signature Books.

Powles, Sir G. Richardson and Dumbleton, E. V. (1969) *Report of the Commission of Inquiry into the Hubbard Scientology Organisation in New Zealand*, Wellington, New Zealand: Government Printer.

Wallis, R. (1976) *The Road to Total Freedom: A Sociological Analysis of Scientology*, London: Heinemann.

Wilson, B. R. (1990) 'Scientology: A Secularized Religion', in B. R. Wilson, *The Social Dimensions of Sectarianism: Sects and New Religious Movements in Contemporary Society*, Oxford: Clarendon, 267–88.

ELISABETH ARWECK

HUMAN POTENTIAL MOVEMENT

The Human Potential Movement (HPM) originated in the 1960s as a counter-cultural rebellion against mainstream psychology and organized religion. It is not in itself a religion, but a broad umbrella of theories and practices derived mainly from Abraham Maslow's humanistic psychology (see **Maslow, Abraham**). Maslow influenced a number of major psychotherapies, in particular Carl Rogers's person-centred counselling, Fritz Perls's Gestalt therapy, Arthur Janov's Primal therapy, Eric Berne's Transactional Analysis (TA), and Will Schutz's encounter groups. They shared an optimistic belief in the fundamental goodness rather than sinfulness of human nature, and affirmed the right of the individual to 'self-actualization': the fulfilment of one's highest potential and unique destiny. In a reversal of the Christian polarity, evil and dysfunctionality were projected onto society – which was seen as restricting and controlling individual freedom in order to maintain the status quo.

The HPM was initially a psychotherapy movement, dedicated to exploring the affective domain of feelings and relationships. The aim was the destigmatization of therapy, transformed into a path enabling 'normal neurotics' to achieve health and happiness – via the 'heart' rather than the 'head'. In the 1960s, these techniques were further developed by counter-cultural 'growth centres', of which the largest is **Esalen**, founded in California in 1962 by Michael Murphy and Richard Price. In London, Quaesitor (founded by Paul and Patricia Lowe) and Michael Barnett's Community were the main centres. Books were instrumental in spreading HPM values, in particular *Be Here Now* by Ram Dass (formerly Richard Alpert) and *I'm OK, You're OK* by Thomas Harris. These paved the way for the current boom of bestselling self-help books which comprise the fastest growing publishing genre.

The HPM has been criticized as narcissistic and lacking social conscience. The response of its practitioners is that self-love and self-awareness are essential preconditions for altruism and effective social action. Furthermore, as with magical practice in Paganism, self-development is a positive response to political powerlessness: the individual cannot change the world but at least can change himself. Certainly, encounter groups and other groups pioneered a shift from individual growth not only towards a group praxis but also the creation of a community of kindred spirits.

However, during the 1970s many therapists and their clients became dissatisfied with the perceived limitations of HPM ideology, and began to look outside Western culture for deeper spiritual solutions. Eastern mysticism and meditation seemed to offer a more effective methodology than the 'meaningless' ritual of Christianity; it provided a path to self-transcendence and ultimately enlightenment. Therapists began to utilize meditation as an adjunct to 'personal growth'. The most significant developments happened in the **Rajneesh Movement**, which attracted many of the leading British and American HPM therapists, including the founders of Quaesitor and Community. Together with the movement's leader **Osho**, they created a synthesis of therapy, **Dynamic Meditation** and other Eastern meditations, which became known as Rajneesh therapy. In the 1970s–1980s it was considered the cutting edge of psychospirituality, and has influenced other therapies and spiritual praxes.

Various fusions of psychotherapy and meditation include Assagioli's Psychosynthesis, Ken Wilber's transpersonal psychology, and Jack Kornfield's interpretation of Buddhism. Even Christianity has been influenced, such as the Alpha courses. The New Age can be seen at the direct heir of the HPM (see **New Age Movement**); its beliefs and values closely reflect HPM philosophy. **Neo-paganism** and **Shamanism** also owe much to it; self-development and empowerment are key concepts in magical ritual. Reciprocally, some shamanic healing techniques have been taken up by psychotherapists, although shamans interpret spirits and the 'non-ordinary reality' in which they are encountered as ontologically more 'real' than the material world, whereas psychologists tend to interpret these experiences as elements of the personal psyche or archetypes.

Nowadays the HPM has expanded in many directions into mainstream society, and become routinized in representative councils and associations such as the Association of Humanistic Psychology (AHP) and hundreds of self-development centres and training organizations worldwide. Esalen itself now offers over 400 courses and programmes. Its influence can be traced in both secular and spiritual developments.

The most interesting and significant secular development of the HPM is its impact on business philosophy, practice and training. Personnel and management training, and teacher training are increasingly focused on the affective domain, utilizing frameworks such as Transactional Analysis and techniques including sensitivity training, role-play, feedback, and group dynamics. Business philosophy is influenced by 'soft' HPM values, such as the widespread emphasis on stress management as an alternative to rampant ambition and competition.

Despite the HPM's emphasis on personal development extending into spiritual growth, it has been largely pro-business and entrepreneurial; many of its practitioners have amassed large personal fortunes and founded successful commercial organizations. Some founders of self-development groups are from a sales background, and their groups have become involved in business consultancy and management training, such as Landmark Forum (formerly *est*), Scientology's subsidiaries WISE and Sterling Management Programmes Ltd, MSIA's Insight Seminars, Lifespring, and Silva. These organizations are sometimes classified sociologically as new religions, though they tend to describe themselves in secular terms.

Most of these trainings do not focus on spirituality directly, but some business leaders are becoming interested in spirituality and inculcating these values into their organizations, such as Richard Barrett at the World Bank. Hundreds of Japanese companies have implemented corporate meditation programmes through the Maharishi Corporate Development International (see **Transcendental Meditation**), which has several multinational corporations as clients. Conversely, therapy and spiritual centres regularly present events and workshops on prosperity consciousness and other approaches to money and spirituality.

The HPM has given a powerfully cohesive framework and set of values to the counter-culture, the NRMs linked to it, the New Age and other alternative spiritualities. The widespread interest of contemporary mainstream society in personal development in the workplace as well as private life, the growth of holistic health, and the replacement of hard political causes with softer issues such as environmentalism, also owe much to HPM values. It can thus be seen as one of the most significant and influential forces in modern Western society.

Further reading

Maslow, A. (1998) *Towards a Psychology of Being,* London: Wiley.

Puttick, E (2000) 'Personal Development: The Spiritualisation and Secularization of the Human Potential Movement', in S. J. Sutcliffe and M. Bowman (eds) *Beyond New Age*, Edinburgh: Edinburgh University Press.

Rowan, J. (2001) *Ordinary* Ecstasy, London: Routledge.

ELIZABETH PUTTICK

HUMANISTIC JUDAISM

Humanistic Judaism originated in 1965 when the Birmingham Temple in Detroit Michigan began to publicize its philosophy of Judaism. In 1966 a special committee for Humanistic Judaism was organized at the Temple to share service and educational material with rabbis and laity throughout the country. The following year a meeting of several leaders of the movement met in Detroit, issuing a statement which affirmed that Judaism should be governed by empirical reason and human needs: in addition, a new magazine, *Humanistic Judaism*, was founded.

Two years later, two new Humanistic congregations were established: Temple Beth Or in Deerfield, Illinois, and a Congregation for Humanistic Judaism in Fairfield County, Connecticut. In 1969 the Society for Humanistic Judaism was established in Detroit to provide a basis for co-operation among Humanistic Jews; the next year the first annual conference of the society met in Detroit. During the next ten years new congregations were established in Boston, Toronto, Los Angeles, Washington, Miami, Long Beach and Huntington, New York. In subsequent years, Secular Humanistic Judaism became an international movement with supporters on five continents. The National Federation, consisting of thirty thousand members, currently comprises nine national organizations in the United States, Canada, Britain, France, Belgium, Israel, Australia, Argentina and Uruguay.

In 1986 the Federation issued a proclamation stating its ideology and aims:

> We believe in the value of human reason and in the reality of the world which reason discloses. The natural universe stands on its own, requiring no supernatural intervention. We believe in the value of human existence, and in the power of human beings to solve their problems both individually and collectively. Life should be directed to the satisfaction of human needs. Every person is entitled to life, dignity and freedom. We believe in the value of Jewish identity and in the survival of the Jewish people. Jewish history is a human story. Judaism, as the civilization of the Jews, is a human

> creation. Jewish identity is an ethnic reality. The civilization of the Jewish people embraces all manifestations of Jewish life, including Jewish languages, ethical traditions, historic memories, cultural heritage, and especially the emergence of the state of Israel in modern times. Judaism also embraces many belief systems and lifestyles. As the creation of the Jewish people in all ages, it is always changing. We believe in the value of a secular humanistic democracy for Israel and for all the nations of the world. Religion and state must be separate. The individual right to privacy and moral autonomy must be guaranteed. Equal rights must be granted to all, regardless of race, sex, creed or ethnic origin.

This ideology of Judaism is based on a radical reinterpretation of the tradition. According to the major exponent of Humanistic Judaism, Rabbi Sherwin Wine, the traditional conception of Jewish history is mistaken. In his view, Abraham, Isaac and Jacob never existed. Further, the Exodus account is a myth. Moreover, Moses was not the leader of the Hebrews, nor did he compose the Torah. In this light, it is an error to regard the biblical account as authoritative. Rather it is a human account of the history of the Israelite nation whose purpose is to reinforce the faith of the Jewish nation. Humanistic Judaism, however, rejects this presupposition of traditional Judaism and insists that each Jew should be free to exercise his own personal autonomy concerning questions of belief and practice.

Dedicated to Jewish survival, Humanistic Judaism emphasizes the importance of Jewish festivals in fostering Jewish identity. Yet, for Humanistic Jews they must be detached from their supernatural origins and be reinterpreted in the light of modern circumstances. As Wine explains:

The Jewish holidays have no intrinsic divine connection. They derive from the evolution of the human species and human culture ... For Humanistic Jews the holidays need to be rescued from rabbinic tyranny and given a secular language and a secular story.

Humanistic Judaism thus offers an option for those who wish to identify with the Jewish community despite their rejection of the traditional understanding of God's nature and activity. Unlike Reconstructionist Judaism, with its emphasis on the observances of the past, Humanistic Judaism fosters a new approach. The Jewish heritage is relevant only in so far as it advances humanistic ideals. In addition, traditional definitions and principles are set aside in the quest to create a Judaism consonant with a scientific and pluralistic age. Secular in orientation, Humanistic Jews seek to create world in which the Jewish people are dedicated to the betterment of all humankind.

Further reading

Wine, Sherwin T. (1994) *Basic Ideas of Secular Humanistic Judaism*, Ithaca, NY: SHJ.

DAN COHN-SHERBOK

I

I-CHING

The *I-Ching* or *Book of Changes* is an ancient Chinese divinatory and philosophical system that gained popularity and prestige within western culture during the second half of the twentieth century, attracting among others many who have influenced or are involved in the **New Age Movement**s and alternative **spirituality**.

The *I-Ching* is a book consisting of sixty-four six-line figures called 'kua' or 'hexagrams': all possible combinations of whole *yang* lines, _____, and divided *yin* lines, __ __ (see **Yin-Yang**). Each hexagram has a name and is related to various texts. When using the *I-Ching* as an oracle, one first frames a question and then, by the random but ritualized division of forty-nine yarrow stalks or the throwing of three coins, one arrives at a response in the form of one of the sixty-four hexagrams. This hexagram with its appended texts comments, sometimes explicitly and sometimes symbolically,

on the situation contained within one's question.

According to the traditional Chinese account, the *I-Ching* was discovered and written down by a series of legendary culture heroes, Fu Hsi, King Wen, and the Duke of Chou, towards the end of the second millennium BCE, with commentaries later added by Confucius (551–479 BCE). Modern sinological scholarship suggests that the earliest layers of the text may indeed date from this period and that they did subsequently receive a Confucian reinterpretation. However, there is no evidence that any of the above mentioned culture heroes or sages had anything directly to do with it. In the second century BCE, the *I-Ching* was canonized as one of the five Confucian classics and became prescribed reading for all who wished to take the civil service exams and achieve prominence in public life. Official and popular traditions of both divining and philosophizing with the *I-Ching* flourished side by side for the next two millennia until the collapse of the Chinese imperial system in the twentieth century. During the twentieth century, discoveries and developments in archaeology and palaeography greatly advanced the academic study of the *I-Ching*, while its translation into western languages has also given rise to a prospering western tradition of work on and with this text.

Although there had been earlier translations, the seminal event in the introduction of the *I-Ching* to the West was the German translation of Richard Wilhelm, rendered into English by Cary F. Baynes with a foreword by C. G. Jung (see **Jung, Carl**) (Wilhelm, 1980). As a result of this edition, the *I-Ching* became a staple diagnostic tool for many Jungian analysts and was also widely adopted by countercultural movements in the 1960s and after. By the 1980s and 1990s numerous further translations and versions had appeared, many of them written specifically for a New Age market. At this popular level, the *I-Ching* has been related to, among other things, transpersonal psychology, **Shamanism**, **T'ai Chi Ch'uan**, creative visualization, the structure of DNA, quantum physics, women's movements, and decision-making in business.

The *I-Ching*, as received and practised in the West, expresses in particularly clear form a range of qualities and themes that may account for its attraction to those involved in New Age and alternative spirituality. To those dissatisfied with modern western traditions, the *I-Ching*, which is pre-modern, non-western, and esoteric, presents an alluring otherness. It offers an aid to decision-making that is based neither on sheer subjectivity (as in the case of simply trusting intuition) nor on institutionalised authority (as is required in much traditional religion). When, as practitioners frequently report, the *I-Ching*'s seemingly chance answers to questions hit the nail on the head with uncanny precision, the effect can be of a direct, personal experience of the operation of paranormal or spiritual reality. With its concern to provide symbols that will help inquirers to harmonize themselves with the process of reality (*Tao*), the *I-Ching* can be used as a method of pursuing psycho-spiritual transformation. Rather than promote a one-sided emphasis on certain privileged qualities such as masculinity or rationality, the divided and whole lines of the *I-Ching* hexagrams, and the concepts of *yin* and *yang* with which they are correlated, provide a model of how reality and human psychology can be composed of interacting pairs of opposites, neither member of which (e.g., the masculine, light, active, rational) is more valuable than or can do without its complement (e.g., the feminine, dark, passive, irrational).

Further reading

Wilhelm, R. (trans.) (1980 [1951]) *The I Ching or Book of Changes*, rendered into English by Cary F. Baynes, foreword by C. G. Jung, 3rd ed., London: Routledge & Kegan Paul.
Karcher, S. (1997) *How to Use the I Ching: A Guide to Working with the Oracle of Change*, Shaftesbury: Element.

RODERICK MAIN

IDENTITY MOVEMENT
(a.k.a: Christian Identity)

A white supremacist, Christian movement, with radically conservative political opinions, the Identity Movement teaches that the Anglo-Saxons – descendants of the ten lost tribes of Israel said by the Second Book of Kings (chapters 17:6, 18:11) to have been enslaved by the King of Assyria in 721 BC – are the true

Children of Israel. This movement preaches racial purity, and teaches that the Jews, the offspring of the illicit relationship between Eve and the serpent in the Garden of Eden, are the children of Satan. The Identity Movement is vehemently opposed to racial integration and interracial marriage and to immigration. It categorizes Africans as pre-Adamites in origin and, therefore, with no part in the divine covenant made by God with human beings. The mission of Jesus Christ is limited to the salvation of white, Anglo-Saxon, Germanic, and related peoples. 'Israel' is taken to mean a federation of white, Christian nations. It is predicted that there will be an End-Time battle between whites and Jews ending in victory for the former.

Its prominent spokespersons include the defrocked Methodist minister Wesley Swift (1913–70) who established the Church of Jesus Christ Christian. Other Identity churches include the Christian Identity Church, founded in 1982 by Charles Jennings in Harrison, Arkansas. This fundamentalist Christian Church teaches the Identity message as outlined above. It also believes that the one true God, YHVH, has become manifest as the Father, Son (Yashua), and Holy Spirit, and that the Bible is infallible. The problems of the world, it maintains, are the result of failure to obey the laws of God. One of its pastors was Thom Robb, the highly controversial chaplain of the Ku Klux Klan.

The movement derives many of its ideas from British or Anglo Israelism which dates back to the seventeenth century and was given a new lease of life in the late nineteenth century. Its three main tenets are: that God's promise to Abraham (Genesis, 17:3–8) that he would father a great nation was to be fulfilled literally and physically, that the Ten Lost Tribes of Israel continued to exist as a nation during the reign of King David (2 Kings, 17:6., 18:11) and that Britain and America are descended from the lost tribes and constitute the 'New Israel'. Unlike the British Israelites the Identity Movement is active in pursuit of its goals and many of its members endorse the use of militant means to achieve these. It is also anti-government claiming that its laws are inspired by Jewish interests and are for the sole benefit of the Jews.

Further reading

Barkum, Michael (1997) *Religion and the Racist Right*, North Carolina: University of North Carolina Press.

PETER B. CLARKE

IGLESIA NI CRISTO
Founder: Felix Manalo Isugan (b. 1886; d. 1963)

Felix Manalo Isugan (1886–1963) was born and raised as a Catholic. As a young man, he became a spiritual seeker, joining first the Methodist Church, then the Churches of Christ. He later became a Seventh-day Adventist, although in 1913, during the course of a mystical experience, he felt called to leave the Adventist Church and establish his own denomination. He proceeded to gather some followers and found a new church, simply known as 'Iglesia ni Cristo' (Church of Christ), registered with the Philippine government on 27 July 1914. The fact that the date coincided with the start of World War One was later regarded as a prophetic omen by Manalo's followers.

The growth of the new church (known as 'the Manalist Church' in the Philippines) was initially quite slow, and plagued by more than one schism. Later it progressed very rapidly, within the framework of the Philippine's post-World

War Two religious revival. Manalists experienced remarkable success and, currently led by the founder's son Erano Manalo (1925–) who took over the leadership on his father's death in 1963, represent the third largest Christian denomination in the Philippines. With some two million members (although the Church claims five million, and statistics are a matter of speculation in the Philippines), it follows in term of size both the Roman Catholic Church and the Aglipayans (i.e. the Philippine Independent Church founded by Gregorio Aglipay (1860–1940), a Catholic splinter group). Branches have been established in the US in response to the large Filipino population settling there (eighty congregations), and in Australia and Europe. The European headquarters are located in Italy, with branches in Spain, the UK, Norway, Poland, Sweden, Switzerland, and Germany, with several thousand members, mostly from the Philippines but also from Sri Lanka and other Asian countries. There are a very limited number of European converts.

Iglesia ni Cristo rejects the traditional doctrine of the Trinity as a dangerous 'thriteism'. In order to avoid the conclusion that there are, in fact, three Gods, Manalo taught that Jesus Christ is indeed the Redeemer and the elected 'Son of God', but not 'God Himself'. A particular status is attributed to Felix Manalo, who is believed to be the 'angel rising from the East', as mentioned in *Revelation* 7. His title in the Iglesia ni Cristo is *sugo*, meaning 'messenger', a word with prophetic and messianic connotations in the language of the Philippines' NRMs. According to Manalo, the Bible's authentic interpretation should be seen as being reflected in the message of the *sugo*. In order to be saved, it is necessary to join the one true church, i.e. the Iglesia ni Cristo. This explains the great importance attributed to pro-

selytization, and the frequent controversies with the Roman Catholic Church. In other respects, the Manalist Church's theology is close to US-style **fundamentalism**, and like the latter gives active support to conservative politicians.

Further reading

Tuggi, A. L. (1976) *Iglesia ni Cristo. A Study in Independent Church Dynamics,* Quezon City: Conservative Baptist Publishing.

MASSIMO INTROVIGNE

IGREJA CATÓLICA APOSTÓLICA BRASILEIRA (ICAB)

Founder: Carlos Duarte Costa
(b. 1888; d. 1961)

The Brazilian Apostolic Catholic Church was founded in 1945, by the former Roman Catholic bishop Don Carlos Duarte Costa, constituting the first schism in the Catholic Church in Brazil. D. Costa was born in Rio de Janeiro (1888), studied at seminaries in both Brazil and in Rome, and was ordained a Roman Catholic priest in 1911. He worked in the diocese of Rio de Janeiro until his episcopal consecration, in 1924, when he was named bishop of the Botucatu diocese, near the city of São Paulo. He was removed from his episcopal post in 1937, when he received the honorary title of Bishop of Maura, the name by which he came to be known throughout the country. In 1944 he was suspended from his sacerdotal duties and in 1946 he was publicly excommunicated by the Holy Office in Rome.

Still acting as Roman Catholic bishop, he assumed clear and belligerent political postures during moments of national crisis. He defended the Constitutionalist Revolution in São Paulo

(1932), a movement aimed at ousting the dictator Getulio Vargas who had taken power using the armed forces, interrupting the democratic process of presidential succession (1930). During the Second World War, he openly opposed fascism and Nazism, at a moment when the Brazilian government and the Roman Catholic Church maintained an ambiguous stance on these issues.

The disagreement between the Bishop of Maura and the Roman church was fundamentally on disciplinary and moral issues, and these same issues inspired his church's principal innovations. Among them, we may cite: the acceptance of divorce, the abolition of ecclesiastic celibacy, permission granted priests to exercise a civil or military profession, and the celebration of mass in the vernacular. According to his *Manifest to the Nation* (1945), 'the Brazilian Catholic Apostolic Church is a religious society, structured on the biblical teachings of the Old and New Testament. It is Catholic because it professes the Christian faith throughout the world, embraced by all Christians, considering brothers in Christ all those who love Christ and respect him as God, Man, and Philosopher. It is apostolic because I am the successor of the apostles and all acts practiced by me are valid and licit. It is Brazilian because it is separated from the Roman church, respecting the direction of the national episcopate, conserving the traditional uses and customs of our land.'

Upon founding the ICAB, Don Costa conferred episcopal consecration on a number of Roman Catholic priests and some protestant pastors who were accompanying him in his rupture with Rome, and ordained several of his lay followers as priests, thus forming his own clergy destined to implant the ICAB in various regions of the country. As the Primate of his church, D. Costa established his residence in Rio de Janeiro where his religious movement met with certain success in the city's suburbs. Other important nuclei sprang up in the states of Santa Catarina, São Paulo, Goiás, Minas Gerais, and Maranhão. The movement penetrated into other Latin American countries, giving rise to national churches in Venezuela and Guatemala.

The ICAB is structured along the lines of the Roman Catholic Church, with dioceses and parishes. Its pastoral activities are oriented fundamentally toward administering the Christian sacraments, often responding to a demand by people who have not been able to marry or baptize their children in the Roman Catholic parishes because they are divorced or not married in the church. Another significant activity of the ICAB is in the realm of popular devotion, as it honors saints and rituals that are considered superstitious or syncretic by the Roman Catholic Church.

If, on the one hand, the path chosen by the ICAB makes it a rival of the Roman Catholic Church, on the other, this same path is responsible for ICAB's scant visibility, given that it is easily confounded with the original church. This absence of a doctrinal or ritual identity has created obstacles to the development of sense of community and strong belonging among the church's members. Despite this fact, in the 2000 demographic census, 500,000 Brazilians (0.29 per cent of the population) declared themselves members of the Brazilian Catholic Apostolic Church in a population estimated at 170 million inhabitants of which 125 million are Roman Catholics (73.5 per cent).

Further reading

Hortal, J. (1990) 'As igrejas brasileiras', in *Landim, Leilah. Sinais dos Tempos.*

Diversidade religiosa no Brasil, Rio de Janeiro: ISER, pp. 19-35.

Costa, C. D. (1945) *Manifesto à Nação*, Diário de São Paulo, 19 de agosto de 1945.

CARLOS ALBERTO STEIL

IKEDA DAISAKU
(b. 1928)

A well known religious leader throughout the world, Ikeda Daisaku is third president and honorary international president of **Soka Gakkai**, the largest of the Japanese new religions or *shinshukyo* (see **New Religion (Japan)**). Ikeda Daisaku was born in 1928 in Tokyo to a seaweed processing family. His father was both poor and suffered from ill health. After finishing primary education, he studied at night schools while working at different times in an ironworks, printing shops and in other employment. He met **Toda Josei** in 1947, and became a member of the Soka Gakkai. From 1949 while he was working for Toda's company selling educational materials his involvement in and commitment to Soka Gakkai deepened. His talent was recognized by Toda, and he was appointed as the director of the general affairs division of Soka Gakkai after Toda's death, and became the third president in 1960.

The rapid expansion of the organization continued for a decade after Ikeda's becoming the president. Officially the membership was said to have exceeded 3 million households by 1962, and 7.5 million by 1970. In the mean time, Soka Gakkai also made ground in the political arena: the Komei Political League was established in 1961 followed by the Komeito party in 1964. In 1967, it won seats in the House of Representatives, and increased its number of seats to 55 in the 1976 election. Ikeda advocated 'Human Revolution' and 'The Third Civilization' as ideas to connect the reform in individual persons and social reform.

However, when Soka Gakkai prevented the proposed publication of *Soka Gakkai o Kiru* (Criticizing the Soka Gakkai) by Fujiwara Kotatsu in 1969 it was not only accused of infringing the freedom of the press but also for its closeness to the Komeito party, thus contravening the principle of separation between politics and religion. Ikeda was forced to resign as its president and become honorary president. This incident was a turning point in the history of Soka Gakkai in Japan and its expansion there began to slow rapidly. Its serious disagreement sometime later with the traditional Nichiren Shoshu priesthood, also damaged its growth, and relations between the two groups were completely broken off in 1991.

Meanwhile, the Soka Gakkai International (SGI) became increasingly active abroad. It has attracted a relatively large following in several countries outside Japan including Korea and Brazil, and has engaged in and promoted numerous humanitarian activities and projects including the destruction of all nuclear weapons and the establishment of peace between nations. Ikeda retains the respect even veneration of followers everywhere overseas.

SUSUMU SHIMAZONO

IKIGAMI

Ikigami is a Japanese term which literally means a 'living god'. He (or She) is usually a very charismatic individual who has some extraordinary knowledge and insight, and possesses supernatural ability, such as mediating between god and humans. Many founders and successors of new religions in Japan many of whom are female, have been called *ikigami*, or *ikibotoke* ('living buddha'), or *arahito-gami* (*kami* that emerges in a human body) or other names, meaning a living god. These figures are not exclusively found in NRMs, but might be spiritual teachers, shamans, and healers who give advice and solutions to individuals on some domestic problems in a rural village. Ikigami are charismatic and their claims to supernatural agency are believed to be real and sacred, and accepted by their believers. Ikigami possess some 'extraordinary' attributes, although they may not be highly educated in a formal sense or successful from a worldly point of view. They can be farmers, old women, or housewives. Ikigami possess amazing knowledge and attract large numbers of people, sometimes even millions of followers. In order to become ikigami, however, they have to enter into a trance state and act as a medium (Shimazono, 1979). Sometimes with, sometimes without shamanic rites, they can either manifest as or communicate with a god. When people gather for a consultation with the ikigami a relationship is established and usually, although the latter may not be in trance the former came to regard her/him as being continuously in a mystical state. This is how they come to be seen as ikigami (Shimazono, 1979).

Ikigami can prophesy and like prophets can offer solutions to life's difficulties. In some cases they are looked up to as models resembling prophets of, what Weber calls, the 'exemplary type'. For example, one of the two founders of **Risshô Kôsei-kai**, Myôkô Naganuma (1889–1957), was regarded as *ikibotoke* due to her frequent divine possession, and she gave spiritual guidance to her adherents. Sayo Kitamura (1900–67) of **Tenshô Kôtai Jingû-kyo** (or the 'Dancing Religion') was a famous ikigami called the 'Dancing God', and attracted a large following.

Further reading

Shimazono, S. (1979) 'The Living Kami Idea in the New Religions of Japan', *Japanese Journal of Religious Studies*, 6(3) September, 389–411.

MASAKI FUKUI

IMPLICIT RELIGION

The concept of Implicit Religion has been popularized through the activities of the Network for the Study of Implicit Religion (which was registered as a charity in 1985) and the Centre for the Study of Implicit Religion and Contemporary Spirituality (registered, 1995). Its prevailing usage dates from 1969, although the odd precursor can of course be found.

The term has been defined in terms of 'commitments', or 'integrating foci', or 'intensive concerns with extensive effects'. So it refers to commitments that are unconscious as well as deliberately chosen; to nodal points within social life, as well as in the lives of individuals; and to influences that may be low-key but are all-pervading, rather than those that are dramatic, but self-contained.

Its initial conceptualization in terms of 'secular religion' (1967–9) indicates its discourse of origin. On the one hand, observation of ordinary life-situations (as an assistant curate in a working-class parish) had shown how real could be the influence of religion (whatever its 'truth' or 'value'). On the other hand, the parallel attempt to understand those who were not religious in the conventional terms of the day, suggested the need to 'credit' them with matching commitments in order to comprehend their motivation. In other words, religion, whether or not it was *sui generis*, was sometimes (indeed often) a reality, not merely an epiphenomenon; and secularity could itself be a 'religious' phenomenon, even if of a different sort of religion.

The concept therefore straddles various frontiers. These include the various levels of consciousness (the sub-, and un-, as well as the conscious itself – and those heightened moments that might be termed 'sur-conscious'); and the differing widths of sociality (the intra- and inter-individual, the social of all widths, and the species, the cosmic and the corporate); as well as the putatively ontological division between the religious and the secular.

In view of this catholicity of interest, and a reluctance to see useful distinctions become assumed divorces, it is important to say what the concept does not suggest, as well as what it does.

First, and most obviously (but it still sometimes needs saying), the concept of implicit religion does not mean 'implicit Christianity', or 'implicit any-other-religion'. In the same way, no value judgement is assumed regarding any particular form of implicit religion that might be discovered. At the same time, it has to be acknowledged that 'the great religions of the world' must relate in some way, be it confirmatory or contradictory, to their adherents' needs, or else cease to function. So it is not altogether surprising to find Religious Education syllabuses in the UK placing Implicit and Explicit Religion on facing pages. The problem only arises when they are assumed to be a simple match.

Second, and most insidiously, to suggest that phenomena (albeit in an unexpected setting) which we may wish to describe as religious in character, may appear anywhere, is not the same as saying that all behaviour is religious. '*Any* thing *may* [upon consideration] turn out to be religious', is a million miles away from saying '*every* thing *is* religious'. Indeed, the appellation is far more focused than the conventional usage of 'religion' itself. For, far from resting content with some actor's or observer's division into the religious and the secular, it ventures the phenomenological question, 'How meaning-full is it?' Recognizing that subjectivity is involved in the (humane) study of all that is distinctively human, it invites dialogue based on inter-subjectivity, rather than resting content with anyone's *diktat*.

Third, and most generally, the concept of Implicit Religion no more assumes that 'everyone has a religion', than it assumes that religion is 'a good thing' or is 'everywhere'. What it does, is to open up the possibility that those who lack [conventional] religion may yet be understood 'better' (more deeply and widely, more fully as persons) through the lenses provided by what we now know about religion(s). They may be seen to have parallel structures of beliefs, activities and solidarities; or they may be found to have a different set of characteristics, which can still be seen as collectively 'religion-making'. Thus the concept avoids the eschatological notion of the Semitic religions, whereby conversion to belief in a single God is assumed to expunge all other traces of religion. Rather, it echoes the East Asian assumption, whereby individuals in practice use different religions for different purposes. Religiosity may be implicit within all prioritization, and so be a human universal, like sexuality, politics or economics; but the purpose of the concept is heuristic, not the proof of any such dogma.

The need for attention to this underlying but oft-hidden congeries of world-views, attitudes and identities has been expressed by scholars and practitioners of all sorts (Bailey, 1997: 10–44). Students of religion, however, will be most familiar with 'invisible religion' (Luckmann, 1967) and 'civil religion' (Bellah, 1967). The latter was necessarily restricted by its brevity to description and consideration of the 'civic theology' aspects of civil religion, but was pregnant with suggestions that were frequently overlooked by its critics in the 1970s. The former's phrase and meaning differed mainly from the one used here in that its author seems to have left its testing in the field until after his retirement.

The current concept was used in three studies (each of which, it was subsequently realized, had drawn mainly upon a different one of the three verbal 'definitions'). The first asked individuals a series of open-ended questions, beginning with, 'What do you enjoy most in life?', and ending with 'Who are you?' The second took the form of participant observation (as a barman) in a public house. The third (which is ongoing) could be described as 'observant participation' (as Rector) in the life of a local community. Perhaps the key finding was the apprehension of 'self' as sacred (see **Self-religion, the Self and Self**). Together, they have allowed (Bailey, 2001) the integration of the concept of Implicit Religion within a developmental model of society, and of consciousness, religious experience, and secular **Spirituality**. Not, of course, itself a religious movement, the concept of Implicit Religion has facilitated consideration of a propensity towards religiosity, which seems to ever anew express itself in both the religious and the secular fields.

Further reading

Bailey, E. I. (1997) *Implicit Religion in Contemporary Society*, Kampen: Kok Pharos (Re-printed by Peeters, Leuven, 2001).

Bailey, E. I. (2001) *The Secular Faith Controversy: religion in three dimensions*, London and New York: Continuum.

Bellah, R. N. (1967) 'Civil Religion in America', *Daedalus: Journal of the American Academy of Arts & Sciences*, XCVI (1).

Luckmann, T. (1967) *The Invisible Religion: the problem of religion in modern society*, London: Macmillan.

EDWARD BAILEY

INDEPENDENT EPISCOPAL CHURCHES

The more deeply one examines Old Catholic, Liberal Catholic, Independent Catholic, British Orthodox, Celtic Orthodox, Catholic Apostolic (etc.) Churches, the more confusing the picture becomes. Some are small but recognizable denominations; others appear to have more clergy than members. Some may be a century or more old; others may have sprung up last year. Their tendency to fission only adds to the complexity. To attempt to cut through the confusion, it may help to establish some defining characteristics.

First, such Churches are independent of the organization and hierarchy of what might be called the well-established historic Churches, i.e. the Roman Catholic Church, the Greek and Russian Orthodox Churches, and the mainstream Anglican/Episcopalian Churches. Some use the term 'autocephalous', meaning 'self-headed', to emphasize this independence.

Second, such Churches claim to be firmly within the *tradition* of (usually) the Catholic or Orthodox churches, with a strong emphasis on the liturgy, robes and ritual, and the sacrament of the Eucharist.

Third, they have priests and bishops (many have archbishops, and some have patriarchs or even popes), hence the overall label of independent *Episcopal* Churches.

Fourth, such Churches invariably claim the authority of *apostolic succession* for their clergy. In most cases they are at least technically correct to do so, to the discomfort of the mainstream Churches.

As this is what gives them their legitimacy (at least in their own eyes), the historicity of this concept must be outlined.

Apostolic succession is the claim of an unbroken line of bishops consecrated through the laying on of hands by other bishops, going right back to the apostles, and thus to Christ. Bishops, again through the laying on of hands, confer a lesser authority on priests, giving them the power to administer the sacraments of communion, absolution of sins, baptism, and so on.

The Roman Catholic Church, at least in part, claims its supremacy through the Petrine succession, Peter traditionally having been the first bishop of Rome, and hence the 'first pope'. The Orthodox Churches also trace their apostolic succession back to the apostles, including James, Thomas, Andrew, Bartholomew, and others, thus creating further complications (see below). Clergy in the Anglican/Episcopalian Churches have apostolic succession because, when the Church of England began, its bishops seceded from the Roman Catholic Church, in which they had been consecrated. They were thus able, quite legitimately, to consecrate further bishops within the Anglican Church.

In fact, in what is known as the Augustinian doctrine of orders, anyone consecrated by a bishop who has the apostolic succession will have it himself, and can then pass it on by consecrating further bishops. Over the centuries many bishops have left the established Churches; even bishops with 'heretical' beliefs (remembering that heresy, like history, is defined by the winners) may validly pass on the apostolic succession. The official position of the Roman Catholic Church is that any such consecrations are 'valid but illegal'. They are 'illegal' because they are outside the proper jurisdiction of the Roman Catholic Church – but they are valid.

The majority of independent Catholic or Orthodox Churches in Britain, Europe and North America trace their apostolic succession through one of three men: Jules Ferrette (1828–1904) who claimed a consecration from the Jacobite or Syrian Orthodox Church; Joseph Villatte (1854–1929), who was consecrated by the Independent Catholic Church of Ceylon and who, through the many consecrations he performed, was instrumental in the birth of numerous American independent Churches; and Arnold Harris Mathew (1852–1919), an English Roman Catholic priest who in 1908 persuaded the Dutch Old Catholic Church to consecrate him a bishop on the false pretext that there were many disenchanted Catholic and Anglican priests in Britain who would gladly join a British branch of the Old Catholics.

The Old Catholic Church began with a schism in Utrecht in 1724, after three bishops with Jansenist beliefs were consecrated against the declared will of the pope. Other Old Catholic Churches in Germany, Austria, and Switzerland seceded from Rome after the proclamation of papal infallibility at Vatican I in 1870; their new bishops were consecrated by bishops of the Church of Utrecht. The continental Old Catholic Churches have been in communion with the Anglican Church since 1932.

In 1914 Mathew consecrated Frederick Samuel Willoughby, who had Theosophical leanings (see **Theosophy**), and who consecrated three further bishops in 1915–16, including a Theosophist, James Wedgwood, who became presiding bishop of the Church. In 1917, accepting that most of the Church had moved considerably away from the Dutch Church, it reformed as the Liberal Christian Church, and in 1918 as the Liberal Catholic Church. Wedgwood then consecrated Charles Leadbeater (the discoverer and main promoter of Krishnamurti) who in turn became leader of the Church. It is through the Liberal Catholic Church that the founders or leaders of some esoteric movements today are priests or bishops (see **Esotericism**; **Servants of the Light**).

The Liberal Catholic Church, which today claims around forty bishops and several thousand members worldwide, is, as its name suggests, liberal in its theology; for example, it does not regard the Bible as verbally or uniformly inspired, and it believes in reincarnation. Some of the other independent Episcopal Churches are also liberal in their beliefs or practices; the Catholic Apostolic Church of Antioch Malabar Rite, for example, welcomes members of any sexual orientation, and not only has women priests but a matriarch at its head.

Others, however, are extremely strict in their theological interpretation; for example, the Celtic Orthodox Christian Church, based in Ohio, condemns many other 'false Celtic Churches' for heretical beliefs including Montanism, Pelagianism, Nestorianism, Monophysitism, Druidism (see **Druidry**) and **Neo-Paganism**.

One term often used of independent clergy is Wandering Bishops, or *episcopi vagantes*. In one sense these have a long tradition, right back to the earliest centuries of Christianity, when the basic beliefs of the religion were still being argued out in Church Councils. Many bishops who held deviant or 'heretical' beliefs, particularly on the nature of Christ or on the issues of sin, grace, and redemption, wandered freely outside the diocesan jurisdiction of the nascent Church, preaching, teaching and gathering followers. Much the same applied in the Middle Ages, though many of these were wandering monks rather than bishops. Today the term is applied, often in a derisory way, to those independent bishops who collect several different lines of transmission of apostolic succession, and who will happily (and sometimes for a fee) consecrate anyone who requests it. One of the best known of these was Hugh George de Willmott Newman, first consecrated in 1944, who swapped consecrations with as many other bishops as he could to increase his legitimacy. As Mar Georgius (and with titles including Patriarch of Glastonbury, Apostolic Pontiff of Celtia, etc.), he was the leader of the Catholicate of the West, which became the Orthodox Church of the British Isles. Under Newman's nephew and successor, William Newman Norton, this Church was eventually brought under the legitimate jurisdiction of the Coptic Orthodox Church of Cairo in 1994. Following a common schismatic pattern in such Churches, some of its priests rejected this new alliance and split off to form the British Eparchy of the Celtic Orthodox Church, giving their allegiance to a French Primate. Both of these British Churches are tiny.

Other groups are larger and claim different heritages. Based in America, the Catholic Apostolic Church of Antioch Malabar Rite takes its legitimacy from several sources, including a Liberal Catholic bishop. But its founder was also consecrated by several bishops from much older eastern traditions, including the Malabar Christians of India, who claim to be descendants of a first century Church established by the apostle Thomas; a more likely history is that they came from sixth century Syrian Nestorian Christians. There are many other ancient Christian traditions and rites; in the western part of the Roman and post-Roman empire, Rome was paramount; but in the eastern part, there were major Christian centres in Antioch, Alexandria, Constantinople, and Armenia. From the Antiochan tradition came the Syrian, Malankarese, Maronite, Chaldean, and Malabar rites; from Alexandria came the Coptic and Ethiopian rites; from Constantinople came, amongst others, the Greek and Russian Orthodox Churches; while today's Armenian Church is perhaps the oldest continuing Christian tradition in the world. Many independent Episcopal Churches, especially those with Orthodox in their names, claim validity by tracing their apostolic succession, their ritual and in some cases their slightly heterodox theology, from one or more of these ancient traditions.

The picture is complicated still more by recent defections from the mainstream Christian Churches. Following in the footsteps of the post-Vatican I rebels, more clergy left the Roman Catholic Church in the early 1960s, in protest at the liberal reforms of Vatican II, and joined or formed new independent Churches. More recently some disaffected Anglican clergy, usually in favour of the Book of Common Prayer and against the ordination of women, have left the Church of England, some joining the Roman Catholic Church (some of these, rarely, as married priests) and others following an independent path as 'continuing Anglicans'.

New independent Churches are being founded all the time. In 2001 the Open Episcopal Church was created in Britain by Archbishop Richard Palmer, who had been consecrated as a Liberal Catholic bishop in 1997, but resigned from that Church in 1999. It views itself as the legitimate successor in Britain to Mathews' Old Catholic Church. By 2003 it had around thirty clergy including four bishops, one of them female, and was beginning to expand into the USA. Although it claims that its clergy have conducted over a thousand baptisms since it began, its actual membership is thought to be small.

Further reading

Fenwick, John (2004) *The Free Church of England: The History and Promise of an Anglican Tradition*, London: Continuum.

DAVID V. BARRETT

INFORM

INFORM (Information Network Focus on Religious Movements) was founded in 1988 by Professor Eileen Barker at the London School of Economics, part of the University of London, England. Barker, a sociologist of religion specializing in new religious movements (NRMs), found that one of the greatest problems in the field was misinformation and disinformation, whether promulgated by the movements themselves or by anti-cultists and counter-cultists. She set up INFORM as an independent charity, with the help of British Home Office funding and the support of the mainstream Churches, in order to help people by providing them with accurate, balanced, up-to-date information about new and/or alternative religious or spiritual movements.

This means, in their own words, 'avoiding making unfounded generalizations about religious movements, avoiding scaremongering and instead looking at each particular group and situation and sifting the facts from the mass of opinions, assumptions, anecdotes and hearsay'.

INFORM has faced considerable opposition from certain anti-cult groups (see **Anti-Cult Movement**, and **Cult and New Religions**), who have accused it of being a 'cult apologist', if not actively 'pro-cult', because it doesn't automatically say that all new religions are cults, and all cults are dangerous. It is also distrusted by anti-cultists because it is prepared to talk with NRMs to find out what they actually believe and do, rather than depending on the accounts of their opponents, the tabloid press, or disenchanted former members. But INFORM does not only rely on the movements themselves for information about them; it is also the hub of a network of academics, writers on religion, members, ex-members, families of members, counsellors, clergy, government officials, police, and others who have encountered NRMs in their personal or professional lives, all of whom can provide information from different viewpoints. In this way a rounded picture is built up of each movement.

The small staff at INFORM, most of whom have academic training in the sociology of religion, collect, analyse, and provide a wide variety of information about the diverse beliefs, practices, membership, organization, and whereabouts of NRMs, and the consequences of their existence. As well as the files on individual movements compiled by the staff, INFORM has a large collection of videos, tapes, newspaper clippings, books, and publications from movements themselves, as well as scholarly studies. It is both a research centre and an information resource for external researchers, and is open to the public with prior appointment.

Part of the aim of INFORM is to make the results of scholarly research into NRMs available to the general public, without academic jargon, and so to counter sensationalist misinformation.

Like many other 'cult-watching' organizations, INFORM operates a telephone helpline, dealing with enquiries from concerned friends and families of people who have joined movements. Although it does not provide counselling itself, it can put callers in touch with trained counsellors. It also handles enquiries from official bodies such as government departments and the police, and from students and scholars wanting factual information about a particular movement, or about trends in different movements. As well as comprehensive files on over 2,000 individual movements, it also maintains 'theme files' on subjects as diverse as Authority, Women in NRMs, and the Satanic Ritual Abuse scare. Many enquiries come from the media, both from journalists following up the latest 'cult' story, and from radio and TV news and documentary producers and researchers, looking for factual information and for useful contacts.

INFORM also provides speakers for schools, universities, religious and other institutions. They present basic information about what NRMs appear to be offering converts, some of the practices involved in their methods of proselytizing, and some of the potentially negative consequences of joining a movement. It has also produced a number of factual leaflets, some about individual movements, and some specifically aimed at students who may encounter NRMs.

INFORM runs one-day seminars twice a year, with themes including NRMs and Violence, NRMs and Sexuality, NRMs and the Millennium, and also Law Enforcement, Parenting, Higher Education, Mental Health, the Internet, and many others. Attendees include members and ex-members, parents, academics, clergy, social workers, journalists, and sometimes staff from other 'cult-watching' organizations. In association with **CESNUR** it has also run two major international three-day conferences in London.

Further reading

Barker, E. (1989, 1995) *New Religious Movements: A Practical Introduction*, London: HMSO.
Barrett, D. V. (2001) *The New Believers*, London: Cassell.
www.infom.ac

DAVID V. BARRETT

INFORMATION AND RESEARCH CENTRES ON NRMS

In the 1980s, the existence of several thousand religious minorities and NRMs generated requests for information from the mainline churches, governmental authorities, law enforcement agencies, the media, and concerned relatives of NRMs members. In the early 1980s, the only centres offering information on NRMs were those associated with the **Anti-Cult Movement**. Their analysis was based on **Brainwashing**, and they claimed to criticize only deeds, not creeds. Although some Christian critics of 'cults' did cooperate with the anti-cult centres, differences between the secular anti-cult approach and the Christian counter-cult criticism, which was also based on a critique of doctrines and creeds, ultimately made the co-operation difficult. Primarily pastoral services and ministries, such as the group 'Pastorale et Sectes' organized in the 1980s by the French Catholic Bishops, or the Italian Catholic group GRIS, 'Gruppo di ricerca e informazioni sulle sette' (later, 'Gruppo di ricerca e informazione socio-religiosa'), act as counter-cult organizations rather than as information and research centres. Some Christian centres, however, were research-oriented, closely cooperating with academics, open to non-Christians, and strongly critical of the anti-cult perspective.

The first of such centres, representing a transition between the purely counter-cult and the non-sectarian academic models, was the Centre d'information sur les nouvelles religions, established in 1983 in Montreal, Quebec, through the efforts of both academics and the local Franciscans led by Fr Richard Bergeron. The Montreal centre emerged as a vocal critic of the Anti-Cult Movement, and later cooperated with independent centres such as CESNUR. Ultimately, however, tension developed between those favouring an evolution towards the non-sectarian academic model, and those insisting that the centre should voice criticism, however respectful, of NRMs from a Roman Catholic point of view. In 2000, the centre merged with the Centre Nouveau Dialogue (originally created by Roman Catholics to engage Quebec atheists and secular humanists in a dialogue) into the newly established Centre de spiritualité et religions de Montréal, the aim of which is to explore religious pluralism in general in Quebec, and to educate Roman Catholics to live with such pluralism, without limiting its interests to 'new religions' or NRMs.

A number of the academic centres which emerged beginning in the late 1960s were established with some cooperation from the mainline churches, although they differed from Bergeron's centre in Montreal, since their by-laws were explicitly non-sectarian and their purpose was (as long as this was reasonably possible) to offer value-free information based on social science. The oldest such organization was ISAR, the Institute for the Study of American Religion, founded in 1969 in Evanston, Illinois, by J. Gordon Melton, a Methodist minister whose large collection on minority religions later became nationally famous and made him the most well-known religious encyclopedist in the United States. In 1985, Melton's centre became associated with the University of California, Santa Barbara, to where the Melton collection of more than 40,000 volumes was transferred from Illinois. It is when headquartered in California that ISAR started cooperative efforts with European scholars, extended its interests beyond the US, and started supplying information to the media and to governmental authorities on a regular basis, although it always remained primarily research-oriented. ISAR continues as an independent organization, while its book collection became the world famous 'American Religion Collection' at the Davidson Library of the University of California, Santa Barbara. In the 2000s, ISAR further extended its international activities and eventually produced the four-volume encyclopedia *Religions of the World*, based on the methodology successfully followed by Melton for his *Encyclopedia of American Religions*. In 1982 The Centre for New Religions at King's College, London was established by Peter Clarke for research and teaching. It introduced courses on New Religions for masters and undergraduate students in 1984. In the same year it began publishing *Religion Today* in 1984 which became the *Journal of Contemporary Religion* in 1995. This centre has carried out major research projects on Japanese, African and Islamic NRMs and some twenty doctoral students completed their research there. The centre, which closed in 2003, also hosted some fifteen international conferences on NRMs.

The model for most information-oriented non-sectarian centres throughout the world is INFORM (Information Network Focus on Religious Movements). Eileen Barker, a professor of sociology at the London School of Economics, conceived the idea of INFORM in 1986, faced with increasing requests for information about NRMs, and an awareness that only the NRMs themselves and the Anti-Cult Movement were engaged in systematic efforts to spread information in the field. INFORM was set up on 1 January 1988 with the support of the mainline British churches and the Home Office. The first office was within a Methodist centre in North London, but after one year INFORM was able to move to the London School of Economics, where it maintains an affiliation with the Department of Sociology, although remaining independent. Governors of INFORM come from the academic world and the mainline churches. The centre organizes seminars, lectures, and conferences, and has been very active in supplying information to media, law enforcement (with an ongoing relationship both with Scotland Yard and the Special Branch), and concerned relatives of NRM members. Although it has also sponsored research in connection with its seminars and lectures, and through its connection with the London School of Economics, INFORM remains the international model structure as far as information-oriented centres are concerned. It has not produced the kind of huge reference works ISAR is famous for, nor does it have a comparably large library, but it has built a substantial data base of information, coupled with an extensive network of international contacts, ready to be accessed when the need arises. Several information centres in countries such as Latvia, Lithuania, and Hungary, although with their own national distinctiveness, are trying, on a smaller scale, to build information-oriented centres based on the INFORM model.

In between the information-oriented INFORM model and the ISAR research-oriented model is **CESNUR**, the Italian centre based in Turin. CESNUR started as a research-oriented facility, hosts a large library, and sponsors several book projects. After the ideas of the Anti-Cult Movement were all but officially adopted by some European governments, however, CESNUR strengthened its information services and developed, in particular, an important international Internet presence. In many countries, academics interested in developing similar centres have sought the assistance of either (or both) INFORM and CESNUR, although financing is a problem almost everywhere.

Further readings

Barker, E. (1989) *New Religious Movements: A Practical Introduction*, London: HMSO.

Melton, J. G. and Baumann, M. (eds) (2002) *Religions of the World: A Comprehensive Encyclopedia of Beliefs and Practices*, Santa Barbara, CA/Denver: ABC-CLIO.

MASSIMO INTROVIGNE

INNEN

One of the most important concepts of Buddhism, the term *innen* refers to cause and effect operating in every event in one's life, and throughout the three worlds of the past, the present and the future. The term *innen* is originally a combination of two words, *in* and *en*. *In* refers to the direct cause of an effect, while *en* refers to indirect causes which effect the relation of the direct cause to the result. Thus, the combination of *in* and *en* produces every event. Realization of this fact is a means of enlightenment in Buddhism.

Following the acceptance of Buddhism in Japan, the concept of *innen* spread widely among the Japanese and became interpreted in a specific way as part of the process of the historical development of Japanese Buddhism. The concept was particularly focused on the relationship between parents and children, and more generally between ancestors and descendants. The meaning of *innen* also tended to be restricted by the idea that certain events were brought about because of certain causes.

Based on this unique kind of interpretation, Japanese new religions (see **New Religion (Japan)**) often adopt the concept of *innen* as an explanation of unhappy accidents or diseases. Typically,

when someone becomes ill or suffers from an accident, the interpretation is offered that such events represent specific messages from ancestors, who are desirous of spiritual salvation in the other world. Descendants are thus encouraged to hold Buddhist memorial services, chant religious slogans such as the the 'daimoku' or 'nenbutsu' before a family Buddhist altar, change their patterns of thinking or living; or engage appropriate religious authorities for the holding of religious services. Conversion to a certain religious sect itself is often considered to be a result of one's *innen*.

Although the term originally referred to the cause–effect relationships involved in both good and evil events, within the Japanese new religions it has been applied primarily to the explanation of unlucky events. In extreme cases, groups may use the threat of *innen* to encourage followers to make donations to religious teachers or groups, namely, as a means of avoiding future misfortune.

Since most Japanese religious groups display a certain degree of eclecticism, the idea of *innen* tends to be accepted widely, no matter whether the group be Buddhist in origin or not.

NABUTAKE INOUE

INTERNATIONAL CHURCH OF CHRIST

The International Church of Christ (ICOC) is an Evangelical Church (see **Evangelical Christianity**) with certain distinctive emphases, which have attracted a great deal of criticism from other Churches and from the anti-cult movement.

The Church grew out of the established American denomination, the Church of Christ. In the 1960s, a Florida Church of Christ set out to evangelize students in what was known as the Crossroads movement. Kip McKean led one such outreach, initially at East Illinois University, then moving to Boston in 1979, where he established the Boston Church of Christ, from which ICOC developed. The Church always takes its local name from its location, so its London Church, established in 1982 (and the first outside the USA), is called the London Church of Christ. There is now no connection between ICOC and the Church of Christ denomination from which they were born.

In practice, ICOC's theology differs from that of most Evangelical Churches in a number of ways. Baptism is essential to salvation, and new members must be rebaptized on joining the Church. This has led to the charge that in effect the Church teaches that salvation can only be found in ICOC. Members who wish to leave have reported that they are warned, implicitly or explicitly, that they could lose their salvation by doing so, even if they maintain their Evangelical beliefs. Evangelical counter-cultists such as the **Christian Research Institute** argue that this, along with the emphasis on obedience, means that ICOC is teaching salvation at least partly through works, rather than wholly through faith.

ICOC follows the practice of discipling, whereby newer or younger members are 'shepherded' by older or more senior members (see **House Church Movement**), who have a great deal of influence over them, including where they should live and who they should have relationships with. Although ICOC sees this as loving guidance, there is no doubt that at times it has led to abuse. Similarly, its practice of members confessing their sins to their discipler has allegedly led to written 'sin lists' being passed on to other leaders.

ICOC still specifically targets students. Because it encourages new members to move into single-sex communal homes with other members, and to spend a great deal of their time evangelizing, a number of British universities have banned it from their campuses.

In November 2002, following a year's sabbatical, Kip McKean resigned as leader of ICOC, confessing that 'my leadership in recent years has damaged both the Kingdom and my family. My biggest sin is arrogance – thinking I am always right.' At the time of writing this appears to be having a major effect on ICOC, with a review of both the leadership structure and the 'culture' of the movement, and a move away from authoritarian discipling.

At the end of 2002 ICOC claimed a worldwide membership of 137,000, 'with typical attendance at our worship services in November 2002 of 193,000'. There are 49,000 members in the USA, 3,000 in the UK and 9,900 in Europe, and a total of 437 congregations in 171 countries.

Further reading

Barrett, D. V. (2001) *The New Believers*, London: Cassell.

DAVID V. BARRETT

INTERNATIONAL SOCIETY FOR KRISHNA CONSCIOUSNESS

The International Society for Krishna Consciousness or Hare Krishna movement has centres in eighty-six countries and publications in over seventy languages. It is a modern, globalized offshoot of the Gaudiya Vaishnava Math, a Bengali mission founded in the 1880s to revitalize the practices of the sixteenth century mystic, Chaitanya, a devotee of Krishna. ISKCON's founder, **Bhaktivedanta Swami** (generally known as 'Prabhupada'), brought Vaishnava teachings to the West in the mid-1960s where he soon found a receptive audience among those young Americans disaffected by the values of their parents and the war in Vietnam.

The first followers were initiated by Prabhupada in a small New York storefront in 1966. Soon after, they took part in their first public *sankirtan* (chanting the names of Krishna), an activity that was to become the movement's trademark. They acquired a knowledge of Vaishnava worship and Bengali culture from their guru, and began to take his teachings across north America, to San Francisco, Buffalo, Boston, and Montreal, and then to England in 1968. There they captured the imagination of The Beatles, particularly George Harrison who helped them to produce a chart-topping record of the Hare Krishna **mantra** (1969) and to buy the house that was to become Bhaktivedanta Manor (1971). The devotees preached in Europe, Australia and Africa, and also in India where, as young, white disciples in Indian attire, they were met with both interest and suspicion.

Prabhupada opened up what had been a movement exclusively for Indian men to all men and women, irrespective of nationality, allowing them an equal opportunity to serve Krishna and take initiation as Hare Krishna *brahmins*. Later he encouraged some of his more committed male followers to give up family life as he had done and become *sannyasi* or ascetics. Eager to transmit the spiritual and cultural traditions of Bengali Vaishnavism, he did not always foresee the consequences, many of which only became apparent after his death in 1977 when the administration of the movement passed to its Governing Body Commission, and the spiritual leadership became the responsibility of eleven initiating gurus, a number of whom failed to live up to ISKCON's moral and spiritual principles and were

later removed from office. The focus in the 1980s on the exalted role of the celibate male – whether young initiate, *sannyasi* or guru – and the emerging culture of gender separation and animosity to family life often led to the undermining of women's status and opportunities and to a lack of protection for children.

Since the late 1980s, the movement has made efforts to address the pressing need for reform, of spiritual leadership, the position of women, the abuse of children, and the contribution of householders and congregational members to ISKCON's mission and culture. At times these problems have led to disaffection or disaffiliation, even to legal action. External relations, which in early years were marked by media interest in celebrity involvement, some attempts at devotee **Deprogramming**, and concern over book distribution and the soliciting of donations, focused in the 1990s on lawsuits involving child abuse.

On the positive side, food distribution programmes, educational outreach, and participation in inter-faith encounter have enabled ISKCON members to engage with external agencies. The inward-looking monasticism of the 1970s, which cast outsiders in the role of demons, has been replaced by a greater awareness of the movement's frailty, its place in society, and need for support. This has been accelerated by the growing role of devotee families, including many Indian Hindu families living in diaspora, who engage in the wider world through work, their children's schooling, and use of public services and facilities. By the late 1990s, in America and Europe – including Eastern Europe where ISKCON grew rapidly following the fall of communism – the number of devotees living in households outside ISKCON centres exceeded those living within them.

Central to daily spiritual life is the chanting on beads of the *maha mantra* – 'Hare Krishna, Hare Krishna, Krishna Krishna, Hare Hare, Hare Rama, Hare Rama, Rama Rama, Hare Hare' – and the practice of the four regulative principles: no meat, fish or eggs; no intoxicants; sex only for the procreation of children; and no gambling. Worshipping Krishna and his consort, Radha, in the temple, and attending festivals is popular. Singing, dancing, and preparing and eating vegetarian food in the name of Krishna are encouraged, as is reading Prabhupada's books, particularly his translation and commentary of the *Bhagavad Gita* and *Srimad Bhagavatam*, and the life of Chaitanya. A devotee's spiritual objective is to serve and remember Krishna at all times and in all activities, whilst the movement's goal is to follow Chaitanya's call to spread Krishna consciousness to every town and village.

Further reading

Knott, Kim (1986) *My Sweet Lord: The Hare Krishna Movement*, Wellingborough, Northants: Aquarian Press.

KIM KNOTT

ISLAMISM

Islamism is a modern version of a political philosophy which makes the case for applying Islamic principles of *shari'a* law to the practice of government in the modern world.

Numerous movements have been established for this purpose and to take the necessary action to ensure that the goal of an Islamic state is achieved. They do not all agree either on the nature and precise structure of an Islamic government or on the means that are necessary to achieve it.

Islamists do agree that Islam is a total way of life and, thus, to live as a true Muslim it is necessary to live in a society in which the legal system, the educational system indeed all the main institutions of government and the economic system are run according to Islamic principles. Islamists for whom 'real' Islam is not possible under secular or corrupt Muslim leadership are motivated in their struggle by both this-worldly and other-worldly desires being convinced that an Islamic society will also be a prosperous and harmonious one and one that will guarantee to all its members a place in paradise.

Many Muslims would agree with Islamists that secular, political systems introduced from the West are seen to have failed to provide a solution to serious social and economic problems and to have had damaging effects on the moral fabric of Muslim society. They would attribute the plight of most of the Muslim world – its poverty and tyranny – to western, economic exploitation, for which the term globalization is a disguise. Where the majority of Muslims differ from the Islamists is in the solution to the problem. The former does not believe the answer lies in direct confrontation. Islamists are divided into two main groups in terms of their response: those who promote *daw'a* (calling) – missionary activity that enjoins all Muslims to live according to Islamic principles – as the most effective means of transforming Muslim society. These Muslims oppose the use of force against civilians of any religion or society. Others believe in the necessity of *jihad* and are often referred to as jihadis, meaning here those who have taken to military means to achieve their objectives. One such group is Islamic Jihad which united with **Al-Qaeda** in 1998 to from the Islamic Front for Jihad on the Jews and the Crusaders. Another is the Lebanese Shi'ite movement **Hizbollah (Party of God)**.

There can be little doubt that the Middle East conflict between the Israelis and Palestinians in which the Americans are seen as the principal allies of the latter, the establishment of foreign military bases in Muslim lands including Saudi Arabia, and the invasions of predominantly Muslim countries the first of which was the Soviet invasion of Afghanistan in 1979 followed by those of the United States and its allies of Afghanistan in 2001 and Iraq in 1991 and 2003 have increased support among Muslim activists for the jihadi approach.

Further reading

Zahab, M. A. and Olivier, R. (2002) *Islamist Networks*, London: Hurst and Company.
PETER B. CLARKE

IVI – INVITATION À LA VIE
Founder : Yvonne Trubert (b. 1932)

IVI is the acronym of Invitation à la Vie, 'Invitation to Life', rather than (as many anti-cult sources mistakenly report) of 'Invitation à la Vie Intense' (Invitation to Intensive Life). It claims not to be a religion, but rather a spiritual movement open to members of all religions. The association was founded in France in 1983 by popular Paris healer Yvonne Trubert (born in Laremans, France, in 1932). A Roman Catholic, Trubert became a full-time healer in 1976, and by 1982 she had gathered seventeen devoted followers to assist her in her healing activities, with the number of 'helpers' rising to more than sixty by 1983. Trubert's teachings are a form of metaphysical Christianity. The majority of IVI's members regard themselves as Roman Catholic, although there are also Protestants, Muslims, Jews, and some secular humanists among them.

The movement has three aims: prayer, 'harmonization', and 'vibrations'. Prayer is centered on the Rosary, obviously a Catholic devotion, although its interpretation by IVI is somewhat non-sectarian. 'Harmonization' is normally interpreted by those scholars who have studied IVI as a healing ritual, but IVI itself insists that it is no therapy. Anyone who has requested harmonization simply lays in bed with his or her eyes closed, while IVI's 'harmonizer' prays silently, kneeling by the bed, and administering a gentle massage designed to create a feeling of well-being and peace. All IVI members who have taken the time to learn the technique are empowered to 'harmonize' others. 'Vibrations' comprise collective songs and chants aimed at transmitting peace and harmony by sending appropriate 'good' energy to Planet Earth. Good energy is best transmitted in sacred places, and IVI often gathers its members in the form of pilgrimages, usually led by Yvonne Trubert herself, to Catholic shrines such as Lourdes, Fatima, or the Mont Saint Michel.

From its native France, IVI spread to Belgium, Brazil, Canada, Germany, Greece, Mexico, Spain, and Italy. It currently has chapters in some seventy countries, with 4,000 members. It is led by an eight-member Board of Directors, elected for three years, and by an Executive Board. It is organized by 'homes' (named after a Catholic saint, and responsible for the movement within a specific geographic area), and 'missions' (devoted to specific aims, such as organizing pilgrimages, or supervising the correct practice of harmonization).

Harmonization, in particular, became quite fashionable in France in the 1990s. The media devoted great attention to the fact that former President François Mitterrand (1916–96), although a secular politician, requested to be 'harmonized' in his final illness. Several hospitals welcome IVI involvement, and have reported positive results, at least psychological, deriving from the harmonization technique. On the other hand, others have regarded harmonization as 'quack medicine', and IVI became a frequent target of opposition in France's 'cult wars' between 1996 and 2002. Some Catholic priests have denounced IVI as a non-Catholic, syncretistic movement, although other priests have maintained an on-going dialogue. As the intensity of the anti-cult campaign decreases in France, IVI looks forward to more peaceful times.

MASSIMO INTROVIGNE

J

JAKOB LORBER ASSOCIATION

Born near Maribor (now in Slovenia), Jakob Lorber (1800–64) trained as a teacher and for a while intended to become a priest, but in the end he decided to dedicate himself entirely to music. Greatly influenced by the violinist Niccolò Paganini (1782–1840), he composed various chamber music works in romantic style. He lived most of his life in Graz, Austria. Interested in spiritual matters, he read the works of various authors, including Jacob Böhme (1575–1624) and **Emanuel Swedenborg** (1688–1772). He was still in bed, early on the morning of 15 March 1840, when he heard a voice order him: 'Get up, take your pen and write!' From then on, he dedicated the rest of his life to transcribing the revelation he received – as he asserted – from God Himself. These dictations covered about 10,000 pages. Some of his friends learned about them and eight volumes were published dur-

ing his lifetime, although they received little mention. Lorber died without completing *The Great Gospel of John*, the missing chapters of which (making up the eleventh volume) would be revealed later by Leopold Engel (1858–1931), co-founder, with Theodor Reuss (1855–1923), of an Order of the Enlightened. On his deathbed, Lorber received the last sacraments from a Catholic priest: like Swedenborg, he never abandoned his Church of origin.

Lorber's writings include various categories of texts. *The Great Gospel of John* was intended to complete the canonical Gospels, and takes the form of a detailed story of the life of Christ, narrated by Jesus Himself: 'The time has come to show the true inner meaning of such texts to all who are worthy of participating in this knowledge,' Jesus explains; God Himself delivers the complete version of the Gospels to mankind. Other teachings on human history develop the opening chapters of *Genesis*. Human history is an ascent through matter, starting from the mineral, plant, animal, and human kingdoms. In truth, the creation was a result of the fall: in the end, even Lucifer – the fallen angel – will be able to return to the source. Another category of Lorber's writings takes the form of the restitution of some allegedly lost early Christian texts. Lastly, there are a few works on the creation of the universe.

During the nineteenth century, there was significant interaction between Lorber's readers and spiritualists. Lorber's works were progressively published, thanks mainly to the support of an ardent reader – Gottfried Mayerhofer (1807–77) – who in turn received divine messages from the Inner Word. The spread of Lorber's works was promoted in particular by a publishing house active in Bietigheim (Württemberg) for over a hundred years. Repressive measures during the Nazi period and World War II drastically interrupted the movement's work: in 1935, there were between eighty and one hundred 'Lorber circles' in Germany, although the number dropped significantly after the war. According to a survey conducted by Matthias Pöhlmann, in 1993 there were – in Germany – fourteen 'Lorber circles,' plus others active in other countries. The 'Lorber circles' do not regard themselves as a separate religious denomination, and do not require any break from original religious affiliations, even if occasionally – in some circles – the Last Supper is celebrated. As Kurt Hutten has noted, all sorts of groups are interested in Lorber, from practising Christians to believers in aliens, from vegetarians to fans of the occult. Moreover, with his model of the Inner Word, Lorber has become a role model for many subsequent revelations in the German-speaking world (*Neuoffenbarungen*).

JEAN-FRANÇOIS MAYER AND
PIERLUIGI ZOCCATELLI

JEHU-APPIAH
Prophet Jemisimiham (b. 1893; d. 1948)

Born at Abura Edumfa, a town in the Central Region of Ghana, Jehu-Appiah's parents were Mr Kwaa Dum and Madam Abena Esuon. He was trained in the Methodist tradition and after his elementary education he became a teacher-catechist of that Church.

In 1919 while he was in charge of the Methodist Society at Gomoa Dunkwa, Jehu-Appiah had a series of visions, which changed his life. He claimed to have received power to heal people of their sicknesses and perform miracles. Together with some friends, he founded the *Egyidifo Kuw* (Faith Society) in 1922, which met weekly to seek the Holy Spirit in prayer. In 1923 he was dismissed from the Methodist Church. He was accused of practising occultism. But the members of his *Egyidifo Kuw* supported him and he continued to heal the sick and perform miracles. The Faith Society was later turned into the *Musama Disco Christo Church* (Army of the Cross of Christ Church) with Jehu-Appiah as leader. His name Jemisimiham Jehu-Appiah, like the name of the Church, divinely revealed to him. His original name was Joseph William Egyanka Appiah.

Although, Jehu-Appiah had a first wife, in obedience to guidance received through prophecy, he also married Hannah Barnes who had been his helper. Hannah was named *Nathalomoa* (Queen mother) Jehu-Appiah and was given the title, *Akatitibi* I, while her husband became *Akaboha* I.

Jehu-Appiah showed great interest in national politics. He was a member of the Aborigines' Rights Protection Society and was consulted by Dr Kwame Nkrumah, the first president of Ghana.

Prophet Jehu-Appiah was succeeded by his second-born son, Kwesi Nyame whose revealed name was Moses Mata-poly Jehu-Appiah. The birth of Matapoly was prophesied and his birthday, 24 August marks the annual 'peaceful Year' which is the most important feast of the Church.

Matapoly's reign as king and prophet of the Church saw very important developments and growth of the Church. Its doctrines and practices were properly set out and the church spread beyond the borders of Ghana. Mata-poly's Son, Miritaiah Jonah Jehu-Appiah is the current head of the Musama Disco Christo Church.

Further reading

Baeta, C. G. (1962) *Prophetism in Ghana*, London: SCM.

ABAMFO O. ATIEMO

JESUS ARMY, THE
(THE JESUS FELLOWSHIP CHURCH)

Founder: Noel Stanton

Country of origin: UK

The Jesus Army is a Christian group called the Jesus Fellowship Church which was founded by Noel Stanton, a Baptist, in 1974 in Bugbrooke, a small village which is located a few miles west of Northampton, England.

After the Second World War, Noel Stanton studied in a Bible college and spent some time working in business, before accepting a call to become a part-time minister to the small congregation of Bugbrooke in 1957. In 1969 he claimed that he received an experience of Baptism in the Holy Sprit and he inspired members of the congregation to speak in tongues and to accept baptism in the Spirit. The congregation grew in numbers and people of the congregation became interested in the idea of a

Christian community. The first commu-nity house was inaugurated in 1974.

By 1981, there were 600 members in community houses, and in 1982 the Jesus Fellowship Church joined the Evangeli-cal Alliance. In 1986, only four years after joining it, the church was asked to resign from the umbrella organization of the Evangelical Alliance on the grounds that it was isolationist and had poor relationships with other churches. Later in the same year the church was also compelled to leave the Baptist Union of Great Britain on the grounds that owing to its nationwide activities and its form of government, it could no longer be recognized as a local Baptist Church.

In 1987, the Jesus Army was estab-lished as the evangelizing wing of the Jesus Fellowship Church to mobilize outreach work for those in need in towns and cities. They formulated their community house programme and had additional houses in Northampton, Kettering, Hastings, Hinckley, Leicester, and London. The Jesus Army sought to improve its relationships with other churches and launched the 'Multiply Christian Network' in 1992, which is a network of independent Christian chur-ches and groups in the UK and overseas. The Jesus Army rejoined the Evangeli-cal Alliance in October 1999.

Because of its historical background, the Jesus Army is sociologically classed as new religious movement. On the other hand, however, it describes itself as an orthodox evangelical and charis-matic Christian church, upholding the universally accepted creeds of the Chris-tian faith: the Apostles' Creed, the Nicene Creed and the Athanasian Creed. The members of the Jesus Army believe in the Trinity that is in the three persons of the one Godhead, the Father, the Son and the Holy Spirit; in the full divinity, atoning death and bodily resurrection of

Jesus Christ; and in the Bible as God's infallible word, fully inspired by the Holy Spirit. The members believe that Jesus has established his rule and now is establishing the Kingdom of God. The Jesus Army campaigns against such social ills such as drugs, racism, homelessness, and prostitution.

The members of the Jesus Army are recognizable on the streets by their military uniform and by the painted double-decker buses and minibuses, as well as by the banners and flags used on marches through towns and cities. They baptize people in rivers, the sea, and even at the fountains in Trafalgar Square London. The Jesus Army makes particular efforts to evangelize those in need, especially homeless young people, those involved in drug or alcohol abuse, prisoners and ex-prisoners.

The Jesus Army runs various businesses, such as farms, health food shops, and garages, and members live in community houses of between six and sixty people. They live as a large family and share possessions. Leaders of community houses are usually men and there is a strict supervision of members' lives. Single men and women are carefully segregated. Although marriage in the community is allowed, nearly 300 men and women are committed to celibacy. Today there are around 2,500 members who are involved in the Jesus Army in different ways and about 700 of them live in sixty or so community houses around the UK.

Further reading

Inaba, K. (2000) 'A Comparative Study of Altruism in the New Religious Movements: With special reference to the Jesus Army and the Friends of the Western Buddhist Order', PhD thesis of King's College, University of London.
Newell, K. (1997) 'Charismatic Communitarianism and the Jesus Fellowship' in S. Hunt, M. Hamilton and T. Walter (eds) *Charismatic Christianity: Sociological Perspectives*, New York: St Martin's Press.

KEISHIN INABA

JESUS MOVEMENT

There have of course been many 'Jesus movements' through the centuries, if the phrase is taken to mean a major and highly visible resurgence in personal devotion to and active witnessing about Jesus – for example, Wesley's eighteenth century revivalism, the several waves of evangelism in nineteenth century USA, the great campaigns of Moody and Sankey, or of Billy Graham, and so on. Some of these revivals are also 'Holy Spirit movements' in that they are Pentecostalist or charismatic in nature (see **Charismatic Movements**).

The Jesus Movement of the late-1960s and 1970s was different from these in several respects. First, it was not due to the work of any individual evangelist, but many joined in; second, as it spread it involved many different 'flavours' of Christianity (though mostly within Evangelical Protestantism) (see **Evangelical Christianity**); third, it seemed to spread like wildfire on both sides of the Atlantic simultaneously; fourth, it was more a grass-roots movement than one led from above; and fifth, it was very much a youth movement.

This was the era of hippies, of 'Peace and Love', of long hair and flamboyant clothes, of convention-challenging folk music by young and vibrant poets/singer-songwriters, of rebellion against authority, of protest, of peace demonstrations, of draft dodging, of psychedelic drugs and of relative affluence. Thus when young people were converted to born-again Christianity, it was natural that they would express their new faith in similar ways. Day-glo orange

287

Jesus stickers were everywhere. Bikers wrote 'Jesus' in studs on their leather jackets, and converted Hell's Angels wrote 'Heavenly Angels'. The Marxist slogan 'The Permanent Revolution' was appropriated by self-proclaimed 'Jesus Freaks'. Christian tracts became lively instead of solemn. Christian comic books appeared. The New Testament was published as a paperback entitled *The Jesus Book*. Christian folk groups and rock bands sprang up in every town, and Christian coffee bars or youth clubs where they could play. Street witnessing became commonplace.

There were larger-scale events as well. In Britain the 1972 Festival of Light was a campaign for Christian values and morality; the following year saw Spre-e 73 (based on Explo 72 in Dallas, Texas), a three-day festival of Spiritual Re-emphasis at Wembley Stadium in London, with Billy Graham preaching and Cliff Richard singing, amongst many others.

One of the hallmarks of the Jesus Movement was its grass-roots ecumenicalism. Young Christians might go to their own church on a Sunday morning, but in the evening they would descend *en masse* on whichever local church had the most interesting visiting preacher. Anglicans, Methodists, Baptists, United Reformed, Christian Brethren, Pentecostals, Salvation Army – the denominational distinctions of their parents were irrelevant although this was less true of Roman Catholics.

Added to the mix were House Churches (see **House Church Movement**), non-denominational groups with leaders who might or might not be ministers from established denominations. Whether or not they were charismatic in the Holy Spirit sense, the leaders were often charismatic personalities, and just sufficiently older than most of those who attended that they commanded respect, but not so old that they were of the parental (conventional and dull) generation. It was an environment with potential for abuse; and there is no doubt that some occurred.

The basic theology of the young Christians caught up in the Jesus Movement was a stripped-down version of **Evangelical Christianity**, and for some it was very simplistic: reading a tract with three proof-texts, then signing on the dotted line at the end, brought salvation from sin and eternal life with Jesus.

What many didn't realize at the time was that they were being exposed to a huge and often conflicting range of theological interpretations, even from the mainstream denominations. The many books which were available on church bookstalls and in Christian bookshops included the perennial favourites, David Wilkerson's *The Cross and the Switchblade* and Hal Lindsay's *The Late Great Planet Earth*, enthusiastic books on the Baptism in the Holy Spirit, or warning against it, books on healing, books against witchcraft and the Jehovah's Witnesses, books by the nineteenth-century evangelist Charles Finney, Corrie Ten Boom, Frank Buchmann (Moral Rearmament), Watchman Nee (the Local Church), and many others. It was often a confusing mixture of Dispensationalism, End-Time teaching, Creationism, Holiness, Word of Faith, Calvinist theology, Arminian theology, and much more.

In the **House Churches**, some of the teachings became quite unusual. Being outside the discipline of denominations with ministerial hierarchies and settled doctrinal stances, and with a strong emphasis on small group and personal Bible study and interpretation, heterodox doctrines surfaced (some of them echoing 'heresies' of the Early Church) on, for example, the nature of Christ, the nature of sin, salvation, universalism, and the End Times.

The strong emphasis on the imminent return of Christ was reflected in groups such as the Children of God (see **Family, The**), which began as an orthodox youth mission on a Californian Beach. The new emphasis on the Baptism in the Holy Spirit resulted in a number of individual movements, such as the **Jesus Army (The Jesus Fellowship Church)**, and also in the spread of Charismatic Christianity (see **Charismatic Movements**) into the mainstream denominations, perhaps the most significant and lasting effect of the Jesus Movement.

Further reading

Inaba, Keishin (2004) *Altruism in New Religious Movements: The Jesus Army and Friends of the Western Buddhist Order in Britain*, Okayama: University Education Press.

DAVID V. BARRETT

JIHADI MOVEMENTS

The concept of *jihad*, means simply struggle or exertion to the best of one's ability. Legally, there are two main types of jihad: greater jihad or jihad of the heart, tongue and hand which aims at the spiritual and intellectual development of the individual, and lesser jihad or jihad of the sword. The direct purpose of the latter has been widely understood to be the strengthening of Islam, the protection of believers and the elimination of unbelief. Closely linked with this notion of jihad is the division of the world into two realms the realm of Islam (*dar al-Islam*) and the realm of war (*dar al-harb*). Some schools of Islamic law also mention a third category or realm, the territory of treaty, which refers to an area whose non-Muslim inhabitants have concluded an armistice or treaty with Muslims and have agreed to pay the latter an annual sum in cash or kind. Twelver Shi'ite Islam (the type of Shi'ism that prevails for example in Iran and most of southern Iraq) holds that the obligation to undertake jihad is conditional on the manifest presence of the Imam. However, since their Imam went into hiding or concealment in 873 CE and though he is expected to return one day, the doctrine of jihad has no meaning in practice until that return takes place. This notwithstanding, the duty of defending Muslim lives and property remains. For jihad to be undertaken legally many requirements must be fulfilled including the obligation not to kill women and children unless they are actively fighting for the enemy. In the opinion of some schools of law only those who are fit and able to fight can be killed.

Countless movements in modern times, one of the most influential being the **Muslim Brotherhood** or Ikhwan founded by **Hassan al-Banna** (1906–49), have undertaken jihad and are frequently referred to as jihadi movements. **Sayyid Qutb**, a prominent member of the Brotherhood, is one of the most influential of the modern theorists of the use of jihad. Many of the modern writings on jihad have more of a mobilizing character than anything else, as do those that extol the bliss of martyrs in the Hereafter. Such writings appeared regularly during the 1967 Arab–Israeli conflict and were replete with feats of Islamic heroism and contempt for death.

It is also important to note that in modern times *fatwas* or pronouncements concerning jihad tend to emphasize much more than in the past that it is an individual rather than a collective obligation and give as one of the reasons the invasion of Islamic territory by non-Muslims. They see the struggle therefore as a defensive war, an explanation given by Osama bin Laden for his declaration of war against the United States and its allies. However, these fatwas do not give to any and every Muslim the right to wage jihad. Often they will stress that rules laid down by the Arab League for participation in jihad must be observed.

Contemporary Islamic reform movements are not all of a kind. So-called radical, Islamist groups active today do not all espouse militancy, though in recent times there has been a growing tendency among such movements to turn themselves into jihadi movements and support the use of force (Zahab and Roy, 2002). However, the most important concern of some these movements is the reform of Islam by peaceful means to enable Muslims to embrace in a positive and constructive way the modern world. Others remain determined to throw a 'cordon sanitaire' around Islam and protect it by jihad or holy war, if necessary, from what they perceive as the corrosive influences of modernization, which for them is synonymous with westernization. For the latter an essential part of this defence of Islam is the restoration of authentic Islam which includes the establishment of an Islamic state, as was attempted by the Taliban with the support of Al-Qaeda in Afghanistan, that is a state in which Shari'a law is recognized as the law of the land.

Further reading

Roy, Olivier (1998) 'The Divergent Ways of Fundamentalism and Islamism among Muslim Migrants' in Peter B. Clarke (ed.) *New Trends and Developments in the World of Islam*, London: Luzac, pp. 41–58.

Voll, John. O. (1991) 'Fundamentalism in the Sunni Arab World: Egypt and the Sudan' in Martin E. Marty and R. Scott Appleby (eds) *Fundamentalisms Observed*, Chicago: Chicago University Press, pp. 345–403.

Zahab, Mariam Abou and Roy, Olivier (2002) *Islamist Networks*, London: Hurst and Company.

PETER B. CLARKE

JUNG, CARL
(b. 1875; d. 1961)

Carl Gustav Jung, the son of a Protestant pastor, was brought up and educated in Basel, Switzerland, and spent all of his working life in and near Zurich. He trained as a psychiatrist and worked for nine years at Zurich's prestigious Burghölzli Mental Hospital before devoting himself exclusively to his private practice. Between 1906 and 1913 he collaborated with Sigmund Freud and was prominent in the development of the psychoanalytic movement. However, various theoretical and personal differences eventually led to the two psychologists' estrangement. After a period of reorientation, Jung developed, by 1921, his own distinctive theory, which was partly a return to traditions of psychological work that had influenced him before his collaboration with Freud. He developed and refined this theory for the remaining forty years of his life, influenced not only by his continuing clinical work but also by extensive studies of mythology, Gnosticism (see **Gnostic Movement**), alchemy, and eastern religions; by travels in India, Africa, and America; and by personal contacts with scientists (such as the physicist Wolfgang Pauli), theologians (such as the Dominican Father Victor White), and scholars of religion (such as the Sinologist Richard Wilhelm, the Indologist Heinrich Zimmer, and the theorist of myth Mircea Eliade).

Several features of Jung's theory make it distinctive from other depth psychological theories, such as Freud's psychoanalysis. For example, Jung postulates not just a personal unconscious, consisting of contents acquired in the course of one's personal life, but also a collective or transpersonal unconscious, consisting of contents that have not been personally acquired but are inherited by all humans. In addition to personal complexes, therefore, the psyche contains impersonal complexes or archetypes, which Jung defines as innate dispositions to apprehend the world in particular ways and which he considered to be as much spiritual as instinctive. Common archetypes are the persona, the shadow, the anima and animus, and the self. Unknowable in themselves, archetypes appear to consciousness in the form of personally and culturally conditioned archetypal images (often mythic personifications), identifiable by their spontaneity, autonomy, and numinosity. The archetype of the self occupies a special place as at once the symbol of psychic totality, the central archetype of the collective unconscious, and the goal of psychic development. The self is realized through the process Jung termed individuation, which involves the union of psychic opposites and the continual, arduous integration of unconscious contents into consciousness. Two other distinctive features of Jung's psychological theory are his insistence on the primacy of psychic reality (the view that other realities, whether material or spiritual, are only known to us as mediated through the psyche) and his notion of synchronicity (the view that psychic and physical events that are not connected causally can nevertheless be connected acausally through shared meaning).

The influence that Jung's personality and work have exerted on the **New Age Movement** and alternative **Spirituality** is widely acknowledged by participants and scholars. Jung's wide-ranging interests included magic, alchemy, astrology, **I Ching**, eastern religions, indigenous worldviews, myths, the feminine aspect of divinity, holistic science (see **Holistic Health Movement**), creative visualiza-

tion, hauntings, communications from discarnate spirits (see **Channelling**), and **UFOs**, and his example has undoubtedly helped to legitimate for many participants of New Age and alternative spirituality their own involvement in these and related areas. Moreover, in some of his later works, Jung explicitly drew attention to the inauguration of a new era with the imminent precession of the spring equinox into Aquarius (see **Age of Aquarius**). At a more conceptual level, the above-mentioned Jungian notions of the collective unconscious, archetypes, the self, individuation, the union of opposites, the primacy of psychic reality, and synchronicity have provided inspiration and support for New Age and related concerns with an inner spiritual dimension, autonomous inhabitants of that spiritual dimension, a higher self (see **Self-religion, The Self, and self**), **self-transformation**, holism, the participation of consciousness in the construction of reality, and the significance of paranormal events. Above all, Jung's psychology has been welcomed by many involved in alternative spirituality for its prioritizing of personal experience over institutionalized beliefs and its location of authority in the individual, spiritual self.

The affinities between Jung's work and New Age and alternative spirituality may be the result of shared heritage and shared contemporary concerns as well as of direct influence. Also, where there has been direct influence, this has often involved imperfect understanding and selective appropriation of Jungian ideas.

Further reading

Jung, C. G. (1995 [1961]) *Memories, Dreams, Reflections*, recorded and edited by Aniela Jaffé, translated by Richard and Clara Winston, London: Fontana.

Tacey, D. (2001) *Jung and the New Age*, Hove and Philadelphia: Brunner-Routledge.

RODERICK MAIN

K

KABBALAH

The term Kabbalah derives from the old Hebrew meaning 'received' or 'tradition', and has many variant spellings. It is a mystical Jewish system, developed gradually between the third and twelfth centuries CE, which attained its flowering in Moorish Spain. After the expulsion of the Jews from Spain in the late fifteenth century, it spread all over Europe including Israel, eventually becoming a major influence on Hasidism. According to hermetic tradition, Kabbalah originated as a direct transmission from God to his angels to Adam, and was then handed down orally to the Old Testament prophets.

Traditionally, access to the study of the Kabbalah has been very restricted. Requirements included being a Jewish male aged over 40, fluent in Hebrew, competent with the Torah and Mosaic law, and finding a willing teacher. In effect, it was mainly the preserve of rabbis. However, since the Middle Ages

its appeal has been growing beyond Judaism, and it filtered into Christianity through a Latin translation. Since the 1970s esoteric revival (see **Esoteric Movements**), there has been a big increase in numbers of people studying the Kabbalah. Few are able to meet the original entry requirements, but most contemporary groups outside orthodox Judaism teach simplified versions that do not require fluency in Hebrew or mastery of the complexities. Many of the older school of Kabbalistic students are unhappy about these developments, particularly orthodox rabbis.

Kabbalah teaches a mystical, holistic philosophy with a multilevel model of the universe and an immanentist view of God. Its main sacred text is the Zohar (Book of Splendour), a mystical commentary on the Torah. The aim is reunion of God with the world, a journey also undertaken by the student. The process is illustrated diagrammatically by Kabbalah's main symbol system, a complex variant of the tree of life, an ancient symbol found in many pre-Christian traditions. The journey begins with an emanation or 'lightning flash' from *Ein Sof* (boundless light), which flows through the *sefirot* (potentialities, vessels of divinity), down to Earth. There are similarities between the kabbalistic tree and the chakra system in **yoga**. Contemporary Kabbalah groups use the teachings for both philosophical enquiry and as a path of spiritual self-development relevant to daily life. In this respect they are in line with the **New Age Movement** and **Neo-Paganism**, which both incorporate Kabbalah into their teachings.

Currently, there are many groups and independent teachers of the Kabbalah all around the world. It is also still taught in some rabbinical schools in Israel and elsewhere. There is no central organization and it cannot be called an NRM. However, the Kabbalah Centre, based in Los Angeles with many branches worldwide including London, has been widely described as 'cultic' (see **Cult and New Religions**) and accused of various abuses and financial misdemeanours by some rabbis and journalists. It is led by the charismatic Rabbi Philip Berg (formerly Feivel Gruberger, insurance salesman) and its membership includes high-profile celebrities from the film and music industries. However, the Centre is unrepresentative of Kabbalah, and its success has triggered further popular interest in the teachings.

ELIZABETH PUTTICK

KARDEC, ALLAN
(b. 1804; d. 1869)

Kardecism was created in France during the nineteenth century around the figure of Allan Kardec. Kardec, the pseudonym used by Denizard Hippolyte Léon Rivail, was in no way exceptional nor did he display any mystical flair or eccentric attitudes. He was an extremely mundane figure, and played an organizing role within a spiritual movement. Though he was the center of a system based on the notion of 'mediumship', he was never himself a 'medium'. What he did do was affirm the fundamental importance of human intervention in a doctrine based on 'spirits'.

Rivail was born in Lyon, in 1804. His education was significantly marked by the period he spent in Switzerland at the school directed by J. H. Pestalozzi, a disciple of Rousseau's ideas. From 1820 onward, he lived in Paris, and dedicated himself to a career as an educator, teaching classes and composing educational manuals. It was not until the 1850s that circumstances led him to become the leader of a spiritual movement. During that time, he was studying magnetism and attending sessions with turning tables. Motivated by a group that habitually attended those sessions, he systematized a set of spiritual messages. The result is *The Spirits' Book*, which set out 'the principles of the spiritist doctrine (...) received and coordinated by Allan Kardec'. Rivail adopted the druid pseudonym that would have been, according to a spiritual revelation, his name in a previous incarnation.

The Spirits' Book, published in April of 1857 gave rise to a great deal of controversy and debate. In 1858 Kardec founded *La Revue Spirite*, in which he continued to compile spiritual messages, and the Spiritist Society of Paris, where sessions were held. Beginning in 1860, he started taking his ideas across France, and dedicated himself to guiding the groups that were multiplying within and outside the country. Kardec published four more principal works: *The Medium's Book* (1861), *The Gospel – Explained by the Spiritist Doctrine* (1864), *Heaven and Hell* (1865), *Genesis, Miracles and Predictions* (1868). He died in 1869, after which his wife and a group of collaborators took leadership in the movement.

EMERSON GIUMBELLI

Further reading

Vieira, Waldo (1971) *Allan Kardec. La Naissance du Spiritisme*, Paris: Hachette.

KARDECISM

Kardecism refers to the writings of Allan Kardec (see **Kardec, Allan**), beginning with the publication of *The Spirits' Book*, in 1857, in France. These works became a reference for a specific set of practices, doctrines, groups, and institutions, and influenced various other spiritist movements and currents that developed later.

The Spirits' Book sets out a system of doctrine that ranges from cosmological issues to what are called 'moral laws', maintaining as its core notion 'spirit', from whence the term 'spiritism' is derived to designate the new system. The authorship of these teachings is attributed to 'higher spirits', while Kardec is presented as a 'codifier', responsible for the organization of and commentary on messages obtained through the 'mediums' with whom he worked. This triad structures the practice of Kardecism, which takes 'spirits' as the primary source of teachings, but depends on intermediaries to materialize them and on human intervention to systematize them.

In the codification proposed by Kardec, the 'spirit' category fulfils a dual role. It first of all designates a principle prior to and opposed to 'matter'. Kardecism oscillates between a monist conception where the spirit is condensed in matter and needs it in order to purify itself; and a dualist conception where matter itself appears as an ontological domain, separate from that of the spirit. 'Spirit' is also understood as the base of individuality: each person is a spirit, created by God, originally ignorant, and destined to perfect itself morally and intellectually. All spirits, therefore, undergo a necessary evolution, and this conception places Kardecism within one of the dominant paradigms of nineteenth century thought: evolutionism. Thus, the spirit can always be evaluated with respect to its degree of spiritual evolution and its actual condition, whether incarnated or disincarnated.

Kardecism is not only devoted to shedding light on the human condition, conceived according to the possible relations between visible and invisible dimensions, but also to offering the keys to spiritual evolution, condensed in moral principles. In this respect, it may be seen from three perspectives. As a religion, once it is accepted as a 'revelation', offered by 'higher spirits', capable of adapting Christianity to modern times. That aspect, which provoked condemnations from various Christian churches, is already present in *The Spirits' Book*, but is fully developed in another work by Kardec, *The Gospel – Explained by the Spiritist Doctrine*. It can also be seen as a philosophy, in that it seeks to know the causes and nature of things, and the principles governing existence, albeit from a spiritualist as opposed to a materialist perspective. Finally, as a science, since it maintains that spiritual interventions may be proven through experimental means similar to those used to prove physical realities. Spiritists have also been attacked for making these claims and accused of dishonesty and even of scientific fraud.

'Mediumship' is seen as an attribute that allows disembodied spirits to intervene in the world where incarnate embodied spirits live. That intervention is permanent in its diffuse form, but may be canalized with the help of persons, the 'mediums', that display a capacity to materialize these interventions through the voice, through writing or in other physical ways, and to use it for specific aims, such as healing.

Kardecism is part of the spiritualist field of the nineteenth century, a field where **Theosophy** also originated, and where Occultism was revitalized. It also interacted with philosophical and scientific conceptions on the relationship between the physical and the moral. In this sense, it represents a specific elaboration of notions and practices associated with spiritual communication and disseminated throughout North America and Europe since the 1850s. Kardecism has had a profound impact on a number of new religions (see **New Religious Movements**) including **Santeria**. In Brazil, Kardecism became important in at least two senses. As a specific religious movement, Kardecism has developed into a sizeable movement with numerous institutions and provided ritual and cosmological material for movements from Umbanda to the New Age (see **New Age Movement**).

Further reading

Aubrée, M. and Laplantine, F. (1990) *La Table, le Livre, les Esprits*, Paris: J. C. Lattes.

Hess, David J. (1991) *Spirits and Scientists*, Pennsylvania: Penn State University Press.

EMERSON GIUMBELLI

KARINGA

Country of origin: Kenya

Karinga was the first anti-colonial religious movement to persist among the Agikuyu (Kikuyu).

Karinga was the name of one of two initiation guilds in alternating generation-sets, into which youths were accepted in mass circumcision ceremonies. The Ukabi guild comprised descendants from long interactions between Agikuyu and Maasai. Even the Gigikuyu word for God came from the Maa Engai and Ukabi is their name for Maasai.

Kenyatta's monthly journal, *Muigwithania* (*The Reconciler*) carried an article in 1928 requesting members of the politico-economic Kikuyu Central Association to call themselves '*Mugikuyu Karinga*' (real or indigenous Gikuyu).

Origin

The precipitating factor was the 'female circumcision controversy', which started in 1920, when the committee at the Church of Scotland mission at Tumutumu divided between the Kirore, those who put their thumb-print to the resolutions demanding abolition, and the Karinga, those who refused. This division was reinforced by pressure on Christians to make the Thogoto Declaration of 1929 renouncing the practice under oath and on pain of excommunication. To abolish the initiation rite was seen as tantamount to the extermination of the people.

In the late 1920s the Irungu generation-set was due to take over from the Mwangi, but the missions were very much against Christians being pressed to provide goats for sacrifice. Even the liberal missionary collaborated with the district commissioner to have police standing over the killing of goats to ensure that it was merely a culinary affair. For the Agikuyu, 'it became a kind of useless thing'. With the suppression of initiation guilds, Karinga was freed to be used in the new religio-political way.

The crisis of 1929 began a split between those who would form in 1934 the Kikuyu Independent Schools Association, which became associated with the African Independent Pentecostal Church, and the Kikuyu Karinga Educational Association founded in 1933. Kenyatta associated himself with the Karinga churches without publicizing his churchmanship. The Karinga anthem, the *Muthirigu*, fostered an ethos of primary resistance to state government, nourishing independency for the **African Orthodox Church**, **Mau Mau**, and at the turn of the millennium, **Mungiki**.

Current organization and practice

Karinga churches combine Anglican liturgy with Gikuyu social institutions. They chant canticles and the Lord's Prayer and appoint 'Bishops', 'Archdeacons', and 'Rural Deans'. A need for training pastors has long been acknowledged and a college is now being started. Karinga cannot be distinguished by their dress, apart from their leaders in church. Their distinctive emphasis still concerns rites of passage, especially polygyny and female circumcision which, though covert in society happens much more frequently than the 5 per cent that the abolitionist churches estimate, and as the upsurge in Mwea in 2002 and its continued practice in Nairobi suggest. Even with an enormous state school system Karinga again have started independent schools, and from 2001 have been appealing for the return of their schools allegedly taken over by the mission schools with the support of the government in the Mau Mau emergency.

BEN KNIGHTON

KHAN, PIR VILAYAT INAYAT

Khan was born in London in 1916. His father Pir-o-Murshid Inayat Khan was the founder of the Sufi Order International, and his mother Ora Baker was a cousin of Mary Baker Eddy, founder of the Christian Science Movement. The young Khan was educated in Paris and London, studying philosophy, psychology, and musical composition. In 1926 he was designated by his father to be his successor as head of the International Sufi Movement. Khan served as an officer in the British Navy in the Second World War. His sister Noor-un-Nisa Inayat Khan served in the French Resistance as a radio operator, liaising with the Allies until killed in Dachau concentration camp. After the war, Khan travelled widely in India and the Middle East, pursuing his spiritual training, studying under various teachers, seeking to find a contemporary perspective on Sufi teachings.

Lineage is considered all-important in Sufism, and Pir Vilayat Inayat Khan is the thirty-seventh Hazrat (leader) in the lineage of the Chishti Sufi Order of India. Recently, his son Pir Zia Khan succeeded him as the thirty-eighth leader. The Sufi Order International has benefited from a strong western interest in Sufism, in particular the poems of Jalalludin Rumi, the Anatolian mystic. It is a non-Islamic school, so members are not required to be Muslims before joining, unlike the majority of orders including Idries Shah's order.

The Sufi Order International has five main branches of activity:

1. An esoteric school, the main activity of the movement. This uses asceticism as its main means of spiritual development. There are no authoritative gurus, but rather teachers.
2. A healing order, operating in fourteen countries. This is devoted to spiritual healing methods, and anyone can apply for a free healing session.
3. Ziraat, an initiating practice.

4. Universal Worship, a form of non-denominational worship, based on Sufi precepts
5. Kinship, or community spirit.

ELIZABETH PUTTICK

KIMBANGU, SIMON

Simon Kimbangu was born at N'kamba in the Lower Congo in 1887. He appears to have received a 'call' in 1918, at the time of both the worldwide flu epidemic and the construction of a railroad between Kinshasa and the coast which were causing severe loss of life. Kimbangu tried to run away from the persistent call, but he eventually responded. On 6 April 1921, the date regarded by his followers as the founding of the **Kimbanguism** movement, Simon entered the house of a woman called Nkiantondo who was critically ill in bed at Ngombe Kinsuka opposite N'kamba. He is said to have laid hands on her and healed her. Other miracles apparently followed, including the lame walking, the blind seeing, and even a dead child being raised. People were convinced that God was doing an extraordinary work through this man, and they flocked to the village in vast numbers to seek healing, and to listen to his teaching.

The Belgian authorities quickly became alarmed. The colonial administrator of the district, Léon Morel, went to N'kamba to interview Kimbangu. But the latter, along with his followers, broke out in tongues (glossolalia). In his report Morel declared that Kimbangu and his followers were not in possession of their right senses, and that he was creating a new religion with elements of Protestantism blended with fetishism. Such was the widespread uproar that a state of emergency was declared. In September 1921 Simon Kimbangu was arrested, as were his wife and three children, who

were all then split up. Kimbangu was accused of sedition and hostility towards whites and was sentenced to death. After lobbying by the Baptist Missionary Society the sentence was commuted to life imprisonment. He was given 120 lashes and transported to Lubumbashi (formerly Elizabethville) in the deep southeast of the country – over 1,500 miles from his home. He spent the next thirty years in solitary confinement and never again saw his wife, his children, nor his home. He died in prison on 12 October 1951, and on his death his relatives were not informed.

RICHARD HOSKINS

KIMBANGUISM

Kimbanguism originated in the Democratic Republic of the Congo (formerly Zaire), and has spread to many countries in Africa and beyond. The movement takes its name from the founder Simon Kimbangu (see **Kimbangu, Simon**). It claims to have some 15 million followers worldwide, although this is unproven.

Origins

Simon Kimbangu was born at N'kamba near MbanzaNgungu in the Lower Congo in 1887. Simon received instruction from Baptist missionaries, and was baptized in July 1915 along with his wife Mivulu Marie near NgombeLutete. In 1918 Kimbangu believed he received a call from God to go and look after his people for the Europeans had been unfaithful to the call of Christ.

On 6 April 1921 Kimbangu began his ministry of healing, and extraordinary scenes are said to have followed, with vast numbers flocking to N'kamba to hear his message and to be healed. But this was too much for the Belgian colonial power who feared a political uprising. A state of emergency was declared, and in

September 1921 Kimbangu was arrested, flogged, and sent into exile to what is now Lubumbashi: 1,500 miles from his home. He died in solitary confinement on 12 October 1951.

Between his deportation and death Kimbangu was not able to see his wife and three sons again. But Kimbanguists are convinced of a rash of miraculous appearances by Simon to people all over the Congo, and beyond, whilst he was still technically in prison. These are not simply visitations through visions and dreams (although Kimbangu is said to appear to them in these ways too) but actual fleshly manifestations.

Persecution

The persecution of Kimbanguists in the period of Kimbangu's solitary confinement was severe. Wherever Kimbanguists were found throughout the Congo there were deportations to other areas, so that an oft-quoted figure of 37,000 deportations of heads of families (meaning at least 100,000 people in total) between 1921 and 1959 is possible, although this may be exaggeration. During those years Kimbangu's wife, Mivulu Marie, effectively helped run the movement. Following her death in 1959 the third son, Joseph Diangienda, was appointed Spiritual Head, something which Kimbangu himself had instructed shortly before being deported.

Diangienda's leadership was an important period for the Kimbanguists. It was a time of expansion and conscious unification. Diangienda himself travelled widely around the Congo and beyond. In addition he presided over the vital decision of the Kimbanguists to join the World Council of Churches – something which took place on 16 August 1969. They are now officially known as The Church of Jesus Christ on Earth through his Special Envoy Simon Kimbangu: the term 'Special Envoy' replacing a previous title of 'Prophet', probably to confer a more pneumatological title on the founder.

Practices today

Kimbanguist practices are a blend of different influences. Main church services take place on Sundays. However, prayers are also held on other days: officially five times a day, though the morning and evening prayers are the most publicly attended of these. Polygamy, smoking, drugs, alcohol, the eating of pork, sleeping naked, and trading on Sundays are all forbidden. Wailing at the time of death is also forbidden, as is dancing unless confined to a gentle rhythmic movement. But marching, especially during collections when there is a formal march-past in front of the most senior person present, is very much encouraged. Among other positive obligations, Kimbanguists have to pray and read the Bible regularly. Shoes are removed before entering places of worship because they are said to be holy ground. All women are required to cover their heads, and are required to dress modestly (e.g. to cover their legs). Kimbanguists prefer the colours of green and white, and most of their churches, and indeed the believers themselves, are decked out in these two colours. Green is said to represent hope, and white purity. Kimbanguists have their own alphabet: a language which they believe has been given to them miraculously by Kimbangu known as Mandombe.

Services close out with major social collections, known as *nsinnsini* for which there are often specific projects directed by the leaders of the Church. These include the running of a hospital in Kinshasa and medical dispensaries elsewhere. The temple at N'kamba is the most famous example of such a project.

The 37,000 capacity temple was built with the help of ordinary believers, many of whom carried rocks and stones several kilometres to the site on the hill at N'kamba. The village itself, known by believers as 'N'kamba New Jerusalem', has regular numbers of visitors. Many of them go to bathe in a site where they believe there is holy water: and both this water, and the very soil from N'kamba, are taken elsewhere for healing.

A more recent major project has been the building of a substantial number of luxury apartments near N'kamba at Kendolo. These appartments have been constructed in response to a prophecy 'received' by the Church that many Afro-Americans will return to Africa – and specifically to N'kamba. Great financial sacrifice has been extracted from ordinary believers for this project, but it has also had the benefit of bringing in considerable interest, and with it money, from the United States.

Doctrinally, and after much thought, the Church eventually settled on the doctrine that Simon Kimbangu is the 'Holy Spirit made flesh' and, as such, the Special Envoy of Christ. However, controversy was sparked when the late leader of the Church, Diulangana Kuntima, the only surviving son of Kimbangu, not only announced that he was Christ returned, but also moved the date of Christmas to 25 May, which happened to be his own birthday. On his death in 2001 he was succeeded by the oldest surviving grandchild of Simon Kimbangu.

The Kimbanguists are strongest in the Congo area, but have members in other central African countries, as well as France, Belgium, the United Kingdom, and the United States.

Further reading

Hoskins, R. (2002) *Kimbanguism*, London: Hurst & Co Ltd.

Martin, M.-L. (1975) *Kimbangu: An African Prophet and His Church,* Oxford: Blackwell.

RICHARD HOSKINS

KOFUKU-NO-KAGAKU

The literal translation of this movement's Japanese name is the 'science of happiness', but it generally means *The Institute for Research in Human Happiness* (or IRH), and this is its official English name. IRH was established in October 1986 in Tokyo by the 30-year-old former businessman, **Ryuho Okawa** (1956–). In 1981, just before graduating from Tokyo University in Law, Okawa's spiritual experiences suddenly began; he is said to have been contacted by a number of spirits, many of whom were extremely well known religious figures, such as Jesus, Moses, Confucius, and the Buddha. After continuous discourses with the spirits, Okawa gradually became aware of his mission to save the world, and of his identity as the reincarnation of Gautama Buddha and the embodiment of *El Cantare*, or the 'Grand Spirit of the Terrestrial Spirit Group' (Okawa, 1994). His discourses with high, divine spirits were taped, edited and published by his father, Saburo Yoshikawa, whose influence on Okawa becoming a religious leader is said to have been significant. Yoshikawa, who had studied various religious ideas in the Christian Church, in Seicho-no-Ie, and in **God Light Association** (GLA), taught his two young sons the basics of the Bible, Zen Buddhism, Kantian thought and the Communist Manifesto. Despite his continuous religious experiences, Okawa carried on his business life with considerable success in one of Japan's major trading houses, and was later sent to the firm's US Headquarters in New York. However, after strong 'persuasion' by many divine spirits, including the spirits of Jesus, **Nichiren** and Amaterasu O-mikami, he finally left the trading house in July 1986 and established his religious movement three months later. During the first three years Okawa concentrated on educating his followers. He limited the number of members by assigning an entrance exam, and only started missionary activities in 1990. In July 1991, IRH held its first 'Birthday Festival' for its founder in Tokyo Dome (a major indoor baseball stadium in Tokyo) and claimed that the number of members had reached 1.5 million (IRH claimed ten million followers worldwide in 1995). During the Festival, Okawa revealed his true identity as El Cantare for the first time. In the same year, the movement officially became a 'religion' by obtaining Religious Juridical Persons status. IRH's purpose built Head Office is in central Tokyo, and it has built a number of retreat centres, called *Shoshin-kan*, across Japan; it has major temples in Utsunomiya City and in Tokyo.

The members study and put into practice IRH's fundamental doctrine, called the Fourfold Path, which consists of 'love', 'knowledge (of the truth)', 'self-reflection' and 'development'. The two most important tasks for the members are to practise the 'Quest for the Right Mind' or the mind of the Buddha, and to establish the 'Buddha Land – Utopia' on earth. IRH's doctrine became more Buddhist orientated after 1992, and especially after 1994, devotion to the Buddhist concept of the 'Three Jewels', in this case the Buddha (El Cantare/ Okawa), Dharma (Okawa's teaching) and Sangha (IRH) have been of supreme importance to the believers. According to Kofuku-no-Kagaku, humans are reincarnated on earth on an average of about every 300 years in order to 'polish' their souls and to work towards establishing Utopia on earth. The power

of the Three Jewels is considered vital in achieving these objectives.

In 1991 IRH was severely criticized by *Kôdan-sha*, one of the largest publishing companies in Japan, and a number of court cases took place between them. The Publisher was accused of publishing magazines that printed 'fabrication and slander' about IRH and Okawa, but after a number of court cases, the Japanese Supreme Court ordered the Publisher to pay a total of three million yen (*c*. £16,000) to IRH in 2001.

Further reading

Astley, T. (1995) 'The Transformation of a Recent Japanese New Religion: Okawa Ryuho and Kofuku-no-Kagaku', *Japanese Journal of Religious Studies*, 22(3–4), 343–80.

Fukui, M. (1999) 'Kofuku-no-Kagaku: The Institute for Research in Human Happiness', in Peter B. Clarke (ed.) *A Bibliography of Japanese New Religious Movements with Annotations*, pp. 149–67.

Okawa, R. (1994) *The Laws of the Sun. The Revelation of Buddha that Enlightens the New Age*, London: Penguin Books.

Yamashita, A. (1998) 'The "Eschatology" of Japanese New and New New Religions: From Tenrikyo to Kofuku-no-Kagaku', *Japanese Religions*, 23(1–2) January, 125–42.

MASAKI FUKUI

KONKOKYO

Founder: Kawate, Bunjiro
(b. 1814; d. 1883)

Founded in 1859 by the peasant farmer Kawate Bunjiro (1814–83) in Okayama prefecture Konkokyo's (Religion of Golden Light) mission is to pray and search for peace and happiness for humanity. Its founder was 'called' to undertake this mission by the malevolent golden Kami or God Konjin whom, according to the movement's accounts of his life, he had offended. This deity inflicted on Kawate an illness before requesting him to retire from farming and devote himself to the work of peace and the performance and teaching of *toritsugi*-meditation. From 1959 Kawate came to regard Konjin not as a malevolent deity but as the Golden Kami of Heaven and Earth (Tenchi Kane No Kami) or Konko Daijin (the Great Kami of Golden Light) who had taken possession of his body.

Although the God it worships, Konko Daijin, was not a recognized Shinto deity nor toritsugi a recognized Shinto practice, Konkokyo was employed by the Meiji government (1868–1912) to support its endeavour to promote **State Shinto**. In 1900 the Government recognized Konkokyo as a Shinto sect and in furthering the goal of promoting Shinto Hagio, son of the founder, became a national evangelist in 1900 of State Shinto. Much later in the 1980s Konkokyo was to reject the label Shinto and its role in advancing State Shinto prior to 1945.

In Konkokyo's teachings God and human beings are seen as interdependent and their relationship is reciprocal leading to the fulfilment of both.

The deity known as Principle Parent of the Universe or Tenchi Kane no Kame is believed to be the source of all life in the Universe. Access to the Principle Parent for the purpose of spiritual counselling (toritsugi) can be had through the mediation of a priest who experiences the feelings and desires of both the God and the worshippers. Through toritsugi people are connected to the Principle Parent and receive the power to overcome human sorrow and pain.

As in the case of many Japanese new religions (see **New Religions (Japan)**) the leader or *kyoshu* of the movement is chosen from among the founder's descendents. The movement's headquarters is in Okayama and there is an international Centre in Tokyo. In Japan Konkokyo is divided into administrative districts each with their own local church. The number of adherents is around 400,000.

The membership overseas, for example, in San Francisco, remains small and continues to consist for the most part of ethnic Japanese.

Further reading

Inoue, N. (1991) 'The Dilemma of Japanese-American Society – A Case Study of State Shinto in North America', *Japanese Journal of Religious Studies*, 18(2–3), 133–50.

McFarland, H. N. (1967) *The Rush Hour of the Gods: A Study of New Religious Movements in Japan*, New York: Macmillan.

PETER B. CLARKE

KRISTO ASAFO (CHRIST REFORMED CHURCH)

Kristo Asafo (Christ Reformed Church) is an African Independent Church (see **African Independent Churchs**) founded in 1971 in Accra capital of Ghana. The church is a member of the Sabbath Association of Ghana. This is an ecumenical organization that unites churches that identify and recognize Saturday as the Sabbath. The most distinctive features of Kristo Asafo, which sets it apart from other African Initiated Churches in Ghana, are its investment in agriculture, manufacturing and industry and its philanthropy. The founder, Apostle Dr Kwadwo Safo has received many honors including a State honor in Ghana.

Kristo Asafo was started as a prayer group in 1969 and was transformed into a Church on 3 February 1971. Currently, the church has 140 branches throughout Ghana with an approximate membership of about 6,000. It also has congregations in Verona and London.

The founder, Apostle Kwadwo Safo was born in 1948 in the Ashanti Region of Ghana. A welding technician by profession, he has received several awards including an honorary Doctorate Degree from the University of Ghana, Legon; and the Grand Medal, Civil Division of the State of Ghana for his exemplary leadership and remarkable philanthropy.

Kristo Asafo church holds worship services at 3 p.m. on Saturdays. The liturgy consists of praises from various choirs, a sermon, followed by prayers and announcements. Participants worship barefooted. Though women participate in Church activities and sit on the National Executive council of the church, they are not allowed to preach. Women wear veils during worship.

Fundamental to Kristo Asafo beliefs are biblical injunctions on Christians to care for the needy. The motto of the Church is 'Service to mankind is service to God'. The church regularly visits hospitals, prisons, orphanages and educational institutions, etc. and makes substantive donations to them. In 1997, for instance they made a large donation to the University of Ghana, Legon towards the building of a students' hostel.

Kristo Asafo is also renowned for its agricultural activities. Each congregation has a farm where youth volunteer and go through a regimented period of training and farming. This creates employment opportunities on farms for members and is seen as stemming the drift from rural farming communities to the urban towns. The Church also trains members and non-members in various kinds of professions and trades such as carpentry, welding, and mechanics. It manufactures and markets electronic, agricultural and other equipment at affordable prices for small-scale businesses.

The major public celebration of the church is an annual food, technology and charity exhibition in support of the needy. It showcases farm produce and other products of the Church during the exhibition. At the end of the fair, farm produce and machinery are distributed to selected needy persons and institutions.

The church and the founder run a group of companies. Kristo Asafo Farms Ltd produces pineapples and papaws for export to Europe. Other businesses distinct from the Church but associated with the founder include the Great Kosa Herbal Clinic (which produces and dispenses herbal medicine), Great Kosa Company Limited (an engineering company) and the Great Imperial Company Limited (runs long distance transport). These businesses also provide training and employment avenues for members of the church and the public.

The church also has an award winning entertainment group, the Kristo Asafo Concert Party group. Concert Party is a popular form of entertainment in Ghana dating back to the 1950s. Drawing on folklorist ideas, the group performs comedy sketches often with moral teaching of Christian revivalist character interspaced with urban popular music. Kristo Asafo is the main Church in Ghana that explores this avenue of popular drama to reach out with the Gospel.

A National Executive Council (NEC) and other subsidiary councils of pastors and elders at the regional, district and branch levels run the church under the overall leadership of Apostle Dr. Kwadwo Safo.

Further reading

Website http://www.kristoasafo.com

ELOM DOVLO

KUROZUMIKYÔ

Founded in 1814 by the Shinto priest Kurozumi Munetada (1780–1850), Kurozumikyô is one of the oldest Japanese new religions. Mainly a rural group, it also commands a significant urban membership, amounting to about 20 per cent of its total membership of 220,000. Its founding illuminates the process by which sectarian forms of Shinto came into being as new religions (see **New Religion (Japan)**).

Kurozumi believed filial piety to be the highest good. He contracted tuberculosis following the 1812 death of his parents, but worship of the sun restored him. The sun seemed to come down from the sky, enter his body, and pervade his entire being, as if he had swallowed it. This was an experience of union with the Sun Goddess Amaterasu, which he called the Direct Receipt of the Heavenly Mission. This experience awakened Kurozumi to humanity's essential oneness with Amaterasu, the source of all life in the universe. He came to believe that worship of the rising sun promotes health by strengthening humanity's unity with Amaterasu. Kurozumi saw all existence pervaded with vitality, which he called *yôki*, literally '*yang* essence', which humanity may acquire through worship of the rising sun, the central practice of Kurozumikyô. Called *nippai*, sun worship consists of inhaling the rays of the sun as it rises, with a swallowing motion.

Recognizing the religious aspirations and abilities of women, Kurozumi emphasized human equality in a distinct departure from the widespread denigration of women typical in other religions, and from the rigid class structure of the day. Kurozumi received all who came to him for healing, but charged no fees, thus undermining the livelihood of local healers, some of whom retaliated against him violently. Though he was originally attached to a Shinto shrine, increasing numbers of followers and his distinctive doctrine led to the establishment of a separate movement outside shrine Shinto (see **State Shinto**). Kurozumi was succeeded by his son. During the Meiji period (1868–1912), Kurozumikyô grew rapidly, establishing branch churches throughout Japan.

Further reading

Hardacre, H. (1986) *Kurozumikyô and the New Religions of Japan*, Princeton: Princeton University Press.

HELEN HARDACRE

303

L

LATIHAN

'Latihan' (from the Indonesian, meaning 'practice' or 'exercise') is the core spiritual activity of **SUBUD**, an international movement that originated in Java in the 1920s. The practice, preformed in gender-segregated groups twice weekly for half an hour and privately at home for an additional half hour, involves an act of profound surrender to the will of God and acceptance of the divinely-inspired involuntary movements and sounds that the body then makes. These are understood as signs of purification occurring in the practitioner's physical, emotional, mental and spiritual bodies and as indications of the practitioner's opening to the action of God's will in her everyday life. More subtle spiritual experiences may then follow.

SUBUD's *latihan* (short for *latihan kejiwaan*, 'spiritual practice') came to the movement's founder, Muhammad Subuh Sumohadiwidjojo, in 1925 as a revelation from God while he was still a young civil servant and student of a Naqsyabandi Sufi master. Late one night, Bapak (I., 'Mr', 'father') Subuh was struck by a marvellous ball of white light (*wahyu*), such as, in Javanese tradition, bestows supernatural power upon gurus and princes destined to assume authority. He surrendered to God (honouring the fundamental requirement of the Islamic faith) and felt his being fill with light. He was then mysteriously propelled to arise and perform two sets (*rakaat*) of the basic Muslim prayers.

For several years thereafter he was miraculously wakened at night in the hours when Sufis do their *dzikir* (rhymic spiritual exercises) and was moved to perform not just conventional acts of Muslim prayer and *dzikir*, but martial arts (*pencak silat*) movements and even dancing and singing. Visions and other wonderful experiences followed.

Bapak Subuh then began teaching the practice to others. He emphasized that what happens following the act of surrender to God differs from individual to individual, according to their character and God's will for them.

Prospective members of SUBUD wishing to learn the *latihan* go through a probationary period of three months. Then a 'helper' (an experienced and authorized member of the organization) 'opens' the new member by performing the *latihan* together with the new person.

JULIA DAY HOWELL

LEARY, TIMOTHY
(b. 1920; d. 1996)

Proponent of 'psychedelic religion', Timothy Leary lectured in psychology at Harvard University. In 1960 a Mexican anthropologist introduced him to tioanactyle, which resulted in his first 'trip'. Together with his colleague Richard Alpert (a.k.a. **Baba Ram Das**), Leary experimented with LSD and other hallucinogenic drugs, and was finally dismissed from his post in 1963. Leary and Alpert moved to the Ananda Ashram, in Millbrook, New York, owned by William A. Hitchcock, where they continued their experiments under the name of the Castalia Institute. Unlike some other psychedelic experimenters, Leary advocated the use of drugs in a supervised, controlled environment. Leary founded the League for Spiritual Discovery (LSD), which had the declared aim of using psychedelic drugs for religious purposes. *The Psychedelic Experience* was co-authored with Richard Alpert and Ralph Metzner, and appeared in 1964. From the mid-1960s Leary appeared at musical and public meetings promoting LSD.

Also in the Ananda Ashram was Art Kleps, who founded the Original Kleptonian Neo-American Church in 1964 (incorporated in 1967). Kleps, together with Leary, Alpert, Hitchcock, Joseph Gross, and William Haines (a.k.a. Sri Sankara), formed the original Board of Directors – 'Board of Toads', as they called themselves – for the purpose of campaigning for the legalization of drugs for religious purposes. Leary authored *The Neo-American Church Catechism and Handbook* (1967), which identified four religious organizations that used drugs as sacraments: the Neo-Kleptonian Church, the Church of the Awakening, the Native American Church, and the League for Spiritual Discovery.

In 1966, LSD was declared illegal in the USA, except for authorized research. Leary continued to promote its use, and having been described by US President Richard Nixon as 'the most dangerous man in America', he was arrested and imprisoned. He escaped from prison in 1970, and sought asylum in Switzerland; however, he was recaptured in 1973. His book *Jail Notes* (1970) was written during the early months of his sentence, and bears an introduction by Allen Ginsburg. His sentence was finally commuted in 1976.

Leary claimed to perceive affinities between psychedelic experiences and eastern religions, regarding *The Tibetan Book of the Dead* and the *Tao Te Ching* (1966) in particular as psychedelic works. (He claimed that numerous verses by Lao Tzu were drug-induced.) His best known writing, *Psychedelic Prayers after the Tao Te Ching* (1966) develops this thesis, and was regarded as the principal spiritual manual by his followers.

Further reading

Leary, T. R. (1966) *Psychedelic Prayers after The Tao Te Ching*, New Hyde Park, NY: University Press.

Leary, T. R. (1967) *The Neo-American Church Catechism and Handbook*, Millbrook, NY: Kriya Press of the Sri Ram Ashrama.

Leary, T. R. (1970) *Jail Notes*, New York: Douglas Book Corporation.

Leary, T. R. (1983) *Flashbacks: An Autobiography*, Los Angeles: Houghton Mifflin, (York: University Books, 1964).

Leary, T. R., Alpert, R. and Metzner R. (1995) *The Psychedelic Experience*, New York: Citadel Press.

GEORGE CHRYSSIDES

LECTORIUM ROSICRUCIANUM

Founder: Jan van Rijckenborgh

The Lectorium Rosicrucianum is one of the largest Rosicrucian organizations in the world (see **Rosicrucian Order, Crotona Fellowship**). In the 1920s, Jan Leene (1896–1968), who wrote under the pen name of Jan van Rijckenborgh, and later emerged as a noted author of writings on the German mystic Jacob Böhme (1575–1624), and his brother Zwier Wilhelm Leene (1892–1938) became the two most important leaders in the Netherlands of the Rosicrucian Fellowship, which had been established ten years before in California by Max Heindel (pseudonym of Carl Louis von Grasshoff (1865–1919)). The spiritual experience regarded as the birth of the movement dates back to 24 August 1924. However, the Leene brothers, who were joined in 1930 by Henny Stok-Huyser (1902–90, pen name: Catharose de Petri), only declared their independence from the Rosicrucian Fellowship in 1935, when they established an independent Rosicrucian Society (Rozekruisers Genootschap.) When the Nazis occupied Holland the movement was forbidden, its possessions confiscated, its temples razed, and several members arrested (some died in the concentration camps, including several Jewish members). Re-emerging from the aftermath of the war, the movement adopted the name Lectorium Rosicrucianum in 1945.

Through their interest in Catharism, the Dutch founders met Antonin Gadal (1871–1962) in France in 1948. Gadal was a key figure in the modern Cathar revival, and in 1957 he became the first president of the Lectorium's French branch. At the same time, the Lectorium began to spread from Holland to a number of other countries. The most notable success came, however, after the death of both Van Rijckenborgh (1968) and De Petri (1990) (Zwier W. Leene died in 1938), and an International Spiritual Directorate was established in their place. The approximately 15,000 adherents are divided into 14,000 'pupils' and about 1,000 'members' (i.e. candidates awaiting admission as pupils.)

Only the pupils, at the end of their probationary period, are allowed to attend monthly services in the Lectorium's temples and engage themselves in a way of life presented as a search for mental, emotional and physical purification, encouraged by vegetarianism, and abstinence from alcohol, tobacco and drugs. There is also a clear reticence with regard to 'unhealthy influences', including the more obvious ones transmitted by the media (television, in particular, is regarded as suspicious,) and the more subtle influences coming from the world of the dead (with a strong rejection of spiritualist and occult practices).

The Lectorium proposes a classical gnostic dualism (organized according to a language and models often taken directly from the Cathar tradition) between the divine world (static) and the natural world (dialectic), of which the true God is not the creator. Humans are believed to be divine in origin, but have forgotten their true source. The path of transfiguration, as proposed by the Lectorium, aims to find and awaken the divine spark ('the rose of the heart', i.e. the residual divine component of each human being), and to lead humans back to their original condition.

Further reading

Rijckenborgh, J. Van (1980) *The Gnosis in Present-Day Manifestation,* Harlem (The Netherlands): Rozekruis Press.

MASSIMO INTROVIGNE

LEFEBVRE MOVEMENT

The Lefebvre movement is a group of traditionalist Roman Catholics, regarded by the Vatican as being in schism from the official Church. It takes its name from the French Archbishop Marcel Lefebvre (1905–91). He had studied for the priesthood in Rome and then served for a time in a parish in an industrial suburb of Lille before deciding to become a missionary. He joined the Holy Ghost Fathers (the Spiritans) and was sent to work in Gabon. He became the first Archbishop of Dakar in Senegal, and Apostolic Delegate (papal representative) for the whole of West Africa. He resigned the see in 1962 to allow the appointment of a black bishop, and Pope John XXIII appointed him to the diocese of Tulle in France

The same year he was elected Superior General of his Order. During the Catholic Church's Second Vatican Council (1962–5) he was a founder member of the 'International committee of fathers' (*Coetus Internationalis Patrum*), a group which vigorously opposed some of the reforms which the Council eventually put in train. He took a strong stance against, in particular, the Declaration on Religious Liberty. The Church, he later claimed, had finally embraced the principles of the French Revolution, of liberty (religious liberty), equality (the teaching on the collegiality, i.e., co-responsibility for the governance of the Church), and fraternity (ecumenism). 'The Church consummated marriage with the Revolution' he said in a speech at Lille in 1976. 'I do not reject everything about the Council', he once wrote, 'but I still think it is the greatest disaster not only of this century but of any century since the foundation of the Church'. Unlike some of the other dissident groups which arose after the Council, the Lefebvre movement constitutes a clear group.

In 1970, before his formal separation from the Church, Lefebvre created the Society of St Pius X, named after the Pope who had conducted a campaign at the beginning of the twentieth century against the heresy of Modernism into which, in the Archbishop's view, the Church had fallen after Vatican II. The Society of Pius X was, and is, a society of priests who share the views of their founder on the departure of the Catholic Church from its traditional teaching on a whole manner of issues. Although Lefebvre himself took issue with the Church on doctrinal matters, like other dissident Catholic groups Lefebvrist hostility to the Vatican has tended to focus on the new liturgy of the mass imposed on the whole Church by Pope Paul VI soon after the Council had ended. Shortly after the Society of St Pius X was founded, Lefebvre opened a seminary at Ecône in Switzerland where the first priests of his Society were ordained in 1976. This ordination, illicit in the Vatican's eyes, led in the July of that year to the suspension from his priestly role of Lefebvre himself.

Shortly after Pope John Paul II was elected in 1978 he met the Archbishop, and it for a time seemed that the schism would be resolved. A decade later, however, Lefebvre finally rebuffed Rome's overtures and in June 1988 ordained four bishops to ensure the survival of his Society. He was then declared formally to be in schism. His seminary continues to flourish, claiming some 150 seminarians and, worldwide, 420 clergy, with about 150,000 adherents to the movement's brand of traditional Catholicism.

At the time of the split with Rome a number of priests left the Society of St Pius X in order to remain linked to the papacy. For them a 'Fraternity of St Peter' was established. Its members were allowed to continue using the old (Latin or 'Tridentine') rite of the liturgy, sometimes known as the 'order of St Pius V', the form of the liturgy imposed on the Western Catholic Church in the sixteenth century in the aftermath of an earlier Council, the Council of Trent. It is part of the Lefebvrist argument against official Roman Catholicism that the Roman Catholic Church is an unchanging institution, with a divine and unchanging constitution, and consequently the reforms introduced at Vatican II were illegitimate. No pope, they argue, can oblige Catholics to accept something which is doctrinally unsound such as the new liturgy, but the pope is not technically an apostate, simply wrong on this and other (such as the treatment of Archbishop Lefebvre himself) issues. The pope has therefore not forfeited all his authority and they still name the pope in their liturgical worship. In this they are at odds with the rather more consistent **Sedevacantists** who believe that there is no pope.

Further reading

Vatican Encounter with Archbishop Marcel Lefebvre (1978) Kansas City: Sheed, Andrews and McMeel.

MICHAEL WALSH

LEGIÃO DA BOA VONTADE

Founder: Alziro Zarur

Country of origin: Brazil

Legião da Boa Vontade (Good Will Legion) was founded by Alziro Zarur (1914–79) on 1 January 1950, in Brazil. Zarur claimed that he had created an ecumenical organization that aimed to promote universal solidarity. A reader and follower of the ideas of **Allan Kardec**, Zarur contended that Kardec had not finished his mission and that he had come to complete it. Regarding this claim to continuity, LBV is considered as *a quarta revelação de Deus aos homens* (the fourth revelation of God to men).

Supported popularity by the ideas of ecumenism and charity LBV has built over a period of time, a network of social services. Its beginnings were announced in a radio program controlled by Zarur, called *Hora da Boa Vontade* (Time of Good Will), broadcast by a radio station called Radio Globo, in Rio de Janeiro, and transmitted for the first time on the 4 March 1949. The movement's connection with the media has been an important factor in the consolidation of its infrastructural development and its national and international expansion.

By the end of the 1960s, LBV had a significant presence in the Brazilian media, published a review called *Revista Boa Vontade* (Good Will Review), and was broadcasting such TV programs, as *Um Homem e a Multidão – O show é Zarur* (A man and the crowd – The show is Zarur). Zarur also promoted what was known as *sopa dos pobres* (poor people's soup). *Sopa dos pobres*, which popularized LBV and its founder, became a target for his critics, who denounced it as populist. Zarur was also accused as having accumulated a fortune, while claiming to be commited to ending poverty.

On the death of Zarur in 1979 Jose de Paiva Neto assumed the presidency of LBV and in response to the continued allegations made by the media and the public about financial irregularities he created two separate organizations, one concerned with charitable activities and the other, The Temple of Good Will (Templo da Boa Morte), with religious and spiritual matters. The Temple was built in Brasilia, the capital of Brazil and was intended as a national monument, providing ecumenical space to people of all races and creeds. It is a seven sided building with a huge crystal rock on the roof. Inside rising from the floor are two spirals one black and one white. While no set ceremonies or rituals have been prescribed by the movement over time visitors have created their own informal rituals.

This movement, initially confined to the south of Brazil, has now spread to most parts of the country. It has also spread to other Latin American countries including Paraguay, Uraguay and Bolivia, and to the United States and Europe. In 1999 it was granted the status of general consultant by the Economic and Social Comittee of the United Nations.

ALBERTO CROISMAN

LEGIO MARIA

This schismatic Catholic movement of East African origin is a breakaway from the Legion of Mary, a lay association founded in 1921 in Dublin, Ireland. The founding aims of the larger body were to develop a Christian spirituality by small group organization and to encourage participation in pastoral and missionary work by lay people under the guidance of priests. It spread to Africa and encouraged the recruitment of catechists in Catholic missions.

The founder of Legio Maria, Simeon Ondeto, a Kenyan, had been a catechist in a section of the Legion already regarded by headquarters as deviant. He met Gaudencia Aoko, a young mother who, after losing her two children to disease in circumstances which made her suspect occult influences, became a visionary.

In 1963, the year of Kenyan independence, the two gained prestige as prophets and a following among people who wanted a ministry aware of their needs in traditional society, including deliverance from the evils of witchcraft. These were also people who wanted to retain their Catholic devotions. Within two years the two had gathered about 100,000 followers and had an organized hierarchy. They worked in different areas and gradually grew apart. Gaudencia did not approve of Simeon calling himself 'Pope'.

As it developed, the new church, in worship and teaching, held on to Catholic language and symbolism, retaining Latin as a sacred language. But it was also traditional in responding to concerns about healing and spirit possession. One prominent feature, noticed many observers, was an element of divination, the 'chief sniffers', whose task is to discern evil.

A strength of the movement was its way of organizing small groups, so as to relate their religious practice to relations within the community. A number of Catholic missionaries, while regretting the divisiveness of independency (see **African Independent Churches**), sought to find practical lessons on building 'basic communities' from the study of this movement.

Further reading

Dirvan, P. J. (1970) *The Maria Legio: the dynamics of a breakaway church among the Luo in East Africa*, la Pontificia Università Gregoriana, Rome.

Perrin-Jassy, Dr M.-F. (1973) *Basic Community in the African Churches*, Maryknoll New York: Orbis Books.

RALPH WOODHALL

LEKHRAJ, DADA
(b. 1876; d. 1969)

Dada Lekhraj (born in 1876 in the Sindh community of what is now Pakistan) founded the Hindu-derived millenarian movement (see **Millenarianism**), the **Brahma Kumaris**. At the age of 60, Lekhraj, then a wealthy diamond merchant, began experiencing dramatic visions, first of the Hindu god Vishnu, and then of the god Shiva. Lekhraj also saw horrifying scenes of world destruction, followed by a vision of a heavenly world of peace and beauty. Transformed by these experiences, Lekhraj divested himself of his business and fully committed himself to spiritual life.

Thereafter Shiva began to descend regularly into Lekhraj, speaking through him at the *satsang* (devotional meetings) held in his home. Lekhraj became known as 'Prajapita Brahma', 'Adi Dev' or, familiarly, 'Brahma Baba' in recognition of the divine presence in him. As news of this spread, the group grew rapidly. Many experienced spiritual ecstasies at his satsang, particularly when he chanted the 'om' mantra, giving rise to the group's popular name, the 'Om Mandali' ('Om Circle').

In 1937 Lekhraj gave the formal direction of the group over to a 'Managing Committee' headed by his principal disciple, Om Radhe, and eight other women. The movement then assumed its present name. A year later Lekhraj devolved the remainder of his fortune on this body.

As medium for 'The Supreme Soul' (Shiva), Lekhraj nevertheless remained the source of spiritual direction for the group. Shiva's messages (*murli*), spoken daily through Lekhraj, became the basis of the movement's understanding of the divine plan of world history encapsulated in his early visions.

Even after his death in 1969, Lekhraj as 'Brahma Baba' has remained central to the spiritual life of the Brahma Kumaris. Soon after his passing, senior 'sister' Dadi Gulzar began functioning as the authoritative medium for his spiritual presence, and thus for Shiva. Brahma Baba's posthumous murli are disseminated to all branches of the organization where they are read at morning devotions. Lekhraj, as beloved 'Baba' (father) to his spiritual 'daughters' (*kumari*) and 'sons', frequently appears in their visions, and as 'Bap Dada', is the point of connection for them with The Supreme Soul.

JULIA DAY HOWELL

LI HONGZHI

Li Hongzhi is the founder and most important teacher of the **Falun Gong** movement. He was born in a small township in Jilin Province in China on 13 May 1951, which happens to coincide with the traditional Chinese festival for the birth of the Buddha. Opponents of the Falun Gong have made much of the hagiographic nature of Li Hongzhi's biography, arguing for instance, and probably truthfully, that he was born on 7 July 1952 and altered the date on his birth certificate much later for religious reasons.

Li led an ordinary life until 1992. He came from a family of office workers and received some secondary education near and in the large city of Changchun. Although he grew up in the heavily industrialized north-east (better known as Manchuria), he himself never worked in the industrial complex. Instead, he held low-level positions in the army and police, followed by an equally modest post in the state-run Cereals and Oil Company of Changchun, until he left voluntarily in 1991. Judging from his teachings, his knowledge tends to come from secondary digests of original materials, coupled with some exposure to Qigong and/or martial arts practices (see **Chi'i Kung** (Qigong)). There is no indication that he ever practised as a lay believer of established Buddhist or Daoist traditions or that he ever belonged to older 'new' religious groups.

Given the nature of his jobs and the highly politicized era in which he grew up, we can surmise that Li Hongzhi received basic literacy teaching, but that his education like that of most of his contemporaries was of a very elementary level. Through the Maoist mass-campaigns of the 1950s and 1960s, he was taught to see the world in terms of violent conflict, with highly polarized definitions of friends and enemies and with both symbolic and real life violence seen as an appropriate and legitimate means of dealing with one's opponents. In his teachings, where he stresses morality and non-violence, Li Hongzhi consciously reacts against this worldview, but preserves its polemical language.

Like all of his contemporaries, Li Hongzhi was exposed to extensive propaganda concerning the 'feudal' and 'superstitious' nature of all religious culture throughout his formative years. In urban China, this is still the dominant way of looking at religion and it is not surprising that this is also the attitude taken by Falun Gong followers of Chinese descent, though their self-definition as scientific kexuede) has been challenged, for instance when the Qigong Research Association in 1996 cancelled the Falun Gong's membership. All in all, Li Hongzhi and his close followers certainly see their beliefs as a modern way of looking at the problem of life and death, even though in many respects they implicitly build on old traditions.

Since 1992 oral lectures and meetings (whether with live audiences, taped or over the phone) have been the main medium for Li Hongzhi to express his views on teachings. He has not been much of writer himself. Close followers then turn these oral messages and lec-tures into writen form. They were first disseminated mainly in print and increasingly through the Internet. In 1992, he also founded the Falun Xiulian Dafa Research Society in Beijing, which joined the Qigong Research Society the following year. In 1994 his main doctrinal work, the the Zhuanfalun (Turning the Dharma Wheel), was published, in the form of nine lectures and in highly colloquial language. Since then, this book has become the core text of the movement, with translations in most modern foreign languages. From 1999 Li's public appearances became extremely rare and new pronouncements were mainly made from a distance, though in 2001 he began again to appear in public more frequently.

In his writings, Li states that his teachings already existed since time immemorial and that he has merely recovered them in this time of the decline of the teachings. He does not explicitly call himself a Buddha, but all Falun Gong materials – including Li's formal portrait, videos of him performing the Falun Gong exercises, and pictures on the Internet – suggest to the follower that he actually is on that enlightened level. In his writings he mixes a degree of tolerance for other teachings with vehement attacks, stressing that this method only works when it is practised consistently. Whatever the historical origins of Li's teachings and practice, they are presented to the practitioner as the revelations of Li Hongzhi in the sense that he was the first to reveal them.

Further reading

Penny, B. (2003) 'The Life and Times of Li Hongzhi: Falun Gong and Religious Biography', forthcoming in *China Quarterly*, 175, 643–61.

BEREND J. TER HAAR

LIBERATION THEOLOGY

Liberation theology has its origins in the reality of the premature and unjust death of many people, as one of the founders of liberation theology, Gustavo Gutierrez, has put it. The struggles of millions, linked with, and inspired by, catholic social teaching prompted priests and religious to think again about their vocation. In so doing, they have learnt afresh from the poor. The starting place of theology is not detached reflection on scripture and tradition but the life of the shanty towns and land struggles. In many ways liberation theology parallels the very earliest years of Christianity's presence in South America when priests like Bartolomé de las Casas took up the cause of the oppressed indigenous people of the sub-continent. The meaning of the Christian faith is illuminated in the very context in which the world's wretched condition is confronted and alleviated. Liberation theology is above all an approach to theology in which the emphasis is on God in history who calls men and women to identify with the poor and marginalized and to understand that commitment in the light of the Christian tradition. Liberation theology harks back to earlier theological methods when worship, service to humanity and theological reflection were closely integrated. Commitment to the poor and marginalized is a determining moment for theology rather than the agenda of detachment and reflection within the academy.

Liberation theology emerged within the wider context of catholic social teaching and, in particular, the significant development of Roman Catholic theology based on the Second Vatican Council, and the encyclicals associated with it. The decisions taken by the Latin American bishops at their epoch-making meeting at Medellín (1968), reaffirmed at Puebla (1979), with the explicit commitment to take a 'preferential option for the poor' were reaffirmed at the conference of Latin American bishops at Santo Domingo (1992).

Liberation theology developed in the context of the emergence of the Basic Ecclesial or Christian Communities (the CEBs). The basic communities are a significant component of the contemporary political as well as ecclesiastical scene, particularly in Brazil. In the CEBs an alternative space opened up to reflect on the way of Christ over against prevailing ideology, thus empowering all people of God to share in the task of bringing the transforming power of the gospel to every part of an unjust world. Among these groups the Bible has become a catalyst for the exploration of pressing contemporary issues relevant to the community. To enable the poor to engage with the Bible has meant the development of programmes of education, in which full recognition is given to the experience of life. Understanding the Bible takes place in the dialectic between the literary memory of the people of God and the issues of the contemporary world. So, the emphasis is not placed on the text's meaning in itself but rather on the meaning the text has for the people reading it.

The contributions of liberation theologians form a small part of a long debate within Christianity, both modern and ancient, about appropriate attitudes and responses to the poor and vulnerable and the church's relations with the political powers. Liberation theologians are engaged in mediation between the poor, church teaching and appropriate 'secular' wisdom which contributes to an understanding of the reality of a life of suffering and facilitates theological reflection, though with a clear commitment to the poor rather than being neutral theological brokers.

There have been significant differences of opinion over the years between the Congregation for the Doctrine of the Faith and certain Latin American theologians, particularly in the encyclicals 'Instruction On Certain Aspects of the Theology of Liberation' and 'Libertatis Nuntius'. Criticisms include the concentration on narrative and prophetic texts in liberation theology, which highlight situations of oppression and which inspire a praxis leading to social change. The use of Marxist analysis of social reality as a frame of reference for reading the Bible is often questioned, as is Liberation Theology's emphasis on a hope for God's reign on earth to the detriment of the more transcendent dimensions of scriptural eschatology. Many liberation theologians have suggested that their use of Marxism does not imply an acceptance of a Marxist Leninist philosophy. What they borrow is an analysis and not a strategy for transforming the world, nor an all-encompassing philosophy.

The emphasis on the experience of the everyday world and its injustices as an essential part of the knowledge of God is also a recurrent theme in a small but growing grassroots theology in Europe. Often such examples are only, at most loosely, related and lack the institutional networks of the liberation theology of Latin America or the Ecumenical Alliance of Third World Theologians (EATWOT). Liberationist perspectives have a long pedigree in Christian theology. There has been a long line of radical exponents of the Scripture whose myth-making and creative use of Scripture is filtered through personal experience and social upheaval.

Further reading

Ateek, N. (1989) *Justice and Only Justice: A Palestinian Theology of Liberation*, New York: Orbis.

Bradstock, A. and Rowland, C. (2002) *Radical Christian Writings: A Reader*, Oxford: Blackwell.

Gutierrez, G. (1988) *A Theology of Liberation* (rev. ed.), London: SCM.

Hennelly, A. T. (ed.) (1990) *Liberation Theology. A Documentary History*, New York: Orbis.

Mesters, C. (1989) *Defenseless Flower*, New York: Orbis.

Nolan, A. (1988) *God in South Africa. The Challenge of the Gospel*, London: CIIR.

Rowland, C. (1999) *The Cambridge Companion to Liberation Theology*, Cambridge: Cambridge University Press.

Sugirtharajah, R. (ed.) (1992) *Voices from the Margins*, London: SPCK.

West, G. (1998) *The Academy of the Poor. Towards a Dialogical Reading of the Bible*, Sheffield: Sheffield Academic Press.

Witvliet, T. (1985) *A Place in the Sun*, London: SCM.

CHRIS ROWLAND

LITERATURE IN FRENCH ON NRMS

This entry introduces the institutional context in which literature in French on New Religious Movements (NRMs) is written, gives a brief note on French terminology and examines key works in French on NRMs in general and on one NRM, New Age (see **New Age Movement**), in more depth as an example.

Literature in French on NRMs is concerned to a much greater extent than literature in English with questions of state. These concerns may owe much in France to Article 10 of the Declaration of the Rights of Man and the Citizen of 1789 which guarantees freedom from public interference in religious opinions, and related provisions such as the separation of Church and State achieved in the Law of 9 December 1905 – but it is interesting to note that the debate on NRMs is not framed to such an extent in this way in the United States of America, a country with similar constitutional guarantees.

This French interest in questions of state is manifested in a fundamental institutional hostility to NRMs. The French Prime Minister ordered a report by Alain Vivien, published in 1985 as 'Les sectes en France: Expression de la liberté morale ou facteurs de manipulation' (Sects in France: Expression of moral liberty or agents of manipulation). A second report 'Sur les sectes' (On sects) was presented to the French National Assembly by Alain Gest and Jacques Guyant in 1995, and published in early 1996. This second report was affirmed by the larger but more limited report of 1999 by Jacques Guyard and Jean-Pierre Brard on the financial situation of sects. The French Act No 2001-504 to reinforce the prevention and suppression of sects which infringe human rights and fundamental freedoms became law on 12 June 2001.

The 1995 report acknowledged the difficulties in defining the area of concern and adopted an approach which explicitly assumes that sects are dangerous, evidenced by indices such as mental destabilization, exorbitant financial demands, a break with the environment in which the sect originated, infringements of personal space, indoctrination of children, anti-social discourse, public order difficulties, legal proceedings, possible embezzlement and attempts to infiltrate public authorities. Based on twenty interviews held in secret and a number of dated publications on NRMs, the report lists 172 'mother organizations' (173 together with **Jehovah's Witnesses**) in France, and claims there are over 800 'satellite' organizations, totalling 160,000 members (of which 130,000 are said to be Jehovah's Witnesses) and 100,000 'sympathizers'.

Another study in French on NRMs which was commissioned by the state is the Swiss report by Jean-François Mayer on 'Les Nouvelles Voies Spirituelles: Enquête sur la religiosité parallèle en Suisse' (New Religious Movements: Inquiry into parallel religiosity in Switzerland) (1993), which was part of a national Swiss research programme (PNR 21) on 'Cultural pluralism and national identity'.

This work takes an approach much more similar to the sociological stance of much English-language literature on NRMs. After discussing problems of definition and method, an overview of parallel religiosity is given, with a historical description of non-conformist spiritualities, an emphasis on the importance of the East and science fiction and a considered conclusion on the implantation of NRMs in Switzerland. A large appendix gives basic information on forty-nine NRMs in Switzerland, including addresses, details of the Swiss operation of each NRM, publications by each NRM and literature on each NRM (which is a good place to start for bibliographic details of further reading in French although see also Champion and Cohen, 1999).

The Swiss National Council Commission produced a further report on NRMs in Switzerland in 1999. Jean-François Mayer founded the website, *www.religioscope.com*, which is the foremost Internet source in French for scholarly information on religion, including NRMs. The Belgian Chambre des Réprésentants also produced a parliamentary inquiry in French on sects in 1997.

Unofficial documents further demonstrating the focus on questions of state in French works on NRMs include: 'Sectes et démocratie' (Sects and Democracy) by Françoise Champion and Martine Cohen (1999, Paris: Seuil); 'Face aux sectes: Politique, Justice, État' (Confronting sects: Politics, Justice, State) by Georges Fenech (1999, PUF), a magistrate proposing measures to prevent the infiltration of sects into mainstream society; and 'Les sectes et le droit en France' (Sects and the Law in France), Francis Messner, (1999, PUF).

Champion and Cohen (1999) is one of the foremost studies in French of NRMs. It contains chapters on **Jehovah's Witnesses**, **Hassidism**, the Catholic Charismatic movement (see **Charismatic Movements**), **Soka Gakkai** and the Solar Temple. This is set within a context of globalization and there is extended discussion of the relation of NRMs with public opinion and democracy. Importantly, the work opens with an introductory chapter on NRMs in France which acknowledges difficulties of terminology.

The conventional terminology in French literature for New Religious Movements is 'les sectes' which, although technically translating Max Weber and Ernst Troeltsch's term 'Die Sekten' (sects), is more akin to English usage of 'cults' with pejorative overtones. Some French sociologists acknowledge the difficulties in using popular language for technical purposes and adopt the more neutral term 'les nouveaux mouvements religieux' (New Religious Movements). One other important French term is 'la nébuleuse mystique-ésotérique' ('the mystic-esoteric nebula'), coined by Françoise Champion (pp. 17–70 in Françoise Champion and Danièlle Hervieu-Léger (eds), *De L'Emotion en Religion*, 1990, Centurion) which approximates Colin Campbell's English term, 'cultic milieu' (see **Cult and New Religions**), and is used to describe New Age and related phenomena (see **New Age Movement**).

This entry now moves on to consider French literature on New Age as an indepth example of French literature on NRMs in general, starting with the work of Jean Vernette (1929–2002). Vernette was adviser on NRMs for the French National Conference of Catholic Bishops and published a number of influential Christian examinations of NRMs in French, including *Sectes et réveil religieux: Quand L'Occident s'éveille* (Sects and Religious Awakening: When the West Awakens), (1976, Mulhouse, Salvator), *Les Sectes, L'Occulte et L'Etrange* (Sects, the Occult and the Mysterious) (1985, Salon de Provence, Editions du Bosquet), and an early French Christian critique of New Age, *Le Nouvel Age: A l'aube de l'ère du Verseau* (The New Age: At the Dawn of the Age of Aquarius) (1989, Paris, Téqui).

New Age is described by Vernette as an Anglo-Saxon movement which is beginning to 'invade' France. Its constituent elements are thus consonant with prior English language descriptions of New Age, and include Thomas Kuhn's idea of a new paradigm, Marilyn Ferguson's *The Aquarian Conspiracy* (1980) (the French translation was entitled *Les Enfants du Verseau* (The Children of Aquarius) (1981, Paris, Calmann-Lévy)), a change in consciousness, the importance of *gnosis* (knowledge), alternative therapies, Holistic Health (see **Holistic Health Movements**), Transpersonal education, and the concept of a global village. Vernette presents conservative Christian evaluations of New Age, asking whether it represents the coming of the Anti-Christ, a Jewish conspiracy, or a project for a global government – and drawing attention to its parallels with Nazism. A final chapter gives a more balanced evaluation for 'discernment' of New Age by Christians.

Other French Christian studies of New Age include *Une religion américaine* by Claude Labrecque (1994, Liana Levi) and Bernard Bastian's *Le New-Age, D'où vient-il? Que dit-il?* (The New Age: Where does it come from? What does it say?) (1991, Paris, OEIL). Christian journals devoted (critical) special editions to New Age, including *Christus* (153, January 1992) and *Fêtes et saisons*

(475, May 1993). A more sympathetic Christian approach to New Age (see **Christaquarians**) was undertaken by Michel Anglarès in his *Nouvel Age et Foi chrétienne* ('New Age and Christian Faith') (1992, Paris, Centurion).

Non-Christian popular works in French by journalists on New Age include Sylvie Grossman and Edouard Fenwick's wide-ranging *Le Nouvel Age* (1981, Paris, Seuil), Michel Lacroix's *La spiritualité totalitaire* ('Totalitarian Spirituality') (1995, Plon) and his *L'idéologie du New-Age* ('New Age Ideology') (1996, Flammarion), Renaud Marhic and Emmanuel Besnier's *Le New Age* (1999, Le Castor Astral) and Jean-Luc Porquet's *La France Des Mutants: Voyage au cœur du Nouvel Age* (France of the Mutants: Voyage to the heart of New Age) (1994, np, Flammarion, reissued in 2001).

Porquet's book is mocking in tone but generally well-researched with first-hand observations throughout – for example at a channelling session, at a New Age fair, a psychic workshop, at the **Findhorn Community** in Scotland, and with a French shaman. An eleven-point 'credo' of New Age is suggested. New Age in France is said to have begun at the beginning of the 1980s among esotericists, ecologists, vegetarians, Holistic Health aficionados and graduates of the 1968 student movement. By 1988, several major publishing houses had dedicated New Age series, including Belfond's 'L'âge du Verseau', Presses Pocket's 'L'âge d'être', J'ai lu's 'J'ai lu-New Age' and Laffont's 'Les énigmes de l'univers' – not to mention a myriad of small independent New Age publishing houses.

Academic studies of New Age in French are not as numerous as their English counterparts, and include works by Marie-Jeanne Ferreux, Sônia Weidner Maluf and Erica Guilane-Nachez. Their most striking feature is that they generally do not reference the now burgeoning literature on New Age in English.

Le New-Age: Ritualités et mythologies contemporaines by Marie-Jeanne Ferreux (2000, Paris, L'Harmattan) sets out to answer the question: Is there a major modern myth? New Age is situated as a non-religious imaginal form in continuity with modern values and in the context of the decline of Christianity and the rise of secularization. New Age is said to have been exported to Europe from California, and is studied in its 'political' and 'representational' aspects before considering New Age approaches to death.

Source, Mythes et Pratiques du New Age: De ses Origines à Nos Jours by Erica Guilane-Nachez (1999, Villeneuve d'Ascq, Septentrion) is the original text of a doctoral thesis. Roots of New Age are discussed – historical, philosophical, socio-cultural, artistic, scientific and Christian – before sketches of twenty-five New Age informants are given. The material is analysed in terms of the tools of New Age such as shamanism, meditation and channelling and invisible guides such as angels and power animals. A final chapter looks at archetypes and myths in New Age.

Les Enfants du Verseau au Pays des Tereiros, Sônia Weidner Maluf (1996, Villeneuve d'Ascq, Septentrion) is a French language study of alternative spirituality in Brazil which does not deal explicitly with New Age and appears to be sourced from one central informant.

The limited number of French journal articles on New Age are typically generalistic, concerning the movement as a whole without many articulations of concrete examples in French-speaking countries – a notable exception being Valérie Rocchi and Françoise Champion's 'Du Nouvel Age aux Réseaux Psychomystiques' (*Ethnologie Française*

2000 30.4 583–90). Key themes identified in English language studies of New Age are generally absent – there is almost no reference to the esoteric foundations of New Age or to its neo-pagan aspects (see **Neo-Paganism**), with the importance of nature religion traditions and the notion of the Self only mentioned in passing. However, the theme of the commercialization of spirituality is taken up, especially in the issue of *Social Compass* (1999, 46(2)) devoted to New Age (with a number of articles in French).

Literature in French on New Age has, then, developed largely in isolation from English language scholarly studies, despite the oft-held assumption in French studies that New Age is an import from the English-speaking world. More generally, literature in French on NRMs has also developed in manifestly different ways to the larger body of English language literature, demonstrated for example in the focus on questions of state and in the hostile, non-sociological stance of most French studies.

Further reading

Assemblée Nationale (1995) *Rapport ... sur les Sectes*, 22 December, http://www.assemblee-nationale.fr/rap-enq/r2468.asp (document d'information no 2468).

Champion, F. and Cohen, M. (1999) *Sectes et Démocratie*, Paris: Seuil.

Kemp, D. (forthcoming) 'Non-English Language Studies of New Age', *Journal of New Age Studies*.

Mayer, J.-F. (1993) *Les Nouvelles Voies Spirituelles: Enquête sur la religiosité parallèle en Suisse*, Lausanne: L'Age d'Homme.

DAREN KEMP

LITERATURE IN GERMAN ON NRMS

The term New Religious Movements (NRMs) is not popular in German-speaking countries. Its use is confined to certain areas of academic literature and to occasional political discussions that wish to avoid the term 'sect'. Nevertheless information about NRMs is available in a number of handbooks and other publications.

Handbooks and monographs

Among the handbooks and monographs are the following: Gasper, H., Müller, J. and Valentin, F. (eds) (1999) *Lexikon der Sekten, Sondergruppen und Weltanschauungen* (Encyclopedia of Sects, Special Groups and Weltanschauungen) (6th edn), Freiburg: Herder; Eggenberger, O. (1994) *Die Kirchen, Sondergruppen und religiösen Vereinigungen* (Churches, Special Groups and Religious Communities) (5th edn) Zürich: Theologischer Verlag; Reller, H., Krech, H. and Kleiminger, M. (eds) (2000) *Handbuch Religiöse Gemeinschaften. Freikirchen, Sondergemeinschaften, Sekten, Weltanschauungsgemeinschaften, Neureligionen* (Handbook for Religious Communities. Free Churches, Religious Groups outside the Churches, Sects, Communities with a particular Weltanschauung, New Religions) (5th edn) Gütersloh: Gütersloher Verlagshaus; Klöcker, M. and Tworuschka, U. (eds) (1997, supplements 1998ff) *Handbuch der Religionen, Kirchen und andere Glaubensgemeinschaften in Deutschland* (Handbook of Religions, Churches and other Religious Communities), München.

Still highly esteemed and influential is Kurt Hutten's (1984) *Seher, Grübler, Enthusiasten* (Seers, Thinkers, Enthusiasts) (13th edn), Stuttgart: Quell Verlag, which started in 1950 as 'Buch der traditionellen Sekten', later editions adding the words 'und christliche Sondergemeinschaften' (special Christian groups) or 'Sonderbewegungen' (special movements) to the title. In 1960 Hutten became the first director of the 'Evangelische

Zentralstelle fur Weltanschauungsfragen' (EZW). Although 'The Hutten', as the book has been called, belongs to pre-NRM-times (only the Baha'i-religion and the Unification Church have been included in some editions) it has been influential in building up an atmosphere of tolerance towards religious minorities. This more liberal and tolerant approach was carried on by the 'Evangelische Zentralstelle fur Weltanschaungsfragen' (EZW) (Protestant Centre for Worldview Questions) and became influential through the publications of its experts (e.g. Mildenberger, Michael (1979) *Die religiose Revolte* (The Religious Revolt) Frankfurt/M.: S. Fischer Verlag; and especially the *Materialdienst*, the monthly magazine of the EZW. In later years the atmosphere changed to some extent, when opposition to NRMs from F.W. Haack and others increased. As Elisabeth Arweck has shown in her dissertation (1999/2005), the Protestant churches in Germany had, already before the emergence of NRMs, created institutions and a network of experts to deal with the growing religious pluralism. The NRMs were easily slotted into the existing framework. A considerable part of the research as well as the literature on NRMs and most of the authors of it have come from this background.

Literature on particular movements, especially in Central Europe

Hans Hemminger (1994) produced VPM – Der 'Verein zur Forderung der psychologischen Menschenkenntnis' und Friedrich Lieblings Zurcher *Schule'*, Munchen: Evangelischer Presseverband Bayern. This is a critical presentation of a controversial therapeutic organization founded in 1986 and active mainly in Switzerland and Germany.

Some authors have written dissertations on NRMs and afterwards added a more popular presentation of the same movement.

Joachim Suss' dissertation (1994) analysed the **Osho** movement *(Zur Erleuchtung unterwegs. Neo-Sannyasin in Deutschland und ihre Religion* (On the way to Enlightenment. Neo-Sannyasin in Germany and their Religion) Berlin: Dietrich Reimer. It was followed by a more popular presentation: (1996) *Bhagwans Erbe. Die Osho-Bewegung heute* (Bhagwan's legacy. The Osho-Movement today), Reihe Claudius Kontur, Munchen: Claudius Verlag. Suss narrates the story of the Osho movement after his demise (1990), analyses what he calls 'sannyatic religiosity' and pleads for a more tolerant and understanding way of dealing with NRMs.

Wolfram Mirbach produced a thesis (1994) *Universelles Leben. Originalität und Christlichkeit einer Neureligion* (Universelles Leben. How original and christian is this New Religion?) Erlangen: Verlag der Evangelisch-Lutherischen Mission. This dissertation analyses '**Universelles Leben**' (UL), previously 'Heimholungswerk Jesu Christi', one of the few NRMs originating from Germany and more or less confined to that country. Mirbach focuses on the attitude of UL towards Christianity. In 1996 he added a second book on the same subject: (1996) *'Universelles Leben'. Die einzig wahren Christen? Eine Neureligion zwischen Anspruch und Wirklichkeit* ('Universelles Leben'. A New Religion between Pretention and Reality) Freiburg i. Br.: Herder, published in the series 'Sekten, Sondergruppen und Weltanschauungen'. In both books theological apologetics prevail, although the information offered is reliable. Mirbach describes and criticizes UL-activities in the fields of healing, education and economy and in its dealing with children and couples. He strongly rejects its claim to represent true and better Christiany. He considers it a 'Neuoffenbarungsbewegung', a movement based on what it believes to be a new revelation.

Matthias Pohlmann (1994) published *Lorber-Bewegung – durch Jenseitswissen zum Heil?* (Lorber-movement – Salvation through knowledge of the Beyond?) Konstanz: Friedrich Bahn. This is a biography of Lorber, and provides an account of his technique and of the **Jacob Lorber Association** in Germany and Austria. There are several studies of Mormonism (see **Church of Jesus Christ of the Latter Day Saints (Mormons)**) including an unpublished dissertation written by Rudiger Hauth (1986) *Der Mormonentempel und seine Rituale* (The Mormon Temple and its rituals) Aarhus/DK. On a more popular level Hauth has combined an overall presentation of the 'Church of Jesus Christ of Latter-day Saints' with a critical presentation and theological assessment of its temple worship (1995) *Die Mormonen, Sekte oder neue Kirche Jesu Christi?* (The Mormons, Sect or New Church of Jesus Christ?) Freiburg i. Br.: Herder.

A dissertation on neogermanic and neo-pagan ideas and groups (see **Neo-Paganism**) has been written by Stefanie von Schnurbein (1992) *Religion als Kulturkritik. Neugermanisches Heidentum im 20. Jahrhundert* (Religion as Cultural Criticism. Neogermanic Paganism in the 20th Century) Heidelberg. A second title on the same subject is: von Schnurbein (1993), *Gottertrost im Wendezeiten. Neugermanisches Heidentum zwischen New Age und Rechtsradikalismus* (Divine Solace in Times of Change. Neogermanic Paganism between New Age and Rightist Radicalism) München:Claudius Verlag (see **New Age Movement**). Information and insight is provided about persons and organizations involved in the neo-pagan ideology, about their links to Theosophy and Nazism, and also about feminism and ecology.

Jena-Francois Mayer (1998) is the author of *Sonnentempel. Die Tragödie einer Sekte* (The Solar Temple: Tragedy of a Sect), Friburg (Switzerland): Paulusverlag. This monograph provides a well documented history and analysis of the rise and fall of this movement.

Martin Repp's (1997) **Aum Shinrikyo** (Marburg: Diagonal-Verlag) focuses on the interaction between the movement and the wider Japanese society and highlights the almost total lack of communication between the young and the old and between mainstream and marginal religions.

Two of the publications on the New Age in German deserve mention. These are:

- Christoph Bochinger's (1994) '*New Age' und moderne Religion: religionswissenschaftliche Analysen* (New Age analysed from the perspective of the study of religion) (Gütersloh: Kaiser/Gütersloh Verlagshaus) which suggests that the term New Age is little more than a popular label applied to the ideas of thinkers such as **Emmanuel Swedenborg** and William Blake and contributes little to their theories.
- Horst Stenger's (1993) *Die soziale Konstruktion okkulter Wirklichkeit. Eine Soziologie des 'New Age'* (The Social Construction of Occult Reality: A Sociology of the New Age) (Opladen, Leske and Budrich) which looks at the New Age phenomenon from the perspective of sociology and identifies its modern origins and impact as a social phenomenon.

Joachim Stiss and Renate Pitzer-Reyl (eds) (1996), brought out *Religionswechsel. Hintergrunde spiritueller Neuorientierung* (Conversion. Backgrounds of Spiritual Reorientation) Reihe Claudius Kontur,

München: Claudius. Eight authors discuss why people (or the authors themselves respectively) have turned to other religions: to Islam, Buddhism, **Rajneesh**, **Anthroposophy** and to the spirituality of Native Americans, the final conclusion being that a new type of person-centered or self-centered religiosity (see **Self-religion, the Self, and Self**) has emerged and that religions are found attractive that offer ways of growth to the individual.

F.-W. Haack and 'Youth Religions'

The appearance of NRMs in the 1960s and 1970s was perceived as a new experience in the realm of religion and provoked a new response – new compared to the 'soft' approach as promoted by K. Hutten. F.-W. Haack, a Bavarian pastor and 'Weltanschaungsbeauftragter', dominated the public discussion on NRMs for many years. He differed from the average ACM-ideology in that he took the NRMs seriously as religion, although, in his view, a dubious form of religion. In many of his books, e.g. (1979) *Jugendreligionen. Ursachen – Trends – Reaktionen* (Youth Religions. Causes, Trends, Responses) München: Claudius, he employed the term 'Jugendreligion' to describe NRMs which he accused of soulwashing (Seelenwasche) rather than **brainwashing**. Haack's book on **Scientology** (1982) *Scientology – Magie des 20. Jahrhunderts* (Scientology – The Magic of the 20th Century) München: Claudius, was as he described it himself the 'result of 10 years of confrontation'. It is a critical presentation of Scientology's theory and practice and a highly effective collection of incriminatory evidence. By contrast Werner Thiede (1992) *Scientology – Religion oder Geistesmagie?* (Scientology – Religion or Spiritual Magic?) Konstanz: Friedrich Bahn, abstains from polemics

but is also unwilling to concede to Scientology the status of a religion.

Religionswissenschaft and Missiology

In the field of Religionswissenschaft (Science of Religion) and missiology the emergence of NRMs caught the attention of scholars including Ernst Benz (1971) *Neue Religionen* (New Religions) Stuttgart; Gunter Lanczkowski (1974) *Die neuen Religionen* (The New Religions) Frankfurt: Fischer Taschenbuch Verlag, and Peter Gerlitz (1977) *Gott erwacht in Japan. Neue fernostliche Religionen und ihre Botschaft vom Gluck.* (God is awakening in Japan. New far-eastern Religions and their message of happiness (see **New Religions (Japan)**).) Freiburg i. Br.: Herder. The primary concern of these authors was not the reception of NRMs in the West but their emergence as part of the renaissance of religion all over the modern world (mostly in Asia) and as countermovement to secularization. My postdoctoral thesis (Hummel, Reinhart (1980) *Indische Mission und neue Frommigkeit im Westen* (Mission from India and new piety in the West) Stuttgart: Kohlhammer), was an attempt to combine both aspects, the awakening of Asian religion (Hinduism) to a new sense of worldwide 'mission' and how this awakening corelated with spiritual developments in Western culture.

A considerable part of research on NRMs has been done and is still being done by university departments of missiology, ecumenics and church-history in Germany. Helmut Obst is an example. While East Germany was still under Communist rule he was writing about NRMs there, publishing in 1984 *Neureligionen, Jugendreligionen, destruktive Kulte* (New Religions, Youth Religions, Destructive Cults) Berlin: Union. In a later edition a chapter on the New Age was added. For the series 'Kirchengeschichte in Einzeldarstellungen' he authored a volume (1990) *Außerkirchliche religiose Protestbewegungen der Neuzeit* (Religious Protest-movements outside the Church in modern times) Berlin: Evangelische Verlagsanstalt. There was one chapter on Apostolic Protest-groups, a second one on Religious Protest-movements of north-American origin, and a third one on 'Spiritualistic Protest-movements of German origin' including Christengemeinschaft and Evangelisch-Johannische Kirche. Obst added an excellent monograph in 1996 *Neuapostolische Kirche – die exklusive Endzeitkirche?* (**New Apostolic Church** – the exclusive Church of the End Times?), Reihe Apologetische Themen, Neukirchen-Vluyn: Friedrich Bahn. The Neuapostolische Kirche is not a NRM in the strict sense of the word, but it has 400,000 members in Germany, more than 8 million world-wide, and has given rise to problems and controversies similar to some of the NRMs.

NRMs from India

Joachim Finger (1987) provides a survey of movements from the Indian province. His publication bears the name *Gurus, Ashrams und der Westen. Eine religionswissenschaftliche Untersuchung zu den Hintergrunden der Internationalisierung des Hinduismus* (Gurus, Ashrams and the West. The Background of the Internationalization of Hinduism examined from the perspective of Religionswissenschaft), Studia Irenica Bd. 32, Frankfurt/M: Peter Lang. Reinhart Hummel wrote on the same theme in his 1996 volume *Gurus, Meister, Scharlatane. Zwischen Faszination und Gefahr* (Gurus, Masters, Charlatans. Between Fascination and Danger) Freiburg i.Br.: Herder.

In 1999 Peter Schmidt published *A. C. Bhaktivedanta Swami im interreligiosen Dialog. Biographische Studien zur Begegung von Hinduismus und Christentum* (A. C. Bhaktivedanta Swami in Interreligious Dialogue. Biographical Studies on the Encounter of Hinduism and Christianity), Theion. Jahrbuch fur Religionskultur, Bd. 10, Frankfurt/Mua: Peter Lang. Leaving aside all controversies surrounding the **ISKCON** the author deals with the 'strategy of interreligious dialogue' of the ISKCON-founder and with its transformation by Subhananda Das (St Gelbert), who has been ISKCON's 'director for interreligious affairs' for some years. Schmidt's analysis of the source material reveals the often overlooked fact, that Prabhupad took an interest in Christianity and in dialogue with it. Schmidt traces its roots back to Prabhupad's religious education under Vaishnava influence but also to the Scottish Church College in Calcutta.

Stephan Nagel (1999) published *Brahmas Geheime Schopfung. Die indische Reformbewegung der 'Brahma Kumaris'. Quellen, Lehre, Raja Yoga* (Brahma's secret creation. The Indian Reformmovement of the 'Brahma Kumaris'. Sources, Teachings, Raja Yoga) Theion, Jahrbuch für Religionskultur Bd. 11), Frankfurt/Mua: Peter Lang.

The greater part of this book is devoted to the Indian sources of the Brahma Kumaris (the *murlis* and *vanis*), their translation from the Hindi-Original and their interpretation. The western part of the movement, its history, the reformulation of the teachings in the western context, its controversial involvement with the peace-movement and its western sources (mostly in English) are not dealt with.

Horst Hüttl (1998) wrote *Die Sri Chinmoy-Bewegung im deutschsprachigen Raum* (The Sri Chinmoy-movement in German-speaking areas) Kalsdorf/

Osterreich: Eigenverlag. Hüttl's dissertation, accepted in Graz (Prof. Manfred Hutter), paints a sympathetic portrait of the history, teachings and practice of the Sri Chinmoy movement, which is perceived as a 'legitimate branch of neo-hinduistic spirituality inculturated in the west' (see **Neo-Hinduism**) and a 'spiritual peace-movement' rather than a religion. A more critical perspective prevails in Hüttl's paper read some time later at a congress in Graz and printed in: Hutter, Manfred (ed.) (2001) *Buddhisten und Hindus im deutschsprachigen Raum* (Buddhists and Hindus in the German-speaking world), Akten des Zweiten Grazer Religionswissenschaftlichen Symposiums, 2.-3. Marz 2000, Religionswissenschaften Bd. 11, Frankfurt/Mua: Peter Lang (see **Buddhism in the West**).

The Rajneesh- (Bhagwan- or Osho-) movement (see **Rajneesh Movement**), especially its Oregon-crisis has provoked heaps of literature but not much serious research among scholars writing in German. Joachim Suss' publications on this subject have already been mentioned. Huth, F.-R. (1993) has written a dissertation on one of the theological aspects of this movement: *Das Selbstverstandnis des Bhagwan Shree Rajneesh in seinen Reden uber Jesus* (The Self-Understanding of Bhagwan Shree Rajneesh in his discourses about Jesus), Frankfurt/Mua: Peter Lang. A much quoted book on this NRM was written by a young psychiatrist and psychologist: Klosinski, Gunther (1985) *Warum Bhagwan? Auf der Suche nach Heimat, Geborgenheit und Liebe* (Why Bhagwan? In search of a Home, a Sense of Belonging and Love) München: Kosel. Klosinski has explored the effects of conversion to Rajneesh and its consequences for psychological stability with much sensitivity. Some of his results can also be found in a small book too: Klosinski, G.

(1996) *Psychokulte. Was Sekten für Jugendliche so attraktiv macht* (Therapy cults. What attracts young people to Sects) München: C. H. Beck. The psychiatrist has observed that frequently it is lack of knowledge about physiological processes that misleads meditators to interpret their inner perceptions as 'mystical' experiences.

Religionswissenschaft and the Unification Church

Rainer Flasche has written a number of articles on NRMs from the Religionswissenschaft perspective including (1978) *Neue Religionen als Forschungsgegenstand der Religionswissenschaft* (New Religions as the subject of research in Religionswissenschaft) in Zeitschrift fur Mission 164–73; '(1984) *Religiose Neugrundungen: Ihre Entwicklungsstrukturen und Entstehungsbedingungen am Beispiel der Vereinigungskirche (T'ong'ilgyo)* (Newly founded religions: Structures, Development and Conditions of their Genesis – The Example of the Unification Church, T'ong'ilgyo) in *Zeitschrift für Missionswissenschaft und Religionswissenschaft*, 24–51. Flasche is primarily interested in how new religions emerge out of old ones. In his view the study of New Religions is a way to understand the genesis and consolidation of new religious communities. New Religions react to what Flasche calls religion-immanent and religion-transcendent conditions, i.e. to problems from within and from outside their own religious continuum. He distinguishes between two types of new religions, the first ('Fusionstypus') that fuse elements of two or more religions with a universalistic tendency, the second ('Reduktionstypus') that reduce their religious content to a small number of elements.

Rainer Flasche has also produced a number of studies on NRMs from the perpective of the science of religion including (1978) *Neue Religionen als Forschungsgegenstand der Religionswissenschaft* (New Religions as the Subject of Research in the Science of Religion) (*Zeitschrift für Mission*, Basle, 4, pp. 164–73). He also examined (1983) the question from this perspective of whether the Tong-II-Kyo (**Unification Church** and/or Moonies), could be called a Christian church and concluded that given its synthesis of Eastern and Western ideas it was more appropriate to describe it as a **New Religion** ('Ist die Vereinigungskirche ('Mun-Sekten') eine christliche Kirche?' (Is the Unification Church (the Moonies) a Christian Church?) (*Blick in die Welt (Monatliche Beilage zu den Nachrichten der Evangelisch-Luterischen Kirche in Bayern*, IV (V)).

The contribution of the Science of Religion to the debate on New Religions has consisted entirely in critiquing popular notions of cults (see **Cult and New Religions**) and sects and in fighting the dominance of Theology in this field which some authors (Usarski, 1988) believe has distorted the public's perception of these movements.

The two NRMs most written about in Germany are the Unification Church/Moonies and Scientology and both have been severely criticized. Both movements have changed considerably over the years. The new image of the former is depicted in Reinhart Hummel's *Vereinigungskirche* (Unification Church), Neukirchen-Vluyn: Friedrich Bahn.

Further reading

Arweck, Elisabeth and Clarke, Peter B. (1997) *New Religious Movements in Western Europe. An Annotated Bibliography*, Westport, CT: Greenwood Press.
Usarski, Frank (1988) *Die Stigmatisierung neuer Spiritueller Bewegungen in der Bundesrepublik Deutschland*, Koln/Wien: Kalner Veroffentlichungen zur Religionsgeschichte.

REINHART HUMMEL

LITERATURE IN ITALIAN AND SPANISH ON NRMS

Literature on NRMs can be classified into four general categories:

(a) academic literature, intended either for scholars and students, or for the general public, which maintains a value-free attitude and complies with the usual academic standards;

(b) anti-cult literature, derived from the **Anti-Cult Movement** and aimed at alerting its readers to the 'dangers of the cults';

(c) counter-cult literature, which (unlike its anti-cult counterpart) focuses on the doctrines of the 'cults' from a religious point of view, and exposes them as heretic from a Christian (or Jewish, or Islamic) point of view;

(d) official reports emanating from governmental, parliamentary, or police bodies. The latter assumed some importance in Europe after the controversial French parliamentary report of 1996, and extended to Latin America through the Chilean report of 2002; we will try to analyze in some depth Italian and Spanish language documents which fall into this category.

(a) Academic literature in Italian is in no way comparable to the large body of published material in English, but is more important than its French, Spanish, or German counterparts. Among the first Italian scholars to apply contemporary social science methods to the study of NRMs was Maria Immacolata Macioti, a sociologist at the University

La Sapienza in Rome. In 1980, she published *Teoria e tecnica della pace interiore – Saggio sulla Meditazione Trascendentale* (Naples: Ligori), a monograph on Transcendental Meditation (see **Transcendentalism**), which she followed by a series of important studies on popular magic and **Soka Gakkai**. Macioti was also instrumental in opening the pages of *La Critica Sociologica*, Italy's most distinguished journal of sociology, to articles on NRMs. Sociologists primarily interested in mainline religion, such as Enzo Pace, also devoted some attention to NRMs, and the same is true for historian Giovanni Filoramo (particularly his *I nuovi movimenti religiosi: Metamorfosi del sacro*, Rome – Bari: Laterza, 1986), and philosopher of religion Aldo Natale Terrin (see his *Nuove religioni: Alla ricerca della terra promessa*, Brescia: Morcelliana, 1985) who, although a Catholic priest, did not write from a counter-cult perspective.

The production of scholarly studies on NRMs became more systematic after the establishment of **CESNUR** in 1988. CESNUR entered into agreements with several publishers, both secular (SugarCo, Mondadori) and Catholic (Elledici, Piemme), and between 1988 and 2003 has produced some fifty books, from monographs on all the largest (and some small) NRMs to the huge *Enciclopedia delle religioni in Italia* (Leumann (Torino): Elledici, 2001), which remains the only European attempt to reproduce a comprehensive survey of religions, large and small, in a single nation. J. Gordon Melton published for the USA CESNUR's *Religioni e Movimenti* collection under the editorial direction of Masssimo Introvigne who in 1989 also authored the influential *Le Nuove Religioni* (Milan: Sugar Co.). CESNUR also commissioned some forty monographs written by Ita-

lian and foreign scholars on NRMs between 1997–2004. Almost all the texts written were published in Italian prior to being published in another foreign language. Among the monographs were Melton's on Scientology which was published in Italian as *La Chiesa di Scientology* by Elledici. While CESNUR's publications defined the field in the 1990s and the 2000s other social scientists and historians, including Macioti and Terrin, also wrote important books on NRMs, and almost without exception they were critical of the Anti-Cult perspective (see Anti-Cult Movement). Silvio Ferrari, a professor of Law at the University of Milan, organized the publication of a series of books on issues such as religious liberty in relation to NRMs.

In contrast to the rich Italian situation, not much has so far been produced in Spain in terms of academic literature on NRMs. Manuel Guerra Gomez, a professor at **Opus Dei**'s University of Navarra, published two important reference works in 1993 and 1998, *Los nuevos movimientos religiosos (Las sectas): Rasgos comunes y diferenciales* (Pamplona: Ediciones Universidad de Navarra) and *Diccionario enciclopédico de las sectas* (Madrid: BAC), both of which however remain somewhere midway between strictly academic and Catholic counter-cult literature. A legal scholar, Augustín Motilla, has also written several noted articles on NRMs and the law in Spain. Unlike Spain, however, several books based on extensive fieldwork have been published in Latin America. A school of NRMs studies, including several graduate students writing significant dissertations, developed in Argentina in the 1990s around Professors Alejandro Frigerio, Jorge Soneira, and Fortunato Mallimaci. Frigerio, for instance, edited *Nuevos movimientos religiosos y ciencias* *sociales* (Tucumán – Buenos Aires: Centro Editor de America Latina) in 1993. Another important center of NRM studies is Mexico, where Renée de la Torre Castellanos studied the local Luz del Mundo movement, while other authors including Cristina Gutiérrez Zuñiga mapped the Mexican scenario in general (see her *Nuevos movimientos religiosos: la Nueva Era en Guadalajara*, Zapopan: El Colegio de Jalisco, 1996), whilst Elio Masferrer Kan increasingly gravitated towards the anti-cult movement.

(b) Anti-cult literature is limited in quantity in Italy, particularly when compared with French and German publications. In fact, for several years a law professor, Michele Del Re, starting with his book *Culti emergenti e diritto penale* (Naples: Jovene, 1982), was the only significant Italian representative of the anti-cult movement. Several journalists and activists joined the fight in the second half of the 1990s, however, but most published only on the Internet, while CICAP, an organization of 'professional skeptics' generated literature critical of religion, miracles, and the supernatural in general, rather than focusing on NRMs only.

Spain, on the other hand, has produced several internationally famous contributions to the anti-cult literature, particularly by journalist Pepe Rodriguez, whose 1989 book *El poder de las sectas* (Barcelona: BSA) created a new anti-cult sub-genre of sensational 'investigative journalism'. In Argentina, psychologist José-Maria Baamonde, who moved to Spain in 2002, although a Catholic often working with Church organizations, resorted more to secular anti-cult **Brainwashing** models than to theological criticism in works such as *Sectas y lavado de cerebro* (Buenos Aires: Editorial Bonum, 1991). In Mexico,

several anti-cult activists work in close cooperation with US organizations.

(c) Much richer than the secular anti-cult literature is a plethora of Christian counter-cult books and pamphlets, both in Italian and Spanish. Most of them are Roman Catholic, although counter-cult works by César Vidal Manzanares (see his *El infierno de las sectas*, Bilbao: Mensajero, 1989) are popular among Spanish-speaking Evangelicals, with Italian Evangelicals publishing a counter-cult magazine known as *Ricerche*. Catholic production has been massive since the 1950s and even earlier, when criticism focused on the **Jehovah's Witnesses** and the **Church of Jesus Christ of the Latter Day Saints (Mormons)**. Monsignor Giovanni Marinelli (1914–2000) emerged as a pioneer in the Catholic counter-cult field in Italy and was instrumental in the foundation of the Catholic counter-cult organization GRIS. His most important work was *I Testimoni di Geova: Storia – Dottrina – Problemi – Prassi* (Ferrara: The Author, 1988), which was a summary of Catholic criticism of the Jehovah's Witnesses. Marinelli's activities were continued by Monsignor Lorenzo Minuti and Fr. Antonio Contri, both authors of anti-Jehovah's Witnesses books and subsequent presidents of GRIS. Jehovah's Witnesses remain the focus of most Catholic counter-cult activity in Italy; Mormons are a distant second, and on other groups counter-cult literature is quite scarce and often drawn from the international anti-cult movement. In this respect, one prolific author is Cecilia Gatto Trocchi, a Catholic counter-cultist and an anthropologist at the University of Chieti, who has emerged in popular TV talk shows as a vitriolic opponent of both 'cults' and psychics. A position paper by the Ecumenical Department of the Italian Catholic Bishops Conference (*L'impegno pastorale* *della Chiesa di fronte ai nuovi movimenti religiosi e alle sette*, Torino: Edizioni Paolime, 1993), on the other hand, is widely regarded as quite balanced and moderate.

Catholic counter-cult literature is also widespread in Spanish, both in Spain and Latin America, and with a Spanish Catholic politician, Pilar Salarrullana, as one of its most well-known authors. In Latin America, an important Catholic counter-cult collection was published in 1985 by CELAM, the Latin American Catholic Bishops' Conference, under the title *Las sectas en America Latina* (Buenos Aires: CELAM – Editorial Claretiana). Fr. Franz Damen in Bolivia, and Francisco Sampedro Nieto in Chile, are also prolific counter-cult authors. Italian-born Fr. Flaviano Amatulli Valente in Mexico, and professor Juan Bosch in Argentina, represent two opposite extremes of the Latin American Catholic counter-cult spectrum. Whilst Bosch uses an academic approach in the service of a counter-cult agenda, Amatulli has produced controversial popular literature intended for the barely literate Latin American country's Catholics, in which complex issues are reduced to very simple slogans.

(d) Finally, official reports have been produced by various governmental bodies in both Italian and Spanish, in an effort to mediate between the academic and anti-cult perspectives. They have not been as influential as their French or German counterparts, although they no doubt express opinions prevailing in certain political and law enforcement circles.

In 1998, the Italian Police Department produced the report *Sette religiose e nuovi movimenti magici in Italia* (Rome: Ministero dell'Interno). This was initially prepared for internal use by police and intelligence agencies, although it was eventually published. It did access considerable scholarly work, and indeed made good use of the **CESNUR** library on new and minority religions. It also contained some blatant mistakes, however, in its discussions of some groups, most notably The Family/The Children of God (see **Family, The**), and received widespread criticism as a consequence.

While the introduction to the 1998 report shows some familiarity with academic literature, chapter three contains a discussion of **Brainwashing** and mind control, offering in a footnote a standard anti-cult oriented reconstruction of the brainwashing process allegedly used by NRMs. The footnote discusses three major processes that are supposedly involved in recruiting and maintaining members. These include isolation, indoctrination, and maintenance, according to the model presented by Italian anti-cult scholar Michele Del Re. The report also includes a discussion of *plagio*, a term close to what some people mean by brainwashing, and which used to be referred to as such in Section 603 of the Italian Criminal Code. The report correctly notes, however, that the offence was declared unconstitutional in 1981 and is no longer part of Italian law. This point notwithstanding, there are several uses of the term later in the report, with claims that members of certain groups are 'submitted to *plagio*'. It is clear that brainwashing notions serve to underpin this report, even though the report contains some thoughtful and informed sections. Such underlying ideas have thus survived the infusion of other scholarship into the report, and confirm that this literary genre attempts, at best, to use *both* academic and anti-cult literature.

In 1988, the Department of Institutions of the Italian-speaking Swiss Canton of Ticino also published a report on *Interrogazioni sulle sette religiose* (Bellinzona: Dipartimento delle Istituzioni,

Repubblica e Cantone del Ticino). This report was apparently influenced by criticism by scholars directed against some earlier reports from France, Belgium, and the French-speaking Canton of Geneva, which simply adopted the anti-cult perspective. Indeed, it even mentions possible problems with 'anti-cult terrorism' against newer faiths, which suggests a different approach in this report. However, there were again signs that the brainwashing themes were accepted by the report's authors. There was also evidence of possible cross-fertilization between this report and the Italian police report of 1998.

The report's section on 'How People Join' is replete with language indicating acceptance of the brainwashing theory. Readers are told that the 'dangers are numerous and treacherous' for young people, who are the main target of the cults. The process of joining the Solar Temple, for instance, is described as a 'seduction exerted on the public by means of a manipulative process'. Of participants, we are told that 'their vulnerability and sense of not being loved are exploited.' There is a discussion of 'affectivity bombing', which would seem to be a reference to the 'love bombing' once practiced by the **Unification Church/ Moonies**. We are told that the recruitment process becomes 'more and more exacting both psychologically and financially', i.e. that recruits then embark on a 'slippery slope that can break them'. The report also says that 'at times the movement will threaten the member's family, in order to put a stop to efforts to lure the adept away from the sect.'

Another footnote discusses more particularly the Unification Church methods, after which we are told that 'it is almost impossible for the person to leave the group. *The submission is complete.*' Quoting Italian anti-cultist Michele Del Re, the report goes on to claim that this technique has three major steps (similar to those outlined in the Italian police report), including:

1. isolation of the person;
2. indoctrination; and
3. keeping him or her in a state of absolute dependence.

The report closes with a familiar anti-cult litany of what should be done about the menace of sects and cults. Here again, some concessions to the academic literature hardly counter-balance the report's heavy reliance on the theories propagated by the anti-cult movement.

Whilst the Italian police report resulted in provoking more criticism against the police from religious liberty activists, than in exerting any degree of influence, and the Ticino report remained a fairly local document, the Chilean report of 2002 was quite influential all over Spanish-speaking Latin America. In part, the report is the result of attempts by the French governmental Anti-cult Mission (MILS) to expand its activities abroad and influence foreign governments (at the end of 2002, due to political changes in France, MILS was replaced by a reformed institution known as Miviludes, with a reduced budget and very limited activities outside of France). MILS focused on Chile as the first country in Latin America interested in amending its laws and setting up a MILS-style anti-cult national agency, following a particular incident involving a small local NRM, the Center for Tibetan Studies.

The Parliamentary mandate of the Chilean commission (created by the law of July 22, 2000) expressly mentioned 'brainwashing' as allegedly taking place within the Center for Tibetan Studies. A 'Commission to Investigate the Existence and Activities of Cults' was then established. Only MPs were members, but two experts worked permanently with the Commission: a lawyer who also has a sociology degree, Humberto Lagos (in turn author of several works quite critical of 'cults'), and a legal scholar, Jorge Precht. The Commission interviewed police officers, journalists, psychiatrists, and the leading Roman Catholic counter-cult expert. It also heard the leadership of the Center for Tibetan Studies. The Commission also solicited written reports from several law enforcement and other governmental agencies, and collected press clippings and court decisions. It claimed to have read both the French 1996 report and **CESNUR**'s criticism of it.

A written report sent to the Commission by the Carabineros, or Military Police, claimed that mind control was a key feature of 'cults' and listed (among 150 religious groups reportedly active in Chile) seven as worth watching: three 'pseudo-Christian' groups – the Mormon Church, the Jehovah's Witnesses and the Unification Church – as well as four 'dangerous religious groups': the Brazilian Universal Church of the Kingdom of God; The Family; Scientology; and the local Theocratic Movement. Several other answers received by government departments and police and military bodies derived their approach from the French reports of 1996 and 1999, occasionally even borrowing literally from them without mentioning the source.

The Commission in its final report dated 7 March 2002, published as a book under the title of *Informe de la Comisión investigadora sobre la existencia y actividades de las sectas religiosas* (Santiago: Cámara de Diputados, 2002,) did not entirely follow these suggestions. On the one hand, many parts of the report used an unmistakable anticult language: the Commission believed that 'destructive cults' do exist in Chile

and that something variously called brainwashing, mind control or mental manipulation may well be taking place within them. On the other hand, examples focused on the much talked-about Center for Tibetan Studies and juvenile Satanism, rather than on the most usual anti-cult targets. The Commission remarked on the controversies raised by the publication of a list of sects in France and recommended against drafting any similar list in Chile.

Generally speaking, the Commission did not recommend any special law on cults, but rather a strict enforcement of the existing laws. It remained doubtful about the French law of 2001 and its anti-brainwashing provisions. The report recommended that further study be conducted, but argued that such study should consider the objections against the French law and the fact that the French position on brainwashing has been criticized not only by scholars but also 'by all the traditional European churches' (with objections by authoritative Catholic agencies listed in detail: clearly, they did not fail to impress the Catholic members of the Commission). The report commented that anti-brainwashing provisions might endanger religious freedom and also be too vague to be really enforceable. Less problematical solutions to the alleged evil of cults may lie in making it more difficult for religious entities to achieve legal registration; in creating an Observatory of Cults; in spreading information (apparently, including very critical comments on specific groups); and in liaising with other Latin American parliaments.

The French impact was felt, but more in the reports the Commission received from several agencies than in the report itself (although a peculiar Latin American approach regularly mixed Catholic and secular criticism). The report did take into account the French diagnosis, but hesitated in recommending the same therapy and was aware that scholars and (apparently, more importantly for several Commissioners) Catholic Church authorities do not favor anti-brainwashing statutes. The enclosures show that an anti-cult sentiment was predominant within several Chilean law enforcement, military and other bodies (and may ultimately lead to anti-cult legislation), but this sentiment failed to completely inspire the report. Ultimately, the Commissioners did not entirely accept the anti-cult model of brainwashing, and showed a surprising awareness of how controversial the concept is, although they were not prepared to discard it entirely, either.

MASSIMO INTROVIGNE

LITERATURE IN JAPANESE ON NRMS

New religious movements (see **New Religious Movement** and **New Religion, Japan**) have become an accepted focus of research within the study of religion in Japan since the 1970s. Previously seen as 'quasi-religious', or even fraudulent, not worthy of serious scholarship, from around the 1970s it became a common assumption that these groups have a connection with the folk religious tradition in Japan and that research on these movements could contribute greatly to the understanding of popular religious expressions in that country. Consequently, there have been a great many works published on new religious movements in Japan in the last decades. This review will not try to be comprehensive in introducing these works, but rather will concentrate on some of the major developments in literature in Japanese on new religious movements. Some of

the works published by NRMs themselves will also be introduced.

Perhaps the first major work appreciative of the new religions as an object of study to appear was *Nihon no kindaika to minshu shiso* (Japanese Modernization and Popular Thought) by Yasumaru Yoshio, published in 1974. In this book, Yasumaru explores the dissemination of what he terms a 'popular morality' (*tsuzoku dotoku*), teaching values such as hard work, thrift, humility, filial piety, and so on. This morality was popularized by itinerant preachers such as Ninomiya Sontoku, a preacher active in the early nineteenth century. As the social order imposed by the Tokugawa shoguns in the early seventeenth century began to unravel in the late eighteenth century, several popular movements emerged among the merchant and peasant classes emphasizing personal morality as the solution to social problems. Yasumaru identifies the common dynamic of these movements as a 'philosophy of the heart' (*kokoro no tetsugaku*). This philosophy of the heart, as described by Yasumaru, identifies inner spiritual activity as the foundation for all change. It posits an essentially unlimited potentiality to the human heart, and offers a means to the realization of the power of the human spirit through the practice of the popular morality mentioned above. The cultivation of the virtues of filial piety, loyalty, thrift, frugality, diligence, and so on was offered as the answer to the social problems caused by the economic upheavals of the latter part of the Tokugawa shogunate, in essence reducing these problems to a matter of personal ethics. These movements spread throughout the countryside in the nineteenth century, becoming firmly implanted in the popular culture by the end of that century. Yasumaru's work contains an extended study of Maruyamakyo, one of the early new religious movements that emerged in the late nineteenth century, indicating how this popular morality becomes the basis for the teachings of many of these new religious movements.

Building on this seminal work by Yasumaru, a group of young scholars began to share the fruits of their research on popular religion, and more specifically new religious movements, through the organization of the *Shukyo shakaigaku kenkyukai* (Sociology of Religion Research Group). The research group edited several volumes in the 1980s in which this research was presented, including *Shukyo: Sono nichijosei to hinichijosei* (Religion: The Ordinary and Extraordinary) (1983) and *Kyoso to sono shuhen* (Founders and Disciples) (1987). The first volume explores the roots of the new religious movements in the traditional shrine and temple organizations as well as popular religiosity in the established Buddhist sects. In addition, a section on religious experience offers several case studies of NRMs. The second volume explores the role of the founder in these new groups, offering a development of Max Weber's theory of charisma that emphasizes the interactional aspect of this quality of religious leadership, that is, that the group of disciples also plays a role in developing the charisma of the founder.

Some of the members of this research group also contributed to a volume titled *Gendaijin no shukyo* (Contemporary Religion) published in 1988. This book seeks to explore the so-called 'religious boom' that started in the 1970s, a phenomenon that was taken as a sign of the return to religious belief despite the expectations of those who had propounded the secularization theory in the 1960s. Perhaps most notable regarding NRMs is an influential article by Nishiyama Shigeru, one of the editors of the above mentioned volume, that presents a schema for analyzing new religious movements in Japan as emerging in four distinct periods: the late Tokugawa and early Meiji periods (roughly the second half of the nineteenth century), the late Meiji and Taisho periods (the first quarter of the twentieth century), much of the Showa period (1925–70), and the period from the 1970s. The first and third of these periods are marked by the emergence of new religions that emphasize the cultivation of the popular morality explored by Yasumaru, whereas the second and fourth periods are marked by the emergence of movements that emphasize spiritism, mysticism, and magic.

Other members of the Sociology of Religion Research Group have also written influential studies on NRMs. For example, Shimazono Susumu published *Gendai kyusai shukyo ron* (The Study of Contemporary Salvationist Religions) in 1992, and a smaller volume titled *Shin-shinshukyo to shukyo bumu* (The New New Religions and the Religious Boom) in the same year. The first volume offers a general theory of new religious movements in Japan, pointing out their roots in the folk religious tradition and the Nichiren or Lotus Sutra schools of Buddhism, as well as more recent developments, including the spread of Japanese new religions abroad and the emergence of what Shimazono calls a 'new spirituality movement', sharing many of the features of the New Age in the West. The second volume is a study of new religious movements that have emerged or become popular since the 1970s, groups that are commonly called 'new new religions' in Japan. Shimazono points out both the continuity of these groups with earlier new religions, as well as the features that set them apart, features that can be found more broadly in the 'new spirituality movement' and New Age explored in his earlier work. A later volume by Shimazono, *Seishin sekai no yukue* (1996), with the English title of 'New Spirituality Movements in the Global Society', further develops his theories on these new movements and their international character.

Shimazono has also published two analyses of Aum Shinrikyo, the new religious group that released the poison gas sarin on the Tokyo subways in 1995: an early work titled *Aum Shinrikyo no kiseki* (The Development of Aum Shinrikyo) (1995), and a more thoroughly researched later work, *Gendai shukyo no kanosei: Aum Shinrikyo to boryoku* (The Promise of Contemporary Religion: Aum Shinrikyo and Violence) (1997). These two works are perhaps among the best analyses of this group that have appeared in Japanese.

Another member of the research group who has published extensively on the Japanese new religions is Inoue Nobutaka. Among his work we can mention a thorough study of early Shinto-based new religious movements, *Kyoha Shinto no keisei* (The Development of Sect Shinto) (1991) and *Shinshukyo no kaidoku* (Deciphering the New Religions) (1992), a general introduction to the study of Japanese new religious movements.

Inoue was also one of the editors of the *Shinshukyo jiten* (New Religions Encyclopedia) (1990), the most comprehensive resource on new religions, including topical introductions to general issues, such as the origin and development of new religions, founders, teachings, practices, new religions and society, etc., as well as individual entries on over three hundred groups and short biographies of several hundred founders. This book has become a standard for reference books on NRMs in Japan.

Numerous longer case studies of individual groups are also available. Particularly worthy of mention here is Morioka Kiyomi's detailed study of developments in Rissho Kosei-kai in the first thirty years of its history, *Shinshukyo undo no tenkai katei* (The Development of a New Religious Movement) (1989), where he argues for a 'lifecycle theory' to describe the transformation of a movement as it matures and becomes more concerned with attaining social respectability.

There are also several series available that offer somewhat more detailed descriptions of individual movements. For example, *Shinshukyo no sekai* (The World of New Religions) (5 volumes, 1979) offers studies of nineteen groups. More recently, *Shinshukyo no jidai* (The Age of New Religions) (5 volumes, 1994–7) presents an equal number of individual studies.

Finally, among more popular works on the new religions we can mention a series of five volumes titled *Shukyo wo gendai ni tou* (Questioning Religion Today) (1976), *Shukyo wa ikiteiru* (Religion Lives) (3 volumes, 1980), and the single volume *Seikimatsu no kamisama* (Gods at the End of the Century) (1993), the first two published by the Mainichi Shinbunsha, and the third written by the religion reporters of the same newspaper group. All three of these provide personal accounts of contemporary religious believers, many of them members of groups commonly recognized as NRMs.

In addition to these works on Japanese new religions, some of the groups have developed their own scriptures, often based on the private revelation of their founder or some other charismatic personality within the group. Although believers of the particular groups are generally the only ones familiar with these texts, works of the founders of some of the earlier new religions, such as the *Ofudesaki* (The Tip of the Writing Brush) of **Tenrikyo** or the *Reikai*

Monogatari (Tales of the Spirit World) of Omotokyo are somewhat better known. I will briefly mention some of these works below.

Tenrikyo, founded in 1838, is generally recognized as one of the oldest of the Japanese new religious movements. Its founding is traced back to the possession experience of Nakayama Miki (1798–1887), a farmer's wife living in the area of Nara, the ancient capital. In 1869, the year following the institution of the new imperial government, Miki, who is supposed to have been illiterate, took up writing and composed the *Ofudesaki*, the record of the revelations she had received from God, which has become one of Tenrikyo's scriptures. The *Ofudesaki* is written in traditional verse and was composed over the course of the years from 1869 to 1882. It consists of 1,711 verses divided into seventeen parts. Miki composed the text in accord with the traditional poetic style known as *waka*, a thirty-one syllable poem transcribed into two lines of verse. The vast majority of the verse is written in the Japanese syllabary writing of *hiragana*, with only minimal use of Chinese characters, a style that would have made it easy to read by her many peasant followers. The situations presented in the text are also often taken from the lives of the peasants, craftsmen, and housewives that constituted the membership in Tenrikyo.

Another scripture of Tenrikyo is called the *Osashizu*. Iburi Izõ, a carpenter and one of the early followers, began to deliver divine messages shortly before Miki's death in 1887, a role that he continued to play in the group until his own death in 1907. These messages are collected in the *Osashizu*. The *Osashizu* contained two kinds of messages, a regular message delivered every evening, and other messages meant to address specific situations or problems that the group faced. It was through the means of this latter type of revelation, for example, that Tenrikyo's decision to do what was necessary to be recognized as a religious group by the government was sanctioned. Although Miki had rejected any compromise of the faith and practice that had gradually been revealed to her in various early attempts to attain recognition and protection from either an established Shinto or Buddhist institution, by means of the continuing revelation mediated by Iburi Izo, Tenrikyo aligned its doctrine and practice to the increasingly rigid religious policy of the national government in order to obtain recognition as the thirteenth sect of Shinto in 1908 (see **State Shinto**).

A final scripture in Tenrikyo is the *Mikagura uta*, also written in verse like the *Ofudesaki*. Miki gave voice to a new revelation that identified the Yamato region in Japan as the center of the world, and developed a liturgy that both reenacted God's original creation and contributed towards the realization of the perfect, joyous life that is God's intention for his children. This liturgy, called the Kagura Service, is performed on the 26th of every month, the day on which both the original possession experience (26 October) and Miki's death (26 January) occurred, around a pillar called the Kanrodai, set up in the center of the main Tenrikyo church, built on the site of the Nakayama residence. The *Mikagura uta*, written between 1866 and 1882, serves as the text of this liturgy.

Omotokyo (see **Omoto**) was a religion founded in 1898 by **Deguchi Nao** (1837–1918) and Ueda Kisaburo (1871–1948), who later married into the Deguchi family and took the name Onisaburo. In many respects Omotokyo bears a resemblance to Tenrikyo, founded by a peasant woman who experienced severe poverty, based on a unique experience of the divine in a state of possession, preaching the imminent establishment of a new order in which all will share equally in the earth's benefits. One of the sacred texts of Omotokyo even bears the same name as that of Tenrikyo, the *Ofudesaki*. Like Miki, Nao is also said to have been illiterate, even though she took up writing the revelations she had received in a trance state. Omotokyo's *Ofudesaki* was written between 1892 and 1918, eventually reaching tens of thousands of pages. This work was edited by Onisaburo and parts of it were published after Nao's death. However, more than the *Ofudesaki*, the *Reikai Monogatari* written by Onisaburo is more readily identified as the scripture of Omotokyo, and more widely know, even outside the circle of Omotokyo believers. The *Reikai Monogatari* is also an extensive work, comprising eighty-one volumes. It is meant to be the collection of the revelations received by Onisaburo while he underwent ascetic training in the mountains, a common practice in Japanese religiosity, before meeting Nao in 1898. The volumes recount a wide variety of events in the spirit world with an enormous cast of deities, humans, mythological, and historical figures. It deals with the creation of the universe, social problems, the teachings of other religions, as well as theories of love and marriage. The imagery of cosmic battles and other epic events in the spirit world have inspired contemporary popular culture, including the *manga* and *anime* culture.

Finally, some other works by founders of new religious movements that have achieved some notoriety in Japan would include works such as *Shinji no kenko* (True Health) by Okada Mokichi, the founder of **Sekai Kyusei Kyo**, and *Seimei no shinso* (The Truth of Life), a forty-volume work by Taniguchi Masaharu, the founder of **Seicho-no-Ie**. The work

by Okada lays out his unconventional ideas regarding the maintenance of health. Sickly from a young age, his own extensive experience with illness had convinced Mokichi of the ineffectiveness of modern medicine. After the medical establishment declared that he had incurable tuberculosis, he felt he was able to cure himself with a vegetarian diet. Further, he came to believe that medical practice was not only ineffective but actually harmful. For a long time he had had severe pain in his teeth, and no dental treatment seemed to be able to alleviate the pain. In desperation he turned to a faith-healer, and stopped taking the medicine prescribed by his dentists. Almost immediately the pain began to subside, and when he stopped going to the faith-healer but continued to recover he attributed the success to the fact that he was no longer being poisoned by the medicine. He developed his own method of faith-healing called *jorei*, or the purification of the spirit, involving the channeling of light energy through the palm of his hand. This method has become influential in several of the new religions popularized since the 1970s in Japan. The later work by Taniguchi is an extensive explanation of this own spiritist beliefs, covering topics such as traditional Buddhist doctrines, the spirit world, a rather conservative ethic, and even practical issues such as education in the home.

ROBERT KISALA

LITERATURE IN PORTUGUESE ON NRMS

This account concentrates mostly on Brazil. The literature published in Brazil on NRMs includes general characterizations of the **New Age** universe, its insertion in the Brazilian religious field and the results of research on groups and particular aspects of that universe.

Diffuse field, emergent literature

In Brazil, a set of institutions, groups, events, services and products corresponding to the universe of NRMs developed sociologically clear though conceptually imprecise features beginning in the 1980s. Though various aspects of the NRM phenomenon refer back to previous periods, it was only in the last two decades when Paulo Coelho's literary output began to become widely known with the publication of *The Alchemist* (1988), that it really took off. It was then that the capital of the country, Brasilia, became famous as a 'mystical city'. Paulo Coelho and Brasilia became the icons of a fluid universe, referred to using the sometimes competing, other times interchangeable adjectives, 'alternative', 'holistic', 'mystical' and 'esoteric'.

With respect to its religious panorama, Brazil may be sociologically characterized by the predominance of Christian religion. On one hand Catholicism is associated with the cultural roots of the country, and has played a key role in the country's modern history. Though Catholicism has always been the majority religion, in the last decades, it registered a progressive decline among its followers. On the other hand, Protestants ('Pentecostalists and Evangelicals'), have in recent times begun to expand both inside and outside Brazil. The decade of the 1980s saw the growth of Neo-Evangelical Christianity (see **Evangelical Christianity**), particularly in its Pentecostalist form, which was accompanied by a significant controversy about the expansion in the number of followers and their incursion in the fields of politics and the media.

The 'mystical' or 'esoteric' universe and new religions account for only a small minority of the population. This has meant that compared with elsewhere there has been little controversy over NRMs in Brazil.

In the 1980s, there was a basic tripartite division of the Brazilian religious field: Catholicism, Protestantism, and medium based cults (a term which covers African traditions and **spiritualism** of European origin). In the 1980s NRM terminology was initially used in studies that sought to map and characterize what did not fit into this three way division. The majority of these studies were linked to church initiatives and fit into the general discussion on 'new religions' and 'sects'. It is important to note that in Brazil, the term 'sects', though it is often used in a prejudicial manner, never acquired the weight or severity it holds in countries where the controversy surrounding NRMs is strong (see **Anti-Cult Movement** and **Cult and New Religions**).

Changes had occurred by the 1990s. On one hand, Pentecostalism had become integrated into the field of Protestantism and had become the most researched subject among religious scholars. At the same time, a corresponding category pertaining to medium based cults was established, and though these were less studied than before, they continued to be studied following a specific research agenda. What had previously been considered under the original label of NRMs came to be treated under the headings: 'alternative complex', 'new mysticism', 'neo-esoterism' and, above all, New Age (Nova Era).

What follows considers only that which has been published in books and articles, taking the 1990s as the starting point. Among the principal writings of the 1990s are the works of L. E. Soares ('Religioso por natureza' ('Religious by nature'), *Cadernos do ISER*, 22, 1989), J. Russo (*O Corpo contra a Palavra*, ('The Body against the Word') 1993: Rio de Janeiro) and L. R. Vilhena (*O*

Mundo da Astrologia, ('The World of Astrology') 1990: Rio de Janeiro).

D. Siqueira's 'Psicologização das religiões: religiosidade e estilo de vida' ('Psychologizing religions: religiosity and lifestyle'), *Sociedade e Estado,* 14, 1999, examines 'mystical-religious groups' in the region of Brasilia, and considers; the link between religion and psychological phenomena, the privatization of faith, which confers on the individual the capacity to compose his/her own religiosity, and the goal of self-knowledge and self-improvement. A similar emphasis on the central place of the individual and the consequent weakening of institutions is found in C.R. Brandão's 'A crise das instituições tradicionais produtoras de sentido' ('The crisis of traditional, sense-producing institutions'), and in his *Misticismo e Novas Religiões*, 1994: Petrópolis (Mysticism and New Religions). The definition of the NAM (see **New Age Movement**) as a sacralization of the principle of self-autonomy, is offered by M.J. Carozzi 'Nova Era: a autonomia como religião' ('New Era: autonomy as religion'). This text is included in her *A Nova Era no Mercosul* ('The New Era in the Mercosur'), 1999: Petrópolis.

J.G. Magnani's *O Brasil da Nova Era*, 2000: Rio de Janeiro maps out the 'neo-esoteric circuit' in the city of São Paulo, and evaluates the spatial distribution of a diverse set of institutional forms. The author provides a classification of practices and an outline of participants, as well as pointing to the doctrinal sources that influence this universe. Though the text agrees that this is a heterogeneous universe, it asserts that participants share a lifestyle, in terms of preferences, concerns, and values, which distinguishes them within urban culture. From another perspective, the author develops a general grammar that, instead of enthroning just the individual, situates the indivi-

dual on the vertex of a relationship that includes the notions of totality and community.

That relativization of the centrality of the individual is deepened by L. Amaral *Carnaval da Alma* ('Carnaval of the Soul'), 2000: Petrópolis. Based on her research in holistic centers and events, she suggests that the New Age be seen as a 'syncretism in movement'. The drifting she perceives among believers also marks doctrinal elaborations and rituals, since they emerge without depending on a fixed place of hybridization. In this way, a de-substantialization of the religious sphere and a relativization of the domains of experience are produced. The New Age, as a way of dealing with the sacred, is thus a religiosity without foundation. Not even the individual serves as a foundation: though the New Age denounces a discontent with the disappearance of the subject, it conceives of the self (see **Self-Religion, The Self and Self**) as a being in search of spiritual communication.

Other works that attempt to characterize the universe of NRMs and their mode of insertion in Brazilian society include articles by C. Steil 'A Igreja dos Pobres: da secularização à mística' ('The church of the poor: from secularization to mysticism'), *Religião e Sociedade*, 19(2), 1998 and M. Camurça's 'A Nova Era diante do Cristianismo Histórico' ('The New Era in relation to Historical Christianism'), *Atualidade em Debate*, 50, 1997. This focuses on the relationships between the New Age and Catholicism. A.B. Fonseca's 'Nova Era evangélica, confissão positiva e o crescimento dos sem-religião' ('Evangelical New Era, positive confession and the growth of persons without religion'), *Numen*, 3(2), 2002, notes the influence of the New Age on this world of literature and the Evangelical media. M.B. Guimarães's 'Umbanda e Santo Daime

"Lua Branca" de Lumiar' ('Umbanda and Santo Daime "Lua Branca" of Lumiar'), *Religião e Sociedade*, 17, 1996, discusses the relationship between African–Brazilian movements such as **Umbanda** and **Santo Daime**.

J.J. Carvalho's 'Características do fenômeno religioso na sociedade contemporânea' ('Characteristics of the religious phenomenon in contemporary society'), *O Impacto da Modernidade sobre a Religião* (The impact of Modernity on Religion), 1992: São Paulo; 'O encontro de velhas e novas religiões: esboço de uma teoria dos estilos de espiritualidade' ('The meeting of old and new religions: outline of a theory of styles of spirituality'), *Misticismo e Novas Religiões* (Mysticism and New Religions), 1994: Petrópolis, all relate NRMs to general tendencies, such as the direction of modernity and the spiritual traditions of the new world. In any case, Carvalho examines traits that mark the current situation. His interest, like that of P. Sanchis's 'O campo religioso contemporâneo no Brasil' ('The contemporary religious field in Brazil'), *Globalização e Religião*, 1997: Petrópolis, focuses on what disposes people to associate with NRMs and the NAM in the Brazilian context.

Among the unpublished works, there are a few texts concerned with institutions, groups or specific features of the world of NRMs in Brazil. Towards the end of the 1980s, an initiative undertaken to map the religious diversity of the country led to the publication of small descriptive texts, authored by a diverse set of researchers, and included presentations on the Igreja da Unificação (Unification Church), **Seicho-no-Iê** (House of Growth), the Perfeita Liberdade (Perfect Liberty), **Hare Krishna**, **Rajneesh**, Ananda Marga, and **Santo Daime** (*Cadernos do ISER*, 23, 1990).

Another collective endeavor of an interdisciplinary character extensively explored the uses of ayahuasca, a hallucinogenic drink around which various native groups gravitate, such as the **Santo Daime** movement, W. Araújo and B. Labate (eds.), *Os Usos da Ayahuasca* ('The Uses of Ayahuasca'), 2002: São Paulo. Some works specifically analyze other groups also created in Brazil. These include A. D'Andrea's *O Self Perfeito e a Nova Era* ('The Perfect Self and the New Era'), 2001: São Paulo, and of A. L. Galinkin's 'Vale do Amanhecer: um caso de milenarismo no Distrito Federal' ('The Sunrise Valley: a case of millenarianism in the Federal District'), *Religião e Sociedade*, 16(1–2), 1992. The scene in this case is a religious complex in the proximities of Brasilia. Texts that focus on groups originating abroad include S. Guerriero's ISKCON au Brésil' ('ISKCON in Brazil'), *Social Compass*, 47(2), 2000, A. Osorio on **Wicca** ('O Corpo da Bruxa' ('The Witch's Body'), *Nus and Vestidos*, 2002: Rio de Janeiro) and F. Usarski's *O Budismo no Brasil* ('Buddhism in Brazil'), 2002: São Paulo.

Finally, there are texts that focus the universe of the New Age in Brazil. Included among these are the articles by F. Tavares on therapeutic activities 'O "holismo terapêutico" no âmbito do movimento Nova Era no Rio de Janeiro' (' "Therapeutic holism" in the context of the New Age movement in Rio de Janeiro'), *A Nova Era no Mercosul*, 1999: Petrópolis, and on learning tarotism 'Tornando-se tarólogo: percepção "racional" versus percepção "intuitive" entre os iniciantes no tarot no Rio de Janeiro' ('Becoming a tarotist: "rational" perception versus "intuitive" perception among the beginners in tarot in Rio de Janeiro'), *Numen*, 2(1), 1999. Other articles on New Age practices include S. Guerriero's 'Os Jogos Divinatórios na

Virada do Milênio' ('Divining Games at the Turn of the Millennium'), *Religião e Cultura*, 1, 2002, on divining games at mystical fairs, and P. Semán's 'Literatura e religião na sociedade contemporânea' ('Literature and religion in contemporary society'), *Imaginário*, 8, 2002. The focus here is on Paulo Coelho's readers. These specific case studies have contributed to the more general discussion of the form, content, style and overall character of the NRM and NAM universes.

Further reading

Amaral Leila (2003) 'Un Espírito Sem Lar: sobre uma dimensão "nova era" da religiosidade contemporânea', Otavio Velho (ed.) *Circuitos infinitos*, Sao Paulo: Attar Editorial, pp. 17–58.

EMERSON GIUMBELLI

LORD'S RESISTANCE ARMY
Founder: Alice Lakwena

In Acholi in northern Uganda several self-proclaimed prophets emerged in the 1980s announcing as their mission the overthrow of the National Resistance Army (NRA) which was under the command of Yoweri Museveni later to become President of Uganda. Among these prophets was Alice Auma from Gulu in Acholi who claimed to be possessed by a previously unknown Christian spirit named Lakwena, meaning messenger or apostle in Acholi. Alice Lakwena (she is known by the name of the possessing spirit) declared that her mission was to heal society. In pre-colonial and pre-Christian times possession by *jok* (spirit) of humans, animals, and material objects could endow them with the power to heal or make the land fertile and turn an immoral, decadent society into a moral and upright one. Such possession could also result in

harm in the form of moral, social, and natural catastrophes.

The arrival of Christianity in the twentieth century eventually gave rise to the emergence of a spirit world in which Christian spirits were thought to heal and purify from witchcraft without harming the one who was responsible for bringing it about and thus breaking the cycle of retaliatory bewitching. This came to be contrasted with the traditional spirits or *joki* (plural of jok) who were believed not only to heal and release from witchcraft but also to kill the one who had perpetrated the affliction.

It was this new, Christian understanding that, under Lakwena's guidance, Alice tried to advance by working as a healer and diviner. In August 1986 she organized the 'Holy Spirit Mobile Forces' (HSMF) a movement that was joined by many regular soldiers for the purposes of waging war on the government, witches, and 'impure' soldiers. Initial successes against the NRA were attributed by Alice Lakwena to 'Holy Spirit Tactics' – a method of warfare that combined modern techniques with magical practices – and led to further support for her armed resistance among the general population.

In 1987 Lakwena's army of around ten thousand soldiers who in theory were under the command of spirits reached within thirty miles of the Uganda capital Kampala before being defeated by government forces. While many of the rebel soldiers were killed Lakwena escaped to nearby Kenya where she continues to reside.

The spirit Lakwena then took possession of Alice's father Saverino Lukoya who for a short time led the various remaining HSMF forces – these were never fully united into one movement – until the one-time soldier in another of Acholi's rebel groups, Joseph Kony, took over. Kony was also from Gulu and claims to be a cousin of Alice.

Sometime after Joseph Kony took over from Severino Kony, Joseph Kony renamed the movement the Lord's Resistance Army (LRA). Though he sought to distance himself from Alice Kony he has retained many of the rites and ritual techniques that she had devised including the same rite of initiation for army recruits. He likewise has endorsed the Holy Spirit Safety Precautions, a set of behavioural rules drawn up by Alice, and has used as she did the Holy Spirit Tactics and fought as vehemently as she did against witchcraft and pagan spirit mediums or *ajwakas*.

However, there are marked differences between Kony and Lakwena which the former has used to highlight the discontinuity between his movement and that led by Alice. For example he claims to have been possessed not by Lakwena but by the spirit Juma Oris who replaced Lakwena as chairman and commander of his army. Another of his spirits is Silli Sillindi (St Cecilia) from the Sudan who leads the Mary Company which consists of the women soldiers of the movement and acts as commander of operations. Kony has established an international network of spirits that goes well beyond Africa to China, Korea and the United States and though their names are new the functions they perform are very often the same as those undertaken by Alice's spirits.

Where Joseph Kerry seems to have made a clear break with Alice is in the area of army discipline and recruitment. Under him abduction of children for initiation in to the army is seemingly commonplace as is drug use by soldiers and the practices of torture, rape and pillaging.

Thus, a movement that began with the aim of healing and unifying society and of reconstituting the moral order has turned into one of random violence and killing.

Further reading

Behrend, H. (1999) 'Power to Heal, Power to Kill. Spirit Possession and War in Northern Uganda' in H. Behrend and U. Luig (eds) *Spirit Possession. Modernity and Power in Africa*, Oxford: James Curry, pp. 20–34.

PETER B. CLARKE

LOVE, SPIRITUAL

Spiritual love is different from all other forms of love because it does not directly involve relationship with anyone or anything. It is not a personal love, nor is it self love. In seeming contradiction, when experienced, this love can encompass everyone and everything, its source and strength being beyond comprehension, a power that the Sufi poet Jelaluddin Rumi describes succinctly: 'And don't look for me in human shape. I am inside your looking. No room for form with love this strong'.

As far as it is possible to say, spiritual love is 'available' before an individual experiences it and continues to exist unchanged if the experience ends – its existence is not dependent on the individual. This means that spiritual love exists as a constant regardless of whether the individual experiences it or not. When human individuality (the mind) is quietened (see **Silence**), the fullness of spiritual love is revealed. This experience is, perhaps, what all women and men who lead spiritual lives ultimately desire and aim towards.

Theists would say that spiritual love is God-given, the *Agape* that Anders Nygren has described, or the *Qalb* (mind within the mind) of the **Sufi**s. In a different vein, it is *Metta* (loving kindness), the first of four *Brahma Viharas* (highest attributes) in Buddhism (see **Buddhism in the West**) of which the 14th **Dalai Lama** speaks so often. Spiritual love is of the highest importance in many

NRMs, particularly **A Course of Miracles**, **Creation Spirituality**, **ISKCON** and Sai Baba's teachings (see **Sai Baba, Sathya**). Philosophers, too, have attempted to describe spiritual love from various directions and many – from Plato to Kierkegaard – have concluded its source is beyond human understanding. Psychologists concentrate more on the study of relationships as, in the main, they have been unable to arrive at any conclusions about love (Carl Jung in *Memories, Dreams, Reflections* saying that he has 'never been able to explain what it is' (1971: 387)) (see **Jung, Carl**).

It is not altogether certain whether there are different forms of love or just one which manifests in different ways, the highest or most pure being spiritual love. This is a love which is not dependent on the transience and changeableness of any external influence. Its foundation appears completely unshakeable, no matter what event might occur and it seems to exist without definable limits. These characteristics make spiritual love the strongest form of love and possibly the most rare, at least in its fullest experience.

Spiritual love is at the heart of most spiritualities, whether old or new. Perhaps it is fair to say that it is the most important element in religious and spiritual beliefs – without it most would fail. However, while there is no overall agreement between religions as to what spiritual love might entail, among priests and the like (reported in Rose, 2004) there is some agreement on certain facets. These are that it is unconditional – that is, it cannot be tailored to fit circumstances; it is central to belief; it is in all types of spirituality; it includes all neighbours; and it is more important than law. There is no agreement that particular faiths are all a reflection of one ultimate spiritual love because each group sees itself as distinct from each other.

Words cannot fully describe spiritual love. Understanding it is much more a matter of inner experience and inner knowing than of dogma and ritual – both of which may be enriched by such insight.

Further reading

Happold, F. C. (1970) *Mysticism: A study and an Anthology*, London: Pelican.
Jacobs, A. (ed.) (1997) *The Element Book of Mystical Verse*, Shaftesbury, UK: Element.
Jung, C. (1971) *Memories, Dreams, Reflections*, London: Collins.
Rose, S. (2004) 'Spiritual Love: Questioning the Unquestionable', *Journal of Contemporary Religion*, 19(2), 205–17
Underhill, E. (1923) *Mysticism: A Study in the Nature and Development of Man's Spiritual Consciousness* London: Methuen.

STUART ROSE

LOVELOCK, JAMES E.
(b. 1919)

Lovelock is a pioneer in the development of environmental awareness and originator of the 'Gaia hypothesis'. British chemist James Lovelock's conjecture (known as the **Gaia** hypothesis) is that the Earth along with its inhabitants is a single living organism. Lovelock was educated at the University of London and Manchester University and received a PhD in medicine. During his work for NASA in the 1970s, he developed the notion of the planet as a self-regulating, self-changing living being. Lovelock's original motivation was to question the prevailing concepts of theoretical ecology, Darwinism and planetary instability. He publicly presented his new idea of the earth as a coherent system of life in his 1979 book, *Gaia: A New Look at Life on Earth*. The central thesis holds that the interlocking self-regulation of climate and chemical composition maintains the earth as a place conducive for life and that the planet behaves as if it were a living super-organism. Rather than owner, tenant, or passenger, the human individual is an integral component of the living whole. Lovelock's breakthrough innovation was to see and understand the planet not as passive matter with regard to existential threat (the conventional view of science), but as a living creature that actively engages with its changing surroundings and conditions and forever seeks regulation and equilibrium.

According to Lovelock, the largest and most irreversible geo-physiological change that humans have made is to have tampered with the original climatic and chemical geo-physiological or homeostatic balance by transferring virtually 75 per cent of the fertile land in the temperate and tropical regions of the planet to agricultural use. This shift he fears might disrupt the ecological equilibrium of the natural ecosystems unless we develop 'a drastic change of heart and habits' and learn to use land not only to feed us but concurrently to sustain the by-production of rain and carbon dioxide that are equally necessary for planetary life.

This concept that the planet is a complete, self-sustaining and self-regulating system has been translated into the idea of **New Age** holism. As part of the impetus to ecological awareness that Lovelock has helped to foster, he favours the use of clean nuclear energy out of respect for the environment. His hypothesis is further linked to current chaos, catastrophe, or complexity theory that pictures the quantum development of consciousness as part of natural evolution. Lovelock has been joined in his theoretical work by American scientist Lynn Margulis, and together they have further refined the notion of the earth as

a closed-loop self-regulating system that produces emergent properties in which the whole becomes more than the sum of its parts. Lovelock and New Age thinkers such as William Bloom understand the evolution of technology – particularly telecommunications, electronic networks, and information processing – as part of this same development. There is a parallel here in the sequential process described by **Teilhard de Chardin** in terms of the geosphere to biosphere to noosphere. While Lovelock's hypothesis is now accorded the status of a theory, it was not originally intended to suggest teleology or self-conscious purpose. Nevertheless, the holistic ontology of Gaia theory has appealed to environmentalists and ecological activists as well as the spiritual reformist movements collectively known as New Age. The more popular vernacular understanding has translated Lovelock's earth as a living organism into earth as a conscious living organism.

The Gaia hypothesis and now theory have provided much of the impetus behind Earth-based spirituality, Earth Religions, the Green Movement and New Age concepts of Gaia consciousness. It contends in essence that life is a planetary-wide happening and that self-regulation of the environment depends on a sufficient number and range of living organisms. Moreover, since the physical and chemical environment is directly affected by the growth of any organism, it is not simply a Darwinian question of the adaptation and survival of the fittest but that the entire environment is interdependent and co-dependent.

Lovelock has further expanded his ideas in *The Ages of Gaia: A Biography of Our Living Earth* and *Gaia: The Practical Guide to Planetary Medicine.* His autobiography is *Homage to Gaia: The Life of an Independent Scientist.* Lovelock was elected a Fellow of the

Royal Society in 1974. He serves as President of the Marine Biology Association and was awarded the first Amsterdam Prize for the Environment by the Royal Netherlands Academy of Arts and Sciences in 1990.

Further reading

Lovelock, J. (1979) *Gaia: A New Look at Life on Earth*, Oxford: Oxford University Press.
Lovelock, J. (1991) *Gaia: The Practical Guide to Planetary Medicine*, London: Gaia Books.
Lovelock, J. (2000) *Homage to Gaia: The Life of an Independent Scientist*, Oxford: Oxford University Press.

MICHAEL YORK

THE LUCIS TRUST

The Lucis Trust was set up in the 1920s in New York by Alice Bailey as a financial and legal parent company for disseminating her work through smaller organizations and publishing her books. It was originally called the Lucifer Trust, then became the Lucis Publishing Company, World Goodwill, and Triangles, and finally the Arcane School. Lucis Productions produces radio and video programmes. Alice Bailey subsequently set up further headquarters in London and Geneva, and it currently works in eight regional languages. It is largely funded through voluntary donations.

The London branch defines its aims as: 'Such charitable objects as shall advance education and learning in general and in particular in the fields of comparative religion, philosophy, science and art. Such charitable objects as shall relieve human suffering and promote mental and moral improvement in the human race. Such charitable objects as shall on a non-sectarian basis promote the advancement of religion.'

Whilst claiming not to be a religion, Lucis Trust is clearly an organization for the advancement and practice of its founder's spirituality mission, and its divisions have separate functions. The Lucis Publishing Company of New York and Lucis Press Ltd of London publish Alice Bailey's twenty-four books, while *The Beacon* magazine is devoted to esoteric philosophy. These are still widely read, and have been influential in the forming of the central tenets of the **New Age Movement**, as well as informing the wider work of the Trust. The overall purpose of World Goodwill (1932) is the establishment of right human relations through the practical applications of the principle of goodwill. It produces correspondence courses on the issues facing humanity, and works with the United Nations as a non-governmental organization.

The Arcane School (1923) is its best known offshoot, dedicated to meditation and esoteric studies, including distance learning courses. It claims to be non-political and non-sectarian, and the emphasis is on students remaining in their own religions but seeking the deeper spiritual meanings within them. However, it is apparent that there is a strong Christian component, as well as one based on the Indian religions, and an attempt to blend both into a coherent whole with elements from several other religions, especially Zoroastrianism. Meditation is an important part of the educational work, and is seen as a science central to all the work of the Lucis Trust.

Triangles (1937) are the spiritual expression of groups of three people 'of goodwill', by power of prayer and meditation, and by using the visualization of light. This is a global network, and a core practice is the recitation of the 'great invocation' which includes a calling for a new avatar, or world teacher. Triangles are also symbolic of the Christian trinitarian principle of the Godhead. Alice Bailey's husband Foster also created a multi-coloured triangle as 'a symbol of the new age'. Lucis Productions make audio and video tapes furthering the aims of the Trust.

The common theme of the Trust's work is described as a deepening of a person's relationship with God. The principle is that all beings move towards the light in their own ways (e.g. plants through photosynthesis), and humans towards God. The minds of human beings should be seen as outposts of the mind of God, and humans have the task of uplifting the natural world – that is, a bridge between God and earth. Shambhala is the centre where the will of God can be known, a focal point of energies; it is a widely defined concept, not unlike enlightenment in Buddhism. Alternatively, some see it as analogous to the 'bindu point' in Hinduism. Although most people are not perfected yet, each has 'the seeds of light' in them. A key belief is the imminent coming of a world teacher, or avatar, 'the Maitreya', who will redeem humanity, and usher in the new age. To some extent then, this can be seen as a millenarian movement (see **Millenarianism**), although there is also a belief that the world can become a better place for all in our time.

The religious teachings of the Lucis Trust are summarized in 'The Great Invocation' which is both a concise statement of beliefs and values, and a prayer, comparable perhaps to the Christian Nicene Creed. It is quite short, with four three-line stanzas.

ELIZABETH PUTTICK

LUMPA CHURCH IN ZAMBIA

Founder: Alice Lenshina Mulenga

The Lumpa Church in Zambia provides very interesting data for understanding the complex relationship between church and state in post-independence Africa.

The Lumpa Church of Alice Lenshina Mulenga (*c.* 1919–78) demonstrates the conflict between prophetic visions and political structures. The acerbic and sometimes violent struggle between the two forces underscores the religio-political dimension within African Christianity. It is also possible to locate the Lumpa Church under the rubric of **millenarianism**. The millennial vision entails the prophetic prediction of a new age in which all the ills of the society are going to be eliminated. The new age will usher in a period of profound spiritual transformations. This perspective often calls for a withdrawal from the society, which is described as a sinful world. The Lumpa Church was based on this millennial vision and this was one of the reasons why this religious movement was at constant loggerheads with the government and all forms of political machinations. The millennial fervor is often antagonistic to existing political dispensations, because it offers a radical perspective on the way things should be within the society. The estrangement that developed between the Lumpa Church and Kenneth Kaunda's United National Independence Party (UNIP) was fueled by conflicting ideologies and worldviews.

Lenshina established the Lumpa Church after recovering from a near-death experience in 1954. She was propelled by a divine revelation and a spiritual injunction to preach the gospel. She could not resist the divine charge to establish a church on 'a rock'. She studied at the same Primary school as Kenneth Kaunda, who later became the Zambian president. She started the Lumpa Church within the Presbyterian Church of Zambia, but within two years, Lenshina's radical message led to a break from the Presbyterian Church. Lumpa in Bemba language means the highest, to excel, the supreme, to be superior, and to go far.

Lenshina emphasized the sanctity of the home and conjugal fidelity. She described the home of Jesus, Mary, and Joseph as an ideal example of a good home.

The racial element in Lenshina's message was very clear. She believed that white people had kept the secret of how to become wealthy and powerful from Africans. The secret has however been given to the prophetess. The secret to success and the power over all the negative forces of this world are contained in a special book that God had given to the prophetess.

The prophetic movement that was started by Lenshina promised spiritual growth and wholeness to those people who abandoned sorcery and witchcraft. Through her passionate hymns, she was able to convince people about the negative consequences of polygamy and divination. Her followers described her as a female John the Baptist or as *tondwe* (the woodpecker), the bird that proclaims the arrival of a visitor by pounding on a tree. Lenshina established a holy village in Kasomo. The village was called the New Zion, the place of refuge and spiritual succor.

Lenshina's Christological ideas were firmly rooted in the historical Jesus as the Messiah who would soon return. She described Jesus as the quintessential man, her younger brother, and the suffering one who had an unparalleled compassion for women. She described Jesus as the *mulonge*, the perfect weaver-bird or the perfect husband; the *shinwinga*, the bridegroom; *kanabesa*, provider of food; and *imfumu mulope*, the kind master. Her conceptions and ideas about Jesus vigorously accentuate the indigenous sagacity that informs theological constructs at the grassroots in many places in Africa. Lenshina further defined Jesus as a constant helper and as someone that was extremely sensitive to the needs of people.

The Lumpa rebellion started in 1963. The confrontation with the government reached a crescendo in 1964 when between 800 to 1,500 people – most of them members of the Lumpa movement – were killed. Lenshina's committed followers believed that the government's bullets could not harm them. If one cried out 'Jericho', one was miraculously protected! The Lumpa Church was officially proscribed in 1964. Alice Lenshina died in detention in 1978. Shortly before her death, she concluded that the political undercurrents in her message had obscured her original message of spiritual wholeness and integrity.

Further reading

Garvey, B. (1994) *Bembaland Church: Religious and Social Change in South Central Africa, 1891-1964*, Leiden: E. J. Brill.

Hinfelaar, H. F. (1994) *Bemba-Speaking Women of Zambia in a Century of Religious Change, 1892-1992*, Leiden: E. J. Brill.

Isichei, E. (1995) *A History of Christianity in Africa*, Michigan: Wm. B. Eerdmans Publishing Co.

AKINTUNDE E. AKINADE

M

MACEDO, EDIR

(b. 1945)

Founder of the Universal Church of the Kingdom of God

Edir Macedo was born in Brazil into a poor family of seven children. A loud and violent explosion of a boiler at the local dairy on the day of his birth is claimed to have been an auspicious sign, foretelling his future destiny; that he would be dynamic, controversial and explosive. This accident was to leave a lasting mark in the small city, but Macedo was also born with another mark, a congenital defect on his hands – atrophied thumbs. However, and in compensation, he was gifted Weberian attributes of a great charismatic leader. Although the cultural context is different, Lévi-Strauss's theory can be applied here – almost all mythological beings are born with some type of physical defect, but also, in compensation, with extraordinary human capabilities and even super-human ones.

Macedo's adolescence was not easy; to survive he had to work and study at the same time. Despite being born into a Catholic family, he assiduously attended Afro-Brazilian cults during his youth, which he was later to vehemently denounce, especially Umbanda. Later, he became a Pentecostal protestant attending and taking an active role in two evangelical churches – *Casa da Benção (House of Blessing)* and *Nova Vida (New Life)*. In 1977, under 'divine inspiration', he started his own evangelical movement the **Universal Church of the Kingdom of God** (Igreja Universal do Reino de Deus – IURD). In 1992 he decided to move to the USA.

Macedo has written many books, which have sold extremely well and constitute the theological basis of the Church, and hundreds of articles in *Folha Universal* (Universal Newspaper), the official church newspaper.

With the rapid growth of his Church in Brazil and abroad, Macedo is now in the position of an executive of a multinational holding company. He now controls a number of television and radio stations and companies and has dealings with numerous others both in Brazil and abroad. He travels in an executive jet and owns houses in São Paulo, Rio de Janeiro, New York and Los Angeles.

Further reading

Rodrigues, D. (2002) *The God of the New Millennium* (preface: Bryan Wilson), Lisbon: Colibri.

DONIZETE RODRIGUES

MAHĀYĀNA BUDDHISM

Mahāyāna (the 'Greater Vehicle', or 'Great Way') Buddhism is not a sect or school. It was not the result of a schism. Mahāyāna represents a particular vision of what the final goal of Buddhism should be, and the practices that are conducive to bringing about this goal. The final goal is said to be complete *Buddhahood*, the perfection of wisdom (*prajñā*) and compassion (*karuṇā*). It is sought not solely as personal liberation from suffering and the cycle of rebirth (i.e. *nirvāṇa*) but rather in order to be able to help more effectively all sentient beings. In ancient times Buddhist monks in India holding this perspective could be found in monasteries together with those who rejected its authenticity as the true intention of the Buddha.

Our earliest sources for Mahāyāna ideas are the Mahāyāna *sūtras*. Sūtras are texts that claim to be the word of the Buddha himself, although the earliest extant Mahāyāna sūtras actually date from perhaps the second century BCE. Sometimes the Buddha is said in these sūtras to have hidden them until the appropriate time for their promulgation. Traditions of Buddhism associated with non-Mahāyāna perspectives, such as **Theravāda**, do not accept the Mahāyāna

sūtras as the word of the Buddha. There is evidence from these sūtras themselves that some may have been the result of visionary experience. Another justification given is that whatever is well said is the word of the Buddha. There is a large number of these Mahāyāna sūtras (such as the 'Perfection of Wisdom' (*prajñā-pāramitā*) sūtras, or the 'Lotus' (*Saddharmapuṇḍarīka*) sūtra, and some are extremely long. There are also composite sūtras, sūtras composed of many shorter sūtras. The Mahāyāna sūtras may not all have been composed in India. They were certainly added to, both within and outside India, particularly in Central Asia.

A feature of many Mahāyāna sūtras is the praising of the sūtra itself and its miraculous effects, together with penalties that come from its disparagement. Sūtras often exhort their advocates to copy and enshrine them, worshipping them with incense, flowers, lamps and so on – the same form of offering traditionally made by Buddhists to *stūpas*, the relic shrines originally associated with the Buddha and his principal disciples. This practice may reflect something in the cultic origins of Mahāyāna. Sometimes Mahāyāna sūtras refer to themselves as the 'Dharma-body' (*dharmakāya*) of the Buddha, superior to his physical body just as his Doctrine (*Dharma*) is superior to the Buddha's corporeal person.

To attain Buddhahood out of compassion for all sentient beings is thought to be immensely superior to attaining *nirvāṇa*, merely freedom from *one's own* suffering and rebirth. Buddhahood should be the final goal of every practitioner. Those who aim for the goal of mere enlightenment (i.e. *nirvāṇa*, as it had previously been understood, rather than full Buddhahood) are referred to derogatorily as followers of a *'Hīnayāna'* – an inferior (*hīna*) way. Thus Mahāyāna

345

Buddhism is finally thought by its followers to be a matter of motivation for following the Buddhist path.

In Mahāyāna ultimately all beings should aim to obtain this supreme goal of Buddhahood for the benefit of others. That is, all should take the vow of a *bodhisattva*. A bodhisattva is one who has taken the vow to attain perfect Buddhahood, and one who is actually on that path. All Buddhist traditions accept the concept of the bodhisattva, but in Mahāyāna Buddhism this is seen as being the highest aspiration. It is often stated that all sentient beings will eventually become bodhisattvas and finally fully enlightened Buddhas. Thus the higher aspiration of a bodhisattva who aims for Buddhahood for the benefit of all sentient beings is contrasted with what for Mahāyāna is a lower aspiration. This is the 'Hīnayāna' *Arhat* who aims simply for *nirvāṇa*, that is, his own personal freedom from suffering and rebirth.

The Buddha in Mahāyāna is particularly characterized by infinite compassion. Through this compassion a Buddha continues to help sentient beings (perhaps remaining on another plane, a 'Pure Land') even after his apparent death. In infinite time and space there must be infinite Buddhas all helping out of compassion and capable still of entering into relationship with sentient beings. Perhaps the most well known of these Buddhas is Buddha Amitābha (known in Japan as *Amida*), compassionately dwelling in his Pure Land of *Sukhāvatī* (the 'Happy Place') somewhere in the west of the Buddhist cosmos. Especially important in east Asian Buddhism, Amitābha is said to help people in myriad ways, particularly aiding those who call on his name to come to his Pure Land after death. There they can practise directly with him the most effective way to attain the universal goal of Buddhahood.

The Mahāyāna path of the bodhisattva is stated to be very long (often given as three incalculable aeons), and begins with the 'enlightenment mind' or 'thought of enlightenment' (*bodhicitta*), portrayed as a revolution in the mind from self-cherishing to altruistic compassion. In Mahāyāna bodhisattvas too are thought to be present and actively engaged in benefiting the world. Some, such as Avalokiteśvara (the 'bodhisattva of compassion'), Mañjuśrī (the 'bodhisattva of wisdom'), or the female Tārā, are said to have attained great powers through their meditations and merit. They use these powers further to help others. But there are infinite other bodhisattvas well advanced on the path to Buddhahood and engaging in compassionate acts for the benefit of beings.

Mahāyāna Buddhism developed a number of philosophical schools although all took as a starting point the philosophy of 'emptiness' (*śūnyatā*). At the same time they offered interpretations that were quite diverse. Common, however, is the idea that the way we see and think things to be differs from the way they really are. Thus, depending on the philosophical school, 'emptiness' could refer to the very conditionality, the property of lacking intrinsic existence – and hence, we might almost say, the quicksilver 'fluidity' – of all things. Or it could be the lack of any independence of objects from the perceiving consciousness. All is really a flow of non-dual awareness. Or 'emptiness' could refer to the truly enlightened and primordially pristine and unsullied state of the mind itself. The philosophy of emptiness provided the basis for an essential equality and therefore equality of potential. All (including women such as Tārā, or laypeople) could in theory become fully enlightened Buddhas.

Mahāyāna scriptures also developed the doctrine of 'skilful means' (or 'skill-in-means': *upāyakauśalya*), whereby the

Buddha or an advanced bodhisattva adapts his teachings to the level of his hearers. This helps explain the diversity of Buddhist teachings, which are each appropriate to a particular level of practice. This also supplies a basis for Mahāyāna ethics, which involves a bodhisattva adapting his or her conduct to the situation in the light of great wisdom and compassion, and therefore not always acting in the way that would be expected. It may be partly the adaptability of Mahāyāna which led to its predominance as a final aspiration for Buddhists in Tibet, Mongolia, China, Japan, and East Asia.

Further reading

Williams, Paul (1989) *Mahayana Buddhism*, London: Routledge.

PAUL WILLIAMS

MAHDIA (MAHDIYYA) MOVEMENT, THE

Founder: Muhammad Ahmad
(b. 1844; d. 1885)

Proclamations of the advent of the Mahdi (God-guided one) have been numerous in Islamic history and while some have met with little response others such as that made by the Sudanese Muhammad Ahmad, a shyakh of a sufi and/or or mystical brotherhood, on Aba Island on the White Nile in June 1881 had widespread social and political as well as religious repercussions not only in the Sudan but across the Muslim world.

Although politics and religion are not easily separated from each other in the particular context of the rise of the Mahdia in the Sudan, as in others, the religious motives were more evident at the beginning of the Mahdi's revolt than secular ones. The primary goal at the outset was, as in the case of so many other **jihadi movements**, the reform of Islam both in the Sudan and beyond. Closely linked to this objective was the ousting of the Turco-Egyptian regime, which at the time was administering the Sudan. The Mahdi finally accomplished this with the defeat in January 1885 of General Gordon at Khartoum, who having withdrawn from the Sudan in 1882, had returned to quell the Mahdist uprising.

With this victory Muhammad Ahmad and his followers believed they had put an end to the tyranny of Turco-Egyptian administration and military. Turco-Egyptian forces had conquered the Sudan in 1821 mainly for financial reasons and had divided it into two provinces administered and garrisoned by Turco-Egyptian officials and troops. The frequent imposition of heavy taxation and attempts to alter the character of Sudanese Islam which included attempts to replace the existing Maliki school of Islamic law with the Hanafite school led to frequent revolts which culminated in the Mahdi's revolution.

Having overthrown Turco-Egyptian rule the Mahdi was persuaded that he was now in a position to spread his purified form of Islam to North Africa and beyond. But first his plans were to create a theocracy in the Sudan. This was to take the form of a state modeled on that of the Muslim community that had existed in the early days of Islam during the period of governance of the first four Caliphs and known as the Golden Age of Islam. As to his own position and claim to authority his letters stress that he believed himself to have been divinely chosen as Mahdi and successor of the Prophet Muhammad. He also believed that his chief followers were divinely chosen to be the successors of the Prophet's companions (*ansar*).

The Mahdi established his headquarters at Omdurman just north of Khartoum which became a large, sprawling camp city and one that depended greatly for security on his revolutionary army which was largely tribal in origin and consisted of three divisions under three commanders. After his death in 1885 in Omdurman Abd Allahi, known as the *khalifa al-Mahdi* (successor of the Mahdi), prosecuted jihad or holy war along the Egyptian and Ethiopian frontiers and in Darfur to the West but with little lasting success. Though internal dissention and revolts weakened the Mahdist theocracy they were not sufficiently well supported to undermine it and it only finally collapsed when conquered by the British in 1898.

The response from African societies outside the Sudan varied. Hundreds of thousands of mainly peasant farmers from as far afield as northern Nigeria were to accept Muhammad Abmad as the Mahdi and laid down their tools to go East to live under the system of theocratic rule which he had established. Influential scholars (*ulama*) including those of Al-Azhar university in Egypt, denounced the revolt as 'sectarian'. Innumerable treatises were composed by the learned to refute Muhammad Ahmad's claims to be the Mahdi, treatises which he then rejected on the basis that the rational arguments which they contained were greatly inferior to the revelations he had received from Allah. As to the colonial authorities in the Sudan, East and West Africa, they were to remain in constant fear of Mahdist uprisings until well into the twentieth century and devoted considerable resources to the task of curtailing what they referred to as Mahdist propaganda.

Further reading

Holt, P. M. (1970) *The Madhist State in the Sudan*, London: Oxford University Press.

PETER B. CLARKE

348

MAHIKARI

Mahikari is one of numerous religious movements which emerged in Japan after the Second World War. It was founded in 1960 by Okada Yoshikazu, who changed his name to Okada Kotama, 'Jewel of Light,' and is called Sukuinushisama or 'Lord Savior' by his disciples. The movement is usually classified among the 'Shinto' derived new religions which emerged out of **Omoto**, a new religion dating back to the end of the nineteenth century. The beliefs and practices of Mahikari are in fact derived from Shinto, Buddhist, Shamanistic, Confucian, and Christian sources. While most of its members are Japanese, Mahikari has established centers in Korea, North and South America, Europe, and Africa. Its headquarters and world shrine are in Takayama, Japan.

The core belief of the movement is based on the idea that the world is assailed by impurities which cause disease, poverty, and unhappiness. These impurities may be brought about by material causes ranging from chemicals to moral shortcomings, but the predominant cause of all misfortune, according to Okada, is spirit possession. The main focus of the movement is thus the restoration of health, wealth, and happiness through purification. The practice of purification is called *okiyome* and consists of the channeling of the divine Light through the palm of the hand of an initiated member to any other individual or object. The power to administer the Light is mediated by a sacred amulet, the *omitama*, received during initiation and surrounded by numerous taboos. When administered to another person, okiyome is usually directed to the forehead, the neck, the kidneys, and any other point of ailment in the body. The forehead is a particularly vital point in the body, since it is believed to be the dwelling place of the spirits. During the transmission of the Light to this point, possessing spirits may manifest themselves through subtle or violent movements of the body, or through speech in a foreign voice or language. This 'manifestation' requires the interrogation of the spirits by a leader of the movement, who implores the spirit to return to the spirit-world. In addition to freeing the person from possessing spirits, the practice of okiyome is also believed to melt impure substances or 'toxins' which coagulate in the body. Okiyome may also be used to purify rivers, houses and food, and may be applied as a preventive as well as a curative device.

In addition to the practice of okiyome, the ritual life of Mahikari is centered on monthly celebrations of thanksgiving called *mimatsuri* and the worshiping of ancestors. The *mimatsuri* consist of the offering of prayers and gifts to Su-God, the supreme God at the summit of Mahikari's hierarchy of spirits and gods, and elaborate testimonies of the miraculous healing effects of receiving the Light. Prayers are generally recited in Japanese, or in *kotodama,* which is believed to be 'the language of the Gods'. One of the most important prayers, or incantations, pronounced before every session of okiyome is the *Amatsunorigoto*, an ancient Shinto prayer. Most members of Mahikari own an altar for the ancestors to which daily offerings of food and prayers are directed for the appeasement of the spirits of the dead and the protection of the living.

After the death of the founder in 1974, a protracted dispute erupted over leadership, resulting in the splitting of the movement into two groups: Mahikari Bunmei Kyodan, led by Sekiguchi Sakae, one of the closest disciples of Okada, and Sukyo Mahikari, headed by the adopted daughter of the founder, Sachiko or Keiju Okada. It is to the latter group that the term Mahikari generally refers. In addition to the Keiju Okada, who is called Oshienushisama by her followers, and her immediate board of five governers, there are regional directors, called *shidobucho*, directors of larger centers, *dojochos*, and leaders of the local groups, called *hancho*. There are also special celibate officers and missionaries in the movement, called *doshi*. The total number of members of Sukyo Mahikari is very difficult to estimate due to a large turnover. It grew quite rapidly in the 1970s and 1980s to number more than 500,000 members or *kamikumite*. But the number of members seems to have stagnated or declined since then.

Further reading

Davis, W. (1980*) Dojo, Magic and Exorcism in Modern Japan,* Stanford: Stanford University Press.
McVeigh, B. (1997) *Spirits, Selves and Subjectivity in a Japanese new religion: the cultural psychology of belief in Sukyo Mahikari,* Lewiston, NY: Edwin Mellen Press.

CATHERINE M. CORNILLE

MAJI MAJI

Founder: Kinjitikile
Country: Tanzania

Though shortlived (1905–7) Maji Maji (in Swahili Maji means water) was the most widespread primary resistance movement in the history of East Africa and it resulted in the largest number of deaths. An explosion of hatred against white rule, like **Mau Mau** it has been enlisted for the cause of African nationalism, but this would be to ignore its religious elements.

Setting

The causes have been contested from the beginning. Maji Maji, a sacred battle cry, arose suddenly in the context of resentment to German rule that had taken two decades to impose by force, and was taken up across 100,000 square miles of the south and east of what is now Tanzania. Hut tax, seen by the Matumbi as an offering that the strangers should give to propitiate the gods, was vigorously imposed from 1897 and forced labour of at least 25,000 men was required to cultivate cash crops.

The Bantu peoples of east-central Tanzania were not culturally separate and shared a belief in the Kolelo divinity. During the nineteenth century it had expanded cross-culturally with the spirit of Kolelo possessing ordinary people who then exorcized it, thus giving a sense of control over change. In particular the cult of Bokero's shrine on the upper Rufiji River had spread to other places. Maji was taken to sprinkle on the land during the drought of 1903–5 and as a panacea. The Zaramo, for instance, who were angry with cotton planting, also acknowledged the Kolelo shrine in Uluguru.

Prophets and meaning

Another shrine was at Ngarambe where the prophet-medium Kinjitikile received the Hongo (messenger) of God, a river-snake spirit, and sent out his own hongo far afield. Having themselves been 'baptized' by drinking the maji medicine, they carried it to peoples for their unity and invulnerability. Hongo were believed because they operated within the known parameters of religious tradition necessary for a mass movement. As people came to hear of the shrine and its hopes, so local leaders sent emissaries to meet the ancestors there in the huge spirit-hut (Kijumba-Nungu), where clients offered them rice, millet, salt, and money to find out just what was happening. He combined pre-existing knowledge about divinity, possession, and medicine for the current exigency. Like the Bokero prophets he gained his knowledge under water (maji), anointed followers with a medicine of water, maize, and sorghum, which would turn the bullets of the enemies into water, protect the women and children, and multiply their grain. It was this religious belief that persuaded people to join and fight despite the previous failures of armed resistance. Among the Ngindo, who knew little of Kinjikitile or the Bokero cult, the hongo spread a millennial message of an epoch of peace and prosperity without white rule. Anti-witchcraft messages helped the cause.

Kinjikitile prophesied the Germans would leave after a war, but for the time-being Africans should work, while a whispering campaign was mounted. Anti-colonial defiance broke out prematurely for him. Matumbi warriors wearing blue American calico and millet heads around their forehead marched to the coast to uproot cotton and burn an Asian trading centre on 31 July 1903. Bokero and Kinjitikile were hanged by the Germans three days later. However the maji medicine had already been spread far and wide and there were many to distribute it.

Military outcomes

Though fighting occurred over a very broad area, so that it was felt on the farthest borders of what was at the time German East Africa, it was organized on a tribal basis with no massing of forces. Indeed there could be internal rivalries in stateless societies or between aspiring chiefs. A few mission stations and small posts were taken, but only fifteen Europeans died. Wherever German forces could bring to bear volleys of fire or machine-guns, the rebels soon suffered many casualties. Since the maji medicine was shown to be ineffective, morale and organization were diminished, though lack of immunity to bullets could be attributed to the failure of the fighters to keep to the tabus against sex, sesame, and pigeon peas. Those who had trusted their lives to Kinjitikile's maji or holy water dubbed him a traitor, and others named the movement Hongo-Hongo (hongo in English means blackmail), or Pahongo as in Uzungwa.

It was not very difficult for Germans to regain control. In rebel areas a scorched earth policy induced dreadful famines that reduced human capacity to keep the elephant and the tsetse-fly at bay. Some 250,000–300,000 Africans died in all, a third of the affected areas and about 7 per cent of the colony's total population. Without diminishing hatred of the colonialists, all plans for further resistance were shelved and means sought for appropriating opportunities brought by a reforming colonial power. Many flocked to the Christian churches and Islam. Yet Maji Maji was remembered by the nationalists of the 1950s, though there had been no concept of nation, just a common aspiration to drive out the Europeans.

Further reading

Wright, M. (1995) 'Maji Maji: Prophecy and historiography' in D. A. Anderson and D. H. Johnson (eds) *Revealing Prophets: Prophecy in East Africa today*, London: James Currey

BEN KNIGHTON

MAKIGUCHI, TSUNESABURO
(b. 1871; d. 1944)

Founder of Soka Kyoiku Gakkai, predecessor of **Soka Gakkai** (Value Creation Society), Makiguchi Tsunesaburo was the son of a shipping agent and was born in 1871 in Niigata prefecture. Upon graduating from school, he went to Hokkaido where he attended part-time a teacher training college and became a primary school teacher. While teaching, he continued his study in geography. In 1901, he resigned his teaching profession to go to Tokyo where he published *Jinsei Chirigaku (Geography of Human Life)*. He worked as an editor and also as a principal for several schools. His main interest was in the relationship between human beings and nature. Highly motivated to study and research, he became a member of a research group on rural life studies led by Nitobe Inazo and Yanagita Kunio. He wrote several books on geography, extended his interests to anthropology and folklore, and conducted studies of rural community life in Yamanashi prefecture and Kyushi among other places.

During his twenty years as a school teacher Makiguchi developed his interests in educational theory. He was dissatisfied with the theory and practice of education current in Japan at the time which he believed were too heavily dependent on European philosophical idealism. As a response to this he devised a unique educational method which he described as 'value-creating theory' (*soka kyoikugaku*). Together with **Toda Josei**, his chief disciple who opened Jishu Gakkan school, Makiguchi tried to put his theory into practice. Between 1930–34 he published his life's work, a four volume educational treatise called *Soka Kyoikugaku Taikei (The Value-Creating Pedagogy System)* in which he explains the theory of 'value-creation education' as a way of education that positively engages students in learning, enables them to make their own judgements regarding value, and discover their own goals. Along with the crystallization of the value-creation theory, Makiguchi was a devout student and practitioner of Buddhism. On the recommendation of Mitani Sokei, the principal of a high school that specialized in commerce, he joined the Nichiren Shoshu sect.

Gradually, he began to integrate the theory of value-creating pedagogy and the beliefs of the Nichiren Shoshu.

In 1932, Makiguchi resigned as a teacher, organized roundtable meetings for school teachers at his house and at Jishu Gakkan tutoring school with a view to starting a movement that would offer education based on the theory of value creation. This would later be developed into a movement aiming to live in accordance with the beliefs of the Nichiren Shoshu sect. In 1937, Sokka Kyoiku Gakkai was inaugurated, and its magazine *Kachi Sozo*(Creation of Values) was first published in 1941. Makiguchi was arrested in 1943 for refusing to accept State Shinto, and died in prison at the age of 73 in 1944.

Further reading

Bethel, Dayle, M. (1973) *Makiguchi the Value Creator*, New York: Weatherhill.

SUSUMU SHIMAZONO

MANTRA

This term, which derives from early Indian religious thought and practice, is frequently used in eastern-oriented NRMs to refer to the sonic focus of meditation or chanting. A mantra is a word, phrase or formula with spiritual power. In some movements its repetition is held to lead to this worldly benefits; in others it provides the means to self-realization or God-consciousness.

Mantras are important in both Hindu and Buddhist traditions. The *Veda*, revered by Hindus, contains hymns of praise, ritual utterances, and magical formulae all of which are referred to variously as mantras. They are *sruti*, which means they are believed to be revealed by the Divine to the hearer, a *rsi* or wise one. This tradition, of hearing sacred sounds, remembering and repeating them, con-

tinues today in the relationship between a guru and a disciple. A guru, as one who leads others from spiritual darkness to light, initiates a follower by revealing a mantra in the ritual of *diksa*. The sacred word (a *bija* or seed mantra such as 'Om') or formula (often a phrase containing the names of God) is whispered in the ear of the disciple. Once repeated and remembered correctly – for the power of a mantra depends upon its accurate repetition – it is used daily as a focus for inner or outer spiritual practice, whether as an act of divine recollection or invocation, to realize the self, to obtain rewards, or to improve karma. It is kept secret as to reveal it would deplete its power.

Mantra repetition is an important ritual activity in **Mahayana Buddhism**, particularly in Tibet where 'Om mani padme hum' is perhaps the most commonly recited. Tantric teachers use mantra meditation to enable initiates to affirm their identity as divine, whilst Hindu and Sikh devotees chant and sing mantras to keep God at the centre of their busy lives. Contemporary NRMs in which the use of mantras plays a part include Tibetan Buddhist and Japanese groups (e.g. **New Kadampa Tradition**, **Soka Gakkai**) (see **New Religions (Japan)**), and Hindu-related movements (e.g. **Transcendental meditation**, **ISKCON**).

Further reading

Coward, H. and Goa, D. (eds) (1991) *Mantra: Hearing the Divine in India*, Chambersburg, PA: Anima Books.

KIM KNOTT

MARANATHA CHRISTIAN CHURCHES
(a.k.a Maranatha Campus Ministries)

Maranatha (the Lord has come) Christian Ministries started in 1971 at Murray

State University in Paducah, Kentucky, as Maranatha Campus Ministries. Its founder was Bob Weiner, who experienced the baptism of the Holy Spirit while serving in the United States Airforce and who with Bob Cording established in 1971 Sound Mind Inc., a ministry for the evangelization of youth. From this ministry emerged Christian Life Center at Long Beach California. By 1972 Weiner had shifted the focus to a campus ministry to university students. In time Maranatha Campus Ministries was absorbed into the larger body of the Maranatha Christian Churches.

The Maranatha Churches derived from the **Assemblies of God** and as an organization bases itself on the various offices described in the Apostle Paul's letter to the Ephesians 4:11. Special emphasis is laid on prophecy by members who also speak in tongues and on discipleship and charismatic leadership. Prophecy is regarded as the means whereby God confirms his present activity in the Church. There is a Maranatha Leadership Institute in Gainsborough, Florida and a world leadership conference is held there every two years. Other activities include interactive televised prayer meetings during which viewers make their requests by telephone.

The Churches like the Campus Ministries continue to concentrate on College and University campuses. The intense nature of the crusading has led to complaints from parents that undue pressure was being placed on their children. The controversy between parents and churches was partially resolved by the creation of a parent–student contact programme, which provided parents with a better understanding of the aims and strategy of the ministry.

At the local Church level activities consist of weekly general meeting in addition to which most members also participate in smaller fellowship sessions.

There are 150 Maranatha Churches in the United States and membership there stands at around 7,000. The movement also exists in Europe.

Further reading

Chryssides, G. (2001) *Historical Dictionary of New Religious Movements*, Lanham, Maryland and London: Scarecrow Press.

PETER B. CLARKE

MASLOW, ABRAHAM

Abraham Maslow (1908–70) was the founding father of the **Human Potential Movement** (HPM), and therefore a major influence on the **New Age Movement**. The most celebrated of his many ideas and discoveries remains his 'theory of human motivation', popularly called the 'hierarchy of needs'.

Post-war psychology was dominated by the two (usually opposed) schools of behaviourism and psychoanalysis. Maslow criticized the mechanistic beliefs of behaviourism and the biological reductionism and determinism of psychoanalysis, and helped create humanistic psychology as a 'third force'. He thus became part of a new movement, a 'middle way', which included luminaries Stanislav Grof, Carl Rogers, and Rollo May. This group produced a radical and cohesive matrix of theories which effectively challenged the established order in psychology. It was formally launched in 1961 as the Association for Humanistic Psychology, which is still the core institution.

Maslow wrote several books, and published over thirty main papers on emotional issues, creativity, personality problems, and religious experience. Underpinning his approach was a belief that the main role of psychotherapy should be the integration of the self; to develop this theory he drew on literary and religious sources, as well as existential philosophy. Today, he is also appreciated as a philosopher, bridging psychology, social science and philosophy. A major feature of his later work was his insistence on the importance of values, in opposition to the many social scientists promoting a strictly value-neutral approach. He argued that without values, it was impossible to give an adequate account of human life. To this end, he studied exemplary leaders such as Einstein and Eleanor Roosevelt, and produced a list of the 'being values': wholeness, perfection, completion, justice, aliveness, richness, uniqueness, effortlessness, playfulness, truth, self-sufficiency, simplicity, and goodness. He used these as a yardstick against which to assess the health of an individual or community.

Maslow is best known for his 'hierarchy of needs' model. This describes how humans need to first meet their basic needs, before achieving higher 'being' values. The model is represented as a pyramid, beginning at the base with physiological and survival needs, then progressing through security, love and belonging, and self-esteem, culminating in 'self-actualization'. Self-actualization is an empirical principle and ethical idea underpinning a vision of human nature as intrinsically good. The self-actualized person displays most of the positive traits Maslow found in his ideal subjects, and is also more likely to have 'peak experiences' – a term which encompasses the spectrum of mystical states of consciousness. It is also possible to see the hierarchy as a table of values, since an individual (or group) at a certain level of need will probably have beliefs and values which facilitate their obtaining or realizing these needs.

Maslow's approach in studying high-achieving people was also intended as a criticism of both Freud and the leading behaviourist B. F. Skinner – Freud, for basing his conclusions on case studies of disturbed people, and Skinner for using rats and birds in laboratory conditions, performing simple tests, and then drawing conclusions about humans. Both ways led, he said, to a pessimistic or reductionist view of human life, as opposed to his own optimistic one. An outspoken atheist, he was also critical of mainstream religions for imposing a uniform set of values, 'one size fits all'.

A central theme in humanistic psychology is the individualized search for 'the true self', and this finds resonances in the Indian religions, as well as native American and tribal **Shamanism**. It also resonates with post-modernism, and Maslow and his school are clearly moving away from communal values towards personal ones.

Although Maslow burnt most of his personal papers, it does seem that later in life he began to have doubts about his advocacy of personal development, and the effect it was having on people. The story is told of how Carl Rogers' daughter, who was studying for a degree with Maslow, was so determined to become self-actualized that she left her young family. Bertrand Russell proposed that human life is a struggle between individual expression and social obligations. If so, Maslow may have felt that he had moved too far in one direction. Nevertheless, he was one of the most significant figures in the creation of contemporary ethics and values, whose influence can be discerned in fields as diverse as the psychology of religion, education, management training, marketing, and pre-eminently psychotherapy.

Further reading

Maslow, A. (1998) *Towards a Psychology of Being*, London: Wiley.

Puttick, E. (1997) 'A new typology of religion based on needs and values', *Journal of Beliefs and Values*, 18(2), 133–46.

ELIZABETH PUTTICK

MAU MAU

Mau Mau was an insurgent religio-political movement of the 1950s that was ended by military force. There is little agreement as to what was the original meaning of Mau Mau, perhaps code for the warning 'Uma!' (Get out!) or a double mishearing of *muma* (oath). All would accept that the term referred to a more radical and underground version of the Kenyan African Union formed in 1946. A most logical meaning then of Mau would be the plural form of the diminutive KAU (pronounced Kau), a perfect expression of the aims of its first organizers. Members referred to it obliquely as *Uiguana (wa Muingi)* (Unity of the Community), Gikuyu (na Muumbi) the proto-ancestral Agikuyu, or *Muma (wa Uiguano)* (Oath of Unity).

Origin

Gikuyu elders in Kiambu made contact with the younger, more radical trade unionists in Nairobi, who would only agree to take the secret oath of the covertly revived Kikuyu Central Association (KCA), if the oath was made more militant and offered to many more Agikuyu, a term used traditionally to describe the people whose homeland is in the central region of the country extending from Mount Kenya to Nairobi. They took the oath (*muma*) at chief Koinange's home in late 1948, but Fred Kubai, Bildad Kaggia, Stanley Mathenge, and others, soon split from the older generation, taking effective control of a widespread secret organization with connections between Nairobi and Kiambu, Muranga, and Nyeri. Mau Mau was proscribed in August 1950.

Oathing

Gikuyu traditional associations and churches used oaths to prevent deception in critical issues. An oath was sworn by the Kikuyu Association in 1920, an oath largely continued when the KCA was formed in 1926, though swearing on the Bible was dropped as ineffectual. When Mau Mau took over the oathing, they operated from a secret central committee or *muhima* in Nairobi, sending out oath administrators as far as Embu or the Rift Valley without fostering any local organizations, simply using social pressure to enforce oath taking. Before the worst atrocities mission and independent Christians regarded the oath as a religious duty. It became customary to open a ceremony with prayers to the missionaries' 'Mwathani Ngai' (the Lord God), whenever possible by a robed **Karinga** clergyman to optimize the blessing on proceedings. A goat was sacrificed at night. Candidates had to remove all metal, shoes, even clothes from their persons. A cross was drawn on the forehead, 'May this blood mark the faithful and brave members of the Gikuyu and Mumbu Unity ...'

Thus baptismal symbolism was combined with the tradition of cleansing from contact with human blood. Blood brotherhood, a regional Arab symbol of friendship was effected by smearing each other's blood on a piece of goat meat and eating it. Candidates had to pass through an arch of sugar-cane and banana leaves seven times, investing the ceremony with all the identity-forming solemnity of initiation (*kurua*).

The candidates had to face Kirinyaga (Mount Kenya), holding balls of damp soil to their navels and to swear many oaths of loyalty before Mwene-Nyaga, the distinctively Gigikuyu name for Ngai (God), ending 'May this oath kill me', if it be broken. More stringent and dangerous oaths were used for higher degrees of commitment, yet all were new combinations of old Gikuyu or Christain rites. There was no 'perversion' beyond bricolage.

Trusting in the oath, the young radicals were able to build a secret, yet mass, movement on the oath. It was Ngai who gave them their fighting power. Church women regarded caring for Mau Mau as a Christian vocation. One could hardly be a 'Mugikuyu karinga' without swearing the oath. Between 75 and 90 per cent of the one million Agikuyu population, besides large numbers of Embu, Meru, Akamba, Maasai, and others took the oath of unity. The political strength of the oath outlasted Mau Mau as Kenyatta showed by his anxiety that it not be used against him in 1964 and then reviving it in 1969.

Songs and prayers

In nine months from November 1951 the Mau Mau published no less than four hymn books which stressed hard work and unity as much as their political pamphlets had. They protested against the evictions of tenants and land alienation, while celebrating education, independent schools, the Kenya Teachers College, political rallies, and KAU leaders. The hymns gave Mau Mau a unity of mind and purpose that politically it lacked, not least because of organizational secrecy.

Songs then, as in traditional and Christian religion, were highly motivating. They reached Gikuyu hearts, quickly moving them to happiness. Songs were prayers that reached Ngai at once, so that he would come to their aid. The British were suspicious of Gigikuyu newspapers, but not of the tune of 'Abide with me', 'Onward Christian soldiers' and 'God save the Queen', however devoted to insurrection and Kenyatta as king. Prayers morning and night were also a part of Mau Mau life, even when dodging the security forces in the mountain forests. Bibles were read there too, so that Kimathi and Kenyatta became Moses and messiah.

The 'Creed of Gikuyu and Muumbi' asserted belief 'in the holy ceremonies of Gikuyu and Muumbi ... and the everlastingness of the Gikuyu tribe. God let it be so!' It sold 20,000 copies, mostly at oathing ceremonies.

Insecurity in land

The owners of the land were the guardians of the ancestral spirits who dwelt in it, and a larger tract of land represented a greater concentration of spiritual powers. The cry of the landless was for *ithaka na wiathi* (lands and moral responsibility). Mau Mau was not merely a moral economy, but divinely authorized by ancestor, prophet, prayer, song, and oath. Its failure was the political aspiration of trade unionism that assumed all Agikuyu could be forcibly united for concerted action, when the house of Muumbi had long had many fractious sons vying for land. Some would become **Mungiki**.

Further reading

Maloba, W. O. (1998) *Mau Mau and Kenya*, Oxford: James Currey
Odhiambo, E. S. A., and Lonsdale, J. (eds) (2003) *Mau Mau and Nationhood*, Oxford: James Currey

BEN KNIGHTON

MAZDAZNAN
Founder: Otto Hanisch (b. 1844; d. 1936)

Mazdaznan is a neo-Zoroastrian group founded in the US between the two

World Wars, which claims, somewhat controversially, to represent a genuine Western branch of ancient Zoroastrianism. Otto Hanisch (1844–1936), later to be known under the pen name of Otoman Zar-Adusht Ha'nish, was born in 1844, probably in Teheran, to a Russian father and a German mother. His place of birth was later disputed, and nothing certain is known about his life until he surfaced in 1900 in Chicago. There, he claimed to have been initiated into a mysterious Zoroastrian order whilst in Iran (and/or Tibet). This order, according to Ha'nish, taught him that, some 3,000 years before the coming of the prophet known as Zarathustra or Zoroaster, another prophet called Ainyahita (later to be worshipped in Persia as the goddess Anahita) spread her teachings from Tibet to the Middle East, Egypt, Greece, India, China, and even pre-Colombian America. Ainyahita's teachings, thus, form the basis of most world religions, including Christianity, since the three wise men taught them to Jesus' family. Thanks to Zarathustra's revival of the original Ainyahita teachings, and to Ha'nish's contemporary revival of Zarathustra's teachings, this original religion of the world is now available again in its most pristine form.

Ha'nish quickly gathered a number of American followers and in 1917 established, in California, an organization known as Mazdaznan, which claimed to offer 'the Eternal Religion that stands behind all other religions', 'the oldest and most comprehensive system ever devised by man or revealed by God'. Among the early followers were Maud Meacham (1879–1959) and Swiss-born David Ammann (1855–1923), who was instrumental in spreading Mazdaznan into Europe. Ha'nish died in 1936, and his successors are known as 'Electors'. Whilst in the US Mazdaznan led a comparatively quiet existence, the organization became quite controversial in Europe. Critics claimed that Mazdaznan was not a genuinely Zoroastrian religion, and put great stress on Ha'nish's idiosyncrasies. His ideas about the Aryan race, for instance, brought accusations in several European countries of his being racist and anti-semitic, although he was also critical of Nazism. The Mazdaznan organization was banned in Nazi Germany in fact as early as 1935.

Crucial to Mazdaznan philosophy is the idea of converting Earth into a garden again, where God would converse and cooperate with humans. Breathing exercises are also very important, and in fact their practice spread from Mazdaznan to a number of other groups, in German-speaking Europe particularly (together with Mazdaznan songs and ideas about food and diet, which in turn attracted a number of medical doctors to the movement). At the end of the 1990s, Mazdaznan launched the 'Life4-Sys' programme, which proposes a combination of breathing practices, exercise and diet, which, although obviously rooted in Ha'nish's teachings, is presented as inherently secular and available to people of all faiths. Mazdaznan's headquarters are currently located in Bonita, California.

Further reading

Ha'nish, Otoman Zar-Adusht (1946) *Avesta in Songs*, Los Angeles: Mazdaznan Press.
Ha'nish, Otoman Zar-Adusht (1960) *The Philosophy of Mazdaznan*, Los Angeles: Mazdaznan Press.

MASSIMO INTROVIGNE

MELANESIA – MILLENARIAN ('CARGO') MOVEMENTS

The first Europeans to arrive in Melanesia, in the late nineteenth century, reported various movements which looked forward to the imminent end of the world. Indigenous religions varied considerably, but often included the myth that, as a result of some primal sin, 'heroic' ancestral figures had disappeared from the world of the living. The arrival of the Whites marked the beginning of a new epoch: not just the return of the mythological heroes, but of all the dead ancestors, who would bring with them everything people needed without their having to work to produce them, whether in their gardens or as wage-labourers on European plantations and in mines. Nor, any longer, would they suffer or die. Nature itself would be transformed: valleys would become mountains, and vice-versa.

Colonial Europeans called them 'Cargo' cults, from the Neo-Melanesian ('pidgin') term, 'cargo', used for material goods. They also called them 'madness' cults, especially when people began shaking or speaking in tongues and when some leaders claimed to have been reborn. Yet a lot of cult ideas were based on empirical experience. The goods the Whites acquired simply arrived from a world outside, and were taken by them simply by handing over pieces of paper. Melanesians now sought to explain how this mysterious exchange worked.

At first, traditional myths were used to explain the European monopoly of the 'cargo'. The goods with which the White man's ships were filled with had been made in the Land of the Dead, by the spirits of the dead ancestors, but had been misappropriated by the Whites.

European missionaries professed to possess ultimate knowledge embodied in the Bible. What impressed their pupils (and their parents), however, out of the entire corpus of ideas contained in the Bible, were the passages about the Apocalypse: about the return of the dead at the millennium, when the virtuous would receive rewards for proper behaviour in this life and for the sufferings they had undergone. To Melanesians, this meant recompense for the exploitation they had suffered on the plantations and in the mines, and for the many-sided inequality between White and Black in social life as a whole. A wonderful future was now assured; so people ceased working on the land and even threw away valued possessions, including European money.

The natives concluded that there must be secret parts of Christian knowledge which gave the Whites this special power over the world. Despite the formal equality of all believers in Christianity, this secret knowledge was being withheld from them. Contemporary anthropologists, therefore, have shown how these cult beliefs constitute a critique of European values, which the natives see as both hypocritical and inhumane.

Movements of this kind rose and fell in one area after another, though not necessarily continuously, throughout the inter-War period, and still do. Yet though the prophecies were falsified, and many people were consequently disillusioned, they were fuelled by unfulfilled hopes, so that the central ideas did not disappear entirely but were kept alive by a core of convinced believers and persisted underground (often literally, when, in many cults, it was believed that the ancestral spirits lived inside the earth).

Melanesians thus drew upon both traditional and Christian ideas in creating their models of the world. They also used their empirical experience of a rapidly-changing world, including new kinds of technology. The original notion that the ancestors would return from the Land of the Dead by canoe, for example, was displaced by a new belief that they would come back by ship, and, later, by aeroplane. So airstrips were built to receive the planes, and lianas served as radio antennae.

There were also different versions of White Christianity, from the larger Catholic and Lutheran missions to the fundamentalist sects which attracted people who already believed that the world would come to an end. Rival mission offshoots; cults which disowned their original European or US origins; and new syncretic cults co-existed alongside persisting paganism: in a recent survey, up to ten denominations were present in some villages, with an average of three. All versions of Christianity, though, subscribed to a belief in the coming of the millennium, the return of the dead, and judgement: reward for righteous behaviour, and punishment for sinners.

After Independence, new charismatic religious leaders emerged to challenge White missionaries, often controlling the lives of whole villages in a 'totalitarian' way, demanding not only conformity of belief and ritual, but also strict adherence to a puritanical code of conduct that regulated every aspect of daily life, from smoking tobacco to wearing new shoes.

But the millennium still did not come about, so cult movements lost members or even disappeared. Yet the key ideas could still be re-awakened by charismatic 'big men' such as Paliau (see **Paliau movement – Melanesia**), and reappear after many years, often in new organizational forms and with novel elements in their ideologies injected by the new charismatic leaders who demanded that their followers adhere to these shifts in doctrine.

After Independence, with increased involvement in the world market, cult movements borrowed modern forms of economic organization: village-level 'community development'; cooperatives and commodity production for the market; and participated in village, regional, and national government. These new ideas co-existed with older, millenarian ones, though the latter were now often hidden because they were thought to be 'pagan'

or 'primitive', and their protagonists lost their appeal, especially among the 'Angry Young Men' in the towns who had access to modern sources of information such as newspapers and radio, and who regarded the new governing elite as 'Lucifer'. But most villagers were still restricted to mission literature and broadcasts for information about the world. So cult leaders (often illiterate) developed their own garbled versions of world and regional events: Chinese communism, the Gulf War, conflict in the Holy Land, space exploration, the election of Lyndon Johnson, or visits to the Pacific by people like Prince Charles, or the devastation of Nature by logging companies or natural disasters such as earthquakes. Contemporary cults, therefore, may retain a diffuse belief that great changes are coming, but this does not necessarily include the coming of the cargo, particularly in areas most subject to Western influence.

Further reading

Worsley, P. (1968) *The Trumpet Shall Sound. A Study of 'Cargo' Cults in Melanesia*, New York: Schocken Books.
Worsley, P. (1999) 'Cargo Cults: Forty Years On', in *Expecting the Day of Wrath. Versions of the Millennium in Papua New Guinea*, K. K. Schmid (ed.), National Research Institute Monograph no.36, Port Moresby.

PETER WORSLEY

MESSIANIC JUDAISM

Messianic Judaism has its roots in both 1960s **Evangelical Christianity** and Biblical Judaism. It has a world wide presence as an organized religion, incorporating both Jewish and Christian religious symbols, prayers and festivals. Members are both Jews and Christians who believe that Jesus is the Jewish Messiah.

There have been Jewish people who believe in *Yeshua* (Jesus) from the first Messianic Congregation in Jerusalem in 40 AD and until 1960 any Jew who believed in *Yeshua* as the Messiah and retained a Jewish identity was referred to as Hebrew Christian. From the middle of the nineteenth century, numerous Christian missionary organizations sought to bring Jewish believers into full membership of one of the denominations of Christianity whilst accepting they also shared a fellowship with one another in heir Jewish identity. The modern Messianic Movement is different in that it lays claim to a continuation of the original Jewish movement of the first-century believers in *Yeshua*. Messianic Judaism sees itself as an indigenous movement within the body of *Yeshua* the Messiah, one in faith with gentile brothers and sisters yet maintaining congregational independence and autonomy as a continuation of the true meaning of Judaism.

The term Messianic Jew therefore refers to a Jew who accepts *Yeshua* (Jesus) of Nazareth as the Messiah but more importantly, they assert their right to live as Jews and believe that God wants the Jewish People to remain a distinct and obedient nation until the end of time. Thus Messianic Jews retain their Jewish symbolism, heritage culture, and religious observances. They also regard themselves as an integral part of the Body of Messiah, what Christians refer to as the Body of Christ, followers of Jesus who have accepted him as their Lord and Saviour.

The present form of Messianic Judaism started in the 1960s in America when Martin Rosen, a missionary with the American Board of Mission to the Jews, formed Jews for Jesus, a Christian missionary group focusing on the Jewish population. By 1970 Rosen adopted the up-front evangelical style of the **Jesus Movement** and had set up a full-scale street outreach, maintaining that one could still believe in Jesus and retain a Jewish cultural identity. Members strongly identified with the group rather than the Church, and there was a strong commitment to Christian values coupled with an insistence that ethnic identity should be a vital part of that faith.

In 1975, during the 'Messiah Conference' chaired by Manny Brotman and Martin Chernoff, the Hebrew Christian Alliance of America changed its name to the Messianic Jewish Alliance of America (MJAA). This signified a clear generational difference in lifestyle between Christians of Jewish origin who were happy to be identified with the world-wide gentile dominated Church, and Jews who followed the Jewish Messiah *Yeshua* and saw themselves as his disciple and a 'fulfilled Jew'.

Issues over the extent of Jewish practice and ideology and the role of the gentiles were frequently debated by members of Messianic Congregations and have never been resolved. Many of the congregations were far more Jewish orientated than others, especially those congregations where leaders raised within Judaism advocated use of traditional Jewish symbols such as *tallit* (prayer shawls) *tefillin* (phylacteries), *tzitzit* (an undergarment with fringes) *davening* (daily chanting from a prayer book), kosher laws, Shabbat services, and the use of Hebrew.

In 1974 there were five messianic congregations in America. By 1993 there were three congregational organizations which represented nearly two hundred Messianic congregations, synagogues and fellowships, the International Alliance of Messianic Congregations and Synagogues (IAMCS), the Union of Messianic Jewish Congregation (UMJC) and the Fellowship of Messianic Congregations (FMC). Their existence has helped to give international legitamcy to the Messianic Movement.

Messianic Judaism has a large international presence, from Israel to America, Europe, Russia, Australia, and in 2000 it established itself in Japan. In 2001 it was claimed that there were over 100,000 Messianic Believers in the USA. Despite this, Messianic Judaism is not a homogeneous group or movement. It does not have a uniform set of practices or a formalized theology that's common to national or international groups. Moreover, it has advanced more rapidly in different parts of the world. For example, the UK is at least twenty years behind North American Messianic Judaism in terms of its organization, structure, support and community.

In 1995 the British Messianic Jewish Alliance (BMJA) recorded twenty-eight Messianic Congregations in the UK and eleven Messianic Jewish Associations of Great Britain, including a number of Congregational Alliances. Messianic Judaism in the UK has attracted many gentile and Hebrew-Christian followers in higher proportions than Messianic Groups in America. The presence of Christians in Messianic groups in the UK means that there is a variety of different perceptions of what it means to be a Messianic Congregation. While there are certain common theological beliefs such as belief in the Trinity, the virgin birth, original sin, resurrection, ascension and the future second coming, salvation through *Yeshua*, infallibility of the Bible, the eternity of the Jewish Race and Israel as the chosen land of God, there is a difference in practice. Some adhere more to Christian prayers and Charismatic style of worship (belief in the gifts of the Holy Spirit such as **glossalalia**, dancing and healing) (see **Charismatic Movements**) and others adopt a more Rabbinical Jewish approach. However most congregations will also recognize Jewish festivals such as Shabbat, Passover, Rosh Hashonnah, and Shavout, and traditional Jewish life ceremonies such as circumcision, Bat' mitzvahs, and Bat' hales. Services are also conducted in a mixture of Hebrew and English, incorporating a number of adapted traditional Jewish and Christian prayers.

A typical Messianic Congregation will therefore be composed of Christians who are not Jewish, Messianic Jews who do not practise Jewish customs, Torah observant Jews and gentiles, who follow Jewish orthodox practices and believe in Jesus as the Jewish Messiah, and members who fall between all of these categories.

While the relationship between the Christian Church and Messianic Judaism has generally been good, the Jewish community from the Orthodox to the Liberal has been fairly united against it. Messianic Jews are seen as apostates, automatically renouncing their right to be considered part of the Jewish Community. However the utilization of Jewish and Christian symbols and belief by both Jews and Christians has meant that Scholars are divided as to whether to call Messianic Judaism a Christian or Jewish Sect.

Further reading

Cohn-Sherbok, D. (2000) *Messianic Judaism*, London: Cassell.
Feher, S. (1998) *Constructing the Boundaries of Messianic Judaism*, Walnut Creek, CA: AltaMira/Sage Publications.
Harris-Shapiro, C. (1999) *Messianic Judaism*, Boston USA: Beacon Press.

ESTHER FOREMAN

METROPOLITAN COMMUNITY CHURCHES, UNIVERSAL FELLOWSHIP OF (UFMCC)

The Universal Fellowship of Metropolitan Community Churches (UFMCC), more commonly termed the Metropolitan Community Church (MCC), may be described as a denomination of the wider religion of Christianity, although some Christians would be keen to see it as a heretical New Religious Movement. The group has spread worldwide, having originally being founded in Los Angeles in 1968 by a Pentecostal pastor who was instructed to leave his denomination because of his sexual orientation. He became certain that homosexual Christians needed their own church.

The original aim, continuing to today, was to establish a Christian group that welcomed all people, especially non-heterosexuals. It is not uncommon to see discreet homosexual affection between couples during the service, in much the same way, as one would expect to find between heterosexual couples in other Christian meetings. It is also not uncommon to see transvestites present at meetings.

Unlike some Christian groups, MCC believe fully in gender equality and in equal opportunities for non-hetero-sexuals and their right to exercise the ministry and live according to their sexual orientation. These churches have female ordained ministers, and they adapt Biblical passages and hymns to use neutral, or sometimes feminist, terminology. The Bible followed in services is the Inclusive NIV, where, for example, 'mankind' is changed to 'humankind'. While this is pleasing to many, others remain frustrated that God is still depicted in perceived masculine terms.

Meetings are often held in church halls, or occasionally in church sanctuaries. MCC congregations have often had great difficulty in finding churches, which will happily share their space with them, for the reason that they do not wish to be seen as condoning homosexuality.

Because of the settings in which meetings take place, at first glance MCC appears to have something of a house or community church flavour to it, especially in its informal sermons and notices, and 'pick up band' feel of the sung worship. Yet other aspects of worship are very similar to that of High-Church Christianity: the liturgy and choral are considered very important by some congregations. This said, it is very difficult to attempt to make any form of generalizations regarding the worship at MCC. For there are often quite substantial differences between that of different congregations, and this in itself is dependent upon the traditions to which both leaders and congregation members have been exposed, and therefore bring with them to the congregation. Lay involvement is key to MCC worship.

MCC Sunday worship is rich in symbolism. A key part of the Sunday liturgy is the lighting of the AIDS candle (a traditional 'church' candle with an AIDS ribbon pinned on) during the time of prayer. Whilst this is highly symbolic, it is mentioned without explanation (usually announced after a time of structured prayer along the lines of 'Now we will light the AIDS candle'). This is because the meaning, it seems, is clear to members and adherents of MCC. The purpose of this ritual is to intercede for those who have been affected by HIV and AIDS, as well as their families. The pride flag is displayed prominently showing the marriage of faith and homosexuality in MCC. A priestly shawl is worn only to celebrate communion, displaying equality amongst all.

MCC identifies with Christianity, and the urban homosexual scene, as a place where Christianity and non-heterosexual sexual identities can meet and be acknowledged without fear of religious recrimination. Some congregations will outreach into their local homosexual scene in order to attract people to become Christians. But this is generally done a lot less often than in mainstream Christianity, and is mostly achieved through more subtle methods of, for example, a float at Pride or Mardi Gras. This said, there is much less proselytizing than in Evangelicalism (see **Evangelical Christianity**); instead most members arrive from mainstream Christianity because of perceived or actual difficulties regarding their sexual orientation. Gender behaviour is typical of that of the national urban homosexual scene, with camp tolerated, if not celebrated.

MCC therefore serves as a centre for healing for homosexuals who have been hurt in other Christian settings and a place where women and men can feel equal in religious involvement. It is also a place where rites of passage can be marked freely acknowledging the places both of religion and homosexuality in a person's life.

Further reading

Euroth, Ronald M. and Jamison, Gerald E. (1974) *The Gay Church*, Grand Rapids, MI: Wm. B. Eerdmans.

JASON PELPLINSKI

MILINGO CULT

'Milingo cult' is a journalistic expression for the network of organizations, religious orders, and foundations founded and headed by the controversial Catholic archbishop Emmanuel Milingo (see **Milingo, Emmanuel**). In fact, the expression 'cult' is inappropriate, since most of these organizations are officially recognized by the Roman Catholic Church, and none of them followed Milingo when he briefly left the Catholic fold for Reverend Moon's **Unification Church/Moonies** in 2001. Some of these organizations remain controversial nonetheless.

Milingo founded the Zambia Helpers Society when he was a parish priest in Chipata, Zambia, from 1963–6. A charitable organization, the Society raised funds in Europe to help humanitarian projects in Zambia, including a farm and a hospital. Later, when Milingo came to Italy in 1983, the Society was helped by nationally famous businessmen, including Giuseppe Volonterio, who came in touch with Milingo through his healing ministry. They helped Milingo in 2000 to reorganize his various fund-raising and charitable activities (including an Emmanuel Milingo Foundation, then headquartered near Milan) under the umbrella of a non-profit company known as Pamo. The Zambia Helpers Society and Pamo managed to avoid most of the controversies associated with Milingo, although they receive a significant amount of funding from Milingo's other organizations. Milingo founded his first female religious order, the Daughters of the Redeemer, between 1966 and 1969. It was duly recognized by the Catholic Church in Zambia, and currently includes some thirty Sisters working in schools and hospitals. A male branch, the Brothers of St John the Baptist, is still awaiting full recognition in Zambia, although most of the Brothers of this small order currently live in Italy.

More controversial is the Pious Union of the Daughters of Jesus, the Good Shepherd, founded in Kenya and recognized by the Catholic diocese of Muranga. In addition to their presence in Kenya, these Sisters have a small convent in Zagarolo, near Rome, where Milingo took residence in 2002. One of the Kenyan Sisters, Sr Anna Ali, claimed from 1987 on to have received hundreds of messages from Jesus Christ, known as 'Divine Appeals'. Some of them express conspiracy theories about the Catholic Church being under threat by Satanists, and by 'Freemasons and their apostate priest-collaborators', who have so angered the Lord that a time of 'Divine Justice' is at hand. Both the Satanist and Freemason conspiracy theories, and the apocalyptic and millenarian prophecies, were typical of Milingo's Italian preaching in the 1990s. Although Milingo's theology has never been subject to in-depth studies (including by Catholic authorities, who have preferred to focus instead on his 'strange' liturgical practices and public exorcisms), it appears that some of his ideas on the Second Coming were, at that time, closer to Evangelical millenarianism (see **Millenarianism**) than to Catholic orthodoxy. Milingo's ideas about a Satanist and Masonic takeover of the Catholic Church, also led him to participate in the activities of Father Nicholas Gruner, the leader of the International Fatima Rosary Crusade (IFRC), a fringe Catholic group repeatedly denounced by Rome as a non-Catholic cult (see **Cult and New Religions**). The same apocalyptic ideas may have played a role in Milingo's contact with Reverend Moon and the Unification Church, which led to the incidents of Summer 2001 described in the entry on Milingo (see **Milingo, Emmanuel**).

Well beyond his religious orders and the charitable foundations, Milingo established a large network of followers in Italy in the 1990s, quite independent of the Roman Catholic hierarchy, and often very critical of Catholic bishops who tried to restrict his public healing and deliverance activities in their dioceses. During the events of summer 2001, it became clear that there were three factions among the followers of this controversial Archbishop. Only a handful were in favour of Milingo's relation with the Unification Church, while a large majority, including the leadership of the various associations and foundations, advocated his return to the Catholic Church. A third party,

however, wanted Milingo to denounce as equally manipulative both the Unification Church and the Catholic hierarchy who had 'persecuted' him. This seems to have been the agenda of painter Alba Vitali and businessman Maurizio Bisantis, who literally 'kidnapped' Milingo upon his arrival in Italy from the US in August 2001. Eventually, after meeting Pope John Paul II on 7 August, Milingo returned to the Catholic fold. Under Vatican supervision, what some media still call the 'Milingo cult' was slowly integrated into Catholic orthodoxy during 2001–2, although not all theological problems connected with some of his teachings appear to have been fully resolved.

Further reading

Mbukanma, J. O. (1990) *On the Eucharist: A Divine Appeal. Revelations from Jesus Christ to Sr Anna Ali*, Cross Junction (Virginia): M.E.T. Publishers.

MASSIMO INTROVIGNE

MILINGO, EMMANUEL
Controversial Roman Catholic Archbishop (b. 1920)

Emmanuel Milingo was born in rural Zambia in 1930, and was ordained a Catholic priest in 1958. He served as the parish priest of Chipata, Zambia, from 1963 to 1966, and as secretary of the national mass media department of the Zambian Catholic Church between 1966 and 1969. In 1969, he was consecrated Archbishop of Lusaka, Zambia's capital, serving there from 1969 to 1983, during which time he became both internationally successful and controversial as a result of his very popular healing and exorcism ministry. In fact, Zambian bishops were trying to modernize the local Catholic Church, and Milingo was so close to popular religion that there were widespread concerns that he was encouraging, rather than suppressing, superstition. In 1983, the Vatican intervened and called Milingo to Rome, asking him to serve on the Pontifical Council for the Pastoral Care of Migrants and Itinerant Peoples.

To the surprise of many, Milingo restarted his successful healing and exorcism ministry in Italy, becoming a popular media figure, but generating among Italian bishops the same degree of opposition he had encountered in Zambia. Feeling persecuted, he started to work with controversial movements, including the Unification Church led by Reverend Moon (see **Unification Church/ Moonies**). His presence at one of Moon's mass weddings in Seoul in 1999 was largely ignored, but the Catholic Church was shocked when Milingo himself was married by Moon to Korean acupuncturist Dr Maria Sung in New York on 27 May 2001. While Milingo initially defended his choice in theological terms, he was later persuaded by his Catholic friends to return to Italy for a personal meeting with Pope John Paul II, in a last minute attempt to avoid excommunication. After the meeting, on 7 August 2001, Milingo announced his return to the Catholic fold, while expressing his 'brotherly' love for Maria Sung. Catholics and Unificationists traded quite liberally accusations of brainwashing back and forth, and the melodrama turned to comedy when reporters discovered that Maria was in fact still legally married to a Naples Unificationist, and not divorced. After a year of silence and meditation in Argentina, Milingo was allowed to return to Rome in September 2002, and to resume his healing ministry under Vatican supervision.

MASSIMO INTROVIGNE

MILLENARIANISM

Millenarianism originally referred to a prophecy about the end of times, derived from the apocalyptic literature of Judaism and from the Book of Revelation. It expressed the belief that a saviour (messiah) would come (or return) to Earth to establish a one-thousand-year-long messianic kingdom, before the Final Judgement of all humanity. The millennium thus installed has been called The Golden Age or the Earthly Heaven. In the history of Christianity it has been the object of diverse interpretations. The dangers of an Anti-Christ, the early resurrection of the Christian martyrs, the characteristics proposed for the Golden Age are different elements of concurrent interpretations. The time of the occurrence of the millennium – in a distant or near future – and the criteria for the salvation of the chosen ones have been the two main points by which these interpretations can be distinguished from one another.

Since 1891, when J. Mooney wrote on the Ghost Dance of the Sioux, the word millenarianism has been used by social scientists and historians as a conceptual tool with which to interpret a particular type of salvationism.

Basing himself on his own thorough analysis of European medieval millenarianisms, Norman Cohn formulated a typology which is still largely used to identify the phenomenon. According to Cohn, millenarians see salvation as

(a) collective, in the sense that it is to be enjoyed by the faithful as a collectivity;
(b) terrestrial, in the sense that it is to be realized on this earth and not in some other-worldly heaven;
(c) imminent, in the sense that it is to come both soon and suddenly;

(d) total, in the sense that is utterly to transform life on earth, so that the new dispensation will be no mere improvement of the present but perfection itself;

(e) miraculous, in the sense that it is to be accomplished by, or with the help of, supernatural agencies (Cohn, 1974: 15).

Although this typology has its source in Christianity, it is broad enough to encompass creeds and movements of other cultural traditions, in or from Africa, Melanesia, North and South America, Asia, in historic and contemporary times (see **Rastafarian Movement, Sekai Kyûsei Kyô, Mucker Movement, Rajneesh Movement, Unification Church/Moonies**).

When millenarian beliefs concur with the arrival of a saviour (a cultural hero, an incarnation of a deity, a sacred persona, etc.) who activates the millenarian hope by revealing the message of salvation and by inaugurating the construction of the Earthly Heaven, we are in the presence of messianism. Prophetism is a millenarian movement led by a prophet who announces the coming of the messiah and the millennium and whose role is to mediate between the sacred and profane.

The emergence of millenarian movements may occur where there is the experience and consciousness of a crisis, a consequent questioning of the established truths, and a cultural background of millenarian cosmology. As the product of collective action such movements structure social relations.

The type and course of millenarian movements relate inextricably to the socio-historic context in which they rise. Creatively, the selective appropriations/interpretations of cultural elements produce a coherent world view. Myth and ritual strengthen specific forms of social/

hierarchical organization and set paths to be followed. Millenarian movements can take the form of a nativistic, a revitalization or an ethnic movement; a revolutionary, or an anti-colonial movement or a liberation struggle; a **cargo-cult** or a particular combination of all of these.

As processes with goals set and pursued millenarian movements can have profound (and often radical) consequences for those involved. They may be effective instruments of social change, even though many of the known cases have either been suffocated or have had a different social effect from the original one intended. The kind of change these movements actually propose is constantly being reformulated in the course of the movement's history. Thus typologies must be complemented by a processual analysis.

The importance of cultural factors to the motivation and action in pursuit of social change, to conceive of millenarian movements as *concrete utopias*. Different from the classic utopias, millenarian movements not only express the possibility, but are projects conceived and constructed by social groups (dispossessed, oppressed, colonized, troubled in any way) who believe in the real possibility of an earthly paradise.

In urban societies of post-modern times millenarian beliefs can provide individuals with an alternative world view and a structured environment which gives meaning to their existence, in place of their experience of the world as fragmented and individualistic. They also define programatic paths to salvation, in a spectrum that ranges from Christian derived churches of a conservative tradition (**Neo-Pentecostalisms**) to the early twenty-first century **Raelian Church** whose salvation doctrine relies on the cutting edge technology of cloning (see **New Age Movement**). For individuals, conversion to a millenarian movement can lead to self-empowerment. The case of Neo-Pente-costalisms in Latin America is an example in which the direct relevance of a religious work ethic and of moral teaching come close to giving rise to utopian communities in which individuals develop a new conception of the **self**.

Further reading

Lanternari, V. (1965) *The Religions of the Oppressed,* New York: Mentor Books.
Cohn, N. (1974) *The Pursuit of the Millenium. Revolutionary Millenarians and Mystical Anarchists of the Middle Ages*, New York: Oxford University Press.
Barabas, A. (1986) *Utopias Indias*, Madrid: Grijalbo.

MARIA AMELIA S. DICKIE

MONTGOMERY, RUTH
(b. 1913; d. 2001)
Journalist and New Age author

Ruth Montgomery, a former White House correspondent, discovered the gift of automatic writing and became a prolific author of spiritual books. Her 1966 bestseller *A Search For The Truth* launched her career in alternative spirituality and her eventual acknowledgement as 'The First Lady of the Psychic World'. Influenced by Nostradamus, Levi Dowling, Arthur Ford, Edgar Cayce, and Hugh Lynn Cayce, her central 'spirit message' is an insistence on oneness with God and our unlimited inner capacity. The fuel for soul advance depends on the good one does during his/her terrestrial existence.

Montgomery denies the reality of death and places a strong emphasis on the efficaciousness of prayer as a psychic experience similar to meditation and dreams. She also accepts the notion of reincarnation or a succession of terrestrial lifetimes all designed and chosen to encourage 'spiritual progress'. In fundamentals, this is a gnostic position in which each created entity or person, despite the obstacles, seeks re-union with its 'Maker'. However, Montgomery interprets her psychic worldview within a decidedly Christian and biblical framework. In the soul's quest for eternal truth and 'Oneness with God', she argues, the material has no importance and physical incarnation represents only a minor segment of in the soul's millennia-long ascent. However, in expressing a common New Age sentiment that physical hardship and deformity are 'chosen' by those who suffer from them in order to progress their souls more rapidly, Montgomery has received criticism.

Among her fifteen publications, including *Here and Hereafter, A World Beyond, Born to Heal, Companions Along the Way, The World Before, Strangers Among Us, Threshold to Tomorrow, Aliens Among Us, Ruth Montgomery: Herald of the New Age*, and her 1999 *World To Come: The Guides' Long-Awaited Predictions for the Dawning Age*, Montgomery explores the compatibility of Christianity and Judaism with Eastern philosophy, the therapeutic value of understanding past lives, postmortem existence in the astral plane, co-creation, earth changes in the coming planetary axis shift, magnetic healing, Lemuria/Mu and Atlantis, extraterrestrial space visitors, the intergalactic universe-federation, Walk-ins, and the millennialist conformity of the New Age transition with the apocalypse of the Book of Revelations.

Further reading

Montgomery, R. (1966) *A Search for the Truth*, New York: Ballantine.

MICHAEL YORK

MOORISH SCIENCE TEMPLE

Timothy Drew or Noble Drew Ali established, with the assistance of Dr Suliman, the first African American Islamic organization, called the Caanite Temple, in Newark in 1913. He claimed that while on his visit to North Africa he received a commission from the king of either Egypt or Morocco to teach Islam to African Americans. Drew asserted that African Americans as a result of being enslaved, were forced to adopt a false cultural identity and religion. Drew taught his followers that they along with North Africans, Arabs, Turks, Japanese, Chinese, Hindus, and Latin Americans were descendants of the ancient Moabites – the founders of the Moroccan empire. Following the destruction of the white people, the Moors will establish a world of love, peace, freedom and justice. Drew bolstered the new Asiatic identity of his followers with a rich array of national symbols, including a national flag depicting a star within a crescent on a field of red, the wearing of red fezzes and long beards, and membership cards. Drew blended together elements from Islam, Christianity, Judaism, Free-masonry, **Theosophy**, and pan-African-ism. In 1927, he published a short book called the *Holy Koran* which drew upon the Quran and the *Aquarian Gospels of Jesus Christ*, and a Rosicrucian (see **Rosicrucian Order, Crotona Fellowship**) tract. Drew asserted that whereas Christianity is the religion of the Europeans, Islam is the religion of Asians, which for him included African Americans. He established a number of small businesses where his followers could work. The Moorish Science Temple was divided into the Bey and El clans. Drew asserted that he embodied the spirits of Jesus, Muhammed, Buddha, Zoraster, and Confucius.

By 1916, the Caanite Temple had split into two factions, the Holy Moabite Temple of the World which remained in Newark and the Moorish Science Temple of America which remained loyal to Drew Ali and relocated its headquarters to Chicago and established branches in Pittsburgh, Detroit, Philadelphia, and a number of other cities, including in the South. In Chicago, he became an even more outspoken 'race man', apparently modelling himself on Marcus Garvey, the founder of the Universal Negro Improvement Association.

Under the sponsorship of the Moorish Manufacturing Association, Drew allowed entrepreneurs to sell various magical potions, such as Moorish Herb Tea for Human Ailments, Moorish Body Builder and Blood Purifier, Moorish Mineral and Healing Oil, and Moorish Antiseptic Bath Compound, to his members. Moors taught numerology as part of religion, a phenomenon that overlapped with illegal lotteries that promised hope to poor blacks. A power struggle, perhaps related to an effort to purge the racketeers within the sect, resulted in the murder of Sheik Claude Green and the subsequent arrest of Drew Ali, even though he was not in Chicago at the time of the crime. Drew Ali died in mysterious circumstances a few weeks after being released on bond. The council of governors of the Temple elected C. Kirkman Bey, Ali's former secretary, to the position of Grand Sheik.

After Drew's death, the Moorish Science Temple split into numerous factions. John Givens-El, Ali's former chauffeur, claimed that he was the reincarnation and assumed leadership over one of the factions. The FBI capitalized upon factionalism within the Moorish Science movement by infiltrating its temples during the 1940s, but continued its program of systematic harassments in the 1970s. The two principal Moorish

Science sects at the present time are the Moorish Science Temple of America and the Moorish Science Temple Divine and National Movement of North America. Muhammed Ezaldeen, an early member of the Moorish Temple in Newark, lived in Egypt from 1929 to the late 1930s, reportedly learning Arabic and studying Islam. Upon returning to the United States, he discovered that the Moorish Science Temple had been in large measure supplanted by the **Nation of Islam**. In response, he started an organization called the Adenu Allahe Universal Arabic Association which promoted the establishment of self-sufficient rural communities.

Grand sheiks serve as leaders of temples. They are assisted by ministers, elders, and stewards. Moorish Americans pray in the direction of Mecca three times a day – at sunrise, noon, and sunset. They observe Friday as their holy day and celebrate Drew's birthday on 8 January, New Year's Day on 15 January, Flag Day in August, and Christmas. Only some Moors celebrate Ramadan. They abstain from meat, eggs, alcohol, and tobacco and are urged not to serve in the military. The Moorish movement has over the course of its history published several newspapers. It has also been involved in various social outreach programs, including feeding the poor and operating drug and alcohol recovery programs.

Further reading

Fauset, A. H. (1971) *Black Gods of the Metropolis,* Philadelphia: University of Pennsylvania Press.

Turner, R. M. (1997) *Islam in the African-American Experience*, Bloomington: Indiana University Press.

HANS A. BAER

MORAL RE-ARMAMENT (MRA)

A moral and spiritual renewal movement, whose aims are defined as a 'hate-free, fear-free, greed-free world', Moral Re-Armament was established by Frank Nathan Daniel Buchman (1878–1961), a Lutheran pastor who received a spiritual experience in Keswick, Cumbria in 1908. In 1921 Buchman set up the First Century Christian Fellowship, a group of Oxford students who became popularly known as the Oxford Group. Launched in 1938, MRA's programme declared that estrangement from God was caused by moral shortcomings, that the human will – rather than the intellect or the heart – was crucial in establishing a relationship with God, and that moral strength was needed for a just society. The movement taught four 'absolutes': honesty, purity, unselfishness and love.

The movement regarded itself as an 'ecclesiola' – a church within the Church – although MRA's principles were offered beyond Christianity, and have been taken up variously by Hindus, Buddhists and Shintoists. In its early years, it organized 'house parties', either in the homes of affluent supporters, or in good hotels. Sharing and guidance have served as important principles, and a frequent practice involved eliciting confessions of sins from members, and offering encouragement for better living. Public testimony meetings were the means of disseminating MRA's ideas to a wider audience, and, particularly after Buchman's death, plays written by Peter Howard served as a vehicle for their propagation.

MRA has sought to exert moral influence rather than to proselytize, and has exercised considerable influence on a number of organizations seeking to improve human behaviour. One example is Alcoholics Anonymous (founded in 1935), and Mary Whitehouse, the first chair of the (British) National Viewers' and Listeners' Association (NVLA), is said to have belonged to MRA.

During World War Two (1939–45/46), MRA was criticized for alleged pro-Nazi leanings, no doubt because of its firm opposition to communism. Buchman sought to influence Nazi policy by arranging meetings with leaders such as Himmler; he attempted unsuccessfully to gain an audience with Hitler himself. MRA, however, proved unpopular with the Third Reich, and its ideas were openly rejected.

After the War, MRA focused on healing and reconciliation. Buchman's death in 1961 left the organization without a clear successor, and it began to decline in the early 1960s. It continues to exist as a network, with the aim of 'remaking the world'. A worldwide movement, it has a presence in twenty-eight countries.

Further reading

Buchman, F. N. D. (n.d.) *Remaking the World*, Washington, DC: Mackinac Press.
Williamson, G. (1954) *Inside Buchmanism: An Independent Inquiry into the Oxford Group Movement and Moral Re-Armament*, London: Watts.

GEORGE CHRYSSIDES

MOTHER MEERA

One of several Indian female gurus who became popular in the West in the second half of the twentieth century, mother Meera may be characterized first by her style of being and teaching. She has no systematic teachings, no communal ritual and no ashram or community of followers. Yet an estimated 30,000 people come to visit her every year at her center in Thalheim, Germany.

Devotion to mother Meera is focused on the belief in her supernatural power to transform the individual and the world.

Mother Meera was born in 1960 as Kamala Reddy into a poor family in the state of Andhra Pradesh. At the age of 12, she was 'discovered' by Mr. Venkat Reddy (no family relation), a religious seeker with a close affiliation to the tradition of Aurobindo (see **Aurobindo, Sri**) and a special attraction to female sages and gurus. Mr. Reddy believed Kamala to be the incarnation of the original and supreme divine energy, the Adiparashakti, and devoted the rest of his life (he died in 1985) to making her known to the world. He took her to live at the ashram of Aurobindo in Pondicherry, where her basic world-view and self-understanding came to develop. She adopted the name 'mother Meera' (after the medieval Bhakti saint Mirabai) and was regarded as an avatar or divine incarnation who descended into the world to bring down the divine Light and continue the work of Aurobindo and Mira Alfassa. One of her earliest disciples at the ashram was Adilakshmi, a woman about twenty years her senior, who continues to be her closest associate and manager. Having failed to receive general support from the members of the Aurobindo ashram, Mr Reddy, Adilakshmi and mother Meera traveled through India, Canada, and the United States and settled in Germany in 1982. Here mother Meera gives *darshan* four nights a week to visitors who come from all over Europe, the United States and Australia.

Darshan, or the grace-filled moment of beholding the divine reality in an image or in a person, forms the essence of mother Meera's mission in the world. It takes place in complete silence. While some visitors meditate, others line up to kneel in front of mother Meera. She then holds the bowed head of the devotee between her hands, pressing it slightly on the sides. This is called *pranam* and is believed to awaken the divine energy in the person and to dissolve mental blockages. It is followed by darshan proper during which mother Meera looks sharply into the eyes of the devotee. This is said to bring about the infusion of the divine Light leading to spiritual transformation. The focus of darshan is thus exclusively upon the individual person and his or her relationship to mother Meera. This relationship may continue after darshan by mail or phone. It is rare, however, to have actual contact with mother Meera herself. While no systematic teaching or explanation of the process of darshan is offered, answers to many of the devotees questions is offered in the literature of the movement: *The Mother* (a hagiography of mother Meera written by Adilakshmi), and *Answers I and II* (dialogues with mother Meera focusing predominantly on concrete issues of practice).

Much of the popularity of mother Meera in the West is due to the fame of one of her earliest devotees, the English writer Andrew Harvey, who in his book *Hidden Journey*, elaborates at length on his experiences with mother Meera. While Harvey has broken ties with mother Meera, she has developed a sufficient following to require several months' advance booking to attend darshan. Mother Meera seems to cater to the Western desire for spiritual growth as a good in itself.

Further reading

Harvey, A. (1992) *Hidden Journey: A Spiritual Awakening*, Harmondsworth: Penguin.
Goodman, M. (1998) *In Search of the Divine Mother*, New York: Thorsons.

CATHERINE CORNILLE

MOVEMENT FOR THE RESTORATION OF THE TEN COMMANDMENTS

Founder: Credonia Mwerinde and Joseph Kibwetere

One of the most widely known new religions in the African context in recent times is the Movement for the Restoration of the Ten Commandments of God (MRTCG). On 17 March 2000 several hundred members of this movement died in an explosion near the village of Kanungu, Uganda, in what appeared to be a mass suicide. Later hundreds of other bodies were discovered in other locations.

The MRTCG grew out of a Marian apparition movement in Rwanda in the 1970s. While visions of the Virgin Mary, many of them concerning the devastation being wrought by Aids, were not uncommon in Uganda and nearby Rwanda of the 1980s, two principal visionaries are closely associated with the origins and development of the MRTCG. One was the dedicated and active Catholic who was heavily involved in local politics Joseph Kibwetere (b. 1932), and the other Credonia Mwerinde (b. 1952) who claimed that she had been in contact with the Virgin Mary since 1984. Prior to this date in 1960 her father Paulo Kashaku claimed to have been the recipient of a vision in which his daughter Evangelista disclosed to him that he would be visited by further apparitions from heaven. According to MRTCG sources he was visited in 1988, a year before the movement began, by Jesus, the Virgin Mary and St. Joseph. These heavenly visitors told him that his family would be blessed if he allowed his land near the city of Kanungu to be used as a meeting place for believers.

Joseph Kibwetere, a father of sixteen, was noted by his neighbours for his

371

piety and good works, which included the founding of a Catholic school. He was also the supervisor of other schools in the region. He also allowed his farm to be used as the headquarters of the nascent MRTCG until these were moved in 1992 to Kanungu where Mwerinde's family lived and where relations with villagers but not the civil authorities were at times tense. The group experienced rapid growth at this point with several hundred members living an austere, communal life. Collectively they built dwellings, a church and a school and established centres at strategic points for the evangelization of the surrounding villages and towns. In 1998 the first serious clash with the civil authorities occurred when the latter took away the movement's school operating licence for the reason that it was violating public health regulations. It was also suspecting of maltreating pupils.

Even before the MRTCG moved to Kanungu it had begun to attract a number of clergy including Fr Dominic Kitaribaabo who had been a postgraduate student in religious studies in the United States. Kitaribaabo had begun to reject some of the liturgical reforms of the Second Vatican Council while still recognizing the authority of the pope.

As MRTCG distanced itself from mainstream Catholicism and the local community it came increasingly to turn in on itself in the manner of an introversionist movement believing that salvation was only available within the walls of its own community. Moreover, this growing isolation reinforced by the apocalyptic messages emanating from the numerous Marian apparitions that had recently occurred, reinforced the belief in the end of the world. Immediately prior to the tragedy of March 17th members were reported to be actively

preparing for the end by preaching and calling all those who had left the movement to re-enter the fold. Furthermore, by way of preparing for their deliverance they were said to have slaughtered cattle and stored away large supplies of Coca-Cola. Reports of activities on the two days prior to the explosion claim that members spent the time feasting on beef and Coca-Cola and praying in their newly built church. At the time of the fire the members were gathered in the old church which had become the dining hall. After consuming the dining hall the fire spread rapidly throughout the headquarters razing to the ground everything in its wake and leaving no one with any chance of escape.

The MRTCG came to depict itself as the Ark of salvation, the vessel which would save those who repented from the coming apocalypse, and carry them to a place that would resemble Heaven on Earth. Its teachings, based principally on revelations received by its leaders were set out in the document A Timely Message from Heaven: The End of the Present Times. Those who sought membership of the MRTCG were required to have read this document several times before being admitted to the movement during a period of between four to six days. They were then admitted as novices and were obliged to wear black during their novitiate. After their novitiate they advanced to the second level of membership which consisted of those who those who had vowed to follow the commandments. This group wore green. The next level was that of the fully professed who wore green and white and had expressed their willingness to die in the ark. Other requirements of membership included the promise to renounce material possessions, abstain from sexual relations, and observe the rule of silence. Sign language was to be the main means of everyday communication between the members.

Different estimates have been given of the number of those who died in this tragic event which resembles the mass suicides that occurred at Jonestown Guyana in 1978 (Chidester, 1988) in which over 900 members of the Peoples Temple died and that of 1993 in Waco Texas in which some seventy-four members of the Branch Davidians were engulfed in flames and died putting an end to over fifty days of stand-off with the FBI (Hall, 2002). The total of MRTCG members who died either in the March 17th inferno or from other causes is not known. Subsequent investigations by the Ugandan police in March and April 2000 reportedly (Mayer, 2001: 204) uncovered graves in various locations around the country containing the corpses of MRTCG members who had been murdered. According Mayer (2001: 204) the Ugandan police estimated that there were 780 victims in all, while Levinson (2001: 198) gives the total number of victims as 925 adding 'perhaps all were murdered'.

Further reading

Chidester, David (1988) *Salvation and Suicide: An Interpretation of the Peoples Temple and Jonestown*, Bloomington: Indiana University Press.

Hall, John, R. (2002) 'Mass Suicide and the Branch Davidians', in David Bromley and J. Gordon Melton (eds) *Cults, Religion and Violence*, Cambridge: Cambridge University Press, pp. 149–70.

Levinson, David (2001) 'Movement for the Restoration of the Ten Commandments of God' in Stephen D. Glazier (ed.) *African and African American Religions*, New York, pp. 198–99.

Mayer, Jean-François (2001) 'Field Notes: The Movement for the Restoration of the Ten Commandments of God.' *Nova Religio: The Journal of Alternative and Emergent Religions* 5(1), 203–10.

PETER B. CLARKE

MOVEMENT OF SPIRITUAL INNER AWARENESS (MSIA)

A syncretistic religious organization, founded by John-Roger Hinkins (b. Roger Delano Hinkins, 1934), usually referred to as 'John-Roger' by his followers, MSIA, pronounced 'Messiah', is also known as John-Roger Insight Seminars. Born in Rains, Utah, of a **Mormon** family (see **Church of Jeses Christ of Latter-Day-Saints (Mormons)**), Hinkins completed a psychology degree at the University of Utah in 1958. In 1963, while undergoing surgery for a kidney stone operation, he entered a nine-day coma, in the course of which he claimed a Near Death Experience. John-Roger is said to have spiritually met Sawan Singh (1858–1945), a past leader of the Radhasoami sect in the same year and received initiation as 'the Mystical Traveller'.

From 1968 John-Roger organized a series of six seminars in a friend's home; as interest grew, he was unable to lead every group, and hence some seminars used tapes. These tapes were transcribed and named *Soul Awareness Discourses*. In 1971 MSIA was incorporated, and the magazine *On The Light Side* was launched; its name was later changed to *The New Day Herald*. Hinkins purchased a large house in Los Angeles, which was named Prana (meaning 'wisdom'), and at its height there were 130 residents. Dissemination of teachings is now mainly by seminars, correspondence courses and Internet contact.

Hinkins studied the teachings of **Eckankar**, and is also said to have been influenced by Lifespring Seminars. Similarities between the teachings of Eckankar and MSIA have caused critics to accuse Hinkins of plagiarism: Hinkins denies having been initiated into Eckankar, however, but acknowledges similarities between the two sets of teachings, arguing that 'Traveller Consciousness' is revealed by many religious leaders, including Moses, Buddha, Mohammed, Lao-Tzu, Confucius, and St Francis. John-Roger claims to synthesize the various 'cosmic energy routes to soul transformation', but does not claim exclusivity, contending that his teachings are compatible with all other faiths. He does not claim to be a **guru**, but a 'way-shower'. A distinctive element in his teachings is the role ascribed to Jesus Christ, who is claimed to be the ultimate head of MSIA, a Mystical Traveller, whose work potentially enables humankind to enter the heart of God.

MSIA's fundamental aim is 'Soul Transcendence'. John-Roger teaches that creation emanates from God, and that each soul has the task of recognizing its oneness with God, 'practically', as well as theoretically. Individuals have chosen the particular physical bodies, which their souls currently inhabit, but this physical existence is an illusion, which one should endeavour to transcend, enabling the soul to return to God, experiencing its true reality. The soul undergoes various births, gaining experience and dealing with the karma it has accumulated in past and present lives, progressing through higher levels of existence towards this greater reality.

Important in MSIA teaching is the 'sound current', into which John-Roger initiated his students from the organization's early years. There are five levels of initiation, which are explained in John-Roger's *Q & A from the Heart*: the astral, the causal, the mental, the etheric, and the Soul, relating respectively to the imagination, the emotions, the mind, the unconscious, and one's true self. The astral initiation is said to occur in a dream in which the seeker encounters the Mystical Traveller; the other four initiations work by means of MSIA's teachings and spiritual exercises. These exercises consist of mantras which followers chant or meditate on, principally 'Ani-Hu' and 'Hu', both of which lead to the 'attunement with Spirit'.

John-Roger describes his path as 'practical spirituality'. It is said to yield pragmatic benefits, such as 'health, wealth, happiness, abundance, and joy', as well as virtues such as 'unconditional love' and service to others, and techniques for dealing with imperfections such as guilt, temptation, resentment and indecision. These techniques and teachings are addressed in John-Roger's many writings, tapes and electronic resources. John-Roger's fifty books include *Do It! Let's Get Off Our Buts* (co-authored with John McWilliams, and later renamed *Do It! A Guide to Living Your Dreams*), first published in 1992 and a best-seller in the USA. John Morton, who became MSIA's Spiritual Director in 1988, has authored *The Blessings Already Are* (2000).

In 1976 John-Roger founded the University of Santa Monica, of which he is Chancellor, and which offers 'soul-centred education'. He is also founder and President of the Peace Theological Seminary and College of Philosophy, which offers Masters' and doctoral degrees in Spiritual Science.

MSIA is not a membership organization, but there are some 5,000 subscribers to *Soul Awareness Discourses* worldwide, mainly in the USA but also in Canada, Latin America, Britain, France, Japan, Australasia, and West Africa.

Further reading

Hinkins, J.-R. (1997) *Inner Worlds of Meditation*, Los Angeles: Mandeville Press.
Lewis, J. R. (1998) *Seeking the Light: Revealing the Truth about the MSIA and its Founder, John-Roger*, Los Angeles: Mandeville Press.

GEORGE CHRYSSIDES

MUCKER MOVEMENT

This movement started in the South of Brazil in 1869 over a dispute over the biblical interpretations of Jacobina Maurer and the healing remedies developed by her husband. Most of the estimated five thousand followers were of German ethnic origin from a largely German colony in Sao Leopoldo. German peasants began arriving in the south of Brazil in 1824 in response to a government colonization initiative. A minority prospered mainly through farming and small-scale family enterprises. The people spoke a dialect of German and lived according to German traditions and rules – much in the same way as the Japanese immigrants were to live when they began to arrive in Brazil to work on the coffee plantations in the early years of the twentieth century. Divorce and remarriage were common among the early German settlers despite the fact that the Canon Law of the Catholic Church was the official law at the time in Brazil. Moreover, Catholics and Lutherans mixed easily and intermarried paying little attention to the rules of their Churches.

Moreover, as the Churches – mainly the Catholic and Lutheran Churches – provided little assistance by way of counseling and guidance the local population selected their own religious guides, specialists, preachers and teachers, the result of which was the formation of a variety of distinctive and different religious communities offering a variety of different biblical interpretations. When the Jesuits arrived in the 1850s they were allegedly shocked by the absence of true religion.

The German peasants were joined by German intellectuals from the late 1840s many of them having immigrated to Brazil after the revolutions of the 1840s in Europe. They were bound together by Masonic ties and struggle to acquire the right to participate in the political process in Brazil, a right reserved for Brazilian born citizens only. Believing themselves to be enlightened and rational, they also set about dispelling what they saw as the superstitious beliefs and practices of their peasant neighbours.

Moreover, economic and social differences began to appear relatively quickly among the population with the rise of Sao Leopoldo from a small rural backwater to a market. This was the cultural, religious and socio-economic background to the rise of Mucker movement and the proclamations of Jacobina.

When defending her behaviour to the police authorities in 1873 Jacobina claimed to be inspired by the Holy Spirit whom she visited during trances. While in trance received knowledge and learnt to interpret the Bible correctly and how to prescribe the appropriate potions to the sick and needy.

Jacobina's message was **millenarian.** In a manner not entirely unlike the Japanese female founder of **Omoto, Deguchi Nao,** she opposed modernity. Among other things she foretold the coming of a New World where barter would replace money as the means of exchange. She also proclaimed that new marriage laws would be introduced and denounced the Jesuits as the Anti-Christ. Her ideal community was one that shared its resources and many of her followers came to live in or close to her compound. Collectively the Muckers built a home for the sick and shared labour and crops.

The community was accused of murdering dissidents in 1873, prison warrants were issued and the army called in and others in the wider community who opposed the movement joined in the attack on its properties. The Muckers put up fierce resistance and only after forty-five days of fighting and much slaughter on both sides were Jacobina and some seventeen of her followers trapped by the army and killed. Other adult survivors were imprisoned only to be found innocent of any crime six years later.

Over time Jacobina's teachings and healing practices were abandoned, although pro and anti-Mucker factions can still be identified today through family names.

The Mucker movement bears many of the characteristics that Cohn (1970) associates with millenarian movements in Medieval Europe.

Further reading

Cohn, Norman (1970) *The Pursuit of the Millennium*, London: Paladin.

MARIA AMELIA SCHMIDT DICKIE

MUNGIKI

Founders: Maina Njenga and Ndura Waruinge
Country: Kenya

Mungiki (Muingiki to be accurate) is a popular, illegal movement, mainly of marginalized young Agikuyu, for whom the modern church and state of Kenya has afforded little hope. The lexical root of Mungiki is the Gigikuyu, *muingi* (the public) and –ki (fully), or the whole Gikuyu community. 'Mungiki means the masses,' says the leader. It is at once ethnic, but more significant is its use in Mau Mau politics, when Muingi was itself used as a synonym for the unity movement. In 1958 the *Kiama Kia Muingi* (Council of the Community) was proscribed, but a series of ethnic opposition movements evolved.

Origin

In 1987 a sect called the Tent of the Living God started to salvage Gikuyu culture from 'confusion by Christian missionaries'. This at once influenced two schoolboys Ndura Waruinge, the grandson of Mau Mau General Waruinge whom he consults on Kirinyaga, and Maina Njenga, who saw a vision in which, he says, Ngai (God) ordered him to lead his people out of bondage to Western ideologies.

Association and aims

Most Mungiki are between 15–25 years old with little education, because they are unable to afford school fees. Some were street-children. They have successively claimed a registered membership of 1.5 million, rising to 6 million, with a third being female. No one would deny them 300,000, and they are capable of raising 700 in any highland town. They seek to convert three-quarters of Kenya, that is 'the masses'. Uniting the Agikuyu, as all tribes of Kenya should unite, is for a grander purpose. 'We (Mungiki) have Mau Mau blood in us and our objectives are similar. The Mau Mau fought for land, freedom and religion ... and so do we.'

Traits and tactics

Mungiki have been blamed for some 110 deaths and raiding police-stations among other things. Their dominance in a locality may lead to control of thieving and thuggery. Any means may be used to 'improve' their 'discipline', including male and female genital cutting campaigns which force Agikuyu women off the streets to avoid being forced to undergo these risky and dangerous punishments. Those caught wearing miniskirts or trousers may be stripped and whipped to prevent the evil of prostitution. Spokepersons explain that Mungiki is a morally upright movement and totally opposed to the satanic western culture.

Males wear dreadlocks, take a non-alcoholic drink (*mukara*) and snuff kept in dry banana skins, when not hiding from the armed forces. They avoid all European-type beer and tobacco. Illicit sex is forbidden. They feel they have no more freedom than in the 1950s with land again being taken from them by foreign interests.

Bitter diatribes against the immorality of school, church, and even the Bible have provoked mainstream churches to respond with descriptions of them as Satanist and devil-worshippers. Since Ngai is seen as God of the nations, there is no conceptual barrier to sharing beliefs, but as the church is seen always to have been importing mental slavery (*gikonjo*), Islam is perceived to be a more congenial resource.

Ceremonies

Seeing themselves as the sons of the Mau Mau movement, they use an oath, but it presupposes initiation as a Mugi-kuyu by genital cutting. The dominant meaning of this rite of *guthera* is one of cleansing from the pollutions of the West, and may include baptism by immersion, demonstrating bricolage.

Oathing is illegal, so oath-takers are sworn to secrecy. Like Mau Mau it may be forced and registers have been kept. Naked men have been discovered, sacrificed lambs, and bowls of blood. Wherever Gikuyu independence is alive, Christians see allies in a more traditional religion such as Mungiki. A senior clergyman with the African Independent Pentecostal Church of Africa allegedly attended several Mungiki oathings. The priest himself had at one meeting been given water and a piece of meat. Dual belonging is still possible.

Prayers and songs

Mungiki prayers are interspersed with traditional chants of 'Thaai, thathaya Ngai, thaai!' (Mercy, pray to God for mercy, mercy!), beseeching him to hear their prayer as they face Mwene-nyaga on his snow-capped seat of Kirinyaga (Mount Kenya). Communication with Ngai is vital to the movement since it 'was started by God. He is our chairman and decision maker.'

Their songs are a mixture of Kikuyu traditional and Mau Mau protest songs. Some of the music in a cassette released in 2002 describes their battles with the police. If blood has to be mixed with soil to achieve justice, then it will be little more than following the tradition invented by the grandfathers.

Further reading

Last, Murray (ed.) (1990) 'Africa' *Journal of the International African Institute*, 60(1).

BEN KNIGHTON

MURID MOVEMENT

This movement is a Sufi order (*tarīqa*) of Muslims, concentrated in north-western Senegal but also with a trading diaspora now extending to the European Union and the United States of America. Followers of this movement, disciples or *talibés*, look to the leadership of their spiritual guides or *marabouts*, guides in worldly as well as religious matters. Mouride *marabouts*, and in particular the movement's supreme leader or Khalifa-General, are seen in Senegal as important political brokers, men with the power to deliver the votes of their disciples in national elections, men who are therefore courted by the national political parties. In recent times however the Khalifa-General has withdrawn from giving electoral advice to the disciples: some of the *talibés* had grown restless at the *marabouts*' apparent subservience to the then governing Parti Socialiste (Socialist Party), with serious rioting after the 1988 elections. After those riots, at the next national elections, Serigne Saliou Mbacké, the Khalifa-General in 1992, withdrew from giving his electoral advice, his *ndiggel* (Wolof for instruction or order). The Mourides present themselves as obedient to spiritual authority, but there is a concealed democracy also within the movement.

The origins of the movement take one back to the late nineteenth century, the time of French conquest of Senegal, a key date being the year 1886, when the Wolof armies were routed. The movement grew rapidly in the social turbulence following French conquest, the focus of devotion being a Wolof Muslim cleric, **Ahmadu Bamba Mbacké**. The new French government of Senegal twice sent Ahmadu Bamba into exile (1895–1902, 1902–7) and miraculous achievements in the face of French colonial persecution were credited to the saintly hero. These miracles remain at the core of Murid belief, remembered in songs and in paintings. The movement appealed notably to the lower orders of Wolof society, to casted persons and to ex-slaves, a charismatic clientele who saw their hero as one who could promise paradise to his followers. Ahmadu Bamba was also a guide in matters of this world, repudiating the idea of armed resistance to the French, of *jihad*. He suggested rather that Murids should adapt to French conquest by giving themselves over to hard agricultural work as well as to prayer.

The colonial government of Senegal kept Ahmadu Bamba in what amounted to house arrest until his death in 1927, but the government also welcomed the Murids' commitment to farming, to growing the peanuts upon which the colonial economy depended. The Murid movement came to occupy a well-recognized position under colonial government. There Marabouts were recognized intermediary powers. When Senegal became independent in 1960 Murid leaders were to continue to be given important symbolic as well as substantial recognition by central government. The great mosque at Touba, the Murid capital, was completed in the year 1960, built by Murid devotion, labour and donations, also facilitated by the support of national politicians and bureaucrats. Touba since that time has grown from a large village to being Senegal's second city in population size. The annual Murid pilgrimage to Touba, the Great Magal (q.v.) is a national as well as a Murid event – the symbolic assertion of Murid power within the state of Senegal.

Murids have moved on from their early agrarian vocation as they increasingly take to trading in the cities of Senegal, then France, then Europe and the USA. The disciples organize themselves in groups for weekly singing of their founder's holy verses, in the 'circle' or *dā'ira*. They remain devoted to the movement's leadership, in particular to the Khalifa-General, but now the urban disciples organize their own spiritual lives. They are also formidable in matters of business, of street trading: the principal market in the Senegalese capital, Dakar, is now seen to be largely a Murid preserve. Murids are powerful in trade and in national politics, their focus still on the leadership of the Mbacké family, Ahmadu Bamba's descendants. They probably number more than two million, they count because of their number, their votes and their productivity, but they count politically above all because they are the best organized Muslims in Senegal.

DONAL CRUISE O'BRIEN

MUSAMA DISCO KRISTO CHURCH

Musama Disco Kristo Church (meaning the Ministry for the Defence of the Cross of Christ or Army of the Cross of Christ Church) is one of the oldest **African Independent Churches** (AICs) in Ghana. Joseph William Egyanka Appiah, a Methodist Catechist founded the Church. He began a prayer group known as the Faith Society in the Methodist Church in the Gomoa District of the Central Region of Ghana in 1919. In 1922, the Methodist Church expelled the group and Appiah. On divine inspiration he formed the church at Gomoah Oguan that year. He also upon divine revelation changed his name to Prophet Jemismiham Jehu Appiah with the title of Akaboha (meaning king). His wife the Prophetess Natholomoa was designated Akatitibi, the queen mother of the Church. Prophet Appiah also founded a holy city, Mozano (meaning 'my town') at Gomoa Fomena. The holy city, relocated after the death of the founder to Gomoa Eshiem in 1951 is called New Mozano and serves as the Headquarters of the church.

The teachings of the Church derive, it is believed, from God's communication through scriptures, the thoughts of the worshipper, dreams, visions and signs. MDCC teachings are based on the belief that the Holy Spirit is the power directing its Prophets and prophetesses, is a source of miraculous power, and bestows gifts and fruits. The Church also believes in a complex angelology and demonology of its own making. The principal ritual is faith healing which can be achieved through prayer and fasting. The Church has healing camps where people can seek spiritual healing. The Prophet also practised telling the spiritual state of a person and fore-telling the future by the laying on of his hands.

The Church teaches that God does not only cater for the spiritual needs of His children but also for their material needs citing Mark 10:28–30 that whatever is given up for Christ will be regained a hundred times over. Tithes and offerings are encouraged in the Church.

The church is strongly influenced by Old Testament rituals. Among its sacred objects is 'The Ark', a box containing the Ten Commandments, and copies of promises God made to the first Akaboha and his vows in respect of these promises known as the 'Book of the Holy Covenants'. This ark has become a ritual object that is used to avert disaster when it is carried in procession. Two major sacrifices are also observed at the Peace festival (24 August) and the Love festival. The Peace festival, which marks the birth of Manapoly son and successor of the prophet/founder, is marked by a whole burnt offering. At the second festival, the Love festival, the sacrifice involves a sharing in a sacrificial meal by all to enhance good neighbourliness.

MDCC uses the vernacular in all services wherever possible. The church has developed a rich liturgy of traditional Fanti musical styles and chants in addition to the use of the Fanti Methodist Hymns. A cantor for instance recites her history in song with responses coming from the congregation using the traditional method of singing known as the Asor Ndwom. They also use Asafo Music, the martial music and dance of the Akan.

The founder introduced a sacred language to members and new members are also given heavenly names and learn the heavenly language. Members use a fifteen-bead rosary (Inaabi) to pray. There is a heavenly name for each bead which has its own meaning and function and copper rings and crosses are kept as protective charms.

The Church encourages temperance in Christian life and members are forbidden to drink or trade in alcoholic beverages. The MDCC permits polygamy because it teaches that it is not a sin, it is better than secret concubinage, and it should be accepted in societies like Africa where it already exists. There are, however, controls on multiple marriages including the requirement that members must have a convincing reason to seek an additional wife. Men who already have several wives are discouraged from marrying new wives. The Church does not allow divorce.

The founder of the Church established a family line of succession. His son Prophet Matapoly Moses Jehu Appiah as Akaboha II thus succeeded Akaboha I. The present Head of the Church is Prophet Miritaiah Jonah Jehu Appiah, Akaboha III. There are two hierarchical strands of leadership in the Church. There is a spiritual line of grades of prophets and healers and an administrative strand of pastors and Catechists under the leadership of the general Head Prophet and the Queenmother. One peculiar element in the MDCC organization is that the leadership is organized along traditional Akan chieftaincy lines. Since the founder of the Church founded a new community he is regarded as a Chief and his descendants form the royal lineage. The installation of a new head prophet therefore has elements similar to the installation of an Akan chief. Divisions of the Church are patterned along Akan chieftaincy divisions. During festivals such as the Peace Festival, the entire church sits in various divisions as will happen at an Akan State durbar when seating will be in accordance with Akan chieftaincy divisions.

The church has links with the **Unification Church** whose members attended the 1995 Peace Festival. They are also linked with the Ascension Presbyterian Church in Columbus, Ohio. Nana Aba Kweiba, an African American who holds an honorary chieftaincy title Nkosuahema (queen of Development) in the Church led some members from Columbus to attend the 1995 Peace Festival. In recent times, the Church has maintained good links with the Methodist Church from which it emerged. At her peace festival in 1995 the renowned African theologian Rev. Prof. Kwesi Dickson, then President of the Methodist Conference of Ghana preached the Sermon and in 2002 it was the Rev. Dr Emmanuel Asante, a Methodist Minister and President of Trinity Theological Seminary, Legon.

The church, the largest AIC in Ghana, has over 800 congregations spread all over Ghana and has branches in Nigeria, the Ivory Coast (Côte d'Ivoire), the Republics of Togo, Benin, Gambia, Sierra Leone, the US, Jamaica, and in the UK.

Further reading

Baëta, C. G (1962) *Prophetism in Ghana*, London: SCM Press.

ELOM DOVLO

MUSLIM BROTHERHOOD
(Ikhwan al Muslimin)

One of the most active and influential movements engaged in the struggle for the creation of an Islamic state, the Muslim Brotherhood was founded in 1928 by **Hassan Al-Banna** (1906–49), an Egyptian primary school teacher. Closely associated with Al-Banna's teachings and ideas is **Sayyid Qutb** (1906–66), also an educationist by profession, who became one of the movement's principal ideologues. The latter's treatise *Ma'alim* *fi al-tariq* (*Milestones*) (1965) has assumed the status of a classic text among contemporary Muslim militants on the rationale for and the means to be adopted for the purpose of creating an Islamic state, the goal of the Brotherhood.

The Brotherhood which began as a youth movement soon became the main inspiration behind the new Islamic radicalism that began to sweep across Egypt in the late 1920s and which became more widespread, determined and committed to bringing about change in the 1930s. It was fed chiefly by the deepening disillusionment with the secular nationalism and liberalism of the political elite which was accused of failing to address the extreme poverty of the masses, and by the global economic crisis caused by the Great Depression (1929).

The Brotherhood linked the serious decline of Islam as a religion and culture for which it held secularism and liberalism responsible to the poverty and economic hardship suffered by the majority of Egyptians. It described what it believed was happening to the Muslim world in apocalyptic terms. Al-Banna's experiences in Cairo and Ismailia in the Suez Canal zone prompted him to speak of the 'devastation' of religion and morality. He became convinced that for Egypt the only escape from the impending catastrophe was through the radical renewal of Islam. This would also be the most effective weapon against the West which he believed had embarked on a new crusade to destroy Islam, this time by corrupting the morals of its leaders and its young and by undermining their faith.

Al-Banna adopted the *dawa* (calling) or bottom up approach in that he sought to reform Islam by calling Muslims to a life lived according to Islamic orthodoxy. It was through Self-change and changing the local community and Islamic society, Al-Banna was persuaded,

that a genuinely Muslim society would emerge. His Islam was an 'engaged' Islam, one that was to be applied to all aspects of life. In addition to spiritual training, the Brotherhood sought to provide for the social and educational needs of Muslims. Organizationally, the Muslim Brotherhood resembled in several ways that of the mystical or Sufi orders. Though a powerful critic of various popular forms of *Sufism* which mixed Islam with what he regarded as non-Islamic practices Al Banna was himself a committed member of the Sufi order the Hasafiyyah. As in the Sufi orders Muslim Brotherhood members were obliged to swear an oath of allegiance and to perform regular spiritual exercises including *dhikr*, the ritual of remembrance of God, the main religious practice of *Sufism*. Daily readings selected from the Qur'an by Al-Banna as well as the five daily prayers (*salat*) were also an integral part of Brotherhood practice.

Over time the structure of the Brotherhood became more complex and formal with the setting up of the General Guidance Council, partially elected by a Consultative Assembly, to advise the final authority known as the General Guide. Organization at the regional level reflected that at the centre and at the local level the basic unit was the small group referred to as the 'battalion' or 'family' within which regular members worked. The publications department performed the role of spreading the movement's philosophy and its objective, which as was previously mentioned was the creation of an Islamic state, and a secret and/or special department defended it from the police and secret service.

During its early years the principal arm of the Brotherhood's campaign to reform Islam was education. As numerous schools for both male and female students – some vocational and/or technical and some academic – were established the movement spread rapidly in and around Ismailia, the Nile Delta, Cairo and further afield. It became largely an urban-based form of fundamentalist Islam. The idea was to lay the foundations of a self-sufficient Islamic society and extricate it from what was perceived as the suffocating stranglehold caused by its dependency on the West.

From the late 1930s and during and after the Second World War (1939–45) the Muslim Brotherhood became increasingly engaged internally in a debate over the use of violence until then never formally endorsed as a tactic by Al-Banna. This period saw a rise in the number of public demonstrations against corrupt local politicians many of whom belonged to the nationalist political party the Wafd (delegation), and against the British government which, though it had unilaterally declared Egypt to be independent in 1922, continued its military occupation of the country and exercised a decisive influence over major domestic and foreign policy issues.

A turning point was reached in the history of the Muslim Brotherhood with the declaration of the State of Israel in 1947, which it regarded as an integral part of the Western, Christian conspiracy to undermine Islam. Relations with the Egyptian government worsened with the assassination by one of the Brotherhood of the Egyptian Prime Minister in 1948. This led by way of retaliation to the murder of Al-Banna in 1949. A brief truce began in 1952 with the overthrow of King Farouk by the Free Officers led by Gamal Abdel Nasser whose new Revolutionary Command Council (RCC) adopted a modern secular version of Islamic socialism as its ideology.

The uneasy alliance between the Brotherhood and the RCC ended in 1954 when the Brotherhood allegedly attempted to assassinate Nasser who had just assumed the presidency of the country. Nasser reacted by executing many of the Brotherhood's leaders and by imprisoning others including Sayyid Qutb. He failed, however, to silence the movement as the prisons became the breeding ground for a new and ever more implacable radicalism. While in jail (1954–64) Sayyid Qutb developed his devastating critique of Nasser's regime and of all liberal, secular, western, non-Islamic governments. This as was previously mentioned was published, as *Milestones* (1965), and has become one of the core texts of all radical Muslims bent on the creation of an Islamic state by both violent and other means. Qutb among others was arrested for conspiracy in 1965 and in 1966 was executed.

The Brotherhood's mainly urban version of Islamic fundamentalism has and continues to exercise a decisive influence on the thinking of radical Muslim activists across the Muslim world. Though autonomous and not necessarily committed to every aspect of its ideology, strategy and tactics versions of this movement can be found in many parts of the Middle East, North Africa, the Sudan, South and Southeast Asia, and the West.

The ideological impact of the Muslim Brotherhood on radical Muslim groups in the contemporary world can hardly be exaggerated. Its main goal of the creation of an Islamic state by the application of Islamic law continues to inspire such Muslim groups as does its emphasis on *jihad* as a defensive weapon and the responsibility of every individual Muslim rather than as a collective duty. Also inspirational for such groups are notions of this age as the age of *jahiliyya* or ignorance of Islam and one therefore which imposes on Muslims the duty to spread their faith, and its explanation of death by martyrdom as a vital weapon in the struggle for the cause of Islam.

Further reading

Qutb, S. (1991) *Milestones*, Burr Ridge, IL: American Trust Publications
Voll, J. O. (1991) 'Fundamentalism in the Sunni Arab World: Egypt and the Sudan' in M. E. Marty and R. S. Appleby (eds) *Fundamentalisms Observed*, Chicago: University of Chicago Press, pp. 345–403.

PETER B. CLARKE

MYOCHIKAI KYODAN

Founder: Miyamoto Mitsu

Myochikai is one of a number of Japanese new religions that started as a splinter group from **Reiyukai**. The founder, Miyamoto Mitsu, was the leader of one of the largest branch churches of Reiyukai and broke away from the larger denomination with about three hundred other followers to form Myochikai in 1950, in the wake of scandals involving tax evasion and other charges. Presently the group claims a membership of about one million.

Mitsu and her husband, Kohei, were both members of Honmon Butsuryuko, an early **New Religious Movement** in the Nichiren Buddhist tradition, before joining Reiyukai in 1934, when the ailing Mitsu was cured through the practice of ancestor veneration taught by Reiyukai. Two years later Kohei was appointed the head of the Seventh Branch Church in recognition of his success as a missionary for the group, and later became a member of Reiyukai's board of directors. Following his death in 1945, Mitsu succeeded him as the leader of the Seventh Branch Church.

Like its parent organization Reiyukai, Myochikai teaches a lay form of Nichiren Buddhism, with a strong emphasis on ancestor veneration. In addition to ancestor veneration, the other pillars of its teaching are a calm endurance of all misfortune for the sake of doing good, repentance for sin, and thanksgiving. Although the group maintains its headquarters in Tokyo, in 1973 new facilities were established in Chiba, outside of Tokyo, the site of both Kohei's and Mitsu's birth and Kohei's grave. Members are encouraged to make pilgrimages to this site, as well as to Mt Minobu, where the monk Nichiren established his temple in the thirteenth century.

Myochikai has been active in peace and interreligious circles practically from its foundation. Within Japan it has been a member of the Federation of New Religious Organizations of Japan since 1953, and on the international level it has also been active in the World Conference on Religion and Peace since the foundational meeting in Kyoto in 1970. Since 1960 it has organized an annual memorial service for war victims at Chidorigafuchi in Tokyo, an alternative memorial site to the controversial Yasukuni Shrine, which is identified with Japanese militarism. Myochikai has participated in international anti-nuclear activities since the 1960s and has cooperated with the Federation of New Religious Organizations of Japan in organizing youth trips to Southeast Asia to promote international understanding.

The group has also cooperated in charity and relief activities in Japan and abroad, participating in the annual community chest drive since the 1950s, contributing towards the relief of earthquake victims in Japan, and participating in leprosy relief in India and famine relief in Africa. On the occasion of its fortieth anniversary in 1990, Myochikai established the Arigatou Foundation to organize its relief and interreligious activities, with a special emphasis on activities directed towards the aid of children in need. 'Arigatou' is the Japanese for 'thanks', and contributions to the foundation are meant to be a concrete expression of the members' faith in action. In May 2000 the Arigatou Foundation, with the cooperation of the Japan Committee for UNICEF and the World Conference on Religion and Peace Japan Committee, established the Global Network of Religions for Children to encourage interreligious work to aid children.

In 1986, two years after Mitsu's death, Miyamoto Takeyasu took over as the leader of Myochikai. Takeyasu was adopted into the Miyamoto family on the occasion of his marriage to Kohei and Mitsu's daughter Aiko in 1945, and he became the chairman of the board of Myochikai in 1957. In this role he was able to reorganize Myochikai's structure, moving away from branch churches based on personal contacts – one factor that contributed to continuous splits within Reiyukai as particularly successful missionaries would move away from the group with some of their converts to establish independent denominations – towards territorial churches and national organizations such as the Young Adults' Group, Women's Group, etc.

In several respects Myochikai is representative of characteristics found broadly in new religious movements in Japan (see **New Religion (Japan)**): in its promotion of an ethic of common virtues such as endurance, repentance, and thanksgiving; in its participation in local and international charitable activities; in its emphasis on world peace and interreligious cooperation; and in the succession of leadership within the family of the founder.

Further reading

Kisala, Robert (1999) *Prophets of Peace. Pacifism and Culture Identity in Japan's New Religions*, Honolulu: Univesity of Hawai'i Press.

ROBERT KISALA

N

NAMDHARI
(a.k.a. Kuka)

A Sikh sect, founded in 1857 by Ram Singh (1816–85) in the Punjab, the Namdhari are recognizable by their white homespun clothing, a turban (*dastar*) tied flat across the forehead, and a woollen cord (*mala*) with 108 knots around the neck, which functions as a rosary. The name *Namdhari* means a 'Sikh who has adopted the name of God in his or her life', and the alternative designation *Kuka* alludes to their ecstatic cries during worship, in which music is especially important. One distinctive practice is their *havan jag* (fire ceremony), and the circumambulation of fire features in their marriage rites. They adopt a pure vegetarian diet, and have a strong concern for cow protection. Equal importance is assigned to the *Adi Granth* and *Dasam Granth,* and the *Chandi di Var*, which is contained in the latter, features in their daily *nitnem* (personal devotion).

Doctrinally, they differ from mainstream Sikhism in their acknowledgement of a lineage of human gurus after Gobind Singh (1666–1708), the founder of the Sikh Khalsa, and – according to the majority of Sikhs – the last of the lineage of human gurus. The Namdharis hold that Gobind Singh did not die at Nander in 1708, as traditionally taught, but lived on until 1812, assuming the name of Baba Ajapal Singh, and aiding Sikhs in distress. Namdharis hold that he appointed Balak Singh (1784–1862) as his successor, whom they regard as the reincarnation of Nanak (1469–1539), the first human guru. Balak Singh's succession is legitimated by a claimed vision of Guru Gobind Singh and his five principal disciples.

Balak Singh was succeeded by Guru Ram Singh (1816–85), who established the Namdhari movement. Ram Singh was a political as well as a religious leader, and assisted the freedom movement in India in its fight against British colonization. A champion of women's rights, he opposed infanticide (frequently practised on females), the selling of young girls into servitude, and the dowry system. He endeavoured to achieve higher standards of literacy, and campaigned against the slaughtering of cows: a Namdhari raid on the Amritsar slaughterhouse resulted in the hanging of several Namdharis in 1871. Namdharis joined the movement of Boycott and Non-Co-operation against the British, refusing to participate in government service, British-run schools, British law courts, and the purchase of imported goods; they refused to comply with laws that were contrary to their consciences. Namdharis claimed that it was not possible to be a Kuka and subject to British imperialism. The British government exiled Ram Singh to Burma on 18 January 1872. His successor Hari Singh (born Budh Singh, 1819–1906) taught that Ram Singh had not died, but could be expected to reappear – a belief that continues to be held by present-day Namdharis.

Guru Pratap Singh (1889–1959) continued with his predecessors' social reforms, successfully introducing the Anand Marriage Act, which abolished the dowry system: simple, affordable marriages are thus the norm among Namdharis. Pratap Singh made several important contributions to Namdhari religious life: he established the Namdhari Darbar (temple) in 1920, and undertook various endeavours to establish inter-religious understanding among different Sikh sects, and among Hindus, Muslims and Sikhs. In 1933 he convened a Gurmat Sangheet Sammelan ('gathering together of Sikhs') and in 1934 representatives of these three religions came together at the Sri Guru Nanak Naam Leva Conference. Keen to improve the Namdharis' own spiritual life, Pratap Singh recommended *nam japo* (meditation on God's name – a practice taught by Nanak) to be practised for one hour each day.

Pratap Singh's successor, Guru Jagjit Singh (b. 1920), has continued the leadership of the tradition, affirming Nanak's three principles of Sikhism: meditation on the name of God (*nam japo*); earning one's living through honest work (*kirat karo*); and sharing with the poor (*wand chakho*). He continues the movement's enthusiasm for inter-faith dialogue, and has a particular interest in Hindu philosophy, especially the Vedas and the Upanishads. As well as a teacher and leader, Jagjit Singh is an accomplished musician – he plays the *dilruba* (a stringed instrument) – and encourages the Namdhari musical tradition. He is also keen on the promotion of sport among the Namdharis.

The Namdharis undoubtedly had an impact on the Independence movement that went beyond their civil disobedience. In 1981, Indira Gandhi, the late Prime Minister of India, stated: 'Our freedom movement gathered strength by attracting every important section of society from every region. The contribution of the Namdhari sect of Sikhs to the movement has been specially significant and unique in its own way.'

Further reading

Kaur, B. (1999) *The Namdhari Sikhs*, London: Namdhari Sikhs Historical Museum.
Jolly, S. K. (1988) *Sikh Revivalist Movements: the Nirankari and Namdhari Movements in Punjab in the Nineteenth Century: a Socio-religious Study*, New Delhi: Gitanjali.

GEORGE CHRYSSIDES

NATION OF ISLAM (NOI)
Founder: Wallace Farad and/or Fard (c. 1887–1934)

Of the many Muslim organizations in the United States, including those organizations that call themselves Muslim but may not be recognized as such by Sunni or orthodox Islam, the largest is the Nation of Islam (NOI). This is the only organization to generate mass appeal based on its own version of Islam's teachings and championing of black nationalism which advocates the unity of all black people, emphasizing their distinctiveness from and superiority to whites (Taylor, 1998: 177). The first significant Black Nationalist movement was the Universal Negro Improvement Association (UNIA) founded in 1914 by the Jamaican Marcus Garvey (1887–1940). Garvey, the inspiration behind the **Rastafarian movement** sought to build an African state on the African continent for all diaspora Black people.

NOI has historical links with several earlier religious movements that preached the message of Black Nationalism including the **Moorish Science Temple** founded in 1913 in Newark, New Jersey, by the African American Noble Ali Drew (1866–1922) from North Carolina. Drew believed that connections could be established between African-American and Oriental peoples, and claimed that he was a reincarnation of the prophet Muhammad, an event heralded by Garvey among others. In 1927, after moving to Chicago, he produced the *Holy Koran of the Moorish Temple of Science*. There are clear differences between this version of the Qur'an and the orthodox Qur'an, the former following more closely Levi Dowling's *Aquarian Gospel* of 1911. Drew died mysteriously after being implicated in a murder that occurred during a struggle over the leadership of his movement.

Suffering even greater economic misery on account of the Depression (1929) and from racial discrimination African-Americans responded with considerable enthusiasm to the message of Wallace D. Fard (pronounced Fa-ROD) (*c*. 1887–1934), whose ethnic origins and rise to the leadership remain largely unknown, but who claimed to come from Mecca. Fard used the Bible, which he saw as a stepping stone to the Qur'an, as the basis for persuading his African-American listeners that Islam not Christianity was the true religion of Africa and Asia.

The NOI under Fard began organizationally as a House Church until a temple in the form of a hall was hired in Detroit and named the Allah Temple of Islam. Fard became increasingly anti-white and encouraged African-Americans to understand and appreciate the glorious history of the African-Asian races. The end of Fard's leadership is as mysterious as its beginnings and as his own ethnic identity. He was arrested, imprisoned in relation to the conviction of a sacrificial killing by a member in 1932 and then ordered out of Detroit and eventually disappeared. Fard was later deified as Allah, and Elijah Muhammad (1897–1975), son of a Baptist minister from Georgia and one of Fard's officers, controversially assumed the leadership and took the title of Prophet and 'sole messenger of Allah'. A leadership struggle soon followed and the movement split, some members moving with Elijah Muhammad to Chicago where he became known as 'Spiritual Head of Muslims in the West', 'Divine Leader' and 'Reformer'. His ministers referred to him as 'The Messenger of Allah to the Lost Found Nation of Islam in the Wilderness of North America'. He named his faction 'Muhammad's Temples of Islam'.

In 1942 Elijah Muhammad was imprisoned for preaching that African-Americans had an obligation not to serve in the Armed Forces, and while in prison he began what became one of the NOI's principal activities, the conversion of prisoners and former prisoners. It was in prison that Malcolm Little, alias Malcolm X Shabazz, from Omaha,

Nebraska, also son of a Baptist minister, was converted and recruited in 1947. This former Garveyite, later to be appointed by Elijah Muhammad as his personal assistant, experienced the worst of racism as he witnessed the Ku Klux Klan burn down his father's home when he was six years old, and later encountered his father's dead body mangled by a train on the railway tracks.

While Elijah Muhammad aimed his message mainly at African-Americans Malcolm X sought to turn the NOI in to a thoroughgoing Black Nationalist movement by involving Africans everywhere. A long running dispute with Elijah Muhammad concerning the propriety of the comment made on the assassination of President John F. Kennedy in 1963 by Malcolm X eventually led to the latter withdrawing and founding the Mosque Inc and its secular counterpart the Organization of Afro-American Unity. Malcolm X's perception of whites changed as a result of his travels to Mecca and elsewhere which convinced him that they were not intrinsically racist. He was assassinated in February 1965, one of the assassins being a member of the NOI.

The transition to a more orthodox Muslim community by the NOI came with the confirmation, after much wrangling and opposition, of Wallace D. Muhammad as the successor to Elijah Muhammad who died in 1975. The changes involved giving the NOI a new name, the 'World Community of al-Islam in the West', calling ministers imams, and reducing Fard's status from Allah to that of an ordinary mortal. Wallace also placed less stress on the ideology of Black Nationalism. These reforms created further division with Louis Farrakhan (b. 1933), then an imam, from the Bronx, New York, leaving the movement with the intention of reconstituting the old NOI. Though other factions also emerged to restore the NOI Farrakhan,

who has acquired a reputation for anti-Jewish rhetoric and who is strongly opposed to Christianity, though not to Black Christians, has done most to refashion the movement in line with the teachings of Elijah Muhammad.

NOI teachings are many and complex, and the following is but the briefest of summaries. The teachings are as they were formulated under Elijah Muhammad and those which Louis Farrakhan was determined to uphold in the 1970s when he rejected Wallace D. Fard's reforms. At the core of these teachings there is a distinctive cyclical notion of God who is not considered to be immortal. Every 25,000 years one God dies and passes on his knowledge and 'godship' to another. There is a 'God of gods' and the idea that different gods perform different functions, one creating the sun, another, the moon, and so on. Gods resemble human beings and like the Greek gods and the Traditional gods of Africa they marry, enjoy normal human pleasures and make mistakes, such as marrying a non-African woman. The first God was a man and all Gods are 'Blackmen' (Taylor, 1998: 190). Human beings are divided into two races one black and one white, the former being self-created, and the 'Original Man' and the 'maker and owner of the universe'. The authentic, original religion of the Black race was Islam, and all Black men are 'god'. Allah is the supreme Blackman and, therefore, God of gods. Black people are believed to be the 'descendants of the Asian black nation and of the tribe of Shabazz' (Taylor, 1998: 190). The beginning of all of this was sixty trillion years ago. Whites, who are evil by nature, were invented by a Dr Yakub, of the black race, and were taught to rule that race. Their religion is one of self-interest, and their rule will last for 6,000 years.

The millenarian (see **Millenarianism**) theme is strongly present in the teachings on the ending of white dominance, and, it is important to note, it is pacific in content. White rule will end with the arrival of a prophet sent by Allah – prophets are sent frequently by Allah – to predict 'the coming of God' who will appear at the 'end of the world' which is understood by NOI to mean the 'end of the white race'. Although there has been some reinterpretation of Fard as God, originally Allah is believed to have come to Wallace Fard from Mecca on 4 July 1930 and from that point on Fard took the place of Allah, and Elijah Muhammad became his prophet in the place of the Prophet Muhammad. It was Elijah's mission to teach Africans the 'knowledge of Self', which is the essence of their redemption, their real identity as members of the Nation of Islam, their true place of origin Asia/Africa, their true God, Allah, and their true religion Islam. In authentic millenarian fashion, all of this is taught in relation to this world, with little speculation about the afterlife.

The NOI provides unusual example of religious change this time from heterodoxy to a more orthodox position, and back again, in contrast with the transition undergone by the **Worldwide Church of God**/Armstrongism in relation to mainstream Christianity. This notwithstanding, the NOI is now considered more orthodox than in the days of Ali Drew and Wallace Ford, and with greater orthodoxy has come an increase in membership. The NOI has grown from a small group of some eight thousand African Americans in the 1950s to around two million members today.

Further reading

Evanzz, K. (1999) *The Messenger: Rise and Fall of Elijah Muhammad*, New York: Pantheon.

Taylor, M. (1998) 'The Nation of Islam' in P. B. Clarke (ed.) *New Trends and Developments in African Religions*, Westport, CT: Greenwood Press, pp. 177–221, .

Gardell, M. (1996) *Countdown to Armageddon. Louis Farakhan and the Nation of Islam*, London: Hurst and Company.

PETER B. CLARKE

NATION OF YAHWEH

(a.k.a. Temple of Love, Black Hebrew Israelites, Tribe of Judah)

This movement is a black supremacist organization, founded by Hulon Mitchell Jr. (b. 1935), known to his followers as Yahweh ben Yahweh ('God, son of God'). Son of a Pentecostalist minister, and an erstwhile football player, Mitchell studied economics and law at Phillips University, the University of Alabama, and Oklahoma University. He joined the United States Air Force, becoming a tactical instructor. For a short period Mitchell was a member of the **Nation of Islam**.

In 1979 Mitchell changed his name to Brother Moses, and came to Miami with his companion Linda Gaines (a.k.a. Judith Israel), where they established the Temple of Love the following year. Gaines was responsible for the Temple's finances, which flourished during the early 1980s, aided by a number of businesses that operated in the Temple's premises. The Temple of Love professed belief in the oneness of God, the Bible, and in himself as the 'Great Light and rule and guide for faith'. The organization taught Yahweh was the 'terrible black God' and Jesus was also black; God's son Yahweh ben Yahweh had come as the saviour of the African Americans, who constituted Israel's lost tribes, and to release them from 400 years of white oppression, and more recently from racial discrimination, police harassment and brutality. Whites were described as 'white devils', and 'white America' was said to be cursed by God. The organization campaigned for electoral reform, and for better education, employment, housing and health care.

Between 1981 and 1982 there were changes in the Temple administration, and during this period Mitchell changed his name to Yahweh ben Yahweh. Followers were encouraged to renounce the 'immoral world' and to live in the Temple's premises, donning African clothing – traditional white robes and turbans. Members were required to give up their legal names ('slave names') and assume Hebrew ones, with the surname 'Israel'. Ben Yahweh kept strict control over rights of entry to the Temple and the behaviour of members. Armed guards – known as the 'Circle of Ten' – protected the premises, and dissenters could be publicly humiliated and beaten. The period from 1982 to 1985 saw the expansion of the movement, with five satellite organizations in other US cities.

During this period a clandestine group known as the 'Brotherhood' developed within the organization. This group turned to physical violence against the white population, and between April and October 1986 Ben Yahweh sent members into Miami's white community as 'death angels', who engaged in random killings of whites at ben Yahweh's command. Membership of this inner circle allegedly required evidence of having killed at least one white person, the killer having to bring to ben Yahweh a trophy consisting of a body part from the victim, such as an ear or the head. Fire-bombings were also carried out, with the aim of terrorizing Miami's white population, and, more specifically, as a warning to whites who had physically attacked ben Yahweh's followers. These activities led to an FBI raid on the Temple in 1990, when some 300 federal agents entered the premises and arrested ben Yahweh, together with six others.

At their trial in 1992, Robert Rozier, a member of the Brotherhood, who had been arrested in 1988 and confessed to several murders, struck a deal with the judiciary, and became the government's star witness. Although ben Yahweh did not personally commit any of the killings, he was nonetheless convicted, together with six other Brotherhood members, who were accused of fourteen killings in all. It was declared that the Nation of Yahweh's activities constituted a RICO (Rackeeting Influenced Corrupt Organizations) conspiracy. Ben Yahweh was given an eighteen-year sentence, but was released in September 2001.

The Nation of Yahweh continues to protest the innocence of ben Yahweh and the others. On their web site he is compared with Jesus, and a parallel is drawn between ben Yahweh's sentence and Jesus' crucifixion. Followers have drawn comparisons between Rozier and Judas Iscariot, Jesus' traitor. The organization claims that it no longer teaches hatred of whites, and that any war between blacks and whites is a 'war of words'. It professes commitment to the ideals of 'character, integrity and morality', emphasizing the virtues of benevolence, charity, chastity, and support for the poor and the oppressed. The organization aims at gathering together, first the lost tribes, and subsequently all God-fearing people, to establish a theocratic government in which God's statutes will be obeyed and immortality offered.

Membership statistics are unavailable; however, the Nation of Yahweh claims to have a presence in seventeen different countries, and 1,300 US cities.

Further reading

Freedberg, S. P. (1994) *Brother Love: Murder, Money, and a Messiah*, New York: Pantheon Books.

GEORGE CHRYSSIDES

NATIVE AMERICAN RELIGION

Native American religions comprise an ongoing, living tradition, though much has been lost in the last three hundred years. As well as being a central part of the identity of many indigenous people, these religions have played a key part in the formation of many shamanic (see **Shamanism**), neo-pagan (see **Neo-Paganism**), and new age (see **New Age Movement**), and movements in America and throughout the West including Europe.

The membership of Native religions is hard to establish, because they are so diverse and so many people have become partly or wholly Christian. The most recent Canadian census estimates 11,000, which may be an underestimate. There is increasing recognition of the importance of central and south American native religions, although there are significant differences, particularly regarding the use of plant substances in the south (see below). New religions based on native traditions from both continents are growing fast, primarily as 'weekend' courses, although many practitioners are trying to 'walk their talk' by living the principles full-time.

There is no system of beliefs and practices common to all the indigenous religions of the Americas, partly because they are still mutating, also because the impact of Christianity has been extensive, and many native American practitioners combine Christian worship with ancient tribal religious practices. In this context it is worth noting that in many states of the USA all Indian religious practices were illegal until as recently as 1978, and penalties were severe. The Freedom of Religions Act eventually cleared the way for open acceptance of the old customs. Even so, there has been considerable hostility from some Christian groups, as well as from within the Indian population. However, some core themes can be identified, shared by many if not all these traditions as well as most non-native new groups. These have many similarities with shamanism, though some Native Americans object to the comparison.

1. Sacred rituals, particularly dance, and purification procedures (e.g. Lakota sweat lodges).
2. The use of psychotropic plant preparations in ceremonies of shamanic nature. Some of the more widely-used substances are peyote (see **Peyote Cult**) and San Pedro (mescaline), from Peru and Mexico, ayahuasca (sometimes called yagé) from the Amazon basin, strong tobacco from both North and South America, and psilocybin mushrooms. One of the major distinctions between North and South American traditions is the featuring of these plant compounds in ceremonies. Apart from tobacco, common to both continents, psychotropic substances were not known in North America. The Native American Church (northern Indian tradition) ceremonies using peyote did not begin until the late nineteenth century, having long been a preserve of Mexican tribes.
3. The use of animal spirits as individual and tribal guardians and guides was widespread across both continents. These could be contacted or invoked either by shamanic means (soul flight of the shaman to the spirit world) (see **Shamanism**) or by **Channelling** (whereby the spirit comes to and through a medium). It seems likely that originally belief in local spirits of place, plants and animals was

prevalent. Nowadays, belief in an overriding 'great spirit' may accompany or replace this animistic worldview, perhaps influenced by Christian monotheism.

4. Vision quests are an important ritual and initiation rite in the Native American tradition, which have been appropriated by contemporary shamanic, neo-pagan and New Age movements and even by some business training schools. Traditionally, vision quests are solo expeditions undertaken to attain spiritual insight by spending several days and nights alone in the wilderness. Experiences are validated by elders, or sometimes kept private. By contrast, in new religions and business any experience, or none, is normally considered valid.

5. Many Native American traditions (north and south) have a concept of 'power' as a force obtainable from the spirit world which enables survival, success, and healing. Power has also been adopted as a key element in contemporary shamanism.

6. Ancestor veneration, together with belief in the sacredness of tribal territory, is a common feature of Native American tradition, as for many other tribal peoples, and once again has been widely adopted in neo-paganism.

The biggest growth in interest in Native American religions was triggered by the books of the Mexican anthropologist Carlos Castaneda, based on the teachings of Don Juan, a Yaqui shaman. Although their authenticity has been challenged, Castaneda's own teachings have been developed since his death by his followers, and there are many other native and non-native teachers spreading these practices throughout the West. Many native North Americans object to

the appropriation of their spiritual traditions by non-natives, though some prefer this to losing them altogether. There are also some successful collaborations between natives and non-natives for the preservation of this rich heritage.

Further reading

Cooper, Guy (1991) 'North American Traditional Religion', in Stewart R. Sutherland (ed), *The Study of Religion, Traditional and New Religion*, London: Routledge, pp. 115–24.
Hultkrantz, A. (1978) *The Religions of American Indians*, Berkeley: University of California Press.

ELIZABETH PUTTICK

NATURE RELIGION

A relatively recent academic construct, nature religion has been used since the 1970s as an umbrella concept under which to group a variety of earth- and nature-centred spiritualities believed by practitioners to have been prevalent before the rise of monotheistic religions. Such religions are often portrayed as remnants which have survived the repression of monotheism, particularly Christianity, and which are now re-emerging or being recreated or revived through imaginative reconstruction. Nature religions thus tend to include animistic, pantheistic and polytheistic religions, varieties of **Neo-Paganism**, eco-spirituality such as Deep Ecology, indigenous, shamanic, or tribal religions, and some New Age beliefs and practices.

Nature religion focuses on religions that revere nature and consider it to be divine, sacred, or populated by spiritual beings. Current academic use of the term 'nature religion' has developed from Catherine Albanese's (1990) usage in *Nature Religion in America: From the Algonkian Indians to the New Age*, in which she defined nature religion as beliefs, behaviours, and values which make nature a 'symbolic centre'. While recognizing the value of the construct in bringing to light the diversity of religious practices which do take nature as a symbolic referent, Albanese's term has been criticized as too broad to be of practical use. Some academics suggest instead that phrases such as 'the natural dimension of religion', or 'nature influenced religion' be used to distinguish those religions which see nature as important but not sacred, and keeping 'nature religion' exclusively for reference to religions which regard nature as sacred.

As well as resisting the domination of monotheisms and their perceived desacralization of nature, practitioners of nature religion also see themselves as critiquing secularization and the centralized authority of global capitalism. Such a stance has led to involvement in anti-globalization and protests against the World Trade Organization, often taking the form of non-violent direct action, as well as protesting against the destruction of the environment. Spiritual intimacy, connection, and harmony with nature is held up as the ideal position for humanity. There is, however, a negative side to nature religion that exists not in harmony with, but in control, mastery, and manipulation of nature and other people, either through magical or mystical means, or through the politics of racist and far right movements which are based on a connection to the land. These might include Nazism and some heathen organizations such as Hammarens Ordens Sällskap ('In the Company of the Order of the Hammer'), who consider multiculturalism and homosexuality to be the cause of confusion and problems, and seek an end to immigration since they believe that a people's identity derives from the land.

On the more positive side, nature religion often inspires practitioners to actively concern themselves with environmentalism, although this is not necessarily a greater concern than that of the population at large. Pro-environmental practices and an ethic of care for the earth are tied in with the idea of communion with a nature imagined to exist beyond civilization or at least beyond mechanized, urban living, both of which are seen as environmentally destructive. Political consciousness is thus derived from, or seen to go hand in hand with nature as an instructive spiritual or religious metaphor. This relationship is, however, often imbued with ideas of 'supernature', in terms of a dialogical communion between humans and a nature populated with powers, deities or other beings. Boundaries between the 'natural' and the 'supernatural', between the religious and the non-religious, are thus made permeable and crossed in the imagining of nature religion and the action which its beliefs inspire. Such ambiguity is not regarded as problematic by practitioners, who seek to overcome dichotomies between nature and culture and embrace an idea of immanence.

Further reading

Albanese, C. (1990) *Nature Religion in America: From the Algonkian Indians to the New Age*, Chicago: Chicago University Press.
Taylor, B. and Kaplan, J. (eds) (2004) *The Encyclopedia of Religion and Nature*, London and New York: Continuum.

JO PEARSON

NEO-CATECHUMENAL WAY

NCW is an organization within Roman Catholicism, started in Madrid in the early 1960s by two lay people, Kiko Arguello and Carmen Hernandez, which soon spread to Rome and beyond. It was their conviction that Catholics are ill-prepared for life in a secularized, even pagan, society. To become better able to withstand and to evangelize the modern world all Catholics in their parishes need to undergo the thorough process of conversion, learning, and liturgical celebration (lived out through regular meetings in small communities) which the NCW provides and which it believes reflects the practice of the early Church. The process of renewal is in stages: with emphases on listening to the 'Word of God', in the scriptures and in the traditions of the Roman Catholic Church; on personal prayer, reflection on the great phases of the 'history of salvation' and on the Church's central beliefs as found in the Creeds; on sharing the faith with others; and finally on learning to 'abandon themselves to the will of the Father' and live in a spirit of praise and thanksgiving to God. Each stage is marked by special liturgies and the whole process can take up to twenty years to complete. The parish priest is at the centre of the NCW communities, thereby putting the NCW at the centre of parish life. This makes it difficult for those who do not wish to be part of the NCW to continue as active members of the parish community. Non-NCW members say they are made to feel like second class Catholics. As a result, some diocesan bishops have banned the NCW from meeting on Church premises. To take an example, one practice that has caused division is that, unlike the two or three hour service in most Roman Catholic parishes, the service for the Easter Vigil in NCW parishes begins at midnight and continues until dawn on Easter Day. NCW has over 500,000 members located in about ninety countries. It runs some forty international seminaries and in Rome has charge of over a quarter of the parishes. It is a leading member of the group of about fifty 'new ecclesial movements and communities' in the Roman Catholic Church which meets regularly under the auspices of the Vatican.

KATHLEEN WALSH

NEO-HINDUISM

The term 'Neo-Hinduism' has been used to describe the worldviews of various Hindu thinkers associated with the Hindu or Indian Renaissance and the organizations they created. It thus refers to a distinct expression of Hinduism that co-exists with other forms of contemporary Hinduism.

The Hindu Renaissance conventionally is regarded as embracing developments within Hinduism from *c.* 1830 until Indian Independence in 1947, although historians have debated whether the achievements of this period did constitute a 'renaissance'. Some commentators have placed it more narrowly between *c.* the 1870s and the end of the independence movement, distinguishing between the 'revivalism' of this later period and the 'reformist' concerns and lack of overt Indian nationalism said to characterize the period *c.* 1830–1870s. Hindu thinkers responsible for this Renaissance would include Raja Rammohun Roy (*c.* 1772–1833) who founded the **Brahmo Samaj**, if the earlier period is included, Bankim Chandra Chattopadhyay (Chatterjee) (1838–94), Swami Vivekananda (1863–1902) (see **Vivekananda, Swami**) who organized the **Ramakrishna Mission**, Sri Aurobindo Ghosh (1872-1950) (see **Aurobindo, Sri**) in whose name **Auroville** was created, Mahatma Gandhi (1869–1948), and Sarvepalli Radhakrishnan (1888–1975). Many of these figures have been revered for contributing to the revival of Hindu self-confidence that fed the nationalist movement or providing political as well as spiritual leadership for the Hindu wing of the nationalist movement. The identification of common elements in the experiences, ideas and strategies of these and other thinkers has prompted their categorization as proponents of 'Neo-Hinduism'. 'Renaissance Hinduism', 'reform Hinduism', and 'modern Hinduism' have been used as overlapping terms. Similarly, some Neo-Hindu thinkers have been described as Neo-Vedantins because of their extensive re-working of ideas taken from the Advaita Vedanta philosophical tradition.

The term Neo-Hinduism has been increasingly used in scholarly writing since the 1950s. The label 'Neo-Hindu', however, was in circulation in India at least by the last decade of the nineteenth century and had pejorative overtones. For example, in 1893 critics of Swami Vivekananda questioned his fidelity to earlier Hindu tradition by placing him with 'Neo-Hindus', those attempting to reform Hinduism on the basis of criteria adopted from European and specifically Christian criticisms. In recent scholarly writing, the term Neo-Hinduism is generally used to describe Hindu thinkers who typically:

(a) have been concerned with the relationship between religion and nationalism;
(b) have been exposed to western ideas and education, and have confessed to having undergone a crisis of confidence in the value of Hinduism;
(c) have voiced a critical attitude to the worship of images;
(d) have placed a heightened reliance upon the *Bhagavadgita*, in spite of its traditional classification as a text of lesser importance than the Veda, the ultimate scriptural authority;
(e) have been willing to re-interpret concepts and traditional philoso-

phies, particularly Advaita Vedanta, in the light of new circumstances and influences external to Hinduism;
(f) have been committed to organized, practical service to humanity.

Drawing selectively on earlier Hindu traditions and western learning, including Christianity, Neo-Hindu thinkers have extended existing understandings of concepts such as *karma* (action) and *dharma* (law, duty, general morality). In seeking more general and flexible interpretations of these principles, they have tended to enhance the role of personal conscience, rather than emphasizing traditional authorities and responsibilities. Their insistence upon the need for social activism frequently has been supported by a social ethic derived from Advaita Vedanta philosophy. The movements they developed, influenced by their encounter with European and American Christian groups, have been marked by modern organizational features and philanthropic activity. While working on behalf of women and low-caste groups, Neo-Hindu groups have tended to attract more members from higher castes and generally have been led by men. Both the Ramakrishna Mission and Sri Aurobindo have attracted western followers.

It is not uncommon to find scholars who use the term Neo-Hinduism, or synonymous labels, claiming that this style of Hinduism is peripheral or even inauthentic, when compared with 'traditional' Hinduism, and that its influence has been exaggerated. Although Neo-Hindu thinkers and the organizations they created have not attracted large numerical followings in India, and some have significantly diminished in influence since the nineteenth century, their indirect influence has been considerable. This was most apparent in the promotion of social activism and the shaping of new Hindu ideologies during the campaign for Indian Independence. It is evident today in many of the practices and beliefs popularized by more recent Hindu sectarian movements both in India and the Hindu diaspora.

Further reading

Hacker, P. (1995) *Philology and Confrontation: Paul Hacker on Traditional and Modern Vedanta* (W. Halbfass ed.) Albany: State University of New York.

GWILYM BECKERLEGGE

NEO-PAGANISM

Neo-paganism is a complex phenomenon. It has no known or uncontested starting point and no single founder or originator, but in the form recognizable today, Neo-paganism originated in 1940s Britain in the form of Gerald Gardner's **Wicca** (see **Gardner, Gerald B.**). From this, other neo-pagan traditions and other varieties of witchcraft derived. Neo-paganism today includes a variety of traditions, such as neo-pagan witchcraft, neo-pagan **Druidry**, Asatrú/Heathenism, neo-shamanism (see **Shamanism**), 'non-aligned' Paganism, and initiatory Wicca. However, the antecedents of neo-paganism can be found in the late nineteenth century, in academic developments such as Egyptology, the rise of tourism to sites of ancient civilizations such as Greece and Rome, the rise of occult/magical secret societies, and literature. The turn of the twentieth century saw the founding of societies such as the Theosophical Society (see **Theosophy**) and the **Hermetic Order of the Golden Dawn**. Influenced by the close-knit secrecy of Freemasonry and its claims to be the guardian of a powerful ancient secret, these societies set about popularizing their own claims to ancient wisdom.

The term itself is, however, contested, and has multiple uses. It is used by some scholars and practitioners to differentiate between ancient and contemporary Paganism, or between broken, or disrupted, religious traditions (e.g. Asatrú, Druidry) and unbroken, or continuous ones (e.g. Hinduism), indigenous peoples such as Australian aborigines or Native Americans (see **Native American Religions**). Neo-paganism is contested by both academics and practitioners, with practitioners assuming that context makes it apparent whether they are talking about their own contemporary practices or ancient Greco-Roman worship. The prefix 'neo' is sometimes regarded as dangerous because it is easily associated with 'neo-Nazi'. It is also seen as a trivializing modifier which is disrespectful. The term is particularly popular in North America and continental Europe, but is not in common usage within the UK. Where it is commonly used, there are several permutations of capitalization and hyphenation, for example neo-Paganism, Neo-paganism.

The term is variously applied to

1. the romantic revival of pagan religions dominant in the classical ancient world, particularly of Egypt, Greece and Rome, interest in which was revived in the nineteenth century;
2. the indigenous peoples of Asia, Africa and the Americas;
3. the powerful rural myth of pastoral innocence pre-World War One epitomized in the writings of, for example, Walt Whitman and Edward Carpenter;
4. a variety of contemporary traditions and practices which revere nature as sacred, ensouled or alive, draw on pagan religions of the past, use ritual and myth creatively, share a seasonal cycle of festivals, and tend to be polytheistic, pantheistic and/or duotheistic rather

than monotheistic, at least to the extent of accepting the divine as both male and female and thus including both gods and goddesses in their pantheons.

Neo-pagan groups take many forms, from Wiccan covens to Druid groves, from Heathen hearths to magical lodges, and entry into them may be by formal rituals of initiation or informal groupings based on friendship. Some groups may practise magic, while others do not. Many use ritual, and almost all make use of myth, celebrating the eight seasonal festivals which together constitute a mythic-ritual cycle, usually referred to as The Wheel of the Year. These festivals are the so-called Celtic fire festivals or cross quarter days of Imbolc/Candlemas (*c.* 2 February), Beltane (*c.* 30 April), Lughnasadh/Lammas (*c.* 31 July), and Samhain/Hallowe'en (*c.* 31 October), plus the Winter and Summer Solstices (*c.* 21 December and *c.* 21 June) and the Spring and Autumn equinoxes (*c.* 21 March and *c.* 21 September). These are the traditional dates for each festival, but they are not fixed; many groups often find it easier, for the practical purpose of getting everyone together, to work to a set date (usually the nearest Friday or Saturday to the dates given), while smaller groups or individuals working alone may choose to wait for a specific sign of nature (e.g. first snowdrop for Imbolc) and celebrate on that day. In the southern hemisphere, the festivals are reversed in line with the seasons, celebrating the autumnal equinox, for example, whilst northern hemisphere neo-pagans celebrate the vernal equinox. Rites of passage have also been developed to mark the birth of a new child, menarche, manhood, marriage, menopause, ageing and death, and initiation rituals and rites to celebrate the phases of the moon are also popular in some Neo-Pagan groups.

Further reading

Harvey, G. and Hardman, C. (eds) (1996) *Paganism Today: Wiccans, Druids, the Goddess and Ancient Earth Traditions for the Twenty-First Century*, London: Thorsons.

Pearson, J. E. (2002) *A Popular Dictionary of Paganism*, London: RoutledgeCurzon.

JO PEARSON

NEO-TEMPLARISM

The Knights Templars, a Catholic military-religious order whose history is linked to the Crusades, was dissolved by Pope Clement V (1260–1314) in 1307, following its cruel persecution by King Philip IV of France (1268–1314). After its suppression, the Order survived for a few decades outside France, but by no later than the early fifteenth century the templars had disappeared completely. The theory of their secret continuation has been denounced as 'completely crazy' by medieval scholars such as Régine Pernoud (1909–98).

The idea that the templars, officially suppressed, secretly continued their activities well into the eighteenth century, spread mainly in French and German Freemasonry, and was based on the legend of persecuted knights templars who had 'hidden' themselves in English and Scottish guilds of Freemasons in order to continue their activities. This is the origin of the Masonic templar grades which – created in Europe – are now found in both the Scottish rite and in the York rite, and also of the current Encampments of Knights Templars, quite popular in Anglo-American Freemasonry (its membership being restricted to masons only).

During the years of the French Revolution, a particularly convulsive period for Freemasonry, not everyone agreed with the idea that the complex of templar grades constituted only a part of the Masonic system and that they had to remain subordinate to Freemasonry as a whole. The controversy was created by an adventurer active in the period, a former seminarian named Bernard-Raymond Fabré-Palaprat (1773–1838) who, in 1804, declared that he had discovered documents proving the uninterrupted lineage of clandestine templar 'Grand Masters' from the suppression of 1307 up to 1792. In 1805, Fabré-Palaprat was appointed Grand Master and re-established the Knights Templars. The idea of independent Knights Templars (i.e. independent of Freemasonry – as opposed to templar grades) was attractive, and even interested Napoleon Bonaparte (1769–1821), who authorized a solemn ceremony in 1808. But Fabré-Palaprat's idea was not simply to establish a knightly order destined to rapidly re-enter the fold of the Catholic Church. His much more ambitious idea, which began to take shape in 1812, was to link the neo-templars to a new religion.

The most direct lineage of the Knights Templars founded by Fabré-Palaprat, is the Belgian 'lay' branch (the only one still active), which in 1894 promoted the formation of an International Secretariat of Templars in Brussels. In 1942, the Order's archives were entrusted to Antonio Campello Pinto de Sousa Fontes (1878–1960) in Portugal, and Fontes thereafter proclaimed himself Grand Master, thus assuring the neo-templar movement international diffusion. In 1948 he designated his son Fernando Campello Pinto de Sousa Fontes to succeed him as Grand Master. On his death, Fernando assumed the title of 'Prince Regent'. There were, however, several independent national branches that had not recognized Antonio's authority, and other national branches declared themselves independent when Fernando took over. At a 1970 meeting in Paris, a number of Grand Priorates rejecting Antonio Sousa Fontes' authority, appointed Polish marshal Antoine Zdrojewski (†1988) as Grand Master. Since then, there have been two main international organizations: OSMTH (Ordo Supremus Militari Templi Hierosolymitani), under Sousa Fontes' leadership, and OSMTJ (Ordre Souverain et Militaire du Temple de Jérusalem), under the authority of Zdrojewski, even if – complicating the matter even further – Sousa Fontes also occasionally uses the French name as well as the acronym OSMTJ. Zdrojewski (succeeded by Georges Lamirand (†1994) in 1988), however, became entangled in political controversies, while Fernando de Sousa Fontes was unable to control all of the priorates he had authorized. As a result, a dozen other organizations and numerous 'independent' national priorates sprang up alongside OSMTH and OSMTJ. Various federations were later formed, such as the OIMT (Ordo Internationalis Militiae Templi Confederationis), which was founded in Rome in 1979, and the IFA (International Federative Alliance, 1989). In 1994–8, there were various attempts to reduce the number of acronyms (including one following the merger of OSMTJ and IFA in Turku, Finland, in 1998), and also to bring about reconciliation between OSMTJ and Sousa Fontes' OSMTH. All these attempts failed for various reasons, and new splits emerged. The only moderately successful result was an agreement signed in London on 12 May 2000 by OSMTJ and OIMT, which was intended to achieve an actual association. In recent years, however, the schisms have been complicated by the desire – and necessity – for all the neo-templar groups to distance themselves from a crazed splinter group, the Order of the **Solar Temple**, involved in group suicides and murders in 1994–7.

Further reading

Le Forestier, R. (1987) *La Franc-Maçonnerie templière et occultiste au XVIIIe et XIXe siècles*, Paris: La Table d'Émeraude.

PIERLUIGI ZOCCATELLI

NEURO-LINGUISTIC PROGRAMMING (NLP)

Described by practitioners as 'the art and science of excellence', NLP ('Neuro-Linguistic Programming') is a series of psycho-therapeutic techniques developed in the 1970s. The term NLP was first coined in 1976 by Richard Bandler and John Grinder, the co-creators of the system. Bandler was then a psychology student at the University of California, USA, while Grinder was Assistant Professor of Linguistics, specializing in Chomskyian transformational grammar.

In creating their system the pair studied the work of Fritz Perls, originator of Gestalt therapy, Virginia Satir, famous family therapist, Milton Erickson, the renowned hypnotherapist and the insights of British anthropologist Gregory Bateson. They isolated a code of effective communication skills used by successful therapists and developed a series of applications using cognitive behavioural techniques and drawing on ideas from humanistic psychotherapy and hypnotherapy. Their key proposals were outlined in *The Structure of Magic Volumes I and II*.

NLP is based on the theory that life experiences condition the way humans perceive their worlds and that changing perceptual habits can correspondingly change thought and emotion patterns. The techniques make use of the sensory faculties as core representation systems for human thought and experience, with the aim of changing the 'submodalities' or qualities of sensory memories and the 'metaprograms' or filters of perception.

Sensory acuity is prioritized in NLP, as the ability to analyse and imitate non-verbal behaviour is used as a means to enhance communication. Practitioners of NLP work either on a one-to-one basis or with groups, explaining and demonstrating techniques, sometimes using hypnotic or trance states during sessions.

NLP has grown rapidly since the 1970s, particularly in the Western hemisphere, having gained a strong foothold in the fields of business, education, therapy, and communication. It has also been developed and applied for particular uses, for example in curing problems such as stammering and phobias. It is a growth industry in the USA and the UK, where the largest associations of practitioners and the greatest number of consultancies have been formed. Influential practitioners run seminars in a number of trademarked NLP techniques such as 'Persuasion Engineering', 'Neuro-Hypnotic Patterning' and 'Business Magick'. At the beginning of the twenty-first century, NLP also has a significant presence in South Africa, India, Pakistan, Hong Kong, Malaysia, Singapore, Thailand, Japan, Brazil, Australia, and New Zealand.

NLP forms part of the **Human Potential Movement** and can be classed as a mainstream psychological and therapeutic tool; for example, it is grouped along with Personal Construct Psychology in the 'Experiential Constructivists' branch of the United Kingdom Council for Psychotherapy. It has also been presented and promoted in the 'psychic fringe' of hypnotism shows and psychic performances. It is difficult to locate NLP in relation to other New Religious Movements (see **New Religious Movement**), as it has become established within the largely secular fields of consumer sales and management training. Hence it is rarely seen as an explicitly spiritual venture, although the enhancement of personal power can easily be divinized and harnessed to the aims of business.

Further reading

Bandler, R. (1975) *The Structure of Magic: A Book About Language and Therapy (Structure of Magic)*, Palo Alto, CA: Science and Behavior Books.

Alexandra Ryan

NEW ACROPOLIS

Founder: Jorge Angel Livraga Rizzi
Country of origin: Argentina

Jorge Angel (Giorgio Angelo) Livraga Rizzi (1930–91), an Argentina-born schoolteacher of Italian origin and nationality, established an association known as New Acropolis in 1957 in Buenos Aires, introducing it as 'a classic school of philosophy'. Between 1957 and Livraga's death in Madrid, in 1991, the association expanded throughout Latin America, and achieved some success in Europe, although it never had a large following in North America. The international headquarters were moved to Bruxelles in 1990 and then to Spain, under the leadership of Delia Steinberg Guzman (while Livraga's widow, Ada Albrecht, founded the rival Fundación Hastinapura).

New Acropolis is now active in forty-two countries, with some 20,000 members. In some countries, including France and Belgium, it has become quite controversial as a 'right-wing' and even 'fascist' organization. Writings by Livraga dating back to the 1960s (some of them denounced by the current leadership as apocryphal) have been quoted in support of the thesis that New Acropolis criticizes modern democracy, and advocates authoritarianism based on the ideas of the Greek philosopher Plato

(428/427–347 BC). In the 1990s, the French branch, which had been specially targeted by anti-cult campaigns (see **Anti-Cult Movement**), made some efforts to rid itself of right-wing extremism and distance itself from politics. Outside France, old tirades by Livraga are more easily forgotten, whilst New Acropolis activities supporting emergency relief, archaeology, the preservation of cultural and historical monuments, and ecology, are widely appreciated.

New Acropolis particularly resents being called 'a religion' or 'a cult' (see **Cult and New Religions**), and insists that philosophy and religion are indeed different. Livraga's thinking is in fact quite complicated and eclectic. It calls for a renewed appreciation of classical Greek philosophical thinking, although its classicism is interpreted through the lenses of modern Western esoteric teachers such as Madame Helena Blavatsky (1831–91) (see **Blavatsky, Helena**), who founded the **Theosophical Society**, and René Guénon (1886–1951). The movement teaches that awakening is possible, and that its tool is a sacred tradition which lies behind all individual traditions and religions, a *philosophia perennis* in the sense of Guénon, although it was expressed with admirable precision by Greek philosophy, and particularly by Plato. Both Christianity and modernity are seen, from this point of view, as involving some decadence, and New Acropolis is often critical of modern organized religion and the Christian churches. An **Age of Aquarius** is approaching, but its beginnings will be harsh and difficult, rather than the easy triumph of peace as promised by the New Agers (see **New Age Movement**). Human rights are seen as a central point of the New Acropolis cultural plan, with the figure of Giordano Bruno (1548–1600), the philosopher critical of Roman Catholicism burned at the stake in Rome in 1600, being frequently mentioned. New Acropolis, thus, is able to advocate both a criticism of modernity and an appreciation of quintessentially modern values.

Further reading

Livraga Rizzi, J. A. (1999) *The Alchemist: In the Footsteps of Giordano Bruno*, Madrid: New Acropolis.
Livraga Rizzi, J. A. (1999) *Thebes*, Madrid: New Acropolis.

MASSIMO INTROVIGNE

NEW AGE MOVEMENT (NAM)

New Age is an umbrella term applied to a vast array of groups, communities, and networks that are engaged in the process of a transformation of consciousness that will give rise to the **Age of Aquarius**, the period of history when the Sun will be in the sign of Aquarius at the Spring equinox. For some New Age practitioners this has already happened; for others it is still some three hundred years off.

History of New Age ideas

While united by this common belief in transformation the New Age Movement embraces a vast range of ideas including the belief that the Self (see **Self-religion, the Self, and Self**), to be distinguished from the ego, is divine, evil is an illusion of the mind and Jesus is a 'Way-shower'. The sources of New Age opinions include the writings of Emmanuel Swedenborg (1688–1772) (see **Swedenborg, Emmanuel**) on the spiritual sense of the Scriptures and his 'science of correspondences', Franz Mesmer's (1734–1815) theory of healing by means of a mysterious cosmic force which came to be known as 'animal magnetism', and to the idealism of the New England Trans-

cendentalist (see **Transcendentalism**), Ralph Waldo Emerson (1803–82) (see **Emerson, Ralph Waldo**). Emerson, along with Emma Curtis Hopkins (1853–1925) and Phineas Parkhurst Quimby (1802–66) provided **New Thought**, a late nineteenth century forerunner of the modern New Age Movement, with its core idealistic perspective which contends that the highest reality and the basis of existence itself is mental.

Ideas such as these were to spread far and wide, and their influence can be seen not only in the idealism of New Thought but also in the development of twentieth-century Japanese spiritual and esoteric teachings such as those found in the writings of Masaharu Taniguchi (1893–1985) who, in 1930 founded the Japanese movement **Seich-no-Ie** (the home of infinite life, abundance and wisdom), and in those of Mokichi Okada (1881–1958) founder in 1935 of **Sekai Kyûsei Kyô** (Church of World Messianity). By the 1980s there had emerged a convergence of New Thought and New Age movements each appropriating the literature, therapies, rituals and music of the other.

It is usual to think of the New Age as having several overlapping dimensions one of the most important of which is its occult wing which owes much to the co-founder of **Theosophy**, the Ukranian born Helena Petrovna Blavatsky (1831–91) (see **Blavatsky, Helena**). At first a spiritualist who was preoccupied with communication with the dead, Blavatsky turned to receiving messages, written mostly on pieces of paper, from the mahatmas or masters of the Great White Brotherhood, the spiritual hierarchy that mediates between the human and divine realms. Blavatsky's goal was to ensure that the plans of these masters were fulfilled in preparation for the coming of the Lord or Bodhisattva Maitreya, the Future Buddha, whom she identified with the Christ of the Second Advent. Annie Besant (1847–1933) who, after Blavatsky's death became the international president of the Theosophical Society, founded the Order of the Star of the East as the vehicle for launching Jidhu Krishnamurti as the Lord Maitreya, who, it was expected, would initiate a new cycle in human evolution, the New Age.

Another integral part of the esoteric/ Christian dimension of the New Age is the Association for Research and Enlightenment, Inc. (ARE) founded in 1931 by Edgar Cayce (1877–1945). The ARE, an open, unstructured movement characteristic of the New Age as a whole, has its headquarters in Virginia, which networks with several hundred inclusive, non-denominational, study groups throughout the United States. There are no prescribed rituals nor is there a prescribed set of beliefs. There is, on the other hand, a common text in the form of *A Search for God* (Books I and II) that proclaims the supreme ideal of love of God and love of neighbour. Personal transformation through the Christ-within can only be obtained by meditating on this ideal and acting accordingly. In a state of self-induced hypnosis, which explains why he is known as the Sleeping Prophet, Cayce produced his readings, invariably Christ-centred and expressive of what might be termed New Age Christianity or the Christian New Age.

Another important New Age thinker is the English-born Theosophist Alice Bailey, the stenographer of the Tibetan ascended master Djwhal Khul who dictated through her nineteen lengthy volumes, the most widely read being *The Reappearance of Christ* (1948). Alice and her husband established various organizations including the **Lucis Trust** (1922), the Arcane School (1923), the New Group of World Servers (1932), the Men of Goodwill, known since 1950 as **World Goodwill**, and Triangles, all with the purpose of bringing people of goodwill together.

Bailey's teachings speak of a 'divine evolutionary plan motivated by love' that can only work out through the efforts of human beings, of a World Teacher whom Christians call Christ, and others by other names including Imam Mahdi and Lord Maitreya. She also believed strongly in reincarnation, in karma, and in a spiritual hierarchy of mahatmas.

Many of the above ideas are found in the writings of more contemporary representatives of New Age thought including those of Ruth Montgomery (see **Montgomery, Ruth**). Several of Montgomery's New Age books including *Companions Along the Way* (1974) and *Strangers Among Us: Enlightened Beings from a World to Come* (1979) that explore the core New Age themes of Atlantis, Lemuria and reincarnation have resulted from conversations with the medium Arthur Ford, cofounder of the Spiritual Frontiers Fellowship that speaks of the infinite capacity within every individual for growth grounded on altruism, and of karma and reincarnation. Montgomery also developed the concept of walk-ins which became popular in New Age and UFO literature (see **UFOs**).

Other formative New Age concepts include the **Gaia** hypothesis of James Lovelock (see **Lovelock, James**) according to which the planet earth is a complete and self-regulating system, and along with its inhabitants comprises a single, living organism. This supposition forms the basis of New Age holism (see **Holistic Health Movement**). The ideas of **Teilhard de Chardin** on the evolution of the cosmos have greatly influenced New Age thinking.

The New Age and Neo-Paganism

Parallels exist not only between New Age and New Thought but also between

New Age and **Neo-paganism**. Both emphasize that human beings are potentially divine or godlike, and both are loosely structured. Neo-paganism, however, is more Goddess centred (see **Goddess Movement**) than New Age and criticizes what it sees as the patriarchal character found in some of its ideas and expressions. Moreover, the New Age belief that 'darkness' is evil and to be eradicated conflicts with the Neo-pagan view that it is necessary for life. Neo-paganism is also critical of what it sees as New Age rejection of this world, of matter and of its concentration on the discarnate, the pure, that which has been unsullied by matter. Ironically, it is New Age immanentism that has prompted conservative Christianity to attack the movement as a form of **Satanism**. Its beliefs in reincarnation, the portrayal of Jesus as a Way-shower and not as a Saviour, and the occult and psychic emphasis found among some branches of the New Age movement have likewise come under attack from the same source.

Exemplary centres of New Age thought

Although the New Age is not a Church or Community with a central bureaucracy and authoritative set of beliefs and rituals, a number of New Age communities have come to be recognized as exemplary centres of New Age thought and activity. Two of the longest established, most reputable and most widely known are Esalen in Big Sur California and the **Findhorn Community** in Northeast Scotland. Other widely known New Age centres are the Naropa Institute in Boulder, Colorado, Interface in Newton, Massachusetts, Holy Hock Farm near Vancouver in Canada, the Omega Institute for Holistic Studies in Rhinebeck New York, the Wrekin Trust in Malvern,

Worcestershire, England, and the Skyros Centre on the Greek island of the same name. These centres offer a varied range of courses from 'Crystals, Magnets and Vibrational Healing', 'Cooking and Spiritual Practice', Kabbalistic Astrology', 'Aromatherapy', 'The joy of Self-Loving', to 'Know Your Car: Basic Automobile Preventive Maintenance'.

New Age communities

In line with the generally held New Age view that co-operation is to be preferred to competition, a number of communal organizations have grown up including the Lama Foundation of New Mexico, and the **Church Universal and Triumphant** (CUT), formerly known as the Summit Lighthouse, founded by Mark Prophet in 1958. The last mentioned is one of the more controversial of the New Age communities. Much of its teaching derives from Theosophy and the I AM movement and includes such New Age beliefs as reincarnation, the role of 'ascended masters', the idea of a divine spark within every individual, and the goal of uniting this divine element of the individual with the Divine source of all and everything. As the end of the second millennium approached CUT became stridently apocalyptic and unambiguously millenarian, predicting that Armageddon would occur on earth sometime between 1989 and 2000. To ensure the survival of its members the community under its leader Mrs Prophet, known by followers as Guru Ma or Mother, authorized the building of underground shelters at its Inner Retreat centre in Montana and elsewhere.

It would be misleading to equate New Age with liberalism in every sphere. CUT, for example, is strongly conservative on many moral and ethical questions: it opposes abortion, the consumption of alcohol, smoking, drug use, and extramarital sex. On the other hand, one would expect to find New Age participants deeply committed to conservation of the environment and opposed to nuclear warfare.

New Age communities appear to be driven more by a concern for individual spiritual growth than by collective concerns. A majority focus on teaching the various techniques for improving the quality of one's life and greater effectiveness by kindling the divine spark within. **Transcendental meditation**, the Self-religions (see **Self-religion, The Self, and self**) including The Forum, formerly *est*, Insight, The Life Training, the **Silva Method** of Mind Control, based largely on New Thought, Mind Dynamics, an offshoot of Silva Mind Control fall into this category. Silva Mind Control gives examples of how its courses changed for the better the attitudes and outlook of top executives, scientists, researchers, laboratory assistance, personnel managers, and secretaries of such companies as the giant pharmaceutical manufacturers Hoffmann-La Roche.

The New Age as a vision

The New Age Movement taken as a whole is more a vision than a coherent system of beliefs and practices. As a movement it is acephalous though, as we have seen, the opinions of a number of its exponents, among them those of **Baba Ram Das** (Richard Alpert), are widely respected and have acquired a form of scriptural authority. What more than anything else gives a degree of unity to the New Age Movement is the goal aspired to by all participants which is transformation of consciousness.

Such a transformation will, it is believed, provide the trigger for a quantum leap of collective consciousness that will usher in the New Age. Thus, New Age salvation or liberation comes through the discovery of the transformative power of consciousness. In order to achieve this salvation much recourse is had to channelling – the process by which information is accessed and expressed by a source that is other than one's own ordinary consciousness – and to alternative therapeutic techniques such as acupuncture, acupressure (shiatsu), iridology, and reflexology. Alternative and/or complementary medicine is part of the bedrock of the New Age culture (see **Holistic Health Movement** and **Gaia**).

Ferguson (1980) uses the concept of the paradigm shift to describe the way in which individual consciousness will arrive at a totally new way of thinking about old problems. The present time is the most opportune age for this shift to occur. First of all, it is an age of unprecedented stress which motivates people to seek for a new paradigm. It is also the age that has access to more liberating technologies than any other. Never before, Ferguson believes, has there been such an opportunity to explore the innate human capacity for mystical experience and never before has this occurred on such a large scale. A vast variety of aids or psycho-technologies exist to facilitate this exploration, among them, **yoga**, meditation and the martial arts, and there exists the material freedom to make use of these.

These are the principal reasons why the present age is unique and why it is seen as the foundation for the cataclysmic, mystical revolution in consciousness that is shortly to occur. Although they may use different techniques New Age participants believe they draw on the same source of spiritual power which will unite the world in the same understanding.

Further reading

Heelas, P. (1997) *The New Age Movement*, Oxford: Blackwell.

Ferguson, M. (1980) *The Aquarian Conspiracy*, Los Angeles, CA: J. B. Tarcher.

Hanegraaff, W. (1996) *New Age Religion and Western Culture: Esotericism in the Mirror of Secular Thought*, Leiden: Brill.

Kemp, D. (2004) *The New Age. A Guide*, Edinburgh: Edinburgh University Press.

Melton, J. G. (1990) *New Age Encyclopaedia*, Detroit: Gale Research Inc.

Montgomery, R. (1974) *Companions Along the Way*, New York, NY: Fawcett Crest.

Montgomery, R. (1979) *Strangers Among Us: Enlightened Beings from a World to Come*, New York, NY: Fawcett Crest.

Spangler, D. (1976) *Revelation: The Birth of a New Age*, San Francisco: Rainbow Bridge.

Sutcliffe, S. (2003) *Children of the New Age: A History of Spiritual Practices*, London: Routledge.

York, M. (1995) *The Emerging Network. A Sociology of the New Age and Neo-pagan Movements*, Lanham, MD: Rowman and Littlefield.

PETER B. CLARKE

NEW APOSTOLIC CHURCH

The New Apostolic Church grew out of a crisis in the **Catholic Apostolic Church**, a British revivalistic millennial group. Believing that some unusual occurrences, including miraculous healings and speaking in tongues, were signs of the imminent return of Christ, the group concluded that the main factor delaying the event was the establishment of a biblical church, signaled by the leadership of twelve apostles. By the end of the 1930s, the apostolic leadership was in place and the church began to spread from England to other European countries and to North America.

The crisis for the group came in the 1860s when Apostles began to die and there had been no provision made to appoint new ones. In 1860, in Germany, a move began to call additional Apostles. When the third such apostle was called in 1863, the church excommunicated the dissidents. Under the leadership of Heinrich Geyer, the New Apostolic Church was formed and the structure of the parent body duplicated. The church grew steadily for two generations, but faced severe persecution under the Nazis. Recovering after World War Two, the church has spread rapidly. It currently has some nine million members in almost 200 countries.

Church beliefs are very similar to those of other Christian churches. God has made provision for salvation through Christ's death and resurrection. It differs in that members believe that it is necessary to be endowed with the Holy Spirit by an Apostle in order to have fellowship with God. Recognizing not only the need to replace any apostles who die before Christ's return, but the problem of the growing church being served by only twelve men, the church has moved to multiply the apostolic office. The New Apostolic Church continues the emphasis on the Second Coming of Christ. When that event occurs, all who believe in Christ will be taken to heaven. Christ will establish the millennial kingdom on Earth and those who remain will be offered God's grace and redemption.

Ultimate authority in the church is in the hands of the Chief Apostle, currently Richard Fehr, a Swiss citizen. International headquarters are located in Zürich. A web site is maintained at http://www.nak.org/.

Further reading

Guide for the Administration of the New Apostolic Church, Frankfurt am Main, Germany: Apostles College of the New Apostolic Church, 1967.

Questions and Answers Concerning the New Apostolic Church, Frankfurt am Main, Germany: J. G. Bischoff, 1978.

J. GORDON MELTON

NEW CHRISTIAN RIGHT

Rather than a single organization, the New Christian Right (NCR) is an umbrella term for the resurgence of mass political activity by conservative Protestants in the United States beginning in the late 1970s. It arose primarily as a reaction among certain evangelical and fundamentalist Protestants (see **Evangelical Christianity**; **Fundamentalism**) against many of the political, social, and cultural developments of the preceding years that were associated with the decline of morality, family, and religion. These developments included disillusionment resulting from the Watergate scandals, fear that America was going soft on communism, anger toward increasingly aggressive gay and women's rights movements, Supreme Court decisions sanctioning abortion-on-demand, and a pervading belief that secular humanism was increasingly dominating the public schools and government. Specific battles over abortion, pornography, and the Equal Rights Amendment convinced many conservative Christians that only political activism could save the nation from secularism and rampant immorality. These threats to what were perceived to be fundamental values and lifestyles, along with a surge in confidence that came with the election of Jimmy Carter, a born-again Christian, to the presidency, led to the emergence of the NCR, a sometimes uneasy political alliance built on a basic foundation of economic libertarianism, social traditionalism, moral conservatism, and militant anti-Communism.

After being actively involved in American politics throughout the nineteenth and early twentieth centuries, after the Scopes trial of 1925 and the repeal of prohibition in 1933, conservative Protestants largely retreated from the public sphere to become custodians of a private morality that was largely divorced from any political agenda. After remaining 'underground' for some five decades, fundamentalists exploded back into American public life in the 1970s through the mobilization of an already existing network of conservative Protestant churches, primarily in the southern United States. A number of grassroots political organizations emerged, such as the Moral Majority, founded in 1979 by televangelist Jerry Falwell, minister of the nation's largest independent Baptist church, in Lynchburg, Virginia. With the help and guidance of professional conservative political strategists, the NCR emerged as the alliance of the Moral Majority, Religious Roundtable (later just the Roundtable), Christian Voice, and other Christian lobbying organizations.

The platform of the NCR went beyond the single-issue politics of many of its component parts, as it fought not just for political victories but for the establishment of its worldview – its definition of America as a 'Christian nation'. In addition, the NCR was largely successful at transcending theological differences among its members, promoting a social and political program based on a moral vision common to all its constituents, regardless of denomination. Falwell's 'Christian Bill of Rights', a kind of charter document for the movement, opposed abortion, supported voluntary prayer and Bible reading in public schools, encouraged the government to take steps to protect the sanctity of the 'traditional family', and resisted government intrusion in Christian schools. Other standard targets included the teaching of evolution, pornography, the moral decline in television programming, and alcohol and drug abuse. Nonetheless, the NCR always represented a coalition rather than a monolith, and the movement was never entirely free from infighting and factionalism. Moreover, not all conservative American Protestants joined or even actively supported the NCR, as many preferred instead to remain relatively insulated from the public sphere and focus almost exclusively on the saving of souls.

The NCR became nationally known during the 1980 presidential campaign of Republican candidate Ronald Reagan, who specifically endorsed the political activism of conservative religious leaders. NCR organizations mobilized churchgoers by impressing upon them that going to the polls was a religious duty, resulting in a substantial bloc of votes for Reagan from evangelical Protestants in 1980 and 1984. In return, the Republican Party gave the Christian Right significant recognition in its local and national conventions, and included many of the NCR's goals on its official party platform. However, once in office Reagan gave only *pro forma* support to specific conservative Christian initiatives, and by the end of his second term it became clear that the NCR represented a junior partner in the Reagan coalition. At the same time, a number of scandals involving prominent evangelical televangelists sullied the movement's reputation, and by 1988 the NCR had fractured, with its presidential hopeful Pat Robertson faring poorly in that year's presidential primaries. This led many observers to suggest that the Christian Right was effectively dead.

However, the movement transformed itself in the early 1990s, placing less emphasis on changing national policy at the top and concentrating more on state and local levels. The largest and most influential conservative Christian political organ in this 'second generation' was the Christian Coalition, founded by Pat Robertson and led by strategist Ralph Reed. They sought to build broader alliances by reaching out to Catholic, Jewish, and Mormon conservatives, overlooking theological differences for the sake of common moral causes, including protests against abortion and homosexual marriage. As part of their broad-based approach, the Christian Coalition retreated from some of the more strident and sectarian language that had characterized the previous decade, which led some fundamentalists to criticize them for being overly secular.

Although the NCR was often defined by what it stood against, it also offered a positive and comprehensive worldview based on conservative Christian beliefs and values that brought fulfillment to many Protestant Americans both as believers and as political actors. However, despite mobilizing millions of voters over the course of more than two decades, in the end the Christian Right has been forced to settle for regional victories rather than achieving a significant restructuring of national politics or the fulfillment of their vision of a 'Christian America'.

Further reading

Wald, K. D. (2003) *Religion and Politics in the United States*, 4th ed., Lanham: Rowman & Littlefield.

Lienesch, M. (1993) *Redeeming America: Piety and Politics in the New Christian Right*, Chapel Hill: University of North Carolina Press.

Bruce, S. (1988) *The Rise and Fall of the New Christian Right: Conservative Protestant Politics in America 1978–1988*, Oxford: Clarendon Press.

Wilcox, C. (1992) *God's Warriors: The Christian Right in Twentieth-Century America*, Baltimore: Johns Hopkins University Press.

R. SCOTT APPLEBY

NEW KADAMPA TRADITION

The New Kadampa Tradition (NKT) is a western form of Tibetan Buddhism related to the Tibetan Gelugpa. It was founded in England, in 1991, but has since expanded to thirty-six countries, mainly in Europe and North America but also to among other countries Hong Kong, India and Brazil. The NKT remains most significant in the UK where it now has a presence in many towns and cities and runs several residential centres. It is one of many western Buddhist groups which operate under the guidance of a teacher who received a traditional Tibetan Buddhist training but came to the West because of the socio-political situation in Tibet

The founder and director of the NKT is Geshe Kelsang Gyatso (b. 1931) who was ordained as a child and studied Buddhism in Tibet until 1959. He subsequently continued his studies in Nepal before, in 1976, accepting an invitation, from Lama Thubten Yeshe, to run a centre in Ulverston, Cumbria owned by the Foundation for the Preservation of the Mahayana Tradition (FPMT) (see **Mahāyāna Buddhism** and **Vajrayāna Buddhism**). A conflict of loyalty to these two charismatic lamas with contrasting leadership and teaching styles led to a split between the FPMT and Geshe Kelsang's followers during the early 1980s.

Geshe Kelsang's tradtitional monastic training and the emphasis he places on study is evident in the structure of the movement. All serious practitioners, including beginners, embark on one of three training programmes which are graded according to the commitment of the individual but are all based on Geshe Kelsang's writings. These are, the General Programme, the Foundation Programme and the Teacher Training Programme. Geshe Kelsang has written eighteen books which range from introductions to Buddhism and meditation, to tantric texts designed for advanced practitioners. The books were written in English but have been translated into other European languages. The movement regards these training programmes and the books on which they are based as Geshe Kelsang's unique and vital contribution to Buddhism.

Teacher Training Programme students are selected to teach on the other two programmes according to their perceived understanding of Geshe Kelsang's teachings. Study is closely tied to the text under discussion and practitioners work systematically through the books often taking an examination at the end of a course. Integral to the study programmes are training in Buddhist doctrine but also meditational and devotional techniques. As practitioners learn about Buddhism they are therefore encouraged to put it into practice in ways which are regarded as relevant for twenty-first-century western living. Most of the texts are accompanied by *sādhanas* (liturgies or ritual manuals) which are recited, often on a daily basis, in the vernacular but with Tibetan style cadences. Geshe Kelsang gives communal empowerments or initiations for these practices at regular events which take place at the major residential centres. Once initiated in this way, the practitioner is committed to regular recitations of the *sādhana*. Such empowerments are readily available as are the books and printed *sādhana*s. These are produced and distributed by Tharpa, the NKTs exclusive publication wing. NKT practitioners are warned that their Buddhist practice should be based only on Geshe Kelsang's writings if it is to be effective.

Central to the self-identity of the NKT is the idea that Geshe Kelsang is presenting an authentic and pure form of Buddhism which has not been corrupted by 'mixing' with other practices and doctrines. This form is considered to be relevant and meaningful to westerners while retaining proven techniques for attaining enlightenment. Many western Buddhist groups present Buddhism as rational or scientific and often downplay elements of traditional practice. The NKT, however, presents some of the darker elements of traditional Tibetan Buddhism. Examples are teachings about death and possible future rebirth realms – which can be presented in graphic ways – and the centrality within the movement of protector deity practices. It is the latter which have been the focus of a significant split within the Tibetan Gelugpa lineage between Geshe Kelsang and his followers and the Dalai Lama. In 1978 the Dalai Lama banned Gelugpa followers from carrying out communal practices based on the protector deity, Dorje Shugdan. This practice is central to the NKT because Dorje Shugdan is thought to be the deity most able to help contemporary practitioners in their journey to enlightenment. This has been a source of tension and has tended to isolate the NKT within Gelugpa Buddhism, leading to mistrust in certain areas of western Buddhism where the Dalai Lama enjoys high status. Traditional elements are also to be found in NKT temples. Iconography is regarded as precious and inherently meaningful and offerings are made regularly to the images which are represented in carefully constructed wall paintings and images.

There are also aspects of the NKT which are less traditional. Monks and nuns wear traditional maroon and yellow robes and are given Tibetan names and, in common with many monastics in Tibet, they take a form of novice ordination rather than extensive precepts. However, the NKT ordination vows have been developed specifically for the western context. Ordination requires that individuals demonstrate their commitment to Geshe Kelsang and to his organization but, in comparison with certain other Buddhist movements operating in the West where the ordination process is protracted (e.g. the **Friends of the Western Buddhist Order** (FWBO)), it is readily available to those who request it.

The ordination process for men and women is identical and lay and monastic men and women play very similar roles in the administration and running of the centres and of the organization as a whole. Many intelligent and able women have been attracted to this movement. Nuns and other women in the NKT, as well as leading men, recognize the importance of women's contributions and their status is high.

Further reading

Kay, D. (1997) 'The New Kadampa Tradition and the Continuity of Tibetan Buddhism in Transition', *Journal of Contemporary Religion*, 12(3), 277–93.

Kelsang, G. G. (2001) *Introduction to Buddhism: An explanation of the Buddhist Way of Life*, London: Tharpa.

Waterhouse, H. (1997) *Buddhism in Bath: Adaptation and Authority*, Leeds: The Community Religions Project, University of Leeds.

HELEN WATERHOUSE

NEW RELIGION (JAPAN)

The new religions of Japan include a variety of newly established religious groups. It has been estimated that some 10 per cent of the Japanese population currently have some degree of adherence to or membership in a new religion (see **New Religious Movement**). New religions are often contrasted with what are called 'established religions', namely the various earlier sects of Buddhism and shrine Shinto (see **State Shinto**). Although they possess deep connections with the established religions in terms of teachings and rituals, the new religions reveal new features in the ways in which they cope with changes in lifestyle resulting from such factors as urbanization and industrialization, the growth of knowledge with the spread of secondary and higher education, and other changes in modern Japanese social life.

The founders of the new religions are mostly laypersons rather than clergy. Most founders expounded their teachings using the ordinary vernacular, and this accessibility of thought has allowed them to attract large numbers of followers in relatively short periods of time. More than 1,000 such groups have been established up to the present day, and while many have died out, some have grown into much larger organizations. Several hundred new religions were estimated to be active in 2002.

The largest of the groups, those with memberships in excess of one million, include **Soka Gakkai**, **Rissho Kosei-kai**, **Reiyukai**, and **Tenrikyo**. Of these, Soka Gakkai is a very large group with some four million members. Groups with memberships in the hundreds of thousands include Shinnyoen, **Sekai Kyusei Kyo** (Church of World Messianity), **Perfect Liberty**, Bussho Gonenkai, Sukyo Mahikari (see **Mahikari**), **Myochikai**, Seicho-no-Ie, and Ennokyo. On the other hand, many smaller groups also exist, each with memberships between several hundred and several thousand.

One of the characteristics of new religions is the strong trust placed by members in the founder. Followers obey the founder's directions during life, and frequently treat deceased founders as deities or buddhas. Another remarkable characteristic is the high number of women founders and current leaders of new groups. The most famous female founders would include Nakayama Miki of Tenrikyo, **Deguchi Nao** of Omotokyo, Fukada Chiyoko of Ennokyo,

Kitamuara Sayo of Tensho Kotai Jingukyo, and Sugiyama Tatsuko of Daijokyo.

New religions can be divided into two main groups, depending on their origin from either Shinto or Buddhism. Very few new religions are of Christian origin, and those that exist are quite small in scale. New religions of Shinto origin include Tenrikyo (established 1838), **Konkyokyo** (1859), Seicho-no-Ie (1936), Sekai Kyusei Kyo or Church of World Messianity (1935), Tensho Kotaijingukyo (Dancing religion) (1945), Sekai Mahikari Bunmeikyodan (1959), and Sukyo Mahikari (1978). New religions of Buddhist origin include Reiyukai (1928), Nenpo Shinkyo (1928), Rissho Kosei-kai (1938), Gedatsukai (1929), Sokagakkai (1930), Shinnyoen (1936), Myochikai (1950), Bentenshu (1952), and Agonshu (1954). Based on a comparison of memberships of the two types, groups with Buddhist origin possess more members than groups with Shinto origin. Both categories, however, are roughly equal in terms of the total number of groups involved.

New religions were treated differently under prewar Japanese law. Some groups such as Tenrikyo and Konkokyo were able to become independent Shinto denominations, and others found approval as branch churches of Shinto denominations. Some Buddhist groups likewise were legally recognized as branch churches of Buddhist denominations. Most other sects, however, were considered quasi-religious, and while being permitted to engage in proselytization, did not receive the preferential tax treatment like that given to recognized religious groups. Too much stress placed on faith healing or political pronouncements, moreover, would result in oppressive treatment from the government.

Under the postwar principles of separation of Church and State and religious freedom, new religions have been granted the same legal protections given to long established religions. This makes it much easier for new movements to gain status as independent religious juridical persons, although the standards of approval became considerably stricter after the **Aum Shinrikyo** affair in 1995.

Viewed overall, the activities of new religions have become socially more influential in postwar Japan. Some have branched out into education, establishing junior high schools, high schools and colleges. Some have established hospitals, and some are promoting peace movements in cooperation with the traditional religions. Against this background of growth in socio-religious activities by the new religions, a large number of scholars have since the 1960s carried out research on the new religions. The term 'new religion' itself became widely accepted among academics in the 1970s, and the many new studies published to date have led to a better understanding of this phenomenon.

NABUTAKE INOUE

NEW RELIGIOUS MOVEMENT

The term New Religion came into use among social scientists in the 1960s. It was regarded as a controversial notion from the outset with researchers, practitioners of the so-called new religions and their opponents, including the **Anti-Cult Movement** (henceforth ACM), questioning both its usefulness and suitability. Some scholars were concerned that the term 'new' gave a misleading impression of the movements many of which derived their core teachings and practices from older traditions, while some practitioners regarded themselves as following an old tradition, and the ACM for its part maintained that to

apply the term religion to what in its view were in reality authoritarian, totalitarian, secretive and sinister cults (see **Cult and New Religions**) that engaged in the practice of **brainwashing** recruits not only gave a distorted version of the meaning of the term religion but also lent to them both status and credibility.

The term New Religion is applied differently in different cultural contexts. Whereas in the United States and Europe it is widely used of innovative religious and spiritual movements that have emerged since the end of World War Two (1945–6), or of movements such as the **New Age Movement** that developed out of all recognition in terms of their appeal, force, and scope, in Japan scholars date the rise of new religions, *shinshukyo*, back to the early nineteenth century. Japanese scholars also write of new, new religions or *shin shinshukyo*, a term they use to distinguish the new movements of the 1970s, among them **Kofuku no Kagaku** (Institute for Research in Human Happiness), which make great use of the most advanced technology to disseminate their beliefs, from pre-1970s movements such as **Omoto**. Some Japanese scholars also prefer the term New Spirituality Movements to that of New Age Movements.

Despite the differences over its usefulness and suitability the term New Religion continues to be very widely used and is best understood if seen as an umbrella concept that is applied to a vast array of spiritual and religious phenomena, by no means all of which are original in the beliefs and practices they espouse. Some New Religions claim to be new, including the Japanese *Shingon* Buddhist movement **Agon Shu**, in the sense of providing for the first time the most complete and authentic interpretation of what are very old teachings. The social and political impact of a doctrinally conservative religious movement, can lead to it being designated a New Movement. The so-called **New Christian Right** in the United States contained few if any new doctrines and practices. This movement is best described as a resurgence of conservative, evangelical (see **Evangelical Christianity**), and fundamentalist Christianity that so powerfully impacted on the political process that it appeared to represent something new and different when compared with the more liberal Christian movements of the 1960s, and against the background of the American Constitution which insists on the separation of Church and State.

Other New Religions, among them the Self-religions (see **Self-religion, the Self, and Self**), can be considered new in the way they fuse to an unprecedented extent the spiritual and the psychological. They reflect the development of a concern with the subjective foundations of personal identity and, more generally with the subjective experience of life as society becomes increasingly fragmented and the moral absolutes imposed from without more contested and problematic with the advances of greater cultural and religious pluralism, and the revolutionary impact of technology and science. These changes have resulted in the search for new models of authentic, individual selfhood, which many of the New Religions have sought to provide. New Religions can also be seen, paradoxically, as part of the pursuit, perhaps largely unconscious, of a shared understanding of the Absolute as national, regional, cultural and political boundaries are prised open under the impact of globalization. This is one way of understanding the new in the **New Age Movement**, as its presence and appeal spread ever wider transforming it into an international, if not global movement.

As we have seen, both the meaning and the application of the term New Religion can vary from culture to culture and region to region. While a religious phenomenon may appear new in a Western context it may be seen as belonging to an old religious tradition in another. With globalization and the revolution in communications religious ideas and practices, once largely confined to and associated with particular cultural and geographical regions, have spread to parts of the world where they were previously largely unknown, or little more than exotic appendages to the mainstream religious traditions. In this way an old religious system becomes new in a new context, an example being the presence in the West since 1969 of the **International Society for Krishna Consciousness** (ISKCON), or as it is popularly known, the Hare Krishna movement. In terms of its teaching and practices this movement claims to date back to the Bengali saint and avatar of *Krishna*, *Chiatanya* (1486–1533), founder of the reformed *Vaishnava* tradition known as Gaudiya Vaishnavism or *Vaishnava Bhakthi*, and even further to the most popular book of Hindu scripture, the *Bhagavadgita*, composed sometime between the second century BCE and the second century CE.

Many social scientists have ruled out the application of the terms sect and cult to the religious phenomena collectively known as New Religions, maintaining that these labels tend to be widely understood by the media and the public at large in a negative sense and, hence, can obstruct the pursuit of objectivity and give rise to distortion and prejudice. Moreover, very few of the religions designated new are sectarian or cultic in the classical sociological meaning of these terms which describes a sect as essentially a breakaway movement from a mainstream religion and a cult as a loosely knit, doctrinally open ended formation or group in which the individual decides what to believe and when to practise.

The concept New Religion, then, was devised in the 1960s to describe the emergence of a vast number of what were widely perceived to be new religious and spiritual movements which were characterized by their unconventional symbols of the sacred, their novel understanding of the relationship between the religious and/or spiritual, and the psychological, their new interpretations of the transcendent, and the new principles of belonging to and/ or membership of a religion or spiritual movement which they exposed.

Further reading

Beckford, J. (ed.) (1986) *New Religious Movements and Rapid Social Change*, London: Sage/Unesco.

Clarke, P. B. (ed.) (2000) *Japanese new Religions. In Global Perspective*, Richmond, Surrey: Curzon.

Robbins, T. (1988) *Cults, Converts and Charisma*, London: Sage.

PETER B. CLARKE

NEW RELIGIONS AND VIOLENCE

A number of serious cases of violence involving loss of life, sometimes on a large scale and involving New Religions (see **New Religion**), have occurred over the past thirty years. The first incident was **The Peoples Temple** at Jonestown Guyana in November 1978 when over 900 followers lost their lives mostly through suicide committed at the behest of the leadership (Hall, 1987). This was followed by the tragic loss of life, albeit on a lesser scale, at Waco, Texas when on 19th April 1993 after over fifty days of stand-off the United States Bureau of Alcohol, Tobacco and Firearms invaded the compound of the Branch Davidian community, a **millenarian** movement under the leadership of David Koresh. As the invasion got under way a fire broke out and razed most of the compound to the ground, taking in its wake the lives of seventy-four members of the community (Hall, 2002). Some eighteen months later, in October 1994, the first of several tragedies – the last occurring in 1997 – afflicted a number of communities of the **Order of the Solar Temple** in Switzerland, and Canada. Some 48 members died in all, some by means of suicide, which may well have been involuntary, others were murdered by poison or shot as 'dissidents' and 'untrustworthy members' by the leadership and core members (Introvigne and Mayer, 2002). The fourth of the notorious cases of violence involving NRMs was the **Aum Shinrykyo** incident on the Tokyo underground on 20th March 1995 when poisonous sarin gas was used against communters, killing twelve members of the public and wounding over five thousand others. Prior to this incident the movement had murdered a number of its opponents.

To give religious legitimation to these acts of murder and elevate them to the status of acts of salvation the leadership had reinterpreted the ancient Tibetan Buddhist (see **Vajrayana**) doctrine of *poa* according to which departed souls could be assisted by the living to attain a higher spiritual status in the spiritual realm. In Aum's interpretation of the concept, killing became a means of liberation for the killer and those killed (Shimazono, 1995, Reader, 2000: 200). The mass suicide by all thirty-nine members of the **UFO** movement **Heaven's Gate** in March 1997 (Balch and Taylor, 2000) again gave rise to worldwide consternation and seemed to provide the **Anti-Cult Movement** in particular with further proof of the validity of their claim that recruits to NRMs were thoroughly brainwashed (see **Brainwashing**). While violence is a regular feature of life and an important

413

part of the recruitment strategy and means of control over members to counter attempts at desertion in the **Lord's Resistance Army**, the other Uganda movement that has received even closer attention and scrutiny from the world's media and scholars in recent times, for obvious reasons, is **The Movement for the Restoration of the Ten Commandments** (MRTC). This apocalyptic movement which traced its formal origins to 1981 when one of its founders Credonia Mwerinde (1952–2000) was gifted with visions of the Blessed Virgin Mary also ended, like Waco, with most of its members (an estimated 800 in all) being engulfed in flames on 22 March 2000 (Mayer, 2001).

While the incidents of violence involving NRMs occurred at different times and in very different contexts it is possible none the less to identify some common characteristics without implying direct links between the tragic events. For example, all of the above mentioned movements were to a greater or lesser degree hostile to the wider society. All, moreover, were driven on by an apocalyptic, millenarian vision, not that a direct link can be made between millenarianism and violence. Many millenarian movements have espoused pacificism, a point sometimes overlooked in discussions of NRMs and the roots of violence. The movements, further, were under the control of a charismatic leader and this in itself, as Wallis (1984; 1993) and Robbins (2002), have shown can be a source of considerable volatility, insecurity and uncertainty. Such leadership can also come to rely on an external threat or enemy for legitimacy and encourage the demonization of the world outside the walls of the community. Focusing on the leader, however, as Dawson (2002) points out can obscure the real causes of violence and can fail to address the question why so

many people were prepared in the first place to entrust themselves to the leader in question. Although it can be manipulative and highly unstable, and indeed needs to be if it is to survive, (see **Osho** and **Gurdjieff**) charismatic authority is by definition relational and demands an act of faith and commitment on the part of the follower in the claims made by or on behalf of a leader.

Common elements are one thing, direct links between the tragedies are another. There is one incident where one of the movements that came to a violent end, the Order of the Solar Temple, viewed the actions of another, Waco, which it does not appear to have fully understood, as a challenge to engage in even greater horrors (Mayer, 2003: 208). As far as is known, the Waco tragedy was not intentional, but the result of mistakes on the side both of the movement and the authorities, the United States Bureau of Tobacco, Alcohol and Firearms. The latter used tactics which backfired in trying to get the members to leave their compound. These included, among other things, the threat of the use of weapons, armed incursion and even siege music. External pressures on the Order of the Solar Temple were far less frightening although this movement, as Robbins (2002: 60) points out, 'did experience agitation by apostates, and anti-cult activists, negative media attention and a governemental investigation prior to the violence'. The right to investigate cannot be denied, but it is the manner in which an investigation is carried out that can push leaders and communities that feel under serious threat from a world they have rejected and demonized to prefer death to surrender.

While in the Waco case account needs to be taken of both internal and external factors when explaining the violence (Hall, 2002) external influences were largely absent in the case if the Heaven's Gate mass suicide in 1997 (Balch and Taylor, 2002). Given the complexity of the issues involved it would seem that any research involving NRMs and violence could do no better than to begin with the principle formulated by Bromley and Melton (2002: 241) that 'violent episodes are fundamentally interactive in nature. That said, it is equally true that the primary impetus toward violence may either emanate from movement or control agents.'

While the ACM's accusation that NRMs brainwashed recruits seemed to be supported by Jonestown, Waco, the Order of the Solar Temple, Heaven's Gate and the Aum Shinrikyo tragedies, it remains the case that such a claim has never been substantiated by solid evidence. When the brainwashing thesis eventually lost much of its credibility other highly emotive allegations came to the fore including the abuse of children. Both sets of allegations suggest that the ACM and those who supported it saw NRMs as posing a threat to the very foundations of society.

Further reading

Balch, Robert W. and Taylor, David (2002) Making Sense of Heaven's Gate' in David G. Bromley and J. Gordon Melton (eds) *Cults, Religion and Violence*, Cambridge: Cambridge University Press, pp. 209–29.

Dawson, Lorne L. (2002) 'Crisis of Charismatic Legitimacy and Violent Behaviour in New Religious Movements', in David, G. Bromley and J. Gordon Melton (eds) *Cults, Religion and Violence*, Cambridge: Cambridge University Press, pp. 80–102.

Hall, John H. (1987) *Gone From the Promised Land: Jonestown in American Cultural History*, New Brunswick, NJ: Transaction.

Hall, John H. (2002) 'Mass Suicide and the Branch Davidians' in David G. Bromley and J. Gordon Melton (eds) *Cults, Reli-gion and Violence*, Cambridge: Cambridge University Press, pp. 149–70.

Introvigne, Masssimo and Mayer, Jean-François (2002) 'Occult Masters and the Temple of Doom: The Fiery End of the Solar Temple' in David, G. Bromley and J. Gordon Melton (eds) *Cults, Religion and Violence*, Cambridge: Cambridge University Press, pp. 170–89.

Mayer, Jean-François (2001) 'Field Notes: The Movement for the Restoration of the Ten Commandments of God', *Nova Religio: The Journal of Alternative and Emergent Religions* 5(1), 203–10.

Mayer, Jean-François (2003) '"Our Territorial Journey is Coming to an End": The Last Voyage of the Solar Temple' in Lorne L. Dawson (ed.) *Cults and New Religious Movements*, Oxford: Blackwell, pp. 208–27.

Reader, Ian (2000) *Religious Violence in Contemporary Japan. The Case of Aum Shinrikyo*, Richmond: Curzon.

Robbins, Thomas (2002) 'Sources of Volatility in Religious Movements' in David G. Bromley and J. Gordon Melton (eds) *Cults, Religion and Violence*, Cambridge: Cambridge University Press, pp. 57–80.

Shimazono, Susumu (1995) 'In the Wake of Aum: the Formation and Transformation of a Universe of Belief', *Japanese Journal of Religious Studies* 22(3–4) pp. 381–415.

Wallis, Roy (1976) *The Road to Total Freedom: A Sociological Study of Scientology*, London: Heinemann.

Wallis, Roy (1984) *The Elementary Forms of the New Religious Life*, London: Routledge and Kegan Paul.

Wallis, Roy (1993) 'Charisma and Explanation' in *Secularization, Rationalism and Sectarianism*, ed. Eileen Barker *et al.*, Oxford: Clarendon Press, pp. 167–81.

PETER B. CLARKE

NEW THOUGHT

New Thought emerged in the context of the spread of Christian Science and the interest in alternative healing it generated in the last decades of the nineteenth century. Its origins can be traced to Emma Curtis Hopkins (1853–1925), a close associate of **Christian Science** founder Mary Baker Eddy (1821–1910) and former editor of the *Christian Science Journal*. Hopkins and Eddy had a disagreement in 1885 that led to Hopkins leaving Boston and establishing an independent school, the Emma Hopkins College of Metaphysical Science which over the next years evolved into the Christian Science Theological Seminary. Hopkins taught her own brand of Christian Science, but more importantly opened avenues for the teaching of metaphysical healing apart from the rigid controls demanded by Eddy and the organizational structure of the Church of Christ, Scientist.

During her ten years in Chicago (including her trips around the country), the somewhat shy and retiring Hopkins would train most of the individuals who later founded the major churches that constituted New Thought – Charles and Myrtle Fillmore (Unity School of Christianity), Melinda Cramer (Divine Science), Annie Rix Militz (Homes of Truth), and Helen Van Anderson (Church of the Higher Life). After retiring to New York City, she would accept as her last student Ernest Holmes who founded Religious Science. The name New Thought, to include these related but diverging groups was suggested in the 1890s.

As New Thought struggled to establish itself, it moved to differentiate itself from Christian Science. Concurrently, Mary Baker Eddy was struggling to separate her beliefs from that of her former teacher, Phineas Parkhurst Quimby (1802–66). In this context, some suggested that Eddy had plagiarized her writings from Quimby and that New Thought had in fact derived directly from Quimby. This view was championed by New Thought's first historian, Horatio Dresser. Later historians would accept Dresser's view through most of the twentieth century, and the role of the self-effacing Hopkins was largely forgotten until rediscovered in the 1990s.

Common to New Thought is a belief in the One Reality of God and the possibility of healing by attunement with that one reality. Humans as an individualized expression of God may manifest God's perfection, health, and abundance. To assist individuals in manifesting God, the various New Thought churches provide the services of practitioners who have been trained in the art of healing prayer and have demonstrated abilities in attuning with the One. Apart from this common core, New Thought groups vary widely on different issues, not the least being their relation to Christianity. Some groups, such as Unity emphasize their Christian heritage and their similarities with traditional Christian thought. Others, such as Divine Science are more distant, emphasizing what they see as a more universal spirituality.

Already in the 1890s, leaders began to suggest the desirability of the different New Though groups to make common cause. After several false starts, an organization of what became the International New Thought Alliance was founded in 1914.

New Thought expanded rapidly, reaching England in the 1880s and over the next decades finding its way primarily to various English-speaking countries – Australia and South Africa most prominently. The movement was introduced to England by Frances Lord, one of Hopkins' students and author of *Christian Science Healing* (1988). In England, New Thought produced one of its most important early theoreticians in Thomas Troward (1847–1916). Among the early organizers were F. L. Rawson, founder of the Society to Spread Knowledge of True Prayer, and Henry Thomas Hamblin (1873–1958) whose work continues in the Hamblin Religious

Trust and its *New Vision* magazine. In the 1950s, Bro. Mandus (1907–88) founded the World Healing Crusade whose publications circulate internationally.

The most active South African New Thought Groups has been the School of Truth founded in the 1950s by Nicol Campbell. The Australian work was begun by Veni Cooper-Matheson in 1903, but greatly encouraged by the several visits of Julia Seton beginning in 1916. New Thought suffered greatly during World War Two, but has recovered in recent years, the largest group being affiliated with the American-based Unity School of Christianity.

While spreading through the English-speaking world, New Thought has had its greatest success in Japan where Masaharu Tanaguchi appropriated the Religious Science writings of Ernest Holmes to create **Seicho-no-Ie**, currently the largest single New Thought group in the world. It blossomed in the years immediately after World War Two and has been carried worldwide by the migration of its adherents. Today, over half of all New Thought adherents belong to Seicho-No-Ie (House of Growth).

Further reading

Braden, C. S. (1963) *Spirits in Rebellion*, Dallas: Southern Methodist University Press.

Harley, G. (2002) *Emma Curtis Hopkins: Forgotten Founder of New Thought*, Syracuse, NY: Syracuse University Pres.

Satter, B. (1999) *Each Mind a Kingdom*, Berkeley: University of California Press.

J. GORDON MELTON

NIGRITIAN EPISCOPAL CHURCH

Founder: Jacob Benjamin Anaman (d. 1939)

This church was founded in 1907 by Jacob Benjamin Anaman, a former minister of the Methodist church. He broke away from the Methodists partly as a result of disagreements he had with the leadership over the attempt by the church to disband singing bands who used songs in the mother tongue. Their singing was sometimes accompanied by dancing which was offensive to the church hierarchy but which the members found meaningful. Consequently, the first congregation of the Nigritian Episcopal Church was made up of members of the singing band who had been expelled from the Methodist church at Anomabo, an important coastal town in the Central region of Ghana.

The Nigritian Church, together with two other churches – the African Methodist Episcopal (AME) Zion Church and the National Baptist Church – came to represent the earliest attempt to give religious expression to Gold Coast nationalism and the search for African identity. The name of the Church 'Nigritian' is derived from the word 'Negro'. Its name in Fanti, the mother tongue of the founder is *Ebibir Asor* (African Church). The nationalist and African orientation of the church is given expression in its constitution:

> Christianity has been introduced among the black races ... long enough that it is now time and also quite possible for some of them to build up for themselves an independent Christian Church upon the lines of the teaching of the New Testament, governed by themselves independently of supervision from any foreign ... country for the practice of the faith and worship of the most High God.

The founder, Rev. J. B. Anaman was associated with movements that played significant pioneering roles in the nationalist movements such as the African Society and the Aborigines' Rights

417

Protection Society. Famous Gold Coast nationalist leaders, such as John Mensah Sarbah, Attoh Ahuma and Casely-Hayford, supported his Church. Atto-Ahuma was a regular preacher at special meetings of the church and Casely-Hayford paid for the first set of choir robes worn by the church's choir. Rev. Anaman also joined in the protest against the Land Bill and was the first to publish a book suggesting a link between modern Ghana and ancient Ghana.

The Nigritian church, like its two contemporary counterparts mentioned above, was not significantly radical in the sense of expressing African cultural identity or pursuing political self-determination through the use of relevant indigenous religious symbolism.

In doctrine and liturgy, the Nigritian Church does not depart significantly from the Methodist church. Apart from its nationalist orientation and its claim to be an indigenous missionary enterprise, there is little to distinguish it from the Methodist church. Its distinguishing characteristics are, mainly, the freedom of self-expression allowed in worship and the use of the mother tongue in worship. Following the example of the missionaries, the Nigritian Episcopal Church, in its early years, embarked on vigorous evangelistic activities, planting churches and establishing schools in many parts of the country. However, unlike the mission-instituted churches, the Nigritian Church had no foreign financial support and most of the members were not high-income earners. So it was plagued with serious financial difficulties, which led to the closure of all its schools in 1929.

After the death of the Rev. J. B. Anaman in 1939, his son, Amos W. Anaman succeeded him. Amos worked hard to reopen most of the schools that were closed down in 1929 and establish new ones. The Church also grew in membership and the number of congregations increased. In 1965, in keeping with its professed Episcopal polity, the church consecrated the Rev. Amos W. Anaman as its first Presiding Bishop.

Although the Nigritian church in many ways held on to the Methodist church's tradition, it shed quite early, the gender prejudices which were so common in all the mission-instituted churches. In 1967 three female leaders – prophetess Anna Ainooson-Noonoo, prophetess Leah Ainooson-Noonoo and Rev. Mother Dorcas – were consecrated as assistant bishops. When the Rt. Rev. Amos W. Anaman died in 1974, Assistant bishop Anna Ainooson-Noonoo became the Presiding Bishop.

The Nigritian Church, in the twenty-first century, has branches in many of the major cities and towns in Ghana. It also has a few schools in Cape-Coast and Kumasi; however, it has not overcome its financial difficulties and most of its congregations continue to worship in classrooms.

Further reading

Ayegboyin, D. and Ishola, S. A. (1997) *African Indigenous Churches, An Historical Perspective*, Lagos: Greater Heights.

ABAMFO O. ATIEMO

NINE O'CLOCK SERVICE

The Nine O'Clock Service, otherwise known as 'NOS', emerged as a radical Christian collective in Sheffield, England during the mid-1980s. A group of young evangelical musicians, including one Chris Brain, had begun attending St Thomas's, Crookes, a thriving evangelical Anglican church led by Revd Robert Warren (see **Evangelical Christianity**). While embracing its charismatic spirituality (see **Charismatic Movements**), they criticized its middle class values as complicit in the power, greed and consumerism rife in the wider church and contemporary culture. Seeking to challenge this, and following a model of radical Christian living popularized by David Watson, they styled themselves as the Nairn St. Community. Remaining a fellowship group within St Thomas's, they lived communally in local houses, were supported by a common purse and followed Brain as spiritual leader.

In 1985, John Wimber brought his 'signs and wonders' theology to a conference in Sheffield City Hall. The Nairn St. fellowship attended the meetings and from then on embraced the charismatic teachings of the **Vineyard ministries**. At the same time, Robert Warren claimed to have received a prophecy from God, urging the Nairn St. community to draw more young people into the church. It was decided that the community would run a new service at nine o'clock each Sunday, aimed at fostering orthodox Christianity among unchurched youth aged 18–30. NOS would also be multimedia, employing the audio-visual technology common to dance night clubs and using music that would appeal to the young clubbers.

Regular attendances at NOS trebled in its first year and by the late 1980s, hundreds travelled to Sheffield each week to take part in its cutting edge worship. Some made a more radical commitment by moving to Sheffield and becoming full-time members of the community. They typically tithed a portion of their salaries, in addition to offering their services for the good of the project and submitting themselves to a strict and highly regimented organizational structure. Many were disillusioned charismatics who had become tired of the jaded, complacent and triumphalistic tone of the evangelical mainstream. By contrast, NOS offered a vision that challenged the complacency

of culture, and worship that appealed to the aesthetic tastes of youth. By 1988 there were 400 members, and the following year, Rt Revd David Lunn, the Bishop of Sheffield, confirmed almost 100 young people at a special NOS service. The hierarchy of the Church of England was forced to take note of NOS as an innovative and highly successful initiative in youth evangelism.

In the early 1990s, there was a marked shift in the theology of NOS, from Wimber and the Vineyard tradition to the **creation spirituality** of Matthew Fox (see **Fox, Matthew**). Around the same time, the community moved from St Thomas's to hold their services in the underground rotunda at the Ponds Forge Leisure Centre in the centre of Sheffield, becoming the first Anglican Extra-Parochial parish. It was in this vast arena that NOS held its weekly Planetary Mass, an alternative celebration of Holy Communion. The Planetary Mass used images inspired by the environmental crisis and echoed Fox's attacks on sexism, patriarchy, and ecological apathy, while calling for a renewed mysticism in a post-modern church. Some church leaders expressed concern that NOS was verging on the boundaries of **Neo-paganism** and the '**New Age Movement**'. Controversy also surrounded the group's Passion in Global Chaos set, performed at the Greenbelt festival in 1992, particularly its use of erotic lyrics and bikini-clad dancers. The NOS leadership explained this as a 'post-modern' attempt to engage with the intuitive and sexual alongside rational media.

In August 1995, several members approached diocesan authorities about a long-standing abuse of power at NOS. The leadership team were confronted and resigned, and the service collapsed. Chris Brain – by now an ordained clergyman – was at the centre of the

419

accusations, and eventually admitted intimate and improper contact with twenty female members. His abuse was evidently more widespread, as eighty members, mostly women under 35, sought counselling from a special team set up by the Church. Investigations by the Church of England found no financial improprieties. Rather, the problems of NOS were identified as a lack of accountability within its leadership and the manipulative conduct of Chris Brain, who later resigned as an Anglican priest.

After NOS collapsed, many of its members became disillusioned with Christianity and abandoned the church. However, some of the survivors have continued to meet on a more low-key basis, as the Nine O'Clock Community (NOC). While its abuses are universally deplored, the positive innovations of NOS also live on in the alternative worship movement, a widespread network of groups which practise creative, multimedia worship geared to a post-modern culture.

Further reading

Howard, R. (1996) *The Rise and Fall of the Nine O'Clock Service*, London: Mowbray.

MATHEW GUEST

NIPPONZAN MYOHOJI

Founder: Fujii Nichidatsu

Nipponzan Myohoji, founded in 1918 by Fujii Nichidatsu, is a small group of both lay and monastic Nichiren Buddhists, numbering about 1,500 people. Although small in number, they are well known in peace circles both in Japan and internationally, where they advocate a strictly pacifist, non-violent position.

Fujii was born in 1885 in Kumamoto Prefecture, in the southern part of Japan. At the age of 19 he decided to become a Nichiren Buddhist monk and studied extensively in Tokyo and Kyoto before leaving on a missionary trip to China in 1917. Following the establishment of his first temple the following year, Nipponzan Myohoji temples were established in five other places in Manchuria within the next six years. The order was started in Japan in 1923, with the establishment of a temple at the foot of Mt Fuji.

In 1930 he embarked upon his next, and what he himself considered his most important, missionary endeavor, the return of Buddhism to India, the land of its birth. In October 1933 he arranged for a short stay at Wardha, Mahatma Gandhi's ashram. While there he had two brief audiences with Gandhi, and in later years Fujii often identified his own philosophy of non-violent activism with Gandhi's example.

One of the primary activities of Nipponzan Myohoji is the erection of *stupas*, or Peace Pagodas, throughout Japan and the rest of the world. Construction work on the first such stupa was begun in Kumamoto City in the early postwar period, and this was completed in 1954. To date, more than seventy Peace Pagodas have been erected, mostly in Japan but also in India, Ceylon, England, and the United States. The first Peace Pagoda abroad was dedicated in 1969 in India, to mark the hundredth anniversary of the birth of Gandhi, an example of their identification with his non-violent activism.

Nipponzan Myohoji is perhaps better known for its social activism in the cause of world peace. Since the mid-1950s it has been active in opposing United States military bases in Japan, organizing protests and fasts outside the bases. In the 1970s, members of Nipponzan Myohoji participated in activities obstructing the construction of the New Tokyo International Airport at

Narita, on the grounds that it could also be used for military purposes. In 1981–2, the monks and nuns of Nipponzan Myohoji participated in a walk across the United States, culminating in the 12 June 1982 mass demonstration against nuclear arms in New York City. During the Persian Gulf War in 1991 some members of this group staged a hunger strike in the square in front of Shibuya Station, one of the major commuter stations in Tokyo, in protest against the war. The monks and nuns have been active in places as diverse as Cambodia, Sri Lanka, and Nicaragua, often engaged in prayers and fasts for peace.

Although thus engaged in high-profile peace activities in the postwar period, there is some dispute regarding Fujii's claim that he and his followers have always been pacifist. Some have claimed, for example, that the monks of Nipponzan Myohoji gave their blessing to the Japanese invasion of China by performing functions comparable to that of army chaplains, and specifically that Myohoji monks accompanied Japanese troops in their conquest of Nanking in 1937. Fujii himself in his autobiography states that he made repeated trips to China during the war years and met with many of the top Japanese military personnel, but claims that these meetings had a religious purpose and that he used his influence to argue for peace.

Each of the Nipponzan Myohoji temples is nominally independent, and the group appears to have a rather loose organizational structure. Although one of the monks is appointed as leader of the group, some of the monks report that their activities are coordinated by discussion among the members. The lay members usually participate in the activities of one of the Myohoji temples, while the monks and nuns are more prominent in the group's activities both nationally and internationally.

Further reading

Fujii, N. (1975) *My Non Violence: An Autobiography of a Japanese Buddhist*, (Yamaori Tetsuo, trans.) Tokyo: Japan Buddha Sangha Press.

Kisala, R. (1999) *Prophets of Peace: Pacifism and Cultural Identity in Japan's New Religions*, Honolulu: University of Hawaii Press.

ROBERT KISALA

NIWAMO NIKKYÔ
(c. 1906–1999)
Founder of Risshô Kôsei-kai

Niwano Nikkyô was born in 1906 in a village in Niigata Prefecture, in northern Japan. His large family were farmers and as a child, he was said to have been deeply impressed by his grandfather's and parents' kindness to others, which is believed to have instilled in him a love of peace and harmony and of service to others.

The harmony and compassion cultivated in his childhood were reinforced by Buddhism particularly by the Lotus Sutra. Niwano made the Lotus sutra the basis of **Risshô Kôsei-kai** and established as the goal of this movement the bringing of peace to members, their families and communities, nations and the world.

When Niwano left his village in Niigata Prefecture to find work in Tokyo at the age of 17, he began studying and practising various spiritual disciplines such as fortune-telling. He got married to a second cousin in 1930. In 1935 when his second daughter fell ill with a very high fever and lost consciousness, Niwano joined **Reiyukai** to seek a cure for her illness. After several years in Reiyukai as a missionary, Niwano Nikkyô seceded from Reiyukai and with Naganuma Myôkô founded Risshô Kôsei-kai in 1938.

Niwano dedicated himself to help free people from suffering and to assist in establishing a peaceful world through the teachings of the Lotus Sutra. Believing that all religions derive from the same source, Niwano met with religious people in various countries for the attainment of world peace through inter-religious dialogue. Niwano served as an honorary president of World Conference on Religion and Peace (WCRP) and the International Association for Religious Freedom (IARF) and as chairman of the Board of Directors of *Shinshuren*, Federation of New Religious Organizations of Japan. He died in 1999 at the age of 92.

Further reading

Kisala, Robert (1999) *Prophets of Peace*, Honolulu: University Press of Hawai'i.

Niwano, N. (1976) *Niwano Nikkyô jiden* (the Bibliography of Niwano Nikkyô), Tokyo: Kosei Publishing Company.

KEISHIN INABA

O

ODUNLAMI, SOPHIA

A Yoruba woman whose visions are associated with the beginning of the **Aladura movement** in Western Nigeria in the early twentieth century, Sophia Odunlami first became widely known locally in 1918 on account of her visionary experience during the influenza epidemic that ravaged South-Western Nigeria. When western medicine failed to hold back the disease or offer any help to those afflicted, the British colonial administration closed down some schools and churches to prevent its continuous spread. As a result of a dream, **Joseph B. Shadare** (his name later changed to Eshinsinade), a member of the Diocesan Board and a leading member of St Saviours Anglican Church, Ijebu Ode, started regular prayer meetings to seek divine intervention to halt the epidemic. One of those who joined the prayer meetings was Sophia Odunlami (later Mrs Ajayi), a relative of Shadare, then a young woman in her early twenties who was

teaching in an Anglican school in a village near Ijebu Ode. Following a vision, she proclaimed that God would send rain that would cure those afflicted with the flu, and anyone using any other medicine whatsoever would die. This brought much public to the prayer meetings attention was drawn to the prayer group, which became known as Egbe Okuta Iyebiye (the Precious Stone or the Diamond Society). This society assumed a semi-autonomous existence as a Pentecostal group within the Anglican Church. Its doctrinal emphases included the rejection of all medicine and reliance on faith **healing** alone, the rejection of infant baptism – an issue that brought them into sharp disagreement with the Anglican clergy – and the importance of dreams and visions. Odunlami was a charismatic leader, a prophet and a visionary. When the Precious Stone Society severed its connection with the Anglican Church which had made life very difficult for members of the new society, Odunlami was one of those who in 1921 affiliated with the **Faith Tabernacle Church**, a holiness church based in the United States of America. Throughout her life, Odunlami was active in a leadership role and provided spiritual guidance to the group. In 1930, she condemned Josiah Ositelu's use of some strange holy names (see **Ositelu, Josiah**) and thus distanced the Ijebu Ode group from Ositelu. Odunlami's charismatic personality helped to break down the restrictive cultural barriers that confronted Yoruba women, and thus created more opportunities for women in church life in the early twentieth century.

Further reading

Turner, H. W. (1967) *History of an African Independent Church: The Church of the Lord (Aladura)* (2 vols.), Oxford: Clarendon Press.

MATTHEWS A.OJO

OKAWA, RYUHO
(b. 1956)

Ryuho Okawa (Founder of Kofuku-no-Kagaku, IRH) was born as Takashi Nakagawa in Tokushima Prefecture in Japan on 7 July 1956. He came from neither a particularly wealthy nor poor family background. Okawa was a lively student; he was the editor of the school journal, enjoyed tennis and fishing, practised *kendô* (a martial art), and graduated from Tokyo University where he read law and politics. He married another Tokyo University graduate, Kyoko (1965–), with whom he has five children. On 23 March 1981, just before graduating from University, Okawa suddenly began to receive messages from a high spirit, and many more divine spirits started to contact him. In July 1981, he became aware of his mission to bring happiness to all humanity and of his identity as the incarnation of the grand spirit, El Cantare. Instead of immediately starting a religious movement, however, he worked in one of Japan's major trading houses and was sent to its US head office in New York, where he also studied international finance at New York City University. Even during his secular life in the financial world his spiritual experiences continued. His father, Saburo Yoshikawa, taped the dialogues held between Okawa and various spirits and edited a vast amount of recordings. Over four years after Okawa's religious experiences had first started, the first volume of these spiritual messages was published. It was entitled *Nichiren no Reigen* (The Spiritual Messages of Nichiren) and appeared under Yoshikawa's name (1985). In 1986, at the age of thirty, Okawa left his firm and established **Kofuku-no-Kagaku** (The Institute for Research in Human Happiness), which obtained official religious body status in Tokyo in 1991. According to Kofuku-no-Kagaku, the number of Okawa's publications exceeds 400; these include booklets, and audio books. His trilogy *The Laws of the Sun*, *The Golden Laws* and *The Laws of Eternity*, are his principal writings.

Further reading

Astley, T. (1995) 'The Transformation of a Recent Japanese New Religion: Okawa Ryuho and Kofuku-no-Kagaku', *Japanese Journal of Religious Studies*, 22(3–4), 343–80.

Fukui, M. (1999) 'Kofuku-no-Kagaku: The Institute for Research in Human Happiness', in Peter B. Clarke (ed.) *A Bibliography of Japanese New Religious Movements*, Eastbourne, Kent: Japan Library, pp. 149–67.

Yamashita, A. (1998) 'The "Eschatology" of Japanese New and New New Religions: From Tenrikyo to Kofuku-no-Kagaku', *Japanese Religions*, 23(1–2), 125–42.

MASAKI FUKUI

OMOTO (GREAT ORIGIN)

A new religion of syncretic Shinto organized in Ayabe, a small rural city near Kyoto in the 1890s, and which gathered strength between 1915 and 1935. As of 2001, it has headquarters in Ayabe and Kameoka, claiming a membership of 172,000.

The founders of Omoto are Deguchi Nao (1836–1918) and Deguchi Onizaburo (1871–1948). Nao was the wife of a poor carpenter. As her husband was a heavy drinker who did not care for the family, Nao had to bring up seven children by trading rags and other jobs. In 1892, she began to claim that a god spoke to her and that she wrote down the god's words (*Ofudegaki*), which later became the Omoto scripture *Omoto Shinyu*. Nao said that the god of the primordial ages was oppressed, and prophesied the god would reappear to rebuild and reform this world. The religious group formed around Nao was small, but in 1898, when Ueda Kisaburo (later Deguchi Onisaburo) joined her group, Nao welcomed him as her collaborator and had her daughter Sumi marry him.

Deguchi Onisaburo was born to a poor farming family in Anao in Kyoto prefecture. He had basic education in Japanese classic literature, and underwent an intensive religious training of syncretic Shinto. He introduced a training method *Chinkon Kishin* (repose of souls, coming closer to gods) to help individuals talk in trance about the spiritual beings related to themselves. He sympathized with the theory of the Soul of Words that all the entities in the universe consist of spiritual power of the phonemes of the Japanese language, and incorporated this theory into the doctrine.

In 1908, he began organizing Omoto as a religious body. Onisaburo incorporated the doctrines of State Shinto (*Kodo*) and named it *Kodo Omoto* (Omoto of Royal Way). He invited military leaders and intelligent people as members, purchased an influential daily newspaper the *Taisho Nichi Nichi Shimbun*, and the land of the Kameoka Castle ruins. He advocated the Taisho Restoration. While apparently hosting emperor worship, Omoto advocated to transfer the capital of Japan to Ayabe, and regarded Onisaburo as the Messiah. Because of this, the police arrested Onisaburo and other leaders in 1921 for the charge of lese majesty. This is called the 1st Omoto Incident.

After the incident, Onisaburo began writing *Reikai Monogatari (Stories of the Spiritual World)* through dictation as the second scripture after *Ofudesaki*, promoted the spread of Esperanto and religious cooperation, and built partnerships with political forces in Manchuria in response to the expansion of the Great Japan Empire onto the China continent. The trial for the 1st Omoto Incident was dismissed in 1927. Omoto organized Miroku (Maitreya) Festival in 1929, and Onisaburo claimed to be a personification of Maitreya Bodhisatva urging the followers to worship him as their Messiah.

However, Omoto emphasized emperor worship after this event, advocating the "Showa Restoration" to build a state centering on the emperor. It strengthened its tie with fascist groups. In 1934, he organized Showa Shinsei-kai with right-wing leaders, which was reportedly said to have 8 million members. In 1935, the government oppressed the Kodo Omoto and destroyed its facilities in Ayabe and Kameoka, and arrested about 300 leaders. Onisaburo was released on bail in 1942, and the organization remained inactive. After the war, Omoto rapidly recovered its strength and promoted a peace movement and a religious cooperation movement. After the 1990s, it placed emphases on the opposition to the manipulation of human life by medical treatment and life science.

The teachings of Omoto are to worship the supreme god, and to realize a life in which a follower can be united with god while being aware of god's blessings. It considers that each person arrives at a certain place in the spiritual world after death depending on what he had done in this world. It teaches the followers to live a "Spirit First and Body Second" life and encourages them to resurrect in a higher position in the spiritual world. It also preaches that while living in this world, one should make every effort to realize heaven on earth. The **Sekai Kyusei Kyo** and **Seicho-no-Ie** are new religions created by leaders who departed from Omoto. The aggregate of Omoto-line new religions can be a large force next to the Soka Gakkai and Reiyukai-line organizations.

Further reading

Berthon, J.-P. (1985) *Ômoto, Espérance Millenariste d'une Nouvelle Religion Japonaise*, Paris (Atelier Alpha Bleue): Cahiers d'Etudes et de Documents sur les Religions du Japon.

Hino, I. P. (1974) *The Ofudesaki: The Holy Scriptures of Ômoto*, Kameoka: Ômoto Foundation.

Ooms, E. G. (1993) *Women and Millenarian Protest in Meiji Japan. Deguchi Nao and Ômotokyô*, New York: Cornell Univerrsity East Asia Program.

PETER B. CLARKE

ONISABURÔ, DEGUCHI

Deguchi Onisaburô (1871–1948) was a co-founder with **Deguchi Nao** (1836–1918) of the Japanese new religion Ômotokyô (f. 1892) (see **Omoto**). Born Ueda Kisaburô, he changed his name to Deguchi Onisaburô upon marriage to Nao's daughter Sumi (1882–1953). Widely experienced in the religious world of his day, Onisaburô had undertaken mountain austerities, headed a confraternity dedicated to the rice god Inari, and had served as a Shintô priest. He systematized Nao's on-going revelations to convey her message of world renovation to a wider, urban, educated spectrum of Japanese society, especially during and after World War One. Following the great loss of life in the Sino-Japanese War and the Russo-Japanese War, an interest in spiritualism arose in Japan, which harmonized with Onisaburô's interpretation of Nao's teachings. He identified Nao's god Ushitora Konjin as a Shintô deity and prophesied that this deity would displace the evil gods ruling Japan, and thereby restore the country to divine rule under an unbroken imperial line. He called for a reformation of society and politics in strong, apocalyptic language. Ômoto published journals and purchased a national newspaper to promulgate Onisaburô's prophecies, which provoked the state to suppress Ômoto-kyô in 1921 on charges of lèse majesté and violation of the Newspaper Law. At this time the religion was garnering many followers among the military and the educated middle class in response to its energetic proselytizing in the cities. Onisaburô and other group leaders were imprisoned.

After this first suppression, Onisaburô began to record his experiences in the spiritual world in *Stories from the Spiritual World* (*Reikai monogatari*), a massive work of more than seventy volumes, written in artful language and parables. Ômoto was suppressed again in 1935, but this time more than 200 of its leaders were arrested, its facilities confiscated and destroyed, and Onisaburô was imprisoned until the end of World War Two. After his release, he dedicated himself to artistic pursuits and the theme of universal brotherly love.

Further reading

Deguchi, Kyotaro (1998) *The Great Onisa-buro Deguchi*, translated by Charles Rowe, Tokyo: Aiki News.

HELEN HARDACRE

OPUS DEI

Opus Dei ('the Work of God', shortened by adherents to 'the Work') is an organization with the Roman Catholic Church. From 1983 it has, juridically, been a 'Personal Prelature', a structure created by Pope Paul VI in 1966. This was originally intended to provide for pastoral ministries within the Church which did not have clear-cut geographical boundaries, such as military chaplaincies or chaplaincies to travellers. The structure has never been used for these purposes, however, and Opus Dei remains as the only one of its kind within the Church. It is, effectively, a diocese, presided over by a 'prelate', customarily a bishop. Members of Opus Dei, wherever they are in the world, belong to this quasi diocese. As with any Roman Catholic diocese, it embraces priests as well as lay men and women, some as full members (the term used is 'numerarii') others as associated members ('supernumerarii'). The former are full-time, celibate members, commonly living in Opus Dei houses, the latter are usually married, or intending to marry. The numerarii members make 'fidelities' which have much in common with the traditional vows of poverty, chastity, and obedience taken by members of religious orders.

They are adamant, however, that Opus is not a religious order, and that its members (other than priests belonging to the Priestly Society of the Holy Cross and Opus Dei, as it is formally known) remain fully lay men and women. There is also a rank called 'co-operators', sympathizers (not necessarily Roman Catholic) with the spiritual ideals and manner of life of Opus Dei, but not formally members of the prelature. The common feature in their lives is that they place themselves under the spiritual direction of Opus Dei clergy, and take as their spiritual guide the writings of the founder of Opus Dei, St Josemaría **Escrivá de Balaguer**.

The inspiration for Opus Dei came to the founder on 2 October 1928, the Feast of the Guardian Angels, while he was making a retreat at a house on the outskirts of Madrid. He began to work with a group of lay men, who shared with him his house, as a small university hostel. Though he began with men, he early conceived the idea of a parallel organization for women. It was not until the early 1940s that he determined to found a society of priests, schooled in his own spirituality, who might look after the spiritual well-being of the members of Opus.

The development of the organization was severely interrupted by the Spanish Civil War, in the course of which Escrivá had to flee Madrid to France, returning soon afterwards to Burgos, which was in the hands of the Nationalist forces. Franco's victory, and the need to re-establish higher education in Spain, gave members of Opus Dei an opening to enter the university sector, where they became an important influence, and an opportunity for recruitment. As the organization grew, Escrivá became dissatisfied with the purely diocesan status which had been formally granted to it by the bishop of Madrid.

In 1947 the headquarters moved to Rome and, in the same year, the Vatican granted the status of a 'secular institute', the first of its kind, which enabled it to spread worldwide. It was also in 1947 that married members (the 'supernumerarii') were admitted.

Opus Dei now operates in a great many countries. It has some 80,000 members in the various branches, only a small and undisclosed proportion of them full-time members. There are among them some two thousand priests, and though Opus Dei claims to be, basically, a lay organization, the central governance is in the hands of clergy. Though it has some institutions of its own apart from residences – the University of Navarre at Pamplona in Spain is its flagship enterprise – many of the undertakings which are described as being of Opus Dei are the responsibility of groups of members, not of the organization itself. Opus Dei has been much criticized within the Roman Catholic Church for its apparent secrecy – though this appears to have been mitigated in recent years – for its recruitment techniques, for its spirituality based, in particular, upon Escrivá's little book of 999 maxims, *Camino* ('The Way'), which to some seems too reminiscent of the Spanish mentality of the Franco regime. Under General Franco a group of members came to prominence in the government, and Opus Dei has also been accused of being close to right-wing regimes in Latin America. The recruitment techniques allegedly employed by Opus were expressly criticised by Cardinal Basil Hume, Archbishop of Westminster, in 'Guidelines for Opus Dei within the Diocese of Westminster', which he published in 1981. Opus Dei is also regarded as theologically very conservative.

Further reading

Walsh, M. (1989) *The Secret World of Opus Dei*, Grafton Books, London, published in the USA as *Opus Dei – An Investigation into the Secret Society within the Roman Catholic Church*, San Francisco: Harper-Collins, reprinted with a new introduction in 2004.

MICHAEL WALSH

ORDER OF THE SOLAR TEMPLE

Founders: Joseph Di Mambro (b. 1924; d. 1994) and Luc Jouret (b. 1947; d. 1994)

Like other New Religious Movements or NRMs (see **New Religious Movement**) that draw on the western esoteric tradition (see Esoteric Movements, the **Rosicrucian Order, Cretona Fellowship** and **AMORC:** Ancient and Mystic Order of the Rosy Cross) the Order of the Solar Temple emphasized the link between itself and a much older tradition dating back to medieval times. The inspiration behind the founding of the Solar Temple movement, Joseph Di Mambro (1924–94) was born in France and was once a member of AMORC (1956–69), whose ideas continued to exercise a strong influence on him even after he left that movement. He also had links with the esoteric renewal movement, the Arginy movement, founded by the French writer Jacques Breyer (1922–96).

In difficulties with the French authorities over allegations of fraud Di Mambro left France for Switzerland where he established himself as a teacher and spiritual master and founded (1976) the Centre for Preparing the New Age. His followers who had purchased a house in France near Geneva lived a communal life and performed esoteric rituals. In 1978 Di Mambro started the Golden Way Foundation in Geneva, an organization that was to remain the centre of his esoteric interests for some years. In the 1980s he met Luc Jouret, also an esotericist and at first member and then Grand Master of the Renewed Order of the Temple, a movement that was based on Templar (see **Ordo Templi Orientis**) and Rosicrucian ideas. In 1982 Jouret joined Di Mambro's group and was to provide the charismatic leadership that it had been lacking. Both men founded the Order of the Solar Temple in 1984 with Jouret assuming the more prominent public role as the movement's principal spokesperson and theorist.

There were several levels of membership beginning with the Amanta group, which consisted of those who attended public lectures and seminars. The next level had direct involvement in the esoteric Achedia Clubs and the top tier consisted of the initiated who were members of the International Chivalric Organization of the Solar Tradition.

Discontent and disillusionment began to surface among members in the early 1990s and accusations were made of fraud and quackery on the part of the leadership, and the among critics was Di Mambro's own 'cosmic child' Emmanuelle, whose origins lay it was claimed in a mystical act of intercourse between Di Mambro's mistress and a discarnate Master. Emmanuelle and others became seriously disillusioned with Di Mambro's leadership when they discovered that what he claimed to be visible manifestations of Masters of the Temple were in fact the product of electronic and other devices installed by the leadership. It was this discovery in particular that led Emmanuelle and some fifteen members to leave the movement. Di Mambro and Jouret were also encountering problems both from members and with the police in Canada. In 1993 their small group of followers led by Jouret had been investigated concerning allegations that they were stockpiling semi-automatic weapons. Jouret and two members who had been arrested briefly were fined. There were also police investigations of financial irregularities in France and Australia following money transfers by Di Mambro, which never reached any conclusion.

Disposed to interpreting misfortune in apocalyptic terms, and suffering from various illnesses, Di Mambro began composing Tracts on the subject of the 'Transit' in 1993. Police investigations and internal discontent and disaffection would seem to have fostered in him the conviction that the End of Time was imminent. With Jouret with whom he also seems to have been in frequent disagreement, Di Mambro began preparing his remaining followers for 'transit' to another world. The sense the movement had of being persecuted by external enemies heightened when the French police refused to renew Di Mambro's wife's visa in 1994.

That the time had come for 'transit' was confirmed by messages from discarnate beings channelled by Di Mambro and the prominent Swiss businessman Camille Pilet (1926–94) who had joined the OTS in 1987. Tragedy soon followed. In the towns of Cheiry and Granges-sur-Salvan in Switzerland on the night of 4 October 1994 fires broke out as part of a planned suicide mission by the leadership of which most of the others who died were unaware. The latter were possibly expecting to be conveyed by supernatural means – perhaps by means of a space ship – to another planet (see **Heaven's Gate).** Some days previously in Quebec two Swiss members had executed the Dutoit family for being untrustworthy. Their principal 'crime' was to have been unprepared to remain silent about the electronic devices used to produce manifestations of the Masters. Their executioners committed suicide two days before the Swiss tragedy in which an estimated forty-eight members died. Of those who died at Cheiry some were classified as traitors and most did so after consuming a sleep-inducing drug before being shot, while most of those at Salvan – the majority of whom were part of the leadership and core membership – were poisoned. Some appear to have perished directly in the flames. By no means all of the membership, therefore, had opted for suicide and certainly not the children who were simply murdered. The tragedy did not end there. On 23 December 1995 sixteen members of OTS including children were found dead in the mountains of Vercours near Grenoble and on 21 March 1997 five members of the OTS committed suicide in St Casimir, Quebec, their children in this case being allowed to choose whether to 'transit' with their parents or to decide not to take part.

Further reading

Introvigne, Massimo and Mayer, Jean-François (2002) 'Occult Masters and the Temple of Doom: The Fiery End of the Solar Temple', in David G. Bromley and J. Gordon Melton (eds) *Cults, Religion and Violence*, Cambridge: Cambridge University Press, pp. 17–188.

PETER B. CLARKE

ORDO TEMPLI ORIENTIS (OTO)

The tradition based on the doctrinal and organizational legacy of **Aleister Crowley** (1875–1947), a controversial English magician, must be considered to be among the most important international currents or systems of ritual magic in the world. Raised in the rigorous fundamentalist orthodoxy of the Plymouth Brethren, Edward Alexander (these were his real Christian names) abandoned strict Christianity while still a youth, soon taking great interest in the occult. Thus, in 1904, after a period in the **Hermetic Order of the Golden Dawn** (founded in London in 1888), Crowley received *The Book of the Law* in Cairo by means of mediumistic evocation. *The Book of the Law*, the true doctrinal code of the subsequent Crowleyan system, announced the advent of a new era marked by the 'Law of Thelema', summed up in the code of conduct 'Do what

thou wilt shall be the whole of the law! Love is the law, love under will.' In 1911 (or 1909, the year is uncertain), Aleister Crowley finally made contact with the Ordo Templi Orientis (OTO), a movement founded in 1906 by Theodor Reuss (1855–1923), and noted for its elaboration of a system of sexual magic and transmission of the tantric teachings of Carl Kellner (b. Austria, 1850–1905).

Among the many controversies that stirred the Thelemite movement after Crowley's death, the Ordo Templi Orientis (then called 'of the Caliphate') was certainly the group that gained the greatest international visibility and importance, although there were scores (if not hundreds) of movements and groups that declared that their 'Thelemite' affiliation or inspiration derived from Crowley's philosophy of magic.

The OTO was able to establish itself in the United States in 1921 as a result of Theodor Reuss's granting of a licence to Crowley's 'magic son,' Charles Stansfeld Jones (1886–1950).

The United States and particularly California remained the movement's hub after Crowley's death, especially when Karl Germer (1885–1962) decided to make his home there. Germer became the first leader of the post-Crowleyan order, holding the key to the future until 1962 (even though he did nothing in particular during his term in office).

Germer's succession was claimed by one of the members of the old Agapé Lodge established by Wilfred Talbot Smith (1888–1957) in Pasadena. This was one of the first, if not the first Crowley inspired movement in the United States. One of its members was the soldier Grady Louis McMurtry (1918–85), who in 1977 began the administrative reorganization of the OTO, becoming its OHO (Outer Head of the Order) under the name Hymenaeus Alpha and registering it as a religious organization (tax-exempt in the USA) in 1982. On 21 September 1985, William Breeze, a French-born New Yorker, succeeded McMurtry (who had won a court case contesting the OTO's legitimacy), taking the esoteric name Hymenaeus Beta.

The OTO's current structure, ritually divided into thirteen esoteric grades, is composed of 'Camps,' normally containing fewer than eleven individuals, empowered to perform the initiation rituals of the 0 and 1st grade; 'Oases' are concerned with initiations up to the 3rd grade; 'Lodges' perform all grades up to the 7th, and 'Grand Lodges' are assigned initiations in the 'Sanctuary of the Gnosis' (8th, 9th, 11th) and control of a Province. There are more than 3,000 OTO members world-wide, divided into about 150 official groups in over forty countries.

The OTO's leadership consists of the ninth grade, which relates to a secret instruction called *Liber Agapé* and this is read together with the commentary written by Crowley and entitled *De Arte Magica*. It reveals the OTO's secret, which, according to Crowley, is the secret of alchemists, of Freemasons, and of esoteric Christianity, which supposedly masked it under eucharistic dogma (see **Esoteric Movements**). After having prepared himself by fasting (which nevertheless does not exclude the use of alcohol and certain drugs), the OTO initiate celebrates the 'eucharistic sacrifice' which, is at the centre of a magic ritual that features sexual intercourse followed by the preparation, 'solemnly and in silence,' of the 'Elixir' (a mixture of the man's and woman's secretions) that is 'immediately consumed'. The Crowleyan rite also requires a temple and scrupulous respect of the formulae and magical invocations which accompany the ritual act. Lastly, the secret instructions of the ninth grade also include a *De Homunculo Epistola*, which resembles ancient legends that are concerned with the possibility of 'manufacturing' an artificial man, albeit in a different environment. The supposition behind the entire procedure, is the idea that a wandering human soul takes possession of a fetus only when the fetus is three months old, and that a magician can keep human souls away from the fetus and attract, in their place, the type of spirit he wants, thus becoming its master and it becoming his servant.

Further reading

Crowley, A. (1973) *Magick*, York Beach, ME: Samuel Weiser.
Symonds, J. (1997) *The Beast 666. The Life of Aleister Crowley*, London: The Pindar Press.

PierLuigi Zoccatelli

ORIMOLADE, MOSES TUNALOSE
(c. 1879–19 October 1933)

Moses Tunolase Orimolade reverently called *Baba Aladura* (the praying father) and venerated as a saint by his followers was born in Ikare in Western Nigeria of Yoruba parents who were Ifa worshippers. Ifa is a complex system of divination practiced among the Yoruba and other peoples of western Africa. Lame in both legs as result of an undisclosed illness in his childhood, Orimolade was frequently carried about on his evangelistic tours. Converted into the Anglican Church in the 1890s, he embarked on itinerant preaching and visited several towns in Western and Northern Nigeria during the influenza epidemic of 1918–19.

In early July 1924 Orimolade arrived in Lagos evangelizing and praying for people with various needs. In June 1925, after praying for a teenage girl, Abiodun

Akinsowon (see **Akinsowon, Christiana Abiodun (Mrs Captain)**), who subsequently regained consciousness from a prolonged trance, more people flocked to him. After Abiodun joined him, both held regular prayer meetings for enquirers, who later became the nucleus of *Egbe Serafu* (the Seraph Society), organized in September 1925 initially as an interdenominational group. Renamed Cherubim and Seraphim (C&S) by 1927 (see **Cherubim and Seraphim Churches**), its activities centred on prayers as the remedy for all human ills and problems.

Orimolade was intensely religious and cultivated a fervent prayer life. He wore a simple white long robe, which later became a distinguishing characteristic of **Aladura** prophets. His message centred on the efficacy of prayers, faith in God, and the renunciation of idolatry and other evil acts. About 1926, Orimolade organized a Praying Band comprising active C&S members who were sent out in groups of three to pray for the sick without charging or collecting any fee.

Differences in personality between the illiterate and aging Orimolade, and the young educated beautiful Abiodun led to a split in the group in March 1929. Thereafter, Orimolade led his own group, the Eternal Sacred Order of the Cherubim and Seraphim until his death.

He was a celibate, ascetic and also poor but surmounted the temptation of ever taking money for prayers. Orimolade's charisma impacted positively on C&S and fostered a significant religious movement in Nigeria.

Further reading

Omoyajowo, J. A. (1982) *Cherubim and Seraphim: The History of an African Independent Church*, New York: NOK Publishers International Ltd.

MATTHEWS A. OJO

OSHO (BHAGWAN SHREE RAJNEESH)

Osho was the founder and leader of the **Rajneesh Movement**. He was a significant if controversial figure in the history of Eastern spirituality in the West, pioneering the synthesis of Eastern mysticism with Western psychology. He did this primarily through the use of his **dynamic meditation**s and his radical innovations in psychotherapy which hundreds of thousands of people have participated in.

Osho was born Rajneesh Mohan Chandra into a Jain business family in northern India. In 1953 he underwent a personal transformation, during which he claimed to have become enlightened. He then obtained a Master's degree in philosophy, and became a professor at the University of Jabalpur for nine years until 1966. He also began his spiritual teaching career, and was visited at the university by the first known Westerner in his life, Dennis Lingwood (Sangharakshita), founder of the **Friends of the Western Buddhist Order**.

After 1966 he moved to Bombay and developed his religious work, assuming the title of Acharya ('spiritual teacher'), and taking on disciples. A charismatic speaker, he gave talks in sports stadiums to huge audiences, exploring controversial topics such as the need for sexual liberation or the alleged shortcomings of Gandhi, which often shocked conservative Indians. Nowadays, he is seen as an important teacher within India itself.

By 1968 Western disciples started coming to him in some numbers, and stories about this rebellious new guru began circulating around the **Human Potential Movement** (HPM), then taking off in the USA and Britain. Leaders of the HPM came to India to investigate, followed by thousands of people interested in personal development. At this time he took on a new name, Bhagwan

Shree Rajneesh. In Sanskrit, Bhagwan means (approximately) God, a claim which shocked some people. In 1974 Osho moved to Pune and formed an ashram (retreat community). A major factor attracting so many disciples was his powerful daily lecture, combining erudition, inspiration, and entertainment.

He produced no formally coherent philosophy, despite his academic background – rather, he delighted in inconsistency and contradiction. His roots can be traced back to India's old antinomian tradition **Tantra**, which advocates the breaking of taboos as a method of attaining non-attachment. He also read widely, maintaining a vast library; other sources of his teachings can be found in Eastern mysticism, particularly the Upanishads, Buddhism, Taoism, and Sufism, as well as Western mysticism, philosophy and psychology. Osho saw in Western writers such as Reich, Nietzsche and D. H. Lawrence the possibility of developing an East–West intellectual synergy. He borrowed especially from Reich in developing his dynamic meditations. From around 1978 he was an outspoken atheist, although still maintaining a doctrine of the soul and reincarnation. He also produced a large body of work in Hindi, most of which has not been translated, which reveals his specifically Indian heritage.

Osho was a very reclusive person, suffering from ever-worsening health. There have been suggestions that because of this and his increasing dependence on medication, his judgement deteriorated with age, leading to uncharacteristically bizarre pronouncements, and a declining sense of responsibility for his actions. However, many followers would dispute this view.

The ashram expanded rapidly, but new land could not be obtained in India. In 1981 he moved to the United States with his disciples – a strategic decision which was to prove disastrous. For several years, he largely withdrew into silence and reclusion, avoiding meeting disciples, giving lectures and the day-to-day administration of the community. Authority was delegated to subordinates, giving them free rein to deal with the mounting problems, although he appears to have still been involved to some extent. The ashram in Oregon soon fell foul of the planning authorities: there were charges of corruption in local elections, immigration violations on a large scale, and many other such issues. Matters came to a head.

Whilst trying to escape the United States, Osho was arrested on immigration charges but released later, and returned to the ashram in Pune. He resumed his programme of lectures and darshans (master–disciple meetings), and died in 1990. Officially his death was due to complications from diabetes and asthma, but his personal staff maintained that he had been poisoned whilst imprisoned in the USA with a slow-acting poison, thallium.

His ashram continues to attract large numbers of participants.

Osho is increasingly being recognized as a major spiritual teacher of the twentieth century, at the forefront of the current 'world-accepting' trend of spirituality based on self-development.

Further reading

Gordon, J. (1988) *The Golden Guru*, New York: The Stephen Greene Press.

Osho (2001) *Autobiography of a Spiritually Incorrect Mystic*, New York: St Martin's Press.

ELIZABETH PUTTICK

OSITELU, JOSIAH OLUNOWO
(b. 15 May 1902; d. 12 July 1966)

Josiah Olunowo Ositelu, son of Ijebu parents who were adherents of African

Traditional Religion, was converted and baptized into the Anglican Church in 1914. He had his elementary education from 1913 to 1919, and thereafter taught in several Anglican schools.

Intense visionary experiences that began in June 1925 led to his dismissal from teaching and the Anglican Church in April 1926. After a period of spiritual preparation he began public preaching in June 1929 at Ogere in the Ijebu province, southwestern Nigeria and in the following month inaugurated a group, which in 1931 was named **Church of the Lord (Aladura)**. His preaching centered on the renunciation of idolatry, the imminence of God's judgment, promises of divine healing, and faith in God alone. His early activities in Ogere consisted of healing services, giving of prophecies and unmasking of witches. Besides, he claimed to have received in visions certain holy words, the obscure meaning of which was interpreted by his assistants. With Ogere as a base, he traveled to many Nigerian cities establishing branches of his church.

Within a year, his fame as a prophet had spread throughout Ijebuland in southwestern Nigeria, attracting the attention of other Aladura revivalists in Western Nigeria. However, from 1931 other Aladura leaders distanced themselves from Ositelu on account of the 'strange' and unintelligible holy names that he was using, the witch-hunting episodes associated with his ministry, and his toleration of polygamy. Between 1929 and 1949, Ositelu married seven wives claiming divine authorization for this.

Ositelu's religious experiences and activities were grounded in local religious culture and were largely free of foreign missionary influence, although he was literate and had a good knowledge of the Bible. His church spread to other West African countries from the late 1940s. He died at Ogere in 1966, and was succeeded by Adeleke Adejobi, his best-known follower, who had joined the church in 1939.

Further reading

Turner, H. W. (1967) *History of an African Independent Church: The Church of the Lord (Aladura)* (2 vols), Oxford: Clarendon Press.

MATTHEWS A. OJO

OUSPENSKY, PIOTR DEMIANOVICH
(b. 1878; d. 1947)

Piotr Demianovich Ouspensky – Russian philosopher, journalist, ardent esotericist, and incontestably G. I. Gurdjieff's most famous pupil (see **Gurdjieff, George Ivanovitch**) – was born into an artistic and intellectual Moscow family on 5 March 1878 Old Style. His father died when Ouspensky was young, bequeathing him an interest in the 'Fourth dimension'. Naturally rebellious, Ouspensky's formal education ended with his expulsion, aged 15, from the Second Moscow Gymnasium: he resolved to spurn examinations and degrees; gradually assumed a scholar-gypsy role; and ended an impressive autodidact.

Ouspensky wrote altogether ten broadly mystical books. His first and only fictional piece, *The Wheel of Fortune*, was drafted in 1905. In quasi-filmic scenarios depicting 'Ivan Osokin' it exhibits Ouspensky's deepest and life-long preoccupation – Eternal Recurrence: 'if a man was born in 1877 and died in 1912, then, having died, he finds himself again in 1877 and must live the same life all over again'. This theory explained the déjà vu he had felt from childhood, yet (because the same blunders were inescapable) the redemptive inutility of déjà vu. Ouspensky would spend colossal energy in meditating this paradigm, in correlating it with the Fourth dimension, and in seeking escape from the trap.

In 1907 Ouspensky contacted the Theosophical Society (see **Theosophy**) and its literature – all the more enticing because prohibited in Russia. In 1908 he was in Constantinople, Smyrna, Greece, and Egypt. Early in 1909 he returned to St Peterburg where he plunged recklessly into a study of occult, Yogic (see **Yoga**), and magical methods and gave public lectures on the Tarot, Superman, Yogis, etc. In 1912 he unexpectedly sprang to fame through *Tertium Organum* a thesis of daunting opacity which, invoking the Fourth dimension, challenged constraints on consciousness implicit in Aristotle's Organon and Bacon's *Novum Organum*. In 1913 and 1914 he was in Egypt, Ceylon, and India; the war found him in Colombo, from where he returned home through London. Huge audiences at his lectures in the Petrograd Duma included the Junoesque widow Sophia Grigorievna Maximenko who became his common-law wife.

In April 1915, following a pivotal meeting in Moscow, Gurdjieff (49) and Ouspensky (37) became respectively teacher and pupil. With unique acuity Ouspensky quickly mastered Gurdjieff's cosmological and psychological ideas. His radical exposure to The Work's praxis (see **Work, The**) came in mid-July 1917 during Gurdjieff's six-week 'intensive' at Essentuki in the Caucasus. By May 1918, however, Ouspensky had reacted against a perceived religious orientation in Gurdjieff and temporarily separated from him. In summer 1920 Ouspensky and Gurdjieff renewed amities in Constantinople attending Mevlevi dervish ceremonies and working together on the scenario of Gurdjieff's ballet *The Struggle of the Magicians*.

Despite various haphazard attempts at rapprochement, Ouspensky progressively crystallized his resolve to differentiate 'The System' from Gurdjieff the man. In January 1924 – now promisingly established in London – he forbade his pupils even to mention Gurdjieff's name and effectively presented himself as The Work's protagonist and leader. He nevertheless completed, by 1925, the first draft of *Fragments*, his lucid and vivid account of his three-year tutelage under Gurdjieff.

Altogether Ouspensky lived 20 years in England propagating and financially dependent on Gurdjieff's ideas. Missing personal liaison with Gurdjieff himself, he vainly sought contact with 'School' or 'Higher Source' (supposedly in Asia or on the supernal plane). His disappointment was offset by alcohol, by the enthusiastic reception given *A New Model of the Universe* (1931), and by his crowded weekly meetings at 38 Warwick Gardens, Kensington. In 1935 he bought Lyne Place, an imposing Regency House at Virginia Water; and in 1938 formed the Historico-Psychological Society, which promptly added the elegant Colet House at 46 Colet Gardens, Kensington. Enjoying the allegiance of 1,000 pupils, Ouspensky at 60 seemed magisterially established: however, following an erroneous political analysis, he left war-time England in January 1941 for America, where his ensuing six years, centred on Franklin Farms, Mendham, New Jersey, saw a poignant decay in his hopes, health, and integrity.

Returning to England in January 1947, Ouspensky held six momentous meetings at Colet Gardens in which he disavowed The System. After assigning his last reserves to visiting locales he would need to recognize 'next time', Ouspensky died from kidney failure at Lyne place on 2 October 1947. Despite his gravitas and literary exertions, his final reputation seems inextricably bound up with Gurdjieff's.

Further reading

Ouspensky, P. D. (1950) *In Search of the Miraculous: Fragments of an Unknown Teaching*, London: Routledge & Kegan Paul.

Webb, J. (1980) *The Harmonious Circle: The Lives and Work of G. I. Gurdjieff, P. D. Ouspensky, and Their Followers*, London: Thames and Hudson.

JAMES MOORE

P

PAGAN FEDERATION

Founder: multiple

Country of Origin: Great Britain

The first representative body for Pagans (see **Neo-Paganism**), the Pagan Federation was founded in 1989 on the basis of an older organization, the Pagan Front. This earlier organization had been established by John Score in September 1970. It developed from a small-circulation inter-coven newsletter called *The Wiccan*, which had first been published in 1968 with the aim of fostering communication between Wiccan covens (see **Wicca**) and had an initial print run of just twelve. The Pagan Front aimed to bring together people from different Pagan religions, to provide information on Paganism to the general public, and to counter misconceptions about Pagan religions. Its inaugural meeting was held in London on 1 May 1971, and was chaired by founder member Doreen Valiente (see **Valiente, Doreen**).

During the 1970s and 1980s, subscriptions to *The Wiccan* varied from fifty to 100, but 1988 saw a new trend, with the October printing more than doubling from that of May, to 240. From that point on, numbers have continually increased. By 1989, the Pagan Front had 250 members, and was renamed the Pagan Federation, with the aims of promoting contact between Pagan groups, providing information for seekers, providing practical and effective information on Paganism to members of the public, the media, teachers, etc., and working for the rights of Pagans to worship freely and without censure according to Article 18 of the Universal Declaration of Human Rights.

Three principles were formulated to which Pagans are supposed to adhere. The first principle is 'Love for and kinship with nature: reverence for the life force and its ever-renewing cycles of life and death'. The second is the Wiccan Rede, renamed the Pagan Ethic: 'An it harm none, do what thou wilt'. The third is 'Honouring the totality of Divine Reality, which transcends gender, without suppressing either the female or male aspect of Deity' (*Pagan Dawn* issue 126, Imbolc 1998, page 14).

Even after promoting Paganism for almost twenty years, however, the newly constituted Federation still saw itself as a mouthpiece for Wicca in the UK, offering a referral service between covens and those seeking initiation into Wicca, and providing a forum for dialogue between Wiccans of different traditions. It was not until the mid-1990s that the Pagan Federation officially recognized the wider boundaries of the constituency which it represented. In 1994, the Pagan Federation's role had to be reformulated to take account of the diversity within Paganism, most notably through the renaming of its journal, which changed from *The Wiccan* to *Pagan Dawn* in Issue 113, Samhain (31 October). It was felt that the former name gave the misleading impression that the Pagan Federation was a purely Wiccan organization, and *Pagan Dawn* was selected by the Pagan Federation committee from suggestions sent in by readers. However, discussions still continue as to the nature of the three principles, particularly the second which was instituted in the early 1970s, when Wicca and Paganism were more or less synonymous because non-Wiccan forms of Paganism (apart from **Druidry**) were still emerging. With the increasing diversity within Paganism, and since the Pagan Federation can no longer be considered a Wiccan organization, using what is considered by many Pagans to be a 'Wiccan commandment' seemed inappropriate.

In 1997, the Pagan Federation International (PFI) was set up, initially as a pen-pal service and swiftly becoming a cyber-network. Its aims are to foster networking and to counter defamation through media campaigns, and it is regarded as a lifeline by Pagans, particularly in countries where fellow Pagans are few and spread over a wide geographical area. Originally European in focus, the PFI is now truly international, run by local national co-ordinators who work on a voluntary basis. By 2003, such local co-ordinators were established in Australia/New Zealand, Austria, Belgium, Brazil, Canada, France, Germany, Scandinavia (including Finland), Portugal, The Netherlands, and the USA. There is also a category of 'The World', which represents smaller numbers of Pagans in, for example, South Africa, Japan, Hong Kong, Greece, Spain, and Bulgaria.

The membership of the Pagan Federation numbered around 6,000 in 2003, plus approximately a further 350 members of the Pagan Federation International. *Pagan Dawn* is published quarterly, and in addition many Pagan Federation Regions publish their own newsletters containing contacts, events, and articles. Regions have their own conferences, and there is an annual Pagan Federation conference in London. Other events, either regional or national, are sometimes open to the public, though some remain open to members only.

Further reading

Pengelly, J., Hall, R. and Dowse, J. (1997) *We Emerge: The History of the Pagan Federation*, London: The Pagan Federation.
www.paganfederation.org

JO PEARSON

PALIAU MOVEMENT – MELANESIA

Though the islands of Melanesia possess an extraordinary diversity of cultures and languages (Papua New Guinea alone has more than over 750 languages and 2,000 'tribes'), a series of remarkably similar movements – usually dubbed 'Cargo cults' – have occurred across the region (though not everywhere) from the late nineteenth century onwards (see **Melanesia – millenarian ('Cargo') movements**). They were syncretic movements which, despite this multiplicity of societies and cultures, drew upon certain themes which were widespread in many pre-colonial belief-systems of the region, notably the belief in a lost 'Golden Age', which would, however, be re-established when the dead ancestors returned – which was likely to be soon. At first, the ancestors were expected to return by canoe; then by ship; then in aeroplanes. (Reports of space rockets have even circulated in recent times.)

These traditional millenarian ideas were reinforced with the arrival of dozens of proselytizing Christian missions, from the large and more socially conservative Lutheran and Catholic congregations to smaller and often fundamentalist sects. Between them, they came to control not only most of formal education (usually little more than catechism, anyhow) but also much of village social life, down to enforced conformity in details of dress and everyday personal behaviour.

The fusion of these two sets of millenarian beliefs – the one indigenous, the other imported – now gave rise to a new doctrines which looked to the end of the world and the end of death, illness, and hard work.

The material goods which the White man monopolized – without doing any hard work – would now accrue to the natives. Even Nature would be transformed: mountains would become valleys, and vice versa.

Such ideas – labelled 'madness' by the colonialists – seemed perfectly possible to the people of the Admiralty Islands in the north of New Guinea at least, when, after experiencing massive and brutal invasion by a new and hitherto unknown people – the Japanese – another wave of unknown foreigners, this time a million US troops – many of them Black – arrived in Manus, in the north of New Guinea, inhabited by a few tens of thousands, late in World War Two.

A remarkable leader – Paliau Maloat – who had served in the colonial police force and been awarded the British OBE, and had then held office under the Japanese occupation – now organized a movement opposed to the colonial Government and, later, to the new government of independent Papua New Guinea – which was labelled as 'Lucifer' (much as Rastafarians (see **Rastafarian Movement**) call the secular governments they live under 'Babylon'). All its works, including its development, education and health systems, were denounced.

Paliau had been arrested twice by the colonial government, and had used every available resource, from participation in local and regional government to lobbying UN Visiting Missions, to fight back.

At Independence, in 1975, Paliau had at first been an active member of Pangu, the first political party, and a Member of the House of Assembly. But he soon became an intransigent opponent of a new governing elite, which was spending three-quarters of the national budget on a wildly over-developed machinery of government and administration, and was (and still is) dependent on 'aid' and military support provided by Australia. Now, he opposed the new elite not only politically, by forbidding his followers to participate in elections at all levels, but by setting up new counter-cultural institutions, based on indigenous values: local production for use instead of commodity production for cash; new versions of abandoned social institutions such as men's houses; and indigenous medical practices, such as midwifery, in lieu of Western medicine.

Similar movements, with sizeable regional followings, led by other remarkable 'prophets' such as Yali, on the Rai Coast of northern New Guinea, emerged in other parts of Melanesia.

The base of the movement (renamed Makasol, or 'Wind Nation'), was Paliau's home area, Manus. Government now tried to replace the structure of local government institutions on Manus, which were under the control of Makasol, with new, rejigged institutions. Makasol members then withdrew their cooperation from the State at all levels, including withdrawing their savings from the state-sponsored national bank and transferring them to a new bank of their own.

These political and economic policies, however, were only part of an overarching and complex ideology, invented and constantly changed, by Paliau himself, centring round a new kind of Holy Trinity – three beings named Wing, Wang and Wong – and enforced by twenty young 'teachers', and by obligatory attendance at interminable 'study groups', at which only Paliau was allowed to speak, and by study of audio cassettes of Paliau's rhetoric, which used (in 'pidgin'– Neo-Melanesian) *tink tink* (feeling, understanding) in place of the White man's rationality (*save*). The older 'cargo' idea of a coming epoch of plenty, though not abandoned, gave way to a new ethic of *hatwok* (hard work) modelled on agricultural labour in village gardens, which was to replace both *malolo* – the idle life of rest and leisure practised by the White man (and the new national elite) – and the cash-crop-based community development programmes of the Government.

Paliau, now designated 'the Last Prophet of the World', even announced his own crucifixion (which was postponed). He died in 1991. An extraordinary *bricolage* of ideas borrowed from dimly-understood world events (Paliau himself did not speak English and was illiterate), such as news of the Cultural Revolution in China, war in the Holy Land, or a visit to New Guinea by Prince Charles, was constantly added to, and altered, by Paliau. Followers were expected, and made, to follow these ideological twists and turns.

All this has to be seen against the background of the virtual absence, at village level, where most national communications are rudimentary, to say the least, of information about the world outside, with the major exception of a (variable) 'Christian view of reality' preached by the missions, mainly by word of mouth or, occasionally, by radio, plus some government-controlled radio and a few newspapers which, if they reach the villages, are used to roll tobacco. TV and videos are unknown; and the more widely-used audio cassettes are mainly mission-produced religious material or Australian pop music.

Some villages have been virtual totalitarian regimes; others, where mission control has weakened, have become more pluralistic, as ambitious young New Guineans, often better-educated, have either become leaders in older, more orthodox missions, or have established new sects to compete with the older, usually White-controlled denominations.

A new and serious challenge has come from gangs of criminal 'rascals' in the towns, and, intellectually, from the more educated 'Angry Young Men', whose world-view is not necessarily religious at all. Some have even gone back to the villages, where they challenge established orthodoxies of all kinds, even cults like Paliau's.

Further reading

Wanek, A. (1996) *Fighting Lucifer. The State and its Enemies in Papua New Guinea*,

NIAS Monographs in Asian Studies, RoutledgeCurzon.

PETER WORSLEY

PEACE AND JAPANESE NEW RELIGIOUS MOVEMENTS

In the postwar period many new religious movements in Japan have specifically identified themselves as pacifist, and have adopted activity aimed at the establishment of world peace as one of their primary goals. Entries contained in the *Shinshukyo Jiten* (New Religions Dictionary), for example, make explicit reference to such activities in over forty cases.

Various explanations can be offered to account for this widespread interest in peace. Certainly the experience of World War Two itself is a major contributing factor in the concern for peace seen broadly in Japanese society and reflected in many religious groups. The public expression of dedication to peace can also help to enhance their image in Japanese society, a matter of no small concern. Within the doctrine and self-understanding of these groups, however, peace is seen as a natural concern of religion, and work towards its establishment is accepted as a truly religious social concern.

The activities to promote world peace undertaken by these groups are varied. **Byakko Shinkokai**, for example, promotes the Prayer for World Peace – whose opening words, 'May peace prevail on earth,' can be found on stickers and poles across Japan and in many unexpected places throughout the world – as its primary peace activity. Meanwhile, the monks and nuns of **Nipponzan Myohoji** engage in nonviolent direct action, protesting against United States military bases in Japan and staging hunger strikes for peace.

Soka Gakkai, on the other hand, has published numerous volumes of recollections of World War Two, as part of their campaign to educate the postwar generations on the reality of war. **Rissho Kosei-kai** and Shoroku Shinto Yamatoyama have been active in interreligious efforts at promoting peace, such as the World Conference on Religion and Peace, which has held a major interreligious conference every four or five years since the initial conference in Kyoto in 1970.

Postwar Japan is generally assumed to have adopted pacifism as its national policy, and many religious groups see themselves as the defender of this position against those at home and abroad who would have the country rearm in order to play a more active role in international politics. One needs to question, however, just what is meant by pacifism here. Often pacifist rhetoric is used without a clear understanding of its implications, leading to contradictions in Japanese society as well as in these groups.

An analysis of the meanings attached to the peace activities of these groups also leads to questions of how these are tied up with Japanese cultural identity. There is an emphasis on individual moral cultivation in Japanese society reflected in the doctrine of many new religious groups (see **New Religion, Japan**), and such cultivation is often seen as the primary means to the establishment of world peace. In addition, work towards world peace is sometimes identified as a unique national or ethnic mission of Japan, with its postwar pacifist ideal.

Pacifism and its limits

Pacifism is a position adopted on the basis of an absolute moral decision. It allows for no compromise with the principle that human life is not to be taken under any circumstances. Within the Christian tradition, pacifism was replaced as the mainstream position early in the fourth century by the just war theory. This position is based on the premise that the proscription against the taking of life is not absolute; that there are other values in competition with the preservation of life whose preservation can on certain occasions require the sacrifice of life.

Heiwashugi, the Japanese term, is translated as pacifism, but in its popular usage it often refers to a presumption against the employment of force, rather than its absolute rejection. The pacifist ideal is enshrined in Article 9 of the Japanese constitution, which renounces war and the threat or use of force as a means of settling international disputes. However, this is not normally interpreted to be an absolute rejection of force, and military spending on 'Self-Defense Forces' is among the highest in the world.

It can be argued that strict pacifism can be maintained only by those who have in some way removed themselves from society and thus do not have to contend with issues of national defense. Nipponzan Myohoji, for example, a monastic order, can be described as pacifist, as can Byakko Shinko Kai with its thoroughgoing spiritism. One needs to question, however, if Soka Gakkai is strictly pacifist as it has increasingly become a mainstream group.

Peace and cultural identity

In line with the common worldview of many Japanese new religions, the establishment of world peace is often described as dependent on the internal change of heart of each individual human being. Although international agreements, confidence building activities, economic development, and social structural changes might all contribute to building a world at peace, unless people themselves change, it is argued, these will all ultimately fail. This idea is perhaps most clearly present in Shuyodan Hoseikai. Shuyodan is a subcategory of Japanese new religions, and it literally means Association for the Cultivation of Morals. In the postwar period Hoseikai explicitly made the establishment of world peace its primary goal, a goal that is to be achieved specifically through the individual moral cultivation of the members of the group.

Echoing Japanese popular culture, the establishment of world peace has also been promoted by many of these religious groups as the unique mission of Japan in the postwar era. Occasionally this is tied to a notion of cultural superiority, that it is specifically Japanese culture, with its postwar pacifist ideal, that will bring about world peace. In some of the new religions, Nipponzan Myohoji for example, this is described as a clash between religious or spiritual civilization and material civilization, the latter identified with the West, or more specifically the United States.

Further reading

Kisala, R. (1999) *Prophets of Peace: Pacifism and Cultural Identity in Japan's New Religions*, Honolulu: University of Hawaii Press.

ROBERT KISALA

PEACE MISSION

Father Divine's Peace Mission is one of the most studied groups in the African American religious experience. Although recent evidence strongly suggests that Father Divine or George Baker was born in Rockville, Maryland, and reared in the Methodist tradition, he moved to

Baltimore in 1899 where he worked as a gardener and jack-leg preacher. He met Samuel Morris, who referred to himself as Father Jehovia, and St John the Divine Hickerson in 1906. Baker viewed himself as a harbinger of Morris and referred to himself as 'the Messenger.' Whereas Morris was the incarnation of God the Father, Baker was the incarnation of God the Son. Baker's exposure to various religious traditions prompted him to develop a new syncretic religion that incorporated elements of **New Thought**, messianic-nationalism, and the Holiness-Pentecostal movement.

Following a preaching tour of the South, Baker established a congregation in Brooklyn where he began to conduct his famous communion banquets. He and his first wife (Pinninnah) lived communally in a house with his followers, operated a job-placement service for them, and administered their earnings. In 1919, Baker and Pinninnah became the first black residents of Sayville, Long Island, and established a congregation and commune there. He signed the deed of sale with the name 'Major J. Devine' and began to refer to himself as Father Divine in 1930. Divine drew busloads of followers to his services, much to the annoyance of local residents. The police raided his services on 15 November 1931, and arrested him and some eighty members. Judge Lewis J. Smith found Father Divine guilty but died of a sudden heart attack after having pronounced sentence. Divine served 33 days in jail before an appellate court reversed the decision. Nevertheless, he moved the headquarters of the sect to Harlem.

Father Divine evangelized up and down the East Coast and established residences, hotels, grocery stores, barber shops, restaurants, and a coal operation. His sect became incorporated as the Peace Mission in 1941, and he moved his headquarters to Philadelphia in 1942. Father Divine's movement emerged largely as a response to the hardships of African Americans during the Great Depression. He was an outspoken critic of racism and a staunch supporter of Franklin D. Roosevelt. Father Divine was committed to a wide range of social reform programs. He regarded his movement as a practical program that would provide his followers with health, food, clothing, shelter, and employment. In addition to establishing schools for both children and adults, Divine urged his followers to register and vote. He supported the Harlem Political Union and in 1936 helped to form the All People's party, a coalition of eighty-nine Harlem-based organizations that endorsed a small slate of radical candidates, including white Communist Vito Marcantonio and black Communist and labor organizer Angelo Herndon. The Peace Mission cooperated with the Communist party in Harlem between 1934 and 1936 because Divine viewed it as much more progressive on racial issues than both the Democrats and Republicans.

Despite his sponsorship of cooperative ventures and flirtation with the Communist party, Father Divine was a reformer committed to working within the framework of the capitalist system. He staunchly advocated the Protestant work ethic, self-support, savings, investments, and the sanctity of private property. The Peace Mission stressed salvation through profound change in oneself. Members were also expected to abide by a strict code of conduct prohibiting alcoholic beverages, smoking, social dancing, gambling, theatergoing, and most notably, all forms of sex. Father Divine claimed that he maintained a life of total celibacy during his two marriages.

The Peace Mission attracted many white people, some of whom assumed positions of leadership in the sect. Indeed, Divine's second wife was white. In reality, the Peace Mission consisted of three movements in one:

1. an African–American Eastern section, composed largely, but not exclusively of poor blacks;
2. a Western section, based primarily in California, that catered to a predominantly white membership (many of whom were middle class); and
3. a foreign section that appealed especially to urban working-class people in Canada, Australia, and Western Europe.

Women constituted between 75 and 90 per cent of the membership. Since the death of Father Divine, the remnants of the group have been under the guidance of Mother Divine. The Peace Mission still conducts communion banquets, services, and anniversary celebrations, and even operates some businesses, but has adopted a much more introversionist stance.

Further reading

Watts, J. (1994) *God, Harlem, USA: The Father Divine Story,* Berkeley: University of California Press.
Weisbrot, R. (1983) *Father Divine and the Struggle for Racial Equality,* Urbana: University of Illinois Press.

HANS A. BAER

PEOPLES TEMPLE

A self-proclaimed prophet from Indiana, James Warren Jones (1931–78), who experienced considerable economic deprivation as a child, founded this movement. Jones though attracted to Communism also found the emotional style of worship and preaching of the Pentecostalists appealing. He began as a preacher at the age of twenty. His speeches and sermons contained ideas from liberal Methodist social thought, Communism and Pentecostal **millenarianism**. His aim was to promote socialism and racial integration within a religious framework constructed of Methodism and Pentecostalism. He was particularly attracted to such ideas as faith healing, speaking in tongues and the gifts of the spirit generally. He was soon accused of being a charlatan for claiming to have cured the sick without proof or evidence.

He founded his first church called the Community Unity in Indianapolis in the early 1950s and used it as a platform to preach racial integration and the social gospel. He and his followers led by example. They established a nursing home for the elderly and adopted children orphaned by the Korean War and African-American children. He also made contact with such Black Messiahs as Fr Divine whose methods of evangelization and recruitment he was to imitate (see **Black Jewish Movements** and **Black Muslim Movements**).

Jones' opposition to segregationist policies led to strong opposition in Indianapolis and in the early 1960s he went to live for a short period in former British Guyana – later to be called the Promised Land – and then for two years in Brazil. In 1965 full of hostility to what he saw as the racism of Indianapolis and loudly proclaiming the imminent arrival of Armageddon Jones decided to emigrate and moved to northern California with about seventy families, half of them black and the other half white. The Peoples Temple as his church had become known was organized hierarchically with Jones, now known as Reverend or Dad, occupying the top tier. His socialist gospel slowly took hold. People of white and black working and middle class background joined him and engaged in social activities in care homes for the elderly and juvenile delinquents from which the Temple reaped considerable profit without having to pay taxes. Other sources of income in addition to members' donations included those derived from the Temple's radio ministry and profits from real estate investments.

Branches of the Temple were established in San Francisco and Los Angeles and by the early 1970s Jones was ministering and preaching to thousands.

Jones, a volatile charismatic leader, while maintaining his socialist ideology increasingly turned to the use of miracles and other spiritual means to sustain and enhance his power and authority. He also used spiritual techniques such as 'discernment' to gain information about members he suspected of being difficult and used it to silence criticism and maintain control. In time the Temple became a total institution, the leadership under Jones using monitoring, catharsis sessions, physical punishment and emotional abuse and humiliation to consolidate its power over the membership (see **New Religions and Violence**).

During the summer of 1977 Jones migrated with over one thousand members to the Promised Land of Guyana and the location he choose to settle his Peoples Temple became known as Jonestown. This followed the defection of a handful of 'apostates' from among the inner core of the leadership in 1975 and 1976. What possibly worried Jones more than anything else and strengthened his resolve to 'emigrate' was the decision of the 'apostates' to air their grievances in public and this at a time when the **Anti-Cult Movement** lobby who insisted recruits to New Religions had been brainwashed (see **Brainwashing**) was growing in influence in the United States. In early 1977 the United States Treasury department had promised the 'apostates' that the leadership of the Peoples Temple would be investigated. Beginning in July 1977 a whole series of negative newspaper articles about the Peoples Temple began to appear accusing it of brainwashing and financial irregularities among other things. Financial difficulties were also looming for earlier in March 1977 the Inland Revenue Service had turned down the Peoples Temple's request for tax-exemption status.

All of this motivated Jones to increase the apocalyptic content of his teachings and to elaborate the concept of 'revolutionary suicide' which Jones had borrowed from the Black Panther leader Huey Newton.

In 1978 opposition to Jones from several quarters included the association known as the Concerned Relatives increased and this led to the fatal journey by Senator Ryan to the Peoples Temple in Guyana, ostensibly on a fact finding mission but also to try to obtain the release from Jonestown of a member of the community whom the latter's father and the Concerned Relatives claimed was being held there against his will. While at Jonestown a number of the members contacted Ryan and his entourage several of whom belonged to the Concerned Relatives association and asked for his help to escape.

Ryan's visit to Jonestown ended in tragedy. Just before departure Ryan there had been an altercation with a would-be assailant who attempted to stab Ryan. This was followed by an airstrip attack on Ryan that left him and four others of his entourage dead and ten wounded. Rather than wait for the community to be dismantled by his opponents Jones ordered his followers to dismantle it themselves and had distributed drums of Fla-Vor acid adulterated with cyanide and tranquilizers. In all some 913 people died—whether willingly or not is something that will never be known—in this act of mass suicide. This act of violence in particular (see **New Religions and Violence**) did more than anything else to strengthen the cause of the Anti-Cult-Movement.

Further reading

Hall, John R. (1987) *Gone from the Promised Land: Jonestown in American Cultural History*, New Brunswick, NJ: Transactional Books.

PETER B. CLARKE

PERFECT LIBERTY KYODAN
Founders: Tokuharu Miki (b. 1871; d. 1938) and Tokuchika Miki (b. 1900; d. 1983)

The Japanese New Religion (Shinshukyo) (see **New Religion (Japan)**) Perfect Liberty Kyodan derives from **Honmichi**. There are two founders, the first being Tokuharu Miki (1871–1938) who is regarded as the first founder or Oshieoya of this movement, and the second his son Tokuchika Miki (1900–83). The former was once a Zen Buddhist priest who in 1912 was allegedly cured of asthma by the rite of *ofurikae* (power of temporarily curing illness) which was administered to him by the Reverend Tokumitsu Kanada. Tokuchika Miki had been imprisoned for his refusal to obey government orders issued in 1937 to disband the movement on account of some of its beliefs including the belief that the spirit of the deity and that of human beings was the same spirit and for regarding the Imperial Rescript on Education of 1892 as a sacred text. He re-established the religion after his release from prison in 1946.

Perfect Liberty Kyodan teaches that 'Life is Art' in the sense that the former like the latter must be balanced, harmonious, and expressive. The movement's mission is to teach others the correct mental attitude necessary for living life according to the rules of the Universe.

There exists, Perfect Liberty is persuaded, a fundamental unity between the individual and the world or society and the bringing together in harmony of individual and social freedom is the basis for a truly fulfilling life. By coming to understand its teachings and by applying them to one's life it is possible, Perfect Liberty maintains, to reach a state where living becomes a continuous form of conscious self-expression accompanied by total mental freedom.

The sacred scripture of Perfect Liberty Kyodan consists of the Twenty-one Precepts, which were received from 'God' by the founder and his successor. They provide guidelines on how to lead a fulfilling life. Twenty-one Principles lend support to these Precepts in this aim. It is claimed that by following the Precepts and the Principles one's life will eventually be transformed into a series of self-expressions that will eventually resemble a masterpiece of art. The achievement of turning life into a work of art is known as *makoto* or sincerity and those who have arrived at this stage of development are said to be living in Perfect Liberty.

Illness and misfortune are seen as forms of divine warning or *mishirase* to a person that he/she is in need of divine instruction or *mioshie*. This instruction consists of an explanation of the cause of illness and misfortune, which attributes them to negative or inappropriate states of mind and ways of thinking. Through *mioshie* a person learns to transform a negative into a positive state of mind.

Practices consist of the recitation of daily prayers which include the *Oyashikiri* (literally strong faith (shikiri) in the parent (oya) prayer). This prayer is recited in front of the prayer symbol (*omitama*) consisting of twenty-one petals which symbolize the Twenty-one Precepts and at the centre of which is a circle that represents the window to Mioya Ōkami (God, Creator of the Universe).

In addition to prayers there are ceremonies including the Thanksgiving Day Service on the twenty-first day of each month. The purpose of this occasion is to express gratitude and appreciation to the leader known as the Oshieoyasama, for his personal sacrifice on behalf of the members. The leader (Oshieoyasama), it is believed, takes on as form of expiation to God for wrongs that have been committed all the misfortunes of his followers. There are also Day of Peace and Ancestors' Day ceremonies on the first and eleventh day of each month respectively.

The principal annual ceremonies are Founders' Day festival which takes place on 1 August each year, PL Establishment Day on 29 September, the leader's birthday on 2 December. On the occasion of Founders' Day all the participants receive purification by means of the ritual known as the Rite of Blessing. A fire service is also held at this event as a symbol of hope for world peace.

Perfect Liberty places great emphasis on the rearing and education of children who are seen as a mirror of their parents. Education in Perfect Liberty values begins for the children of adepts with Kindergarten. The movement has a number of schools and colleges in Japan where there are an estimated 300,000 members. Its headquarters are at Tondabyashi near Osaka. There are also branches of the movement overseas in North and South America and Europe. The largest of the overseas branches is in Brazil where the membership stands at around 70,000.

Further reading

Clarke, P. B. (ed.) (1999) *An Annotated Bibliography of Japanese New Religions*, Eastbourne, Kent: Japan Library, pp. 194–200.

PETER B. CLARKE

PEYOTE CULT

The term 'Peyote Cult' was first coined early in the twentieth century to describe the use of peyote amongst the Winnebago, and later applied to peyote use among other tribes and the Native American Church (NAC). The word 'peyote' is a variation of 'peyotl', the Nahuatl (Aztec) term for the cactus lophophora williamsii, native to Mexico. It contains many alkaloids, but the main psychoactive ingredient is mescaline. Another psychotropic cactus is San Pedro (trichocereus pachanoi), which grows in the mountains of Peru. Other psychotropic plants are found in the Amazon rainforest, of which the best known in the West is ayahuasca or yagé. Peyote and other plants are important ingredients in native ceremonies throughout the Americas, as well as within contemporary **Shamanism**.

The Native American Church (NAC) (see **Native American religion**) began using peyote ritually in the early twentieth century, although archaeologists have discovered that the ritual use of peyote and San Pedro in Mexico and Peru goes back thousands of years. The first Europeans to encounter and describe the peyote ceremonies were Spanish missionaries in sixteenth-century Mexico. From the outset, the response was uniformly hostile; it was seen as the 'devil's tricks', giving rise to 'diabolical visions and evil heresies', and users were persecuted by the Holy Inquisition for nearly two centuries. This negative view is still prevalent amongst local government, the police, religious leaders, and even some Native Americans. The use of mescaline-containing plants is illegal, except for registered members of the NAC in the United States and certain tribes in Mexico. In Europe, plants containing mescaline are illegal for everyone. The NAC obtained legal recognition of their ceremonial use of the plant in the USA in the 1978 Act of Religious Freedom.

Two main themes are common to rituals using psychotropic plants. First, powerful visions are associated with mescaline, illustrated in native art such as the celebrated wool yarn pictures of the Mexican Huichol Indians. These often depict the spirits of the cactus and power animals, especially eagles, deer, and jaguars, as well as numerous tribal and ancestral spirits. One well known spirit is Mescalito, a mischievous, imp-like apparition seen as the soul of peyote. Native shamans or *curanderos* (medicine men) claim to be able to prophesy or contact spirits for information under the influence of mescaline. The other major use is for healing, and a wide range of curative powers are claimed for these plants, provided they are used sacramentally under the guidance of a healer. These powers account for the appeal of psychotropic plants within Western spirituality, where their use is seen as a fast track to spiritual experience and knowledge.

Traditional ceremonies have strong regional variations. The NAC typically starts with a purification process such as a sweat lodge, after which a circle is formed, perhaps inside a tepee. A medicine man (or woman) presides, assisted by a 'keeper of the fire' and other helpers. The carefully-tended fire is in the centre of the circle, and participants sit straight-backed, looking into it. Dried peyote is passed around on a tray, dosage being normally the choice of the individual. Another important part of the ceremony is the passing round of the sacred tobacco pipe. Participants may only speak if holding the pipe, or sometimes a 'talking stick'. The ceremony is very orderly, continuing for over twelve hours, during which participants are requested not to leave the circle. Mexican and South American Indian ceremonies are usually much less formal, as noted by even the earliest seventeenth-century commentators. The medicine man is often a musician, accompanied by other musicians. After the peyote is passed around, the circle group dances all night. Again, strong tobacco is an important feature. Ayahuasca ceremonies are generally more austere with little ritual. After ingesting ayahuasca, participants lie down in the dark and let the plants do the work. The ayahuasquero functions mainly as a medicine man, working also with healing songs called *icaros*.

In modern times, the main central American tribes maintaining the tradition are the Cora, Huichols and Tarahumara, whose ceremonies are still mainly unchanged. In Peru, while many curanderos conduct traditional ceremonies, others have been influenced by Christianity. There are various 'churches' in Brazil combining ayahuasca with Christian ritual. The two best known are **Santo Daime** and the Uniao do Vegetal, which have branches worldwide. As with tribal use but unlike secular and New Age groups, these churches emphasize communal worship more than individual spiritual experience.

Further reading

Schultes, R. E. and Hoffman, A. (1992) *Plants of the Gods, Their Sacred Healing and Hallucinogenic Powers*, Rochester, VT: Healing Arts Press.

ELIZABETH PUTTICK

PRINERMS

(New religious movements in primal societies)

The term PRINERMS was first used in Harold W. Turner's research project (see **Turner, Harold W.**). It designates, in the first place, a historical phenomenon: after Columbus' voyage to America and similar voyages of discovery, there was a long period of missionary activity from Europe to the other continents. In the nineteenth century, this activity was developed even more intensely by Catholics and Protestants. As a result there has been a significant growth in the numbers and influence of Christianity in the southern hemisphere. But a more perplexing result for those engaged in Christian mission is the proliferation of religious movements that represent reactions, from within the resources of tribal cultures, to the preaching of the gospel, to the availability of the Bible and to examples of Christian life.

There is a great variety of movements within this category but it has usefully defined a field of inter-disciplinary research involving many studies from the points of view of history, sociology, and theology. The common features in the category derive from a similar origin. When Christian teaching comes into contact with primal religion, whether in dialogue or in controversy, it is not the same as contact between world faiths. Primal religion generally is not missionary. It is for a particular ethnic group or for the people of a particular locality. It seems that many founders of religious movements of this kind have, in varying degrees, overcome this limitation: they have been struck by the universality of biblical teaching with its wider horizons and have been open to accepting all or part of the new vision but have been unwilling to admit that there was no wisdom at all in the religious traditions of their own culture. With hindsight, today, many Christian scholars and missionaries would now recognize that this attitude, very often throughout these centuries but with some honourable exceptions, was trea-ted without sensitivity: so, in consequence, they now recognize the study of PRINERMs as a source of practical wisdom providing lessons on how the gospel can be related to various cultures.

This large group of religious movements, as a historical phenomenon, is quite different from that other phenomenon, the appearance of religious movements in Europe and North America in the second half of the twentieth century (by many loosely characterized as 'sects and cults') (see **New Religious Movement**), although there has been some limited interaction between these two groups of movements.

Some PRINERMs can be recognized as new Christian churches: for instance, **Kimbanguism** and other African initiated churches have been received, after negotiations, into the World Council of Churches. There are also movements, like Jamaa, which have remained within the denominations. On the other hand, there are some that have taken up elements of Christian teaching or practices in conscious opposition to the Christian presence in primal culture (e.g **Godianism** and **Dini ya Musambwa**). Turner calls these 'neo-primal'.

Between these two extremes, there are movements which may be termed 'syncretist' in the sense that they combine elements from different sources. For example, in central Africa, Kitawala ('Watchtower') is an offshoot of the Jehovah's Witnesses, but combines their teaching with indigenous mythology, certainly not derived from the Witnesses. Turner, in his typology, suggests a further sub-division: 'Hebraist', where we can recognize the influence of Old Testament teaching that God is not aloof from daily life but works through prophetic figures. This would include, for example, Mgijima's Israelites in South Africa, the Bayudaya (People of Judah) in Uganda and perhaps also

AmaNazaretha. From the point of view of Christian theology, this suggests appreciation of the mission of the Spirit, influencing the life of the community through prophetic figures, but not that of the Word or Logos.

Many Christian missionaries and scholars have tried to find meaning in this proliferation of movements. They have noted that often Christianity has been associated with domination and imperialism. This is often an important factor. But perhaps it is more significant that missionaries often have criticized the culture of those they are evangelizing without adverting to the faults of the western culture they have brought with them. More recently and more positively, it is increasingly accepted in mission studies that faith must find expression in different cultural environments and, consequently, the gospel message always needs the process which has come to be known as inculturation or contextualizing. Many see PRI-NERMs as a useful reminder of this.

Further reading

Turner, H. W. (1981) 'Religious movements in primal (or tribal) societies', *Mission Focus* 9(2), September, 45–55, Elkart (Mennonite Board of Missions).
Further material can be found in the CES-NERM Research Centre, School of Mission, Birmingham University.

RALPH WOODHALL

PROCESS CHURCH OF THE FINAL JUDGEMENT

a.k.a. The Process.

This organization developed from Compulsions Analysis, established around 1963 by Robert De Grimston Moore (b. 1935) and his wife Mary Ann MacLean (b. 1931). De Grimston (he dropped the surname 'Moore') and MacLean met at a Dianetics auditing session in the L. Ron Hubbard (see **Hubbard, L. Ron**) Institute of Scientology (see **Scientology**) in London, England. Compulsions Analysis was set up as a human potential therapy organization (see **Human Potential Movement**), drawing on the teachings of L. Ron Hubbard, and Freudian psychologist Alfred Adler. Moore introduced religious ideas into his writings, and the name 'Process Church of the Final Judgement' was adopted in 1969. De Grimston was known as 'The Teacher' and MacLean 'The Oracle', and members were called 'Processians', whose aim was to improve their selves with a view to escaping the imminent world judgement.

The religious dimension stemmed from De Grimston's taking Compulsions Analysis to Xtul, Mexico, in 1966, when he witnessed a hurricane. This experience caused him to view God's nature as combining love and violence, symbolized in the notions of God and Satan/Lucifer (see **Satanism**). Between 1964 and 1974 De Grimston and his followers proselytized extensively in the United States and Europe, establishing their headquarters in Washington DC, with several chapters in the USA, Europe and Canada. They also engaged in various community action programmes, working alongside the Red Cross and the Salvation Army. In 1968 de Grimston met Anton LaVey, the founder-leader of the Church of Satan, but LaVey refused to recognize The Process as a properly Satanist organization.

De Grimston was the organization's principal theologian, although other leaders contributed writings. The most important of these were *The Gods on War, The Devil,* and *As It Is*. The organization circulated two journals: *Process* and *The Processeans*. The teachings drew primarily on the Gospel of Matthew, focusing on Jesus' instruction to love one's enemies. Since Satan is identified in the Bible as God's adversary, De Grimston reasoned that love of enemies must include love of Satan – not of his deeds, but of his being. God and Satan were not to be regarded as opposing forces: Jesus would be the world's judge, while Satan would be its executioner. The Process's theology was constantly in a state of evolution, eventually proclaiming the existence of four forms of deity: Jehovah, Lucifer, Christ, and Satan. Members were asked to identify with one of four 'god patterns': Jehovian–Christian, Jehovian–Satanic, Luciferian–Christian, and Luciferian–Satanic. 'Jehovian' connoted discipline, authority and puritanical values; 'Satanic' violence, lust and disorder; 'Luciferian' self-indulgence and sensuality; while 'Christian' entailed an endeavour to unify the other three divine forms. Outside the organization were 'The Greys': everyone else, who were characterized by compromise, conformity and mediocrity.

The Process Church's holy day was Saturday, when they held their Sabbath Assembly; Sunday was regarded as a day of rest. At the Sabbath Assembly a round altar was situated in the centre, with four candles marking out the four compass directions, and members sat around it, on cushions in concentric circles. Women, as well as men, were allowed to officiate as ordained priests. On one wall was a picture of Christ, and on another the goat of Mendes; at a later stage of development, however the goat was removed. In the early years, members dressed in black capes and turtle necks, and wore silver crosses and badges portraying the goat of Mendes.

The movement obtained negative publicity on account of alleged associations with the serial killers Charles Manson and David Berkowitz ('Son of Sam'). Such allegations were the subject of two books: *The Family: The Story Of*
Charles Manson's Dune Buggy Attack Battalion* by Ed Sanders (1971) and *The Ultimate Evil: The Truth About the Cult Murders: Son of Sam & Beyond* by Maury Terry (1999). Such claims are largely unfounded, however. No links have ever been established between The Process and Berkowitz, whom the police agreed operated on his own in 1976 and 1977. Manson never joined The Process, although members did visit him in prison after his conviction.

In 1974, a split emerged between Robert and Mary Ann. De Grimston relinquished his authority and returned to England, while The Process was dissolved. Mary Ann attempted to reconstitute the organization as the Foundation Church of the Millennium, renamed the Foundation Faith of God in 1980. In 1979, de Grimston attempted to revive The Process. A campaign for expansion in 1987 led to the formation of the Society of Processians in 1988, but in 1993 the teachings were declared obsolete, and the organization was once again dissolved.

Further reading

Sanders, E. (1971) *The Family: The Story Of Charles Manson's Dune Buggy Attack Battalion*, New York: Dutton.

Bainbridge, W. S. (1978) *Satan's Power*. Berkley: University of California Press.

Richardson, J. T., Best, J. and Bromley, D. G. (eds) (1991) *The Satanism Scare*, New York: Aldine de Gruyter.

Terry, M. (1999) *The Ultimate Evil: The Truth About the Cult Murders: Son of Sam & Beyond*, New York: Barnes & Noble.

GEORGE CHRYSSIDES

PROMISE KEEPERS
(PK)

Founded by Bill McCartney in 1990, the organization is an exclusively male

American Protestant movement, whose mission statement describes it as 'a Christ-centered ministry dedicated to uniting men through vital relationships to become godly influences in their world'. Promise Keepers believe that the Church has become 'feminized', with female leadership roles within the churches, and that recent trends towards feminism, which have enabled women to secure greater equality, merely reflect the world's ever-changing values. Instead, PK seeks to return to 'biblical' values which they believe entail male leadership in the home, churches, and communities. PK seeks to encourage men to accept Jesus Christ as their Lord and Saviour, and to enable men to grow spiritually, displaying integrity, commitment and action within their male leadership.

The name 'Promise Keepers' derives from the psalmist's words, 'The Lord is faithful to all his promises' (Psalm 145:13). Reciprocally, PK is committed to seven promises:

1. honouring Jesus Christ and obedience to God's Word;
2. establishing 'vital relationships' with a small number of other men for spiritual support;
3. 'spiritual, moral, ethical and sexual purity';
4. strong marriages, based on love and biblical values;
5. support for one's pastor, offering one's prayers, time and resources;
6. demonstrating 'biblical unity', transcending race and denomination;
7. obedience to Christ's 'Great Commandment' to love God and one's neighbour (Mark 12:30–31) and his 'Great Commission' (Matthew 28: 19–20) to make disciples throughout the world.

Members are committed to keeping and propagating these seven promises.

PK accepts the principles of biblical **fundamentalism**, and, additionally, defines the following seven key theological tenets:

1. The triune God of the Bible is the only true God.
2. The Bible is God's written word, the infallible guide on all matters of teaching and morals.
3. Adam and Eve's Fall from grace resulted in the alienation of humanity from God, for which death is the just penalty.
4. Christ's substitutionary sacrifice for sin made God's grace available through faith, not works. (Additionally, PK affirms the traditional doctrines of the Virgin Birth, Christ's sinlessness, his power to work miracles, his resurrection, bodily ascension to heaven, and imminent second coming.)
5. The Holy Spirit affords regenerative power, enabling followers to lead the Christian life.
6. Christ is the head of the universal Church, uniting all believers, and transcending the boundaries of race and denomination.
7. This gospel must be proclaimed worldwide until Christ's return.

A further eight 'biblical principles of reconciliation' support these aims:

1. The call – the belief that God has summoned men to their various ministries;
2. Relationships – commitment to the need for reconciliation;
3. Intentionality – the need for perseverance and planned activities;
4. Sincerity – entailing the self-disclosure of one's feelings and attitudes;
5. Sensitivity – acquisition of knowledge to enable empathy to people and organizations;

6. Sacrifice – preparedness to give up time, resources and status;
7. Empowerment – through repentance and forgiveness; and
8. Interdependence – recognizing diversity, by means of which difference can bring different qualities into a relationship.

The ideas of Promise Keepers are encapsulated in several key publications. Its manual, written by Geoff Gorsuch and Dan Schaffer, is entitled *Brothers! Calling Men into Vital Relationships* and its magazine is entitled *New Man*. Other publications include *What Makes a Man? What Makes a Man?* by Leighton Ford, and *The Masculine Journey* by Robert Hicks. Additionally, considerable emphasis is given to PK's 'men's conference ministry', which consists of large-scale all-male gatherings, aiming to promote the organization's principles. Several of these conferences have attracted hundreds of thousands of attendees throughout the United States. Additionally, PK organizes 'catalytic events', designed to support pastors, male leaders and congregations that wish to share its values. One of PK's projects is 'A Million Men at the Cross' campaign, which sought to bring one million new male converts to Christ by around 2005; although targeted specifically at men, it is expected that male converts, through their leadership roles, would facilitate the conversion of wives and families also.

A number of PK members' wives have called for a women's counterpart organization, but this has been rejected on several grounds. PK believes that there are particular problems experienced by men in fulfilling their male leadership roles today, and that it is important to focus on these, and to continue to create all-male environments for its events. PK holds, however, that the reconciliation for which it aims also includes women and families, and that the spiritual welfare of women and families are enhanced by the transformation of men that it seeks to effect. Members are committed to respecting and honouring women. PK has therefore no current desire to address specifically women's issues.

Further reading

Claussen, D. S. (ed.) (1999) *The Promise Keepers: Politics and Promises,* Lexington, MA: Lexington Books.

Gorsuch, G. and Schaffer, D. (1993) *Brothers! Calling Men into Vital Relationships*, Boulder, CO: Promise Keepers.

Jansen, A. and Weeden, L. K. (eds) (1994) *Seven Promises Of A Promise Keeper,* Colorado Springs, CO: Focus on the Family.

GEORGE CHRYSSIDES

PROSPERITY THEOLOGY

Prosperity Theology, a form of conservative Protestantism, is also termed 'Word of Faith', **Health and Wealth** or 'Faith-Formula' teaching. It has been espoused by congregations and Bible schools throughout the world, but its epicentre has traditionally been located in the United States, in the ministries of such preachers as Kenneth Hagin Sr, and Kenneth and Gloria Copeland. Prosperity theology parallels classical Pentecostalism in its emphasis on the second baptism of the Spirit and charismatic gifts, but is distinctive in the degree to which it focuses on three specific areas of Christian life: divine healing, material prosperity, and so-called 'positive confession'. In each of these areas, believers emphasize the goodness of God, alongside the idea that the faith of the born-again person can activate divine favour in predictable and tangible ways. The Old Testament covenant that made blessings available to the chosen people is said to have been extended to all peoples by virtue of Christ's atonement on the cross.

While Prosperity adherents usually emphasize the importance of a literal interpretation of the Bible, they also stress the authority and inspiration of the spoken word, as deployed either by God or by believers themselves. Key to this assumption is the doctrine, based in part on Romans 10:8, that whatever is spoken by faith can address and have an influence on all situations. So-called positive 'confession' is therefore not an admission of sin (as in Roman Catholic confession to a priest) but rather a statement that lays claim to divine beneficence, giving prosperity to the person but also equipping them to be more effective in converting others to the faith. Inspired words are therefore seen as literally creative, so that the believer must be careful to speak positively at all times in order to avoid the dangers of 'negative confession'.

The historical and ideological roots of Prosperity Theology are complex and disputed, reflecting the controversial nature of its adherents' claims. The influence of Pentecostal revivalism (see **Azusa Street Revival**) seems evident, particularly through the activities of the North American healing movement of the 1940s and 1950s. Important figures in this post-War revival, such as William Branham, Oral Roberts, A. A. Allen and T. L. Osborn, promoted a prosperity message that eventually encompassed both physical and financial aspects of the believer's life. Some of these preachers were later able to become high-profile participants within the burgeoning revival of independent charismatic ministries that marked the latter decades of the twentieth century.

Some scholars claim that many of the most distinctive themes of Prosperity Theology can also be traced to metaphysical cults that flourished in the US in the late nineteenth and early twentieth centuries, and in particular to the **New Thought** ideas of Phineas P. Quimby (1802–66). Quimby's teachings were important to the foundation of **Christian Science**, but a key figure in the mediation of his ideas to Prosperity Theology appears to have been E. W. Kenyon (1867–1948), a preacher and prolific writer, born in New York, who taught that 'revelation' knowledge could be distinguished from 'sense' knowledge. Only the former was regarded as enabling contact with a higher realm, so that commonsense and the human mind were seen as inferior to comprehension of divine truth through the spiritual dimension of the person.

The extent to which Kenneth Hagin Sr. (1917–) borrowed from Kenyon's writings or simply came independently to very similar conclusions is open to dispute. In any case, Hagin's childhood years were marked by severe illness, and he claims to have become convinced of the reality of divine healing through Mark 11:24. According to his interpretation of this verse, absolute belief in the certain reception of blessings precedes the physical manifestation of such blessings. After becoming a minister in the **Assemblies of God** and participating in the post-War healing revivals, Hagin formed an independent ministry and moved in 1966 to Tulsa, Oklahoma. Besides using various communications media to broadcast an increasingly prosperity-oriented message, he formed the Rhema Bible Training Center in 1974. By the turn of the century, the Center had trained more than 16,000 students, many of whom went on to found their own ministries in other parts of the United States and throughout the world as a whole. Hagin and other Prosperity teachers have also been active in various significant charismatic networks such as the Full Gospel Business Men's Fellowship International, the Association of Faith Churches and the International Convention of Faith Churches and Ministers.

As Prosperity Theology has spread round the globe, it has taken on numerous guises in such diverse locations as West and South Africa, Latin America, South Korea, and Western and Eastern Europe. Promoting organizations and preachers have developed relatively autonomous, idiosyncratic, and often diffuse spheres of influence, appealing in some contexts to urban middle-class constituencies, in others to the aspirant poor, and in yet others to ethnic enclaves situated in migrant diasporas.

This variant of conservative Protestantism has proved highly controversial in many of the contexts in which it has appeared. It has variously been accused of promulgating Gnosticism, undiluted forms of American capitalism, New Age (see **New Age Movement**) individualism, naïve trust in faith-healing, and acceptance of, rather than revolt against, conditions of racial and economic inequality.

Further reading

Coleman, S. (2000) *The Globalisation of Charismatic Christianity: Spreading the Gospel of Prosperity*, Cambridge: Cambridge University Press.

Coleman, S. (2002) 'The Faith Movement: A Global Religious Culture?', *Culture and Religion Special Issue* 3(1), 3–128.

Hollinger, D. (1991) 'Enjoying God Forever: A Historical Profile of the Health and Wealth Gospel in the USA', in P. Gee and J. Fulton (eds) *Religion and Power, Decline and Growth*, London: Sociology of Religion Study Group, BSA.

McConnell, D. R. (1988) *A Different Gospel: A Historical and Biblical Analysis of the Modern Faith Movement*, Peabody, MA: Hendrickson.

SIMON COLEMAN

PROTESTANT BUDDHISM

The term Protestant Buddhism was first used by Obeyesekere in 1970 in preference to Buddhist-modernism, which it was argued then is more concerned with Buddhism's relationship to politics than religion. Gombrich and Obeyesekere (1988: 216) describe Protestant Buddhism in this way:

> The hallmark of Protestant Buddhism, then, is its view that the layman should permeate his life with his religion; that he should strive to make Buddhism permeate his whole society, and that he can and should try to reach nirvana. As a corollary, the lay Buddhist is critical of the traditional norms of the monastic role; he may not be positively anticlerical but his respect, if any, is for the particular monk, not for the yellow robe as such.

This kind of Buddhism is Protestant, then, in its devaluation of the role of the monk, and in its strong emphasis on the responsibility of each individual for her/his 'salvation' or enlightenment, the arena for achieving which is not a monastery but the everyday world which, rather than being divided off from, should be infused with Buddhism.

Gombrich and Obeyeseke (1988) point to Anagarika Dharmapala (1864–1933) as the quintessential Protestant Buddhist. From a wealthy business family and educated in Christian schools Dharmapala was later to be initiated into the Theosophical society (see **Theosophy**), a movement which exercised considerable influence over modern Buddhism in Sri Lanka. Initiated in Madras (now known as Chennai) he became the manager of the Buddhist Theosophical society in Sri Lanka. Later Dharmapala was to seek to purge Buddhism of all traces of Theosophical influence, and to display contempt for Hindus and Muslims alike. Widely travelled, Dharmapala visited

Japan, the United States where he represented Buddhism at the Parliament of World Religions in Chicago in 1893, and many other countries.

Dharmapala founded the Maha Bodhi society in 1891, today a worldwide movement with particular responsibility for Buddhist missionaries in the West. Protestant Buddhism opposed colonial rule and Dharmapala, who might be described as a Buddhist nationalist, was exiled to India for his campaign against British imperialism.

The mission of Protestant Buddhism, thus, was to fashion Buddhists who had internalized the teachings and ethical precepts of their religion, believed in the fundamental equality of all believers, and the practical relevance of religion to every aspect of life.

Further reading

Obeyesekere, G. (1970) 'Religious Symbolism and Political Change in Ceylon', *Modern Ceylon Studies*, 1(1), 43–63.

Gombrich, R. and Obeyesekere, G. (1988) *Buddhism Transformed. Religious Change in Sri Lanka*, Princeton, NJ: Princeton University Press.

PETER B. CLARKE

PSYCHOSYNTHESIS

Psychosynthesis is a school of spiritually-oriented psychology aimed at integrating the many facets of the human personality into a unified self who would therefore be a more authentic and functional person. It is broadly based to include the personal, educational and interpersonal dimensions, although nowadays it is best known as a school of psychotherapy. As such, it was one of the main influences on the **Human Potential Movement**. Psychosynthesis believes that each human being has a vast potential that generally goes largely unrecognized and unused. It also believes that we each have within ourselves the power to access that potential. Psychosynthesis is often seen as an unfolding process where the person actually possesses an inner wisdom or knowledge of what is needed for that process at any given time.

Psychosynthesis was founded in Italy around 1910 by Roberto Assagioli (1888–1974). He was a medical doctor whose formative years were spent in the heyday of psychoanalysis of the Vienna school. He was a student of Freud who also worked with **Jung**, and was much influenced by Jung's theory of the collective unconscious. In the 1960s he was active in the humanistic psychology movement led by Abraham Maslow (see **Maslow, Abraham**, **Holistic Health Movement**) and others. His students claim that he was the only known therapist whose professional career spanned psychoanalysis and humanistic psychology – the two greatest psychological traditions of the twentieth century. Certainly the historical importance of psychosynthesis lies in its pioneering synthesis of Jungian analytical psychology, humanistic psychology and mysticism into a system of psychotherapy and self-development. His books, still in print, are regarded as key historical texts.

Assagioli was a close friend of Foster and Alice Bailey, and a member of the Sundial group. He was committed to their spiritual vision, which gave rise to the **New Age Movement**. In her autobiography, Alice Bailey describes him as 'our representative in Italy'. His books were published by the **Lucis Trust**, the business organization of Alice Bailey. While he did not subscribe to all aspects of the Bailey world view, the idea that human beings have a higher spiritual or transcendent self remained a core part of psychosynthesis. Assagioli further believed that people had their own 'inner wisdom' that could inform their personal development, and the task of the guide or therapist is to help identify these inner resources, support the process, and be attentive to what is happening.

Assagioli stated that psychosynthesis has two main aims. The first is 'the elimination of the obstacles and conflicts that block the complete and harmonious development of the personality'. The second is 'the use of active techniques to stimulate the psychic functions that are weak and immature'. He emphasized the need to develop the body as well as the mind and spirit, although nowadays his school does not stress the physical dimension much. He held that psychosynthesis was essentially a self-help method for personal and spiritual development, rather than a professional therapy practice. This is perhaps unsurprising given his connections with Alice Bailey. He went on to define the core features of 'true' psychosynthesis: dis-identification, recognition of the personal self, the importance of the will, an ideal model, the need for synthesis of techniques, and recognition of the transpersonal or spiritual self (see **Self-Religion, The Self and self**).

Psychosynthesis has been often criticized for being too broad in its aims and lacking a clear focus. In reply, its proponents point out that humans are very diverse in their needs, no single method suits everyone, and nowadays the emphasis is on therapy. It is also claimed that psychosynthesis can act as a framework in which other therapies such as Jungian and Gestalt can operate. Assagioli held that psychosynthesis was not a school, had no orthodoxy, and that no one could claim to be a founder or leader, even himself.

Nowadays there is a vast range of schools and trainings in psychology and psychotherapy, but psychosynthesis courses are still popular. Many developments in the ongoing synthesis of psychotherapy and spirituality owe much to the work of Assagioli. Foremost among these is the transpersonal psychology movement which he helped found. Its best known member is Ken Wilber, author of many influential books including the groundbreaking *No Boundary* (1979). **Wilber** also drew inspiration from the Indian guru **Ramana Maharshi**, whom he described as 'the greatest sage of the twentieth century'. The Indian guru **Osho** also synthesized Eastern and Western methodologies, though he perceived meditation as primary and therapy as simply clearing the way for spiritual experience.

Further reading

Assagioli, R. (1993) *Psychosynthesis: A Manual of Principles and Techniques*, London: HarperCollins.

Wilber, K. (1979) *No Boundary: Eastern and Western Approached to Personal Growth*, Boston, MA: Shambhala.

ELIZABETH PUTTICK

Q

QUTB, SAYYID
(b. 1906; d. 1966)

A leading theorist of the **Muslim Brotherhood** (Ikhwan al-Muslimin) founded by Hassan Al-Banna (see **Al-Banna, Hassan**), Sayyid Qutb was born in a village in Upper Egypt and like Al-Banna became a teacher before joining the ministry of education which sent him to the United States for further study from 1948–50. While in America he was stunned by what he saw as the high level of support for the newly established State of Israel which had recently been victorious in the first of a series of Arab–Israeli wars. Qutb interpreted this support as a Jewish engineered attack on Islam in which Christianity was complicit. He was also greatly disturbed by what he described as the degeneracy of the American way of life and in particular its materialism and lust.

From Qutb's perspective there were two interrelated threats to the Muslim world, the external enemy – the corrupting and corrosive influence of the United States and western culture generally – and the internal enemy to which the external enemy had given birth, and which he termed the new *jahiliyya* or age of ignorance, characterized by the debauchery and indifference to the Islamic way of life that had gripped Islamic society and its new Pharaohs or rulers.

On returning to Egypt from the United States in 1952 Qutb left the ministry of education and joined the Muslim Brotherhood. Greatly influenced by the ideas of Al-Banna and the Indian/Pakistani reformer Sayyid Abul Al'a Mawdudi (1903–79), founder of the Jamaat-i-Islami (Society of Islam) his many articles as editor of the Brotherhood's journal insisted that Islam was and must become once again for Egyptian and other Muslims a complete way of life.

The Muslim Brotherhood saw an opportunity to make this something of a reality in Egypt with the military coup

458

carried out in 1952 in which King Far-ouk was overthrown by the so-called Free Officers prominent among whom was Gamel Abel Nasser (1918–70), the future president and inspiration for nationalist movements in the Arab world and elsewhere. First as prime minister and later from 1954 as President of Egypt Nasser sought to govern according to what he termed the principles of Islamic socialism which to many Islamists including Qutb was largely secular, western socialism. It is not surprising, therefore, that Nasser failed to convince the Brotherhood that he seriously intended to establish an Islamic state and an attempt was made to assassinate him in 1954. Nasser reacted by banning the movement and executing many of its leaders and imprisoning others. Qutb spent the next ten years, until 1964, in prison – a venue for the education of hundreds of potentially radical thinkers and future activists – where he composed his major treatise *Ma'alim fi al-tariq* (Milestones) (1965). Among other things, this treatise con-demned Nasser's government as un-Islamic and laid out the broad principles of an Islamic state and the strategy for achieving this.

Qutb who was previously open to the possibility of some kind of relationship between Islam and the West had hardened his position by 1965 and while he did not call explicitly for the continuous use of violence he did imply that this could in certain situations be justified. He argued, for example, that Islam could not coexist with *jahiliyya* (unbelief) and that the latter must, therefore, be eliminated by jihad if necessary.

Suspicious that it was conspiring to overthrow the government Nasser had hundreds of Brotherhood members arrested in 1965 and a number of the leaders including Qutb executed.

Further reading

Haddad, Y. Y. (1983) 'The Quranic Justification for an Islamic Revolution: the View of Sayyid Qutb', *The Middle East Journal* 37(1), 14–29.

PETER B. CLARKE

R

RADHASOAMI MOVEMENTS

The Radhasoami religion emerged in the nineteenth century with Shiv Dayal Singh at its head ('Soami Ji Maharaj,' 1818–78). Its origins – and even its organization – have been surrounded by heated controversies. For some, it was a new religious current that emerged from Sikhism, and evolved until it separated completely, thereafter becoming a creative synthesis of Hinduism and Sikhism. For others, the Sikh religion and the Radhasoami religion are two independent and different versions of the Sant Mat current ('the way of the saints': an important movement that developed within Hinduism from the thirteenth century on), both defined more by non-Hindu influences. For others, Radhasoami is not a real religion, and the expression 'Radhasoami religion' is fiercely disputed by them.

During his life, Dayal Singh formed a *satsang* ('teaching community') at Agra, with a few thousand followers. He was undoubtedly a charismatic guru, although not all that different from other Sant Mat gurus, and certainly not perceived in India at the time as the founder of a new universal religion that would gain millions of followers in the next century. Singh taught a version of shabd yoga, Surat Shabd Yoga, a **yoga** of light and sound that teaches its initiates to achieve harmony with the luminous and sonorous current emanating from God's creative essence, and to continuously return to this essence. In the Sant Mat tradition in general, at least one living guru is always available to those who seek him with a true heart: a guru who, by means of initiation, can put the faithful into contact with the luminous current and with the divine sound. Dayal Singh was relatively popular during his lifetime and became even more so after his death, with six different groups claiming succession. With these groups – many of which continue to this day, with varying degrees of success – the Radhasoami school of Dayal Singh began to be represented as a universal religion that expanded beyond India's borders and even beyond the Sant Mat current.

For at least twenty years after Dayal Singh's death, the largest groups remained in the Agra area, while the satsang organized by another of the gurus claiming his legacy – Jaimal Singh (1839–1903) – based on the banks of the Beas river in Punjab, attracted a smaller number of followers. Jaimal Singh's group, known as Radha Soami Satsang Beas, owes its success to the problems of the rival Agra groups, which tried to unite in 1902. When the Radhasoami religion began to be known in England and the United States in the early twentieth century, it was already divided into about ten rival branches, including the Radha Soami Satsang Beas of Jaimal Singh, the Soami Bagh and Dayal Bagh groups, and other smaller groups.

Before the leader of the Beas organization, Charan Singh (1916–90), visited the United States, he had been preceded by his fiercest rival for the legacy of Sawan Singh (1858–1948), successor to Jaimal Singh: Kirpal Singh (1893–1974), founder of Ruhani Satsang, and destined to become the most popular Radhasoami guru in the West. After Kirpal Singh's death, there were the usual splits in the Ruhani Satsang as well. As had occurred with the Radha Soami Satsang Beas group, the name of Kirpal Singh's organization remained in its founder's family, with Darshan Singh (1921–89) and now Kirpal Singh's grandson, Rajinder Singh (1946–), at its head. This group is known as Sawan Kirpal Ruhani Mission, or by the Western name of Science of Spirituality. The name Ruhani Satsang has remained the legal property of a Californian organization, with headquarters in Anaheim, which now says it follows no guru and is dedicated exclusively to spreading the teachings of Kirpal Singh. Nevertheless,

there are other gurus who claim Kirpal Singh's legacy: the most important of these are Ajaib Singh (1926–97), founder of Sant Bani, Thakar Singh (1929–), founder of the Kirpal Light Mission, and Harbhajan Singh ('Bhaji', 1932–95), founder of Unity of Man.

There are now scores of organizations in India and in the West, therefore, that trace their family tree back to the Beas branch of the Radhasoami religion (together, of course, with others that refer to other branches). In this lineage, apart from Radha Soami Satsang Beas, we also have to include all of the many groups that claim Kirpal Singh's legacy. There is also a third 'family' deriving neither from Kirpal Singh nor from his Radha Soami Satsang Beas rivals in the line of Jagat Singh (1884–1951) and Charan Singh. This family is the Hans Maharaj Ji (1900–66) family, an Indian guru who broke away in 1949 after having been linked to the Beas group. His son, Prem Pal Singh Rawat ('Maharaj Ji', 1957–) brought the **Divine Light Mission**, later called Elan Vital, to the West. For a few years, this name was also used by the – in some ways rival – organization of Bruce K. Avenell, which now uses the name The Eureka Society. This, at least, is the version of the origins of the Divine Light Mission – one of the 1970s most typical religious movements, intensely studied by sociologists – offered by various scholars and outside observers. The movement's members claim lineage from a separate Sant Mat tradition dating back to at least the eighteenth century completely independent from the various Radhasoami groups.

Among other developments in the Radhasoami sphere, the influence of a whole series of American and European religious movements should be mentioned. Paul Twitchell (1908–71), the founder of **Eckankar**, was initiated by Kirpal Singh in 1955, although his movement derives its teachings from a variety of different sources and cannot be regarded exclusively as a Radhasoami group. The same is true of the various groups created after the splintering which occurred later in Eckankar's history, such as ATOM (Ancient Teachings of the Masters) and MasterPath, as well as groups influenced by Radhasoami techniques and ideas such as MSIA **(Movement of Spiritual Inner Awareness (Insight))** or the new Taiwanese religion of Supreme Master Ching Hai (Hue Thi Thanh, 1951–). There are those who speak of a wider, very 'fluid' and independent satsang movement, thereby referring to oriental or even to Western gurus active in the West who borrow freely from Radhasoami or **Theosophical** themes, or from elements derived from **Osho** Rajneesh. At any rate, the Radhasoami religion disproves the commonly-held idea that fragmentation and division necessarily prevent the success of a spiritual path. On the contrary, the abundance of gurus seems to have guaranteed continuous growth of the Radhasoami movement as a whole.

From the statistical standpoint, there is no doubt that Radha Soami Satsang Beas has had the greatest success. Out of about 3,000,000 Radhasoami followers worldwide, almost 2,000,000 belong to the Beas group. The salient features of Radha Soami Satsang Beas are similar to those of other Radhasoami groups. These have, in common with the Sikhs – and with the entire Sant Mat or Surat Shabd Yoga tradition – a concept of God 'without qualities' (*nirguna*). Although contrary to many Sikh groups they insist particularly on the cosmic current of sound and light, with which initiates make contact by means of meditation, repetition of holy names, and their personal relationship with the living guru. Moreover, unlike the Sikhs, the followers of Radhasoami do not

have a sacred book, although they do honor the writings of the living guru and his predecessors. Radhasoami demands a vegetarian diet, and – with regard to morality – emphasizes the importance of chastity, and condemns premarital sex as well as homosexuality. In Europe, the best known form of religion based on Radhasoami is Science of Spirituality (Sawan Kirpal Ruhani Mission): it has about 300,000 followers worldwide, and its main publications are translated into some fifty languages. The Kirpal Light Mission of Thakar Singh has been very successful in the West: despite opposition from the **Anti-Cult Movement**, the organization has grown in many countries – especially in Germany, where there are about 20,000 initiates – and now exceeds 100,000 members in the West.

Further reading

Juergensmeyer, M. (1991) *Radhasoami Reality: The Logic of a Modern Faith*, Princeton, NJ: Princeton University Press.
Lane, D. C. (1992) *The Radhasoami Tradition: A Critical History of Guru Successorship*, New York and London: Garland.

PIERLUIGI ZOCCATELLI

RAËLIAN CHURCH

Founded in 1974 as the Mouvement pour Accueil des Elohim Créateurs de l'Humanité (MADECH), the Raëlian Church is a **UFO**-religion, originating from a claimed encounter by its founder-leader Claude Vorilhon (a.k.a. Raël, b. 1946) and an extra-terrestrial near the volcanoes of Clermont-Ferrand in France on 13 December 1973. This encounter is described in Raël's first book, *The Book Which Tells the Truth* (1974), in which it is claimed that the Elohim, who come from another planet, created the human race as a genetic experiment, and return periodically to assess their work. Much of Raël's teaching claims to be derived from the Bible, and the book offers sustained biblical exegesis, claiming that its references to gods and chariots are allusions to extra-terrestrials and spaceships.

A further encounter with the Elohim led to Raël's second book *Extra-Terrestrials Took Me To Their Planet* (1975). As the title implies, the work describes how he visited the Elohim's planet, and met their leader, Yahweh. In 1978 the two books were published in Canada as a single volume, *Space Aliens Took Me To Their Planet,* and in 1986 the British edition was entitled *The Message Given To Me By Extra-Terrestrials: They Took Me To Their Planet.*

The Elohim have highly advanced technology, which Raël experiences in his space journey. In the Elohim's planet, all the menial work is carried out by robots, leaving the inhabitants free to enjoy intellectual and sensual pursuits. The Elohim are prepared to share their technology with humankind; however, they have no wish to force their lifestyle or government on Earth's inhabitants, and await a time when they will be freely received on the planet. To this end the Raëlians plan to build an embassy to receive the Elohim, who are expected to arrive around the year 2035. The preferred location for the embassy is the State of Israel, being the country in which the first messiah – Jesus of Nazareth – was born. Raël is hailed as the new messiah, who claims to have been born not of normal human birth, but as a result of a sexual union between Yahweh and his human mother. The Raëlians anticipate that the Jews may once again reject their messiah, and that they may have to approach other governments for land on which to build their embassy.

The government that the Elohim will establish will be a 'geniocracy'. Since Raëlians emphasize intellectual and technological advance, society will be governed only by those whose intelligence is at least 50 per cent higher than the human average. Sensual enjoyment is encouraged, and the Raëlian Church teaches that people should do what they see fit with their bodies. The Raëlians have attracted media publicity for their 'sensual meditation': their annual workshops aim to induce 'cosmic orgasm', which involves a feeling of oneness with the infinite universe.

Since humans were originally created as a genetic experiment, Raëlians have consistently encouraged genetic experimentation, and are in favour of genetically modified crops. They also advocate human and animal cloning, and in 1977 the Raëlian Church established Clonaid, under the directorship of Dr Brigitte Boisellier, a Raëlian 'bishop'. The project originally aimed at enabling clients to bank a DNA sample to enable them to be re-cloned after death, thus ensuring personal survival. Raël teaches that, after death, the Elohim's Council of the Eternals will decide which humans are worthy of recreation, and will ensure that their DNA samples are cloned. Clonaid has also offered services to infertile couples, and in December 2002 Boisellier claimed to have cloned the first human baby from its mother's DNA. Other Raëlian organizations include Ovulaid, which unashamedly encourages the creation of 'designer babies'; Clonapet aims to offer pet owners the opportunity to clone replicas of deceased pets; and Insuraclone stores samples of human cells for the purpose of therapeutic cloning for the treatment or prevention of certain diseases.

Further reading

Chryssides, G. D. (2000). 'Is God a Space Alien? The Cosmology of the Raëlian Church', *Culture and Cosmos,* 4(1), 36–53.

Rael (1998) *The Final Message*, London: Tagman Press.

GEORGE CHRYSSIDES

RAINBOW COALITION

The Rainbow Coalition under the leadership of Rev. Jesse Jackson illustrates the strong protest tradition that has been a central component of African American religion. Jackson, a minister affiliated with the Progressive National Baptist Convention, USA, served as one of Martin Luther King, Jr.'s chief lieutenants during the Southern Christian Leadership Conference's desegregation campaign in Chicago in 1966. He coordinated the SCLC's Operation Breadbasket, which served as his political base when he broke with the SCLC following King's assassination in 1968. Using Operation Breadbasket as a springboard, Jackson created Operation PUSH as a national religious reform organization in 1971. Although he initially espoused black capitalism during the 1970s, he shifted the group's efforts more to the promotion of consumer rights.

On 3 November 1983, Jackson announced his decision to run as a Democratic candidate for the US presidency. Wile Jackson's agenda has been largely reformist in a left liberal or social democratic vein rather than a revolutionary one, many progressives, not only among African Americans but also among European Americans, Hispanic Americans, Asian Americans, and Native Americans rallied under the organizational umbrella of the Rainbow Coalition, particularly during the 1980s. Jackson inspired millions of African American voters in the 1984 and 1988 Democratic primaries for the Presidential nomination. By utilizing the sermonic folk discourse of black political revivalism, Jackson thrust himself, his organization, and African Americans into electoral politics in a way that no African American either previously had been able to do and subsequently has been able to do. Initially Jackson focused on empowering African Americans by relying upon themselves rather than white corporate and political leaders. He later extended the same message to working-class people regardless of their race or ethnicity.

As in the civil rights movement of the 1950s and 1960s, black churches served as the support base of the Rainbow Coalition. Jackson's political rallies were well attended by black ministers and were conducted in a style modeled after African American Baptist services. Members of local Operation Push branches served as coordinators of about half of the state Rainbow Coalition organizations in the 1984 Presidential campaign. Along with many other black ministers, T. J. Jemison, the president of the National Baptist Convention, USA – the largest African American religious body in the country – endorsed Jackson's candidacy. During the 1988 Presidential campaign, Jackson greatly broadened his appeal outside the black community. The Rainbow Coalition presented itself as the voice of the powerless – the poor, small farmers, working-class people, women, gays, and lesbians, and ethnic minorities. As an African American populist *par excellence*, Jackson exuded a charisma generally lacking in mainstream politicians and routinely kept his audiences waiting for his arrival.

As a result of his coalition-building abilities, Jackson received 18.2 per cent of all the votes in the 1984 Democratic primaries and 19.3 per cent of all the votes in the 1988 Democratic primaries. On Super Tuesday in March of 1988, he garnered 26 per cent of the popular vote and 353 delegates in the Democratic primaries in twenty states, fourteen of them in the South, compared to Dukakis'

26 per cent and 356 delegates. Jackson called for a defense budget freeze, full employment, self-determination for Palestinians, and the empowerment of African Americans and other working-class peoples. He also lambasted the exploitative practices of US corporations. Despite his popular appeal and the fact that Jackson trailed only Michael Dukakis in delegate votes at the 1988 Democratic convention, the Democratic Presidential nominee chose Lloyd Bentsen, a conservative white US senator for Texas, as his running mate.

In 1989, Jackson moved the headquarters of the Rainbow Coalition from Chicago to Washington, DC. Since that time, he has focused on addressing inner-city crime, violence, drug abuse, teenage pregnancy, voter registration, health care reform, affirmative action policies, the anti-apartheid movement, and the struggle for democracy in Haiti. Since its highpoint in 1988, the Rainbow Coalition has undergone decline due to serious organizational and financial difficulties. Some critics have argued that Jackson has functioned in a top-down mode that has shut the rank-and-file membership of the Coalition out of decision-making. In reality, this is a pattern not unique to Jackson but rather one inherent in the role of the African American minister and perhaps that of religious leaders around the globe. Since his bids for the Presidency, he has continued to promote the cause of ordinary Americans and has served as a self-designated ambassador-at-large around the globe.

Further reading

Frady, M. (1996) *Jesse: The Life and Pilgrimage of Jesse Jackson,* New York: Random House.
Reynolds, D. (1997) *Democracy Unbound: Progressive Changes to the Two Party System,* Boston: South End Press.

HANS A. BAER

RAJNEESH MOVEMENT

The Rajneesh movement was one of the largest and most influential NRMs of the 1970s, founded by the charismatic guru **Osho** (1931–90), formerly called Bhagwan Shree Rajneesh. In its heyday it may have had up to 200,000 members, although numbers are hard to estimate accurately. Active membership at the time of writing is probably only a fraction of this. The main centre is in Pune in Western India, where Osho lived for several years, and where he died. Additionally, there are around twenty other centres worldwide.

The history of the movement began in 1966, when Osho left his university post, and toured India as a spiritual teacher, taking on disciples. In 1970, this relationship was formalized as *sannyas,* adapted from an ancient Hindu tradition of world-renunciation. Osho reinterpreted sannyas as a life-affirmative spiritual path requiring the renunciation of the ego, symbolized by taking on a new Sanskrit name, wearing orange and a *mala* (locket with a photo of Osho). Osho was introduced to the West by Dr Shyam Singha, a London society naturopath, who promoted him to clients active in the **Human Potential Movement** (HPM), including several American therapists resident in the UK. These HPM leaders met Osho in India, and decided that his blending of personal charisma, Indian mysticism and Western humanistic psychology could transform the HPM into a spiritual movement. Thousands of **Self-Transformation** seekers followed them eastwards, and by the late 1970s it had become the most popular and fashionable NRM (see **New Religious Movement**) among the counterculture and intelligentsia. The profiles of the seekers were varied, but most were in their late twenties to mid-thirties, middle class, university educated, about 60 per cent female.

A typical ashram day started with an energetic dynamic meditation at 6 a.m. for one hour, followed by a two hour spiritual discourse by Osho. For the first few months the novice **sannyasin** (disciple) participated in various full-time therapy and meditation groups, such as encounter, primal therapy, enlightenment intensives and traditional *zazen* or *vipassana* meditation. There was a further 'active meditation' at 6 p.m. for one hour. After 'graduating' from months of this regime, a sannyasin could apply to work in the ashram. Many stayed for years, working in an environment which was intentionally modelled by Osho along the lines of Gurdjieff's community in 1930s France (see **Gurdjieff, George Ivanovitch**). Common to both communities were hard work without pay, and supervision by people with abrasive personalities – a strategy for self-transcendence.

During the 1970s the HPM (Human Potential Movement) groups were considered controversial for their inclusion of physical violence, although there were no serious injuries, and all violence was prohibited after criticisms by the founders of Esalen. Nowadays, Rajneesh therapy is recognized as a pioneering approach to psychotherapy and self-development, which has influenced other therapies and encouraged other Eastern-based NRMs to integrate therapy with spiritual praxis. The movement was famous for its ultra-liberal attitude to sexuality, drawing on Tantric tradition (see **Tantra**) to develop an approach of sacred sexuality. Again, this is now an approved praxis in other NRMs and new age groups.

The main motivation for seekers who joined the Rajneesh movement was neither therapy nor sex, but the prospect of becoming enlightened, in the classical Buddhist sense (see **Buddhism in the West**). Very few sannyasins have been recognized as enlightened (some have declared themselves enlightened), but most current and ex-sannyasins claim to have undergone progress in self-actualization, as described by Maslow and the HPM (see **Maslow, Abraham**). Several writers have classified the Rajneesh movement as a new age movement (see **New Age Movement**), but it was also very Indian in character, with Osho drawing heavily on the tantric and upanishadic traditions, as well as Buddhism.

As the numbers of disciples grew, the availability of Osho to meet people on an individual basis was inevitably reduced, and the solution applied has been described by the sociologist Max Weber, as the 'routinization of charisma'. The charismatic leader (Osho) gradually delegated his functions to subordinates. For example, initially he personally led the dynamic meditations, but after the move to Pune they were led by sannyasins. Over time, all his functions were delegated except for his lectures and *darshan* (evening meetings). It was believed that the guru was present in spirit at all significant events, and that leading sannyasins were vessels or mediums for him. Indeed, the purpose of discipleship was to become open to the direct transmission of energy and spiritual transformation from the guru to the disciple (*shaktipat* in Hinduism).

The most dramatic stage of the history of the Rajneesh movement unfolded after the move in 1981 to Rajneeshpuram, a huge ranch in the high desert of Oregon, USA. Osho was impatient to build a city, and became frustrated by the many laws and regulations applying to such an enterprise. This quickly led to prolonged legal battles, and serious hostility from the local residents, as well as internal disputes in the community. Most of the original disciples left in disillusionment, and Osho himself withdrew from public appearances. Finally, the acting leader, Sheela, left suddenly, and Osho was arrested on charges including immigration offences and tax evasion. Osho was deported, and returned with his closest disciples to the Pune ashram. The multi-million dollar ranch was used to pay off creditors.

Osho lived quietly in Pune until his death in 1990, leaving no spiritual successor. Osho Commune International, as the movement is now known, is directed by a group called the Inner Circle, led by a Canadian called Jayesh. The Inner Circle has been riven by serious disputes and power struggles, some of which have been commented on by the Indian press. A legal struggle is (at the time of writing) taking place in the US courts over the use of the 'Osho' name in a website address, and it seems this is an attempted precedent to underpin the copywriting of the name in all circumstances. There are still many resident members and short-term visitors, though considerably fewer than in Osho's lifetime. However, the therapy and meditation centre is flourishing, and has become a popular 'self-development holiday' destination on the international new age circuit.

Further reading

Carter, L. (1990) *Charisma and Control in Rajneeshpuram*, New York: Cambridge University Press.
Puttick, E. (1997) *Women in New Religions*, London: Macmillan/St Martin's Press,
ELIZABETH PUTTICK

RAMAKRISHNA MISSION

The Ramakrishna Mission is a modern Hindu movement created in 1897 by Swami Vivekananda (see **Vivekananda, Swami**) in the name of his *guru*, Sri Ramakrishna (see **Ramakrishna, Sri**).

It aims to promote harmony between religions as forms of one eternal religion, to train workers to improve the spiritual and material conditions of the masses, and to propagate Vedantic and other ideas elucidated in the life of Ramakrishna. 'Ramakrishna Mission' sometimes refers collectively to the Ramakrishna Math, the monastic order also organized by Vivekananda, and the Ramakrishna Mission, which is open to monastic and lay followers. In practice, the Ramakrishna Mission is subject to the authority of the President of the Ramakrishna Math, although it has enjoyed a legally separate status since 1909. Belur Math, Howrah, is the headquarters of the movement.

Rapidly becoming involved in relief-work, by 1910 the Ramakrishna Mission had established four major 'Homes of Service' and other smaller centres. It currently maintains sixty-four centres (fifty-six in India) and twenty-five combined Math and Mission centres (nineteen in India). There are fifty-nine Math centres (thirty-five in India) and twenty-nine sub-centres (nineteen in India). Those outside India are scattered worldwide, including more recently Russia and Japan. In India and other countries where material development is a recognized priority, the Ramakrishna Mission undertakes medical service, educational work, activities for young people, work for women, work in rural and tribal areas, mass contact, spiritual and cultural work, relief and rehabilitation work, and celebrates religious festivals. The largest centres in India are extensive, often with educational institutions, and provide a complex range of services. Centres in the United States and Western Europe have restricted their activities to teaching, publishing and spiritual guidance. The centres are generally managed by a member of the Math, a *sannyasin*, who holds the title of Secretary. The Secretary is assisted by other sannyasins, lay volunteers and, in some cases, by salaried workers, depending on the size of the centre and its projects. Centres are expected to be financially independent and are supported by private donations, and grants from national and international funding agencies and philanthropic organizations. Demands on the services of the Ramakrishna Mission, and consequently the supply of funding, increased considerably after Indian Independence when both central and regional governments looked to its centres as potential providers of educational and welfare services. In 1998 the Ramakrishna Mission was awarded the Gandhi Peace Prize by the Indian Government for its focus on action and service. The movement's reputation for activism and the popular regard in which Ramakrishna and Vivekananda are held have made it attractive to many Hindus not directly involved in its activities. It has continued to command the respect of English-educated, middle-class Hindus both in India and the Hindu diaspora, especially those with links to West Bengal and the city of Calcutta.

The Ramakrishna Mission points to Ramakrishna as its model and in particular to his reported exhortation to 'serve *jiva* (the human being) as Shiva (the deity)'. At the same time, he is said to have affirmed that such service was superior to self-interested charitable activity. The record of Ramakrishna's teaching, however, shows him to have been a fierce critic of popular philanthropic activity, judging it to be a distraction from the priority of God-realization. Although incidents of philanthropic intervention are attributed to Ramakrishna, their relative paucity and the thrust of his teaching suggests that both the shape and priorities of the Ramakrishna Mission owe much to Vivekananda's concern to galvanize and transform Hindu India. Under Vivekananda's influence, the disinterested service of humanity has been promoted as a *sadhana* ('spiritual discipline') in its own right as the Math and Mission have co-ordinated their efforts under the motto of 'For Liberation and the Good of the World'.

The Ramakrishna Mission displays many characteristics of a modern, voluntary, social service organization. Its reformulation of Hinduism and its appeal to a global audience also has much in common with other movements described as **Neo-Hinduism**, again suggestive of Vivekananda's influence. Its message about the validity of all religions and celebration of festivals from many religions, however, recalls a constant refrain in Ramakrishna's teaching, which the mature Ramakrishna Math and Mission have systematized and presented as thoroughly non-dualist in character. Through their publications, the Ramakrishna Math and Mission have exerted a powerful influence upon depictions of Ramakrishna's life and teaching.

Further reading

Beckerlegge, G. (2000) *The Ramakrishna Mission: The Making of a Modern Hindu Movement*, New Delhi: Oxford University Press.

Gambhirananda, S. (1983) *History of the Ramakrishna Math and Ramakrishna Mission*, Calcutta: Advaita Ashrama.

GWILYM BECKERLEGGE

RAMAKRISHNA, SRI

Sri Ramakrishna (born Gadadhar Chattopadhyay, *c.* 1836–86) was one of the most charismatic and influential Hindu personalities of the nineteenth century. Constantly lapsing into altered states of consciousness, he claimed direct experience of the ultimate reality. Many of his discourses, largely triggered by devotees' questions, were recorded by Mahendranath Gupta ('M') in *The Gospel of Sri Ramakrishna* (*Srisriramakrishnakathamrita*). Ramakrishna's name has been perpetuated in the **Ramakrishna Mission** and Math, founded by his disciple, Swami Vivekananda (see **Vivekananda, Swami**), although that movement substantially reflects the latter's direction. The wider dissemination of Ramakrishna's influence owed much to the many, prominent Hindus who came to hear him, including members of the **Brahmo Samaj**.

Brought up in the village of Kamarpukur north of Calcutta, Ramakrishna gained a reputation for spiritual precocity as a child. After the death of his father, in 1855 he followed his brother to Calcutta where both served as brahmins in the newly built temple to Kali at Dakshineshwar, and where Ramakrishna resided until struck down by terminal illness. His anguished attempts to experience directly Kali, the Divine Mother, led him to accept a succession of spiritual teachers over a period of some thirteen years, including an Advaitin who probably initiated him as a *sannyasin* and gave him the name of Ramakrishna. In 1859, fearing for his sanity, his family arranged his marriage to Saradamani Mukhapadhyay who as Sarada Devi became the holy Mother of the Ramakrishna movement.

Based on his experiments with various Hindu disciplines and certain Muslim and Christian practices, Ramakrishna affirmed the validity of all ways to God. He emphasized that God-realization should be put before all else, stressing to his male followers the dangers of attachment to 'women and gold'. Although portrayed in the later Ramakrishna movement as a non-dualist, Advaita Vedantin, Ramakrishna's repeated assertion of the equal validity of personalist views testify to the enduring influence upon him of Tantra and the worship of Shakti, traditions centred on the Mother Goddess.

Further reading

Kripal, J. J. (1995) *Kali's Child: The Mystical and Erotic in the Life and Teachings of Ramakrishna*, Chicago: University of Chicago Press.

GWILYM BECKERLEGGE

RAMANA MAHARSHI

Ramana Maharshi (1879–1950) was a revered figure in contemporary religious history, who has influenced many later teachers. He was born near Madurai, in southern India, and led an introspective and solitary youth. At the age of 17 he had a strong spiritual experience, confronting the reality of his own mortality and realizing that there was nothing to lose, therefore nothing to fear. This insight caused him to give up formal education and live as a hermit in a cave of Arunachala, one of the two most sacred mountains of India. Arunachala is a major place of pilgrimage, home to many saints and sages, but Ramana is the most renowned.

Ramana was an exemplary teacher who never called himself a guru, though he attracted many disciples who eventually formed an ashram around him. He was known as the 'silent sage', and his only writings were devotional poems to Arunachala. However, his peaceful yet powerful presence transformed many lives. Later he began to teach. The essence of his approach is that through observation or witnessing, the meditator will perceive the illusory nature of the false self (ego) and become reintegrated with the true self. His philosophy is in line with the non-dualistic *advaita Vedanta* tradition of *Janana* **yoga**, with the important addition of a simple but powerful technique: the repeated question 'Who am I?', which will eventually reveal truth. This technique has been widely adopted within the **Human Potential Movement** and other spiritual groups, and comprises the core of the enlightenment intensives created by Charles Berner.

Ramana Maharshi was important as a sage who helped make Hindu spirituality accessible and transformative to Westerners, and is admired by many teachers and psychologists. He can also be seen as a harbinger of the self-development movement. One of his most successful disciples was Poonja, who attracted many Western students, some of whom became **guru**s themselves, such as Andrew Cohen (see **Cohen, Andrew**). Although Ramana was not part of a lineage, he appears to have founded one. His combination of simplicity and charisma charmed all who met him, and there are many stories of healing and miracles, including animals attracted by his compassion.

ELIZABETH PUTTICK

RASTAFARIAN MOVEMENT

The Rastafarian movement began in the 1920s during the time of the Great Depression and was inspired by the Jamaican Marcus Garvey's Back to Africa movement in the United States and his call for 'Africa for the Africans'. The fledgling movement was uplifted and energized by the occasion of the accession of Ras Tafari (Ras meaning Prince, and Tafari, Creator) to the imperial throne of Ethiopia in 1935. Haile Selassie was seen as the fulfilment of Psalm 68, which was interpreted to mean that God, Jah had singled out the black race, for special attention. Its thinking was greatly influenced by the tradition of resistance to foreign dominance found in such indigenous move-

ments as Myalism, one of whose purposes was the counteracting of the 'sorcery of the slave masters', by the resistance to cultural imperialism offered by the African-Christian religions including the Native Baptist movement, by the pan-Africanist philosophy of thinkers such as Edward Wilmot Blyden and by notions already long established in Caribbean society and in particular, by the notion of Ethiopianism – an idea that conflates Ethiopia meaning black with the entire continent of Africa and fills the imagination with dreams of freedom and liberation.

'Ethiopia, Thou Land of Our Fathers', was the title that Garvey gave to the anthem of his Universal Negro Improvement Association (UNIA) whose mission was to inform the world about Africa's great civilization and undermine such assumptions of cultural imperialism as the Hamitic hypothesis, an hypothesis used by among others the ruling minority to underpin and legitimize apartheid in South Africa. More generally, the hypothesis assumed that anything of excellence, refinement and of great beauty found in Africa was the creation of the white race. All the different elements of Biblical messianism and Ethiopianism were joined together by Garvey's movement whose mission it was to rebuild Africa destroyed by slavery and colonialism, a mission foretold, it was believed, by the psalmist in the words 'Princes shall come out of Egypt; Ethiopia shall soon stretch out her hands to God' (Psalms, 68:31).

Using the Bible as a historical text that contained the true history of the Black Race as opposed to that disseminated by colonialists early Rastafarians identified themselves as one of the twelve tribes of ancient Israel and some came to have faith in Haile Selassie as the Messiah who would redeem them from white oppression (Babylon) and return them to their homeland, Africa (see **Black Jewish Movements**, **Black Muslims**). While some have returned to Ethiopia to live in the black paradise of Shashemane, this return is now widely interpreted in a psychological sense to refer to a journey of self discovery leading to an authentic understanding of oneself as an African entrusted with a mission to protect African culture and the African way of life, by 'living naturally' (Clarke, 1986) and by ensuring that Africans are fully aware of the threat from Babylon, white society, to their freedom.

Although it assumes responsibility for the African race as a whole Rastafarianism can be also aptly described as a 'self religion' (Heelas, 1991) (see **Self-Religion, the Self, and Self**). Everything about the movement from its rituals – taking the chalice, another expression for the ganja weed – its language – the use of I and I for We – to its songs and music and its theology in the broadest sense of the term is meant to facilitate the discovery of the God within, Jah, who constitutes one's inner, divine self. This not only empowers the individual – in part of the Caribbean, for example in Dominica, Rastas are known as 'Dreads', meaning the power that lies within every individual – but will also enable Africans to purify their minds and their whole personality of the stains of inferiority and self doubt left by colonialism and slavery.

The music and fame of Bob Marley and the Wailers in particular brought the movement to the attention of the world in the 1970s. Rasta communities emerged in Bahia, Brazil, and in other parts of Latin America, North America, Australia, and New Zealand where it influenced the Maoris in particular. White people were also attracted to the movement, which made for if not a change then a modification of its philo-sophy. Initially, fearing exclusion some whites would claim to have been African in a previous existence, but as their numbers increased the 'check on the colour of the skin' was dropped leaving only the 'check on the spirit', implying that what was required in a 'brother' or 'sister' was the African spirit. Not only has there been a change in the social composition and ethnic background of the membership worldwide but there has also been an improvement in the socio-economic circumstances of a substantial number of followers in the Caribbean.

Two aspects in particular of Rastafarianism have come in for sustained and widespread criticism and those are its patriarchal structure and the related issue of gender inequality. Obiagele Lake (1998) has provided one of the more serious academic critiques of the position of women in the movement showing how they are marginalized and objectified, a position which would appear to be the very antithesis of what the movement aims to achieve for men. Lake believes that the Rastafarian movement cannot be considered to be in this respect at least a force for positive social change in the Caribbean or elsewhere since it simply lends legitimacy to the traditional patriarchal structures that ensure the subordination of women. On the same topic Austin-Broos (1987) compares and contrast the male-centred attitudes of the Rastafarian movement with those of the Pentecostal churches in Jamaica.

Other critics from among the growing intellectual wing of the movement range much wider taking as their unit of analysis the whole social and religious character and aims of Rastafarianism. While most would agree that Rastafarianism has been concerned with the restructuring of African-Caribbean and African diaspora identity from an African perspective, there are those who are concerned to see the movement function less as a religion preoccupied with legends and myths surrounding Marcus Garvey and one that regards the Bible as the source of infallible truth rather than simply an interesting book, and that believes in Haile Selassie as Creator and Messiah, rather than as a symbol of divine-human unity. What is being suggested is that Rastafarianism be developed as a social theory that provides an agenda for social, political and economic action that would lead to true self-understanding for all human beings and to solidarity among all peoples (Semaj, 1985). Others, following the greatly respected, even revered, historian Walter Rodney, also want to rid the movement of its quietist, pacifist, escapist image by emphasizing the role it has played in Jamaica, the Caribbean and beyond both as a resistance movement and as an instrument of social and cultural change. Although the movement will, doubtless, be taken in these directions by some, being a global concern with no central authority, it seems destined to acquire a multiplicity of identities.

Further reading

Austin-Broos, D. J. (1987) 'Pentecostals and Rastafarians: Cultural, Political and Gender Relations of Two Religious Movements', *Social and Economic Studies* 36(4), 1–39.

Barrett, L. E. (1988) *The Rastafarians. Sounds of Cultural Dissonance*, Boston: Beacon Press (2nd revised edition).

Campbell, H. (1987) *Rasta and Resistance: From Marcus Garvey to Walter Rodney*, Trenton, NJ: African World.

Clarke, P. B. (1986) *Black Paradise: The Rastafarian Movement*, London: The Aquarian Press.

Edmonds, E. B. (2003) *Rastafari. From Outcasts to Culture Bearers*, Oxford: Oxford University Press.

Lake, O. (1998) 'Religion, Patriarchy and the Status of Rastafarian Women' in P. B. Clarke (ed.) *New Trends and Developments in African Religions*, Westport, CT: Greenwood Press, pp. 141–58.

Semaj, L. T. (1985) 'Inside Rasta: The Future of a Religious Movement', *Caribbean Review* 14(1), 8–11 and 37–8.

PETER B. CLARKE

RAVIDASI

A.k.a. Ad Dharm ('original or primal religion')

This Sikh-derived movement was started by the Sikh guru Ravidas, or Raidas. Little firm biographical details are available about him. He belonged to the chamar caste, and learned his family trade of tanning hides and making shoes. He is said to have been a worshipper of Rama, and began to mix with *sadhus* during his adolescence. Tradition states that he was a disciple of Ramanand (1366–1467), who also taught the famous poet-mystic Kabir (trad. 1398–1518).

Ravidas taught the irrelevance of caste to the attainment of liberation. In common with Guru Nanak (1469–1539), Sikhism's first human guru, Ravidas rejected austerity, and other outward manifestations of religiosity, such as pilgrimages and ritual ablutions. Deeply influenced by the Sant tradition, he taught devotion and surrender to God, the repetition of his name, and the free availability of grace through the guru. Ravidas is accredited with many miracles, and he was a composer of hymns, forty of which found inclusion in the Sikh holy book, the *Guru Granth Sahib*. Ravidas travelled widely in India, spreading his message. A number of his shrines survive, and, ironically, have become places of pilgrimage.

The veneration of Ravidas was revived as a twentieth-century movement in the

Punjab by Sant Hiran Das and others, who established the Ram Das Sabha. The movement came to Britain between 1950 and 1968, with the substantial immigration that took place in that period. Ravidas temples practise the same type of worship as mainstream Sikh gurdwaras, offering *kirtan* (a worship service with singing), followed by *langar* (communal food offered in the kitchen area). They differ from other forms of Sikhism in their veneration of Ravidas, who is not included as one of the ten Sikh human gurus in the lineage from Guru Nanak to Guru Gobind Singh (1666–1708). Ravidas's picture is usually prominent in a Ravidas temple: in contrast with mainstream Sikh gurdwaras, where pictures are normally prohibited in the temple area. Ravidas is given equal status to Guru Nanak by his followers, and his birthday is celebrated annually.

Further reading

Mahi Mukandpuri, N. S. (1985) *The Teachings of Guru Ravidass*, Birmingham: Guru Ravidass Cultural Association.

GEORGE CHRYSSIDES

REBIRTHING

Devised in 1974 by Leonard Orr, its practitioners claim that rebirthing is not a religion but a particular set of breathing techniques, akin to *prana yoga* or *kriya yoga*. The practice stemmed from an experience of Orr's in which he remained in a sauna for more than the recommended time: the change in his breathing allegedly caused him to recollect his own birth in remarkable detail, and to re-enact the process. In the early stages of the technique's development, practitioners were placed in hot tubs, where they claimed to recollect their births, as well as their time in the womb.

It was later judged that water was not as important as the breathing technique itself. The altered breathing induced by a rebirthing session increases the body's oxygen intake, and this is said to release toxins, taking energy (*prana* or *ch'i*) into the body.

The technique gained in popularity in the 1970s. At a time when the use of recreational drugs gained publicity, rebirthers claimed that the benefits of their practice resembled those claimed for drug-induced states (higher levels of consciousness), but went far beyond these. Dr Stanislav Grof, an American psychotherapist, claimed in 1976 that LSD was effective for narcotics and alcohol addiction, but was prevented from offering LSD-assisted psychotherapy. Grof developed 'Holotropic Breathing', a technique similar to Orr's, as a form of 'drugless psychedelic therapy'.

Rebirthing teachers claim that birth is traumatic, instilling pent-up emotions, which need to be released. Skill is needed in assisting this process, hence qualified counsellors, known as 'rebirthers', were trained. Rebirthing clients are recommended to undergo at least ten sessions with rebirthers, before continuing unsupervised.

The claimed beneficial result is a transformation of one's life – inner cleansing, a recognition of inner blocks and better inter-personal relationships, as well as therapeutic benefits: all disease is said to have an emotional cause. Benefits are not confined to the physical. Rebirthers have claimed that the breath is 'the umbilical cord to the divine' and hence harmonizes one's inner and outer energy, and a much enhanced awareness of life's purpose and why one has been born.

Further reading

Begg, D. (1999) *Rebirthing: Freedom from Your Past*, London: Thorsons.

Holland, C. (1993) *Rebirthing: Introducing a Skill which Enables us to Live in the Past*, Solihull: Lifeworks.

GEORGE CHRYSSIDES

RECLAIMING

Founder: Starhawk (b. 1951)

(and her teaching coven)

Reclaiming is a feminist Witchcraft movement that arose in the 1970s in California out of a teaching coven founded by **Starhawk**, the name used by Miriam Simos, a leading public spokesperson particularly in the fields of feminism, environmentalism and contemporary expressions of Neo-Paganism and modern Witchcraft or **Wicca** in the United States.

The immediate beginnings of this movement's political engagement were its involvement in the civil action in the 1970s known as the Diablo Canyon protest which attempted to prevent the construction of a nuclear power plant. From then on it has continued to attach great importance to political activism and regards this as an important bonding element.

Reclaiming teaches magic to political activists and political activism to the practitioners of magic. Spiral dances, one of Reclaiming's principle techniques, have been performed at protest meetings against the World Trade Organization (WTO) and other agencies of globalization, and classes are provided for cells such as Earth First on the issues in locations where political protests are envisaged. Literature is also made available including such writings as Starhawk's *Dreaming the Dark* (1982) which offer a Reclaiming explanation of the notion of individual empowerment and a faith based critique of the current practice of Capitalism.

This political dimension to Wiccan life is seen to flow from faith and also to act as a form of social cement in that it binds the Reclaiming community together and the community to the wider society. Starhawk is a popular author with a long list of publications on topics that are widely read by both Wiccans and non-Wiccans. Her first book, *The Spiral Dance: A Rebirth of the Ancient Religion of the Great Goddess* (1989), which appeared in 1979, established her reputation as a leading theorist of Goddess Spirituality (see **Goddess Movement** and **Goddess Feminists**) and provided a serious challenge to the male bias of traditional mainstream religion. Her later writings, not only continued with these themes but also placed great emphasis on 'practical' magic, affirmative celebration and political engagement particularly in relation to social, environmental causes and the cause of justice for all.

Starhawk's previously mentioned *Webs of Power: Notes from the Global Uprising* (2002) presents her activist commentary concerning non-violent civil disobedience and details her role in protest movements in various North American and European cities including Seattle, Washington DC, Quebec City, Genoa, and New York. These objectives are furthered by courses in direct action training given in North and South America and Europe which focus on ending war, poverty and racism.

Reclaiming, which shares much in common with the Wicca movement that emerged in the 1940s in Britain, a movement characterized by its stress on ritual, nature veneration, and by its polytheistic, magical, and religious system, has become an international movement with specialist teachers providing organized courses. It has also become one of the most dynamic forms of politically engaged Witchcraft.

Reclaiming is not an exclusive movement but encourages members to look beyond its borders for knowledge and enlightenment. Many of its teachers belong not only to Reclaiming but also to one or more different movements, and some of its practitioners also belong to such movements as **Santeria**.

Reclaiming tends to adapt, where it believes this can be of benefit, the techniques leant from other movements and incorporate them in its own repertoire. This Goddess-based witchcraft movement leaves the question of the reality or otherwise of the deity up to the individual practitioner. Starhawk has expressed the view in her *The Spiral Dance* (1979: 8) that 'The Goddess has infinite aspects and thousands of names. She is in reality behind many metaphors.' Notwithstanding its strong feminist convictions, Reclaiming theology teaches that myriads of both female and male deities arose from the act of creation. However, rather than focusing on its own theology it places the stress on what it shares in common with the rest of the Wiccan tradition.

Further reading

Salomonsen, J. (2002) *Enchanted Feminism: The Reclaiming Witches of San Francisco*, London: Routledge.
Starhawk (1979) *The Spiral Dance: A Rebirth of the Ancient Religion of the Great Goddess*, San Francisco: Harper and Row.
Starhawk (1982) *Dreaming the Dark*, Boston: Beacon Press.
Starhawk (2002) *Webs of Power: Notes from the Global Uprising*, Gabriola Island, BC, Canada: New Society Publishers.

PETER B. CLARKE

RECONSTRUCTIONIST JUDAISM

Unlike **Reform** and Conservative Judaism, Reconstructionist Judaism developed out of the thinking of an individual scholar. Born in Lithuania in 1881, Mordecai Kaplan had a traditional education in Vilna and came to New York City as a child in 1889. After graduating from the City College of New York and the Jewish Theological Seminary, he received a master's degree from Columbia University in 1902. He then became associate minister of Rabbi Moses S. Margolis at New York's Orthodox Kehilath Jeshurun. Although officially Orthodox, Kaplan increasingly became disenchanted with traditional Jewish doctrine. In 1909 he was invited by Solomon Schechter to direct the Teachers' Institute of the Seminary. The following year he became Professor of Homiletics at the Seminary's rabbinical school where he taught philosophy of religion.

During the 1910s and 1920s, Kaplan engaged in wide-ranging congregational work. In 1915, together with several former Kehilath Jeshurun members who had moved to the Upper West Side, Kaplan organized the New York Jewish Center where he experimented with the concept of Judaism as a civilization. Two years later the first stage of a million-dollar synagogue-centre was completed on West 86th Street where Kaplan officiated as rabbi. In addition to overseeing religious worship, he implemented a programme of activities. During these years Kaplan supported controversial political issues and challenged traditional Jewish belief. When the Board of Directors demanded strict Orthodoxy in 1921, Kaplan resigned and founded the Society for the Advancement of Judaism.

Reconstructionism as a movement began in 1922 when Kaplan initiated a policy of reconstructing Judaism to meet the demands of modern life. This was followed in 1934 by the publication of *Judaism as a Civilization* in which Kaplan formulated the principles of the movement. In this work, Kaplan began by evaluating the main religious groupings of American Jewry. In his view, Reform had correctly recognized the evolving character of Judaism, yet it ignored the social basis of Jewish identity as well as the organic character of Jewish peoplehood. Neo-Orthodoxy, on the other hand, acknowledged Judaism as a way of life and provided an intensive programme of Jewish education. Nonetheless, it mistakenly regarded the Jewish religion as unchanging. In contrast, Conservative Judaism was committed to the scientific study of the history of the Jewish faith while recognizing the unity of the Jewish people. Conservative Judaism, however was too closely bound to the *halakhah* and thus unable to respond to new circumstances. All of these movements failed to adjust adequately to the modern age – what was needed, Kaplan argued, was a definition of Judaism as an evolving religious civilization.

In the light of this vision of a reconstructed Judaism, Kaplan called for the re-establishment of a network of organic Jewish communities that would insure the self-perpetuation of the Jewish heritage.

Membership of this new movement would be voluntary; leadership should be elected democratically, and private religious opinions would be respected. In addition, Kaplan proposed a worldwide Jewish assembly which would adopt a covenant defining the Jews as a transnational people. According to Kaplan, religion is the concretization of the collective self-consciousness of the group which is manifest in *sancta* (spiritual symbols such as persons, places, events). Such *sancta* inspire feelings of reverence, commemorate what the group believes to be most valuable, provide historical continuity, and strengthen the collective consciousness of the people. In order for the Jewish community to survive, Kaplan believed it must eliminate its authoritarian, dogmatic features. In particular, Judaism must divest itself of supernatural belief – the spiritual dimensions of the faith should be reformed in humanistic and naturalistic terms.

Many of the ideas found in *Judaism as a Civilization* were reflected in religious literature that appeared during this period including the New Haggadah and the Sabbath Prayer Book. Later in the 1940s and 1950s the leaders of Reconstructionism insisted that they were not attempting to form a new branch of Judaism. Yet, by the 1960s the Reconstructionist movement had become a denomination: it had created a seminary to train Reconstructionist rabbis and had instituted a congregational structure. Regarding halakhah, the Reconstructionist Rabbinical Assocation issued a statement at its 1980 convention that placed authority in the Jewish people (as opposed to the rabbis) and created a process whereby each congregation would be free to evolve its own *minhag* (customs). Three years later the Association produced guidelines on intermarriage, encouraging rabbis to welcome mixed couple (a Jew and non-Jew), permit them to participate in Jewish synagogue life, and recognize their children as Jewish if raised as Jews. In addition, the Association decreed that rabbis could sanctify an intermarriage as long as it was accompanied by a civil, rather than a religious ceremony. Today the Reconstructionist movement has become a central element of the Jewish establishment in the United State with its own leaders and institutional structure.

Further reading

Rosenthal, Gilbert S. (1979) *The Many Forces of Judaism; Orthodox, Conservative, Reconstructionalist, Reform*, Springfield, NJ: Behrman House.

DAN COHN-SHERBOK

REFORM JUDAISM

This is a post-Enlightenment Jewish movement that attempts to develop a form of the Jewish faith that is more relevant to the modern world. The Reform movement began in the 1820s at the Sephardic Congregation, Beth Elohim, in Charleston, where younger members desired a liturgy that made more use of English, rather than Hebrew, which many did not understand. Their petition was rejected, and in 1824 they seceded to form the Reform Society of Israelites, under the leadership of Isaac Harby.

A similar movement was already taking place in Germany, and in 1846 Rabbi Isaac M. Wise – Bohemian by birth – came to live in Albany, New York and subsequently Cincinnati, to minister to the German Jewish settlers. In 1857 Wise published a revised prayer book, which made use of German as well as Hebrew.

A number of rabbinical conferences in the nineteenth century pioneered the Reform movement. Of central importance to the establishment of Reform Judaism in the USA was the Pittsburgh Declaration of 1885, where the attending rabbis affirmed that Judaism was 'a progressive religion, ever striving to be in accord with the postulates of reason', and declared acceptance only of those laws and rituals that were morally and spiritually improving, and consistent with modern lifestyle. In Britain, the Reform movement affirmed the authority of the Tanakh (Jewish scripture), rather the Talmud. However, increasingly there was a trend towards theological conservativism, which was particularly evident at a conference in Columbus, Ohio in 1937.

The main innovations in Reform Judaism have included the use of the vernacular in worship, the ordination of women rabbis, and bat-mitzvah ceremonies for girls as well as for boys. The liturgy uses shorter Torah readings than those of Orthodox synagogues, and there is greater use of inclusive language. The covering of the head in worship was declared to be outmoded, although the practice can still be found in British Reform congregations. Originally anti-Zionist, this stance has now been officially abandoned.

Wise founded the Union of American Hebrew Congregations, with its headquarters in Cincinnati, in 1875, and the World Union for Progressive Judaism is the organization to which Reform congregations collectively belong. In 1877 the Hebrew Union College was established for the training of Reform rabbis. In 1956 the Jewish Theological College was founded in Britain for this purpose, later renamed the Leo Baeck College.

Further reading

Cronbach, A. (1963) *Reform Movements in Judaism*, New York: Bookman Associates.

Philipson, D., and Philipson, F. (1967) *The Reform Movement in Judaism*, New York: Ktav.

GEORGE CHRYSSIDES

REFORMED CHURCH IN JAPAN

During the late nineteenth and early twentieth centuries American Reformed and Presbyterian missionaries played a significant role in all aspects of the development of the Protestant movement in Japan. In 1877 the Reformed and Presbyterian groups joined together to form the *Nihon Kirisuto Ichi Kyokai* (United Church of Christ in Japan). This amalgamated church, later known as the *Nihon Kirsuto Kyokai* (Church of Christ in Japan), remained with the *Nihon Kumiai Kirisuto Kyokai* (the Congregational

Church in Japan) and the *Nihon Meso-jisuto Kyokai* (Japan Methodist Church), one of the three largest Protestant denominations in Japan until the union of all Protestant denominations into the *Nihon Kirisuto Kyodan* (**United Church of Christ in Japan**) in 1941. Prior to Protestant union, the *Nihon Kirisuto Kyokai* had, at its height, some 62,000 members and over 600 ordained ministers. As well as having an extensive network of affiliated secondary schools and theological seminaries in Japan, the Church also maintained overseas missionary work in Manchuria, China, Korea, Taiwan, and Singapore.

A new era in Japanese Christian history opened with the end of the Second World War in East Asia in 1945 and the beginning of the Allied Occupation of Japan. The surrender of Japan brought about an end of Emperor-centred militarism and opened the way for a broader range of beliefs and practices under a new postwar constitution that guaranteed complete religious freedom. The Occupation years between 1945 and 1951 saw a Christian boom and rapid growth. In part, this was caused by the social upheaval and disillusion brought on by Japan's defeat which drew many Japanese to look to Christianity for spiritual fulfilment. Further, the relief efforts of Christian agencies and churches in helping to alleviate the physical suffering of Japanese led to the creation of a positive image of Christianity.

The repeal of the 1940 Religious Bodies Law also allowed Protestants to decide whether they wished to remain within the *Nihon Kirisuto Kyodan*. Many left the union church to re-establish their former denominations including Anglicans, Lutherans, Baptists, and those belonging to Evangelical and Holiness churches. While the majority of Presbyterians chose to remain in the *Kyodan*, some also left, most notably churches of the southern Presbyterian tradition.

The Reformed Church in Japan (*Nihon Kirisuto Kaikakuha Kyokai*) was founded in April 1946 in Tokyo by nine teachers and three elders from the pre-1941 *Nihon Kirisuto Kyokai* and *Nihon Choro Kyokai* (Presbyterian Church in Japan). The new church adopted the Westminster Standards (with Larger and Shorter Catechisms) as its doctrinal standards. It was structurally organized along Presbyterian lines. It quickly received missionary support from the Christian Reformed Church in North America. In 1950 the Cumberland Presbyterian Church, which had conducted missionary work in Japan between 1877 and 1906, returned to support a congregation led by Yoshizaki Tadao, a former *Kyodan* pastor. In 1951 a number of churches with a Reformed-Presbyterian background separated from the *Kyodan* and formed a new *Nihon Kirisuto Kyokai*. Also in 1951, the *Nihon Kirisuto Kaikaku Choro Kyokai* (the Reformed Presbyterian Church in Japan) was founded in Kobe by American Presbyterian missionaries who had left China on account of the Chinese Revolution. In 1956 the *Nihon Fukuin Kaikakuha Kyokai* (Japan Evangelical Reformed Church) was formed. In 1978 the *Seisho Kirisuto Kyokai* (Biblical Church) became a Presbyterian-Reformed denomination. In 1993 a new *Nihon Choro Kyokai* was created through the union of two smaller Presbyterian groups.

The majority of these churches remain very small. The largest are the *Nihon Kirisuto Kaikaku Choro Kyokai* with over 13,000 members and 150 ordained clergy; and the *Nihon Kirisuto Kaikaku Kyokai* with close to 10,000 members and 130 ordained clergy. The tantalizing possibility of rapid growth in Christian numbers, which appeared in the Occupation period, proved a chimera for increase in size has been slow. Between 1970 and 1990, rooted in past history and practices, the Reformed Churches and other mainline Protestant groups appeared unresponsive to changes in Japanese religiosity, such as those indicated by the popularity of new new religions (*shin shin shukyo*) (see **New Religion (Japan)**). In the new millennium, the Protestant movement faces many challenges in postmodern Japanese society, including becoming effectively connected to the concerns of the contemporary generation. Yet the many branches of the Reformed Church illustrate that there is a rich diversity within the Protestant movement from which new responses can emerge.

Further reading

Mullins, M. (2000) *Christianity Made in Japan. A Study of Indigenous Movements,* Honalulu: University of Hawai'i Press.

Drummond, R. H (1971) *A History of Christianity in Japan,* Grand Rapids: Eerdmans.

A. HAMISH ION

REIKI

(a.k.a. Usui Shiko Ryoho System of Healing)

Founder: Usui, Mikao

Reiki is the art of applying by means of a technique the ki or unversal life energy for the purpose of healing and wholeness. As a system of healing reiki is traced back to Usui Makao who was a Christian minister in Kyoto, Japan, in the late nineteenth century. While in Chicago studying for his doctorate, at Loyola University, Usui became interested in Buddhist teachings and in particular in those relating to healing. Back in Japan he came across a discussion in the sutras on healing power and how to activate and apply it. Usui then made a retreat lasting twenty-one days before proceeding to apply what he had discovered and the result was a number of miraculous healings.

A core idea of Usui's was that the one who administers reiki should act as a channel allowing the energy to flow through her/his hand to the patient. Moreover, practitioners were to follow five principles which he enunciated as gratitude for the blessings of the day, the decision each day not to worry on that day, the pledge each day not to be angry, to daily pledge to work honestly, and the promise made each day to be kind to neighbours and every living thing.

Reiki theory, history and techniques including the technique of the laying on of hands, are taught in workshops. The initial stages of the teaching focus on hand placement. Students are shown the method to use when placing the hands on the four points of the three parts (head, front, and back) of the body. There are also special hand placements for specific physical conditions and for the curing of animals. The master leading the workshop will activate the *ki* or universal energy in the students present and teach them how to use this energy whenever necessary. This initial training takes on average two days. A later stage of training is concerned with the methods used to activate the energy needed to heal patients who absent and with those developed for the purpose of healing deeply rooted emotional and psychological illnesses.

Grand masters provide a third level of training by teaching others to become reiki masters and teachers. Much of the emphasis at this stage is on the trainees' inner development growth.

Once initiated as a reiki master it is possible to go beyond this third stage of training by acquiring, again at the hands of a grand master, the knowledge and skills necessary for initiating another person, who must have already completed the second stage, into the third level.

Usui was succeeded as grand master first by Hayashi Chijuro who was followed by Takata Hawayo, a Japanese-American who had been living in Hawaii. Takata developed cancer, returned to Japan where she met several reiki practitioners who allegedly healed her before she returned to the United States.

In the later 1930s Takata succeeded Hayashi as grand master and worked on in Hawaii from where she spread reiki across the United States initiating reiki masters and teaching others to initiate masters. The American Reiki Association (now known as the Radiance Technique Association International (RTAI)) was founded in 1980, the year of Takata's death. Others whom Takata initiated have formed the Reiki Alliance. By the time of her death Takata Hawayo had trained no less than twenty-two grand masters of reiki.

Further reading

Lubeck, Walter (1998) *Complete Reiki Handbook*, Delhi: MLBD.
Petsch, Rahim (2002) *Reiki: A Way of Life*, New Delhi: B. Jain Books.

PETER B. CLARKE

REIYÛKAI

Founded in 1930 by Kubo Kakutarô (1892–1944) and Kotani Kimi (1901–71), Reiyûkai Kyôdan is a lay Buddhist movement based on the Lotus Sutra and the example of the monk Nichiren Daishonin (1222–82). Its primary practice is the veneration of ancestors, believed capable of simultaneously bringing about the salvation of their spirits, one's own spiritual development, and the betterment of society. One of the largest of Japan's new religions (see **New Religion**

(Japan)), it is significant in representing a contemporary, urban adaptation of ancestor worship, and as the matrix of many similar movements.

The huge death toll of the 1923 Taishô earthquake in Tokyo awakened Kubo to the need to enshrine spirits of the dead as ancestors, to ensure their attainment of Buddhahood. This he saw as a duty of lay people, which could not be entrusted to the Buddhist priesthood, as was the long-established custom in Japan. Kubo believed that lay people are fully capable of performing all religious services and rejected all clerical mediation. Kubo's sister-in-law Kotani Kimi was a skilled organizer who proselytized widely and taught her followers to chant the **daimoku** (the title of the Lotus Sutra) and to recite an abridged version of the sutra before a simple home altar. Individual ancestors' names were to be collected and recorded in a Register of Posthumous Names. Under her presidency (1930–71), the group expanded dramatically.

Reiyûkai developed largely as an urban group, centering on the self-employed or those engaged in small businesses. Its small-group counseling provide a rare source of ethical guidance in Japanese urban society. Women are a majority of the membership and are prominent as branch leaders and local organizers. Local leaders have considerable autonomy, creating the possibility for the more than twenty large-scale schisms Reiyûkai has experienced, leading in the case of **Risshô Kôsei-kai**, to a larger organization than the parent group. Nevertheless, the fact that most of the schisms have maintained Reiyûkai's main beliefs and practices intact is eloquent proof of Reiyûkai's widespread appeal and strong connection with foundational elements of the Japanese religious tradition. At the beginning of the twenty-first century, Reiyûkai has roughly 2,500,000 members worldwide.

Further reading

Hardacre, H. (1984) *Lay Buddhism in Contemporary Japan: Reiyûkai Kyôdan*, Princeton: Princeton University Press.

HELEN HARDACRE

RESOURCE GUIDE TO NRM STUDIES

The contemporary study of New Religions grew from two roots, the study of 'cults' (sects in Europe) early in the twentieth century (see **Cult and New Religions**), and the burst of religious life in Japan following World War Two. As early as the 1890s, church leaders concerned with the emergence of heretical minority religions in the atmosphere of religious freedom produced the first writings about 'cults'. Through the twentieth century, a set of Christian counter cult literature would begin to circulate in conservative Protestant circles and occasionally, as both the psychology and sociology of religion developed as distinctive areas of research, scholars would try their hand at tackling the subject – favored targets being independent African American groups (**Father Divine's Peace Mission**, Church of God and Saints of Christ), proselytizing Christian sectarian groups (Jehovah's Witnesses, Seventh-day Adventists) and alternative religions with distinctive practices (Spiritualism, **Christian Science**).

Notable among the early studies are Elmer T. Clark, *The Psychology of Religious Awakening* (New York: Macmillan, 1929); Louis R. Binder, *Modern Religious Cults and Society* (Boston: R. G. Badger, 1933); and Arthur Huff Fauset, *Black Gods of the Metropolis, Negro Religious Cults of the Urban North* (Philadelphia: University of Pennsylvania Press, 1944).

These early volumes led to the pioneer studies in what would emerge in the 1970s as New Religions Studies. In America, several scholars went about the work of surveying and cataloging all the divergences in American sectarian religion, which prior to 1965 included few overtly non-Christian groups. Elmer T. Clark's *Small Sects in America* (1937, 1949) remains a useful survey of the spectrum of religions in the United States prior to World War Two (and more complete than the last government census in 1936). Clark's work influenced F. E. Mayer, a theologian at Concordia Theological Seminary (sponsored by the Lutheran Church-Missouri Synod), to produce several editions of his *The Religious Bodies of America* (1954).

Clark's and Mayer's work would lead in two very different directions. They provided material from which Christian counter-cultists (see **Anti-Cult Movement**) could begin to produce the wealth of material decrying different religions as heretical and unchristian (the subject of an insightful recent study by Douglas Cowan, *Bearing False Witness? An Introduction to the Christian Countercult* (Westport, CT: Praeger, 2003)). They also led to a generation of scholarship, which has specialized in the attempt to survey and understand the emerging religious pluralism in the West following the 1965 change in immigration laws in America. Following Mayer's death, colleague Arthur C. Piepkorn picked up his work and produced what was to be a multi-volume survey. His untimely death as the work was being finished resulted in only the first three volumes of *Profiles in Belief* (New York: Harper 1977, 1978, 1979) appearing. These were limited to the primary Christian bodies. However, Piepkorn's work was then assumed by the Institute for the Study

481

of American Religion, which in 1979 published the first edition of its *Encyclopedia of American Religions*. Now in its eighth edition (Detroit: Gale Group, 2002), the *Encyclopedia* has become a standard reference work offering basic information on all of the known New Religions operating in North America. The *Encyclopedia* has stimulated similar works in other countries and languages (including an Italian religions encyclopedia by Massimo Introvigne and his colleagues at the Center for Studies on New Religions in Torino), and undergirds the forthcoming *Encyclopedia of Canadian Religions* by James A. Beveley.

The pioneering social science work on 'cults' led directly to the groundbreaking work of sociologist Bryan Wilson whose numerous papers and several books on British sects provided a new legitimacy for the study of New Religions in the academy. His observations on their role in society provided scholars with a new agenda quite apart from attacking 'cults' as deviant or even harmful religion. Wilson's *Sects and Society* (Berkeley: University of California Press, 1961) and *Religious Sects: A Sociological Study* (London: Weidenfeld and Nicolson, 1970) remain essential reading for any who would master the field.

Meanwhile, in Japan, the introduction of an American-style religious freedom during the post-war occupation, led to a burst of religious activity that was keynoted by the revival of religions suppressed by the Meiji government and the emergence of a host of newly founded religions. Most of these groups were variations on the established Buddhist, Shinto, and Christian religions of Japan, though some were attempts at combining several traditions. Japanese scholars took note and by the 1960s had dubbed these groups the *New Religions of Japan*, (see **New Religion (Japan)**) the title of an early volume by Harry Thompsen (Rutland, VT/Tokyo: Charles E. Tuttle, 1963), which provided sketches of the most successful of the new movements. Equally important in catching the attention of Western scholars would be Clark B. Offner's *Modern Japanese Religions* (New York: Twayne Publishers, 1963) and H. Neill McFarland's *Rush Hour of the Gods: A Study of New Religious Movements in Japan* (New York: Macmillan Company, 1967).

New religions in the West

Two events stimulated the rise of the community of scholars who now specialize in New Religions Studies. In 1965, the United States passed a new immigration law that allowed for the first time in half a century the movement of large numbers of Asians to the United States. The several Asian teachers who arrived with the tens of thousands of Asians over the next few years encountered the large number of Baby Boomers just coming of age (Roof, Wade Clark (1999) *Spiritual Marketplace. Baby Boomers and the Remaking of American Religion*, Princeton, NJ: Princeton University Press). The Baby Boomers provided a wealth of recruits for the new religions and allowed an initial burst of growth that caught the attention of both the media and scholars.

Hippie religion, with its most visible phase in California, would provide the problem out of which New Religious Studies would emerge. By the end of the 1960s, scholars in the San Francisco Bay area would be hard at work and the 1969 volume by Jacob Needleman, *The New Religions* (New York: E. P. Dutton) would generate a new level of interest among North American scholars. Through the early- and mid-1970s, a host of significant papers and books would be generated by a cadre of studies based at the University of California and the adjacent Graduate Theological School. Still worth perusing are Charles T. Gloch and Robert N. Bellah (eds), *The New Religious Consciousness* (Berkeley: University of California Press, 1976), Robert Wuthnow, *The Consciousness Reformation* (Berkeley: University of California Press, 1976); Robert Wuthnow, *Experimentation in American Religion: The New Mysticisms and Their Implications for the Churches* (Berkeley: University of California Press, 1978), and Stephen Tipton, *Getting Saved from the Sixties: Moral Meaning in Conversion and Cultural Studies* (Berkeley: University of California Press, 1982).

The Berkeley studies had a double-edged effect. While stimulating interest in New Religions, they tied the phenomena to the unrest associated with the counter-culture (thus suggesting an ephemerality) and to California as a unique generating location. Only later, when scholars were surprised by the steady creation of new religions decade by decade long after the counterculture had died did they develop a more historically sophisticated view of the emergence of new religions as part of the overall twentieth-century trend toward greater religious pluralism. In Europe, the Berkeley studies also led to a popular view that the parallel emergence of new religions was due to their importation from America. See, for example, the essays in John Coleman and Gregory Baum, *New Religious Movements* (Edinburgh: T. T. Clark, 1983) and Allan P. Brockway and J. Paul Rajashekar (eds) *New Religious Movements and the Churches* (Geneva: World Council of Churches, 1987).

Working in southern California at the same time that the Berkeley studies were occurring, Robert Elwood, Jr. emerged as one of the most important thinkers about New Religions as the author of a series of books including *Alternative Altars* (Chicago: University of Chicago Press, 1978) and with Harry B. Parrin, *Religious and Spiritual Groups in Modern America* (Englewood Cliffs, NJ: Prentice Hall, 1983).

Often overlooked in New Religious Studies is the development of research in Europe and especially the United Kingdom, most of which can be traced to Bryan Wilson and his students. Rising to the top in England through the 1970s and 1980s were Eileen Barker, James Beckford and Peter Clarke all of whom took a more theoretical approach than the Americans, though not to be forgotten among the early studies is Geoffrey K. Nelson's still valuable research on British Spiritualism, *Spiritualism and Society* (New York: Schocken Books, 1969) that went a long way to removing misconceptions of cults as one-generation phenomena.

The brainwashing controversy

The emergence of New Religions Studies in the 1970s was intimately tied to the public controversy over the movement of many young adults into the groups in spite of parental disapproval. While a longstanding Christian countercult movement had been publishing literature for many decades, the 1970s saw the birth of a new set of anti-cult literature that attempted to attack the new religions from purely secular grounds. The controversy appeared to be dying out when in 1978 the tragic incident at Jonestown, Guyana occurred in which over 900 people lost their lives. In response, the cult awareness movement experienced a rebirth and adopted as a tool in its attack the idea that the new religions succeeded by using **brainwashing** techniques to recruit and hold members against their better judgment and free will.

Brainwashing was offered as a questionable justification in court for the practice of coercive **deprogramming**, in which people were removed from groups and forced to undergo an intensive counter indoctrination program to convince them to renounce their membership. It was subsequently introduced into the court system as a justification for civil suits by former members who claimed to have been damaged by their association with cults. The brainwashing debate would draw several hundred scholars into New Religions Studies in the 1980s. It would lead to advocates of brainwashing preparing a report for the American Psychological Association, the rejection of that report by the APA, and the subsequent end of testimony on that issue in court by the two most prominent proponents – psychologist Margaret Singer and sociologist Richard Ofshe.

For an overview of the brainwashing controversy see J. Gordon Melton 'Brainwashing and the Cults: The Rise and Fall of a Theory' originally published in German in J. Gordon Melton and Massimo Introvigne (eds), *Gehirnwäsche und Secten. Interdisziplinäre Annäherungen* (Marburg, Germany: Dialogonal-Verlag, 2000). It is posted in English at http://www.cesnur.org/testi/melton.htm. The earlier phase of the controversy is highlighted in greater depth in James T. Richardson and David G. Bromley (eds), *The Brainwashing/Deprogramming Controversy* (Lewiston, NY: Edwin Mellen Press, 1983).

For an early statement of the pro-brainwashing position, see John G. Clark, Michael D. Langone, Robert E. Schacter, and Roger C. B. Daly, *Destructive Cultism: Theory, Research, and Treatment* (Weston, MA: Center on Destructive Cultism, 1981). *The Cultic Studies Journal* was founded in 1984 to publish research supportive of the brainwashing

hypothesis (along with other anti-cult perspectives). A more recent summary of negative psychological approaches, with essays gathered after Singer and the refusal of the court to hear testimony on brainwashing in 1990, can be found in Michael D. Langone (ed.), *Recovery from Cults: Help for Victims of Psychological Abuse* (New York: W. W. Norton & Company, 1993). For a psychological perspective, not using a brainwashing approach, see Marc Galanter, *Cults: Faith, Healing, and Coercion* (New York: Oxford University Press, 1989).

Most scholars of New Religions have opposed the brainwashing hypothesis as having no empirical base, but more importantly, from its lack of usefulness in explaining the phenomena they were observing in the New Religions. Important statements of that opposition can be found in Thomas Robbins and Dick Anthony, 'The Limits of "Coercive Persuasion" as an Explanation for Conversion to Authoritarian Sects,' *Political Psychology* 2, 22 (Summer 1980): 22-37; Eileen Barker, *The Making of a Moonie: Choice or Brainwashing* (Oxford: Blackwell, 1984); Dick Anthony, 'Religious Movements and "Brainwashing" Litigation: Evaluating Key Testimony,' in Thomas Robbins and Dick Anthony (eds), *In Gods We Trust: New Patterns of Religious Pluralism in America*, 2nd edn (New Brunswick, NJ: Transaction Press, 1989): 295–344; and James T. Richardson, 'A Social Psychological Critique of "Brainwashing" Claims about Recruitment to New Religions,' in David G. Bromley and Jeffrey K. Hadden (eds), *The Handbook of Cults and Sects in America. Religion and the Social Order,* Vol. 3 (Part B) (Greenwich, CT: JAI Press, 1993).

In spite of the recent attempt by several scholars to reopen the brainwashing debate at the end of the 1990s, it remains largely separated from the main thrust of New Religions Studies and does not appear to have informed researchers on New Religions since the 1980s. Brainwashing remains a hypothesis with a few advocates but little data to commend it to those studying the different New Religious Movements. On the latest attempt to again raise the issue, see Benjamin Zablocki and Thomas Robbins (eds) *Misunderstanding Cults: Searching for Objectivity in a Controversial Field* (Toronto: University of Toronto Press, 2001).

The brainwashing controversy did highlight the many legal issues surrounding New Religions as they negotiate their place in the pluralistic work. Sociologist and legal scholar James T. Richardson has taken the lead in this area. The author of numerous papers, his most recent contribution is *Regulating Religion: Case Studies from Around the Globe* (New York: Plenum Publishing, 2004). Also worthy of note is Derek H. Davis and Barry Hankins (eds), *New Religious Movements & Religious Liberty in America* (Waco, TX: J. M. Dawson Institute of Church–State Studies, 2002), and Derek H. David and Gerhard Besier (eds), *International Perspectives of Freedom and Equality of Religious Belief* (Waco, TX: J. M. Dawson Institute of Church–State Studies, Baylor University, 2002).

New religions: a basic library

Over recent decades the field of New Religions Studies has produced a wealth of material, amply demonstrated in the number of book length bibliographies that now provide entrances into all the works from which this essay can at best only pick and choose. However, anyone wanting to have a basic overview of what is available would do well to become aware of the several bibliographies, of which four stand out: John

A. Saliba, *Social Science and the Cults: An Annotated Bibliography* (New York: Garland Publishing, 1990); John A. Saliba, *Psychiatry and the Cults: An Annotated Bibliography* (New York: Garland Publishing, 1987); Elizabeth Arweck and Peter B. Clarke, *New Religious Movements in Western Europe: An Annotated Bibliography* (Westport, CT: Greenwood Press, 1997); and Peter Clarke, *A Bibliography of Japanese New Religions* (Richmond, Surrey, UK: Japan Library, 1999).

Over the last two decades a variety of volumes have appeared that offer an overview of the field with more or less attention to prominent examples of the hundreds of new religions. Many of these have found their way into use as textbooks. They include volumes by sociologists Eileen Barker, *New Religious Movements: A Practical Introduction* (London: Her Majesty's Stationary Office, 1989); David G. Bromley and Jeffrey K. Hadden (eds) *Religion and the Social Order: The Handbook on Cults and Sects in America* (Greenwich, CT: JAI Press, 1993); William Sims Bainbridge, *The Sociology of Religious Movements* (New York: Routledge, 1997); and Lorne L. Dawson, *Comprehending Cults: The Sociology of New Religious Movements* (Toronto: Oxford University Press, 1998). Religious studies scholars have contributed: J. Gordon Melton, *The Encyclopedic Handbook of the Cults* (New York: Garland Publishing Company, 1992); John A. Saliba, *Perspectives on New Religious Movements* (London: Geoffrey Chapman, 1995) published in a revised edition as *Understanding New Religious Movements* (Walnut Creek, CA: Alta Mira Press, 2003); Timothy Miller (ed.), *America's Alternative Religions* (Albany, NY: State University of New York Press, 1995); and James R. Lewis, *Cults in America: A Reference Handbook* (Santa Barbara, CA: ABC-Clio, 1998).

Saliba's and Dawson's texts have proved the most popular textbooks in recent years and Dawson has edited a helpful supplementary reader *Cults and New Religious Movements: a Reader* (Malden, MA: Blackwell Publishing, 2003). Also, just released is James R. Lewis' compilation of articles from a number of outstanding scholars for the *Oxford Handbook on New Religions* (New York: Oxford University Press, 2003).

Other works of a general nature that deserve mention include: Eileen Barker and Margit Warburg (eds), *New Religions and New Religiosity* (Aarhus, Denmark: Aarhus University Press, 1997); David V. Barrett, *Believers: Sects, Cults and Alternative Religions* (London: Cassell & Company, 2001); George D. Chryssides, *Exploring New Religions* (London: Cassell, 1999); Peter Clarke (ed.), *The New Evangelists: Recruitment, Methods and Aims of New Religious Movements* (London: Ethnographica, 1987); Geoffrey K. Nelson, *Cults, New Religions and Religious Creativity* (London: Routledge & Kegan Paul, 1987); and Bryan Wilson and Jamie Cresswell (eds), *New Religious Movements: Challenge and Response* (London: Routledge, 1999).

In addition to the survey texts, a variety of books have attempted to approach particular problems highlighted by the existence of the New Religions. Philip Jenkins has, for example, inquired into their role in the American past in his outstanding study, *Mystics and Messiahs: Cults and New Religions in American History* (Oxford: Oxford University Press, 2000). Catherine Wessinger and Susan J. Palmer have taken the lead in looking at women and children caught up in NRMs: Catherine Wessinger (ed.), *Women's Leadership in Marginal Religions: Explorations Outside the Mainstream* (Urbana: University of Illinois Press, 1993); Susan J. Palmer (ed.), *Moon Sisters, Krishna Mothers, Rajneesh Lovers. Women's Role in New Religions* (Syracuse, NY: Syracuse University Press, 1994) and Susan J. Palmer and Charlotte E. Hardman (eds), *Children in New Religions* (New Brunswick, NJ: Rutgers University Press, 1999). David Bromley pulled together an important set of papers on the role of former members on the life of religious groups in *The Politics of Religious Apostasy: The Role of Apostates in the Transformation of Religious Movements* (Westport CT, London: Praeger, 1998). Earlier mention was made of the critique of assumptions built up over the years concerning NRMs, and in 1991, Timothy Miller dealt in depth with one of those truisms, the supposed crisis when a founder dies, in the essays collected for *When Prophets Die: The Postcharismatic Fate of New Religious Movements* (Albany, NY: State University of New York Press, 1991).

During the 1990s, the successive violent incidents of the Branch Davidians, the Solar Temple, **Aum Shinrikyo**, **Heaven's Gate**, and the Movement for the Restoration of the Ten Commandments brought the issue of violence and the New Religions again to the fore, especially in light of speculation about the approaching Millennium. Among the best texts discussing violence are Catherine Wessinger (ed.), *Millennialism, Persecution, and Violence: Historical Cases* (Syracuse: Syracuse University Press, 2000); John H. Hall (2000) *Apocalypse Observed: Religious Movements and Violence in North America, Europe, and Japan* (London: Routledge, 2000); Catherine Wessinger, *How the Millennium Comes Violently: From Jonestown to Heaven's Gate* (New York: Seven Bridges Press, 2000); and David G. Bromley and J. Gordon Melton (eds), *Cults, Religion and Violence* (Cambridge: Cambridge University Press, 2002).

Turning from the general to the particular, observation has been made elsewhere that only a modest number of the New Religions, the more controversial and a few believed to have particular value in highlighting theoretical concerns have been studied to the point that a book has been written about them. Beginning with the **Unification Movement** led by the Rev. Sun Myung Moon, different groups have spent time at the top of the list of the more controversial groups. That list would include the **International Society for Krishna Consciousness**, the **Church of Scientology**, the **Church Universal and Triumphant**, The Children of God (now known as **The Family**), and **Soka Gakkai**. Each has been the subject of book-length studies

Concerning the Unification Church, Barker's *The Making of a Moonie: Choice or Brainwashing* (Oxford: Blackwell, 1984) remains an important source, though dated in many respects concerning the fast paced group, as is the other early volume, David G. Bromley and Anson Shupe Jr., *Moonies in America* (Beverley Hills, CA: Sage, 1979). An updated study has appeared from Massimo Introvigne, *The Unification Church.* (Salt Lake City, UT: Signature Books, 2000).

Because of their sexual teachings and the resultant scandals, as series of books have appeared on The Family. Of these, three rise to the top, James D. Chancellor, *Life in the Family: An Oral History of the Children of God* (Syracuse, NY: Syracuse University Press, 2000); William Sims Bainbridge, *The Endtime Family: Children of God* (Albany: State University of New York Press, 2002); and J. Gordon Melton, *The Children of God/The Family* (Salt Lake City, UT: Signature Books, 2004).

The Krishna Consciousness Movement was the focus of an important ex-member court case in the 1980s and has more recently been beset with problems of widespread schism, the conviction of one of its former gurus for murder, and an ongoing lawsuit growing out of some child abuse that occurred at one of its schools. Early research on the Krishnas was summarized in E. Burke Rochford, Jr., *Hare Krishna in America* (New Brunswick, NJ: Rutgers University Press, 1985); Kim Knott, *My Sweet Lord: The Hare Krishna Movement* (Wellingborough, UK: Aquarian Press, 1986); Larry D. Shinn, *The Dark Lord: Cult Images and the Hare Krishnas in America* (Philadelphia: Westminster Press, 1987); and David G. Bromley and Larry D. Shinn (eds), *Krishna Consciousness in the West* (Lewisburg: Bucknell University Press, 1989). Rochford has continued to study the Krishnas over the years and most recently has prepared a lengthy article concerning the movement's current problems 'Child Abuse in the Hare Krishna Movement: 1971–1986', *Cult Studies Review* 1(1) (2001) (and posted at http://www.cultsandsociety.com/csr_articles/rochford_burke_heinlein_p1.htm.

The controversy surrounding the group that gathered around **Bhagwan Rajneesh** (later known **Osho**) quieted considerably following his death, but memory of the community he built in rural Oregon lingers as does his movement. The best coverage is provided by Lewis F. Carter, *Charisma and Control in Rajneeshpuram* (Cambridge: Cambridge University Press, 1990) and Judith Fox, *Osho Rajneesh* (Salt Lake City, UT: Signature Books, 2003). Soka Gakkai went from being one of the most controversial of the New Religions to part of the religious establishment in Japan when the politics aligned with it became part of the ruling power structure. In the meantime it had become the subject of a spectrum of studies in Europe and America, including Bryan Wilson and Karel Dobbelaere, *A Time to Chant: The Soka Gakkai Buddhists in Britain* (Oxford: Oxford University Press, 1994); Philip Hammond and David Machacek, *Soka Gakkai in America: Accommodation and Conversion* (Oxford: Oxford University Press, 1999); David Machacek and Bryan Wilson (eds), *Global Citizens: The Soka Gakkai Movement in the World* (Oxford: Oxford University Press, 2000); and Karel Dobbelaere, *Soka Gakkai: From Lay Movement to Religion* (Salt Lake City, UT: Signature Books, 2003).

Western esotericism

By far the largest number of New Religionists are attached to the many groups of the Western Esoteric tradition. These groups flow out of the history that can be traced to modern Rosicrucianism (see **Rosicrucian Order**, **Crotona Fellowship**), Speculative Freemasonry, and Theosophy. While strides have been made in understanding this most ahistorical tradition in recent decades, many who have done otherwise fine studies remain unaware of the historical background. Help with placing esoteric (or as they are sometimes known, occult, psychic, or New Age) groups on the religious landscape begins with J. Stillson Judah, *The History and Philosophy of the Metaphysical Movements in America* (Philadelphia: The Westminster Press, 1967) and the more recent volumes by Antoine Faivre and Jacob Needleman (eds), *Modern Esoteric Spirituality* (New York: Crossroad, 1992) and Wouter J. Hanegraaff, *New Age Religion and Western Culture: Esotericism in the Mirror of Secular Thought* (Leiden: Brill, 1996).

The Church of Scientology exists as both one of the most controversial of the New Religions and a representative of the Western Esoteric tradition. At its heart is a Gnostic-like myth utilizing space age metaphors. It has been the subject of a series of scholarly studies though not as many as its prominence merits, especially since the dramatic change at the beginning of the 1980s when the entire movement was reorganized from the top down. Roy Wallis' early volume *The Road to Total Freedom: A Sociological Analysis of Scientology* (New York: Columbia University Press, 1976) remains an important source. Studies since the reorganization include Harriet Whitehead, *Renunciation and Reformulation: A Study of Conversion in an American Sect* (Ithaca, NY: Cornell University Press, 1987), and J. Gordon Melton, *The Church of Scientology* (Salt Lake City, UT: Signature Books, 2001).

Work on Esoteric groups has been concentrated in several areas, most noticeably Witchcraft and Paganism, where three recent books have superseded earlier texts: Graham Harvey, *Contemporary Paganism: Listening People, Speaking Earth* (New York: New York University Press, 1997); Ronald Hutton, *The Triumph of the Moon: A History of Modern Pagan Witchcraft* (Oxford: Oxford University Press, 2000); and Sarah M. Pike (ed.) *Earthly Bodies, Magical Selves: Contemporary Pagans and the Search for Community* (Berkeley: University of California Press, 2001). The vast literature that Wicca/Paganism has generated is surveyed in J. Gordon Melton and Issota Poggi, *Magic, Witchcraft, and Paganism in America: A Bibliography* (New York: Garland Publishing 1992).

Competing for interest with Wicca is the **New Age Movement**. The early work from the 1980s has now been superseded by several newer studies such as Paul Heelas, *The New Age Movement* (Oxford: Blackwell, 1996); Richard Kyle, *The New Age Movement in American Culture* (Lanham, MD: University Press of America, 1995); and Mikael Rothstein (ed.), *New Age Religion and Globalization* (Aarhus, Denmark: Aarhus University Press, 2001).

As a subclass of New Age studies, the phenomenon of channeling has received some attention, though often by scholars not otherwise connected with New Religions Studies. A most sympathetic study was done by psychologist Jon Klimo, *Channeling: Investigations on receiving Information from Paranormal Sources* (Berkeley, CA: North Atlantic Books, 1987, 1998). Slightly less enthusiastic is Arthur Hastings, *With the Tongues of Men and Angels: A Study in Channeling* (Fort Worth, TX: Holt, Rinehart and Winston, 1919), but both have been overshadowed by Michael F. Brown's *The Channeling Zone: American Spirituality in an Anxious Age* (Cambridge, MA: Harvard University Press, 1997). The only study of a channeling group yet to be published is J. Gordon Melton, *Finding Enlightenment: Ramtha's School of Enlightenment* (Hillsboro, OR: Beyond Words, 1998).

Further resources

In doing a bibliography in this day and age, one is remiss without mention of the Internet. In the case of New Religions, two excellent sites supplement the scholarly material on New Religions cited above. The New Religions Movements Page originally created by the late Jeffrey Hadden at the University of Virginia is now continued by Douglas Cowan from his base at the University of Missouri-Kansas City. It provides a range of resources, but has become best known for its sketches of several hundred New Religions. It may be accessed at http://religiousmovements.lib.virginia.edu/.

Also of immense value is the site sponsored by the Center for Studies on New Religion (CESNUR) in Italy. While some pages are in French or Italian, the great majority of the materials, including papers from the annual CESNUR conferences, are in English. Access the material at http://www.cesnur.org/. A third site of note, 'Alternative Considerations of Jonestown and Peoples Temple,' sponsored by the Department of Religious Studies at San Diego State University, under the direction of Dr Rebecca Moore and Fielding McGehee, continues the dialogue on this watershed incident

CESNUR is home to the largest research library on New Religions in Europe at its headquarters in Turin, Italy. A slightly larger selection of materials is now included as the American Religions Collection at Davidson Library of the University of California in Santa Barbara. It was donated by the Institute for the Study of American Religion (ISAR), which is located several blocks off of the UCSB campus. CESNUR and ISAR are but two of a growing number of centers that focus research on New Religions. In 1993 ISAR opened a second office in Toronto.

In England, two similar centers have emerged in the 1980s: The Centre for New Religions at King's College (1982) headed by Peter Clarke and no longer functioning since 2003 and INFORM (1988) (Information Network Focus on New Religions) headed by Eileen Barker. INFORM holds conferences on New Religions and maintains an extensive database on groups operating in the United Kingdom and elsewhere. Peter Clarke at the Centre for New Religions founded one of the two main journals covering New Religions, the *Journal of Contemporary Religion*, which continues to be published by Taylor & Francis and is co-edited by himslef and Elisabeth Arweck (http://www.tandf.co.uk/journals). The second journal, *Nova Religio*, is published by the University of California Press, and has the endorsement of the New Religious Movements Group of the American Academy of Religion (http://www.clas.ufl.edu/users/gthursby/aar-nrm/).

J. GORDON MELTON

RISSHÔ KÔSEI-KAI

Founder: **Niwano Nikkyô, Naganuma Myôkô**

One of the largest new religions in Japan (see **New Religions (Japan)**), Risshô Kôsei-kai was founded in 1938 by **Niwano Nikkyô** (1906–99) and Naganuma Myôkô (1889–1957) after they seceded from **Reiyukai**.

In 1935, seeking a cure for his second daughter's illness, Niwano Nikkyô joined Reiyu-kai and began to offer reverence to the spirits of his ancestors and then became active in Reiyu-kai as a missionary. He happened to meet Naganuma Myôkô in 1936 who at the time was suffering from a weak heart and an unhappy family life. Niwano Nikkyô advised her to pay reverence to the ancestors and persuaded her to become a member of Reiyu-kai. Both were later to oppose the proposal that the study of the Lotus Sutra should be abandoned and founded *Dai Nippon Risshô Kôsei-kai* in 1938. The name of the group was changed to Risshô Kôsei-kai and incorporated as a religious juridical person in 1952.

Naganuma Myôkô was of primary importance in the early years of Risshô Kôsei-kai, because of her shaman-like qualities and healing powers. Risshô Kôsei-kai rose to prominence after the Second World War when complete religious freedom was granted in Japan. The movement claimed in 1955 to have over 700,000 members. After the death of Naganuma Myôkô in 1957, the shamanistic practices ceased and great emphasis was placed on the study of Buddhist doctrine, especially the Lotus Sutra as religious practices, and on social activities.

In 1969, Risshô Kôsei-kai launched *Akarui Shakai zukuri Undo*, the Brighter Society Movement for fostering community-based voluntary activities, and in 1975 set up *Ichijiki wo Sasageru Undo*, sponsoring the Donate One Meal Campaign, whose participants forgo three meals a month and contribute the money to the Risshô Kôsei-kai Fund for Peace (see **Peace and Japanese New Religious Movements**). In recent years, Risshô Kôsei-kai has sponsored international movements such as the World Conference of Religions and Peace which seeks to promote world peace through inter-religious dialogue. Since the passing of Niwano Nikkyô in 1999, Risshô Kôsei-kai has been led by his son, Niwano Nichikô, who succeeded him as president in 1991.

The Lotus Sutra is the main scripture of this lay Buddhist movement. According to Risshô Kôsei-kai, the heart of the Lotus Sutra is divided into the three major concepts of **Mahayana** Buddhism:

1. All sentient beings can attain perfect enlightenment, that is, buddhahood, and nothing less than this is the appropriate final goal of believers;
2. the Buddha is eternal, having existed from the infinite past and appearing in many forms throughout the ages to guide living beings through the teaching of the Wonderful Dharma; and
3. the noblest form of Buddhist practice is the way of the bodhisattvas (see **Mahayana Buddhism**), those who devote themselves to attaining enlightenment not only for themselves but for all sentient beings.

Daily recitation of excerpts from the Lotus Sutra is one of the most essential practices of the members. The main chant is *Namu Myôhô Renge-kyô*, meaning 'to take refuge in the Lotus Sutra'. Members also recite *Kaiin Kôryô*, or vow: 'We, members of Rissho Kosei-kai, take refuge in the Eternal Buddha Shakyamuni, and recognize in Buddhism the true way of salvation, under the guidance of our revered founder, Nikkyo Niwano. In the sprit of lay Buddhists, we vow to perfect ourselves through personal discipline and leading others and by improving our knowledge and practice of the faith, and we pledge ourselves to follow the bodhisattva way.'

One of the most important activities of members is a unique form of group counselling called *hoza*, in which the members listen to each other and try to solve each others' problems according to Buddhist teachings. According to Rísshô Kôsei-kai, the purpose of *hoza* is to help all the participants reveal and develop the spark of divinity that dwells in everyone by working together with compassion to solve the problems of those who are troubled. Ancestor worship is encouraged as means of eliminating negative karmic effects.

Rísshô Kôsei-kai claims that there are some 6.5 million members in 239 branches throughout Japan as well as in six branches overseas. The president, other leaders and some 800 staff members are working at the headquarters in Wada, Suginami-ku, Tokyo.

Further reading

Clarke, P. B. (1999) *A Bibliography of Japanese New Religions*, Eastbourne (Kent): Japan Library, pp. 211–18.
Baumann, M. and Melton, G. (eds) (2002) *Religions of the World: A Comprehensive Encyclopedia of Beliefs and Practices*, Santa Barbara, CA: ABC-Clio, pp. 1084–6.

KEISHIN INABA

ROSICRUCIAN ORDER, CROTONA FELLOWSHIP

Founder: G. A. Sullivan
Country of origin: England/UK

The Rosicrucian Order, Crotona Fellowship (ROCF) was a neo-Rosicrucian group active in England in the 1920s and 1930s, first on Merseyside and subsequently in Christchurch and Southampton. The group was founded by George A. Sullivan (1890–1942) and its ritual practices were largely restricted to a circle of family and friends, although a correspondence course was devised for solitary members and there was a small London contact group. The group is of intrinsic interest as an English expression of neo-Masonic, neo-Rosicrucian values and practices in the interwar period, and its intimate, esoteric small group format illustrates a seminal lay response to the perceived stagnation of contemporary 'organized religion'. Furthermore the ROCF has had a diffuse and attenuated impact upon the development of **New Age Movements** and **Wicca** through the involvement of Peter Caddy and Gerald Gardner in its activities in the late 1930s (see **Caddy, Peter**; **Gardner, Gerald B.**).

The ROCF revolved around the charismatic leadership of its 'Supreme Magus', Sullivan, an amateur actor, poet and playwright who was active in occult networks of the day including **Theosophical** and Co-Masonic circles: Mabel Besant-Scott, daughter of Annie Besant, and leader of Co-Masonry in the UK, was a key ROCF member. Its origins are obscure: Sullivan claims that he founded the group in 1911 as 'The Order of Twelve', reviving it around 1920 under its present name, although in another pamphlet it is said to have existed in its present form for 'at least one hundred years' and to be descended from ancient Rosicrucian teachers. Its 'Grand Chapter' first operated in Birkenhead (*c.* 1924) and Liverpool (*c.* 1927) before moving to Christchurch in late 1935 and entering its most productive period. A wooden meeting hall was erected here in the garden of Sullivan's benefactor and thirty-six members – barristers, solicitors, small business operators, teachers, and clerical workers – attended its annual gathering in 1937 (Heselton 2000: 72*ff*). In 1938 a private theatre was built (Heselton 2000: 78*ff*) and some dedicated members bought bungalows nearby. The Order began to unravel after Sullivan's death, although Heselton (2000: 89) traces the group to Southampton in the early 1950s.

The Order's ritual practice required a small altar, a cloth with the Rosicrucian emblem, incense, candles, literature, and ritual regalia of the 'degree' attained by each member in the neo-Masonic hierarchy. Weekend activities and the annual gathering at the 'grand chapter' in Christchurch included communal worship, practical tasks and lectures. A 1925 pamphlet lists over 130 lectures in the Order's syllabus incorporating a wide range of occult and metaphysical material including 'positive thinking, healing techniques, empowering others, and growing into self-possession and self-control' (Caddy 1996: 33–4).

Despite intrinsic interest, the legacy of the ROCF is largely a product of the spiritual biographies of two participants: Peter Caddy and Gerald Gardner. Caddy (1996) makes no secret of his indebtedness to Sullivan and the Order. In the 1960s and early 1970s he sought to transfer the spirit of the ROCF to **Findhorn community** discourse and practice, renewing contact with surviving Order members and passing on some teachings at Findhorn. Caddy's own salience in New Age networking in the 1950s and 1960s, and the importance of Findhorn for international New Age culture from the 1960s onwards, means that a 'Rosicrucian' factor in New Age culture (in the UK at least) cannot be discounted. Gardner's case is more complex: he became involved with the Order briefly in 1938 and was largely sceptical, yet claims to have met a faction within the ROCF which belonged to a local witch coven, into which he was duly initiated and from which he subsequently fashioned Wicca. The historicity and mythic function of this surviving coven in legitimizing Wicca is the subject of a complex debate: the more immediate material influence of the ROCF's initiatic structure and esoteric fellowship upon Gardner's syncretic system has been less widely considered. Nevertheless, given Peter Caddy's prominence in the genealogy of New Age from the 1950s onwards, and Gerald Gardner's role in the creation of Wicca in the late 1940s, the ROCF has had an indirect impact on alternative spirituality in the UK out of all proportion to its slight historical and sociological profile.

Further reading

Caddy, P. (1996) *In Perfect Timing: Memoirs of a Man for the New Millenium*, Forres (Moray): Findhorn Press.

Heselton, P. (2000) *Wiccan Roots: Gerald Gardner and the Modern Witchcraft Revival*, Chieveley (Berkshire): Capall Bann.

McIntosh, C. (1987) *The Rosicrucians: the History and Mythology of an Occult Order*, Wellingborough (Northants): Crucible.

STEVEN J. SUTCLIFFE

S

SACRED NAME MOVEMENT

The term designates a number of organizations, originating in the 1930s in the USA, deriving from Seventh Day Church of God in Arkansas, and insisting on the importance of employing the original Hebrew names for God and Jesus (generally, but not exclusively, Yahweh and Yahshua). The Movement views the Old Testament as the key to interpreting the New, and celebrates the Jewish festivals of Passover, Pentecost and Tabernacles, as instructed in Leviticus 23. They reject the mainstream Christian festivals of Christmas and Easter on account of their pagan origins. They are non-Trinitarian, and other tenets include tithing, conscientious objection to military service, and the observance of the sabbath (Saturday) for rest and worship.

In 1937 C. O. Dodd, another early exponent, launched the magazine *The Faith*, which advocated the celebration of the Jewish feasts, and the following year he established the Faith Bible and Tract Society, which was continued by Dodd's family. The first of the Sacred Name organizations was the Assembly of Yahweh, in Eaton Rapids, Michigan – originally founded as the Assembly of YHWH in 1939.

The largest Sacred Name organization is the Assemblies of Yahweh, founded by Jacob O. Meyer in 1969. Meyer moved to Idaho in 1964, where he became Assistant Editor of the *Sacred Name Herald*. He was consecrated for ministry the following year, and began a radio ministry – 'Sacred Name Broadcast' – in 1966. This was followed by a television ministry, 'Sacred Name Telecast'.

Other early pioneers of the Sacred Name were Lorenzo Dow Snow (b. 1913) and his wife Icie Lela Paris Snow (b. 1912). Snow joined Dodd's Assemblies of Yahweh, and was licensed to preach in the 1940s. However, following a disagreement about the spelling of the divine name, Snow, together with E. B. Adam, formed a rival organization, the Assembly of Yahvah in Emory, Texas, in 1949. Snow published *The Yahwist Field Reporter,* which he edited from 1945 to 1961. The Assembly of Yahvah set up the Missionary Dispensary Bible Research, which brought out the *Restoration of the Original Sacred Name Bible,* a version of the scripture that restores the Hebrew names for God and Jesus.

Other Sacred Name communities include the Scripture Research Association (founded in 1950 by A. B. Traina), the Bible Study Association (established by David B. Northnagel in 1980), the Assembly of Yhwhhoshua (in Colorado), the Assemblies of the Called Out Ones of Yah (founded by Sam Surrat in 1974), and the House of Yahweh (originally founded in Nazareth, Israel in 1973 by Jacob Hawkins).

Further reading

Meyer, J. O. (1978) *The Memorial Name – Yahweh,* Bethel, PA: Assemblies of Yahweh.

Snow, E. D. (1982) 'A Brief History of the Name Movement in America', *Faith* 45 (January–February).

GEORGE CHRYSSIDES

SAHAJA YOGA

Sahaja Yoga was founded in 1970 by Sri Mataji Nirmala Devi (b. 1923), who is known simply as Mataji or the Divine Mother. She was born into a Protestant family in central India, and her husband is a high-ranking official in the United Nations, but Sahaja Yoga is in many ways a traditional Hindu path. Mataji was originally a disciple of **Osho** Rajneesh, but fell out with him and set up her own movement. She teaches mainly in Britain and India, but also has disciples worldwide and travels extensively. The movement claims approximately 20,000 members worldwide, half in India, with another 100,000 loosely associated.

Sahaja Yoga is unusual among religions generally and NRMs with the exception of Japanese NRMs (see **New Religions (Japan)**) in being founded and led by a woman, but the movement is not feminist or matriarchal, and women are encouraged to be meek, submissive, and 'feminine' in imitation of traditional Indian wives (see **Gender and NRMs**). Leadership positions are held almost exclusively by men. There appears to be a fairly high turnover among the membership, which is no longer growing. There have been no public scandals, but there have been various charges of financial misdemeanours, sexual abuse, threatening and violent behaviour towards ex-members and critics. It is claimed that demonic possession is believed to be the root cause of various medical conditions including cancer and mental illness, and even homosexuality, and that medical help has been delayed and refused as a result. There is also concern about separation of the children from their parents at the movement's school in India and the strictness of the discipline there, although it is not compulsory for children to be educated there.

Sahaja means spontaneity, and the basis of Sahaja Yoga is spontaneous union with the divine. This is accomplished through kundalini **yoga**, which is claimed to awaken a powerful spiritual energy (the kundalini) located at the base of the spine. The core technique is to simply put a hand over one's chakras, repeat 'Mother, forgive me', and the *kundalini* will be activated. It is believed that with Mataji's help, kundalini can be awakened in anyone. When it happens, practitioners are said to feel a cool breeze on the palms of their hands and above their heads. The experience also produces deep peace and happiness, and leads to enlightenment when it reaches the crown chakra. As they develop 'vibratory awareness', devotees can tell from feelings of coolness and heat and from discomfort in their own chakras (energy centres on the central nervous system) where their own or other people's chakras are blocked and learn to heal themselves and others. They believe in deities who personify the qualities of the chakras. The ultimate aim, as with most yoga-based teachings, is self-realization or enlightenment, although the praxis is primarily devotional, in line with the bhakti yoga of traditional Hinduism. Concern has been expressed at the high level of commitment demanded by Mataji, although this is typical of the guru-disciple relationship in India and in NRMs.

Traditional imagery of the divine drawn from Hindu and Tantric (see **Tantra**) sacred texts is important in Sahaja Yoga. Mataji herself is believed to be the Supreme Goddess by her followers, and she claims to be an incarnation of the *shakti* or original feminine principle. As Laxmi, the wife of the God Vishnu, she is the model of the ideal wife upon which female disciples are expected to model themselves, and which Mataji herself is seen as exemplifying perfectly. As an enlightened guru and the Adi Shakti she also represents the divine feminine. Photographs of Mataji are also used as symbols in meditation. Devotion may also be expressed through the ancient Hindu ritual of pouring a 'nectar' of honey and ghee over Mataji's feet, which is kept and drunk. The symbolism of kundalini yoga is also central.

Further reading

Coney, Judith (1999) *Sahaja Yoga: Socialization Processes in a South Asian New Religious Movement*, New Delhi: Oxford University Press.

ELIZABETH PUTTICK

SAI BABA MOVEMENT

Founder: Sathya Sai Baba
Country of origin: India

The following of the contemporary, miracle working guru Sathya Sai Baba (see **Sai Baba, Sathya**) constitutes a universalist, modernist and international neo-Hindu movement (see **Neo-Hindism**). The movement follows the style of Hindu *bhakti* devotionalism, emphasizing the individual's personal commitment to a personified deity. Love of god is emphasized over scriptural learning or renunciation; the worshipper is encouraged to transcend desire but remain socially engaged. The movement promotes compassion and charity rather than withdrawal from the world. The teachings are ecumenical and proclaim that there is a single godhead, which is the source of all religious traditions. Although Sai Baba has encouraged the establishment of a world-wide Sai Baba organization, he also insists that the true devotee is one who returns to his own religion and learns to practise it well rather than converting to any other. Though all religions are claimed to be paths to the same single divine source, the fact that divinity is currently manifest in the Hindu form of Sai Baba proposes the primacy of Hinduism.

The following includes influential devotees from the worlds of politics, business, the sciences, and the professions. As of 1995, almost 1,700 Sathya Sai Baba centres and groups were registered in over 130 countries, in all continents. The global organization is administered from its headquarters in Puttaparthi, India, and is pyramidally structured with regional, national and local chairmen. A registered centre must have a chairman, secretary and treasurer and must provide three activities – worship, spiritual education, and charity. The organization is supported through anonymous donations and there are no membership fees. In Puttaparthi, various institutions have been established with funds raised by the organization: a school, a college and a palatial hospital.

The total number of devotees is difficult to estimate as many worship Sai Baba without registering as members or necessarily even attending the centres. Sai Baba altars may include a range of images from several of the world religions, usually with a picture of Sai Baba or his feet in the centre. However, a Sai Baba image may simply be included at the periphery as one among many objects of worship, as is the case on many Malaysian Hindu and Chinese altars. At the Sai Baba centres, worship is generally modelled upon Hindu *puja* worship and usually includes offerings of flowers to the image of Sai Baba, chanting of Sanskrit mantras, singing of devotional songs (*bhajans*) in Sanskrit and other languages, recitation of prayers and the offering of burning camphor to the altar. Offerings that obligatorily include the sacred *vibhuti* ash are then distributed to the congregation. At some centres, individuals recite personal experiences of miracles to the audience or deliver messages taken from the Sai Baba literature.

The literature used by the movement is not written by Sai Baba himself but consists of his numerous speeches, noted down and published by devotees (e.g. The Sathya Sai Speaks series). Sai Baba also frequently refers to the Bhagavadgita and occasionally, and somewhat unsystematically, to other religious scriptures, from both Hinduism and other world religions. In general, his speeches, though often eclectic and ambiguous, reiterate the eternal verity of the principles of Hinduism – in particular, the notion of *dharma*, meaning righteousness or duty. They are also consistently modernist inasmuch as they reconcile capitalist interests with the ideal of detachment; accumulation of wealth is not forbidden, it is even encouraged as long as it is coupled to selfless giving,

One should respect all others as one's own kin, having the same Divine Spark, and the same Divine Nature. Then there will be effective production, economic consumption and equitable distribution, resulting in peace and the promotion of love. Now, love based on the innate Divinity is absent, and so there is exploitation, deceit, greed and cruelty (Sathya Sai Speaks Series, Prashanti Nilayam: Sri Sathya Sai Books and Publications Trust. n.d.: X: 9).

Nor does Sai Baba oppose extant power holders, as have some *bhakti* leaders. He urges his followers to support their leaders and contribute to nation building, though their ultimate devotion must be to him.

His imagery of worldly-asceticism and his intellectually undemanding teachings appeal to the cosmopolitan middle-classes, particularly among diasporic Indian communities in which Indian culture and religious practice is often leached, but also among Europeans and North Americans. These, he claims, are the people currently most in need of spiritual regeneration. He also has a relatively wide following in South America.

Sai Baba education programmes have been set up by devotees to promote a set of 'universal human values' that emanate from the Hindu principles of *prema*, *shanti*, *ahimsa*, *sathya* and *dharma* (love, peace, non-violence, truth and duty) but are also said to underlie all religions. The symbol of the Sai Baba organization is a lotus flower in whose five petals these terms are written. This kind of symbolism, the teaching and Sai Baba himself, give precedence to Hinduism as generative and subsuming of other religious forms.

The Sai Baba movement has prompted some controversy. At least one organization in India has launched a vitriolic crusade against Sai Baba in particular and also other miracle-workers. It has released video films showing Sai Baba performing 'faked' materializations and also books containing evidence that contradicts some of the devotees' claims of miracle experiences. Rumours have also circulated about Sai Baba sexually harassing or even abusing devotees. In general, however, the movement has been unmarred by these accusations and it continues to attract influential members to its following.

Further reading

Babb, L. (1983) 'Sathya Sai Baba's Magic', *Anthropological Quarterly,* 56(3): 116–24.

Bowen, D. (1988) *The Sathya Sai Baba Community in Bradford: Its Origin and Development, Religious Beliefs and Practices.* Monograph Series, Community Religions Project, Leeds: Department of Theology and Religious Studies, University of Leeds.

Kent, A. (2000) 'Ambiguity and the Modern Order: The Sathya Sai Baba Movement in Malaysia', PhD dissertation, Department of Social Anthropology, Göteborg University.

Klass, M. (1991) *Singing with Sai Baba: The Politics of Revitalisation in Trinidad,* Boulder, CO: Westview Press. Reprint, Prospect Heights, IL: Waveland Press, 1996.

ALEXANDRA KENT

SAI BABA, SATHYA

The contemporary Indian, miracle working guru, Sathya Sai Baba, ranks as one of modern India's most important and charismatic religious figures. His claim to be a universal godhead also provides a certain re-ennoblement of Indian culture, allowing Indians all over the world to claim that 'God lives in India'.

Sathya Sai Baba was born to a non-Brahmin, *kshatriya* family on 25 November 1926 in the village of Puttaparthi, not far from Bangalore in India and was named Sathya Narayana Raju. The birth was reputedly heralded by mysterious happenings and later, the young Sai Baba began demonstrating extraordinary powers. As a child, he would materialize objects for his friends and mysteriously locate lost items. At the age of 14, sometime after a seizure that may have resulted from a scorpion bite, he suddenly called his family and neighbours to his bedside and declared that he was Sai Baba. With this, he claimed to be the reincarnation of the Maharashtran ascetic saint Sai Baba of Shirdi, who died in 1918. The contemporary Sai Baba, Sathya Sai Baba (Sai Baba of truth), now claimed to be the second of three Sai Baba incarnations. His successor, he has declared, will be known as Prema Sai Baba (Sai Baba of love).

Sathya Sai Baba has a distinctive appearance that combines erotic and ascetic symbolism. He wears the ascetic colour orange or occasionally white, but his long robes are of glimmering silk. His hair is neither long and matted in the style of Hindu renunciants, nor is it cropped, oiled and controlled like that of ordinary Indian men. It is mid-length and fuzzy – almost 'Afro'. He is often portrayed smiling in indulgent, movie starlet poses: sitting on a swing, surrounded by flowers, eating a banana. His lifestyle, however, is patterned on that of the ascetic; he is unmarried and is said to spend his time in meditation or delivering blessings. His ambiguous symbolism recalls the great Hindu deity, Siva, the erotic ascetic. Indeed, he declared himself the incarnated form of the Siva-Sakti (great god/great goddess) couplet on Guru Purnima day in 1963.

Sai Baba's following began developing in India when he was a young man, but his declaration in 1963 led to a dramatic increase in numbers of devotees, both in India and abroad. By the 1970s, the movement was taking root in various countries and becoming formalized. Sai Baba has travelled extensively in India but only once abroad, when he visited his Gujerati followers in East Africa.

Devotees' publications are numerous and describe his extraordinary cures, resurrections from the dead, materializations of religious trinkets, mind reading and astral travelling. His most commonly reported miracle is his manifestation of ash known as *vibhuti,* which he performs with a circular movement of his right hand. Usually he gives the ash to devotees, often with instructions to use it medicinally. His miracles mark his superhuman status and establish the possibility for human beings to engage in a devotee–deity relationship. It is above all the conviction about Sai Baba's paranormal powers that is the hallmark of a devotee.

Today, Sai Baba resides mainly at his ashram in Puttarparthi, or sometimes in Bangalore. The Puttaparthi ashram is surrounded by a wall and occupies the major part of the village. Inside it are accommodation blocks for devotees, the main worship hall, shops, canteens and several shrines. Sai Baba makes two regular daily appearances known as *darshan*: the opportunity for devotees to meet the gaze of their Lord and in this way participate in divinity. Devotees are encouraged to wear Indian clothing in the worship hall, regardless of their origins.

At *darshan,* Sai Baba wanders slowly through the crowd, stopping sometimes to receive some of the letters people have brought for him. He may call some for an interview after *darshan*. His behaviour is notoriously unpredictable and capricious; he cures some but not others, receives some letters but rejects others and so on. Devotees interpret this as using the *karma* theodicy. They believe he knows how a person's condition relates to their remote past and future

and that he may, in their own spiritual interests, ordain that they repay some *karmic* debts by suffering. For devotees, Sai Baba is omnipresent, omnipotent and omniscient.

Further reading

Haraldsson, Erlendur (1987) *Miracles Are My Visiting Cards*, London: Century Press.
Kasturi, N. (1973–1975) *Sathyam, Sivan, Sundaram: The Life Story of Bhagavan Sri Sathya Sai Baba,* 3 vols, Prasanthi Nilayam, A.P.: Sri Sathya Sai Books and Publications Trust.
Swallow, D. A. (1982) 'Ashes and Powers: Myth, Rite and Miracle in an Indian God-man's Cult', *Modern Asian Studies,* 16: 123–58.

ALEXANDRA KENT

SAINT GERMAIN FOUNDATION

Founder: Guy W. Ballard (b. 1878; d. 1939)

The Saint Germain Foundation is one of the independent movements which derive their core doctrines from the Theosophical Society (see **Theosophy**), whilst adding its own new revelations and insights. In 1930, Master Saint Germain manifested himself to Guy Ballard (1878–1939) on Mount Shasta, California, appointing him and his wife Edna (1886–1971) as the 'authorized messengers' of the Masters. The idea that hidden Masters, mostly human in origin, reside in inaccessible locations from which they direct human affairs, was originally put forward by Madame Helena Blavatsky (see **Blavatsky, Helena**), co-founder of the Theosophical Society. The Count of Saint Germain (1710–84) was a legendary figure in eighteenth-century esotericism who, according to Blavatsky, later became the hidden master Rakoczy. Ballard, however, operated independently of Blavatsky's Society, and in the 1930s received no less than eleven volumes of revelations from Saint Germain, mostly centering on the 'I AM Presence', the energy supporting all the manifested world, on a 'violet flame' of energy surrounding all humans, and on 'decrees', or specially effective prayers which redirect this energy. Ballard proceeded to publish them under the pen name of Godfrey Ray King, and to organize the Saint Germain Foundation, which recruited students mostly through correspondence courses, using a method popularized in the American occult milieu by **AMORC**. In 1939, when Guy Ballard died, the number of students enrolling in correspondence courses reached close to one million.

Ballard's death was unexpected, and caused considerable succession turmoil. Disgruntled students took advantage of the situation to sue Edna Ballard and the Foundation's leadership for mail fraud, claiming that Saint Germain was just a figment of the Ballards' imagination. Edna and other defendants were found guilty of mail fraud in 1941, although in 1944 the US Supreme Court reversed the verdict in the landmark *Ballard* decision, thus establishing once and for all that neither the US Mail nor the courts are competent to decide whether or not supernatural beings, including Saint Germain, really exist. Notwithstanding the final victory against a decision which would have ruled a movement operating primarily through the mail out of existence, the court case, and other problems connected to Guy's succession, swallowed the best part of the Foundation's energies in the 1940s. Many students discontinued the courses, and recovery after the Supreme Court decision was slow.

Chapters were, however, opened in several foreign countries, and in 1978 the headquarters were moved from Mount Shasta to Schaumburg, Illinois, a suburb of Chicago. Mount Shasta remains the seat of a popular yearly pageant on the life of Jesus Christ. The Foundation has not been able to prevent the appearance of Saint Germain as an entity being channelled outside its boundaries. Independent movements which combine the Foundation's doctrines with other elements, and other organizations in which new messages of Saint Germain have appeared, such as the **Church Universal and Triumphant**, now have a larger following than the Foundation itself.

Further reading

King, G. R. (pseud.) (1987) *The Saint Germain Series*, 12 vol., Schaumburg, Ill: Saint Germain Press.

MASSIMO INTROVIGNE

SANDERS, ALEX
(b. 1926; d. 1988)

Alex Sanders was born Orrell Alexander Carter in Birkenhead UK to unmarried parents, and was one of thirteen children. On moving to Manchester, his father adopted the surname Sanders, which Alex took as his legal name by deed poll in 1970.

Sanders was initiated into **Wicca** in Derbyshire in 1963 and went on to act as high priest to a coven in Nottinghamshire. After the group dissolved in 1964, he began running a coven with Maxine Morris in 1965. Media attention led to them becoming the most famous witches in the world by 1966. Many interested people contacted them and a network of 'Alexandrian' covens sprang up, despite longer-established Wiccans denouncing Sanders as a charlatan. In response, he claimed to have been initiated by his maternal Welsh grandmother at the age of seven. By the close of the 1960s, Alex Sanders had established his own version of the Craft, which became known as Alexandrian Wicca. It was, however, quite clearly based along older Gardnerian lines (see **Gardner, Gerald Brosseau**), with the addition of a greater emphasis on magical healing, high ceremonial magic, angels and spirits.

Sanders and Maxine moved to London in 1967 and were married on May Day 1968. Media appearances continued and in 1969 Sanders was publicized in June Johns' romanticized biography, *King of the Witches*, and in the film *Legend of the Witches*. As Sanders' fame reached its peak Alexandrian Wicca grew exponentially and he indeed became known as 'the King of the Witches'. The marriage between Alex and Maxine broke down in 1973 though they did not divorce until 1982 and always remained friends. Sanders retired somewhat from the limelight to Bexhill and then St Leonards, Sussex, where he continued to teach Wicca, and initiated people from continental Europe. He died of lung cancer in Hastings on Beltane Eve (30 April), 1988 and his pagan funeral took place at Hastings crematorium on 11 May. His death certificate gave his occupation as 'occultist'.

Further reading

Hutton, R. (1999) *The Triumph of the Moon: A History of Pagan Witchcraft*, Oxford: Oxford University Press.

John, J. (1969) *King of the Witches,* London: Peter Davies.

JO PEARSON

SANGHARAKSHITA, VENERABLE

Sangharakshita is the founder and spiritual inspirator of the Buddhist organization **Friends of the Western Buddhist Order** (FWBO). Born Dennis Lingwood in 1925 in South London, he considered himself a Buddhist since the age of 16, having studied Buddhist texts. At 18 years old he was conscripted to the British army and sent to Sri Lanka. After the war Lingwood stayed in India as a wandering mendicant and was ordained as a monk in the **Theravada** order in 1950. He received the Buddhist name Sangharakshita ('protector of the order') and settled down in Kalimpong in the Darjeeling district of northeast India where he became very active in publication activities. Enjoying close contact with Tibetan refugees in the area, he studied Tibetan Buddhism (see **Vajrayāna Buddhism**) and received initiations in its different traditions. As a Theravada monk he conducted preaching tours throughout India and engaged himself in the conversion movement of the ex-Untouchables, initiated by B. R. Ambedkar in 1956.

After twenty years of life in India, Sangharakshita returned to England in 1967. There he started the Buddhist movement FWBO, holding that existing Buddhism offers in Britain did not match the interest of spiritual seekers of the then flourishing counter-culture. Sangharakshita disrobed and started to conduct meditation classes, organized study groups and designed the FWBO as a spiritual movement to practise Buddhism under the conditions of a secularized and industrialized society.

Sangharakshita's interpretation of Buddhism strives to discern the so-called 'core of the Buddhist tradition', favouring no organizational, doctrinal or practice-wise ties to any Buddhist tradition. Sangharakshita claims to realign to 'the spirit of the Original teaching', considering himself a translator to communicate the 'spirit' of Buddhist teachings to western people. During the three decades of rapid growth of the FWBO Sangharakshita served as lecturer, instructor, prinicipal ordainer and prolific writer.

In 1997, Sangharakshita handed over the responsibility for ordination and spiritual leadership to Order members living at the Preceptors College Council, based in Birmingham (UK). In 2000, he appointed senior member Dharmachari Subhuti (Alex Kennedy) as the first chairman of the Council. Sangharakshita lives in Birmingham where he spends his time writing and receiving visitors.

Further reading

Sangharakshita (1988) *The History of My Going For Refuge*, Glasgow: Windhorse.

Sangharakshita (1997) *The Rainbow Road: From Tooting Broadway to Kalimpong: Memoirs of an English Buddhist,* Birmingham: Windhorse.

Dharmachari, S. (1995) *Bringing Buddhism to the West. A Life of Sangharakshita*, Birmingham: Windhorse.

MARTIN BAUMANN

SANNYASIN

'*Sannyasin*' is a Hindu term for a man who has renounced worldly ties in order to seek union with the absolute or God. Hinduism divides the life of men (but not women) into four stages: *bramacharya*, childhood and youth, occupied with education; *grihasta*, the householder stage of raising of a family and building a business; *vanaprasta*, a gradual retirement in which worldly and financial responsibilities are passed to the sons while their father moves towards the spiritual life. Finally comes *sannyas*, where the spiritual life becomes primary and all worldly attachments are dropped. Traditionally *sannyasins* left home to lead a wayfaring life on the road, or in a forest or hermitage, dependent on charity. They often dressed in orange robes, and were treated with great respect as wise elders. However, by the mid-twentieth century this ancient institution began to decline, as India became part of the modern world. Nowadays it is uncommon for men to take *sannyas* literally as a forms of worldly renunciation, particularly in the cities.

In the late 1960s, the Indian guru **Osho** reinterpreted and expanded the concept of *sannyas,* enabling serious spiritual seekers of any age, gender or nationality to become *sannyasins*. Osho defined *sannyas* as essentially a spiritual renunciation – not of the world but of the mind or ego obsessed with worldly desires and ambitions. He recommended that rather than renouncing the material world and becoming celibate itinerants, *sannyasins* should fully embrace and experience all aspects of life, within a much broader concept of spirituality. In sociological terms, *sannyas* was therefore transformed from a world-rejecting to a world-accepting spiritual path. The aim, however, in line with Hindu and Buddhist meditation practice, was to witness the mind with its thoughts and desires, and through understanding to become free of attachment. Osho taught that this was the path to true liberation and enlightenment. Originally he called his approach neo-*sannyas*, to distinguish it from the traditional Hindu path, but the 'neo' prefix was later dropped. This revisionism attracted criticism from both traditionalists and secularists, especially as the traditional orange robe was retained but symbolizing celebration rather than renunciation. Following Osho's death, red robes are only worn within the ashram in India, but not otherwise. However, the term *sannyas* is still applied.

Further reading

Zaehner, R. C. (1966) *Hinduism*, Oxford: Oxford University Press.

ELIZABETH PUTTICK

SANTERIA

Throughout the Caribbean, Central, and South America new, distinctive, hybrid religious forms have arisen out of the encounters of indigenous Amerindian peoples, European settlers, and imported Africans and Asians as Europe colonized the Americas. Santeria's hybrid heritage comprises the *orisha* worship practiced by the Yoruba peoples of West Africa; elements of Roman Catholicism; and the Spiritism developed by *Allan Kardec* in France (see **Espiritismo**; **Kardec, Allan**) and promoted throughout the Caribbean and Latin America during the nineteenth century. Santeria makes Cuba one of the outposts of the Yoruba gods in the New World.

The history of Santeria begins in West Africa where the Yoruba had evolved their own religious and social traditions. The Yoruba kingdom was set in a network of political and cultural interaction with the old kingdom of Benin in Nigeria and the kingdom of Dahomey in what is now the Republic of Benin. In the eighteenth and nineteenth centuries all three of these kingdoms battled against each other and were involved in the Atlantic slave trade. Yorubas were a small segment of the enslaved Africans brought into Cuba at the beginning of the slave trade but later at the height of the warfare that fed it (1840 through 1870) more than one-third of the Africans brought into Cuba were Yorubas.

The Cuban Catholic church attempted to guide the African population away from their traditional religious beliefs towards complete conversion to Christianity but in a gradual fashion that tolerated some mixing of religions during the process. Over the course of time, however, it became clear that the African cultural and religious traditions, even in this mixed form, were not about to disappear, and both the Catholic

church and the colonial government joined hands to try and stamp them out. In Cuba waves of persecution aimed at Santeria have alternated with periods of relative tolerance ever since the late nineteenth century; as a result, Santeria became clandestine.

The spiritualist literature of Allan Kardec began to arrive in Cuba in the 1850s. Between 1870 and 1880 the teaching of this French engineer who claimed his books were dictated to him by spirits became a veritable rage throughout the French and Spanish Caribbean and Central and South America where it became known as *Espiritismo* (Spiritism). Some Cuban Santeria priests came to view an apprenticeship in Espiritismo as a valid, even necessary, prerequisite for Santeria practice and became adepts in both systems. Despite the impact of Espiritismo and Christianity, Yoruba religious conceptions dominate Santeria's pantheon, ritual and world view.

Santeria is neither a salvation religion that rejects the world nor a revealed religion with an authoritative founder or holy book in which a new world-changing truth is claimed to have been unveiled. For Santeria devotees spiritual beings and religious truths do not exist in a world apart from the natural and social world known to our senses; instead, they reside within it. Hence Santeria is human-centered, Earth-centered and concerned primarily with the self (see **Self-Religion, The Self, and Self**) and with ritual mastery of the natural, social and spiritual forces affecting daily life. In Cuba Santeria has been transmitted primarily by oral tradition since at least the eighteenth century.

Santeria theology recognizes a somewhat distant Supreme Being, called by various Yoruba names, such as *Olodumare*, *Olorun*, and *Olofi* or simply *Dios* (God) in Spanish. The Supreme Being created a number of lesser deities (called alternately *orichas* or *santos*) to populate and civilize the earth and endow it with the essential powers necessary for the harmonious existence of all living things. (Each oricha corresponds to a saint known and venerated in Cuba's Catholic churches.) When the first human beings were formed by the orichas, they were taught how to access each oricha's powers and energies in order to achieve harmony with the orichas and Supreme Being, and to maintain a balance with nature and within themselves. This knowledge, transmitted down to the present day by countless generations of priests, is believed to constitute the core of Santeria's religious traditions.

Communal worship is highly participatory and features ritual dance; call and response chants performed in Yoruba and accompanied by drums; ceremonial spirit possession; ancestor veneration; and, on occasion, animal sacrifices. Lay devotees carry out a round of private offerings to the santos in their homes; priests and priestesses perform rituals and provide herbal medicine, counseling and symbolic healing to devotees and the general public. There is also a cycle of annual festivals coordinated with the Catholic saints' feast days.

Santeria's attitude toward religion is basically instrumental – that is, 'if it works for you, believe it' – and, despite a history of persecution by both the Cuban government and the Catholic church, Santeria priests and devotees are generally tolerant of other religious systems.

The spread of Santeria outside of Cuba mainly owes its origins to those Cuban exiles who left in 1959 and also to those who were part of the exodus from the port of Mariel in 1980. They brought Santeria to the United States, where it spread to other Latino communities, and to African-American, White, and Asian communities as well.

From these contacts in the United States Santeria has made its way back into the Caribbean to Puerto Rico and the Dominican Republic. Cubans transplanted the religion to Mexico, and also to Venezuela. A small number of exiled santeros made their way to Europe and established Santeria in Spain, spreading it from there to other European countries.

At the dawn of the twenty-first century a Santeria revival began in Cuba, fueled by increased tolerance from the government, and increased contacts within the Santeria diaspora created by the Revolution. Aided by high speed travel and the Internet, there is greater intercommunication between the growing numbers of people inside and outside of Cuba who see themselves as devotees of the orisha.

Further reading

Brandon, G. (1993) *Santeria from Africa to the New World: The Dead Sell Memories*, Bloomington: Indiana University Press.
Cabrera, L. (1983) *El Monte* (The Forest), Miami: Coleccion del Chihereku
Murphy, J. (1993) *Santeria: African Spirits in America*, Boston: Beacon.

GEORGE BRANDON

SANTI ASOKE

Founder: Phra Bodhirak and/ or Photirak (formerly Rak Rakpong) (b. 1950)

Santi Asoke is a politically radical, utopian Buddhist movement founded in Thailand in 1973 by the monk Phra Bodhirak or Photirak (here Bodhirak) meaning the preserver of Enlightenment, who has been a severe critic of the Thai Sangha or monastic community for over a quarter of a century. Bodhirak has repeatedly claimed that the Sangha not only engages in various activities that have nothing to do with Buddhism – the making of amulets, the use of lustral water, the veneration of statues and the use of money but is also subservient to the rich for the reason that it accepts their expensive gifts, a practice that is contrary to its teachings and spirit.

In 1975 Bodhirak committed, in the view of the Thai political and religious establishment, two major errors, the first of which consisted of declaring himself independent of the Association of the Ancients, thus placing himself outside the three legally recognized Buddhist religious groups or orders in the country, the Thai, Chinese, and Vietnamese. Then, without himself being one of the 'Ancients', Bodhirak started to ordain monks, an act of defiance which, in Gabaude's words, constituted an 'unpardonable crime for a Buddhist religious' (1997: 167). This notwithstanding, individuals both male and female continued to join the Santi Asoke community some as ordained monks and nuns and others as lay members.

The anti-establishment Santi Asoke community strives to live according to the Buddhist rule, *vinaya*, as it was laid down and practised by Buddha Gotama, and this, they insist, entails the renunciation of the use of money, of meat eating, smoking, amulet making, and the veneration of icons of the Buddha himself, among other things. This style of life it is believed is the only sure means of saving Buddhism from total decline. Followers are divided into two categories, ascetics (the ordained) and lay people. The ascetics consist of both male and female monks who in order to be accepted for ordination must pursue a rigorous course in asceticism and spiritual development. All members are vegetarians and are committed to living lives of chastity and poverty. Santi Asoke communities also strive to be self-reliant in everything. Images of the Buddha are not allowed in their temples or communities.

Ironically, Bodhirak was defrocked in 1992 for violating the monastic precepts. Some would argue that the real motive for his dismissal, which he has never accepted, was his close association with the now defunct, radical political party, the 'Force of the Dharma' (Thai: *Phalang Tham*).

The main centre of the Santi Asoke community is in Bangkok. Several branches exist elsewhere in the country including one in Nakhon Ratchasima province.

Further reading

Gabaude, L. (1997) 'Le Renouveau Bud- dhiste en Thaïlande est-il possible? Le case de l'ascétisme social,' in C. Clém- entin-Ojha (ed.) *Renouveaux Religieux en Asie*, Paris: École francaise d'Extrême- Orient, pp. 155–75.

Heikkilä-Horn, M.-L. (1997) *Buddhism with Open Eyes: Beliefs and Practices of Santi- Asoke*, Bangkok: Fah Apai Co.Ltd.

PETER B. CLARKE

SANTO DAIME

Founder of the first group: Raimundo Irineu Serra

Country of origin: Brazil

Santo Daime is a term that refers to a plant-based psychoactive substance used by adherents of Brazilian religious sys- tems especially in the Amazon region of the country. The first Santo Daime group emerged in the Amazonia in the 1920s. The word *santo* means *saint*, indicating and emphasizing the adher- ents' belief in the sacredness of the sub- stance. The word *daime* is usally mentioned in the Santo Daime followers' (who use to call themselves *daimistas*) oral tradition as having two possible origins. On the one hand, it might come from the expression *dai-me* (*to give* + *me*), in a metaphorical reference to the biblical passage in which Jesus Christ asked for water, and gall was given to him. In this sense, it would be a reference to the bitterness of daime and its connection with *Christianity*. On the other hand, and according to a more common explanation given by daimistas, the origin of the expression is attributed to a ritual prayer asking for light and spiritual knowledge, that would be asked from daime – also considered a *divine being*.

Daime and Ayahuasca

Daime and analogous substances used mainly in South America are generally included among the so-called plant-teachers and are particularly called *ayahuasca*. Ayahuasca is a word in *Quechua* – an idiom used in Peru – that means 'vine of the souls'. The expression *vine of the souls* is a reference to the plant *Banisteriopsis caapi*, a vine used as the basis for the preperation of ayahuasca, and daime. The term ayahuasca could also refer to symbolic elements, such as the spiritual force that is considered to be inside the substance.

The preperation itself – the product of the stew of *B. caapi* along with other plants is also known in South America among indigenous groups as *yagé*, *caapi*, *natema*, *kamarampi*, *pildé*, *hoasca*, and *vegetal*.

The psychoactive effects of daime come from the ingestion of a combination of alkaloids: the most refered to are harmine, contained in *B. caapi*, and *DMT* (*N,N*–dimethyltryptamine) present in the plant *Psychotria viridis*. The two plants are the most used in Santo Daime tradition, being called *jagube* and *folha rainha* (*Queen Leaf*, in a reference to the Virgin of Conception, or the Queen of the Forest) respectively.

In pharmacological terms, the effects of daime have been regarded in different ways: hallucinogenic, psychedelic, psychotomimetic, entheogenic, psychointegrator, sacramental.

In addition, in some Santo Daime groups, mainly in countries where its use is not strongly repressed or prosecuted, the plant *Cannabis* is also added to ritual proceedings, drawing particular attention to the fact that their psychoactive properties are also manifestations of the divine and regarded as permitting the contact with spiritual forces that teach and heal.

The use of daime in the Santo Daime religious network context has been scrutinized by drugs agencies worldwide, mainly because of its ritual–religious character and control system. It has not been regarded as a threat to public health, therefore in countries like Brazil and The Netherlands, authorities have permitted the use of the substance in a ritual–religious context.

The religious system

The emergence of the religious group known as Santo Daime in Brazil happened in the second half of the 1920s. It was directly related to the influx of migrants to Acre, in Brazilian Amazonia, who were motivated to settle there by the boom of latex production, at the beginning of the twentieth century.

The founder of the first group in Brazil was Raimundo Irineu Serra (1892–1971), from Maranhão, Brazil. He and the majority of the first Santo Daime adherents were previously involved with activities related to rubber extraction. They had moved to the periphery of Rio Branco, the capital of Acre, in different periods, as the production of latex declined. Serra, confronting current social conditions, invested in a collective organization and used it as a way of dealing with problems such as poverty and disease associated with the decline and decadence of latex production. Later on, in the early 1930s, with the consolidation of the groups, Serra and his followers founded a religious organization called *Centro de Iluminação Cristã Luz Universal* (CICLU) (Centre of Christian Illumination and Universal Light), also known as *Alto Santo*. A group derived from Serra's spiritual trunk is known as *A Barquinha* (The Little Boat). It was founded by Danial Pereira de Mattos in 1945 and also use daime calling it *Santo Daime* in their ritual practices.

Over time Serra developed ritual proceedings for the use of daime. These ritual proceedings together with doctrinal principles were developed from the daime experiences, and particularly from sacred songs, called hymns by daimistas, which were believed to have their origins in the spiritual world.

With the death of Serra in 1971, a political division of the main centre of Santo Daime in Rio Branco gave rise to a new group led by Sebastião Mota de Melo (1920–90). This centre was later called *Centro Eclético de Fluente Luz Universal Raimundo Irineu Serra* (CEFLURIS), and it was the followers of Mota de Melo who promoted the expansion of Santo Daime when he died in 1990 and his son Alfredo Gregório de Melo succeeded him and led the process of expansion.

In the 1980s, the religious movement started to expand nationally to urban and industrialized centres, such as Rio de Janeiro, São Paulo and Brasília, and later, internationally. In 1987, a group in Boston (USA) started its activities. In 1989, daimistas organized the first official rituals in Europe. In 1996, daimistas organized the first European meeting, in Gerona, Spain. The meeting was organized in order to consolidate a process of institutionalization, which was expected to expand control and supervision of European centres. At this meeting, twenty-nine Santo Daime groups representing eleven European countries (Spain, Portugal, France, Italy, The Netherlands, England, Wales, Germany, Switzerland, Austria, Belgium) were represented. Santo Daime groups have also been encountered in Argentina, Uruguay, Japan and the USA.

It was also in the 1980s that interest among social scientists in investigating Santo Daime was triggered. In general their approach regarded Santo Daime as a religion influenced by culture of the Amazon and particularly by shamanism. Later with expansion middle-class individuals, connected with the spirituality practiced among New Age participants joined Santo Daime. In terms of its religious practices and doctrine, Santo Daime has also been considered to have been influenced by elements from Esotericism, Espiritismo, Brazilian Popular Catholicism, African-Brazilian religious tradition (see **Candomblé** and **Umbanda**) and New Age.

Further reading

Araújo, Wladimir S. (1999) *Navegando sobre as ondas do Santo Daime: História, Cosmologia e Ritual da Barquinha*, Campinas: Unicamp.

Groisman, Alberto (1999) *Eu Venho da Floresta: Um Estudo sobre o Contexto Simbólica do Uso do Santo Daime*, Florianópolis: Edufsc.

MacRae, E. (1992) *Guiado pela Lua: Xamanismo e Uso Ritual da hoasca no Culto do Santo Daime*, São Paulo: Brasiliense.

ALBERTO GROISMAN

SARVODAYA MOVEMENT
(Sanskrit: The Welfare and/or Awakening of All)
Founder: Dr A. T. Ariyaratna

The Sarvodaya Movement – its full name is the Lanka Jatika Sarvodaya

Sramadana Movement – was founded by A. T. Ariyaratna in December 1958 in the belief that the condition of the less fortunate people of rural Sri Lanka could be greatly improved. While Gandhi used the term Sarvodaya to mean the welfare of all Ariyaratna's reading of the Buddha's teaching led him to reinterpret it to mean the 'awakening of all'. By this Ariyaratna meant the awakening of all from an introverted, subjective outlook to one that embraced the whole of humanity. It was his view that the teachings of the Buddha about the four Sublime Abodes – loving-kindness, compassion, sympathetic joy, and equanimity – and that concerning the four Modes of Social Conduct – the absence of desire, fear, hatred and delusion – supported this interpretation.

This was an awakening that took place on many levels including the social, economic, and political levels as well as the moral, spiritual and intellectual ones.

The term Sramadana in the movement's full title describes its main objective. This concept means the unselfish act of sharing one's labour, thought, efforts, ideas, and other assets and resources with the world community.

The Sarvodaya movement provides one of the clearest expressions in the form of an organized movement, of **Engaged Buddhism** and in particular of its ethical and social philosophy of compassion and kindness-empathy leading to selfless labour.

Concerned with the alleviation of poverty and the ills attendant upon it the movement has provided a model of nonviolent revolution based on Buddhist ethics and teachings. Grounding itself on the twin pillars of agricultural collectives and altruism the movement proposed that communities should farm as a unit on communal, village farms and offer their labour selflessly – the Buddhist term for this would be *dana* or giving – through the medium of communal work groups known as *kayiya* for the betterment of the poor. As Gombrich and Obeyesekere (1988: 245) comment with regard to Ariyaratna's Buddhist philosophy of selfless labour:

> It was a profound vision of involvement in the world, expressed in Buddhist terms ... Undoubtedly this is the major and truly significant innovation of Ariyaratna and the high point of **'Protestant' Buddhism** – to inculcate in the laity a sense of Buddhist work for the welfare of others by the donation of selfless labour.

The Sarvodaya movement is active in more than 11,000 villages in Sri Lanka and though its basic philosophical tenets are Buddhist it is both ethnically and religiously inclusive. It also has a North American branch, the Mission of Sarvodaya, USA.

Although criticized for attempting to impose middle-class, urban, bourgeois values on the rural population of Sri Lanka the Sarvodaya movement inspired the creation of other similar groups which together have contributed significantly to the advancement of the ideals of socially Engaged Buddhism.

Further reading

Gombrich, R. F. and Obeyesekere, G. (1988) *Buddhism Transformed: Religious Change in Sri Lanka*, Princeton, NJ: Princeton University Press.

PETER B. CLARKE

SATANISM

Accusations of Satanic worship or activity have been levelled against others (real or imagined) for centuries. Although rarely tested against the kind of evidence to be expected in modern law courts, they have frequently led to acts of violence against the accused. In the past it was equally rare to find people claiming or admitting to being Satanists unless they had been subjected to torture. However, there are now some self-identified Satanist organizations.

The classic accusations of Satanism are those that were rife in certain periods of European Christian history against Jews, heretics, lepers, and others. Putative refusal to be properly Christian led to accusations of serving a devil who opposed God and godliness. The character of this tempter and corruptor of humanity evolved dramatically within European Christianity alongside fears about and persecution of minority populations. If nascent Christianity had denied creative power to the devil and made it illegal to accuse others of witchcraft (understood here to be the ability to harm others by magic), medieval Christianity became 'a persecuting society' in the eleventh century (Moore, 1987). Magic was now accepted as a real possibility and threat. Opposition to Judaism provided the language for alleged gatherings or 'sabbats' of Satan-worshippers.

The transition from the medieval to early modern period was marked by an increased popularity of the notion of a 'pact' made between the devil and his worshippers, exchanging the individual's eternal 'soul' for this-worldly material benefit. This is part of a wider concern with more mundane, perhaps religio-political, commitments illustrated by the rise of various 'Congregations' and 'Covenants' throughout this transitional period, and an increasing number of accusations made by one kind of Christian against another. In the days leading up to the French Revolution and the Enlightenment various libertarian social currents were manifest in clubs and gatherings that adopted the trappings of Satanism to provoke and

satirize polite society. It has been alleged that the Black Mass (inverting or reversing Christian liturgy and symbols) was celebrated by aristocrats in this era.

In the 1890s a hoax that spread across Europe alleged that Freemasonry was a front for a Satanic conspiracy in which human sacrifices and sexual perversions were committed. While this scare reiterates earlier themes, those accused may represent a new target: **Esoteric movements**. Within the **Hermetic Order of the Golden Dawn** but creating a style unwelcome by the Order, Aleister Crowley (see **Crowley, Aleister**) made playful use of accepted images of Satan to attempt to provoke radical rethinking and imagination. His legacy survives not among self-identified Satanists but among esotericists and among those willing to accept his projected image at face value.

More recent scares involving allegations of Satanism include the spread of a conspiracy theory in 1990s asserting that children were likely to be abused and sacrificed by teachers and careworkers with the collusion of Satanic law-enforcement agents and others (see Richardson *et al.*, 1991). Contemporary witchcraft eradication movements in various parts of Africa (including South Africa and Nigeria) elaborate syntheses of Christian notions about the devil and traditional African understandings of harmful magic. Their current form often implicates educationally and economically successful elites as beneficiaries of a Satanic pact. These and all accusations about Satanism tend to say more about the accusers and changes in their surrounding society than about any Satanic reality. They are interesting as social movements but only background to explicitly self-identified Satanism.

In the context of an expectation of the imminent demise of Christianity, rather than in opposition to Christianity itself, Anton LaVey founded the **Church of**

Satan in California in 1966. This did not require belief in, worship of or obedience to an actual entity beyond the individual Satanist. Rather, it used the image of an archetypal rebel and opponent to provoke people to attempt radical self-awareness, personal growth and individualism. That is, the Church was a self-religion (see **Self-religion, the Self, and Self**) using the form of esotericism and Satanism to generate change. Although LaVey disestablished the Church of Satan in 1975, it continues in the form of a loose network of individuals inspired by its image and ethos. However, some former members took a new direction following a revelation from **Set**, sometimes otherwise understood to be an ancient Egyptian deity or as Satan in a complex misunderstanding, that led Michael Aquino to found the **Temple of Set**. Temple members (Setians rather than Satanists perhaps) are divided about whether Set really exists or not (officially he does) but agree that their aim is to 'become' (a Temple buzz-word) more fully individual human selves. The Temple aligns itself more fully with more traditional esoteric movements in its teachings about magic but maintains LaVey's stress on the need for transgressive performance to inspire change.

Satanic organizations publish voluminously within the Internet, but remain a small minority. Estimates alleging that 10 per cent or more of any population are Satanists are wildly inaccurate, the truth being that there are probably fewer than 100 Satanists in, for example, Britain. This does not include those teenagers who claim to be Satanists in a phase of adolescent rebellion but, almost without exception, make no contact with any group.

In short, there are two kinds of Satanism. There are accusations that reveal something about the accusers and wider society but are rarely based on truth. These perennial polemics have now, within a more secular and pluralist world that is perhaps more accepting of satire and sinister postures, been met by self-identification by a very small minority as Satanists. For such people, Satanism is a self-religion that utilizes sinister self-representation and transgressive performance to discover and fulfil individual self-identities. This Satanism is not about anti-social and cosmic rebellion but a means of self-affirmation.

Further reading

Harvey, G. (1995) 'Satanism in Britain Today', *Journal of Contemporary Religion* 10: 283–96.

La Fontaine, J. S. (1998) *Speak of the Devil: Tales of Satanic Abuse in Contemporary England*, Cambridge: Cambridge University Press.

Moore, R. I. (1985) *The Formation of a Persecuting Society*, Oxford: Blackwell.

Richardson, J. T., Best, J. and Bromley, D. G. (eds) (1991) *The Satanism Scare*, New York: de Gruyter.

GRAHAM HARVEY

SCHOOL OF ECONOMIC SCIENCE

The School of Economic Science (SES) was founded in London in 1937 by the Labour MP Andrew MacLaren (d. 1975), to teach economic and political theory. His son Leon MacLaren (1910–94), a barrister, gradually took over the running of the School. Leon MacLaren shifted the focus to a study of the laws governing human nature, and hence philosophy, and a search for spiritual wisdom. Sources included the Bible, Plato and his successors, the great poets such as Shakespeare, and the Hindu scriptures, the Upanishads.

In 1960, through another group called the Study Society to which he belonged, MacLaren heard the Maharishi Mahesh

Yogi when he first came to London. The Study Society, originally the Society for the Study of Normal Psychology, had been founded by Dr Francis Roles on the basis of P. D. Ouspensky's teachings (see **Ouspensky, Piotr Demianovich**); Ouspensky had studied with G. I. Gurdjieff (see **Gurdjieff, George Ivanovitch**). Roles travelled to India and met Sri Santanand Saraswati, the Shankaracharya of the North, who had studied alongside the Maharishi Mahesh Yogi under the previous Shankaracharya, Guru Dev (1869–1953). Shortly after Roles's return, Leon MacLaren also journeyed to meet Saraswati.

The Shankaracharya of the North is one of four successors to Shankara (or Samkara), a Hindu philosopher who probably lived from 788 to 820 CE (or possibly a century earlier), who was the founder of Advaita Vedanta, a major Hindu philosophical school based on the Vedas.

MacLaren's School and Roles's Society jointly set up the School of Meditation to study and teach the principles and practical use of meditation. MacLaren began using the Shankaracharya's teachings in the SES. Every two years for the rest of his life he would go to India and hold conversations with the Shankaracharya through an interpreter; these were taped and transcribed, and became the basis of the teaching material in the SES.

Leon MacLaren died in 1994 aged 84. He appointed 38-year-old Donald Lambie, also a barrister, to succeed him as senior tutor. Sri Shantanand Saraswati died in 1997. Lambie established contact with the new Shankaracharya of the North, Sri Vasudevananda Saraswati, who has taken on the role of guru to SES.

Teaching at the School is done in small groups, in the form of a dialogue between teacher and students. All the SES teachers are advanced students; none is paid. Courses include Philosophy, Economics, Art, Vedic Mathematics, and Practical Philosophy in Business.

In addition, the School runs four private schools in London, the St James schools for junior and senior girls and boys, and schools in Leeds and Manchester. As well as the standard curriculum, the pupils are taught Sanskrit and Philosophy.

The SES was hit by major controversy in 1984, with the publication of the book *Secret Cult* by two journalists from London's right-wing newspaper, the *Evening Standard*, Peter Hounam and Andrew Hogg. Hounam and Hogg had smelt a potential political scandal in that several leading members of the Liberal Party were members of the SES, and their exposé of this was timed to coincide with the 1984 General Election. They lost a certain amount of credibility when it was revealed that the spokesman for the SES had been, until the previous year, Director of Press and Public Relations at the Conservative Party's Central Office, and a close adviser to Prime Minister Margaret Thatcher. *Secret Cult* was a sensationalist account containing many inaccuracies, and was harmful to the SES. In one respect, however, it had been quite accurate: the SES had been secretive, to the extent that new students were not told that courses in Economics and Philosophy were based on the teachings of a Hindu guru, and parents of some children at the St James schools did not know that the schools were connected to the SES. The SES consulted the Shankaracharya for guidance, and were advised to be more open in all their operations. The School's leaflets and website now clearly state the spiritual underpinnings of the SES.

Since its founding, over 100,000 students have taken courses at SES and its associated schools. In assessing current active membership, however, SES only counts students who continue after their first year's course. The SES currently has around 5,000 members in the UK, 1,400 of them in London, and the remainder in twenty other branches around the UK. There are related schools, independent but using teaching material from the London HQ, in North and South America, Australasia, South Africa, the West Indies, and several European countries.

Further reading

Hounam, P. and Hogg, A. (1984) *Secret Cult*, Tring: Lion.
Barrett, D. V. (2001) *The New Believers*, London: Cassell.

DAVID V. BARRETT

SCIENTOLOGY
(Church of Scientology)
Founder: L. Ron Hubbard
(b. 1911; d. 1986)

Scientology began not as a new religion but as a new system of mental therapy with the publication in 1950 by the American **L. Ron Hubbard** (1911–86) of *Dianetics: The Modern Science of Mental Health*. This publication which sold widely in the United States became the core text of the movement. It detailed mental techniques that could be used to clear away all negative fears, feelings, sensations, and psychosomatic illnesses. After successfully applying these techniques under the guidance of a counsellor or auditor in sessions known as auditing sessions an individual would experience a transformation from a pre-clear to a clear state in which everything became possible.

Continuing his research Hubbard had by 1952 developed his religious philosophy in relation to mental health problems and in particular to those obstacles to

rational thought described as engrams. In 1954 the first Scientology Church was established in Los Angeles, California, and in 1959 Howard moved the headquarters to Saint Hill Manor in Sussex, England. In 1969 the 'Sea Organization' was formed which allowed Hubbard with his closest followers to carry on his research and writing on board several ships. In 1975 Hubbard returned to land at Clearwater in Florida.

Like other systems of thought both western and oriental including that espoused by **Christian Science** and the **Brahma Kumaris** movement, Scientology rejects the idea that the individual is her/his body. In Scientology's teachings the body is simply a vehicle that houses the 'thetan' which is essentially an individual expression of an ultimate reality, the theta or primary substance of thought, life source, ground of all Being. The thetan being the real being which transcends the body, which it inhabits, is not only immaterial and immortal but also possesses infinite creative powers and a capacity to control the universe. Hence the belief that anyone who becomes a 'Clear' by means of auditing comes to enjoy total freedom.

Originally, it is believed, thetans created the world as a plaything in a manner similar to that of the Greek gods or the adolescent Krishna. However, through inattention they allowed themselves to be overwhelmed by the physical universe and thus lost their powers and creative capacities. This resulted in the development of a reactive mind that gives irrational and emotional responses to reality and in particular to whatever leads to a recall of painful and traumatic experiences in the past. Such experiences treated in this way give rise to the previously mentioned engrams, which prevent rational thought in relation to any issue that reminds an individual of the original experience.

Scientology's mission, then, is to rationalize the path to salvation or wholeness by essentially eradicating engrams, which prevent individuals from achieving their full potential. By using a simply device known as an E-Meter to register the emotional response of clients to questions which highlight the engrams present the auditing process can then begin leading to a rational discussion and elimination of engrams acquired either in the present or in some past life and thereby setting the person free to be her/his thetan.

A controversial movement throughout its history, many have questioned Scientology's methods of recruitment, its allegedly authoritarian style, and some of the methods it has used for uncovering information about its activities. Scientology has been strongly opposed in Europe particularly in Germany and its American missionaries were banned for a time by the Home Office from missionizing in the United Kingdom. Nevertheless, at Howard's death in 1986 Scientology was an international movement with some 3,000 churches and missions worldwide.

Further reading

Wallis, R. (1976) *Road to Total Freedom: A Sociological Analysis of Scientology*, London: Heinemann.
Wilson, B. R. (1990) *The Social Dimensions of Sectarianism*, Oxford: Clarendon Press (especially chapter 13).

PETER B. CLARKE

SEA OF FAITH

The Sea of Faith (SoF) Network takes its name from the 1984 TV series and book of the same name written and presented by Don Cupitt.

In this six-part series, the philosopher, theologian, Anglican priest and one-time Dean of Emmanuel College, Cambridge surveyed western thinking about religion and charted the transition from traditional realist religion to the twentieth-century view that religion is simply a human creation.

The name *Sea of Faith* is taken from Matthew Arnold's nostalgic nineteenth-century poem *Dover Beach* in which the poet expresses regret that belief in a supernatural world is slowly slipping away; *the sea of faith* is withdrawing like the ebbing tide.

Following the TV series a small group of radical Christian clergy and laity began meeting to explore how they might promote this new understanding of religious faith. Starting with a mailing list of 143 sympathizers they organized the first UK conference in 1988. A second conference was held in the following year shortly after which the *SoF Network* was officially launched. Annual national conferences have been a key event of the network ever since.

In addition to national conferences, a number of regional conferences and promotional events are held each year. There is an active network of local groups who meet regularly for discussion and exploration. In the UK a high-quality magazine is published bi-monthly, which has a circulation beyond its membership, and the network runs a web site (http://www.sofn.org.uk) and an on-line discussion group. Currently there are national networks in New Zealand and Australia with scattered membership in the USA, Northern Ireland, South Africa, and France. The world-wide membership, as of 2004, stood at about 2,000. Each national network is run by a steering committee elected from its members.

SoF has no official creed or statement of belief to which members are required to assent, seeing itself as a loose network rather than a formal religious movement or organization. Its stated aim is to 'explore and promote religious faith as a human creation'. In this it spans a broad spectrum of faith positions from uncompromising non-realism at one end to critical realism at the other. It possesses no religious writings or ceremonies of its own; some members remain active in their own religion (mainly but not exclusively Christian) while others have no religious affiliation at all.

SoF is most closely associated with the *non-realist* approach to religion. This refers to the belief that God has no 'real', objective or empirical existence, independent of human language and culture; God is 'real' in the sense that he is a potent symbol, metaphor, or projection, but He has no objective existence outside and beyond the practice of religion. Non-realism therefore entails a rejection of all supernaturalism – miracles, afterlife, and the agency of spirits.

> God is the sum of our values, representing to us their ideal unity, their claims upon us and their creative power.
>
> Cupitt (1980)

Cupitt calls this 'a voluntarist interpretation of faith': 'a fully demythologized version of Christianity'. It entails the claim that even after we have given up the idea that religious beliefs can be grounded in anything beyond the human realm, religion can still be believed and practised in new ways.

Since he began writing in 1971 Cupitt has produced thirty-six books and during this time his views have continued to evolve and change. Thus, in his early books such as *Taking Leave of God* and *The Sea of Faith* he talks of only God as *non-real* but by the end of the 1980s he had moved into all-out postmodernism, describing his position as *empty radical humanism* – there is nothing but our language, our world, and the meanings, truths, and interpretations that we have generated.

While Cupitt was the founding influence of SoF and is much respected for his work for the network it would not be true to say that he is regarded as a guru or leader of SoF. Members are free to dissent from his views and Cupitt himself has argued strongly that SoF should never be a fan club. Both Cupitt and the network emphasize the importance of autonomous critical thought and reject authoritarianism in all forms.

Further reading

Cupitt, D. (1980) *Taking Leave of God,* Canterbury: SCM.

Freeman, Antony (1993) *God in Us*, Canterbury: SCM.

Leaves, N. (2004) *Odyssey on the Sea of Faith: The Life and Writings of Don Cupitt*, Santa Rosa: Polebridge Press

ROB WHEELER

SEDEVACANTISTS

From the words 'sede' meaning a 'seat' or 'see' of a bishop, and 'vacante', meaning 'being vacant', 'sede vacante' is the term formally applied to the period between the death of one pope and the election of another. This period has, over the last couple of centuries at least, been relatively short, but in the past there have been papal elections which have lasted nearly three years. The term 'sedevacantist' is applied to those people – it is hardly a movement in any technical sense – who hold that there is currently no legitimate pope and that the present incumbent is an apostate. The argument for this stance arises from the belief that the Church cannot fall into error – this is a maxim of traditionalist Catholics (and, to be fair, in some form is held by all Catholics). But because traditionalists believe that the changes brought about by the Second Vatican Council (1962–5) are errors, therefore those who sanctioned the conclusions of

Vatican II must be in error and have as a consequence forfeited their ecclesiastical authority. Chief among these must be numbered the Pope. He is regarded as an apostate for the same reasons that members of the **Lefebvre Movement** withdrew their allegiance from the papacy, although Lefebvrists are not strictly speaking sedevacantists. Two things in particular are cited as evidence of papal 'apostasy', support for the order of mass as it was introduced after Vatican II, and papal sympathies for the ecumenical movement. Much of the hostility to Vatican II arises from a conviction that the Roman Catholic Church cannot, and has not, changed. The papacy, therefore, has separated itself from the dissidents, not *vice versa*. Specifically, the dissidents point to the introduction of the new liturgy, not only on the grounds that it is new, but because they claim that it is Protestant in inspiration. The objection to ecumenism is based upon the fact that anyone entering into ecumenical dialogue necessarily accepts that the religion of the dialogue partner has in it some elements of truth. This the traditionalists deny. The Vatican Council's Declaration on Religious Liberty, therefore, is a document which they find particularly objectionable. One rigorous sedevacantist, for example, claims that there is a direct and explicit contradiction between that Declaration and the 1864 encyclical *Quanta Cura* of Pope Pius IX condemning the errors of the age – specifically liberalism in all its forms. The French priest Abbé Georges de Nantes wrote in his monthly newsletter *La Contre Réforme Catholique*, 'Freedom of conscience and of religion is an error, insulting to God and pernicious for all human society' – a view which can certainly be found in several papal encyclicals in the nineteenth century. De Nantes' belief that the Pope (Pope Paul VI in this instance) had

fallen into heresy did not, however, arise expressly from the documents of Vatican II but from the promulgation of the new liturgy in 1969. De Nantes himself eventually came to the conclusion that a strict sedevacantism was impracticable, and argued that though the Pope had erred he had done so only in a personal capacity and not as Pope. Even strict sedevacantists admit there is a practical problem with their stance because, if the Pope (and, one should add, the bishops for they all accept the new liturgy and the changes brought about by Vatican II) can no longer be regarded as true Catholics, where then is the visible Church? Some respond rather along the lines of de Nantes that the election of popes and the appointment of bishops are themselves valid, but because the office-holders accept doctrine incompatible with true Catholicism they have no jurisdiction over the Church. Others reject this view as a fudge. They argue on the contrary that what is essential is the Catholic faith itself which ecclesiastical structures only serve to promote, but the faith may survive at least for some time without these structures, until the Pope and bishops see the error of their ways and repudiate the decrees of Vatican II and the new liturgy.

MICHAEL WALSH

SEICHO-NO-IE (HOUSE OF GROWTH)

Founder: Taniguchi Masaharu (b. 1893; d. 1985)

Seicho-no-Ie was founded in Tokyo in 1930 by Taniguchi Masaharu, a graduate of Waseda College Tokyo and former member of **Omoto**. He was also an avid reader of both Eastern and Western philosophy and alternative ideas on health and personal growth. Along with Omoto **New Thought** ideas proved to be particularly influential in shaping Taniguchi's thinking.

Like many other **New Religious Movement**s (NRMs) Seicho-no-Ie is non-denominational in accordance with its belief that all religions emanate from one universal God and that human beings are children of that God and, therefore, divine in nature. However, human beings need to be made aware of their divinity and of the divine attributes, which they possess.

Seicho-no-Ie also teaches that evil, suffering and difficulties in life are illusory and can be overcome through self-reflection. Through the power of the mind and the substitution of positive for negative thoughts people can transform their spiritual condition.

Though it teaches about the power of thought to heal in both a psychological and physical sense Seicho-no-Ie also advises members to visit their doctor when necessary.

The movement is concerned to spread the message that everything in life is a manifestation of God and, therefore, good in principle. The following constitute the core tenets of Seicho-no-Ie:

1. one truth, one God, one religion;
2. human beings are children of God;
3. perfect harmony in the universe is made possible by the reconciliation of all things;
4. and there is an obligation to show gratitude to everyone and for everything.

Gratitude to parents both living and dead receives particular emphasis. Our ancestors are described as our roots, the trunk of the tree represents our parents, the branches present day fathers and mothers and the leaves or fruits or flowers today's children.

Seicho-no-Ie's main scripture is the Sutra known as the Nectarean Shower of Holy Doctrine which the founder received from God while in meditation in 1931. The founder also was deeply interested in Christianity and wrote commentaries on St John's Gospel, which his followers study with great interest. He also developed the notion of the Eternal Christ a statue of whom can be found in Seicho-no-Ie places of worship. Apart from the founder's birthday there are no religious festivals.

A form of meditation known as *shinsokan* or meditation to visualize God aids self-reflection and spiritual advancement. While meditating an invocation is recited which attributes all actions to God and a meditative thought which speaks of the six attributes of God is dwelt upon.

Often regarded as a philosophy of life rather than a religion, Seicho-no-Ie has an estimated 900,000 members in Japan. It has enjoyed little success outside Japan apart from Brazil where the membership is estimated to be around two million.

Further reading

Clarke, P. B. (1999) (ed.) *An Annotated Bibliography of Japanese New Religions*, Eastbourne, Kent: Japan Library, pp. 219–25

PETER B. CLARKE

SEKAI KYUSEI KYO
(Church of World Messianity)
Founder: Okada Mokichi (b. 1882; d. 1955)

One of Japan's many new religious movements (NRMs) Sekai Kyusei Kyo (SKK) or Church of World Messianity (referred to henceforth simply as Messianity) was founded in 1935 by Okada Mokichi (1882–1955), a former associate of **Omoto** (Great Origin).

Messianity's primary goal is the building of paradise on earth principally through the performance of the *johrie* healing ritual which consists of the transmission of divine light. Johrei is administered by a member who, wearing an amulet or ohikari, raises the palm of her/his hand over the recipient, who may nor may not be a believer, and imparts to her/him the divine light of healing.

Okada developed a theory of illness that linked it to spiritual clouds which could be dispersed not only by the practice of johrei but also by the use of herbal remedies. He was also persuaded that certain kinds of illness were beneficial. For example, the common cold served to cleanse the body which would otherwise be rendered dysfunctional by toxic substances. *Shizen noho* or natural farming is also a fundamental part of Messianity's teachings and practices.

There are various views among followers as to whether Okada is divine or human. For example, some members, particularly in Brazil, equate him with Jesus, others see him as the Messiah of the present age. Initially Okada proclaimed himself to be the Boddhisatva Kannon (see **Mahāyāna Buddhism**), long venerated in Japan as the very essence of compassionate mercy, and later as the Messiah of the New Age. Regardless of whether they regard him as divine or human, all refer to Okada as Meishusama, *sama* being an honorific title such as Sir or Lord.

Messianity, as is the case with many other Japanese new religions (see **New Religions (Japan)**), is emphatically millenarian and preaches the coming of an earthly paradise by means of an ever-increasing outpouring of divine light by means of johrei and shizen noho or natural farming. This approach to agriculture is based on the belief that Nature possesses its own intrinsic resources which are sufficient in themselves to bring forth wholesome crops and plants in abundance.

The movement has an estimated 900,000 members in Japan and is present in many parts of the world. It is particularly strong in Brazil and Thailand where the membership is over 300,000 in both countries. Messianity is inclusive where belief and practice are concerned. It does not demand of new members who belong to another faith that this be abandoned on joining.

Messianity has sympathizers and practitioners among some of the Catholic clergy of, for example Brazil and Bolivia, and in recent times it has attracted some 300 Theravada Buddhist monks in Sri Lanka who now both receive and transmit johrei.

Organizationally, Messianity consists of two main institutions, the Church of World Messianity and the Mokichi Okada Foundation, the former focusing on spiritual matters and the latter on cultural activities including *sangetsu* or flower arranging and horticulture. Differences between the two branches are becoming increasingly blurred as the leadership attempts to present johrei not as the core practice of the Church of World Messianity as such but as a non-denominational healing ritual that can be effectively administered by any religious or secular institution that has the necessary 'faith' in its curative powers. 'Faith' here does not mean a belief in a non-empirical, supernatural order, for in the case of johrei the recipient is provided with proof of its beneficial effects before being asked to accept that it has the power to produce such effects.

While at present united, Messianity has experienced serious internal divisions and this has meant the establishment of a number of different branches each with its own headquarters. Today the main headquarters are at Atami, and the World President is the Reverend Tetsuo Watanabe who is also President of Messianity in Brazil. Among those who hold the highest positions of spiritual leadership is the grandson of Mokichi Okada, the Reverend Yoichi Okada

Further reading

Clarke, P. B. (2000) 'Modern Japanese Millenarian Movements: Their Changing Perception of Japan's Global Mission with Special Reference to the Church of World Messianity', in Peter B. Clarke (ed.) *Japanese New Religions in Global Perspective*, London: Curzon Press, pp. 129–82.

Ellwood, R. S. (1974) *The Eagle and the Rising Sun: Americans and the New Religions of Japan*, Philadelphia: Westminster Press.

Okada, Mokichi (1984) *Foundations of Paradise*, Los Angeles: Church of World Messianity, USA.

PETER B. CLARKE

SEKHIYATHAM MOVEMENT
Founder: Sulak Sivaraksa (b. 1945)

The Sekhiyatham movement, more an association of individuals who network among themselves and with the wider society than an organized body with administrative structures, was started in Thailand in 1989 by the scholar-monk Sulak Sivaraksa. Its aim is to promote greater awareness among Buddhists of the misguided policies and inverted set of priorities of secular rulers in relation to development policy, welfare, culture, and the protection of the environment. The Thai government is also perceived to be over anxious to embrace westernization in education, which Sekhiyatham believes fosters materialism, and in other areas of life, to the detriment of Thai values. The movement has also been highly critical of the Sangha or monastic community.

Though twice charged with lese-majesty for attempting to undermine the State but never actually prosecuted Sivaraksa spends less time on directly criticizing the Sangha as an institution than, for example, Bodhirak (see **Santi Asoke**). He does, however, appear to doubt the Sangha's ability or even desire to reform itself, and he is also doubtful whether the State is seriously interested in such reform.

It is in this context that the Sekhiyatham movement attempts to provide a form of engaged asceticism that not only contributes to the reform of Buddhism but also provides all citizens with a model of how to protect the environment and enable society to retain its essential identity under the impact of westernization.

Though he describes himself as a 'Buddhist with a small b', who is open to the values of other faiths and cultures, Sivaraksa stresses the fundamental necessity of providing an alternative to western education which he describes as a system which places the emphasis on property, money, power, and the ability to consume.

What Sivaraksa, and reformers like him, are seeking to promote is learning for life, which involves learning about what separates people from one and another and what blinds them to the natural 'inter-relatedness' between themselves, and between themselves and other beings. The principles of this kind of education – promoted in seminars and workshops on 'Humans and Their Learning' – will, it is envisaged, advance the cause of **Engaged Buddhism** by making for greater awareness of social inequalities and of the need for social solidarity with those affected by venture Capitalism, which Sivaraksa attacks for its profit only mentality which militates against the interests of the underprivileged. This philosophy lies behind Sivaraksa's involvement in campaigns such as the attempt to prevent the construction of the Pak Moon dam on the Mekong river, the

Yadana gas pipeline, and the Thai-Malaysian gas pipeline schemes.

Further reading

Gabaude, L. (1997) 'Le Renouveau bouddhiste en Thaïlande est-il possible? Le cas de l'ascétisme social' in C. Clémentin-Ojha (ed.) *Renouveaux Religieux en Asie*, Paris: École Française d'Extreme-Orient, pp. 155–75.

PETER B. CLARKE

SELF TRANSFORMATION

Self transformation is the aim of religious, spiritual, and existential practices and a general expression for other personal modifications. The term has no agreed meaning because it depends on how its component words are interpreted. It usually refers to practices derived from Eastern religions with a conception of self (see **Self-Religion, the Self, and Self**) very different from western understandings. Its various uses carry assumptions about the nature of human existence and the final purpose of human life.

All current uses of the term suggest a desire for self improvement. It can happen as a developmental process aided by social rites of passage (e.g. graduation, marriage, divorce); through fashion, body modification (e.g. bodybuilding, tattoos, body piercing, weight loss, cosmetic surgery) and artistic creativity including writing. It can be self-repair or liberation in the face of physical and emotional suffering: healing without cure is one of its forms. Several websites describe it as 'inner alchemy'. It is the aim of psychoanalysis and psychotherapy. It sometimes refers to the personal component in wider changes of social consciousness (e.g. towards care for the environment or action against consumerism). For followers of Nietzsche, it is an achievement of the will to power:

the creation of the ideal self, or over-man. Like literary uses of the term metamorphosis, each of these aims can be seen as metaphors for other changes a person consciously or unconsciously desires, so that even its most mundane forms can be considered 'pre-spiritual'.

The term is not synonymous with the related New Age (see **New Age Movement**) expressions self-help, self-actualization and self-empowerment, all of which imply individual responsibility for self-fulfilment. Even New Agers disagree about the place of the (socially conditioned) ego in their quest for Enlightenment. Most seek to transcend it (through meditative practices and/or work benefitting people and nature) but for those on the 'prosperity wing' of the movement, ego is unproblematic. Self-**spirituality**, a similar New Age term, is directed towards self-perfection (or salvation) through discovering a spiritual 'essence' within the self. It presupposes that the resulting transformation will cast off the effects of social conditioning. It does not recognize that even this view of the self is a social construction.

The expression is most often found in explicitly religious texts. It is always related to a growing awareness of truth, through study, meditation, or other disciplined practice. In Buddhism it is the path towards liberation from suffering and to personal and community peace. It is the underlying project of Taoism which encourages turning to others to learn about self. In Judaism it begins with the recognition that each person is guilty of sin. In Christianity, this sinful and suffering self can be transformed through love; not to transcend self, but to become a new, truer self. Mahatma Gandhi used the expression to mean self-transcendence for the good of the larger community. In Hinduism, self-transformation comes about through increasing awareness of the transience of physical phenomena. It is effected at the levels of *karma* (action), *jnāna* (wisdom) and *bhakti* (devotion), all of which require dedicated practice. In **yoga**, transformation (*parināmā*) is a qualitative change towards one-pointed attention leading to an ultimate state of refinement in which the yogi reaches Self (*ātman*): oneness, soul, Lord, truth. It is probably through the translation of this word (parināmā) that these meanings of self transformation became known in the west (e.g. through Gurdjieff (see **Gurdjief, George Ivanovitch**)).

There is evidence of attempts to link the religious meaning of the term with secular 'stress management'. For example, Sethi (1990–1) describes a wide variety of religious meditation practices as 'techniques of self-transformation' (which they are) but primarily as 'strategies for coping with stress and burnout' (which was never their main intention). This illustrates the problems associated with the phrase 'self-transformation'. Its meaning slides between antithetical world views: the western materialist understanding of the individual as having a real existence through time (and sometimes eternity) and the eastern conception of self as an illusion to be overcome by deeper awareness that there is only one reality, which is Self. When self-transformation is taken in its eastern sense, it is not usually connected with ideas of social transformation or transformation of consciousness beyond the individual. Yet in some New Age thinking self transformation is a part of a wider change of consciousness that is leading to a new era for humanity.

Further reading

Garrett, C. (2001) 'Transcendental Meditation, Reiki and Yoga: Suffering, Ritual and Self-Transformation', *Journal of Contemporary Religion,* 16(3), 329–42.

Sethi, A. S. (1990-1991) 'Self transformation', *Journal of Comparative Sociology and Religion*, 17–18, 1–56.

CATHERINE GARRETT

SELF-REALIZATION FELLOWSHIP
(SRF)

Founded by Swami Paramahamsa Yogananda (q.v.) (1893–1953), the organization was originally known as the Yagoda Satsanga Society, founded in India 1917, and brought to the United States by Yogananda in 1920. It was incorporated in the USA in 1935 as the Self-Realization Fellowship, while retaining its original name in India. Its present headquarters are in Los Angeles.

SRF seeks to promote 'scientific' techniques for the acquisition of spiritual knowledge, principally through kriya yoga, an advanced form of raja yoga promoted by Yogananda (see **Vivekananda, Swami**). Through this method SRF aims to bring humanity from 'mortal consciousness' to 'God consciousness', achieving liberation from physical illness, mental disharmony, and spiritual ignorance. Additionally, the organization aims to bring harmony between original Christianity as taught by Jesus and original yoga as Yogananda believed Krishna taught.

Yogananda's followers are committed to the realization of the oneness of all things, recognizing that divisions between East and West, or between individuals or religions, are human constructs, and are part of *maya* (illusion) which characterizes the physical world. SRF seeks to reconcile the different philosophical ideas that have found expression in various world teachers. Although Yogananda's teachings were based on the *advaita* (monist, or non-dualist) teachings of the medieval Indian scholar

Shankara (trad. 788–820), Yogananda sought to reconcile Shankara's *advaita* with the *dvaita vedanta* (dualist) teachings of the later sage Ramanuja (eleventh/twelfth centuries), claiming that the Absolute could be regarded as either personal or impersonal. SRF therefore allows the possibility of God being regarded as separate from human beings and the physical world, consistent with most Christian teaching and worship, as well as the Hindu *bhakti* (devotional) traditions.

The techniques of kriya yoga are disclosed only to practitioners, who are required to embark on a six-stage training course, completion of which leads to *diksha* (first initiation) and eligibility to learn the practices. Its methods are said to be empirical and experiential, involving breathing and body control, thus slowing down one's breathing and pulse rates. This is said to lead to higher levels of perception in which the practitioner experiences subtle energies, recognizing spiritual laws that govern the universe and afford special spiritual and yogic powers.

SRF's activities are conducted in temples, ashrams, fellowship centres and meditation groups, and meetings are held mainly on Sundays and Thursdays. A week-long annual convocation is held in Los Angeles. Activities are co-ordinated by Orders of monks and nuns, who live in the ashrams and travel throughout the world to give classes, lead retreats and offer guidance and counselling. In accordance with SRF's aim of 'plain living, high thinking', monastics follow a simple lifestyle: they are vegetarian, do not consume alcohol, and are committed to a four-fold vow involving simplicity, celibacy, obedience and loyalty.

For those outside the Self-Realization Order, activities include attending meetings, which are conducted by the monks and nuns, and which are generally held on Sundays and Thursdays. At these meetings Yogananda's writings are read, and attendees pray, meditate and chant. In addition to learning kriya yoga, members may follow a home study course, the contents of which are based on Yogananda's personal instruction and compiled in this mode under his direction. Contents include instruction on spiritual practices, principally meditation, concentration, and 'energization', as well as philosophical teachings such as karma and reincarnation, and ways in which spiritual practice can be applied to everyday life. These include interpersonal relationships, marriage and the family, healing, relaxation, finding a vocation, and improving one's mental powers. There is also a worldwide prayer circle to which members belong.

The Society works in conjunction with other organizations that seek to improve humankind's moral and spiritual condition. The **Yogoda** Satsanga Society, whose headquarters are in Dakshineswar, near Calcutta, has had close contact with Mother Theresa's Missionaries of Charity in the city.

After Yogananda's death in 1953, his followers regarded themselves as Yogananda's body, and continued his work. The leadership passed to James J. Lynn, known to members as Rajarsi Janakananda, who died two years later. The present leader is Sri Daya Mata, born Faye Wright in 1914. Born of a Mormon family, she met Yogananda in Salt Lake City in 1931. At that time she was believed to be suffering from a blood disease, and attributes her cure to Yogananda's powers. She assisted him in the establishment of the Self-Realization Order, and is known as Sanghamata ('Mother of the Society'). She has undertaken much travel and attends to the administration of the Society. She is currently preparing for publication more of Yogananda's teachings, which she wrote in shorthand during his life time, including his commentaries on the Christian New Testament. Daya Mata is also preparing her own memoirs for publication.

The Self-Realization Fellowship does not give information on its numerical strength. However, it currently has some 500 centres, in fifty-four countries.

Further reading

Walters, J. D. (Swami Kriyananda) (1966) *The Path: One Man's Quest on the Only Path There Is*, Nevada City, CA: Crystal and Clarity.
Yogananda (1990) *Autobiography of a Yogi*, Los Angeles: Self-Realization Fellowship.

GEORGE CHRYSSIDES

SELF-RELIGION, THE SELF, AND SELF

The self is individual. The Self is universal and incorporates all gods, including the Christian, Islamic, and Jewish God. Self-religion is the absorption of the self into the Self. The difference between Self-Religion and other religions is that the former is based on experiential knowledge while the latter are based primarily on belief.

Being individual, the self appears separate from other selfs – in fact, from all things. The person (self) is alone among all others who also see themselves to be alone. Throughout history, this situation has given rise to various religious and philosophical ideas which attempt to satisfy the human predicament of selfhood. Included in this predicament are psychological problems encountered by the personality or ego.

Very early in history, the Buddha called the nature of this selfdom suffering (*Dukkha*) in the Four Noble Truths and other religions, too, speak of suf-

fering and its cessation. Latterly, from either a theistic or atheistic viewpoint, existentialists identified the same as a sense of alienation in terms of problems involved in self-authentication and described it as anguish, anomie, or *Angst*. The continual rise of new religious movements across the centuries represents yet other attempts to resolve the problems found in selfhood and its concomitant all-embracing characteristic of suffering.

Although some people appear to suffer less and others more, no one escapes suffering's grasp. This is because the contents of life are transient – everything must end and suffering is inevitable. Old and new religious movements and philosophies all fail to provide an escape from it except by insisting variously on beliefs in unproven or eschatological ideas. Most people live their lives in simple acceptance or forgetfulness of the inevitable, enjoying what they can and hoping or praying for more highs than lows during its course. Psychotherapies have been developed to expand the potential of the self (see **Human Potential Movement** and for self-actualization see **Maslow, Abraham**).

The self is a fragile concept, full of insecurities because of the knowledge of its immanent extinction.

The term universal is insufficient to describe the Self. In fact, no words are of use to describe it. The Self is not an it and has no name or form; as Jiddu **Krishnamurti** describes in *Time and the Timeless*, 'God is not something projected by the mind, so the mind cannot possibly at any time comprehend God' (Krishnamurti Foundation, 1997: 13). Swami Vivekananda (see **Vivekenanda, Swami**), in *Vedanta: Voice of Freedom*, believed that the Self is 'the most glorious God that ever was, the only God that ever existed, exists, or will ever exist' (Advaita Ashrama, 1996: 66). The word Self is used because we need to distinguish what we talk about; it is not the same as such terms as God, Allah, Yahweh, Rama, Great Spirit, Universal Being, etc. if they are used within particular meaning systems – the Christian God is not the same as the Self, it is within the Self.

In fact, all life takes place within the Self. There are no bounds to it and it cannot be partitioned or contained in any way. The Self is described as existence and consciousness or awareness with the characteristic of bliss because of its absolute freedom. The Self exists in everything – beings or otherwise – without exception. In a person, the Self can be described as veiled by the self which, through thought (extension of the ego), thinks itself to be individual and separate, hence it suffers. This is an illusion as, in reality, the self is impermanent and its existence is only sustained by the Self. The self is wholly dependent on the Self.

The Self is proved to exist and so can be experienced through knowledge, not belief – this is the difference between Self-Religion and all religions and philosophies. This knowledge is found in everyday occurrences. For example, in deep dreamless sleep we are not conscious of anything and have no memory of this state when we wake. Yet we know there was continued existence because we can remember events before sleep occurred. Thus, existence without mind and body occurs daily. What is more, through training, existence can be experienced and this training is the substance of Self-religion.

The Self is seen as unending continuity where suffering has no place, where no event – thought, action, object – has a place. It is existence itself and that which ultimately enables all events and experiences to occur.

The Self is also completely impersonal and it is this aspect which makes it unappealing for many people who want a personal God to satisfy their individual desires and to provide salvation.

What is more, we make the Self sacred and are reverential to it although ultimately it is not sacred nor do we need to revere it. This is because in absolute terms there is no other than the Self, no duality, and so nothing other than it to make sacred in the first place. However, as most people live a dualistic existence, Self-religion has developed.

The key identifying feature of Self-religion is, above all else, its direct relationship with the Divine in the form of the impersonal Self. Each person's relationship is unique which means that systems and methods of practice play a secondary role – scriptures, etc. or teachers are important as guides, although not essential. The principal method of practice is to quieten the mind (memory, senses, intellect, and ego), so removing the veil of ignorance or illusion, as it were, in order that the self can merge into the Self. The most used method for achieving this is meditation in its many forms (see **Transcendental Meditation**) – all religions and spiritualities incorporate methods of quietening the mind (see **Silence**) and which method is chosen is entirely dependent on the aspirant. There is no particular 'church' in Self-religion.

Many recent teachers (**Adi Da**, J. Krishnamurti, Nisargadatta Maharaj, Ramakrishna Paramahansa (see **Ramakrishna, Sri**), **Ramana Maharshi**, and Swami Vivekananda (see **Vivekananda, Swami**) and others) have taught and written about this path and some 'students' have become teachers in their own right (Ramesh Balsekar, Wayne Liquorman, Robert Adams, Gangaji, John de Ruitter, Francis Lucille, and others). No one teacher's path is the correct one, all paths lead towards Self-realization of which, according to this philosophy, all people already 'have' but are unaware.

Further reading

Krishnamurti, J. (1997) *Time and the Timeless*, Krishnamurti Foundation.
Vivekenanda, S. (1996) *Vedanta: Voice of Freedom*, Advaita Ashrama.

STUART ROSE

SERVANTS OF THE LIGHT

Servants of the Light (SOL) is an Esoteric Movement (see **Esoteric Movements**) or school of occult science based in Jersey, Channel Islands. It was founded in 1971 by W. E. Butler (1898–1978), based on the Helios Course, which was set up by Butler, Gareth Knight (b. 1930) and John Hall of Helios Book Service, in 1965.

Both Butler and Knight have written significant books on various aspects of the Western Mystery Tradition. Butler was succeeded as SOL's Director of Studies in 1976 by Dolores Ashcroft-Nowick (b. 1929), who has also written numerous books on esoteric subjects, including Tarot, and has designed two Tarot packs.

Butler, Knight and Ashcroft-Nowicki had previously been initiated members of the Fraternity of the Inner Light, the Inner Court of the Society of the Inner Light, founded by Dion Fortune. Butler was also an ordained priest in the Liberal Catholic Church.

Like several other schools of occult science, and modern Rosicrucian movements, SOL runs a correspondence course for its initiates, with the Entered Novice beginning a fifty-lesson main course which lasts for four or five years. The first six lessons are based on *The Art of True Healing* by Israel Regardie, a former member of Stella Matutina, which grew directly out of the **Hermetic Order of the Golden Dawn**. The remaining lessons of the course are based on *Practical Guide to Qabalistic Symbolism* by Gareth Knight. If progress is satisfactory, the Novice will become a Fellow around the tenth or twelfth lesson, entering the First Degree. At a later point on the course, having taken part in several practical ritual workshops, the Fellow may enter the Second Degree as a Frater or Soter of the Fraternity of the SOL, and may then help teach Novices and lead Fellows in their ritual work. Entry to the Third Degree is by invitation only.

SOL is firmly within the Western Mystery Tradition, with a strong emphasis on the symbolism of Tarot and the use of the Tree of Life of the Kabbalah. 'Owing to its simplicity, the glyph is easily committed to memory; and because of its profundity, from this sparse simplicity can be derived a complete and satisfying philosophy and knowledge of life in both its inner and outer aspects.'

There is also a strong emphasis on mythology, both the Matter of Britain – Celtic mythology and the Arthurian cycle – and that of other Western religions and cultures. SOL students are required to make a detailed study of at least two pantheons in addition to their own native tradition: 'Any mythological knowledge you acquire will not be wasted. The ability to cross-index the legends and god forms can be of immense value in the understanding of the ancient past.'

SOL believes that such ancient traditions hold 'a timeless key' which may be applied to the complexities of modern life. As with the original Rosicrucian ideals, the intention is that SOL members, through their intense training, will be of service in the wider world, enabled to help others to achieve inner serenity.

The aim of the studies is to balance the inner and outer selves and to give the student a comprehensive theoretical and practical understanding of the ancient Mysteries. SOL says that if the student shows any psychic talents, the courses will stimulate them into activity and polish them. In this way the student may make his or her own inner contacts.

SOL claims to be a 'contacted' school, in that it is 'in close psychic touch with the overshadowing Hierarchy on the Inner Planes'. First and Second Degree students are in the Outer Court. The Inner Court of Third Degree initiates, also known as the House of the Amethyst, is where the real power is believed to reside: 'from there it is mediated in various ways to its counterpart on the physical level'. SOL's 'contact' is from the ancient esoteric school of Alexandria, from the Temple of On, or Heliopolis. The Alexandrian Fraternity, or *Fraternitas Alexandrae*, is the inner fountainhead from which SOL's teaching stems; 'it is a withdrawn Order under whose authority the whole school works, teaches and has its existence.' SOL is its earth-level expression.

As well as the UK, there are SOL Lodges in Australia, Canada, Mexico, Netherlands, Sweden, and the USA. SOL has 2,600 members in twenty-three countries. 'A wide range of traditions are represented within the school: we count ourselves fortunate to have Wiccan witches, Pagans, Christian nuns and priests, Shamans, Hermetists, Kabbalists, Buddhists, Isis-worshippers and many others among our students. All paths to the Light are worthy of respect.'

Further reading

Regardie, F. I. (1932) *The Art of True Healing* (1997 edn ed. M. Allen), Novato, CA: New World Library.
Knight, G. (2001) *Practical Guide to Qabalistic Symbolism*, Boston, MA: Red Wheel/Weiser.

DAVID V. BARRETT

SET

Set was a beneficent sun god in predynastic Egypt but become negatively

associated in later tradition. He is often represented as the opponent of the chaos serpent Apophis, and was brother of Osiris whom he killed in a jealous rage. Following the revenge of Osiris's son Horus, Set degenerated into an unwelcome and hostile deity of thunder storms and the desert, and the unpleasant ruler of the underworld. His ambiguous and changing roles are suitably entangled with the ambiguities and indeterminacy of his physical form or representation.

Members of the **Temple of Set**, perhaps the largest international organization of Satanists (see **Satanism**), consider Set to be the real name of the being mistakenly identified by Christians and others as Satan. Far from being an angel whose responsibility it is to bring accusations before God (Satan's role in the biblical book of Job), and even further from the later Christian and popular notion that Satan is the opponent of God and godliness, Set is understood by these Satanists (or Setians) to be the prime example of self-fulfilment and self-realization. Some members of the Temple of Set say, for example, that 'as Set was, we are, and as Set is, we will be'. Beyond his exemplary role as one who experimented and expressed his true self, Set may be considered to be the giver of a gift that distinguishes humanity from animality. This gift, 'the Black Flame', is self-consciousness and the desire to continuously 'become' more fully one's self. Humans are able, and therefore to be encouraged, to act freely and even transgressively not only in social but also in cosmic contexts. That is, Set and his gift encapsulate a strong notion of freewill with this self-religion (see **Self-Religion, the Self, and Self**). Not all members of the Temple of Set consider that Set really exists, some are uninterested in the question. While all agree that Set is the archetypal provoker and generator of dynamic change in societies and individuals, only some accept at face value the claim of the Temple's founder that Set offered a new self-revelation that inspires all other selves to continue freely evolving.

GRAHAM HARVEY

SHAMANISM

The term 'shaman' originated with the Tungus tribe of eastern Siberia, but is now widely applied to the role of the seer, medicine man, or 'witch doctor' in traditional tribal societies. Shamanism is found among most indigenous peoples, and has become one of the fastest growing spiritual movements in the West. Modern shamanism is sometimes classified under the umbrella of **Neo-Paganism**, but is actually an ancient spiritual methodology predating this socially constructed movement though often incorporated into neo-pagan praxis.

The main function of shamans is the service of mediating between the community and the spirit world. They achieve this by 'soul flight': entering a trance through different methods including rhythmic drumming, chanting, dance, and psychotropic plants. In this altered state of consciousness, the shaman's spirit travels out of his body to any of three realms – the upper, middle, and lower worlds – each with its own topography and spirit denizens. Here the shaman obtains knowledge and power which is used to help the individual or the whole tribe – traditionally with practical concerns such as hunting, medicine, and war. However, in the West shamanic power is used primarily for self-development, healing, and spirituality. Shamans are aided in the spirit world by spirit helpers and allies, with whom they have an ongoing relationship. In the Native American tradition, these guides often take the form of

'power' or 'totem' animals, particularly Bear, Coyote, and Eagle.

The Western shamanic revival originated with the historian of religion Mircea Eliade, who hypothesized a universal shamanism with shared core features. Eliade's ideas were developed and distilled in the 1960s by the American anthropologist Michael Harner into 'core shamanism'. Harner's influential book *The Way of the Shaman* (1992) describes his programme of key common practices stripped of the cultural embellishments carried by tribal shamanism. The Foundation for Shamanic Studies in California has become the largest shamanic organization, offering a wide range of courses. Some of the teachers have become well known in their own right, particularly Sandra Ingerman who teaches soul retrieval: a shamanic technique for healing physical and psychological illness that is beginning to rival Western psychotherapy in its success rate. Jonathan Horwitz, an American now living in Denmark, has adapted the principles of core shamanism into a more European approach which he calls modern Western shamanism in preference to the somewhat derogatory term neo-shamanism. The main British organization is Eagle's Wing, a 'centre for contemporary shamanism' run by Leo Rutherford and Howard Charing.

Some contemporary anthropologists believe that the differences between traditions are as important as the similarities, but the majority of Western teachers have been trained in core shamanism, which has become the most influential and popular approach. However, it has been accused by some members of native American tribes of appropriating the cultural heritage of indigenous peoples. While there is undoubtedly truth in this, some Western practitioners collaborate with tribal groups to conserve their heritage, while some native teachers are happy to share their wisdom with sympathetic Westerners rather than see it die out. Furthermore, many shamanic customs are so universal that they are in the 'public domain'.

The second most significant teacher in the shamanic revival was Carlos Castaneda, a Mexican anthropologist. His influence spread mainly through his books, purporting to be an account of the teachings of Don Juan, a Yaqui shaman; these were enormously popular in the 1960s–1970s counter-culture. Don Juan's magical world view was at complete odds with post-enlightenment rationalism, which was a factor in their appeal. Another major influence was Terence McKenna, whose popular books describe his experimentation with South American psychotropic plants. The combination of powerful shamanic techniques with psychotropic plants creates a very high-octane spirituality. 'Technoshamanism' is a post-modern blend of internet and rave culture, which seeks altered states through the 'ritual' of trance dance and music, sometimes with the aid of psychotropic substances.

The current shamanic revival may be seen as a rebellion against both organized religion and scientific materialism. Its emphasis is on the human being as an embodied soul, living in a world where animals, plants, even rocks have souls or spirit, and the world itself has an 'anima mundi'. This perception enables practitioners to connect and communicate with other life forms and to live in harmony with nature. Shamanism is therefore widely considered the most significant and effective contemporary nature religion, to the extent that some Druids and Wiccans are relocating themselves from the neo-pagan into the shamanic tradition. Western psychology has identified a range of similar phenomena to the soul journey, such as out-of-body experiences, near death experiences, and past life regressions. Psychologists interpret shamanism as an inner psychological journey encountering archetypes created by the mind. However, shamans insist on the reality of the spirit world as a separate parallel universe (termed 'non-ordinary reality by Castaneda), peopled by real life forms.

Further reading

Eliade, M. (1989) *Shamanism – Archaic Techniques of Ecstasy*, London: Penguin
Harner, M. (1992) *The Way of the Shaman*, San Francisco: HarperSanFrancisco
ELIZABETH PUTTICK

SHAMBHALA

Originally an Indian concept, adopted and given prominence in Tibetan Buddhism. In the twentieth century Shambhala had also become a key notion of New-Age thought (see **New Age Movement**).

The term first appeared in the *Mahābhārata* and the *Purāna*s as the place where the future Kalki will be born at the end of the present eon. The significance of Shambhala within Indo-Tibetan Buddhism is traced to the appearance of the first *Kālacakra* texts in the eleventh century. From then onwards, a vast literature in Tibetan on Shambhala has been written (see **Vajrayāna Buddhism**).

According to the *Kālacakra* tradition, there is a close relationship between the *Kālacakra* and Shambhala which operates in the past, present and future. *Kālacakra* teachings are said to have been taught in the past by the Buddha upon the request of Suchandra, King of Shambhala. In the present, Shambhala is said to be the place where the *Kālacakra* teachings are preserved and practised. The *Kālacakra* literature also contains an eschatological account describing the great war to come between the twenty-fifth ruler of Shambhala (T: *rig ldan*) and the barbarians (T: *kla klo*) who will be ruling the earth. The Shambhala army will defeat the barbarians and following that, the twenty-fifth ruler of Shambhala will rule over the entire earth. He will propagate the teachings of the Buddha in general, and the *Kālacakra* specifically.

The first known western reference of the term was made in 1627 by two Portuguese Jesuit missionaries, Estevão Cacella and João Cabral, who heard of the name in Bhutan. Shambhala became more widely known in the west through the writings of Madame Blavatsky in the late nineteenth century (see **Blavatsky, Helena**). Blavatsky refers to Shambhala in her *The Secret Doctrine* and in *The Voice of the Silence*.

Another figure who was very influential on the way views on Shambhala evolved in the west was the Russian painter, mystic master, founder of the Agni Yoga movement and peace activist, Nikolai Roerich. Roerich (1874–1947) had a strong belief that the current cosmic era was coming to an end and that Maitreya, the future Buddha, was about to appear in Shambhala. The Roerich family, Nikolai, his wife Helena and son George (Yuri) believed that through a careful study of the myth of Shambhala along with an actual geographical search, they would be able to find the real location of Shambhala, somewhere in the Altai Mountains. These speculations eventually fuelled the two major expeditions of the Roerich family to central Asia, sponsored by the Roosevelt administration.

Some of Blavatsky and Roerich's ideas are echoed in James Hilton's notion of Shangri-la, the western variation of Shambhala, as described in his 1933 novel, *Lost Horizon*. The book was later adapted into a popular Hollywood film by the same name, directed by Frank Capra (1937). Hilton depicted Shangri-La as a repository of knowledge, with a specific Christian-Buddhist orientation.

The notion of Shambhala was given a non-Buddhist perspective in the teachings of Chogyam Trungpa (see **Trungpa, Chogyam**). Trungpa, born in Tibet in 1939, was an incarnate Buddhist lineage holder and an abbot of a monastery in Tibet. Following the Chinese invasion of Tibet, Trungpa fled to India and later came to the UK. In the 1970s he became a popular teacher in the US, combining Buddhist teachings with other spiritual aspects. In his very influential *Shambhala: the Sacred Path of the Warrior* Trungpa presented Shambhala within a general spiritual perspective, quite removed from Buddhist sources.

Especially as a result of the Tibetan exile since 1959, various inter-connections have developed between perceptions of Shambhala, Shangri-La and Tibet. The view of Tibet as a respiratory of knowledge and as the cure for the declining western culture has its resonance both in New Age thinking and in the way Tibetan Buddhist themselves, and most notably the Fourteenth **Dalai Lama** present Tibetan Buddhism.

With a wish to cash in on the Shangri-La legacy, in March 2002 China's state council announced that the Zhongdian County in Yunnan, which borders Tibet, has been renamed as 'Shangri-La County'.

Western New Age adaptations on Shambhala from the 1990s include Victoria Le Page's *Shambhala: the Fascinating Truth behind the Myth of Shangri-La* and James Redfield's *The Secret of Shambhala: In Search of the Eleventh Insight*. In these sources Shambhala is treated in a pan-religious context.

Further reading

Bernbaum, E. (1980) *The Way to Shambhala*, Garden City, NY: Anchor Books.

Kollmar-Paulenz, K. (1992–93) 'Utopian Thought in Tibetan Buddhism: A Survey of the Śambhala Concept and its Sources', *Studies in Central & East Asian Religions*, 5/6: 78–96.

Le Page, V. (1996) *Shambhala: the Fascinating Truth behind the Myth of Shangri-La*, Chennai (Madras): Quest Books.

McCannon, J. (2001) 'Searching for Shambhala', *Russian Life*, 44(1), 48–57.

Redfield, J. (1999) *The Secret of Shambhala: In Search of the Eleventh Insight*, New York: Warner Books.

RONIT YOELI TLALIM

SHEPHERDING

Also known as discipling, shepherding refers to the practice whereby believers submit themselves to spiritual overseers that originated within certain forms of charismatic **Evangelical Christianity** in the 1970s.

Shepherding can be traced to diverse earlier evangelical groups. In its contemporary form, three influences are relevant. First, the writings of Watchman Nee, Chinese church leader of the Little Flock movement who was imprisoned under communism, whose books, notably *Spiritual Authority* (1972), were widely read. Nee taught that church life should be structured through relationships of 'delegated authority', in which believers should be obedient to those with a 'covering' of 'spiritual authority' over them. Rebellion against God's delegates was tantamount to rebellion against God. A second influence is Argentinian pastor Juan Carlos Ortiz, author of *Disciple* (1975), whom Andrew Walker (1985: 66) calls 'the father of discipling and shepherding doctrines in their modern Protestant form'. Ortiz's church had experienced rapid growth through the implementation of authority and submission doctrines. He believed that only by submitting to authority could believers possess authority. A third influence was a group of independent American Pentecostalist leaders known as the 'Fort Lauderdale Five'. Don Basham, Ern Baxter, Bob Mumford, Derek Prince and Charles Simpson are the founders of Christian Growth Ministries. They taught that Christians should renounce individualism in favour of 'covenant relationships' in which shepherds held a benign authority over other Christians to encourage their progress in both faith and lifestyle. Derek Prince's book *Discipleship, Shepherding, Commitment* (1976) expresses this view.

At its most stringent, each believer had a shepherd or discipler. In the networks where these teachings were most enthusiastically adopted, notably the British **House Church Movement**, a pyramid-style system evolved, with apostles at the top, church leaders below, then 'house group' leaders and finally individual believers. Followers were asked to submit voluntarily to the suggestions and advice of those placed in authority over them. Submission potentially extended to decisions about marriage, finance, career, and leisure. Children submitted to parents, wives to husbands, and all to elders (church leaders), who submitted to apostles, who, finally, submitted to each other.

The shepherding movement received criticism from outsiders, former members and many within evangelical Christianity. Shepherding was regarded as unduly authoritarian and liable to abuse. However, it is important to note that while the shepherding movement was paternalistic, this paternalism was generally benign. In the mid-1970s the Fort Lauderdale Five admitted that their teaching had, interpreted wrongly, been used to exert unreasonable control over believers' lives. They since have tried to distance themselves from negative images of shepherding. Today in the British House Churches, shepherding has, in the groups where it still exists, been moderated substantially. It is now present most notably in the discipling practices of the **International Church of Christ**.

Further reading

Ortiz, J. C. (1996) *Disciple*, Lake Mary, FL: Charisma House.

Prince, D. (1976) *Discipleship, Shepherding, Commitment*, Ft. Lauderdale, FL: Derek Prince Publications.

Tomlinson, D. (1997) 'Shepherding: Care or Control?' in L. Osborn and A. Walker (eds) *Harmful Religion: An Exploration of Religious Abuse*, London: SPCK.

Walker, A. (1985) *Restoring the Kingdom: The Radical Christianity of the House Church Movement*, London: Hodder and Stoughton.

KRISTIN J. AUNE

SHINNYO-EN

Founder: ITÔ Shinjô, ITÔ Tomoji
Country of origin: Japan

Shinnyo-en, a Buddhist order of Japanese origin, was founded in 1936 in Tachikawa city, Tokyo by Itô Shinjô (1906–89) and his wife, Tomoji (1912–67). Itô Shinjô was brought up in Yamanashi prefecture where he 'inherited' a divination called *Byôzeishô* passed down for generations of the family with the instructions that it should not be used for personal gain. While Itô Shinjô was working for an aircraft company in Tokyo, he continued the study of the divination system mentioned above and started studying esoteric Buddhism of the Shingon school. In December of 1935 Itô Shinjô and Tomoji enshrined the image of *Dainichi Daishô Fudô Myô-Ô* 'Great and Holy Mahavairochana Achala' in their house, which was said to have been made by Unkei (?–1223), the famous sculptor of Buddhist images.

In commemoration of its enshrinement, in January of 1936, Itô Shinjô and Tomoji began the thirty-day ascetic practices, and Itô Tomoji inherited the spiritual faculty from her aunt on 4 February, which flowed from Tomoji's grandmother. On 8 February, Itô Shinjô quit his job, and together with Itô Tomoji founded a Buddhist order called Risshôkaku.

In 1939 the name of the order was changed to Tachikawa Fudôson Kyôkai and Itô Shinjô trained at Daigoji in Kyoto, the head temple of Daigo school of Shingon Buddhism, where he attained the qualifications to become a Great Acharya, or Great Master in 1941. With the end of the Second World War, the Japanese government's policy of restrictions on religious affiliation was lifted and Tachikawa Fudôson Kyôkai became independent of Shingon Buddhism with the new name, Makoto Kyôdan, which was changed to Shinnyo-en in 1951. Although it became a religious juridical person in its own right in 1953, Shinnyo-en has maintained its lineage relationship with the Daigoji school of Shingon Buddhism up to today. Itô Shinjô died in 1989 and his daughter, Itô Shinsô, the most qualified disciple, is the current head.

The main canonical sutra of Shinnyo-en is the Mahaparinirvana Sutra, or the Great Nirvana Sutra, which is considered to contain the last teachings of Gautama Buddha and the essence of all his previous teachings. Itô Shinjô judged that the Shingon esoteric teachings continued the essence of Buddhism, although these teachings are to be revealed only to the initiated. Being eager to make the essence of esoteric Buddhism accessible to all and believing that the Mahaparinirvana Sutra was the teaching to make it possible, Itô Shinjô decided to base his teachings on the Mahaparinirvana Sutra.

Followers of Shinnyo-en practice a type of meditation called *sesshin*. While there is also a meditation known as sesshin in Zen Buddhism, sesshin in Shinnyo-en is practised in a relatively short time with the aid of other followers who have already cultivated their spiritual faculty to a high degree. Sesshin in Shinnyo-en is considered to help followers to look at themselves more objectively and realize the Buddha's compassionate heart. Followers are encouraged to practice sesshin regularly and apply the teachings of harmony, gratitude, and loving kindness to their daily lives, in order to guide themselves, as well as others, to the state of eternal bliss and the pure self, which is the aim of the Mahaparinirvana Sutra.

While following Buddhist tradition, Shinnyo-en has developed its own rituals. *Saito-Homa* is an outdoor grand fire ritual which was originally started in *Shugendô* 'ascetic mountain training' in the eighth century. According to Shinnyo-en, the *Saito-Homa* of Shinnyo-en nourishes all living beings, gives rise to their pure nature, destroys evil, strengthens goodness, and heightens one's level of aspiration for enlightenment. Another important ritual is *Tôrô-Nagashi*, 'lantern-floating'. *Tôrô-Nagashi* is a rite believed to comfort the spirits of the deceased by ferrying spirits on the lanterns from the shore of delusion to those of salvation, and was originally associated with *Urabon-e* 'the Bon Festival', a Buddhist observance honouring the spirits of ancestors.

Social activities based on altruistic practice of **Mahayana** teachings are encouraged, and there are activities that contribute to society, such as cleaning public places and providing quick disaster relief. Early morning cleaning of such places as railway stations and public parks is conducted regularly at around 6,000 sites in Japan and several hundred sites outside Japan.

Shinnyo-en has constructed over sixty temples and propagation centres in Asia, North and South America, Europe and Oceania. There are around 800,000 followers in total in various countries.

Further reading

Clarke, P. B. (1999) *A Bibliography of Japanese New Religions*, Eastbourne, Kent: Japan Library, pp. 231–4.
Itô Shinjô (1997[1957]) *Ichinyo no Michi 'The Way to Nirvana'*, Shinnyo-en.

KEISHIN INABA

SHRINE OF THE BLACK MADONNA IN DETROIT

The Shrine of the Black Madonna in Detroit, a black nationalist Christian movement, traces its origins to 1953 when the Reverend Albert Buford Cleage, Jr. (b. 13 June 1911, Indianapolis, Indiana – d. 20 February 2000, Beulah Land, South Carolina) and 300 parishioners withdrew from Saint Mark's Presbyterian Church to form a new congregation that eventually became known as Central Congregational Church (United Church of Christ). The organization of this congregation allowed Reverend Cleage to develop his concept of the church as a focal point for community, especially with respect to education and politics. Throughout the 1950s and early 1960s, Central Congregational Church created strong youth programs, supported the civil rights movement, and provided leadership for local political issues including opposition to racially segregated schools and attempts to dilute the black vote by rezoning congressional districts. In 1962, Reverend Cleage was the Freedom Now party candidate for governor of Michigan.

With the emergence of black power, liberation theology, and religious leaders such as Malcolm X, Revered Cleage began to formulate a new theology and vision of the church. On 22 March 1967, Easter Sunday, he preached a sermon that became the basis of the Black Christian Nationalist Movement and unveiled Glanton Dowdell's fifteen-foot 'Black Madonna and Child'. The painting, hung over the altar at the front of the sanctuary, replaced a stained glass window showing the Pilgrims at Plymouth Rock. Central Congregation Church became the Shrine of the Black Madonna, and in 1970 Reverend Cleage changed his name to Jaramogi Abebe Agyeman, Swahili for 'Defender/Holy Man/Liberator of the People'.

As the movement grew, it established nine additional Shrines. In 1975 the Southern regional headquarters opened in Atlanta, and in 1977 the Southwest regional headquarters in Houston. At a 1978 meeting in Houston, the group proclaimed itself a new denomination, the Pan African Orthodox Christian Church (PAOCC), with Jaramogi Abebe Agyeman its Founder and Holy Patriarch. The church's hierarchy includes cardinals, bishops, and other officials. In its support of gender equality, it ordains women as ministers and consecrates them as bishops. People who complete the church's basic twelve-month training course become full participating members with voting rights. Others are contributing and associate members. Although independent, the domination maintains a weak affiliation with the United Church of Christ, and is a member of the National Council of Churches.

The PAOCC's defining symbols, the Black Madonna and Christ, were also significant in the African Orthodox Church founded in 1921 by George McGuire, Chaplain-General in Marcus Garvey's Universal Negro Improvement Association from 1920–2. PAOCC beliefs begin with God as cosmic energy and creative intelligence from which everything was created. Humans, as a part of God's creation, have a spark of divinity; and the PAOCC, as a sacred circle where the power of God is concentrated, is an instrument of radical social change. Central to PAOCC teachings is that Jesus was the revolutionary black Messiah who came to liberate the black nation of Israel from oppression and exploitation by the white gentile world. Jesus, therefore, is Messiah not because of his death on Calvary, but because of his dedication to the struggle for his people. Today, the revolutionary spirit of God that Jesus embodied is still at work in the liberation of black people from a world system that dominates and exploits them and that perpetuates the myth of their inferiority, all of which is in opposition to the will of God and the divine system.

The PAOCC emphasizes that survival of black people and salvation are dependent on working for the good of the community and rejecting individualism. To this end, the church seeks to build a nation within a nation, where black people can create institutions to promote and sustain their economic, political, social, and psychological well being. Therefore, the church has established centers that focus on community service, day care, youth, education, technology, and culture. Lay ministries promote social action, wellness, benevolence, creative arts, and fellowship. The church's purchase of 2,600 acres of land in Abbeville, South Carolina, along with plans to expand to 5,000 acres, is an effort to rebuild black civilization. The Beulah Land Farm Project is designed not only to grow, process, and distribute food to black people elsewhere, but to promote the communalism that the church sees as an essential part of its teachings.

PAOCC worship consists of elements found in all denominations: meditation, hymns, prayers, responsive readings, choir selections, scripture, offerings, announce-ments, and preaching. Everything that occurs in worship reinforces the theol-ogy of the church: the Lord's Prayer is reworded as the Prayer of the Black Messiah; Holy Communion is the Sacra-ment of Commitment. In addition to Christianity, PAOCC beliefs and rituals reflect other sources, including African, in the offering of libations to the ances-tors, and Asian, in meditation techni-ques that emphasize breathing and opening the body's *chakras*.

The Shrine of the Black Madonna has played a major role in Detroit politics. As supporters of the Black Slate, mem-bers worked for the election of Coleman Young to be mayor of Detroit, and Barbara Rose Collins and Carolyn Cheeks Kilpatrick to become members of the US House of Representatives. Although the Shrine's membership is not in the thousands as when the move-ment began in the late 1960s and was a focal point for much of Detroit's black community, the church attracts several hundred people to its Sunday service and sizable numbers to its cultural programs.

Further reading

Cleage, A. B., Jr. (1972) *Black Christian Nationalism: New Directions for the Black Church*, Detroit: Luxor Publishers.

Cleage, A. B. Jr. (1989) *The Black Messiah*, Trenton, NJ: Africa World Press.

Ward, H. H. (1969) *Prophet of the Black Nation*, Philadelphia: Pilgrim Press.

CLAUDE F. JACOBS

SIDDHA YOGA DHAM

An organization in the Hindu tradition was founded in 1975 by Swami Mukta-nanda Paramahansa (1908–82) as the Siddha Yoga Dham Associates Foun-dation. Its teachings and practices draw mainly on Kashmir Saivism and Advaita Vedanta (non-dualist) Indian philosophy.

The principal practice is kundalini yoga (see **Sahaja Yoga**), enabling the practi-tioner to progress towards the realiza-tion of his or her Inner Self as the Hindu high deity Lord Shiva.

Muktananda's teacher was Nitya-nanda (d. 1961), reportedly born in the first half of the nineteenth century in South West India. He lived as a wan-dering *sadhu*, and founded a monastic order, moving to Ganeshpuri in Mahar-ashtra, some fifty miles from Bombay. Ganeshpuri gained a reputation as a place of pilgrimage, where Nityananda gave *darshan* (divine appearance). Muk-tananda met Nityananda in 1947, hav-ing left home and taken up the life of a wandering saddhu. Nityanada gave him *shaktipat* (spiritual initiation): Mukta-nanda attested that it was at this point that his spiritual energy (kundalini energy) was awakened, and that he reached profound meditative states, finally lead-ing him to enlightenment. Following Nityananda's death, he established the Gurudev Siddha Peeth Ashram near Ganeshpuri.

Being a blend of Kashmiri Saivism and Indian Vedanta (one of the six classical schools of Indian philosophy), Siddha Yoga Dham draws on a variety of Hindu texts. From the Vedanta tra-dition it acknowledges the four ancient Vedas, the Upanishads, Shankara's Viveka-Chudamani (*The Crest Jewel of Discrimination*), Patanjali's Yogas, as well as the Vaishnavite text, the *Shrimad Bhagavatam,* which recounts the exploits of Krishna. Kashmiri texts include the Shiva Sutras, the *Pratyabhijnahridayam*, the *Spanda Karikas*, and the *Vijnana Bhairava*.

The organization combines the two main sources of ideas in its core teach-ing that nothing exists that is not Lord Shiva – an assertion which combines Vedanta's *advaita* (non-dualist) philoso-phy with the personalism that is entailed by worship of Shiva. If everything is Shiva, then one's goal is to recognize oneself as Shiva, dispelling the illusion of separateness between the self and God. Equally, other living beings are Shiva, and hence are also worthy of ultimate respect. Siddha Yoga Dham encapsulates these ideas in the aphorism: 'Honour your Self, Worship your Self, Meditate on your Self, God dwells within you as you.'

Siddha Yoga Dham's principal practice is *guru-kripa yoga*. This entails spiritual practice in the presence of one's guru, since the master's charisma is deemed to be more important than the technique itself. The student is said to receive spiritual energy, transferred from the guru: since the teacher is regarded as divine, the student progressively gains recognition of his or her divinity, as feelings of separation between the self and the divine disappear.

The technique of *kripa yoga* involves the awakening of *kundalini* energy in the body. Kundalini literally means 'serpent', since it is believed that kundalini energy is coiled like a snake around one's body, in the lowest *chakra*. The chakras are points in the body, defined by an occult anatomical system.

The 1960s saw the rise of western interest in Muktananda's ashram, with American seekers arriving, include Werner Erhard, founder of *est*. In 1974 Erhard invited Muktananda to visit the West, and he embarked on a world tour, accompanied by **Baba Ram Das** (Richard Alpert), and including parts of Europe, New York, Dallas, Los Angeles and Australia. Siddha Yoga Dham is now a worldwide movement, with followers principally on these three continents.

Following his death in 1982, Muktananda was succeeded by Swami Chidvilasananda (b. 1955), known to followers as **Gurumayi**, and her brother Swami Nityananda. In 1985 Nityananda resigned from the movement, and went off to form his own organization, Shanti Mandir (Temple of Peace) Seminars in 1987. Swami Chidvilasananda is now in sole charge of the organization. She travels around the world, giving teaching and initiation.

There are currently two main temples belonging to Siddha Yoga Dham, both dedicated to Bhagawan Nityanada, who is regarded as the source of the movement's spiritual energy. The Shree Muktananda Ashram is located in upstate New York, and the Gurudev Siddha Peeth continues to be used in Ganeshpuri, India. The latter has two main areas. There is a public area, which is said to be its 'spiritual heart', and which includes the temple of Bhagawan Nityananda and the *samadhi* ('resting place') of Swami Muktananda: this is a pilgrimage place for their followers. A residential area exists for seekers: residents are expected to spend at least one month, absorbing the spiritual atmosphere and engaging in the organization's daily schedule, which includes meditation, chanting the divine name and the organization's ancient Sanskrit scriptures, practising hatha yoga and contemplation, as well as offering service to the community.

Further reading

Muktananda, Swami (1978) *I Am That: The Science of Hamsa from Vijnana Bhairava*, South Fallsburg, NY: SYDA Foundation.

Muktananda, Swami (1981) *Guru*, New York: Harper and Row.

GEORGE CHRYSSIDES

SILENCE

In a noisy, busy and fast-moving world, it is not surprising that the quality of silence has become increasingly important. This is particularly true of spiritual concerns where many activities place great emphasis on the practice of silence, for example, in communion with God, meditation, **T'ai chi ch'uan** and **Yoga**. Silence is one of the few – perhaps the only – common experience to be found across all religions, both traditional and new. Calmness and peacefulness usually accompany silence.

There are four possible inter-related types of silence. First, silence infers cessation of speech. In spiritual terms, this implies a solitariness within which thoughts are concentrated on particular aspects of an individual's path. The Trappist monk Thomas Merton (1915–68) and the spiritual educationalist Rudolf Steiner (1861–1925) both wrote on this subject, the Amish and Quaker communities practise it and it plays a significant part in classical Yoga and Buddhist meditations (see **Buddhism in the West**). Most forms of private prayer and contemplation also fall within this type of silence.

Second, more comprehensive than the first type is physical silence. However, although it is scientifically possible to create complete silence in an anechoic chamber, it does not exist naturally on the Planet and probably not in the Universe as a whole; experience of it is impossible except via the fourth type. The American minimalist composer John Cage (1912–92) heard two sounds in an anechoic chamber – the higher pitched was the working of his nervous system and the lower pitched his blood circulating. In spiritual terms, retreats and renunciation are examples of ways in which the physical noise of an individual's world is reduced to a minimum as they often act as aids to deeper contemplation.

Third and even more comprehensive is mental silence, that is, the absence of thought or inner speech, emotions and intellectual activities. This type links directly with the fourth type, absolute silence. The objective of many forms of deep meditation is to reduce thoughts completely in order to experience this silence. In such practices, thoughts of individuality cease and the person is said to merge into the Oneness that is infinite and eternal. Absolute silence represents another way of characterizing God, *Brahman*, Self (see **Self-Religion, the Self, and Self**) or whatever term is used and, seemingly a contradiction, absolute silence also includes all sounds and thoughts, because that is the nature of God. This means that attaining physical silence is unnecessary for the experience of absolute silence. God, we are told, has no beginning or end and so, too, with silence: sound and thought always have a beginning and always end, whenever a sound or thought ceases (relative) silence is revealed.

Sri **Ramana Maharshi** (1879–1950) was a living demonstration of this silence, found in the Hindu philosophy of *Advaita Vedanta* (non-dualism), a silence he called the perfect teaching.

Scriptures and contemporary teachings tell us that mental silence cannot be complete or maintained except in states where the mind and body are fully transcended. Enstasy (standing within one's authentic being) or liberation then occurs, giving the qualities of complete freedom and bliss.

STUART ROSE

SILVA METHOD
a.k.a. Psychorientology, and formerly known as Silva Mind Control

Part of the **Human Potential Movement**, the techniques of the Silva Method were devised by José Silva (1914–99). Born in Laredo, Texas, Silva set up his own business as a repairer of electronic equipment. Struck by the way in which electrical impulses affected brain activity, he brought together, largely by self-teaching, a number of subject areas, including western science, alternative healing, psychology, eastern gurus and their philosophies. Silva may also have been influenced by the writings of Norman Vincent Peale, **Christian Science**, Couéism and biofeedback. Particularly impressed by Roger Sperry's 'split brain' theory, Silva developed the technique of 'alphagenetics', which aimed to develop the 'right hand side of the brain', as opposed to the left. Silva believed that 90 per cent of people were 'left-brained', relying on their brain's beta-waves, and on their logical, rational abilities. Alphagenetics sought to develop alpha-waves in the brain, enabling the development of intuition and imagination, allowing practitioners to take control of their lives, surmount personal problems, and develop psychic powers.

Silva's researches started in 1944 initially as a series of experiments with friends and family, in which he used hypnosis, claiming to raise participants' IQs and develop their clairvoyant powers as a result. In 1953 he wrote to the parapsychologist J. B. Rhine, seeking to gain his interest, but without success; in contrast with Rhine, Silva believed that clairvoyance could be developed, and that any individual could acquire extra-sensory perception. In 1964 Silva established his own Laredo Parapsychology Foundation, and in 1966 his 48-hour Silva Method Course was made available to the public. In the same year Silva was invited to address the Area Arts Association in Amarillo, where a number of artists who were sympathetic to 'right brain' activity were persuaded to use his methods and to propagate them in surrounding cities.

Silva Method courses are currently taught in 107 countries in twenty-nine languages, and by 1989 around six million students had completed the basic Silva programme. This two-day seminar, entitled the Basic Lecture Series (BLS), is the recommended introduction, which offers 'self-empowerment' through the development of alpha brain-waves. The claimed benefits are positive thinking, the ability to relax, control of one's ability to sleep and wake, dream control for the purposes of self-improvement, improved health, ability to address unwanted habits, and the power of psychic healing. Other benefits are said to include giving up smoking, curing insomnia, greater confidence, better ability to relax, improved memory and creativity, as well as the development of extra-sensory powers. Silva's basic technique is known as 'dynamic meditation', and involves visualization and 'projection' (mentally placing oneself in appropriate hypothetical situations), which allegedly lead into paranormal activity.

Graduation from BLS enables the practitioner to enrol in the Graduate Program. This two-day seminar develops the techniques learned in BLS, and also addresses the question of how and why they work. Also included is the 'Center of the Galaxy Technique' in which one is believed to receive guidance from 'Higher Intelligence'. Practitioners also gain the ability to teach a modified version of the techniques to their family and friends. Two further programs are offered to graduates: the Ultra Programme, which aims to 'heal' aspects of life, including personal health, business success and personal relationships, and Mind 2.0, which is taught by the most senior Silva instructors, and aims to gather together all aspects of the other programmes, combining the spiritual with the scientific.

The basic principles and applications of the Silva Method are set out in José Silva's principal text, *The Silva Mind Control Method,* co-authored with Philip

Miele, and first published in 1977. Silva has authored numerous other books, including his autobiography, *I Have a Hunch: The Autobiography of José Silva* (1983).

Although the Silva Method is sometimes classified as one of the 'self religions' (see **Self-Religion, the Self, and Self**) and regarded as part of the New Age, its practitioners deny that they are following a religion. However, unlike Mind Dynamics and Landmark Forum (formerly *est*), both of which are believed to be partly derived from Silva, the Silva Method at times appears to use distinctively religious language and ideas. For example, the Silva Method is professedly 'God-oriented', 'striving towards the attainment of Christ consciousness', and 'ushering in a new age of spiritual development and understanding'.

The Silva Method has been criticized from a number of standpoints. Evangelical Christians have objected to Silva's concept of Christ, who offers a model of perfectibility to which all can attain. Others have pointed to Silva's lack of formal qualifications, sometimes describing his work as an inappropriate synthesis of scientific and spiritual sources, placing undue reliance on Sperry's 'split brain' concept. Some have questioned whether the Silva Method's achievements can be scientifically verified, pointing to a lack of evidence of greater success, for example, in intelligence tests.

Further reading

Silva, J. (1980) *The Silva Mind Control Method*, London: Grafton.

Silva, J. (1983) *I Have a Hunch: The Autobiography of José Silva*, Laredo, TX: Institute of Psychorientology

Stone, R. B. (1990) *Jose Silva: The Man Who Tapped the Secrets of the Human Mind and the Method He Used*, Tiburon, CA: H. J. Kramer.

GEORGE CHRYSSIDES

SOCIETY OF THE INNER LIGHT

The Society of the Inner Light is the creation of Violet Firth, better known in occult circles as Dion Fortune (1890–1946). In a certain sense – as has often been noted – she was the female version of Aleister Crowley (1875–1947) (see **Ordo Templi Orientis**).

Violet Mary Firth had a passion for psychoanalysis from a very early age, and by the age of 23 had become one of London's highest-paid analysts. In the years immediately preceding the First World War, and after an early interest in **Christian Science**, she made contact with the **Theosophical Society**. During the war, she took part in efforts for 'national farming', later becoming one of the most enthusiastic disciples of Theodore William Carte Moriarty (1873–1923). Moriarty's teaching was founded on a sort of 'Atlantis-based Christianity', and gave great importance to the mysteries of Atlantis and to the continuous appearance of incarnations of the 'Christ-principle' throughout history, each with its priests and priestesses, within an essentially gnostic cosmology that is the basis of Dion Fortune's *The Cosmic Doctrine*.

In 1919, Violet Firth was initiated into the London Alpha and Omega temple of the Golden Dawn, where she assumed the initiatory motto and name 'Deo, non Fortuna', from which she derived her later pseudonym Dion Fortune. Expelled from the Golden Dawn in 1924 for allegedly having revealed some of its secrets, she began to receive revelations from various masters, including Melchisedec, Socrates (470–399 BC), and Lord Thomas Erskine (1749–1823). In 1927, Dion Fortune married Dr Thomas Penry Evans (1892–1959), a union which brought somewhat pagan interests and trends into the group. In

1928, the Community (later Fraternity, then Society) of the Inner Light was founded, with a centre in London and another in Glastonbury. In the organization's early years (1928–38), Dion Fortune published a large part of her teachings in the form of novels. During this period, she had experiences of magical invocation and evocation. Around 1935 – the year in which she published *The Mystical Qabalah*, which many consider her masterpiece – she began to officiate over the 'rites of Isis' (later described in literary form in her novel *Moon Magic*) in the former Presbyterian church of Belfry.

With the start of the Second World War, Dion and her group lost several important members. In 1932, she had managed to interest Christine Campbell Thomson (1897–1985) in her magical movement. It seems that Dion quickly noted a developing sympathy between her husband Thomas and Christine, and that this observation had something to do with her decision to induce her new pupil to practise her magic paired with Colonel Charles Richard Foster Seymour (1880–1943). Despite these precautions, however, Thomas Penry Evans left Dion Fortune (and the Society) in 1939. Seymour and Christine (having become Hartley by a second marriage) became the Society's most brilliant magicians: their 'dance of the Gods' (of which transcriptions remain) remains one of the most impressive examples of evocatory magic in the twentieth century. Dion did not, however, appreciate Seymour and Christine's excessive independence and, in the last years of her life, she returned to a more Christianized view of the occult, although still 'celtic' and reincarnationist. Seymour, Christine Hartley and Dion Fortune also collaborated in a great magic battle, led from Glastonbury, to help Allied troops in the war against the Third Reich.

Dion Fortune's final years were lived in twilight: obese, bizarrely dressed, adored by pupils who perhaps were not of the same calibre as those of the 1930s, she was described by more than one visitor as being in decline. She died suddenly of leukemia in 1946. The Society of the Inner Light has since continued its activities under the guidance of Arthur Chichester, an Irish Catholic. After its founder's death the Society was actually directed by her spirit, which continued to speak through a medium, until Chichester decided to 'retire' her from her managerial duties in 1950.

Although some adherents criticize the group's new direction (which, at some points also seemed to be influenced by Alice Bailey (1880–49) and by **Scientology**), the Society continues to grow in membership. The Christian orientation of the Guild of the Master Jesus (an inner circle composed of the more Christian inclined members of the Society's 'pagan' period, with which Dion had become reconciled in her last years) continues as well, as does celebration of its peculiar version of the mass.

Further reading

Richardson, A. (1987) *Priestess: The Life and Magic of Dion Fortune*, Wellingborough (Northamptonshire): Aquarian Press.

Chapman, J. (1997) *Quest for Dion Fortune*, York Beach (Maine): Samuel Weiser.

PIERLUIGI ZOCCATELLI

SOKA GAKKAI (VALUE-CREATION)

The largest new religious organization in Japan Soka Gakkai was founded in 1931 when **Makiguchi Tsunesaburo** published volume one of his four volume work *Soka Kyoikugaku Taikei* (The System of Value-Creating Pedagogy) under the auspices of Soka Kyoiku Gakkai (Value-Creation Educational Academic Society). This movement was renamed Soka Gakkai by **Toda Josei** in 1946. It rapidly increased its membership during the 1950s and 1960s, and at the time of writing claims to have a membership of 8.21 million households in Japan and 1,502,000 individuals overseas.

The founder Makiguchi Tsunesaburo (1871–1944) after graduating from school worked part-time and became a primary school teacher. While serving as the principal of a primary school in Tokyo, he devised a unique form of pedagogy which was later crystallized as the concept of value creation. He then attempted to apply this theory in practice, with the assistance of his disciple Toda Josei at his Jishu Gakkan school which prepared students for their university entrance examinations. In the book, *Soka Kyoikugaku Taikai* the theory of value creation education is explained as a form of education which enables students to engage constructively in learning, make value judgements for themselves, and discover their purpose and goals. In 1929, Makiguchi became a member of the Nichiren Shoshu sect, and conscientiously studied and practiced Buddhism. Over time he integrated the beliefs and practices of Nichiren Shoshu with his educational theory of value creation.

In 1932, Makiguchi resigned as a teacher and began promoting his movement among teachers, and the organization Soka Kyoiko Gakkai was formally launched at the first general meeting in 1937 in Tokyo's Azabu district with an estimated sixty people in attendance. By 1941 the organization claimed 3000 members and began to publish its magazine *Kachi Sozo* (Creation of Values). By 1940 with the coming of World War Two the Japanese government took control of religion and was determined to make it contribute to the war effort. To this end it sought to create a single outlook among the people and as part of this endeavour decided that Buddhist schools should overlook all differences between them and merge. At the same time it declared Shinto worship to be compulsory for every Japanese citizen regardless of the personal beliefs or the religious tradition of their family. The majority of Nichiren Shoshu members decided against merging with othe closely related Buddhist schools. They also objected to worshipping the sun goddess Amaterasu declaring that there was no other object of worship than Nichiren and that the State would be successful and prosper only when it recognized this. This was in keeping with the attitude of the founder of the Nichiren Shoshu sect, the monk Nichiren Daishonin (1222–88) who in his time warned the nation that if it failed to worship true Buddhism it would experience a series of national disasters including civil war and foreign invasion.

Kachi Sozo was banned in 1942 but this did not prevent Makiguchi, Toda and other ardent members of the movement from continuing their aggressive proselytizing campaigns known as *shakabuku* (literally break and subdue (false teaching)). Others, including some of the priests of Nichiren Shoshu began to make compromises. Among the more hardline members some were arrested for using the shakabuku approach to spreading the movement's teaching. Makiguchi and Toda were arrested on 6 July 1943 for refusing to follow State Shinto. Makiguchi died in prison in 1944.

Toda Josei (1900–58) was released just before the end of the war, and began to reconstruct the organization. He became the second president of what became known as Soka Gakkai in 1951. Like Makiguchi Toda had also studied while working to become a school teacher. He excelled in organization management. While chanting Daimoku (the invocation Nam-myoho Renge Kyo: Devotion to the Wonderful Law Lotus Sutra) in prison, he discovered that the Buddha was the meaning of life and was inspired to develop his Theory of Life to be formulated later and which included the conviction that happiness and wealth would come through worshipping the *Gohonzon* or sacred scroll inscribed by Nichiren and the principal object of worship for Soka Gakkai members. Indeed, he once referred to the *Gohonzon* as a 'machine that makes you happy' (Murata, 1969: 108).

When Toda became its second president in 1951, Soka Gakkai had a membership of around 5000 and he set the target of increasing this to 750,000 households by 1957 by using the *shakabuku* method. Toda published *Shakubuku Kyoten* (*Manual for Forcible Persuasion*) to explain the modernized doctrines based on his Theory of Life which contained material which he believed useful for criticizing other religions and sects. His aim was to save Japan by reforming society at large and he sought to gain further access to the world of politics.

It is **Ikeda Daisaku** (1928–) who has led this the most successful of Japanese new religious movements (see **New Religion (Japan)**) since the death of Toda Josei, as its third and then honorary president studied part-time while working with a view to discovering the true meaning of life. He met Toda Josei in 1947, and became a member of the Soka Gakkai.

The rapid expansion of the organization continued for a decade after Ikeda became president in 1960. According to official estimates the membership had exceeded 7.5 million households by 1970. In the meantime, it was also advancing in the political arena through

the Komei Political League which was established in 1961. This developed into the Komeito party in 1964 and by 1976 it had 55 seats in the House of Representatives. Ikeda advocated "Human Revolution" and "The Third Civilization" as ideas to connect the reform individual, personal reform with and social reform.

However, when in 1969, it was releaved that Soka Gakkai had successfully stopped the proposed publication of *Soka Gakkai o Kiru* (Criticizing the Soka Gakkai), it was charged with infringing the freedom of the press. It was also forced to separate the organizational structures Soka Gakkai and the Komeito party. Ikeda had to resign at this point as the president and become the honorary president. Also it was from around this time that the growth of Soka Gakkai in Japan began to plateau out. Furthermore, its conflict with the Nichiren Shoshu high priest led to a break between the clerical and lay sides of the movement which was finalized in 1992.

This dispute slowed everything down and caused confusion among members both at home and abroad. Soka Gakkai International (SGI) has experienced mixed fortunes overseas in recent times. While it continues to be the most successful Japanese new religion abroad, generally it has experienced mixed fortunes including decline in the United States and stagnation in Brazil. In other parts of the world, however, including Korea it has continued to gain ground. Everywhere, like other Japanese new religions it has promoted and continues to promote peace initiatives and human rights and to engage in and sponsor research on environmental issues.

Soka Gakkai, inheriting the tradition of the Nichiren Shoshu that advocates exclusive devotion to the Lotus Sutra has linked this to its own modern ideas of self-reform and social reform. The Theory of the Creation of Values developed by Makiguchi and the Theory of Life by Toda have served as a bridge between the teachings of the Nichiren Shoshu sect and the movement's modern ideas. Followers undertake self-reform in small discussion groups (*zandankai*) and in this way receive emotional support from their fellow members. This style was devised by Makiguchi and has become a way of promoting lay participation from below. It encourages among members a strong sense of fellowship which has become typical of new religions in Japan in the latter half of the 20th century.

The Soka Gakkai's idea of reforming the world began to increase its appeal at a time when Japan had lost its pride and confidence after the war. However, its exclusivism, its use of shakabuku, a tactic it has now abandoned, and its stridently critical attitude toward other religions, also less evident in recent times, have given rise to distrust and even strong opposition among non members. Moreover, it is obvious that the Komeito is dependent on the support of the Soka Gakkai. This party now competes with the Communist Party for the position of third largest party in parliament, and at times is perceived to exercise a considerable influence on the political situation, and this is also a reason for the opposition the movement encounters.

Further reading

Clarke, Peter B. (ed.) (2000) *Japanese New Religions. In Global Perspective*, Richmond: Curzon Press.

Dator, James A. (1969) *Soka Gakkai: Builders of the Third Civilization: Japanese and American Members*, Seattle: University of Washington Press.

Metraux, A. (1988) *The History and Theology of Soka Gakkai*, Lewiston, NY: Edwin Mellen.

SUSUMU SHIMAZONO

SPANGLER, DAVID
(b. 1945)
New Age activist and writer

David Spangler was born in Columbus, Ohio and spent formative childhood years in Morocco where his father worked as a US scientist. Here Spangler developed a 'deep interest in the nature of spirituality and the role of the invisible, formative side of life' (Spangler 1984: 24). His family resettled in Phoenix, Arizona, in 1959, where they became interested in the emerging 'new age subculture', exploring UFOs, parapsychology and 'a belief in the imminent dawning of a new age' and reading **Edgar Cayce**, **Alice Bailey** and **Rudolf Steiner** (Spangler 1984: 17ff, 26). By 1965 Spangler had abandoned his college science degree to teach and counsel on the nature of the **New Age Movement** with a family friend, Myrtle Glines. Between 1966 and 1970 Spangler led a local small group which studied New Age ideas in the context of Alice Bailey's books. In 1970 Spangler and Glines came to the **Findhorn Community** where they spent three years helping to formulate the practical management and outreach of a rapidly-expanding colony. Here Spangler composed his early 'manifesto' *Revelation: the Birth of a New Age* (1971). This text included channelled material from a source he called 'Limitless Love and Truth'; later he contacted a more homely, democratized source he called, simply, 'John'. In 1973 Spangler returned to the USA and with Dorothy Maclean (a Findhorn co-founder) and others set up the Lorian Association. Later Spangler contributed to summer conferences at the Chinook Learning Centre near Seattle, of which *Reimagination of the World: A Critique of the New Age, Science and Popular Culture* (1991) forms a vivid dialogical record. Spangler is perhaps the most persistent and self-reflexive popular theorist of New Age, instrumental in negotiating the key hermeneutical shift in the emblem in the 1970s from other-worldly apocalypse to this-worldly transformation. He describes himself as a 'free-lance mystic' teaching a devolved message of 'everyday spirituality' (Spangler 1996: 46, 53).

Further reading

Spangler, D. (1984) *The Rebirth of the Sacred*, London: Gateway Books.
Spangler, D. (1996) *Pilgrim in Aquarius*, Forres: Findhorn Press.
Spangler, D. and Thompson, W. I. (1991) *Reimagination of the World: A Critique of the New Age, Science, and Popular Culture*, Santa Fe: Bear and Co.

STEVEN J. SUTCLIFFE

SPIRIT OF JESUS CHURCH
(Iesu no Mitama Kyokai)

The Spirit of Jesus Church is a Japanese Christian movement that represents an independent and indigenous response to the transplanted mission churches from the West. The founder, Jun Murai (1897–1970), was the second son of a Methodist minister who studied theology at the Methodist-related Aoyama Gakuin University in Tokyo. He was deeply troubled during his student days and even considered suicide. In 1918, while riding a ferry boat in Okayama Prefecture, Murai made the decision to jump overboard and end his life. It was at this moment that he experienced the presence of the Holy Spirit in a powerful way and began speaking in tongues. This experience erased all of Murai's doubts concerning religious faith and gave him a new strength and vision for evangelistic work.

Murai dropped out of Aoyama Gakuin and became an evangelist, eventually becoming a pastor in the Japan Bible Church. In 1933, the pentecostal experience that had changed his life spread throughout the membership of his small congregation in Nishisugamo, Tokyo. This pentecostal movement gained a distinct identity in 1941, when Murai refused to have his congregation absorbed into the **United Church of Christ in Japan**, a church organized as a result of the government's attempt to control religious minorities in Japan during the Second World War. This was also the year that his wife, Suwa Murai, received a revelation from God in which the name Iesu no Mitama Kyokai (Spirit of Jesus Church) was given to them as an official church designation.

Like other pentecostal groups, the Spirit of Jesus Church rejects intellectualism and emphasizes the importance of religious experience. Speaking in tongues, anointing with oil, dancing in the spirit, miracles of healing, and revelations from God are all basic components of everyday religious life. To such pentecostal characteristics and a strong eschatological orientation (emphasis on the Second Coming of Christ), Murai and his followers have added a theology that addresses Japanese folk religious concerns, particularly with regard to the ancestors. While this church rejects the traditional practice of ancestor veneration, it is deeply concerned with salvation of the household and practices baptism for the dead (I Cor. 15). According to Murai, the Biblical teaching of the salvation of the dead has been hidden from the church since the second century. The authority to forgive sins has been forgotten by the modern church along with all the signs, miracles, and wonders that characterized the early church. Through the ritual of vicarious baptism, the good news of the forgiveness of sins is communicated to the dead and their spirts are transformed from Hades to Heaven. This ministry to the dead is regarded as a continuation of the work begun by Jesus Christ when he descended into Hades and preached to the imprisoned spirits (I Peter 3:18–22). Members can request baptism for ancestors at the time of their own baptism or later when they become concerned about the salvation of those who have gone before. One simply states the name and one's relationship to the ancestor and then receives baptism by immersion on their behalf. Concern for the dead is also expressed in the *godo iresai*, an annual festival for the comforting of the spirits.

This movement did not experience significant growth until the postwar period. In 1950 the head church in Tokyo was built and two years later a Bible school established to train pastors. By 1958 it had grown to a membership of 28,000, with churches organized throughout Japan. According to the *2002 Christian Yearbook*, the Spirit of Jesus Church currently has 236 churches, a membership of 56,288, led by 333 ministers (60 per cent women). Field research indicates that the active membership is about 20,000. Leaders of this movement maintain that they are neither Catholic nor Protestant and insist that their church has recovered authentic apostolic Christianity. The Spirit of Jesus Church is best understood as an indigenous Christian sect: it is indigenous in that it has been transformed through contact with native culture and it is sectarian in that it conceives of itself as uniquely legitimate and continues to exist in tension with the larger society. Established churches in Japan consider it to be heretical because it rejects trinitarian theology and practices baptism for the dead.

Further reading

Ikegami Yoshimasa (2003) 'Holiness, Pentecostal, and Charismatic Movements in Modern Japan', in M. R. Mullins (ed.) *Handbook of Christianity in Japan*, Leiden: EJ Brill.

Mullins, M. R. (1998) *Christianity Made in Japan: A Study of Indigenous Movements*. Honolulu: University of Hawaii Press.

MARK R. MULLINS

SPIRITUAL HUMAN YOGA

Spiritual Human Yoga (SHY) was originally known as Universal Human Energy and uses today the name of Mankind Enlightenment Love (MEL) as well. It is a far-Eastern movement founded in 1989 by Luong Minh Dang, born in Vietnam in 1942. From 1961 to 1975, he was an officer in the Vietnamese Navy. After years of difficulty following the communist takeover, he finally emigrated to the United States, becoming a citizen in 1985. Taking residence in St Louis, Missouri, he later became known as a healer. In addition to North America, Mexico and Brazil, SHY is active mainly in the Germanic and Latin countries of Europe, in Hungary, Poland, Romania, Belarus, Ukraine, and Russia, as well as in Turkey, Israel, and Thailand. In 1998, about 10,000 people of all nationalities reached level 6, the movement's then highest level.

Dang states that he inherited his technique from previous masters: the founder of the Human Energy spiritual school allegedly was a certain Dasira Narada (1846–1924) from Sri Lanka. The founder's successor, an Indian, is reported to have initiated Luong Minh Dang in Vietnam in 1972, and to have died in Sri Lanka in 1980. Spiritual Human Yoga claims to develop techniques that control Human Energy so that it can be used for the well-being of mankind (for example, to heal a sick person). Compared with other techniques, Human Energy's supporters say it is simpler to use and quicker. Up to level 5, Energy is transmitted through the hands; at higher levels, telepathically. Advanced students also use small pyramids to gather Energy. Since late 1999, there has been a level 7, and since January 2000 the first three levels have been taught in a single session.

SHY does not have the structure or functions of a religious group: there are none of the classic ceremonies or rites of passage marking the milestones of existence. Nevertheless, Master Dang's message contains a spiritual teaching, which starts beginning at level 4. This eclectic and non-dogmatic teaching combines many of the themes currently popularized by alternative religions. Dang expresses special respect for Buddha and Jesus, and declares that he is guided by Higher Beings who constantly provide him with new information. At times he is fairly critical of established religions.

In Europe, Spiritual Human Yoga has had some problems: in January 1999, Dang was arrested by the Belgian police and spent sixty-five days in jail before being released on bail. Although the charges against him were mainly financial in nature, the media stressed the movement's apocalyptic language. In effect, Dang is certain that the twenty-first century will be a turning-point for humanity, and has often implied that major upheavals are imminent. SHY claims that it can overcome the difficulties of the transitional period, and can develop unprecedented abilities in the control of matter. Dang's teaching includes a clearly millenary dimension (see **Millenarianism**): at its advanced levels, SHY is presented as a technique that can contribute to the establishment of a new earthly paradise in which an ideal climate will reign for eternity, in which all illnesses will be curable, and in which death will be almost entirely eliminated.

Further Reading

Mayer, J.-F. (2000) 'Healing for the Millennium: Master Dang and Spiritual Human Yoga', *Journal of Millennial Studies*, 2/2: posted at www.mille.org/publications/winter2000/winter2000.html.

JEAN-FRANÇOIS MAYER
AND PIERLUIGI ZOCCATELLI

SPIRITUALITY

Spirituality encompasses all ideas and beliefs which involve a transcendence of the individual person (body and mind). This transcendence is of two types, restricted to humanity or that which goes beyond the purely human. The term includes traditional religious beliefs and the beliefs of NRMs, as well as less formalized notions which do not include much in the way of dogmas, institutions, and rituals. All people can experience spirituality and most claim to, although the experience is not usually constant. The term is widely used and analysis of what it needs to entail suggests that a religious belief is not essential, what is essential is a continuous reverential or equivalent experience, maintained effort or practice, and the experience of love (see **Love, Spiritual**).

Each person has a physical body and a mind; the mind does not exist apart from the body, although at times it may seem to. There exists the idea that the person also has a spirit which extends in different dimensions from those of the body and mind in that it transcends or goes beyond and exists apart from them. Without the belief in the transcendence of the individual body and mind, the concept of a spirit cannot be held.

There is a minority of people who believe that the spiritual in humankind does not exist, that it is a mental illusion. In this regard, therapies of the **Human Potential Movement** seek to find the highest that an individual can achieve with the mind. However, opinion polls regularly show that the large majority of people have some belief in a transcendent God or some sort of spirit or life-force, although there is no factual evidence which can be verified to support the existence of spirit.

Some humanistic ideas suggest that spirituality does exist and can be experienced in terms of the sum of humanity being greater than its parts – that is, more than the individual but extending no further than humanity as a whole. The Religion of Humanity or Cult of Man and civil religions are examples of this. Most often, spirituality is based on ideas which transcend humanity, for example in terms of a personal or impersonal God or Goddess, the transcendence of the individual self to higher levels of consciousness, or the notion that all is one non-dual Reality. This vast range of disparate ideas encompasses varieties of traditional and new religions together with, for example, **Shamanism** and aspects of the paranormal, the **New Age Movement**, psycho-spiritual therapeutic ideas (e.g. **Psychosynthesis**) and transpersonal psychology, deep ecology, and matters which relate to a person's ultimate concern.

Spirituality indicates a similar meaning to the term religious, although it is more expansive and incorporates ideas falling beyond the notion of what a religion might comprise. Additionally, it gives voice to unstructured beliefs, for example, where a direct relationship is developed with what is considered divine or particularly meaningful (see **Self-religion, the Self, and Self**). The Fourteenth **Dalai Lama**, in *Ancient Wisdom, Modern World: Ethics for the New Millennium* (1999: London), believes there is an important distinction between the two. Religion he sees is to do with matters of salvation, while spirituality is more to do with qualities of the human spirit such as love and compassion, tolerance, forgiveness, contentment, etc. He says we can do without religion but not without the qualities of spirit. In this description, while not excluding religious qualities, spirituality adds the highest personal qualities thereby suggesting a more comprehensive individual experience than that which the term religious implies.

There is significant interrelation between some humanistic and the transcendent notions of spirituality. The dividing line between the two is a grey area and there is no universal agreement as to what spirituality entails. This situation raises the question: Is the experience of spirituality the same regardless of the ideas each person may hold? In answer, what can be said is that while each person's experiences are unique, there is wide acknowledgement that in absolute terms there can be just one spirit to experience, although this is described in different ways – the God of Judaism is no different from the God of the Jesus Movement, ISKCON (International Society for Krishna Conciousness), or the unity consciousness of transpersonal psychology. We can conclude, therefore, that most, if not all, varieties of spirituality which might be experienced are based on individual interpretation of this one spirit.

Spirituality is usually experienced discontinuously, although its existence may be continuous. The busy mind and life distract attention; it is only by individual effort – discipline, endeavour, aspiration, and desire – that contact with what is deemed spiritual can be maintained. The triggers for spiritual experience are many and varied; they are unique to each person and to particular circumstances. Some events trigger the experience more than others and these are likely to be exceptional life occurrences, for example, birth, illness, death – moments of intense joy or sadness. Ordinary events also act as triggers, for example, walking in nature, witnessing a sunrise, a poem, painting, or piece of music, the list is endless. What shrouds the experience is primarily forgetfulness and this is caused through life's vicissitudes and distractions.

A number of Buddhist, Christian, Hindu, Jewish, and Muslim professionals (priests etc.), together with non-traditional professionals, were asked what spirituality entailed (reported in *Journal of Contemporary Religion* 16(2)). While there was little agreement between the different groups there was an underlying accord in their answers. First, affiliation to a particular religion was not found to be prerequisite for the experience. What was found prerequisite was some form of continued reverential experience, maintained effort with regard to a related practice, for example living in accord with the Ten Commandments or the Noble Eightfold Path, and living a life imbued with love – that is, altruistic activities and loving kindness.

Further reading

Mahony, W. K (1987) 'Spiritual Discipline' in M. Eliade (ed.) *Encyclopedia of Religion* Vol. 14, New York: Macmillan.

Rose, S. (2001) 'Is the Term "Spirituality" a Word that Everyone Uses, But Nobody Knows What Anyone Means by it?' *Journal of Contemporary Religion*, 16(2): 193–207.

STUART ROSE

STARHAWK
(b. 1951)

Born Miriam Simos, Starhawk is one of the most prominent feminist Pagan activists in the United States, although she has also actively reclaimed her Jewish roots, an exploration which has led to her to sometimes refer to herself as a 'Jewitch'. An involvement in feminist activism in the 1970s led her to the **Goddess movement**, and she studied feminist witchcraft with Z. Budapest and Faery Witchcraft with Victor Anderson. After practising as a solitary witch, Starhawk formed Compost, her first coven, from participants in an evening class on witchcraft. A second for women only, named Honeysuckle, followed shortly after. In 1976, she was elected president of the Covenant of the Goddess and in 1979 she published her first book, *Spiral Dance*, a popular volume which sold over one hundred thousand copies in its first ten years of publication. *Spiral Dance*, now in its third edition, is based on the Faery Tradition but also incorporates strictly feminist principles into modern witchcraft (see **Goddess Feminists**). These principles were expanded in Starhawk's later books *Truth or Dare* and *Dreaming the Dark* .

In 1980, Starhawk was one of the founders of the **Reclaiming** Collective in San Francisco, a community for feminist spirituality and counselling based largely on Faery **Wicca**, feminism, and environmental and political activism. Reclaiming offers classes, counselling, public rituals, witchcamps and workshops, seeking to reclaim the image of the witch and empower women (and men) with the Goddess in order to effect political, environmental and social change. The 1998 Reclaiming 'Principles of Unity' explicitly sets out these aims, claiming to 'work for all forms of justice: environmental, social, political, racial, gender and economic'.

The themes of nature worship, politics, activism, psychology, and Goddess worship conjoined in an attempt to heal spiritual and political divisions in society and individuals are strongly expressed in Starhawk's two novels published in the

1990s, *The Fifth Sacred Thing* and *Walking to Mercury*. European Wiccan attitudes towards Starhawk's redirection of witchcraft into political activism tend to be cautious.

Further reading

Starhawk (1999) *Spiral Dance: A Rebirth of the Ancient Religion of the Great Goddess*, New York: HarperCollins (twentieth anniversary edition).

JO PEARSON

STATE SHINTO

The term State Shinto is used to describe state financial support for, and selective ideological appropriation of, Shinto in Japan's modern period from the Meiji Restoration (1868), until this union of religion and state was dissolved by the Allied Occupation with the 'Shinto Directive' of 1945. State Shinto encompasses diverse phenomena: government funding for and regulation of shrines and priests, the emperor's supposed divinity, state creation of Shinto doctrine and ritual, construction of shrines in imperial Japan's colonies, compulsory participation in shrine rites, teaching Shinto myth as history, and suppression of other religions that contradicted some aspect of Shinto. Because the term designates a political manipulation of Shinto, State Shinto was not a 'natural' evolution of Shinto itself. Its chief significance for the study of new religious movements lies in its use before 1945 to suppress new religions.

State Shinto began with a failed attempt to make Shinto a state religion in the years following the Restoration. The Meiji constitution of 1889 granted the Japanese people limited freedom of religious belief, to the extent that the exercise of religion did not interfere with their duties as subjects. Article one stated that the emperor was 'sacred and inviolable'. Shrine priests held that Shinto constituted a supra-religious entity responsible for carrying out the rites of state. On this view, religions were the 'mere' creations of human founders, and it was these which subjects were free to follow. The implication was that Shinto shrine observances, unlike those of Shinto sects, Buddhism, and Christianity, were obligatory for everyone. Buddhism, Christianity, and thirteen sects of Shinto were officially recognized, allowing them to undertake missionary activities freely, but the numerous new religious movements of the era fell outside this framework, leaving them vulnerable to harassment and suppression.

Several aspects of State Shinto posed difficult contradictions for adherents of new religious movements (and Christianity). State Shinto's glorification of death in battle was enacted at Tokyo's Yasukuni Shrine, which came to serve as a national shrine for the war dead, but those whose religious beliefs precluded assent to the apotheosis of the war dead as national gods were suspected as traitors. Similarly, the custom of home worship of a talisman from the Ise Shrines came to have a semi-obligatory status under State Shinto, but the beliefs of new religions such as **Sôka Gakkai** conflicted with that observance, causing members to be viewed with suspicion when they would refuse to enshrine an Ise talisman. Likewise, ritual surrounding the Imperial Rescript on Education (1890) forced members of new religions to choose between their faith and social ostracism. This document, which functioned as a sacred text of State Shinto, painted an ideal of a state built on the model of a family, with the sacred emperor at its head. School pupils and military personnel were expected to bow in reverence as it was ceremonially read, and related ceremonies required reverence of the emperor's portrait.

State Shinto shaped the suppression of religions through charges of lèse-majesté. In a celebrated event of 1890, when Uchimura Kanzô (1861–1930) declined on Christian principles to pay obeisance at a ceremonial reading of the Imperial Rescript on Education, he was accused of lèse majesté, precipitating widespread debate on Christianity and patriotism. The Home Ministry ordered the dissolution of a new religion called Honmichi (f. 1913) and charged 180 of its members with lèse-majesté in 1928 when its founder Ônishi Aijirô (1881–1958) publicly denied the emperor's divinity. In a similar incident of 1936, the new religion Hito no Michi (f. 1931) was disbanded on charges of lèse-majesté, stemming from a doctrine identifying the Shinto goddess Amaterasu Ômikami (the first ancestor of the imperial house, according to Shinto mythology), with the sun, a position taken to slander the imperial house.

The Peace Preservation Law of 1925, which gave the state wide-ranging powers to restrict speech and public assembly, was used in combination with charges of lèse-majesté to suppress minority religions conflicting in some way with Shinto. Three new religious movements were effectively silenced and their leaders jailed until the end of the war through the combined charges of lèse-majesté and violating the Peace Preservation Law: Ômotokyô (f. 1892) in 1935 (see **Omoto**) (following an earlier suppression of this religion in 1921 under the Newspaper Law), **Honmichi** in 1938 for pacifism and renewed denial of imperial divinity, and **Sôka Gakkai** (f. 1930) in 1943, when its leaders refused to enshrine a talisman from the Ise Grand Shrines. There were also some cases targeting traditional Buddhist sects, but the majority of prewar incidents of religious suppression involved either Christianity or new religious movements. The highly repressive Religious Organizations Law of 1940 labeled all religious organizations except Buddhism, Shinto sects, and Christianity, 'pseudo-religions' (*ruiji shûkyô*), greatly curtailing the freedom of new religions to assemble, publish, or proselytize.

State Shinto came to an end with the Shinto Directive of December, 1945 issued by the Allied Occupation, which prohibited all state support for and patronage of Shinto and required that all Shinto influence be removed from the public schools. The emperor renounced the idea of his divinity in a rescript of 1 January 1946. The postwar constitution of 1947 grants freedom of religion and mandates separation of religion from state (article 20) and prohibits state patronage of any religion (article 89).

Further reading

Lokowandt, E. (1981) *Zum Verhältnis Von Staat und Shintô im Heutigen Japan* (On the relation between State and Shinto in modern Japan), Wiesbaden: Otto Harrassowitz.

Holtom, D. C. (1963) *Modern Japan and Shinto Nationalism, A Study of Present-Day Trends in Japanese Religions*, New York: Paragon Book Reprint Corp.

Hardacre, H. (1989) *Shinto and the State, 1868–1988*, Princeton: Princeton University Press.

HELEN HARDACRE

SUAN MOKKH

Founder: Buddhadasa Bikkhu
(b. 1906; d. 1992)

Anyone who described as 'mindless' and an 'obstacle to spiritual liberation' the way in which Thai Buddhists venerated the Lord Buddha, the Dhamma and the Sangha was inevitably going to meet with strong opposition, and this was to be the fate of Buddhadasa Bikkhu

(1906–92) founder in 1932 of the Forest monastery of Suan Mokkh in the province of Surat Thani in southern Thailand.

Buddhadasa sought to free Buddhism from the constraints of Thai culture and to open it up to other religions, and in particular Christianity, albeit mainly to better understand Buddhism. At the same time others in power were seeking the exact opposite in the form of an even closer overlap between Buddhism and Thai culture. One of Buddhadasa's dictums – if a rite is not Buddhist let it fall into disuse (Gabaude, 1990: 215) – reveals his passionate concern to purify Buddhism of all non-Buddhist practices, especially the veneration of spirits, widespread practices such as *sadokroh*, a rite by which a bad destiny is replaced by a more favourable one, and every form of merit making for a better next life.

Buddhadasa believed that by uncovering the core truths of Buddhism he would also reveal its universal character. He, thus, sought to strip away what he believed to be the myths that obfuscated the essence of Buddhism. In this he alarmed the Thai Buddhist hierarchy and many ordinary Buddhists. Particularly traumatic for the elders of the Sangha was his assertion that the words and content of the Pali Canon were not necessarily those of the Buddha. By demythologizing the Canon Buddhadasa believed he would lay bare Buddhism's foundations in those 'natural truths' which were the spiritual and intellectual property of all human beings regardless of race, nationality or creed. In line with this attempt to display this universal character of Buddhism he made use of the concept *sunyata* or voidness to explain the fundamentals of the modern revolution in communications and how human beings should respond to both the contents and effects of that revolution.

Buddhadasa, who was greatly influenced by Zen, also broke with conventional wisdom by insisting on the possibility for everyone, including lay people, of attaining enlightenment in this life, thus rejecting interpretations of nirvana as an extremely vague and distant possibility.

Not only was Buddhadasa's teaching or *sasana* doctrinally radical in the Thai context, it was also perceived as socially radical in that same context, especially in the way it attacked the widespread understanding of *kum* (karma) which people used to make sense of inequalities of all kinds. As in the **Protestant Buddhism** of Sri Lanka he placed the emphasis on each individual's moral responsibility for their own condition.

The response to Buddhadasa's radical if unsystematic reinterpretation in the Thai context of Buddhism has taken one of two exaggerated forms: extremely positive or totally negative. There are those who greatly appreciate what they see as his attempt to present Buddhism in a new, but authentic light, as a culture of awakening from 'greed' (capitalism), and ignorance (conservatism, traditionalism)'. His great achievements are seen as having been his teachings on the identity of Nature and *Dhamma*, his creation of a middle way between the vocation of books (*gantha-dhura*) and/ or dedication to the intellectual and/or textual dimension of Buddhism and the vocation of meditation (*vipasana-dhura*). Others speak of the balance he achieved between the attention he gave to wisdom or knowledge (*panna*) and the importance of the observance of the rule (*vinaya*).

Buddhadasa's intellectual approach to reform, the emphasis he placed on intellect or wisdom (*panna*) at the expense of morality (*sila*), has met with criticism from many on the grounds that he was overly academic and elitist. Bodhirak (see **Santi Asoke**), for example, believed Buddhadasa's teachings would destroy rather than revive true Buddhism.

Further reading

Gabaude, L. (1990). 'Thai Society and Buddhadasa: Structural Difficulties', in S. Sivaraksa (ed.) *Radical Conservatism. Buddhism in the Contemporary World*, Bangkok: Thai Inter-Religious Commission for Development – International Network of Engaged Buddhists, pp. 211–29.
Thipaythasana, M. P. and Progosh, D. (2000) *The Natural Truths of Buddhism*, Surat: Thani: Buddhadasa Foundation.

PETER B. CLARKE

SUBUD

(Susila Budhi Dharma)
Founder: R. M. Muhammad Subuh Sumohadiwidjojo (b. 1901; d. 1987)
Country of origin: Indonesia

SUBUD is an international movement that supports people in a spiritual practice (*Latihan*) conceived in Java in the 1920s. It is the only movement carried by an Indonesian mystical group (*aliran kebatinan*) to have attracted substantial numbers of followers overseas and to operate as a fully international organisation.

SUBUD's founder, known informally as 'Bapak Subuh' or simply 'Bapak' (I., 'Mr'; lit., 'father') was born in Semarang, Central Java, in 1901 into a family of lesser aristocrats steeped in Javanese high culture. Deeply pious, their Islam nonetheless emphasized, in the manner of Islam's Sufis, the cultivation of 'inner' (I., A., *batin*) spiritual life rather than outward (I. *lahir*, A. *zahir*) expressions of faith. The formal obligations of praying five times a day, attending the mosque on Fridays, etc., were not observed; nor did Bapak Subuh, a frequent world traveller in his later years, ever make the pilgrimage to Mecca.

Privileged with a Dutch education, Bapak Subuh trained as a bookkeeper and took up that occupation at the Semarang City Hall in the 1920s. Already at the age of 17, however, he had begun seeking out instruction from masters (*kiai*) of spiritual knowledge in the Javanist traditions of Islam: first techniques for acquiring invulnerability, including the martial art *pencak silat*; and then the spiritual regimes of the *tarekat* (Sufi orders) for ascent to ultimate knowledge.

In 1925, at the age of twenty four, his search bore remarkable fruit: he received as a divine revelation not some words or images embodying a teaching or truth, but a 'spiritual practice' (I., *latihan kejiwaan*) through which one's own 'inner guide' would work God's. The *latihan* involved a simple but profound attitude of surrender to the Divine, and acceptance of the involuntary physical movements that followed as a form of spiritual purification and empowerment. He gradually began teaching this practice to others, first his *tarekat* friends, and then, in the 1930s, his own students in independent groups.

Those groups grew significantly after the liberation of the Indies from Japanese occupation and the declaration of Indonesian independence in 1945. Growth was particularly rapid in Yogyakarta (an old court city and locus of the new Republican government) to which Bapak Subuh moved in 1946. Then, on 1 February 1947, while the war of independence was still raging, the movement first came together as an organization under the name 'SUBUD'. (SUBUD is an acronym for 'Susila Budhi Dharma', Sanskrit words that the movement renders with strong Islamic coloration as denoting surrender to the will of God.)

After full independence in 1949, SUBUD grew rapidly, like many other Javanese mystical groups (*aliran kebatinan*) originating in that era. The Constitution encouraged 'Godliness' (*Ketuhanan Yang Maha Esa*) and provided for state support of religions (*agama*), but legislation had not yet clarified what constitutes 'religion'. Many *kebatinan* groups sought recognition as religions. Under pressure from strict Muslim and Christian groups, however, the so-called 'new religions' (*agama baru*) were rebuffed by a Presidential Decision in 1965 recognizing only six world religions. Although SUBUD does not present itself as a religion and encourages its members to follow a recognized religion as well (many members become Muslims if they are not Muslims already), it has nonetheless suffered some of the stigma associated with the mystical groups.

This parlous status in Indonesia since the mid-1960s has been counterbalanced by its early and sensational success overseas. The Belgian journalist Husein Rofe discovered SUBUD in Yogyakarta in 1950 and carried it abroad in 1955–6, in England introducing the *latihan* to JC Bennett's Gurdjieff circle. Bapak Subuh was able to make his first world tour in 1957, meeting numerous Gurdjieff groups recently bereft of their original teacher. By the 1970s, SUBUD was one of the most populous movements identified as a 'new religion' by Westerners and had branches in sixty countries.

Since its overseas expansion, the SUBUD movement has been administered through the World Subud Association, which has local, regional, and national 'committees'. Its headquarters are in Jakarta. Every four years a world congress is held in a different city. Clerical roles are limited to that of the 'helpers', who induct new people and support the members' practice. Members finance the Association through individual donations but are also encouraged to join together to form businesses that tithe to the organization. The Association reported having about 385 Subud groups around the world in 2003.

Further reading

Geels, A. (1997) *SUBUD and the Javanese Mystical Tradition*, Richmond: Curzon.
Longcroft, H. (1993) *History of Subud*, Volume I. Houston: Al-Baz.

JULIA DAY HOWELL

SWADHYAYA MOVEMENT (DISCOVERY OR STUDY OF THE SELF)
Founder: Pandurang Shastri Athavale (b. 1920; d. 2003).

Swadhyaya (the discovery of self movement) was started by Pandurang Shastri Athavale (1920–2003). Though a largely unstructured movement, Swadhaya has been one of the more intellectually creative and socially radical of the Neo-Hindu movements (see **Neo-Hinduism**) that include the **Brahmo Samaj**, **Sathya Sai Baba Movement** and the **Brahma Kumaris** movements.

The main ideas of the Swadhyaya movement could be said to encapsulate the core notions of the **New Age Movement** and the so called Self-religions (see **Self-Religion, the Self, and Self**). Athavale, who was born into a wealthy Brahmin family, and attended a traditional Sanskrit school, taught what he regarded as a universally valid truth: that the discovery of the real self would lead individuals to find a god within who would lead them to develop constructive and mutually beneficial relationships with others.

This, Athevale's guiding principle, is the one which, perhaps more than any other, lies behind much of the new, socially concerned spirituality found in the Neo-Hindu movement. He was also greatly concerned, in the manner of the reformist branch of the Neo-Hindu movement, to make practical use of his knowledge of the Bhagavad Gita, to improve the condition of the poor, rejecting both Capitalism and Socialism on the grounds that both systems undermined in their own different ways human dignity. Athevale's movement has provided assistance for millions of the materially deprived especially in the area in and around Mumbai (Bombay) through its social action programs which include the sponsoring of housing and agricultural projects.

Further reading

Srivastava, Raj Krishnan (ed.) (1998) *Vital Connections: Self, Society and God: Perspectives on Swadhyaya*, New York: Weatherhill Publishers.

PETER B. CLARKE

SWAMINARAYAN HINDUISM

Founder: Sahajanand Swami
Country of origin: India

Sahajanand Swami (1781–1830), a religious reformer in a time of great social and political change in what is now the State of Gujarat, established a new Hindu movement (see **Neo-Hinduism**) that is strong, wealthy, and growing among Gujaratis abroad. Estimates of followers range up to five million worldwide.

Sahajanand was born to a Brahmin family in Chhapia near Ayodhya and, following a period of study and pilgrimage, accepted initiation in the Vaishnava tradition and settled among Gujaratis in Ahmedabad. Beginning in 1802, he attracted *sadhus* (world-renouncing ascetics) and householders who accepted his authority, teachings, and discipline and came to worship him as Swaminarayan, the final, perfect manifestation of god.

Gujarat suffered a breakdown of social and religious order at the beginning of the nineteenth century. Sahajanand opposed violence, brigandage, *sati* (self-immolation of widows), infanticide (drowning of infant daughters), and the opium trade, which was prominent in Gujarat as a monopoly of the British. Swaminarayan discipline involved five rigorous vows for sadhus:

1. celibacy and avoidance of contact with women;
2. renunciation of family ties and social status;
3. subduing the sense of taste and attachment to the objects of the senses;
4. poverty and avoidance of greed and avarice; and
5. humility and avoidance of the pride of ego.

Initiation of householders included the formula, 'I give over to Swaminarayan my mind, body, wealth, and the sins of previous births', a brief ritual of pouring water over the right hand, and the Swaminarayan *mantra* (chant). Householders also took five vows: not to eat meat, not to take intoxicants, not to commit adultery, not to steal, and not to defile themselves or others. This discipline of personal purity and non-violence is similar to that taught later in Gujarat by Mahatma Gandhi.

Swaminarayan theology reflects the philosophical non-dualism of Ramunaja and Vaishnava *bhakti* (devotion) to Krishna. Swaminarayan is worshipped as the earthly manifestation of *Purushottam* (the highest form of divinity), so, although images of other Hindu deities and saints are prominent in the temples, primary devotion is given to Swaminarayan. He taught that Purushottam and *akshardham* (the eternal abode of Purushottam) are the only realities that transcend the flux of the world and are unaffected by it. The goal of devotees in their devotion, discipline, and service is release and rebirth in akshardham.

Followers accept the authority of the basic Hindu texts, including the *Vedas*, *Vedanta Sutra*, *Bhagavata Purana*, and *Bhagavad Gita*. The specific theology and discipline of Swaminarayan Hinduism are in sacred texts related to Sahajanand Swami: *Shikshapatri*, 212 Sanskrit verses containing duties of followers; *Vachanamritam*, a collections of sermons by Sahajanand; and *Satsangijivan*, a compendium of teachings, history, and legends from his life.

Sahajanand and his sadhus built temples and traveled throughout Gujarat gathering followers. He establish a permanent organization by appointing two nephews as householder *acharyas* (religious specialists) over two dioceses located in Ahmedabad and Vadtal and establishing their authority in an administrative text, the *Lekh*. The twentieth century brought divisions. The Bochasanwasi Shri Akshar Purushottam Swaminarayan Sanstha (BAPS) began when a sadhu, Yagnapurushdas (1865–1951), called Shastri Maharaj, left the Vadtal temple with a group of followers in 1906. They believed that the 'most perfect devotee' who is 'the abode of god' (i.e., *akshar*) should be the administrative and religious leader. The Swaminarayan Gadi began when a sadhu, Muktajivandas (1907–79), left the Ahmedabad temple in 1947 and rejected the authority of the acharya. The Ahmedabad and Vadtal dioceses and the Swaminarayan Gadi initiate females as ascetics, but BAPS does not.

Swaminarayan Hinduism is a transnational movement with headquarters in Gujarat and many temples and centers wherever Gujaratis have migrated. First developments abroad were in East Africa early in the twentieth century, and then through major migrations of Gujaratis to Britain and North America in the last quarter of that century. Swaminarayan sadhus were once restricted to living in India, but now sadhus reside in major temples abroad. The temples and centers sponsor major festivals and distribute their texts, arts, and teachings in publications and electronic media. They also maintain an active presence on the Internet.

Further reading

Dave, H. T. (1974) *Life and Philosophy of Shree Swaminarayan*, London: George Allen & Unwin.
Williams, R. B. (2001) *An Introduction to Swaminarayan Hinduism*, Cambridge: Cambridge University Press.

RAYMOND BRADY WILLIAMS

SWEDENBORG, EMANUEL
(b. 1688; d. 1772)

All researchers are agreed that the ideas and writings of the Swedish engineer, mystic and occultist Emanuel Swedenborg (1688–1772) have had an important influence on the **New Age Movement** and on other forms of contemporary new religion including **Transcendentalism**.

Although a scientist Swedenborg believed he was 'called' by 'the Lord Jesus' to receive the doctrines of the New Jerusalem and to publish these. Over a period of more than twenty years (1749–71) he wrote, in Latin, eighteen treatises in thirty volumes, including *Secrets of Heaven* which ran to eight volumes and was written between 1749 and 1756 and the *True Christian Religion* (1771).

Swedenborg's 'realized eschatology' – he believed that the Second Coming of Christ began in the spiritual realm in 1757 – his interest in healing associated with his theory of correspondences between the spiritual and material realms summarized in the adage 'as above so below', his depiction of the Afterlife in his *Heaven and Hell* (1758), his liberal moral views, his belief in the essential spiritual nature of human beings and his search for ancient wisdom – are all echoed in New Age and/or Aquarian discourse (see **Age of Aquarius**).

While Swedenborg who was born in Stockholm and died in London did not regard himself as the founder of a movement some of his English and Swedish disciples established the Church of the New Jerusalem, also known as the Swedenborgian Church or New Church for the purpose of preserving his teachings. From very early on the Swendenborgian movement has been international in character. Although the adult membership worldwide is still relatively small – just over 1,300 – Swedenborgian churches exist in more than thirty countries including most European countries, Australia, New Zealand, Kenya, Nigeria, and South Africa.

The church engages in the promotion of environmentally friendly politics and tends to lend its support to liberal ideas.

Further reading

McDannell, C. and Lang, B. (1988) *Heaven: A History*, New Haven: Yale University Press (especially chapter 7 'Swedenborg and the Emergence of a Modern Heaven').
Taksvig, S. (1948) *Emanuel Swedenborg: Scientist and Mystic*, New Haven: Yale University Press.

PETER B. CLARKE

SYNAGOGUE CHURCH OF ALL NATIONS

This new Charismatic/Pentecostal independent healing church was founded by Prophet Temitope Balugon Joshua in the 1990s in Lagos, Nigeria. Although little is known about its foundation, the Synagogue Church is one of the most controversial and high profiled of the rapidly growing new churches in Nigeria. It has attracted great attention in the national and international press, most notably when Prophet T. B. Joshua had Zambia's President Chiluba as his special guest during a private visit in November 2000 for 'spiritual renewal'. The church building holds some 5,000 worshippers, including hundreds of foreign visitors, and is known for its claims of miraculous healings of cancer and AIDS through the hands of Prophet Joshua. The church has been the subject of virulent criticism and shunning by other Nigerian churches, who have declared its leader to be using 'occult' and 'Satanic' powers to perform his healings, which allegedly can only be carried out in the church sanctuary. Joshua himself in news interviews declares that he does not heal and attributes his healing power to Jesus.

Further reading

Anderson, A. (2001) *African Reformation: African Initiated Christianity in the 20th Century*, Trenton, NJ and Asmara, Eritrea: Africa World Press.

ALLAN ANDERSON

T

T'AI CHI CH'UAN
(Taijiquan)

T'ai chi ch'uan (translated as 'supreme ultimate fist') is a Chinese martial art which became prominent in China and later in Europe during the twentieth century. The art is conceptually linked to the **Yin Yang** theory of cosmic emergence in the Confucian text **I-Ching**, later developed in Taoism and **Neo-Confucianism**. Despite some gaps in the known lines of transmission, most practitioners believe the founder of the art to have been a fourteenth-century Taoist boxer named Chang San-feng from the Wudang mountain region.

In practical terms, *t'ai chi ch'uan* involves the practice of a 'form', a flowing sequence of movements and postures, plus **ch'i kung** (Qigong) exercises, training in the use of various weapons and partnered sparring practice. It shares with *ch'i kung* the aim of refining the quality of human '*ch'i*' or energy, in order to enact greater harmony between earth, man and heaven. *T'ai chi ch'uan* is taught by practical transmission from master to student, although more often in a liberal class format, rather than the traditional discipleship mode.

Yang Lu-chan, head of the Yang lineage, popularized a form of the art based more on health exercise and less on martial technique, and taught his style in late nineteenth-century Beijing, from where it spread through mainland China. In 1925, *t'ai chi ch'uan* was adapted as a national sport and incorporated into the Chinese curriculum. During the twentieth century it also flourished in neighbouring countries such as Taiwan and Malaysia, which had become the home of many masters whilst Communism suppressed traditional arts. The most common family lineages surviving are the Yang, Chen, Wu, Sun, and Hao styles.

Yang style was the first to be exported to the West, notably via Cheng Man-ch'ing, a popular Chinese master teaching in America from the 1960s onwards.

As Yang style became well known, *t'ai chi ch'uan* was largely perceived as 'moving meditation', part of the **Holistic Health Movement** or the New Age subculture (see **New Age Movement**). It was widely adopted as a spiritual discipline throughout late twentieth century Europe, but this was complemented by the uptake of more traditional martial styles during the 1980s and 1990s.

Further reading

Hong, Tan and McFarlane, Stewart, *Tai Chi*, Oxford: Blackwell.

ALEXANDRA RYAN

TANTRA

Tantra originated in India, as a revolt against the caste-bound hierarchy of orthodox Hinduism; it was later developed by Buddhists, particularly in Tibet (see **Vajrayāna Buddhism**). Tantra has mostly been an antinomian movement, sometimes suppressed though also revered as an effective alternative to **yoga**. It contains a wealth of practices and rituals, comprising a non-dualistic spiritual methodology. The core belief is that the higher is hidden in the lower, for example spirituality within the energy of sexuality. Therefore the lower should not be condemned but transformed, from poison into nectar, through a range of Tantric techniques. Sexuality is only one strand of Tantra – but the one that has been seized upon with most interest by Westerners. The aim is to awaken the *kundalini:* an energy contained in the base chakra, which can be activated and released naturally through orgasm. Tantric practitioners are taught to direct the energy towards higher states of consciousness, which ultimately leads to enlightenment. Unlike most world religions, women have often played a leading role in both traditional and contemporary Tantra.

Some gurus of NRMs have worked with tantric techniques and kundalini energy. The best known was **Osho**, sometimes known as the 'sex guru'. However, his teachings were not simply a licence for 'free love' but a synthesis of psychology with Tantra, which made it accessible to Westerners: 'People think that I teach sex. I am one of the persons who is teaching God. If I talk about sex there is a reason for it – I would like you to know it before it is too late. Know it totally, go into it headlong and be finished with it. Go into it meditatively, alert – that is the approach of tantra. If you know something well, you are free of it.' Osho developed a four-stage model of sexuality designed to transform sexual energy into higher consciousness.

Nowadays, Tantra has been appropriated by the New Age as the basis of sacred sex workshops. Personal development centres offering courses are found worldwide, particularly in the USA and Germany. The largest and best known centre with eight branches is the SkyDancing Institute, founded by Margo Anand, a disciple of Osho (as are a number of other Tantric teachers) and author of the bestselling book *The Art of Sexual Ecstasy*. Well known British teachers include Alan Lowen, who runs the Art of Being in Hawaii, Caroline Aldred, a disciple of Shunyata (Robert Ferris), the 'Laughing Guru' in Bali, David Howe, head of the Institute of Higher Sexology in South London, and Sarita and Geho, former Osho disciples who run Transcendence in Wiltshire.

The main difference between traditional Asian Tantra and 'neo-Tantra' is that the former uses sexuality and relationship as a means towards enlightenment, whereas the latter mostly uses Tantric techniques to enhance sexual relationships.

Neo-tantra has been criticized for diluting and distorting the tradition in the service of Western hedonistic materialism with its predilection for instant gratification and quick-fix techniques. In traditional Tantra, practitioners spend many years training in techniques which require maximum dedication and discipline, whereas some sacred sex workshops encourage the belief that it is possible to become an accomplished tantrika after one weekend workshop. On the other hand, it can be argued that Asian Tantra is impoverished by its neglect of relationship skills. Neo-Tantra emphasizes safe, responsible sex, commitment to one partner, intimacy, and gender equality. This is in line with the holistic philosophy of the **Human Potential Movement**: spirituality grounded in the body; intimate relationship as a valid spiritual path; and emotional health as a precondition for meditation.

Tantra is also an influence on (see **Neo-Paganism**) Paganism. Aleister Crowley (see **Crowley, Aleister**) developed a sex magick partly based on tantric texts in order to create altered states of consciousness. Sacred sexuality is an element of Goddess spirituality, which affirms the female body. In the words of **Starhawk**: 'Sexuality is sacred because it is a sharing of energy, in passionate surrender to the power of the **Goddess**, immanent in our desire. In orgasm, we share in the force that moves the stars.'

The myth of the Sacred Marriage between king and priestess to ensure good harvests and control of the land is fundamental in Paganism, and its reenactment is the basis of the Great Rite: ritual sex between the high priest and priestess. However, the evidence suggests that the Great Rite is usually symbolic, unless the participants are already partners. Some witches (see **Wicca**) compare it to Tantra as a sacred ceremony to raise and release power, and channel it for the purposes of healing, consecration, creativity and inspiration.

For many centuries, the West has perceived sexuality and spirituality as incompatible polarities. On balance, despite criticisms of vulgarization, Tantric teachings can be considered to have played a major role in creating a new body-positive spirituality that counteracts the misogynistic, life-negative attitudes endemic in monotheism.

Further reading

Anand, M. (1991) *The Art of Sexual Ecstasy*, New York: Tarcher.
Cozart, D. (1986) *Highest Yoga Tantra*, Ithaca, NY: Snow Lion.
Shaw, M. (1994) *Passionate Enlightenment: Women in Tantric Buddhism*, Princeton: Princeton University Press.

ELIZABETH PUTTICK

TEILHARD DE CHARDIN, PIERRE

Pierre Teilhard de Chardin (1881–1955), a French Jesuit, was a distinguished scientist of human origins, a prolific religious writer and fervent Christian mystic. Published posthumously, he became internationally known for his controversial ideas which relate Christian beliefs to contemporary scientific thinking, especially the theory of evolution.

Born into an old aristocratic family and brought up in a traditional Catholic milieu marked by a vibrant faith and strong religious practice, Teilhard was endowed with deeply pantheistic and mystical leanings, evident since childhood. He entered the Jesuit order at 18 and was ordained in 1911. From 1905–8 he taught science in a Jesuit school in Cairo where he discovered his great attraction to nature, the desert, the East. This experience made him later write with great lyrical beauty about cosmic and mystical life, culminating in his spiritual classics *Mass on the World* (1923) and *The Divine Milieu* (1927).

Through reading Bergson's *Creative Evolution*, Teilhard discovered the meaning of evolution for the Christian faith. Evolution made him see the world anew, immersed in an immense stream of unfolding creation where everything is animated by a 'christic element' and the heart of God is found at the heart of the world, so that we are surrounded by a 'divine milieu'. His scientific studies in Paris were interrupted by the First World War where he served as stretcher bearer at the front. There he discovered a pluralistic 'human milieu' not met before; this led to speculations about the oneness of humanity and eventually to the idea of the 'noosphere' (sphere of mind) as a layer of thinking which connects people around the globe and hails a new stage in human evolution. Almost daily encounters with death gave him an extraordinary sense of urgency to write a series of deeply stirring essays, only published after his death as *Writings in Time of War*. Relatively little known, these contain the seeds of all his further writings.

After the war he obtained his doctorate in science and was appointed lecturer in geology at the Institut Catholique, Paris, where he could expound his ideas about evolution and the Christian faith. This soon led to difficulties with his church which continued throughout his life. In 1923 he was glad to join a fossil expedition in China, and the discovery of Asia was another decisive experience shaping him for the rest of his life.

China became a place of almost permanent exile where he spent the greatest part of his scientific career (1926–46), regularly interspersed with expeditions and travels in East and West. It was in China that he wrote most of his religious essays and also his best known, but most difficult, work *The Phenom-enon of Man* (1938–40), now retranslated under the more accurate title *The Human Phenomenon* (1999).

After the Second World War Teilhard returned to Paris; further difficulties with his superiors made him accept a research post in the United States. Lonely and marked by suffering, he spent the last four years of his life mostly in New York where he died on Easter Sunday 1955. His large corpus of writings took over 20 years to be published.

Teilhard de Chardin's method consists of a specially understood phenomenology, combining the outer and inner seeing of all phenomena, leading to a profound transformation of the world as seen, so that *seeing more* also implies *being more*. Such seeing involves all the knowledge that science has to offer, but this is combined with a unifying inner vision whereby the world is held together by Spirit. Teilhard's vision brings together cosmic, human, and divine dimensions, all centred in Christ, and each involved in a process of becoming or genesis. Whereas cosmogenesis refers to the birth of the cosmos, anthropogenesis and noogenesis relate to the human dimension and the birth of thought. Christogenesis or the birth of God in Christ, an event of cosmic significance and proportion, can only be seen through the eyes of faith. For Teilhard, cosmic and human evolution are rising and moving onwards to an ever fuller disclosure of the Spirit culminating in 'Christ-Omega'.

This rise is not automatic but involves human responsibility and co-creativity in shaping the future of humanity and the planet. Humans are fully responsible for their own further self-evolution, for a higher social and cultural development and a greater unification of the human community, but ultimately these goals are only achievable through the powers of love. Central to Teilhard's thinking are the ideas of the 'noosphere' and the 'divine milieu'. The first belongs to a more secular, the second to a deeply religious context. The noosphere is a thinking layer which arises out of the biosphere and is intimately connected with it. It is also an active sphere of love which provides a new context for human relationships by creating greater bonds of unity between individuals and groups. The noosphere provides Teilhard with a particularly creative perspective in approaching racial, cultural and religious pluralism within the new context of global complexity, and in relating it to the unitive powers of all-transforming love. He was convinced that humankind must study the powers of love as the most sacred spiritual energy resource in the same way that all other forces in the universe are studied.

Teilhard's thought represents a unique blend of science, religion and mysticism. The essayistic, fragmentary nature of his work marks him more as a postmodern than a traditional thinker. His work contains challenging reflections on God and the world, science and religion, ecological responsibilities, interfaith encounter, the greater unification of humanity, the place of the feminine and of love in creating greater unity, the central importance of **spirituality** and mysticism. Teilhard de Chardin's ideas have influenced several New Age thinkers just as he influenced earlier the Second Vatican Council, Christian-Marxist dialogue, debates about futurology and now about the significance of the worldwide web. Unfortunately his ideas are often taken out of context without acknowledging the profoundly Christian core of his vision.

Further reading

King, U. (1996) *Spirit of Fire. The Life and Vision of Teilhard de Chardin*, Maryknoll, NY: Orbis Books.

Samson, P. R. and Pitt, D. (eds) (1999) *The Biosphere and Noosphere Reader. Global Environment, Society and Change*, London: Routledge.

Teilhard de Chardin, P. (1968) *Writings in Time of War*, London: Collins.

Teilhard de Chardin, P. (1999) *The Human Phenomenon* (trans. Sarah Appleton-Weber), Brighton and Portland: Sussex Academic Press.

URSULA KING

TELEVANGELISM

Televangelism is the generic term that refers to a loose alliance of conservative Protestant Evangelicals (see **Evangelical Christianity**) and Pentecostals who practise their ministry through television programmes and TV channels. The advent of satellite and cable TV has made the production of evangelistic programmes comparatively inexpensive to produce and air. However, the phenomenon remains part of what media scholars call 'narrow-casting' rather than broadcasting. Televangelism is largely a product found within a conservative Protestant ghetto: it has little impact beyond its followers.

Although Televangelism is a phenomenon that is mostly associated with North America, it is important to recognize that it now enjoys a modest global profile. Few countries in the world will be without access to a range of 'God Channels', even if the access is through cable and satellite rather than public broadcasting.

The history of Televangelism belongs to a wider social and cultural chronicle, and several preliminary points need making before describing the phenomenon in more detail. First, the roots of Televangelism belong to a broader historical milieu of radio preaching and other attempts by Evangelicals to reach the public through mass media. Arguably, TV evangelism belongs to the same tradition that prints tracts by the million (and this perhaps stretches back to the Reformation), to those who now run influential web sites. Second, Televangelism has developed in direct proportion to the rise of Evangelicalism and the 'new right' (see **New Christian Right**) in the USA; as the political, social, and economic power of Evangelicals has grown, so has the range of programmes and volume of channels. Third, because of the decline of mainline denominations – which is also reflected in the amount of time given to religion in public sector broadcasting – Evangelicals have shown more willingness to invest both time and money in their own brand of television. Fourth, Televangelism continues to elicit support from its (loyal) followers, who perceive this as a primary means of competing with secular alternatives in the media. Fifth, despite the narrow but ultimately intense support for Televangelism, research continually shows that few outside the churches or religion are persuaded or converted by the offerings of televangelists. Sixth, Televangelism nonetheless continues to thrive as a brand of 'narrow-casting' within the world of television, but has yet to show that it can sustain interest in the highly competitive world of 'default' viewing – programmes people watch, normally in public sector broadcasting, when they have not consciously chosen to view anything else. Seventh, Televangelism is now an established American religious 'tradition', and this has prompted a number of mainline denominations to launch their own programmes on the airwaves, albeit with limited success.

The reputation of North American Televangelism suffered considerably in the 1990s, following a series of high profile financial and personal scandals that engulfed some of its 'household names'. Oral Roberts was widely ridiculed for locking himself away in his purpose built prayer tower (located in Oklahoma – a bizarre structure that resembles a cocktail shaker crossed with a Sputnik), declaring that unless his followers gave more money to underwrite his television ministry, 'God would call him home'. He had prayed and fasted for some weeks, but was able to stop when a local business man and racehorse owner donated several million dollars. Jimmy Swaggart and Jim Bakker had their reputations ruined by well-publicized stories of sexual impropriety, but both have since been rehabilitated as televangelists.

Despite the garish portrayal of televangelism in the secular media, it is important to recognize that the phenomenon operates on a number of levels. First, there are established programmes that have been running for decades – such as *Old Fashioned Revival Hour* and *Old Time Gospel Hour* – which have, in their heyday, drawn audiences of more than 20 million. These programmes are 'folksy' in their allure, and clearly appeal to a constituency that enjoys the singing of hymns and a traditional talk or sermon that calls on the viewer to be 'born again'. The timbre of the programme for the target audience is one of reassurance – armchair revival, with slippers.

Second, there are those programmes that are simply a televised extension of an existing ministry. The programmes are uncomplicated in format or in technical production, and will often be a televised service or rally. Televangelists such as Benny Hinn, who are skilful 'live performers', and whose ministry depends to some extent on creating a 'divine dramaturgy', tend to suit this medium better than those programmes that might utilize a studio audience. Either way, these programmes are unlikely to be seen by many, beyond those who support such ministries already.

Increasingly, these programmes are available through satellite, cable and video.

Third, there are specific programmes and channels that broadcast almost continually, with a simple cycle or spiral of appeals: for converts (who may be casual viewers); for money from donors to carry on broadcasting, so there can be more converts; for more converts; for more money, so the televangelists can broadcast at more sociable hours so they can reach a wider public, and make more converts; and so on. Such programmes and channels have developed a range of unusual (or even notorious) practices that have elevated the television itself to a level of apotheosis, or at least conferred a sacramental status upon it. Instances have included viewers being encouraged to hold up handkerchiefs, hands, wallets, and other items that may need blessing, up against their own television screen, with the televangelist then praying a 'personal' prayer for each respondent. In this theological construction of reality, viewers are being invited to believe that divine power flows from the televangelist, through the TV set, and finally into the viewers' homes and personal life.

This is perhaps not quite as absurd as it may sound to some, when one considers the recent but explosive growth of interactive television. A number of the better-funded and more sophisticated channels that offer televangelism are now able to interact 'live' on TV with prayer partners, supporters, donors, and viewers. The possibility of viewer–televangelist conversations and 'real time' ministry have now become an actuality. With the advent of digital TV, viewers can 'phone, text or e-mail prayer requests during a broadcast, and then invite others to join in these prayers. Instead of being a lone spectator witnessing a religious programme in isolation, the viewer can now become part of a larger network of active worshippers, and indeed participate 'live' within an act of worship or large evangelistic rally. Active spiritual communion is now possible beyond the constraints of the spatial; and all of this is enabled by the gift of technology. The television has been co-opted into armoury of the Lord; it has become a divine instrument for defending the saints and attacking all kinds of foes, and rebuking all manner of evil. The age of the interactive armchair churchgoer has truly arrived. The only difference now is that there is no collection plate. But there will be a free-phone credit card hotline to which believers can pledge.

Televangelism, then, has travelled a long way since its genesis. From being an expensive status symbol for the very few well-funded expansive international itinerant ministries, it has developed into a medium of communication that is now within the grasp of most moderate sized mega churches. These churches can afford to make and air programmes that have a dedicated regional appeal. They can in turn syndicate their distinctive style of televangelism through established Christian TV channels the world over, that will then ensure their audience is global as much as much as it is local. As TV religion enters the third millennium, it is adopting a mercurial role as an agent of globalization and interactive ministry.

The impact of these changes upon 'traditional' televangelists has yet to be assessed. But it appears that the big names of televangelism over the last thirty years are slowly being crowded out of a market that has not expanded in quite the way that many anticipated. Pat Robertson, Oral Roberts, and Jerry Falwell still vie for the position of principal *eminence grise* in the televangelism firmament, but in truth the phenomenon is now prey to one of its own parents –

choice. With more channels and media output to choose from, all religious broadcasters need to work harder and harder just to retain their market share. Were it not for the comparative fall in production costs, a number of televangelism networks would now be out of business.

The future of televangelism appears to be less and less with household name 'holy rollers', and more with bespoke productions that provide a better fit for their target audiences. The days when developing nations imported the offerings of American televangelists wholesale are more or less gone. At the beginning of the third millennium, African and Asian televangelists – such as Dnakararn in India – now produce their own material for their own contexts. At the same time, there continues to be a certain degree of public unease surrounding televangelists. Typically, and especially in America, most are allied to right-wing political concerns, and are wedded to agendas such as the 'moral majority' and other conservative or neo-traditional moralistic crusades. Whilst this undoubtedly pleases many of the traditional supporters of televangelism, it can cause problems for the wider public. In the wake of the terrorist attacks on New York and Washington on 11 September 2001, Jerry Falwell appeared on a TV show hosted by Pat Robertson. Falwell suggested that the reason for 'God allowing the attacks' – 'lifting the veil of protection' is how he described it – was that America was being punished for her sins: 'letting the abortionists and homosexuals' into government, and driving moral standards down. Such comments have done little to enhance the reputation of televangelists in the eyes of most. But in the eyes of their followers, they can say or do little that is not compelling and convincing. Ironically, it is their courting of theological and political controversy, coupled to an extreme social conservatism, that continues to keep them in the public eye, and thereby maintains their solid if small support base.

Further reading

Bruce, S. (1990) *Pray TV: Televangelism in America*, London: Routledge.
Hadden, J. and Shupe, A. (1988) *Televangelism: Power and Politics on God's Frontier*, New York: Henry Holt.

MARTYN PERCY

TEMPLE OF SET

The Temple of Set is an international organization which was incorporated as a non-profit Church in California in 1975, receiving state and federal recognition and tax-exemption later that year. It probably has the most members of any kind of **Satanism** but is far from being a popular or mass movement. It was founded by Michael Aquino following a vision of **Set** who revealed the inadequacy of the **Church of Satan** and indicated the structure and nature of its replacement, the Temple. For Aquino and many (but by no means all) members of the Temple there is a real being, popularly named Satan, but more properly named Set. This person achieved a high degree of self-realization and continues to offer humans encouragement to 'become' (a buzz-word of the Temple) more truly human. 'As Set was, we are; As Set is, we can be' might represent the views of many Temple members.

The Temple of Set is a self-religion (see **Self-religion, the Self, and Self**) that encourages personal growth within the tradition of **esoteric movements**, especially in its elaboration of various forms of magic and ritual. The Temple draws on ancient Egyptian terminology for some of its most distinctive expressions.

Its local groups and/or Internet based networks are called Pylons after Egyptian temple gateways. However, its organization derives from European esotericism and is comparable to that of the **Hermetic Order of the Golden Dawn**. It divides magic into 'lesser' and 'higher' forms. The first aims to change the surrounding world (to some degree) according to the will of the practitioner. The latter attempts to achieve a greater realization of the individual's true will and thus effects changes in the self. The Temple offers members the opportunity of engaging with a wide range of different styles of practice and areas of study, e.g. Celtic mythology or post-modernist philosophy. Advancement within the Temple's series of hierarchical degrees and orders is marked by changes of title and symbol that are, again, recognizably inheritances from previous esoteric movements.

Further reading

Harvey, G. (1995) 'Satanism in Britain Today', *Journal of Contemporary Religion* 10, 283–96.

GRAHAM HARVEY

TENRIKYO

(Religion of Heavenly Wisdom)
Founder: Nakayama Miki (b. 1798; d. 1887)

One of the first of Japan's new religions or shin shukyo (see **New Religion (Japan)**), Tenrikyo was founded in 1838 by Nakayama Miki (1798–1887) a farmer's wife with shamanistic attributes, from a village close to Tenri city, which is situated in the Yamato basin, only a short distance from the historic city of Nara. In 1838 Tenri-O-no-Mikoto (the God of Heavenly Reason), also known as Oyagami, God the parent, is believed to have taken possession of Nakayama

Miki, also called Oyasama (Worthy Parent), for the purpose of revealing to her his divine plan and her role therein, and to bestow upon her the gift of healing.

Nakayama Miki's mission was to consist of delivering people from suffering in preparation for the coming of a perfect divine kingdom (*kanrondai sekai*) in which human beings would enjoy the joyous and blissful life (*yoki-gurashi*) in union with Tenri-O-no-Mikoto. On becoming the shrine of Tenri-O-no-Mikoto, Nakayama Miki was also provided by this same deity with a plot of ground known as the *jiba*, believed to be the place of origin of the human race and its spiritual home (*oyasato*). On this land stands the principal place of Tenriko worship (Shinden) at the centre of which is the kanrondai or sacred pillar. Both the *Shinden* and the *Kyosoden*, the sanctuary of the foundress, are centres of pilgrimage. It is believed that Nakayama Miki continues to dwell in the Kyosoden where she is attended to as if still physically present by devotees who dust and clean her bedroom, prepare her food and look after her every need.

As in the case of other Japanese new religions founded by women (see **Omoto**) Nakayama Miki was also greatly helped by a dedicated male disciple in the person of Iburi Izo, a poor carpenter whose wife she had healed of childbirth fever. Iburi Izo displayed his gratitude for this cure by dedicating himself to *hinokishin* or volunteer work for the church, including the construction of a model of the first kanrondai in 1873, and a sanctuary for Tenri-O-no-Mikoto. Iburo Izo became the joint leader of Tenrikyo on the death of Nakayama Miki in 1887 and in his capacity as *Honseki* or oracle he spoke through the spirit of the foundress to God. His pronouncements were written down and came to constitute a set of sacred writings known as the *Osashizu*.

These supplement the two most important sacred scriptures, the Ofudesaki (Tip of the Divine Writing-pen), transmitted to by God to Nakayama Miki, a transmission that was not completed until 1882, and the divinely inspired Mikagura-uta or poems which are used as the text of Tenrikyo's worship.

The major Tenrikyo sacred ritual, the dance of creation, the *Kagura Tsutome*, takes place around the *Kanrodai* and is performed by dancers in masks led by the head of the Church who is known as the Shimbashira, a descendent of the foundress. The masks represent figures in the cosmogonic myth developed by Tenrikyo. This dance performed on the 26th of each month is believed to hasten the fulfilment of God's plans and is given as the main reason for Tenrikyo's existence. On the day prior to the performance the Shinbashira 'ordains' in a brief ceremony known as the *honseki* those who have completed the course of *besseki* lectures (the nine lectures required for initiation) and the *Shuyoka* course (three months' intensive training). They are given by the *Shinbashira*, the sacred grant of *Osazuke* or healing and these graduates or *yobuku* (literally timbers) are now empowered to perform healing rites using a particular form of hand gesture known as *teodori* or hand dance, the gesture used in Tenrikyo worship.

The major festival for which members from all over the world come to Tenri City is the birthday of the foundress celebrated at the Oyasato or headquarters on 18 April. Other important services include the *Tai-sai* or great services held on 26 January and 26 October. There are memorial services for the dead in March and September and a monthly service, the *Tsukinami-sai*. Three times a month there is the popular sacramental rite of *obiya yurushi* or easy childbirth which involves the consecration of white rice which is then placed on the Kanrodai during the *Obiya Tsutome* service in which the creation is ritually re-enacted.

Regarded as a dissident religious movement Tenrikyo suffered increasing government probes and harassment, and the foundress, while proud of her country, was critical and at times even scornful of its of its ruling elite –as were other women founders of Japanese including **Deguchi Nao**. Nakayama Miki was frequently interrogated and imprisoned on seventeen occasions for among other things blasphemy and obstructing the public highways by performing elaborate ritual dances of the village on the outskirts of where she lived.

The movement's fortunes changed and in 1908 it was recognized as one of the thirteen 'Sect Shinto' organizations, autonomous organizations authorized by the Government between 1868 and 1945.

In 1947 Tenrikyo, believing its teachings had become distorted by **State Shintoism**, launched the campaign for the Restoration of the Original Teachings (Fukugen). In 1970 it withdrew from the Association of Shinto Sects, and had itself placed in the category of 'Other Religions'. It is one of the largest movements in this group with a membership of over one million in Japan. Tenrikyo is also present in many countries outside Japan including Korea, Taiwan, India, Nepal, the Democratic Republic of the Congo, the United States, France, and Great Britain, but in every case with the exception of Korea it has remained numerically small.

Tenrikyo has a number of important cultural and educational institutions including Tenri University founded in 1925, and the very valuable Tenri Library and Tenri Sankokan Museum. It has also established a publishing house and built a very modern hospital. In the latter both spiritual and scientific methods of healing are used together.

The structure and organization of Tenrikyo while formally bureaucratic is essentially based on the principle of the *ie* or family system and the *Honbuin* or central administration consists of descendants of the families of Nakayama Miki and Iburi Izo, or of families very close to theirs. The headquarters are in Tenri city and are known as Oyasato or Village of the Parent

Further reading

Clarke, P. B. (1999) *A Bibliography of Japanese New Religions*, Eastbourne, Kent: Japan Library, pp. 254–65.

Ellwood, R. S. Jr (1982) *Tenrikyo. A Pilgrimage Faith*, Tenri City: Oyasato Research Institute.

Oyasato Reseach Institute, Tenri University (1986) *The Theological Perspectives of Tenrikyo*, Tenri City: Tenri University Press.

Tenrikyo Church (1971) *Ofudesaki. Tip of the Writing-Brush*, Tenri City: Tenrikyo Church Headquarters.

PETER B. CLARKE

THEOSOPHY

The Theosophical Society was founded in America in 1875 by Helena Blavatsky (1831–91) (see **Blavatsky, Helena**) and Henry S. Olcott (1832–1907). It later established its headquarters in Madras, India. The Society estimates around 5,000–10,000 members worldwide (1,000 in Britain), but in its heyday was much larger and is the most important influence on the early growth of Eastern spirituality in Western society. During the nineteenth century, scholars had begun the process of discovering and translating Indian religious texts, but these had been confined to a small circle interested in philosophy. Theosophy was the first movement to make Asian religions, particularly Hinduism and Buddhism, accessible to Western seekers.

Theosophical doctrine is largely a synthesis of Hindu and Buddhist mysticism with Western occultism. Blavatsky claimed to have channelled most of the teachings from Ascended Masters and Mahatmas in Tibet, particularly Kuthumi and El Morya, who represented the wisdom of the ages. She later described these beings as an association called the Great White Brotherhood, who mediate between humanity and the divine, occasionally incarnating to found new religions. Blavatsky and Olcott were the first Westerners to popularize Indian religion for Western seekers, including the now widespread twin doctrines of karma and reincarnation. The Society's motto is 'there is no religion higher than truth', and it claims that all religions have the same goal. Its three objectives are:

1. To form a nucleus of the universal brotherhood of humanity, without distinction of race, creed, sex, caste, or colour;
2. To encourage the study of comparative religion, philosophy, and science;
3. To investigate the unexplained laws of nature and the powers latent in man.

Theosophical symbolism is highly esoteric and complex, drawn from Eastern mysticism and Western occultism. It is believed to comprise a secret body of doctrine open only to the elite few, though it has been collected in various books of which the best known are Blavatsky's *Isis Unveiled* (1877) and *The Secret Doctrine* (1889). Since it also takes members from all religions, it is open to the imagery of ritual of other traditions, particularly Hinduism, Buddhism, Jainism and **kabbalah**, interspersed with the mythology of Atlantis and Lemuria. These symbols and rituals were further developed in a subgroup called the

Esoteric Section. In the early days the key goal of Theosophy was to discover the Maitreya: a Buddhist title for the forthcoming Buddha, whom Theosophists believed would be the World Teacher. Around 1900, Leadbeater believed he had discovered the Maitreya in the person of a young Indian boy, Krishnamurti. After Krishnamurti publicly rejected this role, it became less prominent in their teachings and Theosophy began to dwindle in numbers and influence.

Several schismatic offshoots occurred after Blavatsky's death, including the Theosophical Society International and the United Lodge of Theosophists. Theosophy was also the main influence on Rudolf Steiner, who broke away from the Theosophical Society in 1913 to found **Anthroposophy**. Blavatsky's successors were **Annie Besant** and C. W. Leadbeater, who further developed the teachings. The Society has been attacked for fraudulence since its early days, and its decline was further hastened as a result of various exposés. After the Second World War it was largely superseded by the Indian gurus. Nowadays it is generally perceived as old-fashioned and its membership is largely elderly, although in its heyday it was considered revolutionary. However, it still has centres in forty-eight countries organized by its Indian headquarters.

Further reading

Washington, P. (1993) *Madame Blavatsky's Baboon: Theosophy and the Emergence of the Western Guru*, London: Secker & Warburg.

ELIZABETH PUTTICK

THERAVADA BUDDHISM

Theravada Buddhism, known as the smaller vehicle in contrast with **Mahayana Buddhism**, is the dominant Buddhist tradition in Southeast Asia particularly in Sri Lanka, Myanmar (Burma), Laos, Thailand, and Cambodia. It has its origins in the teaching of the historical Buddha, the Enlightened One, known as Siddharta Gotama who was born in the republic of the Sakka people possibly in their capital at Kapilavathu which has been renamed Lumbini and is situated in present day Nepal. The date of the Buddha's birth is disputed some sources placing it in *c.* 556 BCE and others in 448. All are agreed that he lived to be 80 and therefore died in either 486 or 368 BCE.

Theravada or the teachings or doctrines of the elders remains the only surviving tradition of more than thirty different schools of early Buddhism and claims to be the authentic vehicle of the teachings of the historical Buddha who preached in India some two thousand five hundred years ago.

Some five hundred years after the Buddha's death his teachings were collected in three baskets or Tripitaka and written down in Pali on palm leaves. The three baskets known as the Tripitaka contained the *Vinaya* pitaka or basket of monastic discipline, the *Sutta* pitaka or basket of doctrinal teachings and the *Abhidhamma* pitaka or basket of philosophical teachings. Together these baskets or collections form the Pali Canon. Also important to the understanding of Buddhism are the commentaries on the Canon and in particular that known as the Vissudhi-magga (Path to Purity) composed in the early years of the fifth century CE by the Sri Lankan monk Buddhagosa.

The Sangha or monastic order of ordained monks is one of the three refuges (Tiratana) or spiritual treasures of supreme worth, the other two being the Buddha – not only Siddhartha Gotama but past and future Buddhas – and the Dhamma or body of teachings and practices and the goal of Buddhism, enlightenment or *nirvana*. They are seen as representing the ideal of Buddhism, which is freedom from the desire for and all attachment to worldly, material things, relations and values. This rejection of the world should be seen as more than simply a rejection of its material comforts and values. It is more importantly about not committing actions, which lead to being reborn, *samsara*, and thereby further suffering. The one who successfully renounces the world escapes the cycle of rebirth and in this sense is free.

Thus, monks do not work to maintain themselves and acquire possessions and wealth. Instead they beg and it is the duty of the laity to support them by donating gifts of food, shelter and clothing in return for which they receive merit which removes some of the *karma* attached to past transgressions. Historically there was once an order of lay nuns or a *bhikkhuni Sangha* also, but this became largely extinct. Attempts are being made to revive this order in Thailand and elsewhere including the United States.

After his awakening the Buddha promulgated the doctrine known as the Four Noble Truths which contains the essential teachings of Buddhism. The first of these Truths is the Truth of Suffering (*dukkha*), that it exists. The second is the Truth of the Arising of Suffering that explains its causes. The Third is the Truth of the Cessation of Suffering which teaches that there is a cure for suffering and the fourth is the Truth of the Path that leads to the cessation of suffering. The last mentioned Truth is usually referred to as the Eightfold Path which is reduced in Canonical texts to three constituent elements: moral self-discipline, meditation and wisdom, all of which are interconnected and lead when practised correctly to a calm way of life lived with single mindedness.

All schools of Buddhism (see **Mahayana, Vajrayāna Buddhism**), includ-

ing the Theravada school, are now less associated with particular geographical regions and more global than was the case in the first half of the twentieth century. Theravada Buddhism began to spread slowly West from the nineteenth century, and even a little earlier, and in more recent times, mainly on account of improved communications, enforced exile, immigration and conversion, the number of Buddhists and Buddhist institutions not only in the West but also in Africa, South America, and Oceania has greatly increased (see **Buddhism in the West**). Such expansion has contributed, along with the rapid processes of modernization, to a revival of meditational practices including **vipassana** (insight meditation). The Buddha while teaching the value of such meditational practices, offering as they did 'comfortable abidings in the here and now', also pointed out that they were not a substitute for following the elaborate path which he promulgated, and which has been briefly described above, after his awakening or sambodhi.

Further reading

Harvey, P. (1990) *An Introduction to Buddhism*, Cambridge: Cambridge University Press.

PETER B. CLARKE

THICH NHAT HANH
(b. 1926)

The Vietnamese Buddhist monk, Thich Nhat Hanh is a leading exponent of **Engaged Buddhism**.

One of the founders in 1964 of the Van Hanh University in Saigon and the School for Social Service, which did much to promote Engaged Buddhism during the Vietnam War, Thich Nhat Hanh founded in 1965 a new branch of the Lam-Te movement known as the

Order of Interbeing (*Tiep Hien* Order) which is composed of monks and lay people. The purpose of this new foundation was to further the cause of Engaged Buddhism. He has ordained over 100 monks into the Lam Te order since its foundation.

Prior to going into exile in 1966 Thich Nhat Hanh played a prominent role as strategist and spokesperson for the Struggle Movement which sought to make known the Buddhist perspective on peace in Vietnam without supporting either North or South. He was also one of the more prominent leaders of the **Unified Buddhist Church of Vietnam** which came into existence in the 1960s to coordinate the Buddhist response to the American and/or Vietnam war and to bring relief to those injured, impoverished, and made homeless by that war.

While in exile Thich Nhat Hanh has become engaged in numerous contexts with the resolution of conflicts advocating consistently the use of peaceful means. He made it part of his mission to influence in this respect the Civil Rights Movement in the United States. He has also established the Unified Buddhist Church of Vietnam outside Vietnam, for example in France in the form of the *Église Buddhique Unifiée*.

Thich Nhat Hanh has not only acquired a large following among Vietnamese abroad but has also attracted North Americans and Europeans to Buddhism. While people have converted to Buddhism under his influence, Thich Nhat Hanh does not himself seek to proselytize, but rather encourages inquirers to take Mindfulness Training courses in an ecumenical spirit, seeing in them guides for mindful living.

Further reading

King, S. (1996) 'Thich Nhat Hanh and the Unified Buddhist Church: Nondualism in Action' in S. B. King and C. Queen (eds) *Engaged Buddhism: Buddhist Liberation Movements in Asia*, Albany: State University of New York Press, pp. 321–63.

PETER B. CLARKE

TIAN DAO
(*The Way of Heaven*) (*originally*
Yiguandao: Way of Pervading Unity)
Founder: Zhang Tianran (b. 1889; d. 1947)

While its historical and social origins are rooted more in local conditions of socioeconomic deprivation in the second half of the nineteenth century Tian Dao's spectacular growth in the 1930s and 1940s is best understood from a sociological perspective if seen as a response to unprecedented levels of political and social turmoil in China. The movement was effectively eliminated after the establishment of the People's Republic of China in 1949. Some of its leaders were able to leave China at that time and establish Tian Dao in Taiwan, Hong Kong, and in parts of Southeast Asia where Chinese had settled.

Tian Dao teaches that initiation ensures an individual's entry into Heaven and liberation from the endless round of rebirth (*samsara*) constitutes an important part of the reason why many decide to join the movement. This belief which gives a sense of being one of the elect and free of the cycle of rebirth is given tangible form by issuing a passport to Heaven to all members.

Under the leadership of Zhang Tianran (1889–1947) this small, highly ritualistic, puritanical movement was transformed from a minority group known until the 1940s as Yiguandao (the Way of Pervading Unity), into a mass movement. Changes in the rules governing diet and conduct which resulted in a more liberal regime and the reduction to essentials of long drawn out, elaborate rituals led in part to this improvement in the movement's fortunes. Thus, while vegetarianism was retained as an ideal, meat eating was allowed, celibacy was dropped as a requirement for membership and ancestral rites simplified. Essential rituals include the invitation to the movement's numerous deities to visit its altar, repeated bowing and saluting to each of the deities, the lighting of incense, and the giving of offerings.

Tian Dao, with its strong millenarian strain (see **Millenarianism**), places at the centre of all worship the veneration of the Ancient Mother, Lao Mu, who is said to have ordered the future Buddha, Maitreya, to return to earth to enable lost souls to enter heaven and sit at her right side. The Ancient mother is believed to be present in the flame of the oil lamp which stands in the centre of the temple altar. Other icons on the altar include an image of Maitreya and of the highly popular boddhisattva of compassion Guan Yin who appeals widely across East and Southeast Asia. As with most, if not all, Chinese NRMs the sources of Tian Dao's teachings are many and varied reflecting the desire to appeal widely across different belief systems in order to ensure that religion fulfils its function of ensuring harmony and stability. Thus, ideas and practices from Buddhism, Confucianism, Taoism, and Chinese Folk religion are all present. Though the obstacles to actively participating in community life in a modern, urban setting are affecting temple going, communal meals and attendance at lectures continue to be the principal activities.

Just as important in reversing the movement's fortunes as the changes in diet, life style and ritual introduced by Zhang in the 1930s and 1940s was the stress placed on recruitment, which he promoted as one of the most effective ways of gaining merit for one's family. For example, by recruiting one hundred

members it became possible to have a rite performed which would ensure that the soul of a departed relative would be drawn or pulled up to heaven. Thus, as a more highly motivated, more flexible and more rational movement Tian Dao began to establish a network of temples across China in the 1930s focusing in particular on cities and towns undergoing rapid modernization and industrialization. A similar development was taking place at the same time in Japan where NRMs such as **Soka Gakkai** (Value Creation Society) were beginning to attract the new urban dwellers who had left the rural areas for work in the towns. In the case of Tian Dao, which was to enjoy the favour of the puppet Chinese government installed by the Japanese in Nanjing (1937–45), people leading busy lives in a new and unfamiliar environment were able to fulfil their traditional ritual obligations to their ancestors, now greatly simplified, and find lay friendly, stable communities in a situation of rapid change and social and political upheaval.

Its close contacts with the Japanese and later with the Nationalists in China, and the new Communist government's campaigns against 'superstitious movements', made it impossible, as we have seen, for Tian Dao to function in China after 1949. At that time virtually leaderless – Zhang having died in 1947 – it sought a new future in Taiwan where it also came under suspicion as a Trojan horse for Communist spies seeking to infiltrate the country. In the case of Taiwan hostility from the government and law enforcement agencies were counterproductive. Though it suffered repeated harassment and was several times suppressed by the Taiwanese police, Tian Dao developed close links with local business and commerce during the period of economic prosperity (1960s–1980s) and by the time it was eventually legalized in 1987 it had become the second largest NRM in Taiwan. Once again in Taiwan, as in the 1930s and 1940s on the mainland, Tian Dao provided a streamlined, efficient, rational way of fulfilling traditional ritual obligations to family, and through its temples and adult education courses in the Chinese classics and Buddhism, and offered community and continuity to many who were having to face urban life without the traditional support of their extended family.

Further reading

Jordan, D. D. and Overmyer, D. L. (1986) *The Flying Phoenix: Aspects of Chinese Sectarianism in Taiwan*, Princeton, NJ: Princeton University Press.

PETER B. CLARKE

TODA, JOSEI
(b. 1900; d. 1958)

Toda Josei helped **Makiguchi Tsunesaburo** to form the movement known as Sokka Kyoiku Gakkai. After World War II, he succeeded the late Makiguchi president and began to revive the movement under the name of **Soka Gakkai**. He is cheifly responsible for the movement's phenomenal growth immediately after World War II.

Toda was born in Ishikawa prefecture in 1900, studied while working in Hokkaido, and became an elementary school teacher. He went to Tokyo to work at the school where Makiguchi Tsunesaburo was serving as principal. Entirely in agreement with Makiguchi's educational philosophy and practice, he became his disciple.

In 1923, Toda opened a cram school in Tokyo, Jishu Gakkan, and tried to apply Makiguchi's value creation theory as he prepared students to study for entrance examinations to universities and other institutions of higher education. He also became a member of the Nichiren Shoshu sect in 1928, and when Makiguchi began promoting the movement of Soka Kyoiku Gakkai, he helped with its expansion. In 1943, he was arrested together with Makiguchi for rejecting State Shinto faith, and was released on bail immediately before the end of the war. While in prison he regularly chanted the **Daimoku**, that is the invocation of the Lotus Sutra in the form of the Mystic law which is comprised in the the mantra *Nam myoho renge kyo* (literally: Devotion to the Wonderful Law Lotus Sutra). Toda is said to have chanted this invocation more than one thousand times in a day, and after two million repetitions to have been seized by an extremely strange sensation. Ecstatic, he exclaimed that he had now at the age of forty-five discovered the true meaning of life. He came to understand that the Buddha is Life and this served as the source of his Theory of Life to be formulated later.

In 1946, Toda organized the first national assembly of Soka Gakkai, and became the second president in 1951. At this point in time the membership was estimated to be around 5000, and Toda set it a target of increasing this to 750,000 households using aggressive methods of evangelization based on *Shakubuku Kyoten* (*Manual for Forcible Persuasion*). This manuscript also contained information on how to criticize other religions and sects.

Toda's aim was not limit the spread of religion in any narrow sense of the term but the salvation of Japan by reforming society at large, promoting cultural movements and by political involvement. Soka Gakkai members were selected as candidates for local assemblies in 1955, and three members for the National Diet in 1956. These were the driving force behind the Komeito political party (see **Soka Gakkai**). Toda died in 1958; his leadership had a very profound and long lasting influence on the form, content and ethos of Soka Gakkai.

SUSUMU SHIMAZONO

TOLLE, ECKHART

Eckhart Tolle was born in Germany in 1948 and educated at the Universities of London and Cambridge. At the age of 29, as he was completing his doctorate at Cambridge, a profound spiritual transformation virtually dissolved his identity and radically changed the course of his life. The next few years were devoted to understanding, integrating and deepening that transformation, which bears the hallmarks of the classic enlightenment experience, as described by Indian gurus.

Eckhart Tolle is the author of several bestselling self-development books, which have catapulted him into the position of arguably the most influential western non-Christian guru (not a title he claims personally). He gives talks to gatherings both large and small, and holds retreats that combine talks with periods of contemplation and meditation. He is a charismatic speaker, with the authority of personal revelation, but without being overbearing. Many of his audiences are from the 1970s counter-culture, but there are also younger people present. His ideas are increasingly reaching into the business training arena, helped by the combinations of radical thinking with simple language. This is the goal of many spiritual teachers, but few succeed.

Tolle describes spending much of his early years in an almost suicidal depression. His revelation came about after he decided 'I can no longer live with myself', followed by the question: 'Who is it that cannot live with himself?'. The question itself sparked the transformation, and the elimination of duality. This is classical self-realization philosophy, as exemplified by **Ramana Maharshi**, whose teaching was also based on the question 'Who am I?'. Tolle's answer is that true being can only be experienced by living entirely in the present moment, without the burden and affliction of constant thinking. The past is just a memory, the future a fantasy, and only the present – the now – is real. Hence the title of his first book, *The Power of Now*, the basis of his philosophy and teaching.

Further reading

Tolle, E. (2001) *The Power of Now,* London: Hodder & Stoughton

ELIZABETH PUTTICK

TORONTO BLESSING

Dating from 1994, 'The Toronto Blessing' is the name for a phenomenon that is associated with the Toronto Airport Christian Fellowship. From its very foundation, the Vineyard Christian Church in Toronto had experienced many of the things that would be typical for Christians within the fundamentalistic–revivalist tradition (see **Fundamentalism**, **Evangelical Christianity**): miracles, healings, an emphasis on deliverance, speaking in tongues, and a sense of the believers being in the vanguard of the Holy Spirit's movement as the millennium (see **Millenarianism**) neared.

However, what marks out the 'Toronto Blessing' for special consideration is the more unusual phenomena that occurred. A number of followers trace the initial outpouring back to 'Father's Day', a secular festival in the USA; the result being that some prefer to call the movement 'the Father's Blessing'. There was an unusually high *reportage* of people being 'slain in the Spirit'. A number would laugh uncontrollably, writhing on the floor (the leaders of the movement dubbed this 'carpet time with God'), make animal-like noises, barking, growling, or groaning as the 'Spirit fell on them'. Others reported that this particular experience of God was more highly-charged than anything that had preceded it. Thus, the 'blessing' became known by the place where it was deemed to be concentrated. To date, well over a million visitors or 'pilgrims' have journeyed to Toronto to experience the blessing for themselves. Many of these pilgrims report dramatic miracles or supernatural interventions, substantial changes in their lives, and greater empowerment for Christian ministry. More unusual claims have included tooth cavities being miraculously filled with gold, and 'dustings' of gold on the hair and shoulders of believers, indicating a specific spiritual anointing. Some have even claimed that children born to believers will have supernatural resurrection bodies.

In spite of the extraordinary success of the church, John Wimber, a founding pastor of the Vineyard network, excommunicated the Toronto fellowship for '(alleged) cult-like and manipulative practices'. Some evangelical critics of the Toronto Blessing Movement cited the influence of the Rhema or 'Health and Wealth' (see **Health and Wealth**) movement, through the Toronto Fellowship's connections with Benny Hinn and Rodney Howard-Browne, as another reason for Vineyard-led secession. In January 1996, the Toronto Vineyard became independent. Under the leadership of its pastor, John Arnott, it has flourished, and continues to exercise an international ministry in the fundamentalist–revivalist tradition. More unusually, the leadership consists almost entirely of married couples.

The anatomy of the movement

The Toronto Airport Christian Fellowship meets in a converted trade centre on an industrial estate that is less than a mile away from the main city airport. The building is functional in every respect. For example, at the back of the church there was once a large area that was segregated into track lanes. This is where worshippers, following the end of a service, could stand waiting for individual ministry to take place. A minister stood in front of the worshipper, and a 'catcher' at the back. When or if a worshipper fell to the ground – 'slain in the Spirit' – they were caught, and the minister moved on to the next worshipper on their track, leaving the previous one on the floor to 'marinade in the Spirit'. Typically, worship or revival meetings can last several hours.

To understand the place of the Toronto Blessing as a phenomenon within the wider milieu of global charismatic renewal (see **Charismatic Movements**), close scrutiny of the metaphors used by followers to describe the blessing is helpful. These metaphors mostly occur in the shared grammar of assent that is present in the worship songs, which are a distinctive feature of the tradition; but they are also present in preaching and teaching. The metaphors tend to revolve around concepts of liquidity (or water) and fire, and then bodily intimacy as a means of personal and communal empowerment. When the Toronto Blessing first emerged as a major force within contemporary revivalism, leaders were careful to 'position' the commodity in the 'charismatic market'. It was variously described as a 'spiritual top-up', 'in-flight re-fuelling', 'refreshing, not revival', 'latter rain', and the like. In other words, the Toronto Blessing was a fillip for a flagging (charismatic) movement.

Allied to the liquid or watery metaphors, there are also analogies concerning drunkenness. Because one of the distinguishing features of the 'blessing' is 'holy' and 'uncontrollable' laughter, some within the movement have inevitably linked their experience to the account of the outpouring of the Holy Spirit described in Acts 2, where the apostles are accused of being drunk. Randy Clarke, one of the revivalist leaders closely associated with the Toronto Fellowship, talks about dispensing the Holy Spirit like a drink: pilgrims are encouraged to 'have a double, not a single'. Clarke is known within the movement as 'God's bartender'. The metaphors of fire are generally used to describe the purging and refining that charismatic movements bring, as well as the passion and excitement that revival ensures. 'God's Fire' is also, like water, somehow uncontrollable. The intimacy (with God) is located in the rhetoric of worship, and is sometimes pseudo-erotic. Believers are to know Christ's physical nearness, and even to experience the 'kisses of his mouth'.

In the thinking, grammar and rhetoric of the Toronto Blessing movement, the task of the individual and church, (which is simultaneously soaked with rivers or waves of revival [water], and on fire), as well as being uncontrollably drunk, is to strive for greater intimacy with God, which will lead to the acquisition of enhanced spiritual power. Individuals, as part of the celebrating revivalist community, are being asked to acknowledge their hunger and desperation for God, and then to become (spiritually) hot, wet, powerless, passionate open and responsive, as a prerequisite to experiencing more of God's power.

Conclusion: interpreting the movement

Sociologically, the Toronto Blessing has been studied by a range of scholars who have assessed its vitality, but also predicted its eventual atrophy. It does seem to be important that the movement is partly understood as a resource or commodity within the wider global charismatic and revivalist market. As a cultural creature of its time, the Toronto Blessing placed less emphasis on power (a particular feature of John Wimber's teaching in the 1980s), and through its distinctive grammar of worship, put more accent on concepts such as 'softness' and 'the gentle touch' of God, and the desirability of acquiescence in the believer. The popular worship song 'Eternity' (by Brian Doerksen, 1994, Vineyard/Mercy Publishing) perhaps captures this best, sung many times over by followers, and set to a soft melody:

> *I will be yours, you will be mine.*
> *Together in eternity*
> *Our hearts of love will be entwined.*
> *Together in eternity,*
> *Forever in eternity.*
> *We will worship you forever.*
> *No more tears of pain in our eyes;*
> *No more fear or shame.*
> *For we will be with you,*
> *Yes, we will be with you,*
> *We will worship,*
> *We will worship you forever.*

The Toronto Blessing was one of the first revivalist movements to be promoted through the Internet (see **Cyberspace Religions**). It could spread its message and testimonies quickly and easily, and speedily developed into becoming an 'internet-ional' movement. The experiences of those attending Toronto Blessing meetings since 1994 seem to have been primarily cathartic; one could almost describe the effect of the blessing upon worshippers as something like a spiritual cleansing. However, the influence of the Toronto Blessing has steadily waned since the late 1990s, and its position and prominence in the charismatic market place quickly forgotten.

The movement has been subject to serious atrophy. There are now comparatively few visitors to the fellowship in Toronto, and the phenomenon is rarely mentioned in revivalist circles. An air of cognitive dissonance has set in.

Further reading

Hilborn, D. (ed.) (2001) *Toronto in Perspective*, Carlisle: Paternoster.

Percy, M. (1996) *The Toronto Blessing*, Oxford: Latimer House.

Percy, M. (2005) 'Adventure and Athrophy in a Charismatic Movement: Returning to the Toronto Blessing', *Journal of Contemporary Religions* 20(7), 71–91.

Poloma, M. (1995) *A Preliminary Sociological Assessment of the Toronto Blessing*, Bradford-upon-Avon: Terra Nova.

Richter, P. and Porter, S. (eds.) (1995) *The Toronto Blessing – Or Is it?*, London: DLT.

MARTYN PERCY

TRANSCENDENTAL MEDITATION

Often referred to as TM, transcendental meditation is a technique for mental and physical well-being and rejuvenation which, for some committed meditators, leads on to programmes for higher spiritual development (e.g. *sidhi yoga*), alternative medicine (*ayurveda*), and Vedic astrology. It was introduced to the West in the late 1950s by Maharish Mahesh Yogi (1911–), a physics graduate who then studied with Swami Brahmananda Saraswati (1869–1953) at the Sankaracarya Jyotir Math in north India where he was introduced to the teachings and practices of *advaita vedanta*, a monistic system associated with the early Indian philosopher, Sankara. The Maharishi, as he later became known, found that Westerners were more receptive to his ideas than Indians, particularly in the 1960s after he had cultivated the interest of several celebrities, including The Beatles, Mia Farrow and Jane Fonda,

and attracted media attention. From the mid-1960s to the end of the 1970s the popularity of the Spiritual Regeneration Movement, as it was called, grew enormously, with nearly one million people learning the TM technique in the USA alone. It also grew in respectability, with American veterans and the public school system promoting the practice as a means of reducing stress and developing health and well-being. By the end of the twentieth century, TM had established centres in 108 countries, with six million people having taken the basic meditation course.

During the 1970s Maharishi Mahesh Yogi founded the Maharishi International University (now the Maharishi University of Management, in Fairfield, Iowa), the World Government of the Age of Enlightenment, and the World Plan for spiritual regeneration. More recently Maharishi Corporate Development International has introduced courses for business executives and managers, and the Natural Law Party has been formed to take the Maharishi's message into the political arena. The basis for all these projects is the 'Science of Creative Intelligence'. It is in this process that the Maharishi yokes his earlier education in scientific language and methodology with his later spiritual training, and it is this amalgamation that has led the movement to advertise its benefits in scientific terms, and to encourage scientific research into its effects. The scientific nature of TM was challenged, however, in the late 1970s in the New Jersey courts where it was declared that the teaching offered by the movement in public schools was unconstitutional given its 'religious' nature. Other criticisms have focused on whether the movement's practices actually deliver the stated benefits, on the financial costs of the techniques, and the dependency of practitioners upon them.

The practices and institutional developments associated with TM stem from the idea that changes at the micro-level – in terms of the individual's stress reduction, spiritual growth, and development of yogic powers – can be successfully multiplied to bring about transformation at the macro-level, whether that be crime reduction in the local neighbourhood, improvements to a nation's health, or world peace. This creative multiplication effect is possible, according to the Maharishi, because of 'the Unified Field of the Natural Law'. Personal and social problems arise because this law is violated; the appropriate response to this violation is spiritual regeneration, first of the individual and then, as the number of individuals increases, of the whole planet.

The process starts with mantra meditation, taught individually to a beginner in a ceremony (closely akin to Hindu *diksa* initiation (**Mantra**) in which a disciple makes offerings and is initiated by a guru). The secret, personal mantra then becomes the focus of twice-daily meditation, which is expected to lead to various physical, mental, and spiritual benefits. Once an individual has mastered this process, other techniques may be offered, principally the TM-Sidhi programme – often referred to as 'Yogic flying' – in which a practitioner is taught to levitate by harnessing and channelling spiritual energies. With attention to physical as well as spiritual health, the movement has also developed medical centres and alternative, *ayurvedic* therapies and remedies.

Those committed to disseminating the Maharishi's teachings have found that politics is a viable addition to the normal means of lectures, publications, and electronic communication. Begun in 1992, the Natural Law Party has been active in sixty countries, and contested elections in over thirty. This has pro-vided it with a platform from which to articulate the theory of the Unified Field (with its roots in Hindu *advaita vedanta*), and its ideas about the sources and solutions to national and global problems. The Maharishi has offered the movement's spiritual services in the fight against global terrorism, which he believes can be eradicated if sufficient numbers of people practice yogic *sidhi* practices simultaneously.

Further reading

Wallis, Roy (1984) *The Elementary Forms of the New Religious Life*, London: Routledge and Kegan Paul.

KIM KNOTT

TRANSCENDENTALISM
Founder: Ralph Waldo Emerson
(b. 1803; d. 1882)

Transcendentalism is closely associated with the ideas and philosophy of Ralph Waldo Emerson (1803–82) (see **Emerson, Ralph Waldo**) whose father was the theologically and morally conservative vicar of Boston's First Church. Later at Harvard he was to be greatly stirred by the ideas of Emmanuel Swedenborg (1688–1781) which he learned about through contact with the young Swedenborgian enthusiast Sampson Reed who published in 1826 *Reflections on the Growth of Mind*, a study of Swedenborg's writings.

Though never a numerically large movement, Transcendentalism has been described as 'the single most provocative spiritual movement in American history' (Ahlstrom, 1985: 29). It arose out of Unitarianism as an anti-materialist, anti-rationalist, and anti-Enlightenment movement. Emerson its 'founder' was also greatly influenced by the talented religious innovator Mary Moody Emerson

(1774–1863) through whom he came to know about the many and varied spiritual influences that were in vogue in alternative circles including mystical Catholicism, Oriental religions, Swedenborg's (see **Swedenborg, Emmanual**) (1688–1771) teachings – in particular his doctrine of Correspondence according to which Nature is a symbol of the spirit – the Neo-Platonism of Jacob Boehme (1775–1642), and the Hermetic and/or Secret Traditions. All of these sources offered alternatives to the biblical orthodoxies which Emerson and his friends severely criticized. The more he read the more Nature became for Emerson a holy thing.

In his own mind a seer, prophet and teacher, Emerson was determined not to replace the biblical orthodoxies that he had rejected with a new set of dogmas and for this reason, and to encourage self-reliance, he adopted an aphoristic style of teaching and lecturing that was rich in metaphor and paradox. This led to frequent misunderstanding and confusion. Gurdjieff (see **Gurdjieff, George Ivanovitch**), among other thinkers who have greatly influenced the development of contemporary forms of religion, adopted a similar rhetorical style, contradicting the day after what they had stated categorically to be true the previous day. A bitter critic of what he saw as the evils of American society and in particular of its dehumanizing economic system Emerson did little to bring about change but remained a romantic idealist.

This notwithstanding, Emerson's thought has influenced several important currents in modern American alternative spirituality. For example, his lectures and seminars on the gnostic and esoteric aspects of religion (see **Esoteric Movements**), and on Eastern religions, proved a valuable source for such movements as **Theosophy**. His stress on self-realization, on the importance for individuals of fulfilling their potential, places him in the long tradition of 'Positive Thinking' from **Christian Science** and **New Thought** that were concerned with health, happiness and human well being to Norman Vincent Peale. Also influential for the history of ideas in America has been his critique of the rational and the instrumental culture of the time which he believed was the main reason for the growing disenchantment and disillusionment that many felt so strongly, for the alienation and disaffection arising from the pursuit of materialism, and for the dissatisfaction with the increasing commercialism of American life which he believed was undermining the relationship between human beings and Nature. All of this resonated with many of those who joined the counter-culture or sought an alternative lifestyle in the world transforming NRMs (see **New Religious Movement, Introduction**) and **New Age Movement** of the 1960s, 1970s and 1980s.

Further reading

Alhstrom, S. E. (1985) 'Ralph Waldo Emerson and the American Transcendentalists', in *Nineteenth Century Religious Thought in the West*, Volume II (eds) N. Smart, J. Clayton, P. Sherry and S.T Katz, Cambridge: Cambridge University Press, pp. 69–111.

Cole, P. (1998) *Mary Moody Emerson and the Origins of Transcendentalism. A Family History*, Oxford and New York: Oxford University Press.

PETER B. CLARKE

TREVELYAN, SIR GEORGE

Sir George Trevelyan (1906–96) was a very influential and revered British new age thinker and teacher (see **New Age Movement**), who influenced the lives of thousands of people. He summed up his life's work as 'an exploration into God', and became a leading figure in the quest to bring science and spirituality together. Trevelyan came from an old aristocratic family, noted for its many members who held radical political and social ideas. His uncle was the famous historian G. M. Trevelyan, of Trinity College, Cambridge. It has been suggested that this inherited aristocratic independence of mind gave him the confidence to promote new age ideas that flew in the face of conventional opinion and entrenched cynicism.

Trevelyan studied history at Trinity, and planned to go into politics, like his father who had been a minister in a Labour government. Instead, he moved into arts and crafts, making furniture in the Cotswolds under a well known designer. This experience was integrated into his holistic philosophy and alternative lifestyle. In this respect he followed in the footsteps of Rousseau, who in his treatise on education *Emile*, advocated carpentry as the ideal career for his student. At the same time, Trevelyan was learning the Alexander Technique (a method of postural training), then in its early days, and this too was to become part of his vision.

Trevelyan then met Kurt Hahn, the charismatic founder of Gordonstoun School, and accepted a teaching post there. In Denmark he studied a teaching method which encouraged 'speaking from the heart' instead of from notes, and he came to believe that ideas, like human beings and nature, had a life and vitality of their own, and that they should always be communicated freshly to avoid becoming stale.

In 1942, whilst in the army, Trevelyan had a strong spiritual experience at a talk by Walter Stein, a student of Rudolf Steiner (the founder of **Anthroposophy**). The topics included 'man as a spiritual being' and 'the earth as a training ground for souls'. Trevelyan had hitherto been an agnostic materialist, uninterested in such matters, but now became involved in anthroposophy for several years.

Subsequently, Trevelyan became drawn to adult education, and after demobilization from the army was appointed principal of Attingham Park Adult Training College in 1948. In his twenty-four years there he taught many subjects, notably 'spiritual knowledge as adult education', also a course on the meaning of death – a taboo subject in those days. His courses were usually popular and fully booked, which prevented sceptics from silencing him. Attingham also gave him the opportunity to fulfil his dream of opening English country house culture to a broader spectrum of people in a more educational context.

Trevelyan had a very wide range of interests, and was active in many other new age enterprises, such as the **Findhorn Community** and the Lamplighters movement. He strongly advocated organic farming before it became well known, as well as food production reform. Other projects included community living, the development of arts and crafts, and new age beliefs such as the healing properties of crystals, the power of ley lines (invisible geo-magnetic energy lines), the lost civilization of Atlantis, the Arthurian legends, angels and unicorns. He saw death as an important teacher, and often said that he looked forward to his own death. He was famous for his well attended annual 'round table' conferences bringing together leaders of holistic medicine, spiritual communities, and sympathetic scientists. The theme of the round table was personally significant for him, as the Trevelyan family coat of arms shows a linkage to King Arthur and his knights.

On his retirement from the college in 1971 he was invited to found the Wrekin

Trust, as a vehicle to continue his new age teaching. It is still active, and at the time of writing is in the process of collaborating with other organizations to create a 'University for Spirit': an institute with a mission to provide education to counter-balance the prevailing materialistic philosophy of the modern world, as it was seen by Trevelyan. Its goal is to restore the original meaning of 'university', literally 'turned towards the one'. Currently it has reached the stage of setting up a 'Centre for Spiritual Values in Education' with the aim of bringing holistic and spiritual values into education at all levels.

Trevelyan left a substantial body of lectures, articles and books, covering the whole range of his interests. Most of the books are only available as Internet downloads, free of charge.

Further reading

Farrer, F. (2002) *Sir George Trevelyan and the New Spiritual Awakening*, Edinburgh: Floris.

ELIZABETH PUTTICK

TRUE TEACHINGS OF CHRIST'S TEMPLE

Founder: Daniel Himmans-Arday

The True Teachings of Christ's Temple is the oldest African-initiated church in the Netherlands. It is based in the Bijlmer district of Amsterdam and has branches in Hamburg and London. There is no mother church in Ghana.

The church owes its existence to the circumstances of the diaspora, which has brought many Africans as labour migrants to Europe in recent years. It was founded in the 1970s by the Ghanaian Rev. Daniel Himmans-Arday, who came to the Netherlands in response to a divine calling following a profound experience of illness and healing. In a vision he was told to preach the gospel and heal others as he had been healed himself. Brother Daniel, as he is known, is considered a prophet by the members of the church. He is believed to have received charismatic gifts, notably the gift of healing. Many people come to consult him, including people from outside the church and including non-Africans. As part of its mission, the church aspires to be an international church that is open to people of all races.

The True Teachings of Christ's Temple is an evangelical church (see **Evangelical Christianity**) that bases itself explicitly on the teachings of Christ and the values associated with these, as handed down through the generations. The name of the church points to the importance attached to the undilutable character of biblical truth and the exemplary life of Christ. It also highlights the sacred character of the place where He is worshipped, which should be entered with due mark of respect. The church attaches much importance to biblical symbols as an expression of divine power. This includes the use of blessed water and oil, and of candles and incense.

Sermons take place in the form of lessons delivered not only by the senior pastor, but also by the second in rank, known as the Apostle; by some junior pastors, known as the Holy Children; and by the evangelists, known as Faith Brothers. The Church Mother and other women, known as Divine Sisters, are largely responsible for the general welfare of the church. They also preach on occasion. In all activities, divine inspiration through the working of the Holy Spirit plays an important role. Bible study is a central feature of the life of the church, combined with a strong belief in the power of prayer. During their annual convention church members spend a week of prayer and fasting to build themselves spiritually. The end of the fasting is marked by an appeal to social action, during which money is collected in support of the work of charitable organizations in Ghana and the Netherlands. 'Service to fellow human beings is service to God' is one of the church's mottoes.

The church has a well developed ritual practice. Healing rituals (see **Healing**) are particularly important, while other rituals are related to important phases of life, such as birth and death. An important ritual takes place every year on New Year's Eve to mark the transition from the old to the new year. During an all-night service the senior pastor ritually washes and anoints the feet of all church members. There is a general concern with purity and purification in the church, connected to a keen awareness of the pervasive presence of evil. The sense of evil is heightened by the precarious conditions in which many African migrants live as a result of European immigration policies. Among the church members there is a considerable number of Africans who have been in the Netherlands for many years but still lack official papers. The church helps them to survive spiritually and materially.

The life of this church must be understood in the light of the social and political conditions of the Netherlands today. The social function of the church is of prime importance. People come for personal consultation, seeking concrete advice on spiritual and social problems or a cure for their social ills. The church is a place for exchanging information on housing or jobs, and provides child care for working parents. It helps its members to integrate into Dutch society through a number of activities, including training for young people, computer lessons and various social services. Due to the strict separation between church and state in the Netherlands, the church receives no official support for any of its activities.

From its humble beginnings as a house congregation in the late 1970s, the church experienced its largest growth in the mid-1990s, when it became known as one of Amsterdam's 'car-park' churches, so-called from their location in the parking areas under the residential blocks of the Bijlmer district. In recent years, the church has been relocated to a newly built cultural and educational centre.

Further reading

Haar, G. ter (1998) *Halfway to Paradise: African Christians in Europe*, Cardiff: Cardiff Academic Press.

Haar, G. ter (ed.) (1998) *Strangers and Sojourners: Religious Communities in the Diaspora*, Leuven: Peeters.

GERRIE TER HAAR

TRUNGPA, CHOGYAM

Chogyam Trungpa (1939–87) was a Tibetan lama (priest) who became one of the most renowned but controversial **guru**s of the 1970s counter-culture. Born in Tibet, Trungpa was hailed at an early age as the eleventh *tulku* (incarnation) of the Trungpa lineage, and underwent a traditional boyhood monastic training. After fleeing the Chinese invasion of Tibet in 1959, he arrived in England in 1964 and won a scholarship to Oxford University where he studied comparative religion and fine arts. With Akong Rinpoche he co-founded Kagyu Samye Ling in Scotland, the first Tibetan meditaton centre in the West which now has an international reputation.

Trungpa soon gained notoriety for his tantric approach (see **Tantra**), more attractive to the mainly counter-cultural seekers around him than the drier traditional style. It was also known as 'crazy wisdom', and his flamboyant antics scandalized the community and eventually caused a rift with Akong. In 1969 Trungpa renounced his monastic vows, married an Englishwoman, and went to live in Boulder, Colorado. He was immensely popular in America and founded many organizations, including the Dharmadatu meditation centre with branches worldwide. The Naropa Institute has become a distinguished liberal arts college, attracting around a thousand students a year. The Shambala Training Program claims to be a complete path to enlightenment, while Shambala Publications has become a successful independent publisher.

However, Trungpa's personal behaviour in America scandalized the Buddhist community the wider public, and some of his own followers. It included heavy drinking, drugs, sexual promiscuity, and violence – rationalized as the tantric master path to enlightenment. He died aged 47 from alcohol-related illness. Controversy continued when his appointed successor Ozel Tendzin (Thomas Rich) died of AIDS, accused of knowingly infecting his male students.

Trungpa polarizes opinion more than any other guru apart from **Osho**, with whom he is sometimes compared. Despite the scandals, many Buddhists revere him as a brilliant scholar and poet, an original and highly charismatic teacher. He simplified the arcane complexities of Tibetan Buddhism without losing its integrity or exoticism, and led many Westerners to profound experience of one of the world's richest spiritual traditions. His books brought the teachings to an even wider audience, the best known being *Cutting through Spiritual Materialism*. He also attracted some of the most illustrious poets, philosophers and mystics of the time, including Allen Ginsburg, Thomas Merton, and Shunruyu Suzuki.

Further reading

Trungpa, C. (2002) *Cutting through Spiritual Materialism*, Halifax, Nova Scotia: Shambhala.

ELIZABETH PUTTICK

TURNER, HAROLD W.
(b. 1911; d. 2002)

Brought up in the Presbyterian Church of New Zealand, Harold Turner very early felt called to Christian mission service overseas. Throughout life he reflected on the relation between missions and culture. As a student, he encountered the Oxford Group (Moral Re-armament): this was his first contact with a controversial new movement. He came to recognize their work as a form of mission reaching out in unconventional ways to all classes in society (as, for example, in the work of Alcoholics Anonymous).

He decided his own mission was in teaching. In 1955, while at Fourah Bay College, Sierra Leone, he had a chance encounter with members of an African Initiated Church (at a baptismal ceremony on Lumley beach, which he happened to observe) started him on the speciality of his research career (see **African Independent Church**). He first made a detailed study of how this church, known as '**Church of the Lord Aladura**', used scripture in preaching and then he published an account of its history and contemporary practice. His interest from the first was not merely theoretical: he wanted both to help the church leaders undertake bible study and theological training and to promote ecumenical understanding.

In 1963 he moved to Crowther College, Nsukka, Nigeria. Here his special practical and pastoral concern was reinforced by his work in collaboration with a group of Mennonites whose mission board in America had quite recently responded to an appeal for help from a number of independent churches in Uyo. The missionaries who arrived were anxious to help without adding to the fragmentation of the Christian presence; their declared policy was to respect peoples in their distinctive cultures; so, in addition to offering courses of bible study and leadership training, they did a comprehensive study of churches in the Uyo region, seeking to further Christian unity in diversity. Turner, coming from Nsukka University, contributed to this study. Then, with the Mennonites, he had experience in helping an independent church to set up its own training institution.

In the long term, this work led, as he had hoped, to conciliar developments among the small churches and to better ecumenical relations between them and churches founded by missionaries. In his later teaching career in British and American universities, he retained this pastoral interest in the African movements, relating them to movements among African and Caribbean immigrants in Britain. About this time, he noted a similarity between the African movements he knew and movements among the Maori in his own country. This led him to gather information about movements that have arisen in all the continents through contact between Christian missionary outreach from Europe and local cultures (see **PRINERMs**).

He proposed that this world-wide phenomenon was a field of study that deserved serious research and theological reflection. He was able to induce many members of the movements to write their own histories; one of his aims, in fact, was to help them to 'speak for themselves'. At the same time, he was developing a bibliography of all the literature on the subject, historical, sociological and theological.

While teaching in British universities and for a short period in America, Harold Turner sought to establish a permanent study centre on prinerms. In his final teaching post at Aberdeen, 1972, he was able to get this project going. He produced his 'world survey tables' with lists of relevant movements, wrote a number of articles for *Encyclopaedia Britannica*, did a lecture tour in the South Pacific and made a number of journeys where he was able to expand his collection of documents.

Harold Turner was teaching at Aberdeen until the age for retirement and continued as research fellow for a few years. He was looking for a suitable home for his documentation and a base to continue research. He eventually donated his documents to the library of the Selly Oak Federation of mission colleges, Birmingham, in 1981. There he continued his work with the aid of scholars seconded by missionary associations. He wanted his resources to be available for missionaries and leaders in the independent churches and did in fact, with financial support from various missionary associations, distribute copies of his documentation to teaching institutions throughout the world.

The colleges at Selly Oak, Birmingham, UK to which he left his research and documentation became part of the School of Mission and World Christianity, Birmingham University in 1998.

Further reading

Walls, A. F. and Shenk, W. R. (eds) (1990) *Exploring New Religious Movements. Essays in Honour of Harold W Turner*, Mission Focus Publications, Elkhart Indiana.

Turner, H. W. (1998) *The Roots of Science. An Investigative Journey Through the World's Religions*, Auckland, NZ: Deepsight Trust.

RALPH WOODHALL

TWITCHELL, PAUL
(b. 1908 or 1910; d. 1971)
Founder of Eckankar

Paul Twitchell founded the Sant Mat-derived Eckankar movement in America in 1965.

Twitchell's early days are quite obscure; the current Living Master of **Eckankar**, Harold Klemp, accepts that there are incompatible different versions of his life and achievements, including a self-penned self-aggrandising entry in *Who's Who in Kentucky*. Instead of trying to cover this up, or to paint a glorified picture of their founder's life, as some new religions do, Klemp is disarmingly open about the fact that Twitchell 'was quite a rascal'. It is known that, like L. Ron Hubbard (see **Hubbard, L. R.**), Twitchell wrote pulp fiction, and also served in the US Navy. It was at this time, in 1944, that Twitchell later claimed he had met a Tibetan Master, Rebazar Tzars, in his soul body – a phrase that usually means in a dream.

Twitchell belonged to several religious movements before founding his own. From 1950 to 1955 he was a member of the Self-Revelation Church of Absolute Monism, a Hindu movement led by Swami Premananda. Apparently required to leave because of misconduct, in 1955 he joined Scientology, becoming an early Clear. In the same year he joined Ruhani Satsang, a Sant Mat movement founded by Kirpal Singh, but, with his wife Gail, later left the movement after falling out with Kirpal.

In 1965 he founded Eckankar, declaring himself to be the 971st in an unbroken line of Eck Masters. His books about his beliefs included *The Tiger's Fang* and *The Spiritual Notebook*.

Twitchell always claimed that the teachings of Eckankar had been revealed to him by Masters on higher planes. However, researcher David Lane has shown clearly that not only do the teachings come from Sant Mat origins, but that much of Twitchell's writing is a direct plagiarization from the work of a Sant Mat teacher, Julian Johnson. In early versions of Twitchell's writings, Lane reveals, Twitchell attributed certain teachings to Swami Premananda and Kirpal Singh, but in later editions he claimed that these same teachings came directly from named Masters such as Rebazar Tzars.

DAVID V. BARRETT

TYPOLOGIES OF NEW RELIGIONS

There have been many efforts to develop classification schemes that encompass what most scholars refer to as New Religious Movements (NRMs) and which are popularly (and negatively) called 'cults' within the popular media (see **Cult and New Religions**). This basic distinction between the terms 'cult' and NRM is perhaps the major dividing line in any discussion of new religious phenomena that have emerged in recent decades. The distinction is not an actual typology, but instead represents an ideological position on the part of those using either term (Beckford, 1985: 12–17; Dillon and Richardson, 1994; Greil, 1996). Those using the term 'cult' (or in the European context, the term 'sect') are, to varying degrees, accepting a normative view of such movements and groups. Such entities are viewed as bad, and to be avoided by individuals and controlled by societies. The term NRM is used by those adopting a more neutral and objective view toward some phenomena, while seeking to understand their development and meaning for contemporary society.

The term 'cult' was not always a term of derision. Indeed, it derives from the classical work of Troeltsch (1931), whose term mysticism serves as the basis of much insightful theoretical and empirical work on marginal religious groups of various types (Richardson, 1978). This tradition contains a number of useful typological developments, such as those of Geoffrey Nelson (1969). However, this early work within the classical tradition of the sociology of religion has fallen into disfavour in recent times in large part because of the usurpation of the term by popular media and opponents of religious experimentation. Indeed, some have recommended against any future use of the term 'cult' by scholars because of the dramatic shift in the meaning of the term (Richardson, 1993a). Instead the term NRM has come to be adopted by those wishing to indicate that they are working from a more scientific perspective on contemporary religious phenomena in the West.

There have been a number of efforts to develop genuine typologies of NRMs, as a part of the effort to explain and understand them. Perhaps the best known such effort is that of Roy Wallis (1978), whose typology differentiates between *world-rejecting, world-affirming,* and *world accommodating* movements. The first type condemns society as a whole, including its institutional structure and values, and wants to replace that world with another set of values and institutions. The third type 'claim to possess the means to enable people to unlock their physical, mental, and spiritual potential, without the need to withdraw from the world' (Wallis, 1978: 7–8). Thus, the world-affirming type focuses on individual changes whereas the world-rejecting type has as a goal redoing society itself. The second type, world-accommodating movements, stress the enrichment of spiritual life of individuals as opposed to the gaining of worldly possessions, and there is often an emphasis on the collective life as an end in itself.

Wallis classifies such groups as the Children of God (see **Family, The**), the People's Temple, the **Unification Church**, and the Hare Krishna (see **International Society for Krishna Consciousness**) as world-rejecting. He categorizes such groups as Silva Mind Control (see **Silva Method**), Transcendental Meditation, est, and Nichiren Shoshu (see **Soka Gakkai**) as world-affirming. World-accommodating movements include Charismatic Renewal (see **Charismatic Movements**) groups and Pentecostal ones as well.

Another oft-used typology was first presented in Robbins *et al.* (1978), and then developed more fully in other publications (Robbins and Anthony, 1979; Anthony and Ecker, 1987). This typology differentiates between *dualistic* and *monistic* movements, and offers several different sub-types within the latter category. Dualistic movements and groups 'affirm traditional moral absolutism and theocentric ethical dualism whilst protecting against permissiveness in all spheres of life' (Beckford, 1985: 74). Examples are neo-fundamentalist Jesus Movement and Charismatic and neo-Pentecostal Christian groups, which have been relatively numerous, at least within the American context, as well as the Unification Church, one of the more notorious of the NRMs.

Monistic movements and groups, which Robbins and Anthony (1979) have divided into four sub-types, affirm the oneness of the universe and disavow moral absolutes. **Scientology**, Silva Mind Control, TM, and other Eastern derived or oriented NRMs (see **New Religious Movement**) would be considered monistic groups of one sub-type or another by Robbins and Anthony (see Robbins, 1988: 136–41 for a summary of these ideas and illustrations).

Another typological scheme of note is that of Stark and Bainbridge (1979), which derives from traditional cult/sect/church theory and includes concepts of *audience cult, client cult,* and *cult movement* that are arranged along a continuum. This approach is built upon a broader theory of religion proposed by Stark and Bainbridge that includes the key concept of *compensators* or supernatural rewards offered by the cult. The authors claim that the generality, clarity, and intensity of the compensators increased as one moves from audience cult to cult movement.

Audience cults involve consumer activity in which individuals occasionally participate in lectures or other presentations offered by someone claiming to have some sort of truth. Such groups have little formal organization and they do not maintain membership criteria or lists. Client cults, of which Scientology is perhaps the best known example, offer more services, and most closely resemble the therapist/patient relationship. Such cult movements are much more organized and demanding of participants, and may involve even communal living experiences and total immersion in a group. Most of the more publicized and controversial NRMs of the past few decades would fall within the cult movement category in the Stark and Bainbridge scheme.

One effort at developing a typology divorced from the traditional church-sect typology and more related to social movement theory has been presented by Lofland and Richardson (1984), and summarized in Beckford (1985: 75–6). This scheme builds on the concept of *Religious Social Movement* (RMO), and focuses on the degree of 'corporateness' of a group or movement, which is defined (Lofland and Richardson, 1984: 32) as, 'the degree to which a set of persons actively promotes and participates

in a shared, positively valued, and collective life.' The most elaborate degree of corporateness would be found in a group which included:

1. income and other sustenance producing work;
2. shelter and residence;
3. food provision and eating organization;
4. family and other emotional support circles;
5. collective promulgation of cognitive orientation; and
6. a belief that the organization itself is ideal.

These basic elements accumulate along a continuum of corporateness, and delineate various types, including *clinic, congregations, collective* (two types – work and household), *corps,* and *colony* as falling along that continuum. For instance, a clinic would involve only the idealization of the philosophy or message being presented, but other basic elements would be missing. A colony would incorporate all six basic elements outlined above.

The Lofland and Richardson approach offers an analytic focus on basic elements, and how they might be constituted to define a certain type of NRM. However, it also offers a *dynamic* approach that attempts to grasp the ever-changing nature of many NRMs, which are constantly evolving, and even different at the same point in time, depending on location and other contextual considerations. The authors discuss the 'recomposing' of RMOs using the six basic elements, and focus on inherent internal and external pressures to change over time, such as the effects of establishing families and having children or the impact of efforts at social control by societal authorities (pp. 40–6).

The dynamic nature of NRMs is illustrated in a number of case studies of such movements and groups which show dramatic changes over time in response to various pressures (see for examples Richardson, 1979; 1985; 1993b). Such studies illustrate that, while developing typological schemes can be a useful analytical and heuristic device, such approaches should be used with caution. No NRM remains unchanged over time, and indeed, few are the same in every location at the same time, for quite understandable reasons. Empirical and theoretical efforts to apprehend the immense plethora of NRMs should be cognizant of this basic truth.

Further reading

Dick, A. and Ecker, B. (1987) 'The Anthony Typology: A Framework for Assessing Spiritual and Consciousness Groups', in D. Anthony, B. Ecker and and K. Wilber (eds) *Spiritual Choices*, New York: Paragon, pp. 35–106.

Beckford, J. (1985) *Cult Controversies: The Societal Response to to New Religious Movements*, London: Tavistock.

Dillon, J. and Richardson, J. (1994) 'The "Cult" Concept: A Politics of Representation Analysis', *SYZYGY: Journal of Alternative Religion and Culture* 3(4), 185–98.

Greil, A. (1996) 'Sacred Claims: The "Cult Controversy" as a Struggle Over the Right to the Religious Label', in D. Bromley and L. Carter (eds), *Religion and the Social Order: The Issue of Authenticity in the Study of Religions*, Greenwich, CT: JAI, pp. 47–63.

Lofland, J. and Richardson, J. (1984) 'Religious Movement Organizations: Elemental Forms and Dynamics', in L. Kriesberg (ed.) *Research in Social Movements, Conflicts, and Change*, Greenwich, CT: JAI, pp. 29–52.

Nelson, G. (1969) 'The Spiritualist Movement and the Need for a Redefinition of Cult', *Journal for the Scientific Study of Religion*, 8, 85–93.

Richardson, J. T. (1978) 'An Oppositional and General Conceptualization of Cult', *The Annual Review of the Social Sciences of Religion*, 2, 29–52.

Richardson, J. T. (1979) 'From Cult to Sect: Creative Eclecticism in New Religious Movements', *Pacific Sociological Review*, 22, 139–66.

Richardson, J. T. (1985) 'The Deformation of New Religions: Impacts of Societal and Organizational Factors', in T. Robbins, D. Anthony, and J. McBride (eds), *Cults, Culture and the Law*, Chico, CA: Scholars Press, pp. 163–75.

Richardson, J. T. (1993a) 'Definitions of "Cult": From Sociological-Technical to Popular-Negative', *Review of Religious Research*, 34, 348–56.

Richardson, J. T. (1993b) 'Mergers, "Marriages," Coalitions, and Denominationalization: The Growth of Calvary Chapel', *SYZYGY: Journal of Alternative Religion and Culture*, 2, 193–204.

Robbins, T. (1988) *Cults, Converts, & Charisma*, London: Sage.

Robbins, T. and Dick, A. (1979) 'The Sociology of Contemporary Religious Movements', *Annual Review of Sociology* 5, 75–89.

Robbins, T., Dick, A. and Richardson, J. (1978) 'Theory and Research on Today's "New Religions"', *Sociological Analysis* 39, 95–122,

Stark, R. and Bainbridge, W. (1979) 'Of Churches, Sects, and Cults: Preliminary Concepts for a Theory of Religious Movements', *Journal for the Scientific Study of Religion*, 18, 117–33.

Troeltsch, E. (1931) *The Social Teaching of the Christian Churches*, New York: Macmillan.

Wallis, R (1978) 'The Rebirth of the Gods', Inaugural lecture delivered before the Queen's University in Belfast.

JAMES T. RICHARDSON

U

UFOs

Stories about UFOs represent a collectively shared narrative, a popular myth, with no formal authority to direct or maintain it. Meaning 'Unidentified Flying Object' the acronym 'UFO' refers to strange things seen in the sky. Its earlier equivalent, the concept of 'flying saucers', was coined in the American news media in the summer of 1947. After a flight over the Cascade Mountains, Washington, on 24 June, private pilot Kenneth Arnold (d. 1984) reported that he had encountered nine strange, flying objects in the sky. Talking to a newspaper reporter about his experience, Arnold said that the objects travelled at a tremendous speed and that they moved 'like a saucer would if you skipped it across the water'. He was referring to the movements of the objects but a headline editor misunderstood him, and the notion of 'flying saucers' was subsequently presented to the public. Arnold, however, described the objects as 'crescent shaped'. During the days following the incident many newspapers carried the story, and apparently many other witnesses had encountered 'flying saucers'. Nothing whatsoever was documented or proven. The 'flying saucer', and subsequently the UFO, consequently, was born from a specific, attention-demanding narrative that still expands and gives life to further mythological creativity.

Quite often the notion of UFOs is related to religious world views. A number of significant UFO-religions operate in different countries (The **Aetherius Society**, The **Raelian Church**, **Heaven's Gate**, Unarius and others), but the ufological impact upon the larger **New Age Movement** is probably more important. People attending New Age seminars or reading New Age materials will over and over again learn about benevolent **extraterrestrials** who come to their rescue one way or another. In most cases the wise extraterrestrials are ufological adaptions of the traditional

Theosophical Adepts (see **Theosophy**) or Mahatmas, but occasionally they are of a more independent nature. Usually, however, the notion of UFO and extraterrestrial visitation appears as a secular myth with close associations to different kinds of conspiracy speculations. A vast number of secular UFO organizations operate in a growing number of countries, each of them trying to solve the riddle of the allegedly strange phenomena. Only a few of them, though, will give credibility to a sociological explanation. The so called 'nuts-and-bolts' interpretation remains the strongest as anyone browsing through the Internet will discover. 'UFOs' is among the most popular subjects on the Internet.

The image of the flying saucer probably arose as a response to the tensions between the United States and the Soviet Union in the wake of World War Two. As the Cold War was building up, people realized that their lives were under permanent threat, and the psychosocial climate became increasingly difficult. The political authorities were unable to curtail the proliferation of nuclear weapons, and a myth of how extraterrestrials prepared to either prevent nuclear destruction, or assist a surviving remnant, developed. The 'flying saucer' or UFO, according to this theory, serves as a symbolic mediator between the two oppositional powers, but also as a mediator between the individual human being and the complex society of which he or she is a tiny part. The belief systems of the actual UFO religions that have developed along with the more general UFO narrative seems to confirm that.

Other things, however, also played an important role in the formation of the UFO myth: Most importantly science fiction, new technologies, the emerging possibility of space travel, and the advancement in sciences such as astronomy. The myth of the UFO fits, in substance as well as in structure, the demands of the modern world. The elves, angels, trolls, and demons of pre-industrialized Europe have been abandoned by the modern imagination, but contemporary mythological creatures are taking over. At this point, when the forests and mountains have no secrets left, the super-human agents come from deep space or other realms beyond human reach. The structure of the stories, however, is largely the same as in traditional popular mythology, but the specific narrative is designed for modern world purposes. Mythological creatures of the past have been replaced by their modern equivalents. Furthermore, the UFO myth addresses contemporary problems: The abduction myth (which insists that humans are being systematically captured and manipulated by alien creatures), for instance, mirrors problems with abortion, prenatal birth, medical technology, gene technology, repressed sexual desires, the dignity of the individual, mother–child relations, pain, and other modern ethical problems.

The presence of UFO narratives is a solid indication that modernity and technology has been unable to stop people from developing mythological worlds inhabited by strange creatures. The monitoring of the UFO scene, therefore, gives the researcher a rare possibility for observing how new religious or semi-religious ideas come into being and how they change. One particularly interesting thing is that people have come to accept 'alien space craft' as the answer to the question: 'How do we identify the strange objects?' The only proof for the space craft hypothesis, namely, is contained in a narrative with no supportive evidence.

Further reading

Lewis, J. R. (ed.) (2000) *UFOs and Popular Culture. An Encyclopedia of Contemporary Myth*, Santa Barbara, ABC-Clio.

Rothstein, M. (forthcoming) *UFO Religions*, Utah, Signature Books.

MIKAEL ROTHSTEIN

UMBANDA

Umbanda started in São Paulo, Brazil in the 1920s which was a time of ever increasing urbanization and industrialization. A doctrinally and ethnically inclusive movement Umbanda drew together teachings and practices from African-Brazilian religions, Kardecist spiritism (see **Kardecism, Kardec, Allan**), Amerindian religion and Catholicism, bring together in this way three of the major ethnic groups that make up the population of Brazil: African, Amerindian, and European.

An Umbanda centre is headed by a *pai* or *mae de santo* (father or mother of the saint) who is assisted by *filhas* and *filhos de santos* (sons and daughters of the saint). The father or mother of the saint has a spiritual parallel known as the *guia-chefe* or chief guide of the centre and together with this guide the former prepares the sons and daughters of the saints for initiation and trains them to serve as ritual assistants and mediums.

The eclectic character of Umbanda and the virtual autonomy of local groups mean that there can be considerable variation in belief and practice from one Umbanda centre to another. There is, however, a federation to which each centre is affiliated and which takes care of the material side of the various centres. The federation consists of a president, vice president and secretaries and treasurers. In theory the father or mother of the saint has little or no influence over the federation for the reason that the spiritual and material side of Umbanda should not be mixed. In practice there is mixing and where a ritual leader is weak the federation assumes control over his territory as well as its own.

Umbanda made rapid strides in São Paulo, the industrial hub of Brazil in the 1950s and continued to do so until the 1990s. More recently there appears to have been a decline in the numbers of those involved. Many who do attend Umbanda centres do so on an irregular basis and learn little about the teachings and rituals.

While the ritual leader has considerable authority over the sons and daughters of the saint he/she has little control over its clients the majority of whom are 'accidental', coming and going at will.

The Umbanda cosmos has three tiers: the astral, the earth and the underworld. The African gods or *orishas* (Portuguese: Orixás) inhabit the first tier, along with Caboclos or Amerindian spirits and the Pretos Velhos or Old Blacks, who are considered to be the founders of Umbanda. The spirits of this sphere are referred to as spirits of the light or right, are considered good and are linked to the 'white' magic of Umbanda. The earth is inhabited by human incarnations who are at the lower stages of spiritual evolution, and the underworld by evil and ignorant spirits such as the trickster god Eshu (Portuguese: Exu) and the Pomba Giras, the female counterparts of Eshu. The spirits of the underworld are known as spirits of the shadows or evil and are associated with the left, are considered immoral or amoral and are associated with evil and 'black' magic (*quimbanda*). Because these spirits are more human-like humans can more easily make use of them to resolve the material problems of everyday life. Their presence at sesssions, therefore, is considered indispensable as the majority of clients' problems are material rather than caused by spiritual agencies.

The Orishas occasionally visit the earth to help human incarnations but are not as active or as important as they are in Candomblé. They rarely possess their mediums and when they do they remain mute. In Umbanda it is the spirits of the dead who function as consulting spirits and who are the main focus of the sessions. When Eshu and his counterparts visit the earth it is to create problems for people.

While Umbanda offers its clients solutions to their material and spiritual problems and mainly the former its teachings on the spiritual evolution of human beings also offer an explanation for human weakness and failure. In this way the movement functions as a form of personal psychology.

Umbanda is characterized as more Brazilian and European than African, although it does make considerable use of African cosmology. The ideas of the French Spiritist Kardec have, however, exercised most influence over its world-view.

Further reading

Brown, D. (1988) *Umbanda: Religion and Politics in Urban Brazil*, Ann Arbor: UMI Research Press.

Jensen, T. G. (1998) 'Umbanda and Its Clientele' in P. B. Clarke (ed.) *New Trends and Developments in African Religion*, Westport, CT: Greenwood Press, pp. 75–87.

PETER B. CLARKE

UNARIUS

Founders: Ernest Norman (b. 1904; d. 1971), Ruth Norman (b. 1900; d. 1993)

Unarius-Science of Life is one of the most well-known religious movements based on **UFOs** and messages from the **extraterrestrials**. Ernest Norman (1904–71) and his wife, Ruth Norman (1900–93) founded it in 1954. As is common in UFO movements, both had had experiences in **Spiritualism** before the UFO theme became common in the late 1940s. In the early 1950s, Ernest started channelling messages from the extraterrestrials, and these were transcribed by his wife, and published as a series of popular books. In 1954, there were enough followers to allow the establishment of an organization, known as Unarius from the acronym of 'Universal Articulate Interdimensional Understanding of Science'. Norman later revealed that he had been in touch since his childhood with extraterrestrials from planets Mars, Venus, Orion, Hermes, Eros, and Muse, all acting as his personal spirit guides before revealing messages intended for humanity as a whole.

The most charismatic teacher in Unarius, however, was Ruth Norman. After Ernest's death in 1970, she assumed the leadership of the movement and went on to become one of the most colourful figures in the international UFO community. For her, reincarnation was indisputable, and she revealed that Ernest was the reincarnation of both the Egyptian pharaoh Amenhotep (who reigned between 1390–53 BCE) and Jesus Christ. Ernest, during the course of his past reincarnations, had also visited Planet Earth on a spaceship, at the time of the lost continents of Atlantis and Lemuria. Ruth, in turn, introduced herself as the reincarnation of Amenhotep's mother, the Egyptian woman who saved Moses, Jesus Christ's lost love, and the Mona Lisa of the famous painting by Leonardo da Vinci (1452–1519.)

According to Ruth, the highest political power in the universe is the Intergalactic Confederation, which includes planets well beyond our Solar System. On 14 September 1973, thanks to Ruth's efforts, Planet Earth was finally admitted into the Intergalactic Confederation, with Ruth (under the sacred name of 'Ioshanna') serving as the Confederation's representative on Earth. Charles L. Spiegel (1921–99), the co-author of several of Ruth's voluminous books, succeeded her as Unarius' leader after her death in 1993. Spiegel died in 1999, and was succeeded by a committee of senior members. Notwithstanding the demise of two charismatic leaders such as Ruth and Spiegel within a few years, Unarius continues to be active both in the US and in several European countries; its headquarters in El Cajon, California is a popular stop for those interested in the messages of UFO contactees. Students can follow a correspondence course, which teaches them about the Intergalactic Confederation, the structure of the universe, reincarnation, and the ultimate divine nature of human beings. The annual gathering to celebrate Earth's admission into the Intergalactic Confederation, in the second weekend of October, also attracts to El Cajon both ardent followers and the merely curious.

Further reading

Norman, R. (1985) *Unarius. A Biographical History*, 2 vols., El Cajon (California): Unarius Educational Foundation.

Unarius (1982) *The Universal Hierarchy. A Pictorial Tour of Unarius*, El Cajon (California): Unarius Educational Foundation.

MASSIMO INTROVIGNE

UNIFICATION CHURCH

(a.k.a. Moonies)

The Holy Spirit Association for the Unification of World Christianity (HSA-UWC) is known by various names, such as the Unification Church and Tong Il, or, despite members' protests, 'the Moonies' after their leader, Sun Myung Moon (1920–), who founded the movement in Korea in 1954. In the mid-1990s, the organization was reconceived as the Family Federation for World Peace and Unification, the Unification Church being simply its religious arm.

Unification theology is based on Moon's interpretation of the Old and New Testaments with further revelations about the role he and his family play in the restoration of the Kingdom of Heaven on earth. It is claimed that, in 1936, Jesus appeared and asked Moon to take on the role of Messiah. After further meetings with religious leaders such as Buddha, Mohammad (and God Himself) in the spirit world, Moon developed a system of beliefs, the *Divine Principle,* a number of different versions of which have been written down by his disciples. According to the *Principle,* the Fall was due to the Archangel Lucifer having a (spiritual) sexual relationship with Eve, who then seduced Adam into having a (physical) relationship with her. As a consequence, their children were born of a Lucifer-centred union. The whole of history is interpreted as God's effort, with the help of several key personages, to establish the ideal, God-centred family. Jesus, although born as a perfect man, was murdered before he could marry, so he was unable to fulfil his mission and could offer only spiritual and not physical salvation through his death.

It is, however, believed that Moon (as the Lord of the Second Advent) established the foundation for the restoration of the earth when he married his present wife in 1960, and in 2003 advertisements appeared in newspapers reporting that statements had been channelled from important personages (including Confucius, Jesus, Luther, Jefferson, Mao, and Pol Pot) to the effect that the

Reverend and Mrs Moon are indeed the True Parents of humanity. Activities in spirit world have always played an integral role in Unification life, as, for example, when Moon's son, Heung Jin, died as the result of a car accident and was then embodied in a young Zimbabwean member who brought about a revival in the movement for a short time, before returning to Africa where he established his own group. Another revival is associated with Mrs Moon's deceased mother, who, it is claimed, channels messages to living members, most particularly at a large centre near Chung Pyung Lake in Korea.

The best-known rite of the Unification Church is the 'Blessing', or mass wedding service at which Moon has married thousands of couples. At the Holy Wine Ceremony held before the Blessing, it is believed that the blood lineage of the participants is purified, enabling children of the union to be born without the original sin inherited since the Fall. In the early days of the movement members were expected to have spent several years fundraising and introducing new members ('spiritual children') to the movement before they could be 'matched' by Moon to their partner. By the late 1990s, however, thousands of non-Unificationist couples were being 'blessed', often with no idea that they were deemed to have taken part in the ceremony.

The largest number of members has always been in Korea and Japan, but missionaries were sent to the West from the late 1950s; then, when Moon himself moved to the United States in the early 1970s, the movement began to grow and achieve international recognition. This was due partly to Moon's public speaking tours, widespread attendance at rallies and the widely publicized 'Blessings', but the conversion of young, well-educated Westerners to the movement and their very visible appearance on the streets selling flowers, literature and candles, and inviting young people to their centres and residential workshops soon became a matter of interest to the media and the growing numbers of 'cult-watching groups' (see **Cult Awareness Network**, **Anti-Cult Movement**, **Deprogramming**) that were concerned about new religions in general, but, quite frequently, the Unification Church in particular. The unexpectedness and rapidity of the conversions gave credibility to the idea that members must have been brainwashed through some irresistible techniques, despite the fact that the vast number of those subjected to the so-called mind-control managed to resist them, and the majority of those who did join left the movement within two years of joining (which helps explain why the core membership has never exceeded a few tens of thousands).

Associated with the Unification movement has been the establishment of a large number of businesses and ventures including fishing, ginseng, small armaments, the purchase of real estate, the production of newspapers and journals (including the *Washington Times* and the *Middle East Times*), the establishment of cultural and educational institutions (such as the Little Angels school in Seoul and the Unification Theological Seminary in New York state), and the organizing of large conferences for academics, clergy of all the world's faiths, the media, politicians, and other notables.

While Moon is accepted as the Messiah by his followers, he has frequently been greeted with suspicion and criticism by the rest of the world. He was imprisoned in Korea on a number of occasions and, in the mid-1980s, in the United States for tax evasion. Allegations have been made about connections with the Korean CIA and various other political intrigues. During the Watergate affair, he engendered a certain degree of notoriety by supporting Nixon. After the collapse of communism, the movement became less aggressively anti-communist, but accusations about Moon's private life and many of his public activities have continued to give rise to public condemnation, although the movement has, generally speaking, become relatively low key since the 1990s.

Further reading

Barker, E. (1984) *The Making of a Moonie: Brainwashing or Choice?* Aldershot: Ashgate.

Inglis, M. (ed.) (2000) *40 Years in America: An Institutional History of the Unification Movement*, New York: HSA Publications.

Introvigne, M. (2000) *The Unification Church*, Salt Lake City: Signature Books.

Moon, S. M. (1996) *Exposition of the Divine Principle*, New York: HSA-UWC. http://www.unification.net/dp96/

EILEEN BARKER

UNIFIED BUDDHIST CHURCH OF VIETNAM

Founders: Thich Tri Quang, Thich Tam Chau and Thich Nhat Hanh.

In the 1930s a 'new' Buddhism in Vietnam began to emerge through organizations such as the Cochin China Buddhist Study Society, the Amnan Buddhist Study Society and the Vietnamese Buddhist Study Society all of which were founded in an attempt to rescue Buddhism from its parlous state and draw on its teachings for the purpose of resolving the cultural crisis of colonialism. This new Buddhism was to seek to 'conscienticize' followers in the sense that it was determined to enable them to become truly aware of themselves and of their situation, an objective that, as

Thich Nhat Hanh later pointed out, had been seriously lacking in Vietnamese Buddhism.

The defining moment for this modern version of Vietnamese Buddhism came in the early years of the Vietnam and/or American War (1963–75) with the persecution and jailing of monks in 1963 by the Ngo Dinh Diem regime, and the self-immolation by fire in protest against this persecution and against the War by several monks including Thich Quang Doc. One of the consequences of this persecution was the establishment of the umbrella organization the **Unified Buddhist Church of Vietnam** (UBC) and/or the United or Unified Buddhist Congregation (UBC) two of the aims of which were the creation of an integrated Buddhist response to the War and the promotion of **Engaged Buddhism**. Buddhism in Vietnam was a strikingly diverse phenomenon both theologically and ethnically embracing as it did **Mahayana** and **Theravada** schools and a number of sects including the **Hao Hoa** movement.

Under the leadership of Thich Tri Quang, Thich Tam Chau and **Thich Nhat Hanh**, the UBC became one of the strongest voices in Vietnamese politics from the mid-1960s. Its independent minded approach to war and peace and relief of poverty ensured that it was never popular with any political or ruling body. In 1966 the UBC was driven underground, from where it continued its engagement with society through relief work among those worst affected by the War.

After the fall of Saigon in 1975 the new, independent, socialist government was unprepared to tolerate such an effective and independent minded institution as the UBC and consequently severely limited its activities. In 1981 the UBC was banned and replaced by a more manageable and compliant Buddhist Church of Vietnam which Buddhist groups were encouraged to join. The UBC continued on its struggle for religious freedom and a more open society under the new socialist regime and this campaign reached the attention of many outside Vietnam as house arrests and imprisonment of monks became more frequent in the 1980s. These reached a turning point, in terms of international publicity, with the house arrest and imprisonment of the UBC leader, the Nobel Prize winner, Thich Quang Do, in 1992.

The Unified Buddhist Church exists outside Vietnam in various forms including that of the Église Buddhique Unifiée set up in France by Thich Nhat Hanh.

Further reading

King, S. (1996). 'Thich Nhat Hanh and the Unified Buddhist Church: Nondualism in Action' in S. B. King and C. Queen (eds) *Engaged Buddhism: Buddhist Liberation Movements in Asia*, Albany: State University of New York Press, pp. 321–63.

PETER B. CLARKE

UNITED CHURCH OF CHRIST IN JAPAN

The ecumenical movement and the desire for church union have deep roots in Japanese Protestantism. In 1872 the first Japanese Protestant church, the *Nihon Kirisuto Kokai* (Church of Christ in Japan) was founded on a non-denominational basis. The Reformed-Presbyterian denominations had formed a union in 1877, the Anglicans in 1887, and the Methodists in 1907. However, the creation of a single Protestant denomination in 1941 with the formation of the *Nihon Kirisuto Kyodan* (the United Church of Christ in Japan) remains one of the most controversial issues in the history of Japanese Protestantism. This Protestant union was seen by some as an answer to prayer with the

fulfilment of a long-term ideal. To others the union was viewed as being the result of bowing to the demands of ultra-nationalism, and of the Christian leadership sacrificing personal principles in the name of national solidarity under government pressure. During the late 1960s, the issue of the war responsibility led to a major crisis within the *Kyodan*.

The formation of the *Kyodan* took place during a dark age in Japanese religious history, reminiscent of the witch hunts of European medieval history, which began after the 1931 Manchurian incident. Paralleling the steady rise of Emperor-centred militarism, there was the callous persecution of religious groups, notably new religions such as **Omoto** but some Christian groups were not spared including the Holiness Church, Plymouth Brethren, the Seventh Day Adventists, the Salvation Army and the *Nihon Seikokai* (the Japan Anglican-Episcopal Church) because they were deemed by the authorities to hold heterodox ideas or were too closely identified with foreign countries. After the opening of the Sino-Japanese War in 1937, the government pressed ahead with the union of religious groups, including Protestant churches, in order to enhance its control over religious organizations. In April 1940, the Religious Bodies Law came into effect and all religious bodies had to obtain new government charters. By late 1940 it was evident that the government's intention was to combine all Protestant denominations together in a single church. This led to the creation of the *Kyodan,* which received government recognition in December 1941.

The new union church had a centralized leadership under a director, a single General Conference and twelve regional conferences, which included Taiwan and Korea, and Manchuria (a missionary conference) as well as metropolitan

Japan. Initially, it possessed a sectional structure that allowed the joining denominations to retain a degree of autonomy. Its creedal commitments maintained the traditional emphasis and basis of Universal Christendom by making the Old and New Testaments its standard of faith and practice, and placing the historic Apostles' Creed at the centre of its Confession of Faith. In the discussions leading to the formation of the new church, its faith had taken second place to the formulation of its organizational structure.

With the end of the Second World War in 1945, a new era began in Japanese Christian history in which there was complete religious freedom. Even though a significant number of former Anglicans, Reformed-Presbyterians, Lutherans, Baptists, and others left to re-establish their former denominations, the majority of Protestants chose to remain within the *Kyodan*. A positive image of the Church was created by the work of its ministers and social agencies in helping ordinary Japanese recover effects of dislocation caused by the war. However, the *Kyodan*'s growth was hampered by its dependency in the early post-war years on overseas financial support and also by the general perception that Christianity was a foreign religion not suited to the religious proclivities of ordinary Japanese. Most Japanese still perceived Christianity as not offering a viable religious alternative. The *Kyodan* continues to wrestle with the question of making its Christian message more relevant to the concerns of a rapidly changing Japanese society. In the past, Christian schools and universities have played a significant role in the Japanese educational system. However, lack of Christian academic staff and shortage of ordained ministers has led to an erosion of Christian influence at *Kyodan* associated universities

and schools like Aoyama Gakuin, Doshisha, Kwansei Gakuin, Meiji Gakuin, and Tokyo Joshi Daigaku. The *Kyodan* faces a serious challenge in attracting young people into it for the church membership is rapidly aging. Even so, the *Kyodan* remains the largest Protestant denomination with over 200,000 members with a nation-wide network of churches and strong international links.

Further reading

Drummond, R. H (1971) *A History of Christianity in Japan,* Grand Rapids: Eerdmans.

Mullins, Mark (2000) *Christianity Made in Japan,* Honolulu: University of Hawai'i Press.

Nihon Kirisuto Kyodan Shi Hensan Iinkai Hen (1967) *Nihon Kirisuto Kyodan Shi (A History of the United Church of Christ in Japan)*, Tokyo: Nihon Kirisuto Kyodan Shuppanbu.

A. HAMISH ION

UNIVERSAL CHURCH OF THE KINGDOM OF GOD

The Universal Church of the Kingdom of God (UCKG) (Portugese: Igreja Universal do Reino do Deus or IURD) was founded in 1977, in Brazil, under the leadership of Edgir Macedo (see **Macedo, Edgir**). The first temple began in a small and modest locale (a funeral parlour), in a poor neighbourhood, in Rio de Janeiro. Like other NRMs (see **New Religious Movement**), it is very difficult to get exact data on the number of members. But in Brazil, with more than two thousand temples distributed over the entire country, it is one of the largest neo-Pentecostal churches. It is also present in every continents in around fifty countries.

The Temple

The buildings used are normally large. They are mostly ex-cinemas, and old factories no longer in use. These buildings have not undergone much change, and the churches are minimally decorated. However, new temples are now being built. The construction of the new 'Cathedrals' of São Paulo, Rio and Salvador, Bolivia, have already been achieved.

Self-presentation

This Church presents itself as open, happy and varied:

- Open: the doors are open permanently, and at all times people can find a pastor available to offer counselling in that it receives everyone, regardless of his or her social class, religion, sex, race/ethnic group, etc.
- Happy: because of the music played, which is usually of the popular kind; the great number and diversity of the hymns sung (accompanied by the clapping of hands), and the collective prayers. The informality of the pastor who seeks to establish direct communication between himself and the his followers also contributes to the happy atmosphere.
- Varied: by virtue of the diversity of the activities during the cult – prayer, sermons, hymns, speaking in tongues, music, dance, dialogue between the congregation/audience, collective exorcisms.

Prayers at the beginning, of a service, are used by the pastor to identify the probable day-to-day issues and problems of those present. The music supports the preacher's management of emotional expression, and also provides a vehicle for the expression of collective unity. The sermons are strongly influenced by the language of televangelism; it is very important to note that the

UCKG is the biggest 'electronic church' in Brazil (in 1989 it purchased the television network, TV Record).

There is a weekly cycle with the following daily themes:

- Monday – prosperity;
- Tuesday – health;
- Wednesday – 'children of God';
- Thursday – family;
- Friday – exorcisms;
- Saturday – Glory of God which addresses financial problems;
- Sunday morning – the Holy Spirit;
- Sunday afternoon – emotional problems.

Theological vision

The world-vision of UCKG in brief is as follows: once the heavens and earth were created by the Lord, creation suffered serious contamination due to the fall of Lucifer, who, with his angels, converted themselves into demons. The demons, who have no bodies of their own, require the bodies of humans. Their aim is to destroy and create difficulties for people. They constitute the general cause of suffering and of the evil in the world. The demonic forces cause people to lose control of their will, and thus, it is necessary to expel the Devil from them. Humans are not seen as sinners, but as the victims of the actions of demons. By means of Jesus Christ, the pastor can overcome demons and release people from their grip by exorcisms.

Another core element of the teaching is the indwelling of the Holy Spirit which fosters faith in the Trinity and in the word of the Bible.

Regarding the relationship between God and his creatures this resembles a contract, according to which the latter pay tithes and make offerings in order to obtain a favourable response from God.

Divine favour comes in the form of: spiritual blessing, physical health and economic well-being.

Sociological perspective

The following are some of the main reasons for the rapid expansion of UCKG:

- The stagnation of the Catholic Church, with the exception of the Charismatic Movement (see **Charismatic Movement**).
- The poverty of so many and its bitter consequences.
- The Church's temples are easily found and are often open with personnel available to attend to whoever wants to enter.
- Efficient marketing of printed material (books and the daily *Folha Universal* with a run of a million copies), radio 24 hours a day, and television programmes.
- The open, happy and varied nature of the ritual.
- The emphasis on physical and psychological illnesses and other real problems of daily life. The church promises to people material and spiritual help, and a radical change in their lives: the poor will have money, the sick will be healed. Furthermore, through the divine cure, all the followers will be freed from evil spirits by means of exorcism.

Conclusion

The Universal Church is the largest and most controversial religious movement in Brazil (see **New Religious Movement**). Moreover, it has also become an international religious phenomenon. In this era of increasing globalization, in the broad, complex, and competitive 'world spiritual supermarket', the UCKG clearly is providing a message, a style of being religious, and set of ritual techniques that millions find appealing.

Further reading

Rodrigues, D. (2002). *The God of the New Millennium* (preface: Bryan Wilson). Lisbon: Colibri.

DONIZETE RODRIGUES

UNIVERSAL HAGAR'S SPIRITUAL CHURCH

George Willie Hurley established one of the earliest African American Spiritual associations, namely the Universal Hagar's Spiritual Church. He was born in 1884, in Reynolds, Georgia. Although reared a Baptist and trained as a Baptist minister, after moving to Detroit in 1919, he joined Triumph the Church and Kingdom of God in Christ, a small black Holiness sect. Hurley was quickly elevated to the position of Elder in the sect and became its 'Presiding Prince' of Michigan. Sometime during the early 1920s, he became a preacher in the International Spiritual Church. Shortly thereafter, he had a vision in which a 'brown-skinned damsel', who turned into an eagle representing the church that he was to establish, appeared to him. Hurley started his church in Detroit on 23 September 1923. At the time of his death in 1943, the Universal Hagar's Spiritual Church had come to include at least thirty-seven congregations (eight in Michigan, eight in Ohio, six in Pennsylvania, seven in New Jersey, five in New York City, and single congregations in West Virginia, Delaware, and Illinois). In addition to fluctuations in membership, it has diffused to various other parts of the country, including California and the Southeast. Over the years, various men and women, including one of Hurley's daughters, have led the sect. Due to its esoteric orientation and emphasis on occult abilities, the Mediums' League is probably the most prestigious auxilary of the association.

Like other Spiritual groups, the Universal Hagar's Spiritual Church incorporates elements of Spiritualism, Catholicism, Protestantism, and possibly **Voodoo**. Hurley also incorporated concepts from the *Aquarian Gospel of Jesus Christ*, astrology, **New Thought**, messianic nationalism, into his sect. Sometime around 1933, if not earlier, he began to teach that his 'carnal flesh' had been transformed into the body of Christ. Just as Adam had been the God of the Taurian Age, Abraham the God of the Arian Age, and Jesus the God of the Piscean Age, Hurley preached that he was born to be God of the Aquarian Age (see **Age of Aquarius**) – a period of peace and social harmony. He taught his followers that the Spirit of God is embodied in every person and that black people were Ethiopians and the first human beings. In contrast to the apolitical stance of many Spiritual groups, Father Hurley took unequivocal stands on various issues, particularly the social structural status of African Americans in US society. At times, his writings suggest that the Aquarian Age will be one of black dominance. Although he was a virulent critic of racism, he rejected intermarriage between blacks and whites. He wanted blacks to obtain equal opportunities for social mobility within the US society and was a strong supporter of President Franklin D. Roosevelt.

Since Father Hurley's death the strong nationalist and reformist rhetoric of his church has not been eradicated but has been considerably muted. While he often cried out against racism, the writings and sermons of those who assumed his mantle of leadership have tended to be more inspirational and less political in tone. Nevertheless, each issue of the church's newsletter still carries one or more of the articles that Hurley wrote, on-going reminders that the sect's founder was a 'race man'.

Despite his passage to the 'spirit plane', Father Hurley's presence is still felt in the Hagar's temples. Members of the Universal Hagar's Spiritual Church direct their prayers, petitions for help and guidance, and hymns before images of their God, as well as to Mother Hurley, his spouse, and other 'patriarchs', and 'prophets' who are now in the spirit world. Although Hurleyites do not wear a distinctive type of garb in everyday settings, as do certain African American Islamic and Judaic groups, they do – like the latter – observe certain strict dietary prohibitions. Included among these are abstinence from pork, black tea, coffee, and tobacco. Conversely, the consumption of alcoholic beverages, which are sometimes served at church banquets, is permissible in moderation. Hurleyites also drink a variety of herbal teas, including a special blend called 'Father Hurley tea'. As Muslims enjoin that a believer should pray to Allah five times a day, Hurley instructed his followers recite the following prayer seven times each day – four times at 7 a.m. and three times at 7 p.m.: 'Saint Hurley is my Lord and the Christ, within him is my Savior and my helper each day in every way. I feel the Christ within St. Hurley's body. Through Saint Hurley the Christ I am headed for success, financially and industrially, and I am now happy through Christ alone. Amen. Amen. Amen.'

Like ministers and mediums in the Spiritual movement, Hurley provided the saints of his earthly kingdom with a wide array of magico-religious rituals by which they could attempt to gain control over their destinies. Instead of political-economic solutions, he promised metaphysical power. Hurley also provided his followers with an elaborate political-religious organization of offices and auxiliaries within which they could achieve a religious status far greater than the humble positions that most of them occupied in the larger society.

Further reading

Baer, H. A. (2001) *The Black Spiritual Movement: A Religious Response to Racism* (2nd edition), Knoxville: University of Tennessee Press.

HANS A. BAER

UNIVERSAL SOUL

Roberto Casarin founder of Universal Soul was born in Turin on 9 April 1963 and experienced unusual phenomena and gifts of healing when still a youth. His most tireless activity was preaching and the public recital of the Rosary, as well as daily meetings with the many sick people who had faith in his thaumaturgical powers. There was also talk of miracles, visions, and contact with the dead. All this was disapproved by the Church in Turin which, in 1982, issued a statement by Cardinal Anastasio Alberto Ballestrero OCD (1913–98) forbidding prayer meetings or religious rites associated with young Roberto Casarin, in diocesan places of worship. The Christ in Man Association – Center of Spiritual Elevation, was founded on 26 February 1984.

During these years, Casarin taught his own form of spiritual thought, which proposed overcoming the concept of religion as a 'division' and a 'cultural barrier,' in favor of an ideal addressed to the 'God of all people'. Starting in 1985, and based on Casarin's own teachings, the movement became more and more explicitly an authentic spiritual experience, with no ties to the Catholic Church. A number of more active members later created the Pledge Community within the Association, thus laying the foundation for the birth of the Church of New Jerusalem in 1989. The movement's separation from the Catholic Church was confirmed by a statement issued on 21 March 1990 by Cardinal Giovanni Saldarini, Cardinal Ballestrero's successor as Archbishop of Turin.

The Church of New Jerusalem was the target of criticism from Catholic circles, including a former member of the movement who became its militant critic, and the press. The role of women and sexual morality are prominent aspects of such hostile reports, although these elements play no major role in the group's publications. In 1996, the Church of New Jerusalem changed its name to one considered closer to the spiritual activities it performed: namely 'Universal Soul – Movement of Spiritual Union'.

The Universal Soul cult is monotheistic. Man is a spiritual being who must rediscover his divine origin beyond the veil of material illusion, seeking to develop goodness, love of God and of others, and his own spiritual growth. Its celebratory rites include baptisms, weddings, funerals, meditation and prayer meetings, 'rituals with the elements' and the 'celebration of mantra'. The ministrants are 'Ramia' (priests of the Universal Soul, both men and women), who live in communities constituting 'Centers of the Universal Soul' where they carry out their mission. The Centers hold prayer meetings, offer help to those who suffer, conduct courses in 'ramiric' meditation and sacred dance, and organize sports, recreational, and cultural activities. The common denominator is considered to be the 'cure of the Spirit,' which leads one to fight suffering and loneliness. The Church's headquarters is in Leinì (Turin), where the faithful, who come from such countries as Switzerland, France and Germany, meet every week. There are two other Centers in Turin and Poggiana di Riese Pio X (Treviso). In 1999–2000, construction of the Temple in Poggiana generated new disputes. To the outside observer, the conflict would appear to be somewhat paradoxical, bearing in mind that Universal Soul and its Catholic critics seem to agree on essentials, i.e. on the fact that the movement founded by Roberto Casarin proposes a religious experience all its own, different and separate from that of the Catholic Church.

Further reading

Roldán, V. (2000) *La Chiesa Anima Universale di Roberto Casarin*, Leumann (Turin): Elledici.

PierLuigi Zoccatelli

UNIVERSELLES LEBEN

Founder: Gabriele Wittek
Country of origin: Germany

Gabriele Wittek (1933–) was born in 1933 near Augsburg, Germany, and raised as a traditional Roman Catholic. In 1970, her mother's death precipitated in her a spiritual crisis of some impact. Later, we are told, Wittek's deceased mother started to appear to her daughter, until on 6 January 1975, Gabriele began to hear the 'internal word'. Within this 'word' she received instructions from 'Brother Emmanuel' and the Christ himself, asking her to spread their teachings (increasingly at odds with Wittek's early Catholicism), at first to small groups, and then in large meetings in Europe's main cities, the first being held in Nürnberg on 22 January 1977. In 1976, her followers founded the *Heimholungswerk Jesu Christi* ('Homebringing Mission of Jesus Christ'), which in 1984 was renamed *Universelles Leben* ('Universal Life').

The movement claims to re-enact the original Christianity of the apostles in the modern world, on the basis of the Ten Commandments and Jesus' Sermon on the Mount. Members believe that the Holy Spirit is speaking again through their new prophet, who teaches what she calls an 'internal way', rooted in the idea of the soul's pre-existence in the spiritual world. Our present material world, ruled by the law of reincarnation, is not part of God's original plan, but the consequence of the sin of a group of angels. Because of their pride, the original souls also fell outside the divine realm, and are now subject to reincarnation in the material world. Based on *karma*, the soul should experience several incarnations, until it becomes purified and able to escape the wheel of reincarnation. In Wittek's universalist theology, mainline Christian notions of eternal punishment and Hell are also rejected.

In order to remind the souls of their divine origin, the Son of God was incarnated as Jesus of Nazareth. Jesus was not originally destined to die, and chose a redemptive death only when he was rejected by the majority of his would-be followers. He will soon become incarnate again. According to Wittek, all these teachings were originally included in the Bible, but have been corrupted by the churches throughout the centuries, thus making it necessary for the Holy Spirit to speak again in our time through Universelles Leben.

Some 700 members of Universelles Leben live communally near Würzburg, Germany, in a large community complex including a school, two hospitals, retirement homes, as well as manufacturing and agricultural facilities. This community is regarded as the first seed of Christ's future kingdom of peace on earth, and includes an international healing center. A further several thousand members, however, do not live in the Würzburg community but regularly visit some eighty centers throughout Germany, other parts of Europe, and the world. Universelles Leben also owns several radio networks worldwide.

Further reading

Universal Life (2001) *This Is My Word, Alpha and Omega: The Gospel of Jesus – A Christ-Revelation which the world does not know*, 2nd English Edition. Guilford (Connecticut): The Word.

MASSIMO INTROVIGNE

V

VAJRAYĀNA BUDDHISM

Vajrayāna, the 'Vehicle' (or 'Way'; *yāna*) of the 'Thunderbolt' (or 'Diamond'; *vajra*) is an expression that overlaps with 'tantric Buddhism' (see **Tantra**). This is in its broadest sense the employment within a Buddhist context of ritual magic to attain worldly goals, and even Buddhahood itself.

As far as we can tell, the use of some forms of ritual magic was always part of Buddhist practice. Buddhist monks were religious specialists who sought to serve their local communities in exchange for material support. With the rise of **Mahāyāna Buddhism**, that doctrinally emphasizes acting for the welfare of all sentient beings, the involvement of Buddhist monks too with ritual magic became more pronounced. Nevertheless at this stage tantric Buddhism was known not as 'Vajrayāna', but simply as *Mantrayana* – the path of using *mantras* (see **Mantra**), verbal formulae considered to have power to bring about

magically certain results such as good health, or the success of the crops. It involved the employment of the full range of techniques to aid the welfare of sentient beings.

The earliest Buddhist written works that might be said to be specifically tantric date from about the second century CE. Already we find here the use of ritual diagrams (*maṇḍala*) and mantras, together with special hand-gestures (*mudrā*), in order to bring about magically a desired result. What marks a great conceptual and practical shift, however, is the appearance within Buddhism (from perhaps the seventh century CE) of texts that specifically employ tantric ritual techniques not only for bringing about worldly goals, but for attaining Buddhahood itself. Hence we come to 'Vajrayāna' properly speaking. These texts are supposedly secret and necessitate initiation and a close relationship with a teacher (***guru***). They centre on identification of the practitioner with a Buddha. In fact, true to their ritual magical context, they frequently employ a whole series of identifications often based on the figure five (microcosmically in the *maṇḍalas*, and hence corresponding macrocosmically in the universe, with the four directions and the Buddha – oneself – in the centre). Tantric texts of this type rest on the idea that all reality is truly the play of the enlightened mind of a Buddha. Thus one's own mind too is actually identical with the Buddha's mind. One is oneself already a Buddha, and all is thereby the play of one's own enlightened awareness. The world can therefore be manipulated in order to assist others. It is sometimes held, or implied, that even suggesting one has to realize this at some deeper level involves a conceptual duality that is unreal and hence blocks Buddhahood. It is only necessary to *express* one's own intrinsic Buddhahood.

It is held that such tantric practice can lead to Buddhahood particularly quickly. This is because here the practitioner visualizes from the beginning that he or she is already a Buddha (= 'deity yoga'), rather than practising in order to become a Buddha. Through learning to work on levels of the human psychophysical organism not normally activated this identity which one has already with the Buddha comes to be actualized through its expression. Features of tantric Buddhism that begin to emerge or become more significant from this time are the employment of transgressive acts, such as ritually consuming impure substances (e.g. various meats, including human flesh, or urine, and faeces), or ritual sexual intercourse. The emergence of these is partly associated with the idea that one is already enlightened and therefore beyond dualistic categories of pure/impure, right/wrong, and so on. But the sexual element is also related to theories concerning the mutual relationship between human physiology and mental states. Its place within the path to enlightenment was linked to ancient Indian speculations on the structure of the psychophysical human organism. Thus certain physical activities, when carried out by one who understands the correct technique, can influence the mind in a way that can be harnessed to the enlightenment path. For example, orgasm properly channelled releases the 'great bliss' (*mahāsukha*) that is, or can be used for generating, the enlightened mind of the Buddha.

It is the whole organism that has to be transformed into a Buddha's body and mind. Three important implications follow: First, the human body becomes revalued, as of crucial importance instead of a hindrance to the spiritual path. Second, women are seen as crucial to practice. And third, with the use of sexuality comes a revaluation of other mental states held by wider Buddhism to be negative, particularly desire. Such mental states are just so much powerful energy that, precisely because they are so powerful, are capable of being harnessed by the one who knows as expressing (or to attain) his enlightened nature. The exact place of tantric sexual practice in realizing or expressing one's enlightened nature was however a subject of intense debate within late Indian Buddhism since in particular it would involve breaking monastic precepts of celibacy.

The Buddhas of these Vajrayāna tantric texts and practices are frequently portrayed as fierce beings, with ornaments of human bones and severed heads. They frequent cremation grounds, and are commonly in sexual union with a female partner. They are surrounded by their *maṇḍala*. This is the world, represented as a palace in a cremation ground, polarized around (or expressing) their own enlightened minds. The imagery shows obvious ('Hindu') Śaivite influence. The female element is a trans-position of Śiva's consort Pārvatī or Kālī in her various forms. The evidence is now convincing that at least some of these Vajrayāna tantric ritual contexts originated among Śaivite ascetics.

The fierce form of these Buddhas was explained through myths by which a normally benign Buddha manifests this wrathful form to bring about a parti-cular beneficial goal. Since tantric prac-tice of this type is held to be particularly rapid means of attaining Buddhahood, there appears also to have been debate within Buddhism as to whether it is necessary at this level to employ any other Buddhist practices and study at all. Hence the notion of 'Vajrayāna' as a self-contained path for the suitably qualified, in specific opposition to other *yānas* within Buddhism, such as Mahā-yāna or the so-called 'Hīnayāna'. Not surprisingly there were also those who felt that the importation of tantric prac-tice into soteriology was simply (mainly Śaivite) 'Hinduism' and not Buddhism at all.

With the notion of intrinsic enlight-enment, the figure of the enlightened *yogin* who is beyond all duality comes to the fore. He (or she) is a *siddha*, 'one who has attained', an expression refer-ring to the attainment not just of Bud-dhahood but also of the ability to manipulate 'everyday reality' in order to bring about miraculous feats. Vaj-rayāna is replete with stories of enligh-tened practitioners whose behaviour is unexpected, indeed apparently crazy, for those still bound to dualistic conven-tions. With the growing assimilation of Vajrayāna into mainstream Mahāyāna we find the idea that although the enlightened practitioner is beyond all duality nevertheless he (or she) is really acting for the benefit of others. He may well behave in an apparently crazy way, or do things normally considered immoral, but this is beyond all judge-ment by the unenlightened.

In the modern world tantric Buddhism is most prevalent within Tibetan Bud-dhism, where it is said to be the esoteric or secret wing of the Buddhist path. It is also found in East Asia, notably in some Chinese Buddhist rituals and in Japan (particularly Shingon). The tantric Bud-dhism that is encountered nowadays in these forms represents the emergence over many centuries of an integration of tantric elements with broader (or 'exo-teric') Mahāyāna Buddhism.

Further reading

Cozort, D. (1986) *Highest Yoga Tantra*, Ithaca, NY: Snow Lion.

PAUL WILLIAMS

VALIENTE, DOREEN
(b. 1922; d. 1999)

Doreen Valiente was one of the key fig-ures in the development of modern **Wicca**, and a well-respected witch. She was born in London and later lived in Sussex with her husband Casimiro Valiente, a refugee from the Spanish Civil War (d. 1972). Aware of her clair-voyant abilities, Doreen Valiente read Dion Fortune (see **Fortune, Dion**) and Aleister Crowley (see **Crowley, Aleister**) before meeting Gerald Gardner (see **Gardner, Gerald**) in 1952. She was initi-ated by Gardner in 1953 and worked with him as his High Priestess in the New Forest Coven. Over time, she revised his Book of Shadows to remove extensive passages written by Crowley, re-writing the Charge of the Goddess to which she added the Charge of the God much later, in 1997. She thus acted as an influential force in the formation of Gardnerian Wicca, but Gardner's increasing seeking after publicity as the

1950s drew on and his attempt to impose self-authored 'Laws' of the craft eventually led to mutiny in the coven; Valiente and other members left and went their separate ways in 1957.

After Gardner's death in 1964, Valiente met Robert Cochrane who claimed to be a hereditary witch, and worked with his Clan of Tubal Cain coven. She broke with Cochrane in 1966 having become disillusioned by his fabrications and annoyed by his attacks on Gardnerian witches through the *Pentagram*, journal of the short-lived Witchcraft Research Association formed in 1964.

Valiente periodically withdrew from the public face of witchcraft, but was consistent in her support for what she called the 'Old Religion'. In 1964 she gave the inaugural speech at the launch of the *Pentragram*, and in 1971 she was a founder member of the Pagan Front, which later became the **Pagan Federation**. In November 1998, just ten months before her death, she spoke at the annual Pagan Federation conference in London. Her life within Wicca, witchcraft and Paganism is documented in her books *The Rebirth of Witchcraft*, *Witchcraft for Tomorrow*, and *Witchcraft: A Tradition Renewed* (with Evan Jones).

Further reading

Valiente, D. (1989) *The Rebirth of Witchcraft*, Washington: Phoenix Publishing Inc.

JO PEARSON

VEDANTA SOCIETY

Founded in 1894 in New York, the Vedanta Society was the only Hindu organization to be established in the West before the twentieth century. Its principles are based primarily on the teachings of Ramakrishna (1836–86) (see **Ramakrishna, Sri**) and Vivekananda (1862–1902) (see **Vivekananda, Swami**).

Ramakrishna was born in a Bengali village, and became a Kali priest in the Calcutta area; he is reckoned to have attained *samadhi* (enlightenment), and continued to quest, using a number of *sadhanas* – spiritual paths to gain a permanently enlightened state. Ramakrishna believed that Kali wanted him to remain on the threshold between the Absolute and the relative (the physical world in which humanity resides) in order to act as a vehicle to draw the human to the divine. He also taught that all spiritual paths, including Hinduism, lead to the same goal, and that all forms of the divine are one and the same. In addition to seeking spiritual enlightenment, Ramakrishna and his followers emphasized the importance of social service.

Vivekananda was a disciple of Ramakrishna, and one of the first Hindu gurus to come to the West. He arrived in 1893, with the aim of spreading Ramakrishna's teachings, and he addressed the World's Parliament of Religions in Chicago in 1893, where he attracted considerable interest. In 1894 Vivekananda founded the Vedanta Society in New York, and within two years two further branches were established in San Francisco and Boston.

Vedanta is one of the six major schools (*astikas*) of Hindu philosophy. The word literally means the 'end of the Vedas', referring to the classical Hindu writings that came after the four ancient Vedic texts (the Rig Veda, the Sama Veda, the Artharva Veda and the Yajur Veda). Vedanta draws primarily on the Upanishads, which the Vedanta Society emphasizes, together with the Bhagavad Gita, and Patanjali's Yoga Sutras. The principal teachings of the Vedanta Society include the classical Hindu teaching that *brahman* (the divine substance that underlies and sustains the universe) is identical with the *atman* (human soul). God is 'being, consciousness and bliss', and, although ultimately impersonal, is capable of taking on personal forms, as is taught by the Hindu *bhakti* tradition. All the different forms of God are ultimately forms of the same divine substance, and hence are all one.

The recognition of the unity between the self and the divine leads to the manifestation of love. Ethically, the notion of oneness provides the key to living: one's actions must be done, mindful of one's oneness with the divine, and also with all living beings, since each is the eternal. As the Isa Upanishad teaches, 'The Self is everywhere'. The failure of humans to recognize this oneness is due to *maya* (illusion), but the mind can be trained to know the absolute reality and to remove the perceived separateness between the divine and human. This is achieved by the purification of mind, principally through four *yogas* (spiritual paths): *bhakti* (devotion), *jnana* (intellectual discrimination), *karma* (unselfish work) and *prana* (psychic control).

The Society does not demand conversion from any other religion or school of Hinduism, teaching, as it does, that all religions are ultimately one. All religions, if understood aright, teach the truth: while it is acknowledged that there are doctrinal differences among religions, truth is filtered through the human mind, and perceived differences are due to *maya*: ultimately, each religion points to the same shared spiritual experience. (However, the Vedanta Society teaches the doctrine of karma and reincarnation.) Each religion has its own distinctive contribution to make: Christianity emphasizes sacrifice, Judaism tradition and wisdom, Islam fraternity and equality, Buddhism mindfulness and compassion, Native American religion respect for the earth, and Vedanta the oneness of all things.

The Society's principles are regarded as more important than a *parampara,* or lineage of gurus, although it permits instruction from accredited teachers, and even the veneration of Ramakrishna as an *avatar* ('descent' or incarnation of the divine), if followers consider it appropriate.

A number of prominent western followers helped to spread the ideas of Vedanta. These include Aldous Huxley (1894–1963), whose edited collection *The Perennial Philosophy* (1955) is regarded as a spiritual classic, Gerald Heard (1889–1971), whose many writings include *The Ascent of Humanity* (1929) and *The Eternal Gospel* (1948), and Christopher Isherwood (1904–86), who wrote *Vedanta for the Western World* in 1945. The Vedanta Society attracts its following principally in the United States and in India: by the end of the twentieth century some 3,000 members were estimated in the USA. The Society also has branches in the Argentine, Bangladesh, Brazil, Canada, England, France, Germany, Japan, Singapore, and Sri Lanka.

Further reading

Huxley, A. (1955) *The Perennial Philosophy*, New York: Harper and Row.
Isherwood, C. (1945) *Vedanta for the Western World*, New York: Viking.

GEORGE CHRYSSIDES

VEGETARIANISM

The avoidance of meat is a common feature of religious practice and observance, from ancient and great religious traditions such as Hinduism to small sects and religious movements. Seventh Day Adventism strongly advocates it, UFO 'cults' such as the **Aetherius Society** practice it as do those New Religious Movements of Indian provenance such as the **International Society for Krishna Consciousness**, and it is extremely prevalent among devotees of **New Age Movement**s. Vegetarianism not associated with any particular set of religious beliefs, especially when motivated by ethical concerns, is also often perceived as having underlying religious, quasi-religious or, at least, spiritual overtones.

Vegetarianism in the general sense is, of course, not an organized movement or activity but a matter of individual, personal choice and practice. However, it exhibits a number of attributes which might be said to be religious or spiritual.

Vegetarianism as taboo behaviour

A striking aspect of accounts of the process of conversion to vegetarianism is the frequently reported experience of revulsion towards meat that accompanies it or results from it (Amato and Partridge, 1989: 70–1; Beardsworth and Keil, 1992: 267–8).

Such sentiments suggest that a type of belief and behaviour commonly regarded as religious in nature that might also be applied to vegetarianism is perhaps that of taboo and ritual avoidance.

A feature of things which are commonly tabooed is that they are anomalous with respect to categories and boundaries (Douglas, 1966) because such things are seen as having a special power associated either with the sacred or with impurity and that which is polluting. Meat, especially red meat and its bloodiness, is, according to Twigg (1979, 1983), a particularly anomalous and powerful substance. This idea might be extended to animals in general situated as they are on the boundary between culture and nature, the human and the non-human, especially mammals which are warm and red blooded, copulate, give birth to live young which they suckle and which manifestly experience pain.

Reverence for life

Ethical vegetarianism expresses a rejection of violence and is traditionally associated with pacifism as well as a host of unorthodox, radical and oppositional stances. It extols reverence for all life like our own by abstaining from acts of violence towards other sentient living things. This might be seen as quasi-religious in that it appears to be as much motivated by the need to define what it is to be human as it is from concern with the welfare of animals. Further, meat in itself may operate for vegetarians as a symbol of violence which in being rejected expresses symbolically a reverence for life.

Denial of death

Vegetarianism may also express a denial and rejection of death. Meat may symbolize not only violence and aggression but also death. Blood and the shedding of blood in particular is a symbol of death. For ethical vegetarians it stands as a horrific reminder of the pain and suffering of the animal. This is, perhaps, why many people stop short of full vegetarianism and only avoid eating red meat.

Death is problematic in a culture which places a heavy emphasis upon this-worldly pleasures and pursuits, bodily health, fitness and attractiveness which the unpalatable fact of inevitable death threatens. That which reminds us of death tends to be tabooed and avoided; meat, from the dismembered carcass, presages one's own death and decomposition.

Discipline and observance

Religions throughout the world impose certain disciplines and observances upon their followers often involving dietary practices. Vegetarianism might be seen as a form of observance that expresses the identity and moral standing of the individual and his or her apartness and distinctiveness. There is a sectarian tinge to vegetarianism associated, perhaps, with a sense of moral superiority. This concern to be among the select is demonstrated in the hierarchy of status and prestige that seems to obtain between vegetarians, vegans, and at the very top fruitarians, reflecting the hierarchy of foods themselves defined by Twigg (1983) in terms of a reversal of the status these foods have in the dominant meat-eating culture.

Rejection of domination and repression

As a symbol of violence meat also symbolizes domination. According to Fiddes (1991) meat symbolizes human power over nature and vegetarianism represents a move away from the desire to subject nature to human control.

Alternatively meat might be thought to symbolize the social power of the wealthy and those with high status since until the modern period it was an expensive food which the mass of the population could rarely afford to eat. In Europe meat was associated with the militaristic and hunting culture of the aristocracy. The rise of vegetarianism may reflect a progressive movement away not only from this culture of violence but from the values of domination and hierarchy.

It is the symbolic association of meat with masculinity and violence which leads Adams (1990) to interpret red meat as a symbol of male dominance over women and of patriarchy. However, this view neglects the fact that meat consumption was a class and status symbol rather than a gender related matter.

In conclusion, while several aspects of vegetarianism may have religious or spiritual associations it has to be acknowledged that such sentiments are clearly not in the forefront of vegetarians' minds nor overt aspects of their motivation, a fact which should make us cautious about the claims outlined previously.

Further reading

Adams, C. J. (1990) *The Sexual Politics of Meat: A Feminist-Vegetarian Critical Theory*, Polity: Cambridge.

Amato, P. R. and Partridge, S. A. (1989) *The New Vegetarians: Promoting Health and Preserving Life*, New York: Plenum Press.

Beardsworth, A. D. and Keil, E. T. (1992) 'The Vegetarian Option: Varieties, Conversions, Motives and Careers', *Sociological Review*, 40(2), 253–93.

Douglas, M. (1966) *Purity and Danger. An Analysis of Concepts of Pollution and Taboo*, London: Allen and Unwin.

Fiddes, N. (1991) *Meat: A Natural Symbol*, London: Routledge.

M. B. Hamilton (2000) 'Eating Ethically: "Spiritual" and "quasi-religious" aspects of Vegetarianism', *Journal of Contemporary Religion*, 15(1), 65–83.

Twigg, J. (1979) 'Food for thought: purity and vegetarianism', *Religion*, 9, Spring, 13–35.

Twigg, J. (1983) 'Vegetarianism and the meaning of meat', in A. Murcott (ed.) *The Sociology of Food and Eating*, Aldershot: Gower.

MALCOLM HAMILTON

VINEYARD MINISTRIES

The Vineyard movement emerged out of California in the 1970s. Kenn Gulliksen launched his church in Costa Mesa in 1974, with low-key, guitar-led worship in members' homes, simple Bible teaching, and a faith in the power of the Holy Spirit to produce both miraculous healings and church growth. Three years later, John Wimber (1934–97), a one-time professional musician and Quaker convert, established a charismatic congregation in Yorba Linda. Wimber had been a church growth consultant for the Fuller Evangelistic Association and, through his contact with C. Peter Wagner, became interested in the role of the Holy Spirit in facilitating the growth and nurture of churches. Moreover, Wimber – like Gulliksen – made sense of the exponential expansion of his own church – ballooning to some 1,500 members in just five years – in terms of the charismatic gifts regularly manifest among the congregation.

Both Gulliksen and Wimber associated themselves with the Calvary Chapel churches, a network led by Chuck Smith which had emerged out of the **Jesus Movement**. Despite his background in the Foursquare Pentecostal church, Smith did not support the expression of **glossolalia**, prophecy and healing in public worship, and in 1982 the two churches formally separated from Calvary. The newly formed Vineyard was to be led by John Wimber, who remained its figurehead and spokesperson until his death in 1997.

The Vineyard has subsequently been marked by rapid expansion both across the USA and abroad. The eight Vineyards of 1982 had grown to 120 within three years, some with congregations of several thousand. According to its website, in 2002, the movement had over 500 Vineyards in the USA and was active in a further seventy countries, boasting thirteen churches in Sweden, twenty-one in New Zealand and seventy in the UK. Wimber's influence has also spread through his 'signs and wonders' conferences and numerous publications, particularly popular among charismatics across the denominations in the UK. In this respect, the theology of the Vineyard has spread far beyond its institutional boundaries.

Popular Vineyard teaching adheres to a fundamentalist framework which stresses the immanence of the supernatural realm. It retains a classically evangelical emphasis upon Biblical authority (see **Evangelical Christianity**), the need for a personal relationship with Jesus and the costly nature of practical Christian living. But while the Bible is generally taken to be without error, the authority of passages is legitimated through the charismatic experience of individuals. Moreover, the Vineyard moves beyond the charismatic renewal movement in linking charismata more explicitly with a theology of mission. In this respect, evangelical strands of Biblical authority, charismatic gifts and evangelism are fused into a radical new package.

This is grounded in John Wimber's teaching which, following George Eldon Ladd's dualistic kingdom theology, places an overriding emphasis upon power. Wimber sees the kingdom of God as an invasive force, to be demonstrated in miraculous deeds as well as verbal preaching. According to Wimber, these 'signs and wonders' demonstrate God's power in the present, serving as a divine witness and opening up outsiders to the truth of the Gospel. Charismatic gifts are also treated as a source of empowerment against evil spirits and physical ailments, enemies to be confronted in 'spiritual warfare'. At Vineyard services, charismatic episodes are often dramatic and emotional, occasionally taking on bizarre forms, and it was at a Vineyard church that the **Toronto Blessing** first emerged in 1994. While the 'blessing' quickly spread all over the charismatic world, its intensity provoked significant suspicion and eventually Wimber dissociated himself and the Vineyard church from the Toronto phenomenon.

Vineyard ministries also reflect a wider evangelical movement, which sees cultural relevance as the key to successful evangelism. Accordingly, while theologically conservative, Vineyards are progressive in their ecclesiology, fostering loose organizational structures and encouraging lay leadership. At services, sung worship is exuberant but laid back, accompanied by light pop music, and sermons are light-hearted, illustrative, and informal. This reflects a conscious effort to engage with popular cultural trends, overcoming the formality and disconnectedness of a moribund mainstream church. Vineyard worship also stresses intimacy and the lyrics of its choruses depict the divine: human relationship in terms that stress feeling, familiarity and emotion. While notably popular (see above), the Vineyard appeals to a rather narrow cohort, resonating most with the culture of middle class, educated professionals. In this it reflects the Neo-Pentecostal movement, while its teachings on 'signs and wonders' place it firmly within the 'third wave' of charismatic renewal.

Further reading

Miller, D. E. (1997) *Reinventing American Protestantism: Christianity in the New Millenium*, Berkeley and Los Angeles: University of California Press.

Percy, M. (1996) *Words, Wonders and Power, Understanding Contemporary Christian Fundamentalism and Revivalism*, London: SPCK.

MATHEW GUEST

VIPASSANA

In contrast with *samatha* meditation, which aims at calming the mind, Vipassana ('insight meditation') is a form of Theravada Buddhist (see **Theravada Buddhism**) meditation, which aims at experiencing the true nature of reality, which is the prerequisite for nirvana. In particular, Vipassana directs the student to meditate on Buddhism's three 'marks of existence' – *anatta* (insubstantiality, the absence of a permanent enduring self or soul), *anicca* (impermanence), and *dukkha* (unsastisfactoriness) – which, according to Buddhist teaching, are the three fundamental characteristics of the world.

Although there is no evidence for the Vipassana movement's claim that the Buddha himself taught the practice, it is an ancient technique, but died out in the fourteenth century. In 1914 it was rediscovered by the Burmese monk, Ledi Sayadaw (1856–1923), who wrote a treatise on it, aimed at European students. Being written in Burmese, however, the treatise made little impact. The practice gained momentum in Burma and Thailand, where U Narada (1868–1955), U Kyaw Din (1878–1952) and U Ba Kin (1899–1971) promoted it. Maharsi Sayadaw (1904–82) and S. N. Goenka (b. 1924) are particularly noteworthy for teaching it to western students, and interest grew from the 1950s. Sayadaw's students included Jack Kornfield, Joseph Goldstein, Sharon Salzburg and Christopher Titmuss, who are the leading exponents of the practice in the West, and who founded the Insight Meditation Society in Barre, Massachusetts in 1976. Other organizations that teach the practice include the Dhiravamsa Foundation (formerly the Vipassana Fellowship of America); the English Sangha Trust, headed by the American monk, the Ven. Sumedho, also teaches Vipassana.

Although the present-day practice is believed to be a revival of the ancient one, there are a number of significant innovations. The Vipassana movement is currently taught by lay Buddhists as well as monks, with female as well as male teachers and practitioners; the practices are available in written form, in contrast with traditional oral teaching.

Further reading

Goldstein, J. (1976) *The Experience of Insight*, Boulder, CO: Shambhala.
Kornfield, J. (1977) *Living Buddhist Masters*, Kandy, Sri Lanka: Buddhist Publication Society.

GEORGE CHRYSSIDES

VISHVA HINDU PARISHAD

The Vishva Hindu Parishad (*World Hindu Council*) is one of the offshoots of the Rashtriya Swayamsevak Sangh (National Volunteer Organization – RSS). Founded in 1925, the RSS evolved a nationalist ideology in which the Indian identity was epitomized by Hindu culture: other communities had to be assimilated into it, or lend allegiance to it. Hindu nationalism (or *Hindutva*), in fact, borrows a great deal from its enemies, Islam and Christianity. This is especially evident from the *modus operandi* of the VHP, an organization which had been formed in the 1960s for federating the Hindu sects in order to resist Islam and Christianity more effectively by emulating them, and then got involved in ethno-religious mobilizations with political overtones in the 1980s.

A nationalist attempt to federate the Hindu sects

The first project director of the VHP, Shiv Shankar Apte, a leader of the RSS and a former journalist, published articles on the necessity of bringing together all the currents of Hinduism in order to effectuate a greater coherence in 1961. The same idea was entertained by another former journalist, Swami Chinmayananda, a *sadhu* (world renouncer)

who had established his *ashram* in Bombay, gate to Westernized India: Chinmayananda was a modern **guru** preaching in English for the urban middle class – he was to lecture throughout the world.

Apte and Chinmayananda, who decided to join hands in 1963, exemplified the two groups which were to form the keystone of the VHP: Hindu nationalists and modern gurus. Apte, in effect, undertook to contact the greatest possible number of sect leaders with a view to founding the VHP, in 1964; but he mostly rallied modern gurus and very few leaders of traditional Hindu *sampradâya* (historical sects).

In August 1964 the Pope announced that the International Eucharistic Conference was to be held in November in Bombay. It had a catalysing effect on the efforts of Apte and Chinmayanana who considered that Christian proselytism constituted a threat to Hinduism, and that it was therefore necessary to endeavour to emulate its techniques so as to offer more effective resistance.

The VHP was created on 29 August 1964. It was then decided to organize a large international conference in Allahabad on the occasion of the Kumbh Mela in 1966, in which 'the learned of all sects' were to participate. However, among the 25,000 delegates, at least as many modern gurus were to be found as spiritual masters initiated and invested according to the rules of sects with an ancient tradition. Despite its poor representiveness, the meeting in Allahabad was intended to be a kind of parliament and consistory of Hinduism. It decided to simplify the rites of purification and to elaborate a Hindu code of conduct. In January 1979, a second World Hindu Conference was once again held in Allahabad, under the auspices of the VHP. This time, the different currents of the 'Hindu nation' were represented: Buddhism by the **Dalai Lama**, who inaugurated the conference; the Namdhari Sikhs (see **Namdhari**) and the Jains by two dignitaries from those communities; the disciples of Shankara by the Shankaracharya of Badrinath; the 'dualists' by two Jagadgurus from Udupi; and the Nimbarkhis, the Vallabhis, the different schools and disciples of Ramanuja, the Ramanandis, the disciples of Chaitanya, those of Kabir, the Naths of Gorakhpur, the Arya Samajists (see **Arya Samaj**), the **Ramakrishna Mission** and the Divine Life Society, by various personalities.

The VHP again proposed a 'minimum code of conduct for the daily life of every Hindu', the objective of which was a unification of religious practices and references. Article 1 called for the veneration by all, morning and evening, of the sun; Article 2, for the systematization of the symbol 'Om' (on lockets, visiting cards, etc.); and, Article 3 was yet more explicit since it intended to transform the *Bhagavad Gita* as *the* book of the Hindus, regardless of their sect. In 1981, the VHP strengthened its Central Margdarshak Mandal (Central circle of those 'who show the way'), the members of which were 'to conduct and guide religious ceremonies, morals and ethics of Hindu society'. The VHP leaders also founded a Sadhu Sansad (Parliament of *Sadhus*) which became, in 1984, a Dharma Sansad comprising hundreds of participants.

The Hindu nationalist identity which developed according to this logic did not appear to be very loyal to Hinduism, insofar as it borrowed from Christianity attributes which are alien to it, such as a centralized ecclesiastical structure, a uniform catechism or proselytizing practices.

However, the VHP succeeded in implanting its network throughout India. Traditional notables agreed to patronize the organization as they had always done with religious figures. Former Maharajahs and industrialists have often been appointed president of the VHP, for instance, a tradition which served to enhance its respectability.

Ethno-religious mobilization and politicization

The Vishva Hindu Parishad became the spearhead of Hindu nationalism in the early 1980s, primarily because the RSS decided to make it the principal means of action in politics after it had distanced itself from its party, the Bharatiya Janata Party, which was too moderate for its taste.

The Allahabad conference, in 1979, inaugurated a long-term strategic reorientation of the RSS. It benefited from the sentiment of Hindu vulnerability resulting from the conversions, in Meenakshipuram (Tamil Nadu) of several hundred Untouchables to Islam in 1981. The VHP sponsored Hindu Solidarity Conferences in order to resist these mass conversions and then organized a pan-Indian campaign in November 1983, the Ekatmata Yatra (literally, 'pilgrimage of unity') consisting of three caravans connecting Kathmandu and Rameshwaram (Tamil Nadu), Gangasagar (Bengal) and Somnath (Gujarat), and Haridwar (Uttar Pradesh), and Kanyakumari (Tamil Nadu). These were joined by sixty-nine other caravans which distributed water from the Ganges and provided everyone with sacred water from local temples or from other sacred rivers encountered on the way. This mingling was intended to symbolize Hindu unity. All the caravans converged, moreover, in Nagpur, centre of the RSS and of India.

This Yatra manipulated symbols very judiciously. The Ganges – river of salvation – constitutes one of the rare symbols venerated by all Hindus. The movement tried to transcend caste and sect divisions by associating with it members from low castes, who were responsible for carrying water just as others did. The movement had considerable success, particularly among women.

The manipulation of religious symbols appeared even more distinctly in the Ayodhya movement. In Ayodhya, the Great Moghol, Babur, had had a mosque built on a site which some Hindus regarded as the birthplace of Ram, the most popular god in North India. In 1984, the VHP started a movement claiming the retrocession of the Ramjanmabhoomi (birthplace of Ram) to the Hindus. In September 1984 the VHP conducted a march, beginning in Sitarmahi (Bihar), in the name of the 'liberation' of the Ayodhya temple, which was reached on 7 October. In accordance with this concern to create a pressure group, the march set out to convey a petition to the government in Delhi, which it should have reached in December, shortly before the elections foreseen for January 1985. However, in the meantime, the assassination of Indira Gandhi completely transformed the political atmosphere and led the VHP to change its plans.

The Ayodhya movement experienced a new development before the next elections, in 1989, when the VHP decided to build a temple on Ram's birthplace. Its Ram Shila Pujans programme consisted in taking the bricks with which this temple was supposed to be built to thousands of towns and villages in order to have them consecrated by *sadhus* and to collect donations. More importantly, this campaign surcharged the atmosphere with communal feelings which were to influence the results of the late 1989 elections. The BJP joined the Ayodhya movement at that stage, realizing its growing popularity among the Hindus of North India. It registered a significant electoral advance (eighty-eight seats as opposed to only two in 1984), which was further strengthened in 1991 (119 seats, of which six were won by 'modern gurus'). In 1991 the BJP also won the state elections in Uttar Pradesh. Its government did not attempt to stop VHP and other Hindu nationalist activists when they started to destroy the Babri Masjid on 6 December 1992. Subsequently, the party adopted a more moderate attitude, especially after taking over at the Centre in 1998, largely because it needed the support of coalition partners which did not share its Hindu militancy. However, the VHP is still lobbying for the building of a Ram temple at Ayodhya.

Entryism

The strategy of mobilization was accompanied by another mode of action on the part of the VHP, which consisted in infiltrating, on the local level, certain institutions, such as temples and festivals.

One of the departments of the VHP is devoted to the training of priests for whom ritual practice has become routinized, and for whom formulas they pronounce have lost all meaning and they themselves have lost all sense of their role as intermediaries between the devout and god. This development has facilitated VHP entry to the temples.

The VHP also takes measures to strengthen its presence on the occasion of Hindu festivals. Hindu festivals constitute advantageous moments, from the point of view of the VHP, to spread its message as, in most cases, all sects are represented on such occasions. It is thus a question, from its perspective, of preventing the reassertion of differences, or indeed rivalries, between *sampradaya*s in order to promote the notion of Hindu festivals as crucibles of national unity.

The VHP, to this end, developed a department for the coordination of Hindu festivals (*hindu parva samnvaya*), the objective of which was 'awakening the love of Hinduism'. Festivals should be vehicles of national fervour which alone would be able to overcome the weaknesses of Hindu societies which derive from their enslavement (*goulabi*), from the time of the Muslim conquest to colonization. Its priority is the standardization of festivals in such a way that they become national festivals (*rashtriya tyohar*). The VHP, therefore, has established societies for the coordination of festivals (*hindu samnvaya samiti*) in as many places as possible, and foremostly in places of pilgrimage.

Conclusion

The VHP can only be described as Hindu in a limited sense of the term. Its attempt at federating sects in a centralized framework and its desire to standardize religion in line with the Hindutva ideology are clear limitations of Christianity and Islam. The VHP has served the Hindu nationalist strategy above all during such campaigns as the Ektamata Yatra Yagna and the agitation in support of the Ram temple in Ayodhya, where *sadhu*s provide valuable support in the instrumentalization of religious symbols for the purpose of political mobilization. The strategy of infiltration, which consists for the VHP in penetrating temples and festivals, though less visible than strategy of political mobilization the VHP may be more effective in the long run.

Further reading

Jaffrelot, C. (1996) *The Hindu Nationalist Movement*, New York: Columbia University Press.

McKean, L. (1996) *Divine Enterprise. Gurus and the Hindu Nationalist Movement*, Chicago: Chicago University Press.
Nady, A., Trivedy, S., Mayaram, S. and Yagnik, A. (1995) *Creating a Nationality. The Ramjanmabhoomi Movement and Fear of the Self*, Delhi: Oxford University Press.
Van der Veer, P. (1993) 'Hindu Nationalism and the discourse of modernity: the Vishva Hindu Parishad', in M. Marty and R. Scott Appleby (eds) *Accounting for Fundamentalisms*, Chicago: The University of Chicago Press.

CHRISTOPHE JAFFRELOT

VIVEKANANDA, SWAMI

Swami Vivekananda (born Narendranath Datta, 1863–1902) created the Ramakrishna Math and Mission (see **Ramakrishna Mission**) and has been regarded as one of the architects of **Neo-Hinduism**. Following the death of Sri Ramakrishna (see **Ramakrishna, Sri**), his spiritual mentor, in late 1886 Swami Vivekananda led a group of Ramakrishna's young disciples through an initiation into the state of *sannyasa* (see *Sannyasin*), the ascetic, last stage of life according to the classic Hindu model. This embryonic monastic community was the beginning of the Ramakrishna Math. The self-conferred nature of this initiation and the direction subsequently taken by Vivekananda have prompted questions about the extent of his continuity with Ramakrishna and earlier Hindu tradition.

After a period of solitary, extended pilgrimage in India, Swami Vivekananda was sponsored by patrons to attend the World Parliament of Religions in Chicago in 1893 to speak on behalf of Hinduism. He did not return to India until 1897, having also visited England and Western Europe. During this period he formulated distinctive theories about practical religion (Practical Vedanta), the evolutionary development of a universal religion prefigured by the Advaita Vedanta tradition of Hindu philosophy, and the relationship between East and West. His modification of Advaita Vedanta philosophy and stress upon practical philanthropy have provided the basis for claims that European and Christian influences played as great a part in shaping Vivekananda's expression of Hinduism as Ramakrishna. Vivekananda created several Vedanta Societies (see **Vedanta Society**) in the United States and England and formed the Ramakrishna Mission on his return to India, characterized by its commitment to serving humanity. Inclined to ill health since childhood, he died in India after a second visit to England and the United States (1899–1900).

Swami Vivekananda's legacy is institutionalized within the Ramakrishna Math and Mission but his reputation as an activist has exercised a wider appeal for many Hindus. His defence of Indian culture and theory of Practical Vedanta has been put to new uses by Hindu religious nationalists, while his ideal of a universal religion continues to attract sympathizers in Vedanta Societies beyond India.

Further reading

Sil, Narasingha, P. (1997) *Swami Vivekananda: A Reassessment*, Selinsgrove: Susquehanna University Press/ London: Associated University Presses.

GWILYM BECKERLEGGE

VOODOO/VODOU

'Voodoo' is a Euro-American term used to describe (often derogatorily) several closely related religions practiced on both sides of the Black Atlantic. In West Africa, the Fon of Dahomey (now called Benin) worship a heterogeneous pantheon of spiritual beings called *Vodun* whom they encounter and manifest in trance-possession. The Kongo people of Central Africa attribute similar supernatural powers to their *nzombi* (dead), and to a complex pharmacopoeia through which the powers of the dead can be engaged. Convulsed into new societies by the trans-Atlantic slave trade, Fon, Kongo and related African peoples pooled those beliefs they held in common – the agency of intermediary spirits; the liturgical efficacy of dance and music, especially drumming; the sacral power of images and spirit infused medicines; the benign orchestration of a distant god – into a number of related syncretic religions: **Santeria** in Cuba; **Candomblé** in Brazil, Shango in Trinidad and, most notoriously, Vodou in Haiti.

Vodou's paradigmatic reputation is closely entwined with Haiti's unique history. Once slaves to France's richest colony, Afro-Haitians rebelled in 1791 and by 1804 established the world's first Black republic. The success of their audacious Revolution is often attributed to Vodou, which had continued to evolve and grow during the colonial period, adapting itself to the existential realities of the New World. African captives who had been forcibly baptized into the Roman Catholic Church admired much of what they encountered, particularly in the cult of the saints. Runaway slaves were introduced to new gods and rituals by Taino shamans surviving in the hills; as those slaves who remained in the towns admired and appropriated the Free Masonic rituals of their French masters. By 1804 elements from these alien traditions had already worked themselves into the house of Africa's gods, one of the greatest and most consistently underrated events in world religious history.

Traces of Vodou's eighteenth century assimilations may still be noted in the continuing popularity of *Poule Noire*, *Dragon Rouge* and other French occult traditions whose charms and curses are readily available in Haitian chapbooks; in the Tarot and Crystal divinatory systems used by Vodou necromancers; and in a demonology of werewolves, changelings, and zombies appropriated from superstitious colonials and now deeply embedded in Haitian folklore. However, the most important appropriations from the colonial period remain those from the Roman Catholic Church and the Free Masons. Every significant *lwa* (divinity) is reified by the image of a corresponding Catholic saint, often adopting the same iconography, prayers and feast days. Likewise, Masonic paraphernalia was quickly absorbed into Vodou ritual. Symbols such as the All-Seeing Eye, Skulls and Bones, and Crossed Compasses pervade its sacred arts. *Oungans* (priests) greet each other with elaborate Masonic handshakes, hardly surprising since most have also been initiated into the secret society, as are two of their *lwa* patrons: Ogou, generalissimo of the pantheon, and Baron Samedi, the divine undertaker who wears the funereal garb of the 32nd degree initiate.

This process of assimilating from parallel religious traditions continues to mark Vodou practice. Many *oungans* and *manbos* (priestesses) have been influenced by the writings of Haitian philosopher Milo Rigaud, whose 1953 book *The Secrets of Vodou* (*Le Tradition Voudoo et le Voudoo Haitien*) bears the hallmarks of New Age philosophy (see **New Age Movement**): the assumption of a universal solar mythology, gnosis, alchemy and secret language. For New Age seekers, these are 'keys' which unlock the hidden meaning of Vodou, including the true identity of the *lwa,* who at some dark level are manifestations of the same universal pantheon to be found in the Tarot, the Kabbalah, the Vedas, and the revelations of Mme. Helena P. Blavatsky (see **Blavatsky, Helena**).

It would be easy to dismiss Rigaud's book as a theosophic farrago (see **theosophy**), but that would be a mistake. The book continues to be an extremely influential source for modern Vodou myth making, especially among the various foreign writers, artists and film makers who discover and incorporate Vodou's traces into their own lives and works. First and foremost among such partisans is dance ethnographer and film maker Maya Deren, whose 1953 book, *Divine Horseman: The Living Gods of Haiti*, is a ringing Jungian defense of the religion (see **Jung, Carl**), as well as a source of inspiration for writers as diverse as Russell Banks (*Continental Drift*), William Gibson (*Count Zero*) and Wade Davis (*The Serpent and the Rainbow*). These artists seem to share in sentiments expressed by Alfred Metraux, another famous ethnographer, who described Vodou as 'the paganism of the West: Many of us go to Haiti in search of our classical heritage, and find in Voodoo the charm of fairy tales. Without compelling us to give up our habits and ties with the present, it take us into a magic realm' (Cosentino, 1995: 53).

Vodou apologetics also extend to the scientific avant garde. Thus in the preface to his 2000 book, *The Vodou Quantum Leap*, physician and poet Reginald Crosley asserts, 'Quantum physics reveals to us that reality has two faces, a visible one and an invisible one. Vodou reveals this hidden face of reality...Vodou accounts of possession, channeling, and zombis all reflect the multidimensional nature of existence.' Likewise Ronald Derenoncourt, Haitian musician and TV personality popularly known as 'Aboudja', uses Hollywood idioms to explain trance possession as a manifestation of Einstein's physics: 'In

Vodou, we consider a human being like a starship. You are a starship and your energy is the captain. You can put yourself in a state where another energy can take control within you. It's the same thing when a person is possessed by a *lwa*. It's like a hit – *plaaak* – it makes a *plaaak* and then it goes, leaving you with an open mind' (Cosentino 1995: 27). Employing this sort of discourse, Vodou morphs once again from its African roots to its New Age destiny.

Further reading

Cosentino, D. (1995) *The Sacred Arts of Haitian Vodou*, Los Angeles: Fowler Museum.

Crosley, R. (2000) *The Vodou Quantum Leap*, St. Paul, Minnesota: Llewellyn Publications.

Deren, M. (1953) *Divine Horsemen: The Living Gods of Haiti*, New York: McPherson & Co.

Rigaud, M. (1969) *Secrets of Voodoo*, San Francisco: City Lights Books.

DONALD COSENTINO

WICCA, CHURCH AND SCHOOL OF

Founded: 1968

The Church and School of Wicca was founded by Gavin and Yvonne Frost (née Wilson) near St Louis, Missouri to practice and teach a form of neopagan witchcraft believed to be subtly different from Gardnerian Wicca (see **Wicca**). English-born Gavin Frost claimed to have been initiated in 1948 into an aristocratic coven of witchcraft linked to the Cambridge student group The Pentangle Society which had attempted to reconstruct witchcraft in the 1930s based on Margaret Murray's 1921 anthropological study, *The Witch-Cult in Western Europe* (see **Gardner, Gerald**; **Wicca**). The coven was also claimed to derive from eighteenth-century Druidry. Yvonne was born in Los Angeles and claims descent from two lines of witchcraft stretching back many generations through the Cumberland Gap of Kentucky and into the Clan Gunn of Scot-

land. The Frosts live under a vow of poverty, with all their material possessions belonging to the Church.

The Church moved in the late 1970s to North Carolina, and again in 1996 to West Virginia, where it now teaches eclectic neopagan witchcraft as well a western form of tantric yoga devised by the Frosts. Much of the teaching takes place via the Church and School of Wicca correspondence courses, the initial one of which was published in 1971 as *The Witch's Bible*; they now run thirteen courses including Essential Witchcraft, Advanced Celtic Witchcraft and Shamanism, Mystical Awareness, and Practical Sorcery. The Church also sponsors large neopagan festivals to celebrate the turning of the seasons of the year – its Samhain/Hallowe'en festival has run continuously since 1972 – and publishes an official journal called *Survival*. The CSW is thus a very accessible and widespread form of witchcraft, and has chartered twenty-eight independent CSW tradition churches, and claims to have brought 200,000 people into Wicca.

The Church and School of Wicca gained federal recognition of Witchcraft as a religion in 1972, and in 1985 was recognized as equal to any other church by a federal appeals court.

Further reading

Frost, Y. and Frost, G. (1976) *The Magic Power of Witchcraft*, New York: Parker.

JO PEARSON

WICCA

Founder: Gerald Gardner

Wicca emerged in 1940s Britain as a highly ritualistic, nature venerating, polytheistic, magical and religious system, which made use of Eastern techniques but operated within a predominantly western framework. It arose from the cultural impulses of the *fin de siècle*, in particular from the occult revival of the 1880s onwards, and was heavily influenced by the theories of Margaret Murray. Murray proposed that witchcraft was the survival of remnants of a pre-Christian, indigenous fertility religion, which worshipped a horned god and was almost extinguished by the Great Witch Hunts of the early modern period. These influences were woven into Wicca in the 1940s by Gerald Gardner (see **Gardner, Gerald**), and developed by Doreen Valiente (see **Valiente, Doreen**). Most, though not all, Wiccans today acknowledge that there is little evidence for a continuous Witchcraft tradition, but claim rather that Wicca is a revitalization and re-invention of ancient folk practices that existed in pre-Christian Britain, even if they were not part of any organized tradition. Some Wiccans today continue to identify Wicca with 'The Burning Times', as they call the witch persecutions, and this is particularly true of feminist Wicca and witchcraft.

By the mid-1950s, Wicca had become relatively popular due to Gardner's love of publicity which drew the religion to the attention of the public, and in the early 1960s it was exported to North America. Gardner died in 1964, but his tradition of Gardnerian Wicca was firmly established. In the 1960s, as Alex Sanders (see **Sanders, Alex**) brought a stronger application of high ritual magic to his branch of Wicca, and outside the UK other traditions have evolved, based on Wicca and drawing in their own local or national folklore and culture, with the USA in particular developing a multitude of derivations, including Faery Wicca, Dianic Wicca and Seax Wicca.

Since Gardner's first covens, Wicca has spread across North America, northern Europe, Australia, New Zealand, and South Africa. Wicca has thus become a global phenomenon and significant Wiccan communities can be found in most countries inhabited by significant populations of people of European descent, but also in countries such as Japan that are closely linked to Western cultures by the global economy and media. Wicca is used to refer to 'covens' of friends who have no initiation or training but gather together to celebrate the seasons or full moons, but it traditionally styles itself as an esoteric religion and mystery tradition, entry to which is solely through initiation ceremonies which include oaths of secrecy and which are designed to trigger personal transformation.

Wicca is organized in small, often intense groups called covens. It does not seek converts but believes that those who are right for the religion, which includes the practice of magic in its rites, holds nature to be sacred, and venerates deity in the form of both gods and goddesses, will find their way to an appropriate coven. Wicca is a religion in which the divine is immanent, being apparent in the earth, the moon, the stars, the bodies of men and women. Humans, nature and deities are all regarded as interconnected and sacred. Wiccans have only a few beliefs that most of them adhere to, and these include 'The Witches Rede: An it harm none, do what you will', and 'The Law of Threefold Effect', the belief that any action a person commits will return to that person threefold.

The etymology of the word 'Wicca' has been hotly debated among practitioners. It has been argued that the word derives from the same root as the Anglo-Saxon word for knowledge, *wit, wittich*, which stems from *weet* meaning 'to know', and such a definition lends itself to modern Wiccan understanding of themselves as 'wise' men and women who practise the 'Craft of the Wise'. Similarly, some suggest that 'Wicca' derives from *wik*, meaning to 'bend or shape', which links nicely with modern Wicca's definition of magic, which is to bend or shape energy through will in order to make manifest something on the physical plane. Wicca in fact derives from 'weik' and 'wicce'. Wicca is actually the Anglo-Saxon word for a *male* witch (female, 'wicce'), the plural form of which may have been 'Wiccan'.

Further reading

Hutton, R. (1999) *The Triumph of the Moon: A History of Pagan Witchcraft*, Oxford: Oxford University Press
Salomonsen, J. (2002) *Enchanted Feminism: The Reclaiming Witches of San Francisco*, London: Routledge

JO PEARSON

WILBER, KEN

Ken Wilber (b. 1949) is an independent American philosopher-psychologist and representative of the Transpersonal Psychology movement that followed the work of Abraham Maslow (see **Maslow, Abraham**). His books have been widely translated and he enjoys a strong following among both lay and academic readers. His debut *The Spectrum of Consciousness* established his reputation, and he has published over twenty books, including *Up From Eden: A Transpersonal View of Human Evolution* and *A Brief History of Everything*.

Wilber's intellectual template is constructed primarily around Madhyamika Buddhism, Advaita Vedanta Hinduism, transcendental structuralism, and developmental psychology. In the 1980s he was associated with the controversial **guru Adi Da** (formerly Da Free John) and spoke in admiration of Da's spiritual wisdom, yet in 1996 he publicly withdrew his support for Da and his community. Wilber acknowledges the influence of Da's thought upon his own theory of stages of psycho-physical development.

His core theoretical framework includes a three-stage model of human development, moving from pre-personal to personal to transpersonal. He insists on a non-reductionist study of religion that recognizes different levels of spiritual engagement and is particularly critical of what he has named the 'pre/trans fallacy', the conflation of pre-personal mythical thought with transpersonal spiritual development. An outspoken critic of alternative spiritualities, he is nevertheless considered to be one of the key intellectual voices of the **New Age Movement**.

As a prominent apologist for a non-dualist perspective, and for meditation as a genuine spiritual methodology, he has been criticized for neglecting cultural relativism and presenting an imported Western vision of meditation alongside an idealized view of ancient mysticism. Critics have also called into question his Atman project theory, inconsistencies in his ideas of the human, his use of the *philosophia perennis* and his representation of evolutionary theory.

Wilber lives in Colorado, USA and has spent much of his life in relative solitude, occupied with writing and studying rather than public teaching. In 1998 he founded the Integral Institute, a non-profit think-tank offering consultancy and training in 'Integral Studies', based on discussions with a number of late twentieth century thinkers including Francisco Varela, Robert Forman, Jeanne Achterberg and Deepak Chopra (see **Chopra, Deepak**).

Further reading

Wilber, K. (2000) *Collected Works*, Boston: Shambhala.

ALEXANDRA RYAN

WINNERS CHAPEL
(a.k.a. *Living Faith World Outreach Centre*)

David Oyedepo, a trained architect, started his 'Prosperity gospel' based Living Faith World Outreach/Winners Chapel in 1981 in northern Nigeria. He moved to his native Yorubaland in the south-west and in 2000 erected a 50,000 seat auditorium called 'Faith Tabernacle', which he designed himself. With five halls radiating from the centre in a star-shaped building, this is one of the largest church buildings in the world, situated in an impressive complex of modern buildings at the 300 acre 'Canaan Land' in Ogun State, outside Lagos, Nigeria, including a Christian university and a children's school. Oyedepo, 'Presiding Bishop' of the organization called the Living Faith World Outreach/Winners, has planted churches all over Nigeria and throughout the sub-Sahara. In 1998 he claimed to have 200 churches in Nigeria with over 400 pastors in forty African nations. Oyedepo's preaching is dominated by the success and prosperity themes of the so-called 'prosperity gospel' (see **Prosperity Theology** and **Health and Wealth**) familiar in US Pentecostalism. His members are promised health and wealth in return for their faith and their contributions. Regular slick conventions are a feature of this movement with visiting guest speakers usually from other parts of Africa, and the church prides itself in being an all-African church. One of the fastest growing churches in Kenya is the Winners Chapel in Nairobi, which dedicated a building in 1998 for its 3,500-member congregation after only one year of existence. This congregation was started by Dayo Olutayo from Oyedepo's church in Nigeria, who arrived in Kenya in 1995. The media advertising hype for the dedication service in Nairobi gushed, 'Winners Chapel, Nairobi was built entirely debt free. No loans of bank borrowing and certainly no begging trips to the West!' The organization had two other 'Winners Chapels' in Kisumu and Mombasa. Similar Winners Chapels exist in several other African states.

Further reading

Anderson, A. (2001) *African Reformation: African Initiated Christianity in the 20th Century*, Trenton, NJ and Asmara, Eritrea: Africa World Press.

ALLAN ANDERSON

WOMEN IN NEW RELIGIOUS MOVEMENTS

Women have often been disparaged, excluded and oppressed by organized religion, their public role limited to the menial. Despite – or because of – their lack of formal status, women have historically been attracted to new religions and sects, sometimes as founders and leaders.

During the 1970s, many women joined NRMs (see **New Religious Movement**). These movements varied widely in their beliefs and behaviour towards women, but can be broadly classified into two groups: traditionalist, and self-development oriented. Traditionalist movements appeal mainly to women who are confused and frightened by the complexity of the modern world. They offer clearly defined gender roles and stable family life, thus fulfilling security needs, though often at a price of limitation and oppression. Examples are the Jesus Movement and ISKCON (see **International Society of Krishna Consciousness**). However, as feminism slowly takes root in Western society, even conservative NRMs are responding as their women members find their voices and demand greater equality. It is significant that these movements tend to have a male majority – sometimes 2:1 or higher – whereas in the more liberal NRMs the ratio is typically reversed.

The appeal of NRMs focused on personal development combines secular opportunities for power and status with spiritual growth and empowerment. They attract both counter-cultural seekers and professional women. Their beliefs and practice on gender are more fluid and flexible, sometimes encouraging androgyny, and usually including women in leadership positions. NRMs such as the **Rajneesh Movement**, the **Brahma Kumaris**, and many Buddhist and Pagan groups offer equal opportunities with no glass ceiling, and possibilities for women to combine work, marriage and motherhood with spiritual growth.

In the Brahma Kumaris movement, gender roles are reversed to the point where women occupy positions of power and status, whereas men both in their secular and religious roles are subordinate to women – looking after the mundane side to free women for higher spiritual duties. However, the BKs do not think of themselves as feminists, and their prominence derives from their mediumistic capacities, channelling sermons from their dead founder.

The Rajneesh Movement also promotes female majority in leadership. Its founder Osho proclaimed his 'vision that the coming age will be the age of the woman. Man has tried for five thousand years and has failed. Now a chance has to be given to the woman. Now she should be given the reins of all the powers.' Although 80 per cent of the top positions in the organization were held by women, discipleship was the path to enlightenment for women and men. The goal was to become totally surrendered to the guru to receive the divine. This belief is in line with *bhakti yoga*, and is found in other eastern-based NRMs such as ISKCON, Elan Vital and the Sai Baba Movement, but is obviously not compatible with feminism. However, most women disciples claim to have found this path of devotion ecstatic and fulfilling. Since Osho's death, leadership roles are shared between men and women.

Buddhism is doctrinally egalitarian, but the patriarchal bias of Asian society has permeated religious practice and been vigorously challenged in the West. Most Buddhist NRMs offer equal opportunities, particularly those led by Westerners. The former abbess of

Shasta Abbey, Roshi Kennett, became a Buddhist because of the then impossibility of female ordination in Christianity. However, the **Friends of the Western Buddhist Order** has been criticized for its under-representation of women in the higher echelons and the reluctance of the movement's leader Sangharakshita to ordain women.

There are few examples of women founders and leaders of NRMs, but paradoxically, in view of the conservatism of Indian society, there are several Indian women leaders, of whom the best known are Amritandamayi (aka 'the hugging guru'), **Mother Meera** (now based in Germany), and Nirmala Devi (aka Mataji, founder of Sahaja Yoga). Like the Brahma Kumaris, these women are not overtly feminist, but are highly charismatic leaders with large followings.

One of the main issues for feminists regarding charismatic authority is sexual abuse. It should be emphasized that overall the problem is no worse in NRMs than within organized religion, and there is less evidence of alleged paedophilia than within Christianity. Sexual scandals were also more prevalent during the 1970s – the heyday of the 'sexual revolution'. Many gurus have been accused of sexual abuse, including the leader of the Family (see **Family, The**), David Berg, who devised the practice of 'Flirty Fishing'.

A distinction should be made between 'abuse' and 'liberation'. The Rajneesh movement was notorious in the 1970s for Osho's encouragement of 'free love' among his disciples, although the practice was voluntary and there is little evidence of his own involvement. His aim was to create a sacramental sexuality based on a synthesis between **Tantra** and Reichian therapy. Tantra has also been an influence on Pagan beliefs and practices on sexuality along with the

mythology of the Goddess (see **Goddess Feminists**). Despite censure for 'sky-clad' (naked) worship, and for the Great Rite – ritual sex between the high priest and priestess – paganism appeals to women in its affirmation of the female body, and rituals for celebrating 'women's mysteries'.

Patriarchal religions sanctify motherhood as a woman's destiny and true vocation. Some traditionalist NRMs, most notoriously the **Unification Church/ Moonies**, advocate arranged marriage. ISKCON also favours arranged marriage, though couples may come to a private understanding beforehand. However, women are perceived as temptresses, and excluded from sharing power with the men so as not to 'sexually agitate them'. In Christian sects such as the London Church of Christ and the **Jesus Army**, marriages are not formally arranged but often rely on the advice and consent of the pastor, and divorce is forbidden except for adultery. The benefits for women are clearly defined gender roles and stable families, but the downside is rigid control of sexuality, work and worship by husband and elders, loss of status and opportunities for spiritual advancement, and a high incidence of wife and child abuse.

The third option encountered in NRMs is asceticism. ISKCON awards the highest status to celibate men. Buddhist monks (male and female), as in Christianity, take vows of celibacy, though often they are encouraged to wait till they are older and have experienced sex and parenthood. The Brahma Kumaris are the most uncompromising example of asceticism, perceiving sexuality as an obstacle to enlightenment, and requiring celibacy for their lay members, even between husbands and wives.

Nowadays, women are more likely to become involved in the New Age, neo-paganism or **Shamanism** than the more structured NRMs of the 1970s. Women co-created the New Age, including Helena Blavatsky (see **Blavatsky, Helena**) and Annie Besant (see **Besant, Annie**) in Theosophy, **Alice Bailey** of the Arcane School, and the magician Dion Fortune. In Paganism, women are perceived as equal if not superior to men. Feminist witchcraft obviously has a female leadership. Wiccan covens are led by a priest and priestess, but the priestess usually takes precedence and controls the ritual. Pagan priestesses gain their power partly from the pre-eminence of the Goddess in neo-pagan groups, the **Goddess movement**, and the women's spirituality movement as a whole.

Further reading

King, U. (1989) *Women and Spirituality*, Basingstoke: Macmillan.

Puttick, E. and Clarke, P. (1993) *Women as Teachers and Disciples in Traditional and New Religions*, Lampeter/Lewiston: Edwin Mellen Press.

Puttick, E. (1997) *Women in New Religions*, Basingstoke: Macmillan.

ELIZABETH PUTTICK

WON BUDDHISM

Founder: Pak Chungbin (b. 1891; d. 1943)

Won Buddhism is strongly millenarian (see **Millenarianism**) in outlook though the version of paradise on earth which it offers is less ambitious than most millenarian movements in terms of the transformation it believes will come about, and more pragmatic, utilitarian and small scale than that envisaged by other Korean movements including **Ch'ondogyo** or the **Unification Church**.

With the collapse of the Yi dynasty in the late nineteenth century Korean Buddhism started to undergo a revival and one of the new forms to emerge was Won Buddhism founded in 1916 by Pak Chungbin (1891–1943), also known by his literary name, Sot'aesan. The position adopted by Sot'aesan regarding his own enlightened vision of the nature of ultimate reality was ambiguous in the sense that he claimed that it was both original and independent of any other religious tradition and at the same time that all the ancient sages and religious thinkers had been aware of its content. He also made the point that the best guide to a clear understanding of the nature of his enlightenment was Buddhism and in particular the Diamond Sutra.

While it derives much from the past, Won Buddhism is new in rejecting the traditional understanding of liberation as nihilistic and in replacing it with the idea of creating paradise on earth by enabling people to develop their talents and abilities. In conventional Buddhism the way to understand the nature of ultimate reality, it is taught, is through the Threefold Learning, *samadhi* (meditation), *prajna* (wisdom) and *sila* (morality). In Won Buddhism these are expressed in modern terms as 'the cultivation of spirit', 'the study of facts and principles', and 'choice of conduct'. Also, Won Buddhism's paradise on earth is unusual in that it promises nothing truly spectacular or idyllic but simply the basic facilities that will help to offset some of the more serious emotional, social and economic consequences of modern living. The provision of such relatively widely available facilities could, of course, lead to some people's world being completely transformed. The promise is of more employment agencies to serve those looking for jobs, and marriage bureaux to assist those wishing to marry, day nurseries in many more places to enable mothers to go out to work and not worry about their children. Old people without a protector will live comfortable lives without anxiety, homes for the aged established by the government or by charitable organizations. Life in even the remotest place will be surrounded by such convenience facilities as fast food restaurants that there will be no need to always cook at home. There also will be many tailors, dressmakers, and laundries to make life easier for families and in particular women.

While many of these facilities are taken for granted in much of the Western world the widepread appeal of Won Buddhism suggests that for many they are hard to come by elsewhere. These promises also suggest that Won Buddhism, a much simplified version of Buddhism, has been greatly influenced by Western culture.

The main sacred texts of Won Buddhism are those written by Sot'aesan, and the transcriptions of his words and of those of his successor Son Kyu (1900–62). Practice consists essentially in reciting, as in the Pure Land Tradition, the name of the Buddha Amitabha, when venerating the One-Circle-Figure and/or Black Circle. This One-Circle-Figure represents the Dharmabody and replaces the widespread veneration of the countless images of the Buddha. In this it resembles the **Santi Asoke** movement in Thailand which also prohibits the installation and veneration of images of the Buddha in its monasteries, shrines and temples. In recent times resources have been put into higher education and the training of leaders and monks who attend the movement's Wonkwang University which houses a College of Won Buddhist Studies.

Mainly an urban phenomenon Won Buddhism attaches great importance not only to inner calm and peace but also to social service. It has enjoyed considerable success especially since the 1950s not only in Korea where it has built many schools and has been activily engaged in various kinds of charitable work but also beyond. In 2000 the membership of the movement was estimated to be over one and a quarter million, and the number of temples around 450 served by more than 1,500 monks, and over 10,000 religious specialists. Won Buddhism, now an international movement, has established branches in, among other countries, Japan and the United States.

Further reading

Kwangsoo, Park (1997) *The Won Buddhism (Wonbulgyo) of Sot'aesan: A twentieth Century Religious Movement in Korea*, San Francisco: International Scholars.

PETER B. CLARKE

WORD OF FAITH MOVEMENT

The Word of Faith Movement is known by a variety of alternative designations including the **prosperity** gospel and the 'health and wealth gospel'. Leading North American figures in the movement include Kenneth Hagin, Kenneth Copeland, Fred Price, and the female evangelist, Marilyn Hickey. Other evangelists with popular international ministries, such as Benny Hinn, Morris Cerullo and Rodney Howard-Brown, subscribe to some of the core teaching of the Faith Movement but by no means all. Each of these advocates of the movement lead individual ministries (with a degree of co-operation between them), rather than 'churches' in the conventional sense. Collectively, it is possible to see these ministries as a strand within the broader **Charismatic Movements** – displaying many of its teachings and practices. Yet, they do not rest easily there and the distinctive Faith gospel is frequently criticized by charismatic Christians and denounced as embracing a theology outside of the 'dogmatic core' of the Christian Faith. It has also brought controversy where it has found its way into the established Pentecostal churches.

The key dogma of the Faith teachers is the belief that God always grants believers health and wealth if they 'step out in faith' and are 'reborn' in the Spirit. According to those such as Kenneth Hagin, nothing is impossible to achieve. Christians can 'write their ticket' with God if they follow the four principles of 'positive confession' which are:

1. say it;
2. do it;
3. receive it;
4. tell it.

In many respects such teaching brings the Faith Movement close to the gnostic strains of Ralph Waldo Emerson (see **Emerson, Ralph Waldo**) and the Unity School of Christianity, and the anti-materialism of Mary Baker Eddy (**Christian Science**). The dogma is also akin to teachings of the power of positive thinking of the cultic Science of the Mind which surfaced in different forms throughout the twentieth century: from the writings of Norman Vincent Peale, to the 'possibility theology' of Robert Schuller. The most important figure in the Faith movement is perhaps Kenneth Hagin and there is strong evidence to suggest that he plagiarized the writings of E. W. Kenyon whose works, in turn, are derived from the metaphysical cults of the late nineteenth century.

Despite these influences, the Faith Movement has its own teachings which amount to a radical dualism that posits spiritual truth as superior to knowledge gained by normal human faculties (McConnell, 1990). Thus, the leading advocates distinguish between *rhema* knowledge and *logos* knowledge. The latter refers to God's revealed written word, the former, stressed by the Faith Movement, suggests that knowledge is conveyed directly to the believer and needs no spiritual mediation. There is also a heightened spiritual dualism in the Faith Movement's teachings, between the powers of good and those of darkness where Satan and his minions battle to take away health and material possessions from the Christian believer.

Word of Faith advocates such as Kenneth Copeland talk of 'victory' which means the overcoming of the physical and material limitations of life through 'faith' that is perceived as the supreme spiritual power or force of the universe. Yet 'faith' may be interpreted as a metaphor for self-driven material ambition and, in the USA, the Faith Movement's popularity clearly reflects the material aspects of the 'American dream'. Thus, it could be said to carry a variant of the Protestant work ethic by advancing teachings of hard work and responsibility. It is a message which has enjoyed a significant global appeal.

The world-wide relevance of the Faith ministries cannot be doubted. Across the world hundreds of people subscribe to those centres in the USA that are identified by their vast scale of organizational structure and financial resources. Hence, the characteristic tenets of the Faith ministries have been exported to very different cultural environments ranging from the advanced economies of Western Europe, to the emerging economies of Latin America and the Pacific Rim, and Third World Africa. The largest church in the world, congregation-wise, it that of Paul Yonggi Cho in Korea. It has a membership varying between 150,000 and several hundred thousand. This church, and others like it, have grown at least partly as a result of Faith gospel teachings. Yonggi Cho has however extended many of the Faith gospel practices including techniques of visualization, where the needs of a believer merely have to be visualized in order to be achieved.

Further reading

Coleman, S. (1991) 'Faith Which Conquers the World', *Ethnos*, 56(1/2), 6–18.

Hunt, S. (2000) '"Winning Ways": Globalisation and the Impact of the Health and Wealth Gospel', *Journal of Contemporary Religion*, 16(2), 85–105.

STEPHEN HUNT

WORK, THE

Many new religious movements (see **New Religious Movement**) refer to their teachings as 'the work', but the title is pre-eminently applied to the body of teachings created by Gurdjieff (see **Gurdjief, George Ivanovitch**) and further developed by Ouspensky (see **Ouspensky, Piotr Demianovitch**) and other teachers. Gurdjieff also called his work 'the fourth way' (aka 'the sly way'): a distillation of the best elements of what he saw as the three main traditional spiritual paths: the ways of the fakir, the monk and the yogi.

The essence of Gurdjieff's philosophy is the idea that humanity is asleep, and the goal is to wake up – hence his favourite slogan: 'the war against sleep'. His key technique for awakening is 'self-remembering': a process of close observation of inner states, especially negative personal traits, in order to attain higher states of consciousness and self-awareness. Since this task is almost insuperable, it requires the supervision of an experienced teacher, whose authority must be recognized. Progress is most effective while working with a group of like-minded practitioners. In Gurdjieff's time, 'the work' was mainly physical, advanced by going outside one's 'comfort zone'. At the Prieuré, this precept was carried to extreme lengths. People who had never before worked manually were given demanding yet futile tasks to provoke them into awareness. Another central practice was the 'sacred dance', demanding immense focus and concentration in order to still the mind into meditation – a process similar to Asian martial arts.

Gurdjieff's teaching style was highly intuitive, even idiosyncratic; for example, he would put people with the most abrasive personality in charge, order vegetarians to eat meat, teetotallers to become drunk – anything to 'wake them up'. His praxis was spontaneous, intuitive, unpredictable, but was later systematized and routinized by Ouspensky. Ouspensky is disowned by the Gurdjieff Foundation, though there are schools that combine both teachings. Gurdjieff did not appoint an official successor, but his lineage has passed through Jeanne de Salzmann, who set up many societies and foundations around the world. In modern Gurdjieff schools the focus is less on physical work and more on dance, other awareness exercises, and mystical teaching.

Nowadays there are many NRMs and other organizations around the world exploring 'the work', but two main groups are identifiable. First, there are those which claim some direct (if often remote) lineage from Gurdjieff and his disciples; these continue the tradition in an evolving, diverging format. Second, there are groups whose main teachers are not in Gurdjieff's lineage at all but have co-opted elements of 'the work' into their own praxis. Regrettably, some of these movements do not acknowledge their provenance. Many of the strands and divisions between the current schools are due to differences over the sources of his work, (especially the **Sufi** connection), which remain largely unknown. It is surprising that the movement has survived and flourished for as long as it has after the death of the charismatic founder, given his highly syncretistic teachings and eccentric teaching style. It could be argued that survival has been attained by constant division and schism, a process undergone by many religious movements.

Membership levels are impossible to establish accurately, though they have been estimated at 5,000–10,000 worldwide and either static or declining. There are various possible reasons. There is little proselytizing, the praxis is rigorous, and membership requirements tend to be selective. Gurdjieff was insistent that 'the work' was not for everyone. People who lacked a strong sense of boundaries, or conversely, were too rigid and set in their ways, were deemed unsuitable. His ideal student was the mature 'householder' who was adaptable and able to function in the working world.

Also spiritual fashions have changed since the movement's heyday, and contemporary seekers are more likely to join Eastern-based, neo-pagan (see **Neo-Paganism**) or shamanic groups (see **Shamanism**).

The main legacy of Gurdjieff's work may well lie in a more pervasive influence on philosophy, psychology, and the arts. In his lifetime many celebrated intellectuals and artists were drawn to him. Amongst the many movements that have been influenced directly or indirectly by the Gurdjieff–Ouspensky teachings are the **School of Economic Science**, and TM (**Transcendental Meditation**). The movement side of his work has influenced the **Holistic Health Movement**, particularly Wilhelm Reich's bodywork, the Feldenkrais method, and the Alexander technique. **Osho** replicated elements of Gurdjieff's methods at his ashram in India, including the performance of 'pointless' tasks and the appointment of aggressive personalities as supervisors. His ideas have also been appropriated by many New Age groups (see **New Age Movement**), the most popular being the **Enneagram**, developed by Oscar Ichazo but apparently first used by Gurdjieff and Ouspensky. Another interesting modern development is a system of self-development known as 'the Michael teachings', originating in the USA and now growing in Europe. It is a highly complex and sophisticated system, which has grown rapidly in recent years, and contains many elements from Gurdjieff's work – plus a great deal more in the same vein that he did not cover.

ELIZABETH PUTTICK

WORLD MATE

The activities of World Mate were started in 1984 by Tôshû Fukami (1951–). Fukami was previously known as Seizan Fukami until 1995. The group has also changed its name to 'Cosmo Mate', then to 'Powerful Cosmo Mate' and finally it became 'World Mate' in 1994.

Fukami was born as Haruhisa Handa in Hyogo Prefecture, west Japan, and when he was at school he affiliated to a Japanese new religion (see **New Religion (Japan)**), Sekai Kyusei Kyo, where his mother was a member. He later affiliated to another Japanese NRM, **Omoto**, when he was reading Economics at Doshisha University, Kyoto. After graduating from university, he continued to pursue his religious interests while working for a construction firm in Tokyo as a member of the sales department. In 1977 Fukami met a female psychic, Kaoru Tachibana (1934–), and left the company to pursue his spiritual life with her, becoming a lodger at

Tachibana's house along with a few others. He then created his own firm and cramming schools in 1978. He started lecturing in 1984 in his newly established religious movement, which was a Shinto study group. In 1985, with his new name, Seizan, he published a religious book which sold well. The group, now called World Mate, is categorized as a Shinto new religion and has about 20,000-30,000 members (World Mate claimed 41,000 members in 2003). The teaching includes the salvation of spirits, in the sense of the comforting of ancestors and other spirits that are negatively affecting the lives of humans on earth; this is believed to be the key to a better life.

World Mate is active in charity and welfare movements; it created a hospital in Cambodia (1996), offers scholarships to support foreign students and aids various research centres overseas, particularly in Australia, China and the UK, to support their research into Shinto and other Japanese religions. As a result, Fukami has been appointed to be a number of honorary positions, including an Honorary Fellowship at the School of Oriental and African Studies (SOAS) of the University of London.

MASAKI FUKUI

WORLD OF YAAD

The World of *Yaad* is a **New Religious Movement** based in London. It centres around the founder whom people believe to be of Divine Nature and an avatar (Divine manifestation) on Earth. This highly unusual charismatic leader was born in 1960 as Medhi Zand. In January 2000, following an intense spiritual experience, he identified himself as what he describes as 'The Divine Exorcitation of Thought – The Living Memory, the Construction Personification of *Esser Yaad*'. Since this date, the

movement has grown around him at an accelerated rate.

The World of *Yaad* does not claim to be a religion, and there are no set rituals, prayers or creeds. Instead the founder *Esser Yaad* teaches, amongst other things, a series of stages based on a set of keys to help the growth of Mystical Consciousness for the individual. By using these keys as the basis for spiritual development, people are given the power to unlock the Divine within. The textual foundation of the Movement is a series of books written by the founder, which describe the history of the Divine and the creation of the Universe. The books and the teachings of *Esser Yaad* form part of the Movement's claim to bring new spiritual knowledge to the World in the form of the Biography of the Cosmos. At the heart of this are the ideas of the growth of individual consciousness and self-development/transformation (see **Self-Transformation**) and the spiritual and social responsibilities that this growth entails. The teachings contain a strong sense of social justice and human rights with a focus on the freedom to choose ones own spirituality. *Esser-Yaad* leads the weekly evening meetings where social and 'spiritual', (esoteric or mystical) knowledge is discussed and occasionally spiritual exercises are practised (see **Esoteric Movements**).

There have been many accounts of miracles, healing, and magic surrounding *Esser Yaad*, including incidences where the founder has produced lumps of gold and silver, stones and chains made of precious metal from his mouth during meetings. Other personal accounts claim that he has also materialized ash, heavenly scent, fruit and water. Even though this is not a healing movement, there have been cases where followers are said to have been healed of illness and disorders such as cancer,

627

leukaemia, and paralysis. The most referred to incident took place in South Africa in 2001 when a comatose woman 'came back' to life after being declared clinically dead. This has been seen as a direct result of the intervention of *Esser Yaad*.

By the end of 2002, over five hundred people had been taught by *Esser Yaad*. Members, or devotees, originate from a diverse range of ethnic, cultural, and religious backgrounds such as Hindu, Christian, Jewish, Zoroastrian, Sikh, and Muslim. Although the Movement is centred in the UK, members come from a variety of other countries including USA, Russia, Japan, India, France, Germany, Iran, Nigeria, Eritrea, and South Africa. However, as there is an absence of ritual practice and ethnic, cultural, or religious focus, the Movement can only rely on its philosophy to aid its world growth and global membership in the years to come.

ESTHER FOREMAN

WORLDWIDE CHURCH OF GOD

(and splinter groups)

The Worldwide Church of God is remarkable for its shift to orthodoxy after the death of its founder, following fifty years of heterodoxy, and for its consequent massive splintering.

The Church, which took its current name in 1966, was founded as the Radio Church of God by former Church of God, Seventh Day (COG7) minister Herbert W. Armstrong (see **Armstrong, Herbert W.**) in 1937. Some of its teachings could be found in COG7, particularly its strong emphasis on not just the Saturday Sabbath, but also on maintaining the Jewish Holy Days and food laws, and the teaching of the imminent return of Christ. In those respects, Radio/Worldwide Church of God was a strict sabbatarian millenarian Christian sect.

But Armstrong focused on a number of elements which were to make the Church distinctive. True Christians must obey God's Old Testament commands not just because they are spiritual descendants of the Jews, but because they are literal descendants. Borrowing wholesale (though without acknowledgement) from J. H. Allen's 1902 book *Judah's Sceptre and Joseph's Birthright*, Armstrong taught a version of British-Israelitism in which Britain and America are descended from Joseph's sons Ephraim and Mannasseh respectively; thus, any prophecy in the Bible referring to these tribes, or to Israel generally, meant present-day Britain and America. Like the Mormon Church (see **Church of Jesus Christ of the Latter Day Saints (Mormons)**), Worldwide Church of God was very much a religion for America. Armstrong and others wrote hundreds of articles analysing world events – wars, earthquakes, famines, etc. – to prove that we were in the End Times.

Armstrong's teaching on the nature of God was unorthodox: God is a family, currently consisting of Father and Son, but true believers will become part of the God-family – part of God. (The Spirit is not a person, so the Trinity was a false doctrine.)

The Worldwide Church of God became a hugely successful broadcasting and publishing operation; its radio and TV programme *The World Tomorrow* aired around the world, and its flagship magazine *Plain Truth* had a worldwide circulation, in several languages, of between six and eight million a month. Worldwide published other magazines, a large number of booklets and a few full-length books, all distributed free to enquirers. All of this was paid for by the tithes of co-workers (members of the

Church) – as were three splendid college campuses in Texas, California and near St Albans, England.

Worldwide was heavily criticized by Christian counter-cultists (see **Anti-Cult Movement**) for its doctrinal heterodoxy, and by anti-cultists for many things, including the heavy tithing (in some years members had to pay three full tithes of their gross income, plus frequent 'freewill offerings'), and the perceived authoritarianism of the Church; Armstrong taught a strictly hierarchical form of Church governance, and at times this led to abuses.

In the 1970s the Church was hit by a number of scandals, including the revelation of sexual impropriety by Armstrong's son Garner Ted Armstrong, who as his father grew older effectively ran the Church. Garner Ted was suspended, then reinstated, but after a furious row with his father, was finally disfellowshipped (i.e. excommunicated) in 1978. He formed his own Church, the Church of God, International.

It was widely expected that Christ would return in the 1970s (there was even a booklet entitled *1975 in Prophecy*), and some members left when this failed to happen. Some ministers left when Armstrong reversed two teachings, on the date of Pentecost and on remarriage after divorce; their offshoot Churches taught a purer, stricter form of 'Armstrongism' than Armstrong was now teaching himself.

After Armstrong's death in January 1986 at the age of 94, his chosen successor Joseph W. Tkach withdrew all the Church's literature, and began a doctrinal review. Over the next ten years, one by one Armstrong's distinctive teachings were dropped, until by 1995 Tkach announced that the Worldwide Church of God was now effectively a standard conservative Evangelical Church (see **Evangelical Christianity**).

During these years many senior ministers left, taking large numbers of members with them. The three largest offshoot Churches, each holding in different ways to Armstrong's teachings, were the Philadelphia Church of God (founded 1989, *c*. 6,000–7,000 members), the Global Church of God (1992, *c*. 6,000–7000 members) and the United Church of God, *an International Association* (1995, *c*. 15,000 members).

But this was not the end of the story. United, the most democratic of the three, demoted its leader David Hulme, who left to found his own Church of God, *an International Community*; most of the British ministers and members of United realigned with Hulme's Church. Roderick C. Meredith, one of Armstrong's earliest students back in 1949, fell out with the board of the Church he had founded, Global Church of God, and left this with about 80 per cent of the members to found the Living Church of God. The remnant of Global, effectively bankrupted, reformed as the Church of God Christian Fellowship, most of which later merged with United, though a further remnant became the Church of the Eternal God, which in Britain is still known as Global Church of God. There was another offshoot from Global, shortly after Meredith left it to found Living; one of its leading ministers, David Pack, left to found the Restored Church of God, sticking very strictly to Armstrong's teachings and accusing all the other offshoots of deviating from the Truth.

Shortly before his death Armstrong had written 'the most important book since the Bible', *Mystery of the Ages*. The Philadelphia Church of God, the first and most dogmatic of the 'big three' original offshoots from Worldwide under its leader Gerald Flurry, reprinted this and distributed it to enquirers. Worldwide, which had denounced the book as 'full of errors', still held the copyright, and took Philadelphia to court. A groundbreaking court ruling in Philadelphia's favour, neatly distinguishing between the Church as corporation and the Church as believers, was overturned by the appeals court. At the time of writing the legal battles are continuing.

Armstrong's son Garner Ted also had his problems. After another sexual scandal in 1995, about two-thirds of his Church of God, International (CGI) left in 1996 to form independent local churches linked loosely as Church of God Outreach Ministries. In 1997 CGI removed Garner Ted Armstrong as leader, and he left his own Church to set up yet another new one, the Intercontinental Church of God.

All of these Churches, and others, have suffered further schisms, so that by 2002 there were over 300 offshoots, some with no more than a handful of members. The continuing story can be followed at the website below, and many others.

Further reading

Barrett, D. V. (2001) *The New Believers*, London: Cassell.
'The Missing Dimension' at http://home-pages.ihug.co.nz/~gavinru/wcg.htm

DAVID V. BARRETT

WOVENU, CHARLES KWABLA NUTORNTI

(Mawu fe Ame Wovenu)

Charles Kwabla Nutornti Wovenu is the founder of the Apostle's Revelation Society (ARS) one of the earliest **African Independent Churches** in Ghana. He was born in 1918 at Anyako in the Volta Region of Ghana to Emmanuel Kofi Nutornutsi Kluvia and Mikayanawo Dzakpata. Both were traditionalists. The mother later married a Christian and Wovenu was baptized by the Reverend Robert Domingo Baeta on 26 December 1926.

Wovenu who did not complete his elementary school education initially worked as a teacher in his hometown Anyako where he helped to establish a school for adults. In 1934 he joined the Gold Coast Prison Service as a Warden in the town of Akuse and later moved to the mining town of Akwatia to work in the Consolidated Amalgamated Selection (Cast) mines. Initially employed as a labourer, he was later elevated to the status of a clerk when the superiors became aware of his level of education. He established prayer cells in these towns and actively engaged in evangelism.

In November 1939, Wovenu went to the town of Tadzevu in the Volta Region of Ghana, where his real father Nutornutsi Kluvia lived. He established a school and a prayer group, on land he bought and worked closely with the Ewe Presbyterian Church (now Evangelical Presbyterian Church, Ghana) whose ministers administered the sacraments to his group. Wovenu later fell out with the Church over funding for the school he established and his healing and prophetic activities. In 1942 he received a revelation and founded the **Apostles Revelation Society**. Another revelation made him add the name Wovenu (one who has received grace) to his other names. He is popularly known by his Ewe title Mawu fe Ame (Man of God).

Wovenu is renowned for his prophetic and healing gifts, and his prognostic prayers. He had a special interest in the inculturation of Christianity introducing liturgy to sanctify African life situations and activities such as widowhood, birth of twins, putting up new buildings, acquiring the spirit of one's profession, etc. He also developed a long list of Ewe language Christian names for Church members. Wovenu gradually turned Tadzevu, a traditional religious community into a Christian Community. He was consulted by some Ghanaian political leaders such as Kwame Nkrumah the first president of Ghana and General J. A. Ankrah who invited him to dedicate Christianborg Castle, the site of Government on 21 May 1966, the first leader of an AIC to fulfil such a public role in Ghana. He was also renowned for his generosity.

He did not only have an impact on the lives of his followers spiritually but also exhorted them to hard work and abjured laziness. He brought socio-economic development to the community of Tadzewu and the surrounding villages. He organized communal labour to build schools, markets, public toilets, potable water, clinics, and farms. Wovenu also brought to these communities by the early 1960s, a Postal Agency, electricity, and telephone; a rare achievement in Ghana at the time. He established a Theological College for the training of pastors at New Tadzewu. He also wrote about thirty books and pamphlets on various topics both in Ewe and English.

The church Wovenu founded spread throughout Ghana and currently has over 683 congregations as well international branches in the US, Canada, Britain Italy, Togo, Benin, and the Ivory Coast. He travelled widely, visiting international branches of his churches, and died in London on 10 April 1999 aged 81 years.

Further reading

Amenumey, D. E. K (2002) *Outstanding Ewes of the 20th Century*, Accra: Woeli Publishing Services.

Fernandez, J. Y (1970) 'Rededication and Prophetism in Ghana', in *Cahier d'Etudes Africaines*, Vol. X, pp. 228–305.

ELOM DOVLO

Y

YIN-YANG

The Chinese terms *yin* and *yang* originally (eighth to fifth centuries BCE) referred to 'a hillside in shade' and 'a hillside in sunlight'. However, they quickly acquired a wider range of dualistic associations: dark and light, moist and dry, earth and heaven, passive and active, female and male, supple and strong, low and high, follower and initiator. In philosophical thought, they came to stand for the primary pair of complementary opposites within the Supreme Ultimate (see Figure 1). In *yin-yang* theory, all

Figure 1. The Chinese symbol of the Supreme Ultimate, commonly referred to as the yin-yang symbol, in which the dark (yin) and the bright (yang) are dynamically interrelated. Each contains the seed of the other (the black spot in the white area and the white spot in the black area).

natural and cosmic phenomena were explained in terms of the changing balance of these two forces. They were early associated with the two basic kinds of divinatory line in the **I-Ching**, the supple, divided line, __ __, and the strong, whole line, _____. *Yin* and *yang* are relational concepts, so that the same person who is passive in one relationship may be active in another. Moreover, each member of this primary pair of opposites contains the seed of the other and spontaneously transforms into it.

The notions of *yin* and *yang* have been adopted in various New Age (see **New Age Movement**) discourses where there is an emphasis on holism and balance, especially when these explicitly include Chinese cultural influences. They are widely used in oriental and complementary medicine, divination, fengshui, Chinese yoga, and martial arts; in comparison with the principle of complementarity in quantum physics; and as a general symbol of the harmonious interplay of opposites. The attraction of the notions of *yin* and *yang* may stem largely from their relativization of traditional western cultural and religious values through according equal status to those terms within pairs of complementary opposites that western culture has tended to devalue (e.g., the feminine, the dark, the passive, and the irrational).

RODERICK MAIN

YOGA, MODERN

The expression 'Modern Yoga' is used as a technical term to refer to those types of yoga that evolved mainly through the interaction of Western individuals interested in Indian religions and a number of more or less Westernized Indians over the last 150 years. It may therefore be defined as the graft of a Western branch on to the Indian tree of **yoga**. Most of the yoga currently practised and taught in the West as well as some contemporary Indian yoga falls in this category. Being only one and a half centuries old, it may well be the youngest branch of the tree of yoga, and it seems to be the only one to have stretched across the oceans to continents other than Asia. The definition 'Modern' seems precise enough to describe its age (it emerged in modern times) and geographico/cultural spread (it is preeminently found in developed countries and urban milieus worldwide). It also seems open-ended enough to allow for further definition and elaboration.

Differences between Modern Yoga and earlier, classical forms of yoga may be usefully discussed under three headings: religio-philosophical beliefs, history, and socio-institutional structures.

Belief structures

In its pre-modern forms yoga was largely associated with South Asian religions (mainly Hinduism, Buddhism and Jainism) and with various types of supernatural endeavours, such as the quest for 'powers' (*siddhis*) and for 'liberation' (*moksha*). This started to change due to the development of two main intellectual dynamics:

(a) the reception of post-Enlightenment thought on the part of the Indian intelligentsia (*c.* 1750 onwards) and

(b) the flourishing of a creative dialogue between western esotericists (see **Esoteric Movements**) and the more liberal branches of **Neo-Hinduism** (*c.* 1820s onwards).

These influences led a number of groups and individuals to attempt a reinterpretation of yoga based on radically novel (*vis-à-vis* older forms of yoga) philosophical presuppositions: crucially, modern scientific on the one hand and universalistic on the other. Thus the now familiar discourses of 'yoga as science' and of 'yoga as experiential foundation of all religions' started to be elaborated. Both of these trends find a common ground in 'secularized' definitions of yoga as a 'philosophy' or as a 'way of life' suitable to anyone, whether religious or not. Such a secularizing approach notwithstanding, whenever religio-philosophical beliefs are expressed in Modern Yoga milieus or literature, they tend to align themselves with New Age forms of religiosity.

History

While the diffusion of post-Enlightenment thought was a natural correlate of colonial enterprises worldwide, the dialogue between western esotericism and Neo-Hinduism was a unique phenomenon, and it was thanks to it that the more popular reaches of esotericism (including New Age forms of religiosity) became heavily tinged with Indian overtones. The shaping of Modern Yoga was central to such developments and a key historical figure here – and the first to define fully-fledged Modern Yoga – was Swami Vivekananda (1863–1902) (see **Vivekananda, Swami**). Gathering in his persona the modernism of the **Brahmo Samaj** – the most influential liberal Neo-Hindu movement of the nineteenth century – the charisma of his saintly teacher Sri Ramakrishna (1836–86) (see **Ramakrishna, Sri**), and the cutting edge esotericism of nineteenth century USA, Vivekananda became the most influential apostle of Neo-Vedanta and of Modern Yoga. His seminal *Raja-Yoga*, first published in 1896, already contains most of the themes which would be later elaborated by different types of Modern Yoga schools. A schematic overview of the latter may be seen in the 'Typology of Modern Yoga' reproduced in Figure 2.

Socio-institutional structures

Thus various forms of Modern Yoga have been flourishing from about the beginning of the twentieth century onward. While assimilations of yoga in 'denominational' contexts (i.e. Modern Denominational Yoga) reflect the peculiar belief system of each group, what is usually referred to as 'yoga' and 'meditation' in everyday English should be understood to fall under the heading of Modern Psychosomatic Yoga, including Postural and Meditational forms. These remained loosely structured and socially fluid up to about 1945, theories and

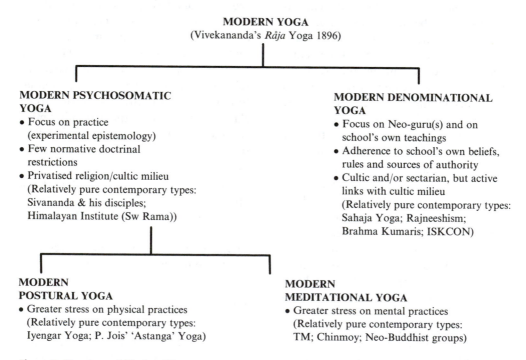

Figure 2. Typology of Modern Yoga.
(Reproduced from *A History of Modern Yoga*, by Elizabeth De Michelis (2004) (Cassell Continuum), with permission from the publishers.)

practices being elaborated and passed on mainly by way of individual lines of teachers and by way of printed texts. From after World War Two onwards, however, we see a progressive process of popularization, professionalization and acculturation: at the level of practice 'yoga' and, to a lesser degree, 'meditation' start to become assimilated into forms of alternative medicine and into psychosomatic 'health and fitness' discourses (see **Holistic Health Movement**), while related professional training courses becomes progressively more formalized. Theorizations and religiophilosophical underpinnings will however retain their strong esoteric (and strongly New Age) leanings: the popularization and acculturation of such ideas and practices still plays a major part in the furtherance of Neo-Hindu, Neo-Buddhist and Neo-Jain groups worldwide.

Further reading

Alter, J. (forthcoming) *Stretching Truth: Yoga, Science and Health in Modern India*, Princeton: Princeton University Press.

Ceccomori, S. (2001) *Cent Ans de Yoga en France* (A Hundred Years of Yoga in France) Paris: Edidit.

De Michelis, E. (2004) *A History of Modern Yoga: Patañjali and Western Esotericism*, London: Cassell Continuum.

Fuchs, C. (1990) *Yoga im Deutschland: Rezeption-Organisation-Typologie* (Yoga in Germany: Reception-Organisation-Typology), Stuttgart: Kohlhammer Verlag.

ELIZABETH DE MICHELIS

YOGA

Yoga is derived from the Sanskrit term meaning 'joining together'; its aim is 'the union of mind, body and spirit with the transcendent (God)'. The origins of Yoga in ancient India are obscure, though it may have begun as a shamanic practice (see **Shamanism**) to attain altered states of consciousness and power. It became systematized around the second century CE when Patanjali's 'Yoga Sutras' were written: a major work still considered essential reading for the advanced yoga practitioner. Yoga is one of the six classic systems of Hindu philosophy. Its key doctrine is that the practice of certain disciplines leads to liberation from karma, the limitations of flesh, the delusions of sense, and the pitfalls of thought. Yoga is an enormously complex system with many schools and branches, the main ones being: *Jnana* yoga (the path of knowledge or wisdom); *Bhakti* Yoga (the path of devotion); *Karma* yoga (the path of action); *Raja* yoga (the royal path of meditation). Raja yoga is considered the most complete path, integrating physical and mental training for spiritual ends.

The main physical praxis of *Raja* yoga is *Hatha* yoga, which forms the basis of most yoga practised in the West. It consists mainly of *pranayama* (breathing exercises) and *asanas* (postures). *Asanas* work on every part of the body, stretching and toning muscles, joints, the spine and the entire skeleton; they also work on the internal organs, glands, and nerves. Through the release of physical and mental tension, vast resources of energy are made available – ideally for meditation, though in the West it may be used for more secular purposes.

Westerners are still interested mainly in hatha yoga, which contains many schools, though only about a dozen are known in the West. Yoga first became popular in the West during the 1960s/1970s counter-culture, introduced mainly by Iyengar. Although yoga cannot be called an NRM (see **New Religious Movement**), it is taught mainly by gurus in India, and Iyengar is still one of the most respected gurus. Another guru who became well known in America after persuading participants at the Woodstock festival to chant *om* for peace was the late Swami Satchidananda. He introduced a more meditative approach known as Integral Yoga. The movement's headquarters is Yogaville, an ashram in Virginia, and it has many branches worldwide. Currently, the most fashionable style is *ashtanga*, a 'serious workout' which has been popularized as 'power yoga' by Beryl Birch. The main representative body for yoga in Britain is The British Wheel of Yoga, a registered charity set up over thirty years ago, and now recognized by the Sports Council. It has a nationwide network of teachers, and offers teacher training and classes.

Yoga has had its critics in modern times, including orthodox religious clerics who see it as opening the way to new beliefs, and from the Indian tantric **guru**, **Osho** Rajneesh. He refused to adopt it in his community at Pune, arguing that yoga's way of disciplining the mind and body strictly, according to an archaic system, was counter-productive to his aim of liberating body and spirit from the tyranny of tradition. He also expressed the view that it is essentially a male-oriented martial art, and therefore unsuitable for most women. Ironically, the most distinguished yoga teacher of modern times, B. K. S. Iyengar, also had his teaching centre in Pune, India, at the same time, and he had many women students. Unsurprisingly, the two famous gurus never arranged a meeting.

Yoga is probably the best example of the '**Easternization** of the West'. It has become firmly rooted in popular culture in many forms, from committed yogis using it as a complete path to enlightenment, to keep-fit classes for the overweight. The final insult or trivialization is the use of yoga to sell insurance, connected by the idea of stress management. On the other hand, it is now being taken more seriously by the medical establishment. Nirmala Heriza, a senior disciple of Satchidananda and associate of Dean Ornish, has pioneered the medical use of yoga as the cardiac specialist for Cedars Sinai Hospital in the USA. It is also the 'market leader' in the health and fitness industry, widely used by physiotherapists and psychotherapists, a staple class in gyms, and adopted by sports trainers to enhance performance. However, its position is now being challenged by pilates, and there have even been attempts at combining the two techniques, resulting in the unfortunately named hybrid yogalates. Numbers of practitioners are impossible to estimate, but they probably run to at least hundreds of thousands. Unlike most fitness techniques, it seems to be more popular with women than men, promoted by women's magazines as a method for enhancing inner and outer beauty.

Further reading

Iyengar, B. K. S (1995) *Light on Yoga*, New York: Schocken Books.

ELIZABETH PUTTICK

YOGANANDA, SWAMI PARAMAHANSA
(b. 1893; d. 1953)

Born Mukunda Lal Ghosh, Yogananda was one of the first Indian swamis to disseminate Hindu teachings in the West, and is the founder of the **Self-Realization Fellowship**. Yogananda came from a lineage of Indian gurus, having been taught by Sri Yukteswar (1855–1936), whose teacher Lahiri Mahasaya (1827–95) is said to have received instruction from Mahavatar Babaji – allegedly born in 203 CE and said to be still alive – who is credited with the revival of kriya yoga.

Yogananda joined Yukteswar's order of swamis in 1914, and was sent to the United States as a delegate to the International Congress of Religious Liberals, held in Boston in 1920. Yogananda commenced a lecturing tour in the USA, and is particularly renowned for his address 'The Science of Religion', delivered on 6 October 1920. In 1922 he established an ashram near Boston, and in 1924 embarked on a major world tour, attracting large crowds. The Yogoda Satsanga Society, founded by Yogananda in 1920, was incorporated as the Self-Realization Fellowship in 1935.

Yogananda's best-known published writing is his *Autobiography of a Yogi,* which first appeared in 1946. It is still in print, having been translated into eighteen different languages, and is widely regarded as a spiritual classic. This autobiography describes some of the ideas underlying the practice of kriya yoga, although much of the practices cannot be revealed to outsiders, being confidential. Yogananda explains that the universe is governed by spiritual laws as well as physical ones, and that those who can learn them can experience special yogic powers such as seeing visions, working miracles and the ability to bi-locate by acquiring a second physical body. The *Autobiography of a Yogi* draws almost as much on Christianity as on Hinduism, with considerable reference to Christian scripture. Yogananda taught the harmony of all religions, and particularly the oneness of Christianity and Hinduism, of Christ and Krishna. Although Yogananda belonged to the *advaita vedanta* (non-dualist) schools, he sought to reconcile the *advaita* and *dvaita* (dualist) traditions, teaching the possibility that the Absolute could be conceived either as impersonal and one with the universe, or as a separate personal being to whom *bhakti* (devotion) could be addressed.

As well as having his own followers, Yogananda's teachings have influenced other religious groups. One example is the Breatharians, led by Jasmuheen, who teaches the possibility of living solely on prajnic (wisdom) energy, without physical food or drink.

Further reading

Walters, J. D. (Swami Kriyananda) (1996) *The Path: One Man's Quest on the Only Path There Is*, Nevada City, CA: Crystal and Clarity.
Yogananda (1990) *Autobiography of a Yogi*, Los Angeles: Self-Realization Fellowship.

GEORGE CHRYSSIDES

YONAOSHI

The literal meaning of this Japanese term is 'reformation' or 'restoration' of the world. The general understanding of the term refers to the numerous riots in Japan from the mid Edo (Tokugawa Shogunate) (1603–1867) to the beginning of the Meiji period (1868–1912). Farmers at this time, who were subjected to abject poverty, started rioting by attacking the wealthy, with the expectation of equalizing the gap between rich and poor. *Yonaoshi* movements became more conspicuous around the end of the Edo period, along with other movements that sought to overthrow the Tokugawa Government. Anxiety and a deep 'sense of crisis' were common at the time, and were to be exacerbated when Japan opened itself up in the 1850s to trade with foreign countries, which was one of the major causes of the yonaoshi movements. In this respect there are similarities between the yonaoshi and the millenarian movements of mediaeval Europe which were caused by political oppression, severe poverty and the lack of representation (Cohn, 1970).

Under strong, charismatic leadership, many religious movements of this period displayed millennialistic features (see **Millenarianism**), in the sense that their objectives were to completely transform the world and live in a state of permanent harmony and happiness by means of the religious faith which supported their activities. Examples of such religions are **Kurozumi-kyo** (1814), **Tenri-kyo** (1838), **Konko-kyo** (1859) and **Omoto** (1899). As researchers point out, the rise of these NRMs coincided with a time of rapid and bewildering social change in Japan (McFarland, 1967), and the vast majority have been motivated by the desire to radically transform the world or yonaoshi.

MASAKI FUKUI

YONO TATEKAE

'*Yono tatekae*' is a Japanese term which means the 'reconstruction of the world'. This concept is the Japanese version of **millenarianism** and hence the most common theme in most (if not all) new religions in Japan (see **New Religions (Japan)**). Most new religions (see **New Religious Movement**) advocate the renewal of the world as the ultimate purpose of their religious movement. The concept was not new but rather became more prominent after the nineteenth century. Millenarian concepts and eschatological expectations existed long before the nineteenth century; for example, the concept of the age of *mappô* (or the last stage of the valid period of the Buddha's Dharma) has been a frequent theme in Japanese history. In particular, the Buddhist monk, Nichiren (1222–82), used it to predict the arrival of a painful period in Japan. The general belief in the arrival of '*Miroku no yo*', or the World of *Maitreya*

(the Future Buddha), was already present as far back as the early eleventh century, as seen in the 'Tales of Genji' (written around 1000 CE).

The idea of *yono tatekae* is a view of collective salvation rather than the salvation of individuals. Like the concept of '**yonaoshi**', this notion became more prevalent when Japanese society was facing rapid social change, for example around the time of the arrival of the Americans and new trade with foreigners, which began in the mid-nineteenth century. These events brought severe economic problems, particularly for the poor and peasants, and generated a high level of anxiety, anger and a sense of crisis in the world.

The notion of world renewal in the nineteenth century, which was generated mainly by nationalism and a sense of anti-establishment by the socially underprivileged class, is not identical to the concept of the creation of a perfect world, which is to be found in new religious groups in the late twentieth century, especially after the 1970s. The idea of 'creating a new perfect world on earth', that is found in 'new' new religions after the 1970s, is not the product of rapid social change or industrialization. By the 1970s Japanese society had long ceased to suffer from material and economic deprivation. However, the modern world was still understood to be in a state of crisis, albeit of a different kind. From the perspective of the new religions of the 1970s its causes are believed to lie in wrong thinking and the modern way of living. People have forgotten, these new religions claim, the true purpose of life and do not know where the heart of God is. As long as people live without spiritual awareness, their lives in this modern, scientific world will soon be subjected to some extremely painful experience, to a 'purificatory period', even to a 'final judgement of

God', 'armageddon', the 'baptism of fire' and so on. Sometimes the name of the sixteenth century French physician, Nostradamus, has been employed in order to support these views on impending disaster. This type of belief system can induce a great deal of fear, and at the same time it can offer hope.

Some of the new religions of the 1970s and later do not predict such apocalyptic periods but rather place more emphasis on the creation of a New Perfect World on earth. Such a Perfect World is to be created by the members of NRMs themselves, for example, simply by becoming good, positive and happy individuals. The process for this may involve studying and practising a group's doctrine, doing voluntary work for a very long time, attending and inviting friends to the group's sessions, and so on. Strictly speaking, the view of 'yono tatekae' within the new religions of Japan of the 1970s and later, is not about renewal of the outer world (political and social), but more accurately, is about the reconstruction of the inner world of individuals which will eventually change the real world.

MASAKI FUKUI

Z

ZAR CULT

The Zar cult flourishes in Ethiopia (whence it may derive its name), Somalia and Djibouti, the Sudan (where the generic spirit is also known as 'red wind'), and to a lesser extent in Egypt, North Africa and the Gulf states (see Lewis *et al.* 1991). Other expressive common names for the spirits and the conditions they cause are 'constitution' or 'power' and in Ethiopia, 'shackles'. It is closely linked historically to the Bori cult in northern Nigeria, Niger, and other parts of Islamic West Africa. In Ethiopia it involves Christian and Muslim populations, elsewhere its setting is entirely Muslim. The cult appeals particularly to urban women, and men of historically low or subordinate status (as in the case of the related Sudanese Tumbura cult), or to powerless individuals who are confronted with seemingly insurmountable identity conflicts. The basic assumption here is that the spirits concerned have the power to invade the bodies of humans who are then 'possessed'. The human vessel incarnates the possessing spirit.

In the Sudan, particularly, the spirit galaxy, whose numbers, like the names of God in Islam, total ninety-nine, are grouped in seven loose categories:

1. the Darawish or 'holy men': Muslim saints (local and international), founders of the Sufi tariqas and teachers of the faith.
2. Al-Habash, Ethiopian spirits, including 'Mimeluk' (Emperor Menelik/Haile Selassie)
3. Al-Bashat, the Pashas: famous colonial administrators and doctors: mainly stereotypes, but includes 'Gordel' (General Gordon) and (Lord) Cromer.
4. Al-Arab, spirits of nomadic desert tribes, some of which are specified, e.g. Beshir Hadendowa.
5. Al-Khawajat, or al-Nasara: Europeans, Christians, Copts, Jews, French and British and includes

640

the abstract spirit of electricity, *kaharla*.

6. Al-Sittat or al-Bunat, 'ladies' or 'daughters', ethnically mixed, includes mermaid spirits of the river Nile.

7. Al-Zurug, the 'blacks', peoples of all the regions from which the Sudanese used to obtain slaves including Zande cannibal spirits and the Tumburani, closely related human and animal spirits such as the crocodile and *al-turabi*, the spirit of death and graveyards. A more recent addition is 'Bokasu' (the notorious Emperor Bokasu of the Congo).

If a person's condition, often initially a minor ailment, is interpreted as evidence of spirit attention, the standard treatment involves placating the spirit concerned, and bargaining with it to reach a mutual accommodation. Thereby the afflicted person accedes to the spirit's demands for delicate foods, perfume, etc. and undertakes to dance in its honour with the appropriate costumes and accoutrements. This requires regular attendance at cult group rituals in the form of seances dedicated to the zar spirits and directed by a shamanic leader (called *alaqa* in Christian Ethiopia, and *sheikha* [female sheihk] amongst Muslims).

These groups and their ritual activities (called 'beating the zar' in Somalia) become an important element in the lives of urban women who may devote as much time to them as their men-folk give to Church or Mosque. In Muslim settings, their organization and ritual vocabulary replicate those of the Sufi religious orders with which, in some cases they merge in common veneration of a spirit-saint.

An alternative treatment, favoured by husbands and other male relatives, is to seek the aid of a cleric exorcist (Christian or Muslim as appropriate) who uses the power of the holy scriptures to expel the spirit which is defined as evil in this context and, amongst Muslims, assimilated to jinns. The spirit is exhorted to leave its human host, usually via the little finger of the left hand. Although initially expensive, exorcism is ideally less costly than the process of initiation into the zar cult which, in the long term, entails repetitive ritual expenditure. (But 'exorcism' may itself become a repetitive ritual addressed to Islamic or Christian saints (See Lewis, 1996: 136–7).)

'Possession' here is not necessarily synonymous with 'trance' since it may be diagnosed in a patient and prospective cult member whose psychic condition is perfectly normal. (See Lewis, 2003: 33–40). In the cult rituals, however, the adept will repeatedly experience trance and, paradoxically, this state is also typically achieved at the height of exorcism, at the point where the possessing spirit is believed to be about to quit its human victim.

In the case of female adherents, the relationship between adept and spirit is conceived as a spiritual marriage which may compete with the woman's human marriage. Such possessed women can, in effect, make a career of their worship, graduating in time to become cult leaders, a position of considerable importance in the world of women. The potential antagonism towards the dominant male world is obvious and finds expression in men stigmatizing zar spirits as irreligious and belief in them superstitious. Men's behaviour, however, is frequently ambivalent. They may be forced by circumstances to compromise with a wife's beliefs in order to ameliorate her pressing problems which, if untreated, risk having major domestic implications.

The male view of zar spirits as primitive superstition, threatening their religious orthodoxy, immediately raises the question of the historicity of the spirits – their temporal as well as geographical provenance. The shared Zar-Bori myth of origin is that the spirits derive from the time of creation when, fearing his jealousy, Eve concealed her most beautiful children from God, and these later became revealed to humans in this spiritual form. In historical time, it seems that, originating in Ethiopia, zar may have spread to north Africa with trade and pilgrimage as early as the fifteenth century where to some extent it was absorbed by the Sufi mystical movement. But the first secure references are in the early nineteenth century when zar appears as well-established and spreading rapidly in the Sudan in the wake of Turco-Egyptian colonization. The personalities of the spirits themselves reflect these derivations.

The origins of the parallel and related bori cult (in the Sudan zar is known as 'zar-bori') are more clearly established. The spirit galaxy, totalling some 130 spirit entities, is even more elaborate and directly associated with he pre-Islamic religion of the Hausa-speaking peoples (See Last, 1991 and Echard, 1991). Here the gender factor is brought to the fore as the wives of Hausa men, who convert to Islam, almost automatically become bori enthusiasts in revenge.

If the spirit cast of these cults is to a certain extent a kind of memory lane of local and regional historical experience, account has also to be taken of the way in which the spirit repertoire expands to absorb 'new' spirits. These include such modern characters as famous sports figures, and even Marxist soldiers. Thus, although the local religious orthodoxies attempt to denigrate zar and bori as 'ancient superstition', both cults are in a sense 'old' and 'new' women's religions whose origins and development appear, as elsewhere, closely linked to social change in the broadest sense.

Further reading

Boddy, J. (1989) *Wombs and Alien Spirits*, Madison: University of Wisconsin Press.

Constantinides, P. (1978) 'Women's Spirit Possession and Urban Adaptation' in P. Caplan and J. M. Bujra (eds) *Women United Women Divided*, London: Tavistock.

Echard, N. (1991) 'The Hausa Bori Possession Cult in the Ader Region of Niger' in I. M. Lewis, A. al-Safi, and S. Hurreiz, *Women's Medicine: the Zar-Bori cult in Africa and Beyond*, Edinburgh: Edinburgh University Press.

Last, M. (1991) 'Spirit Possession as Therapy: Bori among non-Muslims in Nigeria' in I. M. Lewis, A. al-Safi and S. Hurreiz, *Women's Medicine: the Zar-Bori cult in Africa and Beyond*, Edinburgh: Edinburgh University Press.

Lewis, I. M. (1996) *Religion in Context*, Cambridge: Cambridge University Press.

Lewis, I. M. (2003) *Ecstatic Religion*, London: Routledge.

Lewis, I. M., al-Safi, A. and Hurreiz, S. (1991) *Women's Medicine: the Zar-Bori Cult in Africa and Beyond*, Edinburgh: Edinburgh University Press.

Lewis, I. M. (1996) *Religion in Context: Cults and Charisma*, Cambridge: Cambridge University Press.

Lewis, I. M. (2003) *Ecstatic Religion*, London: Routledge.

Makris, G. P. (2000) *Changing Masters: spirit possession and identity construction among slave descendants and other subordinates in the Sudan*, Illinois: Northwestern University Press.

I. M. LEWIS

ZETAHEAL

Founder: Prophetess Lehem

A **new religious movement** Zetaheal founded in 1975. Prophetess Lehem, the founder, was originally known as Comfort Narh, and was once a dressmaker in a garment factory in Accra, the capital city of Ghana. Her father was the custodian of a traditional religious shrine in old Ningo, in the Eastern Region. In 1975 she was possessed by angels who revealed her actual identity and announced her mission in the world. Her real name was said to be Lehem. She pre-existed as an angel in heaven. She is in the world as the link between the earth and a group of angels who, out of compassion, have sought permission from God to act to save the world from imminent catastrophe. She possesses a special soul, which is so pure that it enables her to be possessed by the rest of the angels and other spirits for various purposes, especially, consultation of spirits.

Like the name *Lehem*, *Zetaheal* is of heavenly origin. It means, 'Lean on God and he will save you'. The stated-mission of the movement is twofold: to heal the world of religious conflicts and sectarianism; and to restore truth to the world.

Generally, Zetaheal seeks to promote religious tolerance; it is specifically concerned about the unity of Christians and Muslims. According to *God With Us*, the revealed sacred book of the movement, 'The division between Muslims and Christians is the work of Satan'. Jesus and Muhammad are together in 'the spirit' and they feel sad when their followers fight each other. Zetaheal has come to restore the Children of Abraham to unity in one house. This is captured in the words of one of their most popular hymns:

> *Zetaheal is the family house*
> *of Father Abraham.*
> *Christians and Muslims, come,*
> *Lets us unite to worship God*
> *Let us cast Satan aside.*

Zetaheal seeks to unite the two traditions in such a way that a member of the movement is both a Muslim and a Christian.

In keeping with its stated mission to restore truth to the world, Zetaheal seeks to reform doctrines and practices of both Christianity and Islam, which, from its point of view, are distortions, or misinterpretations of scriptures. It denies the divinity and uniqueness of Jesus, saying, he is the Son of God 'just as you are all children of God'. Zetaheal teaches that it is the ultimate apostasy for orthodox Christianity to interpret the crucifixion as part of God's plan of salvation. The killing of Jesus was a mistake and not part of the plan of God concerning the coming of Jesus into the world. *God With Us* declares, 'In this world you say with conviction that Jesus came to die for you. It is an erroneous thought; a grievous wrong for which you must pray for forgiveness.'

Zetaheal has revealed the actual dates of Christ's birth and the Crucifixion. Christmas must be celebrated on 14 November and the death of Jesus on 11 April. Strict annual observance of these dates by humankind will result in special blessings for the world.

Zetaheal also teaches that monogamy is the norm in Islam for all times and in all circumstances. The Prophet Muhammad had no conjugal relationship with the women he took to his home as wives. He only protected and provided for them. Sexual intercourse at any time in the month of Ramadan defiles the believer and offends the angels who visit in the night to carry prayers to God. So it must be avoided.

Salvation in Zetaheal, is through the mediation of prophetess Lehem who is described as the 'Messiah unto humankind', the 'Mediator between man and God' the 'Centre of Creation' and the 'Torchbearer of the New Age'. The movement's scripture says of her, 'Truly, the human being is in need of

643

forgiveness. If a woman caused the fall of humanity in the Garden of Eden, then naturally, it is expected that a woman will stand in to ask for pardon and repave the way for humanity.' The legitimacy of Lehem's position is based on the claim that she herself is a kinswoman, a close relative of Jesus. The manifestation of angels in her ministry and the miracles she performs are supposed to authenticate her claim to messiaship

Zetaheal worship combines Islam and Christian elements with some African traditional religious practices. A priest and an imam jointly lead services. In addition to the celebration of Christmas and Christ's death, Zetaheal also celebrates all the Islamic feasts. Her members may also join in the pilgrimage to Mecca.

ABAMFO O. ATIEMO

ZIMBABWE ASSEMBLIES OF GOD AFRICA

Zimbabwe Assemblies of God Africa (ZAOGA) is one of Africa's most significant pentecostal movements. It numbers 300,000–400,000 members in Zimbabwe and has branches in at least a dozen other African countries. It was founded by artisans and casual workers living in Zimbabwe's capital, Harare [Salisbury], during the late 1950s. The movement itself emerged from the South African derived pentecostal church, the Apostolic Faith Mission (AFM). A collection of young pentecostal zealots: Joseph Choto, Raphael Kupara, Lazurus Mamvura, James Muhwati, Priscilla Ngoma, Caleb Ngorima, and Abel Sande formed a prayer band and choir around the charismatic evangelist, Ezekiel Guti. This semi-autonomous group were expelled from the AFM in 1959 following a struggle with missionaries and an elder male fraction of the black leadership.

The group subsequently joined the South African Assemblies of God of Nicholas Bhengu in association with the Pentecostal Assemblies of Canada. Once again they were expelled, and in 1967 they formed their own organization, Assemblies of God, Africa (AOGA).

The movement expanded along migrant labour networks into other Zimbabwean towns and cities as well as into Mozambique, Malawi, and Zambia. In the 1970s Guti began to cultivate links with the American Bible Belt after studying at Christ for the Nations Institute (CFNI) in Dallas in 1971. After Zimbabwean independence in 1980 AOGA mushroomed on a transnational scale, renaming itself Zimbabwe Assemblies of God Africa: ZAOGA. Under the guise of Forward in Faith Movement International it established itself in Botswana, South Africa, Rwanda, Zaire, and Tanzania, and sent missionaries to Britain.

Since its founding ZAOGA has undergone a profound transformation. The movement, which had begun as a collection of young zealots rebelling against what they perceived to be corrupt and spiritually dead religious establishments, has changed into a respectable, disciplined denomination with a rich associational life of youth, women's and men's organizations, backed by a complex but personalized bureaucracy. An authoritarian hierarchy has replaced its formerly egalitarian structures of government and personality cult centres on Guti, who, today, is formally addressed as Archbishop but popularly referred to as the 'Prophet and Servant of God'. In the 1990s ZAOGA's leaders made political capital out of their enormous membership. Politicians from the ruling party, ZANU/PF, were invited to church functions and ZAOGA sporadically added its voice to government proclamations on moral issues. Thus, what was once a world-retreating township-based sect with strong links to rural Zionist-type Christian independency has transformed itself into a modern electronic church, part of the global born-again movement. The leadership's former aversion to jewellery, make-up and fancy clothes, which marked out their sectarian status, has given way to embracing the opportunities of the material world, and an espousal of an Africanized prosperity gospel.

These transformations result from a variety of processes. First, ZAOGA has modernized by drawing upon external ideas and resources. From the outset the movement's founders had the support of influential white patrons and pentecostal missionaries. More significant was Guti's period of study at CNFI Dallas, USA. The Institute became a dynamo for global charismatic and pentecostal advance. Guti's stay there gave him a clearer perception of the international born-again movement and its dynamics. It provided him with resources and a range of international contacts, which he used to modernize the movement. ZAOGA has also evolved by virtue of its own doctrines. Its teaching of sobriety and industry, its emphasis on smart attire and respectability, its promotion of self-reliance and entrepreneurial acumen has enhanced the social mobility of its members and attracted aspirant Christians from the historic mission churches.

ZAOGA's phenomenal growth has led to internal conflict. Guti's access to foreign resources provided him with a source of patronage to consolidate his control over the movement. In the 1980s and 1990s he edged out his co-founders and replaced them with his kin and ethnic group. Moreover, as the movement has expanded across social classes it has become a microcosm of wider society

and shares many of its tensions. Conflict between rich and poor is often expressed in theological terms as a clash between the prosperity gospel and an older populist pentecostalism which values the socially humble person as more receptive to the gospel. More sophisticated members of the movement have become increasingly outspoken about the personality cult surrounding Guti.

Further reading

Maxwell. D. J. (2000) '"Catch the Cockerel Before Dawn": Pentecostalism and Politics in Post-Colonial Zimbabwe', *Africa*. 70(2), 249–77

Maxwell. D. J. (2001) '"Sacred History, Social History": Traditions and Texts in the Making of a Southern African Transnational Religious Movement', *Comparative Studies in Society and History*, 43(3), 502–24.

DAVID J. MAXWELL

ZION CHRISTIAN CHURCH

The Zion Christian Church (ZCC) is the largest African Indigenous/Initiated Church in Southern Africa with over 5,000,000 members. It was founded in 1924 by Ignatius Lekganyane (1885–1948), known to many of his followers as Engenas, who was born sometime between 1880 and 1885. He died in 1948 after which two separated churches emerged from the organization he founded.

Lekganyane's mother was the daughter of Marobathota Raphela, a well known traditional healer who many believe was of Swazi descent. After he founded the ZCC critics said that Ignatius was really a traditional healer like his grandfather and not a true Christian. This charge seems totally unfounded.

As a child Ignatius attended school in Matlhanthe reaching grade 3 before having to begin work. By that time he could read and by the standards of the day had a relatively good education for a rural African. Throughout his youth however he was troubled by an apparently incurable eye infection that threatened him with eventual blindness.

Then, in 1912, he had a dream in which he was told that he must go to Johannesburg where he was to join a church that baptized 'three times' in the name of Jesus. If he did this his eye problem would be cured. Ignatius followed the advice he received in his dream and journeyed to Johannesburg to find work in the mines. In Johannesburg he lived in a Black township where he attended numerous churches and Christian meetings before encountering a church that practiced triple baptism. This was the Zion Apostolic Church (ZAC) an offshoot of the Christian Catholic Apostolic Church in Zion (CCACZ).

The CCACZ was founded in 1896 in Chicago, USA, by the English-born Australian evangelist and forerunner of the Pentecostal Movement, John Alexander Dowie (1847–1907) who had visited South Africa in 1888 on his way to America. Emphasizing the importance of healing in Christian ministry he published a magazine the *Leaves of Healing* that was widely read in South Africa.

In 1903 Dowie also commissioned the American Rev. Daniel Bryant, a former Baptist, to a 'prophetic office' and sent him to South Africa. Early in May 1904 Bryant traveled from Durban to the farm of Petrus Louis Le Roux (b. 1864) in Wakkerstroom. Le Roux had resigned as a minister of the Dutch Reformed Church in 1903 following a dispute about his views on spiritual healing and ministry to Blacks. Together they held a revival meeting and began baptizing African converts in the nearby Snake River. A few weeks later, on 31 July, in Pretoria, Bryant ordained

Le Roux as an evangelist in the newly formed Christian Catholic Church in Zion (CCCZ).

Elias Mahlangu (1881–1960) was among the first converts baptized by Bryant and Le Roux and, according to tradition, became Le Roux's interpreter. He traveled to Johannesburg around 1911 to found the ZAC. When Ignatius Lekganyane met him he made a profession of faith and was baptized. From that time on his eye problems were cured. He soon became an evangelist within the ZAC and was ordained probably in 1916. According to a popular, yet disputed, tradition Le Roux was present at the baptism.

Because he had theological problems with Elias Mahlangu's insistence that members of his church remove their shoes during worship, wear special 'heavenly' gowns, and that the men were to grow long beards Ignatius came into conflict with the leaders of the ZAC. These conflicts came to a head in 1916–17 when, encouraged by their leaders, many ZAC openly declared that Germany would defeat Britain in World War One. Ignatius opposed this view claiming that he had received a vision telling him that Britain would be victorious. The defeat of Germany in 1918 enhanced Ignatius' prestige within the ZAC while increasing the tension between him and Mahlangu.

As a result Ignatius resigned from the ZAC to join the Zion Apostolic Faith Mission (ZAFM) led by Edward Motaung. He made a pilgrimage to the ZAFM's headquarters in Lesotho to meet Motaung in 1920 where he was appointed the ZAFM's Bishop for the Transvaal. Problems with the ZAFM's teachings and practices including who appointed ministers and determined their stipends resulted in Ignatius being recalled to Lesotho in 1924. Essentially the dispute was about leadership of the

ZAFM in the Transvaal where Ignatius was seen as a threat to the Lesotho based church hierarchy. Following these conflicts Ignatius decided to form his own Church, the ZCC, which he founded in 1924.

The ZCC was organized in a highly traditional manner with Ignatius performing the functions of a traditional chief. Organizationally it was based on traditional social structure with elders advising the chief. After forming the ZCC Ignatius sought official Government recognition for his church and engaged a firm of lawyers in Pietersburg to carry out the necessary negotiations. Several attempts were made to secure official recognition between 1925 and 1943 when at last the church was given Government approval.

On each occasion that the Church sought recognition they were required to provide accurate membership figures. Thus in 1925 the ZCC claimed to have 926 members of which 411 were female and 515 male. Ten years later the church had 2,000 members. By time of the third application in 1940 the membership stood at 8,500. Two years later when a further application was made the Church had 27,487 members grouped into fifty-five congregations. Finally in 1943 they were able to list over 45,000 members. One of the reasons for the rapid growth of the ZCC during World War Two appears to have been Ignatius' reputation as a prophet capable of foretelling future events. His successful prediction of the outcome of World War One was recalled and used to create confidence in his teachings.

Initially the ZCC grew in and around Lekganyane's birthplace near Pietersburg in the Northern Transvaal where it used buildings that had originally belonged to ZAFM. This led to a dispute about the ownership of the property which Lekganyane eventually won, but the experience caused him to encourage the practice of worship under trees and in the open without the use of a formal church building. This policy was a great success and appears to have attracted many poor people. As a result even today many ZCC congregations do not possess a church building.

Because formal registration with the South African Government required that churches provide the authorities with a written constitution Lekganyane asked his lawyer, P. W. Roos, to help him write one in which the organization and theology of the church was clearly stated. The result was a highly orthodox statement that conformed with the basic tenets of historic Christian theology. Throughout his ministry Ignatius preached from the Bible and taught about Jesus. Oral testimony confirms that he spent most of his spare time reading the Bible and many hours discussing its meaning with his followers.

Within the ZCC healing played a central role. According to Prof. Elias Khelebeni Lukhaimane over 80 per cent of converts joined the church as a result of illness and the promise of healing. Water was frequently used in healing ceremonies. It was sprinkled and poured over people seeking healing and used in baptism as well as being drunk during purification rites. Various types of water were used and many people were asked to go on a pilgrimage to the Orange River or the sea to get the water needed to heal them.

Converts and members of the church who underwent healing rituals were given visible tokens to protect them from attacks by evil spirits. Walking sticks were blessed, straps and special clothing were worn, and copper wire was placed on gates to protect them against lightning. Most important of all the confession of sins was seen as an essential prerequisite to healing and

647

believed to have the power to heal in itself.

So successful was Ignatius Lekganyane's ministry of healing that many people began to attribute divine power to him. As a result some of his followers began calling him 'Messiah' while others seem to have regarded him as God. Not surprisingly critics of the ZCC claimed that it taught and practiced a disguised form of African traditional religion and was pagan at its core. Further, belief in the *badimo*, or spirits of the ancestors and the church's recognition of the power of witchcraft, even though its ministers sought to defeat the power of witches through faith in the Holy Spirit, added to the criticisms. Equally contentious was Lekganyane's decision to allow church members to participate in traditional animal sacrifices to the ancestors and practice polygamy. All of these things created the impression among members of mission churches that the ZCC really was a new religion and not simply an African expression of Christianity.

Members of the church responded by arguing that the leadership should not be held responsible for the beliefs of their followers and that misunderstanding were bound to occur among uneducated and illiterate people. They also claimed that many of the disputed beliefs and practices had a biblical basis and pointed out that the ZCC's firm belief in and reliance on the Holy Spirit was entirely orthodox. Within the church, they stressed, Jesus was referred to as the Son of God, or God, and given the prime place in worship and that while people spoke about of 'the God of Engenas' this was no different from biblical expressions like the 'God of Abraham'.

Further, as proof of their biblical orthodoxy they pointed out that the use of the Bible within the ZCC was governed by the level of literacy in congregations and that as literacy increased so did the use of the Bible in sermons and Church rituals. This interpretation appears to be correct because over time the beliefs of ZCC members seem to have moved closer to its written constitution and the Bible. As a result it is perhaps correct to view Lekganyane's role as that of a spiritual mediator similar to that of the great saints in Roman Catholicism.

Within the ZCC the term used to describe preaching is understood as meaning 'to comfort'. Similarly, both baptism and communion are believed to have the functions that go beyond those normally recognized by most churches. These added spiritual benefits include the forgiving of sins, cleansing from sin, and healing. Baptism is by threefold immersion in running water if possible and takes place immediately after a profession of faith.

From the beginning the church took Paul's injunctions about Government, found in Romans 13:1–7, seriously and prayed for local chiefs and all levels of government. This had the effect of gaining sympathy from local magistrates and eventually the central government. Unfortunately, this teaching created major problems during the liberation struggle when the ZCC rejected the armed struggle and any form of violence. Therefore, it was seen as a pawn of the State by its enemies and many members of the African National Congress. Following the collapse of apartheid and establishment of a Black Government the new rulers found that the Church fully supported them and quickly reached an accommodation with its leaders.

When Ignatius Lekganyane died in 1948 he had left the question of succession unclear while predicting that two churches would emerge after his death. Members of the church and its various congregations soon divided into two main camps, those following his eldest son Edward and those following his fifth and favorite son Joseph. Many rural congregations supported Joseph, while the important Johannesburg area congregations supported Edward. The final split occurred in 1949 with the legal partition of the farms and other property belonging to their father. Following the deaths of Edward and Joseph both churches managed an orderly succession to their sons Barnabas and Ignatius. Throughout this period until the present the ZCC has continued to grow and attract increasing numbers of converts from all sections of South Africa's Black community making it the largest single church in the entire country.

Further reading

Lukhaimne, E. K. (1980) 'The Zion Christian Church of Ignatious (Engenas) Lekganyane, 1924–1948: An African Experiment with Christiantiy', unpublished MA thesis, University of the North, Pietersburg.

Naudé, P. J. (1995) *An Analysis of Some Hymns of the Zionist Christian Church*, Lewiston: Edwin Mellen Press.

Daneel, I. (1987) *Quest for Belonging*, Harare: Mambo Press.

Sundkler, B. (1976) *Zulu Zion and some Swazi Zionists*, Oxford: Oxford University Press.

IRVING HEXHAM

Index

INDEX

INDEX